D1474526

The SAGE Handbook of Organizational Communication

To the memory of Fredric M. Jablin, co-editor, colleague and good friend, whose passionate commitment to teaching and research greatly enriched the field of organizational communication.

The SAGE Handbook of Organizational Communication

Advances in Theory, Research, and Methods

Third Edition

Linda L. Putnam
University of California, Santa Barbara

Dennis K. Mumby
The University of North Carolina at Chapel Hill

Los Angeles | London | New Delhi
Singapore | Washington DC

Los Angeles | London | New Delhi
Singapore | Washington DC

FOR INFORMATION:

SAGE Publications, Inc.
2455 Teller Road
Thousand Oaks, California 91320
E-mail: order@sagepub.com

SAGE Publications Ltd.
1 Oliver's Yard
55 City Road
London EC1Y 1SP
United Kingdom

SAGE Publications India Pvt. Ltd.
B 1/I 1 Mohan Cooperative Industrial Area
Mathura Road, New Delhi 110 044
India

SAGE Publications Asia-Pacific Pte. Ltd.
3 Church Street
#10-04 Samsung Hub
Singapore 049483

Acquisitions Editor: Matthew Byrnie
Editorial Assistant: Gabrielle Piccininni
Production Editor: Libby Larson
Copy Editor: Erin Livingston
Typesetter: C&M Digitals (P) Ltd.
Proofreader: Dennis W. Webb
Indexer: Kathy Paparchontis
Cover Designer: Candice Harman
Marketing Manager: Liz Thornton

Printed in the United States of America

Library of Congress Cataloging-in-Publication Data

The Sage handbook of organizational communication : advances in theory, research, and methods / [edited by] Linda L. Putnam, University of California, Santa Barbara, Dennis K. Mumby, The University of North Carolina at Chapel Hill. — 3e [edition].

pages cm
title: Handbook of organizational communication
Includes bibliographical references and index.

ISBN 978-1-4129-8772-1 (hardcover)
ISBN 978-1-4833-0997-2 (web pdf)

1. Communication in organizations. I. Putnam, Linda. II. Mumby, Dennis K. III. Title: Handbook of organizational communication.

HD30.3.H3575 2014
302.3′5—dc23 2013029379

This book is printed on acid-free paper.

13 14 15 16 17 10 9 8 7 6 5 4 3 2 1

Contents

Acknowledgments

Editing a handbook that attempts to capture the "state of the art" in a field of study is a major responsibility and one not accepted lightly. However, an added sense of responsibility accompanies the editing of this volume of the *Handbook of Organizational Communication* because of its iconic status in the field. Since the publication of the first edition in 1987, the "Org. Comm. Handbook" has been a trusted resource for scholars and students in the field, as well as a staple reading assignment in numerous graduate seminars. As such, the publication of this third edition is met by its editors with equal parts of anticipation, pride, and anxiety.

Since its inception, the *Handbook* has attempted to map the terrain of organizational communication, account for different orientations to the study of the field, and offer both breadth and depth in reviewing the extant literature. As with any volume, it is difficult to do justice to the multiplicity of topics and viewpoints; hence, we recognize that our maps are incomplete. Fortunately, however, a *Handbook* such as this one is, by definition, a collaborative project, and our efforts to bring this new edition to the field benefits from the support of many friends, colleagues, and, of course, our publisher, SAGE.

First, we learned a great deal from scholars who provided feedback on the second edition of the *Handbook*. Fourteen colleagues who had used the book in their courses responded to a SAGE survey regarding the quality, usefulness, and relevance of the second edition. They shared their reasons for adopting it, their views of trends in the field, their recommendations for topics to include in the third edition, and their suggestions for format changes. We are especially grateful to them for their feedback as well as to other colleagues who offered us their insights and advice about the third edition. We also thank SAGE for conducting this survey and consolidating responses that provided guidance in designing the third edition.

Second, a *Handbook* is only as good as the quality of the chapters that contributors write, and in this sense we have indeed been fortunate. The 54 authors who contributed the 31 chapters to this volume have collectively created a scholarly resource that, we think, will endure for many years to come. Taken together, the chapters provide an expansive vision of a field that, while only in its infancy when the first edition of the *Handbook* appeared, is now mature, innovative, and dynamic. Indeed, we would argue that these 31 chapters collectively represent the most complete volume of a communicative view of organizations that is currently available.

Third, we owe a great debt of gratitude to the section editors who helped create a new structure for the *Handbook*, one that reflects current research agendas and problematic issues in the field. Each of the section editors worked closely with chapter authors and greatly enhanced the quality of the final product. The section editors are, in alphabetical order: Jim Barker, Dalhousie University, Nova Scotia; Janet Fulk, University of Southern California; Kathy Krone, University of Nebraska, Lincoln; Steve May, University of

North Carolina at Chapel Hill; and Patty Sotirin, Michigan Technological University.

At SAGE, Matt Byrnie has been a smart, responsive, and capable editor who provided much guidance during the course of the project. The fact that this edition of the Handbook is only 4 months overdue is ample testimony to his ability to keep us on track! Our copyeditor, Erin Livingston, did a fabulous job given the mammoth nature of this project. She turned around 31 chapters in a month, and the quality of the volume has benefitted considerably from her keen editorial eye. We also extend our thanks to Libby Larson, our production editor, for her efficient management of the production details, deadlines, and schedules.

Dennis would like to thank his co-editor, Linda, as well as former SAGE editor, Todd Armstrong, for inviting him to co-edit the volume, and for having the confidence that he could fill the very large shoes of the former co-editor of the *Handbook*, the late Fredric M. Jablin. Linda, in turn, extends appreciation to Dennis for his superb job as a co-editor and his dedication to the quality of this volume.

Finally, we acknowledge our universities, University of California, Santa Barbara and University of North Carolina at Chapel Hill, for their support with this project. In particular, we thank our colleagues, staff, and graduate students who provided assistance and encouragement in this journey.

Above all, we would like to thank the scholars of the interdisciplinary field of organizational communication whose sense of community and connectedness we hope to have captured in this volume.

Linda Putnam
Santa Barbara, CA
Dennis Mumby
Chapel Hill, NC

Introduction

Advancing Theory and Research in Organizational Communication

Linda L. Putnam and Dennis K. Mumby

Twenty-six years have passed since the publication of the first edition of the *Handbook of Organizational Communication.* For scholars who have been in the field since that time, it is hard to believe that organizational communication studies have changed so greatly. Much of what seemed self-evident and apodictic about the field in 1987 is contentious or even anachronistic today. So it is clear that the editorial philosophy and structure used in the first two editions can no longer capture the evolution and current state of the field.

When the first edition appeared in 1987, the field was simultaneously in a period of growth and transition. First, it was small, with only four or five organizational communication doctoral programs in the world. The Organizational Communication Division of the National Communication Association was established only five years earlier, and the first Alta conference occurred in 1981. Second, the 1987 edition of the *Handbook* represented a field that was, on the one hand, struggling with its scholarly identity (especially its links to consulting, management, and practitioners) and, on the other hand, trying to figure out how to embrace the emergent work in interpretive and critical theory (Putnam & Pacanowsky, 1983).

Representing a small but growing area of the field, the first edition had four editors—two from communication (Jablin and Putnam) and two from management (Porter and Roberts)—and was organized around topics that reflected an integration of communication with organizational theory. The sections of the first edition were (1) Theoretical Issues, (2) Context: Internal and External Environments, (3) Structure: Patterns of Organizational Relationships, and (4) Process: Communication Behavior in Organizations.

Reflecting dominant views at the time, the *Handbook* placed an emphasis on organizational structure and the separation between internal/external environments. Despite growing criticism, the *container model* (Axley, 1984) of organizations was the prevailing view of organizational communication at the time. Scholars primarily centered their research on communication processes within an organization, namely, climate, networks, superior-subordinate communication, feedback and performance evaluation, assimilation, and message flow. These processes were skewed toward communication as transmission, information flow, message exchange, message functions, distortion, and overload.

Yet the fundamental tension in the *Handbook*, as evident in Tompkins's (1987) chapter, was that symbolic action was the "substance of organizing and organization" (p. 77); that is, without rhetoric, communication, and persuasion, we would have no organization. This tension, combined with interpretive views of organizational culture and critical notions of power and politics, laid the groundwork for questioning the communication-organization relationship.

Interestingly, the second edition, published in 2001, retained the same overall structure, but with adjustments in many topic areas of the field. The first section morphed into "Theoretical and *Methodological* Issues" and contained chapters on quantitative and qualitative methods as well as one on discourse analysis. Perhaps more significantly, Deetz's (2001) chapter, "Conceptual Foundations," was an important effort to articulate what it meant to engage in theory development and research from a communication perspective. Specifically, it provided an alternative to Burrell and Morgan's (1979) metatheoretical framework, which had dominated the field for over twenty years.

Grounded in new topic areas, the second edition added chapters that focused on organizational learning, wired meetings, new media, and globalization. Other chapters moved away from the notion of communication within the organization to challenge the existence of organizational boundaries, the presumed difference between internal and external communication, and the very nature of an organization (Cheney & Christensen, 2001; Monge & Contractor, 2001). Dropping the classic notion of superior-subordinate communication, the chapter on leadership focused on dualisms between cognitive outcomes and conversational practices and between transmission models and meaning-centered notions in the field (Fairhurst, 2001). Other chapters introduced postmodernism as a new theoretical direction (Mumby, 2001; Putnam & Fairhurst, 2001), signaled the emergence of work-family conflict (Finet, 2001), and unpacked the action-structure dialectic (Conrad & Haynes, 2001). Overall though, the structure of the *Handbook* held to its legacy in the field, even though individual chapters challenged this very foundation.

That the second edition clung to its original structure might indicate that the field was still coming to terms with its identity and the full impact of the linguistic turn.[1] For example, feminist and postmodern theories were prevalent in the landscape of organizational communication studies by the end of the millennium, even though the treatments of these perspectives were relegated to sections rather than separate chapters (Conrad & Haynes, 2001; Deetz, 2001; Mumby, 2001; Putnam & Fairhurst, 2001; Taylor & Trujillo, 2001).

Thus while the chronological gap between the second and third editions is slightly shorter than that between the first and second ones, the conceptual gap is great and reflects not only the exponential growth of the field but also major advances in organizational communication. Although specific topics appear in both editions (e.g., organizational identity, organizational culture, globalization, power, leadership, and organizational socialization), the chapters in the third edition embrace new understandings of the communication-organization relationship.

The most significant theoretical transformation from the second to the third edition is that each chapter is rooted in communicative explanations of their respective domains of study. While each chapter is interdisciplinary in its orientation and draws on literatures from organizational communication, management, and related fields, each one aims to provide communicative understandings of organizational processes and practices.

This theoretical transformation is evident in three important ways. First, the number of chapters has been expanded from 20 in the second edition to 31 in this version of the *Handbook*. This increase not only reflects a proliferation of research topics but also reveals transformations in organizing processes and structures that call for nuanced and more communication-oriented approaches. Second, this edition celebrates a disciplinary identity that is both more communication based and more interdisciplinary than in the past. Over the past decade, the field has grown in numbers of programs, depth and breadth of scholarship, and research domains, and this edition reflects these developments. Finally, the structure of this *Handbook* is a radical break from the first two editions. The format of context, structure, and process has been jettisoned in favor of six sections—each of which represents an important set of issues around which scholarship in the field has developed. The six sections are (1) Theories of Organizational Communication; (2) Research Methods in Organizational Communication Studies; (3) Communication and Post-Bureaucratic Organizing; (4) Organizing Knowledge, Meaning, and Change; (5) Organizations, Stakeholders, and Conflict; and (6) Communication and the Organization-Society Relationship. The remainder of this introduction addresses each of these sections as both the medium and outcome of how the field has evolved over the last 25 years.

Theory Development in Organizational Communication

Several major developments set the stage for theory debates in organizational communication. Historically, the first one came with controversy around competing perspectives. In the early 1980s, Putnam's (1983) essay on the interpretive approach and Pacanowsky and O'Donnell-Trujillo's (1982) article on organizational culture challenged the then-dominant functionalist paradigm and articulated a research agenda for multiple perspectives. Nested in the "paradigm wars" of the 1980s and early 1990s, these debates led to a proliferation of alternative types of inquiry, rooted mainly in various forms of social constructionism.

These multiple perspectives were clearly evident in the public debate between Van Maanen and Bantz (advocating for the role of ethnography in organization studies) and Deetz and Mumby (arguing for the place of critical theory in organization studies) at the 1988 International Communication Association Conference. Framed around the recent publications of Van Maanen's (1988) *Tales of the Field* and Mumby's (1988) *Communication and Power in Organizations,* this debate captured arguments about the relative merits and resultant knowledge claims of descriptive-interpretive versus critical-interpretive organizational research (Putnam, Bantz, Deetz, Mumby, & Van Maanen, 1993). An important understanding that surfaced in this debate was that what counted as knowledge was in itself paradigmatic; that is, each theoretical perspective represented a view of the world that was mediated by its own discursive choices. Knowledge claims, as Van Maanen (1995) argued, were as much about rhetorical style and textual persuasion as they were about the phenomena under study.

With a concern that organizational communication was becoming too theoretically fragmented, scholars revisited the field's focus on multiple perspectives in a 1998 National Communications Association panel that featured three different metatheoretical approaches: post-positivism, interpretivism, and critical theory. Papers from this panel and a set of commentaries were subsequently published in the book, *Perspectives on Organizational Communication: Finding Common Ground* (Corman & Poole, 2000). The upshot of this development, while raising concerns about incommensurate assumptions among perspectives, was the decision to focus on common ground as opposed to the superiority of any one view.

In effect, organizational communication scholars share a common sensibility for the same object of knowledge—organizing as the medium and product of dynamic communication processes. While scholars may differ regarding the best way to investigate the communication-organization dynamic, they agree that communication processes are the *stuff* of organizing and that offering communication explanations for organizational phenomena (i.e., ones that differ from those given by disciplines such as psychology, economics, sociology, etc.) adds something unique and significant to the body of knowledge about people and their organizational lives. In this sense, scholars seem united in their efforts to elevate communication from being just another organizational phenomenon to the means by which organizational structures and processes are constituted.

The first section of this edition, therefore, reflects the diversity of theoretical perspectives that characterize the current terrain in organizational communication studies. From stalwart perspectives such as systems theory, structuration, and critical theory to relative newcomers such as postcolonial theory, institutional theory, and communicative constitution of organization (CCO), the chapters set forth multiple ways of theorizing the communication-organization relationship. The chapters in this section not only overview the history, assumptions, and findings of these perspectives but also offer ways to revitalize theoretical directions in the field.

The multiple metatheoretical views in this section return to the issue of what *common ground* means and how the field should handle the widely disparate ways of examining communication processes as the essence of organizing and organization. For Deetz and Eger (Chapter 1), the danger of multiple approaches is a form of *ecumenical fragmentation* in which each perspective is granted legitimacy but operates in a relatively separatist manner regarding overarching questions that connect different orientations. While a field does not need to privilege a specific perspective, it does need to be self-reflexive about its disciplinary identity and about the consequences of generating questions and making knowledge claims from particular assumptive grounds.

In Chapter 1, Deetz and Eger offer a metatheoretical framework for attending to the complexity and tensions linked to any particular theoretical orientation. Grounded in the belief that all perspectives adopt some form of constructionism in making knowledge claims, they recommend that theorists engage in reflection about the historically and socially situated nature of an approach, the relationship of what is encountered, and the contestable conditions of equality/inequality implicit in a perspective. This framework, then, provides overarching issues and concerns that can lead to comparisons and productive conversations across multiple, diverse perspectives.

Specifically, it might be productive to think about how each chapter in this edition of the *Handbook* situates itself in relation to the key features in this framework. For example, what kinds of knowledge claims does each chapter construct and how are they consistent with or in tension with each other? What implicit or explicit models of equality/inequality are built into various perspectives and research agendas? Moreover, in what ways is communication framed as pivotal (or incidental) to these queries? These questions aid in reflecting on the epistemic assumptions that researchers bring to their work, regardless of their theoretical orientations. The first section of the *Handbook*, then, examines how scholars have explored theory development at the intersection of communication and organization, specifically as it relates to knowledge claims, communicative modes of explanation, and the richness and diversity of research directions.

Research Methods in Organizational Communication Studies

A commensurate broadening of methodological approaches in organizational communication complements the proliferation of theoretical perspectives. This breadth also parallels the linguistic turn, which was a catalyst in the humanities and social sciences for a *crisis of representation* (Jameson, 1984), in which scholars questioned the claims of objective, value-free forms of knowledge.

The linguistic turn, as Mumby (Chapter 4) suggests, does more than signal a turn to the central role of communication in constructing social reality. Rather, it situates language as a mediator that reconfigures the relationships between subject and object and self and the world. In other words, it purports that there is no such thing as direct access to an unmediated world of essence; language constructs the world and our relationship to it. Thus in the wake of the linguistic turn, language and discourse take on a muscular and defining role in constructing reality.

From a methodological perspective, the post-linguistic turn has significantly complicated the relationships among the researchers, the methods they adopt, the subjects of study, and the representational practices used for knowledge claims. This complexity applies to quantitative methods, in which critics have questioned the veracity of objective, value-free data collection and analysis, and also to qualitative methods, in which the researcher simply writes up the data collected in the field. Both perspectives have been challenged on epistemological, methodological, and political grounds.

Organizational communication scholars have shifted rather quickly (certainly in comparison with some cognate fields) from a debate about the relative merits of quantitative versus qualitative research to a recognition that different methods are suited to different kinds of questions about the nature of organizing. Thus any discussion or debate about methods is premature if the researcher is unclear about the empirical context and conceptual issues under study.[2]

The field of organizational communication is clearly pluralistic in its approach to methods. The chapters in this *Handbook* on field research, organizational ethnography, discourse analysis, and mixed methods reflect the diversity of methods used to study organizational life. They demonstrate how the types of participants, data collection methods, types of data, analyst reflexivity, and interpretation/presentation of results have proliferated in the wake of the linguistic turn. Scholars currently examine an array of participants involved in work and nonwork organizations, profit and nonprofit agencies, online communities, occupations, institutions, and social-enterprise organizing. Data collection methods, as Doerfel and Gibbs (Chapter 9) point out, are equally diverse and include surveys, interviews, observations, case studies, and field experiments.

Both the breadth and depth of data collection methods point to the full impact of the linguistic turn in situating types of data (including discourse, symbols, networks, and texts) as both theoretically and methodologically rooted in the research itself. Responding directly to issues of representation, the analyst's role is no longer neutral but varies from an engaged observer to a fully immersed scholar who is reflexively involved with participants in coproducing the research itself (see Fairhurst & Putnam, Chapter 11; Tracy & Geist-Martin, Chapter 10).

The crisis of representation draws attention to tensions between methods and analysis on the one hand and disciplinary norms of textual presentation on the other. In many ways, even qualitative studies are expected to adhere to the standard journal format of problem statement, theoretical framework, literature review, methods, results, and discussion. Thus despite the ostensibly openness to the use of multiple methods, scholars often need to engage in various acts of subterfuge to shoehorn their research into acceptable journal forms (Tracy, 2012). The presentation of research, then, reveals a struggle between the choice of methods and the textual practices for articulating findings.

This struggle points to problems that researchers face in using multiple and mixed methods. Qualitative researchers who employ multiple methods (e.g., ones as diverse as recorded interactions, thematic or contextual interviews, and archival analyses) struggle to fit their complex findings into the standard format of scholarly journals. For instance, research on discourse and materiality, as noted by Fairhurst and Putnam (Chapter 11), captures streams of ongoing actions through shadowing and video-ethnography, in which the researcher examines the interfaces among objects, sites, bodies, and discursive practices. Journal articles often fail to capture the nuances of these interfaces through their standard practices. Similar concerns arise in employing mixed methods (that is, the use of both quantitative and qualitative methods). As Myers (Chapter 12) notes, the dearth of published mixed-methods studies in organizational communication may stem from breaking these projects into multiple publications, since standard formats and journal-length articles make it difficult to integrate these projects.

Moreover, the struggle between choice of methods and textual practices of articulating findings connects poetics to the politics of representation. For example, when Brummans (2007) writes about the death of his father from the perspective of a euthanasia declaration that his family signed, he makes a poetic choice (i.e., the article literally takes the form of a poem) to dramatize how an apparently inert text has an agency that drives family members' interactions and decisions. His choice of a representational form embodies an epistemic function that dramatizes textual agency. In addition, it involves a political function by highlighting how an apparently neutral text constitutes reality in particular ways. Thus regardless of whether investigators are qualitative or quantitative, researchers need to be self-reflexive about the ways in which their textual practices construct knowledge, researchers' subjectivities, and the subjectivities of participants.

In methodology, organizational communication scholars have moved beyond research that takes place within organizations. In keeping with the linguistic turn, current research methods focus on the complex ways in which routine organizing shapes people's lives and, reciprocally, how members' communication practices constitute organizing. Capturing the complexity of this dialectic is one of the most important tasks of organizational communication scholarship. It requires methods that are calibrated enough to enable theoretical sophistication, multiple modes of interpretation, and alternative presentation formats. Regardless of methodological identity (e.g., discourse analysis, ethnography, mixed methods, or variable-analytic approaches), researchers are illuminating the centrality of communication as a defining, constitutive element of organizational life.

Communication and Post-Bureaucratic Organizing

The third section of this edition of the *Handbook* examines the changing character of organizational life in the 21st century. When the first edition appeared in 1987, the standard frame of reference for research was *the organization*, an identifiable structure with relatively distinct boundaries, clearly defined members, and clearly identifiable internal and external communication. This conception paralleled the modernist, bureaucratic form that, in 1987, was beginning to show its cracks as globalization took hold and new systems of production, employee relations, and technology were implemented. Changing economic conditions and global competition pushed organizations to be leaner as well as more flexible and adaptive.

Moreover, the shift from a production-based to a consumption-based economy changed the relationship between employees and organizations regarding the degree to which individuals became subject to corporate control. Traditional distinctions between work and private realms broke down as corporations sought to gain competitive advantage through harnessing the *authentic* employee (Fleming, 2009). As research revealed, however, this shift in employees' relationships to work had a double-edged effect.

On the one hand, employees were expected to do more than show up for work; rather, they were required to enter, body and soul, into the work experience. On the other hand, post-bureaucratic organizing created a work landscape that was much more precarious than bureaucratic work arrangements (Ross, 2003). In this sense, the relationships between *identities* and *insecurities* had become a close one. Specifically, employees continuously sought a sense of security under social and economic conditions that undermined these very possibilities (Collinson, 2003). Based on these changes, Deetz's (1992) arguments regarding the corporate colonization of life are even more salient today than they were 20 years ago. As corporate claims on worker identities have become more intense, managerial discourses define even more spheres of life that were, at one time, traditionally outside the corporate domain.

Section III, then, brings a communication lens to the changing relationships of social actors to organizational life. As Barker notes in introducing this section, *post-bureaucratic* refers both to an ontological condition that describes the character of organizational life in the 21st century and to a lens that allows researchers to problematize organizations in particular ways. From a communication perspective, post-bureaucratic organizing is a dynamic, emergent process in which discursive practices play a central role in configuring relationships among members and organization. The chapters in this section on embedded teams, work-life issues, workplace relationships, leadership, communication technologies, and networks cast post-bureaucratic organizing as complex, emergent, and irreducible to conventional organizational forms. These essays address the shifts in how people organize as well as in their relationships *to* organizations (i.e., work-life issues, technology, networks).

For example, Fairhurst and Connaughton's (Chapter 16) essay on leadership communication captures how this classic topic has shifted dramatically in the last 10 years. In its modernist, bureaucratic form, leadership was considered a capacity or set of behaviors that inhered in specific people and differentiated leaders from followers, whereas in post-bureaucratic organizing, leadership has become an emergent and socially constructed process that revolves around sensemaking and the management of meaning. Similarly, Sias's (Chapter 15) essay on workplace relationships shows how decades of research (largely rooted in managerial assumptions regarding message exchange processes and superior-subordinate communication) has evolved into the study of relational dynamics, including coworker relationships, workplace romances, abusive relationships, sexual orientation, and questions of power and resistance.

The changing nature of post-bureaucratic organizing has also altered the critical role that communication plays in shaping teams, networks, and technology use. Advances in cyber-infrastructure and the Internet have altered the nature of virtual teams and traditional work groups. Embedded teams, as Seibold, Hollingshead, and Yoon (Chapter 13) explain, are communicatively constituted with permeable boundaries that conjoin dispersed members across time, space, and traditional notions of organizations. They form multiplex and multidimensional networks that are no longer limited to individuals but include artifacts and technologies in complex communicative processes that move beyond message exchange and information transmission (Shumate & Contractor, Chapter 18). Unlike the modernist bureaucratic era, changes in communication technologies are rapid, expansive, and transformative, including not only computer-based digital systems but also wired and wireless devices. Rice and Leonardi (Chapter 17) chart the complex processes and contexts that shape the adoption and use of new technologies in this post-bureaucratic era, especially the ways that material features of technology become communicatively and constitutively entangled in people's daily routines.

In these chapters, authors bring a communication lens to examine everyday organizational life in contexts that are dynamic rather than static, emergent rather than fixed, distant rather than close, precarious rather than stable, and intersubjectively constructed rather than objectively existant. In this sense, a communication mode of explanation is well-suited to post-bureaucratic organizing. Indeed, post-bureaucratic organizing is a communication phenomenon just as much as it is an economic, political, and sociological one. The discourses that frame and legitimize a post-bureaucratic form speak of flexibility, mobility, meaningful work, and work-life balance. Organizational communication scholars have a crucial role to play in theorizing and investigating not only these discourses but also the various ways in which they are materially instantiated in everyday organizational life.

Organizing Knowledge, Meaning, and Change

Section IV of the *Handbook* extends many of the issues addressed in the previous section by examining the consequences of post-bureaucratic organizing. Questions of knowledge, meaning, and change, as constitutive features of 21st century organizational life, have been addressed extensively in organizational communication studies. Specifically, in the post-bureaucratic era, no state-of-the-art review of organizational communication would be complete without a discussion of knowledge and knowledge management. In many respects, the idea of the *knowledge-intensive* organization stands as the archetypal post-bureaucratic form, in part, because organizations have shifted over the last thirty years from producing things to producing forms of knowledge. Moreover, the conception of knowledge has shifted from the predominantly cognitive model in which it functioned as a commodity stored in an individual's brain to a practice-based model in which knowledge results from complex webs of communicative activity and systems of meaning (see Kuhn, Chapter 19). Through this shift, knowing becomes a practical accomplishment that is interactively realized.

This movement from knowledge to knowing has profound implications for the role of communication in this process. In the cognitive model, the conception of communication is heavily rooted in an information transmission perspective in which knowledge is extracted, quantified, transferred, measured, bought, and sold. In the practice-oriented perspective, knowing is "indexical, polysemous, processual, and situated in broader discursive/cultural contexts" (Kuhn, Chapter 19, p. 483). In this conception, communication plays a constitutive role in the process of knowing, not just in the sense of creating knowledge but also in shaping the nature of communities who define what counts as knowledge.

Both knowledge management and change have become synonymous with post-bureaucratic forms. In the last 20 years, the vocabulary of corporate life is filled with such terms as *downsizing, rightsizing, reengineering,* and *involuntary exit.* Voluntary and involuntary exit have become critical topics for learning the ropes in organizations (see Kramer & Miller, Chapter 21). Thus socialization and assimilation practices include ways that individuals negotiate their roles; make sense of these changes; and give accounts for individual transitions, transfers, and reduction in force. Newcomers are no longer passive recipients of socialization tactics; assimilation is a highly interactive process in which employees enact, partake, and resist changes.

Indeed, the best-selling late-1990s motivational book, *Who Moved My Cheese?* (Johnson, 1998) captures this corporate philosophy with its injunctions, "Anticipate Change," "Monitor Change," "Enjoy Change," and "Be Ready to Change Quickly and Enjoy it Again." Although this text aims to provide people with skills that are necessary to survive in a volatile economy, managers also use it to minimize resistance to change. Thus as Lewis points out in Chapter 20, conceptions of change have typically been management centered and often cast as natural, inevitable, and beneficial to the company and its employees. Of importance to communication scholars are the corporate discourses that cast change as necessary in an increasingly turbulent and competitive global marketplace, especially for creativity and innovation. The deployment of this discourse often obscures the seamier side of change, in which corporate restructuring favors managerial interests and increases returns to shareholders.

Lewis's chapter reviews research that theorizes change communicatively as a process of sensemaking and interpretation among multiple stakeholders. Thus while a particular stakeholder group may not have significant formal power, they can shape and alter change initiatives through their sensemaking efforts (e.g., developing workplace narratives that question the efficacy of a particular change initiative). Several chapters (Chapter 11, 17, and 20) in this edition reference Leonardi's research on the implementation of a new technology in an automobile manufacturing plant, in which engineers' negative interpretations and interactions about the technology shaped their material engagement with it, thus thwarting a planned change effort (Leonardi, 2008, 2009). This study stands in contrast to the discourses of technological inevitability that often obscure the political choices involved in planned change (Leonardi & Jackson, 2004).

Post-bureaucratic organizing, then, not only creates the context for new forms of knowledge, assimilation, and organizational change, but it also contributes to altering employees' relationships to each other, as is evident in the work on emotions and organizational culture. Twenty years ago, it was rare to read research on emotion and organization that did not embrace a rational, functional view and advocate the use of emotions to promote productivity (e.g., Rafaeli & Sutton, 1988; Sutton & Rafaeli, 1990). Today, scholarship on emotion adopts a broad critical sensibility that examines how emotion management in a post-bureaucratic world has become one of the final frontiers of corporate control. In doing so, scholars have extended Hochschild's (1983) initial work on emotional labor through multiple theoretical lenses (e.g., feminist, critical, post-structuralist) to examine employee identity as the locus of corporate control (Mumby & Putnam, 1992; Tracy, 2000; Tracy & Tracy, 1998).

Moreover, as Miller shows (Chapter 23), organizational communication researchers have shifted from instrumental forms of emotion (construed either positively or negatively) to contexts in which emotion is woven into the fabric of work and work relationships (e.g., human service organizations). Specifically, she notes that recent research on compassion is linked to the increased insecurity of work and the attendant angst and suffering that people experience in a post-bureaucratic world. Compassion is a direct and very human response to suffering, and organizational communication scholars have an important role to play in exploring the interactional dynamics involved in compassionate communication.

The work on emotions and compassion are intertwined with an organization's culture. Keyton's (Chapter 22) review of research on organizational culture provides a strong sense of how studies in the interpretive tradition have evolved in the past 30 years. As Keyton points out, communication scholarship on organizational culture has contributed significantly to viewing organizations as complex sites of symbol systems and meaning formations. Moreover, communication scholars are at the forefront of developing nonmanagerial conceptions, in which culture is a *root metaphor* (Smith & Eisenberg, 1987) of organizing rather than a pragmatic tool used to shape employees' identities.

Questions of knowledge, change, and meaning will continue to be central foci of organizational communication studies. Scholarship in this area has increased our understanding of the communicative dynamics of these key drivers of 21st-century organizational life. Indeed, one of the challenges of our time is to generate insights into the ways that communication processes drive organizational change and knowledge creation. Communication is central to this process, and scholars in our field are well-positioned to examine these drivers.

Organizations, Stakeholders, and Conflict

Section V of the *Handbook* focuses directly on a theme that has become central to organizational communication studies in the past several decades: the organization as a site of power and conflict. This section addresses the topics of power and resistance, organizing and difference, incivility and destructive behavior, and engaged scholarship and democracy. Each chapter examines the various ways in which power is a communicative, constitutive feature of everyday organizational life.

The study of power clearly predated critical theory; indeed, power infused the history of management thought, especially in addressing "the problems of human relations in an authoritarian setting" (Perrow, 1986, p. 53). Traditionally, management thought focused on producing rational, science-based theories of motivation rather than on the increasingly nuanced and sophisticated forms of control that managed alienated labor (Mumby, 2013). Until relatively recently (with a few exceptions; e.g., Pfeffer, 1981; Tannenbaum, 1968), power was an absent presence in management theory and research.

In general, organizational communication scholars conceive of power as a symbolic phenomenon in which discursive practices constructed organizational realities that served certain stakeholder groups over others. Since the interpretive turn, critical studies of power have populated the organizational communication landscape, beginning with the early work of Deetz and Kersten (1983), Conrad (1983, 1988), and Mumby (1987, 1988). These early conceptions of communication, power, and organization were strongly influenced by the neo-Marxist and Frankfurt Schools, especially the work of Althusser (1971), Gramsci (1971), and Habermas (1971, 1984). Scholars drew on concepts such as ideology and hegemony to explore how power was exercised through consent rather than coercion (Deetz & Mumby, 1990).

From this perspective, power functioned through a process of systematically distorted communication (Habermas, 1970) whereby latent conflict was obscured through an ideologically constructed false consensus. Driven by an emancipatory impulse, this work aimed to open up possibilities for alternative forms of organizational decision making and democratic participation through revealing these latent conflicts. In management and organization studies, parallel efforts occurred with researchers exploring power as a symbolic phenomenon (e.g., Alvesson, 1985; Clegg, 1981; Frost, 1980; Rosen, 1985, 1988). Again, the focus was on how discursive processes reproduced prevailing systems of power. For example, Rosen (1985, 1988) explored how corporate rituals in an advertising agency functioned ideologically to obscure underlying asymmetries of power.

In recent years, organizational communication scholars have contributed to a more textured and nuanced picture of organizations as discursive sites of power and conflict. In broad terms, research has shifted from the production and reproduction of extant power relations to the dynamics of control and resistance. This shift has expanded the theoretical landscape of power through an emphasis on post-structuralist and postmodern writings (e.g., Derrida, 1976; Foucault, 1979, 1980). An important consequence of this shift has been an even greater focus on communication and discourse and a closer exploration of the relations among communication, power, and subjectivity.

Organizational communication scholars have contributed significantly to an interdisciplinary body of research that examines the dialectics of control and resistance as well as the subjectivity of the employee as the locus of corporate control. Scholars, such as Deetz (1994, 1998), Murphy (1998, 2003), Ashcraft (2005, 2007), Tracy (2000; Tracy, Myers, & Scott, 2006), and Kuhn (2006, 2009), have examined the complex and often contradictory ways in which employee identity formation becomes implicated in the dynamics of control and resistance (see Zoller, Chapter 24). Indeed, our "flagship" journal, *Management Communication Quarterly,* has played an important role in this research by publishing two special issues on workplace resistance—one in 2005 (Putnam, Grant, Michelson, & Cutcher, 2005) and one in 2008 (Fleming & Spicer, 2008).

This section of the *Handbook* also depicts ways in which scholarship has moved beyond questions of control and resistance to examine issues of incivility and bullying, organizing and difference, and engaged scholarship and democracy. The inclusion of these chapters signals a broader conception of power and conflict as scholars address both the dark side of organizational life as well as its transformative possibilities. Thus Kassing and Waldron's essay (Chapter 26) reviews a large body of research that investigates a disturbing feature of contemporary organizational life: incivility and bullying. It is perhaps no coincidence that this research has flourished in the last decade at the same time that conditions of uncertainty and insecurity have become routine features of organizational life.

Moreover, both Parker's essay (Chapter 25) on difference and Dempsey and Barge's chapter (Chapter 27) on engaged scholarship speak to the possibilities of framing organizations as sites of conflict. While new to this edition, Parker's chapter reflects ongoing efforts to theorize difference beyond gender. Specifically, her chapter, while acknowledging a feminist legacy, examines difference through the lenses of racial, postcolonial, and transnational theories. Consistent with recent trends in the field, her chapter examines a way of complicating difference as both a medium and outcome of intersecting gender, race, class, and sexuality (Mumby, 2011).

Dempsey and Barge's essay (Chapter 27) speaks to the possibilities that power and conflict hold for social transformation. Specifically, they examine what happens when scholars treat theory and research as opportunities for engaged praxis. What happens when researchers conceive of their studies as democratic processes for engaging with participants on equal terms to produce social change? What does it mean to treat knowledge as a cogenerative process? Such epistemological queries are crucial for producing knowledge that leads to social transformation and democratic forms of organizing.

Each chapter in this section, then, adopts a communicative lens to examine organizations as sites of power and conflict. A communication perspective explores how power infuses everyday organizational life in both positive and negative ways—through incivility, control, and bullying on the one hand, and through opening up possibilities for transformation and change on the other hand.

Communication and the Organization-Society Relationship

The final section of this edition focuses on the societal role of organizing and organizations in the 21st century. In the last twenty years, the effects of globalization, communication technologies, and a neo-liberal political economy have significantly reshaped organization as the medium and outcome of social, political, and economic structures. Moreover, the prevalence of anticorporate social movements attests to a growing public concern regarding the power of organizations in contemporary society.

In the last 15 years, the field of organizational communication has embraced these global shifts. Scholars have begun to examine the relationships between organizations and their broader societal structures by exploring such issues as social justice, corporate social responsibility, social movements, and corporate identity in a globalized world.

A central question in exploring these relationships is the increasing fluidity of organizational boundaries. It is no longer easy to identify where an organization begins and ends or to distinguish between work and nonwork in people's lives. As such, the construction of organizational identities and their extensions beyond the boundaries of organizing are critical issues to address. Long-established areas of research, such as organizational identification and assimilation, face difficult questions regarding where personal identity ends and organizational identity begins.

Similarly, the research on corporate social responsibility (CSR) has continued to grow in the wake of efforts to make organizational activities consistent with socially and environmentally responsible practices. As this research shows, brands are no longer merely products that companies develop; they have become an intrinsic feature of an organization's identity (Cheney,

Christensen, & Dailey, Chapter 28). Corporations spend billions of dollars constructing identities that reflect an array of values, including quality, responsibility, community, and democracy. Most corporate CSR efforts are communicative and symbolic as well as behavioral and are designed to evoke positive public responses. The communicative construction of a particular corporate identity, however, is as important as an organization's social actions. Customers and employees engage with the meaning of organizing, not just with what a company does.

In addition to research on corporate identity, organizational communication scholars have developed rich research agendas that focus on community organizing (Ganesh, 2005, 2007). These organizing efforts, as Ganesh and Stohl (Chapter 30) note, are occurring all over the globe. They demonstrate that attaining greater democracy and equality is no longer the exclusive domain of governments and elected representatives but is also the task of social movements that intersect with and become organizations. This research speaks to the possibilities of collective action and the ways in which people can mobilize and transform the conditions of their existence. It also shows how organizational communication scholars have moved away from a parochial, U.S.-centric view of organizing to embrace multiple perspectives in examining globalization processes (Stohl & Ganesh, Chapter 29).

As scholars address the rapidly changing relationships between organizations and society, they continue to show how communication is both the medium and outcome of this relationship. From corporate identity to community-based organizing, communication constitutes the ways that organizations position themselves in social, political, and economic contexts.

Looking to the Future of Organizational Communication

Tracing the changes in organizational communication scholarship across the three editions of the *Handbook* offers some important insights about the field's continuities and discontinuities. In many respects, the field is unrecognizable when compared to its mid-1980s identity. The range of theoretical perspectives has mushroomed, as have the concepts, processes, and practices that scholars employ. Perhaps the most significant transformation is the way that scholars frame the communication-organization relationship.

While the first edition of the *Handbook* touched on the idea that communication was constitutive of organization, the structure and content still held to a container conception of organizations. The third edition of the *Handbook* represents 25 years of evolution that demonstrates the fluidity and fragility of organizations. Embracing a different ontology, scholars increasingly claim that organizations are products of the communication practices of their members. This transformation has spurred research not only in organizational communication but also in management studies.

But what might the next decade of research hold for the field? In what ways might the fourth edition of the *SAGE Handbook of Organizational Communication* differ from its predecessors? In this final section, we engage in speculation about the future of organizational communication.

(Re)Doing Theory

Clearly, the range of theoretical perspectives in organizational communication has increased. However, are we, as a field, too traditional in the kinds of theories that we include in our toolbox? In Chapter 4, Mumby suggests that critical organizational communication researchers typically draw from the same tried-and-tested theorists (e.g., Derrida, 1976; Foucault, 1979, 1980; Habermas, 1971, 1984) while critical management scholars have been more creative in their use of theorists (e.g., Deleuze & Guattari, 1983; Hardt & Negri, 1999; Lacan, 1991; Žižek, 1989). Since choosing a theory hinges on research context and problems, the more choices that scholars have at their disposal, the greater the likelihood that they can capture the complex dynamics of organizing.

Theories, by definition, highlight and hide different elements of a phenomenon under study; thus scholars generate insights and knowledge claims that are as much a product of their own theoretical constructs as they are the phenomenon itself. A larger toolbox of theories offers additional opportunities to conceptualize organizing in rich and diverse ways. Consistently leaning on the same theoretical crutch has the unfortunate effect of transforming it into a hammer.

Moreover, as Deetz and Eger (Chapter 1) point out, researchers need to be politically attentive to and self-reflexive about the assumptions that undergird theory development. Specifically, scholars need to ask the following questions: What problems do theories address? Whose interests are served by these problems? Who gets access to the knowledge produced through a particular theoretical lens? (and, perhaps most significantly) What view of the human condition does a perspective advance? Specifically, does this view enhance our sense of humanity or does it impoverish it?

A final concern that is critical to advancing the field is the need to develop an array of original, homegrown, organizational communication theories. Arguably, the Montréal School's version of CCO is the primary perspective that originates wholly in our field rather than being derivative of other social or organization theories.[3] The Montréal School has developed sophisticated, communication-based concepts that focus on the dynamic relationships among conversation, text, and organization. It is a catalyst for a large body of empirical research and has produced original insights about organizing and organization.

Looking into the future, researchers need to develop additional homegrown theories not simply because they strengthen the field but because they offer communicative modes of explanation and a discipline-based lens to study organizational phenomena. Studying organizing communicatively differs markedly from studying the communication processes of organizations from sociological, psychological, or management perspectives.

Developing communicative modes of explanation can help scholars focus on meaning and sensemaking and especially on how such meanings are communicatively mediated, thus revealing the dynamic, interactional qualities of organizational life. Moreover, homegrown theories illuminate the relationships between everyday, micro-level communication and societal, macro-level meaning systems, particularly as they relate to questions of democracy and decision making. It is difficult to predict the nature or sources of the next theoretical developments, and it usually takes years for them to impact a community of scholars. No doubt, the next *Handbook* will include chapters that center on these contributions.

Rethinking the Individual-Organization Relationship

One arena for both theory development and practice is the degree to which organizations permeate every dimension of our lives. Many chapters in this edition raise concerns about the relationship between our personal and our organizational lives. Specifically, chapters on work-life issues, workplace relationships, socialization and assimilation, organizational emotions and compassion, incivility and destructive workplace behavior, and engaged scholarship address the growing encroachment of organizations into individual lives.

In their recent book, *Dead Man Working*, Cederström and Fleming (2012) paint an apocalyptic image of life in postmodern society, in which every waking moment is co-opted into work; thus we become "dead men [and women] working." They argue that under modernist, bureaucratic organizations, the primary fault line was between capital and labor; however, today "the real fault-line . . . is between *capital and life* . . . the corporation [has] render[ed] our very social being into something that makes money for business" (p. 7, emphasis in original).

Organizational communication scholars, then, need to examine how the production of economic value depends heavily on social reproduction and on communication that occurs outside of the corporate workplace (Hardt & Negri, 1999; Land & Taylor, 2010; Virno, 2004). In this sense, organizations are making porous, if not eliminating, the boundaries between life and work. With its constitutive role in meaning construction, communication lies at the heart of this new relationship. In effect, the power of organizations to discursively name and frame work and nonwork relationships is an increasingly important area of research that scholars need to pursue.

This research requires a more nuanced treatment of the individual-organizational relationship. Rather than viewing employees as *in* organizations and with lives *outside* of them, researchers need to move beyond the work-life dualism. For example, current research on identities and occupations focuses on the discursive and material production of professional bodies and selves rather than on organizations as physical sites in which work occurs (Alvesson, Ashcraft, & Thomas, 2008). In such research, the focus is on the *work of discourse* (Ashcraft, 2007) as it constructs identities, rather than on *discourse at work*. Similarly, recent research on social movements and collective action (see Ganesh & Stohl, Chapter 30) transcends distinctions between work and life by focusing on civil society organizing. This work examines ways in which discourses of change and transformation construct connections across social groups and communities.

The individual-organization relationship has always been a core topic in the field. Indeed, examining how communication mediates this relationship forms a shorthand definition for what organizational communication scholars do. But we need to rethink the dynamics and parameters of this relationship and to reassess how organizations and organizing impact people's lives. Clearly, this topic is an important research agenda item for the next decade.

Rethinking Work, Materiality, and Organizing

In a similar way, organizational communication scholars need to (re)conceptualize the nature of work, particularly its material, economic, institutional, and bodily features. While popular commentators talk about a knowledge economy with its fast-paced capitalism and instantaneous movement of information and wealth, society remains confronted with temporary and precarious jobs. These jobs are often performed by a "body class," whose roles as maids, custodians, taxi drivers, call center employees, nannies, and sex workers provide the infrastructure for the smooth-functioning information economy and the mobile class that runs it (Boltanski & Chiapello, 2005; Castells, 2009; Kang, 2010; Sassen, 1998, 2003).

In responding to this concern, organizational communication scholars need to attend to the materiality of work and the communicative construction of people in various forms of labor. As Kang's (2010) study of Korean employees in nail salons illustrates, the discourses of race, class, and gender intersect in particular ways to construct bodies as having specific skills that become deployed in the service of global capitalism. For Kang, organizing is both material and symbolic as the bodies of employees and the nature of their labors interface with the customers who use these services. In effect, work and organizing are *both* material and discursive; that is, they are socially constructed and embedded in the bodies of those who perform these labors.

Multiple chapters in this edition of the *Handbook* call for rethinking the role of materiality and communication processes (e.g., Chapters 3, 5, 7, 11, 17), especially in their mutually constitutive relationships. Mutuality, however, does not mean equal and symmetrical (Suchman, 2007). Drawing from the work on discourse, technology, and institutions, the authors of these chapters call for scholars to conceive of the communication-materiality relationship in different ways; namely, as constitutive entanglements, as translations or mediations between the two, or as dialectics transcended through an interpenetration of the two. As Fairhurst and Putnam (Chapter 11) point out, researchers are just beginning to understand the relationships among objects, sites, and bodies as they become intertwined in reflexive and discursive actions.

These relationships also produce tensions and disjunctures that create opportunities for developing different modes of organizing.

Thus an important agenda item for future scholarship involves attending to the productive and generative tensions between communication and materiality. Investigating these tensions offers scholars an opportunity to unpack the complex relationships between the symbolic and the material. Organizational communication scholarship is often the most generative when it focuses on complexity and contradiction, and the contemporary organizational landscape provides no shortage of these conditions.

Conclusion

This introductory chapter sets forth conceptual and theoretical developments in the field that laid the groundwork for the third edition of the *Handbook*. By comparing this version of the *Handbook* with previous editions, we show how the field has grown, both theoretically and methodologically, and how communication is no longer treated as a phenomenon that occurs within organizations but is considered the very essence of organizing and organization. In light of these changes, this edition centers on critical themes in the field, including post-bureaucratic organizing, organizational knowledge and change, organizations as sites of power and conflict, and the organization-society relationship. These themes and related topics reveal a unifying focus in the field; that is, the communication-organization relationship. In advancing this relationship, we recommend expanding the field's theoretical toolbox, rethinking the individual-organizational relationship, and focusing on the tensions nested at the intersection of work, materiality, and discourse.

As this edition demonstrates, the field is rich and diverse in scholarly interests and theoretical approaches. The breadth of scholarship included in the six sections of this edition examine profound issues related to the nature of organizing as well as practical problems that impact the daily lives of organizational actors. In reading and editing these chapters, we conclude that the state of the field is strong and getting stronger. The numerous ways that scholars address the intersection of communication and organization in this edition make significant contributions to the body of interdisciplinary knowledge about organizational life. Whether the reader is a seasoned researcher or a neophyte scholar, we think you will find much to interest and excite you in this third edition of the *Handbook*.

References

Althusser, L. (1971). *Lenin and philosophy*. New York, NY: Monthly Review Press.

Alvesson, M. (1985). A critical framework for organizational analysis. *Organization Studies, 6*(2), 117–138.

Alvesson, M., Ashcraft, K. L., & Thomas, R. (2008). Identity matters: Reflections on the construction of identity scholarship in organization studies. *Organization, 15*(1), 5–28.

Ashcraft, K. L. (2005). Resistance through consent? Occupational identity, organizational form, and the maintenance of masculinity among commercial airline pilots. *Management Communication Quarterly, 19*(1), 67–90.

Ashcraft, K. L. (2007). Appreciating the "work" of discourse: Occupational identity and difference as organizing mechanisms in the case of commercial airline pilots. *Discourse & Communication, 1*(1), 9–36.

Axley, S. (1984). Managerial and organizational communication in terms of the conduit metaphor. *Academy of Management Review, 9*(3), 428–437.

Boltanski, L., & Chiapello, E. (2005). *The new spirit of capitalism* (G. Elliott, Trans.). London, England: Verso.

Brummans, B. (2007). Death by document: Tracing the agency of a text. *Qualitative Inquiry, 13*(5), 711–727.

Burrell, G., & Morgan, G. (1979). *Sociological paradigms and organisational analysis*. London, England: Heinemann.

Castells, M. (2009). *Communication power*. Oxford, England: Oxford University Press.

Cederström, C., & Fleming, P. (2012). *Dead man working*. Winchester, England: Zero Books.

Cheney, G., & Christensen, L. T. (2001). Organizational identity: Linkages between external and internal communication. In F. M. Jablin & L. L. Putnam (Eds.), *The new handbook of organizational communication: Advances in theory, research, and methods* (pp. 231–269). Thousand Oaks, CA: SAGE.

Clegg, S. (1981). Organization and control. *Administrative Science Quarterly, 26*(4), 545–562.

Collinson, D. (2003). Identities and insecurities: Selves at work. *Organization, 10*(3), 527–547.

Conrad, C. (1983). Organizational power: Faces and symbolic forms. In L. L. Putnam & M. E. Pacanowsky (Eds.), *Communication and organizations: An interpretive approach* (pp. 173–194). Beverly Hills, CA: SAGE.

Conrad, C. (1988). Work songs, hegemony, and illusions of self. *Critical Studies in Mass Communication, 5*(3), 179–201.

Conrad, C., & Haynes, J. (2001). Development of key constructs. In F. M. Jablin & L. L. Putnam (Eds.), *The new handbook of organizational communication: Advances in theory, research, and methods* (pp. 47–77). Thousand Oaks, CA: SAGE.

Corman, S. R., & Poole, M. S. (Eds.). (2000). *Perspectives on organizational communication: Finding common ground.* New York, NY: Guilford.

Deetz, S. (1992). *Democracy in an age of corporate colonization: Developments in communication and the politics of everyday life.* Albany: State University of New York Press.

Deetz, S. (1994). The micropolitics of identity formation in the workplace: The case of a knowledge intensive firm. *Human Studies, 17*(1), 23–44.

Deetz, S. (1998). Discursive formations, strategized subordination and self-surveillance. In A. McKinley & K. Starkey (Eds.), *Foucault, management and organization theory: From panopticon to technologies of self* (pp. 151–172). London, England: SAGE.

Deetz, S. (2001). Conceptual foundations. In F. M. Jablin & L. L. Putnam (Eds.), *The new handbook of organizational communication: Advances in theory, research, and methods* (pp. 3–46). Thousand Oaks, CA: SAGE.

Deetz, S., & Kersten, A. (1983). Critical models of interpretive research. In L. L. Putnam & M. Pacanowsky (Eds.), *Communication and organizations: An interpretive approach* (pp. 147–171). Beverly Hills, CA: SAGE.

Deetz, S., & Mumby, D. K. (1990). Power, discourse, and the workplace: Reclaiming the critical tradition. In J. Anderson (Ed.), *Communication yearbook* (vol. 13, pp. 18–47). Newbury Park, CA: SAGE.

Deleuze, G., & Guattari, F. (1983). Anti-Oedipus: Capitalism and schizophrenia (R. Hurley, M. Seem, & H. Lane, Trans.). Minneapolis: University of Minnesota Press.

Derrida, J. (1976). *Of grammatology* (G. Spivak, Trans.). Baltimore, MD: Johns Hopkins University Press.

Fairhurst, G. T. (2001). Dualisms in leadership research. In F. M. Jablin & L. L. Putnam (Eds.), *The new handbook of organizational communication: Advances in theory, research, and methods* (pp. 379–439). Thousand Oaks, CA: SAGE.

Finet, D. (2001). Sociopolitical environments and issues. In F. M. Jablin & L. L. Putnam (Eds.), *The new handbook of organizational communication: Advances in theory, research, and methods* (pp. 270–290). Thousand Oaks, CA: SAGE.

Fleming, P. (2009). *Authenticity and the cultural politics of work: New forms of informal control.* New York, NY: Oxford University Press.

Fleming, P., & Spicer, A. (2008). Beyond power and resistance: New approaches to organizational politics. *Management Communication Quarterly, 21*(3), 301–309.

Foucault, M. (1979). *Discipline and punish: The birth of the prison* (A. Sheridan, Trans.). New York, NY: Vintage.

Foucault, M. (1980). *Power/knowledge: Selected interviews and other writings 1972–1977* (C. Gordon, L. Marshall, J. Mepham, & K. Soper, Trans.). New York, NY: Pantheon.

Frost, P. (1980). Toward a radical framework for practicing organization science. *Academy of Management Review, 5*(4), 501–508.

Ganesh, S. (2005). The myth of the non-governmental organization: Governmentality and transnationalism in an Indian NGO. In G. Cheney & G. Barnett (Eds.), *International and intercultural organizational communication* (vol. 7, pp. 193–219). Creskill, NJ: Hampton Press.

Ganesh, S. (2007). Grassroots agendas and global discourses: Tracking a local planning process on children's issues. *International and Intercultural Communication Annual, 30*, 289–316.

Gramsci, A. (1971). *Selections from the prison notebooks* (Q. Hoare & G. N. Smith, Trans.). New York, NY: International Publishers.

Habermas, J. (1970). On systematically distorted communication. *Inquiry, 13*(1–4), 205–218.

Habermas, J. (1971). *Knowledge and human interests* (J. Shapiro, Trans.). Boston, MA: Beacon Press.

Habermas, J. (1984). *The theory of communicative action: Reason and the rationalization of society* (vol. 1, T. McCarthy, Trans.). Boston, MA: Beacon Press.

Hardt, M., & Negri, A. (1999). *Empire.* Cambridge, MA: Harvard University Press.

Hochschild, A. (1983). *The managed heart: Commercialization of human feeling.* Berkeley: University of California Press.

Jameson, F. (1984). Foreword to J-F Lyotard, *The postmodern condition* (pp. vii–xi). Minneapolis: University of Minnesota Press.

Johnson, S. (1998). *Who moved my cheese?* New York, NY: Putnam.

Kang, M. (2010). *The managed hand: Race, gender and the body in beauty service work.* Berkeley: University of California Press.

Kuhn, T. (2006). A 'demented work ethic' and a 'lifestyle firm': Discourse, identity, and workplace time commitments. *Organization Studies, 27*(9), 1339–1358.

Kuhn, T. (2009). Positioning lawyers: Discursive resources, professional ethics, and identification. *Organization, 16*(5), 681–704.

Lacan, J. (1991). *The seminar of Jacques Lacan, book 1: Freud's papers on technique 1953–54.* New York, NY: W.W. Norton.

Land, C., & Taylor, S. (2010). Surf's up: Work, life, balance and brand in a new age capitalist organization. *Sociology, 44*(3), 395–413.

Leonardi, P. M. (2008). Indeterminacy and the discourse of inevitability in international technology management. *Academy of Management Review, 33*(4), 975–984.

Leonardi, P. M. (2009). Why do people reject new technologies and stymie organizational changes of which they are in favor? Exploring misalignments between social interactions and materiality. *Human Communication Research, 35*(3), 407–441.

Leonardi, P. M., & Jackson, M. H. (2004). Technological determinism and discursive closure in organizational mergers. *Journal of Organizational Change Management, 17*(6), 615–631.

Monge, P., & Contractor, N. (2001). Emergence of communication networks. In F. M. Jablin & L. L. Putnam (Eds.), *The new handbook of organizational communication: Advances in theory, research, and methods* (pp. 440–502). Thousand Oaks, CA: SAGE.

Mumby, D. K. (1987). The political function of narrative in organizations. *Communication Monographs, 54*(2), 113–127.

Mumby, D. K. (1988). *Communication and power in organizations: Discourse, ideology, and domination.* Norwood, NJ: Ablex.

Mumby, D. K. (2001). Power and politics. In F. M. Jablin & L. L. Putnam (Eds.), *The new handbook of organizational communication: Advances in theory, research, and methods* (pp. 585–624). Thousand Oaks, CA: SAGE.

Mumby, D. K. (Ed.). (2011). *Reframing difference in organizational communication studies: Research, pedagogy, practice.* Thousand Oaks, CA: SAGE.

Mumby, D. K. (2013). *Organizational communication: A critical approach.* Thouand Oaks, CA: SAGE.

Mumby, D. K., & Putnam, L. L. (1992). The politics of emotion: A feminist reading of bounded rationality. *Academy of Management Review, 17*(3), 465–486.

Murphy, A. G. (1998). Hidden transcripts of flight attendant resistance. *Management Communication Quarterly, 11*(4), 499–535.

Murphy, A. G. (2003). The dialectical gaze: Exploring the subject-object tension in the performances of women who strip. *Journal of Contemporary Ethnography, 32*(3), 305–335.

Pacanowsky, M., & O'Donnell-Trujillo, N. (1982). Communication and organizational cultures. *The Western Journal of Speech Communication, 46*(2), 115–130.

Perrow, C. (1986). *Complex organizations* (3rd ed.). New York, NY: Random House.

Pfeffer, J. (1981). *Power in organizations.* Cambridge, MA: Ballinger Publishing.

Putnam, L. L. (1983). The interpretive perspective: An alternative to functionalism. In L. L. Putnam & M. Pacanowsky (Eds.), *Communication and organizations: An interpretive approach* (pp. 31–54). Beverly Hills, CA: SAGE.

Putnam, L. L., Bantz, C., Deetz, S., Mumby, D. K., & Van Maanen, J. (1993). Ethnography versus critical theory: Debating organizational research. *Journal of Management Inquiry, 2*(3), 221–235.

Putnam, L. L., Grant, D., Michelson, G., & Cutcher, L. (2005). Discourse and resistance: Targets, practices, and consequences. *Management Communication Quarterly, 19*(1), 5–18.

Putnam, L. L., & Fairhurst, G. T. (2001). Discourse analysis in organizations: Issues and concerns. In F. M. Jablin & L. L. Putnam (Eds.), *The new handbook of organizational communication: Advances in theory, research, and methods* (pp. 78–136). Thousand Oaks, CA: SAGE.

Putnam, L. L., & Pacanowsky, M. (Eds.). (1983). *Communication and organizations: An interpretive approach.* Beverly Hills, CA: SAGE.

Rafaeli, A., & Sutton, R. I. (1988). Untangling the relationship between displayed emotions and organizational sales: The case of convenience stores. *Academy of Management Journal, 31*(3), 461–487.

Rosen, M. (1985). "Breakfast at Spiro's": Dramaturgy and dominance. *Journal of Management, 11*(2), 31–48.

Rosen, M. (1988). You asked for it: Christmas at the bosses' expense. *Journal of Management Studies, 25*(5), 463–480.

Ross, A. (2003). *No-Collar: The humane workpace and its hidden costs.* New York, NY: Basic Books.

Sassen, S. (1998). *Globalization and its discontents: Essays on the new mobility of people and money.* New York, NY: The New Press.

Sassen, S. (2003). Global cities and survival circuits. In B. Ehrenreich & A. Hochschild (Eds.), *Global woman* (pp. 254–274). New York, NY: Metropolitan Books.

Smith, R., & Eisenberg, E. (1987). Conflict at Disneyland: A root metaphor analysis. *Communication Monographs, 54*(4), 367–380.

Suchman, L. A. (2007). *Human-machine configurations: Plans and situated actions* (2nd ed.). Cambridge, England: Cambridge University Press.

Sutton, R. I., & Rafaeli, A. (1990). Busy stores and demanding customers: How do they affect the display of positive emotion? *Academy of Management Journal, 33*(3), 623–637.

Tannenbaum, A. S. (1968). *Control in organizations.* New York, NY: McGraw-Hill.

Taylor, B., & Trujillo, N. (2001). Qualitative research methods. In F. M. Jablin & L. L. Putnam (Eds.), *The new handbook of organizational communication: Advances in theory, research, and methods* (pp. 161–196). Thousand Oaks, CA: SAGE.

Tompkins, P. K. (1987). Translating organizational theory: Symbolism over substance. In F. M. Jablin, L. L. Putnam, K. H. Roberts, & L. W. Porter (Eds.), *Handbook of organizational communication: An interdisciplinary perspective* (pp. 70–96). Newbury Park, CA: SAGE.

Tracy, S. (2000). Becoming a character for commerce: Emotion labor, self-subordination, and discursive construction of identity in a total institution. *Management Communication Quarterly, 14*(1), 90–128.

Tracy, S. (2012). The toxic and mythical combination of a deductive writing logic for inductive qualitative research. *Qualitative Communication Research, 1*(4), 109–141.

Tracy, S., Myers, K., & Scott, C. (2006). Cracking jokes and crafting selves: Sensemaking and identity management among human service workers. *Communication Monographs, 73*(3), 283–308.

Tracy, S., & Tracy, K. (1998). Emotion labor at 911: A case study and theoretical critique. *Journal of Applied Communication Research, 26*(4), 390–411.

Van Maanen, J. (1988). *Tales of the field: On writing ethnography.* Chicago, IL: University of Chicago Press.

Van Maanen, J. (1995). Style as theory. *Organization Science, 6*(1), 133–143.

Virno, P. (2004). *A grammar of the multitude: For an analysis of contemporary forms of life.* Los Angeles, CA: Semiotext(e).

Žižek, S. (1989). *The sublime object of ideology.* London, England: Verso.

Notes

1. Indeed, in the treatment of any one topic, handbooks often lag behind the latest developments in a field, and we're sure this third edition will be no different.

2. Of course, if we embrace Deetz and Eger's (Chapter 1) contention that all research, regardless of methodological proclivities, is a form of social construction, then training in particular methods inevitably leads scholars to focus on particular kinds of questions and see organizing processes in certain ways (e.g., as comprised of causal relationships or as constituted through systems of meaning and sensemaking).

3. However, we recognize that all theory development, to some degree, builds on extant theory work.

SECTION I

Theories of Organizational Communication

Patricia J. Sotirin

Theory holds a privileged place in organizational communication scholarship. Over the past several decades, theoretical debates and developments have shaped the field: paradigm contestations among critical, interpretive, and post-positive metatheoretical perspectives; waves of successive theoretical preoccupations—systems, culture, structuration, the communicative constitution of organization (CCO); and the excitement of emerging, politically charged challenges—feminism, postcolonialism, critical race theory, ecocriticism, disability studies, and more. At the center of this ongoing ferment is the organization←→communication dialectic, continually and productively reconceptualized. As the following chapters demonstrate, the theoretical focus has shifted from the constitution of organizations by communicative processes to sophisticated conceptualizations of dialectic tensions and articulations in which neither organizing nor communicating is primary.

The chapters in this section exude a sense of passion and vitality, embracing the plurality, creativity, and energy of theorizing in organizational communication and advocating for multiple research opportunities and trajectories. Yet at the same time, the power of hegemonic incorporation across this seeming diversity is evident, particularly in the consensus that communication and organization are mutually constitutive. By way of introducing this section of the *Handbook*, I will briefly explore five themes that contribute to this tension between plurality and hegemony: eclecticism, inclusivity, exigency, constitutiveness, and timidity.

Thematic Threads

While each chapter narrates a particular theoretical tradition, together, they display the richly textured multitheoretical plurality of organizational communication studies. A long-celebrated aspect of the field, this multiplicity has, at times, been disciplined into "metatheoretical fiefdoms" (Corman, 2000)—post-positivist, interpretivist, critical theory, social construction, critical realism—whose divergences are debated yet deemed productive (cf. May & Mumby, 2005). Indeed, the field is known for creative hybrids and eclectic conceptual borrowing across diverse philosophical and theoretical sources. One thematic manifestation of this eclecticism is the multidisciplinarity of citations in every chapter; another is that chapter authors often illustrate their particular perspective by citing studies that do not use their perspective!

A second theme is inclusivity, evidenced not just by the number of chapters but by their diversity. There is consensus among the chapter authors that the field looks different now—more robust, more inclusive—than it did in the previous two editions of the *Handbook*. Notably, three chapters open with this observation: the critical perspective (Chapter 4), the feminist perspective (Chapter 5), and the postcolonial perspective (Chapter 6). For these authors, being invited to contribute to this edition marks a notable shift in the inclusivity of the field itself. Ironically, all of the authors in this section might make this claim. In the *New Handbook of Organizational Communication* (published in 2001), there was only one chapter devoted to theory *per se*, "Conceptual Foundations" (Deetz, 2001), and two methodological chapters—one on quantitative and one on qualitative methodologies. That there is no longer a preoccupation with differences in methods testifies to the theoretical maturation of the field; instead, differences are couched at the level of metatheoretical commitments and allegiances and are understood not as paradigmatic blinders but as points of potential conceptual articulation producing new interdisciplinary conjunctions (institutionalism and rhetoric in Chapter 8, mathematical modeling in Chapter 2), theoretical hybrids (liberal poststructuralist feminism in Chapter 5; emancipatory postmodernism in Chapter 4; discursive materialism in Chapter 7), and political commitments (postcolonial commitments in Chapter 6, political relationalities in Chapter 1).

As a third theme, all of the chapter authors set this proliferation of concepts and projects in the context of contemporary exigencies. Each chapter reiterates the need and urgency for theorizing that addresses contemporary events, issues, and conditions—recession and employment crises, global markets, technological innovations, democratic revolutions, institutional changes (family, law, education), the new social contracts, ecological crises, changing organizational forms and practices (virtual, digital, fluid, and permeable), the ontological insecurities and existential angsts of fragmentary subjects; neoliberal relations and discourses—in short, "the precarity of the contemporary economic and political landscape" (Mumby, Chapter 4, p. 102). That the stakes entail the well-being and even the survival of social life is a thematic refrain.

Another thematic point is the import of the 20th-century linguistic turn and the accompanying crisis of representation in the human sciences (see explications in Chapters 1, 4, 7, and 11). The received narrative highlights the emergence of an interpretive view of organizational communication that countered the dominance of a systems-functionalist perspective (Putnam, 1983), resituating communication from a medium of control and sociality to the medium of organizing itself. While some authors wax nostalgic over the lost vitality of this moment, all point to the philosophical, political, and ethical insights that continue to enrich the field. The emergence of well-defined communicative perspectives on CCO (see Chapters 3 and 7) attests to the theoretical maturation of the constitutive view from interpretive construction to communicative flows or text-conversation.

Yet consensus on political commitments, constitutiveness, and inclusivity may also affect (ironically) a hegemonic collapse of difference and a creative timidity. Several chapters include a thematic warning about hegemonic constraints on theorizing. For example, in Chapter 1, Deetz and Eger observe that the claim of constitutiveness has become rote, and as a result, organizational communication scholarship often fails to explicate theoretical presuppositions, conceptual specificities, and political responsibilities. Their metatheoretical framework seeks to reinstate explicit attention to theoretical depth and rigor. Several authors warn that hegemonic consensus may be stifling conceptual creativity and innovative theorizing. For example, in Chapter 4, Mumby suggests that "there is room for the field to be more theoretically adventurous" (p. 117). Where are the contemporary philosophers and social theorists (for example, Latour, Rancière, Delueze, and Nancy) and the radical conceptualizations (for example, object-oriented ontology or governmentality) that are energizing other areas of communication scholarship? In Chapter 5, Ashcraft observes, "The vibrant plurality of feminist theory in our field shows some wear, and our diversity and depth of resources for engagement seem to be dwindling" (p. 145). And in Chapter 2, Poole opines that communication researchers have been timid about moving out of their intellectual comfort zones—set largely in subjective and localized forms of systems analysis—in order to explore the potential of abstract systems modeling. Reviving theoretical rigor, curiosity, and innovation is a critical theme and valuable contribution of these chapters.

Overview of Chapters

In the first chapter, Deetz and Eger appeal for a metatheoretical rapprochement among organizational communication theories. Their framework parses the commitments implicit in the consensus that organizations are communicatively constituted and political. Specifically, they propose a politically attentive relational constructionism (PARC) that plumbs the insights of the linguistic turn to address the complexities, tensions, and generativity of communicative constitutiveness. Deetz and Eger argue that despite the acceptance of some version of constitutiveness, much organizational communication scholarship takes for granted the processes of subject-world co-construction in favor of a focus on products (i.e., particular identities, cultures, interactional forms, organizational conditions) and thus can offer little insight into how co-constitution happens or its implications for creativity and change. They contend that the field would have much more to offer organizational practitioners and larger publics if insights that are drawn on the underlying dynamics of constructionism and power were explicitly addressed in organizational communication scholarship.

To this end, PARC proffers a vocabulary and organizing schema that both addresses constitutive processes and facilitates productive conversations across paradigmatic differences in the field. At the heart of this perspective is the concept of *subject-engagements* within various contexts and relations. Such engagements are *situated* (historically, bodily, socially), *relational* (a manifestation of the encounter, what-is-encountered, and the encountering subject), and *political* (contestable and accomplished under conditions of inequality). In effect, Deetz and Eger articulate an overarching agenda for organizational communication studies: to advance inclusive, emancipatory modes of subject-engagement and to critique relational configurations of inequality and discursive closure. Organizational communication in this perspective is committed to a project of intervention in the constitutive communicative dynamics and political relations of organizational life.

While Deetz and Eger promote metatheoretical rapprochement, Poole opens his chapter (Chapter 2) by acknowledging that systems theory has been the site of deep divisions in the field between empirical-analytic and interpretive traditions. Yet most would agree with Poole that a systems vocabulary "is part of the DNA of organizational communication" (p. 50), and his chapter is a convincing argument for the opportunities that contemporary work in systems theory offers organizational communication scholars. The chapter explicates an illuminating typology of current systems models based on the level of complexity and agency attributed to systems and the degree of representational formality (abstract representation) or informality (verbal or metaphoric representation) (pp. 54–60). Using this typology, Poole finds that considerable organizational communication research to date is concentrated in particular systems approaches—traditionally network research but also structural-functionalism, sense-making, metaphoric uses of systems concepts, and self-organizing systems models. Yet there are exciting lines of organizational communication research that are exploring other systems approaches: for example, cellular automata models applied in research on terrorist networks or crazy systems models adopted to study dysfunctional decision-making systems and unusual organizational routines.

The value of systems thinking is the capacity to address real-world complexities and agential interdependencies in rigorous, testable models, so the lack of organizational communication work drawing on abstract systems models is disappointing. Poole suggests that there may be a residual apprehension among organizational communication scholars about learning arcane mathematical and programming languages; yet new software applications have modified these demands so that formal modeling does not require dauntingly steep learning curves. He urges more abstract systems modeling and more dialogue between formal mathematical and informal textual approaches to expand organizational communication systems theorizing.

It is not the dearth of theorizing and research that troubles the authors of Chapter 3; structuration theory (ST) has been central to organizational communication theory since the 1980s. McPhee, Poole, and Iverson characterize ST as "an invaluable metatheory and research enterprise" for organizational communication (p. 93). Their chapter advances the potency of ST to address theoretical issues critical to organizational communication studies: agency and structure, organizations and society, materiality, and communication as constitutive. In a particularly cogent elaboration, the authors advance six ways that ST accounts for the constitutive processes underlying the communication←→organization dialectic and provides a "necessary basis" for CCO conceptualizations (p. 80). However, they caution that the metatheoretical value of ST can be compromised when alternative theoretical projects attempt to synthesize ST concepts without attending in a rigorous manner to its strengths.

The chapter begins with a succinct explication of ST's distinctive conceptual vocabulary. The heart of the chapter is an expansive review of organizational communication research organized in terms of the Four Flows Model. The Four Flows Model theorizes communication as constitutive by expounding ST precepts as the basis for four fundamental structuring processes: communication integrating people as members (*membership negotiation*), communication structuring the organization (*reflexive self-structuring*), communication contextualizing particular coactions (*activity coordination*), and communication positioning the organization in larger social systems (*institutional positioning*). By locating existing research and identifying new opportunities within these flows, the chapter demonstrates the value of ST as a metatheoretical perspective: its explanatory power, its conceptual resilience, and its capacities for generating creative theorizing.

Mumby (Chapter 4) expounds on the theoretical legacies and strengths of the critical organizational communication tradition. Of particular value is his succinct but illuminating discussion of the linguistic turn and the crisis of representation it invoked. He traces the conceptual shifts that transformed organizational communication "from the study of *communication in organizations* to the study of *the communicative politics of organizing*" (emphasis in original, p. 103). Mumby identifies two theoretical strands that contribute to the critical perspective: a critical, emancipatory strand drawn on a neo-Marxist radical humanism and a postmodern, deconstructive strand drawn on the various "post" social philosophies of discourse and power. There are critical continuities and theoretical sympathies between these two perspectives. Both critique modernist conceptions of organizing, control, and meaning; both entail methodological reflexivity and the critique of taken-for-granted understandings; both conceive of organizations as communicatively constructed; and both critique relations of subordination and control and seek alternative modes of organizing.

Turning to the question, "What's critical about critical studies?", Mumby draws together the commitments of the two strands of critical theorizing. He retains the emancipatory ethos of radical humanism along with critical theory's critique of exploitative relations of production and ideological mystification. Yet his agenda also includes an ethics of affirmation and hope for socially just and democratically inclusive organizing forms and conditions along with deconstructive analyses of oppressive disciplinary regimes and apparatuses of governance. This is an agenda for critical scholarship that is responsive to the crises of the lived world and envisions meaningful possibilities for non-repressive futures.

Ashcraft (Chapter 5) offers a perceptive history of feminist organizational communication theorizing focused on conceptual rather than political distinctions and developments. The five perspectives she identifies are familiar: liberal, cultural, standpoint, post-structuralist, and postmodern feminisms. Usefully, each perspective is introduced by an insightful list of characterizing statements. She finds that the fertile intermingling of multiple feminisms over the past 25 years has assured a valued place for feminist critique in organizational communication. Yet she argues that the productively chaotic conceptual ferment of the first decade of feminist organizational communication has been distilled in the past decade into a stagnating consensus and stability.

Specifically, she warns that postmodern feminism has come to discipline feminist organizational communication studies and enjoys a hegemonic status that suppresses theoretical multiplicities and conceptual energies, often by failing to acknowledge divergent traditions and influences. She urges scholars to destabilize this "discursive closure" by revitalizing alternative feminisms and advancing provocative ideas. For example, she proposes drawing on liberal and post-structuralist elements to comprise a hybrid perspective that engages both gendered sameness and difference, affecting a kind of strategic essentialism marked by calculated irony. In addition, she bemoans the arrested development of standpoint feminism and calls for reviving its emphasis on material conditions while shifting focus from individual experiences in socially constructed groups to analyses of the communicative conditions of group solidarity. She also argues for rigorous theoretical work that attends to intersectionality, redresses the persistence of a gender binary, engages materiality, and deals with the multisited nature of contemporary organizing. By the end of Ashcraft's chapter, feminist organizational communication is poised for a revitalized role as a critical, creative theoretical force.

In Chapter 6, "Postcolonial Approaches," Broadfoot and Munshi pose reflexive challenges to the field guided by two key postcolonial questions: "'How can taken-for-granted dominant organizing and communicative practices and outcomes be undone and redone?' and 'What is the alternative?'" (p. 158). Postcolonial scholarship, albeit multidisciplinary and complicated, provides both critical and creative resources for addressing these questions. Drawing on this scholarship, Broadfoot and Munshi identify three dialectical postcolonial commitments and sites of theorization:

1. Disrupting and reimagining organizing space(s);
2. Resisting colonialist discourse and rethinking organizing practices;
3. Decolonizing thought and reconfiguring organizing forms of knowledge (p. 163).

Each commitment entails a deconstructive and a creative impulse, thus addressing both key questions. For example, in illustrating the first commitment, Broadfoot and Munshi charge that Organizational Communication (capitalized) is mired in an Anglo-American cultural context, heeding neither voices nor rationalities from other contexts. Rather than a strict dichotomy between colonialist and counter-colonialist discourses, practices, and spaces, the authors argue for projects reclaiming local epistemologies, histories, and ethics, and reorganizing inequitable practices in global relations. They hold that ferreting out assumptions of cultural neutrality, universal applicability, and benign dictums in organizational scholarship and management practices is a necessary prerequisite to pluralizing the organizational world and realizing imaginative alternatives.

This latter task is addressed in the final section of the chapter in which Broadfoot and Munshi retheorize the *space in-between* to refigure organizational communication scholars and scholarship in terms of postcolonial translation. Translation is not a faithful reproduction of a colonialist narrative but a creative act of meaning making in a hybrid space. They propose organizational communication scholars as translators, positioned to question the privileging of Western managerial forms of knowledge and practices and to reshape the political conditions of meaning making and authority/authorship through creative infractions. In this imaginative refiguring of organizational communication scholarship, the authors posit the integral role of an ethics of intersubjectivity for postcolonial organizational communication. This vision of decolonizing the field's geographic-historic spaces, practices, and knowledge formations in order to create ways to be (academically) postcolonial realizes the radical potential of the organization←→ communication dialectic.

Chapter 7 takes on CCOs most directly. Authors Brummans, Cooren, Robichaud, and Taylor are key theorists in what has come to be known as the *Montréal School.* Although a constitutive view of communication has prevailed in organizational communication for almost three decades, it is only in the last 15 years that there has been intense theoretical elaboration of the CCO perspective. The authors identify three theoretical projects: the Four Flows Model based on ST (see Chapter 3), the Montréal School approach, and the autopoietic systems model of social theorist Niklas Luhmann. While the chapter explains each project and the differences among them, the major focus is on the Montréal School approach.

The Montréal School model of CCO centers on the conversation-text dialectic, co-orientation through interactions, and translation as recontextualizing meaning from one context into another. Organization is constituted as such through an inductive stitching together of communicative practices that occur through interactions and task co-orientation on different scales. Summarily, (1) from a myriad of situated local communicative practices that organize and bind everyday relations, (2) practices of metaconversations and metanarratives map the meanings of collective experience to articulate the organization as an entity. The (3) textualization of organization involves a further abstraction that constitutes the organization as a collective actor enabled to author its own acts of speech (Brummans et al., Chapter 7, p. 177). But (4) to make itself present as an actor, this reification depends on agents who are authorized to act for the organization and in so acting, claim the authority of the organization, a relation that can be thought of as *ventriloquism.* Translating these representations back into the situated practices of everyday interactions is a final and perhaps the most complicated of the translation steps.

The three CCO models are conceptually quite distinct. For example, while the Four Flows Model emphasizes human agency, the Montréal School admits both human and nonhuman agencies. In Luhmann's systems model, communication is the sole agency of an autopoietic system; that is, a self-constituting and self-reproducing system. For Luhmann, "an autopoietic system produces its own order out of the perturbations that constitute its environment, an environment made of mental, psychic, neurophysiological, and chemical processes" (Brummans et al., Chapter 7, p. 185). In this model, organizations are wholly communicative decisional systems. The differences and debates among these three models evidence the vitality, innovation, and sophistication of CCO theorizing.

In Chapter 8, Lammers and Garcia make a strong case for a mutually beneficial rapprochement between institutional theory and organizational communication studies. Throughout the chapter, they identify conceptual overlaps and organizational communication scholarship that addresses—sometimes unintentionally—institutional theory. Current developments in institutionalism that refine interests in symbolic environments and explore issues of language, rhetorical action, and communicative processes as integral to institutionalization and deinstitutionalization have created clear opportunities for organizational communication scholarship.

Perhaps the most intriguing opportunities for rapprochement are those lines of institutional theorizing that engage the agency-structure tension and deal with the problem of embedded agency, to wit: How do actors change institutions if those very institutions limit their actions and rationality? Studies of institutional logics, institutional entrepreneurship, and institutional work have explored the role of strategic rhetorical action and communicative praxis. In turn, organizational communication studies of the professions might integrate institutional concepts such as co-optation, rational myths, institutional fields and logics, and institutional work. In these examples and throughout their chapter, Lammers and Garcia demonstrate that a rapprochement between institutional theory and organizational communication is not only based on compatible concepts and shared theoretical concerns but has potential to enrich the purview of both fields.

The challenge issued by these eight chapters is to engage theorizing as a creative and conscientious exploration into the complexities of communication←→organization, the exigencies of contemporary life, and the worlds we might imagine to be possible. Together, they advance a mandate for theorizing that is rigorous, relevant, ethical, imaginative, and intellectually bold. The goal, as Ashcraft puts it, is communicative: "to honor and [continually] reinvigorate a collective conversation that contributes to a better world" (p. 146).

References

Corman, S. R. (2000). The need for common ground. In S. R. Corman & M. S. Poole (Eds.), *Perspectives on organizational communication: Finding common ground* (pp. 3–16). New York, NY: Guilford Press.

May, S., & Mumby, D. K. (Eds.). (2005). *Engaging organizational communication theory & research: Multiple perspectives.* Thousand Oaks, CA: SAGE.

Putnam, L. L. (1983). The interpretive perspective: An alternative to functionalism. In L. L. Putnam & M. Pacanowsky (Eds.), *Communication and organizations: An interpretive approach* (pp. 31–54). Beverly Hills, CA: SAGE.

CHAPTER 1

Developing a Metatheoretical Perspective for Organizational Communication Studies

Stanley A. Deetz and Elizabeth K. Eger

Ongoing rapid social and organizational changes put great pressure on researchers to continually develop new and useful concepts to match the complex interactions characteristic of diverse workplaces. These changes are many, deep, and much discussed from the political arena to the popular press to organizational stakeholder meetings to shop floors to kitchen tables to the academy (Grant, 2011). Globalization, pluralism, interdependence, new technologies, and various occupational developments are likely to continue to generate changes in our relations to others, how the world is seen, how people do their jobs, and human interaction in organizations and between organizations and external communities. These changes and challenges provide numerous places and spaces of entrée for communication researchers. Additionally, they pose questions about the relevance of the research practices, conceptions, and teaching of organizational communication.

In response, those researching organizational communication have important choices to make in how to move forward. One response would be increasingly more ecumenical fragmentation. This would support a separate but equal world where different approaches are followed and disparate topics studied with little reflection on larger theoretical issues or attempts at integration. Organizational communication studies could become a kind of food fair where we congregate as Teflon-coated cosmopolitans, stopping only to sample the parts of the field with which we identify and admire, ignoring or refuting the rest. In fact, in our relatively comprehensive review of the field's top-tier organizational communication journal articles (e.g., *Management Communication Quarterly, Journal of Applied Communication, Communication Monographs*) and edited volumes from the past decade, we found considerable evidence that ecumenical fragmentation is occurring. We believe that this ultimately reduces the impact and innovation of organizational communication studies.

An alternative to our current approach might begin by considering a more rigorous set of metatheoretical reflections that detail a different background paradigm. If agreement could be reached and past work could be rethought within a new paradigm, this could be used as a way to account for the place of different studies, topics, and approaches and interpret them together into a growing understanding of organizational communication. We would like to engage in such metatheoretical reflections here. We believe that even if we fail to offer a convincing case for a new background paradigm, much can be learned about the field in the process. The goal is not a grand integrative theory but rather a way of attending to and talking about complexity and tensions that can overcome the inevitably situated partiality of any particular theoretical or research practice orientation.

The fear is, of course, that any overarching approach can become a kind of imperialism and a disguised way to elevate certain studies at the expense of others. Certainly, endless critical reflection is essential to guard against this, but the process can also be liberating in that it challenges deep assumptions in existing approaches that are not being currently examined. And we consider this less of an overarching approach than an explication of an organic terrain already widespread in the field.

We believe that both natural and social science in general, and organizational communication in particular, have come to agree on some form of constructionism. This does not mean that constructionism is always accounted for or clearly practiced any more so than the common acceptance that the world is round means that we will take that into account when we measure a room. But what we take to be the case matters, as does any decision to set that aside for purposes of convenience. This is the origin of the many jokes in physics about a "spherical cow" (see Harte, 1988, for example), the punch line being "I know how much hay the cow will consume if we assume the cow is spherical and resides in a vacuum." It takes nothing away from even the most restricted quantitative study to recognize all the constructionist processes in instrumentation and the construction of events into data. Yet recognizing the constructionist activities enables comparison of findings, better applications, and potential integration of differences (see Deetz, 2000, for development). This makes knowledge relational but hardly relativist nor mere opinion. Constructionism, like tolerance, is not advancing one perspective over others, but rather the guarantee of a space for discussion.

From this consensus on some form of constructionism, this essay will build a specific constructionist metatheory of organizational communication. In so doing, we develop how it could allow for integrative translation and interpretation across studies without diminishing difference and maintain a view of the world as fundamentally based on conflict and tension rather than consensus and order. The notion of construction and tension as fundamental is in no way new to organizational communication scholars. But what does it mean to say that organizations are communicatively constructed in spaces of contested meaning or that communicating and organizing are mutually constitutive? Despite the consensus that such claims enjoy among organizational communication scholars, our review of the past decade's scholarship in the field indicates that not only are such conceptions not clearly theorized but their very popularity has also created a danger of muddling and even undermining their significance. This is especially the case given the general failure to either reflect on the philosophical grounding of constructionism and constitutivism or to theoretically engage with and develop these implications.

We advance here a metatheoretical perspective that resituates the communicative construction of organization in the tradition of the linguistic turn and addresses the relational nature, conditions, and products of constitutivism. We advance relational constructionism and tension filled co-constitution as a metatheoretical framework for a communicative understanding of organizations and organizing. This framework promises to create a way of conversing among the disparate approaches to organizational communication and provide a theoretically rich vocabulary for developing the implications of constructionism and constitutivism for the field. We expand on a politically attentive relational constructionism (PARC) that affords an alternative framework for organizing the study and field of organizational communication (Deetz, 2009). We will show that while *communication as constitutive* has become a routine way that constructionism has been addressed, its development has shown insufficient appreciation for the complexity of human interaction in the constitution of human experience and social institutions. As such, it has remained unable to detail processes on construction across aspects of organizational life. And it has overlooked core political concerns regarding equality, reciprocity in constitutive processes, and the difference between more and less generative forms of interaction.

PARC allows for a deeper analysis that can display how research is produced rather than simply reviewing results from different research programs and calling the field eclectic. By developing this view, we advance a useful vocabulary for talking across different programs of research that engages essential issues underlying all of them. We argue that a constructionist metatheory provides a useful way to keep a place for even nonconstructionist orientations while investigating their logic and consequences. We will demonstrate that a relational constructionist view can benefit the field by returning to a deeper account of construction and offering a heuristic model that demonstrates the connections among various issues of interest to the field and the larger communities it serves. This orientation will offer insights into the identity of organizational communication, its contested histories, the (in)coherence of contemporary research, and the potential generativity of its struggles. We will end by looking at how relevancy and engaged scholarship impact the way we think about these conceptions and this research.

How Do We Organize Organizational Communication?

The complexities of conceptualizing organizational communication and the challenges of offering a metatheory of the field partly arise because different conceptualizations offer *very* different metatheories. Our struggle with looking at organizational communication theories and perspectives, then, comes from the contested nature of what organizational communication as a study is, means, does, includes, and excludes to those who have the power to write or define the field. Trying to produce any organizing scheme of these competing discourses accounting for different theoretical conceptions, methodological preferences, and value commitments is filled with difficulties. Each research program may even use different ways of comparing and contrasting itself with other programs. These different perspectives have political consequences. A political attentiveness makes clear that scholars should rightfully ask of any research program the following questions: To solve what and whose problems? To what and whose ends? Whose meanings, experiences, hopes, and dreams are of interest? Whose and what type of knowledge is this? How should organizations function? How well do they function? What do humans become by virtue of having organizations and organizing processes such as these?

In the last edition of the *Handbook*, Deetz (2001) argued that organizational communication is most often delimited from other areas of study in two ways: (1) as a phenomenon and (2) as a self-described community of people. He went on to argue that communication can, in a third sense, be seen as a way to describe and explain organizations. In the same way that psychology, sociology, or economics can be thought of as capable of explaining organizational processes, communication might also be viewed as a distinct mode of explanation or way of thinking about organizations (Deetz, 1994; Pearce, 1989; Putnam & Nicotera, 2009). We will work to show how human interaction explains organizational phenomena, including those that are most often called *communication(s)*. This position is recursive in that both the production of the field as an academic unit and organizing organizational communication as a distinct phenomenon are themselves discursive accomplishments. Communication as an explanation, rather than as a phenomenon or community, is what makes a communicative approach to studying organizations unique. This leads to a distinct contribution to the study of organizations and the individuals connected to them (see also McClellan & Deetz, 2009).

Communication theory, then, can be about ways to explain the production of social structures, psychological states, member categories, difference, knowledge, power, and so forth rather than being conceptualized as simply one phenomenon among these others in organizational life. From such a perspective, the interest is not in theories of organizational communication but in producing a communication theory (or theories) of organizations (Deetz, 1973b, 1994). This in no way denies the existence of things called *structures*, *roles*, *norms*, *knowledge*, *networks*, and *information flow* nor minimizes the benefits of temporarily holding them as stable and studying them as such; rather, it highlights the recognition that these areas were developed, deployed, and rendered significant in complex interaction systems. This recognition is core to communication studies, yet relatively few organizational communication scholars have approached research in this way, and instead, psychological or social-cultural explanations have prevailed. The presence of consideration of constructionism and constitutivism call for more explicit consideration of construction processes in organizations and organizational research and give a stronger place for openness in construction.

Constructionism and Constitutivism in Organizational Communication

Construction and *constitutive* are messy, contested terms. Probably most important terms are. We will not try to sort out all the different usages. In a basic way, the term *construction* appeals to the continental phenomenological tradition as brought forward by sociology. And *constitutive* appeals to the Anglo-conventionalist tradition as brought forward more often by linguists in the concept of the illocutionary force of an utterance. Both traditions try to address the conditions under which something can count as being something else. We will not carefully distinguish the two, rather always referencing the ways "being as" occurs—that is, the fundamental linguisticality of life.

Up until the past 10 to 15 years, most scholarly interest has been in constructionism. Constructionism has been in the organizational communication literature for at least 40 years (e.g., Hawes, 1974). In taking up such a social constructionist approach, organizational communication scholars have tended to focus on the products of construction rather than the processes of construction. This probably largely arose from the popularity of social constructionism as articulated by Berger and Luckmann (1966) that heightened a concern with the product and its institutionalization rather than the process. Generally, attention has been focused on interaction products such as organization, boundaries, culture, identities, structures, and institutions.

Where process has been taken up, it has tended to remain conceptualized in psychological terms, if systemic. From at least Weick (1979) forward, many of those studying organizational communication have seen *organizing* as a better conception than *organization* to capture process over product, as it also eradicates some of the limitations of the transmission framing of our field that seems to inherently contextualize communication as a phenomenon in a contained organization. Weick built the concept of organizing around two key subconcepts: sensemaking and systemic relations. Sensemaking was largely considered to be a psychological or cognitive process of meaning making, and systemic relations were relatively functional relations that existed among the various objects and events in organizational life. Both have provided a heuristic analytic framework for looking at the emergent process aspects of organizational life but rarely have dislodged native theories of organizational communication.

Most of the central lay conceptions of communication and organizational life continued, and they continue to arise from a person-centered or physiological metatheory. Communication difficulties are expressed in terms of influence failures and misunderstandings. *Knowledge* is largely understood as *information*, and agency is located in the person. *Communication* implicitly is viewed as what happened from the personal to the social rather than as the social processes of producing the personal. In contrast, we argue that the sensibility of these conceptions is a product of specific relational construction processes that often remain unrecognized and is consequential. Personal agency, for example, as Laclau and Mouffe (1985) developed, is a necessary illusion to keep hidden the politically laden nature of various constructions.

Nonetheless, since the early 1980s, scholars in communication departments as well as a large number of non-U.S. scholars and some researchers from other academic units have continued to develop a form of product-centered constructionism focusing on organizations as complex discursive formations where discursive practices are both in organizations and produced from them. This conception was adopted most often in structuration, critical, and feminist theories to look at a particular aspect of organizational life, such as identity, power, or rules. During the past decade or so, the concept of the CCO has claimed this space. Allow us to develop the Communicative Constitution of Organization (COO) before we turn to develop a PARC as a more fundamental, radical alternative that will place CCO as a particular theory within this more comprehensive metatheory.

Communicative Constitution of Organizations

Over the past decade, CCO has risen to popularity in the field (see Brummans, Cooren, Robichaud, & Taylor, Chapter 7). With its growing popularity, CCO has, at times, become a catchall term for all sorts of constructionist and constitutive positions. Often, the term *constitution* remains undertheorized and used interchangeably with words such as *constructs*, *produces*, and *creates*, which may differ much in agency and causal force. Sometimes the focus seems to be on something more akin to *constitutive conditions* or on *co-constitution,* although the *co* remains unclear.

Communication as constituting organizations (or organizing) is an ongoing conversation in our discipline, independent of the moniker or metaphor most in vogue (Putnam & Boys, 2006). In the introductory chapter to Putnam and Nicotera's (2009) edited collection *Building Theories of Organization: The Constitutive Role of Communication*, Putnam, Nicotera, and McPhee observe that "for decades, organizational communication scholars have claimed in our scholarship, pedagogy, and practice that *organizations are communicatively constituted*" (2009, p. 1). These authors historicize CCO as being sorted out and (re)-imagined in various interdisciplinary conversations on organization studies and tie CCO's roots to theories ranging from speech act theory to structuration and paradigms from phenomenology to critical theory.

Ashcraft, Kuhn, and Cooren (2009) situate CCO as connected to two strains of prior research in organizational communication. The first is what they term *embedded strains*—similar to some research on organizational culture (Eisenberg & Riley, 2001; Putnam, 1983), power (Deetz & Mumby, 1990), and networks (McPhee & Corman, 1995)—where "their constitutive claims are not their primary focus; hence, they are seldom recognized as CCO 'proper'" (Ashcraft et al., 2009, p. 9). The second encompasses *explicit strains* that "take up the CCO question directly and are overtly marked with the CCO label" (p. 9), including both structuration views of CCO (McPhee & Iverson, 2009; McPhee & Zaug, 2000) and the Montréal School text and conversation orientations to the CCO (Cooren, 1999; Taylor & Van Every, 2000).

Importantly, CCO researchers aim to, and specifically focus on, explicating the relationship between *organization* and *communication* without reducing one term to an unnecessary abstraction in the process (Putnam et al., 2009). CCO research also builds upon and adds to interdisciplinary conversations about the importance of a focus on materiality in communication studies and works to further theorize it in organization studies (Ashcraft et al., 2009). In many ways, then, CCO scholars join and enliven what Ashcraft et al. (2009) term "*Previous* Efforts to Theorize Communication as Pivotal, not Peripheral" (p. 10, emphasis added) for organizational theory writ large.

Furthermore, at times, CCO has become a catchy label without fully unpacking what scholarship on its behalf hopes and claims to uncover. What, exactly, does CCO mean to scholars and for the field as a growing area of emphasis? Despite the new and seemingly uniform moniker, differing perspectives on and conflicting conceptions about understanding communication as constituting organizations exist. A troubling aspect of this heterogeneity is clear as Putnam and Nicotera (2009) focus the aim of their edited volume to better explore what is meant by those claiming CCO research. As the introductory chapter explains, "Namely, we say that communication is constitutive of organizations without fully understanding what this means, conceptually or empirically" (Putnam, Nicotera, & McPhee, 2009, p. 5).

The upshot is that both constitutiveness and constitution in organizing as a crucial forms of organizational communication theorizing are in danger of being muddled and even undermined due to the consensus they enjoy. This consensus, perhaps ironically, contributes to a general failure among organizational communication scholars to reflect on its philosophical grounding in the linguistic turn and to theoretically engage with and develop the implications of the relations of construction and constitutiveness. We begin to assuage this need by offering a focus on organizing as constituted by relational constructionism.

Co-Constitution and a Politically Attentive Relational Constructionism (PARC)

As we briefly introduced, most discussions of construction and constitution have focused on the manufactured products rather than unpacking processes by which *something comes to count as something*. In doing this, the character and politics of the processes are often left unexplored. This has contributed to the common misunderstanding of constructionism as supporting subjectivity and relativity rather than what will be developed here as *relationality*. Here, we wish to return to the more basic descriptions of production processes. This will show that many of the oppositions that have dominated organizational communication writings such as symbolic/material, subjective/objective, qualitative/quantitative, and so on, are produced, rather than inevitable. Treating them as real may be responsible for our ecumenically separate but equal approach to difference.

Husserl's phenomenology (no matter how greatly distorted over time) initially set in play an approach that could enable a discussion in the space that preceded the various produced dualisms without giving up a system based in fundamental conflict and tensions. To abbreviate a century of work, the linguistic turn of Heidegger took Husserl's fundamental relational co-constructionism and described the endless constitutive conditions of something *being-seen-as/being-as* something else (for review of these moves in relation to communication studies, see Deetz, 1973a, 1992, 2003). This turn in thought made possible the various, and often differing, forms of critical, postmodern, and post-structuralist thought. Without an understanding of the common turn, many of these conflicting forms of thought highlight their programmatic differences rather than the common path they enunciate in different ways.

Dualism, for example, separates meaning from the world; hence, the world as produced is treated as a set of objects. The stability is necessary for *representation*. But if representation is seen as only possible because of reproductive processes, an understanding of the embedded earlier production and its fluid contestability is reclaimed. This productivity makes clear that while reproduction is common, meaning is always potentially emergent and contestable. Language is not simply of the symbolic and does not name objects in the world; language is core to the process of co-constituting the indeterminate and ambiguous internal, social, and external world into specific objects and events. Understanding the emergence, potential contestation, and open process systems of particular productions is central, if at times implicit, in all organizational studies grounded in communication.

Much of this has been widely discussed, but the full implications have not often been seen in mainstream work in the field. The social construction conception often still renders invisible the productive direct encounter in a material situation and focuses on reproductions as people are recruited or interpellated into ready-at-hand modes of encounter and construction processes. The focus has been on the constraints experienced rather than on new subject possibilities and the indeterminacy of the material world encountered. The products as constituted—whether they were feelings, identities, rules, or knowledge—became accepted as existing in organizations and, similarly, often became the objects of analysis for organizational communication scholars. The material part of the co-construction got lost.

CCO research, for example, is often grounded in a constructionism that focuses on only one half of a co-constitutive process. Relational constructionism, in contrast, is not a one-way street from the subject to the world but draws attention to the relational aspect of construction and how particular, already created subject/object relational configurations become institutionalized and treated as naturally occurring. The focus is on the moments of co-constitution and the conditions making particular constructions possible as well as the products of this process. Allow us to elaborate.

A relational constructionist view shows that experience arises from relationships *in* the world rather than people looking *at* a fixed, *a priori* world or constituting an empty world. People are not separate from the materiality of the world, others, and institutions. Individuals are always, first and foremost, in the world with real bodies, projects, and activities. The world is always seen/produced from somewhere through some sense or sense-extending equipment, but the world is not without form and demands. The manner of engagement and that which is engaged are both part of the constitutive process, something being-as something.

Any particular way of engaging the world has traditionally been called a *subject position*. Unfortunately, such a term evokes a static image and sometimes implies merely a point of view. To keep the relational connection and active conception more in the forefront, we will refer to the manner of acting in and attending to the world as a *subject-engagement*. A subject-engagement is always realized in relation to something. It is half of a relational co-constitution. A relational construction focuses on the relational product of an engagement and the not-yet-determined stuff engaged—or what we will term the "what" for the lack of a good word for real but not-yet-brought-to-determination internal, social, and external elements. This not-yet-brought-to-determination set of elements has qualities that can be brought to a fixed state in many different ways. But the *what* cannot be left out, or construction becomes abstract, overstated, and without material objection.

Subject-engagements become routinized, sedimented, and institutionalized in practices, language, objects, technologies, and organizational forms. Berger and Luckmann (1966) highlighted this stability in the world at the expense of attending to originality, an emphasis that often prevailed in the field. But subject-engagements are not personal, psychological, or biographic nor fixed in any simple way; rather, they are historically produced, bodily specified, and socially shared ways of engagement. They are socially available ways of attending to the world, but their physical, social, and historical natures are often overlooked; hence, they are experienced as transparent and as one's own experience. Thus those who focus on the products rather than processes of constitution overlook the politics of their formation. A PARC metatheory keeps the processes as well as the politics of the process clearly in focus as products are considered.

PARC and Essential Issues of Organizational Life

A metatheory grounded in communication has to account for the products—the *whats* that various organizational communication theories are about—by taking seriously how the not-yet-determined both effects and comes to be shaped in determination. A PARC metatheory is a way to provide an account of and place for (rather than accept or reject) work in the field conducted from a variety of perspectives as well as to provide a vocabulary for talking about essential organizational life issues based in a communication metatheory (Deetz, 2009; McClellan & Deetz, 2012).

The phenomena that are the usual focus of organizational life and studies of it are outcomes of constitutive relational processes. The relational constructions arising in the encounter of a subject-engagement and that which is engaged make claims *about* the encountered and claims *on* the person embodying the subject-engagement. A claim on and about is the most fundamental relational manifestation. For analytic purposes, organizational life can be considered a constellation of six different types of relational constructions, each based on the "what" that is encountered as a subject-engagement moves in the world. We suggest six relational configurations based on the way the subject engages and is engaged by (1) the inner world, (2) the world of specific others, (3) the world of general others, (4) the external world of elements, (5) the past/future vortex, and (6) the presence of limited resources and interdependence. These are six essential constructions that compose organizational life. Each makes claims on organizational members (and those who study organizing and organizations), and organizational members (and those who study organizing and organizations) make claims about each.

Each of these six kinds of claims could be disagreed with or contested in interactions with others and events. Because (1) they can be disputed, (2) they have implications for the choices we make together, and (3) they were created under conditions of power inequality, we can say that each type of claim provides for a distinct set of politics. As we have explained, relational constructions are outcomes of the politics of their production. All constructions happen in real conditions of inequality, specific historical circumstances, and practical needs. These politics can be named based on the relational issue each is about: (1) *the politics of authenticity* (relation to the inner world), (2) *the politics of identity and recognition* (relation with specific others), (3) *the politics of order* (relation to general others), (4) *the politics of truth* (relation to the external world), (5) *the politics of life narratives* (relation to past/future vortex), and (6) *the politics of distribution* (relation to interdependence and scarcity).

PARC offers a vocabulary that draws attention to underlying communication processes in these politics. Further, these processes can be discussed based on interaction rights, and questions of organizational success can be based on measures derived from different stakeholder perspectives. The political attention allows a vocabulary to describe the different ways power enters into the construction process. In the current context of both corporate and other organizations, interaction processes that generate innovation and creativity are essential for meeting the conflicting goals of multiple stakeholders. Not only is constitutive process itself of importance but so too is developing generativity. Our liberal democratic heritage that grounds much of our native communication theories cannot provide this. Interaction processes differ greatly in terms of the relative degrees of space for the contesting of claims and the invention of new meanings. A vocabulary is needed to discuss how difference can be made productive and how the forces of closure hinder that. PARC provides a vocabulary for this more generative form of democracy.

Consider the following terms we and other researchers have used to theorize the production and contestation of claims: (1) *unwitting consent* (a recognition that organizational members accept as their own feelings, knowledge, and concepts of rightness that are products of unknown construction processes), (2) *systematically distorted communication* (the produced systemic and structural features of interaction processes that arbitrarily constrain attention to parts of the environment and favor some people's knowledge and understanding over others), (3) *discursive closure* (the specific processes by which certain conflicts are suppressed and important discussions not had), or (4) *reciprocity* (interaction systems that assure not just that people have their say but that all positions have had an equal opportunity to influence a decision). Each of these terms help members attend to very real parts of organizational life where core communication conceptions are ignored. They offer an important heuristic when we turn these terms and their issues on ourselves in considering how we construct and conduct studies of organizational communication. In the following sections of the chapter, we wish to develop how each of these politics and their communicative constitutions underlie current work in organizational communication.

Politics of Authenticity

Emotions in organizational life and affective states have long been of interest to organizational communication scholars and members. This interest ranges from concerns with motivation and satisfaction to the presence of the "private" in organizations. Hochschild's work in the late 1970s, widely distributed through her popular book, *The Managed Heart* (2003), set in place much of the field's explicit discussion of emotions. Her vivid descriptions of the relation between social management and spontaneous feelings posed the question of authenticity in a specific way. Mumby and Putnam (1992) extended the analysis with a much more nuanced and communication-based consideration of emotions and their place and management in the workplace. We can state this more generally as *the politics of authenticity*. Questions include the following: What feelings are present and possible? Whose feelings are these? How are they gendered? What are the material and interactive practices required for such feelings to arise? How are feelings and the production of feelings distributed and institutionalized? Is subject-engagement institutionalized in ways that reduce affective conflict and introduce unwitting consent and cultural management? What would be required for reopening the production process so as to reform experience in relation to specific contemporary conditions?

Much research in organizational communication has focused on emotions and emotional labor as well as related thematics (see Miller, Chapter 23, in this volume and the review of emotion literature by Miller, Considine, & Gardner, 2007). For example, Tracy (2000) explored the politics of authenticity in workers' emotion work through the ways in which cruise staff employees became "characters for commerce" in the service of creating pleasurable experiences for travelers on luxury cruise ships. Morgan and Krone (2001) theorized negotiations and improvisations of emotional performances in cardiac caregiving work. Eger's recent research on employees of an international innovation incubator considered the ways in which not only individual employees' emotions are managed but also how entire organizational moods are performed in what she theorized as "mood manufacture" (Eger Rush, 2012). In her extensive ethnography, she found that mood manufacture was used by employees and management to mitigate the uncertainties of innovation work. For example, staff shared cultural and structural rules about how to construct a spatial container for innovation and how to sustain the "mood of innovation" at all hours of the day and night. These employees, like some organizational communication scholars, assumed that feelings enabling innovative work could be controlled for the staff and could be manufactured in entrepreneurial visitors to the incubator. But they seemed unable to articulate the deeper politics of constitution, even when aware of them. Similarly, in addressing such politics, Benson and Kirsch (2010) explored the colonization of emotions, theorizing about capitalism and the politics of resignation as they evaluated corporate responses to societal critique using case studies of harm industries such as mining and tobacco corporations. But even work such as this often fails to detail the interaction processes by which the colonization of emotions occurs.

A PARC account of the relational conditions of the production of the interior does not deny or diminish studies of these internal products and relations; rather, it can add depth and detail to them. The correlation of satisfaction or happiness to various organizational conditions is of great importance. But such studies may uncritically accept the mere existence of these relational products rather than investigate them. Following Becker (1953) and Harré (1986; Harré & van Langenhove, 1999), specific emotions and affective states can usefully be thought of as requiring both a set of engaged practices that produce physiological responses and discursive practices that situate the subject-engagement in relation to the not-yet-determined physiological responses that shape further physiological responses. Focusing on relational construction enables an investigator to hold these products constant, understand the processes by which such constancy can occur, and investigate the communicative co-constitution of them.

The politics of authenticity focuses questions on the subject-engagement in relation to the inner world. PARC details the processes of formation in organizational life, providing an analytic of production processes and an assessment of the quality of the politics. This allows researchers to pose both surface and deeper questions. The issue is not simply about how organizational actors feel and what those feelings correlate to, but how is it that they feel that way? What is the nature of the world in which those feelings are possible? What are the means by which they are expressed?

Politics of Identity and Recognition

As with the inner world, subject-engagement with not-yet-determined others happens throughout organizational life. The engagement co-constitutes an identity for self and others. Organizational communication has long recognized the need for inquiry and scholarship on the topic of identity.

Organizational communication scholars' interest in the encounters of "the world of specific others" continues to be a central thematic in the communicative construction of organizing (see Cheney, Christensen, & Dailey, Chapter 28). This focus is appropriate, given the increasing fluidity and fragility of identity, the often unobtrusive power of communicative processes of identification in organizing (Cheney, 1983; Tompkins & Cheney, 1985), and the colonization of selfhoods (Deetz, 1992; Wieland, Bauer, & Deetz, 2009). The *politics of identity and recognition* thus pose the following research questions: Who are the people in this interaction, organization, and occupation? What are their implied rights and responsibilities with these identities? How strongly do individuals identify with a specific identity? What would challenge that identity? How are identities institutionalized?

Sister fields such as critical management studies have charted these constructionist views on identity and have moved toward a more relational constructionist view. For example, Thomas (2009) reviewed the "dynamic interconnections between (a) identity regulation at work; (b), resistant and resisting identities; and (c) the crafting of identities in contexts of power and knowledge" (p. 170). In works such as this, difference and reclaiming of tension are demonstrated as an active part of the co-constitution process.

Recognizing difference and how it is institutionalized allows us to investigate organizing processes of the communicative construction of identities in order to interrogate this systemic work and production. Exemplary in this regard are organizational communication studies of the professional as both a revered organizational discourse and an identity accessible only to certain privileged occupations, workers, and bodies (Ashcraft & Flores, 2003; Ashcraft & Mumby, 2004; Cheney & Ashcraft, 2007; Nadesan & Trethewey, 2000; Schilt, 2010; Scott, 2011; Trethewey, 1999, 2000). For example, Rumens and Kerfoot's (2009) research on gay male professionalism queries the constitution of the professional identity as the authors challenge constitutive conditions in the United Kingdom—as a sovereign state, the U.K. has more gay-friendly work and life policies than other states, yet the authors found that despite this purported lesbian, gay, bisexual, and transgender friendliness, gay men still struggled with and were unable to have equal access to being "the professional" at work, as they were subjected to heteronormative hegemony. The meanings and influences of work(er) identities continue to captivate our field and offer an important space of furthering the development of the politics of identity.

The Politics of Order

Whereas the politics of identity focuses on subject-engagement with self and other, the politics of order entails the relationship with general others characterized by productions of rules and norms in organizing. Contemporary interest in these productions arises in connection with increased pluralism and intercultural contact as well as with legitimacy and compliance concerns in much of organizational life. Contemporary societies are often characterized by the decline of accepted authority, questions regarding the legitimacy of rules, community surveillance, and reduced voluntary compliance. The *politics of order* focuses on the following questions: What behaviors, actions, and ways of talking are considered appropriate? What norms and rules support these activities? Do individuals consider these norms and rules to be legitimate and applicable to them? How are rules and norms institutionalized?

Such questions continue to be at the heart of the issues of rationality (Mumby & Stohl, 1996) in organizational communication theory and the ways in which order is relationally constructed and becomes rationalized as natural, as in classic theorizing about bureaucracy and its ordering systems as an ideal organizational form (Simon, 1957; Weber, 1947). The rebirth of institutional theory can be seen as a response to questions in this arena. However, much of the work on institutional theory and institutionalization starts with these relational productions of self and general others as given (see Lammers & Garcia, Chapter 8).

Though not often highlighted, issues of relational construction are known. Some institutional theory explores organizations as a stage for institutional rules and the "way things are done" (Meyer & Rowan, 1977) and an important arena for considering the politics, logics, and processes of institutional messages as patterns of beliefs and rules (Lammers, 2011). The range of institutional research considers organizing issues from intentionality of messages (Barley, 2011) to organizational discourse perspectives that question, "How can processes of communicating serve to institutionalize?" (p. 191) to the discursive formation and maintenance of institutions by communication (Suddaby, 2011). Across these research interests, the questions that occupy institutional theorizing can be understood as addressing the politics of order.

The Politics of Truth

Perhaps the most significant, though sometimes implicit, concern of this metatheory chapter is how we as organizational scholars are also positioned in relation to the external world of elements (including people) and the politics of truth that organize our field and the research and teaching we conduct. These concerns are about knowledge claims and the implicit conceptions framing the ways we endlessly attend to, think through, and talk about the world.

Most in the field have long accepted some form of the social construction of knowledge (Corman, 2000). Phrased in terms of relational constructionism, our instruments and forms of observation are particular forms of subject-engagements coproducing in those engagements relatively stable objects out of the open-to-determination elements in the world. Our consensus on the means of knowledge production provides a type of objectivity but frequently at the cost of overlooking the constitutive process and the politics therein (just as in the natural sciences; see Deetz, 2000, for a more complete development). But overall, the field seems much more aware of the relational construction and constitutive processes in regard to knowledge than in regard to other claims.

From the communicative metaperspective taken here, the core process in understanding alternative research programs is to understand their particular manner of subject-engagement. Understanding this includes identification of the object distinctions they make, whose language is used in making those object distinctions, what and whose values and interests are carried with those distinctions, and how the conflicting descriptions of the world are handled as well as exploring their processes of self-justification and distinction from alternative research programs.

Research inquiring into *the politics of truth* confronts organizational life with several knowledge questions: What is worth knowing about and what is ignored, given that organizational "ignorance" is often more about what is ignorance than believing untrue things? What is true? How and by whom is truth to be claimed, verified, and disagreement adjudicated? How is knowledge connected to action? Inquiry into the politics of truth leads researchers to explore such issues that are deeply embedded in the construction and constitution of products such as the accountant's report, knowledge capture systems, and data used to make decisions.

Over the years, various overviews of the discourse of organizational communication itself have attempted to get at constitutive practices. The best-known overviews have focused on the metaphors of organizational communication studies. The metaphor imagery calls forth different ways of viewing, understanding, and problematizing organizational communication. Putnam and her colleagues have framed organizational communication research perspectives through the lens of metaphor in multiple iterations (Putnam & Boys, 2006; Putnam, Phillips, & Chapman, 1999).

Knowledge production and organizing is extensively theorized in Canary and McPhee (2011) and Kuhn (Chapter 19). Kuhn focuses on the politics of truth, especially in using practice theory, to explore how we come to recognize organizing practices and the complexities of organizational knowledge production. In an application of knowledge and practice theory, Murphy and Eisenberg's (2011) theorizing of knowledge in health care organizations as collectively routinized, emergent, and political illustrates the messiness of knowledge work in the applied context of emergency room medicine, where understanding truths and meanings can become life-or-death situations. Reckwitz (2002) theorizes knowledge as cultural production and social order as "embedded in collective cognitive and symbolic structures, in a 'shared knowledge' which enables a socially shared way of ascribing meaning to the world" (pp. 245–246). Similarly, Kogurt and Zander (1996) view organizations themselves as collectives of knowledge, just as Orlikowski (2002) uses "the lens of organizational knowing to understand how members of global production development organizations generate and sustain knowledgability in their distributed operations" (p. 249).

The politics of truth shows that all facts are really artifacts, outcomes of specific social processes of production. The question is not whether knowledge is true, but what we form knowledge about and whose knowledge comes to count as true. This is a question that organizational communication scholars have scrutinized. For example, Ashcraft and Mumby (2004) theorize a feminist communicology of organizational communication, including the ways in which organizing (en)genders discourse and how discourse (en)genders organization. Ashcraft (Chapter 5) and Broadfoot and Munshi (2007; Chapter 6) herein discuss feminist theorizing and postcolonial theorizing respectively to consider these politics of truth in the academy and our field as well as in organizations. The politics of truth invite inquiry at multiple levels in the field, from metatheory to methodologies to practical findings for organizational audiences.

The Politics of Life Narratives

Organizational life also entails a set of constituted, situated notions of the good and beautiful. A subject engages a constant vortex of the past-future, both of which move in front of such engagements. This movement is constituted through narratives of connected re-understanding of past events in light of movement toward a future. Relational constructionism considers how subject-engagements are directed in the world toward some future. This relationship is often best shown in narratives that give an account of ideals and how they are achieved, often as stories of the good life or various forms of tragedy and melodrama.

The *politics of life narratives* poses the following questions: How does the world work for members? What would a good and beautiful future look like? What do they want for themselves in it? What is their preferred or expected way of getting there? What do their favorite stories reveal about how things work? How is the sense of how things move from the past to the future institutionalized?

Certainly, the politics of narratives is readily observed in contemporary scholarship. Lyotard (1979) described grand narratives, which serve to manage culture in ways that support dominant subject-engagements and benefit particular people. As societies became more pluralistic, grand narratives were challenged (e.g., "his-tory" is challenged by "her-story"). The future and the past have become contested, reducing the power and naturalness of the grand narratives and affecting competition among group-based smaller narratives. This does not mean that larger discourses do not exist but that they exist in contestable spaces. Organizational life is filled with various, often competing social narratives—sometimes called big "D" Discourses and everyday small "d" discourses that pull on Discourses—in order to put together accounts and organize sensible responses (Alvesson & Karreman, 2000; Fairhurst & Putnam, 2004; Grant, Hardy, Oswick, & Putnam, 2004).

Narratives and the ways they are assembled are endlessly contested and relationally constituted. Recently, Whittle and Mueller (2011) investigated public hearings in the U.K. involving senior bank executives and analyzed moral stories constructed by public officials and the executives. Such hearings were common throughout the world following the 2008 financial crisis. Their analysis is extraordinarily detailed and revealed two compelling stories constructed in the discourse of the hearings. The public official story was *Bankers are the villains that brought down the world.* The executive story was *Bankers are the victims of a financial tsunami.* Both are distinctly moral tales, built from relational co-constitution.

Since the 1980s introduction of interpretivism (Putnam & Pacanowsky, 1983), organizational communication scholars have illustrated how qualitative methods and also narrative itself can be rich forms of inquiry, reflexively exploring how "[n]arratives are our way of knowing" (Goodall, 2008, p. 15) and how we are *homo narrans* (Fisher, 1984, 1985). Extensive studies of organizational culture consider organizational narratives as incredible communicative processes, investigating relationships of past, present, and future in organizing and the politics of organizational storytelling (Czarniawska, 1998, 2004, 2011; Goodall, 1995; Keyton, Chapter 22; Trujillo, 1992). Beyond organizational narratives and representations of the "good life" at work, research on the politics of life narratives has considered extensively our relationship to work and organizations and their meanings in our lives and hopes for the future.

The Politics of Distribution

Resources are contestable in much the same way as narratives. People engage a world filled with interdependence and scarcity. This engagement situates distribution as an essential element of life. Individual morality in such a context has been challenged by those claiming that all concepts of responsibility have to be rethought relationally (Gergen & McNamee, 1998). The *politics of distribution* focuses on the following questions: What is considered to be the right and appropriate way to distribute resources in organizations? What is just? How are systems of distribution and justice institutionalized? Increasingly, such questions have been addressed by looking more at a procedural than substantive ethics, and the system of determination rather than *a priori* ethics has been central.

Benhabib (1990) advances the importance of researching communication in consideration of justice, ethics, and distribution "in which we exercise reversibility of perspectives either by actually listening to all involved or by representing to ourselves imaginatively the many perspectives of those involved" (p. 26). Rawls, a foundational theorist on justice and distribution politics, in his classic conceptualization, *A Theory of Justice* (1971), theorizes fairness and democracy, the roles of institutions and organizing, and distributive sharing. In 2001, Rawls amended his theory to address the politics of distribution and justice, advocating what he termed *allocative justice* by questioning how institutions can follow a "fair, efficient, and productive system of social cooperation [that] can be maintained over time, from one generation to the next." Hiller (1998) offers an applied example of Rawls' theory in a study of organizing governance evidenced in an urban planning project in Perth, Australia. She identifies a form of communicative justice by exploring the importance of voice, information, feedback, respect, control, and management in organizing and distribution resources in a multi-organizational urban planning process.

Much organizational communication research has approached the politics of distribution through value-based participative decision making using democratic and political theorizing. Cheney and colleagues (Cheney & Cloud, 2006; Cheney, Mumby, Stohl, & Harrison, 1997; Stohl & Cheney, 2001) and Deetz and colleagues (Deetz, 1995, 2008; Deetz & Simpson, 2004) focus on the politics of limited resources, voice(lessness), and interdependence in organizational democracy work. Harter and colleagues also specialize in the politics of distribution and democratic organizing (Harter, 2004; Harter & Krone, 2001; Novak & Harter, 2008), and extensive research has developed connected to participatory organizing (Budd, Gollan, & Wilkinson, 2010; Heath, 2007; Johnson, 2006). Interrogating the complexities and tensions of distribution continues to be an important area of inquiry to consider how rights and justice are constituted and organized by employees, managers, and stakeholders.

The Relation of Relational Claims

While the politics of relational constructions can be distinguished analytically as we did in this chapter, they do *not* stand alone but are articulated or cojoined together in particular ways in particular organizational settings. Thus multiple communicative claims and their contestations are always engaged at once. Claims are *orthogonal*, meaning that no necessary relations exist among them, but, in the frame of a particular context and articulation, the relations become more or less oblique. Hence, action on each of these may have more or fewer implications across the others. Challenging a knowledge claim, for example, has implications for identity, and so forth. In conflict, one face of the configuration or a particular politics is most often salient, but the intensity of the conflict rests in the implications for hidden politics in other relational configurations. Thus surface and interpretive implicative conversations are always being had simultaneously. The articulatory relations always reflect the transformation of an orthogonal relation into an oblique one.

Most community cultural changes occur around reframing or dis- or re-articulating the relations among the political configurations (see Deetz, in press). Disarticulation can come from *difference* within either pole of the relational configuration. Either a difference in subject-engagements makes a different product possible or the indeterminacy of that which a claim is about is reclaimed, denying a particular engagement's hold over it (processes usually referred to as *deconstruction*). *Difference* may form a contestation of a claim within each of these politics or of the articulatory relations among them. The most serious organizational conflicts reside more in the articulatory relations than the particular politics. For example, sometimes the consequences to key players' identities from resource allocation mean much more than the resource allocation itself. As long as resources and identity are articulated together, the dispute over resources intensifies and is more complicated to solve.

Organizational change is difficult because implicit claims about/claims on identity, social order, life narratives, or justice (claims articulated with the explicit claims) will tighten up owing to threats to these that often cannot be brought to discussion. The feeling of threat to these critical underlying claims leads to the tightening of explicit claims and rejection of contesting claims. Lasting change occurs through processes of disarticulation where assumed simple relations are shown to be more complex. Strong forms of collaboration and respect for difference are essential for disarticulation and the invention of new claims to occur. We often lack the patience or reciprocity for such communication and theory building. These are complex relationships addressing knowledge in the field but with a different generative vocabulary, so we will walk it through a current project, and we invite other applications and additions.

An example is the International Atomic Energy Agency (IAEA)'s project on safety culture in the preoperational phase of building nuclear energy plants. Most of IAEA's work on safety has focused on the operational phases of facilities and very little on the preoperational phases. Their central concern is that countries that have not had nuclear energy facilities are beginning to move toward building them. Many of these same countries do not have industries with a history of quality control in building, and some do not have a wider culture supporting such an approach. Similarly, many contractors and subcontractors have not developed a culture of quality and safety; their workers often have a "laboring" mentality; in some places, a culture of corruption exists; and few companies know much about shifting cultural expectations and systems of cultural control and direction. Policy changes alone have not had the impact on the problem that the

IAEA had hoped. Hence, policy has to be placed within a paradigm-level change.

Most of the IAEA's current focus has been on developing safety cultures across these international sites, but there has not been much success in inculcating desired changes. When there have been changes, IAEA members are concerned that their own efforts have been shallow and unsustainable. Much of the blame for this has been placed on surrounding national cultures and historical work practices. While the IAEA knows much about general cultural change (often following psychological models), it has less knowledge about the impact of specific national and company cultures on the process and the mechanisms by which that occurs (see IAEA, 2012).

What can PARC add in bringing a communication perspective to this set of issues? Let us begin with the very definition of *safety culture* and the agency given to it. *Safety culture* is defined as "The assembly of characteristics and attitudes in organizations and individuals which establishes that, as an overriding priority, *protection and safety issues* receive attention warranted by their significance" (IAEA, 2012, p. 14, emphasis in original). And *culture* is defined as "a dynamic concept that encompasses everything that happens in an organization. It affects what people do, what they think and how they make sense of events and information—it is a collective understanding of reality" (p. 14). These conceptions direct the intervention strategies and, to some extent, set up the tension between safety culture and presumed deficient national and organizational cultural characteristics. The very concept of culture as a kind of iceberg with visible surface behaviors and a massive set of assumption and beliefs under the surface represents the difficulty, if not impossibility, of change.

PARC details cultures in a very different way as articulated relationships among a set of claims about and claims on topics that arise in engagement with on-the-ground elements and activities. In contrast to an iceberg, PARC sees an ice field jammed together by situated events with varying thicknesses and sutured at places. Two aspects of this initially stand out. First, culture cannot be understood outside of the concrete aspects of life, which differ greatly across regions. Second, none of the relational configurations can be transformed without evoking a sense of risk and loss, because other configurations are articulated with it. Individuals can easily feel that their identity as well as understandings of justice and the way the world works are challenged in revising building practices. Such issues are endlessly consequential in this environment. But this does not say that work practices cannot be changed, simply that the change must be worked out in articulatory relationships rather than added on or treated as an isolated aspect. Individuals are not just claiming an identity or feeling; rather, work practices make a claim on the individual's constituted identities and feelings. These endlessly arise in everyday activities. But still, these formations are highly contingent and the suturing often weak.

A communication understanding helps detail the processes of experience formation, the various articulatory relationships that are involved, and the interaction processes by which they become challenged or reproduced. Such a perspective affords a more nuanced analysis of complicated interrelations of constitutive activities and highlights formative processes alongside descriptions of social constructions. This can move groups such as IAEA away from a model of outside intervention to a concrete and detailed understanding of interactional designs and processes that can help overcome closure to new relational configurations as industrial needs and risks change. This is a perspective that can work openly with people and companies in specific contexts to rearticulate identities, emotions, institutions, truths, and the like in ways that uphold self-determination.

Where Might We Go? Organizing Organizational Communication's Futures

PARC presents a fundamentally relational conception of experience formation. It offers a relational understanding that works with difference and the collaborative possibility in construction processes as fundamental principles. At the end, we wish to pose two metatheoretical concerns that will do much to direct the future of organizational communication studies. We will be brief in our discussion, but we hope to instantiate an orientation to the area of study that provides different types of theories and new forms of theorizing. The first issue concerns how far organizational communication will move from an implicit metaperspective of strategic communication to more codeterminative and collaborative forms. The second concern will be with how much and in what ways nonacademic communities will be part of the organizational communication conception and research process—that is, how cogenerative the enterprise might be.

From the Discursive to Collaborative Turn

The last couple of decades have shown a clear move in organizational communication studies from a psychological and sociological grounding to a direct interest in language and interaction—what is often called the *discursive turn*, building on conceptions from literatures on the *linguistic turn*. But a somewhat quieter change has also been occurring. This has been a move away from the control revolution (Beniger, 1986) and the information age to a concern with collaborative and emergent forms of decision making based in quite different models and motives for human interaction (Deetz & Putnam, 2001). We see this evidenced in the growth of work in the politics of distribution that we discussed above, in Sections V and VI in this volume, and more generally in the discussion of matrix, polycentric organizational forms and various modes of collaborative and stakeholder-based decision making. Some of the communication theories guiding this work are fairly traditional, but many evidence a deep rethinking of what communication is all about. Much of this was anticipated in Habermas's (1984) contrast between strategic and communicative action—a difference in the focus on influence and control versus a pursuit of understanding.

Koschmann, Lewis, and Isbell (2011) contend that this collaborative turn in communication studies is based in three realities of the 21st century: "(1) The prevalence of intractable, complex 'meta-problems' that are beyond the scope of any single organization or government, yet affect and are affected by multiple stakeholders (i.e., climate change, poverty, HIV/AIDS, disaster preparedness and response, national security)"; "(2) The extensive interdependence that exists between economies, nation states, and local communities in today's global society"; and "(3) Increasing numbers of stakeholders whose interests and contributions are necessary to address key community, national, and international challenges" (p. 3).

They are certainly not alone in this recognition. The *Harvard Business Review* dedicated an entire issue to collaboration in the summer of 2011. The recent increased influence of Ostrom's works (2005; Poteete, Janssen, & Ostrom, 2010) has led many in political science and economics to focus on collaborative institutions and inaction practices. The role of collaborative organizing could continue to become more consequential in organizational communication research in future decades, given our contemporary times of rapid change, interdependence, and pluralism.

The Researcher as Engaged Subject and Cogenerative Theorizing

Despite the potential developments of the collaborative turn, much organizational research is doubly removed from ongoing organizational life. First, theory, concepts, problem statements, and research practices are developed in scholarly communities and taken to external communities. Second, our scholarship talks *about* external sites, people, events, and practices, rather than talking *in* them.

Engaged scholarship has emerged as the term suggesting not only more contact with the outside but a different philosophy of the nature of knowledge, a different metatheoretical orientation. Part of this has to do with what it is about organizational communication scholarship that we believe has an impact. Some years back, Gergen (1978) showed that the major theories that shaped everyday thinking and defined social science problems function mostly to offer compelling conceptions of central life issues and in doing so challenge both existing assumptions and the supporting dominant values. The greatest impact of organizational communication scholarship may come from what he called *generative theories* rather than findings. When these provide a compelling way to think and talk about the world, the impact can be widespread. Deetz (2008) suggested that we might best get this impact through a cogenerative model where theory and concepts are directly co-constructed with members of external communities.

Certainly, many are taking issues of engagement seriously. The Aspen conference on engaged scholarship has taken place for over 10 years now and involved many leading scholars (Barge et al., 2008; Dempsey & Barge, Chapter 27; Simpson & Schockley-Zalabak, 2005). A special issue of the *Journal of Applied Communication Research* in 2008 outlined many of the issues and challenges of doing engaged work, and participatory action research has received much discussion. While not much is published using such an approach, the groundwork is present for a very different approach to theory and research in the future.

In Sum

We have argued that a metatheoretical orientation offers a PARC that facilitates conversations across diverse theoretical and research perspectives. As a framework for addressing relational politics, PARC enables studies of organizing to offer new and more complete explanations of processes related to traditional organizational concerns with reason and emotionality, organizational knowledge, socialization, distribution, and conflict. Interpreting existing studies done from different perspectives into a metatheoretical set of concerns allows these perspectives to be brought to bear on complex problems that do not meet the constitutive parameters of the studies themselves.

While we offer collaborative, cogenerative turns as continuing future possibilities, we recognize that our anticipated and hoped-for trajectories may not materialize. Unforeseen social and political dilemmas around international organizing as well as growth in organizational communication as a field may take shape, shifting our directions entirely. What is for certain is that we await fruitful conversations; more engagement with our differences; and substantial theoretical, methodological, and pedagogical growth. We look forward to watching the ways in which organizational communication grows and continues to organize itself as a discipline in the next decades.

References

Alvesson, M., & Karreman, D. (2000). Varieties of discourse: On the study of organizations through discourse analysis. *Human Relations, 53*(9), 1125–1149.

Ashcraft, K. L., & Flores, L. (2003). "Slaves with white collars": Persistent performances of masculinity in crisis. *Text and Performance Quarterly, 23*(1), 1–29.

Ashcraft, K. L., Kuhn, T., & Cooren, F. (2009). Constitutional amendments: "Materializing" organizational communication. *The Academy of Management Annals, 3*(1), 1–64.

Ashcraft, K. L., & Mumby, D. K. (2004). *Reworking gender: A feminist communicology of organization.* Thousand Oaks, CA: SAGE.

Barge, J. K., Jones, J. E., Kensler, M., Polok, N., Rianoshek, R., Simpson, J. L., & Shockley-Zalabak, P. (2008). A practitioner view toward engaged scholarship. *Journal of Applied Communication Research, 36*(3), 245–250.

Barley, S. R. (2011). Signifying institutions. *Management Communication Quarterly, 25*(1), 200–206.

Becker, H. S. (1953). Becoming a marihuana user. *The American Journal of Sociology, 59*(3), 235–243.

Benhabib, S. (1990). In the shadow of Aristotle and Hegel: Communicative ethics and current controversies in practical philosophy. In M. Kelly (Ed.), *Hermeneutics and critical theory in ethics and politics* (pp. 1–31). Cambridge, MA: The MIT Press.

Beniger, J. (1986). *The control revolution.* Cambridge, MA: Harvard University Press.

Benson, P., & Kirsch, S. (2010). Capitalism and the politics of resignation. *Current Anthropology, 51*(4), 459–486.

Berger, P. L., & Luckmann, T. (1966). *The social construction of reality: A treatise in the sociology of knowledge.* New York, NY: Anchor Books.

Broadfoot, K. J., & Munshi, D. (2007). Diverse voices and alternative rationalities. Imagining forms of postcolonial organizational communication. *Management Communication Quarterly, 21*(2), 249–267.

Budd, J. W., Gollan, P. J., & Wilkinson, A. (2010). New approaches to employee voice and participation in organizations. *Human Relations, 63*(3), 303–310.

Canary, H. E., & McPhee, R. D. (Eds.). (2011). *Communication and organizational knowledge: Contemporary issues for theory and practice.* New York, NY: Routledge.

Cheney, G. (1983). The rhetoric of identification and the study of organizational communication. *Quarterly Journal of Speech, 69*(2), 143–158.

Cheney, G., & Ashcraft, K. L. (2007). Considering 'the professional' in communication studies: Implications for theory and research within and beyond the boundaries of organizational communication. *Communication Theory, 17*(2), 146–175.

Cheney, G., & Cloud, D. (2006). Doing democracy, engaging the material: Employee participation and labor activity in age of market globalization. *Management Communication Quarterly, 19*(4), 501–540.

Cheney, G., Mumby, D., Stohl, C., & Harrison, T. M. (1997). Communication and organizational democracy: Introduction. *Communication Studies, 48*(4), 277–278.

Corman, S. R. (2000). The need for common ground. In S. R. Corman & M. S. Poole (Eds.), *Perspectives on organizational communication: Finding common ground* (pp. 1–15). New York, NY: Guilford.

Cooren, F. (1999). Applying socio-semiotics to organizational communication: A new approach. *Management Communication Quarterly, 13*(2), 294–304.

Czarniawska, B. (1998). *A narrative approach to organization studies.* Thousand Oaks, CA: SAGE.

Czarniawska, B. (2004). *Narratives in social science research.* Thousand Oaks, CA: SAGE.

Czarniawska, B. (2011). Narrating organizational studies. *Narrative Inquiry, 21*(2), 337–344.

Deetz, S. (1973a). Words without things: Toward a social phenomenology of language. *Quarterly Journal of Speech, 59*(1), 40–51.

Deetz, S. (1973b). An understanding of science and a hermeneutic science of understanding. *Journal of Communication, 23*(2), 139–159.

Deetz, S. (1992). *Democracy in the age of corporate colonization: Developments in communication and the politics of everyday life.* Albany: State University of New York Press.

Deetz, S. (1994). The future of the discipline: The challenges, the research, and the social contribution. In S. Deetz (Ed.), *Communication yearbook* (vol. 17, pp. 565–600). Thousand Oaks, CA: SAGE.

Deetz, S. (1995). *Transforming communication, transforming business: Building responsive and responsible workplaces* (pp. 57–78). Cresskill, NJ: Hampton Press Inc.

Deetz, S. (2000). Putting the community into organizational science: Exploring the construction of knowledge claims. *Organization Science, 11*(6), 732–738.

Deetz, S. (2001). Conceptual foundations. In L. Putnam & F. Jablin (Eds.), *The new handbook of organizational communication* (pp. 3–46). Thousand Oaks, CA: SAGE.

Deetz, S. (2003). Taking the "linguistic turn" seriously. *Organization: The Interdisciplinary Journal of Organization, Theory, and Society, 10,* 421–429.

Deetz, S. (2008). Engagement as co-generative theorizing. *Journal of Applied Communication Research, 36*(3), 288–296.

Deetz, S. (2009). Politically attentive relational constructionism (PARC) and making a difference in a pluralistic, interdependent world. In D. Carbaugh & P. Buzzanell (Eds.), *Reflections on the distinctive qualities of communication research in the social sciences* (pp. 32–52). New York, NY: Taylor Francis.

Deetz, S. (in press). Power and the possibility of generative community dialogue. In S. Littlejohn and others (Eds.), *The coordinated management of meaning: A festschrift in honor of W. Barnett Pearce*. Madison, NJ: Fairleigh Dickinson University Press.

Deetz, S., & Mumby, D. K. (1990). Power, discourse, and the workplace: Reclaiming the critical tradition. In J. Anderson (Ed.), *Communication yearbook* (vol. 13, pp. 18–47). Newbury Park, CA: SAGE.

Deetz, S., & Putnam, L. L. (2001). Thinking about the future of communication studies. In W. B. Gudykunst (Ed.), *Communication yearbook* (vol. 24, pp. 1–14). Thousand Oaks, CA: SAGE.

Deetz, S., & Simpson, J. (2004). Critical organizational dialogue: Open formation and the demand of "otherness." In R. Anderson, L. Baxter, & K. Cissna (Eds.), *Dialogic approaches to communication* (pp. 141–158). Thousand Oaks, CA: SAGE.

Eger Rush, E. K. (2012, May). *Innovation incubation as mood manufacture: Investigating the communicative construction and consequences of work to organize and perform an innovation organization*. Paper presented at the annual meeting of the International Communication Association, Phoenix, AZ.

Eisenberg, E. M., & Riley, P. (2001). Organizational culture. In F. Jablin & L. L. Putnam (Eds.), *The new handbook of organizational communication: Advances in theory, research, and methods* (pp. 291–322). Thousand Oaks, CA: SAGE.

Fairhurst, G. T., & Putnam, L. (2004). Organizations as discursive constructions. *Communication Theory, 14*(1), 5–26.

Fisher, W. R. (1984). Narration as a human communication paradigm: The case of public moral argument. *Communication Monographs, 51*(1), 1–22.

Fisher, W. R. (1985). The narrative paradigm: An elaboration. *Communication Monographs, 52*(4), 347–367.

Gergen, K. (1978). Toward generative theory. *Journal of Personality and Social Psychology, 36*(11), 1344–1360.

Gergen, K., & McNamee, S. (Eds.). (1998). *Relational responsibility*. Thousand Oaks, CA: SAGE.

Goodall, H. L., Jr. (1995). Work-hate narratives. In R. Whillock & D. Slayden (Eds.), *Hate speech*. Thousand Oaks, CA: SAGE.

Goodall, H. L., Jr. (2008). *Writing qualitative inquiry: Self, stories, and academic life*. Walnut Creek, CA: Left Coast Press.

Grant, A. (2011, August 9). 6 ways the world of work is changing: These trends will affect both your work and personal life. *U.S. News*. Retrieved from http://money.usnews.com/money/careers/articles/2011/08/09/6-ways-the-world-of-work-is-changing_print.html

Grant, D., Hardy, C., Oswick, C., & Putnam, L. (Eds.). (2004). *The SAGE handbook of organizational discourse*. Thousand Oaks, CA: SAGE.

Habermas, J. (1984). *The theory of communicative action, volume 1: Reason and the rationalization of society* (T. McCarthy, Trans.). Boston, MA: Beacon.

Harré, R. (Ed.). (1986). *The social construction of emotions*. Oxford, England: Basil Blackwell.

Harré, R., & van Langenhove, L. (1999). *Positioning theory*. Oxford, England: Blackwell.

Harte, J. (1988). *Considering a spherical cow: A course in environmental problem solving*. Sausalito, CA: University Science Books.

Harter, L. (2004). Masculinity(s), the agrarian frontier myth, and cooperative ways of organizing: Contradictions and tensions in the experiences and enactment of democracy. *Journal of Applied Communication Research, 32*(2), 89–118.

Harter, L., & Krone, K. (2001). The boundary-spanning role of a cooperative support organization: Managing the paradox of stability and change in non-traditional organizations. *Journal of Applied Communication Research, 29*(3), 248–277.

Hawes, L. C. (1974). Social collectives as communication: Perspectives on organizational behavior. *Quarterly Journal of Speech, 60,* 497–502.

Heath, R. G. (2007). Rethinking community collaboration through a dialogic lens: Creativity, democracy, and diversity in community organizing. *Management Communication Quarterly, 21*(2), 145–171.

Hiller, J. (1998). Beyond confused noise: Ideas toward communicative procedural justice. *Journal of Planning Education and Research, 18*(1), 14–24.

Hochschild, A. R. (2003). *The managed heart: Commercialization of human feeling* (2nd ed.). Berkeley: University of California Press.

International Atomic Energy Agency. (2012). *Safety culture in pre-operational phases of nuclear power plant projects*. Safety Report Series No. 74. Retrieved from http://www-pub.iaea.org/MTCD/publications/PDF/Pub1555_web.pdf

Johnson, P. (2006). Whence democracy? A review and critique of the conceptual dimensions and implications of the business case for organizational democracy. *Organization, 13*(2), 245–274.

Kogurt, B., & Zander, U. (1996). What firms do? Coordination, identity, and learning. *Organization Science, 7*(5), 502–518.

Koschmann, M., Lewis, L., & Isbell, M. (2011). *NSF/SBE White Paper: Effective Collaboration in a Complex and Interdependent Society.* Retrieved from http://www.nsf.gov/sbe/sbe_2020/Abstracts.pdf

Laclau, E., & Mouffe, C. (1985). *Hegemony and socialist strategy: Towards a radical democratic politics.* London, England: Verso.

Lammers, J. C. (2011). How institutions communicate: Institutional messages, institutional logics, and organizational communication. *Management Communication Quarterly, 25*(1), 154–182.

Lyotard, J. (1979). *The postmodern condition: A report on knowledge* (G. Bennington & B. Massumi, Trans.). Minneapolis: The University of Minnesota Press.

McClellan, J., & Deetz, S. (2009). Communication and critical management studies. In H. Willmott, T. Bridgman, & M. Alvesson (Eds.), *Handbook of critical management studies* (pp. 433–453). Oxford, England: Oxford University Press.

McClellan, J., & Deetz, S. (2012). Sustainable change: A politically attentive discursive analysis of collaborative talk. In J. Aritz & R. Walker (Eds.), *Discourse perspectives on organizational communication* (pp. 33–58). Madison, NJ: Fairleigh Dickinson University Press.

McPhee, R. D., & Corman, S. R. (1995). An activity-based theory of communication networks in organizations, applied to the case of a local church. *Communication Monographs, 62*(2), 132–151.

McPhee, R. D., & Iverson, J. O. (2009). Agents of constitution in communidad: Constitutive processes of communication in organizations. In L. L. Putnam & A. M. Nicotera (Eds.), *Building theories of organization: The constitutive role of communication* (pp. 49–88). Oxford, England: Taylor and Francis.

McPhee, R. D., & Zaug, P. (2000). The communicative constitution of organizations: A framework for explanation. *Electronic Journal of Communication,* 10(1–2). Retrieved from http://www.cios.org/EJCPUBLIC/010/1/01017.html

Meyer, J. W., & Rowan, B. (1977). Institutionalized organization: Formal structure as myth and ceremony. *American Journal of Sociology, 83*(2), 340–363.

Miller, K., Considine, J., & Garner, J. (2007). "Let me tell you about my job": Exploring the terrain of emotion in the workplace. *Management Communication Quarterly, 20*(3), 231–260.

Morgan, J., & Krone, K. (2001). Bending the rules of "professional" display: Emotional improvisation in caregiver performances. *Journal of Applied Communication Research, 29*(4), 317–340.

Mumby, D., & Putnam, L. (1992). The politics of emotion: A feminist reading of bounded rationality. *Academy of Management Review, 17*(3), 465–486.

Mumby, D., & Stohl, C. (1996). Disciplining organizational communication studies. *Management Communication Quarterly, 10*(1), 50–72.

Murphy, A., & Eisenberg, E. (2011). Coaching to the craft: Understanding knowledge in health care organizations. In H. E. Canary & R. D. McPhee (Eds.), *Communication and organizational knowledge: Contemporary issues for theory and practice* (pp. 264–284). New York, NY: Routledge.

Nadesan, M. H., & Trethewey, A. (2000). Enterprising subjects: Gendered strategies of success. *Text and Performance Quarterly, 20*(3), 1–28.

Novak, D., & Harter, L. (2008). "Flipping the scripts" of poverty and panhandling: Organizing democracy by creating connections. *Journal of Applied Communication Research, 36*(4), 391–414.

Orlikowski, W. J. (2002). Knowing in practice: Enacting a collective capability in distributed organizing. *Organization Science, 13*(3), 249–273.

Ostrom, E. (2005). *Understanding institutional diversity.* Princeton: Princeton University Press.

Pearce, W. B. (1989). *Communication and the human condition.* Carbondale: Southern Illinois University Press.

Poteete, A., Janssen, M., & Ostrom, E. (2010). *Working together: Collective action, the commons, and multiple methods in practice.* Princeton, NJ: Princeton University Press.

Putnam, L. L. (1983). The interpretive perspective: An alternative to functionalism. In L. L. Putnam & M. E. Pacanowsky (Eds.), *Communication and organizations: An interpretive approach* (pp. 31–54). Beverly Hills, CA: SAGE.

Putnam, L. L., & Boys, S. (2006). Revisiting metaphors of organizational communication. In S. R. Clegg, C. Hardy, T. B. Lawrence, & W. R. Nord (Eds.), *The SAGE handbook of organization studies* (pp. 541–576). Thousand Oaks: SAGE.

Putnam, L. L., & Nicotera, A. M. (Eds.). (2009). *Building theories of organization: The constitutive role of communication.* New York: Routledge.

Putnam, L. L., Nicotera, A. M., & McPhee, R. D. (2009). Introduction: Communication constitutes organization. In L. L. Putnam & A. M. Nicotera (Eds.), *Building theories of organization: The constitutive role of communication* (pp. 1–19). New York, NY: Routledge.

Putnam, L. L., & Pacanowsky, M. (Eds.). (1983). *Communication and organizations: An interpretive perspective.* Beverly Hills, CA: SAGE.

Putnam, L. L., Phillips, N., & Chapman, P. (1999). Metaphors of communication and organization. In S. R. Clegg, C. Hardy, & W. R. Nord (Eds.), *Managing organizations: Current issues* (pp. 125–158). Thousand Oaks, CA: SAGE.

Rawls, J. (1971). *A theory of justice.* Cambridge, MA: Harvard University Press.

Rawls, J. (2001). *Justice as fairness: A restatement* (E. Kelly, Ed.). Cambridge, MA: Harvard University Press.

Reckwitz, A. (2002). Toward a theory of social practices: A development in culturalist theorizing. *European Journal of Social Theory, 5*(2), 243–263.

Rumens, N., & Kerfoot, D. (2009). Gay men at work: (Re)constructing the self as professional. *Human Relations, 62*(5), 763–786.

Schilt, K. (2010). *Just one of the guys? Transgender men and the persistence of gender inequality.* Chicago, IL: The University of Chicago Press.

Scott, J. (2011). Attending to the disembodied character in research on professional narratives: How the performance analysis of physically disabled professionals' personal stories provides insight into the role of the body in narratives of professional identity. *Narrative Inquiry, 21*(2), 238–257.

Simon, H. A. (1957). *Administrative behavior* (2nd ed.). New York, NY: Macmillan.

Simpson, J., & Shockley-Zalabak, P. (Eds.). (2005). *Engaging communication, transforming organizations: Scholarship and engagement in action* (pp. 79–97). Cresskill, NJ: Hampton Press.

Stohl, C., & Cheney, G. (2001). Participatory processes/paradoxical practices: Communication and the dilemmas of organizational democracy. *Management Communication Quarterly, 14*(3), 349–407.

Suddaby, R. (2011). How communication institutionalizes: A response to Lammers. *Management Communication Quarterly, 25*(1), 183–190.

Taylor, J. R., & Van Every, E. J. (2000). *The emergent organization: Communication as site and surface.* Mahwah, NJ: Lawrence Erlbaum.

Thomas, R. (2009). Critical management studies on identity. In H. Willmott, T. Bridgman, & M. Alvesson (Eds.), *Handbook of critical management studies* (pp. 166–185). Oxford, England: Oxford University Press.

Tompkins, P., & Cheney, G. (1985). Communication and unobtrusive control in contemporary organizations. In R. McPhee & P. Tompkins (Eds.), *Organizational communication: Traditional themes and new directions* (pp. 179–210). Beverly Hills, CA: SAGE.

Tracy, S. J. (2000). Becoming a character for commerce: Emotion labor, self-subordination, and discursive construction of identity in a total institution. *Management Communication Quarterly, 14*(1), 90–128.

Trethewey, A. (1999). Disciplined bodies: Women's embodied identities at work. *Organization Studies, 20*(3), 423–450.

Trethewey, A. (2000). Cultured bodies: Communication as constitutive of culture and bodied identities. *Electronic Journal of Communication, 10* (1–2). Retrieved from http://www.cios.org/EJCPUBLIC/010/1/01016.html

Trujillo, N. (1992). Interpreting (the work and the talk of) baseball: Perspective on ballpark culture. *Western Journal of Communication, 56*(4), 350–371.

Weber, M. (1947). *The theory of social and economic organization* (A. H. Henderson & T. Parsons, Trans.). Glencoe, IL: Free Press.

Weick, K. E. (1979). *The social psychology of organizing* (2nd ed.). Reading, MA: Addison-Wesley.

Whittle, A., & Mueller, F. (2011). Bankers in the dock: Moral storytelling in action. *Human Relations, 65*(1), 111–139.

Wieland, S., Bauer, J., & Deetz, S. (2009). Excessive careerism and destructive life stresses: The role of entrepreneurialism in colonizing identities. In B. Sypher & P. Lutgen-Sandvik (Eds.), *The destructive side of organizational communication* (pp. 99–120). Mahwah, NJ: Lawrence Erlbaum.

CHAPTER 2

Systems Theory

Marshall Scott Poole

Systems terminology and the systems metaphor are commonplace in organizational communication theory and research and are a staple of introductory textbooks on organizational communication. For organizational communication scholars, systems theory has many connotations. To some, it is the ideal theoretical framework for the study of organizational communication, capable of capturing the complexity inherent in organizations in a rigorous, empirically testable manner. To others, it serves as a devil term, a conservative, positivistic approach that attempts to objectivize organizations and hides their meaning to their members or their oppressive nature. For the majority of organizational communication scholars, however, systems theory provides some basic terminology, part of the taken-for-granted vocabulary that forms the backdrop to inquiry and teaching.

The goal of this chapter is to review the varied and vibrant scholarship on systems theory in organizational communication and to suggest potential advances. It starts with a brief history of systems theory and its influence on organizational communication research. The second section introduces key systems concepts and principles. Building on this work, the third section explicates a typology for the classification of systems approaches, and the fourth section maps the terrain of past and current systems approaches in organizational communication in terms of this typology. Finally, central issues in systems theory will be considered as well as promising directions for systems theory in organizational communication research.

Systems Theory in Organizational Communication

A systems theory develops a description of real-world phenomena in terms of an abstract logic of explanation that is constructed by the observer. While most organizational communication scholars who implicitly invoke systems concepts focus more on their particular object of study, systems theorists (e.g., Cushman & Pearce, 1977; Krippendorff, 1977; Meehan, 1968; Wolfram 2002) are clear that any systems theory is an abstraction that uses some formal logic and technical terminology—mathematical, simulation, verbal—to develop descriptions, explanations, and understandings. Meehan (1968) argued that a systems model is

> an abstract calculus that is totally unrelated to anything in the empirical world. The system, as a system, says nothing whatever about empirical events; it generates expectations within its own boundaries.... The key to the explanatory process, when the systems paradigm is employed, is the generation of expectations within a formal calculus and the transfer of those expectations, under suitable conditions, to the empirical world. (1968, p. 48)

The appeal of systems theory for organizational communication research lies in its potential to represent the complexity of organizations and organizational communication in a rigorous yet manageable fashion, just as it has done in the natural and biological sciences and in engineering. Another appealing feature of systems theory is its potential to incorporate agency in ways that traditional quantitative methodologies cannot accommodate.

Systems theory has influenced organizational communication research since its inception. Early organizational communication textbooks (e.g., Redding & Sanborn, 1964; Thayer, 1968) draw explicitly on systems ideas conveyed by Barnard (1938), Follett (1941), and March and Simon (1958). During the 1950s and 1960s, general systems theory (von Bertalanffy, 1968), cybernetics (Ashby, 1954), and structural-functionalism (Parsons, 1951) influenced social scientific discourse broadly, and systems thinking via these perspectives was reflected in much of the general literature that early organizational communication scholars drew on. Krippendorff (1977) and Monge (1973, 1982) developed important explications of systems theory for organizational communication, and Thayer (1968), Goldhaber (1974), and Farace, Monge, and Russell (1977) published influential texts that accorded a prominent role to systems conceptualizations of organizational communication.

The interpretive-critical turn in organizational communication in the 1980s and 1990s was, in part, articulated in opposition to systems theory, particularly structural-functionalism (Putnam, 1983). References to systems theory are scarce in major works of this period, including Putnam and Pacanowsky (1983), though it was reviewed in the first edition of the *Handbook of Organizational Communication* in the introductory chapter as the systems-interaction perspective (Krone, Jablin, & Putnam, 1987) and was prevalent in Goldhaber and Barnett's (1988) *Handbook of Organizational Communication*. Interpretive-critical scholarship was also influenced by systems theory through Weick's (1979) model of organizing, discussed later in this chapter.

In the 1990s, the advent of new systems theories (such as catastrophe theory, chaos theory, and complex adaptive systems theory) caught the imagination of organizational communication scholars, just as they did the academic community at large. Poole (1997) argued that these new conceptions of systems could address problems important to interpretive and critical scholars, and some systems research in the 1990s and early 2000s reflected this orientation. Miller (2003) and Salem (2002), for example, applied ideas from new systems theory to communication and organizational change (see Barnett & Thayer, 1997, for other examples). Indeed, systems theory is part of the DNA of organizational communication research and continues to exert a significant, yet subtle, influence on the direction of research.

Basic Concepts and Principles

A *system* is a set of interdependent components that form an internally organized whole that operates as one in relation to its environment and to other systems. Examples of systems include biological organisms, electrical circuits, and organizations. Systems approaches share a core terminology and several central principles. Table 2.1 summarizes basic systems concepts, which are broadly familiar, while Table 2.2 summarizes some principles of systems theory and their implications, which will be discussed subsequently in this chapter. While there is broad agreement that these concepts are central to defining systems, there are differences among systems theories based on diverse interpretations of these terms and varied assumptions about the nature of systems. Krippendorff (1977), Barnett (1997), and Buckley (1968) provide a more detailed discussion of basic terminology and different interpretations of terms.

Table 2.1 Fundamental Concepts in Systems Theory

Concept	**Explication**
Component	Components are the units that compose the system. In the case of organizational systems, common units are individuals, groups/work units, divisions/departments, and entire organizations.
Levels	Systems have multiple levels, with lower levels nested within higher ones (e.g., individuals nested within groups, which are nested within organizations, which are nested within organizational communities). Each lower-level component of a higher level system (*subsystem*) is a system in its own right.
Goals	Systems have *explicit*, specific goals, such as producing goods. Systems also have more universal, *implicit* goals (such as survival, growth, and adaptation) that ensure the persistence of the system.
Interdependence	Components of the system are related to each other by various interdependencies. Dependencies may be one-way or mutual. Common types of interdependencies include workflow, communication, authority, and affect. Interdependencies among components are the basis for the functional and causal effects they have on one another.
Structure	Structure refers to the overall configuration of interdependencies in a system. Each type of interdependency gives rise to different structure, such as workflows, communication networks, or hierarchies of authority.
Feedback	Feedback refers to a circular relationship in which (a) causal processes form a closed loop whereby each cause becomes an effect of the other factors in the loop or (b) information about the past or present influences future states of the system. In positive (deviation-amplifying) feedback, each cycle has reinforcing effects so that the input to each variable in the loop always changes the value of that variable in the same direction (increasing or decreasing). The result is a self-reinforcing loop. In negative feedback, the relations counteract one another, and as a result, the system has the potential to achieve and maintain a stable state or equilibrium. There may be multiple feedback loops in a system, and the stability/change that occurs in a system is a product of how the positive and negative loops interact and their relative strength.

(Continued)

Table 2.1 (Continued)

Concept	Explication
Boundary	The system's boundary marks what is in the system and what is outside it. Boundaries figure in systems theory both as part of the system's reality and as analytical constructs. Organizations and groups explicitly or implicitly define system boundaries. The system boundary is also an important analytical construct, because to study a system, we must define its boundary to give the system a "spatiotemporal reference" and to facilitate "evaluation of the organization by providing a context for the analysis of its communication activity" (Barnett, 1997, p. 6; cf. Krippendorff, 1977).
Environment	The environment is everything outside the system's boundary that is relevant to it. Dimensions of environments include (a) *complexity*, the number of elements in the environment and their interdependence; (b) *unpredictability*, the lack of information about what the elements of the environment are and about how they will impact the organization; (c) *dynamism*, the degree of change in the environment; and (d) *hostility*, the degree to which the environment is potentially harmful to the organization (Burton, DeSanctis, & Orbel, 2006).
Information	Information theory (Barnett, 1997; Krippendorff, 2009; Shannon & Weaver, 1959) has contributed a number of concepts important to systems theory, including uncertainty and information overload. In terms of information theory, *information* is "a change in an observer's state of uncertainty caused by some event in [his or her] world" (Krippendorff, 2009, p. 242). The *uncertainty* in question is related to a set of possible states of the world, and information increases the probability that one or more of these states is the case compared to the others. Information flow through systems enables them to coordinate activities and regulate themselves.
Input	Input is anything that crosses the system boundary from the environment into the system.
Output	Output is anything that crosses the system boundary from the system to its environment.
Process	A process is a coordinated set of changes in the system that are linked to one another either causally or functionally (Poole, 2012; Rescher, 1996). A process consists of an integrated series of developments unfolding over time, driven by some program or generative mechanism. At the most basic level, systems take inputs from their environment and convert them into outputs via processes conducted by their components. Process has also been used to refer to changes in the structure of the system (Barnett, 1997). Finally, process has been used to refer to how systems and their components change and develop over time (Poole, 2012).

Concept	Explication
Equilibrium	Equilibrium is the condition of the system in which competing influences are balanced. Equilibrium may be set at a single point or state or it may shift around a set of points and states that repeat over time.
Coupling	Coupling refers to the degree to which the parts or modules of the system are tightly or loosely connected. In a tightly coupled system, the components are strongly interdependent, while a loosely coupled system can be divided into subsets of tightly coupled components that are loosely connected to one another
Holism	Holism means that the system is qualitatively different from its components, and the interactions among components yield a higher-level entity with its own distinctive properties that cannot reduced to those of the components.

Table 2.2 Systems Principles

Principle	Definition	Implications
Equifinality	Multiple system structures can serve the same goals.	There is more than one way to organize an effective system.
Requisite Variety	To be effective, a system must be at least as complex in its structure and/or behavior as its environment (Ashby, 1962).	Systems adapt to their environments by becoming similar to them in terms of structure.
Complex Causality	Due to feedback loops (sometimes multiple loops), it is impossible to distinguish cause and effect, because each variable in the loops are both. So it is more productive to consider the causal process of the system as a whole.	Complex causal loops can also make it difficult to control the system, because actions taken at one point in the system reverberate through other causal loops to produce unintended consequences.
Emergence	The system and its properties emerge from interactions among components and are fundamentally different from any of the components. In some cases, emergence is assumed to result in a higher-level entity that encompasses and surpasses its components. Emergence also refers to surprising results or outputs of a system.	The system cannot be reduced to its components. Any model of the system must allow for and/or explain emergence.

A system is an organized set of interdependent components that are connected by a variety of interdependencies. Systems have explicit goals that include accomplishment of specific purposes and more general implicit goals such as survival, growth, and adaptation. Information flow throughout the system enables the components to coordinate with each other and to attain the system's goals. The complex of interdependencies among components and the associated arrangement constitute the structure of the system. A system is set off from its environment by a boundary. In a closed system, this boundary is impermeable, but fully closed systems are rare. More common is the open system, in which inputs cross the boundary and are processed by the system to produce outputs and to maintain the internal structure of the system (Farace et al., 1977). Systems are more than the sum of their parts, with unique properties (such as culture) that cannot be reduced to their components.

The systems concept is quite flexible, and scholars can represent organizational systems made of individual members; groups, units, or divisions; entire organizations (in the case of interorganizational systems); industries or economic sectors (in the case of societal systems); and economic/social systems (in the case of global systems). Hence, systems are *multilevel* entities in which each component can itself be viewed as a system.

One important approach to systems analysis focuses on the *functions* that system components fulfill. The functionalist approach posits that systems are wholes and can be understood in terms of the functions they have in constituting and maintaining the organization as it responds to its environment (Parsons, 1951). Functions can be defined as the effect that the component has in the system, such as goal attainment (contributing to the system's ability to meet its goals or purpose). Farace et al. (1977) define several functions of communication in organizational systems (for example, innovation).

A second approach to systems analysis focuses on *causal relationships* within the system and between the system and its environment. In some cases, the analysis examines causal effects among components of the system, while in others, it focuses on causal processes occurring within the system as a whole. An example of this second type of causal analysis, which depicts the burnout process for human service workers in health care organizational systems, is shown in Figure 2.1. As Figure 2.1 indicates, causal processes in systems can be quite complex and may involve causal cycles and positive and negative feedback loops.

A Typology of Systems Approaches

Representations of systems can be differentiated along three dimensions: (1) the degree of *complexity* ascribed to a system, (2) the degree of *agency* that researchers assume a system possesses, and (3) whether scholars take a *formal or informal* approach to description and explanation of the system. These dimensions will constitute the basis for mapping extant systems research in organizational communication and identifying promising directions for future research.

Complexity

The complexity of a system is difficult to define succinctly, because it depends on the interaction of several factors. Symptoms of system complexity include unpredictability, sensitivity to initial conditions (the so-called *butterfly effect*), inability of the system to settle into a simple equilibrium, surprising and unexpected behavior or outcomes, perplexing patterns of change, and what is now popularly referred to as *chaos*. These are manifestations of structural and processual characteristics of the system that render it complex.

It is important at the outset to distinguish between *complication* and *complexity*. The social world and communication are complicated, but

Figure 2.1 A Causal Structure Underlying Burnout in an Organizational System

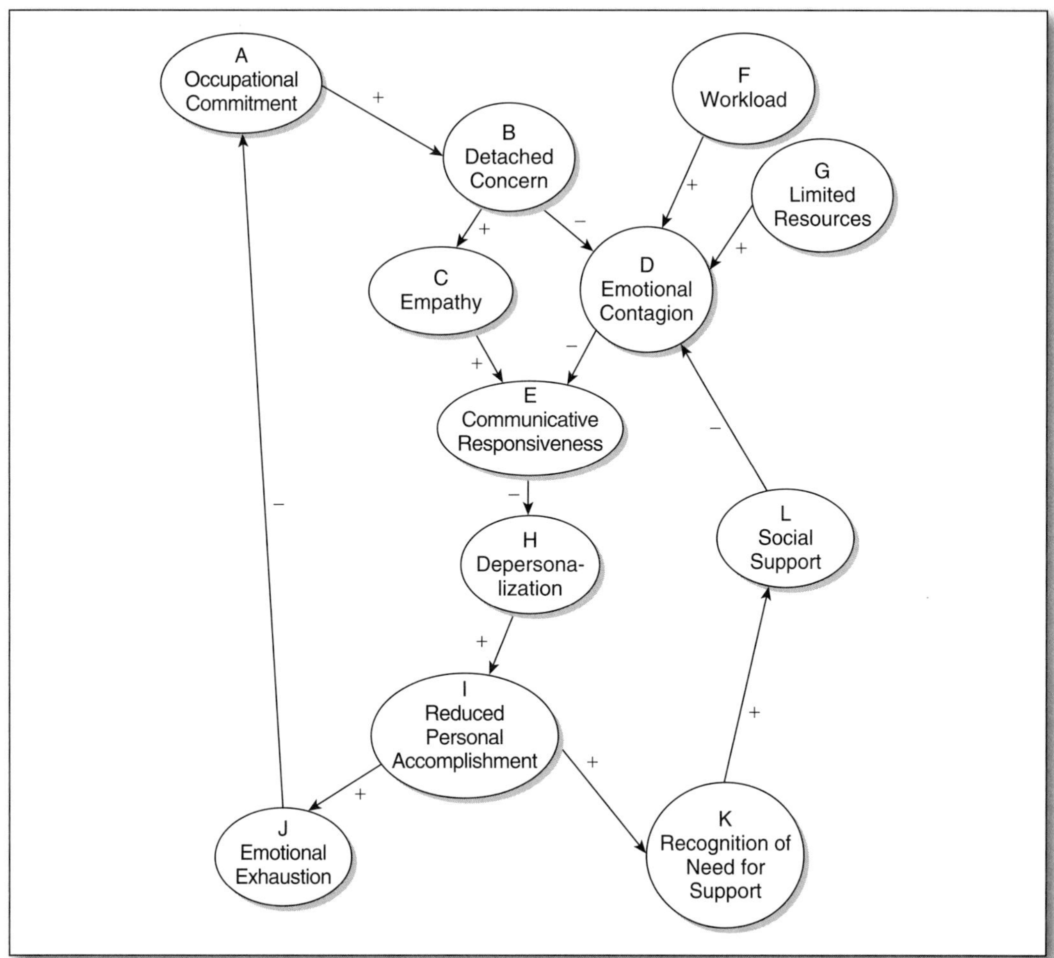

Based on Miller et al. (1988), this model posits that human service workers enter the occupation because they have a desire to help, which creates a high level of occupational commitment (A). In their professional socialization, workers are encouraged to develop an attitude of detached concern (B), which involves caring but keeping a professional distance. Detached concern facilitates empathy with clients (C) and helps the worker avoid negative emotional contagion from clients (D). Empathy and avoidance of emotional contagion increases the ability of the worker to be communicatively responsive to his or her clients (E). However, large workloads (F) and insufficient resources (G) create overload that increases their susceptibility to emotional contagion (D), because they are upset because they cannot give the professional care they desire to give. This, in turn, has a negative effect on communicative responsiveness (E). Burnout consists of three components: (1) *depersonalization* (H), a negative shift in attitudes toward clients that involves blaming them for their problems, expecting the worst from them, and generally developing a poor opinion of them; (2) *reduced sense of personal accomplishment* (I), a sense of their own inadequacy and failure as a caregiver; and (3) *emotional exhaustion* (J), being worn out and depleted, which develop sequentially. The result of this chain of influences is decreased occupational commitment. A positive counter-influence is social support from supervisors, coworkers, or friends. In this system, as emotional exhaustion increases, the worker should recognize her or his need for support and seek it out (K); to the extent social support is available (L), emotional contagion will be reduced.

not all complicated phenomena are complex (Miller & Page, 2007). Complicated systems can be explained by reducing them to simpler parts or modules that stand independent of one another and interact in a relatively straightforward manner, whereas complex systems cannot be understood through reduction. Instead, the parts of complex systems concatenate in intricate and convoluted ways, and their processes are entangled and recursive and may exhibit multiple feedback loops and layers. So we can define a continuum along which conceptualizations of systems vary from somewhat complicated to highly complex. Understanding the complexity of systems is important for organizational communication scholars, because it sheds light on phenomena such as emergence and loose coupling.

Several characteristics determine the complexity of a system:

- *Number of components*: The greater the number of components in a system and the more diverse they are, the greater the complexity of the system, other things being equal. More interacting parts generally increase system complexity.

- *Modularity*: This characteristic refers to the degree to which a system can be decomposed into independent, more-or-less freestanding modules that are influenced by other modules or external forces through their inputs (Simon, 1969). Modules may be composed of basic components that are densely connected to one another within the module but are only loosely connected to the remainder of the system. For example, an organization might consist of modules or subsystems for supply, production, sales, and human resources. Each of these modules might have many employees and subunits within it and be quite complex internally, but for purposes of the larger organization, each module functions as a single whole and relates to other modules. Modules function as coherent units within the system that can be treated as "black boxes" with respect to the system as a whole. The complexity of a system is negatively related to its modularity, other things being equal. Modularity of systems is associated with the property of loose coupling (see *Coupling* in Table 2.1).

- *Aggregativity*: Systems are more complex to the extent that they are not simply the sum of their parts. Systems such as crowds or pure markets whose properties are the product of simple aggregation are less complex than systems whose properties depend on how the system is organized. The level of demand in a market, for example, can be calculated simply by adding the demand of all the market participants. In contrast, the property of being a church is not aggregative but is a function of the nature of its organizational system. In highly complex systems, each component makes a unique, non-substitutable contribution, and removing this component fundamentally changes the system.

- *Nature of interactions among components*: Relationships among the components that compose the system is the fourth determinant of complexity. One relationship is simply the density of connections among system components. *Ceteris paribus*, the higher the density of connections, the higher the complexity of the system. Density is related to modularity of systems. Modular systems tend to have low densities between modules, though within modules, densities may sometimes be quite high.

- *The type of relationships among components*: If relationships among components are nonlinear, such as when the interconnectedness of a network increases as the square of the numbers of network nodes, the complexity of the system is higher. Nonlinear relationships contribute to the explosions or the rapid collapses of system properties, especially ones that have the potential to add complexity to the system. It is also more difficult to predict the system when the processes that produce and maintain it are nonlinear.

• *Positive feedback loops*: These generate complexity. Chaotic systems are an example of positive feedback loops that, over time, lead to self-reinforcing cascades of systems changes that are either explosive growth or dynamic equilibria (e.g., attractors).

Complexity is not a simple additive function of these characteristics. A system with many components that are densely linked in nonlinear relationships with positive feedback that is nonmodular and nonaggregative is definitely complex. However, systems with only a few components that have nonlinear positive feedback relationships can also exhibit complex behavior.

Complexity has two important consequences for systems. First, highly complex systems may be more fragile and brittle than those with low complexity. As Simon's (1969) and Weick's (1979) discussions of loosely coupled systems emphasize, modular systems are less vulnerable to shocks and negative events, because the problems that they cause tend to be localized and do not spread. A highly complex system, however, is more vulnerable, due to interconnections and amplifying feedback. Second, complex systems are more likely to exhibit emergent behavior than systems of low complexity (Sawyer, 2005). The surprising, unexpected results associated with emergence make complex systems good candidates to model human communication phenomena. Emergence also offers an explanation for the constitution of higher-level group, organizational, and social properties and structures by communication and other micro-level activities and interactions.

Complexity also has important implications for research. On the one hand, complex systems are much more difficult to theorize, analyze, and model than systems of low complexity, but on the other hand, they are more interesting to many scholars because they have the potential to exhibit emergence and other nonobvious properties. To study complex systems explicitly requires scholars to utilize approaches such as agent-based modeling and statistical methods that are less common in communication research.

Agency

Systems theories differ in terms of the degree of agency accorded either to the system as a whole or to its components. An extensive literature on agency (e.g., Emirbayer & Mische, 1998) informs our understanding of systems theory through focusing on responsiveness and meaningfulness of an agent's actions. Systems theorists have long been concerned with how to handle agency, tracing this concern back at least as far as Wiener's (1961) cybernetics and the subsequent debate over the nature of intention and action in systems (Rosenbluth, Wiener, & Bigelow, 1968; Taylor, 1968). In a foundational article for communication theory, Cushman and Pearce (1977) distinguished *rules theories*, which were portrayed as primarily focused on human agency, from *systems theories*, which were portrayed as variable-centered formalisms without much focus on issues of agency. The literature on agent-based systems and self-reflexive systems theories (Krippendorff, 2009; Steier & Smith, 1985) represent two lines of inquiry that deal explicitly with agency and have important insights for organizational communication.

For this chapter, the agency of a human being (or other entity) can be defined in terms of the following characteristics:

• *Responsiveness* to internal and external cues for action. At the lowest level, the agent simply responds to cues, and at higher levels, the agent actively monitors its environment for cues.

• *Reflexive monitoring of action* against goals or intentions that allows for changes that align activity better with them.

• Action governed by a *deliberative, problem-solving process* in which the agent considers alternative responses. The stream of mundane activity may be mindless and habitual, but when a novelty or impediment suggests a need to adapt, the agent engages in problem solving. Whatever course of action is taken, the agent could always have done otherwise. The complexity of the problem-solving process may also vary.

- *Awareness of other agents and the environment* through the construction of internal representations or models that enable the agent to predict and understand others and to rehearse and evaluate the outcomes of possible actions. Other persons are not considered simply to be objects but are accorded agency, and action toward them takes their own agency into account.

- *Meaningfulness* is linked to agency through a process of interpretation. Action occurs against the backdrop of the agent's life narrative, and the agent interprets external cues and other agents in light of that narrative, solves problems by drawing on previous episodes, considers how choices fit with the narrative, and monitors actions in terms of the appropriateness of that narrative (Fay, 1996). In this interpretive process, actors consider the past, present, and future and the degree of emphasis placed on the deliberative problem-solving process and reflexive monitoring (Emirbayer & Mische, 1998).

- *Awareness of agency* stems from a sense that one is an agent and an (perhaps mistaken) understanding of the constraints on agency as well as the capabilities of what he/she/it can do.

The agentic continuum in systems theory is exemplified in an influential analysis by Boulding (1956) that Pondy and Mitroff (1979) applied to organization studies. Boulding distinguished nine hierarchically ordered levels of systems based on the degree to which the system resembled living organisms and the degree to which the system's internal processes resembled human cognitive systems (see Poole, 1997, for an in-depth discussion of the implications of this scheme for organizational communication research). Drawing on Boulding's typology and adding insights from social theory, agents can be distinguished along a continuum based on the degree to which they realize the characteristics of agency. As we move up the continuum, each new step incorporates attributes of the previous steps and advances levels in terms of sophistication:

- *Level One: Determined systems.* At the lowest end of the continuum are frameworks that portray the static structure of a system and dynamic models that change it in a deterministic fashion without a hint of agency.

- *Level Two: Reactive systems.* Slightly above this are agents that simply react to their environments in predetermined ways. These agents pick up internal and external signals, process them, react, and then go back into scanning mode. They monitor their internal and external environments in rudimentary ways.

- *Level Three: Goal-driven systems.* At this level of the continuum are agents that add goals and internal mechanisms for adjusting to deviations from those goals and are thus capable of more complex reactions to cues. These systems monitor their activity in terms of preset goals.

- *Level Four: Problem-solving systems.* Agents add more complex internal representations of their environments and other agents and engage in problem-solving processes that involve creativity and improvisation. Reflexive monitoring by these systems is more sophisticated and may include adjustments in goals along with changes in behaviors.

- *Level Five: Self-aware systems.* At this level, agents with self-awareness and reflexivity consciously figure themselves into problem-solving and monitoring processes. These agents live in a meaningful world and view their actions in the context of this world. They dynamically adjust goals and may switch between goals and envision new projects that emerge as they go along.

- *Level Six: Multivocal systems.* At the highest end of the continuum are full-fledged conscious agents who are potentially complicated by having multiple selves that are differentially relevant to various situations. These selves may be constructed dynamically as problem solving and making choices as monitoring unfolds.

The prototypical agent is a human being. However, as this continuum suggests, inanimate objects such as computer programs can also be agents in the sense that they can respond to cues, initiate activity, and bring some end to this process. These simple agents do not exhibit the more advanced characteristics at the high end of the continuum, but as computer applications become more sophisticated, they are likely to perform at higher systems levels. The line between human agency and the agency of things presents a challenging conceptual problem (Pickering, 1995), and systems theory is one area that pushes the boundaries of human-centered views of agency.

Thus far, this discussion has focused on the agency of systems as a whole. This analysis, however, also applies to components of systems or to groups of agents interacting in a larger system. This factor leads to complications, because the interactions of the agents, a component of complexity, may differ qualitatively for different levels of agency represented in the continuum.

Agency has several important consequences for systems. The higher the level of agency a system possesses, the greater its ability to change and adapt. Systems with fixed structures and processes that monitor their environments can change through altering their processes, but a system with higher orders of agency can consciously adapt and even change its structures and processes. Systems with higher levels of agency are also more likely to display inconsistency than those lower in agency. The same inconsistency that may be an advantage in adaptation may also impede interactions with other organizational systems, which may depend on a degree of predictability and consistency in planning their own interactions with the systems in question. Agency also has an impact on emergence in systems. Sawyer (2005) makes a complex and convincing argument that systems higher in agency are more likely to exhibit emergent properties.

Agency also has implications for research. Many communication scholars find systems higher in agency to be more consistent with their views of human participation in organizations. In addition, systems higher in agency are more consistent with interpretive approaches that stress human action as the wellspring of organizing. Systems models high in agency, however, are much more difficult to conceptualize and analyze, especially using formal systems analytic methods. It is challenging to conduct analyses with precision and detail as agency increases.

Formalization

Systems perspectives can also be differentiated in terms of whether they represent the system using *formal* mathematical, computational, or logical methodologies or *informal* verbal terms. *Formal systems representations* emphasize rigorous application of systems models to organizational communication phenomena. A number of formal methodologies may be employed, including cybernetics (Ashby, 1954); systems dynamics (Forrester, 1968; Sterman, 2000); mathematical modeling procedures such as petri nets, systems of differential equations, state space analysis, and Markov models (Fishwick, 2007; Hinrichson & Pritchard, 2010; Leik & Meeker, 1975); statistical approaches such as structural equation modeling (SEM) and time series analysis (Monge, 1982); catastrophe theory (Thom, 1975); chaos theory (Gregersen & Sailer, 1993; Tutzauer, 1997); agent-based models such as cellular automata, deliberative agents, and artificial societies (Miller & Page, 2007; Sawyer, 2005); and logical calculi (Pearce & Cronen, 1980). Fishwick (2007) notes that formal models can be expressed in at least four formats: (1) as *mathematical structures*, "encoded in traditional textually based mathematical notation"; (2) as *physical constructs*, "physical objects made of organic or engineered materials"; (3) in *diagrammatic terms*, pictorial formats that illustrate flows or relationships; and (4) as *linguistic constructs*, "formal languages with syntax, semantics, and pragmatics" (pp. 2–3).

Formal systems models provide an ideal-type representation of the phenomenon; that is, translating it into the formal modeling language extracts essential or interesting features that can be studied through analysis of the model. When verbal theories are recast into formal systems models, theorists often narrow or restrict the meaning of concepts to fit the constraints of the formalism (Leik & Meeker, 1975). While these alterations elide aspects of the phenomenon, they also permit a level of rigor not possible in models expressed in ordinary language. The key to building a good model is to analyze the phenomenon deeply to identify the key aspects to include in a simpler model (Miller & Page, 2007).

Formal models are first and foremost evaluated in terms of whether they measure up to the requirements of the formal method (e.g., Does a system dynamics model converge as it should?). In terms of empirical evaluation, systems modeling yields conclusions about the properties of the system or representations of its behaviors that can be compared to empirical data from real instances of the system (McPhee & Poole, 1980). Such assessments, however, are tricky because the model truly is an abstraction and idealization of any real-world system, and so the model does not always correspond to the empirical data to any degree of precision. In many cases, qualitative comparison of the model with empirical descriptions of the system is the best indicator of fit because of error—random and due to research design issues—in the empirical data. For example, does the empirical organizational system exhibit a qualitatively recognizable discontinuous jump from one state to another (e.g., from supporting a proposed strategy to opposing it), as predicted by a catastrophe model of the system?

Informal systems representations use systems concepts, but describe and explain the system in a verbal expository fashion. Such representations focus primarily on description, explanation, and understanding of the phenomenon under study through application of systems concepts such as boundaries and causal maps to understand and explain organizational phenomena. This approach appropriates ideas from formal systems theories and perspectives and applies them to organizational communication. Miller (2003), for example, drew selectively on concepts from chaos theory, complexity theory, and self-organizing systems to illuminate the situation of nurses compelled to change their roles and practices through modifying processes in health care organizations.

Informal systems analyses do not always present a neat picture of organizational communication systems. They often highlight the fuzziness of systems concepts when applied to empirical organizations that use systems concepts in evocative ways. For example, research in the bona fide group tradition (Putnam & Stohl, 1990) has explicated the notion of boundary in ways that turn it from an arbitrary line around the system into something that members perceive and that is structured dynamically over time. Other informal systems research has combined systems concepts with ideas from other theoretical traditions, as Rice and Cooper (2010) do in their study of dysfunctional routines in organizations. The informal systems approach is used most frequently in interpretive studies of systems, as exemplified by Miller (2003) and Weick (1979).

Formal and informal systems approaches present a dichotomy, but they are also ultimately complementary. Formal approaches develop core ideas in a clear and relatively unambiguous fashion and thus are sources for informal analysts. Informal approaches are more evocative and suggest implications of concepts that originate in the formal realm but are expressed sparsely. Informal approaches also stretch concepts from formal systems and thus suggest new ideas that can enrich formal analysis.

Systems Perspectives in Organizational Communication

This section positions systems approaches to organizational communication using the three dimensions as an organizing framework. Table 2.3 classifies research according to the type

Table 2.3 A Classification of Systems Approaches in Organizational Communication

	Informal Representation			Formal Representation		
	Low Complexity	**Moderate Complexity**	**High Complexity**	**Low Complexity**	**Moderate Complexity**	**High Complexity**
Low Agency Determined Systems Reactive Systems	**1.1**	**1.2**	**1.3**	**1.4** Statistical Models (→)	**1.5** Deterministic Mathematical Models Network Models Self-Organizing Systems (↓)	**1.6** *Catastrophe Theory* *"Chaos Theory"* Cellular Automata (↓)
Moderate Agency Goal-Driven Systems Problem-Solving Systems	**2.1** Structural-Functionalism	**2.2** Organizing/ Sensemaking (Weick) (↓) and (→) Crazy Systems Structuration Theory Luhmann (↓)	**2.3** Informal "Chaos Theory" Analyses Informal Complex Adaptive Systems Analyses	**2.4** Cybernetics (→) *Logic-Based System Models* (→)	**2.5** *System Dynamics Models*	**2.6** *Complex Adaptive Systems* *Agent Based Models* (↓)
High Agency Self-Aware Systems Multivocal Systems	**3.1**	**3.2** Self-Reflexive Systems Theory (→) and (←)	**3.3**	**3.4**	**3.5**	**3.6**

Note: An arrow by an entry indicates that some uses of the approach could fit in the cell(s) it is pointing to.

of representation, the level of complexity, and the level of agency.

Non-italicized entries in the cells represent existing research, while italicized entries represent types of systems analysis that have promising potential for future organizational communication studies. The following discussion identifies lines of research and the dimensions of systems approaches as well as the contributions of this research to organizational communication scholarship. This analysis indicates the degree to which organizational communication scholarship has covered the terrain of systems theories, some predispositions and biases in current thought, and new directions.

Structural-Functionalism (Cell 2.1)

Structural-functionalism was one of the two perspectives that guided the first wave of systems research in organizational communication. Fontes and Guardalabene (1976) argued that structural-functionalism hinged on the "relationship between structures that produce functions facilitating the achievement of some goal" (p. 299) and noted that structural-functional analysis assumes that the system is attempting to maintain equilibrium in the face of environmental demands. For specific functions, Parson's system theory (Parsons, 1951; Skidmore, 1979) from sociology served as an implicit guiding framework. It posited four main functions that must be met in a coherent and effective system: adaptation, goal attainment, pattern maintenance, and integration. Farace et al. (1977) defined three functions of communication within this larger framework: task achievement, system maintenance, and innovation. These three categories were reflected in a great deal of subsequent research, particularly in network analysis.

Structural-functional analysis represents a system informally (even though statistical models are sometimes generated to test verbal hypotheses) and accords a moderate degree of agency to the system, which is presumed to seek goals and be capable of limited problem solving in pursuit of these goals (at least in some subsystems of the overall system). Structural-functional representations are also low in complexity, since they have relatively few components, are assumed to seek equilibrium, and do not interact in particularly complex ways.

Structural-functionalism has been criticized on several grounds, including (1) circular reasoning in the establishment of functions, since they are generally identified *post hoc* and then traced back to establish their effects on the system (e.g., Giddens, 1977); (2) weakness in establishing causal explanation for effects; and (3) a lack of dynamism, since the approach assumes equilibrium as a fixed state. Fontes and Guardalabene (1976) mount a spirited defense against these charges and develop an account of quasi-teleological explanation in response. Pavitt (1994) provides a thoughtful and thorough discussion of the prerequisites for establishing whether a functional explanation holds. Perhaps the most serious indictment of structural-functionalism is its inability to gain much theoretical traction in organizational communication research, especially since its critique in the cultural-critical turn that organizational communication took in the early 1980s (cf. Putnam, 1983).

Cybernetics (Cell 2.4)

Cybernetics (Ashby, 1954, 1962; Barnett, 1997; Buckley, 1968; Krippendorff, 1977; Wiener, 1961) is defined by Wiener as "the science of control and communication" (p. 11). It offers a formal representation of goal-driven systems. Most cybernetic systems are quite simple and fall into the low-complexity range, but some cybernetics models incorporate complex cycles of control and have the potential to achieve moderate complexity. In cybernetic systems, control is managed through gathering information about the performance of the system to compare with its desired goal states. If the performance is within acceptable bounds, then the system maintains its current state. If the performance deviates from acceptable bounds, then the system adjusts itself until performance returns to acceptable levels. As the reader has no doubt noted, cybernetics presents one archetypal account of negative, deviation-correcting feedback.

Cybernetics has provided the foundation for theories of control and for the design of control systems ranging from machines and missiles to organizational controls (Farace et al., 1977) and has had substantial influence on many aspects of life. Formal mathematical and graphical techniques for the analysis of cybernetic systems are described by Ashby (1954, 1962). Krippendorff (2009) synthesizes formal cybernetic analysis and information theory to develop a communicative theory of cybernetics.

Organizing and Sensemaking (Cell 2.2)

Weick's (1979, 1995) application of systems thinking focuses on how organizations are built up through a process of enacting their environments within an evolutionary cycle of variation, selection, and retention of interpretations. Weick's (1979) early work centers on how organizing is possible at all, particularly how organization stems from interlocking behaviors organized through selecting sets of assembly rules that guide interpretations, cycles of actions, and causal maps of an organizing unit (Narayan & Armstrong, 2005). These processes are built up, modified, and retained in the system through multiple cycles of an evolutionary process that shape member understandings of how the organization works. Weick's model of organizing offers one view of self-organizing systems.

Building on his theory of organizing, Weick (1995) turned his attention to sensemaking, which he characterized as an ongoing retrospective enactment of sensible environments by members of an organization. Sensemaking is driven by plausibility rather than accuracy, is triggered by extracting cues from the environment, and is influenced by organizational identity. Controlling key premises and ensuring organizational continuity in the midst of member turnover contribute to the enactment of sensemaking. It occurs through the four processes of "arguing, expecting, committing, and manipulating" (Weick, 1995, p. 170). Hernes and Maitlis (2010) present more recent perspectives on sensemaking. This work is situated in Cell 2.2, because the organizational system is informally represented as a problem-solving entity. Most of Weick's exemplars are relatively simple but have moderately complex implications. However, this approach could support highly complex systems and perhaps even higher levels of self-awareness within the system.

Crazy Systems and Unusual Routines (Cell 2.2)

Kafka (1998) and Heller (1961) were both chroniclers of dysfunctional systems that ostensibly operated normally but trapped their unfortunate occupants in frustrating, sometimes nightmarish dilemmas. Unpacking these chronicles, Rice and Cooper (2010) present a systems-based analysis of "unusual routines" in organizations, "recurrent interaction pattern[s] in which a system allows or requires a process which creates and reinforces, through dysfunctional (nonexistent, obstructive, or deviation-reinforcing) feedback, unintended and undesirable outcomes, either within or across system levels (or both)" (p. 17). They draw on work by Singer (1980) on crazy systems in which conflicting goals, broken feedback processes, manipulative behavior, and willful and unwitting blindness to the nature of the system create frustrating and self-defeating processes. This informal analysis of moderately complex systems in which problem solving has become dysfunctional shows how trying to solve a problem or resolve a seemingly small error generates huge amounts of unnecessary work, elicits no meaningful or effective response from the system, and may perpetuate a cascade of further errors.

Structuration Theory (Cell 2.2)

Structuration theory, discussed in Chapter 3, is also situated in Cell 2.2. Structuration theory is a critical systems theory that accounts for an underlying generative structure and rules and resources of the observable system that are mobilized in action by agents to produce and reproduce the system. This theory accounts for the complexity of a system and system dynamics by using the concept of duality of structure, which argues that action and structure are inseparable parts of the same process. As a result, seemingly separate levels of social systems are encompassed in a single process of structuration (Sawyer, 2005). Stated informally, this theory situates agency with the individual actors in the system.

Informal Chaos Theory and Informal Complex Adaptive Systems Theory (Cell 2.3)

Chaos theory and complex adaptive systems theories include heuristic and powerful concepts that expand the repertoires of systems analysts. Insightful qualitative analyses of the stresses and strains of nurses at the edge of chaos (Miller, 2003), organizational culture (McFarland, 1997), the glass ceiling (Reuther & Fairhurst, 2000), and organizational change (Salem, 2002) use concepts such as fractals, strange attractors, autopoiesis, and self-organizing systems in illuminating qualitative analyses. These studies evoke high complexity and thus are placed in Cell 2.3. The value of these analyses is that they transfer technically obscure insights into general use and expand on the implications of these insights. There are also potential problems. Because formal systems concepts are used metaphorically by studies in this cell, there is a risk that these analyses might inadvertently misinterpret formally stated processes, add meaning that is not justifiable by the original formal analyses, or omit important implications that the original models do not make clear except to those versed in the technical formalisms they are expressed in. However, metaphor has an expansive capacity, and some of these analyses might suggest avenues or implications that could be reformalized and provide new ideas for formal theorizing.

Radical Constructivism and Self-Reflexive Systems Theory (Cell 3.2)

In much of the empirical communication research, the scholar or the observer is regarded as outside the phenomenon of interest. Theories of "the cybernetics of cybernetics" and radical constructivism (Krippendorff, 2009; von Glasersfeld, 1985) explore the position of the observer of a system. Radical constructivism (Krippendorff, 2009) argues that the observer can only construct a model of reality rather than actually getting at this reality. These constructions are not arbitrary but represent what the observer is set up to create by his/her interests and positioning in the world. Constructions are subject to an evolutionary-like process of selection, since some descriptions serve observers better than others. Selection, however, does not guarantee an optimal construction but merely one that is capable of thriving within the constraints of the current situation, including the observer's constraints and the constraints embedded in what is observed.

In this approach, the observer must be part of the system, because he/she affects the construction process. Thus theory or model construction is self-referential and recursive; that is, the observer is reshaped by the construction process. Since the observer is intimately involved with the construction, there is also an ethical imperative that others involved in any construction should be accorded the same authority over the process as the observer is. Research, then, must ultimately be comprised of multiple observers who recursively interact as they participate in constructing the system. To ensure that this process results in a valid representation, the observer should expand the number of choices available to those involved in the construction and place as few constraints as possible on it. Doing this, however, is paradoxical, because construction is necessarily subject to constraints. Hofstadter (2007) examines these paradoxes and related issues in additional detail. Examples of these types of analyses applied to communication in general and to organizational communication specifically are presented in Steier (1991) and in Krippendorff (2009).

The value of radical constructivism is its inclusion of self-reflexivity and paradoxes in working out a logical account of systems observation (Krippendorff, 2009). This research takes an informal approach and represents the clearest example of high levels of agency in organizational communication research. Most analyses that have been advanced imply low to moderate complexity, but in principle, this approach could yield high-complexity representations.

Statistical Models (Cell 1.4)

Theorists have used two types of statistical models to represent organizational systems formally. Structural Equation Modeling (SEM) is commonly used to test causal models of organizational communication systems phenomena, such as burnout (Miller, Stiff, & Ellis, 1988). Monge (1982) explicitly addressed the application of SEM to study systems in detail and concluded that it was appropriate for the study of holistic properties of systems and (if nonrecursive SEM is utilized) causal feedback loops. Monge, Farace, Eisenberg, Miller, and White (1984) proposed the use of time series analysis as a second approach to organizational communication analysis on the grounds that it yields insights into the nature of temporal processes.

While statistical modeling is an important tool for characterizing and testing hypotheses about systems, there are limitations to this approach. Both SEM and time series assume that the system is in equilibrium, and hence, the process applies to only a subset of systems. Second, SEM and time series analysis can only be applied usefully to low-complexity systems (although some time series applications can be used to model nonlinear systems of moderate complexity, as discussed in Poole, Van de Ven, Dooley, & Holmes, 2000). Finally, the insights that statistical modeling provides are based on variance-based analyses of samples of systems rather than on the analysis of the behavior and dynamics of the system per se. Hence, it can only provide synopses of system processes that are one step removed from the processes themselves. Approaches described in the following sections provide different types of insights that can be combined with statistical modeling to yield more complete pictures of systems.

Deterministic Mathematical Models (Cell 1.5)

Scholars have frequently used mathematical models with both continuous and discrete variables to represent organizational systems (McPhee & Poole, 1980). Researchers in management, sociology, and organization studies have advanced a number of continuous mathematical models of organizations and organizational processes, but organizational communication researchers have not used these approaches very often. Continuous mathematical models are used extensively in interpersonal communication, persuasion, and influence (e.g., Hunter, Danes, & Cohen, 1984; Watt & VanLear, 1996), and these applications can serve as useful exemplars for organizational communication scholars. Specifically, researchers have employed Markov chain analyses of discrete variables to model group processes (Hewes & Poole, 2012). Richards and Seary (1997) develop a discrete stochastic model of network convergence in organizational contexts and Poole et al. (2000) describe procedures that use the SPSS statistical package to conduct Markov chain analyses in the study of organizational change.

Both genres of formal mathematical models assume determined or reactive systems with low agency. They are capable of modeling systems of low to moderate complexity. While this may seem to limit their applicability, mathematical models are an important resource for organizational communication scholars. To formulate a workable model, scholars must focus on the essentials and think through the precise nature of relationships among constructs. A well-formulated model can illuminate how the system unfolds over time, and the trajectory of the model can be compared to longitudinal empirical data for qualitative resemblances. Hence, the very sparse nature of mathematical models can yield clear insights of significant parts of a system. Mathematical models can serve as a source of discipline for the sometimes florid and overcomplicated verbal theories of organizational communication. McPhee and Poole (1980), however, register several caveats in the use of mathematical models for communication research. These include the possibility that the model may omit important aspects of phenomena that are not amenable to mathematical representation and that modeling may lead to oversimplification of complex phenomena.

Communication Network Models (Cell 1.5)

The largest body of research associated with systems theory in organizational communication focuses on the analysis of organizational communication networks (Shumate & Contractor, Chapter 18). Network analysis is by far the most common formal method for describing organizational systems. Until around 1995, network mapping was the predominant approach in organizational communication scholarship, and network concepts were derived from the configuration of the network. The major explanatory concepts were network properties (such as density and centralization), properties of individual nodes (such as centrality and connectedness), and network roles (such as liaison and isolate).

Since this early work, scholars have focused on identifying the mechanisms that generate the network processes. Monge and Contractor (2003) identified ten distinct classes of generative mechanisms for networks, including exchange, homophily (like seeks like), balance, contagion, and collective action. They have developed a multitheoretical, multilevel model for communication networks. Methods exist to identify which generative mechanisms operate in a given network and to model network dynamics over time (Shumate, 2010, in Miller et al., 2010; Shumate & Contractor, Chapter 18). Agent-based models that incorporate theoretical assumptions about network mechanisms are also available to simulate network generation (Ahmad et al., 2010). These approaches enable organizational communication scholars to go beyond the descriptions common in traditional network research to test the causes behind network systems.

Self-Organizing Systems Models (Cells 1.5/2.5)

Self-organizing systems theory seeks to explain how order can arise in the face of ever-increasing disorder (*entropy*). The groundwork for this approach was laid in the work of Prigogine (1980) and colleagues on dissipative structures and Varela, Maturana, and Uribe (1974) on autopoietic systems. Self-organizing systems often have goals, but their emergence and existence is dependent solely on self-organizing processes, so they reside at the border of Cells 1.5 and 2.5. Since they are emergent, they are at least moderately complex.

Contractor, Seibold, and colleagues (Contractor, 1994; Contractor & Seibold, 1993) define four requirements that must be met for a system to be self-organizing. First, at least two components of the system must be mutually causal (e.g., there must be a feedback loop). The system must also exhibit *autocatalysis*; that is, the product of the interactions of at least two components must lead to subsequent increases in at least one of the components. Third, the system must be "far from equilibrium" in that it must import

> a large amount of energy from outside the system [and] use the energy to help renew

> its *own* structures—a process referred to as 'autopoiesis' (Varela et al., 1974)—and dissipate, rather than accumulate the accruing disorder (entropy) back into the environment. (Contractor, 1994; Contractor & Seibold, 1993, p. 539)

Finally, the system must be open to external shocks from its environment. This type of system can be self-organizing, given an appropriate set of components and relationships.

Organizational communication scholars have employed the self-organizing systems approach to understand group-decision development (Contractor & Whitbred, 1997), the use of group-decision support systems (Contractor & Seibold, 1993), and the emergence of shared interpretations in organizations (Contractor & Grant, 1996). These applications show the value of this perspective in highlighting the ways in which systems emerge and sustain themselves and the impact of autonomous systems on communication processes and outcomes.

Luhmann (Cell 2.2/3.2)

Luhmann's (1995) influential theory develops informal representations of systems based on formal self-organizing systems theory (see Chapter 7 for a detailed discussion of Luhmann's theory). Luhmann advances a process-based theory that argues that systems self-organize through communicative processes that serve system functions and simultaneously establish the boundary of the system. This demarcation of what is and what is not the system is a foundational act that establishes the system as an ongoing entity in which maintaining its boundary becomes a continual process accomplished through communication. For Luhmann, communication is the selection of a particular state of the world out of a range of possibilities through interactions between senders and receivers (cf. information theory). Schoeneborn (2011) details how this approach enables Luhmann to offer a communicative conceptualization of the constitution of organizations based on the decision as the foundational act. In the tradition of self-organizing systems theorists, particularly autopoiesis, this conceptualization of how communication is constitutive of organization allows Luhmann to tackle the problem of how systems emerge seemingly from nothing and maintain themselves in the face of forces that work to break them down. Luhmann has been criticized for downplaying materiality and placing too much emphasis on communication (Schoeneborn, 2011). Luhmann's work and Leydesdorff's (2001) critical extensions of it remain quite influential among systems and critical theorists.

Cellular Automata (Cell 1.6)

A cellular automaton consists of a grid of cells, each of which can take a limited number of discrete states (e.g., on-off; persuaded-not persuaded; linked-not linked) in addition to rules that specify how the cells influence one another over time. The grid of cells can thus evolve into various temporal patterns, and these patterns can be used to model systems, such as networks or groups of adherents to particular beliefs. Wolfram (2002) groups cellular automata into four classes: (1) those in which the patterns becomes homogeneous and stable over time, (2) those with patterns that oscillate over time in consistent fashion, (3) those which show patterns that are seemingly chaotic and random, and (4) extremely complex yet stable patterns that recycle over time. Numerous examples of cellular automata can be found in Wolfram (2002); Bitstorm's version of Conway's game of life offers an easily accessible online example (http://www.bitstorm.org/gameoflife/).

Corman's (2006) program of research using cellular automata to model network phenomena is an outstanding example of the application of the new science to organizational communication. The starting point of this work is a theory of communication network activation developed by Corman, McPhee, and Scott (Corman & Scott, 1994; McPhee & Corman, 1995) and expanded in subsequent research combining qualitative methods and modeling (Corman, Stage, & Scott, 1997). The basic idea is that networks tend to propagate due to common activities that their members engage in. The cells of the model are the activity foci, and the model simulates their activation and the networks that result from this activation (Corman, 2006). Corman (1996) employs a cellular automaton model to derive unintended consequences as emergent. In subsequent analyses (Corman, 2006), he indicates how overactivating certain activity foci could disable a terrorist network.

Issues and Future Directions

As Table 2.3 indicates, many promising possibilities for applying systems approaches in organizational communication exist. The lack of work in Cells 1.1, 1.2, and 1.3 is understandable, because scholars employing informal approaches have tended to operate from interpretive and critical perspectives. More striking is the relative paucity of formal analyses, especially in Cells 1.6, 2.5, and 2.6, for which there are well-developed bodies of modeling and simulation methodologies. Contrary to predictions that formal systems approaches would show their value by illuminating problems of interest to organizational communication scholars (Poole, 1997), formal systems analysis still seems to be a relatively isolated specialty in organizational communication. It may be that the price of admission to the formal systems club—that is, learning difficult formal systems and software and moving to abstract representations—seems too steep for most communication scholars. Formal systems scholars, for their part, have not framed their work in ways that reach out to other communities of scholars, and so their insights remain for the most part inaccessible. Recent advances in network modeling (Miller et al., 2010) and Rice and Cooper's (2010) intriguing application of dysfunctional systems theory have the potential to bridge the informal and formal traditions.

More dialogue between the informal and formal traditions would be beneficial. While informal systems analyses are messier than formal models, they can contribute to formal systems scholarship in at least two ways. First, they suggest modifications or reinterpretations of formal concepts that can enrich systems theory. Second, they provide empirical examples for model building. These examples present challenges that can stimulate advances in formal modeling and the development of new formal approaches. Formal systems models, in turn, can contribute concepts and ideas for real-world systems analysis, and to the extent that new approaches are added to formal modeling, they hold potential for advancing informal systems studies. The insights derived from chaos theory and the new sciences exemplify the potential of formal models.

Table 2.3 also suggests another key lacuna, a lack of research in row 3. With the exception of the self-reflexive systems theorists and possible extensions of some approaches in Cell 2.2, most systems representations in organizational communication (and systems studies in general) are relatively mindless in the sense that they do not model self-awareness or multiple self-aware voices. Sawyer (2005) argues that formal agent-based models that incorporate self-awareness and other complex agential processes will emerge in the future. However, at this point, formal representations remain simple and mindless.

In formal systems representations, there are impressive advances—some old, some new—that could be used in organizational communication. Several of these are listed in italics in Table 2.3. They include:

- *System dynamics* (Cell 2.5; Forrester, 1968; Sterman, 2000) models causal influences in systems as flows among variables that use specialized algorithms to solve banks of differential equations. It is placed in Cell 2.5 because goals are embodied in cycles of variables that govern system operation in a fashion similar to cybernetic models. System dynamics models are often quite complex, incorporating dozens of variables in multiple causal loops. Sterman (2000) and Senge (1990) offer detailed examples of the insights that this type of modeling (and informal approaches that derive from it) can yield for complex causal processes in systems. The work on system dynamics offers a rigorous complement to informal modeling of complex causal loops that enables the impact of key features to be precisely specified and tracked over time. Software to support system dynamics modeling, such as Vensim (Ventana Systems, 2011), has made this technically difficult enterprise not much more demanding than using traditional statistical packages.

- *Catastrophe theory* (Cell 1.6), developed by Thom (1975), has been applied in management, organizational psychology, and social psychological research (Guastello & Gregson, 2011). It is based on deterministic mathematical models that assume an equilibrium system. Catastrophe models depict the behavior of response variables as a function of two or more control variables. Various types of catastrophe models are used to model *tipping points* (when a sudden change in state occurs), sudden shifts between two or more states (e.g., supportive-unsupportive), and the *butterfly effect* (where small changes in initial conditions can result in significant differences in systems behavior; McPhee & Poole, 1980). Methods for building and testing catastrophe models that use statistical packages and accessible languages are described in Guastello and Gregson (2011).

- Formal mathematical modeling based on *chaos theory* (Cell 1.6) depends on these features: (1) the behavior of the system over time is sensitive to initial conditions; (2) trajectories of systems behaviors mix and overlap over time, creating complex interdependencies of temporal patterns; and (3) highly dense maps of behaviors emerge over time (see Poole et al., 2000, for a description of methods to determine when these assumptions hold). Chaos theory models can capture complex moving equilibria in which behaviors follow qualitatively similar patterns without exact repetition (e.g., strange attractors) and patterns repeat at different scales or levels of the system (fractals). Another model associated with chaos theory is self-organized criticality, which models systems at the edge of transition from one phase (e.g., highly organized and structured) to another (e.g., disorganized and unstructured). Chaos theory is based on deterministic models that recursively develop over time, creating complex dependencies and surprising behaviors such as sudden phase shifts from relatively simple mathematical formulations. Chaos theory captured public imagination in the early 1990s due to Gleick's (1987) book and has been appropriated in informal systems analysis of organizational communication.

- *Complex adaptive systems* modeling (Cell 2.6) uses sets of independent intelligent agents to simulate systems (Holland, 2012; Miller & Page, 2007). The agents differ in their degree of intelligence, from reactive units to adaptive ones (paralleling levels of agency, as each agent is itself a small system). Systems also differ in the variety of agents they incorporate. In some systems, every agent is the same (in basic cellular automata, all cells are identical), while in others, different types of agents emerge. Agent-based models offer a different approach to systems analysis than do mathematical models or variable-based systems simulations, such as systems dynamics which offer synoptic views of the system. Agent-based models are composed of individual components that operate autonomously and interact with other agents, just as individuals, groups, and organizations do. From these interactions, emergent phenomena arise (Sawyer, 2005). Sawyer (2005) argues that as agents become more sophisticated, systems models will be able to simulate organizations composed of a variety of human agents, albeit with more simple agents than actual human beings would be. Corman's (2006) previously noted research with cellular automata represents one exemplar of agent-based modeling. Contractor, Wohlgezogen, and Zhu (2012) have also explored agent-based modeling of organizational networks.

- *Logic-Based systems models* (Cells 2.4 and 2.5), which describe systems and their processes in terms of nonmathematical logical formalisms, have been around for more than half a century (e.g., Lévi-Strauss, 1969) and have been developed in sociology. In communication, Pearce and Cronen (1980) set forth a useful and powerful deontic logic that they apply to interpersonal and organizational communication with some impressive results. This approach models practical reasoning and other purposive processes as well as rules and norms. As such, it falls in Cell 2.4 and, in some cases, Cell 2.5, because these models are generally low to moderate in complexity. These models have great potential, because they are built on rule-based logics of communication.

To use these approaches, researchers need to learn modeling techniques. In the past, this required an extensive background in mathematics and programming, but this prerequisite is no longer the case. Formal analyses that use systems dynamics, cellular automata, and even agent-based modeling can be conducted using software that takes about as long to learn as SEM and network analysis techniques that many organizational communication scholars have mastered (e.g., Mathematica, Vensim, and NetLogo). These methods could be included in graduate methodology courses, just as network analysis approaches currently are.

One reason that scholars do not seem motivated to use formal systems approaches is the lack of useful applications of these methods to important problems in organizational communication. Formal systems studies tend to be written in arcane language so that they are inaccessible and unappealing to most organizational communication scholars. Hence, a critical task is to communicate the results of formal systems studies effectively and to show how they contribute to organizational communication.

The discussion to this point has valorized human agency, as is typical of contemporary organizational communication studies. Relatively simple formal systems models, however, pose a challenge to this presumption. Simple systems models, such as a catastrophe model that has three variables, and basic agent-based models with relatively small sets of identical agents can generate surprises, unintended consequences, emergents, and complex dynamics (Miller & Page, 2007; Sawyer, 2005). This discovery raises a compelling question: If relatively simple models with low levels of agency can generate patterns of behavior similar to those of self-reflexive human agents, then do we really need the complex agency posited by interpretive and critical approaches? It is a question worth pursuing.

A trend that is likely to encourage scholars to use systems approaches is the emerging era of *big data*, huge data sets of digitally captured data from Internet use, online games, digital libraries, digitized pictures, maps, diagrams, online census data, troves of government documents, and many other sources. These data sets contain unprecedented detail and accuracy in the use of present and historical behaviors and offer outstanding new opportunities for research. Pursuing these opportunities requires information technology to capture, store, and process the data and systems approaches to theorize and model processes (e.g., Ahmad et al., 2010). The Virtual Worlds Exploratorium project, for example, is a four-institution project that focuses on the analysis of huge data sets from massive multiplayer online games (Williams, Contractor, Poole, Srivastava, & Cai, 2011) to gain insights into group dynamics, networks, and individual phenomena such as trust and expertise.

Conclusion

The quest of systems theory is to understand complexity and to turn mysteries that seem too difficult to grasp into verbal or formal models. At their best, these models show how relatively simple processes at the level of parts generate unexpected and surprising phenomena at the level of wholes. They illuminate how systems at all levels engage with their environments. They suggest straightforward measures to manage complex processes so that they benefit the organization, its members, and its environment. They motivate scholars to reflect on their own roles in constructing knowledge, especially on the relationship between knower and known. If there is a central lesson in systems theory, it is that everything is a process, a journey into inquiry. Systems research in organizational communication invites scholars to come along on that journey.

References

Ahmad, M. A., Huffakar, D., Wang, J., Treem, J., Poole, M. S., & Srivastava, J. (2010). *GTPA: A Generative Model for Online Mentor-Apprentice Networks.* Paper presented at Twenty-Fourth AAAI Conference on Artificial Intelligence, Atlanta, GA.

Ashby, W. R. (1954). *Design for a brain.* New York, NY: Wiley.

Ashby, W. R. (1962). Principles of the self-organizing system. In H. von Foerster & G. W. Zopf (Eds.), *Principles of self-organization* (pp. 255–278). New York, NY: Pergamon.

Barnard, C. I. (1938). *The functions of the executive.* Cambridge, MA: Harvard University Press.

Barnett, G. A. (1997). Organizational communication systems: The traditional perspective. In G. A. Barnett & L. Thayer (Eds.), *Organization—Communication, emerging perspectives V: The renaissance in systems thinking* (pp. 47–64). Greenwich, CT: Ablex.

Barnett, G. A., & Thayer, L. (Eds.). (1997). *Organization—Communication, emerging perspectives V: The renaissance in systems thinking.* Greenwich, CT: Ablex.

Boulding, K. E. (1956). General systems theory: The skeleton of a science. *Management Science, 2*(3), 197–208.

Buckley, W. (1968). *Modern systems research for the behavioral scientist.* Chicago, IL: Aldine.

Burton, R. M., DeSanctis, G., & Obel, B. (2006). *Organizational design: A step-by-step approach.* Cambridge, NY: Cambridge University Press.

Contractor, N. S. (1994). Self-organizing systems perspective in the study of organizational communication. In B. Kovacic (Ed.), *New approaches to organizational communication* (pp. 39–66). Albany, NY: SUNY Press.

Contractor, N. S., & Grant, S. J. (1996). The emergence of shared interpretations in organizations: A self-organizing systems perspective. In J. H. Watt & C. A. VanLear (Eds.), *Dynamic patterns in communication processes* (pp. 215–230). Thousand Oaks, CA: SAGE.

Contractor, N. S., & Seibold, D. R. (1993). Theoretical frameworks for the study of structuring processes in group decision support systems: Adaptive structuration theory and self-organizing systems theory. *Human Communication Research, 19*(4), 528–563.

Contractor, N. S., & Whitbred, R. C. (1997). Decision development in workgroups: A comparison of contingency and self-organizing systems perspectives. In G. A. Barnett & L. Thayer (Eds.), *Organization—Communication, emerging perspectives V: The renaissance in systems thinking* (pp. 83–104). Greenwich, CT: Ablex.

Contractor, N., Wohlgezogen, F., & Zhu, M. (2012). *Assessing system readiness for the delivery of family health interventions: Agent-based model.* Report prepared for the Bill and Melinda Gates Foundation. Evanston, IL: Northwestern University. Retrieved from http://bit.ly/GatesABM

Corman, S. R. (1996). Cellular automata as models of unintended consequences in organizational communication. In J. C. Watts & A. VanLear (Eds.), *Dynamic patterns in communication processes* (pp. 191–212). Thousand Oaks, CA: SAGE.

Corman, S. R. (2006). Using activity focus networks to pressure terrorist organizations. *Mathematical and Computational Organization Theory, 12*(1), 35–49.

Corman, S. R., & Scott, C. R. (1994). Perceived communication relationships, activity foci, and observable communication in collectives. *Communication Theory, 4*(3), 171–190.

Corman, S. R., Stage, C., & Scott, C. R. (1997, May). *Communication-related activity systems: An empirical description and computational organization model of activity foci in a grocery store chain.* Paper presented at the meeting of the International Communication Association, Montreal, Canada.

Cushman, D. P., & Pearce, W. B. (1977). Generality and necessity in three types of human communication theory: Special attention to rules theory. In B. D. Ruben (Ed.), *Communication yearbook* (vol. 1, pp. 173–182). New Brunswick, NJ: Transaction.

Emirbayer, M., & Mische, A. (1998). What is agency? *American Journal of Sociology, 103*(4), 962–1023.

Farace, R. V., Monge, P. R., & Russell, H. (1977). *Communicating and organizing.* Reading, MA: Addison-Wesley.

Fay, B. (1996). *Contemporary philosophy of social science.* Malden, MA: Blackwell.

Fishwick, P. A. (2007). The languages of dynamic systems modeling. In P. Fishwick (Ed.), *Handbook of dynamic systems modeling* (pp. 1–12). London, England: Chapman & Hall.

Follett, M. P. (1941). *Dynamic administration: The papers of Mary Parker Follett* (H. C. Metcalf & L. Urwick, Eds.). New York, NY: Harper & Brothers.

Fontes, N., & Guardalabene, N. (1976). Structural-functionalism: An introduction to the literature. *Human Communication Research, 2*(3), 229–310.

Forrester, J. W. (1968). *Urban dynamics.* Waltham, MA: Pegasus Communications.

Giddens, A. (1977). *Studies in social and political theory.* New York, NY: Basic Books.

Gleick, J. (1987). *Chaos: Making a new science.* New York, NY: Viking.

Goldhaber, G. M. (1974). *Organizational communication.* Dubuque, IA: Kendall-Hunt.

Goldhaber, G. M., & Barnett, G. A. (Eds.). (1988). *Handbook of organizational communication.* Norwood, NJ: Ablex.

Gregersen, H., & Sailer, L. (1993). Chaos theory and its implications for social science research. *Human Relations, 46*(7), 777–802.

Guastello, S. J., & Gregson, R. A. M. (Eds.). (2011). *Nonlinear dynamical systems analysis for the behavioral sciences using real data.* Boca Raton, FL: CRC Press/Taylor & Francis.

Heller, J. (1961). *Catch 22.* New York, NY: Simon & Schuster.

Hernes, T., & Maitlis, S. (2010). *Process, sensemaking, & organizing.* New York, NY: Oxford.

Hewes, D. E., & Poole, M. S. (2012). The analysis of group interaction processes. In A. B. Hollingshead & M. S. Poole (Eds.), *Research methods for studying groups and teams* (pp. 358–385). New York, NY: Routledge.

Hinrichson, D., & Pritchard, A. (2010). *Mathematical systems theory I: Modeling, state space analysis, stability, robustness.* Heidelberg, Germany: Springer.

Hofstadter, R. (2007). *I am a strange loop.* New York, NY: Basic Books.

Holland, J. H. (2012). *Signals and boundaries: Building blocks for complex adaptive systems.* Cambridge, MA: MIT Press.

Hunter, J. E., Danes, J. E., & Cohen, S. H. (Eds.). (1984). *Mathematical models of attitude change.* New York, NY: Academic Press.

Kafka, F. (1998). *The trial.* New York, NY: Schocken Books.

Krippendorff, K. (1977). Information systems research: Theory and overview. In B. Rubin (Ed.), *Communication yearbook* (vol. 1, pp. 149–172). New Brunswick, NJ: Transaction.

Krippendorff, K. (2009). *On communicating: Otherness, meaning, and information* (F. Bermejo, Ed.). New York, NY: Routledge.

Krone, K. J., Jablin, F. M., & Putnam, L. L. (1987). Communication theory and organizational communication: Multiple perspectives. In F. M. Jablin, L. L. Putnam, K. Roberts, & L. W. Porter (Eds.), *Handbook of organizational communication* (pp. 18–40). Newbury Park, CA: SAGE.

Leik, R., & Meeker, B. (1975). *Mathematical modeling in sociology.* Englewood Cliffs, NJ: Prentice Hall.

Lévi-Strauss, C. (1969). *The elementary structures of kinship.* London, England: Eyre and Spottis-wood.

Leydesdorff, L. (2001). *A sociological theory of communication: The self-organization of the knowledge based society.* London, England: Universal Publishers.

Luhmann, N. (1995). *Social systems.* Stanford, CA: Stanford University Press.

March, J. G., & Simon, H. A. (1958). *Organizations.* New York, NY: John Wiley.

McFarland, S. D. (1997). Ontogeny, structural drift, and self-organizing: An autopoietic perspective of organizational communication. In G. A. Barnett & L. Thayer (Eds.), *Organization—Communication, emerging perspectives V: The renaissance in systems thinking* (pp. 191–211). Greenwich, CT: Ablex.

McPhee, R. D., & Corman, S. R. (1995). An activity-based theory of communication networks in organizations, applied to the case of the local church. *Communication Monographs, 62*(2), 132–151.

McPhee, R. D., & Poole, M. S. (1980). Mathematical modeling in communication research: An overview. In M. Burgoon (Ed.), *Communication yearbook* (vol. 5, pp. 159–191). New Brunswick, NJ: Transaction.

Meehan, E. J. (1968). *Explanation in social science: A system paradigm.* Homewood, IL: Dorsey.

Miller, J. H., & Page, S. E. (2007). *Complex adaptive systems: An introduction to computational models of social life.* Princeton, NJ: Princeton University Press.

Miller, K. I. (2003). Nurses at the edge of chaos: The application of "new science" concepts to organizational systems. *Management Communication Quarterly, 12*(1), 112–127.

Miller, K. I., Stiff, J. B., & Ellis, B. H. (1988). Communication and empathy as precursors to burnout among human service workers. *Communication Monographs, 55*(3), 250–265.

Miller, V. D., Poole, M. S., Seibold, D. R., Myers, K. K., Park, H. S., Monge, P., . . . Shumate, M. (2010). Advancing research in organizational communication through quantitative methodology. *Management Communication Quarterly, 25*(1), 4–58.

Monge, P. R. (1973). Theory construction in the study of communication: The systems paradigm. *Journal of Communication, 23*(1), 5–16.

Monge, P. R. (1982). Systems theory and research in the study of organizational communication: The correspondence problem. *Human Communication Research, 8*(3), 245–261.

Monge, P. R., & Contractor, N. S. (2003). *Theories of communication networks.* New York, NY: Oxford.

Monge, P. R., Farace, R. V., Eisenberg, E. M., Miller, K. I., & White, L. L. (1984). The process of studying process in organizational communication. *Journal of Communication, 34*(1), 22–43.

Narayan, V. K., & Armstrong, D. J. (Eds.). (2005). *Causal mapping for research in information technology.* Hershey, PA: Idea Group.

Parsons, T. (1951). *The social system.* Glencoe, IL: The Free Press.

Pavitt, C. (1994). Theoretical commitments presupposed by functional approaches to group discussion. *Small Group Research, 25*(4), 520–541.

Pearce, W. B., & Cronen, V. E. (1980). *Communication, action, and meaning.* New York, NY: Praeger.

Pickering, A. (1995). *The mangle of practice: Time, agency and science.* Chicago, IL: University of Chicago Press.

Pondy, L., & Mitroff, I. I. (1979). Beyond open systems models of organization. In L. L. Cummings & B. M. Staw (Eds.), *Research in organizational behavior* (vol. 1, pp. 3–39). Greenwich, CT: JAI.

Poole, M. S. (1997). A turn of the wheel: The case for the renewal of systems inquiry in organizational communication research. In G. Barnett & L. Thayer (Eds.), *Organization-Communication, 6* (pp. 47–64). Norwood, NJ: Ablex.

Poole, M. S. (2012). On the study of process in communication research. In. C. Salmon (Ed.), *Communication yearbook* (vol. 36, pp. 371–409). New York, NY: Routledge.

Poole, M. S., Van de Ven, A. H., Dooley, K., & Holmes, M. E. (2000). *Organizational change and innovation processes: Theory and methods for research.* New York, NY: Oxford University Press.

Prigogine, I. (1980). *From being to becoming: Time and complexity in the physical sciences.* San Francisco, CA: W. H. Freeman.

Putnam, L. L. (1983). The interpretive perspective: An alternative to functionalism. In L. L. Putnam & M. E. Pacanowsky (Eds.), *Communication and organizations: An interpretive approach* (pp. 31–54). Beverly Hills, CA: SAGE.

Putnam, L. L., & Pacanowsky, M. E. (Eds.). (1983). *Communication and organizations: An interpretive approach.* Beverly Hills, CA: SAGE.

Putnam, L. L., & Stohl, C. (1990). Bona fide groups: A reconceptualization of groups in context. *Communication Studies, 41*(3), 248–265.

Redding, W. C., & Sanborn, G. A. (Eds.). (1964). *Business and industrial communication: A sourcebook.* New York, NY: Harper & Row.

Rescher, N. (1996). *Process metaphysics.* Albany, NY: SUNY Press.

Reuther, C., & Fairhurst, G. T. (2000). Chaos theory and the glass ceiling. In P. M. Buzzanell (Ed.), *Rethinking organizational & managerial communication from feminist perspectives* (pp. 236–255). Thousand Oaks, CA; SAGE.

Rice, R. E., & Cooper, S. D. (2010). *Organizations and unusual routines: A systems analysis of dysfunctional feedback processes.* Cambridge, UK: Cambridge.

Richards, W. D., Jr., & Seary, A. J. (1997). Convergence analysis of communication networks. In G. A. Barnett & L. Thayer (Eds.), *Organization—Communication, emerging perspectives V: The renaissance in systems thinking* (pp. 141–190). Greenwich, CT: Ablex.

Rosenbluth, A., Wiener, N., & Bigelow, J. (1968). Behavior, purpose, and teleology. In W. Buckley (Ed.), *Modern systems research for the behavioral scientist* (pp. 221–226). Chicago, IL: Aldine.

Salem, P. (2002). Assessment, change, and complexity. *Management Communication Quarterly, 15*(3), 442–450.

Sawyer, R. K. (2005). *Emergence: Societies as complex systems*. Cambridge, UK: Cambridge University Press.

Schoeneborn, D. (2011). Organization as communication: A Luhmannian perspective. *Management Communication Quarterly, 25*(4), 663–689.

Senge, P. M. (1990). *The fifth discipline: The art & practice of the learning organization.* New York, NY: Doubleday.

Shannon, C. E., & Weaver, W. (1959). *The mathematical theory of communication.* Urbana: University of Illinois Press.

Simon, H. A. (1969). *Sciences of the artificial.* Cambridge, MA: MIT Press.

Singer, B. (1980). Crazy systems and Kafka circuits. *Social Policy, 11*(2), 46–54.

Skidmore, W. (1979). *Theoretical thinking in sociology* (2nd ed.). Cambridge, UK: Cambridge University Press.

Steier, F. (Ed.). (1991). *Research and reflexivity: Inquiries in social construction.* Thousand Oaks, CA: SAGE.

Steier, F., & Smith, K. K. (1985). The cybernetics of cybernetics and the organization of organization. *Journal of Strategic and Systemic Therapies, 4*(4), 53–65.

Sterman, J. D. (2000). *Business dynamics: Systems thinking and modeling for a complex world.* Boston, MA: Irwin/McGraw-Hill.

Taylor, R. (1968). Comments on a mechanistic conception of purposefulness. In W. Buckley (Ed.), *Modern systems research for the behavioral scientist* (pp. 226–232). Chicago, IL: Aldine.

Thayer, L. (1968). *Communication and communication systems.* Homewood, IL: Richard D. Irwin.

Thom, R. (1975). *Structural stability and morphogenesis* (W. H. Fowler, Trans.). Reading, MA: W. A. Benjamin.

Tutzauer, F. (1997). Chaos and organization. In G. A. Barnett & L. Thayer (Eds.), *Organization—Communication, emerging perspectives V: The renaissance in systems thinking* (pp. 213–228). Greenwich, CT: Ablex.

Varela, F., Maturana, H., & Uribe, R. (1974). Autopoiesis: The organization of living systems, its characterization, and a model. *Biosystems, 5*(4), 187–196.

Ventana Systems. (2011). *Vensim.* Retrieved from http://www.vensim.com

von Bertalanffy, L. (1968). *General systems theory: Foundations, development, applications.* New York, NY: George Braziller.

von Glasersfeld, E. (1985). Reconstructing the concept of knowledge. *Archives de Psychologie, 53*(204), 91–101.

Watt, J. H., & VanLear, C. A. (1996). *Dynamic patterns in communication processes.* Thousand Oaks, CA: SAGE.

Weick, K. E. (1979). *The social psychology of organizing* (2nd ed.). Reading, MA: Addison-Wesley.

Weick, K. E. (1995). *Sensemaking in organizations.* Thousand Oaks, CA: SAGE.

Wiener, N. (1961). *Cybernetics: Control and communication in the animal and the machine.* Cambridge, MA: MIT Press.

Williams, D., Contractor, N., Poole, M. S., Srivastava, J., & Cai, D. (2011). The virtual worlds exploratorium: Using large-scale data and computational techniques for communication research. *Communication Methods and Measures, 5*(2), 163–180.

Wolfram, S. (2002). *A new kind of science.* Champaign, IL: Wolfram Media.

CHAPTER 3

Structuration Theory

Robert D. McPhee, Marshall Scott Poole, and Joel Iverson

The theory of structuration, rooted especially in the work of Giddens (1976, 1979, 1984, 1987, 1990, 1991), was first applied to organizational communication in the 1980s, a period of theoretical and methodological ferment. Structuration theory (ST) in general, and in communication and organization studies in particular, has evolved since that time (Ahrens & Chapman, 2007; Englund, Gerdin, & Burns, 2011; Haslett, 2012; Poole & McPhee, 2005; Seibold & Myers, 2005; Whittington, 2011) and has influenced parallel schools of self-organizing systems theory (see Poole, Chapter 2), actor-network theory, and critical realism.

In this chapter, we add flesh to two undeniably true skeletal tenets: First, ST addresses, cogently and enlighteningly, the major theoretical issues still roiling organizational communication studies (the relationship of agency and structure, the articulation of organizations and society, the place of material factors in explaining organizational interaction, and the communicative constitution of organizations [CCO]). Second, ST has demonstrated broad applicability and important insights regarding organizational identity and identification, organizational culture/climate, formal and genre-clad discourse, group decision making, information technology use in organizations, and institutional impacts on organizations.

We focus on structuration-based studies in communication but also include relevant work in allied disciplines. We examine work that represents hybrids of ST with the theoretical traditions mentioned above. Our first section reviews the basic concepts of ST. Second, we review ST-inspired organizational communication research, using the Four Flows Model of organizational structuration. The third section discusses critiques, debates, and future directions.

Foundations of Structuration Theory

Although the basic principles of ST were formulated by Giddens (1979, 1984), their application in organizational communication has often generated debate.

System/Practice/Structure

ST hinges on the distinction between system and structure. A *system* is an observable pattern of relationships among actors. Systems are layered and include micro-level interaction; meso-level units such as groups, larger organizations, and networks; and macro-level units such as economic sectors, intersocietal systems, and religions. ST focuses especially on systems of human practices or meaningful patterns of activity that range from narrow micro-level activities, such as problem solving or assimilating a new member, to broader arrays of processes, such as project management or medicine.

Structures are the rules and resources that actors depend on in their practices. Structures underlie the patterns that constitute systems. A *rule* is any principle or routine that can guide activity. In micro-level assimilation, learning the ropes means learning technical rules as well as principles of exchange and reciprocity. A *resource* is anything else that facilitates activities, namely, material (budget, tools) or nonmaterial (knowledge, traditions) items. For instance, the structure implicated in money as a resource is not the coins per se but the action potentials that money affords. Structures are not directly observable, and in fact, the term *structure* is only a useful reification. In the *duality of structuration*, structures are both the medium of interaction and its outcome. As actors draw on rules and resources to participate in a system, they enact and sustain these structures as part of the ongoing organization of the system, thereby reproducing these structures.

Structuration—the production and reproduction of a social system in interaction—is the process through which structures are constituted. Production means that agents draw on rules/resources to act meaningfully; *reproduction* implies that the acts maintain or transform those rules/resources. From its beginning (McPhee & Poole, 1980), ST scholarship reframed organizational interaction as production (i.e., appropriating but transforming rules/resources available in the larger social/organizational context). But perhaps the more important reframing occurs through the concept of reproduction. In effect, members keep the larger organization going as an organization; that is, they reproduce its broad structural properties, but they potentially transform them during productive interaction. The process of structuration is the nexus of several pairs of concepts often counterposed in social analysis, including action and structure, stability and change, and institution and interaction. ST argues that both poles of these pairs are implicated in a continuous structuring process; consequently, good explanations must emphasize both of them.

Two major research approaches focus on the duality of structure. Giddens (1979) argues that institutional reproduction and action are always implicated in a parallel manner during structuration; that is, they are inseparable except analytically, and much scholarship incorporates this Heraclitean, purist assumption (e.g., Corman & Scott, 1994; Orlikowski, 2000; Poole, Seibold, & McPhee, 1985). Another school sees structuration occurring in a cycle between distinct phases dominated by change/action and structure/stability, respectively (Barley, 1986; Jarzabkowski, 2008; Leonardi, 2007; Yates & Orlikowski, 1992; cf. Archer, 1982; Sawyer, 2005). This school avowedly treats action/structure as dualism, not duality, and purists see it as sacrificing the key insight of ST, the idea that relates structure to action. Advocates of the second approach claim that empirical observations show fairly stable social structures with clear change phases. They recognize the existence of a continuous interplay between action and structure, but they argue that the ratio of action to structure varies over time. Purists, in turn, would prefer to explain the cycle rather than assume it.

Agency

Giddens (1979) refers to humans who draw on structural resources as *agents* and treats them as central to understanding organizations. Agents must have the power to make a difference (thereby reproducing structural resources) and must have the *knowledgeability* to use their powers in meaningful, normative ways. There are limits to agency, however, including available structures, other actors, and social-systemic complexity that result in actions that do not follow routines or accomplish plans. This process can lead, either immediately or eventually, to unintended consequences.

Agents then can draw on or *appropriate* (Ollman, 1976; Poole & DeSanctis, 1990) structural resources in interacting. Through appropriation, they put a general structural rule/resource into action in a version adapted to their contexts. Local uses reproduce the structure over time and can gradually alter or drastically transform it.

Agents *reflexively monitor* their actions (usually tacitly) to assess their progress along expected trajectories of action. However, ST decenters rational, goal-directed agency in favor of a routine flow of context-responsive activity that is monitored at several levels of consciousness. *Discursive consciousness* (i.e., formulated in words and accessible to deliberative thought), *practical consciousness* (i.e., nondiscursive knowledge and especially skills that can be used purposefully), and the *unconscious* (i.e., barred from any level of awareness but affecting actors' *ontological security* and *existential anxiety*) interdependently enable action.

Knowledgeable agents routinely navigate their own local worlds. Knowledgeability operates equally but differently in practical and discursive consciousness, but the latter characterizes organizational information gathering, decision processing, and implementation through communication. Greater knowledgeability both leads to and results from greater efficacy and control (Jessop, 1996); but in all systems, knowledge endures alongside incapacity and dissensus.

Dimensions and Modalities of Structuration

ST distinguishes among three dimensions of the duality of structure that appear different at the interaction and institutional levels of analysis. In interaction, the three dimensions are communication, power, and sanction. At the social/institutional level, the dimensions are *signification, domination,* and *legitimation.* The interaction and institution levels interpenetrate in three *modalities* of structuration: interpretive schemes, facilities, and norms, respectively (Giddens, 1984, pp. 28–29). Modalities highlight ways in which the duality of structure works out in practice. For instance, institutions of domination mean that power resources are available as facilities to some agents (e.g., managers) and not others. Moreover, the ways that facilities are applied and maintained help reproduce domination in society and organizations. Different dimensions may be highlighted in certain appropriations, but they are separable only analytically. Every action or utterance and every social system involves varying ratios among dimensions, and each of dimension implicates the others; for example, task-oriented interaction also conveys norms for control, concealed by ideology.

Researchers who focus on discourse have developed classifications of appropriation and structuring moves, partly based on Giddens's three dimensions, to analyze the range of communicative agency. Adaptive ST and Communication Genre Theory (discussed in detail later in the chapter) elaborate broad, rich schemas that reflect the effects of communication acts on the adaptation and reproduction of communication resources. Communication researchers have also articulated more specific domains of modalities (for example, Seibold and Meyers's [2007] work on group argumentation, Corman and Scott's [1994] research on networks, and Canary's [2010a, 2010b] activity system elements).

An important consequence of agency is the dialectic of control in which dominated agents have room to maneuver because power holders depend on their agentive abilities. Through the dialectic of control, agents participate in the production and reproduction of their own action capacities and their own constraints.

Institutions and Action

A central problem in social science is the macro-micro issue. Organizational communication researchers offer conflicting accounts linking micro phenomena (i.e., interactions, decisions) with macro systems such as institutions. ST has increasingly reconceptualized this problem, while shunning the terms *macro/micro*, by framing social structure as (1) an assemblage of rules and resources, including *structural principles* and far-reaching, stable, and consequential rules and resources, and as (2) an order of spatial, temporal, material, and symbolic resource *differences*, reproduced in distributed interaction. McPhee (1988) refers to this process as *systems-structuration* to emphasize that structures are often unequal. For example, a surgeon, in treating patients, can draw on medical rules and resources (i.e., expertise, credentials, and operating room access) in different, often more empowered ways than the patients can.

Institution-level reproduction may simply reiterate this process but may also plant the seeds of institutional change, particularly when a local innovation is reproduced robustly and eventually incorporated into the institution. Specifically, Yates and Orlikowski's (1992) structuration analysis sees genres, such as memos, as part of an organization's institutional fabric. As the memo is transformed into e-mail messages, some conventions are maintained, but others are changed due to novel affordances of the new technology (e.g., smileys and other emoticons). If these novelties are repeated sufficiently over time, they revise the institution. Such phenomena and conditions have received much less attention from communication scholars than they warrant.

Time and Space

ST emphasizes space and time as crucial aspects of social theory. Despite communication's focus on process, most past organizational communication research is atemporal, spatially abstract, and general. ST emphasizes time-space *distanciation*, in which agents bind time-space in practical forms of face-to-face (social integration) or through indirect, mediated organizing processes at greater distances (system integration). Giddens (1984) developed an array of distance ideas (reviewed in McPhee & Canary, 2013), including the virtuality of structure as a Derridean presence/absence process (Bertilsson, 1984), tacit powers of bodily posture and participation (cf. Goffman, 1963), and the power to edge off from one encounter into another and disembed along time-space trajectories between locales.

Mediation/Contradiction

As the modalities imply, agents draw on multiple structures for any practice, and these structures can either mediate or contradict one another. One structure mediates another when its production and reproduction involve the reproduction of the other. For example, in a group decision made using cost-benefit logic, the model of economic rationality mediates group argumentation and choice practices. Structural contradiction is "an opposition . . . of structural principles . . ., whereby those principles operate in terms of each other, but at the same time contravene one another" (Giddens, 1979, p. 141). Contradiction stems from clashes of structural principles (e.g., norms of decision quality and decision speed) whose production and reproduction are connected. Contradictions may result in conflict, but conflicts and contradictions can occur separately of each other.

Communication

Several ST scholars focus on the structurational nature of communication (Bisel, 2010; Heracleous, 2010). Specifically, in Bisel's (2010) *structure in action* model, communication is dually action and structural reproduction; it reflects both skilled, purposeful orientation and conventional routine. Paradoxically, Giddens (1976, 1979) accepts the intentional use of signs but denies that purpose or intention exists as a present idea held in mind and expressed in signs. He also states that interpretive schemes are "standardized . . . stocks of knowledge" that distinguish communication from other actions (Giddens, 1979, p. 83; cf. 1976, 1984). In effect, he seems caught on both horns of the free action/determinism dilemma.

The resolution of this paradox seems to lie in the emphasis Giddens places on the Wittgensteinian sense of meaning as the 'ability to go on' and respond to sense made. But making sense communicatively necessarily involves two features: (1) structurating a *flow of intentionality* wherein the speaker/writer is normatively as well as semantically accountable for being meaningful, that is, communicating rightly (relative to known semiotic systems) given the context and (2) construing, reflexively, an appropriate communicative intent. Communicators therein reproduce the standardized signification system in context, a true duality rather than a text-conversation dialectic. However, Poole et al. (1985) held (as Giddens seems to) that interpretive mutual knowledge generated in local contexts cannot be regarded as logically separable from semiotic systems available to larger groups in society. This stand makes it easier to explicate the CCO (see also Brummans, Cooren, Robichaud, & Taylor, Chapter 7).

Overview of Structuration Research and the Four Flows

Communicative Constitution of Organizations

ST has become prominent in organizational communication research because of its analysis of interaction and its potential to link with higher system-level phenomena. Recently, theoretical debates have shifted to the notion of the *communicative constitution of organizations* (Ashcraft, Kuhn, & Cooren, 2009; Putnam & Nicotera, 2009). This idea assumes that (1) communication has a constitutive, order-producing force (Smith, 1993; Taylor & Van Every, 2000) and (2) the constitutive force of some *specific* communication practices is particularly powerful in generating complex organizations. The idea of the duality of structuration recurs constantly, though often tacitly, in this discussion. Notably, ST accounts for the constitution of organized, coordinated systems of interaction episodes and social practices in at least the following interdependent ways:

1. in equating interaction (i.e., production) with interaction that maintains/transforms the system and its structural resources (i.e., reproduction);
2. in the depth and range of structural resources available to agents. An extreme case of this is *glocalization* or the interweaving of various local practices with global institutions;
3. in the constitutive powers of language (e.g., conlocutions), whereby social subsystems are named, categorized, referentially linked to one another, given legitimacy, and endure despite system changes (Boden, 1994);
4. in the phenomenon of distanciation, where relations in time-space are marked and time-space itself is bound so that interdependence across contexts is contextualized;
5. through the coordination and control powers of language, in which one episode choreographs transactions among other episodes as well as power relations within and between them; and
6. in the concept of discursive/material practice itself as constitutive. The terms *material*, *socio-material*, and *practice* have become foci for theory development across disciplines, including communication (Ashcraft et al., 2009; Kuhn, 2011; Orlikowski, 2007). McPhee and Iverson (2011) array the various ways that materiality is treated in ST.

These implications of system reproduction are logically interdependent in ST's terms. Thus we can understand how ST is described as both *becoming* and *grounded in action* in Fairhurst and Putnam's (2004) schema and how it might fit equally well into their *object* category but also how it transfigures all three categories. Objects, including language, operate in action/appropriation as types of resources and discursive organizing is grounded (i.e., enabled/constrained) in material practice. For instance, Sarason, Dean, and Dillard (2006) note how entrepreneurs, interpretive norms, and economic resources co-evolve in "reflexive, recursive processes of interpretation, action, consequence, and reflection" (p. 295).

Looking at all six implications interdependently avoids some of the critiques leveled at ST. Thus Fairhurst and Putnam note how *becoming* approaches collapse the macro-micro distinction through focusing on organizing. However, if properly developed, the concept of *distanciation*, as well as the notion that institutions are grounded in broad structural phenomena and discursive powers of meaning-coordination, addresses this issue. These implications also address the criticisms that the *becoming* views are antirealist, while *practice-grounded* views can tilt toward social constructionism rather than realism/constraint. The second, fourth, and sixth implications, however, address the critiques of ST by avowed realists.

Some constitutive communication models (ST and non-ST) are very broad, for example, the text-conversation model (Taylor & Van Every, 2000), systems models (Schoeneborn, 2011), Barley's (1986) punctuated model, Jessop's (1996) strategic-relational approach, the reticulation model (Corman & Scott, 1994), the structurational hermeneutic model (McPhee & Iverson, 2009), or the ventriloquism model (Cooren, 2010). A recent, elaborately developed model is the focus of Haslett's (2012) encyclopedic book on ST and Goffman. She emphasizes framing practices and increasingly abstract levels of *frames, frame systems* (frames with shared themes), and *metaframes* (global knowledge structures). In this model, frames include contextualized knowledge that is generally shared and taken for granted; these properties account for organized systems as members interact meaningfully and construct purposeful metaframes. Even though we agree with Haslett on the importance of contextualized, shared meanings in practice, we would place added emphasis on other features that Giddens (1987) draws from Goffman; namely, the time-space coordination of encounters in copresence, which is "never separate from either the ordering of behavior across contexts or . . . of contexts themselves [with] one another" (p. 136). Our stand is that the system of structurational insights outlined above, including many in these models, is a necessary basis for CCO accounts.

The Four Flows Model

As we look at the way structuration informs how communication constitutes organization, we discern four subprocesses that embrace the paradox that communication is at once human and organizational. These four subprocesses include (1) communication integrating people as members (*membership negotiation*), (2) communication structuring the organization (*reflexive self-structuring*), (3) communication contextualizing particular coaction (*activity coordination*), and (4) communication positioning the organization in larger social systems (*institutional positioning*). These processes embody four basic types of communicative *flow*; we contend that no single model, from any source, is sufficient without examining these flows (McPhee & Iverson, 2009; McPhee & Zaug, 2000). We use the four flows to examine the range of ST-based organizational communication research and to indicate integrative potential and neglected topics in the field.

Membership Negotiation

Membership negotiation constitutes the organization as relevant to its individual members. As a social system, every organization includes people. This flow, then, incorporates the practices and strategies that constitute identities, positions, membership boundaries, and status gradations. The membership negotiation concept takes a duality view of traditionally static concepts such as membership, self, and role. Thus as Yberra, Keenoy, Oswick, Beverungen, Ellis, and Sabelis (2009) urge, it balances positioning (Davies & Harre, 1990), reflexivity, and narrative form/process in the structuration of identity and organizational presence.

Often treated as a predesigned or preconceived list of behaviors that members fulfill, the concept of *role* in ST becomes a set of dynamic position-practices or a more agentive version of *subject-positions* (Kuhn, 2009; Kuhn & Nelson, 2002). A *normative role* is structured through enactment, and an individual's career in a role can be vague, highly politicized, or very narrow. Thus the role of an employee in Kirby and Krone's (2002) analysis of work-life conflict encompassed the controversy between workers with children and those without them. Employees without children were more likely to travel in their work, to be overburdened, to feel resentment than were those with children; so employees had to develop coping practices.

A number of communication researchers have focused on identity issues, and many of their insights align with ST theory. For instance, Myers (2005) and Scott and Trethewey (2008) examined how firefighter cultural practices enabled them to cope with the risks and basic insecurities of their jobs. Their accounts demonstrated ST influence by going beyond the agency-devaluing explanations that are typical of post-structuralist research. Specifically, the agency involved in fashioning a self-identity narrative becomes visible when multiple conflicting, fragmented identity sources become available for an agent. Of course, as they communicate identity, individuals are palpably negotiating it with other members as a condition of organization membership.

Scott, Corman, and Cheney (1998) developed a structurational model of organizational identification in which *identity* is viewed as "a set of rules and resources that functions as an anchor for who we are" and *identification* as "interaction or other behaviors illustrating one's attachment" (p. 303). Their model posits a duality of identity and identification in which identity figures both in the process of forming and maintaining attachment to the organization and as the product of this process. Identity is a regionalized structure of resources (e.g., beliefs, work experience, self-knowledge) and rules (e.g., codes of conduct, public habits)—regions that people draw on when they interact in specific social situations.

Haslett's (2012, pp. 192–196) survey of ST-based studies of identity shows the fecundity of analyzing different identities, regionalized sub-identities, and identification targets during situational change and conflict (Scott et al., 1998; Scott et al., 1999) through communication networks and media use (Kuhn & Corman, 2003; Kuhn & Nelson, 2002; Larson & Pepper, 2011; Scott & Fontenot, 1999; Scott & Stephens, 2009) and through self-help books and online professional development sites (Kuhn et al., 2008). Scott et al. (1998), following Goffman (1959), also distinguished front from back regions of identities. Similarly, Kuhn et al. (2008) pointed out how larger societal discourses, such as ones that stress the impermanence of employment or the differences among gender and ethnic groups, shape the structuration of identities and identification.

The idea of multiple identity regions leads to concerns with interregional conflicts. Nicotera and Clinkscales (2003, 2010) developed a theory of structurational divergence (SD) that focuses on individual and work-unit problems that stem from conflicts rooted in broad structural contradictions. SD occurs when multiple incompatible social structures interpenetrate (in an *SD-nexus*) and place contradictory, conflicting demands on individuals, work units, and organizations. For individuals, these contradictions generate a negative communicative spiral through immobilization—members feel paralyzed, stuck, and hopeless and reenact the same problems repeatedly. This process leads to erosion of organizational development and prevents individuals from acquiring needed skills, thus causing poor performance. Poor performance then spawns persisting conflicts due to frustration and a lack of problem-recognition skills and problem-solving skills, which cycle back to immobilization.

The spiral *appears* to result from surface interactions, because its underlying source (i.e., incompatible meaning structure) is unclear, and "the resulting communication difficulties become entrenched" (Nicotera, Mahon, & Zhao, 2010, p. 364). Nicotera and Clinkscales identified 20 potentially contradictory structural interpenetrations that might be embedded in organizations, including unity/hierarchy, shared responsibility/control, and common good/competition. At the organizational level, these interpenetrations are enacted in any of four *problematics*—communication/interpersonal dynamics, cultural identity/human development, leadership/management, and power/authority/control. Individual and organizational levels are connected through specific task orientations and relational orientations toward these problematics. For example, Nicotera and Clinkscales (2010) describe how an SD-nexus between an ethic of shared responsibility and managers' need for control in a nursing unit generated spiraling conflicts over work scheduling.

In addition to identification, communication scholars have also examined socialization and organizational assimilation through the use of ST, especially, for instance, Scott and Myers' (2010) model of assimilation based on membership negotiation and the duality of structure. They contend that members produce and reproduce their own connections, memberships in general, and the larger assimilation dynamic through specific communicative processes. In addition to socialization, researchers have used ST to explore correlated memberships in communities of practice (CoPs; Iverson & McPhee, 2008). Membership in these communities is developed through knowledgeable characteristics of practitioners, such as mutual engagement, repertoire sharing, and negotiating the joint enterprise. Additionally, members of a CoP are enacting their belongingness and identifying with their CoP and the organization (Iverson, 2004).

The membership negotiation flow organizes many currents of identity and socialization-related research. Despite the opening this flow gives to research on the membership of higher-tenure, higher-status, and ambiguous-role members, research on this flow has centered on new member assimilation. The excellent work on that issue needs to be balanced by work on the whole range of membership negotiations.

Reflexive Self-Structuring

Giddens's (1979, 1984) main idea about organizations is that they are founded on institutional reflexivity, that is, surveillance collects information into power containers for use in reflexively steering organizational systems. Communication scholars emphasize that communication does the collecting, the containing, and the steering. Research on these phenomena has focused on the resources crucial for self-structuring; the processes by which those resources are reproduced in self-structuring in many loci and ways; and the communication systems that accomplish forceful, conflicted, and/or ambiguous self-structurings. Perhaps the main contribution of research on this flow is to show how reflexivity and retained structurings are not purely the products of a centralized, purposeful, manipulative authority. Instead, they are dispersed based on multiple media and time frames and are produced through multiple inconsistent social processes—yet they can be seen as building monolithic organizations with fateful enduring impacts.

Organizations are definitely cast by Giddens (1984) as power containers, but the critiques of the container metaphor would seem apt for power, too. Among the raw power resources they contain are humans and their abilities, information/knowledge, material resources, and general relationships (i.e., class, profession); in self-structuring, these are appropriated and organized reflexively and thus not in a container. Among the media of reflexive self-structuring are formal texts, including flyers, forms, and cheat sheets for routine activities (Canary & McPhee, 2009; Iverson, 2004); hierarchies and organizational design; strategies (Jarzabkowski, 2008); building designs (Giddens, 1984; Holmer-Nadesan, 1998); informal interpretations; and routines. Sillince (2007) argues that discursive moves help constitute communication contexts themselves, ones that have impact on later communication that depends on those contexts.

ST research on self-structuring reveals an interesting pattern. Specifically, local, strategic conduct research shows creative and political appropriations of various media of self-structuring, often including conflicts induced by the structuring attempts. More broadly, these appropriations coexist with and even lead to a distanciation pattern in which local variation, and within bounds, allows for less hands-on or intensely *informated*[1] management (Zuboff, 1988). This process, in turn, maintains standards while using distance to absorb the local variation that maintains overall control (but see Jarzabkowski, 2008).

For instance, knowledge of the hierarchy, obsession with it, and its use as a metalanguage decrease as one looks down the hierarchy. Even in traditional bank retail operations, its impact is politically and contextually mediated at all levels. In school policy hierarchies, national and state control over programs is variable and is more of a mediating factor than a constraint or a determinant of relevant school processes (Canary & McPhee, 2009). This pattern is observed for other controlling communication factors in organizations. Adaptive structuration and other technology studies show how variable the impact of purely material technology is. Even for so-called *routines*, their stability is a product of adaptive, knowledgeable agency with broad cultural values (Essen, 2008).

The unintended result is that local structuring allows considerable room for oppositional patterns. For instance, Holmer-Nadesan (1997) describes managerial personnel and training discourses that aim to give motivation, direction, and positive relational attitudes to staff members at a university, but the members use the autonomy consequent to these discourses to construct oppositional identities. Similarly, Ahrens and Chapman (2007) report on a financial management system in which

> day-to-day contests of accountability between restaurant managers and superiors occurred, with the managers justifying deviations from the system in varied ways; the managers traded off various sources of legitimacy in the context of highly asymmetric power relations between the head office and the restaurant managers. (p. 105)

Even Kirby and Krone's study (2002) describes resistance to policies aimed at helping individuals' work/life issues that some employees experienced as unfair. Yet the institutional forms have strong impact, even on resistant self-structuring.

Organizational Formalisms and Policies. The most obvious phenomenon of organizational self-structuring is the process of implementing classic bureaucratic features, such as hierarchy and the division of labor. McPhee (1985; McPhee & Poole, 2001) argued that an organization's communication about its structure is particularly critical in two respects. First, communication related to formal structure substitutes for (and removes the need for) other forms of communication, such as arguments about authority. Second, formal structures provide linguistic resources for metacommunication among members relative to these structures. Authoritative structuring communication varies across a distanciated organization, being explicit at the top but loosely appropriated or resisted elsewhere (McPhee, 1988, 2001). Fordham-Hernandez and McPhee (1999) describe how a food company president and top consultant constructed participatory structures that lower-level participants saw as the work of a highly connected vice president. Banks and Riley (1993) also give an example of a conflict over a career path policy, one that tacitly illustrates McPhee's (1988) theory.

Perhaps the best-known examples of structurational research are the appropriations of formal family leave polices (Golden, Kirby, & Jorgenson, 2006; Kirby & Krone, 2002). Kirby and Krone found that, while policy permitted employees to take leaves, interactions with coworkers about the use of them generated a system of peer pressure that constrains and distorts employees' appropriation of the policies. In a study of requests for accommodating work-life issues, Hoffman and Cowan (2010) explicated six rules (e.g., "Family related requests are appropriate and nonfamily-related requests are inappropriate") and three resources (i.e., family, employee competence, and work experience). They showed how the duality of structure led to institutional changes in corporate stances toward work-life issues and how appropriations of policies affected individual identities by reinforcing some structures but not others.

Canary (2010a, 2010b; Canary & McPhee, 2009) advances *Structurating Activity Theory* (SAT) to examine how policies enter into the structuration process. Organizations respond to policies developed by governments, industry, and other public institutions, and they do so by incorporating them into their structuring processes. By synthesizing ST and activity theory (Engstrom, 1995), SAT casts policy structuration as intersecting with activity systems composed of a subject (agent) who operates on an object via mediating factors, such as material/technical resources, rules, a coacting community, and a division of labor among community members. The mediating instruments interact in the production and reproduction of the system as the agent operates on the object.

SAT (Canary 2010a, 2010b) highlights the contradictions posed by policy implementation as a major source of organizational change. The locus of contradiction may be between the policy and the allocation of the existing rules and resources or between different activity systems. Canary emphasizes four contradiction types: (1) deep primary contradictions, (2) secondary system contradictions that occur when new policy elements are added to a stabilized activity system, (3) tertiary contradictions that occur when a new motive or purpose is introduced into a system, and (4) quaternary contradictions that occur when two or more activity systems come into conflict. The system contradictions interact to promote organizational and policy changes, as illustrated in the policy impacts on an educational program.

In a series of articles, Olufowote (2008, 2009, 2010) applied ST to the development of legal standards regarding informed consent to treatment in court cases and social research. He identified three systems of meaning: the traditional system, determined by consent defined as simple permission (perhaps based on a physician's individual judgment); the liability system, based on state/administrative control of informed consent to treatment practices (despite ambiguous, contradictory normative imperatives); and the decision-making system, ideally based on shared information between physician and patient.

Technology. An alternative way in which organizations structure themselves is through acquisition and deployment of technology. Adaptive Structuration Theory (AST) is concerned with the implementation and use of information and communication technologies (ICT) in groups and organizations (DeSanctis & Poole, 1994; DeSanctis et al., 2008; Poole & DeSanctis, 1990). AST posits that the impacts of ICTs on organizational processes and outcomes depend on the structures incorporated in the technology and the structures that emerge as users attempt to appropriate them for the tasks at hand. AST focuses on two elements of ICT structures: features and spirit. Structural *features* are specific rules and resources that are embodied in the material ICT artifact or the technology itself, while *spirit* is the general intent with regard to the values and goals that underlie a given set of structural features. When features are *faithfully* used, that is, when they are used compatibly with the spirit of the technology, outcomes and use depend on the match of ICTs to the external and internal challenges that the organization faces. However, if ICT features are used in ironic ways that are incompatible with the spirit of the technology (e.g., use of an electronic vote to suppress dissent), outcomes are much less predictable. This finding accounts for ICTs that have failed to deliver intended benefits or that lead to unexpected effects. AST was originally developed to explain the use of group support systems, but it has been applied to a wide array of ICTs, including enterprise-level systems, collaboration technologies, and mobile systems as well as to nontechnical phenomena such as leadership, collaboration procedures (Neiderman, Briggs, de Vreede, & Kolfschoten, 2008), and implementation of innovations.

Appropriation develops interactively in members' attempts to coordinate technology use. When members appropriate structural elements, they may adopt them directly (which involves specifying how the elements fit into the current activity stream), change them, combine them with other structures, or use them ironically. Appropriation occurs in a bid-response-elaborate process in which multiple members construct an object-in-practice (cf. Orlikowski, 2000). AST research has developed a general categorization of 37 distinct types of appropriation moves in nine categories based on two questions: (1) Does the move involve a single structure or more than one structure? and (2) Does the move consist of an active use of the structure, an attempt to understand or clarify it, or a response to another member's appropriation move? Local patterns of appropriation build over time to global patterns that continue to influence multiple episodes of a practice (Poole & DeSanctis, 1992; Yates, Orlikowski, & Okamura, 1999).

Several scholars, some who build on AST, have used ST to explore the use, impacts, and effectiveness of ICTs in organizations. Orlikowski (1992, 2000) developed an analysis that emphasizes how the three dimensions or modalities of structuration are enacted during appropriation. Initially, Orlikowski (1992) argued that institutional features that serve the modalities were built into the technology by designers, but later, she emphasized how the modalities were enacted in practices (Orlikowski, 2000). The latter view was successfully applied to study the structuring of interorganizational networks of sales representatives and customers (Schultze & Orlikowski, 2004).

Orlikowski and Yates (2002) have also applied this approach to the study of how members produce and reproduce multiple different temporal orientations that structure their practices and the relationships among them. Majchrzak, Rice, Malhotra, King, and Ba (2000) applied AST to show how ICTs captured shared knowledge via communication and how a large interorganizational design team adapted collaboration technologies to respond to misalignments between organizational and team structures. They note a two-phase process in which (1) the team reconfigures its practices around the ICT, and then (2) the team redefines and melds the ICT into work practices. Soernes, Stephens, Browning, & Saetre (2005) used AST in a grounded theory analysis of sales representatives' choices regarding technological links to customers. They observed that agents selectively chose communication media based on the task at hand, then they interpreted tasks using available media. Importantly, DeSanctis et al. (2008) integrated a broad literature into an ST-based model of group support systems and the use of collaborative technologies in organizational contexts.

Moving to the interpretation of ICT use, Leonardi and Jackson (Leonardi, 2007, 2009, 2011; Leonardi & Jackson, 2009; Leonardi, Treem, & Jackson, 2010) have developed an impressive research program about how interpretations of ICTs by users, managers, and potential users mediate the technology-organization interaction. These interpretations generally capture only part of the potential of a technology, are often incorrect in their understandings of it, and are shaped by the interpreter's position. Their structuration can result in a self-reinforcing positive process whereby the ICT changes organizational practices and expands possibilities in positive ways while simultaneously enacting a negative, limiting cycle. Interestingly, ICTs have the impacts that they do in part because users, managers, and other stakeholders regard their impacts as deterministic, even though they want to control the use of them. This illusion of determinism encourages users to persist in their cycles and also preserves the aura of technology as a "magic bullet." This stems in part from the ways that technology becomes imbricated or layered in structurational practices (Leonardi, 2011; Taylor & Van Every, 2000).

Communication Genres. Yates and Orlikowski (1992, 2002; Orlikowski & Yates, 1994; Yates, 1989; Yates, Orlikowski, & Okamura, 1999) identified genres of organizational communication, such as memos, e-mail messages, phone calls, and blueprints, as "typified rhetorical action[s] in the context of socially defined recurrent situations" (Yates & Orlikowski, 1992, p. 301). Genres provide expectations about the socially recognized purpose of a practice, about interactions and activities involved with it, about how participants will use the genre, and about the temporal sequencing of the process. They advanced a model with alternating phases of micro-level production and institutional reproduction of genres. Their temporal model resembles Barley's (1986) view of structuring more than it does a constant duality.

Of particular interest is genre analysis of the interplay of ICTs with two or more genres. For example, Dandi and Muzzi (2005) show how the formality and task orientation of the e-mail genre has evolved to match the complexity of tasks performed in a unit. Yates, Orlikowski, and Okamura (1999) describe large-scale explicit and local genres as well as implicit transformation of electronic news genres in a research and development division in Japan. These genres stabilized and directed message flows and guided their own changes as new purposes and problems emerged in the mix of genre use (Pickering, 1995). At both levels, the format, purpose, and even the distribution of the messages changed through explicit structuring, centralized action, and local appropriation regulated by higher-level forces.

Organizational Climate and Culture. In addition to formal policies and technology, self-structuring also occurs through organizational climate and culture. Culture and climate are often regarded as stemming from individuals' free interpretations of their organizational contexts, but they also result from local or imposed interpretations due to self-steering or self-structuring processes. Poole (1985, 1994; Poole & McPhee 1983) applied ST to climate because in prior conceptions, the concept muddled organizational with personal and subjective references. In ST, climate includes rules and resources structurated in varied organizational practices. Thus a risk climate emerges through reflexive interaction about ongoing risk practices and rules, intermingled with kernel climate tenets ("This organization will support members who take judicious risks yet fail").

Communication networks and dominance orders shape the structuration of climate. To illustrate, Bastien, McPhee, and Bolton (1995) studied the structuration of climate during a major change effort in a large municipal bureaucracy. They identified existing kernel themes, such as *secrecy*, reflected in surface themes, such as *intended secrecy*. When a planning director was fired, for example, the informal communication network spread the rumor, but the director asked his employees to keep it secret. These surface themes became sufficiently repeated, *sedimented* the climate kernel, became *inverted* to justify secrecy against planners, and then *spread* to unrelated topics.

Similarly, Riley's (1983) study reveals the multifaceted interpretive, normative, and political implications of structuration and organizational culture. Using structuration notions of routine announcements, Banks (1994) shows how flight attendants give a cultural edge to message situations through enacting performative flexibility and personalism during flights.

Organizational Knowledge. Climate issues also point to structuration practices linked to organizational knowledge. A variety of research lines explore the role of self-structuring in communication-based knowledgeability. Canary's SAT, summarized above, deals with policy knowledge as well as implementation. Similarly, Iverson (2004; Iverson & McPhee, 2008) demonstrates three distinct but interdependent communication-knowledge processes that constitute CoPs: (1) mutual engagement of members in generating, critiquing, and reproducing knowledge; (2) sharing repertoires of practices; and (3) negotiating a collective joint enterprise around the practices.

Moreover, Kuhn and Jackson's (2008) dynamic, practice-based view of knowledge focuses on episodes of knowledge accomplishment that are stimulated by a problematic situation in which organizational members create blocks to activity. Members' claims of being knowledgeable rest on three episodic criteria: identification (Who or what does the member identify with in the situation?); legitimacy (What is the individual's motivation in this situation?); and accountability (Where does the member look for validation?). In highly determinate situations, knowledge is accomplished through information requests and exchanges, while in less determinate situations, instruction, improvisation, and political contestation dominate the process. Kuhn and Porter (2011) argue that heterogeneity, reflected in differential claims on the three criteria and on diverse resources, plays a critical role in the knowledge generation. Further, Leonardi (2011) shows how the same knowledge, documented in a blueprint, gets reproduced differently in three national contexts (ones characterized by different norms regarding knowledge legitimation).

In effect, research on self-structuring has emphasized the local and adaptive powers of communicators to the point that studies portray organizations as assemblages of distanciated, reproductive subsystems. This leads to a criticism of ST, namely, that it emphasizes structural reproduction over system generation. To date, neither research nor theory in communication and structuration has sufficiently addressed the problem of treating organizations as power-containing, reflexive totalities.

Activity Coordination

The third flow, activity coordination, has received considerable attention from organizational scholars (e.g., Burton, DeSanctis, & Obel, 2006; Mintzberg, 1979). It represents a confluence in which self-structuring and membership-negotiation processes must adapt to nonroutine, local, and interdependent contingencies. One picture of activity coordination posits a relatively clear process in which members co-orient to attain a common goal; however, more often, activity coordination involves effortful alignment of actors with disparate goals and inconsistent perspectives. An important foundation of activity coordination is establishing and maintaining mutual knowledge and explaining common ground (Clark & Brennan, 1991; Cramton, 2001), especially in representations of cooperative tasks. Also important are the alignments and structuring conversations that account for the inevitable situation-specific glitches (Boden, 1994). Most current knowledge about activity coordination comes from studies of decision making and other knowledge-based tasks, such as air traffic control and design.

Task representations take several forms, including plans and protocols for carrying out tasks and schemes that specify substantive content or operations. They are often drawn from objects such as ICTs, checklists, and diagrams. Okhuysen and Bechky (2009) note that objects aid coordination by creating a common perspective on the task, channeling information sharing, providing scaffolding for structuring work, allotting responsibilities, allocating resources, and aligning work by signaling what each member needs to contribute and his or her progress. AST focuses specifically on the ways that members appropriate resources as they coordinate activities. The categories of moves and processes of bidding, described above as types of self-structuring, are often initiated in coordination flows.

For example, Faraj and Xiao (2006) analyze how members with different, but well-defined and well-delineated roles, coordinate work in a medical trauma center. Coordination involves expertise-based moves, including invocation of protocols that specify roles, structuring teams based on assigning a set of complementary role slots, invoking professional CoPs to define roles, and sharing knowledge across role boundaries. These strategies are complemented by dialogic coordination moves that are meant to repair problems introduced by expertise-based moves and to adapt to the situation, including epistemic contestation, joint sensemaking, cross-boundary interventions, and protocol breaking. In contrast, Kellogg, Orlikowski, and Yates (2006) analyze how members who do not have well-defined and well-delineated roles coordinate activity in an interorganizational design group. Specifically, they display their work to make it visible to others, represent their work in common formats (boundary objects), and assemble distant work pieces in provisional products.

One basis for collaboration is what might be called *metacollaboration*, which refers to a participatory process of developing and adjusting to the structural bases for combining specific actions. Gastil, Black, and Moscovitz (2008) argue that deliberation is cultivated in a multilayered process in which habits, motivations, and skills are structured over time in mutually reinforcing cycles. This same sort of process can be generalized to explain how collaborative participation develops momentum that persists across episodes.

A key influence on activity coordination is the degree to which self-structuring constrains relevant practices. Kuhn and Jackson (2008) identify a continuum that ranges from determinate situations (which appear routine and require straightforward actions) to indeterminate ones (which appear chaotic). Determinacy stems from several activity and interaction dimensions, including stability of and consensus on the task, role definitions, member identity and identification, and whom members look to for direction and validation (accountability). In more determinate situations, members draw on and reproduce current modes of self-structuring, whereas in less determinate situations, members improvise and negotiate roles that are likely to produce novelties that feed into the self-structuring process to change existing rules and resources.

The dialectic of control plays an important part in activity coordination, which is one flow in which power is overtly produced and reproduced in practices. Many types of structuring moves have implications for power distributions and the exercise of power in practices and, hence, for the long-term structuring of control. Kuhn and Jackson (2008) describe how two moves, classification and discursive closure, shape how members claim identities that give them access to roles with control while other members end up in positions with less capacity.

In general, ST has identified a range of coordination resources and processes, but the very nature of this flow opens it up to disorganization, resistance, and problematic acts that point to a general concern: Given the need to coordinate locally, how does an organization's system derive sufficient integration to ensure that it will remain a powerful entity? Of course, one answer to this issue is that many organizations do not endure. Hence, bankrupt corporations and failed states challenge explanations based on power-containing organizations and thus deserve research attention.

Institutional Positioning

The fourth flow includes, prototypically, interaction with agents outside the organization, especially clients, peers, and powerful parties in the organization's context. This flow, referred to as *institutional positioning*, highlights a fact often overlooked in organizational communication research—that organizations are constituted in institutionally significant contexts. For instance, despite market uncertainties, even individual customers have institutional significance as potential sources of work tasks, income, lawsuits, and marketing information. Lammers and Barbour (2006; Lammers, 2011) articulate a general, ST-relevant institutional theory for organizational communication (see Lammers & Garcia, Chapter 8). Specifically, they cast institutions as larger umbrella systems under which organizations can span boundaries and communicatively align themselves.

Other research related to this flow clusters into the work on identity, especially organizational and professional reputation (thus overlapping with member negotiation); self-structuring links to the environment; and the negotiation of an organization's place in a larger, global network and community of organizations. In its overlap with identity work, "institutional positioning in large measure rests on individuals representing the organization, especially spanning boundaries as representatives communicating with the outside constituencies" (McPhee & Iverson, 2009, p. 83). Organizational members make strategic choices, interact with other organizations, and even straddle organizational boundaries in work-life and gender dilemmas.

For instance, Butler and Modaff (2008) explored home-based daycare ownership, which creates tensions between professional and private identity for the owner as well as other family members. This tension, (re)produced by individuals in their daily practices, enables and constrains individual choices. In a similar way, Norander and Harter (2012) show how institutional contradictions in a multinational feminist organization become problematic on a local, routine basis because of unavoidable differences in perspectives and the reproduction of gender and national institutions. Applying institutional positioning to race, Halone (2008) examined how racialized sports are organized on micro and macro levels simultaneously. Another example of institutional positioning by individuals is the phenomenon of entrepreneurship. When organizational agents make purchases or sales or engage in mergers or acquisitions, they act in an entrepreneurial way. Sarason, Dean, and Dillard (2006) contend that entrepreneurship is not simply waiting for an opportunity to be discovered, but it occurs through engaging in the duality of structure.

Institutional positioning also depends on internal self-structuring to achieve the (positive or negative) linking capacities articulated by the three structurational dimensions. Specifically, Witmer's (1997) classic study of a local chapter of Alcoholics Anonymous (AA) illuminates how the group draws on the national AA organization for structuring principles that set the tone for the chapter's culture and invokes the mediation of a key founding member in the process. However, the chapter also creates its own important local variants in the dimensions of signification, legitimation, and domination; many of these variations revealed resistance to the national organization. The variants of institutional structures that the chapter enacts rendered the principles of AA into locally defined abstractions that enable members to restructure their day-to-day (drinking and participating) practices.

Internal structuring also ties to projections of external legitimacy. For instance, Moll and Hoque (2011) demonstrate that using accounting practices to gain legitimacy is structurated internally and externally before being directed to external perceptions of legitimacy. In addition, Staber and Sydow (2002) explore the ways that organizations could survive turbulent environments by enacting organizational adaptive capacity. They use structuration to examine the multiplex systems that must be managed and enacted by organizations. Also, institutional isomorphism (DiMaggio & Powell, 1983) points to the interinstitutional production and reproduction of rules and resources.

Examining how institutional positioning communicatively constitutes the organization in a multi-organizational environment, McPhee and Iverson (2009) analyzed a *communidad*, La Cucurpe, which was entangled with challenges to its legitimacy; some were specific to it and others were contested in the Mexican legal system. In a major research program, Browning and colleagues (Browning & Beyer, 1998; Browning, Beyer, & Shetler, 1995; Browning & Shetler, 2000; cf. Kellogg, Orlikowski, & Yates, 2006) studied SEMATECH, an interorganizational ICT consortium. The willingness of two powerful members of SEMATECH to share information through embedding it in symbols and procedures generates a self-reinforcing norm of cooperation, despite considerable changes in the parties involved.

In a study of NASA and the interorganizational relations that contributed to its failures, Garner (2006) notes,

> As interorganizational relationships are realized in interactions, they are reproduced, perpetuating inappropriate power imbalances. Any change must be realized using those same interorganizational relationships since the structures are not only the outcome[s] of action, but also the medium of action. (p. 380)

Another arena of institutional positioning is corporate social responsibility (see May & Roper, Chapter 31). Whether examining how for-profit organizations relate to civil society or how a collection of organizations build resources together, organizations are engaging in practices aimed at enhancing their institutional positions. For example, Fichter and Sydow (2002) explore the networking of organizations in global labor markets that led to better corporate social responsibility practices. They state, "inter-organizational cooperation supports the development of shared views and norms (i.e., rules of signification and rules of legitimation in structurationist terms)" (p. 363).

Occasions for public communication also present opportunities for institutional positioning and developing interrelationships among organizations. Lampel and Meyer (2008) introduce a special issue on tradeshows, conferences, and ceremonies as field-configuring events that offer opportunities for organizations to be represented, collaborations to be formed, and ideas to be exchanged. Also, Norton (2007) examined public negotiations of environmental issues through a structuration lens. In this work, ontological security plays a significant role in the ways that multiple stakeholders produce and reproduce structures for organizational participation, even if those structured systems continue to fail.

Analysis of institutional positioning targets the ways that organizations influence the constituting, structuring processes that are central to other flows. Even though research, such as Hoffman and Cowan (2010), examines the micro and macro level connections in work-life balance, these influences are often misrecognized or undertheorized in the literature.

Cross-Flow Phenomena. While a number of topics in this chapter fit multiple flows, several of them demand separate consideration as sites of multiple flows, namely, the group level and communication networks that entail multiple analytic levels.

The Group Level. ST research is as important for group communication as it is for organizations. Many groups are spawned, formally or informally, by organizations, and organizations are often the contexts for group membership, self-structuring, coordination, and positioning. For instance, Silva and Sias (2010) used Scott et al.'s (1998) structurational identification model to explore the ways that groups structure the relationships of their members to organizations. They identify several functions that religious education groups serve in mediating member identification, namely, a connection function that provides members with local linkages and restructuring and buffering functions to help with identity compatibility issues.

Focusing on self-structuring and coordination processes, Poole et al. (1985) have constructed a broad theoretical statement that serves as the foundation for research group decision making and the use of technology in decision groups. In particular, Poole's (1983; Poole &

Doelger, 1986; Poole & Roth, 1989) theory of decision development details multiple discussion paths and cycles. Relatively simple, rational paths occur when members share interpretations and decision-making norms; otherwise, group members engage in redundant, conflict-ridden interactions. To test this notion, Seibold and Meyers (2007; Seibold, Meyers, & Shoham, 2010) conducted an extensive program of research on the structuring of group arguments. SAT views argumentation as a situated practice irreducible to individual reasoning. SAT distinguishes three interconnected mechanisms of structuration in group argument: (1) use of rules of logic, informal arguments, and norms; (2) elaborations by multiple layers or other members; and (3) multiple influence routes that correspond to the three modalities of structuration.

Moving from argumentation to deliberation, Burkhalter, Gastil, and Kelshaw's (2002) structurational model of group deliberation focuses on political discussions and jury decision making; however, it has important implications for organizational democracy and participation (Gastil, Black, & Moscovitz, 2008). In their view, decision making is secondary to deliberation, a continuous process of structurating political community. The model posits four self-reinforcing cycles that occur through participation in effective deliberations, namely, (1) cultivating deliberative habits and values; (2) developing a sense of civic identity and commonality; (3) forming knowledge and competence development; and (4) enhancing motivations to participate.

Communication Networks. Structurational theories of networks (Barley, 1990; Sydow & Windeler, 1998) parallel interpretively oriented network models in organization studies. Corman and Scott (1994; Corman, 2006; Feld, 1981; McPhee & Corman, 1995) introduce a structurational theory of network reticulation to reconcile competing views of networks as grounded in communication behaviors versus developed from beliefs and perceptions. They define a *network* as "an abstract structure of perceived communication relationships that functions as a set of rules and resources actors draw upon in accomplishing communication behavior" (Corman & Scott, 1994, p. 181). Network structuration occurs through three processes: reticulation (of links as resources), activation (of link salience, generated by shared activities or foci), and enactment (use of the link); both network structure and use are explained by underlying activity parameters. Whitbred, Fonti, Steglich, and Contractor (2011) suggest that reticulation and activation can also result from friendship, workflow, physical and social proximity, and power similarity. A test of their model yields support for several of the rules as generative factors of the network.

Critique and Issues

Action-Structure

One common critique of ST is that Giddens (1979, 1984) overemphasizes action at the expense of structure. Rather than a balanced duality, scholars who draw on theorists such as Foucault (1980) and Laclau (1990) have charged Giddens with granting too much power to individual agents. A similar set of issues confronts scholars who have used the practice perspective in structurational studies (e.g., Kuhn & Jackson, 2008; Orlikowski, 2000; Schultze & Orlikowski, 2004; cf. Fairhurst & Putnam, 2004). However, the notion of the duality of structure explicitly incorporates social institutions and material constraints as key parts of communication (McPhee & Iverson, 2011). Moreover, recent works, such as Canary's (2010b) SAT, Jarzabkowski's (2008) model of strategy, and the Four Flows Model, illustrate a balanced emphasis on action and institutions.

Materiality

More recently, ST has been charged with underplaying materiality and material constraints and neglecting the contextual factors that influence actors' abilities to transform or resist structures (Ashcraft et al., 2009; Fairhurst & Putnam, 2004; Stones, 2005). Scholars continue to debate the degree to which structural elements can be materialized and the ontological status of rules and resources whose traces can be seen in material objects. In the area of technology, researchers also contest the spirit-features distinction in AST that revolves around whether structural elements can be incorporated into ICT (Orlikowski, 2000).

Paralleling this discussion is a debate over the status of agency. If rules and resources can be embodied in material artifacts, then can these artifacts also have a type of agency? For Giddens (1979), only individual human beings can act as agents. He argues against functionalism and contends that collectives (i.e., groups, organizations, constellations of organizations) cannot be agents in the literal sense, but he has loosened his discourse in later years in his use of such terms as *institutional reflexivity*.

Some ST scholars, particularly ones who study communication and information technologies, have focused on notions of material agency, namely, the dynamic, mediating, generative character of artifacts (Chae & Poole, 2005; Leonardi, 2011; Pickering, 1995). Yet fundamentally, ST argues that such usage, while enlightening, inevitably glosses, brackets, black-boxes, and risks obscuring the differences between agents, who socially interact in lived contexts, and the constraining/enabling/mediating resources and conditions of such interactions. Glossing and black-boxing are fine—if one remembers and explores the theoretic simplifications that occur.

The Four Flows

A number of critiques of CCO theorizing, and especially the Four Flows Model, have appeared. The most serious critiques are that communication cannot be clearly assigned to specific flows and that the model does not distinguish or give logical conditions for organizational constitution (Bisel, 2010; Browning, Greene, Sutcliffe, Sitkin, & Obstfeld, 2009; Lutgen-Sandvik & McDermott, 2008; Sillince, 2010; cf. Putnam & Nicotera, 2010). However, from the beginning (McPhee & Zaug, 2000), the Four Flows model has emphasized that any communicative interaction is multifunctional and has an organizing place in multiple flows. Moreover, flows usually involve multiple contexts, have no simple location in an organization's time-space, and can be and are theoretically conceived to involve oppositional, disorganizing, and ambiguous episodes. Regarding the second critique, Sillince (2010) offers the example of social movements and questions whether they are organizations. Based on the Four Flows model, if individuals begin to engage in systematic member negotiations and positioning of issues and the group becomes recognizable, then the movement is transformed into an organization (for example, the way Greenpeace developed from the environmental movement). He offers broad rhetorical strategies as an alternative framework, but these strategies fit neatly as examples of the flows and have their own sufficiency-condition limitations.

Critical Focus

Finally, scholars have criticized communication researchers who use ST as lacking a critical edge. Giddens (1979, 1984) is sometimes portrayed as a politically moderate theorist, who glosses over the impact of power relations in organizations, the state, and the economy (Conrad, 1993). Moreover, scholars have criticized Giddens's (1991) account of globalization for de-emphasizing colonialism and for, instead, focusing on how the structural resources of modernity have empowered people and given them new and different ranges of choices with accompanying risks.

Although these criticisms are understandable in view of Giddens's (1990, 1991) more recent writings, we believe they lack inherency and overlook critical structurational studies. ST, with its concepts of interpenetrating signification, regulation, and domination and with its analysis of contradiction as the driving force of organizational and social change, is at heart a critical theory. In fact, a number of structurational analyses in communication employ critical approaches both avowedly (e.g., the Four Flows model; Howard & Geist, 1995; Kirby & Krone, 2002; Kuhn & Jackson, 2008; McPhee, 1985) and implicitly (Burkhalter et al., 2002; Canary, 2010a).

Conclusion

Though clearly at a point of maturation, ST is nonetheless growing both in multidisciplinary research and in its influence on the framing of issues. We contend that as more diverse theories have tried to synthesize the insights of ST, some of the special strengths of this approach have been lost or diluted. When the extensions and repairs of the basic theory that have been advanced over the past 15 are considered, however, ST stands as an invaluable metatheory and research enterprise, one that includes unique productive solutions to problems plaguing other organizational communication theories.

References

Ahrens, T., & Chapman, C. S. (2007). Theorizing practice in management accounting research. In C. S. Chapman, A. G. Hopwood, & M. D. Shields (Eds.), *Handbooks of management accounting research* (pp. 99–112). Philadelphia, PA: Elsevier.

Archer, M. (1982). Morphogenesis versus structuration: On combining structure and action. *British Journal of Sociology, 33*(1), 455–483.

Ashcraft, K. L., Kuhn, T. R., & Cooren, F. (2009). Constitutional amendments: "Materializing" organizational communication. *Academy of Management Annals, 3*(1), 1–64.

Banks, S. P. (1994). Performing public announcements: The case of flight attendants' work discourse. *Text and Performance Quarterly, 14*(3), 253–267.

Banks, S. P., & Riley, P. (1993). Structuration theory as an ontology for communication research. In S. Deetz (Ed.), *Communication yearbook* (vol. 16, pp. 167–196). Newbury Park, CA: SAGE.

Barley, S. R. (1986). Technology as an occasion for structuring: Observations on CT scanners and the social order of radiology departments. *Administrative Science Quarterly, 31*(1), 78–108.

Barley, S. R. (1990). The alignment of technology and structure through roles and networks. *Administrative Science Quarterly, 35*(1), 61–103.

Bastien, D. T., McPhee, R. D., & Bolton, K. A. (1995). A study and extended theory of the structuration of climate. *Communication Monographs, 62*(2), 87–109.

Bertilsson, M. (1984). The theory of structuration: Prospects and problems. *Acta Sociologica, 27*(4), 339–353.

Bisel, R. S. (2010). A communicative ontology of organization? A description, history, and critique of CCO theories for organization science. *Management Communication Quarterly, 24(1)*, 124–131.

Boden, D. (1994). *The business of talk: Organizations in action.* Cambridge, UK: Polity.

Browning, L. D., & Beyer, J. M. (1998). The structuring of shared voluntary standards in the U.S. semiconductor industry: Communicating to reach agreement. *Communication Monographs, 65*(3), 220–243.

Browning, L. D., Beyer, J. M., & Shetler, J. C. (1995). Building cooperation in a competitive industry: SEMATECH and the semiconductor industry. *Academy of Management Journal, 38*(1), 113–151.

*Browning, L. D., Greene, R., Sitkin, S., Sutcliffe, K., & Obstfeld, D. (2009). Constitutive complexity: Military entrepreneurs and the synthetic character of communication flows. In L. L. Putnam & A. M. Nicotera (Eds.), *Building theories of organization: The constitutive role of communication* (pp. 89–116). New York, NY: Routledge.

Browning, L. D., & Shetler, J. (2000). *SEMATECH: Saving the U.S. semiconductor industry.* College Station: Texas A&M University Press.

Burkhalter, S., Gastil, J., & Kelshaw, T. (2002). A conceptual definition and theoretical model of public deliberation in small face-to-face groups. *Communication Theory, 12*(4), 398–422.

Burton, R. M., DeSanctis, G., & Obel, B. (2006). *Organizational design: A step-by-step approach.* New York, NY: Cambridge University Press.

Butler, J. A., & Modaff, D. P. (2008). When work is home: Agency, structure, and contradictions. *Management Communication Quarterly, 22*(2), 232–257.

Canary, H. E. (2010a). Constructing policy knowledge: Contradictions, communication, and knowledge frames. *Communication Monographs, 77*(2), 181–206.

Canary, H. E. (2010b). Structurating activity theory: An integrative approach to policy knowledge. *Communication Theory, 20*(1), 21–49.

Canary, H., & McPhee, R. (2009). The mediation of policy knowledge: An interpretive analysis of intersecting activity systems. *Management Communication Quarterly, 23*(2), 147–187.

Chae, B., & Poole, M. S. (2005). The surface of emergence in systems development: Agency, institutions, and large-scale information systems. *European Journal of Information Systems, 14*(1), 19–36.

Clark, H., & Brennan, S. (1991). Grounding in communication. In L. B. Resnick, J. M. Levine, & S. D. Teasley (Eds.), *Perspectives on socially-shared cognition* (pp. 127–149). Washington, DC: APA Press.

Conrad, C. (1993). Rhetorical/communication theory as an ontology for structuration research. In S. Deetz (Ed.), *Communication yearbook* (vol. 16, pp. 197–208). Newbury Park, CA: SAGE.

Cooren, F. (2010). *Action and agency in dialogue: Passion, incarnation, and ventriloquism.* Amsterdam, the Netherlands: John Benjamin.

Corman, S. R. (2006). Using activity focus networks to pressure terrorist organizations. *Computational and Mathematical Organization Theory, 12*(1), 35–49.

Corman, S. R., & Scott, C. R. (1994). Perceived networks, activity foci, and observable communication in social collectives. *Communication Theory, 4*(3), 171–190.

Cramton, C. (2001). The mutual knowledge problem and its consequences for dispersed collaboration. *Organizational Science, 12*(3), 346–371.

Dandi, R., & Muzzi, C. (2005). Structuring of genre repertoire in a virtual research team. *Communities and Technologies 2005*, 263–282.

Davies, B., & Harre, R. (1990). Positioning: The discursive production of selves. *Journal of the Theory of Social Behaviour, 20*(1), 43–63.

DeSanctis, G., & Poole, M. S. (1994). Capturing the complexity in advanced technology use: Adaptive structuration theory. *Organization Science, 5*(2), 121–147.

DeSanctis, G., Poole, M. S., Zigurs, I., DeSharnais, G., D'Onofrio, M., Gallupe, B., . . . Shannon, D. (2008). The Minnesota GDSS Research Project: Group support systems, group processes, and group outcomes. *Journal of the Association of Information Systems, 9*(10), 551–608.

DiMaggio, P. J., & Powell, W. W. (1983). The iron cage revisited: Institutional isomorphism and collective rationality in organizational fields. *American Sociological Review, 48*(2), 147–160.

Englund, H., Gerdin, J., & Burns, J. (2011). 25 years of Giddens in accounting research: Achievements, limitations, and the future. *Accounting, Organizations and Society 36*(8), 494–513.

Engstrom, Y. (1995). Objects, contradictions and collaboration in medical cognition: An activity-theoretical perspective. *Artificial Intelligence in Medicine, 7*(5), 395–412.

Essen, A. (2008). Variability as a source of stability: Studying routines in the elderly home care setting. *Human Relations, 61*(11), 1617–1644.

Fairhurst, G. T., & Putnam, L. (2004), Organizations as discursive constructions. *Communication Theory, 14*(1), 5–26.

Faraj, S., & Xiao, Y. (2006). Coordination in fast-response organizations. *Management Science, 52*(8), 1155–1169.

Feld, S. (1981). The focused organization of social ties. *American Journal of Sociology, 86*(5), 1015–1035.

Fichter, M., & Sydow, J. (2002). Using networks towards global labor standards? Organizing social responsibility in global production chains. *Industrielle Beziehungen, 9*(4), 357–380.

Fordham-Hernandez, T., & McPhee, R. (1999, May). *Cognitive maps of organizational narratives and processes: Differences across levels of an organizational hierarchy.* Paper presented at the International Communication Association conference, San Francisco, CA.

Foucault, M. (1980). *Power/knowledge: Selected interviews and other writings 1972–1977.* New York, NY: Pantheon.

Garner, J. (2006). It's not what you know: A transactive memory analysis of knowledge networks at

NASA. *Journal of Technical Writing and Communication, 36*(4), 329–351.

Gastil, J., Black, L., & Moscovitz, K. (2008). Ideology, attitude change, and deliberation in small face-to-face groups. *Political Communication, 25*, 23–46.

Giddens, A. (1976). *New rules of sociological method: A positive critique of interpretative sociologies.* New York, NY: Basic Books.

Giddens, A. (1979). *Central problems in social theory: Action, structure, and contradiction in social analysis.* Berkeley: University of California Press.

Giddens, A. (1984). *The constitution of society: Outline of the theory of structuration.* Berkeley: University of California Press.

Giddens, A. (1987). *Social theory and modern sociology.* Stanford, CA: Stanford University Press.

Giddens, A. (1990). *The consequences of modernity.* Stanford, CA: Stanford University Press.

Giddens, A. (1991). *Modernity and self-identity: Self and society in the late modern age.* Stanford, CA: Stanford University Press.

Goffman, E. (1959). *The presentation of self in everyday life.* New York, NY: Free Press.

Goffman, E. (1963). *Behavior in public places.* New York, NY: Free Press.

Golden, A. G., Kirby, E. L., & Jorgenson, J. (2006). Work-life research from both sides now: An integrative perspective for organizational and family communication. In C. Beck (Ed.), *Communication yearbook* (vol. 30, pp. 143–195). Mahwah, NJ: Lawrence Erlbaum.

Halone, K. K. (2008). The structuration of racialized sport organizing. *Journal of Communication Inquiry, 32*(1), 22–42.

Haslett, B. (2012). *Communicating and organizing in context: The theory of structurational interaction.* London, England: Routledge.

Heracleous, L. (2010). *Discourse, interpretation, organization.* Cambridge, UK: Cambridge University Press.

Hoffman, M. F., & Cowan, R. L. (2010). Be careful what you ask for: Structuration theory and work/life accommodation. *Communication Studies, 61*(2), 205–223.

Holmer-Nadesan, M. (1997). Dislocating (instrumental) organizational time. *Organization Studies, 18*(3), 481–510.

Holmer-Nadesan, M. (1998). Time-space distanciation and organizational communication. In G. A. Barnett & L. Thayer (Eds.), *Organization—Communication, emerging perspectives VI: Power, gender, and technology* (pp. 105–119). Greenwich, CT: Ablex.

Howard, L. A., & Geist, P. (1995). Ideological positioning in organizational change: The dialectic of control in a merging organization. *Communication Monographs, 62*(2), 110–131.

Iverson, J. (2004). *Knowing volunteers through communities of practice* (Unpublished doctoral dissertation). Arizona State University, Tempe, AZ.

Iverson, J., & McPhee, R. D. (2008). Communicating knowing in COPs. *Journal of Applied Communication Research, 36*(2), 176–199.

Jarzabkowski, P. (2008). Shaping strategy as a structuration process. *Academy of Management Journal, 51*(4), 621–650.

Jessop, J. (1996). Interpretive sociology and the dialectic of structure and agency. *Theory, Culture, and Society, 13*(1), 119–128.

Kellogg, K. C., Orlikowski, W. J., & Yates, J. (2006). Life in the trading zone: Structuring coordination across boundaries in post bureaucratic organizations. *Organization Science, 17*(1), 22–44.

Kirby, E., & Krone, K. J. (2002). "The policy exists but you can't really use it": Communication and the structuration of work-family policies. *Journal of Applied Communication Research, 30*(1), 50–77.

Kuhn, T. (2009). Positioning lawyers: Discursive resources, professional ethics and identification. *Organization, 16*(5), 681–704.

Kuhn, T. (Ed.). (2011). *Matters of communication/Matters of engagement.* London, England: SAGE.

Kuhn, T., & Corman, S. (2003). The emergence of homogeneity and heterogeneity in knowledge structures during a planned organizational change. *Communication Monographs, 70*(3), 198–229.

Kuhn, T., Golden, A. S., Jorgenson, J., Buzzanell, P. M., Berkelaar, B. L., Kisselburgh, L. G., . . . Cruz, D. (2008). Cultural discourses and discursive resources for meaning/ful work: Constructing and disrupting identities in contemporary capitalism. *Management Communication Quarterly, 22*(1), 162–171.

Kuhn, T., & Jackson, M. H. (2008). Accomplishing knowledge: A framework for investigating knowing in organizations. *Management Communication Quarterly, 21*(4), 454–485.

Kuhn, T., & Nelson, N. (2002). Reengineering identity: A case study of multiplicity and duality in organizational identification. *Management Communication Quarterly, 16*(1), 5–38.

Kuhn, T., & Porter, A. J. (2011). Heterogeneity in knowledge and knowing: A social practice perspective. In H. Canary & R. McPhee, *Communication knowledge: Contemporary issues for theory and practice* (pp. 17–34). New York, NY: Routledge.

Laclau, E. (1990). *New reflections on the revolution of our time.* London, England: Verso.

Lammers, J. C. (2011). How institutions communicate: Institutional messages, institutional logics, and organizational communication. *Management Communication Quarterly, 25*(1), 154–182.

Lammers, J. C., & Barbour, J. B. (2006). An institutional theory of organizational communication. *Communication Theory, 16*(3), 356–377.

Lampel, J., & Meyer, A. D. (2008). Field-configuring events as structuring mechanisms: How conferences, ceremonies, and trade shows constitute new technologies, industries, and markets—Introduction. *Journal of Management Studies, 45*(6), 1025–1035.

Larson, G. S., & Pepper, G. L. (2011). Organizational identification and the symbolic shaping of information communication technology. *Qualitative Research Reports in Communication, 12*(1), 1–9.

Leonardi, P. M. (2007). Activating the informational capabilities of information technology for organizational change. *Organization Science, 18*(5), 813–831.

Leonardi, P. M. (2009). Crossing the implementation line: The mutual constitution of technology and organizing across development and use activities. *Communication Theory, 19*(3), 278–310.

Leonardi, P. M. (2011). Innovation blindness: Culture, frames, and cross-boundary problem construction in the development of new technology concepts. *Organization Science, 22*(2), 347–369.

Leonardi, P. M., & Jackson, M. H. (2009). Technological grounding: Enrolling technology as a discursive resource to justify cultural change in organizations. *Science, Technology & Human Values, 34*(3), 393–418.

Leonardi, P. M., Treem, J. W., & Jackson, M. H. (2010). The connectivity paradox: Using technology to both decrease and increase perceptions of distance in distributed work arrangements. *Journal of Applied Communication Research, 38*(1), 85–105.

Lutgen-Sandvik, P., & McDermott, V. (2008). The constitution of employee-abusive organizations: A communication flows theory, *Communication Theory, 18*(2), 304–333.

Majchrzak, A., Rice, R. E., Malhotra, A., King, N., & Ba, S. (2000). Technology adaptation: The case of a computer-supported inter-organizational virtual team. *MIS Quarterly, 24*(4), 569–600.

McPhee, R. D. (1985). Formal structure and organizational communication. In R. D. McPhee & P. K. Tompkins (Eds.), *Organizational communication: Traditional themes and new directions* (pp. 149–177). Beverly Hills, CA: SAGE.

McPhee, R. D. (1988). Vertical communication chains: Toward an integrated view. *Managerial Communication Quarterly, 1*(4), 455–493.

McPhee, R. D. (2001, February). *Discursive positioning in organizational hierarchies: Four cases.* Paper presented at Western States Communication Association, Coeur D'Alene, Idaho.

McPhee, R. D, & Canary, H. (2013, July). *Distanciation and organizational constitution.* Paper presented at the European Group for Organizational Studies conference, Montreal, Canada.

McPhee, R. D., & Corman, S. R. (1995). An activity-based theory of communication networks in organizations, applied to the case of a local church. *Communication Monographs, 62*(2), 132–151.

McPhee, R. D., & Iverson, J. (2009). Agents of constitution in Communidad: Constitutive processes of communication in organizations. In L. L. Putnam & A. M. Nicotera (Eds.), *Building theories of communication in organization: The constitutive role of communication* (pp. 49–88). New York, NY: Routledge.

McPhee, R. D., & Iverson, J. (2011). Materiality, structuration, and communication. In T. Kuhn (Ed.), *Matters of communication/Matters of engagement.* London, England: SAGE.

McPhee, R. D., & Poole, M. S. (1980, November). *A theory of structuration: The perspective of Anthony Giddens and its relevance for contemporary communication research.* Paper presented at Rhetorical and Communication Theory Division, Speech Communication Association Convention, New York, NY.

McPhee, R. D., & Poole, M. S. (2001). Organizational structures and configurations. In F. Jablin & L. Putnam (Eds.), *The new handbook of organizational communication* (pp. 503–543). London, England: SAGE.

McPhee, R. D., & Zaug, P. (2000). The communicative constitution of organizations: A framework for explanation. *Electronic Journal of Communication, 10* (1–2).

Mintzberg, H. (1979). *The structuring of organizations.* Englewood Cliffs, NJ: Prentice Hall.

Moll, J., & Hoque, Z. (2011). Budgeting for legitimacy: The case of an Australian university. *Accounting, Organizations and Society, 36*(2), 86–101.

Myers, K. K. (2005). A burning desire: Assimilation into a fire department. *Management Communication Quarterly, 18*(3), 344–384.

Neiderman, F., Briggs, B., de Vreede, G-J., & Kolfschoten, G. (2008). Extending the contextual and organizational elements of adaptive structuration theory in GSS research. *Journal of the Association for Information Systems, 9*(10), 633–652.

Nicotera, A. M., & Clinkscales, M. J. (2003). *Understanding organization through culture and structure: Relational and other lessons from the African-American organization.* Mahwah, NJ: Lawrence Erlbaum.

Nicotera, A. M., & Clinkscales, M. J. (2010). Nurses at the nexus: A case study in structurational divergence. *Health Communication, 25*(1), 32–49.

Nicotera, A. M., Mahon, M. M., & Zhao, X. (2010). Conceptualization and measurement of structurational divergence in the healthcare setting. *Journal of Applied Communication Research, 38*(4), 362–385.

Norander, S., & Harter, L. M. (2012). Reflexivity in practice challenges and potentials of transnational organizing. *Management Communication Quarterly, 26*(1), 74–105.

Norton, T. (2007). The structuration of public participation: Organizing environmental control. *Environmental Communication, 1*(2), 146–170.

Okhuysen, G. A., & Bechky, B. A. (2009). Coordination in organizations: An integrative perspective. *The Academy of Management Annals, 3*(1), 463–502.

Ollman, B. (1976). *Alienation: Marx's conception of man in capitalist society.* New York, NY: Cambridge University Press.

Olufowote, J. O. (2008). A structurational analysis of informed consent to treatment: Societal evolution, contradiction, and reproductions in medical practice. *Health Communication, 23*(3), 292–303.

Olufowote, J. O. (2009). A structurational analysis of informed consent to treatment: (Re)productions of contradictory sociohistorical structures in practitioners' interpretive schemes. *Qualitative Health Research, 19*(6), 802–814.

Olufowote, J. O. (2010). Informed consent to treatment's sociohistorical discourse of traditionalism: A structurational analysis of radiology residents' accounts. *Health Communication, 25*(1), 22–31.

Orlikowski, W. J. (1992). The duality of technology: Rethinking the concept of technology in organizations. *Organization Science, 3*(3), 398–427.

Orlikowski, W. J. (2000). Using technology and constituting structures: A practice lens for studying technology in organizations. *Organization Science, 11*(4), 404–428.

Orlikowski, W. J. (2007). Sociomaterial practices: Exploring technology at work. *Organization Science, 28*(9), 1435–1448.

Orlikowski, W. J., & Yates, J. (1994). Genre repertoire: The structuring of communicative practices in organizations. *Administrative Science Quarterly, 39*(4), 541–574.

Orlikowski, W. J., & Yates, J. (2002). It's about time: Temporal structuring in organizations. *Organization Science, 13*(6), 684–700.

Pickering, A. (1995). *The mangle of practice: Time, agency and science.* Chicago, IL: University of Chicago Press.

Poole, M. S. (1983). Structural paradigms and the study of group communication. In M. Mander (Ed.), *Communications in transition: Issues and debates in communication research* (pp. 186–205). New York, NY: Praeger.

Poole, M. S. (1985). Communication and organizational climates. In R. D. McPhee & P. K. Tompkins (Eds.), *Organizational communication: Traditional themes and new directions* (pp.79–108). Beverly Hills, CA: SAGE.

Poole, M. S. (1994). The structuring of organizational climates. In L. Thayer & G. Barnett (Eds.), *Organizations-communication IV* (pp. 74–113). Norwood, NJ: Ablex.

Poole, M. S., & DeSanctis, G. (1990). Understanding the use of group decision support systems: The theory of adaptive structuration. In J. Fulk & C. Steinfield (Eds.), *Organizations and communication technology* (pp.175–195). Newbury Park, CA: SAGE.

Poole, M. S., & DeSanctis, G. (1992). Microlevel structuration in computer-supported group decision making. *Human Communication Research, 19*(1), 5–49.

Poole, M. S., & Doelger, J. A. (1986). Developmental processes in group decision-making. In R. Y. Hirokawa & M. S. Poole (Eds.), *Communication and group decision-making* (pp. 35–62). Beverly Hills, CA: SAGE.

Poole, M. S., & McPhee, R. D. (1983). A structurational analysis of organizational climate. In L. Putnam & M. Pacanowsky (Eds.), *Communication and organizations: An interpretive approach* (pp. 195–220). Beverly Hills, CA: SAGE.

Poole, M. S., & McPhee, R. D. (2005). Structuration theory. In S. May & D. Mumby (Eds.), *Engaging organizational communication theory and research: Multiple perspectives* (pp. 171–196). Thousand Oaks, CA: SAGE.

Poole, M. S., & Roth, J. (1989). Decision development in small groups V: Test of a contingency model. *Human Communication Research, 15*(4), 549–589.

Poole, M. S., Seibold, D. R., & McPhee, R. D. (1985). Group decision-making as a structurational process. *Quarterly Journal of Speech, 71*(1), 74–102.

Putnam, L. L., & Nicotera, A. (Eds.). (2009). *Building theories of organization: The constitutive role of communication.* New York, NY: Routledge.

Putnam, L. L., & Nicotera, A. M. (2010). Communicative constitution of organization is a question: Critical issues for addressing it. *Management Communication Quarterly, 24*(1), 158–165.

Riley, P. A. (1983). A structurationist account of political culture. *Administrative Science Quarterly, 28*(3), 414–437.

Sarason, Y., Dean, T., & Dillard, J. F. (2006). Entrepreneurship as the nexus of individual and opportunity: A structuration view. *Journal of Business Venturing, 21*(3), 286–305.

Sawyer, R. K. (2005). *Social emergence: Societies as complex systems.* New York, NY: Cambridge University Press.

Schoeneborn, D. (2011). Organization as communication: A Luhmannian perspective. *Management Communication Quarterly, 25*(4), 663–689.

Schultze, U., & Orlikowski, W. J. (2004). A practice perspective on technology-mediated network relations: The user of Internet-based self-serve technologies. *Information Systems Research, 15*(1), 87–106.

Scott, C. R., Connaughton, S. L., Diaz-Saenz, H. R., Maguire, K., Ramirez, R., Richardson, B., . . . Morgan, D. (1999). The impacts of communication and multiple identifications on intent to leave: A multimethodological exploration. *Management Communication Quarterly, 12*(3), 400–435.

Scott, C., Corman, S., & Cheney. (1998). Development of a structurational model of identification in the organization. *Communication Theory, 8*(3), 298–336.

Scott, C., & Fontenot, J. (1999). Multiple identifications during team meetings: A comparison of conventional and computer-supported interactions. *Communication Reports, 12*(2), 91–100.

Scott, C., & Myers, K. (2010). Toward an integrative theoretical perspective on organizational membership negotiations: Socialization, assimilation, and the duality of structure. *Communication Theory, 20*(1), 79–105.

Scott, C., & Stephens, K. K. (2009). It depends on who you're talking to . . . : Predictors and outcomes of situated measures of organizational identification. *Western Journal of Communication, 73*(4), 370–394.

Scott, C., & Trethewey, A. (2008). Organizational discourse and the appraisal of occupational hazards: Interpretive repertoires, heedful interrelating, and identity at work. *Journal of Applied Communication Research, 36*(3), 298–317.

Seibold, D. R., & Meyers, R. (2007). Group argument: A structuration perspective and research program. *Small Group Research, 38*(3), 312–336.

Seibold, D. R., Meyers, R. A., & Shoham, M. D. (2010). Social influence in groups and organizations. In C. R. Berger, M. E. Roloff, & D. Roskos-Ewolsen (Eds.), *Handbook of communication science* (2nd ed., pp. 237–253). Thousand Oaks, CA: SAGE.

Seibold, D., & Myers, K. (2005). Structuring. In G. J. Shepherd, J. St. John, & T. Stripha (Eds.), *Communication as . . . : Perspectives on theory* (pp. 143–152). London, England: SAGE.

Sillince, J. (2007). Organizational context and the discursive construction of organizing. *Management Communication Quarterly, 20*(4), 363–394.

Sillince, J. A. A. (2010). Can CCO theory tell us how organizing is distinct from markets, networking, belonging to a community, or supporting a social movement? *Management Communication Quarterly 24*(1), 132–138.

Silva, D., & Sias, P. M. (2010). Connection, restructuring, and buffering: How groups link individuals and organizations. *Journal of Applied Communication Research, 38*(2), 145–166.

Smith, R. (1993, May). *Images of organizational communication: Root-metaphors of the organization-communication relation.* Paper presented at the International Communication Association Convention, Washington, DC.

Soernes, J-O, Stephens, K. K., Browning, L. D., & Saetre, A. S. (2005). A reflexive model of ICT practices in organizations. *Informing Science Journal, 8*, 123–142.

Staber, U., & Sydow, J. (2002). Organizational adaptive capacity: A structuration perspective. *Journal of Management Inquiry, 11*(4), 408–424.

Stones, R. (2005). *Structuration theory.* Basingstoke, UK: Palgrave Macmillan.

Sydow, J., & Windeler, A. (1998). Organizing and evaluating interfirm networks: A structurationist perspective on network processes and effectiveness. *Organization Science, 9*(3), 265–284.

Taylor, J. R., & Van Every, E. J. (2000). *The emergent organization: Communication as its site and surface.* Mahwah, NJ: Lawrence Erlbaum.

Whitbred, R., Fonti, F., Steglich, C., & Contractor, N. (2011). From microactions to macrostructure and back: A structurational approach to the evolution of communication networks. *Human Communication Research, 37*(3), 404–433.

Whittington, R. (2011). Giddens, structuration theory, and strategy as practice. In D. Golsorkhi, L., Rouleau, & D. Seidl (Eds.), *Cambridge handbook of strategy as practice* (pp. 109–126). Cambridge, UK: Cambridge University Press.

Witmer, D. (1997). Communication and recovery: Structuration as an ontological approach to organizational culture. *Communication Monographs, 64*(4), 324–349.

Yates, J. (1989). *Control through communication: The rise of system in American management.* Baltimore, MD: Johns Hopkins University Press.

Yates, J., & Orlikowski, W. J. (1992). Genres of organizational communication: A structurational approach to studying communication and media. *Academy of Management Review, 17*(2), 299–326.

Yates, J., & Orlikowski, W. J. (2002). Genre systems: Structuring interaction through communicative norms. *The Journal of Business Communication, 39*(1), 13–35.

Yates, J., Orlikowski, W. J., & Okamura, K. (1999). Explicit and implicit structuring of genres in electronic communication: Reinforcement and change of social interaction. *Organization Science, 10*(1), 83–103.

Yberra, S., Keenoy, T., Oswick, C., Beverungen, A., Ellis, N., & Sabelis, I. (2009). Articulating identities. *Human Relations, 62*(3), 299–322.

Zuboff, S. (1988). *In the age of the smart machine.* New York, NY: Basic Books.

Note

1. This term refers to the processes mainly performed, controlled, and monitored by information technologies.

CHAPTER 4

Critical Theory and Postmodernism

Dennis K. Mumby

Twenty-five years ago, this chapter would have been much easier to write and probably quite brief. Critical and postmodern approaches to organizational communication were still, relatively speaking, in their infancy. In fact, Cooper and Burrell's series of articles in *Organization Studies* stand as testament to early efforts to bring together sometimes-abstruse philosophical thought and organizational analysis (Burrell, 1988, 1994; Cooper, 1989; Cooper & Burrell, 1988). In organizational communication, the critical perspective informed some theoretical work and a few efforts at empirical analysis (e.g., Conrad, 1988; Deetz, 1982, 1992a, 1992b; Deetz & Mumby, 1990; Mumby, 1987, 1988, 1993). However, most of the organizational communication research coming out of the linguistic turn tradition was focused, at least initially, on organizational culture research (Bantz, 1993; Pacanowsky & O'Donnell-Trujillo, 1982; Putnam & Pacanowsky, 1983), with relatively little attention to the broader implications of critical theory and postmodernism for understanding organizational life. Hence, the first two editions of the *Handbook of Organizational Communication* did not feature a chapter on critical theory and postmodernism, although the *Handbook of Organization Studies* (Clegg, Hardy, & Nord, 1996) did include one (Alvesson & Deetz, 1996).

Today, the picture is quite different. The continental philosophical tradition undergirds a good deal of the scholarship conducted in organizational communication as well as in organization and management studies, with the critical management studies (CMS) group having a strong—if still niche—presence in the Academy of Management. In parallel fashion, critical organizational communication scholarship has taken up this tradition as a way to develop insight into the complex relations among communication, power, and organizing. Thus as a field, we are now—to a greater or lesser degree—comfortable with theorists such as Adorno, Althusser, Bakhtin, Bauman, Deleuze, Derrida, Foucault, Gramsci, Habermas, Lyotard, Marx, Ricoeur . . . all the way to Žižek.

Moreover, just as the theoretical and philosophical landscape of organizational communication has been transformed over the last 25 years, so too has its object of study. The effects of neo-liberal political discourses and global economic markets have dramatically altered the organizational landscape, with particularly profound implications for the relationships among work, identity, and organizing. The emergence of the post-Fordist organization and the so-called *end of work* (at least, in its incarnation of the post-World War II social contract) require different kinds of analyses with different theoretical tools. Indeed, one could argue that the *self* and the anxieties produced by the *precarity* of the contemporary economic and political landscape (Kalleberg, 2009; Neff, 2012; Ross, 2003) have become *the* locus of study for critical organizational communication and organization studies.

In a very real sense, the so-called *linguistic turn* and the myriad approaches that generally are included under its rubric—interpretive, critical, postmodern, post-structuralist, and so on—has enabled the field of organizational communication to come into its own. This is true, I think, for at least three reasons:

1. The linguistic turn repositioned communication as constitutive of organizing rather than as one of its (sometimes peripheral) effects (Ashcraft, Kuhn, & Cooren, 2009). While other, cognate disciplines (management, organizational psychology) had ceded the study of communication to organizational communication scholars in the 1950s (Redding, 1985), focusing on more "consequential" variables such as personality and organizational structure, in the wake of the linguistic turn, it became much harder to argue that communication was merely ancillary to these other, supposedly more central organizational phenomena. Indeed, it could now be argued that such phenomena were only realizable in the context of an organizational system of signification.

2. Related, the impact of the linguistic turn on management and organization studies meant that suddenly we were all studying many of the same phenomena, albeit from somewhat different perspectives. Discourse, narrative, metaphors, power, resistance, identity, and so forth became a lingua franca that created a loose coalition among organizational communication, (critical) management, and organization studies scholars. While, with a few exceptions (e.g., Deetz, 1985, 1992b; Mumby & Putnam, 1992; Riley, 1983), research often occurred in parallel universes, interconnections among the fields have been increasingly commonplace, with a marker of this interconnection being the *Handbook of Organizational Discourse* (Grant, Hardy, Oswick, Phillips, & Putnam, 2004). The linguistic turn has thus (re)positioned organizational communication studies at the nexus of a vibrant interdisciplinary research agenda. Some dissenting voices notwithstanding (e.g., Prichard, 2006), scholars in the field of organizational communication have probably never been as interdisciplinary as they are currently.

3. Finally, the shift in the landscape of organizational life, mentioned above, lends itself especially well to a communicative mode of explanation and, in particular, to communication analyses informed by critical theory and postmodern thought. In the wake of the linguistic turn, phenomena such as identity, subjectivity, knowledge, and even work have been problematized in ways that have destabilized received notions of their meaning (coherence, objectivity, rationality, autonomy, etc.). Such conceptions and analyses have become particularly salient in a political, economic, and social environment where instability, fragmentation, and precarity have come to the fore, and notions of stable, autonomous identities and relationships have receded. In this sense, the field of organizational communication is well placed to explore the complex and contradictory processes and structures through which organizing is accomplished.

In this chapter, then, we will explore some of the contours of critical and post-structuralist approaches to organizational communication. First, I will examine in more detail the significance of the linguistic turn and show how it has shaped organizational communication studies. Second, I will address some of the principal conceptual threads that make up critical theory and postmodernism, at least as they have influenced organizational communication and cognate fields. Third, I will examine organizational communication research grounded in critical and postmodern theory, with particular attention to scholarship that explores relationships among communication, work, identity, and power. Finally, I will delineate some challenges for the development of organizational communication and advocate for critical analyses that provide meaningful contributions to lived concerns about democratic life, consumption, identity, and security.

Organizational Communication and the Linguistic Turn

On one level, the linguistic turn was an effort to take language and communication seriously and involved a conceptual shift from a correspondence, representational view of language as standing for something else (cognitions, behaviors, objects, etc.) to a view in which language and communication make cognitions, behaviors, and objects possible. In the language of the field, the shift was from a conduit and/or representational perspective (Axley, 1984) to a constitutive model of language and communication (Ashcraft et al., 2009).

But the importance of this shift remains misunderstood without an additional, more fundamental piece of the puzzle. Most significantly, the linguistic turn constituted an effort to overcome the hegemony of Cartesian dualist forms of thinking in the humanities and social sciences. As such, it was not just about the place of language in everyday life but, more importantly, reconfigured the relationship between subject and object, mind and body, individual and society, and so forth. In this sense, then, the linguistic turn was not only epistemological—shifting our conception of the relationship between language and truth—but also ontological, axiological, and political. Read through the lens of critical and postmodern theorizing, the linguistic turn opened up various possibilities for rethinking the relationships among communication, power, and identity and for the relationship between individuals and organizing (Deetz, 2003; Mumby, 2011a).

In the specific context of organizational communication studies, the linguistic turn reinvigorated research in ways that no one could have foreseen. Most importantly, it transformed the study of organizational communication from a managerial focus on a relatively narrow set of variables to a communicative focus on everyday organizing processes (Deetz & Kersten, 1983; Pacanowsky & O'Donnell-Trujillo, 1982). For the first time, communication was viewed as epistemic, that is, as creating the possibilities for particular modes of organizing. Moreover, the linguistic turn problematized the very idea of organization, creating the epistemological and methodological frame through which to examine organizing as a precarious, moment-to-moment accomplishment (Mumby & Stohl, 1996). The field of organizational communication was thus transformed from the study of *communication in organizations* to the study of the *communicative politics of organizing*, with a communication mode of explanation front and center in this conceptual shift.

However, scholarship under the rubric of the linguistic turn is by no means a monolithic enterprise. While the variants of the turn might arguably be traced to a common intellectual origin in the works of Kant and Hegel, the 200 years since have spawned a variety of efforts to problematize and overcome Cartesian dualist thinking, including a number of variants of hermeneutics and phenomenology, numerous efforts in critical theory to rework Marxism, and various attempts to reimagine Saussure's (1960) structuralist decentering of the subject, manifest today in a number of variations of postmodernism and post-structuralism.

Given these challenges to Cartesian representational thinking, arguably the most important legacy of the linguistic turn for organizational communication and other subdisciplines in the field is not the privileging of language but rather the "crisis of representation" (Jameson, 1984) that accompanied it. This crisis undermined the status of knowledge and experience as articulated through the Cartesian version of the modernist, Enlightenment project and questioned the bifurcation of a rational, autonomous subject who knows and an object to be known/discovered. In organizational communication, the implications of this crisis were manifested in productive ways across a number of related issues:

1. *The status of knowledge claims.* In a post-crisis world, how do we make knowledge claims if we undermine the foundations that come with an objective world of discoverable facts? What kinds of assumptions should knowledge claims be based upon? Who and what are appropriate subjects of knowledge? Moreover, such subjects of study are undergirded by an even more radical claim that the studies of various phenomena do not need to be justified by demonstrating their causal connection to organizational efficiency. Such a shift entails a movement from an instrumental, managerial view of knowledge to one where insight and understanding of the human condition become central.

2. *The status of theory and theory development.* Post-crisis theory takes on a quite different role in organizational communication and cognate fields. Rather than a Popperian model of theory testing and falsification, post-crisis theory becomes a generative tool (Gergen, 1978) through which different modes of understanding human behavior become possible. In organization and management studies, the tension between pre- and post-crisis models of theory development led to quite vituperative debates (see, for example, the exchange between Jeffrey Pfeffer and John Van Maanen in Pfeffer, 1993, 1995; Van Maanen, 1995a, 1995b). In organizational communication, this debate has not been nearly as polarized; the post-crisis approach to theory development has been to embrace ecumenicism and find common ground (Corman & Poole, 2000).

3. *The role of the researcher and representational practices.* Post-crisis organization scholars have been reflexive not only about theory development but also about the consequences of different kinds of representational practices in constructing accounts of others' meaning-making practices. The question of how we legitimately make knowledge claims about others has been placed front and center, particularly in research contexts where ethnography is practiced (Tracy, 2012). Clifford and Marcus's (1986) widely cited *Writing Culture* highlighted the intimate connection between *poetics* (representational practices) and *politics* (the interests that underlie knowledge claims). Their arguments framed the move in organizational communication studies to undermine the traditional bifurcation of researcher-as-subject and researched-as-object and to situate all research as political, regardless of its theoretical allegiance.

4. *Power and politics.* The crisis of representation placed questions of power and politics at the center of organizational communication and organization studies. Questions of social order have always been at the center of the modernist project; indeed, as a 20th century manifestation of modernity, the entire history of management thought pivots around struggles over who controls the labor process (and where the locus of struggle lies). In a post-crisis context, power is not merely a resource to be accumulated and allocated but is intimately tied to communication and meaning. Communication is no longer a handmaiden of power (Pfeffer, 1981) but instead creates the very possibility for power to be exercised or, indeed, communicatively constructed as something else (thus obscuring its exercise).

5. *Identity and difference.* In the wake of the crisis of representation, the (human) subject of modernity is both decentered and becomes the central problematic of theory and research. That is, the autonomous, rational subject of modernity

is seen less as the wellspring of truth and knowledge and instead as an effect of truth and power (Foucault, 1979a, 1982). For organizational communication and organization studies, the effect of this shift is profound. Increasingly, research has focused on the communicative and discursive processes through which organizational selves are constructed, disciplined, negotiated, and resistant (Collinson, 2003; Fleming & Spicer, 2003; Kondo, 1990; Kuhn, 2006; Tracy, Myers, & Scott, 2006). Moreover, questions regarding the organization of difference have come to the fore, with scholars examining the communicative processes through which identities are constructed around "differences that make a difference"—race, gender, sexuality, able-bodiedness, and so forth (Allen, 2003; Ashcraft & Mumby, 2004; Bateson, 1972; Buzzanell, 2003; Harter, Scott, Novak, Leeman, & Morris, 2006; Mumby, 2011b; Rumens & Kerfoot, 2009). In this sense, critical organization studies writ large has become centrally concerned with the communicative explanation of the relationships among identity, power, and organization.

Of course, the field of organization communication is by no means reducible to research conducted under the rubric of the linguistic turn. Moreover, critical theory and postmodernism represent two different (and by no means exhaustive) trajectories of the linguistic turn and have different implications for organization communication theory and research. In the next two sections, then, I want to explore the implications of these two traditions for organizational communication and attend more closely to the ways each one constructs organizations as discursive phenomena.

Critical Theory and Organizational Communication

In this section, I want to do three things. First, I will address the question, "What's critical about critical theory?" In other words, what are the assumptions, motivations, and goals of a critical approach to organizations? Second, I will provide a brief, highly glossed history of critical organization research, tracing some of the more important influences that have shaped the field. Third, I will examine briefly some of the more recent organization studies scholarship that has been influenced by the critical tradition.

What's Critical About Critical Organization Studies?

Since the late 1970s/early1980s, there have been numerous efforts to define what is critical about critical organization studies. Burrell and Morgan's (1979) landmark volume characterized critical theory as radical humanist in orientation, with its focus on ideology and human consciousness and its privileging of radical change as an undercurrent of capitalism. Other theorists have provided more nuanced characterizations.

One of the earliest efforts to lay out an agenda and framework for critical organization studies is provided by Frost (1980) in an early volume of *Academy of Management Review*: "Critical organization science should attempt a combination of theory and revolutionary action aimed at making individuals fully aware of the contradictions and injustices in their organizational existence and at assisting them to find a path out of these contradictions" (p. 503). In critical organization studies, then, contradiction is not simply a problem to be solved but a generative mechanism that provides the impetus for social change.

Not long after Frost's manifesto, and drawing on a broad range of philosophical perspectives (including hermeneutics, phenomenology, and critical theory), Deetz argued that critical studies of organizing are founded on three goals: (1) *understanding*—developing rich insight into the meaning-based activities of human behavior; (2) *critique*—deconstruction of false consensus and the processes through which it is sustained; and (3) *education*—efforts to expand the conceptual base through which organization members experience the world. In brief, these goals position critical studies as recognizing that organizations (1) are socio-historical creations that are humanly constructed and thus not natural or inevitable, (2) are produced through power and political interests that privilege some forms of social construction over others but that obscure the contested character of these constructions, and (3) embody possibilities for social transformation through human consciousness-raising and emancipation (Deetz, 1982, 1992a; Deetz & Kersten, 1983). Deetz's conception of critical studies emphasizes the recuperation of conflict and struggle inherent in social construction processes, with the goal of the increased democratization of organizing practices. Deetz draws on the Habermasian tradition in arguing that "the role of all [critical-] interpretive research is the undermining of the conditions leading to false consensus" (1982, p. 140).

Extending Frost's (1980) effort to stake out a CMS agenda, Alvesson (1985) explicitly invokes the Frankfurt School tradition of critical theory, focusing heavily on the distinction between technical/instrumental rationality and practical rationality. The former undergirds traditional management theory with its focus on efficiency and maximization of resources, while the latter undergirds critical theory with its goals of maximizing freedom and minimizing repression. Alvesson quotes Marcuse as the touchstone of a critical approach to organization studies: "How can the people who have been the object of effective and productive domination by themselves create the conditions of freedom?" (Marcuse, 1964, p. 6).

Fournier and Grey (2000) provide a more recent effort to delineate a CMS agenda. For them, CMS involves

1. *A (non)performative intent.* While performativity guides traditional management studies, where knowledge production is framed by an imperative toward efficiency rooted in means-end calculation, CMS is nonperformative in its questioning of the links among knowledge, truth, and efficiency. It is concerned with performativity only to the degree that it attempts to expose the ways in which this logic undergirds and shapes decision-making processes.

2. *Denaturalization.* CMS assumes a discourse of suspicion (Mumby, 1997; Ricoeur, 1970) in the process of deconstructing the reality of organizational life. Unlike traditional management studies, it is assumed that things are not as they appear. In this sense, CMS is committed to uncovering the alternate possibilities for organizing that are effaced by management knowledge and practice.

3. *Reflexivity.* CMS assumes a position of philosophical and methodological reflexivity. That is, CMS continually reflects on its own assumptive grounds regarding the character of knowledge claims as well as on the assumptions upon which other perspectives are built.

There is certainly a large body of critical research in both organizational communication and management studies that addresses questions of reflexivity (or lack thereof) and its implications for theory and research (Deetz, 1996; Jones & Munro, 2005; May & Mumby, 2005; Mumby & Stohl, 1996; Van Maanen, 1995b). Much of this metatheoretical work seeks to position a body of scholarship that explicitly politicizes the research process. Given that research is political and not simply the progressive accumulation of knowledge, what, then, is the role of theory and empirical research in its engagement with members of organizations?

For critical researchers, questions of emancipation and democratization loom large in addressing this question. If organizational communication researchers are to stay true to the emancipatory ethos of the critical project, then enabling organization members to develop the conceptual and discursive tools that foment possibilities for emancipation are key to the critical agenda. As Deetz (1985) argues, critical organization research entails "theoretically guided political praxis" (p. 123). Or, to paraphrase Marx, while the traditional role of research has been to describe and explain the world, the point of critical research is to change it. Critical theory is founded on utopian imaginaries whereby the possibilities for rethinking society as more inclusive and emancipatory are defining conditions. While there is much debate about the actual possibilities for critical engagement with such questions in the context of organization life—for example, micro versus macro approaches to emancipation (Alvesson & Willmott, 1992)—critical theory is heavily defined by its investment (epistemological, axiological, and methodological) in such imaginaries.

Finally, and most recently, Spicer, Alvesson, and Karreman (2009) have attempted to present such a vision through their articulation of critical performativity as a model for critical organization studies. Importantly, they attempt to reclaim the idea of *performativity* from managerial notions of instrumentality and technical efficiency and, contra Fournier and Grey (2000), argue that performativity is central to an engaged, affirmative conception of CMS. Spicer et al. argue that the five (non-exhaustive) elements of a critical performativity are (1) an *affirmative stance* toward subjects of study that proceeds from informants' practices and experiences; (2) an *ethic of care* rather than a reflexively oppositional stance in regard to one's objects of study that opens up the possibility of challenge to the researcher's perspective; (3) *pragmatism*, in which organizations are not seen as totalizing institutions but rather as consisting of a plurality of contexts and actors who coexist in tension with one another, constituting the specific micro contexts within which critical research must offer interventions; (4) *exploring potentialities*, which involves moving beyond the critique of extant managerial practices and exploring what could be; and (5) *normativity*, or engaging with organizations, practitioners, and other researchers regarding what counts as ethical organizing practices and being at the center of debates regarding the possibilities for emancipation and autonomy in organizational life.

Having elaborated the commitments and developments that characterize critical organization studies, I turn now to a relatively brief (and necessarily glossed) discussion of the history of critical organization studies, with principal focus on its turning points. This enables us to get at a sense of how the research foci of critical studies have shifted historically.

A Brief History of Critical Organization Studies

While there's a degree of arbitrariness in delineating its history, the work of Marx is an obvious starting point, especially given his defining and ongoing influence on critical organization studies (Marx, 1967; Marx & Engels, 1947). Marx's great contribution to our understanding of social forces was in showing how, while exploitation exists in every societal form, it takes a particular and peculiar shape under capitalism. Through his historical materialist analysis, Marx shows how three factors make the dynamics of capitalism unlike any other economic system. First, workers live under conditions of expropriation, having had their own means of subsistence and reproduction removed from them by the state (e.g., through laws of enclosure). As such, workers are left with nothing but their labor power, which they are "free" to sell on the open market. Second, capitalism is different from other economic systems in that it exists not to turn goods into more goods but to turn money into more money. Indeed, all elements of the capitalist enterprise, including workers, are defined in terms of their exchange (commodity) value and their ability to produce surplus value. Third, and related, capitalism is unique in that it hides its exploitive character and the means by which it produces surplus value. While in other economic systems (e.g., slave or feudal systems), the production of surplus value is visible (e.g., the serf works for or must give part of his yield to his lord; time spent working for his own subsistence is temporally and often spatially separate), under capitalism, the production of surplus value is enfolded into and obscured by the labor process itself.

This analysis of capitalism still lies at the heart of critical organization and organizational communication studies, although the labor process has changed in numerous ways. Critical studies examine the dynamics of control and resistance as they unfold at the point of production (defined broadly) in the effort to secure and obscure the creation of surplus value (see Zoller, Chapter 24, for an extended discussion of workplace power and resistance). While critical studies perspectives run the gamut from neo-Marxism (e.g., Braverman, 1974; Burawoy, 1979; Rosen, 1985) through postmodernism (e.g., Contu, Driver, & Jones, 2010; Fleming, 2009; Fleming & Spicer, 2003; Tracy, 2000) to feminism (e.g., Ashcraft, 2004; Ashcraft & Mumby, 2004) and postcolonialism (e.g., Broadfoot & Munshi, 2007; Prasad, 2003), the kernel of this work is an effort to understand and critique how expropriated labor lies at the heart of the production of surplus value. The goal of critical studies is, in part, to explore the processes of ideological and discursive mediation that maintain the veil between work and the production of surplus value and to examine how workers variously reproduce, negotiate, and challenge that ideological veil.

While Marx's critique of capitalism still remains a fundamental touchstone for critical organization studies, his project has taken various twists and turns in the 130 years since his death. Indeed, much of the reinterpretation of his work during the first half of the 20th century was aimed at understanding how capitalism was able to resist its various legitimation crises and not crumble under the weight of its own contradictions (Gramsci, 1971; Horkheimer & Adorno, 1988; Lukács, 1971). However, much of this reinterpretation of Marx focused not on the labor process but rather on the ideological superstructures that enabled the reproduction of the capitalist mode of production (e.g., the Frankfurt School's focus on the "culture industry" and Gramsci's focus on the role of hegemony at the level of civil society).

It wasn't until the appearance of Braverman's (1974) work, *Labor and Monopoly Capitalism*, that (neo)Marxist thought turned its attention back to the labor process itself as a defining feature of capitalist hegemony. Braverman's thesis is well rehearsed, but in brief, he argued that 20th-century monopoly capitalism reproduced itself via the structural separation of the conception of work from its execution and, as an effect, the deskilling of labor. Hence, the 20th century witnessed the establishment and legitimation of a managerial class that became the custodian of the body of knowledge regarding how work should be accomplished, while workers themselves were degraded to mere executors of the labor process. Braverman sees Frederick Taylor as one of the principal culprits in this deskilling process, framing him not as an efficiency expert but as intervening on the side of the owners of capital in the struggle over control of the labor process. Hence, for Braverman, the widespread implementation of scientific management principles led not just to the separation of hand (execution of work) and brain (conception of work) but to an antagonistic and alienated relationship between them. Thus scientific management was not made anachronistic by other management theories; it became the taken-for-granted system into which other management theories would intervene in order to manage the human element in work.

Braverman's analysis of monopoly capitalism is generally credited with revitalizing the critical study of work and for being the impetus for a loose coalition of scholars engaged in what became known as *Labor Process Theory* (LPT; e.g., Burawoy, 1979; Edwards, 1979; Knights & Willmott, 1990). For the most part, LPT scholars focused less on the structural features of monopoly capitalism and more on the antagonistic relations between labor and capital as they unfolded in the workplace itself. This work is perhaps best exemplified by Burawoy's (1979) ethnographic analysis of the game of *making out* (hitting production rates and earning incentive pay) played by workers on a factory shop floor; he illustrates how the game functions ideologically to both secure and obscure the production of surplus value. Burawoy addresses this issue by reversing the usual managerial question of "Why don't workers work harder?" and instead asking, "Why do workers work as hard as they do?" Following Gramsci (1971), Burawoy frames the creation of surplus value as occurring at the point of production through the subjective experience of work, mediated through the worker-created game of making out.

From the mid-1970s onward, we can see a sustained effort among critical scholars of organization to understand the dynamics of power as intimately connected to interpretive, sense-making processes (e.g., Clegg, 1975; Deetz, 1985; Deetz & Kersten, 1983; Frost, 1980). Much of this early work is theoretical, entailing various efforts to lay out the premises of a critical approach to organizational communication and organization studies as well as to theorize issues such as power, democracy, resistance, identity, and so forth. While Alvesson (1985) bemoans the lack of a sustained body of critical empirical work that explores the dynamics of power and organizing, the 25 years since then have seen an explosion of such research. Two research trajectories stand out in particular because of their efforts to examine the communicative/discursive construction of power and organization.

What Are the Dynamics of Organizational/Workplace Control and Resistance?

A central tenet of the critical perspective is that, within capitalism, power is not distributed evenly but is concentrated with the owners of capital and the managers who mediate between capitalists and workers. This tenet has existed alongside the idea that social actors are agents who can act otherwise (Giddens, 1979) and engage in forms of resistance even in the most oppressive conditions. Thus much critical research has explored the dynamics of control and resistance as it plays out in everyday organizational life.

In critical organizational communication studies, this work has taken on a distinctly meaning-centered orientation with a focus on the communicative constitution of power and resistance (Conrad, 1988; Helmer, 1993; Mumby, 1987). This research has gone through several phases, with power and resistance receiving varying degrees of emphasis. Much of the early work in both organizational communication and CMS tended to adopt what I have elsewhere referred to as a *reproduction* model of power and resistance (Mumby, 2005), whereby worker resistance to workplace regimes of control tended to be interpreted as reproducing extant power relations.

This emphasis on *reproduction* is often undergirded by neo-Marxist thought, with Althusser's (1971) famous conception of ideology as reproducing capitalist relations of production and Gramsci's (1971) articulation of *hegemony* as framing relations of consent both figuring prominently. Burawoy's (1979) study discussed above is a case in point, with resistance through the game of making out obscuring the contradictions in capitalist relations of production rather than exposing and challenging them. Similarly, Mumby's (1987) analysis of the political function of organizational stories highlights their role in symbolically instantiating and reproducing extant power relations rather than undermining them. Other studies that emphasize this reproduction frame include Helmer's (1993) critique of the role of storytelling in reproducing gender relations at a race track, Rosen's neo-Marxist ethnographies of corporate rituals (Rosen, 1985, 1988), and Collinson's (1988) field study of shop-floor humor in a truck factory.

In contrast, an alternate line of neo-Marxist research argues that the increasing influence of postmodern (particularly Foucauldian) analytics has undertheorized worker resistance because of its focus on managerial practices and efforts to create disciplinary regimes that shape employee identities. Ackroyd and Thompson's work is especially critical of this tendency, arguing that the focus on managerial discourses of control (e.g., Casey, 1995; Townley, 1994) has overemphasized the ability of such programs to create a homogeneous workforce that subordinates professional identities to managerialism (Ackroyd & Thompson, 1999; Thompson & Ackroyd, 1995). As they note, "the shift towards the primacy of discourse and the text encourages the removal of workers from the academic gaze and the distinction between the intent and outcome of managerial strategies and practices is lost" (Ackroyd & Thompson, 1999, p. 629).

Ackroyd and Thompson argue for a return to the study of labor and workers themselves and how they strategically misbehave in the face of managerial control efforts. Karlsson (2012) extends Ackroyd and Thompson's theme with a series of workplace narratives that focus on employee efforts to maintain dignity and autonomy in the face of various forms of control.

In recent years, focus has shifted to the examination of the dialectics of control and resistance, with a greater emphasis on the contextual analysis of the control-resistance dynamic (Fleming, 2007; Mumby, 2005). Much of this research addresses the agency of organization members while at the same time avoiding the imputation of some kind of inviolable core sense of agency that is immune to organizational efforts to colonize it (Kondo, 1990). Postmodern and post-structuralist theory is a strong influence here, given the prevailing theme of human subjectivity as decentered and discursive. In this vein, the work of Knights and Willmott has had a foundational influence in both CMS and critical organizational communication studies, particularly in their development of a Foucauldian approach to the control-resistance dialectic (Knights, 1990; Knights & Willmott, 1999; Willmott, 1990, 1994). We will take up this literature in more detail below, when we discuss the relationship between identity and resistance.

In What Ways Are Organizations Implicated in Broader Questions of Democracy?

This question has been addressed both in terms of the possibilities for organizations realizing democratic participative structures (e.g., Cheney, 1995, 1999; Stohl & Cheney, 2001) and in terms of the ways in which corporate forms and discourses have colonized the lifeworld of community and practical reason (Deetz, 1992a; Habermas, 1987).

Arguably the centerpiece of this research is Deetz's (1992a) *Democracy in an Age of Corporate Colonization.* The importance of this work lies in its effort to develop a conception of democracy rooted in the articulation of a communicative politics of experience and identity that draws heavily on the continental philosophical tradition. In opposition to a *politics of expression,* Deetz develops a *politics of experience,* in which democracy is framed as a communicative effort to reclaim hidden conflicts that are typically obscured by processes of discursive closure that legitimate existing (and nondemocratic) relations of power. Deetz argues that the main impediment to the reclaiming of such conflicts is the *discourse of managerialism* that frames all issues as problems of efficiency rather than problems of human identity, work, and participative democracy. Deetz's work stands at the intersection of (Habermasian) critical theory and (Foucauldian) post-structuralism as an effort to articulate a conflict-based model of participatory democracy in tandem with a conception of the human (corporate) subject that owes much to Foucault's conception of disciplinary power. In a subsequent work, Deetz (1995) develops a stakeholder model of organizational democracy that examines the pragmatic possibilities for new forms of organizational governance. In this model, the notion of *stakeholder* is expanded beyond managerial conceptions of corporate governance, and *management* is redefined as a *managing process,* the purpose of which is to coordinate various and conflicting stakeholder groups in order to realize multiple outcome interests.

Other scholars have examined the communicative micro practices that both enable and constrain the possibilities for organizational democracy. Stohl and Cheney (2001), for example, address the *paradoxes of participation,* developing a communication-based approach to the dynamics through which organizations and their employees manage participatory processes. In an extended organizational communication case study, Cheney has examined the Mondragón system of worker-owned cooperatives and the effects of economic pressures and globalization processes on the ability of the cooperative movement to maintain core social values of equality, worker solidarity, and participatory democracy (Cheney, 1995, 1999). Complementing this work, Cloud takes an explicitly Marxist perspective in arguing that the linguistic turn in critical organizational communication studies has led to the neglect of the materiality of work and, more specifically, has ignored possibilities for collective, transformative resistance by workers (Cheney & Cloud, 2006; Cloud, 2001, 2005). Cloud thus makes the case for a dialectical materialist approach to organizing that focuses much more explicitly on questions of economic inequality and justice.

In the last 20 years or so, the critical tradition delineated above has been complicated by the emergence of postmodern thought. In the second half of this chapter, I will address some of the continuities and discontinuities that characterize the relationship between these two research traditions.

Critical Theory and/or Postmodernism: Continuities and Discontinuities

Distinguishing between critical theory and postmodernism is a tricky business these days; in many ways, the two have merged into a broad-based *critical approach* to the study of organizations, with neo-Marxist and post-structuralist theories sitting happily alongside one another in a number of studies (e.g., Deetz, 1992a). Moreover, accompanying the continuities and discontinuities between these two approaches to organization studies is a parallel historical shift in organizational forms, broadly glossed as a transformation from Fordist bureaucratic structures to post-Fordist flexible structures. In this section, then, we will address the emergence of postmodern CMS and organizational communication studies as an effort to extend research on control and resistance in the context of changing organizational forms and practices—changes that, for example, have produced managerial strategies that take direct aim at employee identity as a locus of control.

In many ways, we can think of the relationship between Marxism and critical theory on the one hand and postmodernism on the other hand as characterized by a concern with autonomy and subjectivity, respectively. Taken in this sense, neo-Marxist–influenced critical organization studies challenge and critique capitalist work arrangements by focusing on threats to human autonomy and the individual and collective resistance to such threats in which workers engage. On the other hand, postmodern organization studies take issues of human subjectivity (or, more accurately, *subjectification*—the process of measuring, governing, and constructing the individual through various discourses and disciplinary practices) as the central problem, examining how employees in a post-Fordist, globalized economic environment are subject to, accommodate, and resist corporate efforts to shape selves in a context of increasing workplace precarity (Kalleberg, 2009; Ross, 2003). Given these distinctions, the notions of *ideology* and *consciousness* are terms that one can identify with Marxism and critical theory, while the concepts of *discipline* and *subjectification* more appropriately characterize postmodern theorizing.

Placing these different approaches to work and organizing in the context of a changing economic, political, and cultural landscape, a useful reference point is Bauman's (2000) distinction between *heavy* or *solid* modernity and *light* or *liquid* modernity. For Bauman, the heyday of Fordism is the epitome of solid modernity:

> Fordism was the self-consciousness of modern society in its "heavy," "bulky," or immobile and "rooted," "solid" phase. At that stage

> in their joint history, capital, management, and labour were all, for better or worse, doomed to stay in one another's company for a long time to come, perhaps forever—tied down by the combination of huge factory buildings, heavy machinery, and massive labour forces. . . . Heavy capitalism was obsessed with bulk and size, and, for that reason, also with boundaries, with making them tight and impenetrable. (pp. 57–58)

On the other hand, *liquid modernity* is the era of disengagement and elusiveness; it is "those free to move without notice, who rule" (Bauman, 2000, p. 120). In contrast, "it is the people who cannot move quickly, and more conspicuously yet the category of people who cannot at will leave their place at all, who are ruled" (p. 120). The disembodied labor of liquid modernity no longer ties capital to a specific location: "Capitalism can travel fast and travel light and its lightness and motility have turned into the paramount source of uncertainty for all the rest. This has become the present-day basis of domination and the principal factor of social divisions" (Bauman, 2000, p. 121).

Marxism is the modernist grand narrative par excellence for the critique of heavy capitalism and the processes through which surplus value is extracted from the workers. On the other hand, postmodernism and post-structuralism are the primary analytic tools for liquid modernity, with its destabilization of coherent identities and privileging of consumption over production (Du Gay & Salaman, 1992). This parallel does not fit precisely (e.g., autonomist Marxism and the rejection of work movement is an important critique of neo-liberal capitalism), but it provides a useful way of framing research that adopts—broadly speaking—a postmodern approach to organizations.

Jones's (2003) observation that in recent years, the field of organization studies has "become increasingly attuned to complexity, discontinuity, conflict, resistance, and difference" (p. 503) effectively summarizes the emergence over the last 25 years of postmodernist approaches to organizational life. Postmodern research has focused heavily on organizations as discursive sites through which employees are constructed as objects of managerial knowledge. Within this focus, organizational communication research has addressed both the broad, macro-level discourses of managerialism (e.g., Deetz, 1992b; Nadesan, 2001, 2008) and the everyday, micro-level discursive and material practices through which organization members engage with these broader discourses (Deetz, 1994; Nadesan, 1996; Tracy, 2000; Trethewey, 1997). Accordingly, this section will explore some of the research themes that have emerged out of this shift in emphasis from ideology critique toward analyses of the multiple spheres within which the subject and power intersect in organization studies.

For critical organizational communication studies, the turn to postmodernism and post-structuralism has been particularly fruitful, given the centrality of discourse and communication to organizing processes (Taylor, 2005). In this context, research has focused on the *work of discourse* (Ashcraft, 2007) in constructing organizational identities, regimes of knowledge, and power relations. In this vein, we will look at three different areas of research: (1) deconstruction, (2) processes of subjectification, and (3) identity regulation and resistance. These areas do not exhaust research conducted under the rubric of postmodern analytics, but they provide a sense of the major prevailing research trends in the evolution of the "critical tradition" in organizational communication over the last three decades.

Deconstruction

In the last 20 years, one avenue of post-structuralist and postmodern analyses has been the deconstruction of modernist organization theory itself. Using the work of Derrida as a starting point, much of this research attempts to reveal the ambiguities and internal contradictions that are latent in the texts of canonical works (Calás & Smircich, 1991; Cooper, 1989; Kilduff, 1993; Martin, 1990; Mumby & Putnam, 1992). The principal target of these deconstructive efforts is *logocentrism*—a philosophy of presence that sees language as the externalization of the thoughts of a fully formed and coherent subject. Logocentrism creates the illusion of texts with fixed centers that articulate a safe conceptual world (Jones, 2004). But this world is rooted in violent hierarchies (Cooper, 1989), in which meaning is constructed around binary oppositions where one (present) binary is privileged over its (absent) other but depends on that absent other for its meaning. For Derrida (1976), there is "nothing outside of the text" (p. 158) in the sense that the systems of meaning social actors inhabit consist of intertextual elements (texts referring to other texts, *ad infinitum*) that constitute a complex social reality.

Deconstruction, then, questions these hierarchically structured binaries and attempts to open up texts to other readings. However, deconstruction is not a negative, merely critical enterprise; it is an affirmative process that demonstrates the indeterminacy and undecidability of meaning in any text and engages in an ongoing dialogue with received readings. By breaking down the binary oppositions in texts, it becomes possible not only to develop alternate readings but also to reimagine possibilities for theory and research.

In organizational communication studies and CMS, deconstructive efforts have aimed at both unpacking the discursive moves in particular forms of knowledge and at articulating alternative views of knowledge. In some of this work, modernist conceptions of organizational rationality are the focal point of deconstructive critique. In organizational communication, for example, Mumby and Putnam (1992) engage in a feminist deconstruction of Simon's (1976) notion of bounded rationality, exploring how this notion simultaneously relies on and marginalizes the emotional side of organizational life. As a way to destabilize the principles of bounded rationality, Mumby and Putnam coined the term *bounded emotionality* not to overturn the existing hierarchy but as a way to invoke a more open dialogue between rationality and emotionality. The resulting analysis explores the *rationality of emotionality* and the *emotionality of rationality*. Subsequent research has taken up the ways in which bounded emotionality can extend insights into the relationships among power, discourse, emotions, and organizing (e.g., Jayasinghe, Thomas, & Wickramasinghe, 2008; Martin, Knopoff, & Beckman, 1998; Raz, 2002).

Kilduff's (1993) deconstruction of March and Simon's (1958) classic, *Organizations*, similarly focuses on how the text discursively constructs a particular form of rationality that privileges an "ideology of programming" that "legitimate[s] fractionation of work and restriction of innovation" (p. 27). Moreover, Kilduff argues that while the explicit, present text of *Organizations* "appears to offer a stark contrast between a model of the employee as machine and a model of the employee as decision maker . . . the subtext . . . undermines this dichotomy," with the model of the worker "updated from a laboring machine to a computing machine" (p. 28). Kilduff's goal in this deconstructive analysis is not simply to critique *Organizations* but also "to permanently change the way the text is used in management education and research" (p. 27).

Other deconstructive analyses have taken on various aspects of organizational life, including enterprise discourse (Nadesan & Trethewey, 2000), leadership theory (Calás & Smircich, 1991), gendered management narratives (Martin, 1990), and globalization and patriarchy (Calás & Smircich, 1993), amongst many others. In each case, the process of deconstruction serves as an effort to undermine the reified assumptions of extant theory and research by destabilizing the binary, hierarchical divisions on which it is based and, hence, opening up possibilities for thinking and theorizing otherwise.

Processes of Subjectification

In recent years, scholars in the fields of both organizational communication and CMS have focused heavily on the various ways in which managerial power-knowledge regimes (Foucault, 1980b) have worked to construct employee subjectivities. Research in this area draws heavily on Foucault's work; indeed, Foucault is probably the most dominant intellectual influence in both CMS and postmodern organizational communication studies. Just as the relationship between *the subject* and *power* is central to Foucault's writings (e.g., Foucault, 1979a, 1980a, 1982), so organization scholars have closely examined processes of *subjectification*, that is, studies of the technologies through which—in a liberal society that positions freedom of the individual at its political and moral epicenter—the free subject is constructed and disciplined in specific ways that shape what it means to act as an individual.

Here, we must note the significant difference between a Marxist and a Foucauldian conception of the subject and its implications for the conception of power. For Marxism, the individual as subject is primarily the bearer or supporter of capitalist relations of production and thus largely reducible to its functions therein—worker, capitalist, bourgeoisie, and so on. Foucault explicitly rejects the Marxist idea of the humanist, autonomous subject that struggles against ideological obfuscation and material oppression and instead focuses both on multiple modes and sites of subject formation and on the particular relationships of the subject to itself and others that such modes, sites, and specific practices produce (Miller & Rose, 2008). Thus the focus becomes exploring "how individuals come to see and understand themselves in a particular way and, through this, become tied to a particular conception of their identity or subjectivity" (Townley, 1994, p. 11). Such a conception of subjectivity requires a very different view of power—one that sees it neither as centrally located (in the State, for example) nor as negative, top-down, and prohibitive (what Foucault calls *sovereign power*). Instead, power is conceived as widely dispersed (*capillary*, in Foucault's terms), decentered, and productive of meanings, objects of knowledge, identities, and so forth. In this sense, power and knowledge are not separate (as in the Marxist model), but intimately tied together.

Importantly, in studying processes of subjectification, critical scholars of organization are interested in how, through various discursive and nondiscursive practices, individuals are constructed as subjects and objects of knowledge, that is, as both subject to various technologies and practices that construct specific measurable and governable identities and as self-reflecting agents who are "encouraged or required . . . to compare what they did, what they achieved, and what they were with what they could or should be" (Miller & Rose, 2008, p. 9). Drawing in part from Foucault's (1979b) notion of *governmentality*, or the conduct of conduct, this research examines "those processes through which objects are rendered amenable to intervention and regulation by being formulated in a particular conceptual way" (Townley, 1994, p. 6).

For example, Nadesan's (1997) Foucauldian analysis of the discourses of personality testing addresses precisely this issue. Her analysis focuses on corporations' widespread use of personality tests as a way of measuring and categorizing employees and potential employees in terms of their suitability for specific job roles and forms of employment. Nadesan demonstrates how these tools are not simply technical instruments that measure already-existing skills and personality traits but rather are constitutive processes through which employees are constructed and defined as measurable and categorizable. Moreover, such instruments have the effect of constructing employees as reflexive subjects who continuously engage in process of self-surveillance, measuring themselves against what and who they feel they should be.

At a more macro level, Townley (1994) has provided a Foucauldian analysis of human resource management as a humanist discourse that constructs employees as objects of knowledge and control. And Jacques (1996) has conducted a genealogical historiography of management knowledge in the 19th and 20th centuries, showing how the very idea of *the employee* is a discursive construction, the creation of which provides an object of knowledge, discipline, and normalization for management discourses and practices.

From a Foucauldian perspective, then, studies of micro practices such as personality testing and macro discourses such as human resource theory and management knowledge illustrate the effects of the discourse of humanism in redefining human subjectivity. They illustrate how demands are placed on all of us to be individually self-referential, how we are frequently the target of others' judgments, and how we are responsible for our own well-being. Humanism creates an obsession with discovering the "true" self. Foucault, however, argues that we need to refuse—not discover—what we are. In its production of forms of control and surveillance aimed at measuring human potential, the discourse of humanism reduces self-formation to self-subjugation. Foucault's intervention—and the organization and management research that draws on it—is important for, in part, deconstructing and reimagining humanism and its effects on the human subject in the realm of organizing.

However, an important critique of such work is that it fails to adequately theorize the agency of employees who are subject to such discourses and practices. Newton (1998) provides a particularly trenchant critique of this research, arguing that while it illustrates how managerial discourses construct a particular conception of the employee-as-subject who is amenable to control processes, it ultimately fails to theorize a robust, agentic conception of employee subjectivity through which such control processes are challenged. In the next section, we will examine research that more adequately conceptualizes employee agency in the face of management control processes (for a more detailed discussion, see Zoller, Chapter 24).

Identity Regulation and Resistance

Scholarship on worker identity and subjectivity has emerged as a central theme in postmodern and post-structuralist organizational communication and management research (Alvesson, Ashcraft, & Thomas, 2008). Much of this research is rooted in the perceived inability of earlier critical studies to adequately account for the role of complex subjectivities in the dialectics of control and resistance. Collinson (1992), for example, argues that the work of early labor process theorists such as Willis (1977) and Burawoy (1979) failed to provide a robust theory of subjectivity in their analyses of organizational power relations and, as such, tended to essentialize the subject (particularly in terms of class), presenting it as a self-evident phenomenon.

Much of the research on worker identity rests on the premise that changes in the social contract and the dominance of a neo-liberal economic model has fundamentally shifted both management-worker relations and the nature of work itself. Indeed, while managerial regimes in Fordist organizations focused their attention mainly on controlling worker behavior and attitudes, control in post-Fordist organizations takes direct aim at employee identities and their sense of worth as human beings. The study of such control efforts (along with employee responses to them) becomes particularly important in an economic and political climate where unstable and precarious work is increasingly the norm (Sennett, 1998). Research on identity regulation and resistance thus attempts to problematize the subjectivity of the organizational employee; that is, rather than take worker oppression and/or resistance as given, scholars attempt to explicate the communicative and discursive process through which employee *identity work* is implicated in the dialectics of control and resistance. In short, the employee as subject is examined as a *terrain of conflict* (Jones, 2009).

Alvesson and Willmott (2002) provide a relatively early effort to articulate an agenda for this research, arguing that "identity work . . . is a significant medium and outcome of organizational control" (p. 622). At the same time, they suggest, "the organizational regulation of identity . . . is a precarious and often contested process" in which organization members engage in active identity work in response to such control efforts (p. 621). For Alvesson and Willmott, the organizational construction of identity consists of the interaction of three elements: (1) *identity regulation*—organizational discursive practices that attempt to define and regulate identity construction, (2) *identity work*—the interpretive activity of organization members "involved in reproducing and transforming self-identity" (p. 627), and (3) *self-identity*—a "repertoire of structured narrations" (p. 627) that is the precarious result of identity work. Employee identity, then, involves a struggle between organizational control processes and efforts to establish a coherent narrative of self-identity.

Collinson (2003) extends this analysis by showing how identity work occurs in the face of threat and insecurity. Making a distinction between *ascribed* and *achieved* selves, he argues that it is the latter that characterizes identity work in post-Fordism, where efforts to achieve a coherent self are undermined by the constantly shifting expectations of organizational life. In the face of such insecurity, employees respond with various "survival strategies" that attempt to reassert a coherent life narrative. Collinson asserts that three such survival strategies involve the construction of (1) conformist selves, (2) dramaturgical selves, and (3) resistant selves. Conformist selves "tend to be preoccupied with themselves as valued objects in the eyes of those in authority, subordinating their own subjectivity in the process" (p. 536). Dramaturgical selves are the product of contemporary forms of workplace surveillance, where employees feel highly visible and/or insecure and respond by carefully enacting identities for significant workplace others. Finally, resistant selves involve an effort to construct an alternative sense of self by advancing a counter-narrative in the face of prevailing organizational efforts to regulate employee identities. As Collinson points out, many of these efforts to articulate a resistant self involve discursive practices such as irony, cynicism, and humor (e.g., Fleming & Spicer, 2003; Taylor & Bain, 2003; Trethewey, 1999).

An important aspect of this research is the effort to complicate relationships among discourse, identity, power, and resistance (Mumby, 2005). Rather than treating control and resistance as oppositional, mutually exclusive processes, scholars illustrate the complex and contradictory ways in which employee identities are implicated in the dialectics of power. Examined discursively, power and identity are mutually defining, revolve around the ambiguity of meaning-management, and are open to contestation. Moreover, efforts to articulate resistant selves can often result in the reproduction of existing relations of power and control. A large body of research in organizational communication and management studies has explored these complex processes (e.g., Ashcraft, 2007; Fleming & Spicer, 2007; Hall, 2010; Kuhn, 2006, 2009; Tracy et al., 2006; Tracy & Scott, 2006; Trethewey, 2001; Wieland, 2010). At the heart of this work is an effort to understand identity as agentic, contradictory, contingent, and, above all, lacking any essence. As such, it provides insight into how workplace identities are both subject to and strategically engaged with managerial discourses in complex ways. In CMS, the work of Fleming and Spicer has been particularly insightful in its examination of the relationship between power and identity (Fleming, 2009; Fleming & Spicer, 2003, 2007). For example, Fleming (2005) argues that cynicism as a discourse of resistance does not protect an *a priori* subject that exists behind or beneath such discourse but rather is productive of subjectivity. In other words, cynicism can be read as a performative act that brings a particular organizational subject into being in a specific organizational context.

In organizational communication, numerous scholars have extended the notion of communication as constitutive of organizing by examining how different discourses circulate around the process of identity construction (e.g., Ashcraft, 2007; Kuhn, 2006; Lair & Wieland, 2012; Murphy, 2003; Sotirin & Gottfried, 1999). In this work, organizations *per se* are less important than the discursive organizing and contestation of work identities; research focuses more on the efforts of agents to construct subject positions in the context of larger discourses of subjectification than on the study of organizational contexts *per se*. For example, Ashcraft's (2007) study focuses on the gendered identity work of airline pilots as they attempt to maintain a coherent sense of self in the context of a changing professional landscape. Lair and Wieland's (2012) study examines the intersection of work and education discourses in the phrase, "What are you going to do with that major?" They explore how this phrase invokes particular discursive strategies and identity work among students as they struggle to make sense of the phrase's implicit causal link between education and career. This study is particularly interesting given current conditions of work precarity and ontological insecurity (Giddens, 1991). Finally, Kuhn (2006) explores how lawyers at two different firms deploy a variety of discursive resources as a way to account for workplace time commitments and articulate their identities in response to both the normative control of their profession and the bureaucratic control of the corporate context in which they work.

All of these studies have in common an effort to examine professional identities not simply as effects of macro discourses nor, indeed, as agentic articulations of a fully coherent and autonomous self. Instead, these studies point to the ways in which identities are indeterminate; involve ongoing, situated struggles over meaning; and are communicatively constructed through various discursive resources and articulations.

Summary and Conclusion: Thinking About the Future of Critical Studies

In this chapter, we have explored critical organizational communication studies and CMS as they have developed through two research traditions: (1) critical theory and neo-Marxism and (2) postmodernism and post-structuralism. Both traditions provide important ways to theorize and investigate organizing as the site of complex dynamics of power, resistance, and identity within capitalist relations of production. Through communicative modes of explanation, critical organizational communication researchers have contributed significantly to our understanding of these dynamics. Indeed, contemporary critical research in our field pursues both critical-emancipatory and postmodern-deconstructive lines of research in efforts to explore the relationship between the communication dialectics of everyday organizing and the democratic-participatory potential of organizational forms. Thus it is important that we recognize the continuities between the critical/neo-Marxist tradition and postmodern/post-structuralist theory. Both perspectives engage with and critique the modernist tradition, albeit in different ways; both attempt to reflexively engage with theory and knowledge production; both conceive of organizations as precarious systems of meaning that must be continually produced and managed; and, finally, both seek to critique organizing processes as systems of control and articulate possibilities for alternative modes of organizing.

The last 25 years or so, then, has been a period of epistemological ferment, with multiple efforts to theorize and empirically examine questions of power, identity, discourse, and meaning. The richness of this work has spawned a diverse and exciting set of research agendas that have only strengthened the health and vitality of the field. However, vital and generative research agendas can all too easily become institutionalized and ossified. Given that critical research is, in part, defined through its challenges to the dominant orthodoxy, what challenges exist if it is not to become part of that orthodoxy?

First, while the conceptual terrain of organizational communication has expanded over the last three decades, I think there is room for the field to be more theoretically adventurous. We have tended to stick to a narrow group of tried-and-tested theories and theorists (Giddens, Habermas, Foucault, Derrida, etc.), mostly overlooking ways to expand our conceptual repertoire and empirical insights as we address key issues such as power, discourse, and identity. For example, it is surprising that Jacques Lacan has remained a peripheral figure in organizational communication studies, especially given the place of identity as a central problematic in our field. The same is not true in CMS, where a number of scholars have taken up Lacan's work in efforts to explore questions of identity and power (Driver, 2009a; Harding, 2007; Hoedemaekers, 2010; Jones & Spicer, 2005) and a special issue of *Organization* has been devoted to Lacan (Contu et al., 2010).

Lacan's work is challenging and his psychoanalytic perspective is one that, at first blush, does not necessarily lend itself well to organizational communication studies. However, it presents interesting possibilities for radicalizing how we have typically approached identity studies, particularly given the centrality of language in his work and his exploration of desire and the imaginary. In discussing the possibilities of a Lacanian perspective for identity research, Driver (2009a) observes that while organizational communication and CMS are replete with studies that demonstrate the complexities and contradictions of identity work, these studies "rarely seem to escape from documenting recurring identity themes of coherence and fragmentation" (p. 490), with limited implications for moving beyond extant knowledge.

In this context, Lacan can help critical scholars reframe identity work as the processes through which organization members struggle with lack—with the gap between an imaginary, coherent, construction of self as knowable and self-sufficient and the unlimited system of possibilities that the symbolic order presents. Specifically, "entering into the symbolic register of language produces lack. Lack . . . produces desire and as such is also the source of everything that is potentially innovative about human life" (Johnsen & Gudmand-Hoyer, 2010, p. 338). Lacan therefore sheds light on an underexplored area of identity research—the imaginary character of all organizational identity discourse (Driver, 2009b). Whether viewing identity as coherent or fragmented, both are imaginary constructions that attempt (and fail) to fix identity in a particular way. Ultimately, there is only lack, but it is precisely the recognition of this lack and the ongoing efforts (desire) to overcome it (and the *jouissance* we experience in the effort) that is potentially liberating and empowering.

Another unexplored possibility for reinvigorating radical organization theory is the work of Deleuze and Guattari (Carter & Jackson, 2004; Deleuze & Guattari, 1983; Massumi, 1992). In a sense, Deleuze and Guattari flip Lacan on his head, arguing that desire is not rooted in a subject's sense of lack but rather, "desire lacks a fixed subject" and, moreover, "there is no fixed subject unless there is repression" (Deleuze & Guattari, 1983, p. 26). Thus for Deleuze and Guattari, lack is not natural and desire does not lack anything; it just is. However, the main objective of capitalism is to plan and regulate desire by orienting it toward things that capitalism can provide. Capitalism exercises power through its effort to oedipalize and neuroticize us all. Capitalism thus attempts to create fixed subjects—a state that we desire. In a sense, then, we desire our own repression. Deleuze and Guattari suggest *schizoanalysis* as an antidote to the repression of difference that arises from capitalism's effort to fix subjectivities. Schizoanalysis is rhizomatic, nomadic thought that opens up a plain of infinite possibility and randomness and thus negates the repression of difference.

From a critical organization studies perspective, Deleuze and Guattari present possibilities for exploring how organizations function oedipally to construct lack and the desire that arises out of it. Indeed, both Lacan and Deleuze and Guattari have "clearly established the significance of the unconscious and ostensibly 'irrational' aspects of organizational processes and shown how there is much more to organizational life than meets the eye" (Jones & Spicer, 2005, p. 228). Moving forward, it seems to me that critical researchers need all the tools they can muster to adequately explore the intersections of organizing, power, discourse, and identity. Lacan and Deleuze and Guattari have done much to explain how power and identity intersect through desire, and their work may open up possibilities for us that have hitherto remained unexplored.

A second area of possibility and challenge for critical studies concerns the relationship between the symbolic and the material in conceptualizing organizing processes. Critical organizational communication scholars have embraced with alacrity the notion that communication constitutes organization and that, moreover, there is nothing outside of the text when it comes to explaining organizational life. Indeed, our field has come into its own in the interdisciplinary study of organizations in good part because of its efforts to take this idea seriously. But perhaps it is time to take a step back, not so much to reassess this piece of received wisdom of critical studies but, rather, to provide space to think about the *relationship* between the symbolic and the material. Simply asserting that everything is communication/symbolic does not get us very far and, indeed, runs the risk of leaving unexplained precisely what we need to explain, that is, the ways in which the symbolic *is* material and has real, material effects on people's lives. Concomitantly, we need to pay close attention to the ways in which the material world both mediates (and is mediated by) and constrains the symbolic. Ashcraft et al.'s (2009) call for a greater focus on the objects, sites, and bodies of organization as a way to explore the symbolic-material dialectic is an important step in this direction.

Finally, I think the future of critical organizational communication theory and research is linked at least in part to its ability to make a meaningful contribution to ongoing debates over the meaning of work and its place in our lives and concomitant questions about the relationship between organizations (particularly the corporate form) and the democratic process. Theory and research in the early days of critical organization studies was conducted in a quite different political and economic environment, where the Fordist organizational form and social contract between workers and employers was, if not completely unchallenged, at least the default organizational form. Today's organizational terrain is characterized by work precarity, a breakdown of work-life boundaries, a privileging of consumption over production practices, and, perhaps most importantly, the positioning of individual self-identity (and the meaning thereof) as the central terrain of struggle in organizational life. Corporations are simultaneously divesting themselves of their responsibilities for employees' well-being and making increasing demands on their sense of self (for an insightful analysis of the far-reaching consequences of this development, see Ho's [2009] ethnography of the culture of Wall Street).

As organizations have become more complex and less clearly identifiable as substantive forms, they have simultaneously—and paradoxically—become more central and influential in people's lives. The ongoing challenge, then, for critical organization scholars is to develop theoretical frameworks and engage in empirical work that explores the many ways in which organizing processes intersect with social actors' efforts to create a sense of ontological security (Giddens, 1991). The condition of late modernity and its institutional forms simultaneously destabilize a coherent sense of identity and provide interesting opportunities for reimagining the self and its relationship to wider communities. Challenges have emerged to corporate business-as-usual (e.g., the Occupy movement, UK Uncut), and many communities and consumers are demanding more sustainable and socially responsible practices from companies, even as corporate social responsibility and greening have become fertile ground for new forms of commodification (Cederström & Fleming, 2012).

Critical organizational communication studies play an important role of critique in exposing organizations as discursive sites of contradiction, where systems of power and politics are enacted and reproduced in ways that benefit some stakeholders over others. However, critical organizational communication studies must also play an affirmative role in articulating alternative, more emancipatory possibilities for organizing; developing an active politics of engagement with various stakeholder groups (including management); and generally taking on a more pragmatic, interventionist role in organizational life (Spicer, Alvesson, & Karreman, 2009). It is only through this dual engagement of critique and affirmation that critical studies can meet the challenges of organizational life in the 21st century.

References

Ackroyd, S., & Thompson, P. (1999). *Organizational misbehaviour*. London, England: SAGE.

Allen, B. J. (2003). *Difference matters: Communicating social identity in organizations*. Prospects Heights, IL: Waveland.

Althusser, L. (1971). *Lenin and philosophy*. New York, NY: Monthly Review Press.

Alvesson, M. (1985). A critical framework for organizational analysis. *Organization Studies, 6*(2), 117–138.

Alvesson, M., Ashcraft, K. L., & Thomas, R. (2008). Identity matters: Reflections on the construction of identity scholarship in organization studies. *Organization, 15*(1), 5–28.

Alvesson, M., & Deetz, S. (1996). Critical theory and postmodernism approaches to organizational studies. In S. Clegg, C. Hardy, & W. Nord (Eds.), *The handbook of organization studies* (pp. 191–217). Thousand Oaks, CA: SAGE.

Alvesson, M., & Willmott, H. (1992). On the idea of emancipation in management and organization studies. *Academy of Management Review, 17*(3), 432–464.

Alvesson, M., & Willmott, H. (2002). Identity regulation as organizational control: Producing the appropriate individual. *Journal of Management Studies, 39*(5), 619–644.

Ashcraft, K. L. (2004). Gender, discourse, and organizations: Framing a shifting relationship. In D. Grant, C. Hardy, C. Oswick, N. Phillips, & L. L. Putnam (Eds.), *Handbook of organizational discourse*. Thousand Oaks, CA: SAGE.

Ashcraft, K. L. (2007). Appreciating the "work" of discourse: Occupational identity and difference as organizing mechanisms in the case of commercial airline pilots. *Discourse & Communication, 1*(1), 9–36.

Ashcraft, K. L., Kuhn, T., & Cooren, F. (2009). Constitutional amendments: "Materializing" organizational communication. *The Academy of Management Annals, 3*(1), 1–64.

Ashcraft, K. L., & Mumby, D. K. (2004). *Reworking gender: A feminist communicology of organization*. Thousand Oaks, CA: SAGE.

Axley, S. (1984). Managerial and organizational communication in terms of the conduit metaphor. *Academy of Management Review, 9*(3), 428–437.

Bantz, C. R. (1993). *Understanding organizations: Interpreting organizational communication cultures*. Columbia: University of South Carolina Press.

Bateson, G. (1972). *Steps to an ecology of mind*. New York, NY: Ballantine.

Bauman, Z. (2000). *Liquid modernity*. Cambridge, UK: Polity Press.

Braverman, H. (1974). *Labor and monopoly capital: The degradation of work in the twentieth century*. New York, NY: Monthly Review Press.

Broadfoot, K., & Munshi, D. (2007). Diverse voices and alternative rationalities: Imagined forms of postcolonial organizational communication. *Management Communication Quarterly, 21*(2), 249–267.

Burawoy, M. (1979). *Manufacturing consent: Changes in the labor process under monopoly capitalism*. Chicago, IL: University of Chicago Press.

Burrell, G. (1988). Modernism, postmodernism and organizational analysis 2: The contribution of Michel Foucault. *Organization Studies, 9*(2), 221–235.

Burrell, G. (1994). Modernism, postmodernism and organizational analysis 4: The contribution of Jürgen Habermas. *Organization Studies, 15*(1), 1–19.

Burrell, G., & Morgan, G. (1979). *Sociological paradigms and organisational analysis*. London, England: Heinemann.

Buzzanell, P. (2003). A feminist standpoint analysis of maternity and maternity leave for women with disabilities. *Women and Language, 26*(2), 53–65.

Calás, M. B., & Smircich, L. (1991). Voicing seduction to silence leadership. *Organization Studies, 12*(4), 567–602.

Calás, M. B., & Smircich, L. (1993). Dangerous liaisons: The "feminine-in-management" meets "globalization." *Business Horizons, 36*(2), 71–81.

Carter, P., & Jackson, N. (2004). Gilles Deleuze and Félix Guattari. In S. Linstead (Ed.), *Organization theory and postmodern thought* (pp. 105–126). London, England: SAGE.

Casey, C. (1995). *Work, self and society: After industrialism*. London, England: SAGE.

Cederström, C., & Fleming, P. (2012). *Dead man working*. Winchester, UK: Zero Books.

Cheney, G. (1995). Democracy in the workplace: Theory and practice from the perspective of communication. *Journal of Applied Communication Research, 23*(3), 167–200.

Cheney, G. (1999). *Values at work: Employee participation meets market pressure at Mondragón*. Ithaca, NY: Cornell University Press.

Cheney, G., & Cloud, D. (2006). Doing democracy, engaging the material: Employee participation and labor activity in an age of market globalization. *Management Communication Quarterly, 19*(4), 501–540.

Clegg, S. (1975). *Power, rule, and domination*. New York, NY: Routledge & Kegan Paul.

Clegg, S., Hardy, C., & Nord, W. (Eds.). (1996). *Handbook of organization studies*. Thousand Oaks, CA: SAGE.

Clifford, J., & Marcus, G. (Eds.). (1986). *Writing culture: The poetics and politics of ethnography*. Berkeley: University of California Press.

Cloud, D. (2001). Laboring under the sign of the new: Cultural studies, organizational communication, and the fallacy of the new economy. *Management Communication Quarterly, 15*(2), 268–278.

Cloud, D. (2005). Fighting words: Labor and the limits of communication at Staley, 1993 to 1996. *Management Communication Quarterly, 18*(4), 509–542.

Collinson, D. (1988). "Engineering humor": Masculinity, joking and conflict in shop-floor relations. *Organization Studies, 9*(2), 181–199.

Collinson, D. (1992). *Managing the shop floor: Subjectivity, masculinity, and workplace culture*. New York, NY: De Gruyter.

Collinson, D. (2003). Identities and insecurities: Selves at work. *Organization, 10*(3), 527–547.

Conrad, C. (1988). Work songs, hegemony, and illusions of self. *Critical Studies in Mass Communication, 5*(3), 179–201.

Contu, A., Driver, M., & Jones, C. (2010). Editorial: Jacques Lacan with organization studies. *Organization, 17*(3), 307–315.

Cooper, R. (1989). Modernism, post modernism and organizational analysis 3: The contribution of Jacques Derrida. *Organization Studies, 10*(4), 479–502.

Cooper, R., & Burrell, G. (1988). Modernism, postmodernism and organizational analysis: An introduction. *Organization Studies, 9*(1), 91–112.

Corman, S. R., & Poole, M. S. (Eds.). (2000). *Perspectives on organizational communication: Finding common ground*. New York, NY: Guilford.

Deetz, S. (1982). Critical interpretive research in organizational communication. *The Western Journal of Speech Communication, 46*(2), 131–149.

Deetz, S. (1985). Critical-cultural research: New sensibilities and old realities. *Journal of Management, 11*(2), 121–136.

Deetz, S. (1992a). *Democracy in an age of corporate colonization: Developments in communication and the politics of everyday life*. Albany: State University of New York Press.

Deetz, S. (1992b). Disciplinary power in the modern corporation. In M. Alvesson & H. Willmott (Eds.), *Critical management studies* (pp. 21–45). Newbury Park, CA: SAGE.

Deetz, S. (1994). The micro-politics of identity formation in the workplace: The case of a knowledge intensive firm. *Human Studies, 17*(1), 23–44.

Deetz, S. (1995). *Transforming communication, transforming business: Building responsive and responsible workplaces*. Cresskill, NJ: Hampton Press.

Deetz, S. (1996). Describing differences in approaches to organization science: Rethinking Burrell and Morgan and their legacy. *Organization Science, 7*(2), 191–207.

Deetz, S. (2003). Reclaiming the legacy of the linguistic turn. *Organization, 10*(3), 421–429.

Deetz, S., & Kersten, A. (1983). Critical models of interpretive research. In L. L. Putnam & M. Pacanowsky (Eds.), *Communication and organizations: An interpretive approach* (pp. 147–171). Beverly Hills, CA: SAGE.

Deetz, S., & Mumby, D. K. (1990). Power, discourse, and the workplace: Reclaiming the critical tradition. In J. Anderson (Ed.), *Communication yearbook* (vol. 13, pp. 18–47). Newbury Park, CA: SAGE.

Deleuze, G., & Guattari, F. (1983). *Anti-Oedipus: Capitalism and schizophrenia* (R. Hurley, M. Seem, & H. Lane, Trans.). Minneapolis: University of Minnesota Press.

Derrida, J. (1976). *Of grammatology* (G. Spivak, Trans.). Baltimore, MD: Johns Hopkins University Press.

Driver, M. (2009a). Encountering the Arugula leaf: The failure of the imaginary and its implications for research on identity in organization. *Organization, 16*(4), 487–504.

Driver, M. (2009b). Struggling with lack: A Lacanian perspective on organizational identity. *Organization Studies, 30*(1), 55–72.

du Gay, P., & Salaman, G. (1992). The cult[ure] of the consumer. *Journal of Management Studies, 29*(5), 615–633.

Edwards, R. (1979). *Contested terrain: The transformation of the workplace in the twentieth century.* New York, NY: Basic Books.

Fleming, P. (2005). Metaphors of resistance. *Management Communication Quarterly, 19*(1), 45–66.

Fleming, P. (2007). Sexuality, power and resistance in the workplace. *Organization Studies, 28*(2), 239–256.

Fleming, P. (2009). *Authenticity and the cultural politics of work: New forms of informal control.* New York, NY: Oxford University Press.

Fleming, P., & Spicer, A. (2003). Working at a cynical distance: Implications for power, subjectivity, and resistance. *Organization, 10*(1), 157–179.

Fleming, P., & Spicer, A. (2007). *Contesting the corporation.* Cambridge, UK: Cambridge University Press.

Foucault, M. (1979a). *Discipline and punish: The birth of the prison* (A. Sheridan, Trans.). New York, NY: Vintage.

Foucault, M. (1979b). On governmentality. *Ideology and Consciousness, 6*, 5–21.

Foucault, M. (1980a). *The history of sexuality: An introduction* (R. Hurley, Trans., vol. 1). New York, NY: Vintage.

Foucault, M. (1980b). *Power/knowledge: Selected interviews and other writings 1972–1977* (C. Gordon, L. Marshall, J. Mepham, & K. Soper, Trans.). New York, NY: Pantheon.

Foucault, M. (1982). The subject and power. In H. F. Dreyfus & P. Rabinow (Eds.), *Michel Foucault: Beyond structuralism and hermeneutics* (pp. 202–226). Brighton, UK: Harvester.

Fournier, V., & Grey, C. (2000). At the critical moment: Conditions and prospects for critical management studies. *Human Relations, 53*(1), 7–32.

Frost, P. (1980). Toward a radical framework for practicing organization science. *Academy of Management Review, 5*(4), 501–508.

Gergen, K. (1978). Toward generative theory. *Journal of Personality and Social Psychology, 36*(11), 1344–1356.

Giddens, A. (1979). *Central problems in social theory: Action, structure, and contradiction in social analysis.* Berkeley: University of California Press.

Giddens, A. (1991). *Modernity and self-identity: Self and society in the late modern age.* Stanford, CA: Stanford University Press.

Gramsci, A. (1971). *Selections from the prison notebooks* (Q. Hoare & G. N. Smith, Trans.). New York, NY: International Publishers.

Grant, D., Hardy, C., Oswick, C., Phillips, N., & Putnam, L. L. (Eds.). (2004). *Handbook of organizational discourse.* London, England: SAGE.

Habermas, J. (1987). *The theory of communicative action: Lifeworld and system* (T. McCarthy, Trans., vol. 2). Boston, MA: Beacon Press.

Hall, M. (2010). Re-constituting place and space: Culture and communication in the construction of a Jamaican transnational identity. *Howard Journal of Communications, 21*(2), 119–140.

Harding, N. (2007). On Lacan and the "becoming-ness" of organizations/selves. *Organization Studies, 28*(11), 1761–1773.

Harter, L. M., Scott, J. A., Novak, D. R., Leeman, M., & Morris, J. F. (2006). Freedom through flight: Performing a counter-narrative of disability. *Journal of Applied Communication Research, 34*(1), 3–29.

Helmer, J. (1993). Storytelling in the creation and maintenance of organizational tension and stratification. *The Southern Communication Journal, 59*(1), 34–44.

Ho, K. (2009). *Liquidated: An ethnography of Wall Street.* Durham, NC: Duke University Press.

Hoedemaekers, C. (2010). 'Not even semblance': Exploring the interruption of identification with Lacan. *Organization, 17*(3), 379–393.

Horkheimer, M., & Adorno, T. (1988). *Dialectic of enlightenment* (J. Cumming, Trans.). New York, NY: Continuum.

Jacques, R. (1996). *Manufacturing the employee: Management knowledge from the 19th to 21st centuries.* London, England: SAGE.

Jameson, F. (1984). Foreword. In J-F Lyotard (Ed.), *The postmodern condition* (pp. vii–xi). Minneapolis: University of Minnesota Press.

Jayasinghe, K., Thomas, D., & Wickramasinghe, D. (2008). Bounded emotionality in entrepreneurship: An alternative framework. *International Journal of Entrepreneurial Behaviour & Research, 14*(4), 242–258.

Johnsen, R., & Gudmand-Hoyer, M. (2010). Lacan and the lack of humanity in HRM. *Organization, 17*(3), 331–344.

Jones, C. (2003). Theory after the postmodern condition. *Organization, 10*(3), 503–525.

Jones, C. (2004). Jacques Derrida. In S. Linstead (Ed.), *Organization theory and postmodern thought* (pp. 34–63). London, England: SAGE.

Jones, C. (2009). Poststructuralism in critical management studies. In M. Alvesson, T. Bridgman, & H. Willmott (Eds.), *The Oxford handbook of critical management studies* (pp. 76–98). Oxford, UK: Oxford University Press.

Jones, C., & Munro, R. (Eds.). (2005). *Contemporary organization theory.* Oxford, UK: Blackwell.

Jones, C., & Spicer, A. (2005). The sublime object of entrepreneurship. *Organization, 12*(2), 223–246.

Kalleberg, A. L. (2009). Precarious work, insecure workers: Employment relations in transition. *American Sociological Review, 74*(1), 1–22.

Karlsson, J. (2012). *Organizational misbehaviour in the workplace: Narratives of dignity and resistance.* Basingstoke, UK: Palgrave Macmillan.

Kilduff, M. (1993). Deconstructing organizations. *Academy of Management Review, 18*(1), 13–31.

Knights, D. (1990). Subjectivity, power and the labor process. In D. Knights & H. Willmott (Eds.), *Labour process theory* (pp. 297–335). London, England: MacMillan.

Knights, D., & Willmott, H. (Eds.). (1990). *Labor process theory.* London, England: MacMillan.

Knights, D., & Willmott, H. (Eds.). (1999). *Management lives: Power and identity in work organizations.* London, England: SAGE.

Kondo, D. K. (1990). *Crafting selves: Power, gender, and discourses of identity in a Japanese workplace.* Chicago, IL: University of Chicago Press.

Kuhn, T. (2006). A "demented work ethic" and a "lifestyle firm": Discourse, identity, and workplace time commitments. *Organization Studies, 27*(9), 1339–1358.

Kuhn, T. (2009). Positioning lawyers: Discursive resources, professional ethics, and identification. *Organization, 16*(5), 681–704.

Lair, D., & Wieland, S. (2012). "What are you going to do with that major?" Colloquial speech and the meanings of work and education. *Management Communication Quarterly, 26*(3), 423–452.

Lukács, G. (1971). *History and class consciousness: Studies in Marxist dialectics* (R. Livingstone, Trans.). Cambridge, MA: MIT Press.

March, J. G., & Simon, H. (1958). *Organizations.* New York, NY: Wiley.

Marcuse, H. (1964). *One-dimensional man: Studies in the ideology of advanced industrial society.* Boston, MA: Beacon Press.

Martin, J. (1990). Deconstructing organizational taboos: The suppression of gender conflict in organizations. *Organization Science, 1*(4), 339–359.

Martin, J., Knopoff, K., & Beckman, C. (1998). An alternative to bureaucratic impersonality and emotional labor: Bounded emotionality at the Body Shop. *Administrative Science Quarterly, 43*(2), 429–469.

Marx, K. (1967). *Capital* (S. Moore & E. Aveling, Trans.). New York, NY: International Publishers.

Marx, K., & Engels, F. (1947). *The German ideology.* New York, NY: International Publishers.

Massumi, B. (1992). *A user's guide to capitalism and schizophrenia: Deviations from Deleuze and Guattari.* Cambridge, MA: MIT Press.

May, S. K., & Mumby, D. K. (Eds.). (2005). *Engaging organizational communication theory and research: Multiple perspectives.* Thousand Oaks, CA: SAGE.

Miller, P., & Rose, N. (2008). *Governing the present.* Cambridge, UK: Polity.

Mumby, D. K. (1987). The political function of narrative in organizations. *Communication Monographs, 54*(2), 113–127.

Mumby, D. K. (1988). *Communication and power in organizations: Discourse, ideology, and domination.* Norwood, NJ: Ablex.

Mumby, D. K. (1993). Critical organizational communication studies: The next ten years. *Communication Monographs, 60*(1), 18–25.

Mumby, D. K. (1997). Modernism, postmodernism, and communication studies: A rereading of an ongoing debate. *Communication Theory, 7*(1), 1–28.

Mumby, D. K. (2005). Theorizing resistance in organization studies: A dialectical approach.

Management Communication Quarterly, 19(1), 1–26.

Mumby, D. K. (2011a). What's cooking in organizational discourse studies? A response to Alvesson and Karreman. *Human Relations, 64*(9), 1147–1161.

Mumby, D. K. (Ed.). (2011b). *Reframing difference in organizational communication studies: Research, pedagogy, practice.* Thousand Oaks, CA: SAGE.

Mumby, D. K., & Putnam, L. L. (1992). The politics of emotion: A feminist reading of bounded rationality. *Academy of Management Review, 17*(3), 465–486.

Mumby, D. K., & Stohl, C. (1996). Disciplining organizational communication studies. *Management Communication Quarterly, 10*(1), 50–72.

Murphy, A. G. (2003). The dialectical gaze: Exploring the subject-object tension in the performances of women who strip. *Journal of Contemporary Ethnography, 32*(3), 305–335.

Nadesan, M. H. (1996). Organizational identity and space of action. *Organization Studies, 17*(1), 49–81.

Nadesan, M. H. (1997). Constructing paper dolls: The discourse of personality testing in organizational practice. *Communication Theory, 7*(3), 189–218.

Nadesan, M. H. (2001). Post-Fordism, political economy, and critical organizational communication studies. *Management Communication Quarterly, 15*(2), 259–267.

Nadesan, M. H. (2008). *Governmentality, biopower, and everyday life.* New York, NY: Routledge.

Nadesan, M. H., & Trethewey, A. (2000). Performing the enterprising subject: Gendered strategies for success (?). *Text and Performance Quarterly, 20*(3), 223–250.

Neff, G. (2012). *Venture labor: Work and the burden of risk in innovative industries.* Cambridge, MA: MIT Press.

Newton, T. (1998). Theorizing subjectivity in organizations: The failure of Foucauldian studies? *Organization Studies, 19*(3), 415–447.

Pacanowsky, M., & O'Donnell-Trujillo, N. (1982). Communication and organizational cultures. *The Western Journal of Speech Communication, 46*(2), 115–130.

Pfeffer, J. (1981). *Power in organizations.* Cambridge, MA: Ballinger Publishing.

Pfeffer, J. (1993). Barriers to the advance of organizational science: Paradigm development as a dependent variable. *Academy of Management Review, 18*(4), 599–620.

Pfeffer, J. (1995). Mortality, reproducibility, and the persistence of styles of theory. *Organization Science, 6*(6), 681–686.

Prasad, A. (Ed.). (2003). *Postcolonial theory and organizational analysis: A critical engagement.* New York, NY: Palgrave.

Prichard, C. (2006). Global politics, academic dispositions, and the tilting of organizational communication: A provocation to a debate. *Management Communication Quarterly, 19*(4), 638–644.

Putnam, L. L., & Pacanowsky, M. (Eds.). (1983). *Communication and organizations: An interpretive approach.* Beverly Hills, CA: SAGE.

Raz, A. E. (2002). *Emotions at work: Normative control, organizations, and culture in Japan and America.* Cambridge, MA: Harvard University Asia Center and Harvard University Press.

Redding, W. C. (1985). Stumbling toward identity: The emergence of organizational communication as a field of study. In R. D. McPhee & P. K. Tompkins (Eds.), *Organizational communication: Traditional themes and new directions* (pp. 15–54). Beverly Hills, CA: SAGE.

Ricoeur, P. (1970). *Freud and philosophy: An essay on interpretation* (D. Savage, Trans.). New Haven, CT: Yale University Press.

Riley, P. (1983). A structurationist account of political culture. *Administrative Science Quarterly, 28*(3), 414–437.

Rosen, M. (1985). "Breakfast at Spiro's": Dramaturgy and dominance. *Journal of Management, 11*(2), 31–48.

Rosen, M. (1988). You asked for it: Christmas at the bosses' expense. *Journal of Management Studies, 25*(5), 463–480.

Ross, A. (2003). *No-Collar: The humane workpace and its hidden costs.* New York, NY: Basic Books.

Rumens, N., & Kerfoot, D. (2009). Gay men at work: (Re)constructing the self as professional. *Human Relations, 62*(5), 763–786.

Saussure, F. de. (1960). *Course in general linguistics.* London, England: Peter Owen.

Sennett, R. (1998). *The corrosion of character: The personal consequences of work in the new capitalism.* New York, NY: W.W. Norton.

Simon, H. (1976). *Administrative behavior* (3rd ed.). Glencoe, IL: Free Press.

Sotirin, P., & Gottfried, H. (1999). The ambivalent dynamics of secretarial "bitching": Control, resistance, and the construction of identity. *Organization, 6*(1), 57–80.

Spicer, A., Alvesson, M., & Karreman, D. (2009). Critical performativity: The unfinished business of critical management studies. *Human Relations, 62*(4), 537–560.

Stohl, C., & Cheney, G. (2001). Participatory processes/paradoxical practices: Communication and the dilemmas of organizational democracy. *Management Communication Quarterly, 14*(3), 349–407.

Taylor, B. (2005). Postmodern theory. In S. K. May & D. K. Mumby (Eds.), *Engaging organizational communication: Theory and research* (pp. 113–140). Thousand Oaks, CA: SAGE.

Taylor, P., & Bain, P. (2003). "Subterranean worksick blues": Humour as subversion in two call centres. *Organization Studies, 24*(9), 1487–1509.

Thompson, P., & Ackroyd, S. (1995). All quiet on the workplace front? A critique of recent trends in British industrial sociology. *Sociology, 29*(4), 615–633.

Townley, B. (1994). *Reframing human resource management: Power, ethics and the subject at work.* London, England: SAGE.

Tracy, S. (2000). Becoming a character for commerce: Emotion labor, self-subordination, and discursive construction of identity in a total institution. *Management Communication Quarterly, 14*(1), 90–128.

Tracy, S. (2012). The toxic and mythical combination of a deductive writing logic for inductive qualitative research. *Qualitative Communication Research, 1*(1), 109–141.

Tracy, S., Myers, K., & Scott, C. (2006). Cracking jokes and crafting selves: Sensemaking and identity management among human service workers. *Communication Monographs, 73*(3), 283–308.

Tracy, S., & Scott, C. (2006). Sexuality, masculinity, and taint management among firefighters and correctional officers: Getting down and dirty with "America's heroes" and the "scum of law enforcement." *Management Communication Quarterly, 20*(1), 6–38.

Trethewey, A. (1997). Resistance, identity, and empowerment: A postmodern feminist analysis of clients in a human service organization. *Communication Monographs, 64*(4), 281–301.

Trethewey, A. (1999). Isn't it ironic: Using irony to explore the contradictions of organizational life. *Western Journal of Communication, 63*(2), 140–167.

Trethewey, A. (2001). Reproducing and resisting the master narrative of decline: Midlife professional women's experiences of aging. *Management Communication Quarterly, 15*(2), 183–226.

Van Maanen, J. (1995a). Fear and loathing in organization studies. *Organization Science, 6*(6), 687–692.

Van Maanen, J. (1995b). Style as theory. *Organization Science, 6*(1), 133–143.

Wieland, S. (2010). Ideal selves as resources for the situated practice of identity. *Management Communication Quarterly, 24*(4), 503–528.

Willis, P. (1977). *Learning to labor: How working class kids get working class jobs.* New York, NY: Columbia University Press.

Willmott, H. (1990). Subjectivity and the dialectics of praxis: Opening up the core of labor process analysis. In D. Knights & H. Willmott (Eds.), *Labour process theory* (pp. 336–378). London, England: MacMillan.

Willmott, H. (1994). Bringing agency (back) into organizational analysis: Responding to the crisis of (post)modernity. In J. Hassard & M. Parker (Eds.), *Towards a new theory of organizations* (pp. 87–130). London, England: Routledge.

CHAPTER 5

Feminist Theory

Karen Lee Ashcraft

The appearance of the first *Handbook* chapter on feminist theory is surely a sign of significant growth: the rise of feminism as an important intellectual force in the field, a thriving body of empirical research to review, the diffusion of feminist concerns across the field—or at least, faith that such trends are or should be so. This inaugural chapter answers the guiding question—How has feminist theorizing developed in the context of organizational communication studies?—by considering five perspectives: liberal, cultural, standpoint, radical–post-structuralist, and postmodern feminisms. My main argument is that feminist organizational communication theory has grown more prominent, impactful, and settled, as well as less contested and resourceful, over the past 25 years. I consider associated challenges and how we might meet them to revive the collective vitality of feminist theorizing in our field.

Five Feminisms That Characterize Organizational Communication Studies

It is common for scholars to identify streams of feminist theory operating in a given field of inquiry (e.g., Tong, 1989). Close to home, Calás & Smircich (1996, 2006) offer a comprehensive review of feminisms at work in organization and management studies; and in some ways, the landscape of feminist organizational communication theory looks similar. For example, Buzzanell's (1994) agenda-setting call for feminist work in our field proposed a parallel list of promising catalysts for future scholarship. It was not long after this oft-cited call that feminist theory became a recognized voice in our field, thanks in no small part to several leading organizational communication scholars who championed its rise (e.g., Mumby, 1993; Putnam, 1990; Putnam & Fairhurst, 1985). While feminist theorizing enjoyed a rapid ascent, it is also the case that we have witnessed the distillation rather than proliferation of perspectives along the way. Indeed, I argue that the feminist theoretical resources in play have shrunk and consolidated in recent years.

Before we begin, it is worth noting that most reviews of feminist scholarship in our field trace the evolution of gender as an organizational communication problematic (e.g., from gender *in* organization to gender *of* organization to the *cultural organization* of gender, difference, and work) instead of weighing the fate of particular feminist theories. Reflecting on my experience composing such reviews (e.g., Ashcraft, 2004, 2005, 2006a), I suspect this is because the range and depth of feminist theorizing did not keep pace with the explosion of empirical studies. Explicit reflection on the status of feminist organizational communication *theory* is thus a timely endeavor that can reinvigorate stagnant theoretical energies.

In what follows, I utilize previous reviews by asking what we can learn about feminist theory *per se* from the evolution of gender as an organizational communication problematic. To be clear, I offer the five feminisms framework below as a heuristic device—a helpful way to reframe where we have been in order to make sense of where we want to go. I do *not* claim that this is how it is/was or that the scholars cited would understand their work in the ways proposed. Nor do I claim to provide a neatly chronological account, though I do flag developments over time, as appropriate. Since feminist theory arrived in our field fairly recently, multiple feminisms, which unfolded gradually and independently elsewhere, intermingled here all at once. This high-speed collision enabled feminist theorizing that was admittedly chaotic *and* distinctively nimble, and I seek to address both sides of that coin. As that suggests, I acknowledge that there has been considerable overlap among perspectives, though at times, I accentuate distinctions in order to capture subtleties we sometimes miss. Overall, I offer this framework as a useful way to both read and stimulate theorizing in the field. For each of the five feminisms, I discuss unifying assumptions (about gender, difference, communication, organization, and power), their specific manifestation in our field, and key critiques and future possibilities. To capture how these feminisms interact in our disciplinary ecology, I stress alliances and tensions among perspectives.

Liberal Feminism: Sameness and Standardization

Liberal feminism is perhaps the most familiar stream of feminist theory, present in the early waves of feminism and still on the popular tongue today, especially when it comes to work and organization. This perspective emphasizes equal opportunities based on shared humanity. This is not to say that we are all the same but that what *is* common about our condition supports universal rights and a logic of merit: Namely, we are all autonomous individuals with potential to self-actualize, who bear responsibility for personal success and failure. At a glance, it may seem strange to advocate individualism while fighting for collective rights. But from this view, collective action is imperative when certain groups—namely, women—are routinely denied human fulfillment.

Because our *core* sameness is what matters most, justice is best pursued through standardization. Not surprisingly, then, liberal feminism is comfortable with many bureaucratic principles, particularly the ideal of impartiality through uniform rules and the incentive of career through hierarchical advancement. The trick is to open equal access and remove unfair obstacles to success or, as it is often abridged, "Add women and stir."[1] Liberal feminist politics are, in this sense, conservative: Change is required, but that means reformation, not rejection, of extant systems; tackle individual bias, and you will eventually correct the system distortions it creates.

In organizational communication studies, liberal feminism is most evident in early research attending to gender, especially research that focused on barriers to women's advancement (e.g., the glass ceiling; see Buzzanell, 1995). Many studies examined how male and female managers are seen to communicate differently and how women are deemed deficient by comparison (for a review and current example, see Elsesser & Lever, 2011). Most of this research sought to expose and challenge biased perceptions that block women from climbing the hierarchy (Natalle, 1996)—for example, with "double standards," which interpret similar behaviors differently depending on who does them, or with "double binds," which enforce stereotypes of femininity on women in traditionally male roles. Here, the problem is not that women managers *are* fundamentally different; it is that they are *treated* differently.

In terms of the evolution of gender as an organizational communication problematic, liberal feminism tends to highlight gender *in* organizations and regard communication as an expressive, not constitutive, mechanism. Gender, in this view, is a social identity that fixes nurture (i.e., norms of difference and inequality) upon nature (i.e., natal features that distinguish sex). Every person has a gender, and gender prejudice lies within as a consequence of repetitive messages. This individualistic, psychologized conception of gender relegates communication to a social practice already scarred by bias. Communication is how we learn gender, but it is an outcome or effect of the internalized prejudice of previous generations. Hence, communication is overdetermined for liberal feminism. It is a vehicle for the *transmission* of fully formed attitudes, not a way to explain their formation. Organizations, on the other hand, are settings and structures that bear little to no culpability for gender inequality. Instead, they are useful tools to administer fairness (e.g., bureaucratic standardization). Certainly, there are biases in workplace policy and practice that mark women as different; and these need to be removed. Yet prejudice is assumed to leak from individuals into systems, not the other way around.

Whereas a psychologized model of gender dominated liberal feminism in our field, liberal feminist theory in management and organization studies has a longer history that reflects a diverse array of disciplinary influences (Calás & Smircich, 1996). Management scholars have been slower to abandon liberal feminism, which lives on in the colossal and enduring literature on women-in-management (e.g., Fagenson, 1993). Quickly, however, organizational communication scholars rebuffed liberal feminism for its dull critical edge. Arguments for universality are inadequate for many reasons, elaborated below by other feminisms (see also Buzzanell, 1995; Calás & Smircich, 1996). In brief, matters of difference require far more conceptual nuance and political complexity than liberal feminist theory affords. Liberal feminism treats women as a homogenous category of persons denied their essential humanity yet takes the situation of white, middle-class, heterosexual women (e.g., the plight of educated housewives) as a universal female condition (hooks, 1995). Precisely in its insistence on sameness, then, liberal feminism is complicit in perpetuating gender oppression. It has been used to advance comparatively privileged women on the backs of women who simultaneously bear class and race discrimination, among other disadvantages (Glenn, 1994). For good reason, liberal feminism rapidly fell out of favor in our field.

If it is deemed passé and if little contemporary organizational communication research claims it, why include liberal feminist theory as a major theoretical influence? Because it lives on—and, arguably, *should* live on—in important forms. First, it deserves credit for persuading many audiences (our field included) that gender inequality at work is a real problem in need of redress. Second, our feminist scholarship continues to draw on liberal feminism to formulate rationales, objectives, and measurements of progress (see Ashcraft, Muhr, Rennstam, & Sullivan, 2012). Ubiquitous appeals based on the number of women in certain professions provide an example. Third, liberal feminism still serves as a starting point for exchange between feminist scholars and other audiences, particularly in a cultural milieu where individual achievement and impartial assessment are held as virtues. Finally, liberal feminism supplies an easy target that facilitates exchange among feminists in our field. It is the deficient, abject other whose rejection is a condition for dialogue, the Straw Woman against which we affirm our progressive sophistication.

Mindful of the many earned criticisms of liberal feminist theory, we might fruitfully consider a qualified revival that recognizes *both* the utility *and* shortfall of sameness and standardization, wielding them strategically while holding them critically, without full faith. Some postmodern feminists in our field already advocate "strategic essentialism" (e.g., Edley, 2000), in which claims of difference are marshaled for political effect even as their authenticity is rejected. Can we not also do so with sameness and standardization? Might we exploit the coherent, autonomous subject that allegedly defines the human condition or the supposedly universal category *woman* as temporary strategies for meeting situational exigencies? What I mean to plant here is the possibility of a calculated, ironic liberal–post-structuralist fusion. In the wake of liberal feminism, difference became the fashion *du jour,* as the next four feminisms exhibit. I suspect we might do well to hold difference in check by keeping sameness in play.

Cultural Feminisms: Difference With Value and Variation

In contrast with liberal feminism's informal slogan, which might be summarized "equality for sameness," cultural feminism advocates equity for difference. In this view, women are fundamentally different from men; hence, standardization begets discrimination. Programs such as equal opportunity, merit, and universal rules are inadequate, because their baseline is biased toward men. They privilege the "normal" figure around whom their mold is cast and render "deviant" or "special" those excluded by definition. Justice is best pursued, then, by documenting and revaluating difference. Eventually, reassessment at individual and cultural levels will be reflected in our institutions. In short, equality necessitates being gender conscious, not gender blind.

Cultural feminist politics appear to be more radical in that they regard men and women as beings apart and harbor suspicions of systemic bias. As we shall see, however, cultural feminism can be quite conservative; and claims of difference, like those of sameness, are also problematic. In organizational communication studies, cultural feminist theory can be interpreted to provide two broad explanations of gender at work that reflect divergent politics, which I call "gendered communication expertise" and "gendered organizational culture."

Gendered communication expertise. The first explanation focuses on communication practices deemed relevant to work life, such as conflict, leadership, self-promotion, and so-called strong versus weak speech (e.g., Tannen, 1994). It entails such overlapping claims as

- professional and managerial communications are governed by masculine norms that are difficult, if not hostile, for many women;
- there are "women's ways," or feminine styles, of communicating;
- these alternative norms are of equal, if not greater, value for organizational purposes; and
- women and/or femininity are teeming with underutilized organizational expertise.

The latter two claims exhibit the *revalorist* strain of cultural feminism, which seeks to restore the validity of things denigrated by virtue of their association with women and femininity, as evident in arguments for the so-called feminine advantage (e.g., Helgesen, 1990).

The problem here is not that women are *treated* differently; it is that they *are* different, yet we continue to measure them by male-biased benchmarks not acknowledged as such. Double binds and standards remain vital concerns, but the diagnosis changes. To accentuate what may otherwise seem a subtle distinction, consider the claim that many women are not assertive enough to lead. Through a liberal lens, women need assertiveness training to overcome their socialization in deference, but we must simultaneously tackle the double standard that depicts assertive women as excessively aggressive. Through a cultural lens, the very notion that leadership necessitates self-assertion is partial to masculine communication. Thus training women to emulate masculinity is misguided; it is unlikely to be seen as authentic, because for many women, it *is not,* in fact, authentic. When it comes to double binds, then, the issue is not only that women in managerial roles are squeezed into stereotypes; it is that management is defined around masculinity, such that women's differences—real and imagined—will always appear deficient.

This strand of cultural feminism thus seeks to identify and ease discursive dilemmas that ensue from masculine norms. Wood and Conrad (1983), for instance, identified key paradoxes, such as professional women's struggles for coherent definitions of self and suitable mentor relationships; they also considered specific communicative responses that perpetuate and transcend such paradoxes. Work in this vein also aims to appreciate feminine modes of organizing on their own terms, such as "women's ways" of career building and team building (e.g., Marshall, 1989; Nelson, 1988). Some authors say that actual women and men exhibit such communication differences, while others stress the symbolic division of masculine and feminine communication. Despite the significant distinction, there remains a tendency for slippage between women and femininity, men and masculinity (Ashcraft, 2009). Indeed, the revalorist strain of cultural feminism often conflates communication linked to women with femin*ist* practice (e.g., Marshall, 1989)—a habit rectified in the second strand of cultural feminism.

Much like liberal feminism, the first strand of cultural feminism highlights gendered communication *in* organizations. In contrast with management and organization studies, where cultural feminism largely reflects psychoanalytic perspectives, organizational communication scholars acknowledge such influences yet theorize difference in more intercultural terms, wherein gender is a cultural membership that fosters opposing ways of interacting (e.g., Bate & Taylor, 1988). Lest this be taken for a robust view of communication, I hasten to add that, as in liberal feminism, communication here remains an overdetermined outcome of already internalized difference. Gender enculturation results in deep inculcation, which gets expressed and maintained in communication (more of a social-psychological than psychoanalytic account; see Wood, 2011), but in any case, it is not one in which communication exerts much influence, save its apparent value for economic activity. Particularly in the revalorist strain, communication becomes a marketable skill set, a form of expertise to be commodified. As in liberal feminism, organizations are settings in which gendered knowledge assumes value. Granted, they exhibit systemic bias (i.e., the institutionalization of masculine communication), which must be adjusted to accommodate gender difference. But so too should feminine ways be accommodating (and how femin*ized* is that?) in the service of organizational aims. Therein, the radical potential of cultural feminist theory is arrested.

Such potential is further stunted as gender difference remains binary, secluded from other social identities. As with liberal feminism, the question becomes "*Which* 'women's ways,' *which* femininities, does revalorist cultural feminism promote?" Again, norms ascribed to white, middle-class, heterosexual femininity are extrapolated to all women. Though devalued as weak in public life, this femininity is venerated as sacred and nurturing in the private realm. What this perspective does, then, is revalue an already privileged femininity in a new arena, while what constitutes *the* feminine remains restrictive (Calás & Smircich, 1993). "Gendered communication expertise" thereby appeases the current order of gender-race-class relations. Heteronormativity lurks in its celebration of conventional mothering images. Class and race bias become glaring if we ask why this perspective began by focusing on professional and managerial environments, when women of color and/or lesser means have long been concentrated in working-class settings (Tomaskovic-Devey, 1993), where restrictions on sexism tend to be comparatively minimized. Whereas professional masculinities are reined in by demands for civility, for example, working-class masculinities often entail latitude for "primitive" display, such as aggressive sexuality (Ashcraft & Flores, 2003). In other words, had the first strand of cultural feminism embraced more radical criticism, it might have begun with environments more openly hostile to a diversity of women.

Finally, the conservative politics of "gendered communication expertise" are evident in its thin conception of power. If masculine communication entails doing dominance and feminine communication involves doing deference (Rogers & Henson, 1997), then revaluing difference as currently defined means celebrating inequality and endorsing the gendered division of labor (Ashcraft & Pacanowsky, 1996; Buzzanell, 1995; Calás & Smircich, 1993). After all, if women are in possession of unique skill sets, so are men, though the latter is rarely admitted in the literature. It is a small step to the conclusion that women are more suited for relational work—say, human resources or customer service—whereas men are better equipped for technical, financial, scientific, and other analytical jobs. That the latter are already coded as more knowledge-intensive, strategic, and valuable is a gendered phenomenon too, but cultural feminist theory in this form can say little about it.

Gendered organizational culture. A second strand of cultural feminism begins to explain such phenomena at the organization level, taking a far more radical departure from liberal feminism. This strand emerged at the confluence of two developments: the rise of organizational culture and the insight that organizations, not merely the people who populate them, are gendered. The idea that organization *is* culture, constituted through the negotiation of meaning—for example, in storytelling and narrative, vocabulary, metaphor, and ritual—began to catch fire in organizational communication in the early 1980s (e.g., Pacanowsky & O'Donnell-Trujillo, 1982). A decade later, sociologist Joan Acker (1990) published an influential essay (elaborated later in this essay under *radical feminism*), which recast gender as an organizing principle. Coalescing an idea on the tip of many tongues, her theory of gendered organizations launched a decisive move away from gender as a cultural membership causing individual predispositions (as in "gendered communication expertise") and toward the insight that organizations play a distinctive role in the gendering process. In our field, this insight fused with budding research on organizational culture to yield the following claims:

- Gender difference is a malleable relation formed through situated, collective negotiations of meaning.
- Gender at work must be explained in terms more grounded, relational, and holistic. We should examine organizations as local interpretive communities rather than diagnose communication practices such as leadership in abstract isolation.
- Such ethnographic epistemology enables us to understand gender in all its rich contextual variation, appreciate organizational culture as a political phenomenon, and develop a more constitutive account of organizational communication as it (en) genders difference *in situ.*
- For these reasons, we should be analyzing the gendering *of* organization, rather than merely gender *in* organization.

One of the first published feminist works on organization to appear in a communication journal, a *Communication Yearbook* chapter by Marshall (1993), exhibits the early relation between the first and second strands of cultural feminism. Her chapter begins with a discussion of "male and female values" (p. 124), which lays the groundwork for an assessment of "organizational cultures as high context, preprogrammed with male values" (p. 127). Although organizational culture is central to Marshall's framework, her argument follows the logic of "gendered communication expertise": Broad differences between men and women are salient to communication and power *in* the workplace, which is theorized as an *aggregate* culture. Such logic is reversed by scholars in the second strand, who theorize gender difference as a variable product of *specific* organizational cultures, manufactured through communication. Gender is *not,* in this view, a ready-made cultural difference simply imported from outside of organizations into communication within them.

The work of a few critical management scholars, with whom organizational communication scholars were developing close ties, became influential in the rise of this second strand in our field. Mills (1988; Mills & Chiaramonte, 1991), for example, treated organizational culture as metacommunication—a tailored script for gendering interaction and identity formation, which members constantly enact and improvise. Mills went on to become one of the leading communication-friendly theorists of "gendered organizational culture," and his work is particularly distinctive for its historical lens (Mills, 2002). His extensive empirical work with airline cultures, for instance, documented the evolution of gendered jobs and hierarchies over time, tracking shifting relations among multiple masculinities and femininities (Mills, 2006). Alvesson and Billing (1992), though hesitant to grant communication a strong role, proposed a differentiated understanding of gender that called out the plural, contradictory character of organizational symbolism. This approach is well illustrated by Alvesson's (1998) provocative analysis of the gendered culture of an advertising firm. Likewise, Gherardi's (1995) book, the first extended treatise on gender and organizational culture, foregrounds gendered organizational symbolism as both site of struggle and spring of innovation.

Such efforts were met with an explosion of empirical research in organizational communication that documents the gendering of varied organizational cultures (e.g., Bell & Forbes, 1994; Edley, 2000; Gibson & Papa, 2000). Evident across these studies is growing awareness that women and men are not homogenous categories and that the gender binary unfolds *in situ* in myriad and surprising ways. In response, scholars of "gendered organizational culture" slowly began attending to the intermingling of social identities (known today as *intersectionality*)—especially class, race, and sexuality—although gender tends to remain the primary lens even now.

For this strand of cultural feminism, politics remain a matter of debate. Interpretive scholars of "gendered organizational culture" emphasize *description* and *understanding* of how communication (en)genders realities received as facts (e.g., Alvesson & Billing, 2009), whereas critical scholars stress *critique, deconstruction,* and sometimes *reconstruction* of this process (e.g., Townsley & Geist, 2000). Both can regard communication as constitutive, but the former highlights how communication creates gender difference and the latter how communication is, in turn, distorted by that very creation. Critical research on "gendered organizational culture" wields a sharper feminist edge than interpretive projects, which expose relations of power yet stop short of confronting them. By showing how "women's ways" of communicating contribute to gender oppression, for example, critical approaches temper the revalorist strain of cultural feminism, warning that the femin*ine,* as we yet know it, is far from femin*ist* (e.g., Ashcraft & Pacanowsky, 1996).

Internal debate notwithstanding, the second strand of cultural feminism is more radical than the first with its deeper systemic explanation. It is also more nuanced in its commitment to gender multiplicity (particularly around intersections with other social identities) and contextual variation. Finally, the second strand abandons a psychologized view of communication as reducible to transmission and expression. Indeed, research on "gendered organizational culture" was the first feminist scholarship in our field to claim a generative role for communication; and this research tends to demonstrate the performativity of culture (i.e., its dynamic, evolving enactment, which brings "it" into being) more than other interpretive organizational communication studies (Ashcraft & Mumby, 2004).

In sum, both strands designate culture as a vital companion to feminist theory, albeit in divergent ways. The first takes culture as a metaphor for *gender* (i.e., gender is a societal-level cultural category that demarcates difference), whereas the second views culture as a metaphor for *organization* (i.e., organizations are interpretive communities). For the first, gender-as-cultural-difference is expressed *in* organizational communication; for the second, organization-as-culture constitutes gender difference *through* communication.

The question remains: How have cultural feminisms fared over time in organizational communication studies? "Gendered communication expertise" faded from prominence after criticism of its sweeping abstractions. Two feminisms considered below, standpoint and micro-postmodern, respond to such criticism by thoroughly reworking the notion of feminine knowledge. Although "gendered organizational culture" also redressed many critiques of "gendered communication expertise," it is seldom acknowledged that the latter persists in the former. To the extent that all empirical variants are retained within a dualistic frame, a generic gender binary underlies claims of gender multiplicity. That is, when we speak of masculinities and femininities in the plural, we are still affirming two poles. An abstract cultural binary is summoned to identify gender, for in the face of situated plurality, how else are we to know one from another or to recognize deviation as such when we see it? In sum, a generic notion of binary difference remains essential equipment (i.e., compulsory *and* essentialist) for knowing gender in context. The binary is especially evident in critical studies of organizational culture where researchers claim gendered phenomena not seen as such by participants. However, interpretive studies that instead ground gender claims in participant understandings are, in effect, depending on participants to do the binary dirty work.

Over time, the construct of organizational culture has receded into the background of our field, a presumed phenomenon more than an object of investigation. In a related development, many feminist scholars have moved beyond the lingering container implied by "gendered organizational culture," examining salient cultural phenomena beyond conventional organization boundaries (Ashcraft, 2004). For example, while the second strand of cultural feminism can explain the gendering of certain airlines (Mills, 2006), it cannot explain how constructions external to the airline intermingled with that gendering process (see Ashcraft & Mumby, 2004). The attendant shift in emphasis from the gender *of* organization to the *cultural organization* of gender, difference, and work (see macro-postmodern feminism below) can thus be read as a new face of "gendered organizational culture," though the earlier face has by no means disappeared. The next feminism also exceeds organizational boundaries, though in quite different ways.

Standpoint Feminism: Difference as Social Materialities

Feminist standpoint theory (FST) shares with cultural feminism an emphatic rejection of sameness and dedication to difference, but the affiliation mostly stops there. Generally speaking, FST maintains the following claims:

- Women are indeed fundamentally different, but from one another as much as from men.
- Difference arises from *social location*—the nexus of symbolic and material realities from whence we form a sense of self, other, agency, and ethics. Difference does not stem from our internalization of generic masculine or feminine culture (as in "gendered communication expertise") or from the co-construction of gender in particular organizations (as in "gendered organizational culture"). It emanates, rather, from the specific web of cultural, political, temporal, spatial, and economic relations in which we are embedded.
- Specifically, difference hinges around the historical intersections of class, race, and gender that we live on a daily basis. These trajectories of repetitive injury or privilege

cultivate habits of reading reality and our range of possibility within it. From this recurring experience, we develop expectations and tactics for maneuvering everyday life. We develop, in short, situated knowledge about how the world works.

- With much critical reflection, those who occupy marginalized social locations can hone their lived experience of oppression into a powerful standpoint—a critical exposé or commentary on relations of power.
- Fostering just organizations begins with hearing multiple standpoints, absorbing this knowledge as crucial corrections to dominant versions of reality, and redressing the systemic inequalities they surface.

Several important amendments to other feminisms are noteworthy here. First, FST sharpens cultural feminism's critique of liberal feminist sameness and standardization by extending it to relations *among* women. The autonomous subject of liberal feminism is refigured with a thoroughly socio-material understanding of the self; and cultural feminist claims to an essential or universal sisterhood are flatly rejected. Second, gender difference is no longer treated in isolation—either from other aspects of difference such as race and class or abstracted from the historical, political, cultural, physical, and economic circumstances that give rise to it. As that suggests, context is significantly expanded beyond its meaning in "gendered organizational culture" research, where it primarily refers to specific organizational sites. This enriched definition of context does not exclude the role that organizations play in social location. Indeed, several standpoint theorists examine how gender, race, and class divisions of labor breed distinctive ways of knowing the world (e.g., Aptheker, 1989). But by redefining context so rigorously and concentrating on gender's entanglement with class and race, FST further erodes the gender binary latent in cultural feminism.

Moreover, FST avoids a psychologized version of gendered identity and communication with its insistence on the influence of historical and material relations. For FST, most other feminisms settle for too narrow a scope. The focus on gender *in* organization is overly individual and/or interpersonal, but even those who highlight the gendering *of* organization are missing larger forces and downplaying the extent to which these forces foster multiple and competing organizational realities, some of which (i.e., those of the marginalized) are, frankly, more accurate than others. In a stratified society, objective knowledge of reality is achieved not through the impossible fantasy of a neutral science, which inexorably favors dominant perspectives, but through consciously prioritizing the knowledge endemic to oppressed standpoints (see Harding, 1991). In this way, FST casts difference epistemologically and as a mandate for moral politics.

There is a strong socialist feminist bent to FST, especially evident in its emphasis on the bigger picture (of which organizational life is only a part): public *and* private, production *and* reproduction, capitalism *and* patriarchy, and the ways in which these ideological and material spheres, once conceived as *dual systems,* are not simply interdependent but rather are sides of the same coin, or *unified systems* (Tong, 1989). Critical race research has also had a defining impact on FST, particularly in theorizing the formation of race consciousness in lived experience (Collins, 1991). Vestiges of Marxist feminism are evident in the claim that one's place in the economic order invariably imprints her identity and interests. Also apparent are strains of psychoanalytic feminism, particularly in FST's view of social location as a developmental process that becomes deeply embedded in the psyche and embodied in reflexes of thought and behavior and that can only be brought to consciousness (i.e., standpoint) with a great deal of work (Tong, 1989). Although FST earnestly qualifies the deterministic leanings that once typified some of these feminisms, it risks returning to a view of communication as outcome—this time, not of some psychological predisposition, but of institutional and material forces said to exist outside of communication. In short, our communicative capacities are delimited by social location.

Organizational communication scholars cast FST more communicatively, as both the basis for making the material world meaningful (e.g., anatomical and phenotypical features, physical encounters with task and place) and the means for achieving conscious standpoints. Yet such modifications often stopped short of a constitutive view of communication, in part because our early efforts in FST sought to challenge (but were often difficult to distinguish from) the strain of cultural-revalorist feminism evident in "gendered communication expertise." Dougherty (1999), for instance, invoked FST to analyze women's and men's standpoints on sexual harassment in organizations. As this work minimizes intersectionality in favor of a binary view and highlights gendered perceptions detached from situated socio-material histories, it exhibits a limited application of FST, in which *standpoint* appears synonymous with *perspective.* In contrast, an early attempt to enact FST's commitment to intersectionality and situated experience occurred at a 1995 National Communication Association (then SCA [Speech Communication Association]) panel, later published as a forum in *Management Communication Quarterly* (see May 1998 issue). This collection of personal, critical tales of organizational life is exemplified in Spradlin's (1998) poignant narrative of negotiating lesbian identity in the academy, from which she theorized discursive tactics of *passing,* an agonizing communicative performance in which members collaborate in the institutionalization of heteronormativity.

The panel and subsequent papers illustrate several typifying features of FST in organizational communication studies. First, it tends to emphasize gender and difference *in* organization. In this way, it reflects the residual container metaphor of communication in our field, thereby minimizing customary FST devotion to a broader systemic picture. But standpoint feminism in our field also contests the container metaphor by treating one's accumulation of repetitive experience not only *in* but also *across* organizations as an embodied thread indicative of a larger system. Here, FST's dedication to historical relations becomes highly personal and self-reflexive: History is narrowed to one's recurring experience over time, which yields living evidence of specific legacies of domination and subordination. Given this emphasis on self-reflexivity, it is not surprising that much FST in our field highlights difference in the academy.

With its proclivity for personal history, FST in our field also deviates from standpoint feminisms elsewhere by doing what Collins (1997) cautioned against: highlighting "individual experiences within socially constructed groups" over the "conditions that construct such groups" (p. 375). As Allen (2000) reminds us, however, attention to individual narrative need not be idiosyncratic; FST in our field entails comparison—a search for commonalties as well as openness to disjuncture—between one's own narrative and those of others in similar social locations. In this way, standpoint feminism in organizational communication resists a common criticism of FST writ large: that it grants too much muscle to social location, rendering static and overdetermined depictions of difference that downplay nuance. By stressing the evolving character of communication and its mediating function, we have softened such unilateral tendencies and bolstered the symbolic, discursive, and relational dimensions of social location.

Allen's (1998) work in FST provides a prominent example in our field. In her research, often focused on relations of difference in the academy, Allen places her own experience in varied institutional environments in conversation with a wealth of literature on the organizational experiences of people of color. She has particularly theorized how Black feminist standpoints challenge received models of organizational socialization (Allen, 1996, 2000). Parker's (e.g., 2005) work on leadership offers another exemplar of sustained FST in our field. She directly confronts masculine and feminine leadership, as theorized in the "gendered communication expertise" strain of cultural feminism, with a multicultural reconception. Parker analyzes the narratives of 15 African American women executives, using their life stories of social and material struggle to theorize how race and gender entwine to structure leadership communication. Other projects similarly employ FST to contest and revise current communication theory, for example, of organizational socialization (Bullis & Stout, 2000) and emotionality (Krone, Dougherty, & Sloan, 2001). Consistent with the larger interdisciplinary body of FST, most of these works look to historically marginalized standpoints as sources of corrective knowledge. Against this grain, yet also in its support, Mumby (1998) draws on standpoint logic to argue that privileged men, as "concentric (i.e., common, unmarked) subjects" (p. 167), can play a crucial role in deconstructing dominant standpoints through critical, self-reflexive investigation of hegemonic masculinity.

Arguably, in accentuating the role of communication, we relinquished a vital strength of FST: its quest to explain the social and material together. As in other areas of organizational communication theory, FST scholars let materiality—matters of place, body, economy, and so forth—take a back seat as they made the case for communication. Relative disregard for the material emphasis of FST is evident, for instance, when standpoint theorists position FST as readily compatible with postmodernism (Fletcher, 1994) or as a liberal-postmodern hybrid (Bullis & Stout, 2000). What such portrayals miss is that, for most adherents to FST, women's multiple standpoints emanate from concrete and enduring, albeit socially mediated, circumstances. The socio-material origins of these standpoints are *not,* as postmodern feminism would have it, mere effects of discourses that "form the objects of which they speak" (Foucault, 1972, p. 49). In sum, FST grips the ontology of difference, whereas postmodern feminism releases such foundations (Gherardi, 1995). Both object to the humanist self of liberal feminism, but FST less strenuously. For FST, the notion that we are all autonomous actors is a dominant epistemology enabled by repetitive privilege, a distortion integral to the maintenance of inequality. But the sovereign, knowing subject as a wellspring of knowledge—the very figure rejected by postmodern feminism—can be rehabilitated.

The recent turn toward materiality in our field reframes FST as a unique way to formulate a communicative explanation of how difference organizes social and material systems. Put another way, the case for communicative FST need not diminish the force of materiality. Rather, we can theorize communication as the dynamic site where ideational and material matters meet, commingle, crystallize, and transform (Ashcraft & Harris, 2014; Ashcraft, Kuhn, & Cooren, 2009). Despite this opportunity, FST curiously seems to have withered on the vine of organizational communication theory. In the late 1990s and early 2000s, it appeared to be one of our most popular, promising perspectives, but it quickly faded in the face of a growing collective preference for postmodern feminism. I suggest that this is a case of arrested development and that we would do well to revive and deepen our relation to FST in light of rising concern for materiality. However, we might adjust our original focus on "individual experiences within socially constructed groups" and stress instead the *communicative* "conditions that construct such groups" (Collins, 1997, p. 375). Like FST, the next feminism hails from socialist origins and interrogates difference as an organizing principle, but it gives short shrift to intersectionality for a return to more binary comforts.

Radical–Post-Structuralist Feminism: Bad Bureaucracy, Good Alternatives, and Acceptance of Ambiguity

Radical feminist theory has many branches and applications. Speaking of those most pertinent to organization, we might encapsulate radical feminism as a theoretical position that flies in the face of liberal feminism by maintaining that

- gender is a primary determinant of difference in patriarchal societies;
- masculine ways are irretrievably repressive (i.e., masculin*ist*);
- dominant institutions are premised on masculinist principles;
- a just society requires uncompromising rejection of extant institutions, supplanted by alternatives founded on feminist values; and
- women who actively develop a feminist consciousness are best equipped to generate and enact such alternatives.

Steadfast faith in binary gender identities and relations is notable here, as is the tendency to idealize an essential sisterhood. Yet a critical edge absent from most forms of cultural feminism (save critical approaches to organizational culture) is also apparent. Hardly an endorsement of so-called women's ways, radical feminist theory bestows tough love on femininity, recovering its emancipatory potential by purging the scars of subordination. This critical care, however, is far from that which FST employs to transform social location into standpoint. Whereas FST renounces a mythic feminine essence, radical feminism seeks the restoration of feminine principles that lie beneath the wounds of oppression. Simply put, the goal is women and femininity unfettered through the twin tasks of individual consciousness raising and institutional overhaul.

Applied to organizational life, radical feminist theory can be interpreted to take two broad and related forms. Because these forms can also be found beyond our field and because their development there shaped their manifestation among us, I begin by describing their interdisciplinary evolution. The first form makes the case that *bureaucracy is fundamentally gendered.* Acker and Van Houten's (1974) classic rereading of the Hawthorne studies was among the first to argue that organizations *produce* difference by using gender to divide and control labor. Motivated by a liberal feminist focus on sameness, Kanter (1975) also theorized gender difference as a product of structural relations—the *outcome of,* rather than *reason for,* the concentration of women in lowly roles. Ferguson's (1984) well-known book, *The Feminist Case Against Bureaucracy,* advanced these critiques by contending that bureaucracy institutionalizes male domination by trussing managers, members, and clients alike in dependent relations that effectively feminize them. Acker's (1990) influential essay, mentioned earlier, synthesized these insights to theorize bureaucracy as gendered to its core:

> To say that an organization . . . is gendered means that advantage and disadvantage, exploitation and control, action and emotion, meaning and identity, are patterned through and in terms of a distinction between male and female, masculine and feminine. (p. 146)

Together, these and related works are widely recognized as the ancestry of a radical feminist theory of gendered organization (Mills & Tancred, 1992; Savage & Witz, 1992).

Rarely do we comment on the wild theoretical mix in this lineage, but this is significant, because it helps to explain the continuing debate over whether bureaucracy is salvageable or irreparable. Kanter's (1975) model exhibits a rare moment when liberal and radical feminism become allies in an indictment of organization structure. Ferguson's (1984) book, on the other hand, is avowedly post-structuralist, though it also draws on existentialist feminist theory to treat "second sexing" as a metaphor for bureaucratic relations. In contrast, Acker's (1990) radical analysis employs a heavy structural vocabulary influenced by the shift from dual to unified systems in socialist feminism. Such pronounced theoretical differences yield conflicting evaluations of bureaucracy. For liberal feminists, the flaws of bureaucracy are containable if only organizations would divide and control labor through means other than gender. For post-structuralist feminists, liberation comes not from replacing bureaucracy with a new totalizing form but, rather, from constantly subverting it through alternative feminist discourses. For socialist feminists, hierarchical organization is defective all the way down. Gender is neither a replaceable technology used by bureaucracy nor a mere metaphor for bureaucracy; gender is encoded in bureaucratic DNA, inseparable from the operation itself.

A second and related form of radical feminist theory can be found in research on *feminist organizations.* This work responds to the first form's indictment of bureaucracy with the pursuit of feminist alternatives. It is less related in terms of scholarly community, however. Historically, it has closer ties to feminist and women's studies than it does to organization studies; and it seemed to reach an apex with the publication of Ferree and Martin's (1995) book. Most of this work defines feminist organization as egalitarian, collectivist, participatory—in a word, *counter*-bureaucratic (Ianello, 1992). For those of a radical *separatist* bent, feminist organizations are necessarily by and for women and/or devoid of bureaucratic impurities. Others envision them as separatist only during incubation (e.g., Sealander & Smith, 1986) or capable of colliding with bureaucracy in hybrid forms (e.g., Eisenstein, 1995). Most take the *revalorist* position that feminist forms are morally superior to bureaucracy (the femin*ist* advantage?). However, much of the empirical literature mourns the "unhappy marriage" of feminist theory and practice (Murray, 1988)—predictable pressures that erode pure radical feminist ideology in practice (e.g., Morgen, 1990). Research on radical feminist organization, in this light, might better be described as *thwarted revalorist.* Perhaps for that reason, it seems to be relatively dormant in recent years.

Turning to the specific case of our field, we can say that organizational communication theory creatively blends and transforms both forms. Some of our earliest feminist work weighed the feminist critique of bureaucracy and affirmed the call for alternative forms (e.g., Buzzanell, 1994; Natalle, Papa, & Graham, 1994). Also evident was sympathy with the radical feminist caution that resorting to "women's ways" as currently configured was an unsatisfactory answer (e.g., Ashcraft & Pacanowsky, 1996). Moreover, feminist scholars in our field directly engaged with interdisciplinary feminist organization research as we launched our own empirical studies of feminist practice (e.g., Ashcraft, 2000).

A provocative theoretical fusion cropped up along the way. Even as we embraced radical claims about masculinist and feminist forms—including their robust moral-ethical overtones—and even as we justified our research on socialist grounds (e.g., Acker, 1990), we fused these influences with a post-structuralist understanding of gender and organizational form (Weedon, 1987). I use *post-structuralist* here in a specific way. Radical and socialist feminists often theorize structure in unilateral terms, as if structure yields difference, not the other way around. In contrast, several feminist organizational communication scholars quickly broached the issue with a bilateral view of structure (wherein structure and practice remain analytically separate but mutually constitutive) and, increasingly, with a performative model (which rejects the structure-practice duality and theorizes form as an ongoing accomplishment made real in its enactment). Almost from the beginning, then, communication scholars prioritized feminist organiz*ing* over feminist organizat*ion.*

At least three distinctive twists emerged from this unlikely hybrid. First, we reworked the *separatist* bent of radical feminist organization studies, which judged practical deviations from feminist ideology as a compromise. In place of purity, we developed a tension-centered approach, in which irony and contradiction were not pathologized but, rather, theorized as productive empirical dilemmas to explore through a critical yet ever-curious lens (see Trethewey & Ashcraft, 2004). We also challenged radical separatism with a destabilized view of gender, in which women are not presumed to be the sole experts on, or beneficiaries of, feminist forms. Although most of the communities studied were organized by and for women, we embraced an agenda of dissemination that couched feminist organizing as an important investment for all (e.g., Ashcraft, 2006b; Trethewey, 1999b).

Second, we tempered the *revalorist* claim of radical feminist organization studies with a contingent view of emancipation that allowed for moral ambiguities encountered in context (e.g., Sotirin & Gottfried, 1999). On the one hand, we argued that feminist organizational values, in the abstract, are loaded with empowering promise not (or less) present in bureaucratic tenets. Simultaneously, we recognized that feminist organizing teems with its own oppressive potential and that bureaucracy cannot be discarded, as it has infinite possibilities *in situ.* Emancipatory forms can only be known provisionally, in relation to the demands of specific and ever-changing contexts. Hence, we need not be flustered by impurities. Distortions of feminist ideology in practice are inevitable and productive, for they can yield possibilities not yet imagined in theory. Even when practice yields disempowering effects, it can be read to reveal where theories of feminist organization are inadequate to the tasks of organizing; it need *not* be hastily read as practice disappointing theory. In sum, acceptance of vulnerability supplants faith in utopia. If "forms have tendencies, not destinies," then we would do best to follow their situated twists and turns (Ashcraft, 2006b, p. 78).

Third, as we focused on feminist organiz*ing* right away, we began to develop a genuinely communicative model of organizational form, in which mundane interaction is the site of interest, where form comes to life and evolves in the act of performing it. The difference made by this turn toward the verb is worth underscoring. Prior to our engagement with feminist organizing, most available research treated feminist organizat*ion* as an ideal type of governance. As a noun, feminist structure exists apart from communication. It is imposed on and privileged over interaction, and the latter is measured by its faithfulness to the former. Communication scholars strove to transcend this habit of dividing structure from interaction. We supplanted it with a conception of form as *discourse community* or *gendered rationality* (Maguire & Mohtar, 1994; Mumby, 1996).

Our field's fusion of radical and post-structuralist feminisms is novel indeed, as well as productively ironic in itself. Typically, these feminisms are configured as deeply opposed, for reasons explained further below. Calás & Smircich (1996, 2006) maintain their separation in management and organization studies, depicting radical feminism as thoroughly modernist—ontologically and morally overconfident—and, conversely, post-structuralist feminism as susceptible and amoral, at times to a fault. Our radical–post-structuralist hybrid tempers these tendencies in each.

Moreover, this hybrid overlaps in significant ways with critical versions of the second strand of cultural feminism, "gendered organizational culture." Both harbor a suspicion that mainstream modes of organizing are oppressively gendered and feminist alternatives less so, though they suspend judgment for particular instances and then wield critique with a cautious, contingent spirit. "Gendered organizational culture" locates the problem in the performance of *culture,* which it renders accessible for critique, whereas radical post-structuralism locates the problem in the performance of *governance scripts,* which it seeks to rewrite. In this sense, they can be said to diagnose, respectively, informal and formal dimensions of gendered organizing. Unlike liberal and early cultural feminism, both emphatically stress the gendering *of* organization. Neither, however, can capture the broad array of social and material forces cited by FST. The final feminism endeavors to do so by a dramatically different route.

Postmodern Feminisms: Difference as Multileveled Drag

Postmodern feminism is a catch-all term for what has become the dominant feminism in organizational communication studies. Those who claim this family usually subscribe to a post-structuralist orientation and concur on several anti-foundationalist premises:

- Gender is an unstable notion, not a real thing with independent existence. Except as a social construction, gender does not exist. It has no final origin, no steady nature; it is a device, among an infinite range of possibilities, through which we continually carve up the world into two broad categories of people.
- The central question is not "How are we different?" but rather, "How did/do we come to appear different, as if this were the natural or normal order of things?" The answer is that gender, as with all social identities, is a product of the language, narratives, and embodied practices through which we know people and their essential similarities and differences. Gender is made in discourse, a thoroughly communicative achievement; and we are all performers in perpetual drag.
- Our task, then, is epistemological and genealogical: to trace how discourse generates knowledge about gender and enactments thereof, which activate subjectivities and relations of power among them. Knowledge does not spring from the subject, as in FST; rather, it constitutes the subject.
- Hence, we can never be free of the discourse-knowledge-power triad, for there is neither self nor other to enact without it, no real or authentic condition to be unleashed beneath it. But we can deconstruct the triad, and it is in this continual slackening of certainty that a qualified version of emancipation—localized forms of subversion—can be found. As Butler (1999) declared, "I am not outside the language that structures me, but neither am I determined by the language that makes this 'I' possible" (p. xxiv).
- Of particular interest is the discursive production of difference in and around work and organization, and the performance of gender is inevitably entangled with that of other differences. FST is thus right in this respect: We must look to situated constructions of intersectionality.
- Finally, the notion of organizational boundaries is problematic, because *intertextuality* (i.e., the overlapping presence, fusion, and collision of social texts, such that interpretive communities cannot be regarded as discrete) is a defining condition (Taylor, 1999).

For organizational communication scholars, the arrival of postmodern feminism was a most(ly) welcome development. While many feminists elsewhere resisted the postmodern turn, fraught with understandable anxieties about the political and ethical consequences of ontological instability, organizational communication scholars were decidedly more enthusiastic (Mumby, 1996). For many of us, postmodern feminism was a way to finally make communication pivotal not only as object or site of study, but as a—make that *the*—constitutive force. By the early 2000s, feminist scholars in our field appeared to be making a collective turn toward postmodern theorizing.

In keeping with an ironic postmodern spirit, I invoke a structural vocabulary to characterize a feature of this work that seldom draws notice: Despite its *post*-structuralist bent, the literature reflects clear micro, meso, and macro levels of emphasis. Theoretically, postmodern feminist scholars would concur that these are not discrete levels of discursive activity and that structure-agency divisions and debates are misguided. Nonetheless, a lingering structural lens seems to organize our focus. I opted against a common distinction in organizational discourse studies—the d/D continuum[2]—because it does not hold up well when applied to our field. A more relevant way is to distinguish the object of a post-modern gaze: For what I call *micro-postmodern feminism,* the everyday production of gender/difference *in* organization is the typical object. For *meso-postmodern feminism,* it is organizational form and culture (i.e., gender/difference *of* organization). For *macro-postmodern feminism,* it is the organization-culture relationship in the wake of intertextuality (i.e., the *cultural organization* of gender/difference and work/production).

Micro-postmodern Feminism. A first strand of postmodern feminism is occupied with gender *in* organization. But whereas "gendered communication expertise" emphasizes personal predispositions (i.e., "Do men and women communicate differently at work?"), and FST stresses individual narratives across organizations (i.e., "What standpoints form from cumulative experience in the workplace?"), micro-postmodern feminism highlights mundane interaction or performance (i.e., "How do we enact gender at work, making a fragile binary look fixed or occasionally disrupting it?"). Especially influential in our field is West and Zimmerman's (1987) sociological model, in which they theorize "doing gender" as an ongoing activity we accomplish together—the management of everyday interaction in response to situated expectations for gender difference. To account for intersectionality, the model was later expanded as "doing difference" (Fenstermaker & West, 2002). The revised model holds that gender, race, and class are indivisible because we enact them at once and in light of one another, *not* in addition to one another, as if they are interlocked yet still separable strands. In the varied contexts of everyday life, we craft changing configurations of difference, using resources afforded by our surroundings (e.g., divisions of labor and space, physicality).

West and Zimmerman's (1987) original model pointed to work as a key site of gender negotiation, but it was critical management theorist Gherardi (1994) who first elaborated how we do gender in the context of organization. She theorized the discursive labor whereby we both celebrate sacred gender divisions and repair their transgression. Her account transcended an earlier dispute between liberal and cultural feminism. Namely, women's alleged lack of assertiveness becomes a context-specific tactic. Neither biased perception nor universal trait, it is a way of responding to workplace expectations for femininity that admits its violation of a masculine space without rescinding the violation. Gherardi's work significantly expanded the theoretical resources employed by West and colleagues, whose formulation was ethnomethodological. Gherardi (1995, 2002) integrated works from literary and cultural studies, such as Butler, Irigaray, and other poststructuralist and psychoanalytic influences.

In management and organization studies, social scientific and humanistic influences often remain cloistered. For example, sociological debates over "undoing" and "redoing" gender (e.g., Connell, 2010; Deutsch, 2007) transpire apart from the sort of agency debates surrounding Butler (e.g., Benhabib, Butler, Cornell, & Fraser, 1995). Despite divergent lineage, these theories share meaningful commonalties and differences. West and colleagues, for instance, explain the durability of the normative order with the construct of accountability (i.e., the constant risk of assessment that holds us responsible to expectations). Butler prefers the construct of performativity (in the dual sense of speech acts and dramaturgy), explicitly theorizes subjectivity (ignored by West and colleagues), and leans toward historicity to explain durability. Organizational communication scholars uniquely combine such theoretical resources instead of retaining their separation (e.g., Buzzanell & Liu, 2005; Nadesan, 1996; Trethewey, 1999a).

Meso-postmodern Feminism. A second strand of postmodern feminism shifts attention from the production of gender *in* organization to that *by* organization (i.e., consistent with a focus on the gender *of* organization or gendered organizing). Gender is not displaced as a primary interest; rather, the role of organization in its production now takes center stage. Organization is said to condition gender subjectivities. Specifically, the enactment of organizational forms and cultures is a pivotal way we come to know gendered selves and relations. In this sense, meso-postmodern feminism is more a reversal of emphasis than a departure from micro.

With the notion of meso-postmodern feminist theory, I mean to mark an emerging overlap that we might otherwise miss between two literatures reviewed earlier. The first is radical–post-structuralist theory of organizational form. As detailed above, feminist scholars in our field have developed postmodern conceptions of form that underscore its communicative character: form as text, script, and discourse community or formation (see D'Enbeau & Buzzanell, 2011, for a contemporary example). We have also theorized the relation between postmodern and feminist forms of organizing. Postmodern forms are generally theorized as a *post*-bureaucratic response to the decline of modernist principles such as hierarchy, centralization, standardization, and formalization. Though born of radical feminism's *counter*-bureaucratic impulse, feminist forms often look similar to postmodern forms. Both tend to minimize fixed hierarchy in favor of participative decision making and flexible rules. In other words, feminist organizing has long grappled with, and is thus equipped to illuminate, dilemmas endemic to postmodern organizing (Ashcraft, 2006b).

The second literature stems from "gendered organizational culture." While most early studies in this vein did not reflect a postmodern orientation, increasingly, most now do (Ashcraft & Mumby, 2004). Signs of a postmodern bent include attention to the performativity of culture, to the ways that local co-constructions of meaning summon broader societal discourses, to situated histories of contestation and fragmentation, and/or to the vulnerability of authorial voices. Although focus remains on local realities, cultural boundaries are considered more permeable than in conventional studies of organizational culture (e.g., Bell & Forbes, 1994; Nadesan, 1997).

Macro-postmodern Feminism. A final strand riffs on permeable boundaries to thoroughly reconfigure the relation between organization and culture. While meso-postmodern feminism highlights local formations, the macro approach contends explicitly with the wake of intertextuality. If interpretive communities are increasingly unbounded, we must develop forms of cultural analysis that transcend customary notions of *site*. Here, the narrow scope of *organizational culture* morphs into the *cultural organization* of difference and work (see Carlone & Taylor, 1998). This wider lens enables multiple refractions of the organization-culture relationship and reflects a critical cultural turn from *studies of organizational culture* to *cultural studies of organization*.

Accordingly, macro-postmodern feminist theory takes up with the cultural discourses thought to mutually constitute (gender) difference and organization. Popular and trade cultures as well as organization theory itself attract particular attention (e.g., Dempsey, 2009; Dempsey & Sanders, 2010; Medved & Kirby, 2005). Noteworthy across these works is a growing historical sensibility—a genealogical approach to the evolution of discourse, which challenges our field's tendency to theorize the co-construction of organizational culture in a temporal vacuum (e.g., Ashcraft & Flores, 2003).

Macro scholarship is commonly criticized for treating discourse as a grand, powerful, free-floating symbolic agent, detached from the vested interests of individual and institutional actors and removed from its material consequences in everyday life (see Alvesson & Karreman, 2000). Feminist scholars in our field moved swiftly to address this criticism. Early in the development of macro-postmodern feminism, we began to traverse the d/D continuum, tracing shifts in societal discourses while respecting their local manifestations (e.g., Nadesan & Trethewey, 2000). In such ways, we demonstrated that discursive formations are highly consequential *and* hardly monolithic.

Yet even as macro-postmodern feminism became micro-conscious, the larger discourses under scrutiny seemed to hover in a neverland devoid of actors pulling the discursive strings to pursue their interests amid lived exigencies. That is, we were quick to ask how people *respond* to discursive formations, but the formations themselves seemed to arise from nebulous texts floating above the fray of political economy. With our feminist communicology of organization, Mumby and I (Ashcraft & Mumby, 2004) endeavor to redress this problem. We merge postmodernist and modernist feminist theorizing in order to situate genealogies of discourse in the social, political, institutional, physical, and economic trajectories in which they intervene and to reveal how the struggle over meaning is an embodied, interactive tussle among agents vying to secure their material interests. A communicative explanation of organizing need not entail text positivism; it can incorporate materiality rather than oppose it.

Evoking a satirical postmodern sensibility, I suggest that postmodern feminism on the whole has achieved the kind of hegemonic status in our field of which postmodern perspectives themselves demand suspicion. In terms more consistent with its vocabulary, postmodern feminism exercises evident disciplinary power. *Disciplinary* assumes a double meaning here: a dispersed regulatory (i.e., *disciplining*) practice that defines our collective enterprise (i.e., the *discipline*). Arguably, postmodern feminism has become *the* feminism of organizational communication theory, the utmost in sophistication by which "others" are measured and found naïve. If this is the case, we would do well to honor postmodern feminism by undermining it—an irony it can readily embrace, if not require.

Destabilizing postmodern feminism is further warranted, I believe, because it is suppressing the multiplicity of perspectives that remain in our midst. As others have shown (Fournier & Smith, 2006), postmodern feminist theory is claimed by authors who proceed to reinscribe the gender binary or otherwise violate anti-foundationalist premises. While such habits are typically framed as a function of the theorist's inconsistency, I suggest that they are also a disciplinary problem in our field—the result of pressure to conform, at least nominally, to a collectively preferred feminism. In a self-reflexive application of meso-postmodern feminism, we might put it this way: Our own organizational text conditions the theorist to identify and converse in a postmodern discourse of vulnerability (Mumby, 1997) that has lost *its own* vulnerability. We can lift this discursive closure by resuscitating theoretical "others" in our midst (e.g., traces of liberal feminism as well as FST) and exploring new conceptual inspirations that push against and enrich postmodern feminisms.

Toward Feminist Communication Theories of Organizing

What might we observe about the place and character of feminist theory in our field from this account of its evolution over the past 25 years? We can say, first, that feminist theory has moved from peripheral critic to vital voice whose contributions are established and valued. In itself, this nearly mainstream status distinguishes feminist theory in organizational communication from that in management and organization studies. No longer confined to a silo, feminist theory now circulates within the field, invoked as a productive way to explain organizational phenomena that exceed gender (e.g., Dempsey, Parker, & Krone, 2011). Even this *Handbook* attests to the diffusion of feminist theory across the field, to the extent that gender issues and feminist perspectives appear across the volume and are not relegated to a single chapter. The same cannot be said of parallel anthologies in management and organization studies,[3] though individual (critical) management scholars certainly apply feminist theory to shared concerns (e.g., Thomas & Davies, 2005).

Second, we can observe a steady but sluggish turn toward intersectionality. We seem to now embrace the premise that gender is not fruitfully theorized in isolation from other relations of difference, but we have been painfully slow to make good on this premise as a collective. This crucial work must accelerate if we hope to better grasp and resist the complex ways that differences are wielded in relation to one another (see Ashcraft, 2011).

I would venture a third observation, which I intend *alongside* earlier observations of our creativity: Our feminist theorizing exhibits signs of stagnation. It is not as resourceful (i.e., inventive and resource rich) as it was in earlier moments. Generally speaking, our energy for philosophical, political, and moral debates among diverse feminisms has flagged in recent years. With exceptions, of course, we seldom specify precisely which feminism(s) are at play in our research beyond nodding to broadly postmodern conceptions. In sum, the vibrant plurality of feminist theory in our field shows some wear, and our diversity and depth of resources for engagement seem to be dwindling.

In an effort to rekindle robust deliberation among feminisms, I conclude by marking three major dilemmas apparent in this chapter and suggesting some resources for grappling with them. One dilemma concerns sameness, difference, and the binary. Arguably, feminist organization theory faces a gender paradox akin to the racial paradox debated among critical race scholars (Flores & Moon, 2002): an apparent choice between reproducing difference, ironically in order to deconstruct it, or denying difference and thereby ignoring its pressing reality. Applied here, is justice best pursued by stressing sameness or difference, and how can we move beyond a binary model of gender plurality? Earlier, I suggested a liberal–post-structuralist hybrid that includes, self-consciously, shifting claims of difference *and* sameness. Rather than seeing the dilemma as an ontological question with an either/or answer, we can reframe it as a situational quandary that demands agile tactics, none of which correspond with some "real" condition.

However, as I also argued above, we do well to expand our repertoire of responses beyond such postmodern reflexes. Three diverse ways to upend the binary by enhancing intersectionality in our theorizing seem especially fruitful. With its rich capacity to confuse the binary with a dazzling array of sex-gender-sexuality possibilities, queer theory is one of the most likely sources of productive interventions (e.g., Harding, Lee, Ford, & Learmonth, 2011). Additionally, post/neo-colonial and transnational feminisms are sorely needed in our field (Broadfoot & Munshi, 2007; Dempsey, 2011). For those who might read this primarily as a call for theorizing difference beyond Western contexts, I hasten to stress the importance of interrogating the ways in which colonial relations constitute domestic fronts as well. Finally, there is ample reason to suspect that dis/ability serves as a unifying metaphor of deficiency/wholeness through which all relations of difference are managed (Allen, 2003). Engaging with dis/ability studies thus has the potential to surface the normalization of able bodies and other oppressive dynamics lurking in theories of gender resistance.

A second dilemma concerns the development of feminist communication theory that accounts for materiality, especially embodied experience in space and time, without reducing it to discursive effect. This calls for a more pronounced turn from feminist perspectives *on* organizational communication to feminist *communication* theories of organizing. The feminist communicology approach reviewed above takes steps in this direction, but much remains to be done (e.g., see the final dilemma below). Earlier, I proposed that we resuscitate FST as another promising path toward communicative explanations of materiality, especially as a counterpoint to postmodern theorizing. Divergent theoretical influences might assist in this effort, including the ethnography of communication, phenomenology of the body, feminist psychoanalytic theory, and recent developments in organizational approaches to embodied sociology, practice theory, and socio-materiality.

A third and final dilemma concerns accounting for the multisited character of organizing. Our feminist theories of organizational form and culture remain largely site bound, with the exception of macro-postmodern feminism, and all of these reflect disconcerting degrees of imprecision. For example, radical–post-structuralist feminism often merges competing influences (such as structuration theory, post-structuralist theory, and the Montréal School of thought on the communicative constitution of organization) without acknowledging, much less tackling, tensions among them. Macro-postmodern feminist theory is similarly imprecise about the mechanisms that organize difference across time and place. I suspect that the larger family of theoretical perspectives loosely known as actor-network theory and post-human theories of agency may prove quite helpful here.

Even in this sizeable chapter, however, we have barely scratched the surface of such dilemmas. They are big, and the theoretical resources mentioned here are philosophically diverse and not readily compatible, either—with one another or with the development of communication theory. But these challenges also make the work exciting. My hope is that our conscious commingling and engagement with resources old and new can infuse new energy into feminist organizational communication theorizing. That, after all, is the aim of this chapter: to honor and reinvigorate a collective conversation that contributes to a better world.

References

Acker, J. (1990). Hierarchies, jobs, bodies: A theory of gendered organizations. *Gender and Society, 4*(2), 139–158.

Acker, J., & Van Houten, D. R. (1974). Differential recruitment and control: The sex structuring of organizations. *Administrative Science Quarterly, 19*(2), 152–163.

Allen, B. J. (1996). Feminist standpoint theory: A Black woman's (re)view of organizational socialization. *Communication Studies, 47*(4), 257–271.

Allen, B. J. (1998). Black womanhood and feminist standpoints. *Management Communication Quarterly, 11*(4), 575–586.

Allen, B. J. (2000). "Learning the ropes": A Black feminist standpoint analysis. In P. M. Buzzanell (Ed.), *Rethinking organizational and managerial communication from feminist perspectives* (pp. 177–208). Thousand Oaks, CA: SAGE.

Allen, B. J. (2003). *Difference matters: Communicating social identity in organizations.* Prospects Heights, IL: Waveland.

Alvesson, M. (1998). Gender relations and identity at work: A case study of masculinities and femininities in an advertising agency. *Human Relations, 51*(8), 969–1005.

Alvesson, M., & Billing, Y. D. (1992). Gender and organization: Toward a differentiated understanding. *Organization Studies, 13*(1), 73–102.

Alvesson, M., & Billing, Y. D. (2009). *Understanding gender and organizations* (2nd ed.). London, England: SAGE.

Alvesson, M., & Karreman, D. (2000). Varieties of discourse: On the study of organizations through discourse analysis. *Human Relations, 53*(9), 1125–1149.

Aptheker, B. (1989). *Tapestries of life: Women's work, women's consciousness, and the meaning of daily experience.* Amherst: University of Massachusetts Press.

Ashcraft, K. L. (2000). Empowering "professional" relationships: Organizational communication meets feminist practice. *Management Communication Quarterly, 13*(3), 347–392.

Ashcraft, K. L. (2004). Gender, discourse, and organizations: Framing a shifting relationship. In D. Grant, C. Hardy, C. Oswick, N. Phillips, & L. L. Putnam (Eds.), *Handbook of organizational discourse.* Thousand Oaks, CA: SAGE.

Ashcraft, K. L. (2005). Feminist organizational communication studies: Engaging gender in public and private. In S. May & D. K. Mumby (Eds.), *Engaging organizational communication theory & research: Multiple perspectives* (pp. 141–170). Thousand Oaks, CA: SAGE.

Ashcraft, K. L. (2006a). Back to work: Sights/sites of difference in gender and organizational communication studies. In B. Dow & J. T. Wood (Eds.), *The SAGE handbook of gender and communication* (pp. 97–122). Thousand Oaks, CA: SAGE.

Ashcraft, K. L. (2006b). Feminist-bureaucratic control and other adversarial allies: How hybrid organization subverts anti-bureaucratic discourse. *Communication Monographs, 73*(1), 55–86.

Ashcraft, K. L. (2009). Gender and diversity: Other ways to 'make a difference.' In H. Willmott, T. Bridgman, & M. Alvesson (Eds.), *The Oxford handbook of critical management studies* (pp. 304–327). Oxford, UK: Oxford University Press.

Ashcraft, K. L. (2011). Knowing work through the communication of difference: A revised agenda for difference studies In D. K. Mumby (Ed.), *Reframing difference in organizational communication studies: Research, pedagogy, practice* (pp. 3–30). Thousand Oaks, CA: SAGE.

Ashcraft, K. L., & Flores, L. A. (2003). "Slaves with white collars": Decoding a contemporary crisis of masculinity. *Text and Performance Quarterly, 23*(1), 1–29.

Ashcraft, K. L., & Harris, K. L. (2014). "Meaning that matters": An organizational communication perspective on gender, discourse, and materiality. In S. Kumra, R. Simpson, & R. Burke (Eds.), *The Oxford handbook of gender in organizations.* Oxford, UK: Oxford University Press.

Ashcraft, K. L., Kuhn, T., & Cooren, F. (2009). Constitutional amendments: "Materializing" organizational communication for a management audience. *The Academy of Management Annals, 3,* 1–64.

Ashcraft, K. L., Muhr, S. L., Rennstam, J., & Sullivan, K. R. (2012). Professionalization as a branding activity: Occupational identity and the dialectic of inclusivity-exclusivity. *Gender, Work and Organization, 19*(5), 467–488.

Ashcraft, K. L., & Mumby, D. K. (2004). *Reworking gender: A feminist communicology of organization.* Thousand Oaks, CA: SAGE.

Ashcraft, K. L., & Pacanowsky, M. E. (1996). "A woman's worst enemy": Reflections on a narrative of organizational life and female identity. *Journal of Applied Communication Research, 24*(3), 217–239.

Bate, B., & Taylor, A. (Eds.). (1988). *Women communicating: Studies of women's talk.* Norwood, NJ: Ablex.

Bell, E. L., & Forbes, L. C. (1994). Office folklore in the academic paperwork empire: The interstitial space of gendered (con)texts. *Text and Performance Quarterly, 14*(3), 181–196.

Benhabib, S., Butler, J., Cornell, D., & Fraser, N. (Eds.). (1995). *Feminist contentions: A philosophical exchange.* New York, NY: Routledge.

Broadfoot, K. J., & Munshi, D. (2007). Diverse voices and alternative rationalities: Imagining forms of postcolonial organizational communication. *Management Communication Quarterly, 21*(2), 249–267.

Bullis, C., & Stout, K. R. (2000). Organizational socialization: A feminist standpoint approach. In P. M. Buzzanell (Ed.), *Rethinking organizational and managerial communication from feminist perspectives* (pp. 47–75). Thousand Oaks, CA: SAGE.

Butler, J. (1999). *Gender trouble: Feminism and the subversion of identity* (10th anniversary ed.). New York, NY: Routledge.

Buzzanell, P. M. (1994). Gaining a voice: Feminist organizational communication theorizing. *Management Communication Quarterly, 7*(4), 339–383.

Buzzanell, P. M. (1995). Reframing the glass ceiling as a socially constructed process: Implications for understanding and change. *Communication Monographs, 62*(4), 327–354.

Buzzanell, P. M., & Liu, M. (2005). Struggling with maternity leave policies and practices: A post-structuralist feminist analysis of gendered organizing. *Journal of Applied Communication Research, 33*(1), 1–25.

Calás, M. B., & Smircich, L. (1993). Dangerous liaisons: The "feminine-in-management" meets "globalization." *Business Horizons, 36*(2), 71–81.

Calás, M. B., & Smircich, L. (1996). From 'the woman's point of view': Feminist approches to organization studies. In S. R. Clegg, C. Hardy, & W. R. Nord (Eds.), *Handbook of organization studies* (pp. 218–257). Thousand Oaks, CA: SAGE.

Calás, M. B., & Smircich, L. (2006). From the 'woman's point of view' ten years later: Towards a feminist organization studies. In S. Clegg, C. Hardy, T. B. Lawrence, & W. R. Nord (Eds.), *The SAGE handbook of organization studies* (2nd ed., pp. 284–346). London, England: SAGE.

Carlone, D., & Taylor, B. (1998). Organizational communication and cultural studies. *Communication Theory, 8*(3), 337–367.

Collins, P. H. (1991). *Black feminist thought: Knowledge, consciousness and the politics of empowerment.* New York, NY: Routledge.

Collins, P. H. (1997). Comment on Hekman's "Truth and method: Feminist standpoint theory revisited": Where's the power? *Signs: Journal of Women in Culture and Society, 22*(2), 375–381.

Connell, C. (2010). Doing, undoing, or redoing gender? Learning from the workplace experiences of transpeople. *Gender & Society, 24*(1), 31–55.

D'Enbeau, S., & Buzzanell, P. M. (2011). Selling (out) feminism: Sustainability of ideology-viability tensions in a competitive marketplace. *Communication Monographs, 78*(1), 27–52.

Dempsey, S. E. (2009). The increasing technology divide: Persistent portrayals of maverick masculinity in US marketing. *Feminist Media Studies, 9*(1), 37–55.

Dempsey, S. E. (2011). Theorizing difference from transnational feminisms. In D. K. Mumby (Ed.), *Reframing difference in organizational communication studies* (pp. 55–76). Thousand Oaks, CA: SAGE.

Dempsey, S. E., Parker, P. S., & Krone, K. J. (2011). Navigating socio-spatial difference, constructing counter-space: Insights from transnational feminist practice. *Journal of International and Intercultural Communication, 4*(3), 201–220.

Dempsey, S. E., & Sanders, M. L. (2010). Meaningful work? Nonprofit marketization and work/life imbalance in popular autobiographies of social entrepreneurship. *Organization, 17*(4), 437–459.

Deutsch, F. M. (2007). Undoing gender. *Gender & Society, 21*(1), 106–127.

Dougherty, D. S. (1999). Dialogue through standpoint: Understanding men's and women's standpoints of sexual harassment. *Management Communication Quarterly, 12*(3), 436–468.

Edley, P. P. (2000). Discursive essentializing in a woman-owned business: Gendered stereotypes and strategic subordination. *Management Communication Quarterly, 14*(2), 271–306.

Eisenstein, H. (1995). The Australian femocratic experiment: A feminist case for bureaucracy. In M. M. Ferree & P. Y. Martin (Eds.), *Feminist organizations: Harvest of the new women's movement* (pp. 69–83). Philadelphia, PA: Temple University Press.

Elsesser, K. M., & Lever, J. (2011). Does gender bias against female leaders persist? Quantitative and qualitative data from a large-scale survey. *Human Relations, 64*(12), 1555–1578.

Fagenson, E. A. (Ed.). (1993). *Women in management: Trends, issues, and challenges in managerial diversity.* Newbury Park, CA: SAGE.

Fenstermaker, S., & West, C. (Eds.). (2002). *Doing gender, doing difference: Inequality, power and institutional change.* New York, NY: Routledge.

Ferguson, K. (1984). *The feminist case against bureaucracy.* Philadelphia, PA: Temple University Press.

Ferree, M. M., & Martin, P. (Eds.). (1995). *Feminist organizations: Harvest of the new women's movement.* Philadelphia, PA: Temple University Press.

Fletcher, J. (1994). Castrating the female advantage: Feminist standpoint research and management science. *Journal of Management Inquiry, 3*(1), 74–82.

Flores, L. A., & Moon, D. (2002). Rethinking race, revealing dilemmas: Imagining a new racial subject in *Race Traitor. Western Journal of Communication, 66*(2), 181–207.

Foucault, M. (1972). *The archaeology of knowledge and the discourse on language* (A. M. S. Smith, Trans.). New York, NY: Pantheon.

Fournier, V., & Smith, W. (2006). Scripting masculinity. *Ephemera, 6*(2), 141–162.

Gherardi, S. (1994). The gender we think, the gender we do in our everyday organizational lives. *Human Relations, 47*(6), 591–610.

Gherardi, S. (1995). *Gender, symbolism and organizational cultures.* London, England: SAGE.

Gherardi, S. (2002). Feminist theory and organizational theory: A dialogue on new bases. In C. Knudsen & H. Tsoukas (Eds.), *Organizational theory as science: Prospects and limitations.* Oxford, UK: Oxford University Press.

Gibson, M. K., & Papa, M. J. (2000). The mud, the blood, and the beer guys: Organizational osmosis in blue-collar work groups. *Journal of Applied Communication Research, 28*(1), 68–88.

Glenn, E. N. (1994). Social constructions of mothering: A thematic overview. In E. N. Glenn, G. Chang, & L. R. Forcey (Eds.), *Mothering: Ideology, experience, and agency* (pp. 1–32). New York, NY: Routledge.

Harding, N., Lee, H., Ford, J., & Learmonth, M. (2011). Leadership and charisma: A desire that cannot speak its name? *Human Relations, 64*(7), 927–949.

Harding, S. (1991). *Whose science? Whose knowledge? Thinking from women's lives.* Ithaca, NY: Cornell University Press.

Helgesen, S. (1990). *The female advantage: Women's ways of leadership.* New York, NY: Doubleday.

hooks, b. (1995). Black women: Shaping feminist theory. In B. Guy-Sheftall (Ed.), *Words of fire: An anthology of African-American feminist thought* (pp. 270–282). New York, NY: The New Press.

Ianello, K. P. (1992). *Decisions without hierarchy: Feminist interventions in organization theory and practice.* New York, NY: Routledge.

Kanter, R. M. (1975). Women and the structure of organizations: Explorations in theory and behavior. In M. Millman & R. M. Kanter (Eds.), *Another voice: Femimist perspectives on social life and social science.* Garden City, NY: Anchor Books.

Krone, K. J., Dougherty, D., & Sloan, D. K. (2001). *Gendered emotion and communication in a corrections organization: A test of feminist standpoint theory* Paper presented at the Western States Communication Association Convention, Coeur d'Alene, ID.

Maguire, M., & Mohtar, L. F. (1994). Performance and the celebration of a subaltern counterpublic. *Text and Performance Quarterly, 14*(3), 238–252.

Marshall, J. (1989). Re-visioning career concepts: A feminist invitation. In M. B. Arthur, D. Hall, & B. Lawrence (Eds.), *Handbook of career theory* (pp. 275–291). Cambridge, UK: Cambridge University Press.

Marshall, J. (1993). Viewing organizational communication from a feminist perspective: A critique and some offerings. In S. A. Deetz (Ed.), *Communication yearbook* (vol. 16, pp. 122–141). Newbury Park, CA: SAGE.

Medved, C. E., & Kirby, E. L. (2005). Family CEOs: A feminist analysis of corporate mothering discourses. *Management Communication Quarterly, 18*(4), 135–478.

Mills, A. J. (1988). Organization, gender and culture. *Organization Studies, 9*(3), 351–369.

Mills, A. J. (2002). Studying the gendering of organizational culture over time: Concerns, issues and strategies. *Gender, Work and Organization, 9*(3), 286–307.

Mills, A. J. (2006). *Sex, strategy and the stratosphere: Airlines and the gendering of organizational culture.* New York, NY: Palgrave Macmillan.

Mills, A. J., & Chiaramonte, P. (1991). Organization as gendered communication act. *Canadian Journal of Communication, 16*(3), 381–398.

Mills, A. J., & Tancred, P. (Eds.). (1992). *Gendering organizational analysis.* Newbury Park, CA: SAGE.

Morgen, S. (1990). Contradictions in feminist practice: Individualism and collectivism in a feminist health center. In C. Calhoun (Ed.), *Comparative social research* (s.1, pp. 9–59). Greenwich, CT: JAI Press.

Mumby, D. K. (1993). Feminism and the critique of organizational communication studies. In S. Deetz (Ed.), *Communication yearbook* (vol. 16, pp. 155–166). Newbury Park, CA: SAGE.

Mumby, D. K. (1996). Feminism, postmodernism, and organizational communication: A critical reading. *Management Communication Quarterly, 9*(3), 259–295.

Mumby, D. K. (1997). Modernism, postmodernism, and communication studies: A rereading of an ongoing debate. *Communication Theory, 7*(1), 1–28.

Mumby, D. K. (1998). Organizing men: Power, discourse, and the social construction of masculinity(s) in the workplace. *Communication Theory, 8*(2), 164–183.

Murray, S. B. (1988). The unhappy marriage of theory and practice: An analysis of a battered women's shelter. *NWSA Journal, 1*(1), 75–92.

Nadesan, M. H. (1996). Organizational identity and space of action. *Organization Studies, 17*(1), 49–81.

Nadesan, M. H. (1997). Constructing paper dolls: The discourse of personality testing in organizational practice. *Communication Theory, 7*(3), 189–218.

Nadesan, M. H., & Trethewey, A. (2000). Performing the enterprising subject: Gendered strategies for success (?). *Text and Performance Quarterly, 20*(3), 223–250.

Natalle, E. J. (1996). Gendered issues in the workplace. In J. T. Wood (Ed.), *Gendered relationships* (pp. 253–274). Mountain View, CA: Mayfield.

Natalle, E. J., Papa, M. J., & Graham, E. E. (1994). Feminist philosophy and the transformation of organizational communication. In B. Kovacic (Ed.), *New approaches to organizational communication* (pp. 245–270). Albany, NY: SUNY Press.

Nelson, M. W. (1988). Women's ways: Interactive patterns in predominately female research teams. In B. Bate & A. Taylor (Eds.), *Women communicating: Studies of women's talk* (pp. 199–232). Norwood, NJ: Ablex.

Pacanowsky, M., & O'Donnell-Trujillo, N. (1982). Communication and organizational cultures. *The Western Journal of Speech Communication, 46*(2), 115–130.

Parker, P. S. (2005). *Race, gender, and leadership: Re-envisioning organizational leadership from the perspectives of African American women executives.* Mahwah, NJ: Lawrence Erlbaum Associates.

Putnam, L. L. (1990). *Feminist theories, dispute processes, and organizational communication.* Paper presented at the Arizona State University Conference on Organizational Communication, Tempe, AZ.

Putnam, L. L., & Fairhurst, G. (1985). Women and organizational communication: Research directions and new perspectives. *Women and Language, 9*(1/2), 2–6.

Rogers, J. K., & Henson, K. D. (1997). "Hey, why don't you wear a shorter skirt?" Structural vulnerability and the organization of sexual harassment in temporary clerical employment. *Gender & Society, 11*(2), 215–237.

Savage, M., & Witz, A. (Eds.). (1992). *Gender and bureaucracy* (vol. 39). Oxford, UK: Blackwell/The Sociological Review.

Sealander, J., & Smith, D. (1986). The rise and fall of feminist organizations in the 1970s: Dayton as a case study. *Feminist Studies, 12*(2), 321–341.

Sotirin, P., & Gottfried, H. (1999). The ambivalent dynamics of secretarial "bitching": Control, resistance, and the construction of identity. *Organization, 6*(1), 57–80.

Spradlin, A. (1998). The price of "passing": A lesbian perspective on authenticity in organizations. *Management Communication Quarterly, 11*(4), 598–605.

Tannen, D. (1994). *Talking from 9 to 5: Women and men in the workplace: Language, sex and power.* New York, NY: Avon Books.

Taylor, B. C. (1999). Browsing the culture: Membership and intertextuality at a Mormon bookstore. *Studies in Cultures, Organizations, and Societies, 5*(1), 61–95.

Thomas, R., & Davies, A. (2005). What have the feminists done for us? Feminist theory and organizational resistance. *Organization, 12*(5), 711–740.

Tomaskovic-Devey, D. (1993). *Gender & racial inequality at work: The sources & consequences of job segregation.* Ithaca, NY: ILR Press.

Tong, R. (1989). *Feminist thought: A comprehensive introduction.* Boulder, CO: Westview Press.

Townsley, N. C., & Geist, P. (2000). The discursive enactment of hegemony: Sexual harassment and academic organizing. *Western Journal of Communication, 64*(2), 190–217.

Trethewey, A. (1999a). Disciplined bodies: Women's embodied identities at work. *Organization Studies, 20*(3), 423–450.

Trethewey, A. (1999b). Isn't it ironic: Using irony to explore the contradictions of organizational life. *Western Journal of Communication, 63*(2), 140–167.

Trethewey, A., & Ashcraft, K. L. (2004). Practicing disorganization: The development of applied perspectives on living with tension. *Journal of Applied Communication Research, 32*(2), 81–88.

Weedon, C. (1987). *Feminist practice and poststructuralist theory.* Oxford, UK: Basil Blackwell.

West, C., & Zimmerman, D. (1987). Doing gender. *Gender and Society, 1*(2), 125–151.

Wood, J. T. (2011). *Gendered lives: Communication, gender, and culture* (9th ed.). Boston, MA: Wadsworth.

Wood, J. T., & Conrad, C. (1983). Paradox in the experience of professional women. *Western Journal of Speech Communication, 47*(4), 304–318.

Notes

1. Calás & Smircich (1996) make a similar point in their depiction of liberal feminist organization studies as "thirty years of researching that women are people too" (p. 223).

2. Lowercase d typically refers to highly localized discursive activity, or language in use, while capital D refers to broad societal discourses (Alvesson & Karreman, 2000).

3. See, for example, the 2009 *Oxford Handbook* of *Critical Management Studies.* Issues of gender and diversity are concentrated in a single chapter and barely mentioned elsewhere—in a massive volume dedicated to relations of power, no less.

CHAPTER 6

Postcolonial Approaches

Kirsten J. Broadfoot and Debashish Munshi

> As soon as I desire, I am asking to be considered. I am not merely here-and-now, sealed into thingness. I am for somewhere else and for something else. I demand that notice be taken of my negating activity insofar as I pursue something other than life; insofar as I do battle for the creation of a human world—that is a world of reciprocal recognition. (Fanon, 1967, p. 218)

A desire for the *reciprocal recognition* (Fanon, 1967) of postcolonial approaches that offer a radically different, even insurgent, perspective on organizational communication underlies this chapter. Driven as we are by Shome and Hegde's (2002) call to question "why conditions are what they are and how they can be undone and redone" (p. 250), we have chosen to adopt a reflexive approach to this chapter on postcolonial worldviews, examining how the engagement of such views may help us reframe aspects of organizational communication that many of us take for granted. The challenges of outlining such a scholarly terrain are considerable: It is vast and complicated, inhabited by multiple interdisciplinary others; confusing and contested terms, language, and historicity; and a profound struggle for inclusion. Our focus, therefore, has been to document issues, concerns, thinkers, conversations, and practices that question how contemporary organizing and communicative practices can be undone and redone.

The chapter will demonstrate how postcolonial commitments can blur discursive, spatial, and epistemological boundaries around questions of organizing and communicating as we highlight and open up the *spaces in-between* (Bhabha, 1994, 1996) and their capacity for translation and negotiation. Our goal is to usher in an epistemological, discursive, and physical "spatial politics of inclusion . . . that initiate new signs of identity and innovative sites of collaboration and contestation" (Bhabha, 1994, p. 1). In line with this goal, we spotlight three conceptual commitments of postcolonial scholarship, indicating its deconstructive or critical dimension as well as its creative and reimagining potential, providing exemplars (where they exist) of work in this area. Based on this discussion, we then provide two potential conceptual, empirical, and pragmatic lenses to advance scholarship at the intersection of postcolonialism and organizational communication as it enters an unknown and yet-to-be-imagined future.

The Quandaries of Postcolonial Scholarship

Postcolonial thought was born from the experiences of those who actively opposed colonial rule in the early and mid-twentieth century—thinkers, activists, and freedom fighters such as Césaire, Gandhi, Ho Chi Minh, Lenin, Mannoni, Nyerere, Senghor, and many more (Prasad, 2003). Central ideas in postcolonial thought have been (and in some cases, continue to be) issues of nation-states, citizenship, knowledge production, colonization, empire, otherness/othering, and decolonization. Drawing from a diverse disciplinary and experiential base, postcolonial scholars have made visible the particular histories that have dominated their locales, the impacts of such histories on people, and their current and future self-determinations. These accounts describe the processes that have undergirded uneven social and economic developments across the globe and that continue in the present day and in present forms of governance.

As a result, postcolonial scholarship has been many things to many people. As Moore-Gilbert (1997) explains, "Such has been the elasticity of the concept 'postcolonial' that, in recent years, some commentators have begun to express anxiety that there may be a real danger of it imploding as an analytic construct with any real cutting edge" (p. 11). Admittedly, postcolonial scholarship can be dense, even messy, as scholars negotiate the difficult terrain of resisting colonialist ideas while granting centrality to colonialism as a subject of critique. To complicate matters, their language can be inaccessible, their position elitist and exclusionary, and their work largely made of intellectual formulations. Yet it is the simultaneous heterogeneities and convergences of this complex engagement with colonial experience, both historic and ongoing, that provides postcolonialism with its multifaceted, syncretic, interdisciplinary, productive, and generative power.

Despite this powerful formation, contemporary work in postcolonial approaches to organizational communication remains nascent and embryonic, struggling against the dominance of a Eurocentric (read Anglo-U.S.) stance and its concerns. There are also the unacknowledged but difficult realities of inequality and poverty as both substance and condition of scholarly work by those in *other* and *othered* locales (inside and outside the academy). Although a few communication scholars have taken postcolonial approaches (see e.g., Broadfoot & Munshi, 2007b; Broadfoot, Munshi, & Nelson-Marsh, 2010; Dutta, 2011; Dutta & Pal, 2010; Ganesh, 2011; Munshi, Broadfoot, & Tuhiwai-Smith, 2011; Munshi & Edwards, 2011; Pal & Dutta, 2008; Shome & Hegde, 2002), the use of the postcolonial frame is still limited in organizational communication research.

Postcolonial scholarship, however, has become much more visible in management and organizational studies, especially critical management studies (see Banerjee & Prasad, 2008; Frenkel & Shenhav, 2006; Jackson, 2012; Mir, Mir, & Upadhyaya, 2003; Prasad, 2003; Westwood, 2006). But as Jack, Westwood, Srinivas, and Sardar (2011) argue, postcolonial scholarship in this area needs to be "deepened, broadened and re-asserted in order to contribute to the development of a more critical and heterodox examination of organizations" (p. 275). This lack of deeper postcolonial interventions is due in part to issues of participation: Who is postcolonial? When? Where? According to whom? Who counts? There are also questions over processes and practices: Consider, for example, ongoing debates over whether we are living in postcolonial; neocolonial; or ever-evolving, morphing, colonial times.

In his work exploring the influence of postcolonial theory on organizational analysis, Prasad (2003) suggests that postcolonial theory can defamiliarize organizational phenomena, help scholars excavate and understand the colonial underpinnings of current management and organizational processes and discourse (how subdisciplines may unconsciously sustain the colonial project in particular), and expose the ways in which cross-cultural management and transnational organizations operate. As Prasad (2003) states, "Postcolonial theory is relevant for management and organization studies because it offers a uniquely radical and ethically informed critique of Western modernity and modernity's overdetermined accoutrements like capitalism, Eurocentrism, science and the like" (p. 33). Rao and Wasserman (2007) concur, stating that

> the strength of postcolonial theory is that it provides us with a critical framework that validates the local epistemologies necessary for the formulation of global ethics, and acknowledges the unequal power relationships in which various cultures and nations are historically positioned. (p. 34)

A special issue of *Critical Perspectives on International Business,* edited by Banerjee and Prasad (2008), provides insight into the potential of postcolonial thought to facilitate critical reflection on organizing practices that are soaked in Euro-American traditions but are passed off as universal. Mapping the terrain of the special issue, Banerjee and Prasad discuss a wide range of organizational studies scholars' engagements with "the power dynamics that frame discourses of neoliberal development and knowledge production" (p. 94), highlighting especially the work of de Maria (2008) in exposing the neo-colonial tendencies of constructing discourses around corruption in Africa; Mir, Banerjee, and Mir's (2008) critique of colonial-era assumptions of organizational relationships that characterize interactions between multinational corporations and their subsidiaries; and Cheung's (2008) study of the power imbalance in the business interactions between Western managers of corporations and local employees based in China. The analyses in this special issue exemplify the potential of a postcolonial framework for critical analysis, reflection, and self-reflexivity in organizational studies.

Developing a postcolonial analysis entails drawing conscientiously from the theoretical work that has been foundational to postcolonial theory. Many excellent overviews of postcolonial theory exist, discussing its history and development (see, e.g., Ashcroft, Griffiths, & Tiffin, 1995; Gandhi, 1998; Goldberg & Quayson, 2002; Loomba, 1998; Mongia, 1996; Young, 2003). Prasad (2003), in his own discussion of the connections between postcolonial theory and organizational studies, centers on four scholars—Edward Said, Ashis Nandy, Homi Bhabha, and Gayatri Chakravorty Spivak, all of whom were deeply influential in the past and present of postcolonial inquiry. Nkomo (2011) expands this range by drawing on Francophone scholars from the Caribbean and Africa, such as Fanon, Césaire, and Senghor. Our own work (e.g., Broadfoot & Munshi, 2007a, 2007b; Broadfoot et al., 2010; Munshi et al., 2011) has drawn on (in addition to Said, Spivak, and Bhabha) an array of scholars from across disciplines, especially historiographers from the Subaltern Studies collective, such as Ranajit Guha, Dipesh Chakrabarty, and Gyan Prakash, and Kaupapa Maori scholars, such as Linda Tuhiwai Smith and Graham Hingangaroa Smith. Accordingly, in this chapter, we document the terrain of postcolonial theory and organizational communication in order to chart a way forward for scholars to consider how analyses of organizing and communicative phenomena can be reframed through a postcolonial lens and the potent and influential consequences of such an exercise for the field.

Postcolonial Thought Meets Organizing Practices

In this section, we introduce three central conceptual postcolonial commitments: to disrupt and reimagine organizing space(s); to resist colonialist discourse and rethink organizing practices; and to decolonize thought and reconfigure organizing forms of knowledge. Each commitment entails both deconstructive and imaginative impulses. We elaborate on the epistemological and political foundations of these impulses. We also connect them to specific empirical examinations of communicative and organizational practices, where possible. Some of these exemplars come from work in organizational communication, while others are sourced from organizational communication's cognate disciplines, such as organizational studies and critical management studies.

Commitment #1: Disrupt and Reimagine Organizing Space(s)

Colonization has always been about space and resources, from early voyages of discovery and conquest to the influence of global media and knowledge production. Thus concepts of space and place are central concerns in postcolonial forms of inquiry. Space, Shome (2003) argues, is "a component of power . . . a product of relations that are themselves active and constantly changing material practices through which [space] comes into being" (p. 41). How individuals and organizations are distributed within particular material spatial relations as well as the idea of space as a complex transnational imaginary location have real consequences in terms of mobility, access, exclusion, and inclusion (Shome, 2003).

Organizations/cultures/nations/identities are unstable, historically situated products undergoing constant differentiations and diverse identifications (Shohat & Stam, 1994). Thus reframing organizing and communicative practices through a postcolonial lens asks scholars to take seriously how cultural, national, and international organizing practices and forms are located "in larger, unequal histories and geographies of global power and culture" (Shome & Hegde, 2002, p. 253). It also means moving from representing others to collaborating with them in shared spaces (Shohat & Stam, 1994).

Given colonial history and their experience of it, many postcolonial writers, for example, take issue with the fiction of *the nation* and its corresponding form of being, that is, nationalism itself. As Anderson (1991) has argued, *the nation* is an imagined community that is constructed, inasmuch as people are convinced of the comradeship of unknown fellow compatriots, yet they often ignore any actual inequality and exploitation that exists in such an imagined community. During the 1980s and 1990s, postcolonial scholars such as Chatterjee (1986, 1995) and Bhabha (1983, 1990, 1994) critically interrogated the concept of *nation*, its fictional character, and the forces of nationalism that construct and sustain such a fiction.

While in agreement with Anderson's contention of nations as imagined communities, Chatterjee (1995) extended these ideas to investigate nationalist thought as simultaneously opposing and accepting the "dominating implications of post-Enlightenment European thought" (p. 37). Much of Chatterjee's work, while focused on nationalism, implicates concepts such as *colonialism*, *postcolonialism*, and *modernity*. Chatterjee found the concept of *nation-state* especially problematic due to its fictive construction in European social-scientific thought and its unreflective appropriation by postcolonial administrators so that new possibilities of thinking outside the national box remained obscured. This inability to find a new way to govern also raised questions for Chatterjee over the degree to which those who were governed participated in nationhood.

Postcolonial historian Dipesh Chakrabarty (1992, 2000) critiques the ways in which Eurocentric ideas permeate organizations. In his landmark book, *Provincializing Europe: Postcolonial Thought and Historical Difference*, Chakrabarty (2000) seeks to decenter the universalized notion of Europe, "an imaginary figure that remains deeply embedded in clichéd and shorthand forms in some everyday habits of thought" (p. 4). He argues that Europe is as provincial as any other part of the world, and yet historicist accounts that chart the development of modernity and all its appendages unabashedly claim that Europe was intellectually ahead of other regions. Such an ideology allowed John Stuart Mill to write foundational essays that "proclaimed self-rule as the highest form of government and yet argued against giving Indians or Africans self-rule on grounds that were indeed historicist. . . . Indians or Africans were not yet civilized enough to rule themselves" (Chakrabarty, 2000, p. 8). Indians and Africans (and other colonized peoples) did indeed fight for and get self-rule and, in doing so, upset the historicists' paradigm.

Chatterjee and Chakrabarty have been committed to interrogating unreflective appropriations of Eurocentric ideas and ideals that permeate organizations so that new possibilities of thinking outside the national box remain obscured. This commitment not only enriches the field but also adds an additional layer of political analysis to much of the critical and deconstructive work done by organizational scholars such as Mumby and Putnam (1992) and Mumby (1997), who have focused on genealogies of modernity and their attending forms and effects of hierarchy, rationality, and forms of progress. Similarly, Chakrabarty's discussion of the colonial mindset provides a larger political frame through which to examine how organizations determine who their strategic stakeholders are and what processes count for success and legitimacy (Deetz, 1992).

The political dimension of organizational analysis provided by Chatterjee and Chakrabarty's work comes through in a postcolonial study of the communication between expatriate Western managers of multinational companies and local employees on the ground in China (Cheung, 2008). This study examines how the Western managers use their colonial managerial frames to judge Chinese business customs. Cheung (2008) provides the example of the Chinese tradition of *guanxi,* which forms the basis for business relationships in the country, and how Western managers simply equate this tradition with corruption and that "they have to bribe their way to successful negotiation or business with [the] Chinese" (p. 302). It is only through a postcolonial evaluation of what Cheung calls an "asymmetrical understanding" of organizational behaviors across national spaces that it is evident how dominant frames of understanding prevent the Chinese from "being understood fairly and their voice being heard" (p. 302).

Cheung's analysis highlights the relational and cultural practice of *guanxi* as the personal connection between people that can be deployed to ask one another for a favor or service. It refers to the social benefits people can gain from social connections and, similar to the concepts of *on* and *giri* in Japanese culture, outlines the strong social bonds that exist in collectivistic cultures, where rules of reciprocity are crucial to the cultural fabric and an individual's recognition of and ability to survive in and through an expansive social web. Such cultural concepts of deep relational connection and reciprocity are not dominant cultural characteristics of highly individualized and Western cultures. They are, therefore, not considered part of formal organizing practices governed by particular philosophies of law and economics. These relational and reciprocal behaviors have traditionally been seen as corruptive and disruptive; they have been *othered,* even though most contemporary organizational actors could speak to their necessary presence (often hidden) at work and for effective organizational performance in a globalized world. In Cheung's (2008) example, both Chinese and Western businessmen find themselves *in-between,* caught between ways of organizing and relational practice where two sets of rules are in contest with one another, each requiring the suppression of the other.

This critique of *in-betweenness* draws on Bhabha's (1983, 1990, 1994) rigorous interrogations of nationalism, representation, and resistance, which stress the ambivalence, hybridity, and liminal spaces in which we produce imagined ideas of cultural and national identity. Drawing on Lacan, Foucault, and Derrida, Bhabha's writings argue that *nations* (e.g., China) are narrative constructions that emerge at the intersection of contending cultural populations. This intersection or gap between dominant social formations is, by its very nature, an ambivalent space, filled with a capacity for resistance and performative mimicry. Bhabha argues that this in-betweenness indicates that which has been *othered*, disavowed, or denied authority. Recovering what has been denied authority, or even altering or displacing the language of authority, provides a small space of resistance for those colonized.

Indeed, the critical and deconstructive drives of both postcolonial thought and critical/postmodern/dialogic organizational communication are dedicated to recovering what has been denied authority as well as the consideration of any form of organization (corporation or nation) as a narrative construction. But is it possible to take these ideas further to creatively reimagine organizing spaces, principles, and forms of knowledge?

Take, for example, the spaces from/in which much of organizational communication thought, practices, and principles have emerged. Prior to the linguistic or discursive turn in the field (Deetz, 2001), much of the founding work in organizational communication arose from the study of business management in North American contexts. Heavily pragmatic and normative (Deetz, 2001), this work mainly focused on developing better management practices through communication. Organization was considered a box within which communication happened. The move to a more constitutive view of the organization-communication relationship that emerged in the 1990s, continuing into the new millennium, was heavily influenced by European theorists, but its scholarship was predominantly produced in the U.S. Thus much of the academic work in Organizational Communication (with a capital O and a capital C) has been limited by what Shome (1996) calls *discursive confinement*—a state where scholars work within a narrow space constructed by dominant structures and ideologies (Broadfoot & Munshi, 2007a, 2007b). Despite several superb scholarly works in such areas as gender (e.g., Ashcraft & Mumby, 2004), race (e.g., Ashcraft & Allen, 2003), and globalization from below (e.g., Ganesh, Zoller, & Cheney, 2005; Pal & Dutta, 2008; Stohl, 2001), the field of organizational communication has been stuck in a North American cultural context. Neither the voices from nor the rationalities of other contexts have received much attention (Broadfoot & Munshi, 2007b).

Pluralizing the terms of reference is, therefore, a major objective of postcolonial theorizing in organizational contexts. Empirical questions that might motivate valued and valuable scholarly investigations at the intersection of postcolonial thought and organizational communication include the following: How do we get organizations to move beyond mere demographic diversity to develop epistemological, political, and cultural diversity? How do we, as organizational scholars, study communication and organizations and communication across cultures together, simultaneously? How might explorations of organizational communication processes beyond the Anglo-American context disrupt the embedded notion of nationhood in organizations?

Spivak's (1999) conceptualization of being postcolonial is helpful for organizational communication scholars in answering such questions. For her, a postcolonial being is sensitive to the historical forces and conditions of the emerging global order but is also cognizant of its flows and ephemeral character. A postcolonial approach, therefore, does not essentialize or attempt to locate a stable, singular *other*, nationally or individually, but instead recognizes *othering* practices at work and the ways in which our *others*, just as our postmodern selves, are fragmented, dispersed, multiple, and partial.

We have been inspired by this understanding of *being postcolonial* in our own efforts to construct an alternative space of scholarly community. We organized the COMMUNEcation community (Broadfoot et al., 2010) in response to conferencing practices that made it difficult for scholars from developing nations, or even those who had caretaking duties, to participate in annual disciplinary meetings (where much disciplinary knowledge is created and validated). The COMMUNEcation community was our attempt at creating a *space in-between* (Bhabha, 1994, 1996), a means of harnessing the productive and reflective capacities of a digital space, by which its very character was ambivalent, ambiguous, and ethereal. We believed that this digital space, unmoored from geographical, disciplinary, and temporal constraints, would enable a "spatial politics of inclusion rather than exclusion that initiate new signs of identity and innovative sites of collaboration and contestation" (Bhabha, 1994, p. 1). For us, the creation of such a space, in active reciprocal recognition of all other corporeally bounded spaces in which we exist, was a postcolonial form of organizing and communication.

When conceptualizing and creating the COMMUNEcation community, we were forced to recognize and acknowledge that while all fences/borders/boundaries (be they national, institutional, or disciplinary) serve to define what is inside, it is the "use of space inside and in-between that activates it" (Spivak, as cited in Shome & Hegde, 2002, p. 276). Our initial networks of scholarly friendships, forged through our travels, for example, enabled the initiation of such a community; but what happened next defined it. After the conference, as COMMUNEcation moved to publish work from this conference, we met another set of boundaries erected in the name of form, genre, author-attribution, and citation style. COMMUNEcation was lucky to have allies in its editors and publishers, who negotiated institutional and interdisciplinary rules to create a space and style of publication that honored the creative and postcolonial spirit of the scholarship and scholars. They worked against a discursive and materially constrained elite space to include and recognize a diverse range of communicative and organizing practices.

Deconstructing taken-for-granted configurations of space that privilege certain geographic-historical formations and productively reimagining *in-betweenness* as spaces of postcolonial being is the first of our three commitments in a postcolonial frame. The second entails both discursive resistance and new ways of thinking.

Commitment #2: Resist Colonialist Discourse and Rethink Organizing Practices

The "colonial elite" was of central concern in Edward Said's *Orientalism* (1978), considered by many to be an inaugural text for the study of postcolonial theory and criticism. Said (1978) argued that Western systems of knowledge and representation were tightly connected to colonial control and domination and that Western understandings of scholarship as pure, objective, and disinterested were erroneous (Prasad, 2003). His work has drawn sustained criticism over the years on many fronts, but its central contribution remains untouched—that is, colonialism does not solely function through military and economic controls and oppression but also as a dominating discourse (Prasad, 2003).

The power of colonialism was exercised not only through military might but also by the discourse of what Said (1978) called the *positional superiority* of the West. Hence, the systematic privileging of Western art, literature, and culture over those of the Orient not only valorized European traditions and values but also used these traditions and values to subjugate the colonized. Indeed, as Viswanathan (1987) states, colonial administrators "discovered an ally in English literature to support them in maintaining control of the natives under the guise of a liberal education" (p. 17). In their much-cited work, *The Empire Writes Back*, Ashcroft, Griffiths, and Tiffin (2002) discuss how the oppression of a standardized version of English was resisted by a variety of homegrown versions of English in the Caribbean, the Indian subcontinent, and Africa, and the use of local languages in freedom struggles.

Importantly, just as anticolonial struggles were varied in different locations, the nature of postcolonial discourses is much more than a point of binary opposition to colonial discourses.

As Castle (2001) states, it "is a process in which the native intellectual crafts or forges a new discourse, a new literary style, a way of singing or dancing that expresses a native point of view in contest with colonial discourse" (p. xiii). A contemporary example of such a discourse is evident in the novels of Ghosh (2008, 2011), who exquisitely combines the literary traditions of the English language with its native, even pidgin, variants in India, China, and other Asian locations to weave narratives on the sordid aspects of the colonial era hidden under all the gloss and spectacle. Much like subaltern historiographers, Ghosh's novels rewrite the histories of the time through the voices of ordinary characters and resist imperial narratives handed down through colonial discourses.

This focus on discursive struggle is rightly at the center of critical organizational communication studies, a legacy of the *linguistic turn* (Alvesson & Karreman, 2000). Yet, as Mumby (2011) points out, the "linguistic turn is not simply about the privileging of language or discourse in understanding human behavior" but about "a reconfiguration of how we understand and explore our mediated relationship to the world and each other" (p. 1149). Drawing on his own work and that of Deetz (1992, 2003) he argues that "by examining the ways that particular identities, meanings, institutions, and objects are privileged over other potential formations, it opens up possibilities for rethinking and re-imagining organizing processes and practices" (Mumby, 2011, p. 1149). Such an examination speaks powerfully to the postcolonial commitment to deconstruction and rethinking alternatives. Moreover, as our colleague from Nigeria, Jenks Okwori (personal communication, February, 2008) so insightfully asks, how do scholars investigate the ways in which ideologies categorize and divide forms of knowledge into *mainstream* or *fringe* so that more emotional and mundane subjects (topics) and subjects (people) are not considered worthy of intellectual endeavor? This question encourages scholars to "critique what we are, and, at one and the same time, the historical analysis of the limits imposed on us, and experiment with the possibility of going beyond them" (Foucault, 1984, p. 50). Or, in the words of Spivak's enduring provocation, "What is the alternative?" (as cited in Hegde & Shome, 2006).

Traditionally, organization scholars have rarely taken on such explicit political agendas (Banerjee & Linstead, 2004), so in some ways, postcolonial interventions bring larger political tensions into organization studies. Banerjee and Prasad (2008), for example, bring the politics of organizing to the forefront of their work by showing how seemingly neutral organizing practices are inherently political in as much as they normalize Euro-American political values as universal. In the same trajectory, Parsons (2008) examines how the rhetorical elevation of indigenous communities in Australia to stakeholders did nothing to dismantle the colonial ways of pursuing development—ways that were far removed from indigenous understandings of development. Similarly, Schwabenland and Tomlinson (2008) expose the politics of managing diversity; their UK-based research shows how despite "public policy rhetoric" on celebrating diversity, "practices of funding, accountability and regulation are producing conformity" (p. 331). These findings echo the proposition that "theory and practices of the management of diversity are guided by the terms of reference framed by powerful Anglo-American and other Eurocentric policy makers to keep the non-Western other under control" (Munshi, 2005, p. 51).

Further, the pervasive influence of transnational hegemonies in economics, politics, and business are often translated into organizational practices. Dutta and Pal (2011) demonstrate how a postcolonial lens exposes the ways in which public relations practices (and, we add, organizational communication practices in general) in transnational corporations (TNCs)

> serve the interests of TNCs and the free market logic . . . and maintain the hegemony of West-centric articulations of modernity and development. . . . The modernist tropes of

> capitalism are circulated through mainstream mediated and other communication channels, through knowledge structures, and development-based public relations campaigns (pp. 196–201)

Dutta and Pal draw a powerful connection among discourse, narrative constructions, and organizing practices, such as those discussed in Commitment #1. A postcolonial lens on organizing and communicative practices in their work simultaneously provides us with insight into how hegemonic organizing practices can be, and are indeed, disruptive and disrupted.

Similarly, a recent study by Hall (2010) on leadership in Jamaica sits squarely at the intersection of discourse, culture, and organizing practices. Drawing on insights from postcolonial theory, Hall uses the framework of discursive leadership to examine how narratives of Jamaican managers construct culturally indigenous organizations in a national colonial and neocolonial discursive context. Hall's study focuses on how nationalizing, representing, decolonizing, provincializing, and defamiliarizing processes can work. Leadership in Hall's Jamaican context is thus morphed away from leadership as it may be taught in a textbook or leadership as may be expected in an American corporate context as the leaders came to grips with implementing ideas considered to be colonial in Jamaica, a post-independence nation. Hall's managers struggled with how Jamaica's past and future intersected in the nation's and their organizations' quests for international productivity and over which set of cultured ideas of progress would bring a brighter future. His study is ultimately a study of agents caught between competing discourses and practices, trying to move forward while holding on to who they are.

Gautam's (2008) work on human resources (HR) practices in Nepal is also illustrative of the ways in which wholesale appropriation of Western organizing practices in a non-Western or Eurocentric setting can become disrupted or resisted *in situ*. Mission statements, the establishment of HR departments and personnel or lack thereof, and a lack of connection between business strategy and HR strategy plagued many of the organizations he studied. Most management in these firms held business, economics, or management degrees and were well experienced in their fields. However, recruitment was still considered the role of line management, and practices included hiring through friends and relatives, no uniformity in salary scales, no proper training policies, and job classifications ranging from period contracts to daily wages. Gautam's work considers possible cultured explanations for such gaps among knowledge, strategy, and practice.

The two postcolonial commitments discussed so far highlight the deep connections among space, discourse, and practice. The interconnectedness of these concepts is foregrounded in much of the work discussed, and while much of the literature reviewed has been more heavily set in the deconstructive or critical side of scholarship, more recent scholarship has begun to take into account Jack et al.'s (2011) call for development of a more "heterodox" understanding of organizing (p. 275). In the final commitment, the bond between thought and organizing forms of knowledge, already implicated in the previous two sections, is highlighted.

Commitment #3: Decolonize Thought and Reconfigure Organizing Forms of Knowledge

The impact of transnational hegemonies seeking to impose (actively or passively) the power of neocolonial empires over less powerful national or organizational entities through managerial practices (as demonstrated in Hall, 2010; Gautam, 2008) has been critically interrogated by postcolonial scholars through the frame of decolonization. For scholars such as Frantz Fanon (1965), Martinique-born French psychiatrist-turned-political activist, and Ngugi Thiong'O (1986), Kenyan literary and social activist, the concept of decolonization reflects ways in which an oppressed country or group can become self-determined enough to demand its own liberation. Decolonization, therefore, can be considered the force by which people claim their own future, deciding independently how they wish to live, work, care for others, and express their rights to be free. It means not only the repossession of lands but also the reclamation of cultural identities and forms of representation.

Much of the work on decolonization has been focused on decolonizing mind and thought. Fanon (1965), for example, was critical of the way Europe talked about advances in thought without ever being cognizant of the debilitating impact of such advances on much of the Earth—"the sufferings humanity has paid for every one of their triumphs of the mind" (p. 252). Thiong'O's work (1986) discusses unshackling the mind from an imperialist tradition

> maintained by the international bourgeoisie using the multinational and of course the flag-waving native ruling classes. The economic and political dependence of this African neo-colonial bourgeoisie is reflected in its culture of apemanship and parrotry enforced on a restive population through police boots, barbed wire, a gowned clergy and judiciary; their ideas are spread by a corpus of state intellectuals, the academic and journalistic laureates of the neo-colonial establishment. (p. 2)

Against such an imperialist tradition, Thiong'O (1986) invokes focused attention on the *resistance tradition* shouldered by the working people. This focus on the working class, although Marxist in orientation, is an attempt to insert subaltern histories into social thought and forms of knowledge through the accounts of the lives, struggles, and aspirations of people at the grassroots, rather than elitist versions of realities from above that silence *other* voices. Focusing on the people at the grassroots of society galvanized Thiong'O to support the abolition of the English department at the University of Nairobi. Although an accomplished novelist in English with celebrated novels such as *Weep Not, Child* (1964) and *A Grain of Wheat* (1967), Thiong'O decolonized the influence of English as the central language of literature in Kenya by writing powerful political plays and stories in his native tongue, Gikuyu. In doing so, Thiong'O opened the literary world to not only *other* voices and lives but also provided a path and vehicle for the participation of literary *others* to rebalance representations of life in Kenya.

Resistance to established and taken-for-granted norms and values of organizing knowledge is also well articulated by the postcolonial Caribbean novelist George Lamming (1991), who explains how the "community, not person, is the central character" of his novel, *In the Castle of My Skin:*

> There is often no discernible plot, no coherent line of events with a clear, causal connection. Nor is there a central individual consciousness where we focus attention, and through which we can be guided reliably by a logical succession of events. Instead there are several centers of attention which work simultaneously and acquire their coherence from the collective character of the village. (pp. xxxv–xlvi)

Lamming (1991), as with many other postcolonial Caribbean novelists, focuses on the poor to restore meaning to people disenfranchised by colonialist representations, rebalancing social understandings of Caribbean life in the process. Decentering the individual and diversifying the dominant language forms of knowledge have both proven to be decolonizing methods for postcolonial scholars in these contexts.

In the 1980s, the people of the First Nations took a different route to reclaiming representation. After years of anthropological and scientific abuse, they critically denounced the research processes and practices imposed on their peoples in order to reclaim self-determination and room to participate in larger systems of knowledge production. The silencing of First Nations peoples, both material and discursive, has been perhaps the most insidious and damaging outcome of colonial endeavors. However, the path to reclamation of identity and voice has not been easy. So extensive was the damage to native knowledge that, as Battiste (2008) argues, before even a postcolonial frame could be established from which to reclaim rights and representation, the First Nations had to first renew and rebuild the principles that grounded their worldview, communication forms, language, and very being. As a result, reclaiming the land and resources removed from their possession in colonial times meant that First Nation peoples had to uncover discrepancies, absences, and falsehoods in colonial records. They have also had to recover other forms of knowing and recording based in their own diminished cultures in order to construct political and legal arguments to substantiate their claims. First Nations have also politicized and decolonized the research process writ large to contest the continued consumption of data from their persons and places in contemporary times (Smith, 1999). Their successes in these endeavors have depended on allies in law and policy regulations and shifting understandings of history. As a result, the outcomes for First Nations remain as varied as their socio-political-historical-economic contexts. Nevertheless, several indigenous scholars have started reclaiming indigenous forms of knowledge, ethics, and rights, empowering and transforming their own communities in the process.

Efforts to decolonize and reorganize knowledge forms and organizing practices are also becoming visible in communication, organization, and critical management studies. Dutta (2011) draws on postcolonial studies extensively to map a trajectory of communicating for social change that can resist power structures in oppressive neo-liberal global contexts. Similarly, Munshi et al. (2011) draw on the indigenous research framework of *Kaupapa Maori* from Aotearoa New Zealand to formulate a process of decolonizing ethics. Banerjee and Linstead (2004) refer to the Kaupapa Maori framework as well as other indigenous protocols to chart the resistance of indigenous communities to the norms and processes of the colonizing elite. Illustrating how the postcolonial project of subaltern studies enters into dialogue with dominant organizational discourse, Dutta and Pal (2010) provide examples of the indigenous resistance to free trade agreements in North America by the Zapatista National Liberation Army, a group espousing the cause of subaltern communities in Mexico, and moves by Peruvian indigenous groups to ban the biopiracy of indigenous resources and traditions. Indeed, a small but growing commitment in communication studies exists to insert subaltern voices into the discursive space of organizational scholarship (Dutta & Pal, 2010; Munshi & Kurian, 2007).

As Cao (2007) argues, "opening up new voices or different truths to be in dialogue with existing, often dominant, ones represents a productive and empowering engagement in resisting essentialist representations of the Other" (p. 117). Postcolonial theory can provide scholars with ways to recover local epistemologies and reform global ethics to address the powerful inequality of organizing practices in global relations. This is the ethico-political ambition of the postcolonial project, based in "the desire for a more just and equitable global order not only in political and economic terms but also in terms that are more cultural, psychological, epistemological and so forth" (Prasad & Prasad, 2003, p. 284).

The difficulties of realizing such postcolonial ambitions were discussed in the 2006 *Management Communication Quarterly* Forum. Prichard (2006) from Aotearoa New Zealand, drawing on an example of distance he experienced at a conference on organizational discourse in Australia, described how the U.S. scholars present at the conference enacted a set of assumptions and positions that "were not those that the audience *effortlessly affirmed, emulated or would readily circulate*" (p. 639, emphasis added). Feminist organizational communication scholar Karen Ashcraft (2006) countered his point, stating that organizational communication as a field was itself in the margins of the larger realm of U.S. organization studies. Furthermore, Ashcraft argued, organizational communication scholars were actually outsider refugees rather than part of any dominant collective. Cooren (2006) clarified that the power of the *outsider refugee* allowed scholars to stand at (or in) intersections of perspectives and epistemic choices. He argued that such intersections or spaces in-between (Bhabha, 1996) enable the examination of disciplinary boundaries and the process that sustain them within communities. They also expose the ways in which the outsider refugee may begin to disrupt those same processes through mimicry, multilingualism, and the displacement of linguistic authority, while always remaining an interlocutor. The question of the Forum became whether organizational communication scholars, particularly those based in the U.S., were fully actualizing their role as outsider refugees as both critics of disciplinary boundaries and pathfinders for expanding those boundaries to include other forms of voice, knowledge, and being.

Three years earlier, a similar conversation was held in our cognate discipline of organizational studies. Like Prichard (2006), Frenkel and Shenhav (2003) argued that a greater sensitivity to the colonial elements embedded in organization theory would contribute to its pluralization as well as energize multiculturalism in management. The authors carefully interrogated the distinctly Western cultural roots of management models that promote themselves as culturally neutral and therefore universally applicable, arguing that these hidden assumptions are the major barriers to a "pluralizing of the organizational world and to the possibility of a meaningful multicultural spirit taking root in it" (p. 4). Frenkel and Shenhav (2003) also argued that attempts to impose the "one best way" in other parts of the world without any cultural reflexivity were also imperialist. This point is demonstrated in Long and Mills' (2008) postcolonial evaluation of the organizational practices of seemingly benign but latently colonialist supranational organizations. Their analysis convincingly shows how the West "was complicit in the 1994 genocide in Rwanda" (p. 405), which "was in large part the outcome of imperialist and colonial legacies" manifested in the actions/inactions of organizations such as the United Nations (p. 390).

The unquestioned adoption of ideas and values, as argued by several postcolonial scholars such as Chatterjee and others discussed earlier in this chapter, not only constitute a form of personal control over the *other* but also cultural control, by forcing an internalization of non-indigenous assumptions. Gautam's (2008) study of the imposition of Western human resource practices in Nepalese organizations, referred to earlier, is an example of such control, as is Simpson's (2008) research on how elder care in Aotearoa New Zealand is aligned more with Western models of market and commodification than with indigenous ideas of aging.

Through our discussions of these three conceptual commitments of postcolonial thought and the deep interconnections among ideas of space, discourse, knowledge, and organizing forms and practices, it is clear that while postcolonial thought holds considerable potential for the study of organizing and communicative practices, it is very rarely easy or comfortable. It's not easy to answer Shome and Hegde's (2002) call to examine "why conditions are what they are and how they can be undone or redone" (p. 250). Further, it can be too easy to argue that concerns with postcolonial subjectivity, organizing, and voice rest fully and solely within the empirical domain of sociology, anthropology, literature, political science, economics, and history. However, as Bhabha (cited in Mitchell, 1995) describes, any act of theorizing arises out of the need to create an alternative understanding of particular conditions that people inherit, in order to articulate other forms of emergent social and cultural identification.

Indeed, decolonizing subtle and ephemeral phenomena such as thought, being, discourses, and organizing practices requires time, concerted effort, and an awareness of the imbricated and implicated ways in which we come to know who and how we are as individuals and collectives. In the following section of the essay, we move away from postcolonial concepts to *postcolonial practices and processes,* which may ground further and future postcolonial deconstructive and imaginative intersections in organizational communication.

Organizing and Communicating in the Spaces In-Between: The Journey Continues

In an interview with Hegde and Shome (2006), Spivak contends that postcolonial theory not only examines a globalizing world with historical depth and complexity but also allows us to focus on flows (relying less on more established concepts of nation, state, and citizenship) to instead uncover nexuses, contradictions, and the situatedness of these concepts in contemporary times. Her constant question is, "What is the alternative?"

This is indeed a profound question that we grapple with in this section. In this chapter so far, we have focused on three particular commitments and points of theoretical attention: disrupting and reimagining spaces, resisting colonial discourses to rethink organizing principles, and decolonizing thought to reconfigure organizing forms of knowledge. Our own scholarly focus has grown out of these commitments as we have engaged with other scholars to work toward building more inclusive spaces, accounts, and ways of thinking about disciplinary origins, forms of constructing and disseminating knowledge, and their accompanying discourses. Our conversations and collaborations with a variety of people, both academic and nonacademic, have allowed us to look at the discursive contexts in which we see organizing practices form and transform.

It is in line with these conversations that we look ahead to the kinds of roles organizational communication scholars can play as new models, prototypes, and measures of social progress emerge in the social and organizational theaters of the 21st century. Toward what ends will/can/should scholarly energies be directed? What kinds of organizing and communicative phenomena will/can/should be addressed? With the boundaries between nations, cultures, and ethnicities blurring in a technology-fueled world of globalization as well as the increasing discursive space in the blurred zone, ideologically, theoretically, and practically, we suggest two future postcolonial practices in the following section on which organizational communication scholars could focus: reconceptualizing the theoretical realm of the *in-between* and reframing the practical process of *translation.*

Reconceptualizing the Space In-Between

Amidst the growing complexity of organizational communication, Bhabha's (1994) concept of the *space in-between* is a useful departure point from which to chart future postcolonial possibilities. Spaces in-between can emerge through decolonizing and translating processes, as indigenous thinkers and practitioners of a discipline (re) enter a field through alternative processes that, as Chatterjee (1995) claims, align new forms of knowledge with prior knowledge. Such spaces can be interpreted as either material/physical space, such as a borderland or as a neutral territory; a philosophical space between theories or a discursive space; and/or an opening or pause in a conversation where silence and future and past participants wait at the edges for their turn to speak. The nature of this space is open, inclusive, and yet to be determined. It exists as a multidimensional, unpredictable potentiality—as a forum where organizational meanings can be negotiated from multiple angles of history, culture, and context; a space of translation and negotiation, equal copresencing, and a complex relationality complicated by ambivalence, multiple tensions, and diverse affective dynamics (Bhabha, 1994; de Sousa Santos, 2007; Shohat & Stam, 1994).

Spaces in-between are, however, grounded in reciprocal recognition, dedicated to the question of how conditions can be undone and redone. In an illuminating interview (Mitchell, 1995), Bhabha argues that such productive and generative political and epistemic spaces can insert context into, as well as chronologically and epistemologically realign, events and their narratives, recovering their communal and public agency as well as the ethical-political subject. As a result, individuals and communities become able to rethink issues of social causality, contingency, and referentiality, especially with respect to representation. An interesting example of such rethinking lies in Okwori's (as cited in Nelson-Marsh, Broadfoot, & Munshi, 2008) work at the Theatre for Development in Nigeria. Okwori's work in participatory development communication involves gathering together community stakeholders to engage with a problem that faces them, creating a theatrical event for them that is left open-ended, and then performing it, with the community entering into the evolving improvisational piece to resolve the issues together. In this line of work, Okwori sets the stage through participatory action research with community members, then scripts out situations that the Theatre begins performing, inviting community members to act out possible solutions, decisions, and consequences. This method of encouraging collective voice and decision making enables community-designed and community-owned processes that aid successful development.

Land and language, in particular, are two contested spaces of in-betweenness. Physical space (or its more earthy representation, *land*) has been one of the principal fronts of colonial onslaught. Imperialism spread with the conquest of land across vast swathes of Asia, Africa, and Oceania, depriving multitudes of people of their sense of identity, freedom, and preferred forms of life and livelihood and reorganizing their worlds. Such acts continue in contemporary times and form much of the material with which postcolonial scholars work. Discussing postcolonial ecologies, DeLoughrey and Handley (2011) point out that two foundational postcolonial scholars emphasized the role of the land in anti-colonial struggles. They observe that "Franz Fanon identified the land as a primary site of postcolonial recuperation, sustainability, and dignity" while "Edward Said argued that the imagination was vital to liberating land from the restrictions of colonialism and, we might add, from neocolonial forms of globalization" (p. 3). This *imagined* land is the space in-between—a memory of the struggles that deal with the physical ravages wrought upon the earth by avaricious corporations (Shiva, 2002), the attempts by indigenous communities to reclaim nationhood (Lee, 2008), and the fight for survival by local communities in different parts of the world faced with proxy wars imposed on their lands by external forces.

How can we begin a postcolonial reconceptualization of the space in-between in such a context, recognizing that the act of nation building has always involved imagining land and language in specific ways? Is it as simple as just doing it differently or from another perspective? As Nkomo (2011) states, "Finding alternatives between colonized representations and counter-representations is not an easy project" (p. xx). Given the complexity of reconceptualizing spaces in-between, how can the process of translation further scholarly work done at the intersection of postcolonial thought and organizational communication?

Reframing the Process of Translation

The process of representation necessarily involves some sort of translation or transformation of substance, form, appearance, and/or language. When coupled with the positionality of the *outsider refugee* (Taylor, 2005), a theoretical and empirical focus on translation opens up a space for individuals to question how knowledge is constituted and how that may be different from the ways in which it is disseminated and the exclusionary nature of monolingualism as well as the relationship between processes and practices of management and mediation, especially in regard to cultural and linguistic practices (Srinivas, 2008).

The colonialist process of translation has historically allowed Western tropes and ways of thinking to be disseminated to the far corners of the earth. In organizational settings, the translation of Western corporate ideas has colonialized perceived corporate knowledge in the rest of the world. In fact, as organizational scholars Long and Mills (2008) explain, translation

> is a material phenomenon in which non-western cultures are subordinated and reconstructed to fit superimposed and alienating western ways of thinking and structuring. This is a process of objectification and reductionism; non-western peoples are translated into objects of control that possess a set of universal characteristics that are in opposition to the privileged qualities that the west attributes to itself. (p. 394)

This form of translation is inherently asymmetrical, for one form of knowledge is privileged over another. For example, in a postcolonial ethnographic description of a strategy-planning workshop run by a nongovernmental organization (NGO) in southern India, Srinivas (2008) described how facilitators struggled to get across the key messages of *strategy* and *mission and vision*, because these terms couldn't be easily translated into the local language of the participants: "They were trying hard to use a vocabulary alien to them, rather than develop their own, to describe what they were doing" (p. 340).

Postcolonial interventions provide some space for reframing translation. Successful NGOs, as Srinivas (2008) says, are the ones who "are able to inhabit the 'in-between,' speak two different types of language, perhaps with different emphases (say technocracy as well as community)" (p. 340). Translation, which is at the core of the "hybrid and negotiated quality of management practice" (Srinivas, 2008, p. 341), happens when discursive boundaries are crossed or transgressed (Bhabha in Mitchell, 1995). In this moment, Bhabha explains, neither theory nor experience is more powerful than the other. Instead, they exist in translation, and through their translation, both theory and experience are reconstructed.

Much of Bhabha's work in translation draws on Foucault's (1974) *conditions of emergence*, the point at which some event, object, or discourse becomes authorized and dominant, and Benjamin's (1969) *conditions of translation*, focusing on the ways in which abstract concepts such as identity become materially transformed and exist in a constant state of becoming. For Foucault (1974), the conditions of emergence for any discursive object appear in their overlaps, tensions, and relations between contexts or situations, groups, and communities, authorities of delimitation and grids of specification. As such, to understand discursive objects is to uncover the where, how, and who of constructed events, phenomena, or objects in existence.

Benjamin's (1969) work on the conditions of translation adds another analytical layer to this examination of events, proposing, as does Foucault, that scholars should not analyze individual dimensions or characteristics of a phenomenon but, instead, the totality of linguistic (or discursive) conditions in which it emerges or the multiple points of discursive infractions in a discursive formation. Discussing the process of linguistic translation specifically, Benjamin argued that real translation does not translate meaning but instead attempts to translate a word as close to its original form as possible, transferring not only syntax but its form of expressing a concept. Hence, Benjamin argues, translation is transparent and does not cover the original. In order to accomplish this form of translation, Benjamin proposed the necessity of capturing the ontological and temporal conditions of a word for interpretation and mutual understanding. In this way, difference has a particular specificity.

This form of translation is a conscious, deliberate exploration of difference between linguistic and discursive cultural systems. It encourages an ethic of responsibility (Slater, 2004), through which organizational communication scholars and practitioners can begin to develop

> a perspective which questions conceptualizations of terms such as "modernization," "civilization," "development" and "sovereignty" that fail to discuss the geopolitics of power, profiles the dynamic and relational nature of colonial and global power as continually, albeit differentially, a two-way process; and continues to discuss the centrality of the Third World periphery in the formation of the modern world as we know it. (p. 232)

Such a perspective, Slater (2004) goes on to explain, would recognize and respect other cultures and frames, encouraging a meaningful ethics of intersubjectivity that would enable people to be critical and different no matter their geopolitical positionality. It would also enable discussions of multiculturalism, racism, and colonialism that would highlight the ways in which they may be different according to context and yet relationally and discursively linked, highlighting the interethnic and international contradictions and hybridities that exist on what has, until now, been discussed as the margins or periphery (Shohat & Stam, 1994).

By combining processes of translation and the notion of in-betweenness, the *inter* of international, intercultural, or interaction can be considered a highly charged space, weighted with meaning (Bassnett, 2010). For many postcolonial writers, focusing on the space in-between facilitates the simultaneous reinvigoration of local languages and thoughts and their subversion of dominant languages and, by association, dominant organizational practices. Bassnett's (2010) work, for example, profiles the work of the Ivory Coast writer, Ahgmadou Kourouma, who thinks in his native tongue of Malinke but writes in French, liberating Malinke "through a process of translation that takes place in the act of writing" (p. 80). She cites Kourouma as saying, "I have, therefore, translated Malinke into French by breaking the French in order to find and restore an African rhythm" (as cited in Bassnett, 2010, p. 80).

The postcolonial notion of translation is, therefore, one of empowerment, where new meaning is created in a hybrid space rather than the mere reproduction of a colonialist master narrative. It is "constituted as a mediation that brings subaltern narratives into mainstream structures/sites of knowledge" and becomes a means to "disrupt neoliberal hegemony" and co-create "spaces of praxis in solidarity with subaltern communities" (Dutta & Pal, 2010, p. 364).

This process of translation calls for an expansion of the range of metaphors and language used in organizational settings that can allow multiple ways of crossing discursive as well as practical boundaries. The future of organizational communication, as we see it, lies in such an expansion in the range of metaphors, a range that not only draws on a variety of cultures, nations, and locales but also on the reconstituted metaphors that arise from the contestations of original ones.

Postcolonial Approaches to Organizational Communication: In-Conclusion(s)

> Sonny: Everything will be all right in the end . . . if it's not all right, then it's not the end. (Broadbent, Czernin, & Madden, 2011)
>
> Evelyn: Nothing here has worked out quite as I expected. Muriel: Most things don't. But sometimes what happens instead is the good stuff. (Broadbent et al., 2011)

The philosophical quirkiness of the Indian and English characters in *The Best Exotic Marigold Hotel*, a movie that depicts the interaction of Western and Eastern worldviews in a globalized age, reflects, in some ways, the theoretical complexity that postcolonial approaches bring to contemporary issues of organization and communication. As we have discussed, postcolonial scholarship has been many things to many people and is largely interdisciplinary in nature. Terms, ideas, and examples are complex and contextualized. Analytical concepts are vast and abstract concepts—thought, space, and discourse, for example—are interconnected, as we have shown. And yet this complexity of postcolonial thought, which mirrors the world in which we live, allows us, as Spivak so eloquently suggests, to uncover nexuses, contradictions, and the situatedness of established concepts of nation, state, and citizenship in contemporary times. Postcolonial scholars have focused their efforts on making visible diverse forms of history, nation building, particular and unequal forms of social and economic development, and the ways in which determinations of space, discourse, thought, and knowledge have organized our contemporary globalizing world *until now*. On what issues, contexts, and forces will scholarly attention and energies become focused in the future?

This chapter, at the intersection of postcolonial thought and organizational communication scholarship today, has been guided by two key postcolonial questions: "How can taken-for-granted dominant organizing and communicative practices and outcomes be undone and redone?" and "What is the alternative?" In particular, we have attempted to provide examples of scholarship that focus on the creation of spaces in-between and the examination of both *othering* and *pluralizing* forces at work. However, in our own experiences and as this chapter demonstrates, the dual deconstructive and imaginative impulses of postcolonial analyses in organizational communication remain unbalanced in contemporary scholarship.

Although postcolonial approaches to organizational communication are beginning to surface, these approaches are much more visible in management and organization studies, especially critical management studies. Is there a disciplinary lag in effect? Could postcolonial scholarship in organizational communication be following its cognate disciplines and drawing on their disciplinary credibility to ground its scholarly acceptance? Only time will tell. But as is evident in our own reviews of the literature, postcolonial scholarship, in general, needs to be reinvigorated for an even more critical and contextual look at organizations.

To address this need, we have drawn on Bhabha's concept of *spaces in-between* to focus on three central postcolonial commitments—disrupt and reimagine organizing space(s); resist colonialist discourse and rethink organizing practices; and decolonize thought and reconfigure organizing forms of knowledge. As we have discussed, these commitments are interwoven, implicating each other so that, like multiple facets of a diamond, one turn reveals another face to be explored. Analyses, therefore, cannot be singularly focused but are always already implicative of the other facets. It is this multifaceted nature of postcolonial lenses that simultaneously thwarts concise, linearly written scholarship and yet also creates imaginative alternatives.

The two postcolonial practices of *spaces in-between* and *translation* are paths forward in empirically examining the multifaceted nature of material and discursive flows in a globalizing world and their ontological, epistemological, and pragmatic priorities. Exploring and examining spaces in-between and processes of translation is, however, a genealogical project. Such a project requires scholars to examine conditions of emergence and points of discursive infractions for potential places of transformation and reorganizing, with the caveat that what may emerge at these junctures of time, space, and discourse may not be predictable and will probably be messy. It will be at these junctures that our own disciplinary structures around knowledge production will need to transform in order to capture the indeterminacy of work reflecting a dynamically evolving world. It is therefore our hope that the questions of how phenomena can be undone and redone, as well as the constant committed search for alternatives, will guide future scholarship in postcolonial organizational communication and enable scholars to harness both its deconstructive and imaginative impulses.

References

Alvesson, M., & Karreman, D. (2000). Varieties of discourse: On the study of organizations through discourse analysis. *Human Relations, 53*(9), 1125–1149.

Anderson, B. (1991). *Imagined communities: Reflections on the origins and spread of nationalism.* London, England: Verso.

Ashcraft, K. (2006). Falling from a humble perch? Rereading organizational communication studies with an attitude of alliance. *Management Communication Quarterly, 19*(4), 645–652.

Ashcraft, K., & Allen, B. (2003). The racial foundation of organizational communication. *Communication Theory, 13*(1), 5–38.

Ashcraft, K., & Mumby, D. (2004). *Reworking gender: A feminist communicology of organization.* Thousand Oaks, CA: SAGE.

Ashcroft, B., Griffiths, G., & Tiffin, H. (Eds.). (1995). *The post-colonial studies reader.* London, England: Routledge.

Ashcroft, B., Griffiths, G., & Tiffin, H. (2002). *The empire writes back: Theory and practice in post-colonial literature.* London, England: Routledge.

Banerjee, S. B., & Linstead, S. (2004). Masking subversion: Neocolonial embeddedness in anthropological accounts of indigenous management. *Human Relations, 57*(2), 221–247.

Banerjee, S. B., & Prasad, A. (2008). Introduction to the special issue on 'critical reflections on management and organizations: A postcolonial perspective.' *Critical Perspectives on International Business, 4*(2/3), 90–98.

Bassnett, S. (2010). Postcolonial translations. In S. Chew & D. Richards (Eds.), *A concise companion to postcolonial literature* (pp. 78–96). Chichester, England: Wiley-Blackwell.

Battiste, M. (2008). Research ethics for protecting indigenous knowledge and heritage. In N. K. Denzin, Y. S. Lincoln, & L. T. Smith (Eds.), *Handbook of critical and indigenous methodologies* (pp. 497–509). Thousand Oaks, CA: SAGE.

Benjamin, W. (1969). *Illuminations: Essays and reflections.* New York, NY: Schocken.

Bhabha, H. (1983). The other question. *Screen, 24*(6), 18–36.

Bhabha, H. (1990). DissemiNation: Time, narrative and the margins of the modern nation. In H. Bhabha (Ed.), *Nation and narration* (pp. 291–321). London, England: Routledge.

Bhabha, H. (1994). *The location of culture.* London, England: Routledge.

Bhabha, H. (1996). Culture's in-between. In S. Hall & P. du Gay (Eds.), *Questions of cultural identity* (pp. 53–60). London, England: SAGE.

Broadbent, G., Czernin, P. (Producers), & Madden, J. (Director). (2011). *The best exotic marigold hotel* [Motion Picture]. London, UK: Participant Media.

Broadfoot, K. J., & Munshi, D. (2007a). Afterword: In search of a polyphony of voices. *Management Communication Quarterly, 21*(2), 281–283.

Broadfoot, K. J., & Munshi. D. (2007b). Diverse voices, alternative rationalities: Imagining forms of postcolonial organizational communication. *Management Communication Quarterly, 21*(2), 249–267.

Broadfoot, K., Munshi, D., & Nelson-Marsh, N. (2010). COMMUNEcation: A rhizomatic tale of participatory technology, postcoloniality and professional community, *New Media & Society, 12*(5), 797–812.

Cao, Q. (2007). Western representations of the other. In Shi-Xu (Ed.), *Discourse as cultural struggle* (pp. 105–122). Hong Kong: Hong Kong University Press.

Castle, G. (2001). Editor's introduction: Resistance and complicity in postcolonial studies. In G. Castle (Ed.), *Postcolonial discourses: An anthology* (pp. xi–xxiii). Oxford, UK: Blackwell.

Chakrabarty, D. (1992, Winter). Postcoloniality and the artifice of history: Who speaks for "Indian" pasts? [Special issue]. *Representations, 37,* 1–26.

Chakrabarty, D. (2000). *Provincializing Europe: Postcolonial thought and historical difference.* Princeton, NJ: Princeton University Press.

Chatterjee, P. (1986). *Nationalist thought and the colonial world: A derivative discourse?* London, England: Zed Books.

Chatterjee, P. (1995). *Texts of power: Emerging disciplines in colonial Bengal.* Minneapolis: University of Minnesota Press.

Cheung, L. L. (2008). Let the "other" speak for itself: Understanding Chinese employees from their own perspectives. *Critical Perspectives on International Business, 4*(2/3), 277–306.

Cooren, F. (2006). The organizational communication-discourse tilt: A refugee's perspective. *Management Communication Quarterly, 19*(4), 653–660.

de Maria, B. (2008). Neo-colonialism through measurement: A critique of the corruption perception index. *Critical Perspectives on International Business, 4*(2/3), 184–202.

de Sousa Santos, B. (2007). *Beyond abyssal thinking: From global lines to ecologies of knowledges.* Retrieved from http://www.ces.uc.pt/bss/documentos/AbyssalThinking.pdf

Deetz, S. (1992). *Democracy in an age of corporate colonization: Developments in communication and politics of everyday life.* Albany, NY: SUNY Press.

Deetz, S. (2001). Conceptual foundations. In F. M. Jablin & L. L. Putnam (Eds.), *The new handbook of organizational communication: Advances in theory, research and methods* (pp. 3–46). Thousand Oaks, CA: SAGE.

Deetz, S. (2003). Corporate governance, communication, and getting social value into the decisional chain. *Management Communication Quarterly, 16*(4), 606–611.

DeLoughrey, E., & Handley, G. (2011). *Postcolonial ecologies: Literatures of the environment.* New York, NY: Oxford University Press.

Dutta, M. J. (2011). *Communicating social change: Structure, culture, and agency.* New York, NY: Routledge.

Dutta, M. J., & Pal, M. (2010). Dialog theory in marginalized settings: A subaltern studies approach. *Communication Theory, 20*(4), 363–386.

Dutta, M. J., & Pal, M. (2011). Public relations and marginalization in a global context: A postcolonial critique. In N. Bardhan & K. Weaver (Eds.), *Public relations in global cultural contexts.* New York, NY: Routledge.

Fanon, F. (1967). *Black skin, white masks* (C. Markmann, Trans.). New York, NY: Grove.

Fanon, F. (1965). *The wretched of the earth.* New York, NY: Grove Press.

Foucault, M. (1974). *The archaeology of knowledge and the discourses on language.* New York, NY: Pantheon Books.

Foucault, M. (1984). What is enlightenment? In P. Rabinow (Ed.), *The Foucault reader* (pp. 32–50). New York, NY: Pantheon.

Frenkel, M., & Shenhav, Y. (2003). *Decolonizing organization theory: Between orientalism and occidentalism.* Paper presented at the third Critical Management Studies conference at Lancaster University, Lancaster, Lancashire, United Kingdom.

Frenkel, M., & Shenhav, Y. (2006). From binarism back to hybridity: A postcolonial reading of management and organization studies. *Organization Studies, 27*(6), 855–876.

Gandhi, L. (1998). *Postcolonial theory: A critical introduction.* St. Leonard's, NSW, Australia: Allen & Unwin.

Ganesh, S. (2011). Difference and cultural identities in Aotearoa New Zealand. In D. Mumby (Ed.), *Reframing difference in organizational communication studies* (pp. 173–190). Thousand Oaks, CA: SAGE.

Ganesh, S., Zoller, H., & Cheney, G. (2005). Transforming resistance, broadening our boundaries: Critical organizational communication meets globalization from below. *Communication Monographs, 72*(2), 169–191.

Gautam, D. (2008). A study of developing human resource practices in Nepal. [Part of K. J. Broadfoot, T. Cockburn, C. Cockburn-Wootten, M. do Carmo Reis, D. K. Gautam, A. Malshe, . . . N. Srinivas, A mosaic of visions, daydreams, and memories: Diverse inlays of organizing and communicating from around the globe], *Management Communication Quarterly, 22*(2), 335–338.

Ghosh, A. (2008). *Sea of poppies.* New York, NY: Farrar, Straus & Giroux.

Ghosh, A. (2011). *River of smoke.* London, England: John Murray.

Goldberg, D. T., & Quayson, A. (2002). *Relocating postcolonialism.* Oxford, UK: Blackwell.

Hall, M. L. (2010). Constructions of leadership at the intersection of discourse, power, and culture: Jamaican managers' narratives of leading in a postcolonial cultural context. *Management Communication Quarterly, 25*(4), 612–643.

Hegde, R. S., & Shome, R. (2006). Postcolonial scholarship—Productions and directions: An interview with Gayatri Chakravorty Spivak. *Communication Theory, 12*(3), 271–286.

Jack, G., Westwood, R., Srinivas, N., & Sardar, Z. (2011). Deepening, broadening, and reasserting a postcolonial interrogative space in organizational studies. *Organization, 18*(3), 275–302.

Jackson, T. (2012). Postcolonialism and organizational knowledge in the wake of China's presence in Africa: Interrogating South-South relations. *Organization, 19*(2), 181–204.

Lamming, G. (1991). *In the castle of my skin*. Ann Arbor: University of Michigan Press.

Lee, L. L. (2008). Reclaiming indigenous intellectual, political, and geographic space: A path for Navajo nationhood. *American Indian Quarterly, 32*(1), 96–110.

Long, B., & Mills, A. (2008). Globalization, postcolonial theory, and organizational analysis: Lessons from the Rwanda genocide. *Critical Perspectives on International Business, 4*(4), 389–409.

Loomba, A. (1998). *Colonialism/Postcolonialism*. London, England: Routledge.

Mir, R., Banerjee, S. B., & Mir, A. (2008). Hegemony and its discontents: A critical analysis of organizational knowledge transfer. *Critical Perspectives on International Business, 4*(2/3), 203–227.

Mir, R., Mir, A., & Upadhyaya, P. (2003). Toward a postcolonial reading of organizational control. In A. Prasad (Ed.), *Postcolonial theory and organizational analysis: A critical engagement* (pp. 47–74). New York, NY: Palgrave Macmillan.

Mitchell, W. J. T. (1995). Interview with cultural theorist Homi Bhabha. *Artforum, 33*(7), 80–84.

Mongia, P. (1996). (Ed.). *Contemporary postcolonial theory: A reader*. London, England: Arnold.

Moore-Gilbert, B. (1997). *Postcolonial theory: Contexts, practices, politics*. London, England: Verso.

Mumby, D. K. (1997). The problem of hegemony: Rereading Gramsci for organizational communication studies. *Western Journal of Communication, 61*(4), 343–375.

Mumby, D. (2011). What's cooking in organizational discourse studies? A response to Alvesson and Karreman. *Human Relations, 64*(9), 1147–1161.

Mumby, D., & Putnam, L. L. (1992). The politics of emotion: A feminist reading of bounded rationality. *Academy of Management Review, 17*(3), 465–486.

Munshi, D. (2005). Through the subject's eye: Situating the other in discourses of diversity. In G. Cheney & G. Barnett (Eds.), *International and multicultural organizational communication* (pp. 45–70). Creskill, NJ: Hampton Press.

Munshi, D., Broadfoot, K. J., & Tuhiwai-Smith, L. (2011). Decolonizing communication ethics: A framework for communicating otherwise. In G. Cheney, S. May, & D. Munshi (Eds.), *Handbook of communication ethics* (pp. 119–132). New York, NY: Routledge.

Munshi, D., & Edwards, L. (2011). Understanding 'race' in/and public relations: Where do we start and where should we go? *Journal of Public Relations Research, 23*(4), 349–367.

Munshi, D., & Kurian, P. A. (2007). The case of the subaltern public: A postcolonial investigation of corporate social responsibility's (O)missions. In S. May, G. Cheney, & J. Roper (Eds.), *The debate over corporate social responsibility* (pp. 438–447). New York, NY: Oxford University Press,

Nelson-Marsh, N., Broadfoot, K., & Munshi, D. (2008). COMMUNEcating in the spaces in-between: Creating new understandings of organizing and communicative practice around the globe. *Management Communication Quarterly, 22*(2), 313–321.

Nkomo, S. (2011). A postcolonial *and* anti-colonial reading of 'African' leadership and management in organization studies: Tensions, contradictions and possibilities. *Organization, 18*(3), 365–386.

Pal, M., & Dutta, M. J. (2008). Theorizing resistance in a global context: Processes, strategies and tactics in communication scholarship. In C. Beck (Ed.), *Communication yearbook* (vol. 32, 41–87). New York, NY: Routledge.

Parsons, R. (2008). We are all stakeholders now: The influence of Western discourses of "community engagement" in an Australian Aboriginal community. *Critical Perspectives on International Business, 4*(2/3), 99–126.

Prasad, A. (2003). The gaze of the other: Postcolonial theory and organizational analysis. In A. Prasad (Ed.), *Postcolonial theory and organizational analysis* (pp. 3–43). New York, NY: Palgrave Macmillan.

Prasad, A., & Prasad, P. (2003). The postcolonial imagination. In A. Prasad (Ed.), *Postcolonial theory and organizational analysis* (pp. 283–295). New York, NY: Palgrave Macmillan.

Prichard, C. (2006). Global politics, academic dispositions, and the tilting of organizational communication: A provocation to a debate. *Management Communication Quarterly, 19*(4), 638–644.

Rao, S., & Wasserman, H. (2007). Global media ethics revisited: A postcolonial critique. *Global Media and Communication, 3*(1), 29–50.

Said, E. (1978). *Orientalism*. New York, NY: Vintage Books.

Schwabenland, C., & Tomlinson, F. (2008). Managing diversity or diversifying management? *Critical Perspectives on International Business, 4*(2/3), 320–333.

Shiva, V. (2002). *Water wars: Privatization, pollution, and profit.* Cambridge, MA: Southend Press.

Shohat, E., & Stam, R. (1994). *Unthinking Eurocentrism: Multiculturalism and the media.* London, England: Routledge.

Shome, R. (1996). Postcolonial interventions in the rhetorical canon: An "other" view. *Communication Theory, 6*(1), 40–59.

Shome, R. (2003). Space matters: The power and practice of space. *Communication Theory, 13*(1), 39–56.

Shome, R., & Hegde, R. S. (2002). Postcolonial approaches to communication: Charting the terrain, engaging the intersection. *Communication Theory, 12*(3), 249–270.

Simpson, M. (2008). Voices and visions of organizing elders in Aotearoa New Zealand. [Part of K. J. Broadfoot, T. Cockburn, C. Cockburn-Wootten, M. do Carmo Reis, D. K. Gautam, A. Malshe, . . . N. Srinivas. A mosaic of visions, daydreams, and memories: Diverse inlays of organizing and communicating from around the globe], *Management Communication Quarterly, 22*(2), 328–332.

Slater, D. (2004). *Geopolitics and the post-colonial: Rethinking north-south relations.* Oxford, UK: Blackwell Publishing.

Smith, L. T. (1999). *Decolonizing methodologies: Research and indigenous peoples.* London, England: Zed Books.

Spivak, G. C. (1999). *A critique of postcolonial reason: Toward a history of the vanishing present.* Cambridge, MA: Harvard University Press.

Srinivas, N. (2008). Linguistic mediation in the global construction and dissemination of knowledge [Part of K. J. Broadfoot, T. Cockburn, C. Cockburn-Wootten, M. do Carmo Reis, D. K. Gautam, A. Malshe, . . . N. Srinivas, A mosaic of visions, daydreams, and memories: Diverse inlays of organizing and communicating from around the globe]. *Management Communication Quarterly, 22*(2), 338–341.

Stohl, C. (2001). Globalizing organizational communication. In F. Jablin & L. Putnam (Eds.), *The new handbook of organizational communication: Advances in theory, research, and methods* (pp. 323–375). Thousand Oaks, CA: SAGE.

Taylor, J. R. (2005). In praise of ambiguity. *Management Communication Quarterly, 19*(2), 299–306.

Thiong'O, N. (1964). *Weep not, child.* London, England: Heinemann.

Thiong'O, N. (1967). *A grain of wheat.* London, England: Heinemann.

Thiong'O, N. (1986). *Decolonising the mind: The politics of language in African literature.* Nairobi, Kenya: East African Publishers.

Viswanathan, G. (1987). The beginnings of English literary study in British India. *Oxford Literary Review, 9*(1/2), 2–26.

Westwood, R. (2006). International business and management studies as an orientalist discourse: A postcolonial critique. *Critical Perspectives on International Business, 2*(2), 91–113.

Young, R. (2003). *Postcolonialism: A very short introduction.* Oxford, UK: Oxford University Press.

CHAPTER 7

Approaches to the Communicative Constitution of Organizations

Boris H. J. M. Brummans, François Cooren, Daniel Robichaud, and James R. Taylor[1]

How does an organization come into being? How does it continue, or why does it cease to exist? In other words, what *is* an organization? How does it become an organization and reproduce itself, even as its component members come and go? Following the etymological origin of the word *constitution* (implying *to cause to stand, set up, fix, place, establish, set in order, form something new, resolve,* or *appoint to an office*), a number of scholars have explored these kinds of ontological questions over the past decades by concentrating on the role of communication in the production and reproduction of organizations. In turn, a field of inquiry, now referred to as the *communicative constitution of organizations* (CCO), has been gaining traction in organizational communication studies and beyond (see Ashcraft, Kuhn, & Cooren, 2009; Bisel, 2010a, 2010b; Cooren, 2000, 2007; Cooren, Kuhn, Cornelissen, & Clark, 2011; Cooren, Taylor, & Van Every, 2006; Fairhurst & Putnam, 1999, 2004; Putnam & Nicotera, 2009, 2010; Robichaud & Cooren, 2013; Taylor & Van Every, 2000, 2011). What sets this research apart from other areas of inquiry is its novel ways of theorizing and analyzing how organizations as discursive-material configurations are reproduced and coproduced through ongoing interactions.

In this chapter, we map this emerging field, knowing full well that any such attempt is fraught with difficulties, since any mapping exercise implies representing reality from a point of view that serves certain interests and marginalizes others. With this consideration in mind, we begin by outlining what we consider to be the major trends in CCO research today. CCO scholars may all agree that communication constitutes organizations, but they differ in their understanding and examination of its organizing properties (Bisel, 2010a). Thus we will discuss three different approaches to the study of these properties: (1) McPhee's structurationist approach, (2) the Montréal School approach, and (3) the emerging Luhmannian systems approach. While one of our aims is to show how these approaches vary in terms of their characteristics, assumptions, and influences on the field, the main purpose of this chapter is to explicate and set forth the Montréal School approach as a theoretical lens for understanding CCO; hence, the bulk of it focuses on this perspective. Since other chapters in this volume elaborate on structuration theory and CCO, our discussion of McPhee's approach is reduced (see McPhee, Poole, & Iverson, Chapter 3). Finally, we compare and contrast the three approaches to illustrate the growing theoretical development of CCO as a field in and of itself.

Approaches to CCO Research

McPhee's Structurationist Approach

One approach to understanding what an organization is and what constitutes it draws from McPhee's application of structuration theory (McPhee & Zaug, 2000). This approach begins with the presumption that an organization is constituted by coproducing it "as an ensemble of rules and resources" in which organizational members draw on their interactions with each other (McPhee, Corman, & Iverson, 2007, p. 135). Interactions depend on more or less taken-for-granted routines, which enable members (human agents) to "position themselves, claim knowledgeability, and rationalize their arguments and stands" (p. 136).

McPhee's Four Flows Model

McPhee's Four Flows Model (McPhee & Zaug, 2000, 2009) is grounded in these structurationist assumptions and forms the core of this approach. As we will show in the next section, this model postulates that different interdependent communication processes (flows) constitute an organization.

McPhee and Zaug (2000) set forth four different flows that together produce an organization: membership negotiation, reflexive self-structuring, activity coordination, and institutional positioning. *Membership negotiation* occurs especially during the socialization of newcomers, which involves the negotiation of different kinds of boundaries through instruction, storytelling, and dismissive reactions as well as introduction and initiation (McPhee & Iverson, 2009). Membership negotiation is constitutive of an organization because it "necessarily makes reference, however indirectly, to the organization" (p. 66). For example, during this process, people may impose boundaries by using *we* in an exclusive way or by controlling who can speak on behalf of the organization.

The second flow, *reflexive self-structuring*, occurs through declarative illocutionary acts (utterances inciting certain kinds of action; see Searle, 1995) that enable a group of people "to represent themselves as (part of) an organization" (McPhee & Iverson, 2009, p. 73). This self-structuring has constitutive force, in part, because it produces a system of signs (e.g., jargon) that serve as resources for creating coherence across different discourse episodes.

The third flow, *activity coordination*, involves the negotiation of task roles through self-structuring of interactions as individual members develop a sense of each other's "manifest activity to know what is called for from them, and to make their contributions fit" with each other (p. 79). Hence, the constitutive force of this flow resides in the integration of interactions and work processes.

Finally, *institutional positioning* entails an array of different communication processes through which public relations, investor relations, labor relations, and so on are managed, such as various forms of organizational *face-presentation* (see Cheney & Christensen, 2001), environmental exploration, and negotiation. These processes "constitute the organization as a sign, with a recognizable and significant place in the local ecology of organizations" (p. 82).

McPhee's Notion of "Text"

Similar to other CCO scholars, McPhee emphasizes the importance of texts in the CCO, and grounds his conceptions in Giddens's (1984) work. A text, McPhee (2004) claims, needs to be defined in a rather strict sense as "a relatively permanently inscribed symbolic formulation" (p. 365) and therefore does not include everyday activities or embodied performances. Thus text is distinct form other forms of interaction "because it is a vital precondition for the development and continuing existence of organizations as we commonly conceive of them":

> [As] an enduring inscribed record of organizational arrangements, . . . [a text] is a common if not necessary medium for stability of membership, relationships, and roles. It is the typical medium for organizing and organizational inception. It is the medium for legitimate stipulation of the formal structure, which in turn shapes power relationships and generates multiple sites and perspectives. Finally, enduring formulation is the medium of information storage and processing, which ground the institutional reflexivity that gives organizations their amazing power in society. (p. 365)

To gain insight into the constitution of an organization, McPhee argues that it is important to study how self-reflexive human agents create and use texts but are also constrained by them. "Perhaps the biggest change in organizational life in developed countries," he notes, "is our growing powers and practices to work with texts." Accordingly, our conceptualization of agency needs to account for the "interpretive powers to forge and understand texts," yet also "to act on them and react to them in meaningful ways" (p. 367).

The Influence of the Four Flows Approach

McPhee's approach has had considerable influence on organizational communication scholars' ways of understanding the communicative constitution of organizations. For example, McPhee and Zaug's model provided the organizing framework for Putnam and Nicotera's (2009) often-cited book, *Building Theories of Organization*. This model also offered a basis for Lammers's (2011) research on institutional messages and logics (see also Lammers & Barbour, 2006), Schumate and O'Connor's (2010) research on nongovernmental organization (NGO)-corporate alliance communication, and Ballard and Gossett's (2008) work on nonstandard work relationships, such as part-time employment or telework.

Browning et al. (Browning, Greene, Sitkin, Sutcliffe, & Obstfeld, 2009; Browning, Sutcliffe, Sitkin, Obstfeld, & Greene, 2000) provide some compelling illustrations that demonstrate the value of the Four Flows Model. For example, in a study of an Air Force maintenance squadron, Browning et al. (2009) reveal how *constitutive complexity* (Mitchell, 2003) emerges when one or more of the four flows blend or overlap. To illustrate this claim, the authors describe, for instance, how membership negotiation ("Who are we?") merges with activity coordination ("What are we doing?") when airplane technicians routinely walk around a plane after it has been repaired in order to assure that no objects are lying around that could potentially be sucked into the jet engine. By coordinating their activities in this way, technicians demonstrate their concern for the safety of pilots, who are seen as *blue-suiters* just like themselves, and thereby contribute to the constitution of the Air Force family culture and their own role or position in it. Thus Browning et al. show that the merging of flows may result in "synergistic processes" by combining "methods of controlling structures to produce reliable outcomes with variation to produce new information and learning" (p. 107).

Moreover, Lutgen-Sandvik and McDermott (2008) drew on McPhee's model to investigate how a community women's center came into being and persisted as an employee-abusive organization (EAO) through the flow of abusive messages. In addition to the four flows, their research shows how a fifth flow, referred to as the *syncretic superstructure*, "a shifting macro system of meaning schemas from which organizations emerge and in which they are suspended" (p. 310), contributes to the reproduction of EAOs.

In spite of research like this, Koschmann (2011) notes that McPhee's four flows approach is widely cited, but "only a handful of empirical studies . . . actually engage their work and make a substantive contribution to this line of CCO theorizing" (p. 144). Other scholars critique this approach in terms of its scope and lack of precision as far as theorizing the constitutive force of communication is concerned. For example, Sillince (2010) has argued that the flows model can also apply to markets, networks, communities, or social movements and therefore does "not satisfactorily distinguish between organizational and other collective forms" (p. 134). Bisel (2010a) has made a similar argument by claiming that communication "is a necessary condition for constituting organizing" in this model, "but it is not sufficient to ensure organizing will be called into being" (p. 129). Putnam and Nicotera (2010) maintained, however, that the flows need to be treated as "a texture of practices" and that "any one of them [needs to be envisioned] as a prototype rather than a necessary and sufficient condition of an organization" (p. 161).

Perhaps the strongest critics of McPhee's work are scholars associated with what has come to be known as *the Montréal School* of organizational communication research (Brummans, 2006; see also Fairhurst & Putnam, 1999, 2004). For example, Taylor (2009), the school's founder, believes that the flows model does not provide a precise enough theory of how organization emerges *in* communication (see also Dewey, 1944). As we will show, Montréal School researchers take an inductive approach rather than McPhee's deductive one, demonstrating how an organization emerges through "micro-associations between humans and non-humans" (Cooren & Fairhurst, 2009, p. 142) that scale up through a dynamic of translations.

The Montréal School Approach

The Montréal School dates from the initiation of a new doctoral program in 1987 at the Université de Montréal but is becoming increasingly international in its membership (see below). From the start, the program reflected influences that distinguish it from mainstream perspectives in organizational communication (see Smith, 1993). Its continental influences are evident: Derrida, Greimas, Latour, and Ricoeur. This CCO approach is also distinct in its emphasis on ethnographic methods, appropriation of cybernetics and complexity theory, and continuing focus on narrative and speech act theory. Moreover, it draws on the grounded-in-practice ideas of pragmatists such as Dewey, Mead, and Peirce as well as the ideas of Garfinkel, Labov, Sacks, Schegloff, and Wittgenstein. Perhaps not surprising in a francophone program located in a predominantly English-speaking continent, the role of language and discourse has been a preoccupation of Montréal researchers ever since the school's inception, including an emphasis on the formative influence of language on the processes and structuring of organization.

A convenient starting point in an analysis of some of the core ideas the Montréal School has developed is a model of organization that Taylor (1999, 2000a, 2001a) first proposed and that is shown here, updated to reflect current research, in Figure 7.1. The schema originally appeared in the same issue of the *Electronic Journal of Communication* in which McPhee and Zaug's (2000, 2009) Four Flows Model was published.

Organization as a Dynamic of Four Translations

Taylor's schema differs from McPhee and Zaug's model by focusing on a four-translation image of organizational communication. Translation involves more than a change from one position to another (flow). It implies transformation both in medium and in form, one that becomes a new lexicon (Guralnik, 1964).

Figure 7.1 Organization as a Dynamic of Four Translations

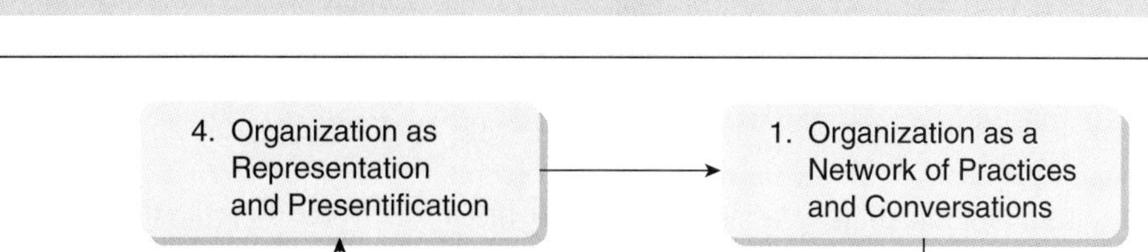

Adapted from Taylor, 1999, 2000b, 2001a, and revised.

Translation loses distinctions but also adds new readings that conform to the realities of the new situation and its favored ways of making sense (Eco, 2003). It is therefore a *betrayal*—in the Italian proverb, "*Tradurre è tradire.*" Transaction-grounded understandings in one context are both lost and added in a new one. Both *upkeying* and *downkeying* (Goffman, 1974) are involved (see also Fauré, Brummans, Giroux, & Taylor, 2010; Taylor & Van Every, 2011; Vollmer, 2007). A focus on translation foregrounds the inductive stitching together of a multiverse of communicative practices that scale up to compose an organization, then to constitute it as a person, whereas an emphasis on flows highlights the deductively derived types of communicative processes that are necessary "for complex organization to exist" and for it to "have the impact it does on society" (McPhee & Zaug, 2000, 2009, p. 29).

Figure 7.1 depicts the four translations that situate the focus of the Montréal School. Which manifestation of organization shown in this schema is emphasized depends on a researcher's point of view. Our explanation begins arbitrarily with organization as a network of situated local practices and their associated conversational patterns (Box 1).

Organization as a Network of Practices and Conversations. The term *network of practices* refers to the situated activities (and their associated conversations) that accomplish the work of the organization. Doing the work of a contemporary organization involves a transactional infrastructure that creates a web of mutual obligations, linking complementary practices of two (or more) human agents who co-orient by focusing on a single (and shared) object (Taylor & Van Every, 2000). For example, surgeons rely on laboratories for their operational data. The laboratories are, in turn, justified by their contribution to the doctors. Physicians need nurses and vice versa. They all count on someone, an administrator, to maintain the facility that they work in, the infrastructure of a hospital. The embedding of these many transactions is predicated on an even more basic one: treating patients, the beneficiaries of medical practice. Complementary interdependencies are not only transactional, they imply a tacit (and sometimes explicit) contract. Obligations are created.

Linkages between the practices also exhibit what Taylor (1995, 2000b, 2005) calls *worldview* (see also Brummans, 2013). Why the *view* in worldview? Because, in Taylor's (2000b) words, "Doctors and patients simply do not see the hospital world in the same way. Nor does a filmmaker have the same take on filmmaking as the lab that processes her film" (p. 1). Nor, he might have added, do professors and students (or parents and children) see things through the same lens. Worldview is thus not a property of a faith or an ideology. It reflects a role that is defined by a two-party transaction. In Taylor's (2000b) words,

> There will *never be less than two* worldviews on any event involving communication, and *never more than two*. Two, and *only* two . . . [W]hen as few as two people engage in communication each participant must independently foreground what is occurring but, in doing so, each brings to the encounter their own background frame, depending on their purposes, their expectations, their previously established assumptions about what to expect. They literally see the conversation in contrasting ways. Thus, although both participate in the "same" event they never experience it as the same. Each interprets it through a different lens. (p. 1, emphasis in original)

Worldview is correlated with a practice and an attitude that are institutionally grounded and require a pattern of communication that candidates must learn if they are to be admitted into the practice (Drew & Heritage, 1992). The view reflects the logic of the activity, that is, dealing with patients that demand communication skills that doctors have to learn.

As Taylor, Cooren, Giroux, and Robichaud (1996, p. 231) wrote, "An organization . . . is a set of transactional relationships, mediated by interaction: people making requests of others, promising things, passing judgment on others' performances, promoting and demoting, hiring and firing, entering into contractual arrangements." Cooren and Taylor (1997) similarly wrote that "there will be no object constituted (and thus no organization) in the absence of its [i.e., the object] being transferred in a transaction, with a source and a recipient" (p. 237).

The connotation of *transaction* or *co-orientation* is that of a two-way or ditransitive set of obligations with respect to a valued object (Taylor & Van Every, 2000). The transaction organizes the performances of members by establishing mutual, if always negotiable, commitments. Not only human agents are involved in maintaining the relationship. Transactions "allow for the possibility of many orders of actant, some individual, some collective or corporate, some human, some nonhuman. The 'organization' is an effect of the 'organizing,' not its progenitor" (Cooren & Taylor, 1997, p. 237; note that *actant* refers to the many agents that enable transactions, not all human).

Transactional protocols, because they link two worldviews (that of an agent and of a beneficiary), have to be negotiated. Güney's research (2006; Taylor & Van Every, 2011), for example, offers an ethnographic account of a dispute involving specialized hardware and software centers, engaged in a contested negotiation over whose function would be primary and whose secondary in the development of a management-inspired new information technology (IT) system. Güney's research confirmed Bateson's (1935, 1972) perception of the *schismogenetic* risks inherent in transactional relations; that is, they can degenerate into either domination or conflict. In a different study, one that focused on local hospital officials and representatives of Doctors without Borders in the Democratic Republic of the Congo, Cooren and colleagues also portrayed tensions as arising from ambiguity regarding whose responsibilities took precedence over whose and who had authority over what (see Benoit-Barné & Cooren, 2009; Cooren, Brummans, & Charrieras, 2008; Cooren, Matte, Taylor, & Vásquez, 2007). Their research illustrated another feature of organization as well in that the boundary between *in* and *out*, internal and external, is fluid. That is, transactional negotiations that spill over the borders to link the organization to its environment are a normal feature of practice (see also Brown & Duguid, 2000).

Organization as Mapping Collective Experience Through Distanciation. A second concern of the Montréal School is to explain how the many situated *local* domains of practice become transformed into a single *collective* actor. Two steps are involved: First, the experience of the many situated practices must be mapped into a verbal representation that will furnish a composite image of the whole organization. Second, the readings thus generated must be transformed again by writing a narrative that expresses the point of view of the organization *itself* as a single unity, where "a collective identity begins to take shape" (Taylor et al., 1996, p. 24). This progressive *distanciation* (Ricoeur, 1981) implies a shift of scale from the many to one that is enabled by *metacommunication*, defined as communication *about* communication (Robichaud, Giroux, & Taylor, 2004; Watzlawick, Beavin, & Jackson, 1967).

The transformation involved is described by Robichaud et al. (2004) this way:

> It is crucial . . . to recognize the progressive construction of the city-as-actor—a voice translating many different voices—as the conversation . . . develops. . . . [W]e are not witnessing merely a succession of multiple opinions and narratives. . . . [W]e take language use to be [the] actual site where organizing occurs. . . . [T]his organizing lies first and foremost in the possibility of meta-conversation—in the process by which the frames are themselves being framed. . . . The recursive property of communication allows each of the participants . . . to take both the subjects of conversation offered by the participants and the narrative frames in which they are embedded and to turn them into a larger meta-narrative constituting the city as a discursive entity. (pp. 629–630)

This research was based on Robichaud's (2004) study of municipal government, in which he recorded a public meeting convoked by the mayor of the borough to allow citizens to air their grievances, based on their own neighborhood's experiences. The mayor listened sympathetically and then spun his own story, involving unions, other municipalities, and state government, with whom he had to deal. He presented himself as a sympathetic ally of citizens; that is, his story was not "a counter-narrative to the citizens' stories; instead he offered a 'meta-story' enfolding them" (p. 630). His sensemaking incorporated the citizens as part of the city.

> In other words, the mayor [did] a lot more than [adjust] his discourse to the expressed preferences of his audience; through the meta-conversation, he reconstruct[ed], along with the citizens, the city as an organization. . . .[Thus] this entity [wa]s brought into existence. (p. 630)

Organization as Authoring the Organization and Its Purposes Through Textualization. To explain how an organization comes to be *authored* or turned into a text, Taylor et al. (1996, p. 24) again drew on Ricoeur's (1981) concept of *distanciation*. Interpretation of action by its translation into text further alienates the *said* from the now-even-more-distant *saying*. The text does this by a decontextualization of actual practices, transforming them into a symbolic equivalent that lends itself to global planning (e.g., see Sergi, 2013; Spee & Jarzabkowski, 2011). A new phenomenon emerges in the construction of an incorporated body whose members are no longer an *I* and a *you* (engaged in a face-to-face conversation) but have been objectified (seen as *us* and *them, the employees, the union*, etc.). The initial grounded-in-practice embedding of the organization in the materiality of work becomes less salient. Codes of conduct emerge, such as those that define professional practice, denuded of what is specific to this situation or that but applicable across the board. Situations are grouped into classes, allowing for bureaucratic instruments, such as manuals of procedure. The text becomes extracted from the tangible realities of local, down-to-earth practice. It is this phase of distanciation that produces "a reified representation of what is no longer a situated set of conversations but what has instead become an organizational template so abstract that it can be taken to represent not just some but all the conversations it refers to" (Taylor et al., 1996, p. 26).

The newly authored text has, however, one key advantage—it enables dissemination of the organization's intentions to a varied population that includes both its own members and other individuals and organizations that make up a larger society. It also serves as a "basis for standardization—and for organization in its contemporary postmodern, globalized guise" (Taylor et al., 1996, p. 25). Distanciation thus leads to the authorship of the purposes of the organization as a whole. The organization is constituted as a *collective* actor (legally speaking, also a person), one that is thereby enabled to issue its *own* acts of speech.

Organization, as Taylor et al.'s 1996 article concludes,

> exists because we, collectively, *will* it to exist. By saying it exists, it exists. . . . The organizational text [therefore] is a (standardized) description of persons, circumstances, objects, intention and conventional procedure now no longer situated circumstantially with respect to a particular context, but categorized, generalized. (p. 28, emphasis in original)

Organization as Representation and Presentification. Once authored, the organization can now be constituted as an actor, capable of *representing* the collectivity and *making itself present* to others and to its own organizational members (see Brummans, 2006, 2013; Brummans, Cooren, & Chaput, 2009; Chaput, Brummans, & Cooren, 2011; Cooren, 2006; Cooren, Brummans, & Charrieras, 2008). It can make its decisions known to its own communities of practice, yet it can also engage in "conversations" with other macro actors (Cooren & Taylor, 1997). Hence, *the* organization becomes one actor among many others and must present itself (its *self*) to these others within the larger scene, similar to Goffman's (1959) idea of the presentation of individual selves. To do this, it is obliged to call on agents, since the organization has no voice of its own. Only through its representatives can it interact with outside bodies, such as boards of governors, government agencies, banks, the press, customers, and its own members. The individuals who play this role claim authority, since it is they who have been authorized to enunciate the purposes of the organization to all (see also Benoit-Barné & Cooren, 2009; Brummans, Hwang, & Cheong, 2013; Taylor, 2011; Taylor & Van Every, 2011).

The mechanism that explains how the organization takes on authority is thus *agency* (Taylor & Cooren, 1997). Agency is an *acting for*, or one actor who voices the position of another, a principal. Consider, for example, how parliamentary procedure acts as an agent. Suppose the Speaker says something such as, "The House recognizes the honorable member from . . . " The words are those of an individual, the *Speaker*, but the authority is actually vested in a collectivity, the *House*. This is how the collective actor, Parliament or Congress, enters the conversation of its own members and is enabled to act, to express *its* point of view. As Taylor and Cooren wrote (1997),

> [the] organization is thereby constituted as an entity. Such entities have, however, *no existence other than in discourse*, where their reality is created, and sustained; to believe otherwise is simply to fall victim to reification. Other than performed in discourse, the one voice very quickly degenerates into many voices. . . . It is the character of all human social organization that its existence be both *conditional on communication* and *a frame within which the latter occurs*. It is through talk that organization is

> constituted, but it is in talk that it is expressed. (p. 429, emphasis in original)

Cooren (2004), in particular, extends this work by demonstrating how different kinds of agents, be they human beings, texts, artifacts (Cooren & Matte, 2010), or even attitudes and emotions (Cooren, 2010; van Vuuren & Cooren, 2010), *matter* in how organizations are discursively and materially constituted and thus are given a voice and a presence (see also Bencherki & Cooren, 2011; Brummans, 2006, 2007, 2011, 2013; Brummans & Cooren, 2011; Cooren, 2006, 2010, 2012; Groleau, 2006). According to Cooren, many kinds of agents can be mobilized to act on an organization's behalf and thereby make it present, again and again. Using concepts such as *incarnation*, *presentification*, and *ventriloquism*, his studies show how organizations (macro actors) speak and act through interactions in which agents (micro actors) enlist other agents. Hence, organizational modes of being are constantly coproduced "for another next first time" (Garfinkel, 1992, p. 186).

Cooren, Matte, Taylor, and Vásquez (2007), for example, studied how the organizational discourse of Doctors without Borders (MSF) traverses space and time. As they showed, MSF's mission is maintained, and reinforced, through interactions between MSF representatives and representatives of other macro actors. The organization's Discourse has to be materialized or incarnated in discourses (i.e., in tokens of talk and text, such as mission statements, protocols, brochures) in order for it to become an *immutable mobile* (Latour, 1987), something that can be transported from one point in space and time to another. Hence, it can only be maintained across space and time if extensive interactive work is done to assure its reproduction in the ordinary, day-to-day conversations and activities of the people and things that embody it.

Cooren's studies of MSF demonstrate that an organization is constituted through communication in such a way that it can communicate with other organizations and individuals. This coproduction is a process of negotiation that plays itself out in concrete situations enacted on the *terra firma* of interactions between different agents, including human beings who are more or less attached to specific positions, ideas, principles, beliefs, values, and so on.

Organization as Translating the One Back into the Many. The Montréal School's research has also addressed the final translation in Figure 7.1—the implementation of corporate policy back into the situated practices of the organization. Two aspects of this translation deserve a brief mention. On the one hand, recent research has shown that members use policy to legitimate their own positioning in the transactional conversation and to establish their own authority (Taylor & Van Every, 2011). To do this, they evoke the position of the organization as an authoritative third person, *they, it,* or *he/she* in what would otherwise be a two-person interaction: *you, we, I.* By aligning themselves with the third person (the organization or its authorized representatives), speakers buttress their own claims to authority. In this case, Cooren (2010, 2012) would say that the speakers establish their authority by *ventriloquizing* the organization, yet at the same time, *they* are also *being* ventriloquized by the organization in that it makes them speak and act in certain ways.

We have described a process involving four steps: practice → voicing the practice → authoring the organization → enunciating the organization's purposes → translating them back into practice. These stages are merely conceptual, though. Had we started with Box 4, the organization as an already existent entity, then the focus would have been on how *it* informs the practices of its members, that is, how its text becomes translated into the conversations of its members. Hence, none of the steps involved in the reconciliation of distributed practice and a single actor's practice, that of the organization itself, are unproblematic, since translation intervenes at every intersection. How, for example, does local practice get translated into subsequent representation in a different context, that of the administration (Fauré et al., 2010; Robichaud et al., 2004)? This supposes a crystallization involving a translation into a single account, that of the organization (Katambwe & Taylor, 2006; Taylor & Robichaud, 2007). The most problematic of all is translating how *the* purposes of the organization are translated into the many conversations of its own communities of practice, where the texts must be made to fit local circumstances. Of course, any of these translations can only be accomplished in, by, and through communication. And how that all takes place is the focus of the Montréal School's ongoing research.

The Influence of the Montréal School Approach

The Montréal School's influence has grown over the past ten years within organizational communication studies as well as in management and organization studies (for the latter, see Cooren et al., 2011; Phillips, Lawrence, & Hardy, 2004; Quinn & Dutton, 2005; Robichaud & Cooren, 2013; Weick, Sutcliffe, & Obstfeld, 2005). Within communication studies, Kuhn's (2008) *communicative theory of the firm* draws on Taylor and Van Every's (2000) conversation-text dialectic to conceive of "firms as textual coorientation systems through which actors engage in 'games' that serve a variety of purposes" (p. 1228). His work shows how communication constitutes intraorganizational power and extraorganizational relationships through the production of an *authoritative text*, an abstract text "that represents the firm as a whole" (p. 1236; see also Kuhn, 2012; Kuhn & Ashcraft, 2003). This dialectic also forms a basis for Kuhn's more recent work with Koschmann on cross-sector partnerships (Koschmann, Kuhn, & Pharrer, 2012; see also Koschmann, 2013). Other scholars have brought attention to the importance of materiality in CCO research by drawing on the Montréal School approach (see Ashcraft et al., 2009; see also Ashcraft et al., 2011). Moreover, this approach has influenced the understanding of leadership as plural and hybridized effects of presence(s) and absence(s) (Fairhurst & Cooren, 2009) as well as our conception of *organizations as discursive constructions* (Fairhurst & Putnam, 1999, 2004).

The main critique of the Montréal School approach focuses on the fact that it does not provide a coherent, unified perspective. For example, Bisel (2010a) noted that Taylor and Van Every's (2000) theory offers "a dizzying number of linguistic, interpretive, and critical theories to argue that communication is the location and manifestation of organization" (p. 126). A similar point was made by McPhee (2008). In addition, McPhee, one of the strongest critics of this approach, especially takes issue with the school's conception of nonhuman agency (see Brummans, 2006; McPhee, 2008; Robichaud, 2006) and claims that the school does not pay sufficient "attention to time and space, as well as to power and large-scale social reality" (McPhee & Trethewey, 2000, p. 334), as structuration theory does.

In line with this, Bisel (2010a) suggested that, from the Montréal School's point of view, "McPhee and Zaug's (2000, 2009) model of CCO is too broad," while McPhee may argue that the Montréal School's approach "is too narrow to account for communication's multifaceted relationship to organization" (p. 126). An even stronger critique was offered by Reed (2010), who argues that

> a process or practice-based conception of organizational power and control fails to access the wider structures of the material, discursive, and relational power within which ongoing political processes and practices are necessarily embedded and from which they take their authorizing and allocating force. (p. 154)

Accordingly, Reed criticized the Montréal School's bottom-up, "*tabula rasa* conception of society and organization," claiming that "*society* (and by logical extension *organization*) is not, only or primarily, the outcome of local construction because the process of local construction is necessarily dependent on nonlocal relationships, resources, and practices that make it possible in the first place" (pp. 154–155, emphasis in original).

Indeed, by our starting with practice, this chapter might leave the impression that members of the Montréal School uniformly adhere to a bottom-up, conversation-to-text constitution of organization. However, the process of organizing can equally be read as the opposite: text first, conversation second (Taylor & Van Every, 2000). A conversation-text emphasis recognizes the need for all of the organization, if it is to continue, to respond to the environment. A text-conversation reading assumes a different starting point, that of preestablished modes of understanding that shape the conversation, by structuring the patterns of talk. The two-way translation conforms to Giddens's (1984) *recursive logic* and resembles Weick's (1979) notion of *enactment*.

As Taylor (1995) wrote, "[U]nder an assumption of conversational autonomy, organization may be generated by communication (i.e., communication → organization) while, under an assumption of heteronomy, organization would be thought of as external to communication and controlling it (i.e., organization → communication)" (p. 5). Taylor (1996) described the alternative images this way:

> Whether the researcher takes conversation as primary focus, and then studies its translation into text or, vice versa, text as starting point and its translation into the conversations of the organization leads to quite different perceptions of the constitutive role of communication as the foundation of organization. . . . Both concepts incorporate a theory of both conversation and text but . . . to give either view primacy would . . . be misguided. . . . Each worldview brings a salient image of communication—and of organization—into view, and simultaneously pushes another into the background. (pp. 29–30)

The conversation-text/text-conversation dialectic as the constitutive basis of organization has led Taylor (1995, 2001a) to explore the concept of self-organizing systems. For this, he drew on the work of Maturana and Varela (1987), who had pioneered the concept of *operational closure* to explain forms of organization that regenerate and reproduce their own identity over successive generations. Maturana and Varela called this phenomenon *autopoiesis*.

It is here that the work of the Montréal School links up with an emerging German school of thought, inspired by the work of Luhmann (1992). In Blaschke's (2008) words, "the theories [of Luhmann and Taylor] are incredibly close in terms of the coherent picture they paint for readers, scholars, and students alike" (p. 6) Our survey of approaches to the CCO thus concludes with a brief examination of this recent development, using the voluminous writings of Luhmann (1995) on social systems as our guide.

The Emerging Luhmannian Systems Approach

Luhmann's (1992, 1995) work has had a profound influence on the German social sciences. A former student of Parsons, the sociologist developed his own social systems theory, inspired (among others) by the work of the mathematician Spencer-Brown (1969), the physicist von Foerster (1992), and the biologists Maturana and Varela (1987). As Seidl and Becker (2006) note in their review of Luhmann's work, we can roughly identify two Luhmanns—the early and late one, just as others identified two Wittgensteins and two or even three Foucaults. The two periods of his career are delineated by his "autopoietic turn" (p. 11), which he explicated in his opus magnum, *Social Systems* (Luhmann, 1995). Here, we will concentrate on the late Luhmann, since this work has the clearest implications for CCO research (see Blaschke, Schoeneborn, & Seidl, 2012). In what follows, we will discuss the implications of his ideas for CCO research, based on the key tenets of his systems thinking.

Organizations as Self-Referential Systems

Although Luhmann (1992, 1995) acknowledges his theoretical debts to cyberneticians, he claims that his own systems theory focuses on the existence and mechanisms of *self-referential* systems, that is, "systems that have the ability to establish relations with themselves and to differentiate these relations from relations with their environment" (Luhmann, 1995, p. 13). What is crucial for Luhmann is that such systems—which comprise *social* as well as *psychic* and *living* systems—are marked by their capacity to produce *by themselves* a difference that distinguishes them from their own environment. For Luhmann (2006), this distinction or boundary makes self-referential systems what they are, which leads him to argue that "a system *is* the difference between system and environment" (p. 38, emphasis in original).

Echoing Spencer-Brown's (1969) *Laws of Form*, Luhmann (2006) maintains that distinctions have the capacity to create boundaries between two sides. One side is marked (the system or *form*) while the other side is unmarked (the environment or *ground*), creating a fundamental asymmetry. Self-referential systems can thus be seen as systems whose main operations consist of demarcating themselves from the rest of the world. In turn, Luhmann invites each of us to become a *second-order observer*, an observer who observes another observer. Self-referential systems, he argues, are systems that actively create distinctions by observing themselves (Seidl & Becker, 2006). They make distinctions in order to reenact or reconstitute their own existence and we can attempt to observe this autopoietic process.

Autopoiesis. According to Luhmann, self-referential activities involve "a *single* operator and a *single* mode of operation" (Luhmann, 2006, p. 46, emphasis added). As he notes, "the difference between system and environment arises merely because an operation produces a subsequent operation of the same type" (p. 46). To explain these circular operations, Luhmann borrows Maturana and Varela's (1987) notion of *autopoiesis*, implying the idea of *self-creation* or *self-production*. For these biologists, all living systems are autopoietic systems, characterized by their capacity to (re)produce themselves within and out of an environment. Living systems are thus considered to be *operationally closed*. Their operations consist of reproducing the conditions that ensure their uninterrupted existence until their demise.

What is perhaps the most counterintuitive about the notion of autopoiesis is that although these systems need the resources of the environment to exist and function, the operations that define how they are organized and bounded are not determined by the environment, but by the system itself. Autopoietic systems are defined by their operational closure, which allows them to establish relationships with themselves by demarcating themselves from their surroundings (Luhmann, 1995). Any reflection on autopoiesis and systematicity therefore also becomes a reflection on individuality and autonomy.

The Self-Production of Social Systems. As a social scientist, Luhmann (1995) conceives of the key operations of social autopoietic systems by emphasizing the importance of communication. In his view, social systems are not constituted by human beings but by *communications*—the *single* mode of operations that makes social self-referential systems what they are. Hence, his famous statement that "only communication can communicate" (Luhmann, 1992, p. 251), which implies that acknowledging another author or agent (e.g., a human being) would compromise a social system's self-referentiality and autonomy. For this reason, human beings are merely *part* of the environment of communication systems (Schoeneborn, 2011).

Luhmann (1995, pp. 140–142) proposes a very specific definition of communication by identifying a three-part selection process, involving *information*, *utterance*, and *understanding*. Communication (1) selects something from its environment (while leaving other things aside), (2) selects what is going to be said about it (triggering questions of sincerity), and (3) selects how what is said is going to be understood. Consequently, "communication happens when information that has been uttered is understood" (Luhmann, 2006, p. 47). Each selection implies an operation of differentiation that marks the autonomous, self-referential character of a communication system (Luhmann, 1995, p. 149). Thus a social system *is* a communication system, and nothing else; "[it] emerges when communication develops from communication" (Luhmann, 2006, p. 47). As Schoeneborn (2011) points out, this kind of system is constituted by interconnected *communicative events*.

What is important for understanding Luhmann's view is that acceptance or rejection of what gets communicated lies *outside* of communication. "[E]very communication invites protest. As soon as something specific is offered for acceptance, one can also negate it" (Luhmann, 1995, p. 173). Communication therefore not only produces redundancy but also difference. It is not inherently directed toward consensus or agreement. Because it has a binding effect that invites positive or negative reactions to what is being communicated, we can never completely predict how things will unfold. As Luhmann states, "[C]ommunication always ineluctably reproduces the freedom to accept or reject" (Luhmann, 1995, p. 149), which explains its eventful character.

To summarize his constitutive view of communication, Luhmann (1995) writes the following:

> In social systems formed by communication, only communication is available as a means of decomposing elements. . . . A social system has no other manner of dissection; it cannot resort to chemical, neurophysiological, or mental processes (although all these exist and play a part). In other words, one cannot bypass the constitutive level of communication. (p. 164)

To claim that communication is constitutive of social systems thus means that it has *its own* operational logic and that anything that is *not* communication is seen as a mere *environmental perturbation* by the communication system itself. What Luhmann posits, then, echoing von Foerster's (1992) *order from noise* theory, is that an autopoietic system produces its own order out of the perturbations that constitute its environment, an environment made of mental, psychic, neurophysiological, and chemical processes.

Organizations as Decision Systems. While Luhmann's (2000) book on organizations is not yet available in English, his ideas about organizations are explicated in several texts (see Luhmann, 2003, 2005). In addition, Seidl and Becker's (2006) article, as well as Schoeneborn's (2011) more recent contribution, provide in-depth insights into Luhmann's conception of organizational systems.

Luhmann views an organizational system as one of the three basic types of self-referential systems (the other being micro-level interactions and macro-level society). That is, organizations are considered to be meso-level systems, characterized by their relative stability and formality. In keeping with his constitutive view, Luhmann argues that communication is an organization's single mode of operations. However, following March and Simon (1958), he claims that an organization is constituted by special types of communication, which he calls *decision communications*.

If communications do not concern decisions, they merely constitute interactions, the social system's micro level. As soon as they involve decisions, they pertain to the organization, reproducing it and assuring its continuity and stability. Decision communications are thus central to an organization's existence and its ability to move forward (Schoeneborn, 2011; Seidl, 2005). As self-referential systems, organizations should be regarded as interconnected communication decisions, one decision communication leading to another, and so on. The forms of communication that lead to a decision do not really count for the organizational system because they are *absorbed* by it and become irrelevant once a decision is made (Seidl, 2005; Seidl & Becker, 2006).

Again echoing von Foerster (1992), Luhmann (2005) goes on to note that decisions are paradoxical in that they are characterized by their *undecidability* (see also Cooren, 2010). Decision communications are marked by selective processes. The identification of alternatives (the marked side) versus non-alternatives (the unmarked side) results in the selection of one alternative (the marked side of the decision) among others (its unmarked side). However, alternatives that are left out when the decision is made are *both* marked and unmarked—hence the paradox. They are marked because they have been selected as alternatives, but they are also unmarked because they were ultimately not selected when the decision was made. In other words, as alternatives, they are *a priori* equally valid possibilities. Yet they are not *real* alternatives, since making a decision means that one alternative was more valid than the others (Seidl & Becker, 2006).

To counter the paradoxical nature of decisions, organizations rely on processes of *deparadoxification* or the practice of absorbing the level of uncertainty produced by the undecidable character of decisions. To produce this absorption, a decision's arbitrariness is concealed or obscured by focusing on past decisions, which now function as decision premises and make the decision seem *decidable*, *predictable*, or *programmable*. *Uncertainty absorption*, a notion Luhmann borrows from March and Simon (1958), therefore constitutes the very logic (i.e., the operational closure) of organizations. Echoing Giddens's (1984) duality of structure, decisions limit and enable future decisions, while also acting as the medium and outcome of decisions. "[I]n contrast to Giddens, the relation between structure and action/operation is not 'mediated' by an agent but by the autopoiesis of the system—it is the network of decision that produces the decisions: 'only decisions can decide'" (Seidl, 2005, p. 28).

The Influence of the Luhmannian Systems Approach

Luhmann's view offers a radically different approach to CCO research, one that has only emerged recently through the work of German scholars such as Blaschke, Seidl, and Schoeneborn. Since their writings have mainly focused so far on translating Luhmann's complex ideas into a theoretical vocabulary that is useful for organizational communication researchers, future empirical studies need to demonstrate the benefits of using this systems approach to gain insight into the communicative constitution of organizations. A good recent example that moves in this direction is Blaschke et al.'s (2012) article on organizations as networks of communication episodes.

As we have explained, for Luhmannian CCO scholars, an organization is *nothing but* a communication system. The character of this constitutive view of organization appears most radical in that no other beings or agents directly and operationally participate in the constitution of this system. As communication systems, organizations are authorless or agentless in that communicative events author other communicative events in a circularity that is typical of self-referential systems. Hence, the three CCO approaches discussed are distinct in their conception of authorship or agency: McPhee's Four Flows approach centers on human agency; the Montréal School's four translations approach highlights multiple kinds of human and nonhuman agency; and the Luhmannian scholars recognize communication as the only author of an organizational system.

Directions for Future CCO Research

As mentioned at the beginning of this chapter, mapping an emerging field such as CCO research is a challenging undertaking. Since the claim that "organizations are communicatively constituted" is highly general, its territory is amorphous. It is thus only natural that different approaches are being developed to investigate this claim. Second, by producing this chapter, the authors and editors inevitably participate in the very emergence of the phenomenon they mean to describe (see Brummans, 2006). Hence, the multiple connections tying the map to the territory amount, at least in this context, to coproduction more than correspondence. Third, postulating that organizations are constituted in and by communication requires us to think deeply about what we mean by *communication* because it profoundly affects our conception of what an organization is.

We have shown that current approaches to CCO research provide different views of communication, grounded in a variety of sources, including structuration theory; various traditions in language analysis, such as narrative theory, speech act theory, and conversation analysis as well as actor-network theory and systems theory. The resulting mix may confront researchers with a *mélange* of terms that require some decoding. We believe, however, that it would be unwise to ignore this diversity in an attempt to look for common ground, as it would lead to oversimplification and reification, which stifle the productive debates that are presently ongoing. In this final section, our aim is, therefore, to discuss promising directions for future research that both exploit but also clarify issues arising out of this diversity of perspectives.

One concern in examining the multiple perspectives is the issue of (communicative) practice and how to approach its analysis. McPhee and Zaug, for example, draw on Giddens's notion of *recursivity*, implying that the collective behavior of people results in patterns of interaction that become, reflexively, their own justification and meaning, thus both framing and structuring subsequent interaction. The initial research of the Montréal School, while coherent with this view, emphasizes more firmly the role of language in explaining self-structuring. Their perspective could be traced back to Saussure's (1959) distinction between *parole* (essentially, *conversation*) and *langue* (*language*, with its own sensemaking patterns of meaning). Once constituted, *langue* has powerful structuring effects because as people use its categories to decode their own activities, they are also buying into a structured pattern of interaction and its interpretation. Language, in this sense, furnishes what Weick (1979) called the *cause map* that people draw on in both acting on their environment and making sense of it. Later work by Montréal School researchers has extended this view to include the structuring properties of not only language but the entire infrastructure of built objects, in all their materiality (buildings, roads, maps, signs, etc.), that serve to reduce complexity to mere complication. A Luhmann-inspired view of interaction emphasizes even further the self-structuring properties of ordinary conversation in that the meaning of a segment of communication is determined, not by how individuals understand what has been said, but rather by ensuing communications that establish retrospectively the meaning of what preceded them.

These observations indicate that each CCO approach acknowledges both the eventful as well as iterable (repeatable) or lasting character of organizing. Specifically, organizations are constituted in and by situated performance (*human action* for McPhee; *conversation* for Montréal School scholars; *communication acts* for Luhmannians) as well as in and by that which appears to transcend or outlive the here-and-now situationality of interactions (*structures* for McPhee; *texts, material artifacts, etc.* for Montréal School scholars; *systems* for Luhmannians). Regardless of their differences, CCO scholars therefore seem to be united in their quest to develop theories that explain how generality emerges from performativity. Language, as the most powerful generalizing and typifying technology at our disposal, is the obvious object of study in this regard and has been looked at in detail by the Montréal School.

More and more scholars, though, are reluctant to investigate language only by zooming in

(Nicolini, 2009) on organizational members' accounting in specific situations and argue that we should not overlook the generalizing effects of practices across sites and episodes of organizing. Actor-network theorists, for instance, have demonstrated how the dissemination of scripts through the delegation of nonhuman agents plays an important role in extending practices across space and time and in enabling certain actors to become more powerful than others (see Latour, 2013). Consequently, future CCO research should investigate how situated performance is transformed into practice by means of "typification materials" *other* than language. This goal will require us to develop new theories for explaining how the virtual and the generic act together in constituting organizations as more or less durable space-time configurations with both symbolic and material features (see Bencherki & Cooren, 2011; Robichaud & Cooren, 2013).

A question that is very much related to our discussion about virtuality and generality is the question of continuity and change. Extant CCO research has sometimes seemed overly focused on studying the continuity of organizations, specifically their self-structuring properties. Yet conflicts and contradictions should be addressed as being of at least equal importance in explaining both continuity and change. For example, recent CCO research suggests that conflicts and contradictions are both constitutive of organization and powerful agents of change (see Chaput, Brummans, & Cooren, 2011; Cooren, Matte, Benoit-Barne, & Brummans, 2013; Taylor & Van Every, 2011). The model we used to outline the key commitments of the Montréal School shows why contradiction is endemic to organizing on a large scale. On the one hand, the conversations of several communities of practice (the right-hand boxes of Figure 7.1) are responsive to the environment that forms their grounding and must continually adapt their modes of interacting and sensemaking to be responsive to its exigencies. This need is particularly prevalent during periods of rapid technological change, where learning is continuous. The left-hand boxes of Figure 7.1, by contrast, reflect preoccupations with fixing the organization's purposes and the continuity of its "personality." The result, as Barley (1996) has pointed out, is *scission*, a division between the authority of expertise (developed locally) and the authority of position (an extension of the already established organization), which is codified in texts of various kinds and which must insist on its continuity in its presentation (or presentification) to others outside the organization. How this contrast of sources of authority is worked out in practice is an area that has hardly received any attention in the existing CCO literature, and given the current pace of technological developments, this is an area that will merit close attention in future research (see Leonardi & Barley, 2011).

To conclude, the emerging Luhmannian approach opens up a promising area for future research. Drawing on Maturana and Varela's (1987) theory of autopoiesis, Luhmann sees communication as its own object, with its own self-structuring properties. Recent work by Blaschke et al. (2012) has extended this idea to portray organizations as networks, not of people, but of conversations. This elaboration resembles, in certain respects, Taylor's (2001b, 2011; Taylor & Van Every, 2011) conception of an organization as a configuration of *imbrications* (i.e., a stitching together of conversations to compose a more complex entity). How this imbrication takes place in practice and what effects it has are questions that need to be examined in greater detail.

One possibility, currently envisaged by some of the Montréal School scholars, is to examine larger organizational constellations as space-time configurations that, when suitably integrated, compose larger units at the national scale or beyond (see Vásquez, 2013; Vásquez & Cooren, 2013). This work also raises important new methodological questions, as it requires us to *zoom in* and *out* (Nicolini, 2009). Thus while it is important to investigate the here-and-now discursive and material accomplishment of everyday organizational practices by zooming in on what people say and do and the active role of tools, materials, and so on, these methods need to be combined with zooming out methods, such as trailing connections between practices through multisited ethnographies (Marcus, 1995), shadowing (Vásquez, Brummans, & Groleau, 2012), and studying the effects of practice-networks (see Nicolini, 2009). What is becoming more and more evident, then, is that scholars need to do both in order to understand "how translocal phenomena come into being and persist in time as effects of the mutual relationships between the local real-time accomplishments of practices, as well as how they make a difference in the local process of organizing" (Nicolini, 2009, p. 1392). In turn, both are necessary for moving CCO research forward.

Our brief reflections on points of convergence and divergence between the current approaches to CCO research show that this nascent field has much to offer because it presents us with innovative ways for theorizing and analyzing the central role of communication in the coproduction and reproduction of organizations. What is most interesting, in this regard, is that although various scholars have been investigating the communicative constitution of organizations for several decades, CCO research is now emerging as a field of inquiry in its own right, becoming increasingly international in character and also attracting the attention of scholars outside organizational communication studies.

References

Aakhus, M., Ballard, D., Flanagin, A. J., Kuhn, T., Leonardi, P., Mease, J., & Miller, K. (2011). Communication and materiality: A conversation from the *CM Café*. *Communication Monographs, 78*(4), 557–568.

Ashcraft, K. L., Kuhn, T. R., & Cooren, F. (2009). Constitutional amendments: "Materializing" organizational communication. In J. P. Walsh & A. P. Brief (Eds.), *The academy of management annals* (vol. 3, pp. 1–64). London, UK: Routledge.

Ballard, D. I., & Gossett, L. M. (2008). Alternative times: The temporal perceptions, processes, and practices defining the nonstandard work relationship. In C. S. Beck (Ed.), *Communication yearbook* (vol. 31, pp. 274–321). Mahwah, NJ: Lawrence Erlbaum.

Barley, S. R. (1996). Technicians in the workplace: Ethnographic evidence for bringing work into organization studies. *Administrative Science Quarterly, 41*(3), 404–440.

Bateson, G. (1935). Culture contact and schismogenesis. *Man*, Article 199, p. xxxv.

Bateson, G. (1972). *Steps to an ecology of mind.* New York, NY: Ballantine.

Bencherki, N., & Cooren, F. (2011). Having to be: The possessive constitution of organization. *Human Relations, 64*(12), 1579–1607.

Benoit-Barné, C., & Cooren, F. (2009). The accomplishment of authority through presentification: How authority is distributed among and negotiated by organizational members. *Management Communication Quarterly, 23*(1), 5–31.

Bisel, R. S. (2010a). A communicative ontology of organization? A description, history, and critique of CCO theories for organization science. *Management Communication Quarterly, 24*(1), 124–131.

Bisel, R. S. (2010b). Forum introduction: Communication is constitutive of organizing. *Management Communication Quarterly, 24*(1), 122–123.

Blaschke, S. (2008, May). *What is organizational communication? A fictitious discourse between Luhmann and Taylor.* Paper presented at the What is an Organization? Materiality, Discourse, and Agency preconference of the annual meeting of the International Communication Association, Montreal, Canada.

Blaschke, S., Schoeneborn, D., & Seidl, D. (2012). Organizations as networks of communication episodes: Turning the network perspective inside out. *Organization Studies, 33*(8), 879–906.

Brown, J. S., & Duguid, P. (2000). *The social life of information.* Cambridge, MA: Harvard Business School Press.

Browning, L. D., Greene, R. W., Sitkin, S. B., Sutcliffe, K. M., & Obstfeld, D. (2009). Constitutive complexity: Military entrepreneurs and the synthetic character of communication flows. In L. L. Putnam & A. M. Nicotera (Eds.), *Building theories of organization: The constitutive role of communication* (pp. 89–116). New York, NY: Routledge.

Browning, L. D., Sutcliffe, K. M., Sitkin, S., Obstfeld, D., & Greene, R. (2000). Keep 'em flying: The constitutive dynamics of an organizational change in the U.S. Air Force. *Electronic Journal of Communication/La Revue Electronique de Communication, 10*(1).

Brummans, B. H. J. M. (2006). The Montréal School and the question of agency. In F. Cooren, J. R. Taylor, & E. J. Van Every (Eds.), *Communication as organizing: Empirical and theoretical explorations in the dynamic of text and conversation* (pp. 197–211). Mahwah, NJ: Lawrence Erlbaum.

Brummans, B. H. J. M. (2007). Death by document: Tracing the agency of a text. *Qualitative Inquiry, 13*(5), 711–727.

Brummans, B. H. J. M. (2011). What goes down must come up: Communication as incarnation and transcension. *Communication and Critical/Cultural Studies, 8*(2), 194–200.

Brummans, B. H. J. M. (2013). What is an organization? Or: Is James Taylor a Buddhist? In D. Robichaud & F. Cooren (Eds.), *Organization and organizing: Materiality, agency, and discourse* (pp. 90–108). New York, NY: Routledge.

Brummans, B. H. J. M., & Cooren, F. (2011). Forum: Communication as incarnation. *Communication and Critical/Cultural Studies, 8*(2), 186–187.

Brummans, B. H. J. M., Cooren, F., & Chaput, M. (2009). Discourse, communication, and organisational ontology. In F. Bargiela-Chiappini (Ed.), *The handbook of business discourse* (pp. 53–65). Edinburgh, UK: Edinburgh University Press.

Brummans, B. H. J. M., Hwang, J. M., & Cheong, P. H. (2013). Mindful authoring through invocation: Leaders' constitution of a spiritual organization. *Management Communication Quarterly, 27*(3), 346–372.

Chaput, M., Brummans, B. H. J. M., & Cooren, F. (2011). The role of organizational identification in the communicative constitution of an organization: A study of consubstantialization in a young political party. *Management Communication Quarterly, 25*(2), 252–282.

Cheney, G., & Christensen, L. T. (2001). Organizational identity: Linkages between internal and external communication. In F. M. Jablin & L. L. Putnam (Eds.), *The new handbook of organizational communication: Advances in theory, research, and methods* (pp. 231–269). Thousand Oaks, CA: SAGE.

Cooren, F. (2000). *The organizing properties of communication.* Amsterdam, the Netherlands: John Benjamins.

Cooren, F. (2004). Textual agency: How texts do things in organizational settings. *Organization, 11*(3), 373–393.

Cooren, F. (2006). The organizational world as a plenum of agencies. In F. Cooren, J. R. Taylor, & E. J. Van Every (Eds.), *Communication as organizing: Practical approaches to research into the dynamic of text and conversation* (pp. 81–100). Mahwah, NJ: Lawrence Erlbaum.

Cooren, F. (Ed.). (2007). *Interacting and organizing: Analyses of a board meeting.* Mahwah, NJ: Lawrence Erlbaum.

Cooren, F. (2010). *Action and agency in dialogue: Passion, incarnation, and ventriloquism.* Amsterdam, the Netherlands: John Benjamins.

Cooren, F. (2012). Communication theory at the center: Ventriloquism and the communicative constitution of reality. *Journal of Communication, 62*(1), 1–20.

Cooren, F., Brummans, B. H. J. M., & Charrieras, D. (2008). The coproduction of organizational presence: A study of Médecins sans Frontières in action. *Human Relations, 61*(10), 1339–1370.

Cooren, F., & Fairhurst, G. T. (2009). Dislocation and stabilization: How to scale up from interactions to organization. In L. L. Putnam & A. M. Nicotera (Eds.), *Building theories of organization: The constitutive role of communication* (pp. 117–152). New York, NY: Routledge.

Cooren, F., Kuhn, T., Cornelissen, J. P., & Clark, T. (2011). Communication, organizing and organization: An overview and introduction to the special issue. *Organization Studies, 32*(9), 1149–1170.

Cooren, F., & Matte, F. (2010). For a constitutive pragmatics: Obama, Médecins sans Frontières and the measuring stick. *Pragmatics & Society, 1*(1), 9–31.

Cooren, F., Matte, F., Benoit-Barné, C., & Brummans, B. H. J. M. (2013). Communication as ventriloquism: A grounded-in-action approach to the study of organizational tensions. *Communication Monographs, 80*(3), 255–277.

Cooren, F., Matte, F., Taylor, J. R., & Vasquez, C. (2007). A humanitarian organization in action: Organizational discourse as a stable mobile. *Discourse and Communication, 1*(2), 153–190.

Cooren, F., & Taylor, J. R. (1997). Organization as an effect of mediation: Redefining the link between organization and communication. *Communication Theory, 7*(3), 219–260.

Cooren, F., Taylor, J. R., & Van Every, E. J. (Eds.). (2006). *Communication as organizing: Empirical and theoretical explorations in the dynamic of text and conversation.* Mahwah, NJ: Lawrence Erlbaum.

Dewey, J. (1944). *Democracy and education.* New York, NY: The Free Press.

Drew, P., & Heritage, J. (Eds.). (1992). *Talk at work: Interaction in institutional settings.* Cambridge, UK: Cambridge University Press.

Eco, U. (2003). *Mouse or rat: Translation as negotiation.* London, UK: Phoenix.

Fairhurst, G. T., & Cooren, F (2009). Leadership as the hybrid production of presence(s). *Leadership, 5*(4), 469–490.

Fairhurst, G. T., & Putnam, L. L. (1999). Reflections on the communication-organization equivalence question: The contributions of James Taylor and his colleagues. *The Communication Review, 3*(1/2), 1–19.

Fairhurst, G. T., & Putnam, L. L. (2004). Organizations as discursive constructions. *Communication Theory, 14*(1), 5–26.

Fauré, B., Brummans, B. H. J. M., Giroux, H., & Taylor, J. R. (2010). The calculation of business, or the business of calculation? Accounting as organizing through everyday communication. *Human Relations, 63*(8), 1249–1273.

Garfinkel, H. (1992). Two incommensurable, asymmetrically alternate technologies of social analysis. In G. Watson & R. M. Seller (Eds.), *Text in context: Contributions to ethnomethodology* (pp. 175–206). London, UK: SAGE.

Giddens, A. (1984). *The constitution of society: Outline of the theory of structuration.* Berkeley: University of California Press.

Goffman, E. (1959). *The presentation of self in everyday life.* Garden City, NY: Doubleday.

Goffman, E. (1974). *Frame analysis: An essay on the organization of experience.* Boston, MA: Northeastern University Press.

Groleau, C. (2006). One phenomenon, two lenses: Understanding collective action from the perspective of coorientation and activity theories. In F. Cooren, J. R. Taylor, & E. J. Van Every (Eds.), *Communication as organizing: Practical approaches to research into the dynamic of text and conversation* (pp. 157–177). Mahwah, NJ: Lawrence Erlbaum.

Güney, S. (2006). Making sense of a conflict as the (missing) link between collaborating actors. In F. Cooren, J. R. Taylor, & E. J. Taylor (Eds.), *Communicating as organizing: Empirical and theoretical explorations in the dynamic of text and conversation* (pp. 37–54). Mahwah, NJ: Lawrence Erlbaum.

Guralnik, D. B. (Ed.). (1964). *Webster's New World Dictionary of the American Language.* New York, NY: The World Publishing Company.

Katambwe, J. M., & Taylor, J. R. (2006). Modes of organizational integration. In F. Cooren, J. R. Taylor, & E. J. Van Every (Eds.), *Communication as organizing: Empirical and theoretical explorations in the dynamic of text and conversation* (pp. 55–77). Mahwah, NJ: Lawrence Erlbaum.

Koschmann, M. A. (2011). Developing a communicative theory of the nonprofit. *Management Communication Quarterly, 26*(1), 139–146.

Koschmann, M. A. (2013). The communicative constitution of collective identity in interorganizational collaboration. *Management Communication Quarterly, 27*(1), 61–89.

Koschmann, M. A., Kuhn, T., & Pharrer, M. (2012). A communicative framework of value in cross-sector partnerships. *Academy of Management Review, 37*(3), 332–354.

Kuhn, T. (2008). A communicative theory of the firm: Developing an alternative perspective on intra-organizational power and stakeholder relationships. *Organization Studies, 29*(8/9), 1227–1254.

Kuhn, T. (2012). Negotiating the micro-macro divide: Thought leadership from organizational communication for theorizing organization. *Management Communication Quarterly, 26*(4), 543–584.

Kuhn, T., & Ashcraft, K. L. (2003). Corporate scandal and the theory of the firm: Formulating the contributions of organizational communication studies. *Management Communication Quarterly, 17*(1), 20–57.

Lammers, J. C. (2011). How institutions communicate: Institutional messages, institutional logics, and organizational communication. *Management Communication Quarterly, 25*(1), 154–182.

Lammers, J. C., & Barbour, J. B. (2006). An institutional theory of organizational communication. *Communication Theory, 16*(3), 356–377.

Latour, B. (1987). *Science in action: How to follow scientists and engineers through society.* Cambridge, MA: Harvard University Press.

Latour, B. (2013). "What's the story?" Organizing as a mode of existence. In D. Robichaud & F. Cooren (Eds.), *Organization and organizing:*

Materiality, agency, and discourse (pp. 37–51). New York, NY: Routledge.

Leonardi, P. M., & Barley, W. C. (2011). Materiality as organizational communication: Technology, intention, and delegation in the production of meaning. In T. Kuhn (Ed.), *Matters of communication: Political, cultural, and technological challenges to communication theorizing* (pp. 101–122). Cresskill, NJ: Hampton Press.

Luhmann, N. (1992). What is communication? *Communication Theory, 2*(3), 251–259.

Luhmann, N. (1995). *Social systems.* Stanford, CA: Stanford University Press.

Luhmann, N. (2000). *Organisation und Entscheidung.* Opladen, Germany: Westdeutscher Verlag.

Luhmann, N. (2003). Organization. In T. Bakken & T. Hernes (Eds.), *Autopoietic organization theory: Drawing on Niklas Luhmann's social systems perspective* (pp. 31–52). Oslo, Norway: Copenhagen Business School Press.

Luhmann, N. (2005). The paradox of decision making. In D. Seidl & K. H. Becker (Eds.), *Niklas Luhmann and organization studies* (pp. 9–35). Copenhagen, Denmark: Copenhagen Business School Press.

Luhmann, N. (2006). System as difference. *Organization, 13*(1), 37–57.

Lutgen-Sandvik, P., & McDermott, V. (2008). The constitution of employee abusive organizations: A communication flows theory. *Communication Theory, 18*(2), 304–333.

March, J. G., & Simon, H. A. (1958). *Organizations.* New York, NY: John Wiley.

Marcus, G. E. (1995). Ethnography in/of the world system: The emergence of multi-sited ethnography. *Annual Review of Anthropology, 24*, 95–117.

Maturana, H. R., & Varela, F. J. (1987). *The tree of knowledge: The biological roots of human understanding.* Boston, MA: Shambhala.

McPhee, R. D. (2004). Text, agency, and organization in the light of structuration theory. *Organization, 11*(3), 355–371.

McPhee, R. D. (2008, May). *A structurational critique of some central Montréal School schemata.* Paper presented at the What is an Organization? Materiality, Discourse, and Agency preconference of the annual meeting of the International Communication Association, Montréal, Canada.

McPhee, R. D., Corman, S. R., & Iverson, J. (2007). "We ought to have . . . gumption": A CRA analysis of an excerpt from the videotape *Corporation: After Mr. Sam.* In F. Cooren (Ed.), *Interacting and organizing: Analyses of a management meeting* (pp. 133–161). Mahwah, NJ: Lawrence Erlbaum.

McPhee, R. D., & Iverson, J. (2009). Agents of constitution in communidad. In L. L. Putnam & A. M. Nicotera (Eds.), *Building theories of organization: The constitutive role of communication* (pp. 49–87). New York, NY: Routledge.

McPhee, R. D., & Trethewey, A. C. (2000). The emergent organization: Communication as its site and surface [Book review]. *Management Communication Quarterly, 14*(2), 328–334.

McPhee, R. D., & Zaug, P. (2000). The communicative constitution of organizations: A framework for explanation. *The Electronic Journal of Communication/La Revue Electronique de Communication, 10*(1/2).

McPhee, R. D., & Zaug, P. (2009). The communicative constitution of organizations: A framework for explanation. In L. L. Putnam & A. M. Nicotera (Eds.), *Building theories of organization: The constitutive role of communication* (pp. 21–47). New York, NY: Routledge.

Mitchell, S. D. (2003). *Biological complexity and integrative pluralism.* Cambridge, UK: Cambridge University Press.

Nicolini, D. (2009). Zooming in and out: Studying practices by switching theoretical lenses and trailing connections. *Organization Studies, 30*(12), 1391–1418.

Phillips, N., Lawrence, T. B., & Hardy, C. (2004). Discourse and institutions. *Academy of Management Review, 29*(4), 635–652.

Putnam, L. L., & Nicotera, A. M. (Eds.). (2009). *Building theories of organization: The constitutive role of communication.* New York, NY: Routledge.

Putnam, L. L., & Nicotera, A. M. (2010). Communicative constitution of organization is a question: Critical issues for addressing it. *Management Communication Quarterly, 24*(1), 158–165.

Quinn, R. W., & Dutton, J. E. (2005). Coordination as energy-in-conversation. *Academy of Management Review, 30*(1), 36–57.

Reed, M. (2010). Is communication *constitutive* of organization? *Management Communication Quarterly, 24*(1), 151–157.

Ricoeur, P. (1981). *Hermeneutics and the human sciences* (J. B. Thompson, Ed. and Trans.). Cambridge, UK: Cambridge University Press.

Robichaud, D. (2006). Steps toward a relational view of agency. In F. Cooren, J. R. Taylor, & E. J. Van Every (Eds.), *Communication as organizing: Practical approaches to research into the dynamic of text and conversation* (pp. 101–114). Mahwah, NJ: Lawrence Erlbaum.

Robichaud, D., & Cooren, D. (Eds.). (2013). *Organization and organizing: Materiality, agency, and discourse.* New York, NY: Routledge.

Robichaud, D., Giroux, H., & Taylor, J. R. (2004). The metaconversation: The recursive property of language as a key to organizing. *Academy of Management Review, 29*(4), 617–634.

Saussure, F. de (1959). *Course in general linguistics* (W. Baskin, Trans., C. Bally & A. Sechehaye, Eds.). New York, NY: Philosophical Library.

Schoeneborn, D. (2011). Organization as communication: A Luhmannian perspective. *Management Communication Quarterly, 25*(4), 663–689.

Schumate, M., & O'Connor, A. (2010). The symbiotic sustainability model: Conceptualizing NGO-corporate alliance communication. *Journal of Communication, 60*(3), 577–609.

Searle, J. R. (1995). *The construction of social reality.* New York, NY: The Free Press.

Seidl, D. (2005). Organization and interaction. In D. Seidl & K. H. Becker (Eds.), *Niklas Luhmann and organization studies* (pp. 145–170). Oslo, Norway: Copenhagen Business School Press.

Seidl, D., & Becker, K. H. (2006). Organizations as distinction generating and processing systems: Niklas Luhmann's contribution to organization studies. *Organization, 13*(1), 9–35.

Sergi, V. (2013). Constituting the temporary organization: Documents in the context of projects. In D. Robichaud & F. Cooren (Eds.), *Organization and organizing: Materiality, agency, and discourse.* (pp. 190–206). New York, NY: Routledge.

Sillince, A. A. (2010). Can CCO theory tell us how organizing is distinct from markets, networking, belonging to a community, or supporting a social movement? *Management Communication Quarterly, 24*(1), 132–138.

Smith, R. C. (1993, May). *Images of organizational communication: Root-metaphors of the organization-communication relation.* Paper presented at the annual meeting of the International Communication Association, Washington, DC.

Spee, P. A., & Jarzabkowski, P. (2011). Strategic planning as communicative process. *Organization Studies, 32*(9), 1217–1245.

Spencer-Brown, G. (1969). *Laws of form.* London, UK: Allen and Unwin.

Taylor, J. R. (1995). Shifting from a heteronomous to an autonomous worldview of organizational communication: Communication theory on the cusp. *Communication Theory, 5*(1), 1–35.

Taylor, J. R. (1996, October). *The worldviews of organization communication.* Invited talk given at the University of Colorado, Boulder, CO.

Taylor, J. R. (1999). What is "organizational communication"? Communication as a dialogic of text and conversation. *The Communication Review, 3*(1/2), 21–63.

Taylor, J. R. (2000a). Apples and orangutans: The worldviews of organizational communication. *Saison Mauve, 3*(1), 45–64.

Taylor, J. R. (2000b). What is an organization? *Electronic Journal of Communication/La Revue Électronique de Communication, 10.*

Taylor, J. R. (2001a). The rational organization re-evaluated. *Communication Theory, 11*(2), 137–177.

Taylor, J. R. (2001b). Toward a theory of imbrication and organizational communication. *American Journal of Semiotics, 17*(2), 1–29.

Taylor, J. R. (2005). Engaging organization through worldview. In S. May & D. Mumby (Eds.), *Engaging organizational communication theory and perspectives: Multiple perspectives* (pp. 197–221). Thousand Oaks, CA: SAGE.

Taylor, J. R. (2009). Organizing from the bottom up? Reflections on the constitution of organization in communication. In L. L. Putnam & A. M. Nicotera (Eds.), *Building theories of organization: The constitutive role of communication* (pp. 153–186). New York, NY: Routledge.

Taylor, J. R. (2011). Organization as an (imbricated) configuring of transactions. *Organization Studies, 32*(9), 1273–1294.

Taylor, J. R., & Cooren, F. (1997). What makes communication "organizational"? How the many voices of the organization become the one voice of an organization. *Journal of Pragmatics, 27*(4), 409–438.

Taylor, J. R., Cooren, F., Giroux, N., & Robichaud, D. (1996). The communicational basis of organization: Between the conversation and the text. *Communication Theory*, *6*(1), 1–39.

Taylor, J. R., & Robichaud, D. (2007). Management as metaconversation: The search for closure. In F. Cooren (Ed.), *Interacting and organizing: Analyses of a management meeting* (pp. 5–30). Mahwah, NJ: Lawrence Erlbaum.

Taylor, J. R., & Van Every, E. J. (2000). *The emergent organization: Communication as its site and surface.* Mahwah, NJ: Lawrence Erlbaum.

Taylor, J. R., & Van Every, E. J. (2011). *The situated organization: Case studies in the pragmatics of communication research.* New York, NY: Routledge.

van Vuuren, M., & Cooren, F. (2010). "My attitudes made me do it": Considering the agency of attitudes. *Human Studies*, *33*(1), 85–101.

Vásquez, C. (2013). Spacing organization (or how to be here and there at the same time). In D. Robichaud & F. Cooren (Eds.), *Organization and organizing: Materiality, agency, and discourse.* (pp. 127–149). New York, NY: Routledge.

Vásquez, C., & Cooren, F. (2013). Spacing practices: The communicative configuration of organizing through space-times. *Communication Theory, 23*(1), 25–47.

Vásquez, C., Brummans, B. H. J. M., & Groleau, C. (2012). Notes from the field on organizational shadowing as framing. *Qualitative Research in Organizations and Management*, *7*(2), 144–165.

Vollmer, H. (2007). How to do more with numbers: Elementary stakes, framing, keying, and the three-dimensional character of numerical signs. *Accounting, Organizations and Society, 32*(6), 577–600.

von Foerster, H. (1992). Ethics and second-order cybernetics. *Cybernetics and Human Knowing, 1*(1), 9–19.

Watzlawick, P., Beavin, J., & Jackson, D. (1967). *The pragmatics of communication.* New York, NY: W.W. Norton.

Weick, K. E. (1979). *The social psychology of organizing* (2nd ed.). New York, NY: McGraw-Hill.

Weick, K. E., Sutcliffe, K. M., & Obstfeld, D. (2005). Organizing and the process of sensemaking. *Organization Science*, *16*(4), 409–421.

Note

1. We kindly thank Linda Putnam and Patty Sotirin for their superb editorial work on this chapter. Since this chapter is a joint effort, the authors appear in alphabetical order.

CHAPTER 8

Institutional Theory

John C. Lammers and Mattea A. Garcia

This chapter contends that the institutional perspective holds tremendous promise for scholars of organizational communication. At its heart, institutional theory seeks to explain the "the elaboration of rules and requirements to which organizations must conform if they are to receive support and legitimacy" (Scott & Meyer, 1983, p. 140). The strength of this perspective today may flow from the fact that that the world is awash in rules and requirements in every sector, industry, and nation-state.

However, we think a case must be made for the relevance of institutional theory to organizational communication. After all, organizational communication frequently focuses on the communicative behavior of individuals in groups and organizations or, more specifically, their "language and social interaction that promote coordinated action toward a common goal" (Eisenberg, 2009, p. 700). It seems appropriate, therefore, to treat the larger institutional landscape as outside and beyond the purview of organizational communication. The reason for the distance between status quo organizational communication and institutionalism probably lies in their roots: the former in practical matters of post-WWII social psychology, the latter in 19th- and early 20th-century sociology. But institutionalism today has grown beyond its sociological field of origin[1], and the vines of organizational communication are also creeping beyond their early managerial concerns. The interpenetration of organizational communication and institutionalism is far from complete, however. Indeed, we believe the opportunities for these fields to inform each other are very exciting. The chapter aims to document the reach of institutional theory into organizational communication and to provide examples of organizational communication scholarship that have special relevance for institutionalism.

Definition and Characteristics

As with many organizational concepts, institutions have been defined in multiple ways (Greenwood, Oliver, Sahlin, & Suddaby, 2008; Scott, 2001). This chapter draws from Lammers and Barbour's (2006) definition of institutions as "constellations of established practices guided by enduring, formalized, rational beliefs that transcend particular organizations and situations" (p. 357). This definition points to a number of key characteristics that scholars draw on to develop institutional theory and situate it as an area of study. First, institutions are enduring social phenomena—they persist across time and space, particularly in comparison to the organizations and conventions observable in any given period (*fixity* is the term used by Giddens, 1984, p. 69). Second, institutions take on lives of their own that have social meaning beyond strict functional requirements (Selznick, 1949). Third, institutions organize social life across and through organizations (Lammers & Garcia, 2009). Fourth, institutions are manifest in a broad range of social phenomena, including "cultural-cognitive, normative, and regulative elements" (Scott, 2001, p. 48). Fifth, institutions take on a subtlety, because they are "more-or-less taken-for-granted repetitive social behavior(s) that [are] underpinned by normative systems and cognitive understandings that give meaning to social exchange and thus enable self-reproducing social order" (Greenwood et al., 2008, p. 5). Sixth, drawing on Commons's (1934) "working rules" (p. 79), institutions reflect a rational purpose that guides behaviors toward certain ends. Perhaps a useful distillation of these characteristics is that institutions are composed of established patterns of communication and conduct that transcend specific organizations.

Though the taken-for-granted features of institutions make them difficult to define, scholars have offered various examples. Weber (1968) identified the church and the state as dominant institutions in the 19th century. In the 18th through the 20th centuries, the family, markets, and political structures (such as representative democracy) arose as institutions (Berger, Berger, & Kellner, 1973; Gehlen, 1988). The idea that a single organization or agency of the government could become institutionalized took root in the 20th century, as documented by Selznick (1949, 1957). Abbott (1988) observed that professions are institutionalized occupations—a topic we pursue in some detail below. Jepperson (1991) identified social objects such as marriage, wage labor, the corporation, and voting as contemporary institutions. Today, when an agency (for example, a government), a practice (for example, racial or gender discrimination), or an organization (for example, the long-lived corporation) becomes institutionalized, we mean that it has become an established and taken-for-granted pattern of practices and communication. Institutional theory aims to explain how these patterns arise and to demonstrate their effects on organizations.

The literature in institutional theory is voluminous and multilayered. Although we cannot review all the literature in this area, we can identify broad philosophical features that make institutional theory distinct and note its compatibility with organizational communication research. We then turn to a discussion of older and newer strands of institutional theory and research. We consider institutionalization as a process that begins with the establishment of institutional patterns across organizational fields. We review three fundamental concepts related to this process: legitimacy, the rational myth, and isomorphism. We then explore four areas of institutional scholarship that share intellectual ground with organizational communication: institutional logics, entrepreneurship, institutional work, and deinstitutionalization. We then turn to the intersections of institutionalism and communication: institutional rhetoric, discourse, and messages. To highlight the possibility of future collaborations between institutionalists and organizational communication scholars, we consider the case of professions. We close this chapter with comments about methods, limitations, and future possibilities for institutional organizational communication.

Distinctive Features of Institutional Theory

Several detailed summaries of institutional theory are readily available (Greenwood et al., 2008; Powell & DiMaggio, 1991). To provide a concise description of institutionalism, we summarize institutional theory in terms of four interrelated constructs: functionalism and limited rationality, external environments, attenuated consciousness, and the symbolic life of organizations. Tolbert and Zucker (1996) observed that the development of institutionalism in the late 1970s was a reaction to the unsatisfying results of research following functionalist assumptions about organizations. Functional analysis assumed that "components of a system must be integrated for the system to survive" (p. 176), that changes in one component necessitated changes in other components, and that change would occur when the dysfunctions of structural arrangements outweighed their functionality. A number of theorists argued that functional rationality had its limits (e.g., Cohen, March, & Olsen, 1972; March & Simon, 1958). Much of institutional theory and research concerned the unintended consequences of action in organizations (Merton, 1936). This thread of antirationalism connected institutional theorists across the decades (DiMaggio & Powell, 1983, 1991; Drori, 2008; Merton, 1936; Meyer & Rowan, 1977; Selznick, 1949, 1957). A hallmark of institutionalism historically, then, was that organized actors' intentions were shaped and even thwarted by their institutional environments. Institutionalists thus began and have continued with a view of rationality as situated (Drori, 2008; see also Kuhn, 2005; Trethewey & Ashcraft, 2004).

This discussion leads to a second fundamental construct in institutionalism: the role of the *external* environment of organizations. As Tolbert and Zucker (1996) observed, institutionalism developed at the same time that other approaches were also taking environments seriously, including population ecology (Hannan & Freeman, 1977) and resource dependency (Pfeffer & Salancik, 1978). Institutional studies focus on the boundary between authority in the organization and legitimacy bestowed by the institutional environment (Meyer & Rowan, 1977; Selznick, 1949). This distinction reaches beyond a micro-macro issue or even an interconnected view of organizations. The insight of institutionalism is that organizations and organizing are transcended by institutional(*ized*) ideas, beliefs, rules, and messages (Lammers, 2011; Lammers & Barbour, 2006; Lammers & Garcia, 2009). Thus with the recognition of a preexisting institutional environment, an institutional perspective complements the root metaphor of communication as constitutive of organizations (McPhee & Zaug, 2000).

The third fundamental construct, *attenuated consciousness*, focuses on the degree to which actors are conscious of institutional conditions. This concern is an empirical question and is at least as problematic for institutional researchers as it is for critical scholars (Deetz & Kersten, 1983; Mumby, 1988). This is because institutions are part of the taken-for-granted conditions on which organizing occurs. As Zucker (1983) said, "The taken for granted quality of institutions . . . implies that participants are not conscious of their central values" (p. 5). Thus the fixed routines that define institutions lead to an attenuation of consciousness such that institutions operate less as visible objects and more as unacknowledged trellises upon which organizing occurs and organizations grow.

Finally, institutionalism emphasizes the symbolic role of formal organizational structures in contrast to informal interactions and specific local or technical interests (Powell & DiMaggio, 1991). For example, *legitimacy* is viewed as social acceptance that results from adhering to regulative and normative organizational policies as well as cognitive norms and expectations (Deephouse & Carter, 2005, p. 332). The current interest in corporate social responsibility (CSR) is viewed by many scholars working from an institutional perspective as an example of what Meyer and Rowan (1977) referred to as "ceremonial activities" (p. 355) that are undertaken to assure access to perceived legitimacy (Bertels & Peloza, 2008; Levis, 2006; Truscott, Bartlett, & Tywoniak, 2009; Winn, MacDonald, & Zietsma, 2008). From an institutional view, organizations in their very structures communicate symbolically with their environments, absorbing information from the environment and signaling their conformity to established norms and values.

These features of institutionalism (namely, limited rationality, external forces, attenuated consciousness, and symbolism) are familiar territory for organizational communication researchers.

Organizational communication scholarship is quite at home in casting rationality as situated (e.g., Meisenbach, Remke, Buzzanell, & Liu, 2008) or problematic (Mumby & Stohl, 1996). Moreover, the concepts, constructs, and arguments of institutional theory offer avenues for research that incorporate cross-organizational variables, such as professional and trade associations, rules and regulations, and market forces. Also, actors' uneven awareness of institutional forces, such as the specifications of standard contract language in health insurance or procurement protocols in government spending policies, creates new opportunities for communication scholars to explore the limits and dynamics of conscious action. Finally, studying the symbolic life of organizations as it is manifested in texts and discourse is a well-established focus of organizational communication scholarship (Cooren, 2000; Cooren, Taylor, & Van Every, 2006). In the next section, we examine the specific concepts that form the institutionalists' armament. Even though institutional scholars share fundamental constructs, the development of the field has not been straightforward. In particular, an older form of institutionalism focused more on specific organizations than on environments.

Old Institutionalism

Weber (1968), typically the earliest scholar to whom institutionalists refer, defined institutions as "involuntary associations," thereby emphasizing an element of control in institutionalized life (p. 52). In the United States, however, Selznick (1949) set forth a sociology of institutions with his observation that "the important thing about organizations is that though they are tools each nevertheless has a life of its own. . . . [T]hey universally resist complete control" (p. 10). Selznick referred to this resistance as "recalcitrance" (p. 10) and noted later that organizational practices could become "infused with value beyond the technical requirements of the task at hand" (1957, p. 17).

One might see the institutional perspective as a focus on larger, distant, or abstract social structures. Selznick, however, was not interested in abstractions. Similar to many organizational communication scholars today, he was interested in actual organizations and communities and deeply concerned about democratic action. His best-known book, *TVA and the Grass Roots* (1949) was a study of a New Deal-era U.S. federal agency designed to maximize citizen participation at the local level.[2] The Tennessee Valley Authority (TVA) was the federal agency created to develop hydroelectricity in the Tennessee River Valley to improve the living standards of the surrounding farming communities. Selznick found that, as with other New Deal social experiments, the actual result of the TVA was not what was planned. He observed a special case of unintended consequences in the development of the TVA: *cooptation*. He defined *cooptation* as "the process of absorbing new elements into the leadership or policy determining structure of an organization as a means of averting threats to its stability or existence" (p. 13). As he noted, "Cooptation tells us something about the process by which *an institutional environment impinges itself upon an organization* and effects changes in its leadership, structure, or policy" (p. 13; emphasis added).

Although cooptation certainly seems to be a powerful mechanism, it has been studied fairly rarely in organizational communication research (for exceptions, see Brimeyer, Eaker, & Clair, 2004; Golden, 2009; Stohl & Coombs, 1988). Stohl and Coombs (1988) used the concept to describe the development of quality circles in U.S. industry and found that training manuals for quality circles advanced managerial interests over workers' interests.

Through Selznick's (1949) analysis of the TVA, and later, the Bolshevik revolution (1952) and administrative theory (1957), he influenced organizational scholarship of the 1950s (Dalton, 1959; Gouldner, 1954) and laid the ground work for later (new) institutional analyses: "(1) seek the underlying implications of the official doctrine . . . ; (2) avoid restriction to the formal structure of the organization . . . ; and (3) observe the interaction of the agency with other institutions in its area of operation" (1949, p. 11). Whereas Selznick focused on a particular organization and its institutional environment, later scholarship placed greater emphasis on the environment rather than a focal organization (Powell & DiMaggio, 1991, pp. 11–15).

A notable exception, and one of interest for organizational communication scholars, is Kraatz and Block's (2008) concern with institutional pluralism, which grows directly out of Selznick's concern with the institutional environment. Kraatz and Block (2008) defined *institutional pluralism* as "the situation faced by an organization that operates within multiple institutional spheres" (p. 243). In this situation, the organization answers to multiple regulatory agencies and follows multiple sets of norms, values, or legal requirements. Kraatz and Block suggested that organizational legitimacy "requires symbolic conformity with cultural norms and expectations" (p. 245). Pluralism, they argued, challenges the idea of organizational stability and makes organizational change less surprising (p. 257). Organizations will have "multiple, institutionally derived identities" (p. 243). Examples of these types of organizations include hospitals, universities, and multinational firms. This type of analysis—examining the multiple entities that constrain or shape an organization—represents an opportunity for communication scholars who are concerned with organizational identities, organizational change, and symbolic transactions.

New Institutionalism

For about 20 years, Selznick's type of analysis lay fallow. It was not until 1977 with the publication of Meyer and Rowan's article on formal organizational structure as myth and ceremony that organizational scholars picked up institutional analysis again. Meyer and Rowan (1977) noted that organizational environments were actually "littered" (p. 345) with values in excess of technical requirements. By then, Selznick's work was called *old institutionalism* and the later analyses were *new institutionalism* (Powell & DiMaggio, 1991). Powell and DiMaggio (1991) saw the new institutionalism as focusing on the symbolic role of formal structure (rather than on the informal organization), and they treated the organization as constituted by the environment in which it was embedded. New institutionalism, they argued, focused on the "homogeneity of organizations" and the "stability of institutional components" (p. 14). Moreover, DiMaggio and Powell viewed the unreflective activity in organizations as evidence for a critique of a utilitarian view of organizations. Organizations receive (perhaps unwittingly) classifications, routines, scripts, and schema, which function as key forms of cognition. Beginning in the late 1970s and continuing to the present day, institutional scholars (mostly in business schools) have developed a range of concepts through which the institutionalization process may be explored. We contend that these ideas map well onto the interpretive (Putnam & Pacanowsky, 1983), constitutive (McPhee & Zaug, 2000), and the Montréal school (Cooren, 2000; Cooren et al., 2006) approaches to organizational communication. In the following sections, we begin with institutionalization and end with deinstitutionalization; in between, we review three concepts used in institutional analysis with particular relevance for organizational communication scholarship: institutional logics, entrepreneurship, and work.

Institutionalization. Meyer and Rowan (1977) described institutionalization as the process by which "social processes, obligations, or actualities come to take on a rule-like status in social thought and action" (p. 342). From their perspective, this process is driven as much by external forces as functional requirements or internal organizational rationality. Their core contribution was communicative; that is, organizations absorb policies and structures to signal to their environments that they are legitimate; *legitimacy*, in turn, serves as a symbolic resource for organizations.

Tolbert and Zucker (1996) hypothesized a series of processes by which organizational practices may become institutionalized or develop *habitualized actions* (Berger & Luckmann, 1967). The processes, which can occur simultaneously and independently in different settings, include innovation, habitualization, objectification, and sedimentation. Tolbert and Zucker did not theorize about innovation, instead noting that it is a "largely independent activity" (1996, p. 181).[3] Indeed, innovation might be best understood in *contrast* to institutionalization, as it may occur as individual organizations seek to solve problems outside established conduct. In contrast, an important aspect of the second process, *habitualization*, is that routine actions take on lives independent of actors and can be classified and typified (Tolbert & Zucker, 1996, p. 180). This observation leads to the third process of institutionalization, *objectification*. Organizational structures that are habitualized and objectified may be said to be "semi-institutionalized" (p. 183), while full institutionalization requires historical continuity or sedimentation (p. 184). It is worth noting that innovation, habitualization, objectification, and sedimentation are essentially communicative processes. Deetz (1992, p. 126) used *sedimentation* with reference to *institutionalization* in essentially the same sense. Kuhn (2005) applied this model to the adoption of interpretive scholarship within the field of organizational communication. Tolbert and Zucker's (1996) framework offers communication scholars an opportunity to unpack the communicative features that underlie the processes of innovation, habitualization, objectification, and sedimentation. In addition to understanding the processes by which practices come to be institutionalized, scholars are concerned with *why* these practices become institutionalized. Meyer and Rowan (1977) contributed insights here by guiding scholars to explore the quest for legitimacy.

Legitimacy and the Rational Myth. Meyer and Rowan (1977) argued that the appearance of legitimacy is an important resource for organizations, particularly in highly regulated environments. They recognized that the structure of organizations is derived not only from the functional requirements of production but also from the external symbolic pressures *perceived* as legitimate, that is, "the extent to which the array of established cultural accounts provide explanations for [an organization's] existence, function, and jurisdiction, and lack or deny alternatives" (Meyer & Scott, 1983, p. 201). Moreover, Meyer and Rowan (1977) suggested that an organization uses rational myths (untestable means-ends statements such as "This organization engages in affirmative-action hiring policies.") to signal its legitimacy. These activities involve the efforts of managers and leaders to persuade workers about the adoption of practices congruent with externally established norms (Deephouse & Carter, 2005).

Several studies in organizational communication illustrate this thread, including O'Connor and Shumate (2010) and Barbour and Lammers (2007). Lammers (2003) argued that the high salaries paid to CEOs reflected established standards of legitimacy that operated in the absence of any evidence for a high correlation between firm performance and CEO salaries. In other words, symbolic, not functional, requirements explained these remuneration practices. Similarly, Zorn, Flanagin, and Shoham (2011) studied the roles of efficiency (functional) and legitimacy (symbolic) goals in the adoption of information technology among nonprofit organizations. They suggested that "efficient use of ICTs [information and communication technologies] may be spurred by institutional isomorphic pressures if organizations have the autonomy (i.e., leadership) and resources (i.e., knowledge and size) to find workable structures to make use of ICTs" (p. 24). These findings explain the ways that certain practices come to be institutionalized and show how these practices are embedded in or influenced by widespread social norms. Thus in the area of legitimacy, organizational scholars should consider the influence of institutional pressures, including hiring practices, wage and benefit practices, and performance evaluations on workplace policies and communication technology decisions. Another institutional insight is that such practices are commonly shared *across* organizations and industries and may therefore be field specific.

Fields and Isomorphism. Organizational fields consist of "those organizations that, in the aggregate, constitute a recognized area of institutional life: [including] key suppliers, resource and product consumers, regulatory agencies, and other organizations that produce similar services or products" (DiMaggio & Powell, 1983, p. 148). Organizations that make up a field are similar in structural and symbolic ways and share similar motivations for gaining legitimacy. DiMaggio and Powell (1983) drew heavily on sources and themes familiar to organizational communication scholars in developing the theory of institutional fields:

> The process of institutional definition, or "structuration," consists of four parts: an increase in the extent of interaction among organizations in the field; the emergence of sharply defined interorganizational structures of domination and patterns of coalition; an increase in the information load with which organizations in a field must contend; and the development of a mutual awareness among participants in a set of organizations that they are involved in a common enterprise. (DiMaggio & Powell, 1983, p. 148)

In brief, DiMaggio and Powell (1983) observed that organizations in established fields were becoming more similar, referring to this as *isomorphism*: "a constraining process that forces one unit in a population to resemble other units that face the same set of environmental conditions" (p. 150). They argued that competition alone could not explain isomorphism but that coercive, mimetic, and normative institutional pressures were at work. *Coercive pressures* are those that involve the influence of more powerful organizations. *Mimetic pressures* lead organizations to imitate others perceived as successful. *Normative pressures* are those associated with practices shared across organizations via trade and professional associations (pp. 150–154). These "mechanisms through which institutional isomorphic change occurs" (p. 150) have vastly influenced organizational studies (see Davis & Marquis, 2005; Green, Babb, & Alpaslan, 2008; Scott, 2001) and remain rich soil for scholars to till, especially by unpacking the processes in which these practices are adopted.

Organizational communication scholarship has participated in the development of these ideas. For example, Berteotti and Seibold (1994) observed isomorphic forces at work in the development of a hospice team. The hospice team "experienced coercive isomorphic processes as it tried to implement a team approach to health care within the context and [the] constraints of hierarchically structured organizations" (p. 127). They also found that the team "had to struggle to avoid modeling itself on non-hospice organizations," and "that normative pressures played a role as the members tried to create organizational norms to define the conditions" (p. 127) of their work. Sheets (2007) argued that scholars should look for signs of isomorphism in the public communication rather than the structures of these companies. She proposed an examination of major oil firms' responses to the Kyoto protocol. Similarly, O'Connor and Shumate (2010) found evidence of mimicry in the CSR statements of Fortune 500 companies. They noted that imitation is "one way corporations reduce the uncertainty of crafting messages for stakeholders" (p. 534).

Despite the uptake of the isomorphic concepts, the central thrust of the DiMaggio and Powell (1983) article—how *fields* are structured (with an emphasis on fields instead of individual organizations)—has yet to be tapped by organizational communication scholars. Yet it is clear that communicative processes are at work in the structuration of fields and that these processes have consequences for organizational members. By emphasizing the broader structures within which organizations operate, institutional scholars have observed that fields not only constrain the appearance of organizations but also shape members' cognitions and perceptions. In other words, *what makes sense* to organizational members is, in part, a function of institutional logics.

Institutional Logics. Both institutionalization and deinstitutionalization involve alterations in underlying ways of doing business or making sense of work. These ways can be thought of as *logics*. Institutional logics are "[sets] of material practices and symbolic constructions—which constitute [an institutional order's] organizing principles and which [are] available to organizations and individuals" (Friedland & Alford, 1991, p. 248). These *logics*, or guiding principles, can "constrain and enable the potential agency of actors" (Suddaby & Greenwood, 2005, p. 37). For example, in the case of DDT disuse, Maguire and Hardy (2009) found that actors, via the creation of discourses that endured over time, had to change the underlying logics of an institution to exert agency and disrupt the prevailing practice.

Of particular interest to communication scholars is that "the interests, identities, values, and assumptions of individuals and organizations are embedded in institutional logics" (Thornton & Ocasio, 2008, p. 103). Logics make certain ways of thinking and communicating possible or unlikely. Institutional logics "provide individuals with vocabularies of motives and with a sense of self" (Friedland & Alford, 1991, p. 251). While these authors do not refer specifically to Mills (1940), they note that vocabularies of motives are analyzable and institutionally specific.

In this vein, Lammers (2011) argued that actors know institutional logics via institutional messages (discussed further below). A communicative perspective suggests examining institutional messages to reveal underlying logics and the ways that actors transmit and take up logics. Regulatory agencies and industry standards transmit logics through written rules and regulations, and individuals may communicate logics via everyday talk or through the creation of texts. A communicative approach to logics would also explore the rhetorical strategies employed to establish certain views or how organizations respond to external pressures. Logics constrain which actions are taken and what actions are even available. To understand how institutional logics may change, scholars often focus on entrepreneurs.

Institutional Entrepreneurship. DiMaggio (1988) asserted that "new institutions arise . . . when organized actors with sufficient resources (institutional entrepreneurs) see in them an opportunity to realize interests that they value highly" (p. 14). Maguire, Hardy, and Lawrence (2004) defined institutional entrepreneurship as the "activities of actors who have an interest in particular institutional arrangements and who leverage resources to create new institutions or to transform existing ones" (p. 657). Research on institutional entrepreneurship considers what types of actors can become entrepreneurs, what field conditions are necessary to allow for change, and the "role of interpretive struggles" and "patterned actions" used to change a field (Hardy & Maguire, 2008, p. 199). Entrepreneurs negotiate and shape boundaries, mobilize resources, and construct logics to create change.

Institutional entrepreneurship strikes at the heart of a classical problem in organizational studies: embedded agency. How do actors change institutions if those very institutions limit their actions and rationality? Seo and Creed (2002) advanced a "dialectical framework" that identified "institutional contradictions and human praxis as the key mechanisms linking institutional embeddedness and institutional change (p. 223). They proposed that the conditions for change include contradictions or "inconsistencies" and a "partially autonomous social actor situated in a contradictory social world" (p. 230). Beckert (1999) argued that an entrepreneur is able to "take a reflective position towards institutionalized practices and can envision" alternatives (p. 786). Hardy and Maguire (2008) suggested that entrepreneurs could be individuals, organizations, professions, or networks. For example, Wijen and Ansari (2007) explored the possibility of "collective institutional entrepreneurship" (p. 1079). They studied state-level actors who developed global climate policies. Even though entrepreneurs may not have a great deal of power, they may hold positions that provide access to other institutional fields and thus other practices (Hardy & Maguire, 2008, p. 201). These actors must "dislodge existing practices (in the case of mature fields), introduce new ones, and then ensure that [the new practices] become widely adopted and taken for granted" (p. 206).

Battilana, Leca, and Boxenbaum (2009) claimed that entrepreneurs craft rhetorical arguments that embody institutional logics and align with "the values and interests of potential allies" (p. 82). Entrepreneurial actors are reflexive about existing logics and develop strategies—for example, texts of recurring patterns to influence existing discourses (Phillips, Lawrence, & Hardy, 2004). Such texts support or reject current institutional logics. Entrepreneurs reframe current problems and offer alternative ideas, as in the case of the Stockholm Convention, when a discursive struggle ensued over the difference between *precaution* and *sound science* (Maguire & Hardy, 2006). Zilber (2007) found that while crisis narratives in a high-tech industry in Israel reinforced the institutional order, counter stories called for change. These stories influenced how other actors understood the institutional order. In another study, Zilber (2002) found that powerful individuals at a rape crisis center controlled institutional meanings "by offering one official account" (p. 237). The struggle over meanings influenced power dynamics and, subsequently, the center's services.

Organizational communication scholars can contribute to research in this area by exploring the narratives, discursive struggles, and textual patterns of institutional entrepreneurship. With the fieldwide forces of isomorphism on the one hand and the individualistic implications of entrepreneurship on the other, institutionalists may appear to have limited room for agency, but an emerging area known as *institutional work* suggests that institutions are constructed, reconstructed, and changed in an ongoing way.

Institutional Work. Institutional work is an alternative approach to understanding agency and institutions. The term refers to the "purposive action of individuals and organizations aimed at creating, maintaining, and disrupting institutions" (Lawrence & Suddaby, 2006, p. 215). Even though institutional entrepreneurship and institutional work share an emphasis on the roles of actors in creating or changing institutions, Lawrence, Suddaby, and Leca (2009) criticized the scholarship on institutional entrepreneurship, arguing that it "[overemphasized] the rational and 'heroic' dimension . . . while ignoring the fact that all actors, even entrepreneurs, are embedded in an institutionally defined context" (p. 5).

An institutional work perspective treats institutions as the products of specific actions, created by a "wide range of actors, both those with the resources and skills to act as entrepreneurs and those whose role is supportive or facilitative of the entrepreneur's endeavors" (p. 217). While institutional studies often "accentuate the role of collective actors" (p. 5), institutional work also considers the role of individual organizational actors in providing a "middle ground of agency" (p. 6). Unlike Tolbert and Zucker's (1996) view of institutionalization in which habitualized actions and processes take on lives independent of actors, institutional work accounts for the "awareness, skill, and reflexivity of individual and collective actors" (Lawrence & Suddaby, 2006, p. 219).

Lawrence et al. (2009) argued that "institutional work highlights the intentional actions taken in relation to institutions" (p. 1). Studies on institutional work recognize that all practices occur within "sets of institutionalized rules" (Lawrence & Suddaby, 2006, p. 220) but also that actors can make intentional efforts to affect institutions. For example, Zietsma and Lawrence (2010) examined how the British Columbia coastal forest industry engaged in types of institutional work to maintain or change existing practices. During periods of stability, institutional work was aimed at maintenance, and during conflict cycles, institutional work included disrupting organizational and industry practices.

The creation and dissemination of texts, narratives, definitions, and other forms of discourse can also be seen as institutional work. Sahlin and Wedlin (2008) argued that ideas, in particular, are "actively transferred and translated in a context of other ideas, actors, traditions, and institutions" (p. 229). For example, actors engage in defining or constructing "rule systems that confer status or identity, define boundaries of membership or create status hierarchies within a field" (Lawrence & Suddaby, 2006, p. 222). These rule systems are communicated formally and informally in a variety of ways. In studies of professions, for example, individuals not only create professional associations and educational requirements to establish membership, they also develop a unique jargon to accompany membership. For example, Garcia (2011) found in her study of librarians that individuals engaged in strategic rhetorical constructions of their profession and individual professional identities. The aforementioned studies of institutional logics, entrepreneurship, and work focus on the creation, change, disruption, or maintenance of institutions. We now turn to the concept of deinstitutionalization.

Deinstitutionalization. Institutional stability requires organizational actors to accept a taken-for-granted legitimacy about certain practices, but deinstitutionalization reflects "a discontinuity in the willingness or ability of organizations to take for granted and continually re-create an institutionalized organizational activity" (Oliver, 1992, p. 564). Political, functional, and social pressures, aggravated by inertia and entropy, can lead to the dissipation or rejection of a practice. The established or institutionalized practice then "erodes or discontinues" (p. 564).

Lawrence and Suddaby (2006) argued that the literature on deinstitutionalization makes room for the possibility that individuals can strategically act to destroy institutions. They borrow from the sociology of practice, which "[focuses] on the situated actions of individuals and groups as they cope with and attempt to respond to the demands of their everyday lives" (p. 218). For example, Maguire and Hardy (2009) found that through the creation, distribution, and consumption of texts of practices, discourses drive the process of deinstitutionalization. They examined texts that problematized current practices associated with DDT use and argued that "individual acts of translation . . . can change discourse" and thus the underlying logics of an institution (p. 149). The idea of deinstitutionalization challenges the idea that practices, once institutionalized, are nigh impossible to alter and instead draws attention to the conditions under which they can be altered or rejected. More broadly, the literature on new institutionalism focuses on how practices and rules come to be taken for granted, altered, or disrupted and the relationship between structure and agency. Organizational communication scholars can contribute to this research by exploring the role of discourse, the creation and circulation of texts, and the communicative strategies actors use to disrupt institutional practices. We turn now to areas of scholarship that organizational communication and institutional studies already share conceptual terrain.

Conceptual Territory Shared by Institutionalism and Communication

The last few years have revealed a turn toward rhetorical and discourse analysis in organization and institutional studies (Green et al., 2008; Hardy, 2011; Phillips et al., 2004; Powell & Colyvas, 2008) and a similar turn among rhetorical and discourse scholars toward institutional analysis (Cheney,

1991; Finet, 2001; Ford, 2003; Hartelius & Browning, 2008; Hoffman & Ford, 2010; Jablonski, 1989; Keranen, 2007; Lynch, 2005; Schwarze, 2003; Sproule, 1988). In particular, institutional scholars have called for considering the role of language in studies on institutionalization. Phillips et al. (2004), for example, criticized the institutional literature for focusing more on social behaviors and structural arrangements than on the discursive elements of social interaction that contribute to institutionalization. In the following section, we show how scholarship in institutional rhetoric, institutional discourse, and institutional messages explicitly or implicitly use institutional concepts and ideas.

Institutional Rhetoric

A focus on rhetoric allows scholars to account simultaneously for the structural elements of institutions and the discursive actions of individual and organizational interactions. Hartelius and Browning (2008) argued that rhetoric serves as a "theoretical lens" as well as "a framework for understanding the role of narrative and rational organizational discourses" (p. 33). Rhetorical analysis of texts produced by actors in institutional environments has led to useful discoveries about the role of language in circulating ideas (Sahlin & Wedlin, 2008), persuading actors to subscribe to new logics or altering current practices or beliefs.

A number of studies in communication have employed the idea of institutional rhetoric (see, for example, Cheney, 1991; Finet, 2001; Ford, 2003; Hartelius & Browning, 2008; Hoffman & Ford, 2010; Jablonski, 1989; Keranen, 2007; Lynch, 2005; Schwarze, 2003). For Sproule (1988), a new type of rhetorical criticism was necessary to account for "institutions, ideologies, media, and audiences" (p. 477). He argued that a "new managerial rhetoric" arose as a way of accounting for the spokespersons of "whole industries" (p. 460), the media as an institution composed of professionals in the "impersonal institutional voice of corporate suasion" (p. 469), and mass audiences. In this rhetorical approach, the institution is an entity that speaks for itself and, by proxy, for its members. For example, Jablonski (1989) and Cheney (1991) examined the rhetoric of the Catholic Church. In both cases, the Church was seen as an institution that rhetorically managed multiple identities and responded to the pressures of a broader socio-political context, including external and internal audiences. While not explicitly drawing from institutional theory, these studies nonetheless make a contribution to our understanding of how institutions work.

Finet (2001) proposed a view of institutional rhetoric that involved the "collective expression [of organizations] intended to influence the larger social normative climate" (p. 274). This approach to organizational rhetoric reveals the "embeddedness of organizations" and the "reciprocal influences" of organizations and their environments (p. 270). An expanding literature has also focused on the rhetoric CSR (Battilana et al., 2009; see May, Cheney, & Roper, 2007). Schwarze (2003) argued that "a rhetoric of CSR must have an interorganizational focus" (p. 625). In this view, he comes very close to the institutional approach. Organizational and institutional research in CSR includes both rhetorical and discourse analysis. We argue that examining institutional rhetoric allows scholars to explore the strategic collective expressions of organizations as they seek legitimacy in their institutional environments.

In addition to CSR statements, scholars have also studied texts of rules and practices that become institutionalized. For example, Keranen (2007) analyzed the institutionalization of resuscitation, demonstrating that code status worksheets (patients' end-of-life documents) served as part of a system of rules that influenced the taken-for-granted status of resuscitation. Green et al. (2008) examined the corporate control rhetoric of board members, arguing that it "shapes the institutional logics of control and thus legitimizes the dominant stakeholder group in the institutional field" (p. 41). Suddaby and

Greenwood (2005) used transcripts from commission hearings. Examining classical categories of rhetoric (e.g., logos), they suggested that "rhetorical strategy is a significant tool by which shifts in a dominant logic can be achieved" (p. 41). In these examples, rhetoric is a tool used by organizational actors to influence logics, and its analysis can account for institutionalization or institutional change.

Rhetorical scholars have much to offer institutional studies. For example, Lawrence and Suddaby's (2006) typology of institutional work lends itself to a communication perspective. The authors describe types of institutional work (e.g., advocacy and theorizing), which are specifically communicative in nature and could be analyzed from a rhetorical perspective. Additionally, evidence of institutional work is found in the texts and conversations that occur in and around organizations. In sum, reframing existing scholarship on organizational rhetoric as explicitly institutional offers rich avenues and new directions for future studies of institutional rhetoric.

Institutional Discourse

Rhetoric and *discourse* are sometimes used interchangeably or indiscriminately, but it is useful to distinguish them for conducting institutional analysis (see Fairhurst & Putnam, Chapter 11). Citing Burke (1969) and Mills (1940), Castello and Lozano (2011) observed that rhetorical analysis "focuses on persuasive texts fostering a specific response to social change," while discourse analysis "examines texts without supposing how recipients of their messages will be influenced" (p. 4). Grant, Hardy, Oswick, and Putnam (2004) included rhetoric as a "domain" of organizational discourse (p. 3). Cheney, Christensen, Conrad, and Lair (2004) suggested that a rhetorical approach is concerned primarily with the strategic dimensions of discourse. At the institutional level, discourses reflect shared management philosophies, procedures, and published texts as well as conversations. Grant, Keenoy, and Oswick (2001) argued that discourse analysis examines "meta-discourses . . . which congregate to form dominant paradigms, institutional practices, and collective social perspectives (p. 11).

Discourse analysis offers a way to get at institutional logics (reflected in institutional work) and even institutional entrepreneurship. For example, Kuhn (2006) studied attorneys and government officials and suggested that these officials drew discursive resources from the social practices around them. Similarly, studies of institutional dialogue show how talk in institutionalized settings—for example, among professionals in health care organizations—contributes to a range of concerns, such as identity, roles, and constraints on behavior (see Grant et al., 2004, p. 11). As Grant et al. (2004) noted, scholars can focus on the "socially situated aspects of everyday talk" (p. 3; see also Drew & Heritage, 1992). Certainly, the institutional context is an important influence on everyday talk, the management of identities, and the performance of organizational tasks.

These issues surface in both organizational and institutional discourse research. For example, Clair (1993) studied the discourse of sexual harassment at large universities. She used *institutional discourse* to refer to relatively established discourses in a large organization, and she did not distinguish the organizational from the institutional arena. However, her work echoes issues related to institutional logics. In particular, the dominant discourses revealed underlying logics that were reflected in established practices and rules. More recent research has identified institutional discourse as a level of analysis. For example, O'Connor and Shumate (2010) studied CSR statements of Fortune 500 companies and found that at both the institutional and economic industry levels of analysis, corporations gave primacy in their CSR discourse to their "ethical and philanthropic responsibilities over their legal and economic responsibilities" (p. 547). As noted earlier, the mimicry found in CSR statements illustrates corporations' attempts to reduce uncertainty and to gain legitimacy.

For practices to change, however, discourse about those practices must also change. Hardy and Maguire (2010) found that less powerful actors influenced change because "field-configuring events," such as the Stockholm Convention, "generate multiple discursive spaces that are governed by different rules and understandings regarding text production" (p. 1365). This analysis of discourse and discursive spaces explains the conditions necessary for embedded agents, *entrepreneurs*, to engage in processes that might lead to change. Institutional discourse attends to the symbolic ways that actors attempt to influence the institutional arrangements around them.

Institutional Messages[4]

A third area in which institutional and organizational communication scholars share interests is in the identification and analysis of institutional messages, "collations of thoughts that are intentional, enduring, have a wide reach, and encumber organizational participants to engage in certain behaviors or to take performative responses" (Lammers, 2011, p. 154). In contrast to discourse or rhetorical analysis, a focus on messages is reductionist rather than holistic, positing that relatively discrete components of communication play a role in the persistence and development of institutions. The analysis of messages offers clues to several institutional issues, such as the institution-organization interface, the question of how institutions endure, and how institutional logics are transmitted.

Institutional messages can be observed at interactional, organizational, and institutional levels of analysis. An important feature of institutional messages is that they can take the form of an implicit command, obligating receivers to engage in some form of action (Lammers, 2011, p. 162). Institutional messages communicate logics, or the "means by which ends are achieved" (Friedland & Alford, 1991, p. 256), as persons draw upon and incorporate them in their speech and established interactions. Such interactions are characterized by an obligatory asymmetry; that is, the disembodied institution speaks for itself, and the rules are followed. At the organizational level, institutional messages aim to align the organization's core values and interests with those of its environment. Such messages are conveyed both to internal (as in the case of policies to which all employees must adhere) and external audiences (as in the case of an organization conveying to a funding agency that its practices are consistent with the agency's aims and goals). As institution-level phenomena, institutional messages project a rational feature of modernity; namely, they are spread across specific organizations and interaction moments through educational practices, consultants, and interagency and interorganizational agreements and are enforced with rules and sanctions.

The variety of settings and levels at which institutional messages may be observed and analyzed led Lammers (2011) to suggest that institutional messages could be understood in four ways: establishment, reach, incumbency, and intentionality. *Established* messages are unequivocal, are sent or exchanged frequently, and are thus enduring. The *reach* of messages refers to the size and number of audiences in which the message may be received. *Incumbency* refers to the duty—implicated in the message itself—of the respondent to heed and comply with the message. Finally, institutional messages can be characterized by their *intentionality*; the message may be varyingly congruent with the conscious, stated purposes of the members of the field in which it is exchanged.

Institutional messages also figure prominently in McPhee and Zaug's (2000, 2009) influential articulation of the communicative constitution of organizations. Of their four message flows, *institutional positioning* bears directly on the recognition that communication constitutes organization when actors recognize the extraorganizational, preexisting constraints on the actions and resources at their disposal (McPhee & Zaug, 2009). The importance and complexity of institutional positioning was described in Browning, Greene, Sitkin, Sutcliffe, & Obstfeld's (2009) description of a United States Air Force maintenance and repair unit's effort to coordinate its activities with external agency rules.

Sahlin and Wedlin (2008) reviewed a concept related to messages in their discussion of the circulation of ideas in institutional fields. Summarizing research in the field of Scandinavian institutionalism, they observed that although organizations embrace ideas for ceremonial and symbolic purposes (Meyer & Rowan, 1977), they also adopt policies, practices, and routines that influence functional activities as well. They noted that organizations adopted ideas because of normative forces ("appropriateness and fashion," p. 222) through imitation and identification processes. One shortcoming of these observations is that the researchers tended to anthropomorphize organizations. Nonetheless, this research and others in this vein have developed a robust set of concepts (including translation, editing, flows, prototypes, and templates) to describe the processes by which ideas spread across fields.

The notion of institutional messages holds considerable promise for organizational communication researchers who work with institutional ideas (Barley, 2011; Hardy, 2011; Suddaby, 2011). However, the concept may be overly deterministic in its emphasis on enduring social structures (Hardy, 2011; Suddaby, 2011). Hardy argued that such messages are in fact the creations of individuals and that institutions gain their power and force through the communicative behavior of individuals. In addition, Barley (2011) pointed out that institutional messages may be vague or ambiguous by design; that is, laws and other policies are often worded imprecisely to allow for a range of interpretations. For organizational communication researchers, research on institutional messages offers the opportunity for scholars to participate in these debates by addressing the structure/agency relationship, the issue of ambiguity, and the types and varieties of institutional messages.

The Special Case of Professions

The concepts reviewed in this chapter can also be used to study communication and the professions in new ways. Abbott (1988) referred to professions as "institutionalized occupations," (p. 323; see also Douglas, 1986). As Lammers and Garcia (2009) pointed out, the profession is part of the (external) institutional environment of work, because professionals bring norms and rules with them into the organizations where they work. Scott (2008) argued that professions are cultural-cognitive, normative, and regulative agents of institutionalization (pp. 224–226). As such, they do much to shape organizations and organizational communication. The concepts generated by institutionalists over the last 50 years can offer organizational communication scholars approaches for studying the professions.

Specifically, conceptual tools such as cooptation, rational myths, institutional fields and logics, and institutional work are available to communication scholars to aid in understanding how professions shape organizational life. An institutionally infused study of communication between professionals and managers is likely to find examples of institutionalized *cooptation*. For example, associate attorneys in large law firms may be understood as coopted by the managing partners of their firms, and physicians may be seen as coopted by the managers of hospitals. The rise of the professions historically (for example, Starr, 1982) and contemporarily (for example, Cheney, Lair, Ritz, & Kendall, 2010) provide accounts of *legitimacy* as part of the adoption of *rational myths* or ways that work should be accomplished. Professionals are also the designers of stable practices and knowledge domains and thus influence the development of recognizable *institutional fields* organized by underlying *institutional logics* (Douglas, 1986; Scott, 2008). The effort to professionalize various fields is an example of *institutional work,* notably characterized as *institutional entrepreneurship.* Cheney and Ashcraft (2007) argue that having professional status is something occupants struggle for control over. Individual or collective struggles to gain professional status represent efforts to institutionalize occupational practices.

Just as the rise of a profession may be understood as a process of *institutionalization*, the demise of a profession may be seen as *deinstitutionalization*. Both of these concepts, as well as the ongoing maintenance or re-creation of professional autonomy and control, provide examples of institutional *rhetoric* and *discourse*. And the presence and dominance of a profession may be recognized by the strength of *institutional messages*, such as "Is there a doctor in the house?" Employing these conceptual tools of communication and institutionalism can advance knowledge about the role of the profession in organizational practices.

Communication scholars have begun to recognize professionals as unique organizational members who play institutional roles (e.g., Cheney & Ashcraft, 2007; Cheney et al., 2010, pp. 123–158; Lammers & Garcia, 2009; Real & Putnam, 2005; Trethewey, 2001). Cheney et al. (2010), in an examination of ethics at work, considered the influence of professionalism on careers and organizations and recognized professions as institutions that organize knowledge in society (p. 129). More commonly, communication researchers have viewed professionalism as a special identity project. Trethewey (2001) considered issues of gender and identity for professional women, and Ashcraft (2005) and Real and Putnam (2005) explored pilots' discourse regarding defense of their profession. Heaton and Taylor (2002) explored how knowledge communities find a "collective identity in professional associations" (p. 212). Although only a few of these scholars explicitly relied on institutional theory, these studies demonstrated how particular occupations served as institutionalized communication. As Cheney and Ashcraft (2007) argued, professionalization is a "rhetorical process" in which identity and status are "constantly negotiated through discursive activity" (p. 165). Their argument points to important connections between communication and professionalization as forms of institutionalization.

A few scholars explicitly relied on institutional theory to explore the relationship between communication and professions. Lammers and Garcia (2009) found that the profession served as an extraorganizational force that influenced veterinarians' work experiences, including their decision making and communication. Barbour and Lammers (2007) also argued that institutional beliefs mediated physicians' responses to managed health care. Further, Barbour (2010) urged scholars to focus on the day-to-day conversations in health care organizations to examine how institutions "control and constrain talk . . . [and how] actors appropriate institutions to their own ends" (p. 450). Dunn and Jones (2010) analyzed medical education and found that the logics of care and science in medical education competed and changed over time. They argued that as logics are thrown "out of balance," the profession becomes "vulnerable to threats from interprofessional rivals, intraprofessional groups, and external invaders like managed care" (p. 140). Communication scholars, then, can examine the creation, maintenance, and change of institutions by following professions and professionals through these processes. This brief overview of the profession serves as evidence of a particularly rich area of mutually informed research in institutional and organizational communication studies.

Conclusion

This chapter has aimed to encourage organizational communication scholars to employ institutional analyses. To this end, we underscore the mutually enriching compatibilities of the institutional perspective, particularly its emphases on limits to rationality, external forces on organizations, socially constructed consciousness, and symbolism as well as its prevailing ideas in organizational communication. We have also pointed to the concepts of legitimacy and rational myth, isomorphism, institutional fields, institutional logics, institutional entrepreneurship, and institutional work as available for organizational communication scholarship. Rhetorical and discourse analysis are already examining how institutions rise, persist, or decline. In this conclusion, we draw attention to methodological considerations and limitations of the institutional approach as organizational communication scholars look to institutional theory as a framework for future studies.

Methodological Considerations

Institutional theory does not privilege a particular methodology, but the task of investigating institutions strongly calls for certain methodological moves and empirical foci. First, studies must adopt diachronic methods (see Barley & Tolbert, 1997). Institutions cannot be captured effectively with the single-point observations that organizational communication studies often employ. Another key feature of institutions is that they transcend individual organizations. This characteristic requires scholars to observe populations, fields, industries, or interorganizational relationships rather than single organizations. In this respect, O'Connor and Shumate's (2010) study of web-based CSR statements is a good example. A third and related point is that an institutional perspective emphasizes external influences on organizations, suggesting that institutionally informed studies should include external sources of information and influence. Fourth, the institutional perspective focuses on rules, norms, and laws more than on interpersonal interactions. With its roots in interaction, organizational communication scholars have typically bypassed archival sources as the basis of meaning in organizations. Few studies focus on the role of contracts and regulations in explaining organizational communication. Geist and Hardesty's (1992) study of hospital workers' reactions to the adoption of a federal Medicare reimbursement scheme, known as *diagnosis related groups*, provides a notable exception.

Limitations of the Institutional Approach

Institutional approaches are often criticized as theoretically imperialistic; that is, they purport to encompass and explain everything about organizations. Thus all external forces are commonly seen as institutional, and all behavior in organizations is held to be a manifestation of institutional forces. Also, institutions in contemporary industrial and postindustrial societies may actually represent a particular type of cultural development. Hence, it is difficult to distinguish analytically between the external cultural environments of organizations and their institutional environments. We also observe that the institutional approach has a tendency to elude straightforward specification and operationalization of terms, including concepts such as *institution* and *rational myth*. And yet this is where organizational communication, with its careful attention to interaction, discourse, persuasion, audience, interpretation, and messages, is able to inform institutional theory.

The institutional perspective is one of the dominant theoretical paradigms in organization studies today (Palmer, Biggart, & Dick, 2008). Under its aegis, a wide range of organizational studies have been and continue to be published. Many of these projects have strong implications for organizational communication, especially in studying how individuals exercise agency while embedded in institutions. As Battilana et al. (2009) observe, "It seems important to develop finer-grained analyses that will account for the actions and values of all of the agents involved in the process of shaping institutions" (p. 95).

Another area ripe for investigation is the use of network analysis to demonstrate the endurance of established institutional patterns (see Pentland, 1999). The current interest in nonprofit and nongovernmental organizations also offers organizational communication researchers an opportunity to examine institutional change and persistence (Doerfl, Lai, Chewning, 2010; Taylor & Doerfl, 2011). Communication studies of organizational change (Lewis, 2007; see also Lewis, Chapter 20) have tended to dwell on intra-organizational issues but have begun to consider institutional forces as well (Lewis, 2011, p. 210). In addition, the core concepts of institutional theory—in particular, legitimacy and logics—need to be unpacked in terms of communication. Both legitimacy and logics are communicatively constructed and implicated in scholars' concerns for uncertainty, identity, and power. With a strong tradition of carefully designed and closely focused research, organizational communication can make a substantial contribution to institutional theory and research. In its most recent manifestations, institutional theory offers a fertile field for reframing organizational communication scholarship and for showing how institutions are communicatively constituted.

References

Abbott, A. (1988). *The systems of professions: An essay on the division of expert labor*. Chicago, IL: University of Chicago Press.

Ashcraft, K. L. (2005). Resistance through consent? Occupational identity, organizational form, and the maintenance of masculinity among commercial airline pilots. *Management Communication Quarterly, 19*(1), 67–90.

Barbour, J. B. (2010). On the institutional moorings of talk in health care organizations. *Management Communication Quarterly, 24*(3), 449–456.

Barbour, J. B., & Lammers, J. C. (2007). Health care institutions, communication, and physicians' experience of managed care: A multilevel analysis. *Management Communication Quarterly, 21*(2), 201–231.

Barley, S. R. (2011). Signifying institutions. *Management Communication Quarterly, 25*(1), 200–206.

Barley, S. R., & Tolbert, P. S. (1997). Institutionalization and structuration: Studying the links between action and institution. *Organization Studies, 18*(1), 93–117.

Battilana, J., Leca, B., & Boxenbaum, E. (2009). How actors change institutions: Towards a theory of institutional entrepreneurship. *Annals of the Academy of Management, 3*(1), 65–107.

Beckert, J. (1999). Agency, entrepreneurs, and institutional change: The roles of strategic choice and institutionalized practices in organizations. *Organization Studies, 20*(5), 777–799.

Berger, P., Berger, B., & Kellner, H. (1973). *The homeless mind: Modernization and consciousness*. New York, NY: Random House.

Berger, P., & Luckmann, T. (1967). *The social construction of reality: A treatise in the sociology of knowledge*. Garden City, NY: Anchor Books.

Bertels, S., & Peloza, J. (2008). Running just to stand still? Managing CSR reputation in an era of ratcheting expectations. *Corporate Reputation Review, 11*(1), 56–73.

Berteotti, C. R., & Seibold, D. R. (1994). Coordination and role-definition problems in health-care teams: A hospice case study. In L. R. Frey (Ed.), *Group communication in context: Studies of natural groups* (pp. 107–131). Hillsdale, NJ: Lawrence Erlbaum.

Brimeyer, T. M., Eaker, A. V., & Clair, R. P. (2004). Rhetorical strategies in union organizing: A case of labor versus management. *Management Communication Quarterly, 18*(1), 45–75.

Browning, L., Greene, R., Sitkin, S., Sutcliffe, K., & Obstfeld, D. (2009). Constitutive complexity: Military entrepreneurs and the synthetic character of communication flows. In A. Nicotera & L. Putnam (Eds.), *Building theories of organization: The constitutive role of communication* (pp. 89–116). Mahwah, NJ: Lawrence Earlbaum.

Burke, K. (1969). *A grammar of motives*. Berkeley: University of California Press.

Castello, I., & Lozano, J. M. (2011). Searching for new forms of legitimacy through corporate responsibility. *Journal of Business Ethics, 100*(1), 11–29.

Cheney, G. (1991). *Rhetoric in an organizational society: Managing multiple identities*. Columbia: University of South Carolina Press.

Cheney, G., & Ashcraft, K. L. (2007). Considering "the professional" in communication studies: Implications for theory and research within and beyond the boundaries of organizational communication. *Communication Theory, 17*(2), 146–175.

Cheney, G., Christensen, L. T., Conrad, C., & Lair, D. J. (2004). Corporate rhetoric as organizational discourse. In D. Grant, C. Hardy, C. Oswick, & L. L. Putnam (Eds.), *The SAGE handbook of organizational discourse* (pp. 79–103). London, England: SAGE.

Cheney, G., Lair, D. J., Ritz, D., & Kendall, B. E. (2010). *Just a job? Communication, ethics, and professional life*. Oxford, UK: Oxford University Press.

Clair, R. P. (1993). The bureaucratization, commodification, and privatization of sexual harassment through institutional discourse: A study of the Big Ten universities. *Management Communication Quarterly, 7*(2), 123–157.

Cohen, M. D., March, J. G., & Olsen, J. P. (1972). A garbage can model of organizational choice. *Administrative Science Quarterly, 17*(1), 1–25.

Commons, J. R. (1934). *Institutional economics: Its place in political economy*. New York, NY: Macmillan.

Cooren, F. (2000). *The organizing property of communication*. Amsterdam, the Netherlands: John Benjamins.

Cooren, F., Taylor, J. R., & Van Every, E. J. (Eds.). (2006). *Communication as organizing: Empirical and theoretical explorations in the dynamic of text and conversation*. Mahwah, NJ: Lawrence Erlbaum.

Dalton, M. (1959). *Men who manage*. New York, NY: John Wiley & Sons.

Davis, G. F., & Marquis, C. (2005). Prospects for organization theory in the early twenty-first century. *Organization Science, 16*(4), 332–343.

Deephouse, D. L., & Carter, S. M. (2005). An examination of differences between organizational legitimacy and organizational reputation. *Journal of Management Studies, 42*(2), 329–360.

Deetz, S. A. (1992). *Democracy in an age of corporate colonization: Developments in communication and the politics of everyday life*. Albany: State University of New York Press.

Deetz, S. A., & Kersten, A. (1983). Critical models of interpretive research. In L. L. Putnam & M. E. Pacanowsky (Eds.), *Communication and organizations: An interpretive approach* (pp. 147–171). Beverly Hills, CA: SAGE.

DiMaggio, P. J. (1988). Interest and agency in institutional theory. In L. G. Zucker (Ed.), *Institutional patterns and organizations: Culture and environment* (pp. 3–22). Cambridge, MA: Ballinger.

DiMaggio, P. J., & Powell, W. W. (1983). The iron cage revisited: Institutional isomorphism and collective rationality in organization fields. *American Sociological Review, 48*(2), 147–160.

Douglas, M. (1986). *How institutions think*. Syracuse, NY: Syracuse University Press.

Doerfel, M. L., Lai, C., & Chewning, L. V. (2010). The evolutionary role of interorganizational communication: Modeling social capital in disaster contexts. *Human Communication Research, 36*(2), 125–162.

Drew, P., & Heritage, J. (Eds.). (1992). *Talk at work: Interaction in institutional settings*. Cambridge, UK: Cambridge University Press.

Drori, G. S. (2008). Institutionalism and globalization studies. In R. Greenwood, C. Oliver, K., Sahlin, & R. Suddaby (Eds.), *Handbook of Organizational Institutionalism* (pp. 449–472). Thousand Oaks, CA: SAGE.

Dunn, M. B., & Jones, C. (2010). Institutional logics and institutional pluralism: The contestation of care and science logics in medical education 1967–2005. *Administrative Science Quarterly, 55*(1), 114–149.

Eisenberg, E. (2009). Organizational communication theories. In S. Littlejohn & K. Foss (Eds.), *Encyclopedia of communication theories* (vol. 2, pp. 700–705). Thousand Oaks, CA: SAGE.

Finet, D. (2001). Sociopolitical environments and issues. In F. M. Jablin & L. Putnam (Eds.), *The new handbook of organizational communication: Advances in theory, research, and methods* (pp. 270–290). Thousand Oaks, CA: SAGE.

Ford, D. J. (2003). *Prism analysis of the debate over the American Medical Association's Health Access America Plan*. Proceedings of the 2004 Alta Conference on Argumentation, National Communication Association, Washington, DC.

Friedland, R., & Alford, R. R. (1991). Bringing society back in: Symbols, practices, and institutional contradictions. In W. W. Powell & P. J. DiMaggio (Eds.), *The new institutionalism in organizational analysis* (pp. 232–263). Chicago, IL: University of Chicago Press.

Garcia, M. A. (2011). *Ask a librarian: The profession, professional identities, and constitutive rhetoric of librarians* (Unpublished doctoral dissertation). University of Illinois at Urbana-Champaign, Urbana, IL.

Gehlen, A. (1988). *Man, his nature and place in the world*. New York, NY: Columbia University Press. (Originally published as *Der Mensch; seine Natur und seine Stellung in der Welt*. Frankfurt am Main: Äthenäum Verlag, 1966).

Geist, P., & Hardesty, M. (1992). *Negotiating the crisis: DRGs and the transformation of hospitals*. Hillsdale, NJ: Lawrence Erlbaum.

Giddens, A. (1984). *The constitution of society. Outline of the theory of structuration*. Cambridge, UK: Polity.

Golden, A. G. (2009). Employee families and organizations as mutually enacted environments: A sensemaking approach to work-life interrelationships. *Management Communication Quarterly, 22*(3), 385–415.

Gouldner, A. (1954). *Patterns of industrial bureaucracy*. New York, NY: Free Press.

Grant, D., Hardy, C., Oswick, C., & Putnam, L. (Eds.). (2004). *The SAGE handbook of organizational discourse*. London, England: SAGE.

Grant, D., Keenoy, T., & Oswick, C. (2001). Organizational discourse: Key contributions and challenges. *International Studies of Management and Organization, 31*(3), 5–24.

Green, S. E., Jr., Babb, M., & Alpaslan, C. M. (2008). Institutional field dynamics and the competition between institutional logics: The role of rhetoric in the evolving control of the modern corporation. *Management Communication Quarterly, 22*(1), 40–73.

Greenwood, R., Oliver, C., Sahlin, K., & Suddaby, R. (2008). Introduction. In R. Greenwood, C. Oliver, K. Sahlin, & R. Suddaby (Eds.), *The SAGE handbook of organizational institutionalism*. Thousand Oaks, CA: SAGE.

Hannan, M. T., & Freeman J. (1977). The population ecology of organizations. *American Journal of Sociology, 82*(5), 929–964.

Hardy, C. (2011). How institutions communicate; or how does communicating institutionalize? *Management Communication Quarterly, 25*(1), 191–199.

Hardy, C., & Maguire, S. (2008). Institutional entrepreneurship. In R. Greenwood, C. Oliver, K. Sahlin, & R. Suddaby (Eds.), *The SAGE handbook of organizational institutionalism* (pp. 198–217). Thousand Oaks, CA: SAGE.

Hardy, C., & Maguire, S. (2010). Discourse, field-configuring events, and change in organizations and institutional fields: Narratives of DDT and the Stockholm Convention. *Academy of Management Journal, 53*(6), 1365–1392.

Hartelius, E. J., & Browning, L. D. (2008). The application of rhetorical theory in managerial research: A literature review. *Management Communication Quarterly, 22*(1), 13–39.

Heaton, L., & Taylor, J. (2002). Knowledge management and professional work: A communication perspective on the knowledge-based organization. *Management Communication Quarterly, 16*(2), 210–236.

Hoffman, M. F., & Ford, D. J. (2010). *Organizational rhetoric: Situations and strategies*. Thousand Oaks, CA: SAGE.

Jablonski, C. J. (1989). "Aggiornamento" and the American Catholic bishops: A rhetoric of institutional continuity and change. *Quarterly Journal of Speech, 75*(4), 416–432.

Jepperson, R. L. (1991). Institutions, institutional effects, and institutionalism. In W. W. Powell & P. DiMaggio (Eds.), *The new institutionalism in organizational analysis* (pp. 143–163). Chicago, IL: University of Chicago Press.

Keranen, L. (2007). "'Cause someday we all die": Rhetoric, agency, and the case of the "patient" preferences worksheet. *Quarterly Journal of Speech, 93*(2), 179–210.

Kraatz, M. S., & Block, E. S. (2008). Organizational implications of institutional pluralism. In R. Greenwood, C. Oliver, K. Sahlin, & R. Suddaby (Eds.), *The SAGE handbook of organizational institutionalism*. Thousand Oaks, CA: SAGE.

Kuhn, T. (2005). The institutionalization of Alta in organizational communication studies. *Management Communication Quarterly, 18*(4), 618–627.

Kuhn, T. (2006). A "demented work ethic" and a "lifestyle firm": Discourse, identity, and workplace time commitments. *Organization Studies, 27*(9), 1339–1358.

Lammers, J. C. (2003). An institutional perspective on communicating corporate responsibility. *Management Communication Quarterly, 16*(4), 618–624.

Lammers, J. C. (2011). How institutions communicate: Institutional messages, institutional logics, and organizational communication. *Management Communication Quarterly, 25*(1), 154–182.

Lammers, J. C., & Barbour, J. B. (2006). An institutional theory of organizational communication. *Communication Theory, 16*(3), 356–377.

Lammers, J. C., & Garcia, M. A. (2009). Exploring the concept of "profession" for organizational communication research: Institutional influences in a veterinary organization. *Management Communication Quarterly, 22*(3), 357–384.

Lawrence, T. B., & Suddaby, R. (2006). Institutions and institutional work. In S. R. Clegg, C. Hardy,

T. B. Lawrence, & W. R. Nord (Eds.), *Handbook of organization studies* (2nd ed.). London, England: SAGE.

Lawrence, T. B., Suddaby, R., & Leca, B. (2009). Introduction: Theorizing and studying institutional work. In T. B. Lawrence, R. Suddaby, & B. Leca (Eds.), *Institutional work: Actors and agency in institutional studies or organizations* (pp. 1–27). Cambridge, UK: Cambridge University Press.

Levis, J. (2006). Adoption of corporate social responsibility codes by multinational companies. *Journal of Asian Economics, 17*(1), 50–55.

Lewis, L. K. (2007). An organizational stakeholder model of change implementation communication. *Communication Theory, 17*(2), 176–204.

Lewis, L. K. (2011). *Organizational change: Creating change through strategic communication.* Chichester, UK: Wiley-Blackwell.

Lynch, J. (2005). Rhetoric and the failure of the Catholic church's pastoral letter on homosexuality. *Rhetoric & Public Affairs, 8*(3), 383–404.

Maguire, S., & Hardy, C. (2006). The emergence of new global institutions: A discursive perspective. *Organization Studies, 27*(1), 7–29.

Maguire, S., & Hardy, C. (2009). Discourse and deinstitutionalization: The decline of DDT. *Academy of Management Journal, 52*(1), 148–178.

Maguire, S., Hardy, C., & Lawrence, T. (2004). Institutional entrepreneurship in emerging fields: HIV/AIDS treatment advocacy in Canada. *Academy of Management Journal, 47*(5), 654–679.

March, J. G., & Simon, H. A. (1958). *Organizations.* New York, NY: John Wiley.

May, S., Cheney, G. and Roper, J., eds (2007) *The debate over corporate social responsibility.* New York, NY: Oxford University Press.

McPhee, R. D., & Zaug, P. (2000). The communicative constitution of organizations: A framework for explanation. *The Electronic Journal of Communication, 10*(1/2).

McPhee, R. D., & Zaug, P. (2009). The communicative constitution of organization: A framework for explanation. In L. L. Putnam & A. M. Nicotera (Eds.), *Building theories of organization: The constitutive role of communication* (pp. 21–48). New York, NY: Routledge.

Meisenbach, R., Remke, R., Buzzanell, P. M., & Liu, M. (2008). "They allowed": Pentadic mapping of women's maternity leave discourse as organizational rhetoric. *Communication Monographs, 75*(1), 1–24.

Merton, R. K. (1936). The unanticipated consequences of purposive social action. *American Sociological Review, 1*(6), 894–904.

Meyer, J. W., & Rowan, B. (1977). Institutionalized organizations: Formal structure as myth and ceremony. *American Journal of Sociology, 83*(2), 340–363.

Meyer, J. W., & Scott, W. R. (1983). Centralization and legitimacy problems of local government. In J. W. Meyer & W. R. Scott (Eds.), *Organizational environments: Ritual and rationality* (pp. 199–215). Beverly Hills, CA: SAGE.

Mills, C. (1940). Situated actions and vocabularies of motive. *American Sociological Review, 5*(6), 904–913.

Mumby, D. K. (1988). *Communication and power in organizations.* Norwood, NJ: Ablex.

Mumby, D. K., & Stohl, C. (1996). Disciplining organizational communication studies. *Management Communication Quarterly, 10*(1), 50–72.

O'Connor, A., & Shumate, M. (2010). Corporate social responsibility communication: An economic industry and institutional level of analysis of corporate social responsibility communication. *Management Communication Quarterly, 24*(4), 529–551.

Oliver, C. (1992). The antecedents of deinstitutionalization. *Organization Studies, 13*(4), 563–588.

Palmer, D., Biggart, N., & Dick, B. (2008). Is the new institutionalism a theory? In R. Greenwood, C. Oliver, K. Sahlin, & R. Suddaby (Eds.), *The SAGE handbook of organizational institutionalism* (pp. 739–768). Thousand Oaks, CA: SAGE.

Pentland, B. T. (1999). Organizations as networks of action. In J. Baum & B. McKelvey (Eds.), *Variations in organization science: In honor of Donald T. Campbell* (pp. 237–253). Thousand Oaks, CA: SAGE.

Pfeffer, J., & Salancik, G. R. (1978). *The external control of organizations: A resource dependence perspective.* New York, NY: Harper and Row.

Phillips, N., Lawrence, T. B., & Hardy, C. (2004). Discourse and institutions. *Academy of Management Review, 29*(4), 635–652.

Powell, W. W., & Colyvas, J. A. (2008). Microfoundations of institutional theory. In R. Greenwood, C. Oliver, K. Sahlin, & R. Suddaby (Eds.), *The SAGE handbook of organizational institutionalism* (pp. 276–298). Thousand Oaks, CA: SAGE.

Powell, W. W., & DiMaggio, P. J. (Eds.). (1991). *The new institutionalism in organizational analysis.* Chicago, IL: University of Chicago Press.

Putnam, L. L., & Pacanowsky, M. E. (Eds.). (1983). *Communication and organizations: An interpretive approach.* Newbury Park, CA: SAGE.

Real, K., & Putnam, L. (2005). Ironies in the discursive struggle of pilots defending the profession. *Management Communication Quarterly, 19*(1), 91–119.

Rogers, E. M. (1962). *Diffusion of innovation.* New York, NY: Free Press.

Sahlin, K., & Wedlin, L. (2008). Circulating ideas: Imitation, translation, editing. In R. Greenwood, C. Oliver, K. Sahlin, & R. Suddaby (Eds.), *The SAGE handbook of organizational institutionalism* (pp. 218–242). Thousand Oaks, CA: SAGE.

Schwarze, S. (2003). Corporate-state irresponsibility, critical publicity, and asbestos exposure in Libby, Montana. *Management Communication Quarterly, 16*(4), 625–632.

Scott, W. R. (2001). *Institutions and organizations.* Thousand Oaks, CA: SAGE.

Scott, W. R. (2008). Lords of the dance: Professionals as institutional agents. *Organization Studies, 29*(2), 219–238.

Scott, W. R., & Meyer, J. W. (1983). The organization of societal sectors. In J. W. Meyer & W. R. Scott (Eds.), *Organizational environments: Ritual and rationality* (pp. 129–153). Beverly Hills, CA: SAGE.

Selznick, P. (1949). *TVA and the grass roots: A study in the sociology of formal organization.* Berkeley: University of California Press.

Selznick P. (1952). *The organizational weapon: A study of Bolshevik strategy and tactics.* New York, NY: McGraw-Hill.

Selznick P. (1957). *Leadership in administration: A sociological interpretation.* Evanston, IL: Row, Peterson & Company.

Seo, M. G., & Creed, W. E. D. (2002). Institutional contradictions, praxis, and institutional change: A dialectical perspective. *Academy of Management Review, 27*(2), 222–247.

Sheets, P. (2007). *Five distinct companies or one 'big oil'? A test of institutional isomorphism in oil communications* (Unpublished manuscript). University of Washington, Seattle, WA.

Sproule, J. M. (1988). The new managerial rhetoric and the old criticism. *Quarterly Journal of Speech, 74*(4), 468–486.

Starr, P. (1982). *The social transformation of American medicine.* New York, NY: Basic Books.

Stohl, C., & Coombs, W. T. (1988). Cooperation or cooptation: An analysis of quality circle training manuals. *Management Communication Quarterly, 2*(1), 63–89.

Suddaby, R. (2011). How communication institutionalizes: A response to Lammers. *Management Communication Quarterly, 25*(1), 183–190.

Suddaby, R., & Greenwood, R. (2005). Rhetorical strategies of legitimacy. *Administrative Science Quarterly, 50*(1), 35–67.

Taylor, M., & Doerfel, M. L. (2011). Evolving network roles in international aid efforts: Evidence from Croatia's post-war transition. *Voluntas: International Journal of Voluntary and Nonprofit Organizations, 22*(2), p. 311–334.

Thornton, P., & Ocasio, W. (2008). Institutional logics. In R. Greenwood, C. Oliver, K. Sahlin, & R. Suddaby (Eds.), *The SAGE handbook of organizational institutionalism* (pp. 99–129). Thousand Oaks, CA: SAGE.

Tolbert, P. S., & Zucker, L. G. (1983). Institutional sources of change in the formal structures of organizations: The diffusion of civil service reform 1880–1935. *Administrative Science Quarterly, 28*(1), 22–39.

Tolbert, P. S., & Zucker, L. G. (1996). "The institutionalization of institutional theory." In S. R. Clegg, C. Hardy, & W. R. Nord (Eds.), *Handbook of organization studies* (pp. 175–190). Thousand Oaks, CA: SAGE.

Trethewey, A. (2001). Reproducing and resisting the master narrative of decline: Midlife professional women's experiences of aging. *Management Communication Quarterly, 15*(2), 183–226.

Trethewey, A., & Ashcraft, K. L. (2004). Practicing disorganization: The development of applied perspectives on living with tension. *Journal of Applied Communication Research, 32*(2), 81–88.

Truscott, R. A., Bartlett, J. L., & Tywoniak, S. (2009). The reputation of the corporate social responsibility industry in Australia. *Australasian Marketing Journal, 17*(2), 84–91.

Weber, M. (1968). *Economy and society* (G. Roth & C. Wittich, Trans.). Berkeley: University of California Press. (Original work published 1906–1924.)

Wijen, F., & Ansari, S. (2007). Overcoming inaction through collective institutional entrepreneurship: Insights from regime theory. *Organization Studies, 28*(7), 1079–1100.

Winn, M. I., MacDonald, P., & Zietsma, C. (2008). The dynamic tension between collective and competitive reputation management strategies. *Corporate Reputation Review, 11*(1), 35–55.

Zietsma, C., & Lawrence, T. B. (2010). Institutional work in the transformation of an organizational field: The interplay of boundary work and practice work. *Administrative Science Quarterly, 55*(2), 189–221.

Zilber, T. B. (2002). Institutionalization as an interplay between actions, meanings, and actors: The case of a rape crisis center in Israel. *Academy of Management Journal, 45*(1), 234–254.

Zilber, T. B. (2007). Stories and the discursive dynamics of institutional entrepreneurship: The case of Israeli high-tech after the bubble. *Organization Studies, 28*(7), 1035–1054.

Zorn, T. E., Flanagin, A. J., & Shoham, M. (2011). Institutional and non-institutional influences on information and communication technology adoption and use among nonprofit organizations. *Human Communication Research, 37*(1), 1–33.

Zucker, L. G. (1983). Organizations as institutions. In S. B. Bacharach (Ed.), *Advances in organizational theory and research* (vol. 2, pp. 1–43). Greenwich, CT: JAI.

Notes

1. It bears mentioning that institutional theory is by far the most invoked approach in organization studies today. Google returns about 342,000 sites in a search for *institutional theory*, and Google Scholar lists 32,100 citations on the same search. A topic search in the ISI Web of Knowledge renders 9,213 citations.

2. Throughout *TVA and the Grassroots*, Selznick quite explicitly embraces the values of democratic action at the local level and includes a discussion of local disenfranchisement of Black farmers and colleges in the region.

3. In an example of the disciplinary distance between institutionalists and other scholars, Tolbert and Zucker (1983, 1996), in their discussion of diffusion, make no mention of Rogers (1962).

4. This section draws upon and summarizes material in Lammers (2011).

SECTION II

Research Methods in Organizational Communication Studies

Linda L. Putnam

This section focuses on the issues, developments, and applications of research methods in organizational communication. The first edition of the *Handbook* did not include a section on research methods, but since 1987, the uses and complexities of data gathering and analytic methods have mushroomed. The second edition, then, contained separate chapters on discourse analysis, quantitative approaches, and qualitative methods, and each chapter championed the methodological pluralism that characterized the field.

Importantly, the authors of the quantitative and the qualitative chapters in the second edition acknowledged that debates about privileging one method over the other had become "tiresome" (Taylor & Trujillo, 2001, pp. 167–168). They readily claimed that the distinctions among methods did not rest on epistemological stance and that no one method had privileged access to organizational reality (Miles & Huberman, 1994). Instead of championing a particular approach, scholars needed to capture the complexity of organizational communication by using different styles of inquiry, matching theory and analysis, and developing a tight interdependence between the various stages of research (Miller, 2001; Taylor & Trujillo, 2001).

A decade later, the third edition of this *Handbook* picks up on many of the themes that surfaced in the second one. Methodology in organizational communication has continued to embrace multiple approaches, and the chapters in this section expand on several themes mentioned in the second edition, namely, the eclecticism of methods in the field, the difficulties of integrating multiple methods, and the role of the researcher. The chapters in Section II also pursue new frontiers in challenging the definition of a field, studying the relationship between discourse and materiality and focusing on mixed methods. The remainder of this introduction addresses these themes and overviews the chapters in this section.

Key Themes in Research Methods

As in the past, organizational communication exhibits a healthy eclecticism in the use of research methods. Investigators employ archival data, observations and field notes, case studies, interviews, field experiments, surveys, websites, and blogs. This eclecticism has moved beyond pluralism, which draws on the strengths and weaknesses of particular methods; rather, it surfaces in the selection of organizational participants, the types of data, and analytical/interpretative approaches.

The selection of participants for organizational communication studies encompasses workers and nonworkers, employees and families, occupational groups, communities, and institutions (see Doerfel & Gibbs, Chapter 9). Moving away from corporate environments, scholars study profit and nonprofit organizations, governmental institutions, environmental groups, community activists, theater groups, and even terrorist networks (Brummans et al., 2008; Stohl & Stohl, 2011). As in the past, types of communicative data include discourse, messages, information, symbols, networks, interaction patterns, and texts but also performances (i.e., creative, local interactions of events) and practices (i.e., routine dimensions of communication acts) that enact meanings. The interpretive/analytic methods that scholars use are complex, as evident by references to multimethod, multilevel, and intertextual analyses (see Tracy & Geist-Martin, Chapter 10; Fairhurst & Putnam, Chapter 11; Shumate & Contractor, Chapter 18).

Finding ways to integrate multiple methods continues to challenge scholars (see Tracy & Geist-Martin, Chapter 10; Myers, Chapter 12). Many ethnographies and case studies employ *multiple methods*, such as field notes, in-depth interviews, and archival data. *Mixed methods* combine elements of qualitative and quantitative approaches to add breadth and depth to findings. In both approaches, scholars have adopted new metaphors, paradigms, and modes of reasoning. Qualitative researchers, who employ multiple methods, engage in *bricolage* or piecing together representations from a variety of data sources, such as interviews, observations, and websites (Tracy & Geist-Martin, Chapter 10). Similar to constructing a quilt, investigators create a *montage* of organizational life, often from multiple paradigms and fragmentary sources. Combining a variety of shapes and substances, they form a crystal rather than a triangle or a tool (Ellingson, 2008). The starting point of a study is often a research question or problem rather than a theory or a perspective. This practice parallels the multiparadigmatic approach that fits the transition zones between diverse schools of thought (Miller, 2001). The mode of reasoning in integrating multiple methods is iterative and dialectical as scholars move back and forth across data sets.

Similarly, researchers who use mixed methods embrace different paradigms and modes of reasoning. Unlike a top-down process driven by theory or a bottom-up approach influenced by method choice, mixed method scholars align with a community of researchers who share beliefs and embrace *pragmatism* (Morgan, 2007; Myers, Chapter 12). Pragmatism is an action-oriented paradigm grounded in practice and committed to exploring ambiguities and uncertainties. Rather than working deductively or inductively, mixed methods scholars engage in *abductive* reasoning, in which they move back and forth in cyclical ways from data to theory construction to conclusions. Similar to multiple methods, the process is iterative and employs designs that are diverse and complex. In an exciting way, mixed methods joins with multiple methods in focusing on continua rather than dualism, context-specific inferences, transferability, and multistrand approaches.

Another theme that surfaces in these chapters is reflexivity or the role of the researcher in producing knowledge. Researchers have become more reflective than in the past about their roles in constructing participants' subjectivities, especially the gender, race, and class of the investigators and the participants. Even though scholars embrace reflexivity, they are often constrained by conventional norms of writing and ideological practices that make it difficult to tell their tales (Tracy & Geist-Martin, Chapter 10). Scholarship, for the most part, adopts a social scientific format rather than narrative or dramaturgical tales of the field (Van Maanen, 1988). As scholars seek to capture both the interactional and the material aspects of organizing, visual and digital formats may emerge and alter standard writing practices and the representation of findings. Research methods such as shadowing and autoethnography are creating opportunities for these developments to occur (Bruni, Gherardi, & Poggio, 2005; McDonald, 2005; Streeck, Goodwin, & LeBaron, 2011). The chapters in Section II expand on these key themes by examining field research, organizational ethnography, organizational discourse analysis, and mixed methods.

Field Research

Doerfel and Gibbs (Chapter 9) introduce this section with a chapter on field research, one that challenges the ambiguous definition of *the field* and classifies *research* into a spectrum of studies. For these authors, field research entails observations that are conducted in value-laden contexts or *in situ*. Embracing reflexivity, the authors treat field research as engaged scholarship that examines how participants constitute space, place, and organizing. Since field research incorporates both social scientific and humanistic approaches, Doerfel and Gibbs contend that it defies classifications into a distinct qualitative or quantitative category; and it is also difficult, if not impossible, to replicate the work in a controlled laboratory environment. As a whole, field studies in organizational communication privilege external validity over control, engaged participants as opposed to passive subjects, and localized rather than general understandings.

In Chapter 9, Doerfel and Gibbs review findings from organizational communication field studies published between 2001 and 2011. Over 57% of the 181 studies in their sample fit their definition of a field study. Moreover, these studies typically used surveys, interviews, and ethnographies to collect data. Even though interviewing surfaced as the most common method of data collection, these studies also entailed content analysis, participant observation, casework, and network analysis. In theoretical foci and topics areas, they cast a broad net across the field and typically embraced problem-driven questions.

To advance field studies, Doerfel and Gibbs advocate classifying research into three types: (1) nominal studies that decontextualize communication through the use of surveys or interviews; (2) middle-ground studies that use multiple methods, maintain some distance from the site, and focus on a given context; and (3) inseparable or immersion studies that employ a variety of field methods to present a story of how communication and organizing shape empirical choices. The three types vary in the degree to which the researcher is immersed in the context, the procedures for data analysis, and the interplay of communication across various levels of analysis. As the authors contend, developing distinctions among these types of fieldwork provides researchers with guidelines for how to conduct studies and how to make choices about methods and data analysis. Doerfel and Gibbs conclude their chapter with insights about the practical issues of doing field research, namely, gaining access to participants; ethical dilemmas; and new frontiers such as e-field, social media, and work-life situations.

Organizing Ethnography and Qualitative Approaches

In Chapter 10, "Organizing Ethnography and Qualitative Approaches," Tracy and Geist-Martin expand on the third level of field studies, inseparable research in which the investigator is fully immersed in the context. In contrast to theory-driven studies, researchers who embrace this approach work inductively and are grounded in the context and in participants' experiences. Organizational communication scholars who employ ethnographies typically rely on sensitizing concepts—for example, gender, identity, or workplace relationships—to narrow their designs and aid in interpretations.

The metaphors of *bricolage* and crystallization govern data analysis as investigators assemble sets of representations and concepts from multiple data sources. As Tracy and Geist-Martin note, sampling differs for full immersion studies in that researchers aim for both breadth and depth; thus they gather data along the way rather than in discrete stages. The goal of this method is to capture how multiple organizational participants understand and narrate their worlds by examining both the performances of organizing and the macro-level processes that enable and constrain them.

Tracy and Geist-Martin track the historical roots and multiple paradigms that shape ethnography in organizational communication. Of particular interest, they focus on *embodied data* or ways in which writing becomes an integral part of the research process. Drawing on reflexivity, they describe how the researcher mediates and constructs the data and how the subjectivities of both the investigator and the participants impact research findings. They treat writing as a form of inquiry that is intertwined with data collection and tailored to a wide range of stakeholders, including participants, academics, policy makers, and lay publics. Finally, Tracy and Geist-Martin urge scholars to move out of their comfort zones and conduct multisite studies, pursue alternative writing styles, develop aesthetic texts that are both creative and evocative, and conduct social justice research that advocates for marginalized participants.

Organizational Discourse Analysis

Multiple methods are also prominent in organizational discourse studies, specifically in examining the mutually constitutive nature of communication, organizing, and organization. Fairhurst and Putnam in Chapter 11 define discourse studies as a set of approaches that focus on the constitutive effects of language, text production and consumption, and socially constructed organizational realities. Unlike the second edition, this chapter adopts a broad-based view of discourse that focuses on three central questions: (1) How does discourse constitute features of organizational life? (2) How does discourse interact with the material world to privilege certain realities over others? (3) How do discourse and materiality mutually constitute one another? These questions function as key concerns for integrating the vast literatures on these topics.

In response to the first question, the authors explore five themes: the organizing potential of language and texts, the social construction of subjectivities, new rhetoric and organization, tensions and contradictions in disorganization, and social poetics as dialogic experiences. The first two themes demonstrate how discourse shapes organizing and organizational subject positions through social and historical texts. The third one, the new rhetoric, focuses on uncertainty, context-dependent persuasion, and interactions with multiple, highly vocal stakeholders that blend internal communication with external branding. Unlike a decade ago, scholars often trace rhetorical practices across events, time periods, and multiple texts.

The research on tensions and contradictions as the fourth theme embraces a logic of difference and focuses on disorganization, order, and disorder. Scholars locate oppositional tensions in problem identification as well as in conflicts and resistance and examine how these tensions become enacted, managed, segmented, or held together in everyday organizational practices. The final theme centers on dialogue as creating the potential for organizational change. Social poetics draws from practice theory to help participants enlarge vocabularies, reflexively co-construct meanings, and alter problematic practices. These five themes, as Fairhurst and

Putnam point out, have guided extensive organizational communication research. One major critique of this work is that there is too much emphasis on human agency and too little on materiality and institutional constraints.

The last two questions address this critique in examining the discourse-materiality relationship. To unpack this relationship, Fairhurst and Putnam recommend that researchers focus on the nature of mutuality, avoid privileging either the symbolic or the material, and avoid using human agency as a prototype for the material. To this end, they show how organizational communication scholars have developed new ways to study this relationship, particularly by focusing on the absence of signifiers that operate just out of reach, hybrid agencies, constitutive entanglements, and the recursive relationships among objects, sites, bodies, and interactions. To advance this work, they call for discourse analysts to ground their studies in practices, focus on translations between the symbolic and the material, treat mutuality as dissymmetry, and employ methods that capture both the discursive and the material.

Mixed Methods: When More Is Really More

Similar to organizational discourse studies, mixed methods has become a research arena in its own right. As noted in this introduction, it focuses on ways to integrate findings from both qualitative and quantitative approaches. In Chapter 12, Myers describes the popularity of this approach across disciplines; specifically, an entire journal is devoted to the topic of mixed methods. Scholars have produced a handbook and considerable research about the approach; hence, it is emerging as a third methodology—one that is separate from qualitative or quantitative approaches alone. As previously noted, scholars who use mixed methods often embrace a pragmatic view of inquiry and employ abductive reasoning. Thus as a hybrid approach, it aims for comprehension, analytical density, and depth of understanding.

Myers's chapter examines the issues, obstacles, and opportunities for mixed methods research in organizational communication. She contends that effective use of this approach should fully integrate both quantitative and qualitative data rather than rely heavily on one method over the other. To this end, she describes four alternatives for conceptualizing mixed methods designs, collecting and interpreting the data, and integrating the two approaches. *Triangulation*, the first type of design, gathers the two data sets simultaneously and compares research findings. Although cast as a validation approach (Taylor & Trujillo, 2001), triangulation in mixed-methods research aims for complementarity and visualization of similarities and differences. Even though convergence is one possible outcome, Myers notes that some scholars believe that complete triangulation is never possible.

The *embedded design* provides an alternative to triangulation and casts one type of data as secondary to the other; hence, scholars often place too much emphasis on the primary method, which defeats the purpose of using the secondary one. An *explanatory approach* collects quantitative data initially followed by qualitative data used to explain the quantitative findings. This design needs to integrate both approaches fully to explain the how and why of the initial investigation. In a similar way, an *exploratory design* employs two phases, but with the qualitative data collected first and then followed by the quantitative study. This design is particularly useful when a phenomenon is unexplored and when scholars want to use qualitative findings to construct survey instruments. Other studies in organizational communication employ a three-phase sequence and use customized embedded designs that combine multiple with mixed methods. For example, a researcher might conduct case studies and interviews and then develop surveys with open-ended responses that are analyzed through thematic coding or grounded theory analysis.

Overall, Myers notes that the number of mixed-methods studies in organizational communication is relatively low in comparison with other fields. One explanation for this shortfall is that scholars break up mixed-methods studies into separate manuscripts for publication. Other reasons might be the time-consuming nature of this work, lack of expertise in both quantitative and qualitative approaches, and difficulty in managing iterative and emergent data. Engaging in collaborations and team research, as Myers points out, can make this method feasible to scholars. Chapter 12 concludes with reasons to embrace mixed-methods designs, namely, their capacity to extend knowledge, their overall impact, and their ease in providing rich understandings of context and experiences, especially for organizationally sensitive issues.

Conclusion

As the chapters in this section illustrate, organizational communication scholars have moved beyond pluralism in research methods to embrace complexity in design, data collection, and analysis. Collectively, they demonstrate how scholars have adopted new metaphors for multiple- and mixed-methods designs, employed iterative and abductive reasoning to integrate data sets, and developed a spectrum of approaches for field studies. They show how researchers function reflexively as engaged scholars who mediate and influence their participants as well as their own subjectivities. Two of the chapters describe how scholars use these methods to examine the mutually constitutive nature of communication, organizing, and organization, especially the discourse-materiality relationship. They also demonstrate how organizational communication scholars create new research designs and are using new technologies, such as shadowing and video ethnography, to capture communicative practices and performances. Overall, they situate organizational communication scholarship as taking a leading role in multiplex and multimethod research, ones designed to bridge paradigms and theoretical domains of the field.

References

Bruni, A., Gherardi, S., & Poggio, B. (2005). *Gender and entrepreneurship: An ethnographic approach* (vol. 1). New York, NY: Routledge.

Brummans, B. H., Putnam, L. L., Gray, B., Hanke, R., Lewicki, R. J., & Wiethoff, C. (2008). Making sense of intractable multiparty conflict: A study of framing in four environmental disputes. *Communication Monographs, 75*(1), 25–51.

Ellingson, L. L. (2008). *Engaging crystallization in qualitative research.* Thousand Oaks, CA: SAGE.

McDonald, S. (2005). Studying actions in context: A qualitative shadowing method for organizational research. *Qualitative Research, 5*(4), 455–473.

Miles, M. B., & Huberman, A. M. (1994). *Qualitative data analysis* (2nd ed.). Thousand Oaks, CA: SAGE.

Miller, K. (2001). Quantitative research methods. In F. M. Jablin & L. L. Putnam (Eds.), *The new handbook of organizational communication: Advances in theory, research, and methods* (pp. 137–160). Thousand Oaks, CA: SAGE.

Morgan, D. L. (2007). Paradigms and pragmatism regained: Methodological implications of combining qualitative and quantitative methods. *Journal of Mixed Methods Research, 1*(1), 48–76.

Stohl, C., & Stohl, M. (2011). Secret agencies: The communicative constitution of a clandestine organization. *Organization Studies, 32*(9), 1197–1215.

Streeck, J., Goodwin, C., & LeBaron, C. (2011). *Embodied interaction: Language and body in the material world.* Cambridge, UK: Cambridge University Press.

Taylor, B. C., & Trujillo, N. (2001). Qualitative research methods. In F. M. Jablin & L. L. Putnam (Eds.), *The new handbook of organizational communication: Advances in theory, research, and methods* (pp. 161–194). Thousand Oaks, CA: SAGE.

Van Maanen, J. (1988). *Tales of the field: On writing ethnography.* Chicago, IL: University of Chicago Press.

CHAPTER 9

Field Research[1]

Marya L. Doerfel and Jennifer L. Gibbs

It is Monday, December 5, 2005, and my trip's success relies on strangers. Three months after Hurricane Katrina and the flooding that devastated New Orleans, non-recovery workers can book hotel rooms. Once I arrive, I learn that the context awaiting me includes electricity that is still spotty [and] most traffic lights don't work, so temporary stop signs [are] attached to white and orange construction [signs]. Horses are scattered around [the] intersections, abandoned cars swamped out by brackish waters are parked in "higher" areas and never to be retrieved by their original owners. It's a ghost town that's buzzing with activity. Cars crawl through intersections tentatively, and their riders are confronted by mountains of garbage piled up in the medians of boulevards (in New Orleans' speak, "neutral ground"). I find myself playing "where's the water line" while gawking at flood-damaged houses and buildings. The sludgy line lower down means "they were lucky" but when it's up above door and window frames, near the blue plastic roof, I stare, silently, and wonder about the people who once called the ruins "home" or those buildings with countless knocked out windows "work." (Doerfel, unpublished raw data, 2005)

Over the years, the field of organizational communication has moved away from static, bounded conceptions of organizations as containers in which communication occurs inside physical offices and buildings to notions of communication as constitutive of organizing (Putnam & Krone, 2006; Taylor, Flanagin, Cheney, & Seibold, 2001). Doerfel's (2005) field notes featured in the opening quote reflect the influence of the interpretive movement (Putnam & Pacanowsky, 1983), which shifted the focus of organizing from topics such as rational models of managerial effectiveness to communication embedded in a value-laden context. In field research, the investigator embodies the role of engaged observer who attends to the constitution of place, space, and communicative interaction. Moreover, driven by workplaces that are becoming increasingly global, flexible, virtual, and multicultural, scholars have expanded their notions of organizations to include both corporate and nonprofit, work and nonwork, and intra- and interorganizational arrangements as well as telework and virtual work, part-time contingent work, online groups and communities, and other nonstandard forms of organizing (Ballard & Gossett, 2007). The changing nature of organizations calls into question the methods that we use and the contexts that we study.

Organizational communication research is characterized by a variety of methods and approaches, but, as this chapter shows, scholars tend to share a commitment to field research, specifically focusing on communication processes in particular contexts. Data such as the quotation from Doerfel's field journal provide thick descriptions (Geertz, 1973) that help scholars understand organizational contexts in ways that other methods cannot. Kerlinger (1986) points out other advantages of field studies; namely, variables become more pronounced, they capture complex influences and processes in more complete ways, and they are helpful in addressing practical questions.

This chapter reviews field research published in organizational communication over the past decade. It does so with an eye to projecting the future that field research holds in organizational communication studies. The chapter is organized as follows. First, we define field research and provide a brief history of its use in organizational communication. Second, we map the topics and methods used by organizational communication field researchers, drawn from an analysis of the published studies. Third, we develop a more nuanced view of *fieldness* than appears in textbook definitions. For example, Kerlinger (1986) contends that anything outside of a controlled laboratory experiment "counts" as field research: "*any* scientific studies, large or small, that systematically pursue relations and test hypotheses, that are nonexperimental, and that are done in life situations like communities, schools, factories, organizations, and institutions" (p. 372; emphasis in original). Such a broad definition does little to tease out the quality, advantages, and contributions of field studies. We outline a spectrum of *fieldness* that ranges from low to high field emphasis. In particular, research that is largely removed from the organizational context (e.g., uses survey methods) anchors the low end, while full-fledged ethnographies anchor the high end of the spectrum. Simply put, not all field research is the same. We use examples from the organizational communication literature to illustrate each type. In this way, the types of scholarly contributions across the spectrum can be explicated, and decisions about research design can be better informed. Fourth, we discuss the core epistemological assumptions of field research, including dilemmas and tradeoffs that investigators must navigate. Finally, we acknowledge the practical challenges that may deter scholars from field studies, including issues of access, data collection, and ethics, and we offer suggestions for handling them. We end the chapter by highlighting the importance of investigating, explicating, interpreting, critiquing, and analyzing organizational spaces, forms, processes, and practices and call for organizational communication scholars to embrace these activities. In doing so, we provide a 21st-century view of organizations as cross-cutting space and time in processes of organizing rather than being confined to a single physical location or bounded entity.

History and Definition of Field Research

The history of field research in communication has its roots in perspectives as diverse as systems theory and cultural anthropology. Drawn from systems thinking, field research has been a part of social scientific organization studies that date back to Taylor's (1911) scientific management, in which he espoused *in situ* experiments to help managers design the best way to structure work. Mayo and his colleagues' research embraced field studies to assess employee productivity in the Hawthorne electrical plant (Mayo, 1945). The goal of these field experiments was to rule out rival hypotheses by finding alternative ways of controlling for changes in the workplace and across different sites.

Along with the interpretive turn in organizational communication (Putnam & Pacanowsky, 1983) came more humanistic approaches that were grounded in cultural anthropology. Organizational communication scholars in the 1980s began to treat organizations as cultures that could be studied through participant observation, interviews, and ethnography. This approach was derived from ethnographers such as Malinowski or Mead, who travelled to distant remote cultures such as the Trobriand Islands or Samoa to become immersed in the context and see life through the eyes of the natives (Geertz, 1973). This movement produced ethnographies of organizations, such as Kunda's (1992) seminal study of the engineering division of a high-tech firm and its subtle yet pervasive forms of control and commitment. This approach developed ways to conceptualize organizational culture (Martin, 1992) and to provide guidelines for reporting field research (Van Maanen, 1988). It also inspired scholars to broaden their notions of organizations and to conduct fieldwork in such varied sites as factories, restaurants, hospitals, prisons, and schools (Burgess, 1984).

Field research in organizational communication thus has its roots in both social scientific and humanistic approaches that embrace the common goal of understanding communication processes in naturalistic organizational settings. Whether treated as the backdrop, the story, the political environment, the locale, or the broader national culture, field research privileges context. It situates observations in organizations as systems of relationships. Methods as diverse as surveys, interviews, observations, case studies, content analyses, and field experiments are employed as field methods to study naturally occurring organizational phenomena. Thus field research does not fit neatly into an epistemological category such as *positivist* or *constructivist*. Moreover, it transcends traditional methodological divides between quantitative versus qualitative approaches. For example, in their edited volume on organizational audits, Hargie and Tourish (2009) feature chapters on methods that range from surveys to critical incident reports as ways to assess communication practices within and across organizations. The case studies in their various chapters detail the contexts that shape communication practices and include studies of health care organizations (e.g., Hargie & Tourish, 2009; Skipper, Hargie, & Tourish, 2009), business entities (e.g., Clampitt & Berk, 2009), a police organization (Quinn, Hargie, & Tourish, 2009), and professional association activities (Downs, Hydeman, & Adrian, 2009). These cases show how organizational communication emerges as something that is difficult, if not impossible, to replicate in a controlled environment (e.g., laboratory setting), although crises and naturally occurring events can set the stage for quasi-experimental designs.

The field can be virtual as well; for instance, online communities enabled by message boards and Web 2.0 technologies provide exciting new sites for examining organizing processes. These sites call for new methods, such as cyberethnography and the mining of large data sets of server-log behaviors, to detect patterns. They are also well-suited to more traditional survey, content analysis, and network analytic methods. For example, Yuan, Cosley, Welser, Xia, and Gay (2009) found that network features influenced Wikipedia editors' adoption of a task recommendation tool that fostered an online community. Aakhus and Rumsey (2010) studied a conflict episode in an online cancer support community and explored its implications for community interactions. Such studies extend our notions of the field to online contexts and broaden the ways that organizations are conceptualized.

Field Research From 2001–2011

Field studies published in organizational communication since 2001 span an array of topics, including socialization, change, identity, power, diversity, and groups as well as new technologies, teams, and networked structures. Data collection methods range from the use of surveys in which qualitative descriptions augment quantitative analyses to ethnographies that develop thick descriptions. Regardless of the particular topic or method, field studies provide rich theoretical understandings of how communication constitutes organizing.

Field research has a strong presence in the discipline. To determine the type of field research published in organizational communication, we sampled the past decade of publications and analyzed a representative group of studies. In the years since the *New Handbook of Organizational Communication* (Jablin & Putnam, 2001) was published, we categorized a total of 181 articles as empirical organizational communication research in seven peer-reviewed journals that routinely publish organizational communication research. Table 9.1 lists the communication journals that were selected, including ones sponsored by the International Communication Association (*Human Communication Research*, *Journal of Computer-Mediated Communication*, *Journal of Communication*), the National Communication Association (*Journal of Applied Communication Research*, *Communication Monographs*), general field journals (*Communication Research*), and ones supported by the International Communication Association/National Communication Association organizational communication divisions (*Management Communication Quarterly*). The table shows the strong presence of field studies; specifically, 103 of the 181 empirical articles (57%) fit along the field research spectrum (see references for the full list of sampled articles).

Of the 103 studies that fit the definition of field research embraced in this chapter, interviews were the most common form of data collection (67%). About one-third of the studies used one or some combination of observations, surveys, and document/content analysis. About 10% used social network analysis, and less than 1% (n=1) used conversation analysis. Interestingly, the list contains very few, if any, explicitly quasi-experimental designs, despite their historical viability in field research (Cook & Campbell, 1979; Kerlinger, 1986). Although more than half of the sites were drawn from English-speaking, American-centered organizations, researchers in countries such as Australia, Canada, China, Colombia, Croatia, India, United Kingdom, Italy, Jamaica, Korea, Malaysia, Norway, New Zealand, and Sweden also employed field studies. Some studies were not located within a particular national context, because they examined online organizing, the virtual activities of particular organizations, networks of organizations, or multinational organizations that spanned multiple countries (e.g., García-Morales, Matías-Reche, & Verdú-Jover, 2011; Shumate & Lipp, 2008).

The types of organizations that were studied included university residential housing and services (e.g., Ballard & Seibold, 2004a), nonprofit and nongovernmental organizations (e.g., Cooren, 2004; Ganesh, 2003), dot-coms and for-profit entities (e.g., Lynch, 2009; Lyon, 2004), governmental organizations (e.g., Chaput, Brummans, & Cooren, 2011), and high-reliability organizations such as fire stations (Myers, 2005; Tracy, Myers, & Scott, 2006; Tracy & Scott, 2006) in addition to emergent organizational forms characteristic of modern technological affordances. Specifically, websites and general online activity provided data for Bennett, Foot, and Xenos's (2011) research on the divergence of fair trade networks; for Tateo's (2005) study on the nature of ties among Italian extreme-right websites; for Gossett and Kilker's (2006) investigation of dissent and voice in blog activity; and for Yuan et al.'s (2009) project that examined activities among online contributors. Another topic of focus was distributed work, whether by teleworkers (e.g., Fay & Kline, 2011; Hylmö & Buzzanell, 2002) or employees who shared knowledge for coordinating work (e.g., Quan-Haase, Cothrel, & Wellman, 2005).

Theories that field researchers embrace reflect the interdisciplinary nature of organizational communication (e.g., structuration, social network, and transactive memory theories) as well as discipline-specific theoretical advances (e.g., constitutive view of communication, communication

Table 9.1 Organizational Communication/Field Research Papers Published in Core Communication Journals, 2001–2011

Journal	Issues Each Year	Approximate Number of Articles per Issue	Number of Organizational Communication Articles From 2001–2011	Number of Field-Based Organizational Communication Articles	Percent of Field-Based Organizational Communication Articles Out of All Organization Communication-Focused Articles
Journal of Applied Communication Research (JACR)	4	6	36	28	77.8
Human Communication Research (HCR)	4	6	13	8	61.5
Communication Monographs (CM)	4	6	24	14	58.3
Management Communication Quarterly (MCQ)	4	8	60	34	56.7
Journal of Computer-Mediated Communication (JCMC)	4	6	24	10	41.7
Communication Research (CR)	6	6	16	6	37.5
Journal of Communication (JoC)	4	8	8	3	37.5
Totals (about 2,000 articles, including symposia, research notes, and discussions, were published from 2001–2011)			181	103	57

design, stakeholder theory, and sensemaking). Studies that focus on understanding structural influences of organizing are also prevalent across topics. In such work, researchers develop theory to make sense of the tensions and opportunities that various types of structures create, whether organizational (e.g., virtual teams), discursive (e.g., norms, identities, control), social (e.g., diversity, culture, power), or a combination of these. Problem-driven research is also well-represented in the form of such topics as organizational technologies, social networks, groups and teams, interorganizational relationships, communities of practice, online communities, voice and gendered communication, emotional labor, resistance and control, leadership, organizational change, assimilation/socialization, and identification.

Interestingly, these categories typically entail multiple authors and thus show that particular scholars are not driving the state of the field. This collective aura may be a by-product of the extensive time commitment required in field research, since these projects often take several years to pass through conception, funding, access, data collection, and analysis and publication. Regardless, within this 10-year time frame, 10 articles categorized generally as *communities of practice* were written by 10 different authors or teams of authors. While there are a few topics on which particular scholars published multiple articles (e.g., work on emotional labor by Miller, 2007; Miller & Koesten, 2008), expertise on these topics seems distributed among multiple scholars who collectively build knowledge.

These observations highlight how field research makes contributions to the discipline. A collection of authors who grapple with the same topic reflects the notion of "work built on the shoulders of giants." These publications from a variety of scholarly perspectives amass knowledge of these topics, support generalizable discovery, and engage in theory building, even though each one may lack the generalizability that is typical of random sample designs. Hence, taken together as a collection of viewpoints on the same communication problem, they develop concepts, integrate knowledge, and build on each other across contexts.

These organizational communication-centered field studies make advances in multidisciplinary theory development as well as discipline-specific arenas. For example, social network research, in general, treats information flows and exchange networks as dichotomous, assuming that either the link between two organizations, groups, or people exists or it doesn't. This view of a link is, in part, shaped by economists and sociologists who consider links as currency flows. Communication network scholars focus on the content or quality of communication that constitutes these links and examine beyond the abstract representation of communication (e.g., financial exchange). These studies reveal how future networks evolve by examining the ways that communication relationships change over time (e.g., Doerfel & Taylor, 2004; Shumate, 2012; Whitbred, Fonti, Steglich, & Contractor, 2011).

In addition to multidisciplinary contributions, field research guides communication theory development. To illustrate, communication scholars have conceptualized virtual teamwork as communicative practices and processes, such as trust, leadership, conflict management, power and control, knowledge sharing, and identification (Gibbs, Nekrassova, Grushina, & Abdul Wahab, 2008). This constitutive approach treats organizations as dialectical and multifaceted, which helps scholars explore the tensions and paradoxes that arise in new forms of organizing, such as telework (Hylmö & Buzzanell, 2002), multinational organizations (Gibbs, 2009; Wieland, 2011), political parties (Chaput et al., 2011), and corporate mergers and acquisitions (Pepper & Larson, 2006). Through their flexibility and depth of analysis, field approaches allow researchers to capture the nuances and complexities inherent in processes of organizing in ways that enrich organizational theory.

Field researchers have also analyzed communication process and content together rather than separating them in reductive operational measures. Aakhus (2001), for example, conducted individual and group interviews with meeting facilitators to advance theory about the interdependent nature of content, action, and interaction of this practice (facilitation). His work went beyond the efficacy of communication practice by examining the moral and interpretive dimensions of this process. Field research also highlights the importance of cultural and historical contexts for organizational communication practices. For example, the finding that gender and ethnicity of a leader moderates the "appropriateness" of his or her communication style (e.g., competitive orientation, feminist orientation; Parker, 2001; Perriton, 2009) draws on cultural context that interfaces with communication practices.

Degrees of Fieldness

Across these contributions, themes of complexity, richness, and context play an integral part in revealing how and why communication processes emerge and the forms that organizational structure takes as a result of them. Although field-based scholarship values context, the intensity with which a study emphasizes context varies. Some field research treats organizations largely as containers in which communication occurs, while other studies value the nuances and interplay between communication and organization. Field research is not a simple dichotomy in that studies are either field based or they are not. Rather, we contend that field research exists on a continuum that ranges from low to high field emphasis. In particular, we outline a continuum and provide specific examples of field studies that vary on three points on this spectrum.

Nominal Field Studies

This type of research ranks relatively low on the spectrum, because it is field research in name only. Nominal field studies offer a paragraph or brief overview of the organization or environment and then use measures that are observational (e.g., surveys) rather than participative engagement. As long as the study takes place in an organization or with a particular sector of professionals, any study could nominally be considered field research. This type of investigation does not delve into granular aspects of the context. In addition, nominal field studies often treat organizations as physical containers in which communication functions as message exchange or information flow (Axley, 1984). Research has continued in this vein, even though it came under wide scrutiny during the *interpretive turn* in the 1980s with the advent of constitutive views of communication (Putnam & Krone, 2006). As an example of nominal field research, McCann and Giles (2006) examined cultural and generational differences in communication accommodation behaviors among younger and older managerial and nonmanagerial bankers in Thailand and the United States. Although their research was tailored to the banking industry, the organizations served mainly as containers for the communication accommodation processes. Interpersonal and intercultural rather than organizational processes provided explanatory mechanisms for their findings.

Other studies that embrace a container view may use surveys or interviews with individuals from a variety of different organizations, sometimes recruited by students in a communication class who distribute surveys to working adults, or content analysis of public data available from online communities or social media applications such as Twitter and Facebook. These approaches may provide useful findings for communication scholars but without additional data, they decontextualize the communities of study and produce limited insights about particular organizations. Research that falls into the container view exhibits its low field research emphasis, since it remains largely decontextualized from the organizational phenomena under study. Although decontextualized studies often adopt a container view, they can lead to studies that can generalize to a variety of organizational contexts but without providing insights into particular organizational processes. To increase the field value of such work, researchers could add site visits, preliminary or follow-up interviews, focus groups, or artifacts (such as memos and handbooks) that could improve the validity of observational tools such as surveys in which the researcher is kept distant from the context (Bradburn, Sudman, & Wansink, 2004).

Middle-Ground Field Studies

Other studies take a middle-ground approach that situates the researcher within a given context while avoiding a specialized focus. To illustrate, Waldeck, Seibold, and Flanagin (2004) surveyed 405 employees from four organizations (i.e., two hotels, a bank, and a professional association of realtors) on their uses of advanced communication and information technologies (ACITS), such as e-mail, Internet, instant messaging, and mobile phones. They conducted preliminary interviews and did extensive pilot testing to refine their survey questions, which included contextualized scenarios of organizational assimilation experiences. Their study exemplified a middle-ground position, because it provided insights about particular organizational contexts while showing how different organizations collectively produced generalizable findings regarding the influence of communication media on the organizational assimilation experience.

Moving further up the middle-ground stage of the continuum, Tracy et al. (2006) conducted a comparative ethnographic study of the use of humor among human service workers from four different organizations and three professions (e.g., correctional officers, 911 call-takers, and firefighters) using observations, ethnographic field interviews, and in-depth formal interviews. The data from the various organizations, which totaled 325 research hours and 1,000 pages of single-spaced transcripts, were collected separately but were merged to yield comparative insights. Their analysis revealed that humor served important functions for human service workers by helping them engage in sensemaking about their work and allowing them to manage their identities during difficult work situations. Even though during data collection, the researchers were fully immersed in their respective research contexts, this study fits a middle-ground field approach, since their analytical procedure relied on "etic-level categories based on extant literature and more specific emic issues that emerged from the data and participants' voices" (Tracy et al., 2006, p. 290). In addition, their comparison across contexts was aimed at producing generalizable findings regarding humor among human service workers.

The essence of middle-ground field studies is that they sample from multiple sites; hence, they sacrifice some of the contextualization that comes from full immersion in a single site. In this sense, they provide more richness about organizational contexts than do nominal studies, while they maintain some distance from the site in order to generalize across contexts. They often draw on multiple methods, such as observation and interviews or interviews and surveys, to add validity to singular methods.

Intertwined and Inseparable Field Studies

At the high end of the spectrum are investigations in which an organization's context is intertwined and inseparable from the communication processes under study. This approach treats communicating as the core organizing process; that is, it views communication and organizations as inseparable and communication as constituting organizations and organizing (Putnam & Nicotera, 2008; Weick, 1979). To illustrate this type, Leonardi (2009) used insider observational methods to study a major automotive company, conducted ethnographic fieldwork on technology and organizational change, and employed both qualitative (e.g., shadowing workers, recording conversations and meetings workers had) and quantitative data (e.g., how much time a project took). With this immersive approach, he developed a case about the ways that interactions with other professionals and with the technology itself thwarted organizational change.

Full-blown ethnographies are not the only type of field investigations that typify this category. In another longitudinal study of organizational change, Kuhn and Corman (2003) relied on a combination of interviews at three points in time, observation, and a network-based discourse-processing technique to study a division of a large municipal government that was going through a planned change. Through this mixed-method approach, they found that members' knowledge structures diverged in some ways but converged in others, due to the change initiative and to unanticipated organizational events, such as a workgroup clash.

The social networks perspective also considers the context fully with generally quantitative methods. Social network scholars examine the context of an organization at multiple levels simultaneously (Monge & Contractor, 2000). Put another way, researchers intertwine individual-level communication data with the broad network of communication processes. For example, Doerfel and Taylor (2004; Taylor & Doerfel, 2011) used longitudinal data that spanned a four-year period to develop a model of cooperation in the context of civil society. They gathered interorganizational network data from organizations in the city of Zagreb, Croatia, and from civil society partners in interorganizational networks. Their findings emerged from the interconnectedness of individual organizations' experiences as well as from the historical backdrop of the political transformation of the country. This research then incorporated data from the broad context of an interorganizational network, data that cannot exist apart from the actions and interactions of its members.

Field research at the high end of the spectrum tells the story of communicating and organizing. These stories are shaped by empirical choices (e.g., observations, artifacts, surveys, interviews), quantitative and/or qualitative data analyses, and a recognition that discoveries should be tempered by specific as opposed to broad, generalizable claims. Some studies in this category, however, provide for generalizability (e.g., Cheong, Huang, & Poon, 2011; Doerfel, Lai, & Chewning, 2010; Whitbred et al., 2011) while others are case specific (e.g., Kuhn & Corman, 2003; Leonardi, 2009; Taylor & Doerfel, 2003). Field studies that describe the context qualitatively offer rich details about the politics of the organization or the nature of work within which organizational activities take place. On the surface, context may appear to be a stable, unchanging environment that shapes what is being studied with empirical observation techniques. Most field research, however, acknowledges (either implicitly or explicitly) that the interplay of communication at various levels of analysis is being shaped by and shaping the context (e.g., the interplay of individual, group, and organizational processes; concerns with agency versus structure; and multilevel/multitheoretical points of view). The interplay of various structures and relationships and the constitutive nature of communication and organization are the driving forces for this research.

Epistemological Assumptions of Field Research

Ways of knowing or understanding communication (epistemology) and the nature of particular views of communication (ontology) are complementary philosophies that help shape scholarship. As Littlejohn (1999) asserts, "actually, epistemology and ontology go hand in hand because our ideas about knowledge depend in part on our ideas about reality" (p. 33). Field research may be characterized by a variety of methods and degrees of *fieldness*, but researchers share several key epistemological and ontological assumptions that drive their investigations.

A common feature of recent field research is an emphasis on interaction and in-context organizational discourses. Given the focus on interaction and context, research findings often support middle-range ontologies by capturing individual (micro-level) acts within a context that influences and is influenced by environmental (macro) factors. For example, in their study of the evolution of the children's media sector, Bryant and Monge (2008) showed how a particular organization's communication ties changed as the competitive environment grew over time. This type of field research emphasizes states of being as dynamic (e.g., longitudinal data collection), context sensitive, and social. As with all types of research, the investigators' choices involve trade-offs that have both advantages and disadvantages and require careful consideration.

Validity Versus Control

Field research tends to privilege validity over control. Whereas controlled contexts such as laboratories are useful for isolating variables and testing for specific effects, fieldwork conducted in organizations is messy and hard to control. As open systems theorists have recognized (e.g., Bahg, 1990; von Bertalanffy, 1968), most organizational activity is complex and interdependent and is not subject to simple causal explanations. Researchers often collaborate with managers and other organizational members to design and conduct studies that are consistent with organizational policies and provide minimal disruption to organizational practices—which explains why controlled experiments are rare. The lack of control, however, is mitigated by researcher knowledge of the setting, which provides greater confidence in what is being studied.

Content validity refers to the representativeness of a sample and thus the extent to which the research captures various meanings within the study (Baxter & Babbie, 2004; Cook & Campbell, 1979; Kerlinger, 1986). Content validity depends on how the researcher gathers data (e.g., in-depth interviews versus surveys), but having field-specific information enhances the validity of measures, which increases *ecological validity*, or a researcher's ability to approximate the phenomena of study (Bradburn et al., 2004). Indeed, having deep knowledge of the context is one way to assess convergent or divergent construct validity (that is, how well constructs and measures represent the concepts under study). If data gathered through conventional methods such as surveys do not fit with insights from participation in the field, the researcher can show validity by relying on thick description of the data (Geertz, 1973) or by triangulating different data sources gathered from the field. Most prominent is the use of member checks to ascertain the extent to which participants deem measures meaningful and/or representative of their experiences. Gathering data within the organizational context gives the researcher the advantage of being close to one's participants while they participate in data collection.

Engagement Versus Objectivity

A second trade-off involves researcher engagement versus objectivity. *Engaged scholarship* refers to a reciprocal relationship between the researcher and the community (i.e., a researcher-community partnership) as opposed to the investigator playing the role of a detached observer. Even though notions of engaged scholarship entered communication discussions only recently (Cheney, Wilhelmsson, & Zorn, 2002; Lewis, 2011; Van de Ven, 2007), field research has a history of connecting theory to practice and demanding closeness to rather than distance from one's research site. Waldron (2007) regards engaged scholarship as a practice of building *virtuous relationships* with research partners in the community. This practice requires the investigator to engage with organizational members in active ways and to view them as collaborative partners who participate in knowledge co-creation, rather than human subjects.

Engagement departs from the traditional positivist view, developed in the physical sciences (Burrell & Morgan, 1979), which aimed for a "complete separation between the investigator and the subject of the investigation" (Miller, 2001, p. 139). In the traditional view, the researcher was distant and detached from the object of study to avoid unduly influencing it. This view has given way to a post-positivist position that recognizes that complete objectivity is impossible because of human judgment and values that enter into the research process. Complete separation has been replaced by the notion of objectivity as a "regulatory ideal" in which the researcher strives to avoid bias as much as possible (Miller, 2001). Interpretive and critical scholars tend to acknowledge the inevitability of subjectivity in their designs and findings, even though research in this vein varies in degrees of engagement with the communities of study.

Particularistic Versus Generalizable

As discussed above, field research privileges particular context-based insights generated from case studies in contrast to generalizable findings drawn from random samples or experimental methods. For example, Wieland (2011) draws on rich ethnographic and interview data from a single Swedish organization to examine how the dialectic of control and resistance is conditioned by cultural norms about work/life balance. Even though field researchers aim to generate thick descriptions and meaningful understandings, this approach is not devoid of explanations aimed at theory building. The immersive and time-consuming nature of field studies, especially ethnographies that require a year or more in the field, makes it difficult to publish many studies on the same topic and to replicate research findings. Having a breadth of scholarship across contexts may increase generalizability through collective or aggregated knowledge produced by a critical mass of scholars who research the same topic in various ways, which Miller (2001) describes as a "healthy eclecticism" (p. 137). Even quantitative methods, which are presumed to be objective, rely on "the critical scrutiny of a community of scholars to safeguard objectivity and maximize the growth of social scientific knowledge" (Miller, 2001, p. 139). This practice of critical scrutiny of a community of scholars applies to field research as well. In short, field research supports the explanatory aspect of theory development (*why*) and does so in a generalizable way.

In sum, the philosophy of field research is driven by the figure-ground interplay of actors, their environments, and the mutual influences of micro and macro levels of communication as process and product of organizing. Field research values real-world contexts while teasing out particular aspects of communication and behavior. It can be used to develop and test theory, but it emphasizes discovery over prediction. Regardless of the goals of particular studies, field research supports theory development and offers the potential to uncover the granular details of *why* an organization functions as it does. Field research may be either qualitative (e.g., ethnography, interviews) or quantitative (e.g., surveys, content analysis, field experiments) or both, but either way, it grounds its discoveries in context-sensitive information.

Practical Issues and Challenges in Field Research

Although field research develops understandings of complex naturalistic organizations, investigators often face practical issues in gaining access to organizations and/or their communities, executing the fieldwork itself, and managing the unintended consequences that research can have on participants. This section details these challenges, provides examples of these experiences, and suggests ways of overcoming them.

Access and Participant Feedback

Gaining access to an organization or a community of organizations can be challenging if the researcher does not have an inside contact. Through reputation and referrals, some researchers are invited into an organization by its leaders. For example, Gibbs was invited to do a small class project in a global software team at a large high-tech corporation and got access to it through a former student of her advisor. Two years later, she reapproached the organization and was able to regain access for her dissertation study. In such cases, the challenges of access are diminished but are still present in contacting particular groups or collecting particular types of data. In an organizational audit of a local government municipality (Liberman & Doerfel, 2012), the town manager and mayor approached the researchers for help in analyzing the municipality's communication problems. Within the first week of the study, the researchers discovered that the employees deeply distrusted the town manager and disliked his projects. Most employees distinguished the field project from the manager, especially as the researchers became more familiar after several months of work in the organization. On the one hand, the researchers' physical presence afforded opportunities for more casual conversation, such as explaining what organizational problems interested scholars and the ways in which research offers insights into organizational processes and relationships. On the other hand, one branch of the municipality did not participate in the study because of issues with organizational power and politics. One informant revealed that his/her manager directly ordered employees not to participate in any research projects.

Personal contacts are helpful in securing access to organizations, but researchers need to have the *right* contact, especially in larger companies. For instance, global teams in the multinational corporation that Gibbs (2009) studied were fragmented into many divisions, departments, and units. Gaining access to an organizational context as specific as global teams required making contact with a person who worked in or supervised a global team and who ranked high enough in the organization's hierarchy to approve the study. Identifying this person may be difficult. Further, initial enthusiasm by organizational leaders for a study may dwindle as requests to conduct the project move up through the management chain. Enthusiasm for the study may ultimately fizzle due to lack of time or interest in the project or concerns about the security and confidentiality of the data.

Finally, research relationships often change over time as key organizational stakeholders leave or get transferred to other parts of the company, and these changes affect the level of support for a research project. For example, Gibbs and her colleagues (Gibbs, Ellison, & Heino, 2006) initially began with one director who valued the research and championed their project, but after several years of a productive relationship, this individual left the company and the researchers were referred to new contacts who were suspicious of the study and the way that it could potentially harm the company's reputation. They stonewalled the project, and the research partnership eventually came to a halt. This example underscores the need for field researchers to cultivate and maintain good relationships with organizational partners and to identify contacts who are likely to support their projects and who have the authority to do so. These particular experiences suggest the need for a checklist or a how-to guide for the novice field researcher. In some ways, the researcher is similar to a politician—a hand-shaker, a trust-builder, and a vote-getter ("Participate in my study, please!"). Yet being too slick, lacking authenticity and concern, or engaging in organizational politics may undermine the study in overt ways (e.g., low participation) and in covert ones (e.g., subversion, participants' lack of candor).

From Hawthorne Effect to Panopticon Effect

Field researchers have traditionally grappled with a phenomenon known as *the Hawthorne Effect*. Stemming from the classic Hawthorne studies, this effect suggests that simply attending to participants in a research project can change their behaviors. Investigators in the Hawthorne studies manipulated various types of material conditions to see which would influence employees' productivity, only to find that participation and interaction itself shaped productivity rates (Roethlisberger & Dickson, 1939). Even though such findings were later discredited (Miller & Monge, 1986), they gave birth to the human relations school and led to an increase in studies on worker participation in decision making. They also highlighted that participants may behave differently when they know researchers are present. Realizing that researchers can affect their own studies might suggest that scholars should maintain distance and be detached from their participants, as described in the section on engagement versus objectivity. However, we argue that the Hawthorne Effect is becoming less of an issue in modern organizations due to the rise of a concept known as *the Panopticon Effect*.

Foucault's (1977) critique of surveillance systems in prisons as an additional form of managerial power (Panopticism) is readily apparent in modern organizations in which perpetual monitoring has become commonplace, in the forms of open office environments created by cubicles, information and communication technologies (ICTs) that record phone calls ("This call may be recorded for customer service training") and track work activity and worker status, e-mail surveillance, and monitoring of employee attitudes through satisfaction and feedback surveys (Stohl & Cheney, 2001). This practice may lead to *the Panopticon Effect*, in which employees' awareness of *the potential* to be under constant surveillance transforms the way they self-police and regulate their behaviors in line with organizational norms. In this sense, the gap between how employees act when they know they are being watched versus how they "normally" act may be reduced, in that they could act as though they are being watched all the time. This finding is consistent with research on unobtrusive control (Barker, 1993; Tompkins & Cheney, 1985), which finds that control in modern organizations is more internalized and subtle. In this sense, the Panopticon Effect may actually render the Hawthorne effect less of an issue, because employees are becoming impervious to the researcher's presence, since they are already constantly monitored. The ongoing tracking of employees, however, may pose new challenges to fieldwork as concerns about employee research fatigue and information overload make managers more reluctant to engage in academic research. Indeed, some companies restrict the degree to which their employees may be surveyed internally as well as externally.

Data Collection and Rights of Research Subjects

Related to these issues are ethical concerns that occur because field research, by definition, enters into people's lives. Specifically, the research itself could put participants at risk on the job. For example, analyses might highlight ineffective or problematic employees or departments that could incur layoffs. Designing research that addresses these ethical concerns is one way to protect participants. Yet risks also occur when participants feel pressured to participate in the project, either from management or from the researchers. Field research involves politicking to recruit participants, and it is far easier to do this in face-to-face settings than to convince individuals to complete a survey. Thus training researchers to recognize the ethical issues that arise in recruiting participants is important.

Field research is a good option when recruiting participants is difficult. Challenges arise from a variety of reasons ranging from workplace politics to busy professionals who cannot carve out time to participate. So while online surveys are easy and attractive, they also yield low response rates (Tuten, Urban, & Bosnjak, 2002; Watt, 1999). In Doerfel's study in New Orleans (Doerfel et al., 2010), she recruited senior-level managers, owners, and executives through face-to-face networking and received a nearly 100% response rate, despite participants' busy schedules. Returning to the quote at the beginning of this chapter, Doerfel was fully aware of the difficulties of being in New Orleans in the time after Hurricane Katrina. From her conversations with participants, she discovered that they wanted to tell their stories and would not have been so eager to fill out a survey. Moreover, the participants valued Doerfel being with them so that she could see, firsthand, what they were facing.

Similarly, in Gibbs's (2009) experience, her position as an intern/consultant gave her increased access to participants, since she had a company badge and was on site several days a week. Because she was viewed as an insider, she established greater rapport with company employees than she would have as an outsider. She found that her insider status influenced the response rate and the quality of her data. She noticed a marked difference between her initial class study, in which her interviews portrayed the company in a superficially positive light, and her subsequent dissertation research, in which she delved deeper and gained greater understanding of the tensions and complexities of global organizing. Her immersion in the field allowed for rich and nuanced insights to emerge from her research. Insider access also facilitated her ability to schedule impromptu interviews with busy managers by stopping by their offices or arranging a follow-up time to return. In both Doerfel's and Gibbs's experiences, busy managers were more open to a 30-minute (or longer) conversation than to filling out a short survey. In comparing these experiences, response rates would have likely been lower if we had used surveys. Immersion brought us closer to participants who were eager to talk about their professional experiences. This immersion stands in contrast to organizational surveys that rely on high response rates and the support of managers (at various levels) to communicate the importance of the project to their employees.

As with any investigation of human subjects, field research has its opportunities and challenges. For example, an informed consent letter seems daunting when it is rife with legalistic phrasing and details, yet those same details can serve as a point of relief to other participants. Informed consent forms convey that the researchers are ethical and concerned about the participants' well-being. In this way, informed consent forms and letters serve as a recruiting tool, not just a legal document.

Conclusion

Field research is an integral part of scholarship in organizational communication. It privileges organizational context, and it represents a spectrum of studies that range from treating organizations as little more than containers to conducting rich, ethnographic fieldwork in which context is inseparable from the phenomena of study. It is used to study a broad range of organizational communication topics. Field research generates and enriches theories as well as addresses practical organizational problems. Although scholars employ a number of methods, such as the ones in studies published from 2001–2011, we see further opportunity to use quasi-experimental methods to develop predictive models of communication behavior.

We encourage field researchers to consider these methods to the extent that they are viable in particular field settings. Field research has expanded beyond bounded physical organizations to examine new sites, such as telework (Hylmö, 2006), online support groups and communities (Aakhus & Rumsey, 2010; Yuan et al., 2009), professional communities of practice (Vaast, 2004), virtual network organizations (Shumate & Pike, 2006), and nongovernmental organization hyperlink networks (Shumate & Lipp, 2008). We see opportunities for scholars to investigate new e-fields enabled by the Internet and social media technology through both traditional (content analysis, surveys, interviews) and new (cyberethnography, hyperlink analysis, big data server-log analysis) methods.

Organizational communication scholars also need to attend to 21st-century issues. Because of the regular use of digital tracking, employee assessments, and ongoing evaluations, employees are becoming accustomed to being observed. Hence, overt observations of work behavior may no longer cause a Hawthorne Effect; but instead, modern field scholars and practitioners may need to grapple with a Panopticon Effect. Indeed, the Panopticon Effect could become a new direction for theory development in field studies. Finally, we recognize the ongoing challenges of securing access to organizations, yet we encourage scholars to conduct immersive field research rather than opt for methods such as student samples or decontextualized surveys, which are much less costly to obtain but also less likely to yield in-depth insights about the organizational contexts that shape communication processes. We also appeal to the organizational communication community to continue to capture the complexity of organizational experiences through collaborative field research. We believe that it is the collective body of scholars that enables discoveries in the field to be aggregated into generalizable theories of communicating and organizing.

References[2]

*Aakhus, M. (2001). Technocratic and design stances toward communication expertise: How GDSS facilitators understand their work. *Journal of Applied Communication Research, 29*(4), 341–371.

*Aakhus, M., & Rumsey, E. (2010). Crafting supportive communication online: A communication design analysis of conflict in an online support group. *Journal of Applied Communication Research, 38*(1), 65–84.

*Ashcraft, K. L. (2005). Resistance through consent? Occupational identity, organizational form, and the maintenance of masculinity among commercial airline pilots. *Management Communication Quarterly, 19*(1), 67–90.

*Ashcraft, K. L., & Kedrowicz, A. (2002). Self-direction or social support? Nonprofit empowerment and the tacit employment contract of organizational communication studies. *Communication Monographs, 69*(1), 88–110.

Axley, S. (1984). Managerial and organizational communication in terms of the conduit metaphor. *Academy of Management Review, 9*(3), 428–437.

Bahg, C-G. (1990). Major systems theories throughout the world. *Behavioral Science, 35*(2), 79–107.

*Bakar, H. A., Dilbeck, K. E., & McCroskey, J. C. (2010). Mediating role of supervisory communication practices on relations between leader-member exchange and perceived employee commitment to workgroup. *Communication Monographs, 77*(4), 637–656.

Ballard, D. I., & Gossett, L. M. (2007). Alternative times: Communicating the non- standard work arrangement. In C. S. Beck (Ed.), *Communication yearbook* (vol. 31, pp. 274–321). Mahwah, NJ: Lawrence Erlbaum.

*Ballard, D. I., & Seibold, D. R. (2004a). Communication-related organizational structures and work group temporal experiences: The effects of coordination method, technology type, and feedback cycle on members' construals and enactments of time. *Communication Monographs, 71*(1), 1–27.

*Ballard, D. I., & Seibold, D. R. (2004b). Organizational members' communication and temporal experience: Scale development and validation. *Communication Research, 31*(2), 135–172.

*Barge, J. K., Lee, M., Maddux, K., Nabring, R., & Townsend, B. (2008). Managing dualities in planned change initiatives. *Journal of Applied Communication Research, 36*(4), 364–390.

Barker, J. R. (1993). Tightening the iron cage: Concertive control in self-managing teams. *Administrative Science Quarterly, 38*(3), 408–437.

Baxter, L. A., & Babbie, E. (2004). *The basics of communication research.* Belmont, CA: Wadsworth/Thomson Learning.

*Bennett, W. L., Foot, K., & Xenos, M. (2011). Narratives and network organization: A comparison of fair trade systems in two nations. *Journal of Communication, 61*(2), 219–245.

*Benoit-Barné, C., & Cooren, F. (2009). The accomplishment of authority through presentification. *Management Communication Quarterly, 23*(1), 5–31.

*Botero, I. C., & Van Dyne, L. (2009). Employee voice behavior. *Management Communication Quarterly, 23*(1), 84–104.

Bradburn, N., Sudman, S., & Wansink, B. (2004). *Asking questions: The definitive guide to questionnaire design—For market research, political polls, and social and health questionnaires.* San Francisco, CA: Jossey-Bass.

Bryant, J. A., & Monge, P. R. (2008). The evolution of the children's television community, 1953–2003. *International Journal of Communication, 2,* 160–192.

Burgess, R. G. (1984). *In the field: An introduction to field research.* New York, NY: Routledge.

Burrell, G., & Morgan, G. (1979). *Sociological paradigms and organisational analysis: Elements of the sociology of corporate life.* London, England: Heinemann.

*Castor, T., & Cooren, F. (2006). Organizations as hybrid forms of life: The implications of the selection of human and non-human agents in problem formulation. *Management Communication Quarterly, 19*(4), 570–600.

*Chaput, M., Brummans, B. H. J. M., & Cooren, F. (2011). The role of organizational identification in the communicative constitution of an organization: A study of consubstantialization in a young political party. *Management Communication Quarterly, 25*(2), 252–282.

Cheney, G., Wilhelmsson, M., & Zorn, T. E. (2002). 10 strategies for engaged scholarship. *Management Communication Quarterly, 16*(1), 92–100.

*Cheong, P. H., Huang, S., & Poon, J. P. (2011). Religious communication and epistemic authority of leaders in wired faith organizations. *Journal of Communication, 61*(5), 938–958.

*Cho, H., Trier, M., & Kim, E. (2005). The use of instant messaging in working relationship development: A case study. *Journal of Computer-Mediated Communication, 10*(4), article17. Retrieved from http://jcmc.indiana.edu/vol10/issue4/cho.html_

Clampitt, P. G., & Berk, L. (2009). A communication audit of a paper mill. In O. Hargie & D. Tourish (Eds.), *Auditing organizational communication: A handbook of research, theory, and practice* (pp. 274–289). New York, NY: Routledge.

Cook, T. D., & Campbell, D. T. (1979). *Quasi-experimentation: Design and analysis issues for field settings.* Boston, MA: Houghton Mifflin Company.

*Cooren, F. (2004). The communicative achievement of collective minding. *Management Communication Quarterly, 17*(4), 517–551.

*Dickson, D., Hargie, O., & Wilson, N. (2008). Communication, relationships, and religious difference in the Northern Ireland workplace: A study of private and public sector organizations. *Journal of Applied Communication Research, 36*(2), 128–160.

*Doerfel, M. L., Lai, C., & Chewning, L. V. (2010). The evolutionary role of interorganizational communication: Modeling social capital in disaster contexts. *Human Communication Research, 36*(2), 125–162.

*Doerfel, M. L., & Taylor, M. (2004). Network dynamics of interorganizational cooperation: The Croatian civil society movement. *Communication Monographs, 71*(4), 373–394.

Downs, C. W., Hydeman, A., & Adrian, A. D. (2009). Auditing the annual business conference of a major beverage company. In O. Hargie & D. Tourish (Eds.), *Auditing organizational communication: A handbook of research, theory, and practice* (pp. 304–322). New York, NY: Routledge.

*Fairhurst, G. T., Cooren, F., & Cahill, D. (2002). Discursiveness, contradiction, and unintended consequences in successive downsizings. *Management Communication Quarterly, 15*(4), 501–540.

*Farrell, A., & Geist-Martin, P. (2005). Communicating social health. *Management Communication Quarterly, 18*(4), 543–592.

*Farrow, H., & Yuan, Y. C. (2011). Building stronger ties with alumni through Facebook to increase volunteerism and charitable giving. *Journal of Computer-Mediated Communication, 16*(3), 445–464.

*Fay, M. J., & Kline, S. L. (2011). Coworker relationships and informal communication in high-intensity telecommuting. *Journal of Applied Communication Research, 39*(2), 144–163.

*Flanagin, A., Monge, P., & Fulk, J. (2001). The value of formative investment in organizational federations. *Human Communication Research, 27*(1), 69–93.

Foucault, M. (1977). *Discipline and punish: The birth of the prison* (A. Sheridan, Trans.). New York, NY: Vintage.

*Ganesh, S. (2003). Organizational narcissism. *Management Communication Quarterly, 16*(4), 558–594.

*Ganesh, S., & Stohl, C. (2010). Qualifying engagement: A study of information and communication technology and the global social justice movement in Aotearoa New Zealand. *Communication Monographs, 77*(1), 51–74.

*García-Morales, V. J., Matías-Reche, F., & Verdú-Jover, A. J. (2011). Influence of internal communication on technological proactivity, organizational learning, and organizational innovation in the pharmaceutical sector. *Journal of Communication, 61*(1), 150–177.

*Gasson, S. (2005). The dynamics of sensemaking, knowledge, and expertise in collaborative, boundary-spanning design. *Journal of Computer-Mediated Communication, 10*(4), article 14. Retrieved from http://jcmc.indiana.edu/vol10/issue4/gasson.html

Geertz, C. (1973). *The interpretation of cultures.* New York, NY: Basic Books.

Gibbs, J. L. (2009). Dialectics in a global software team: Negotiating tensions across time, space, and culture. *Human Relations, 62*(6), 905–935.

Gibbs, J. L., Ellison, N. B., & Heino, R. D. (2006). Self-presentation in online personals: The role of anticipated future interaction, self-disclosure, and perceived success in Internet dating. *Communication Research, 33*(2), 152–177.

Gibbs, J. L., Nekrassova, D., Grushina, Y., & Abdul Wahab, S. (2008). Reconceptualizing virtual teaming from a constitutive perspective: Review, redirection, and research agenda. In C. S. Beck (Ed.), *Communication yearbook* (vol. 32, pp. 187–229). New York, NY: Routledge.

*Gill, R., & Ganesh, S. (2007). Empowerment, constraint, and the entrepreneurial self: A study of White women entrepreneurs. *Journal of Applied Communication Research, 35*(3), 268–293.

*Golden, A. G. (2009). Employee families and organizations as mutually enacted environments. *Management Communication Quarterly, 22*(3), 385–415.

*Gossett, L. M. (2002). Kept at arm's length: Questioning the organizational desirability of member identification. *Communication Monographs, 69*(4), 385–404.

*Gossett, L. M. (2006). Falling between the cracks. *Management Communication Quarterly, 19*(3), 376–415.

*Gossett, L. M., & Kilker, J. (2006). My job sucks. *Management Communication Quarterly, 20*(1), 63–90.

*Grice, T. A., Gallois, C., Jones, E., Paulsen, N., & Callan, V. J. (2006). "We do it, but they don't": Multiple categorizations and work team communication. *Journal of Applied Communication Research, 34*(4), 331–348.

*Hall, M. L. (2011). Constructions of leadership at the intersection of discourse, power, and culture. *Management Communication Quarterly, 25*(4), 612–643.

Hargie, O., & Tourish, D. (Eds.). (2009). *Auditing organizational communication: A handbook of research, theory, and practice.* New York, NY: Routledge.

*Hart, Z. P., & Miller, V. D. (2005). Context and message content during organizational socialization. *Human Communication Research, 31*(2), 295–309.

*Harter, L. M., & Krone, K. J. (2001). The boundary-spanning role of a cooperative support organization: Managing the paradox of stability and change in non-traditional organizations. *Journal of Applied Communication Research, 29*(3), 248–277.

*Heiss, S. N., & Carmack, H. J. (2011). Knock, knock; Who's there? Making sense of organizational entrance through humor. *Management Communication Quarterly, 26*(1), 163–179.

*Hong, J., & Engeström, Y. (2004). Changing principles of communication between Chinese managers and workers. *Management Communication Quarterly, 17*(4), 552–585.

*Hylmö, A. (2006). Telecommuting and the contestability of choice. *Management Communication Quarterly, 19*(4), 541–569.

*Hylmö, A., & Buzzanell, P. M. (2002). Telecommuting as viewed through cultural lenses: An empirical investigation of the discourses of utopia, identity, and mystery. *Communication Monographs, 69*(4), 329–356.

*Iverson, J., & McPhee, R. (2008). Communicating knowing through communities of practice: Exploring internal communicative processes and differences among CoPs. *Journal of Applied Communication Research, 36*(2), 176–199.

Jablin, F. M., & Putnam, L. L. (Eds.). (2001). *The new handbook of organizational communication: Advances in theory, research, and methods.* Thousand Oaks, CA: SAGE.

*Kalman, M. E., Monge, P., Fulk, J., & Heino, R. (2002). Motivations to resolve communication dilemmas in database-mediated collaboration. *Communication Research, 29*(2), 125–154.

Kerlinger, F. N. (1986). *Foundations of behavioral research* (3rd ed.). New York, NY: Holt, Rinehart and Winston.

*Kirby, E. L., & Krone, K. J. (2002). "The policy exists but you can't really use it": Communication and the structuration of work-family policies. *Journal of Applied Communication Research, 30*(1), 50–77.

*Kleinnijenhuis, J., van den Hooff, B., Utz, S., Vermeulen, I., & Huysman, M. (2011). Social influence in networks of practice. *Communication Research, 38*(5), 587–612.

*Kramer, M. W. (2006). Shared leadership in a community theater group: Filling the leadership role. *Journal of Applied Communication Research, 34*(2), 141–162.

*Kramer, M. W. (2009). Role negotiations in a temporary organization: Making sense during role development in an educational theater production. *Management Communication Quarterly, 23*(2), 188–217.

*Kuhn, T., & Corman, S. R. (2003). The emergence of homogeneity and heterogeneity in knowledge structures during a planned organizational change. *Communication Monographs, 70*(3), 198–229.

*Kuhn, T., & Nelson, N. (2002). Reengineering identity. *Management Communication Quarterly, 16*(1), 5–38.

Kunda, G. (1992). *Engineering culture.* Philadelphia, PA: Temple University Press.

*Lammers, J. C., & Garcia, M. (2009). Exploring the concept of "profession" for organizational communication research: Institutional influences in a veterinary organization. *Management Communication Quarterly, 22*(3), 357–384.

*Larson, G. S., & Pepper, G. L. (2003). Strategies for managing multiple organizational identifications. *Management Communication Quarterly, 16*(4), 528–557.

*Larson, G. S., & Tompkins, P. K. (2005). Ambivalence and resistance: A study of management in a concertive control system. *Communication Monographs, 72*(1), 1–21.

*Leonardi, P. M. (2009). Why do people reject new technologies and stymie organizational changes of which they are in favor? Exploring misalignments between social interactions and materiality. *Human Communication Research, 35*(3), 407–441.

*Leonardi, P. M., Treem, J. W., & Jackson, M. H. (2010). The connectivity paradox: Using technology to both decrease and increase perceptions of distance in distributed work arrangements. *Journal of Applied Communication Research, 38*(1), 85–105.

Lewis, L. K. (2011). *Organizational change: Creating change through strategic communication.* Chichester, UK: Wiley-Blackwell.

*Lewis, L. K., Hamel, S. A., & Richardson, B. K (2001). Communicating change to nonprofit stakeholders: Models and predictors of implementers' approaches. *Management Communication Quarterly, 15*(1), 5–41.

*Lewis, L. K., Isbell, M. B., & Koschmann, M. (2010). Collaborative tensions: Practitioners' experiences of interorganizational relationships. *Communication Monographs, 77*(4), 460–479.

*Lewis, L. K., Richardson, B. K., & Hamel, S. A. (2003). When the "stakes" are communicative: The lamb's and the lion's share during nonprofit planned change. *Human Communication Research, 29*(3), 400–430.

Liberman, C. J., & Doerfel, M. L. (2012, January). *Structuring organizational communication: Employees' role and network position as predictive of institutional talk about the adoption of technology.* Proceedings from the Hawaii International Conference on Systems Sciences, Maui, HI.

*Lin, C., & Clair, R. P. (2007). Measuring Mao Zedong thought and interpreting organizational communication in China. *Management Communication Quarterly, 20*(4), 395–429.

Littlejohn, S. W. (1999). *Theories of human communication.* Belmont, CA: Wadsworth.

*Liu, B. F., Horsley, J. S., & Levenshus, A. B. (2010). Government and corporate communication practices: Do the differences matter? *Journal of Applied Communication Research, 38*(2), 189–213.

*Lucas, K. (2011). Blue-collar discourses of workplace dignity: Using outgroup comparisons to construct positive identities. *Management Communication Quarterly, 25*(2), 353–374.

*Lucas, K., & Buzzanell, P. M. (2004). Blue-collar work, career, and success: Occupational narratives of *sisu. Journal of Applied Communication Research, 32*(4), 273–292.

*Lynch, O. H. (2009). Kitchen antics: The importance of humor and maintaining professionalism at work. *Journal of Applied Communication Research, 37*(4), 444–464.

*Lyon, A. (2004). Participants' use of cultural knowledge as cultural capital in a dot-com start-up organization. *Management Communication Quarterly, 18*(2), 175–203.

*Martin, D. M. (2004). Humor in middle management: Women negotiating the paradoxes of organizational life. *Journal of Applied Communication Research, 32*(2), 147–170.

Martin, J. (1992). *Cultures in organizations.* New York, NY: Oxford University Press.

Mayo, E. (1945). *The social problems of an industrial civilization.* Cambridge, MA: Harvard University Press.

McCann, R. M., & Giles, H. (2006). Communication with people of different ages in the workplace: Thai and American data. *Human Communication Research, 32*(1), 74–108.

*McGuire, T. (2010). From emotions to spirituality: "Spiritual labor" as the commodification, codification, and regulation of organizational members' spirituality. *Management Communication Quarterly, 24*(1), 74–103.

*McNamee, L. G. (2011). Faith-based organizational communication and its implications for member identity. *Journal of Applied Communication Research, 39*(4), 422–440.

*Meares, M. M., Oetzel, J. G., Torres, A., Derkacs, D., & Ginossar, T. (2004). Employee mistreatment and muted voices in the culturally diverse workplace. *Journal of Applied Communication Research, 32*(1), 4–27.

Miller, K. I. (2001). Quantitative research methods. In F. M. Jablin & L. L. Putnam (Eds.), *The new handbook of organizational communication: Advances in theory, research, and methods* (pp. 137–160). Thousand Oaks, CA: SAGE.

*Miller, K. I. (2007). Compassionate communication in the workplace: Exploring processes of noticing, connecting, and responding. *Journal of Applied Communication Research, 35*(3), 223–245.

*Miller, K. I., & Koesten, J. (2008). Financial feeling: An investigation of emotion and communication in the workplace. *Journal of Applied Communication Research, 36*(1), 8–32.

Miller, K. I., & Monge, P. R. (1986). Participation, satisfaction, and productivity: A meta-analytic review. *Academy of Management Journal, 29*(4), 727–753.

Monge, P. R., & Contractor, N. S. (2000). Emergence of communication networks. In F. M. Jablin & L. L. Putnam (Eds.), *The new handbook of organizational communication* (pp. 440–502). Thousand Oaks, CA: SAGE.

*Morgan, J. M., & Krone, K. J. (2001). Bending the rules of "professional" display: Emotional improvisation in caregiver performances. *Journal of Applied Communication Research, 29*(4), 317–340.

*Myers, K. K. (2005). A burning desire. *Management Communication Quarterly, 18*(3), 344–384.

*Myers, K. K., & McPhee, R. D. (2006). Influences on member assimilation in workgroups in high-reliability organizations: A multilevel analysis. *Human Communication Research, 32*(4), 440–468.

*Norander, S., & Harter, L. M. (2011). Reflexivity in practice: Challenges and potentials of transnational organizing. *Management Communication Quarterly, 26*(1), 74–105.

*Norton, T., Sias, P., & Brown, S. (2011). Experiencing and managing uncertainty about climate change. *Journal of Applied Communication Research, 39*(3), 290–309.

*Parker, P. S. (2001). African American women executives' leadership communication within dominant-culture organizations. *Management Communication Quarterly, 15*(1), 42–82.

*Pepper, G. L., & Larson, G. S. (2006). Cultural identity tensions in a post-acquisition organization. *Journal of Applied Communication Research, 34*(1), 49–71.

*Perriton, L. (2009). "We don't want complaining women!" A critical analysis of the business case for diversity. *Management Communication Quarterly, 23*(2), 218–243.

*Perry, D. C., Taylor, M., & Doerfel, M. L. (2003). Internet-based communication in crisis management. *Management Communication Quarterly, 17*(2), 206–232.

*Procopio, C. H., & Procopio, S. T. (2007). Do you know what it means to miss New Orleans? Internet communication, geographic community, and social capital in crisis. *Journal of Applied Communication Research, 35*(1), 67–87.

Putnam, L. L., & Krone, K. J. (2006). Editors' introduction. In L. L. Putnam & K. J. Krone (Eds.), *Organizational communication* (pp. xxiii–xliii). Thousand Oaks, CA: SAGE.

Putnam, L. L., & Nicotera, A. M. (Eds.). (2008). *Building theories of organization: The constitutive role of communication.* New York, NY: Routledge.

Putnam, L. L., & Pacanowsky, M. E. (Eds.). (1983). *Communication and organizations: An interpretive approach.* Beverly Hills, CA: SAGE.

*Quan-Haase, A., Cothrel, J., & Wellman, B. (2005). Instant messaging for collaboration: A case study of a high-tech firm. *Journal of Computer-Mediated Communication, 10*(4), article 13. Retrieved from http://jcmc.indiana.edu/vol10/issue4/quan-haase.html

Quinn, D., Hargie, O., & Tourish, D. (2009). Auditing a major police organization. In O. Hargie & D. Tourish (Eds.), *Auditing organizational communication: A handbook of research, theory, and practice* (pp. 346–355). New York, NY: Routledge.

*Riedlinger, M., Gallois, C., McKay, S., & Pittam, J. (2004). Impact of social group processes and functional diversity on communication in networked organizations. *Journal of Applied Communication Research, 32*(1), 55–79.

Roethlisberger, F. J., & Dickson, W. J. (1939). *Management and the worker.* Cambridge, MA: Harvard University Press.

*Rooney, D., Paulsen, N., Callan, V. J., Brabant, M., Gallois, C., & Jones, E. (2010). A new role for place identity in managing organizational change. *Management Communication Quarterly, 24*(1), 44–73.

*Rosenfeld, L. B., Richman, J. M., & May, S. K. (2004). Information adequacy, job satisfaction and organizational culture in a dispersed-network organization. *Journal of Applied Communication Research, 32*(1), 28–54.

*Scarduzio, J. A. (2011). Maintaining order through deviance? The emotional deviance, power, and professional work of municipal court judges. *Management Communication Quarterly, 25*(2), 283–310.

*Scott, C. W., & Trethewey, A. (2008). Organizational discourse and the appraisal of occupational hazards: Interpretive repertoires, heedful interrelating, and identity at work. *Journal of Applied Communication Research, 36*(3), 298–317.

Shumate, M. (2012). The evolution of the HIV/AIDS NGO hyperlink network. *Journal of Computer-Mediated Communication, 17*(2), 120–134.

*Shumate, M., & Lipp, J. (2008). Connective collective action online: An examination of the hyperlink network structure of an NGO issue network. *Journal of Computer-Mediated Communication, 14*(1), 178–201.

*Shumate, M., & Pike, J. (2006). Trouble in a geographically distributed virtual network organization: Organizing tensions in continental direct action network. *Journal of Computer-Mediated Communication, 11*(3), 802–824.

Skipper, M., Hargie, O., & Tourish, D. (2009). A communication audit of a hospital clinic. In O. Hargie & D. Tourish (Eds.), *Auditing organizational communication: A handbook of research, theory, and practice* (pp. 260–273). New York, NY: Routledge.

*Skovholt, K., & Svennevig, J. (2006). Email copies in workplace interaction. *Journal of Computer-Mediated Communication, 12*(1), 42–65.

Stohl, C., & Cheney, G. (2001). Participatory processes/paradoxical practices: Communication and the dilemmas of organizational democracy. *Management Communication Quarterly, 14*(3), 349–407.

*Susskind, A. M. (2007). Downsizing survivors' communication networks and reactions: A longitudinal examination of information flow and turnover intentions. *Communication Research, 34*(2), 156–184.

*Susskind, A. M., Odom-Reed, P. R., & Viccari, A. E. (2011). Team leaders and team members in interorganizational networks. *Communication Research, 38*(5), 613–633.

Tateo, L. (2005). The Italian extreme right on-line network: An exploratory study using an integrated social network analysis and content analysis approach. *Journal of Computer-Mediated Communication, 10*(2), article 10.

Taylor, F. W. (1911). *The principles of scientific management.* New York, NY: Harper & Row.

Taylor, J. R., Flanagin, A. J., Cheney, G., & Seibold, D. R. (2001). Organizational communication research: Key moments, central concerns, and future challenges. *Communication yearbook* (vol. 24, pp. 99–137).

*Taylor, M., & Doerfel, M. L. (2003). Building interorganizational relationships that build nations. *Human Communication Research, 29*(2), 153–181.

Taylor, M., & Doerfel, M. L. (2011). The Croatian civil society movement: Implications, recommendations, and expectations for donors and NGOs.

Voluntas: The International Journal of Voluntary Associations, 22, 311–334.

Tompkins, P. K., & Cheney, G. (1985). Communication and unobtrusive control in contemporary organizations. In R. D. McPhee & P. K. Tompkins (Eds.), *Organizational communication: Traditional themes and new directions* (pp. 179–210). Beverly Hills, CA: SAGE.

*Tracy, S. J. (2004). Dialectic, contradiction, or double bind? Analyzing and theorizing employee reactions to organizational tension. *Journal of Applied Communication Research, 32*(2), 119–146.

*Tracy, S. J. (2005). Locking up emotion: Moving beyond dissonance for understanding emotion labor discomfort. *Communication Monographs, 72*(3), 261–283.

*Tracy, S. J., Myers, K. K., & Scott, C. W. (2006). Cracking jokes and crafting selves: Sensemaking and identity management among human service workers. *Communication Monographs, 73*(3), 283–308.

*Tracy, S. J., & Scott, C. (2006). Sexuality, masculinity, and taint management among firefighters and correctional officers. *Management Communication Quarterly, 20*(1), 6–38.

Tuten, T. L., Urban, D. J., & Bosnjak, M. (2002). Internet surveys and data quality: A review. In B. Batinic, U. Reips, & M. Bosnjak (Eds.), *Online social sciences* (pp. 7–26). Seattle, WA: Hogrefe & Huber Publishers.

*Vaast, E. (2004). O brother, where are thou? *Management Communication Quarterly, 18*(1), 5–44.

Van de Ven, A. H. (2007). *Engaged scholarship: A guide to organizational and social research.* New York, NY: Oxford University Press.

Van Maanen, J. (1988). *Tales of the field: On writing ethnography*. Chicago, IL: University of Chicago Press.

von Bertalanffy, L. (1968). *General systems theory: Foundations, development, applications*. New York, NY: Braziller.

*Waldeck, J. H., Seibold, D. R., & Flanagin, A. J. (2004). Organizational assimilation and communication technology use. *Communication Monographs, 71*(2), 161–183.

Waldron, V. R. (2007). Public scholarship, relational practices: A reflection on "virtuous" partnerships. *Management Communication Quarterly, 21*(1), 118–125.

*Waldvogel, J. (2007). Greetings and closings in workplace email. *Journal of Computer-Mediated Communication, 12*(2), 456–477.

Watt, J. H. (1999). Internet systems for evaluation research. In G. Gay & T. L. Bennington (Eds.), *Information technologies in evaluation: Social, moral, epistemological, and practical implications* (pp. 23–43). San Francisco, CA: Jossey-Bass Publishers.

Weick, K. E. (1979). *The social psychology of organizing* (2nd ed.). New York, NY: McGraw-Hill.

*Whitbred, R., Fonti, F., Steglich, C., & Contractor, N. (2011). From microactions to macrostructure and back: A structurational approach to the evolution of organizational networks. *Human Communication Research, 37*(3), 404–433.

*Wieland, S. M. (2011). Struggling to manage work as a part of everyday life: Complicating control, rethinking resistance, and contextualizing work/life studies. *Communication Monographs, 78*(2), 162–184.

*Yuan, Y. C., Cosley, D., Welser, H., Xia, L., & Gay, G. (2009). The diffusion of a task recommendation system to facilitate contributions to an online community. *Journal of Computer-Mediated Communication, 15*(1), 32–59.

*Yuan, Y. C., Fulk, J., Monge, P. R., & Contractor, N. (2010). Expertise directory development, shared task interdependence, and strength of communication network ties as multilevel predictors of expertise exchange in transactive memory work groups. *Communication Research, 37*(1), 20–47.

*Zorn, T. E., Flanagin, A. J., & Shoham, M. D. (2011). Institutional and noninstitutional influences on information and communication technology adoption and use among nonprofit organizations. *Human Communication Research, 37*(1), 1–33.

Notes

1. The authors wish to thank Seol Ki for her assistance with the literature review and analysis for this chapter.

2. Articles noted with an asterisk were part of the 103 sampled from communication journals for the analyses presented in this chapter.

CHAPTER 10

Organizing Ethnography and Qualitative Approaches[1]

Sarah J. Tracy and Patricia Geist-Martin

Ethnography combines two Greek words: "*graphein*, the verb for 'to write,' and *ethnoi*, a plural noun for 'the nations—the others'" (Erickson, 2011, p. 43). Writing and interacting with other people are core ethnographic activities. Researchers typically immerse themselves in fieldwork, engage in participant observation, and conduct interviews. Additionally, they tend to focus on embodied data, view writing as a core part of the analysis process, and construct creative textual, aural, or visual research representations. This chapter is devoted to ethnography and qualitative methodologies in organizational communication research.

We engaged in a number of methods in writing this chapter. In addition to a critical literature synthesis, we conducted several original data collections and textual analyses. These included e-mail interviews, an examination of several websites, and an analysis of organizational communication qualitative articles published over the last 15 years. By linking this chapter's content to specific people and qualitative data, readers will hopefully gain a sense of the epistemology that undergirds ethnography. Namely, that knowledge—including that presented throughout this chapter—is constructed, relational, and dependent on specific individuals' standpoints. Our practices aim to *show* qualitative methods and not just *tell* about them.

We open this chapter with an explanation of key concepts and markers of quality that are associated with qualitative research in general. Second, we then turn to the way qualitative research has been employed in organizational studies specifically, sketching the history of qualitative approaches and their role in today's organizational communication discipline. Third, we discuss the ways qualitative methods emerge differently depending on paradigmatic affiliation. Fourth, we share our analysis of organizational communication qualitative research over the last 15 years, showing the most common contexts and themes studied and the landscape of high-impact qualitative research. Finally, we offer future directions and conclusions.

Key Characteristics of Qualitative Methods

In order to understand the role of qualitative methods in organizational communication, it helps to be familiar with several key characteristics that set it apart from other forms of research. Here, we discuss how qualitative researchers approach the research design, data collection, and the research instrument. We also discuss writing as a form of inquiry.

Research Design

Context takes a central role in qualitative research. Most studies tend to be inductive or *emic* in nature—meaning that the researcher often begins with collecting data from the ground up and then uses these data to make theoretical claims (Harris, 1976). This is different than deductive or *etic* studies, in which researchers begin with theory, presuppositions, or hypotheses. Qualitative research can be quite open ended—especially when the data available and access granted is contextual and, therefore, largely outside of the control of the researcher. For example, interviewing high-ranking elites, such as organizational executives, can be very difficult (Undheim, 2003). Likewise, many organizational arenas are closed or even hostile to outsiders, and research access requires a mixture of luck, savvy negotiation, and insider contact.

Even though research is contextual, most qualitative researchers bring favorite "sensitizing concepts" with them to the scene (Charmaz, 2006; Glaser & Strauss, 1967). For instance, a research team may begin their study with background knowledge in any number of issues, such as gender, collective action, or social responsibility. These sensitizing concepts serve as interpretive devices—almost like magnifying glasses—that offer frameworks through which researchers see, organize, and experience the data. For instance, Meisenbach, Remke, Buzzanell and Liu (2008) used Burke's pentad to better understand the progress of organizations regarding maternity leave. This sensitizing concept spurred focus on specific acts, agents, and scenes.

Sensitizing concepts are very helpful for narrowing a study. Qualitative researchers, however, tend to hold on loosely to presuppositions and *a priori* theories and remain open to issues that emerge as salient throughout the research journey. In this way, interpretive qualitative research is similar to a funnel; researchers approach the scholarly task with a wide lens and, over time, focus on specific issues that may help explain important theoretical, moral, and practical questions. For example, when Scott and Myers (2005) began their research on firefighters, they knew they were interested broadly in issues of emotion and identity but did not determine a focus on emotional interference and emotion socialization until midway through data collection. This contextual focus affects the way researchers approach data.

Data Collection

Given the contextual focus, qualitative researchers tend to be interested in the influence and juxtaposition of myriad issues together, rather than isolating variables. In other words, even as qualitative researchers funnel in from wider to more specific issues of study, they still typically use a Gestalt approach, examining multiple pieces of data in relation to and in tandem with others. For example, in their field study of firefighters, Scott and Myers (2005) examined socialization in relation to emotional labor, dirty work, and identity, showing how these issues intersect and influence one another. Likewise, rather than isolating one demographic factor, such as gender, qualitative research is primed to help organizational communication scholars examine how various identity characteristics such as gender, race, sexuality, and class are constructed in relation to and together with one another (Ashcraft, 2011).

Relatedly, qualitative researchers tend to be *bricoleurs*. *Bricolage* is a French term that refers to "a pieced-together set of representations that is fitted to the specifics of a complex situation" (Denzin & Lincoln, 2005, p. 4). As bricoleurs, qualitative scholars often piece together data they have collected through a broad variety of data sources, which may include, for example, participant observation field notes, interview transcripts, organizational documents, and websites. By crystallizing data from a variety of sources, they create a meaningful, multifaceted (but still admittedly partial and constructed) understanding of the scene (Ellingson, 2009). For instance, Trethewey (2001) compiled data from advertisements, employee interviews, and her own organizational experience to critically examine the grand narratives that suggest that women's aging automatically equates with professional decline. In order to construct a valuable data set and answer significant theoretical, practical, and moral questions, qualitative researchers must be resourceful, creative, and flexible.

In most cases, qualitative researchers develop a sampling plan along the way, rather than strictly in advance. They make use of the data, perspectives of interviewees, and organizations that allow access. Therefore, rather than justifying the sample based upon research goals, qualitative researchers are just as likely to justify their research goals based upon the sample or site(s) of study, with sampling choices varying from study to study (for a range of sampling plans, see Patton, 2002). Most qualitative scholars do not aim for a statistically random sample that can be formally generalized. Rather, they usually aim for *depth* over *breadth* and ensure the project's goals and claims fit the case at hand. As such, qualitative research gains its resonance (ability to impact other scenes) not through statistical generalizability but through choosing critical cases (Flyvbjerg, 2011) and providing enough rich and thick description that the study's findings can be transferred or naturalistically generalized to other settings (Tracy, 2010).

Discourse scholars use the term *discourses* (lowercase) to refer to everyday talk, action, and text and *Discourses* (capitalized) to refer to larger systems of thought (Alvesson & Karreman, 2000). Qualitative analysis includes the examination of both, usually in tandem. For instance, a researcher interested in line-standing behavior might analyze field data that illustrate the following (small *d*) discourses or actions: "(a) patiently waiting in line at the grocery store, (b) yelling self-righteously at a driver who cuts into our lane, or (c) scolding children who do not wait their turn" (Tracy & Rivera, 2010, p. 6). They may link these data to larger structures, theories, or (big *D*) Discourses—such as to the prevailing assumption that "only rude people cut in line." By examining discourses, qualitative methods are well-poised to identify and offer understanding of the ways grand narratives and societal structures are constructed and, over time, create normalcy and powerful ideologies (Eisenberg, 2007; Giddens 1979, 1981).

Making use of a wide range of data also highlights the ways multiple organizational participants understand and narrate their world. Max Weber brought the concept of *verstehen* to the social sciences to refer to the practice of examining the world from the participants' point of view in order to strive toward empathic insight (Tucker, 1965). This concept passed down through a number of prominent research strains, including those of Husserl, Heidegger, Gadamer, and Habermas (Erickson, 2011) and had significant influence on Geertz's (1973) interpretive methods. As Geertz delightfully explains, in order to be able to differentiate a wink from a twitch from an imitation of someone else's twitch, the researcher must not just observe others but understand the scene from participants' points of view. Qualitative analyses make use of participant observation as well as ongoing participant interaction and member reflection practices in order to access this understanding.

The Researcher as Instrument

In qualitative research, the researcher is, literally, the research instrument. In contrast to studies that rely on external instruments (e.g., a thermometer, a scale, or a sweat-test) for ascertaining the findings, qualitative researchers mediate and construct the data. They use their own bodies, observations, feelings, questions, and interpretations to make research claims based upon what they heard, felt, smelled, and saw. They may also co-construct the research with participants. Such is the case, for example, with Eisenberg, Baglia, and Pynes (2006), who partnered with hospital administrators to improve the flow and speed of patient care. This and other participatory and collaborative research suggests that researchers work *with* participants rather than conduct research *on* them (Reason, 1994).

Because of the central role of the researcher as instrument, good qualitative analysis must be self-reflexive. In other words, researchers carefully consider how their (and any co-participant's) subjectivity impacts the research and writing process. Investigators' demographic characteristics, past experiences, and points of view invariably shape their approach, topics, and goals. Rather than deny this fact or cloak it in a veil of objectivity, qualitative researchers embrace and share this information with readers.

For example, in his analysis of wheelchair rugby, Lindemann (2008) reveals that "as an able-bodied researcher who grew up with a physically disabled father (who was himself a wheelchair athlete), I was reflexive about my assumptions and interpretations and recorded these thoughts in field notes" (p. 103). Self-reflexivity provides the opportunity for the reader as well as the author to mitigate interpretive bias and consider how the author's subjectivity might affect the data collection and analysis. Among other things, Lindemann (2010a) explains how being reflexive regarding his past experience tempered what may have been a tendency to glamorize disabled men. Furthermore, it allowed him to better empathize with participants and their families, which likely prompted more trust and openness (Lindemann, 2010b).

Writing as a Form of Inquiry

Finally, qualitative research is characterized by an analysis process that interweaves data collection, interpretation, and writing. Throughout the research project, qualitative researchers draft and redraft research questions, create data collection plans, write field notes, transcribe interviews, and craft analytic memos about their hunches and interpretations. Writing, from this point of view, is not separate from data collection and analysis but is itself a form of inquiry (Richardson, 2000). As Tracy (2013) states,

> *Qualitative researchers find meaning by writing the meaning into being.* Artists' magic comes in their *process* of creation. Artists don't "paint up" their picture or "sculpt up" their statues. Likewise, qualitative researchers do not "write up." They write. And through writing, they meander, produce crappy sentences, feel stuck, go back and edit, write some more—and through this process they come to *know.* (p. 275, emphasis in original)

Because writing is viewed as a way of knowing, many qualitative researchers emphasize the importance of aesthetic stories and narrative (Goodall, 2008).

Aesthetic texts are interactive, descriptive, and evocative (Scarduzio, Giannini, & Geist-Martin, 2011)—ones that move the "heart and the belly" as well as the "head" (Bochner, 2000, p. 271). For example, in his book-length treatment of democratic systems, Cheney (1999) wove together rich qualitative data to illustrate the successes and challenges of the famous Mondragón worker-owned cooperatives in Basque, Spain. From his participant observation and interviews, Cheney (1999) constructed a compelling case study that shows, rather than tells, the challenges of maintaining democratic organizational systems in a competitive global market. By writing aesthetically, qualitative studies have the potential to reach a wide range of stakeholders, including policy makers, business practitioners, and interested lay publics.

In summary, qualitative researchers tend to focus on context, emic interpretive design, piecing together a wide range of data, being self-reflexive, and approaching the writing process as a crucial form of inquiry. Knowing these key characteristics sets the stage for delving into the role of qualitative methods in organizational communication.

Historical Matters and Key Turning Points

The use of qualitative methods in organization and management studies has a long history. The original Hawthorne Studies, conducted between 1924 and 1933, included qualitative interviews designed to "move away from Taylorist approaches where the worker was seen as a cog in a machine, to the focus on the worker as an emotional human being" (Cassell, 2009, p. 501). In the first phase of the studies, the researchers found that by being observed, employees worked harder. In a second phase, researchers watched a group of male workers wiring up equipment in the Bank Wiring Room (Arnold, Randall, Patterson, Silvester, & Robertson, 2010). Although the workers were initially suspicious of the researchers' presence, after three weeks, they resumed normal behavior, which included talking, game playing, teasing, and fighting.

These studies provide a key insight about the impact of observation on participants: the Hawthorne effect means that the mere observation of a group—or more precisely, the *perception* of being observed and one's interpretation of its significance—tends to change the group. "*When people are observed, or believe that someone cares about them, they act differently*" (Newstrom & Davis, 2002, p. 340, emphasis in original). And, if they are watched over time, the impact of being watched changes. The consistent finding from the Hawthorne studies is that human relations matter (Arnold et al., 2010).

Management scholars continued to use qualitative methods throughout the 1950s and 1960s. Roy (1959) engaged in participant observation on a factory floor for two months, examining the relationship between job satisfaction and informal social interactions such as "banana time." Labor-management relations began to be studied using descriptive accounts of work in a bank department (Argyris, 1954a, 1954b), the work of business executives (Argyris, 1953), and socialization into professions (e.g., Becker & Geer, 1961; Van Maanen, 1973).

The late 1970s and early 1980s represent a time in our history when organizational communication scholars "drew on the unique rhetorical roots of our discipline and applied rhetorical criticism to the study of organizational communication" (Taylor & Trujillo, 2001, p. 164). Weick (1979) explicitly focused on organizational social interaction. Doctoral students in the 1980s began to take seriously the idea that organizations were constructed in and through communication and that they would need interpretive, discursive, and rhetorical research methods that could tap into such organizational rituals, interactions, and processes (Bullis, 2005).

A turning point for qualitative research and organizational communication was the 1981 Alta, Utah, organizational communication conference. Dialogue focused on dissatisfaction with quantitative, rational, and managerial approaches to studying organizations. Participants discussed opportunities to move beyond the transmission model of communication to analyze the ways interaction and communication constructed organizations (Taylor, Flanagin, Cheney, & Seibold, 2001). Although some scholars contend that Alta has become a romanticized story and was not the radical and wholly wonderful change agent retold in classrooms over the years (see Kuhn, 2005), there is no denying that in the mid-1980s, scholars harnessed the interpretive turn to encourage a boom in qualitative methods.

Putnam and Pacanowsky's (1983) edited volume from the Alta conference both signified a methodological shift away from studying communication as a measurable outcome and indicated a fundamental transformation in researchers' ways of building knowledge and knowing the world (Deetz, 2003). Increasing numbers of organizational communication scholars began to question a rationalistic approach that favored managerial interests and realist representations and, instead, became more concerned with everyday workers' ideology, resistance, and stories that were inherently intersubjective and partial.

Drawing from Geertz's (1973) interpretive anthropology, communication researchers began to study organizations as tribes and cultures, viewing organizational phenomena as performances and texts that were strange, exotic, and full of specialized meanings (Pacanowsky & O'Donnell-Trujillo, 1982, 1983). Tompkins and Cheney (1985) developed their theory of unobtrusive control that, in turn, spurred qualitative field studies that examined the ways organizational power emerged in and through communication and identification (Barker, 1993; Bullis & Tompkins, 1989; Cheney, 1983; Geist & Hardesty, 1992). Meanwhile, Riley (1983) and Poole, Seibold, and McPhee (1985) drew from Giddens's (1979, 1981) structuration theory, highlighting how groups and organizational cultures were constructed in and through communication. Deetz (1982) incorporated critical theory into interpretive approaches, suggesting that "knowledge is produced in talk, not simply transmitted or shared" (p. 133). Goodall (1989) embedded himself in a technology company and reimagined the role of researcher as organizational detective and writing as narrative. Howard and Geist (1995) studied downsizing in a merging organization.

Clearly, the role of qualitative methods in organizational communication has a rich history. Organizational communication scholars offered their views of key turning points through our e-mail interviews. Sias sees the role of qualitative methods in organizational communication as having three primary turning points: (a) the publication of Putnam and Pacanowsky's (1983) book, (b) the emergence of critical research, and (c) the role of qualitative methods in understanding communication as constitutive of social reality and experience. Buzzanell echoed the idea that Pacanowsky and O'Donnell-Trujillo's organizational culture work helped launch the critical, postmodern, feminist perspectives in the late 1980s and early 1990s.

Trujillo told us that since the last review of qualitative organizational research (Taylor & Trujillo, 2001), he has witnessed the expansion of this work to autoethnography, performance studies, and his own work in automythyology (The Ethnogs, Fem Nogs, & Rip Tupp, 2011). Goodall echoed these expansions in his e-mail interview and added that the new ethnography work is "still largely insular and outside of the cadre of true believers, more or less discounted as 'not scholarship.'" At the same time, Goodall was heartened by the use of ethnography to reach broader public audiences, including Ho's (2009) ethnography of the experiences and ideologies of Wall Street investment bankers and de Rond's (2008) ethnography of the Cambridge/Oxford boat race as high-performance teams and peak experiences. These viewpoints provide perspective on our history. But what is the role of qualitative methods in today's organizational communication discipline?

Contemporary organizational communication qualitative work is manifested in a variety of representations and tends to be concerned with process, language, and a range of voices—not just those of management (Mumby & Stohl, 1996). For example, organizational communication scholars examine how dialogue reveals and constructs organizational attitudes and norms (e.g., Tracy & Rivera, 2010), how communication is constructed within and impacts larger social structures (e.g., Fairhurst & Putnam, 2004), and the way that communication flows serve to constitute the organization (e.g., McPhee & Zaug, 2000). In locating the frontiers of organizational communication in New Zealand and Australia, Simpson and Zorn (2004) argue that organizational communication scholarship focuses on "messages, interactions, communication behaviours, communication strategies, symbols, and discourses" highlighting "language, discourse, and other symbolic dimensions" (p. 18). In his e-mail interview, Ganesh noted that, compared to those in organization studies, qualitative methods in organizational communication have increasingly featured what he called the "[University of] Colorado model of the late 1990s. . . . These were big, intensive projects that involved collecting a LOT of data, from which people published for years" (e.g., Ashcraft, 2001; Gossett, 2006; Larson & Pepper, 2003; Tracy, 2004).

A number of structural developments indicate the important role of qualitative methods in organizational communication. The establishment of the National Communication Association's ethnography division, led in large part by those who are also organizational communication scholars, has promoted performative and creative nonfiction scholarship (Ashcraft & Flores, 2003; Tracy, 2004). Additionally, qualitative methodology books for the communication discipline at large are (co)authored by organizational communication researchers (e.g., Clair, 2003; Goodall, 2000, 2008; Lindlof & Taylor, 2011; Tracy, 2013). This overlap has the consequence that many of the theories (e.g., structuration, critical cultural studies, and sensemaking) discussed in qualitative methods books and organizational communication overlap in their pedagogy and practice. The opportunity for qualitative methodologies to flourish also has been bolstered by editors at *Management Communication Quarterly* (MCQ), who have regularly published research adopting qualitative methods and interpretive, critical, postmodern, and narrative approaches.

Furthermore, if we examine award-winning organizational scholarship, we see the growing prominence of qualitative methods. From 2001–2010, 11% of *Academy of Management Journal's* articles were qualitative only, and Bansal and Corley (2011) noted that "six of the last eight papers awarded *AMJ*'s 'Best Article Award' were based exclusively on qualitative data" (p. 234). Additionally, more than half of the empirical studies that have received a National Communication Association (NCA) organizational communication research award use qualitative methodologies. Table 10.1 provides a list of these references in chronological order.

Table 10.1 NCA Award-Winning Organizational Communication Studies That Employ Qualitative Methods[2]

Clair, R. (1993). The use of framing devices to sequester organizational narratives: Hegemony and harassment. *Communication Monographs, 60*(1), 113–136.

Fairhurst, G. (1993). The leader-member exchange patterns of women leaders in industry: A discourse analysis. *Communication Monographs, 60*(4), 321–351.

Howard, L., & Geist, P. (1995). Ideological positioning in organizational change: The dialectic of control in a merging organization. *Communication Monographs, 62*(2), 110–131.

Scheibel, D. (1996). Appropriating bodies: Organ(izing) ideology and cultural practice in medical school. *Journal of Applied Communication Research, 24*(4), 310–331.

Fairhurst, G. T., Cooren, F., & Cahill, D. J. (2002). Discursiveness, contradiction, and unintended consequences in successive downsizings. *Management Communication Quarterly, 15*(4), 501–540.

(Continued)

Table 10.1 (Continued)

Kuhn, T., & Corman, S. R. (2003). The emergence of homogeneity and heterogeneity in knowledge structures during a planned organizational change. *Communication Monographs, 70*(3), 198–229.
Boczkowski, P. J. (2004). *Digitizing the news: Innovation in online newspapers*. Cambridge, MA: MIT Press.
Ashcraft, K. L., & Mumby, D. K. (2004). *Reworking gender: A feminist communicology of organization*. Thousand Oaks, CA: SAGE.
Ellingson, L. (2005). *Communicating in the clinic: Negotiating frontstage and backstage teamwork*. Cresskill, NJ: Hampton Press.
Brummans, B. H. J. M., Putnam, L. L., Gray, B., Hanke, R., Lewicki, R. J., & Wiethoff, C. (2008). Making sense of intractable multiparty conflict: A study of framing in four environmental disputes. *Communication Monographs, 75*(1), 25–51.
Lutgen-Sandvik, P. (2008). Intensive remedial identity work: Response to workplace bullying trauma and stigmatization. *Organization, 15*(1), 97–119.
Leonardi, P. M. (2009). Why do people reject new technologies and stymie organizational changes of which they are in favor? Exploring misalignments between social interactions and materiality. *Human Communication Research, 35*(3), 407–441.

Unquestionably, qualitative methods are now common in organizational communication. Next, we discuss how qualitative methods have emerged and continue to emerge from different paradigmatic assumptions and theoretical traditions.

Qualitative Methods Across Paradigms in Organizational Communication

Qualitative methods emerge from a range of paradigmatic perspectives in organizational communication. As noted by Cheney in his e-mail interview, "organizational communication as professional network and a sub-discipline has proven to be more adaptable and open to new ideas . . . in part because of a periodic reexamination of its central tenets, objects of study, goals, and methods." We use the term *paradigm* to refer loosely to the different ways people understand reality (ontology), knowledge building (epistemology), the values they bring to research (axiology), and gathering information about the world (methodology). It's important to note that paradigms are not separate categories but rather indicate different priorities, discourses, and viewpoints that researchers may draw from depending on a particular research project or goal (Deetz, 2009; Ellingson, 2011a).

Qualitative methods from a normative, positivist, or post-positivist point of view begin with specific research priorities in hand and gather data that can provide a clear unified answer. Deetz (2000) notes that

> most of the work on culture, climate, or varieties of total quality management (TQM) in organizational communication are more normative than interpretive owing

to the way culture is treated as a variable or objective outcome within a larger strategic move of cultural management. (p. 20)

He provides an exemplar study by Shockley-Zalabak, Morley, and Dean (1994), who evaluated 52 rule-like statements, generated from interviews and observations, and demonstrated how managers shape workers' values. Likewise, qualitative management research often begins with specific research questions and hypotheses, answers them in the form of models and tables, and concludes by proposing testable postulates and forecasting specific outcomes (e.g., Pratt, 2000).

Qualitative methods from an interpretive framework are similar to those in the positivist camp in focusing on consensus—or telling a single, cohesive story. However, rather than beginning with specific theoretical foci, interpretive studies focus on emergent meanings, considering the ways organizations are cultures accomplished through communicative performance. In this orientation, communicative data narrate how meaning evolves through social interaction and sensemaking activities (Smircich & Calás, 1987). For example, Pacanowsky and O'Donnell-Trujillo (1983) hung out with cops, collecting thick descriptions of cultural performances and scripts, such as the regular routines and dialogue that take place during a traffic violation. Today's interpretive organizational communication research continues to employ narrative, rhetorical, and discursive methods (e.g., Dempsey, 2010), focusing on how communication constructs organizational relationships and structures.

Qualitative methods also commonly emerge from a critical paradigm in which studies examine power, ideology, and hegemony. Central to critical approaches is the idea that research has an ethical obligation—either internally, by helping uncover false consciousness, or externally, such as helping to transform situations that are immoral, unfair, or unethical. As such, through a tandem focus on both action and structure, qualitative methods can reveal how power differences are sedimented and normalized in organizational settings, for instance, how employees voluntarily underreport their work hours (Deetz, 1998), how marginalized groups can act as their own worst enemy (Ashcraft & Pacanowsky, 1996), and how a business case for diversity can restrict discussion of workplace differences (Perriton, 2009). Qualitative methodologies are not only used to critique but to also spur transformation. For example, Eisenberg et al.'s (2006) narrative description of emergency room culture catalyzed practical improvements at the hospital. Critical research such as this is bolstered by the growing discipline of critical management studies in Europe, New Zealand, and Australia (Simpson & Zorn, 2004).

Finally, qualitative methods in organizational communication can emerge from a postmodern or post-structuralist paradigmatic perspective. Researchers from this perspective may piece together qualitative data in a way that shows how reality is partial, fractured, and contested. Their aim is not to tell the whole story but to also show how data can distort and reconfigure the scene. For instance, Trujillo's (1993) postmodern ethnography of the 25th anniversary of John F. Kennedy's assassination revealed how people focused on Kennedy's death, not on his life, and in doing so, Dealy Plaza became a site of simulation and commodification. Indeed, postmodern or post-structuralist research often focuses on issues of reproduction, plurality, decentered subjectivity, and hyperreality (Mumby, 1996), showing how power is fragmented, fluid, and available to all participants (Foucault, 1980). For example, Trethewey (1997) points out through her fieldwork the clever ways women in social service agencies resist the intrusive inquiries of welfare managers.

A postmodern approach is also related to the way research is eventually written or otherwise represented—something we return to in future directions. Certain writing methods help us to viscerally feel and see issues of partiality and the dance of power and resistance. Examples of such qualitative work include Fox's (2010) "auto-archaeology" of gay identity formation in a high school setting, Gunn's (2011) analysis of the discursive construction of care, and Ellingson's (2011b) poetic representation of professionalism among dialysis technicians. Understanding how qualitative methods emerge differently from a range of paradigmatic perspectives helps set the stage for exploring the recent landscape of organizational qualitative research.

The Recent Landscape of Organizational Qualitative Research

In the following section, we provide the results of our close analysis of the last 15 years of organizational qualitative research. Our analysis is based upon a list of 241 journal article citations and abstracts published between 1996 and 2011 that we compiled, read, coded, and categorized. From our analysis, we constructed a numerical synthesis of the articles' context, theme/concept, and contribution. Some readers may find it odd that we counted as one method to analyze qualitative research. However, counting has a long tradition in ethnography (e.g., see Geertz's [1973] use of statistical analysis of betting in Balinese cock fights). Furthermore, mixed methods are increasingly common in a range of research studies (Creswell & Plano-Clark, 2007). The following sections illustrate the common contexts, themes, and contributions of qualitative journal articles over the last 15 years, since the last handbook chapter on qualitative methods appeared.[3]

Context

We found that qualitative research was published by organizational communication scholars in 34 different journals, including 20 in the communication discipline, with most of the others in business, management and organization studies.[4] Our analysis revealed a range of multitextured contextual sites, with many relating to social justice, advocacy, and even co-constructed or participant-constructed paradigms. We used the North American Industry Classification System (NAICS; http://www.census.gov/eos/www/naics/) to classify the contexts. Approximately 10 of the abstracts were coded with two or more contexts, because the data were collected from different sites and a number of the abstracts did not specify context. Table 10.2 offers the list of contexts studied, sequenced from the most to least often studied.

In addition to the NAICS classification system and as represented in Table 10.2, we added a category called *voice* (V) to represent studies (primarily interview studies) where the research featured voices from specific sets of identity groups. Examples include studies of employees of a specific ethnicity (e.g., African American managers), demographic group (e.g., women back at work from maternity leave), or connected to a certain nature of work or concern (e.g., workers caring for an elderly parent at home). Clearly, this was one of the most common types of qualitative organizational communication research, with a total count of 40.

A second frequently studied context was *health care and social assistance* ($n = 40$), which focused on a wide array of research sites, including hospitals, clinics, and community health assistance programs targeting teens, elderly, or a specific illness. The health context, in particular, has been studied every year since 1996, with nurses the most common set of participants. The most recent studies focused on issues of social justice, including a critical examination of pharmaceutical interactions with physicians (Lyon & Mirivel, 2011), a public health campaign targeting a chemical plant (Zoller & Tener, 2010), and health professional and parent collaboration in changing disability policy (Canary, 2010).

The next three most commonly studied contexts included (a) the professions, science, and technical services; (b) community nonprofits; and (c) education. The frequencies in the bottom half of the Table 10.2 indicate contexts that may offer rich directions for future research—*construction*; *finance & insurance*; *real estate, rental, & leasing*; and *utilities*.

Themes/Concepts Studied

The process of identifying dominant themes/concepts began by locating those that appeared multiple times—not only in terms of concepts examined but also in terms of the contributions offered. We determined the key themes/concepts, examined the number of articles that focused on each theme, and the time range that articles featured each theme—available in table form in the endnotes.[5] From this table, and as a method of showing an innovative way to textually analyze data, we developed a word cloud (software available at www.wordle.net) to illustrate the role and relative dominance of each of 35 themes (Figure 10.1). The size of font in the word cloud corresponds with the number of times the theme appeared (e.g., with themes such as work/life/family, identity, health, and emotion work being among most frequent and themes such as bullying, strategic ambiguity, network(s), and social capital among the least frequent). The saturation of font color in the word cloud relates to the number of years the topic appeared in articles over the 15 years. The darker the saturation, the more years the topic appeared. Emotion work, for instance, appeared in the data set across a long span of time (1997–2011), while the topic of masculinity appeared over a smaller span of time (2003–2011).

In 35 of the 241 articles we analyzed, *identity* was the most common theme/concept studied (approximately 15%). Identity was coded separately from *identification*, even though the concepts sometimes overlap. *Health*, as the focus in 27 studies, emerged as the second-most-prominent theme/concept. Its prevalence may also be due to the fact that health is both a context and a theme/concept being investigated. Interestingly, these two themes/concepts were studied throughout a span of 14 to 15 years, where others appear of interest in shorter spans of time.

Table 10.2 Contexts Studied in Qualitative Organizational Communication Journal Articles 1996–2011

Code	Context Description	Count
?	Unspecified in abstract	95
V	Voices of particular groups of people	40
HCSA	Health Care and Social Assistance	40
PST	Profession, Scientific, Technical services	24
CN	Community Nonprofit	22
E	Education	20
AER	Arts, Entertainment & Recreation	15
PS	Public Service [e.g., police, firefighters, 911]	13
MGT	Management of companies and enterprises	9
M	Manufacturing	8
T	Transportation [e.g., airlines]	8
RT	Retail Trade	6
AG	AG, fishing, forestry, hunting	3
ME	Mining, quarrying, & oil/gas Extraction	2
AFS	Accommodation & Food Services	1
C	Construction	0
FI	Finance & Insurance	0
RRL	Real Estate, Rental, & Leasing	0
U	Utilities	0

Figure 10.1 Word Cloud Illustrating Themes and Concepts Featured in Qualitative Organizational Communication Journal Articles Ranging 1996–2011

The third and fourth most prevalent themes/concepts in qualitative organizational communication research were *work/life/family negotiation* and *emotion work*. These themes were studied in a wide array of contexts and, in some cases, were interrelated and connected in single articles. For example, Krouse and Afifi (2007) chose caregiving professionals—who must consistently engage in emotional labor as a core part of their job—as the subject in their study on stress and family-to-work spillover. In a more recent study, Golden (2009) illustrates through the analysis of employee and family interview accounts the ways families and organizations are mutually enacted.

Our analysis of these articles revealed a complexity to each and every theme/concept that goes beyond the word cloud and tables. For example, one fascinating concept that spans over a decade, *knowledge*, we found represented variously as *knowledge*, *knowledge construction*, and *organizational learning*. A wide range of other concepts are often juxtaposed with knowledge, including *cultural*, *expert*, *policy*, *organizational*, *instrumental*, and *technological*.

Based upon our analysis of the articles in organizational communication, we not only see what is present but also what is absent. Themes/concepts that have limited attention in terms of qualitative organizational analyses include *assimilation, bullying, dialogue, social capital, strategic ambiguity*, and *voice*. Even less attention has been paid to issues of *diversity*, empirically explored in only three qualitative studies, spanning four years.

Another group of people whose voices do not often appear in qualitative organizational communication research is that of children. It is clear that children would have much to say about their enculturation into ideas of work as well as their experiences in organizations, including education, social services, and organizations/programs designed for young people to be involved in after school or during the weekend, including those related to the arts, entertainment, and communities (e.g., girl scouts, boy scouts, community theatre, dance, music, film, and nonprofits devoted to specific causes). Although children's voices deserve our attention, too often the constraints that arise from following the university's institutional review board (IRB) guidelines dissuade researchers from pursuing study with young people (Swauger, 2009). Way's (2009) research with a girl's running team is a promising exception and suggests new directions for organizational communication qualitative study with young people.

High-Impact Organizational Communication Qualitative Research

With an increasing technological ease for calculating citation rates and impact factors and institutions' growing reliance on these factors to measure the excellence of research and researchers (Goodall, 2008), one imperfect way to assess the impact of qualitative research in organizational communication is through its citation. Table 10.3 lists the 10 most-frequently cited organizational communication qualitative journal articles (according to Google Scholar in August 2011) published in the last 15 years. Twenty-four additional articles, each with 50 or more citations, are additionally referenced in the endnotes.[6]

In addition to analyzing highly cited journal articles, we also chose a single article to review as an exemplar. We chose Leonardi's (2009) article, "Why Do People Reject New Technologies and Stymie Organizational Changes of Which They Are in Favor? Exploring Misalignments between Social Interactions and Materiality," because it has recently won the NCA organizational communication division's annual research award.

Table 10.3 Top 10 Cited Organizational Communication Qualitative Journal Articles in the Last 15 Years[7]

Times Cited	Journal Article Reference
156	Kirby, E. L., & Krone, K. J. (2002). "The policy exists but you can't really use it": Communication and the structuration of work-family policies. *Journal of Applied Communication Research, 30*(1), 50–77.
137	Tracy, S. J. (2000). Becoming a character for commerce: Emotion labor, self-subordination, and discursive construction of identity in a total institution. *Management Communication Quarterly, 14*(1), 90–128.
132	Trethewey, A. (1999). Disciplined bodies: Women's embodied identities at work. *Organization Studies, 20*(3), 423–450.
123	Sias, P. M., & Cahill, D. J. (1998). From coworkers to friends: The development of peer friendships in the workplace. *Western Journal of Communication, 62*(3), 273–299.
107	Robichaud, D., Giroux, H., & Taylor, J. R. (2004). The meta-conversation: The recursive property of language as the key to organizing. *Academy of Management Review, 29*(4), 617–634.

(Continued)

Table 10.3 (Continued)

106	Shuler, S., & Sypher, B. D. (2000). Seeking emotional labor: When managing the heart enhances the work experience. *Management Communication Quarterly, 14*(1), 50–89.
105	Murphy, A. G. (1998). Hidden transcripts of flight attendant resistance. *Management Communication Quarterly, 11*(4), 499–535.
104	Ulmer, R. R. (2001). Effective crisis management through established stakeholder relationships: Malden Mills as a case study. *Management Communication Quarterly, 14*(4), 590–615.
95	Ashcraft, K. L. (2001). Organized dissonance: Feminist bureaucracy as hybrid form. *Academy of Management Journal, 44*(6), 1301–1322.
82	Scott, C. R., Connaughton, S. L., Diaz-Saenz, H., Maguire, K., Ramirez, R., Richardson, B., . . . & Morgan, D. (1999). The impacts of communication and multiple identifications on intent to leave: A multi-methodological exploration. *Management Communication Quarterly, 12*(3), 400–435.

Moreover, it employs mixed methods—something that we believe will be increasingly common in the discipline. In analyzing the article, we referred to Tracy's (2010) eight big-tent criteria, which include the following end goals of high-quality qualitative studies: worthy topic, rich rigor, sincerity, credibility, resonance, significant contribution, ethical, and meaningful coherence.

Leonardi (2009) engaged in a nine-month study of the implementation of a computer simulation technology entitled *Crashlabs* at an automotive manufacturing firm. The study examines *manufacturing*—one of the contexts midway through our content list—and the common theme/concept areas of *change, resistance,* and *technology*. The article, published in *Human Communication Research,* is cited 17 times between its publication and 2011 (an average of 5+ times a year) and exemplifies criteria for high-quality qualitative research.

First, the focus on change and the implementation of new technology is clearly a worthy area of study—it is a contemporary hot topic and has potential for significant practical and theoretical implications. The analysis provides a fascinating study of performance engineers (PEs) working in the company's safety division, who are charged with the responsibility of conducting crashworthiness engineering of automobiles. Considerations of power and resistance are timely and relevant, particularly in a study of engineers, who we might mistakenly assume would not resist the adoption of new technology. The study focuses upon the complicated interactions among PEs, design engineers, and managers that create resistance, regardless of the material features of the technology. As Leonardi (2009) points out, "in the practice of forming interpretations about a new technology, users act with and in response to each other (social interactions) as they use a new technology, and . . . they also act with and in response to the material features of technologies themselves (material interactions)" (pp. 411–412).

Second, the study exemplifies rigor in terms of the length of time in the field (nine months over the course of two years), 500 hours of observation, and field notes that thickly describe a range of individual and group actions. Meaningfully, the author spent two months on site prior to the implementation of the new technology and then seven months on site as the technology was introduced and utilized. As Leonardi (2009) notes,

> One advantage of this data collection strategy was that I was able to capture an *emic* (insider's) understanding of PEs' work prior to their interaction with the new technology. Because I conducted observations during the implementation period I was able to document how informants struggled to make sense of the technology in the real-time practice of their work rather than having to rely on retrospective accounts of their interpretation formation. (p. 414, emphasis in original)

The rigor of the study spans not only the rich review of literature and methods of data collection but also the complex and interesting forms of data analysis.

Third, Leonardi's (2009) study is credible in a number of ways. The study reaches conclusions by crystallizing (Ellingson, 2009) qualitative field observation analyses with quantitative hierarchical linear regression analysis and analysis of variance. In addition to the 64 observation records of PEs, made by shadowing them throughout the day, Leonardi analyzes field notes and audio recordings of interactions with design engineers, managers, and customers. The credibility of the research is enhanced by multivocality and member reflections throughout the description of findings. These are best exemplified in observation data before and after the implementation of the new technology and Leonardi's collection of *in situ* dialogue, such as the following amongst PEs:

> During the lunch break of one of the training sessions, I overheard two PEs discussing the utility of CrashLab:
>
> **PE1:** I like it [CrashLab]. It's better than what I thought it would be.
>
> **PE2:** I don't know. I mean, it seems ok, but it doesn't seem all that revolutionary.
>
> **PE1:** That's true, but I don't think it's supposed to be this new big thing (*he raises his hands over his head in emphasis*). I got the impression it's supposed to just cut down on the repetition of doing setup stuff. That would be very helpful.
>
> **PE2:** Yeah, I suppose. That would be good. I'd be real happy if it did that. (pp. 417–418)

As these examples illustrate, PEs were, on the whole, quite hopeful that CrashLab would be a useful tool in their work.

Leonardi's (2009) study also provides a significant contribution, offering a model depicting the misalignment and alignment between social and material interactions. In the end, readers learn a great deal about the role of technology interpretations in organizational change and how these findings may be relevant in a range of organizational settings.

Conclusions and Future Directions for Organizational Ethnography

In this chapter, we synthesized the landscape of qualitative methodological work in organizational communication research. We began with a discussion of key characteristics of qualitative research in organizational communication, historical matters, and how qualitative research is represented differently depending on its paradigmatic values. Then, based upon an analysis of 241 journal articles, we traced the landscape of the research over the last 15 years, showing the most common contexts and themes studied and the most impactful studies and provided an in-depth snapshot of a recent award-winning essay. We close here with a discussion of future directions and developments.

Organizational ethnography research has traditionally been associated with long-term immersion in a single, contained community, complete with face-to-face participant observation and interviews (Yanow, 2012). However, qualitative research has broadened to study organizational issues that are more mediated, fragmented, complex, and uncertain (Van Maanen, 2011). A variety of organizational communication scholars have engaged in multisite analyses, including investigation of airline pilots (Ashcraft, 2005), wheelchair rugby teams (Lindemann, 2010a), polar expeditions (Rix-Lièvre & Lièvre, 2010), a French Doctors without Borders team in the Congo (Benoit-Barné & Cooren, 2009), and passengers in airport security lines (Malvini Redden, 2013). As organizational ethnographers continue to focus on topics that are more far reaching, they will travel to diverse organizational spaces over time—rather than arriving at a single organizational site out there.

Along with multisite studies, another burgeoning area is participatory qualitative research that engages with and advocates for people who are marginalized—economically, socially, politically, and/or culturally. Social justice scholars not only study but also take "direct vigorous action in support of or opposition to a controversial issue for the purpose of promoting social change and justice" (Frey & Carragee, 2007, p. 10). Essays included in Frey and Carragee's (2007) volume include examinations of civil rights organizations and sexual assault recovery centers.

Problem-based qualitative research has necessitated an increase in interdisciplinary and transdisciplinary approaches that foreground *phronesis*, or practical knowledge (Flyvbjerg, 2001). Such efforts draw upon music, performance, visual art, film, and poetry—arts-based practices that are attractive to a wide range of stakeholders, including policy makers and professionals (Leavy, 2011b). Frey and Palmer (in press) highlight performance ethnography as a method of understanding and representing organized systems such as Holocaust concentration camps and prisons. Performance is not just a representation but can also constitute a method of organizational intervention (Wimmer, 2002). For example, performance has been used as a method to discourage domestic violence (Walker & Curry, 2007), combat bullying (Thomas, 2008), and promote action to stop South Sudan genocide (Welker, 2012). As researchers utilize alternative representations, they must also engage with special considerations regarding creativity, collaboration, and ethics (Leavy, 2011a; Van Maanen, 2006).

New and innovative approaches to the study of organizational communication include representation of the findings in unique forms, such as problem-solving, brief white papers, website development, and poetry. Tracy and Rivera (2009) wrote and posted a freely downloadable white paper that provides layperson-friendly advice about ways in which executives can influence and ease work-life challenges. Poetry as an innovative method assists researchers in understanding the research and data; it is "built from the *line* rather than the paragraph or block of text . . . to illuminate and crystallize experience" (Willis, 2002, pp. 4–5). In their study of a rehabilitation center, for example, Carless and Douglas (2009) create poetic representations from the words of people with severe mental health difficulties.

More recently, innovation in ethnographic research is represented in digital and visual data, computerized methods of analysis, and electronic representations. Qualitative researchers are turning to social media, webinars, and text messaging as sources of data. They are becoming comfortable with computer-aided data analysis tools such as NVivo or Wordle (the word cloud software that helped construct Figure 10.1). Visual methods—including videos, drawings, photographs, charts, and maps (Guillemin 2004)—are also increasingly common. Harter and Hayward (2010) created a film that combined visual diaries of young cancer patients and their families to reveal the day-to-day realities of living with cancer and receiving treatment at MD Anderson Cancer Center. Another practice is the use of photovoice or photo-elicitation (Wang & Burris, 1997). With the common use of camera phones, researchers can feasibly ask participants to take their own photographs, share them, and reflect. Such was the case with patients who took photos and shared their experiences with hospital medical care (Lorenz & Chilingerian, 2011).

With these innovative forms of organizational ethnography, new journals and writing approaches have emerged to keep up with the groundbreaking work—venues such as the *Journal for Organizational Ethnography, Journal of Ethnographic & Qualitative Research,* and *Qualitative Communication Research Methods.* These outlets, in turn, promote alternative writing styles that challenge the typical four-act play linear journal article format (Brannan, Rowe, & Worthington, 2012). Indeed, despite the central role of qualitative methods in organizational communication, the deductive literary style of most of our communication mainstream journals may still serve as a stumbling block for those who want to publish their inductive qualitative analyses. Qualitative scholars describe engaging in *guerilla scholarship* in which, to get published in mainstream journals, they have cloaked their inductive and artistic qualitative analyses in traditional social scientific literary conventions (Ellingson, 2011a). This conventional writing style foregrounds *a priori* theory over context and sample and theory verification or falsification over extension. This is unfortunate, because the rich particulars of context provide a valuable scholarly contribution of qualitative research, and the theory building available from them becomes limited in a deductive writing logic (Tracy, 2012).

Despite these limitations, the future for organizational qualitative work in organizational communication looks bright. If the past is any prediction for the future, organizational communication will continue to provide a rich and supportive atmosphere for qualitative methodological growth.

References

Alvesson, M., & Karreman, D. (2000). Varieties of discourse: On the study of organizations through discourse analysis. *Human Relations, 53*(9), 1125–1149.

Argyris, C. (1953). *Executive leadership: An appraisal of a manager in action.* New York, NY: Harper.

Argyris, C. (1954a). Human relations in a bank. *Harvard Business Review, 32,* 63–72.

Argyris, C. (1954b). *Organization of a bank: A study of the nature of organization and the fusion process.* New Haven, CT: Yale University Labor and Management Center.

Arnold, J., Randall, R., Patterson, F., Silvester, J., & Robertson, I. (2010). *Work psychology: Understanding human behaviour in the workplace* (5th ed.). London, England: Financial Times Management.

Ashcraft, K. L. (2001). Organized dissonance: Feminist bureaucracy as hybrid form. *Academy of Management Journal, 44*(6), 1301–1322.

Ashcraft, K. L. (2005). Resistance through consent? Occupational identity, organizational form, and the maintenance of masculinity among commercial airline pilots. *Management Communication Quarterly, 19*(1), 67–90.

Ashcraft, K. L. (2011). Knowing work through the communication of difference: A revised agenda for difference studies. In D. K. Mumby (Ed.), *Reframing difference in organizational communication studies: Research, pedagogy, practice* (pp. 3–30). Thousand Oaks, CA: SAGE.

Ashcraft, K. L., & Flores, L. A. (2003). "Slaves with white collars": Persistent performances of masculinity in crisis. *Text and Performance Quarterly, 23*(1), 1–29.

Ashcraft, K. L., & Pacanowsky, M. E. (1996). "A woman's worst enemy": Reflections on a narrative of organizational life and female identity. *Journal of Applied Communication Research, 24*(3), 217–239.

Bansal, P., & Corley, K. G. (2011). The coming of age for qualitative research: Embracing the diversity of qualitative methods. *Academy of Management Journal, 54*(2), 233–237.

Barker, J. R. (1993). Tightening the iron cage: Concertive control in self-managing teams. *Administrative Science Quarterly, 38*(3), 408–437.

Becker, H., & Geer, B. (1961). *Boys in white: Student culture in medical school.* Chicago, IL: University of Chicago Press.

Benoit-Barné, C., & Cooren, F. (2009). The accomplishment of authority through presentification: How authority is distributed among and negotiated by organizational members, *Management Communication Quarterly, 23*(1), 5–31.

Bochner, A. (2000). Criteria against ourselves. *Qualitative Inquiry, 6*(2), 266–272.

Brannan, M., Rowe, M., & Worthington, F. (2012). Time for a new journal, a journal for new times. *Journal of Organizational Ethnography, 1*(1), 5–14.

Bullis, C. (2005). From productivity servant to foundation to connection: One history of organizational communication. *Management Communication Quarterly, 18*(4), 595–603.

Bullis, C. A., & Tompkins, P. K. (1989). The forest ranger revisited: A study of control practices and identification. *Communication Monographs, 56*(4), 287–306.

Canary, H. (2010). Constructing policy knowledge: Contradictions, communication, and knowledge frames. *Communication Monographs, 77*(2), 181–206.

Carless, D., & Douglas, K. (2009). Opening doors: Poetic representation of the sport experiences of men with severe mental health difficulties. *Qualitative Inquiry, 15*(10), 1547–1551.

Cassell, C. (2009). Interviews in organizational research. In D. A. Buchanan & A. Bryman (Eds.), *The SAGE handbook of organizational research methods* (pp. 500–515). Thousand Oaks, CA: SAGE.

Charmaz, K. (2006). *Constructing grounded theory: A practical guide through qualitative analysis.* Thousand Oaks, CA: SAGE.

Cheney, G. (1983). On the various and changing meanings of organizational membership: A field study of organizational identification. *Communication Monographs, 50*(4), 342–362.

Cheney, G. (1999). *Values at work: Employee participation meets market pressure at Mondragón.* Ithaca, NY: Cornell University Press.

Clair, R. P. (2003). *Expressions of ethnography: Novel approaches to qualitative methods.* Albany, NY: SUNY.

Creswell, J. W., & Plano-Clark, V. L. (2007). *Designing and conducting mixed methods research.* Thousand Oaks, CA: SAGE.

de Rond, M. (2008). *The last amateurs: To hell and back with the Cambridge boat race crew.* London, England: Icon Books.

Deetz, S. (1982). Critical-interpretive research in organizational communication. *Western Journal of Speech Communication, 46*(2), 131–149.

Deetz, S. (1998). Discursive formations, strategized subordination and self-surveillance. In A. McKinley & K. Starkey (Eds.), *Foucault, management and organizational theory* (pp. 151–172). London, England: SAGE.

Deetz, S. (2000). Conceptual foundations. In. L. L. Putnam & F. M. Jablin (Eds.), *The new handbook of organizational communication: Advances in theory, research, and method* (pp. 3–46). Thousand Oaks, CA: SAGE.

Deetz, S. (2003). Reclaiming the legacy of the linguistic turn. *Organization, 10*(3), 421–429.

Deetz, S. (2009). Organizational research as alternative ways of attending to and talking about structures and activities. In A. Bryman & D. Buchanan (Eds.), *Handbook of organizational research methods* (pp. 19–38). London, England: SAGE.

Dempsey, S. E. (2010). Critiquing community engagement. *Management Communication Quarterly, 24*(3), 359–390.

Denzin, N. K., & Lincoln, Y. S. (2005). Introduction: The discipline and practice of qualitative research. In N. K. Denzin & Y. S. Lincoln (Eds.), *Handbook of qualitative research* (3rd ed., pp. 1–20). Thousand Oaks, CA: SAGE.

Eisenberg, E. M. (2007). *Strategic ambiguities: Essays on communication, organization, and identity.* Thousand Oaks, CA: SAGE.

Eisenberg, E. M., Baglia, J., & Pynes, J. E. (2006). Transforming emergency medicine through narrative: Qualitative action research at a community hospital. *Health Communication, 19*(3), 197–208.

Ellingson, L. L. (2009). *Engaging crystallization in qualitative research: An introduction.* Thousand Oaks, CA: SAGE.

Ellingson, L. L. (2011a). Analysis and representation across the continuum. In N. K. Denzin & Y. S. Lincoln (Eds.), *Handbook of qualitative research* (4th ed., pp. 595–610). Thousand Oaks, CA: SAGE.

Ellingson, L. L. (2011b). The poetics of professionalism among dialysis technicians. *Health Communication, 26*(1), 1–12.

Erickson, F. (2011). A history of qualitative inquiry in social and educational research. In N. K. Denzin & Y. S. Lincoln (Eds.), *Handbook of qualitative research* (4th ed., pp. 43–60). Thousand Oaks, CA: SAGE.

The Ethnogs, the Fem Nogs, and Rip Tupp. (2011). Performing mythic identity: An Analysis and critique of "The Ethnogs." *Qualitative Inquiry, 17*(7), 664–674.

Fairhurst, G., & Putnam, L. L. (2004). Organizations as discursive constructions. *Communication Theory, 14*(1), 5–26.

Flyvbjerg, B. (2001). *Making social science matter: Why social inquiry fails and how it can succeed again* (S. Sampson, Trans.). Cambridge, England: Cambridge University Press.

Flyvbjerg, B. (2011). Case study. In N. K. Denzin & Y. S. Lincoln (Eds.), *Handbook of qualitative research* (4th ed., pp. 301–316). Thousand Oaks, CA: SAGE.

Foucault, M. (1980). *Power/knowledge.* New York, NY: Pantheon Books.

Fox, R. (2010). Tales of a fighting bobcat: An "auto-archaeology" of gay identity formation and maintenance. *Text and Performance Quarterly, 30*(2), 122–142.

Frey, L. R., & Carragee, K. M. (Eds.). (2007). *Communication activism: Vol. 2. Communication for social change.* Cresskill, NJ: Hampton Press.

Frey, L. R., & Palmer, D. L. (Eds.). (in press). *Teaching communication activism.* New York, NY: Hampton Press.

Geertz, C. (1973). *The interpretation of cultures: Selected essays.* New York, NY: Basic Books.

Geist, P., & Hardesty, M. (1992). *Negotiating the crisis: DRGs and the transformation of hospitals.* Hillsdale, NJ: Lawrence Erlbaum.

Giddens, A. (1979). *Central problems in social theory.* Berkeley: University of California Press.

Giddens, A. (1981). *A contemporary critique of historical materialism* (vol. 1). London, England: MacMillan.

Glaser, B. G., & Strauss, A. L. (1967). *The discovery of grounded theory: Strategies for qualitative research.* Chicago, IL: Aldine.

Golden, A. G. (Ed.). (2000). Communication perspectives on work and family [Special issue]. *Electronic Journal of Communication, 10.*

Golden, A. G. (2009). Employee families and organizations as mutually enacted environments: A sensemaking approach to work–life interrelationships. *Management Communication Quarterly, 22*(3), 385–415.

Goodall, H. L., Jr. (1989). *Casing a promised land: The autobiography of an organizational detective as cultural ethnographer.* Carbondale: Southern Illinois University Press.

Goodall, H. L., Jr. (2000). *Writing the new ethnography.* Walnut Creek, CA: AltaMira.

Goodall, H. L., Jr. (2008). *Writing qualitative inquiry: Self, stories, and academic life.* Walnut Creek, CA: Left Coast.

Gossett, L. M. (2006). Falling between the cracks: Control and communication challenges of a temporary workforce. *Management Communication Quarterly, 19*(3), 376–415.

Guillemin, M. (2004). Understanding illness: Using drawings as a research method. *Qualitative Health Research, 14*(2), 272–289.

Gunn, A. M. (2011). The discursive construction of care when there is no care to be found: Organizational life (re)framed by those on the socioeconomic margins facing job loss. *Culture and Organization, 17*(1), 65–85.

Harris, M. (1976). History and significance of the emic/etic distinction. *Annual Review of Anthropology, 5*, 329–350.

Harter, L. (Producer), & Hayward, C. (Director). (2010). *The art of the possible* [DVD]. Scripps College of Communication, Ohio University. Available at http://www.amazon.com/The-Art-Possible-Casey-Hayward/dp/B003DKJFKK

Ho, K. (2009). *Liquidated: An ethnography of Wall Street.* Durham, NC: Duke University Press.

Howard, L. A., & Geist, P. (1995). Ideological positioning in organizational change: The dialectic of control in a merging organization. *Communication Monographs, 62*(2), 110–131.

Kirby, E. (Ed.). (2006). Communication and the accomplishment of personal and profession life [Special issue]. *Electronic Journal of Communication, 16.*

Krouse, S. S., & Afifi, T. D. (2007). Family-to-work spillover stress: Coping communicatively in the workplace. *Journal of Family Communication, 7*(2), 85–122.

Kuhn, T. (2005). The institutionalization of Alta in organizational communication studies. *Management Communication Quarterly, 18*(4), 618–627.

Larson, G. S., & Pepper, G. L. (2003). Strategies for managing multiple organizational identifications: A case of competing identities. *Management Communication Quarterly, 16*(4), 528–557.

Leavy, P. (2011a). *Essentials of transdisciplinary research: Using problem-centered methodologies.* Walnut Creek, CA: Left Coast.

Leavy, P. (2011b). *Method meets art: Arts-based based research practice.* New York, NY: Guilford Press.

Leonardi, P. M. (2009). Why do people reject new technologies and stymie organizational changes of which they are in favor? Exploring misalignments between social interactions and materiality. *Human Communication Research, 35*(3), 407–441.

Lindemann, K. (2008). "I can't be standing up out there": Communicative performances of (dis) ability in wheelchair rugby. *Text & Performance Quarterly, 28*(1/2), 98–115.

Lindemann, K. (2010a). Masculinity, disability, and access-ability: Ethnography as alternative practice in the study of disabled sexualities. *Southern Journal of Communication, 75*(4), 433–451.

Lindemann, K. (2010b). Self-reflection and our sporting lives: Communication research in the community of sport. *Electronic Journal of Communication, 14*(3/4).

Lindlof, T. R., & Taylor, B. C. (2011). *Qualitative communication research methods* (3rd ed.). Thousand Oaks, CA: SAGE.

Lorenz, L. S., & Chilingerian, J. A. (2011). Using visual and narrative methods to achieve fair process in clinical care. *Journal of Visualized Experiments, 48*, 23–42.

Lyon, A., & Mirivel, J. (2011). Reconstructing Merck's practical theory of communication: The ethics of pharmaceutical sales representative-physician encounters. *Communication Monographs, 78*(1), 53–72.

Malvini Redden, S. (2013). How lines organize compulsory interaction, emotion management, and "emotional taxes": The implications of passenger emotion and expression in airport security lines. *Management Communication Quarterly, 27*(1), 121–149.

McPhee, R. D., & Zaug, P. (2000). The communicative constitution of organizations: A framework for explanation. *Electronic Journal of Communication/La Revue Electronique de Communication, 10*.

Meisenbach, R. J., Remke, R. V., Buzzanell, P., & Liu, M. (2008). "They allowed": Pentadic mapping of women's maternity leave discourse as organizational rhetoric. *Communication Monographs, 75*(1), 1–24.

Mumby, D. K. (1996). Feminism, postmodernism, and organizational communication studies: A critical reading. *Management Communication Quarterly, 9*(3), 259–295.

Mumby, D. K., & Stohl, C. (1996). Disciplining organizational communication studies. *Management Communication Quarterly, 10*(1), 50–72. doi: 10.1177/0893318996010001004

Newstrom, J. W., & Davis, K. (2002). *Organizational behavior: Human behavior at work* (11th ed.). Boston, MA: McGraw-Hill.

Pacanowsky, M. E., & O'Donnell-Trujillo, N. (1982). Communication and organizational cultures. *The Western Journal of Speech Communication, 46*(2), 115–130.

Pacanowsky, M. E., & O'Donnell-Trujillo, N. (1983). Organizational communication as cultural performance. *Communication Monographs, 50*(2), 126–147.

Patton, M. Q. (2002). *Qualitative research and evaluation methods* (3rd ed.). Thousand Oaks, CA: SAGE.

Perriton, L. (2009). "We don't want complaining women!" A critical analysis of the business case for diversity. *Management Communication Quarterly, 23*(2), 218–243.

Poole, M., Seibold, D., & McPhee, R. (1985). Group decision-making as a structurational process. *Quarterly Journal of Speech, 71*(1), 74–102.

Pratt, M. G. (2000). The good, the bad, and the ambivalent: Managing identification among Amway distributors. *Administrative Science Quarterly, 45*(3), 456–493.

Putnam, L. L., & Pacanowsky, M. E. (Eds.). (1983). *Communication and organizations: An interpretive approach.* Thousand Oaks, CA: SAGE.

Reason, P. (1994). Three approaches to participative inquiry. In N. K. Denzin & Y. S. Lincoln (Eds.), *Handbook of qualitative research* (pp. 324–339). Thousand Oaks, CA: SAGE.

Richardson, L. (2000). Writing: A method of inquiry. In N. K. Denzin & Y. S. Lincoln (Eds.), *Handbook of qualitative research* (2nd ed., pp. 923–943). Thousand Oaks, CA: SAGE.

Riley, P. (1983). A structurationist account of political culture. *Administrative Science Quarterly, 28*(3), 414–437.

Rix-Lièvre G., & Lièvre, P. (2010). An innovative observatory of polar expedition projects: An investigation of organizing, *Project Management Journal, 41*(3), 91–98.

Roy, D. (1959). "Banana time": Job satisfaction and informal interaction. *Human Organization, 18*(4), 158–168.

Scarduzio, J. A., Giannini, G. A., & Geist-Martin, P. (2011). Crafting an architectural blueprint: Principles of design for ethnographic research. *Symbolic Interaction, 34*(4), 447–470.

Scott, C., & Myers, K. K. (2005). The socialization of emotion: Learning emotion management at the fire station. *Journal of Applied Communication Research, 33*(1), 67–92.

Shockley-Zalabak, P., Morley, D. D., & Dean, D. (1994). Creating a culture: A longitudinal examination of the influence of management and employee values on communication rule stability and emergence. *Human Communication Research, 20*(3), 334–355.

Simpson, M., & Zorn, T. E. (2004). Locating the frontiers in organisational communication scholarship in New Zealand and Australia. *Australian Journal of Communication, 31*(3), 13–34.

Smircich, L., & Calás, M. B. (1987). Organizational culture: A critical assessment. In F. M. Jablin, L. L. Putnam, K. H. Roberts, & L.W. Porter (Eds.), *Handbook of organizational communication: An interdisciplinary perspective* (pp. 288–263). Newbury Park, CA: SAGE.

Swauger, M. (2009). No kids allowed!!!: How IRB ethics undermine qualitative researchers from achieving socially responsible ethical standards. *Race, Gender & Class, 16*(1/2), 63–81.

Taylor, B., & Trujillo, N. (2001). Qualitative organizational research. In. L. L. Putnam & F. M. Jablin (Eds.), *The new handbook of organizational communication: Advances in theory, research, and method* (pp. 161–196). Thousand Oaks, CA: SAGE.

Taylor, J. R., Flanagin, A. J., Cheney, G., & Seibold, D. R. (2001). Organizational communication research: Key moments, central concerns, and future challenges. In W. Gudykunst (Ed.), *Communication yearbook* (vol. 24, pp. 99–137). New York, NY: Routledge.

Thomas, S. (2008). Art as "connective aesthetic": Creating sites for community collaboration. *LEARNing Landscapes, 2*(1), 69–84.

Tompkins, P. K., & Cheney, G. (1985). Communication and unobtrusive control. In R. McPhee & P. K. Tompkins (Eds.), *Organizational communication: Traditional themes and new directions* (pp. 179–210). Beverly Hills, CA: SAGE.

Tracy, S. J. (2004). The construction of correctional officers: Layers of emotionality behind bars. *Qualitative Inquiry, 10*(4), 509–533.

Tracy, S. J. (2010). Qualitative quality: Eight "big tent" criteria for excellent qualitative research. *Qualitative Inquiry, 16*(10), 837–851.

Tracy, S. J. (2012). The toxic and mythical combination of a deductive writing logic for inductive qualitative research. *Qualitative Communication Research, 1*(1), 109–141.

Tracy, S. J. (2013). *Qualitative methodology matters: Creating and communicating qualitative research with impact.* Hoboken, NJ: Wiley-Blackwell.

Tracy, S. J., & Rivera, K. D. (2009). *Work hard, live hard.* White paper distributed to work-life organizations, their websites, and media outlets internationally. Retrieved from http://humancommunication.clas.asu.edu/files/WorkHardLiveHard-WhitePaperFINAL.pdf

Tracy, S. J., & Rivera K. D. (2010). Endorsing equity and applauding stay-at-home moms: How male voices on work-life reveal aversive sexism and flickers of transformation. *Management Communication Quarterly, 24*(1), 3–43.

Trethewey, A. (1997). Resistance, identity, and empowerment: A postmodern feminist analysis of clients in a human service organization. *Communication Monographs, 64*(4), 281–299.

Trethewey, A. (2001). Reproducing and resisting the master narrative of decline: Midlife professional women's experiences of aging. *Management Communication Quarterly, 15*(2), 183–226.

Trujillo, N. (1993). Interpreting November 22: A critical ethnography of an assassination site. *Quarterly Journal of Speech, 79*(4), 447–466.

Tucker, W. T. (1965). Max Weber's "verstehen." *The Sociological Quarterly, 6(2)*, 157–165.

Undheim, T. A. (2003). Getting connected: How sociologists can access the high tech elite. *Qualitative Report, 8*(1), 104–128. Retrieved from http://www.nova.edu/ssss/QR/QR8-1/undheim.html

Van Maanen, J. (1973). Observations on the making of policemen. *Human Organization, 32*(4), 407–418.

Van Maanen, J. (2006). Ethnography then and now. *Qualitative Research in Organizations and Management: An International Journal, 1*(1), 13–21.

Van Maanen, J. (2011). Ethnography as work: Some rules of engagement. *Journal of Management Studies, 48*(1), 218–234.

Walker, D. C., & Curry, E. A. (2007). Narrative as communication activism: Research relationships in social justice projects. In L. R. Frey & K. M. Carragee (Eds.), *Communication activism: Vol. 2. Media and performance activism* (pp. 345–369). Cresskill, NJ: Hampton Press.

Wang, C., & Burris, M. A. (1997). Photovoice: Concept, methodology, and use for participatory needs assessment. *Health Education & Behavior, 24*(3), 369–387.

Way, A. (2009, November). *There's no "I" in team: Destabilizing the gendered emotions of competition, motivation and social support.* Paper presented to the Organizational Communication Division of the National Communication Association, Chicago, IL.

Weick, K. E. (1979). *The social psychology of organizing* (2nd ed.). Reading, MA: Addison-Wesley.

Welker, L. (2012). Staging Sudanese refugee narratives and the legacy of genocide: A performance-based intervention strategy. In L. R. Frey & K. M. Carragee (Eds.), *Communication activism: Vol. 3. Struggling for social justice amidst difference* (pp. 139–178). New York, NY: Hampton Press.

Willis, P. (2002). Don't call it poetry. *Indo-Pacific Journal of Phenomenology, 2*(1), 1–14. Retrieved from http://www.ajol.info/index.php/ipjp/article/view/65661/53350

Wimmer, C. (2002). "*I dwell in possibility—*": Teaching consulting applications in performance studies. In N. Stucky & C. Wimmer (Eds.), *Teaching performance studies.* Carbondale, IL: Southern Illinois University Press.

Yanow, D. (2012). Organizational ethnography between toolbox and world-making. *Journal of Organizational Ethnography, 1*(1), 31–42.

Zoller, H. M., & Tener, M. (2010). Corporate proactivity as a discursive fiction: Managing environmental health activism and regulation. *Management Communication Quarterly, 24*(3), 391–418.

Notes

1. The authors would like to thank Jennifer Scarduzio and Shawna Malvini Redden for their helpful input and editing on this chapter.

2. In order to save space, we have not duplicated the citation to these in the reference section unless referenced elsewhere in the chapter.

3. We began with a list of qualitative articles constructed by Larry Frey (available at http://comm.colorado.edu/~freyl/Comm_Courses/Qualitative%20Methods%20%28Graduate%29/QualitativeGrad.html) and added to it by specifically searching other journals that we knew published organizational communication qualitative work (e.g., *Management Communication Quarterly, Qualitative Inquiry,* and *Journal of Contemporary Ethnography,* among others). While we are confident that this list of 241 abstracts over these 15 years is not complete, it does offer a comprehensive snapshot of the growing and changing nature of this landscape.

4. Most noncommunicative articles were from business journals (e.g., *Academy of Management Journal, Administrative Science Quarterly,* or *Human Relations*) or journals that are either interdisciplinary or from other fields (e.g., *Sex Roles, Women & Language,* or *Journal of Personal & Social Relationships*). Not surprisingly, at 30%, *Management Communication Quarterly (MCQ)* is by far the leading journal for publishing qualitative organizational communication research during this time period. *Journal of Applied Communication Research (JACR)* is the second most popular outlet with over 19% of the publications. Other top outlets included *Communication Studies, Communication Monographs,* and *Western Journal of Communication,* with approximately 8% of our list of publications appearing in these three journals. Journals that published 5%–7% of the qualitative organizational communication research include *Health Communication, Southern Communication Journal, Qualitative Research Reports, Journal of Family Communication,* and *Qualitative Inquiry.* The *Electronic Journal of Communication,* established in 1990, has published at least one qualitative organizational study every year, including two special issues on work and family (Golden, 2000) and personal and professional life (Kirby, 2006). In addition, outlets have become available for qualitative organizational communication research with the establishment of *Qualitative Inquiry* in 1995, *European Journal of Cultural Studies* in 1998, *Critical Studies: Critical Methodologies* in 2001, *International Review of Qualitative Research* in 2008, and two brand-new journals—*Qualitative Communication Research* and *Journal of Organizational Ethnography*—in 2012.

5. *Themes/Concepts Studied in Qualitative Organizational Communication Journal Articles 1996–2011*

Theme/Concept	Over This Year Span	# of Articles
Identity	1996–2011	35
Health	1996–2010	28
Work/Life/Family	2001–2010	27
Emotion Work	1997–2011	21
Control	1995–2010	17
Change	2000–2009	15
Dialectic	1996–2011	14
Power	1999–2010	14
Roles	2000–2011	14
Sensemaking	1999–2010	14
Contradiction	2002–2010	13
Identification	2000–2010	12
Resistance	1998–2009	12
Feminist	1997–2008	10
Gender	1996–2010	10
Knowledge	1997–2010	10
Paradox	1997–2011	10
Community	1999–2010	9
Technology	1999–2010	9
Conflict	2000–2011	8
Framing	1999–2010	8
Masculinity	2003–2011	8
Agency	1999–2009	7
Empowerment	2000–2008	7
Ethics	2000–2011	7
Spirituality	2000–2008	7
Structuration	1997–2010	7
Humor	1998–2010	6
Metaphor	1996–2006	6
Structure	1997–2008	6
Support	1999–2007	6
Teams	2002–2010	6
Authority	1998–2009	5
Collaboration	1999–2007	5
Decision Making	1998–2006	5
Ideology	1996–2004	5
Sexual Harassment	2000–2008	5
Socialization	2001–2005	5
Caregiving	2001–2009	4
Irony	1999–2006	4
Leadership	1997–2006	4
Policy	2000–2010	4
Diversity	2004–2007	3
Maternity	1999–2004	3
Network(s)	2004	3
Assimilation	2000–2005	2
Bullying	2006	2
Dialogue	1999–2005	2
Social Capital	2004–2010	2
Strategic Ambiguity	1996–2000	2
Voice	2004–2006	2

6. These qualitative empirical studies were excerpted from our master list (described above). Furthermore, we sent out calls on International Communication Association and NCA organizational communication asking participants to add to or amend our list. A total of 34 journal articles published in the last 15 years have a Google Scholar citation record (as of August 2011) of 50 or more citations. In order to save space, we have not duplicated

the citation to these in the reference section unless referenced elsewhere in the chapter. The additional 24 not listed in the body of this chapter are as follows (Note: The bolded number at the beginning of the reference indicates the number of citations through October 2011.):

80: Boczkowski, P. J. (2004). The processes of adopting multimedia and interactivity in three online newsrooms. *Journal of Communication, 54*(2), 197–213. doi:10.1111/j.1460 2466.2004.tb02624.x

80: Boczkowski, P. (1999). Mutual shaping of users and technologies in a national virtual community. *Journal of Communication, 49*(2), 86–108. doi:10.1111/j.1460-2466.1999.tb02795.x

78: Clair, R. P. (1996). The political nature of the colloquialism, "a real job": Implications for organizational socialization. *Communication Monographs, 63*(3), 249–267. doi:10.1080/03637759609376392

75: Tracy, K., & Tracy, S. J. (1998). Rudeness at 911: Reconceptualizing face and face attack. *Human Communication Research, 25*(2), 225–251. doi:10.1111/j.1468-2958.1998.tb00444

74: Tracy, S. J., & Tracy, K. (1998). Emotion labor at 911: A case study and theoretical critique. *Journal of Applied Communication Research, 26*(4), 390–411. doi:10.1080/00909889809365516

73: Jorgenson, J. (2002). Engineering selves: Negotiating gender and identity in technical work. *Management Communication Quarterly, 15*(3), 350–380. doi:10.1177/0893318902153002

73: Zorn, T. E., Page, D. J., & Cheney, G. (2000). Nuts about change: Multiple perspectives on change-oriented communication in a public sector organization. *Management Communication Quarterly, 13*(4), 515–566. doi:10.1177/0893318900134001

72: Ashcraft, K. L. (2000). Empowering "professional" relationships: Organizational communication meets feminist practice. *Management Communication Quarterly, 13*(3), 347–392. doi:10.1177/0893318900133001

69: Papa, M. J., Auwal, M. A., & Singhal, A. (1997). Organizing for social change within concertive control systems: Member identification, empowerment, and the masking of discipline. *Communication Monographs, 64*(3), 219–249. doi: 10.1080/03637759709376418

65: Meyer, J. C. (1997). Humor in member narratives: Uniting and dividing at work. *Western Journal of Communication, 61*(2), 188–208. doi:10.1080/10570319709374571

62: Tracy, S. J., Lutgen-Sandvik, P., & Alberts, J. K. (2006). Nightmares, demons, and slaves: Exploring the painful metaphors of workplace bullying. *Management Communication Quarterly, 20*(2), 148–185. doi:10.1177/0893318906291980

59: Ashcraft, K. L., & Pacanowsky, M. E. (1996). "A woman's worst enemy": Reflections on a narrative of organizational life and female identity. *Journal of Applied Communication Research, 24*(3), 217–239. doi:10.1080/00909889609365452

58: Sias, P. M., Heath, R. G., Perry, T., Fix, B., & Silva, D. (2004). Narratives of workplace friendship deterioration. *Journal of Social and Personal Relationships, 21*(3), 321–340. doi: 10.1177/0265407504042835

58: Witmer, D. F. (1997). Communication and recovery: Structuration as an ontological approach to organizational culture. *Communication Monographs, 64*(4), 324–349. doi:10.1080/03637759709376427

57: Kramer, M. W., & Hess, J. A. (2002). Communication rules for the display of emotions in organizational settings. *Management Communication Quarterly, 16*(1), 66–80. doi:10.1177/0893318902161003

56: Trethewey, A. (2001). Reproducing and resisting the master narrative of decline: Midlife professional women's experiences of aging. *Management Communication Quarterly, 15*(2), 183–227. doi:10.1177/0893318901152002

55: Tracy, S. J. (2004). Dialectic, contradiction, or double bind? Analyzing and theorizing employee reactions to organizational tensions. *Journal of Applied Communication Research, 32*(2), 119–146. doi:10.1080/0090988042000210025

55: Kuhn, T. (2006). A "demented work ethic" and a "lifestyle firm": Discourse, identity, and workplace time commitments. *Organization Studies, 27*(9), 1339–1358. doi: 10.1177/0170840606067249

55: Papa, M. J., Auwal, M. A., & Singhal, A. (1995). Dialectic of control and emancipation in organizing for social change: A multitheoretic study of the Grameen Bank in Bangladesh. *Communication Theory, 5*(3), 189–223. doi: 10.1111/j.1468-2885.1995.tb00106.x

54: Ashcraft, K. L. (2005). Resistance through consent? Occupational identity, organizational form, and the maintenance of masculinity among commercial airline pilots. *Management Communication Quarterly, 19*(1), 67–90. doi: 10.1177/0893318905276560

54: Darling, A. L., & Dannels, D. P. (2003). Practicing engineers talk about the importance of talk: A report on the role of oral communication in the workplace. *Communication Education, 52*(1), 1–16. doi:10.1080/03634520302457

53: Ashcraft, K. L. (1999). Managing maternity leave: A qualitative analysis of temporary executive succession. *Administrative Science Quarterly, 44*(2), 240–280. Retrieved from http://www.jstor.org/action/showPublication?journalCode=admisciequar. doi:10.2307/2666996

53: Ellingson, L. L. (2003). Interdisciplinary health care teamwork in the clinic backstage. *Journal of Applied Communication Research, 31*(2), 93–117. doi:10.1080/0090988032000064579

51: Larson, G. S., & Pepper, G. L. (2003). Strategies for managing multiple organizational identifications: A case of competing identities. *Management Communication Quarterly, 16*(4), 528–557. doi:10.1177/0893318903251626

7. In order to save space, we have not duplicated the citation to these in the reference section unless referenced elsewhere in the chapter.

CHAPTER 11

Organizational Discourse Analysis

Gail T. Fairhurst and Linda L. Putnam

When Putnam and Fairhurst (2001) wrote the first chapter on discourse in the last *Handbook of Organizational Communication,* the field of organizational discourse analysis was still in its infancy. A number of factors were converging to lead a group of international and interdisciplinary scholars to become discourse analysts, many of them from the field of organizational communication. These convergences included organizational culture studies which presaged a role for language in organizations, the rise of sociolinguistics that examined the linguistic repertoires of occupations, the emergence of studies on labor processes, and the growth of critical theory and studies of power and the opacity of language (Deetz & Mumby, 1990). Moreover, the rise of postmodernism and the so-called *linguistic turn* in social theory revealed that language more than mirrors reality; it constitutes it (Rorty, 1967). In the turn toward language, a meaning-centered view of human communication took hold—meanings that are "fluid and fragmented rather than fixed and universal" (Grant, Putnam, & Hardy, 2011, p. xxi).

However, scholars have struggled to reach definitional agreement regarding the term *discourse.* In 2001, Putnam and Fairhurst adopted a more language-centric view of discourse research, which centered on "the study of words and signifiers, including the form or structure of these words, the use of language in context, and the meanings or interpretations of discursive practices" (Fairhurst & Putnam, 1998, p. 79). Meanwhile, European and Australasian scholars gravitated toward a Foucauldian view of discourse rooted in socio-historical systems of thought that simultaneously disciplined social actors while providing them with linguistic resources. Alvesson and Kärreman (2000) labeled the former little "d" discourse and the latter big "D" Discourse to avoid confusion in the burgeoning literature at the time. However, scholars today are as apt to embrace either or both views to examine the multiple levels at which organizational discourse operates (e.g., Cheney, Christensen, Conrad, & Lair, 2004; Fairclough, 2005), and thus they find the distinction less useful (Alvesson & Kärreman, 2011; Hardy & Grant, 2012).

Similar to Grant et al. (2011), we define *discourse studies* as a broad class of approaches that focuses on the constitutive effects of language; processes of text production, distribution, and consumption; and reflexive, interpretive analysis aimed at deciphering the role of discourse in a socially constructed reality (p. xvii). The notion of *text* figures prominently into this definition in that text, unlike language use or conversation, refers to the material representation of discourse in spoken or recorded forms (Taylor &Van Every, 2000). Texts can range from written documents to memory traces to verbal routines—all of which may be reconfigured through continued use (Derrida, 1988). In this sense, discourses represent structured collections of texts (Parker, 1992). Yet discourses exist beyond any given text (Hardy & Maguire, 2010; Hardy, Thomas, & Grant, 2005), since they retain a generative capacity to source new texts and thus stand ready to layer and interweave with current practices, as situations demand (Keenoy & Oswick, 2003).

For many organizational scholars, discourse analysis is primarily a *methodology*, that is, a different way of operationalizing communication-related phenomena than the use of surveys and psychometric scales. As this chapter suggests, discourse analysis is a method or form of data analysis, but it is much more. Since it operates within a broad social constructionist epistemology (Berger & Luckman, 1966; Gergen, 2001), it is a perspective in its own right, one that gained significant momentum with the linguistic turn (Rorty, 1967). As such, the focus in discourse analysis is on the discourse itself, that is, on how it is organized and what it is doing (Potter & Wetherell, 1987). Asking what discourse is *doing* is a very different theoretical question than focusing on how it *represents* ideas and objects. That said, theory-method pairings are not uncommon in organizational discourse analysis, because it incorporates methodological concerns fundamental to its constructionist roots. These concerns include types of data (e.g., meaning-centered), the theoretical and analytical lens, and actor/analyst reflexivity—issues that we address in this chapter.

Putnam and Fairhurst (2001) chronicled at least 10 approaches to organizational discourse

Table 11.1 Putnam & Fairhurst's (2001) Types of Discourse Analysis[1, 2]

Discourse analysis is "the study of words and signifiers, including the form or structure of these words, the use of language in context, and the meanings or interpretations of discursive practices."[3]	
Type	**Definition**
Sociolinguistics	Language is an outgrowth of social categories (e.g., socio-economic class, education, or geographic location) and organizational structures (e.g., occupation, subculture groups, or hierarchical position). The emphasis of sociolinguistics is on the semantics or lexicon that emerges from societal and structural differences.
Conversation Analysis	Conversation analysis focuses on the detailed organization of talk-in-interaction. The goal is to discern how people use various interactional methods and procedures (e.g., turn taking, membership categorization, adjacency pairs, and accounts) to produce their activities and make sense of their worlds.
Cognitive Linguistics	Cognitive linguistics is the study of discourse patterns that arise from mental processes (e.g., scripts, schemata, cause-maps, semantic networks, and frames). The emphasis is on the link between discourse forms and language users' sensemaking.
Pragmatics	This broad category of discourse analyses focuses on the study of language in context, discourse as action, and symbolic action in speech communities.

Type	Definition
Speech Acts	This approach treats language as action in an immediate interactive context (e.g., directives, politeness and face work, accounts and justifications). Speech acts also serve as a building block for viewing organizations constructed through speech agency.
Ethnography of Speaking	This approach examines the expectations and typifications of actors in the everyday routines of organizational life. Studies focus on speech communities, communication rules, conversational performances, storytelling performances, and symbolic interaction.
Interaction Analysis	This method uses standardized procedures for coding verbal behavior to develop categories and meanings embedded in structural patterns of talk. Genres include interaction process analysis, systems-interaction research, structuration studies, and negotiation research.
Semiotics	Semiotics focuses on the way that interpretations evolve from code systems. This approach includes not only discourse but also nonverbal codes, images, actions, and objects. Emphasis is placed on the ways that signs signify, how they associate among codes, and how they develop into a system of signals.
Literary and Rhetorical Analyses	This approach defines rhetoric as the available means of persuasion and draws from classical methods of argumentation to examine corporate messages in crisis situations, organizational decision making, and identification. Emphasis is given to texts and the ways that meaning intertwines with function to shape messages and message responses.
Critical Language Studies	This approach focuses on the power and control issues in language, particularly the ways that individuals or groups compete for symbolic and discursive resources. Discourse is the means of producing, maintaining, or resisting systems of power and inequality through ideology and hegemony. Studies focus on the ideological functions of narrative, rituals, and texts that (re)constitute power relationships and privilege some meanings over others.
Postmodern Discourse Analysis	Postmodern discourse analysis centers on the instability of meaning. Power and knowledge are produced in temporary language games and stories located in space and time. Language functions as a system of difference, devoid of any stable and direct relationship to the natural world, thus texts are meaningful only as different people read and interpret them in multiple ways.

Source: From L.L. Putnam & G.T. Fairhurst (2001). Discourse analysis in organizations: Issues and concerns. In F.M. Jablin & L.L. Putnam (eds.), *The New Handbook of Organizational Communication: Advances in Theory, Research, and Methods,* p. 78–136. (Thousand Oaks, CA: Sage).

analysis, which are defined in Table 11.1. They include sociolinguistics, conversation analysis, cognitive linguistics, pragmatics (e.g., speech acts, ethnography of speaking, and interaction analysis), semiotics, literary and rhetorical analysis, critical discourse analysis (CDA), and postmodern language analysis. While one way to update the field would be a straightforward review of these approaches, such logic would make it difficult to appreciate the stunning complexity of organizational discourse studies today. This complexity includes the crossover among approaches, also called *hybrid theorizing* (Heracleous & Marshak, 2004); the blends in conducting research, especially between critical and postmodern approaches; and the manner in which various approaches either coalesce or diverge to address challenging issues and concerns.

Thus we have selected an issue-based approach to cross the vast body of research that has grown exponentially since 2001. The field has produced a number of literature reviews (Alvesson & Kärreman, 2000; Grant & Iedema, 2005; Putnam & Fairhurst, 2001), commentaries (Alvesson & Kärreman, 2011; Bargiela-Chiappini, 2011; Hardy & Grant, 2012; Iedema, 2011; Mumby, 2011), edited books (Aritz & Walker, 2012; Cooren, 2007; Grant, Keenoy, & Oswick, 1998; Westwood & Linstead, 2001), handbooks (Bargiela-Chiappini, 2009; Grant, Hardy, Oswick, & Putnam, 2004), and even a major works collection (Grant, Hardy, & Putnam, 2011) that indicate that the state of organizational discourse studies is well past its infancy. These venues highlight several issues posed as questions that scholars are addressing.

The first question is deceptively simple: How does discourse constitute the features of organizational life? These features include identities, relationships, cultures, contexts, leadership, organizational units, and other phenomena. Informed by social constructionism, most discourse analysts problematize the taken-for-granted aspects of organizational life, including the very notion of the *organization* itself (Fairhurst & Putnam, 2004). Discourse studies aim to show how the taken-for-granted "could have been otherwise" by highlighting the coproduction of the actors involved (Hacking, 1999). Thus the primary issues concern agency, process, and possibility (Ashcraft, Kuhn, & Cooren, 2009).

The second major question asks, "How does discourse interact with the material world to privilege certain realities over others in organizational life?" Wrought by economic realities and the growing disparities of the market, this genre of research is also constructionist, but with a bent toward critical realism (Bhaskar, 1986; Reed, 2005), such as Marxist dialectical materialism (e.g., Cloud, 2001, 2005) or theories of hegemony (Laclau, 1990; Laclau & Mouffe, 1985). The central concerns are issues of power and the ways that the material aspects of organizations constrain organizational actors. Even though some scholars treat materiality as a "catch-all category for the hard stuff of existence" (Cheney & Cloud, 2006, p. 511), the focus in this work is on the economic and institutional influences as they impact discourse and agency in organizational life.

The third and final question is, "How do discourse and materiality mutually constitute each other in routine practices of organizational life?" Unlike the previous category, this concern centers on physical factors that interface with discourse and the symbolic. It sets forth a posthumanist challenge to social constructionism that stems from the role of technology in society and the difficulty of knowing when technology begins and human beings leave off (Barad, 2003; Latour, 1994; Suchman, 2007). As such, it focuses on the performative nature of discourse and material practices (Orlikowski, 2007).

In posing these three questions, we realize that any program of research can and does address more than one of these issues. To illustrate these concerns, we have selected studies based on their representativeness to communication scholars. For each perspective, we highlight themes, specific areas of work, methodological concerns, and critiques of these areas. We then conclude the chapter with a discussion of the contributions of organizational communication scholarship to discourse studies.

Discourse Constitutes Organizational Realities

One singular achievement of discourse research has been to challenge the modernist view of organizations as rational and reified entities (Putnam, 1983). In doing so, scholars have reexamined positivistic organizational science in which organizations, communication, and discourse are objective realities that call for measurement approaches drawn from the physical sciences (Putnam, Phillips, & Chapman, 1996). Importantly, scholars began to conceive of both discourse and communication in different ways; namely, discourse is not simply an artifact that reflects reality (Chia, 2000). Instead, it reveals the dynamic processes behind the stable and enduring organizational objects, entities, levels, or conditions whose ontologies, heretofore, were largely assumed or rarely problematized (Chia, 2000, 2003). Moreover, with the assertion of a lack of essence in post-structuralist views of reality (Ritzer & Goodman, 2002), discourse scholars aim to counter or qualify the use of essentialism (i.e., ascribing universal properties to persons or entities, thus eliding a dependence on context; Prasad, 2012).

In a similar manner, communication is not merely a conduit or tool for transmitting information (Axley, 1984). Instead, it is the ongoing, dynamic process of actions and interactions aimed at creating, transforming, maintaining, or destroying meanings (Ashcraft et al., 2009). In this definition, communication constitutes social realities through the many entanglements of symbolic and material practices that are activated through interaction.

Unpacking the relationship between discourse and communication seems central to exploring what is unique about a communication focus on organizational discourse. Clearly, not all discourse scholars have an interest in communication *per se*, and many organizational communication scholars take pains to distinguish *discourse* from *communication* (Barker, 2008; Fairhurst & Putnam, 2004; Jian, Schmisseur, & Fairhurst, 2008; Putnam, 2008; Taylor, 2008). For example, Jian et al. (2008) suggest that organizational actors operate *in* communication and *through* discourse. *Communication* refers to the processes of coproduced meaning at unique moments in time, while *discourse* is the medium for social interaction based on the cognitive and linguistic resources supplied. This approach suggests a part-whole relationship between discourse and communication in which discourse is a resource in service to communication.

Other scholars reverse this relationship and make discourse the whole and communication the part or the mediator among multiple types of discourses (Ashcraft, 2007). Another approach views these two concepts as distinct, but symbiotic—that is, they are mutually interdependent and reflexively intertwined. Working from a co-constructive perspective, discourse accomplishes communication that, in turn, reflects back on discourse in ways that redefine or alter communication (Putnam, 2008).

So what does a communication approach offer to the study of organizational discourse? Phillips and Oswick (2012) claim that scholars often differ as to whether *organization* or *discourse* is the figure or the ground of a study. As they note, "there are communication/discourse scholars who do organization(s) and organization/management scholars who do discourse" (p. 461). The contribution of a communication lens to organizational discourse studies, however, should not be based on figure-ground relationships among these concepts. Rather a communicative approach drives the constitutive nature of organization and serves as a bridge for interpenetrating multiple levels of analysis (Putnam & Nicotera, 2009b). In the field of communication, these arguments parallel perspectives on the communicative constitution of organizations (CCO) (Ashcraft et al., 2009; McPhee & Zaug, 2000; Putnam & Nicotera, 2009a).

In these perspectives, organizations become *discursive constructions* that involve complex systems of meaning (Boden, 1994; Chia, 2000; Cooren & Taylor, 1997; Deetz, 1992; Fairhurst & Putnam, 2004; Mumby & Clair, 1997; Tsoukas & Chia, 2002). Discourse, then, is a key building block or foundation on which organizational life is built, even if the discourse-organization relationship is complex, subject to multiple interpretations, and interlaced with a material world (Ashcraft et al., 2009; Fairhurst & Putnam, 2004).

Five key themes characterize the new frontiers that address the question of how does discourse constitute aspects of organizational life. These themes include the organizing potential of language and texts, the social construction of subjectivities, the new rhetoric and organizations, tensions and contradictions in disorganization, and social poetics as dialogical experiences.

The Organizing Potential of Language and Texts

Scholars who focus on the organizing potential of language examine how this process occurs through communication. For Hawes (1974), a focus on organizing is centered on "how organizations organize in the first place, continue to stay organized and sometimes un-organize" (p. 498), while Chia (2003) sees organizing as challenging "the apparent solidity of social phenomena such as 'the organization'" (pp. 111–112). Studies on the organizing potential of language aim to put "abstract structures into live motion" (Ashcraft et al., 2009, p. 4). Theorists, such as Weick (1979, 1995; Weick, Sutcliffe, & Obstfeld, 2005), Giddens (1979, 1984), and Garfinkel (1967), supply key conceptual resources that assist scholars in analyzing this view of organizing.

Examples of studies that focus on the organizing potential of language are certainly present in the literature, although perhaps not as prominent as in our last review (Putnam & Fairhurst, 2001). These studies show how language enacts organizing through (1) what the discourse is doing; (2) how it is doing it, particularly through sequential interactions or patterned redundancies over time; and (3) what it means or how the patterns are interpreted. These processes are often analyzed amid activities of organizing or as the interaction patterns of actors over time coproduce organizing.

Diverse forms of discourse analysis address these topics differently. Table 11.1 provides definitions and explanations of these types of discourse analysis. For example, using *conversation analysis*, Fairhurst and Cooren (2004) found that categorization work in a radio call of an injured police officer signaled how she had joined the search for her own bullet-ridden body, while an *interaction analysis* demonstrated the consistent deferral by the police dispatcher to the commands of police supervisors on the scene that, in turn, paralleled the stand-down by other beat officers (Cooren & Fairhurst, 2004; Fairhurst, 2007).

Shifting to a different form of language analysis, the ordering of *speech acts* in the same scenario led to closing off "spatio-temporal" activities for on-scene tasks and produced attributions of "command presence" for a supervisor. Drawing from *cognitive linguistics*, Brummans et al. (2008) investigated how the framing repertoires of different stakeholder groups fueled the intractability of environmental disputes and created barriers in resolving them. Using *rhetorical analyses* of Total Quality Management discourse, Green, Li, and Nohria (2009) demonstrated how the simplification of argument structures served as robust measures of institutionalization.

Perhaps no other group of researchers has done more to investigate the organizing potential of language than the Montréal School and their work on the role of CCO. Influenced by speech act theory, ethnomethodology, and actor-network theory (among others), Taylor and Van Every (2000, 2011) argued that organizations emerged at the intersection of the conversation-text link (see Brummans, Cooren, Robichaud, & Taylor, Chapter 7, for a discussion of CCO research; Cooren, 2000). *Conversation* is the site of an emerging organization as individuals use the rules and protocols of social interaction to negotiate their needs. In and through conversation, individuals attune to each other and the objects around them. As conversation captures the dynamics of organizing, *texts* are the built-in structures of language from which an organization is read. Texts also form from the residues of past conversations that become resources for future actions across time and space. The text-conversation link becomes embedded in actions and interactions that are imbricated or overlap as practices and structures form both organizing and organization. The seeds of the organization, then, reside in this text-conversation link.

These forms of discourse analysis also vary in how they incorporate text and context; focus on only one or multiple levels of analysis (e.g., interpersonal, organizational, institutional, societal); and examine how meanings are created, contested, and negotiated. They also differ in methodological approaches, although studies that embrace the organizing potential of language rely less heavily on interviews and more heavily on recorded interactions. Researchers typically code interactions, develop discourse themes, or draw from conceptual analyses (such as framing or metaphor) to analyze interaction processes and texts (Putnam, 2005).

The Social Construction of Subjectivities

Postmodernists embrace another theoretical stream in which discourse constitutes organization. Scholars in this stream focus on complex systems of meaning, ones suffused with social and historical practices (Grant et al., 2011, p. xxi). Following Foucault (1980, 1995), discourse is a system of knowledge that creates its own *truth effects* (i.e., the treatment of knowledge as if it were true). Going beyond language use, this approach emphasizes how culturally rooted ways of thinking create various subject positions through the ways that one or more discursive practices (such as talk, text, writing, or cognition) shape an individual's subjectivity (Deetz, 1992).

For example, Tracy and Trethewey (2005) examined identity construction processes associated with the language of "real" and "fake" selves in Western societies. Dichotomizing these concepts produced a powerful discourse that, ultimately, shaped how subject positions favored managerial interests. Other postmodernist studies include Ashcraft's (2007; Ashcraft & Mumby, 2004) investigation of the subjectivities and fallen status of airline pilots; Fairhurst's (2007; Fairhurst, Church, Hagen, & Levi, 2011) study of the discourses of executive coaching aimed at subjugating both female leaders and alpha male leaders; Medved and Kirby's (2005) analysis of corporate mothering discourses that created new subject positions for stay-at-home mothers; Sewell, Barker, and Nyberg's (2012) study of management-training employees as "piggies in the middle"; and Ziegler's (2007) study of organizational discourses that portrayed firefighters as benevolent leaders, heroic saviors, self-aware servants, obedient rule followers, or critical-thinking team members. These studies focus on the power of discourse to influence the subjectivities of organizational actors who have disciplined themselves to its ways.

Research methods for examining the discursive construction of subjectivities differ from ones that focus on the organizing potential of language. Even though both approaches treat discourse and organization as mutually constitutive, postmodern scholars embrace the multiple and diverse ways that discourse constructs subjectivities. To decipher how power works, scholars often analyze *discourse formations* or groups of statements and conceptual configurations embedded in *discourse practices,* which are the rules, routines, and structural principles in organizations. Postmodern scholars also focus on the ways that meanings shift or carry the seeds of their own transformation (Weedon, 1997). Grounded in the belief that macro-level discourses are reproduced in micro-discursive practices, they examine the moments in which sites of discursive construction are contested through struggles among diverse forms of knowing, being, and speaking (Broadfoot, Deetz, & Anderson, 2004).

In addition, researchers strive to hold multiple levels of analysis in conversation with each other as they construct, contest, and create opportunities for organizing. Hence, scholars focus on multilevel, multimethod approaches and treat them as complementary and equally important, often through the use of intertextuality (Kristeva, 1984). In intertextual analysis, researchers examine the interconnectedness of texts, the construction of webs of texts within texts, and the ways that current texts interplay with past conversations (Broadfoot et al., 2004).

The New Rhetoric and Organizations

Intertextual analysis is also a prominent feature in rhetorical approaches to the organizing potential of language and texts. Prior research on organizational rhetoric often treated this approach as corporate advocacy, crisis management, and the study of persuasive arguments (Cheney et al., 2004; Putnam & Fairhurst, 2001). Previous work focused heavily on the strategic functions of rhetoric from a single orator with a sole text in a public forum. These analyses presumed largely undifferentiated audiences and the strategic interplay of ethos, logos, and pathos to maximize persuasive effect. But rhetoric's long-standing association with persuasion has broadened in the past decade, and contemporary organizational rhetoric examines "the dialectical processes that link social actors, texts, and communicative situations" (Cheney et al., 2004, p. 80).

Contemporary rhetorical analyses of organizations embrace a constructionist rather than a functionalist perspective and examine a variety of texts (Heracleous, 2012). Such textual variety includes redefining audiences as multiple groups of stakeholders whose interests may or may not converge. The wide range of symbolic action that contemporary perspectives embrace overlaps with the concepts of *discourse* and *texts,* especially groups of texts that vary across time and context (Heracleous, 2012; Sillince, 2006). This overlap is most dramatic in Sillince's (2006) use of the term *participation rhetorics* and Suddaby and Greenwood's (2005) treatment of rhetoric as a linguistic repertoire.

As Cheney et al. (2004) note, contemporary organizational rhetoric differs from its traditional roots through a number of defining concerns. In particular, it focuses on situations of uncertainty and possibility (Christensen & Cornelissen, 2011; Heath, 2011), situations in which the intent of a message is ambiguous for the speaker and/or audience (Leonardi & Jackson, 2004). It also examines circumstances in which the credibility, or *ethos,* of a source is problematic; the audiences for messages are unclear or complex (Larson & Pepper, 2003; Sillince, 2006); or the nature of persuasion is context dependent (Green et al., 2009; Sillince, 2006; Suddaby & Greenwood, 2005).

Broadening the domain of organizational rhetoric calls for examining how organizations interact with multiple stakeholders to legitimate arguments for decision making (Erkama & Vaara, 2010; Green et al., 2009; Sillince, 1999, 2002); assessing the ethics and values of persuasive campaigns (Heath, 2011; Meisenbach & Feldner, 2011); and situating agency as circumscribed in a material, political, and social world (Cheney & Cloud, 2006; Cloud, 2005; Ziegler, 2007).

Developing a broad-based organizational rhetoric stems, in part, from the turbulence of global environments, shifting market conditions, and rapid technological advances—circumstances that blur the lines between internal and external communication (Cheney & Christensen, 2001). In particular, rhetorical approaches aimed at employee internal communication interface and fuse with the discourses of external branding. Thus organizational actors are continually negotiating tensions between presenting messages that are univocal and ones that are tailored to a broad multivocal group of stakeholders (see Cheney, Christensen, & Dailey, Chapter 28).

Methods for analyzing contemporary organizational rhetoric have shifted from critiques of persuasive strategies nested in particular texts (such as a corporate apology) to focusing on active stakeholders, indeterminate texts, and variable contexts. To investigate active stakeholders, researchers employ focus group interviews or dialogues with multiple audiences (Lindlof & Taylor, 2011). Textual methods use narrative to link past stories with future ones and to show how organizational identity is volatile and subject to change (Browning & Morris, 2012). Finally, Sillince's (2007) context-based framework for studying organizational rhetoric centers on intertextuality and provides a method for tracking changes in discourse and texts across events, time periods, and situations (pp. 368–369). Specifically, he recommends that scholars analyze the who, when, why, and where of situations and how discourses from one context become inserted, reframed, and recursively coupled with another one.

Tensions and Contradictions in Disorganization

Just as research on organizational rhetoric has shifted to examine dialectical processes, organizational discourse studies on contradictions and paradoxes have continued to grow. Drawn from postmodern approaches, this research focuses on how discourse constitutes disorganization as a routine feature of organizational life. Tensions and paradoxes, then, are not just anomalies or ruptures in the social fabric of organizations (Trethewey & Ashcraft, 2004); rather, they are infused into routine processes of organizing. Extant literature typically treats these tensions and paradoxes as problems to be solved, processes that veered from equilibrium, or fault lines that signal resistance (Wendt, 1998). The regular occurrence of these tensions, however, signals the ubiquity of organizational dilemmas, disjuncture, contradictions, and dissonance. Theoretically, then, research on organizational tensions and contradictions embraces a logic of difference in which organizing arises from the collision of order and disorder, rationality and irrationality, and predictable and unpredictable (Clegg, Kornberger, & Rhodes, 2005).

This line of work looks at discourse in the gray zones of organizational dilemmas, specifically, the ways that organizational processes often move in opposite or competing directions. Tensions refer to the push-pull dilemmas among choices that grow out of discontinuities as a result of competing directions. Tensions can evolve into contradictions, dialectics, and paradoxes as they develop in complexity and become intertwined into different types of relationships. For example, Tracy (2004) showed how correctional officers in a prison managed a family of contradictions, namely, having to be respectful but mostly suspicious of inmates, nurturing them while disciplining them, and being empathetic at times while being detached at other times.

A paradoxical situation occurs when these oppositions become constructed in ways that are mutually exclusive, reflect back, and impose on one another. Paradoxes also occur from the simultaneous enactment of two incompatible imperatives. For example, consider a supervisor's command "to participate by not getting involved;" this edict issues an imperative to comply with two seemingly mutually exclusive actions. Paradoxes pervade workplace participation programs when employees become empowered by giving up individual rights (Carroll & Arneson, 2003; Stohl & Cheney, 2001; Wendt, 1998). Particular communicative practices, such as humor and irony, serve as mechanisms to reframe oppositional structures and rise above these dilemmas (Butler & Modaff, 2008; Martin, 2004; Real & Putnam, 2005).

Importantly, the interplay between constituting organization and disorganization is the relationship between binaries and dialectics. *Binaries* emphasize the mutual exclusivity of opposites, while *dialectics* focus on their unity and interdependence. In a dialectical relationship, the opposite pairs need each other, which necessitates holding them together or developing ways to embrace the tensions; hence, dialectical analysis focuses on the dynamic interplay between unified opposites (Baxter & Montgomery, 1996).

Specifically, Jameson (2004) showed how anesthesiologists and nurses held tensions of autonomy and connectedness together through rotating supervision and educational training. In similar ways, negotiating the identities of musicians, board members, and administrators constructed solidarity while creating division among members of a community orchestra (Rudd, 2000), and in a battered women's shelter, the process of working out client independence resulted ironically from increasing client-staff dependence (Vaughn & Stamp, 2003). Equally paradoxical, organizational change processes are often developed by simultaneously embracing and resisting change by protecting core ideologies (Harter & Krone, 2001; Jian, 2007; Kellett, 1999). Hence, a number of discourse studies focus on how organizational members enact tensions, embrace them, derive energy from them, and preserve difference.

Methodologies for dialectical analyses are in their infancy, but some guidelines exist for using this approach (Jian, 2007; Real & Putnam, 2005). Specifically, scholars can locate oppositional discourses in themes or problem identification and then characterize whether the tensions are enacted as single or co-occurring dilemmas, contradictory and mutually exclusive ones, or dialectical and unified tensions. After identifying and situating the tensions, scholars should focus on how organizational members manage them, specifically, the ways that they make choices to favor one pole or the other, to vacillate between them, to integrate them, or to reframe them.

Thus in examining the organizing potential of language and texts, scholars also focus on discourse processes in disorganizing that shape the fragmented and ambiguous actions in organizational life. This approach examines tensions, contradictions, and paradoxes at the intersection of order and disorder that becomes the ground for new possibilities and alternative organizational orders.

Social Poetics as Dialogical Experiences

Closely related to dialectics is a genre of discourse known as *dialogue*. Dialogue refers to the development of mutuality through "questioning, critiquing, reconfiguring interests, and affirming differences" and as such, serves as a way to mediate competing and contradictory discourses (Putnam & Fairhurst, 2001, p. 116). The current work on dialogue and organizational processes privileges the poetics of experience, that is, imagining or "creating possibilities rather than describing actualities [through] . . . multiplicity not specificity" (Cunliffe, 2002, p. 133). Drawn from Bakhtin (1981), Wittgenstein (1953), and Shotter (1996), social poetics is a "relationally engaged dialogic experience" in which the investigator and the participants coproduce the research process as they jointly create meaning through the interplay of language and framing (Cunliffe, 2002). Research thus becomes a reflexive conversation for "seeing connections" (Wittgenstein, 1953, p. 122) produced by the "arresting moments" of dialogue (Shotter, 1996, p. 294). Learning is likewise transformed into a dialogic, embodied, and relational experience (Cunliffe, 2002, 2004; Katz & Shotter, 1996; Shotter & Cunliffe, 2003).

Barge (2001, 2004a, 2004b; Barge & Oliver, 2003) demonstrates how leaders' poetic forms of talk (particularly storytelling, metaphor use, and appreciative inquiry) create new ways of seeing and acting in the world. For Barge (2001), discourse and communication operate as practical theory (i.e., theoretical concepts and ideas that can promote reflexivity through praxis) that restory organizational life in ways more consistent with a participant's value commitments and social ethics (Barge, 2004a; Barge & Little, 2002). Barge's (2007) form of social constructionism promotes systems thinking to help actors understand the connections among persons-in-conversation, actions, meanings, and context that facilitate narratives of change (Barge, 2007; Barge & Fairhurst, 2008). In social poetics, language is alive with the potential for reflexivity and change as meanings evolve from the flows of experience.

Methodology for researchers engaged in social poetics draws on reflexive grammars and rules of practice. Investigators invoke normative models of discourse and communication (e.g., dialogue) and move back and forth between interactions and interpretive findings to enlarge the vocabularies of researchers and participants as they make sense of, reflect back on, and develop new ways to conceptualize their concerns (Barge, 2004a, 2004b, 2007; Craig & Tracy, 1995). Overall, in social poetics, discourse constitutes organization through praxis, reflexivity, and the potential to transform practice.

Critique of the Organizing Potential of Language

Studies that examine the organizing potential of language, subjectivities, new rhetorics, dialectics, and social poetics problematize taken-for-granted worldviews in organizational life and stipulate how they could have been otherwise. Critics of this approach contend that discourse analysts place too much emphasis on organizing and downplay the role of institutional stabilities in this process (McPhee, 2004; McPhee & Zaug, 2000).

Critical scholars, in particular, charge discourse researchers with overemphasizing the role of human agency in constructing the social world and obscuring the real material constraints on agency (Cloud, 2005; Conrad, 2004; Fairclough, 2005; Fleetwood, 2005). The result is that scholars who work within this realm find "it difficult, if not impossible, to deal with institutionalized stabilities and continuities in power relations because they cannot get at the higher levels of social organizations in which micro-level processes are embedded" (Reed, 2000, pp. 526–527). In response to this critique, discourse scholars contend that the material world is always symbolically mediated, since it enters into view through human experience (Chia, 1995; Hardy & Grant, 2012). Even so, discourse researchers know that the material world must assume a greater presence than in the past, because language has "dynamics [that are] often disconnected from other dimensions of the world" (Cheney & Cloud, 2006, p. 512).

Discourses Interacting With the Material World

No doubt, the relationship between the symbolic and the material is one of the most vexing for discourse analysts (Cheney & Cloud, 2006). Research on how discourse interacts with a material world, our second key question, focuses on three central concerns. First, do discourse and the material have separate ontologies? Or, because the material world is symbolically mediated once it enters into human experience, does ontology collapse into epistemology? A raging debate has ensued regarding these questions (Al-Amoudi & Willmott, 2011; Billig, 2008; Cederstrom & Spicer, 2013; Contu & Willmott, 2005; Fairclough, 2005; Fleetwood, 2005; Reed, 2004, 2005).

Second, what is the precise relationship between discourse and the material? Specifically, materialists prioritize the brute facts of a physical and economically structured world over a symbolic one (Ashcraft et al., 2009; Searle, 1995). In contrast, discourse scholars portray symbolic processes as political and material (Burrell, 2012; Cooren, 2006; Cooren, Brummans, & Charrieras, 2008; Taylor & Van Every, 2000) and as having very real consequences (Deetz, 1992; Deetz & Mumby, 1990; Mumby, 1997). For these scholars, power configurations accrue as readily from a discursive struggle (i.e., the ongoing human contest over meaning) as they do from economic forces (Ashcraft et al., 2009, p. 15).

Finally, scholars raise questions about which material features to emphasize, namely, economic, institutional, technical, or physical ones. One response to these questions stems from critical realism, an orientation that purports that an organization is not *just* a discursive construction; *organizing* is constrained by a structured, materially imbalanced, social world (Fairclough, 2005).

Critical Realism

In CDA, Fairclough (1995, 2001, 2005) claims that a real social world exists, even if it is independent of knowing it (Fairclough, 2005, pp. 916, 922). CDA focuses on the relationships among discourse, institutions, and structures of privilege that have material qualities (Chouliaraki & Fairclough, 2010; Fairclough & Thomas, 2004). For example, Fairclough (2006) and Fairclough and Thomas (2004) use CDA to explore the relationship between discourse and globalization by focusing on how the *discourse of globalization* gets translated and crystallized into various texts (e.g., consultant-oriented books) that shape the *globalization of discourse* or how such (textualized) crystallizations influence social practice, including displacing workers through reorganization and downsizing. Fairclough's view of organizational discourse, mainly as *text and talk*, is but one among many elements of the social view (e.g., power or institutions), one that plays a far less central role for him than it does for other discourse analysts.

Cloud (2005) draws from Fairclough (1995, 2003) in her study of dialectical materialism. In her narrative analysis of the newsletters published by locked-out workers in a labor dispute, she shows how a lack of material resources eclipsed labor's fighting words (Cloud, 2005, p. 534). In her study, discourse emerged from the economic resources that shaped it, and agency hinged on the dialectical relationship between discourse and the material contexts of power.

As a method, CDA is well established (Mumby & Clair, 1997) and exists in many varieties (Fairclough & Wodak, 1997). Generally speaking, scholars employ a micro-level analysis, which examines one or more texts vis-à-vis syntax, metaphor, argument structure, or other linguistic features; a meso level that focuses on text production, distribution, and consumption to discern relations of power; and a macro level that examines how intertextual processes shape or are shaped by discursive events formed from socio-cultural practices and real, material qualities (Fairclough, 2001, 2006).

The Laclauian *Real*

A second response to the concerns about discourse and materiality examines how organizing is subject to the conditions of (im)possibility by a real world that lies outside of discourse (Laclau, 1990). Thus the material world enters into the social as an *absence* that is ambiguous and resists symbolization in structuring discourses (Bhaskar & Laclau, 2002; Laclau, 1990). For example, the concept of *workplace spirituality* is an incomplete expression of the phenomenon that it represents (Cederstrom & Spicer, 2013). As Contu and Willmott (2005) suggest, the lack in discourse is some unknown presence that creates the condition of impossibility and the (un) available means by which *the social* reproduces itself.

How exactly does this happen? In Laclau's theorizing, nodal or focal points stand in for the absence associated with any discourse(s). The concept of *articulation* highlights the discursive struggle and transformative moment when a signifier shifts from multiple meanings to a presence or momentary closure by temporarily fixing meaning (Laclau & Mouffe, 1985). To illustrate, Jian (2011) adopted Laclauian discourse analysis to examine the ways that language brought circumstances, identities, and practices into being to enact change. Using the discourses and nodal points deployed during a key management meeting, he focused on the struggles between market-friendly versus family-friendly discourses. Key signifiers in favor of the market to the exclusion of the family temporarily fixed the meanings that emerged from this meeting. In this way, the absent was brought into presence as a material factor that influenced change.

Although Laclau and Mouffe (1985) do not propose a method *per se*, Phillips and Jørgensen (2002) show how scholars can employ discourses, identities, and social spaces to identify key signifiers (e.g., nodal points, master signifiers, and myths) and how they can combine them to create meaning in chains of equivalence.

Critique of the Material as Real

Even though critical realists have brought materiality to the fore (Cederstrom & Spicer, 2013), critics fault this camp for its overly narrow conception of discourse and its lack of reflexivity in the way that language is cast in relation to a materialist world. For example, Cederstrom and Spicer (2013) take Fairclough (2005) to task for his narrow view of discourse as linguistic and semiotic elements of the social. In this rendering, discourse is distinct from material entities, artifacts, and social structures.

Similarly, Conrad (2011) faults critical realists for failing to recognize that rhetoric (i.e., intentional/persuasive symbolic action) plays a vital role in the formation and reproduction of discourses. Moreover, Billig (2008, p. 783) argues that critical realists' use of language obscures agency through the use of passive verbs that turn processes into entities. Contu and Willmott (2005) and Willmott (2005) even suggest that once the sound and fury of the critical realists' argument is stripped away, its structuralist foundation provides little that is really new.

Another way to view this debate is to acknowledge that critical realists and constitutive discourse scholars simply choose different emphases (Al-Amoudi & Willmott, 2011). For the former, materiality *bites back* to shape the social and symbolic (Suchman, 2007), while for the latter, discourse analysts need to construct categories to speak and write about the *bite* and its consequentiality. As an effort to address this bite, research on technology explores how materiality and discourse mutually constitute each other in practice.

Discourse and Materiality as Mutually Constituted

The third question, how do discourse and materiality mutually constitute each other in organizational practices, stems from the study of technology, especially how humans and objects form a *hybrid agency* (i.e., a network of associations) in actor-network theory (Callon & Latour, 1981; Latour, 1994, 2005; Latour & Woolgar, 1979). More recently, Pentland and Singh (2012) refer to this network of associations as an *agency stew*, in which designers and users of technology interact with the material. Since the material can exert multiple practical consequences, it is difficult to parse out the ways that the social and material define each other; hence, scholars should ground discourse and the material in specific practices rather than rely on abstract theorizing or developing categories of material forms.

Other theorists echo this practice-based approach in which subjects and objects form their existence through interactions with one another (Barad, 2003). Mutual constitution, however, does not imply symmetry; that is, "persons and artifacts do not constitute each other *in the same way*" (Suchman, 2007, p. 269; emphasis in original). Rather than focusing on mutuality, Orlikowski (2007; Orlikowski & Scott, 2009) urges scholars to examine *constitutive entanglements* or ways that discourse and materiality enter into new levels of engagement based on technological practices in organizations.

The common ground among these scholars is *practice*, defined as organized activities undertaken with material arrangements in a given setting (Schatzki, 2005). In this way, scholars move from focusing on the material (i.e., its properties or enduring features) to *socio-materiality* (i.e., the development and use of objects, sites, and bodies; Cook & Brown, 1999). Importantly, materiality is not reducible to linguistic constructions but is intertwined with discourse and imbricated in practice (Leonardi, 2012). In the work on socio-materiality, the organization emerges from ensembles of people, discourses, artifacts, equipment, sites, and bodies that are constitutively entangled. To analyze practices, communication serves as the nexus of the discourse-material interface, and objects, sites, and bodies function as the focal points of study (Ashcraft et al., 2009).

Objects

Objects and artifacts are material features that have matter, form, and properties of a temporarily permanent quality (Orlikowski, 2000). Objects then cannot necessarily be categorized by their physical features, since their properties and exact matter often change, as is evident in the physicality of information technology (Leonardi, 2012). Moreover, not all features of objects, especially technology, are relevant to every user or practice; hence, materiality is made applicable through discourse and communication.

For example, in a study of an automotive firm's use of a computer simulation, Leonardi (2008) demonstrated how engineers' interactions with the material features of the technology interpenetrated their communication with managers, coworkers, and customers. In particular, the misalignment of interactions between the social and material stymied planned change, especially when they were less than comprehensive or lacked reflexivity. Similarly, in a merger between two high-technology companies, discourses of technological inevitability and obsolescence favored managerial interests and obscured political choices in justifying the planned change (Leonardi, 2008; Leonardi & Jackson, 2004).

Materiality is also made applicable through the ways that objects exert agency when they become entangled with humans. Even though objects lack the ability to symbolize or be reflective, they exert agency through their capacities to make a difference (Taylor & Van Every, 2000). Hence, organizations are filled with a plenum of human and nonhuman agencies, including *discursive objects* (such as authority), which can become *text objects* (e.g., a memory trace, written or recorded documents, memos, work order, checklists). However, with the exception of studies such as Cooren's (2004, 2006), relatively few researchers grant them agency (i.e., show how text objects participate in the accomplishment of action). In effect, texts do not possess agency *per se*, but they participate in networks in which they guide actions as well as become inscribed with other objects in organizing.

To illustrate, Cooren et al. (2008) focused on the ways that Médecins Sans Frontières (MSF [Doctors without Borders]) presented itself amid a series of human and nonhuman agents in the war-torn Democratic Republic of the Congo. Its Paris headquarters possessed the trappings of a formal organization (e.g., building, signage, bureaucratic forms), while its presence in the Congo did *not* reside in a specific location or with a single (human) agent. Instead, objects such as white Toyotas, the MSF logo, and identity cards incarnated the organization through "*relationships* between interacting spokespersons and 'spokes-objects' that act and/or speak on [the] organization's behalf" (Cooren et al., 2008, p. 1360; emphasis in original).

Sites

In addition to objects, space also functions as a nonhuman agent that speaks on behalf of organizational actors, as Cooren, Fairhurst, and Huët (2012) showed in a study of remodeling a physical location for future business transactions. The building manager served as a "ventriloquist" to speak for the tech room and its physical constraints as human actors envisioned the renovation.

Sites, then, are physical spaces, locations, or the materiality of place. Typically, discourse scholars have treated site as a cultural artifact by segmenting text from context and focusing on its symbolic meaning (Keenoy & Oswick, 2003). Specifically, studies that examine the front and back stages of organizational life (Friedman, 1994), architectural forms or the organization of physical space as cultural landscapes (Gagliardi, 1990), physicality as the aesthetics of organizations (Linstead & Hopfl, 2000), and the division of space as a form of organizational control (Collinson, 1988) provide only a partial view of the relationship between discourse and space.

Moreover, physical spaces are often treated as boundaries or containers in which actions and interactions occur. This practice privileges interaction by reducing space to a backdrop or a container. Yet space is not "simply a flat, pre-existing context for social action" (Halford, 2008, p. 938); rather, it shapes and is shaped by social action. Space, then, needs to be examined through the affordances that it provides, the ways that the social and the material are mutually implicated, and the interconnections of meanings worked out through these entanglements (Burrell & Dale, 2003; Dale & Burrell, 2008).

Research that embraces a reflexive relationship among space, discourse, and social action illustrates how it is difficult to label what is *social* and what is *material*. For example, Dale's (2005) study of a private utility company demonstrated how organizational control over a given space became interwoven with the spatial politics of privatization, reconfiguring workspaces, and dismissing employees. In a study of identity work, Kuhn (2006) showed how two separate locales produced contrasting sets of discursive resources for organization members' time commitments. Similarly, in a study of the British National Health Service, Halford and Leonard (2006) found that specific locales triggered gendered discourses through a repertoire of place-based meanings and organizational practices that shaped doctor and nurse subjectivities. Also drawing on gender discourses, Bryant and Jaworski (2011) observed that the putative use of assessments such as *skill shortages* that characterized the Australian mining, food, and beverage industries stemmed from the gendering of place, work, and organization. In these studies, the physicality of site becomes interwoven with discourse practices, repertoires of meanings, and organizational actions.

Bodies

Gendered discourses and materiality are featured prominently in the research on embodied practices. Organizations, in this view, are socially constructed through and with the body, its practices, and its struggles; hence, the discursive, symbolic, and material are mutually constitutive. Scholarship in this area examines how bodies materialize in discursive struggles of gendered workplace practices (Butler, 1993; Wolkowitz, 2006). Research focuses on the human body and the role of embodiment in three types of discourses: (1) safety and risk, (2) professionalism and embodied practice, and (3) the disciplining of the entrepreneurial body (Trethewey, Scott, & LeGreco, 2006).

Early research on the body at work focused on health, safety, and security, specifically the struggle to protect the body through dangerous use of machinery, equipment, and bodily risk (Levenstein & Wooding, 1997). This work typically presumed a universal, disembodied worker rather than recursive interactions that constituted body, objects, and safety (Wolkowitz, 2006). Recent studies in this area, however, focus on bodies and feelings of insecurities, such as bodily stress in a hypercompetitive, changing marketplace (Collinson, 2003).

Discourses of occupations, professionalism, and embodied practices examined the body politics of professionalism. Research on the social construction of physical work, while yielding classifications of people in occupations, often glossed embodied experiences and the symbolism of the body. Specifically, studies of dirty work, sex work, and gendered occupations highlighted typifications of the body rather than embodied experiences. The outcome for gender was a "glass slipper" effect, "which not only extended (dis)advantage to the occupation as a whole, but also (dis)advantages [to] those who [could](not) embody figurative social identities" (Ashcraft, 2013, p. 20).

For example, Grint (2010) depicted organizational leaders as *THWAMPs* or tall, handsome, white, alpha males of privilege. Moreover, Sinclair (2005) acknowledged a similar bias in her study of female leaders whose raced and gendered bodies positioned them "on the edge of legitimacy" (p. 403), as did Ashcraft and Allen (2003), who asserted that "real" jobs (for senior leaders) were not just figuratively white, but also literally so. Tracy and Scott (2006), however, offered a notable exception in their study of constituting masculine identities through gendered practices among firefighters and corrections officers.

Research on the discourses of professionalism departs from this pattern through examining the interplay of material, symbolic, and political dimensions. Studies on the body politics of professional women (including the aging female body) demonstrated how professional, gendered, and/or age-based discourses inscribed themselves on women's bodies as texts to be read and identities to be shaped (Ainsworth, 2002; Trethewey, 1999, 2000, 2001). Relatedly, there are discourses of entrepreneurialism in which professional employees treated their bodies as "projects" to be developed through consumption (e.g., popular press books on success; Nadesan & Trethewey, 2000) or as discursive practices to discipline and commodify. In particular, Trethewey (1999) showed how women disciplined themselves to achieve a fit body and to minimize the leakages (e.g., tears or blood) or protrusions (e.g., through pregnancy) associated with the female body or, in the case of menopause, leaving them open to subtle practices that defined normalcy of the body (Putnam & Bochantin, 2009).

Historically, studies of the body at work have privileged the ideational over the material features of the body. The body, however, is constitutively entangled in the ways that it shapes work while organizations shape the body (Wolkowitz, 2006). Research on embodied practices captures the mutually constitutive nature of gendered identities, as Ashcraft et al. (2009) nicely summarize, "[I]deas materialize in bodies in un/expected ways; ideas take root or shift in response to bodily resistance; and bodies are experientially and literally altered" (p. 34).

Methodologies for examining the mutually constituted nature of discourse and materiality have become sophisticated, both in data collection and analysis. Techniques such as shadowing and video ethnography make it possible to capture streams of ongoing actions in which objects, sites, and bodies play a critical role in the plenum of agencies. *Shadowing* is a data-collection method that involves following actors and video recording streams of actions and interactions and is aimed at examining how human and nonhuman actors become entangled in events (Czarniawska, 2007; McDonald, 2005; Vasquez & Cooren, 2013). Similarly, video ethnography situates the camera as a participant observer to record human interactions in ways that capture nonverbal behaviors, spatial relations, use of objects, and location in space. Importantly, researchers often employ multiple methods, including thematic and contextual interviews, focus groups, and archival analysis, in addition to participant observation to collect data. Scholars often adopt multiple theoretical lenses that allow them to place different constructs in the foreground and background and to choose different angles for observation (Nicolini, 2009).

Critique of Mutual Constitution

From a perspective of mutual constitution, neither discourse nor the material should be prioritized; they form a dialectic that can be transcended by considering their interpenetration and how they gain meaning *only* in relation to one another. In many ways though, researchers are just beginning to understand the agentic properties of objects, bodies, and sites. The study of place and space, for example, is profoundly undertheorized (Halford, 2008), and while studies of the body at work are certainly on the rise, they remain within the domains of occupational, feminist, and safety/health investigations (Ashcraft et al., 2009).

Likewise, the study of objects, especially among discourse scholars, remains the focus of technology scholars or researchers in the Montréal School who study the interface between human and nonhuman agents. Yet researchers often have difficulty getting past the role of humans as the prototype for understanding objects, so they continue to prioritize the symbolic realm and/or embrace a materialist agenda by cherry-picking physical influences as special cases. The problem with this stance is that "it loses sight of how *every* organizational practice is *always* bound with materiality" (Orlikowski, 2007, p. 1436).

A possible alternative to privileging either the human or the material lies with Suchman's (2007, pp. 269–270) argument that *mutuality* is not necessarily *symmetry*. She suggests that a *durable dissymmetry* must be interrogated for the culturally and historically constituted differences among human and nonhuman agents in ways that do not privilege either one. Suchman (2007) recommends that scholars focus on the translations from the ideational to the material, where other actors "for whom technologies act as delegates, translators, mediators" (e.g., human engineers, designers, and users) lie just offstage (p. 270). Cooren (2008) goes a step further with his work on *ventriloquism*, which captures the translational role from an object's constraints and affordances. Interrogating the processes of translation between the symbolic and the material may be the durably dissymmetrical stance that is needed to develop a mutually constitutive material agency without diminishing the role of humans and their capacities to create meaning.

Conclusions and Contributions

Organizational discourse research is clearly an interdisciplinary enterprise that has mushroomed in the past decade. Communication scholars have played a pivotal role in the growth and development of this area. As this review suggests, scholars continue to investigate what discourse is doing, how it is doing it, and what the complex systems of meaning linked to it are. In the past decade, however, this work has taken some new turns, namely, integrating discourse patterns with social and historical practices, focusing on the transport of texts across time and space, analyzing tensions between order and disorder, and investigating dialogic models through the poetics of experience.

Clearly, the most dramatic turn in organizational discourse analysis is the focus on materiality, especially the ways that discourse and the material mutually constitute each other in routine organizational practices. Moving away from the ontology of critical realists, scholars are exploring new ways to conceive of materiality, particularly as a mode of articulation that operates just out of reach; as hybrid agencies; as constitutive entanglements between the material and the discursive; and as objects, sites, and bodies that become intertwined in reflexive and discursive actions. Finding a way to avoid using humans as a prototype for examining the material continues to be a challenge in this research.

In the past decade, communication scholars have played a significant role in this interdisciplinary pursuit. In particular, they have developed an array of theoretical perspectives grounded in the role of language, action, and interaction in constituting the organization (McPhee & Zaug, 2000; Taylor & Van Every, 2000). In the area of socio-materiality, they have grounded discourse in action, examined the imbrication of texts in practices, and explored the ways that materiality presents and translates the mutual constitutive relationships between the ideational and the material.

The future of this work hinges on examining processes in which discourse and the material come together, such as how organizing occurs across time and space and how interpenetration becomes a way to scale up and down, that is, to span levels of analysis. To illustrate, Vasquez and Cooren (2013) examine space as an ongoing process of multiple and heterogeneous socio-material interrelations. They focus on how the organization is transported to make it materially present in distributed actors and practices across space and time and to interpenetrate the local and the global. Hence, researchers need to focus on the role of communication in instantiating materiality and in interpenetrating macro acting and micro organizing. Overall, scholars can now employ sophisticated modes of data collection and analysis to capture the interpenetration of the material and the social.

In doing so, discourse studies need to create a shared space for research grounded in different traditions and to encourage cross-pollination among them. Scholars might share a focus on big problems or dilemmas using multiple methods and theoretical traditions to promote these conversations. Researchers can draw on the insights of past scholarship and cross-pollination across traditions to concentrate on the structural and material bases that serve as the indispensable guide to the constitution of society and its institutions.

References

Ainsworth, S. (2002). The feminine advantage: A discursive analysis of the invisibility of older women workers. *Gender, Work and Organization, 9*(5), 579–601.

Al-Amoudi, I., & Willmott, H. (2011). Where constructionism and critical realism converge: Interrogating the domain of epistemological relativism. *Organization Studies, 32*(1), 27–46.

Alvesson, M., & Kärreman, D. (2000). Varieties of discourse: On the study of organizations through discourse analysis. *Human Relations, 53*(9), 1125–1149.

Alvesson, M., & Kärreman, D. (2011). Decolonializing discourse: Critical reflections on organizational discourse analysis. *Human Relations, 64*(9), 1121–1146.

Aritz, J., & Walker, R. C. (Eds.). (2012). *Discourse perspectives on organizational communication.* Plymouth, UK: Rowan & Littlefield/Fairleigh Dickinson University Press.

Ashcraft, K. L. (2007). Appreciating the "work" of discourse: Occupational identity and difference as organizing mechanisms in the case of commercial airline pilots. *Discourse & Communication, 1*(1), 9–36.

Ashcraft, K. L. (2013). The glass slipper: "Incorporating" occupational identity in management studies. *Academy of Management Review, 38*(1), 6–31.

Ashcraft, K. L., & Allen, B. J. (2003). The racial foundation of organizational communication. *Communication Theory, 13*(1), 5–38.

Ashcraft, K. L., Kuhn, T., & Cooren, F. (2009). Constitutional amendments: "Materializing" organizational communication. *The Academy of Management Annals, 3*(1), 1–64.

Ashcraft, K. L., & Mumby, D. K. (2004). *Reworking gender: A feminist communicology of organizations.* Thousand Oaks, CA: SAGE.

Axley, S. R. (1984). Managerial and organizational communication in terms of the conduit metaphor. *Academy of Management Review, 9*(3), 428–437.

Bakhtin, M. (1981). *The dialogical imagination.* Austin: University of Texas Press.

Barad, K. (2003). Posthumanist performativity: Toward an understanding of how matter comes to matter. *Signs, 28*(3), 801–831.

Barge, J. K. (2001). Practical theory as mapping, engaged reflection, and transformative practice. *Communication Theory, 11*(1), 5–13.

Barge, J. K. (2004a). Antenarrative and managerial practice. *Communication Studies, 55*(1), 106–127.

Barge, J. K. (2004b). Reflexivity and managerial practice. *Communication Monographs, 71*(1), 70–96.

Barge, J. K. (2007). The practice of systemic leadership. *OD Practitioner, 39*(1), 10–14.

Barge, J. K., & Fairhurst, G. T. (2008). Living leadership: A systemic, constructionist approach. *Leadership, 4*(3), 227–251.

Barge, J. K., & Little, M. (2002). Dialogical wisdom, communicative practice, and organizational life. *Communication Theory, 12*(4), 375–397.

Barge, J. K., & Oliver, C. (2003). Working with appreciation in managerial practice. *Academy of Management Review, 28*(1), 124–142.

Bargiela-Chiappini, F. (2009). *The handbook of business discourse.* Edinburgh, Scotland: Edinburgh University Press.

Bargiela-Chiappini, F. (2011). Discourse(s), social construction and language practices: In conversation with Alvesson and Kärreman. *Human Relations, 64*(9), 1177–1191.

Barker, J. (2008). Directions for thought leadership in discourse and communication: A commentary on Jian et al. *Discourse & Communication, 2*(3), 333–337.

Baxter, L. A., & Montgomery, B. M. (1996). *Relating: Dialogues & dialectics.* New York, NY: Guildford Press.

Berger, P., & Luckman, T. L. (1966). *The social construction of knowledge: A treatise on the sociology of knowledge.* Garden City, NY: Doubleday.

Bhaskar, R. (1986). *Scientific realism and human emancipation.* London, England: Verso.

Bhaskar, R., & Laclau, E. (2002). Critical realism and discourse theory: Debate with Ernesto Laclau. In R. Bhaskar (Eds.), *From science to emancipation: Alienation and the actuality of enlightenment.* London, England: SAGE.

Billig, M. (2008). The language of critical discourse analysis: The case of nominalization. *Discourse & Society, 19*(6), 783–800.

Boden, D. (1994). *The business of talk: Organizations in action*. Cambridge, UK: Polity.

Broadfoot, K., Deetz, S., & Anderson, D. (2004). Multi-levelled, multi-method approaches in organizational discourse. In D. Grant, C. Hardy, C. Oswick, & L. Putnam (Eds.), *The SAGE handbook of organizational discourse* (pp. 193–211). London, England: SAGE.

Browning, L., & Morris, G. H. (2012). *Stories of life in the workplace: An open architecture for organizational narratology*. London, England: Routledge/Taylor & Francis.

Brummans, B. H., Putnam, L. L., Gray, B., Hanke, R., Lewicki, R. J., & Wiethoff, C. (2008). Making sense of intractable multiparty conflict: A study of framing in four environmental disputes. *Communication Monographs, 75*(1), 25–51.

Bryant, L., & Jaworski, K. (2011). Gender, embodiment and place: The gendering of skill shortages in the Australian mining and food and beverage processing industries. *Human Relations, 64*(10), 1345–1367.

Burrell, G., & Dale, K. (2003). Building better worlds: Architecture and critical management studies. In M. Alvesson & H. Willmott (Eds.), *Studying management critically* (pp. 177–196). London, England: SAGE.

Burrell, J. (2012). The materiality of rumor. In P. Leonardi, B. Nardi, & J. Kallinikos (Eds.), *Materiality and organizing: Social interaction in a technological world* (pp. 315–331). Oxford, UK: Oxford University Press.

Butler, J. (1993). *Bodies that matter: On the discursive limits of "sex."* New York, NY: Routledge.

Butler, J. A., & Modaff, D. P. (2008). When work is home: Agency, structure, and contradictions. *Management Communication Quarterly, 22*(2), 232–257.

Callon, M., & Latour, B. (1981). Unscrewing the big leviathan: How actors macrostructure reality and how sociologists help them to do so. In K. D. Knorr-Cetina & A. V. Cicourel (Eds.), *Advances in social theory and methodology: Toward an integration of micro- and macro-sociologies* (pp. 277–303). Boston, MA: Routledge and Kegan Paul.

Carroll, L. A., & Arneson, P. (2003). Communication in a shared governance hospital: Managing emergent paradoxes. *Communication Studies, 54*(1), 35–55.

Cederström, C., & Spicer, A. (2013). Discourse of the real kind: A post-foundational approach to organizational discourse analysis. *Organization, 20*(4). doi: 10.1177/1350508412473864

Cheney, G., & Christensen, L. T. (2001). Organizational identity: Linkages between internal and external communication. In L. L. Putnam & F. M. Jablin (Eds.), *The new handbook of organizational communication* (pp. 231–269). Thousand Oaks, CA: SAGE.

Cheney, G., Christensen, L. T., Conrad, C., & Lair, D. J. (2004). Corporate rhetoric as organizational discourse. In D. Grant, C. Hardy, C. Oswick, & L. Putnam (Eds.), *The SAGE handbook of organizational discourse* (pp. 70–103). London, England: SAGE.

Cheney, G., & Cloud, D. L. (2006). Doing democracy, engaging the material. *Management Communication Quarterly, 19*(4), 501–540.

Chia, R. (1995). From modern to postmodern organizational analysis. *Organization Studies, 16*(4), 579–604.

Chia, R. (2000). Discourse analysis as organizational analysis. *Organization, 7*(3), 513–518.

Chia, R. (2003). Ontology: Organization as "world-making." In R. Westwood & S. Clegg (Eds.), *Debating organization: Point-counterpoint in organization studies* (pp. 98–113). Malden, MA: Blackwell.

Chouliaraki, L., & Fairclough, N. (2010). Critical discourse analysis in organizational studies: Towards an integrationist methodology. *Journal of Management Studies, 47*(6), 1213–1218.

Christensen, L. T., & Cornelissen, J. (2011). Bridging corporate and organizational communication: Review, development and a look to the future. *Management Communication Quarterly, 25*(3), 383–414.

Clegg, S. R., Kornberger, M., & Rhodes, C. (2005). Learning/becoming/organizing. *Organization, 12*(2), 147–167.

Cloud, D. L. (2001). Laboring under the sign of the new: Cultural studies, organizational communication, and the fallacy of the new economy. *Management Communication Quarterly, 15*(2), 268–278.

Cloud, D. L. (2005). Fighting words: Labor and limits of communication at Staley, 1993 to 1996. *Management Communication Quarterly, 18*(4), 509–542.

Collinson, D. L. (1988). "Engineering humour": Masculinity, joking, and conflict in shop-floor relations. *Organization Studies, 9*(2), 181–199.

Collinson, D. L. (2003). Identities and insecurities: Selves at work. *Organization, 10*(3), 527–547.

Conrad, C. (2004). Organizational discourse analysis: Avoiding the determinism-volunteerism trap. *Organization, 11*(3), 427–439.

Conrad, C. (2011). *Organizational rhetoric.* London, England: Polity Press.

Contu, A., & Willmott, H. (2005). You spin me round: The realist turn in organization and management studies. *Journal of Management Studies, 42*(8), 1645–1662.

Cook, S. D. N., & Brown, J. S. (1999). Bridging epistemologies: The generative dance between organizational knowledge and organizational knowing. *Organization Science, 10*(4), 381–400.

Cooren, F. (2000). *The organizing property of communication.* Amsterdam, the Netherlands: John Benjamins.

Cooren, F. (2004). Textual agency: How texts do things in organizational settings. *Organization, 11*(3), 373–393.

Cooren, F. (2006). The organizational world as a plenum of agencies. In F. Cooren, J. R. Taylor, & E. J. V. Every (Eds.), *Communication as organizing: Empirical and theoretical explorations in the dynamic of text and conversation* (pp. 81–100). Mahwah, NJ: Lawrence Erlbaum.

Cooren, F. (Ed.). (2007). *Interacting and organizing: Analyses of a board meeting.* Mahwah, NJ: Lawrence Erlbaum.

Cooren, F. (2008). The selection of agency as a rhetorical device: Opening up the scene of dialogue through ventriloquism. In E. Weigand (Eds.), *Dialogue and rhetoric* (pp. 22–37). Amsterdam, the Netherlands: John Benjamins.

Cooren, F., Brummans, B., & Charrieras, D. (2008). The coproduction of organizational presence: A study of Médecins Sans Frontières in the Democratic Republic of Congo in action. *Human Relations, 61*(10), 1339–1370.

Cooren, F., & Fairhurst, G. (2004). Speech timing and spacing: The phenomenon of organizational closure. *Organization, 11*(6), 797–828.

Cooren, F., Fairhurst, G. T., & Huët, R. (2012). Why matter always matters in organizational communication. In P. Leonardi, B. Nardi, & J. Kallinikos (Eds.), *Materiality and organizing: Social interaction in a technological world* (pp. 296–314). Oxford, UK: Oxford University Press.

Cooren, F., & Taylor, J. R. (1997). Organization as an effect of mediation: Redefining the link between organization and communication. *Communication Theory, 7*(3), 219–260.

Craig, R. T., & Tracy, K. (1995). Grounded practical theory: The case of intellectual discussion. *Communication Theory, 5*(3), 248–272.

Cunliffe, A. L. (2002). Social poetics as management inquiry: A dialogical approach. *Journal of Management Inquiry, 11*(2), 128–146.

Cunliffe, A. L. (2004). On becoming a critically reflexive practitioner. *Journal of Management Education, 28*(4), 407–426.

Czarniawska, B. (2007). *Shadowing and other techniques for doing fieldwork in modern societies.* Malmo, Sweden: Liber.

Dale, K. (2005). Building a social materiality: Spatial and embodied politics in organizational control. *Organization, 12*(5), 649–678.

Dale, K., & Burrell, G. (2008). *Spaces of organization and the organization of space: Power, identity and materiality at work.* London, England: Palgrave Macmillan.

Deetz, S. A. (1992). *Democracy in an age of corporate colonization: Developments in communication and the politics of everyday life.* New York: State University of New York Press.

Deetz, S. A., & Mumby, D. (1990). Power, discourse, and the workplace: Reclaiming the critical tradition. In J. Anderson (Eds.), *Communication yearbook* (vol. 13, pp. 18–47). Newbury Park, CA: SAGE.

Derrida, J. (1988). *Limited Inc.* Evanston, IL: Northwestern University Press.

Erkama, N., & Vaara, E. (2010). Struggles over legitimacy in global organizational restructuring: A rhetorical perspective on legitimation strategies and dynamics in a shutdown case. *Organization Studies, 31*(7), 813–839.

Fairclough, N. (1995). *Critical discourse analysis: The critical study of language.* London, England: Longman.

Fairclough, N. (2001). *Language and power.* London, England: Longman.

Fairclough, N. (2003). *Analysing discourse: Textual analysis for social research.* London, England: Routledge.

Fairclough, N. (2005). Peripheral vision: Discourse analysis in organization studies: The case for critical realism. *Organization Studies, 26*(6), 915–939.

Fairclough, N. (2006). *Language and globalization.* New York, NY: Routledge.

Fairclough, N., & Thomas, P. (2004). The discourse of globalization and the globalization of discourse. In D. Grant, C. Hardy, C. Oswick, & L. Putnam (Eds.), *The SAGE handbook of organizational discourse* (pp. 379–396). London, England: SAGE.

Fairclough, N., & Wodak, R. (1997). Critical discourse analysis. In T. A. Van Dijk (Ed.), *Discourse as social interaction* (pp. 258–284). London, England: SAGE.

Fairhurst, G. T. (2007). *Discursive leadership: In conversation with leadership psychology.* Thousand Oaks, CA: SAGE.

Fairhurst, G. T., Church, M., Hagen, D. E., & Levi, J. T. (2011). Whither female leaders? Executive coaching and the alpha male syndrome. In D. Mumby (Eds.), *Discourses of difference.* Thousand Oaks, CA: SAGE.

Fairhurst, G. T., & Cooren, F. (2004). Organizational language in use: Interaction analysis, conversation analysis, and speech act schematics. In D. Grant, C. Hardy, C. Oswick, & L. Putnam (Eds.), *The SAGE handbook of organizational discourse* (pp. 131–152). London, England: SAGE.

Fairhurst, G. T., & Putnam, L. L. (1998). Reflections on the organization-communication equivalency question: The contributions of James Taylor and his colleagues. *Communication Review, 31*(1/2), 1–19.

Fairhurst, G. T., & Putnam, L. L. (2004). Organizations as discursive constructions. *Communication Theory, 14*(1), 5–26.

Fleetwood, S. (2005). Ontology in organization and management studies: A critical realist perspective. *Organization, 12*(2), 197–222.

Foucault, M. (1980). *Power/knowledge: Selected interviews and other writings 1972–1977.* New York, NY: Pantheon.

Foucault, M. (1995). *Discipline and punish.* New York, NY: Vintage/Random House.

Friedman, R. A. (1994). *Front stage, back stage: The dramatic structure of labor negotiations.* Cambridge, MA: MIT Press.

Gagliardi, P. (1990). *Symbols and artifacts: Views of the corporate landscape.* New York, NY: Aldine de Gruyter.

Garfinkel, H. (1967). *Studies in ethnomethodology.* Englewood Cliffs, NJ: Prentice Hall.

Gergen, K. (2001). *Social construction in context.* London, England: SAGE.

Giddens, A. (1979). *Central problems in social theory.* Berkeley: University of California Press.

Giddens, A. (1984). *The constitution of society.* Berkeley: University of California Press.

Grant, D., Hardy, C., Oswick, C., & Putnam, L. (2004). *The SAGE handbook of organizational discourse.* London, England: SAGE.

Grant, D., Hardy, C., & Putnam, L. L. (Eds.). (2011). *Organizational discourse studies (3 volume set). SAGE major works series.* Los Angeles, CA: SAGE.

Grant, D., & Iedema, R. (2005). Discourse analysis and the study of organizations. *Text: An Interdisciplinary Journal for the Study of Discourse, 25*(1), 37–66.

Grant, D., Keenoy, T., & Oswick, C. (Eds.). (1998). *Discourse + organization.* London, England: SAGE.

Grant, D., Putnam, L. L., & Hardy, C. (2011). History, key challenges, and contributions of organizational discourse studies. In D. Grant, C. Hardy, & L. L. Putnam (Eds.), *Organizational discourse studies* (pp. xvii–xlii). London, England: SAGE.

Green, S. E., Li, Y., & Nohria, N. (2009). Suspended in self-spun webs of significance: A rhetorical model of institutionalization and institutionally embedded agency. *Academy of Management Journal, 52*(1), 11–36.

Grint, K. (2010). *Leadership: A very short introduction.* Oxford, UK: Oxford University Press.

Hacking, I. (1999). *The social construction of what?* Cambridge, MA: Harvard University Press.

Halford, S. (2008). Sociologies of space, work and organization: From fragments to spatial theory. *Sociology Compass, 2*(3), 925–943.

Halford, S., & Leonard, P. (2006). Place, space and time: Contextualizing workplace subjectivities. *Organization Studies, 27*(5), 657–676.

Hardy, C., & Grant, D. (2012). Readers beware: Provocation, problematization and . . . problems. *Human Relations, 65*(5), 547–566.

Hardy, C., & Maguire, S. (2010). Discourse, field-configuring events, and change in organizations and institutional fields: Narratives of DDT and the Stockholm convention. *Academy of Management Journal, 53*(6), 1365–1392.

Hardy, C., Thomas, T. B., & Grant, D. (2005). Discourse and collaboration: The role of conversations and collective identity. *Academy of Management Review, 30*(1), 58–77.

Harter, L., & Krone, K. (2001). The boundary-spanning role of cooperative support organization: Managing the paradox of stability and change in non-traditional organizations. *Journal of Applied Communication Research, 29*(3), 248–277.

Hawes, L. C. (1974). Social collectivities as communication: Perspectives on organizational behavior. *Quarterly Journal of Speech, 60*(4), 497–502.

Heath, R. L. (2011). External organizational rhetoric: Bridging management and sociopolitical discourse. *Management Communication Quarterly, 25*(3), 415–435.

Heracleous, L. (2012). Four proposals toward an interpretive theory of the process of discursive reality construction. In J. Artiz & R. C. Walker (Eds.), *Discourse perspectives on organizational communication* (pp. 9–32). Madison, NJ: Fairleigh Dickinson University Press.

Heracleous, L., & Marshak, R. J. (2004). Conceptualizing organizational discourse as situated symbolic action. *Human Relations, 57*(10), 1285–1312.

Iedema, R. (2011). Discourse studies in the 21st century: A response to Mats Alvesson and Dan Kärreman's "decolonializing discourse." *Human Relations, 64*(9), 1163–1176.

Jameson, J. K. (2004). Negotiating autonomy and connection through politeness: A dialectical approach to organizational conflict management. *Western Journal of Communication, 68*(3), 257–277.

Jian, G. (2007). Omega is a four-letter word: Toward a tension-centered model of resistance to information and communication technologies. *Communication Monographs, 74*(4), 517–540.

Jian, G. (2011). Articulating circumstance, identity and practice: Toward a discursive framework of organizational changing. *Organization, 18*(1), 45–64.

Jian, G., Schmisseur, A., & Fairhurst, G. T. (2008). Organizational discourse and communication: The progeny of Proteus. *Discourse & Communication, 2*(3), 299–320.

Katz, A. M., & Shotter, J. (1996). Hearing the patient's "voice": Toward a social poetics in diagnostic interviews. *Social Science Medicine, 43*(6), 919–931.

Keenoy, T., & Oswick, C. (2003). Organizing textscapes. *Organization Studies, 25*(1), 135–142.

Kellett, P. M. (1999). Dialogue and dialectics in managing organizational change: The case of mission-based transformation. *Southern Communication Journal, 64*(3), 211–231.

Kristeva, J. (1984). *Revolution in poetic language.* New York, NY: Columbia University Press.

Kuhn, T. (2006). A "demented work ethic" and a "lifestyle firm": Discourse, identity, and workplace time commitments. *Organization Studies, 27*(9), 1339–1358.

Laclau, E. (1990). *New reflections on the revolution of our time.* London, England: Verso.

Laclau, E., & Mouffe, C. (1985). *Hegemony and socialist strategy.* London, England: Verso.

Larson, G. L., & Pepper, G. L. (2003). Strategies for managing multiple organizational identifications: A case of competing identities. *Management Communication Quarterly, 16*(4), 528–557.

Latour, B. (1994). On technical mediation: Philosophy, sociology, genealogy. *Common Knowledge, 3*(2), 29–64.

Latour, B. (2005). *Reassembling the social: An introduction to actor-network they.* New York, NY: Oxford University Press.

Latour, B., & Woolgar, S. (1979). *Laboratory life: The social construction of scientific facts.* London, England: SAGE.

Leonardi, P. M. (2008). Indeterminacy and the discourse of inevitability in international technology management. *Academy of Management Review, 33*(4), 975–984.

Leonardi, P. M. (2012). Materiality, sociomateriality, and socio-technical systems: What do these terms mean? How are they different? Do we need them? In P. Leonardi, B. Nardi, & J. Kallinikos (Eds.), *Materiality and organizing: Social interaction in a technological world* (pp. 25–48). Oxford, UK: Oxford University Press.

Leonardi, P. M., & Jackson, M. H. (2004). Technological determinism and discursive closure in organizational mergers. *Journal of Organizational Change Management, 17*(6), 615–631.

Levenstein, C., & Wooding, J. (Eds.). (1997). *Work, health, and environment: Old problems, new solutions.* New York, NY: Guilford.

Lindlof, T. R., & Taylor, B. C. (2011). *Qualitative communication research methods* (3rd ed.). Thousand Oaks, CA: SAGE.

Linstead, S., & Hopfl, H. (Eds.). (2000). *The aesthetics of organizations.* London, England: SAGE.

Martin, D. M. (2004). Humor in middle management: Women negotiating the paradoxes of organizational life. *Journal of Applied Communication Research, 32*(2), 147–170.

McDonald, S. (2005). Studying actions in context: A qualitative shadowing method for organizational research. *Qualitative Research, 5*(4), 455–473.

McPhee, R. D. (2004). Text, agency, and organization in the light of structuration theory. *Organization, 11*(3), 355–371.

McPhee, R. D., & Zaug, P. (2000). The communicative constitution of organizations: A framework for explanation. *The Electronic Journal of Communication, 10,* 1–16.

Medved, C. E., & Kirby, E. (2005). Family CEOs: A feminist analysis of corporate mothering discourses. *Management Communication Quarterly, 18*(4), 435–478.

Meisenbach, R. J., & Feldner, S. B. (2011). Adopting an attitude of wisdom in organizational rhetorical theory and practice: Contemplating the ideal and the real. *Management Communication Quarterly, 25*(3), 560–568.

Mumby, D. K. (1997). The problem of hegemony: Rereading Gramsci for organizational communication studies. *Western Journal of Communication, 61*(4), 343–375.

Mumby, D. K. (2011). What's cooking in organizational discourse studies? A response to Alvesson and Kärreman. *Human Relations, 64*(9), 1147–1161.

Mumby, D. K., & Clair, R. P. (1997). Organizational discourse. In T. A. Van Dijk (Ed.), *Discourse as social interaction* (vol. 2, pp. 181–205). London, England: SAGE.

Nadesan, M., & Trethewey, A. (2000). Performing the enterprise subject: Gendered strategies for success? *Text and Performance Quarterly, 20*(3), 223–250.

Nicolini, D. (2009). Zooming in and out: Studying practices by switching theoretical lenses and trailing connections. *Organizational Studies, 30*(12), 1391–1418.

Orlikowski, W. J. (2000). Using technology and constituting structures. *Organization Science, 11*(4), 404–428.

Orlikowski, W. J. (2007). Sociomaterial practices: Exploring technology at work. *Organization Studies, 28*(9), 1435–1448.

Orlikowski, W. J., & Scott, S. V. (2009). Sociomateriality: Challenging the separation of technology, work and organization. *The Academy of Management Annals, 2*(1), 433–474.

Parker, M. (1992). *Discourse dynamics.* London, England: Routledge.

Pentland, B. T., & Singh, H. (2012). Materiality: What are the consequences? In P. Leonardi, B. Nardi, & J. Kallinikos (Eds.), *Materiality and organizing: Social interaction in a technological world* (pp. 287–295). Oxford, UK: Oxford University Press.

Phillips, L., & Jørgensen, M. W. (2002). *Discourse analysis as theory and method.* London, England: SAGE.

Phillips, N., & Oswick, C. (2012). Organizational discourse: Domains, debates, and directions. *The Academy of Management Annals, 6*(1), 435–481.

Potter, J., & Wetherell, M. (1987). *Discourse and social psychology.* London, England: SAGE.

Prasad, A. (2012). Beyond analytical dichotomies. *Human Relations, 65*(5), 567–595.

Putnam, L. L. (1983). Organizational communication: Toward a research agenda. In L. L. Putnam & M. E. Pacanowsky (Eds.), *Communication and organizations: An interpretive approach* (pp. 31–54). Beverly Hills, CA: SAGE.

Putnam, L. L. (2005). Discourse analysis: Mucking around with negotiation data. *International Negotiation, 10*(1), 17–32.

Putnam, L. L. (2008). Images of the communication-discourse relationship. *Discourse & Communication, 2*(3), 339–345.

Putnam, L. L., & Bochantin, J. (2009). Gendered bodies: Negotiating normalcy and support. *Negotiation and Conflict Management Research, 2*(1), 57–73.

Putnam, L. L., & Fairhurst, G. T. (2001). Discourse analysis in organizations. In F. M. Jablin & L. L. Putnam (Eds.), *The new handbook of organizational communication* (pp. 78–136). Thousand Oaks, CA: SAGE.

Putnam, L. L., & Nicotera, A. (Eds.). (2009a). *Building theories of organization: The constitutive role of communication.* New York, NY: Routledge.

Putnam, L. L., & Nicotera, A. M. (2009b). Introduction: Communication constitutes organization. In L. L. Putnam & A. M. Nicotera (Eds.), *Building theories of organizations: The constitutive role of communication* (pp. 1–19). New York, NY: Routledge.

Putnam, L. L., Phillips, N., & Chapman, P. (1996). Metaphors of communication and organization.

In S. Clegg, C. Hardy, & W. Nord (Eds.), *Handbook of organizational studies* (pp. 375–408). London, England: SAGE.

Real, K., & Putnam, L. L. (2005). Ironies in the discursive struggle of pilots defending the profession. *Management Communication Quarterly, 19*(1), 91–119.

Reed, M. (2000). The limits of discourse analysis in organizational analysis. *Organization, 7*(3), 524–530.

Reed, M. (2004). Getting real about organizational discourse. In D. Grant, C. Hardy, C. Oswick, & L. Putnam (Eds.), *The SAGE handbook of organizational discourse* (pp. 413–420). London, England: SAGE.

Reed, M. (2005). Reflections on the 'realist turn' in organization and management studies. *Journal of Management Studies, 42*(8), 1621–1644.

Ritzer, G., & Goodman, D. (2002). Postmodern social theory. In J. H. Turner (Eds.), *Handbook of sociological theory* (pp. 151–169). New York, NY: Kluwer Academic/Plenum Publishers.

Rorty, R. (Ed.). (1967). *The linguistic turn: Recent essays in philosophical method.* Chicago, IL: University of Chicago Press.

Rudd, G. (2000). The symphony: Organizational discourse and the symbolic tensions between artistic and business ideologies. *Journal of Applied Communication Research, 28*(2), 117–143.

Schatzki, T. R. (2005). The sites of organizations. *Organization Studies, 26*(3), 465–484.

Searle, J. R. (1995). *The construction of social reality.* New York, NY: Free Press.

Sewell, G., Barker, J. R., & Nyberg, D. (2012). Working under intensive surveillance: When does "measuring everything that moves" become intolerable? *Human Relations, 65*(2), 189–215.

Shotter, J. (1996). Living in a Wittgensteinian world: Beyond theory to a poetics of practice. *Journal for the Theory of Social Behavior, 26*(3), 293–311.

Shotter, J., & Cunliffe, A. L. (2003). Managers as practical authors: Everyday conversations for action. In D. Holman & R. Thorpe (Eds.), *Management and language* (pp. 1–37). London, England: SAGE.

Sillince, J. A. A. (1999). The organizational setting, use, and institutionalization of argumentation repertoires. *Journal of Management Studies, 36*(6), 795–831.

Sillince, J. A. A. (2002). A model of the strength and appropriateness of argumentation in organizational contexts. *Journal of Management Studies, 39*(5), 585–618.

Sillince, J. A. A. (2006). Resources and organizational identities: The role of rhetoric in the creation of competitive advantage. *Management Communication Quarterly, 20*(2), 186–212.

Sillince, J. A. A. (2007). Organizational context and the discursive construction of organizing. *Management Communication Quarterly, 20*(4), 363–394.

Sinclair, A. (2005). Body possibilities in leadership. *Leadership, 1*(4), 387–406.

Stohl, C., & Cheney, G. (2001). Participatory processes/Paradoxical practices: Communication and the dilemmas of organizational democracy. *Management Communication Quarterly, 14*(3), 349–407.

Suchman, L. A. (2007). *Human-machine configurations: Plans and situated actions* (2nd ed.). Cambridge, UK: Cambridge University Press.

Suddaby, R., & Greenwood, R. (2005). Rhetorical strategies of legitimacy. *Administrative Science Quarterly, 50*(1), 35–67.

Taylor, J. R. (2008). Communication and discourse: Is the bridge language? Response to Jian et al. *Discourse & Communication, 2*(3), 347–352.

Taylor, J. R., & Van Every, E. (2000). *The emergent organization: Communication at its site and surface.* Mahwah, NJ: Lawrence Erlbaum.

Taylor, J. R., & Van Every, E. (2011). *The situated organization: Case studies in the pragmatics of communication research.* New York, NY: Routledge.

Tracy, S. J. (2004). Dialectic, contradiction, or double bind? Analyzing and theorizing employee reactions to organizational tensions. *Journal of Applied Communication Research, 32*(2), 119–146.

Tracy, S. J., & Scott, C. (2006). Sexuality, masculinity, and taint management among firefighters and correctional officers: Getting down and dirty with "America's heroes" and the "scum of law enforcement." *Management Communication Quarterly, 20*(1), 6–38.

Tracy, S. J., & Trethewey, A. (2005). Fracturing the real-self-fake-self dichotomy: Moving toward 'crystallized' organizational discourses and identities. *Communication Theory, 15*(2), 168–195.

Trethewey, A. (1999). Disciplined bodies: Women's embodied identities at work. *Organization Studies, 20*(3), 423–450.

Trethewey, A. (2000). Revisioning control: A feminist critique of disciplined bodies. In P. Buzzanell

(Ed.), *Rethinking organizational and managerial communication from feminist perspectives* (pp. 107–127). Thousand Oaks, CA: SAGE.

Trethewey, A. (2001). Reproducing and resisting the master narrative of decline. *Management Communication Quarterly, 15*(2), 183–226.

Trethewey, A., & Ashcraft, K. L. (2004). Practicing disorganization: The development of applied perspectives on living with tension. *Journal of Applied Communication Research, 32*(2), 171–181.

Trethewey, A., Scott, C., & LeGreco, M. (2006). Constructing embodied organizational identities. In B. J. Dow & J. T. Wood (Eds.), *SAGE handbook of gender and communication* (pp. 123–141). Thousand Oaks, CA: SAGE.

Tsoukas, H., & Chia, R. (2002). On organizational becoming: Rethinking organizational change. *Organization Science, 13*(5), 567–582.

Vaughn, M., & Stamp, G. H. (2003). The empowerment dilemma: The dialectic of emancipation and control in staff/client interaction at shelters for battered women. *Communication Studies, 54*(2), 154–168.

Vasquez, C., & Cooren, F. (2013). Spacing practices: The communicative configuration of organizing through space-times. *Communication Theory, 23*(1), 25–47.

Weedon, C. (1997). *Feminist practice and poststructuralist theory* (2nd ed.). Oxford, UK: Blackwell.

Weick, K. (1979). *The social psychology of organizing* (2nd ed.). Reading, MA: Addison-Wesley.

Weick, K. (1995). *Sensemaking in organizations.* Thousand Oaks, CA: SAGE.

Weick, K. E., Sutcliffe, K. M., & Obstfeld, D. (2005). Organizing and the process of sensemaking. *Organization Science, 16*(4), 409–421.

Wendt, R. F. (1998). The sound of one hand clapping: Counterintuitive lessons extracted from paradoxes and double binds in participative organizations. *Management Communication Quarterly, 11*(3), 323–371.

Westwood, R., & Linstead, S. (Eds.). (2001). *The language of organization.* London, England: SAGE.

Willmott, H. (2005). Theorizing contemporary control: Some poststructuralist responses to some critical realist questions. *Organization, 12*(5), 95–127.

Wittgenstein, L. (1953). *Philosophical investigations.* Oxford, UK: Blackwell.

Wolkowitz, C. (2006). *Bodies at work.* London, England: SAGE.

Ziegler, J. A. (2007). The story behind an organizational list: A genealogy of wildland firefighters' 10 standard fire orders. *Communication Monographs, 74*(4), 415–442.

Notes

1. Putnam, L. L., & Fairhurst, G. T. (2001). Discourse analysis in organizations: Issues and concerns. In F. M. Jablin & L. L. Putnam (Eds.), *The new handbook of organizational communication: Advances in theory, research, and methods* (pp. 78–136). Thousand Oaks, CA: SAGE.

2. See Putnam and Fairhurst (2001) for a detailed description of these approaches, the research undertaken using them, and a discussion of the implications for studying organizations.

3. This definition can be found in Putnam and Fairhurst (2001, p. 78).

CHAPTER 12

Mixed Methods

When More Really Is More

Karen K. Myers

Mixed-methods research is defined by Johnson, Onwuegbuzie, and Turner (2007) as research in which the investigator "combines elements of qualitative and quantitative approaches (e.g., use of qualitative and quantitative viewpoints, data collection, analysis, inference techniques) for the broad purpose of breadth and depth of understanding and corroboration" (p. 123). This approach to scholarship is being employed increasingly in the social sciences and in the field of organizational communication. Methodologists have noted an energy and excitement surrounding the use of mixed-methods research (Denzin, 2012).

In the past decade, dozens of books, numerous articles, and even a new journal (i.e., *Journal of Mixed Methods Research*) discuss theories related to mixed methodology, issues central to using it, and research reports that demonstrate their value. Creswell and Plano-Clark (2007) argue that at least one reason for the growing popularity of mixed-methods research is that qualitative methods have achieved legitimacy in the social sciences. Funding agencies, such as the National Science Foundation, now conduct workshops designed to instruct researchers in the use of these methods (National Science Foundation, 2004). Indeed, mixed-methods research has been called "*the third major research approach or research paradigm*" (Johnson et al., 2007, p. 112).

Interest in mixed methods dates back to the 1950s, when Campbell and Fiske (1959) recommended that scholars collect multiple forms of data to enable them to triangulate research findings. Campbell and Fiske proposed a multitrait-multimethod matrix (MTMM), a quantitative method for assessing construct-related validity of quantitative instruments. Their method afforded researchers the ability to examine patterns of association between constructs and potential interactions between methods used to assess those constructs. However, MTMM was not a direct call for mixed methods, because the methods that Campbell and Fiske proposed involved only quantitative methodology.

The term *multimethod* is often used interchangeably with mixed methods (Brewer & Hunter, 2006). However, this interchange is a misnomer, since most researchers agree that multimethod actually means using more than one method to collect data, rather than mixing quantitative and qualitative methods of data collection and analysis. Some scholars use other criteria to distinguish mixed methods from other methodologies. For example, Bazeley and Kemp (2012) described mixed-methods research: "[At] a minimum there must be interdependence of component approaches *during the analytic writing process* (i.e., as results *are being formulated* for [presentation]) and, usually, well before that stage" (p. 69, emphasis in original). Although multimethod research is valuable, this chapter focuses on mixed-methods research because of the new opportunities it brings to organizational communication studies.

Mixed methods research became a distinctive approach to empirical investigation in the 1980s and 1990s. Articles by Greene and McClintock (Greene & McClintock, 1985; McClintock & Greene, 1985) and Creswell (1994) in the field of education, by Bryman (1988) in management, and by Morse (1991) in both nursing and anthropology initiated discussions on the value and use of mixed-methods research. In 2003, Tashakkori and Teddlie edited the first edition of the *SAGE Handbook of Mixed Methods in Social & Behavioral Research* (a second edition was published in 2009). In 2007, editors Tashakkori and Creswell, together with Plano-Clark as managing editor and Bazeley as associate editor, launched the *Journal of Mixed Methods Research*. The journal has the following aim:

> to be an impetus for creating bridges between mixed methods scholars, a platform for debate and discourse about important issues in mixed methods research, and a forum for sharing ideas across disciplines, across philosophical and methodological boundaries, and among different cultures around the world. (Tashakkori & Creswell, 2007, p. 3)

This chapter discusses issues, obstacles, and opportunities for mixed-methods research in the field of organizational communication. When possible, exemplars of mixed-methods studies from organizational communication frame those discussions. However, mixed-methods studies remain relatively rare in the field of organizational communication. Locating them is challenging, because the term *mixed-methods* research is rarely used to describe the work. To find mixed-methods studies, I have examined methods sections and descriptions of data analyses and scanned communication journals that span the last four decades. This list of studies, however, may not be comprehensive or inclusive of all research in the field that fit this definition.

The chapter begins with an overview of mixed-methods research, followed by a discussion of data integration in mixed-methods designs and mixed methods use in organizational communication. Next, the chapter reviews three primary perspectives that thrive in contemporary organizational communication research. This section focuses on the characteristics and values of quantitative and qualitative research, ones traditionally associated with the various philosophies. More broadly, it examines how combining methods and interrogating organizational phenomenon can lead to stronger inferences than would be possible from single method research. Next, the chapter reviews several typologies that can be applied to mixed-methods research and introduces four primary mixed-method designs. For each design, I discuss its relative usefulness and review a mixed-method study conducted in the field that used that design. The final portion of the chapter focuses on a discussion of two questions related to mixed-methods use in organizational communication: Why are so few mixed-methods studies conducted in organizational communication? What unique opportunities are available to researchers who adopt a mixed-methods approach?

Defining and Situating Mixed-Methods Research

Social scientists are attracted to this *hybrid approach* (Creswell & Plano-Clark, 2007), because it uses more lenses to interrogate a phenomenon and provides a more comprehensive understanding of it than one method alone can do (Erzberger & Kelle, 2003). Hence, mixed-method studies typically include multiple hypotheses or research questions and often both of them. This combination is important, because mixed-methods research does not mean simply gathering and analyzing both quantitative and qualitative data. Rather, it requires that the data be interrelated or *integrated* so that they can work together to respond to research questions and yield insights that could not be achieved without these comparisons. Beyond deploying different approaches, mixed-methods research also embraces different philosophical assumptions that guide investigations (Van Maanen, 1990). Ideally, mixed-methods researchers use methodological eclecticism to invoke different epistemological paradigms (Morgan, 2007). Teddlie and Tashakkori (2009) suggest that "a researcher employing methodological eclecticism is a connoisseur of methods, who knowledgeably (and often intuitively) selects the best techniques available to answer research questions that frequently evolve as a study unfolds" (p. 8).

Mixed-methods research has become prevalent in disciplines outside of communication and in areas other than organizational research (e.g., Arnault & Fetters, 2011; Van Ness, Fried, & Gill, 2011). When used by organizational researchers, most investigations have been outside the discipline of communication (e. g., Feilzer, 2007; Vitale, Armenakis, & Field, 2008; Wesely, 2010). While still not extensive, interest in mixed-methods designs among organizational communication scholars has increased in recent years (Myers, 2011).

One of the first calls for using mixed-methods research in organizational communication came from Faules (1982), who urged scholars to examine performance appraisals through mixed-methods designs. He recommended that investigators employ surveys, given their widespread use and acceptance, but suggested that they combine surveys with other data collection methods to generate greater understanding. Faules demonstrated this approach in a study conducted with the Center for Public Affairs and Administration in which he promised that the data from a survey would be available to the university. As part of the project, he collected organizational narratives to identify feelings, values, and images that were commonly held among organizational members. His analysis consisted of exploring convergence and divergence in the quantitative and qualitative data. When Faules presented the two data sets to organizational members, he found they were interested in findings from the survey data, but "[d]iscussion about the story analysis represented 90% of their responses" (Faules, 1982, p. 160). The interview data helped the Center's members gain a better understanding of the participants' attitudes and concerns. He concluded by arguing that human behavior is complex and that using only one means to assess that behavior often is inadequate and may yield "more confusion than help" (p. 161).

Data integration in mixed-methods research often requires extra effort but also offers many advantages (Bryman, 2007). Fielding (2012) argues that integration is the essence of mixed methods "because the purpose of mixing methods is to get information from multiple sources" and so how to bring them together is crucial (p. 127). The point is not *what* types of data are used or *when* they are used but *how* various types of data are integrated and for *what purpose*. Generally, integrating data in a mixed-method study is useful for three purposes. First, scholars are drawn to use mixed methods because integrating two or more types of data can demonstrate *convergence*. When data converge, the findings point to the same or very similar conclusions. Because different methods can be affected by different types of measurement error, mixed data that converge are more likely to demonstrate validity than do data collected by a single method. Second, integrating data helps to *illustrate* findings in a better way than does the use of a single method. Qualitative data can bring added life to statistics. Specifically, participant narratives can bring meaning to quantitative data. Alternatively, statistical data can demonstrate concreteness and provide distinctness to the large quantities of data that are common in qualitative research. Third, mixing methods provides *analytic density*. Simply said, using different types of data that were collected from the use of varied methods provides a deep, complex view of the phenomena (Shih, 1998). Such thoroughness can result in definitive findings and implications.

With these potential advantages to data integration, why is it that more organizational scholars do not employ mixed-method studies? The next section addresses this question and explores the paradigms and perspectives that guide research in the field. This section also proposes how these views influence not only how research is conducted but also the ideas and intentions of individual scholars as they conceptualize meaningful investigations. Importantly, I contend that research perspectives influence the goals and assumptions that guide investigators in the designs of their studies. It is these goals and assumptions that lead researchers to choose methods that are commonly associated with a particular perspective.

Paradigms and Perspectives in Mixed-Methods Research

This section presents an overview of three foundational paradigms or perspectives used in organizational communication. I use the term *perspective* to denote a personal viewpoint but also to increase receptiveness to views that others hold. Regardless of the term used, *paradigm* or *perspective*, perspectives can guide the questions that scholars use and the research designs that they develop. Even though the boundaries between perspectives often blur, they continue to influence scholars' objectives and thereby affect their methodological choices. This section addresses the choice between quantitative and qualitative methods and links this choice to a scholar's values and goals for conducting research. Finally, I overview the perspectives, but in doing so, I acknowledge how the boundaries between them are becoming blurred.

Different Goals, Processes, and Data

Traditionally, organizational communicational scholars have conducted their research in either quantitative or qualitative methods. Maxwell (2010) argues that today's reliance on either quantitative or qualitative methods arises from different philosophies or paradigms rather than a preference for using number or texts. His argument is compelling, because most contemporary organizational communication scholars commonly read and appreciate the value of quantitative *and* qualitative studies. Thus the intrinsic value of the data does not appear to be the reason that quantitative researchers do not design studies using qualitative methods or why qualitative methodologists rarely collect quantitative data. Instead, the foundational reason that many scholars rarely venture outside their traditional mode of conducting research is likely related to their preferred ontologies.

Traditionally, methods have been linked to paradigms. Morgan (2007) defines *paradigms* as "shared beliefs within a community of researchers who share a consensus about which questions are most meaningful and which *procedures* are most appropriate for answering those questions" (p. 53, emphasis added). Although a number of contemporary organizational communication scholars do not feel confined by paradigms (Miller, 2000), their perspectives clearly shape their vantage point for viewing the world. This pattern affects scholarship in two interrelated ways. First, most scholars conceptualize studies in accordance with their dominant paradigm or *worldview*. This practice may not be a conscious choice, but it results from training and/or habitual ways of conceiving research and viewing the world. Second, scholars develop ideas and plans for research with particular objectives in mind. Some researchers conceptualize studies with a goal to examine variance and relationships between relevant constructs. They achieve their goals when they are able to generalize findings to a large population. Scholars in the second perspective are driven by a curiosity about meanings that stems from interactions, experiences, and events. Their purpose is to gain an understanding of a phenomenon that their participants share. For them, meaningful insights accrue from gleaning participants' viewpoints. Scholars with a third perspective are driven by concerns for power imbalances. They aim to uncover systems and structures that marginalize or disadvantage some individuals.

Perspectives also are also linked to methodological approaches or to the patterns of reasoning involved in conducting research. Using deductive reasoning, the researcher starts with broad theory, moves to testable hypotheses, and follows with data collection and analyses to confirm or disconfirm initial theorizing (Babbie, 2009). Inductive reasoning moves in the opposite direction, beginning with data, progressing to data analysis, and ending with general theorizing derived from the data (Babbie, 2009). A third and less commonly discussed approach is abductive reasoning. In using abductive reasoning, researchers move back and forth between the data and theory to better understand the data (Morgan, 2007). For example, the researcher may begin with induction by examining data and then move to deduction by drawing on theory to better understand data. The process does not end at theory development because abduction requires action; hence, researchers return to the data once again to bring additional theoretical insights to the study (Morgan, 2007, p. 71). The back-and-forth examination enables researchers to be thoughtful about the data gathered within one worldview but to analyze and interpret it with another perspective. These approaches are commonly linked to different perspectives.

In organizational communication, three perspectives are most evident: post-positive, interpretive, and critical. Next, I review each perspective and the methods commonly associated with it. This review sets the stage for a discussion about the ways that methods, similar to perspectives, can be combined in research and how a pragmatic perspective fosters mixed-methods investigations.

Post-positivist

Much of the early research in organizational communication fit the post-positivist paradigm (e. g., Eisenberg, Monge, & Farace, 1984; Fairhurst, Green, & Snavely, 1984; Infante & Gordon, 1985; Jablin, 1980; Spiker & Daniels, 1981; Sypher & Zorn, 1986). These studies, modeled after the long tradition of natural science (Kuhn, 1962), use deductive reasoning and aim for testable, explanatory theories. Emerging from these foundations, post-positive research uses primarily quantitative methods. Values such as skepticism, objectivity, reliability, validity, and replicability are foundational (Babbie, 2009). Social scientists conduct research to detect patterns of behavior. Their primary goal is generalizability; thus they commonly employ quantitative methods that include large samples and surveys and, at times, observation to assess the widespread nature of their findings (Miller, 2000). Unlike the research in many other disciplines and in other areas of communication, lab and field experiments are not common in organizational communication. Instead, post-positive research typically involves survey or other field methods (see Doerfel & Gibbs, Chapter 9, for more detail of field methods).

As with other approaches, quantitative methods that are frequently used in the post-positivist tradition have several limitations. In particular, they rely on large samples to generalize their findings, which may cause researchers to ignore contextual nuances that affect the data (Levine, 2011). Researchers assess cause-and-effect relationships by measuring variables through validated instruments that effectively measure a construct in a given context and may not generalize across contexts. This process often requires researchers to modify scales to meet their intended needs. In addition, scales can be shortened to reduce respondent fatigue. These modifications can alter the original instrument in ways that make the validity and reliability of it problematic (Hess, Pollom, & Fannin, 2009).

Furthermore, although establishing cause and effect, replicability, and generalizability are noteworthy, these objectives can result in tunnel vision that ignores context and in-depth participant understanding (Tracy, 2013). Another concern is that knowledge claims based entirely on quantitative research make universal claims grounded in probability. Therefore, although quantitative inquiry can provide overarching insights, it is not commonly used for deeper understandings about how and why individuals behave as they do (Levine, 2011).

To address these concerns, some post-positive researchers are collecting supplemental qualitative data. They acknowledge that including participants' insights can add depth of understanding to the quantitative data. An example is Flanagin's (2007) quantitative study about the factors that influence trust and bidding options in eBay auctions. Because some of his findings were inconclusive, he suggested in his conclusion that "using rich qualitative data from users, is required to develop and fully test the novel application proposed here" (p. 419).

Interpretive

Interpretive research emerged in organizational communication in the late 1970s and early 1980s (e.g., Brown, 1985; Riley, 1983; Smith & Eisenberg, 1987; Trujillo, 1992; see Deetz & Eger, Chapter 1, for the historical foundations of this work). Interpretive researchers view knowledge as socially constructed; that is, social reality is co-constructed through interactions and symbols (Putnam, 1983). A primary objective of many interpretive investigations is to understand meanings from the vantage point of participants (Strauss & Corbin, 1998). In the interpretive perspective, collectives perform as "symbolic processes that evolve through streams of ongoing behavior" (Putnam, 1983, p. 35). This perspective acknowledges that individuals act with free will and are able to interpret their actions (Putnam, 1983). Notably, this stance contrasts with assumptions and objectives of post-positive research, which aims to discover general patterns of human behavior. Nevertheless, inductive studies that use qualitative methods also seek to build theory and to identify transferable patterns of behavior, but in a given rather than a general context (Anderson, 1987; Deetz, 1996; Festinger, Riecken, & Schachter, 1956; Putnam, 1982; Tompkins, 1994). Although qualitative-based studies test theory differently than do quantitative methods, potential findings can be theorized through hypotheses and participant responses can be compared to determine if data support hypotheses (Huberman & Miles, 2002).

As in post-positivist research, methods used in interpretive research have limitations. For example, findings may not apply beyond the participants or context of the study, thereby limiting transferability. Another critique is that interpretive studies are not conducive to theory testing (Bansal & Corley, 2011), but many qualitative scholars contest this claim. In addition, some critics argue that qualitative studies are less rigorous than are quantitative ones. However, in recent years, as qualitative methods have become widespread, scholars have developed standardized norms for assessing the rigor of designs, data analysis, and interpretation (Tracy, 2010). Increasingly, organizational communication researchers have called for qualitative reports to include structured formats, propositions, and data illustrations, such as tables, graphs, and diagrams (Tracy, 2013). Some traditionally focused interpretive scholars may question whether these reports are necessarily advancements. Today, interpretive studies have gained widespread acceptance, and few organizational communication scholars flatly dismiss the potential rigor of qualitative research and the contributions of this perspective.

Critical

The third perspective that has influenced scholarship is the critical paradigm. Marx believed that social behavior represented a struggle to dominate others (Hardt, 1992). He focused his ideology and writing on economic strife between social classes, that is, the view that power struggles are at the root of individual and societal behaviors. This philosophy, extended by such theorists as Horkheimer and Adorno (1972), gained popularity in organizational communication by the 1980s (Alvesson & Deetz, 1996; Alvesson & Willmott, 1995; Deetz & Kersten, 1983). Critical research focuses on illuminating injustices, revealing power and abuse of it, and empowering marginalized groups (e.g., Barker, 1993; Murphy, 1998; Tompkins & Cheney, 1985; Tracy, 2000).

Because it advocates change, critical scholarship examines distortions of consciousness, thought, and meaning in communication (Deetz, 2005) and may be seen as prescriptive. Organizational communication scholars who adopt this perspective often advocate for participatory communication to advance democracy in organizations (Cheney, 1995; Deetz, 1992; Forester, 1989). Feminist theory, as a particular type of critical thinking, examines how women are disadvantaged in a world that has been socially constructed and dominated by men and patriarchal worldviews (e.g., Ashcraft, 2005; Buzzanell & Liu, 2005; Trethewey, 1999). Critical and feminist researchers seek to challenge the prevailing assumptions developed and preserved by dominant voices (Blair, Brown, & Baxter, 1994).

With a focus on giving participants voice, qualitative methods are ideally suited for critical scholarship. However, the critical perspective can also employ quantitative research. Feminist scholar Reinharz (1992) reminds researchers that "feminism supplies the perspective and the disciplines supply the method. The feminist researcher [then] exists at the intersection" (p. 243). Nevertheless, scholars must be mindful that the use of methods, such as the development and data interpretation of surveys, can reinforce power and status quo relationships (Hesse-Biber, 2009), which can counter the primary objective of critical research, that is, fostering social change (Deetz & Kersten, 1983).

Mixing Methods and Perspectives

The preceding discussion reviews three commonly held organizational communication perspectives and links them to quantitative or qualitative methodologies. As noted, a primary reason some scholars employ deductive reasoning and quantitative methods while others use inductive reasoning and qualitative methods stems from a scholar's perspective, which drives his or her intellectual curiosity and purpose of research as well as objectives and assumptions. However, the field of communication exhibits an increasing openness to perspectives and methodologies that provide new opportunities to examine longstanding issues in organizational communication.

For example, organizational identification often relies on survey research and a post-positive perspective, but this line of research has begun to employ qualitative methods linked to interpretive and critical perspectives. Recently, Frandsen (2012) investigated organizational identification and distancing among high-prestige workers in an organization that had a negative image. She used an interpretive perspective and relied on interview data, but she also drew on previously collected worker surveys about their job satisfaction and perceptions about the organization's prestige at entry and exit. By combining both types of data, she was able to contextualize the qualitative findings and to provide stronger conclusions about how an organization's image can affect members' connections to it.

Conversely, the topic of *inequality* in the workplace has been traditionally studied by critical researchers who use interviews and observational data. However, workplace inequality could be examined with a post-positivist lens by surveying participants to uncover cause-and-effect relationships. By examining the phenomena with a different set of tools, researchers can reveal the previously unseen and prompt a new view of reality that might shape social change (Mertens, 2011).

At the National Communication Association conference in 2012, a group of scholars convened a preconference to discuss "pressing pragmatic, political, social, and theoretical developments that invite methodological agility in organizational communication research" (Ashcraft et al., 2012). Although a number of approaches were discussed, a central point of the discussion was the use of mixed-methods designs. Researchers felt that multiple perspectives and methods rather than a single approach could provide a more complete understanding of the issues and phenomena they want to investigate.

To interrogate a phenomenon, an investigator should explore its ambiguities and singularities (Greene, 2008; Morgan, 2007; Myers, 2011). Most textbooks on research methods instruct budding researchers to allow their questions to drive their methods. Yet, and as previously mentioned, adopting a perspective can cause scholars to value some qualities and outcomes more than others. At the extreme, perspectives or paradigms can constrain thought when researchers focus on some issues to the exclusion of others, thereby restricting scholars to only certain aspects of a social phenomenon (Feilzer, 2010). As Mills (1959) argued, this practice has the effect of constraining the sociological imagination, a point echoed by Miller (2000) when she claimed that a paradigm "can serve as a straightjacket" (p. 48). Instead, mixed-methods researchers should "choose the combination or mixture of methods and procedures that works best for answering [their] research questions" (Johnson & Onwuegbuzie, 2004, p. 17). This advice not only calls for using mixed methods but also urges researchers to maximize value by integrating perspectives that examine a phenomenon from different worldviews. Often, this process involves abductive reasoning to examine a phenomenon in multiple stages.

Some mixed methodologists rely on a pragmatic perspective. Pragmatic researchers are "anti-dualists" (Rorty, 1999, p. ixx), because they seek to reveal that which is useful and refuse to see the world through only one perspective (Rorty, 1999). In communication, Craig and Tracy (1995) argue that pragmatism is "a process of inquiry that arises within practical situations in response to practical problems" (p. 253). Russill (2004) claimed that communication scholars, while generally open to a pragmatic view, were late to adopt a pragmatic approach formally. Pragmatic scholars, according to Russill, are action oriented and adaptive to problems; therefore, they respond to and address problems associated with incommensurability in the field. In the pragmatic tradition, the basis of scientific theory allows scholars to select the most efficient and effective means to conduct research; hence, the pragmatic perspective is attractive to mixed-methods researchers.

The ultimate goal in pragmatic research is to discover what the investigator wants to know. Researchers must enter an investigation with a commitment to uncertainty. Instead of adhering to a predetermined design, researchers adapt methods, analyses, and the scope of a study when opportunities present themselves during an investigation (Craig, 2007). Mixed-methods researchers are encouraged to think beyond traditional research methods and designs to respond to questions and issues that are unexamined. Bergman (2011) argues that as quantitative and qualitative researchers begin to alter their views about objectivity-subjectivity, types of samples, and generalizability, mixed-methods researchers may become less stringent about study designs. This flexibility encourages pragmatic and mixed-methods approaches.

Fully integrating perspectives through the use of a pragmatic perspective is not a requirement for mixed-methods research. Some scholars primarily rely on post-positivism or interpretive worldviews to guide both quantitative and qualitative elements of their designs. Many of them shift back and forth between perspectives in various stages of the research. The challenge with this double-paradigm approach is in interpreting the data. Effective mixed-methods designs must fully integrate research findings from both data sets. However, when researchers have become accustomed to a paradigm, they may find it difficult to embrace an ontology associated with another approach; thus they may not exploit their results completely.

Primary Designs

Mixed-methods designs can be classified into several typologies. This portion of the chapter describes one primary classification system, even though several others exist (see Greene, Caracelli, & Graham, 1989; Nastasi, Hitchcock, & Brown, 2009; Tashakkori & Teddlie, 1998, 2003; Teddlie & Yu, 2007).

This section elaborates on the Creswell and Plano-Clark (2007) mixed-methods typology and provides an exemplar from organizational communication research of each design category. This typology is the least complex and most commonly used one and is based on three key design criteria: (1) when qualitative and quantitative data are collected, (2) whether one type of data is dominant or both are weighted equally, and (3) when the data are mixed (see Table 12.1 for a summary.) Although it is basic, this typology aids in selecting a design that best suits the purposes of an investigation, fits the researcher's schedule requirements, and draws on the needs and strengths of the researcher.

Triangulation Design

The first and most commonly used mixed-method approach is *triangulation*. The goals of triangulation research are to collect and compare complementary quantitative and qualitative data, to examine the phenomenon in multiple ways, and to gain a more complex understanding than analysis of one type of data would permit. Using more than one type of data enables the researcher to overcome methodological limitations and to draw on the advantages of both quantitative and qualitative data. Triangulation is often the goal when interview or observation data are used in unison with questionnaires. Data are collected simultaneously, analyzed separately, and interpreted simultaneously.

Variations on the triangulation design typically occur when one type of data can be transformed to compare directly to the other (e.g., qualitative data are transformed into quantitative data) or when one type of data can be used to validate the other (e.g., qualitative data are used to support quantitative survey results). For example, in a triangulation study of organizational culture and workgroup innovation, surveys could be distributed to individuals immediately before their participation in focus groups. This procedure would allow researchers to extend their arguments about the strength of the relationship between culture and workgroup creativity. When researchers use triangulation designs, they can interpret quantitative and qualitative data that cross different levels of analysis.

Studies such as Beck and Keyton's (2009) investigation of meeting interactions demonstrate how meaningful integration of data provides researchers with insights about members' strategic communication. Through the process of coding the meeting transcripts into thought units and interviewing participants about their interaction strategies, the investigators ascertain how coded units are related to each participant's perceptions of strategy. Using two types of data allows the researchers to compare members' interactions in the meeting with their intensions regarding these strategies.

Data triangulation can be assisted by various means of visualization. Flow charts can be used to plot data visually and to demonstrate how events and processes relate (Tracy, 2013). In mixed-methods research, these plots can aid researchers in analyzing multiple data sets and explaining complex organizational processes. Concept maps are representations of constructs and other words that demonstrate how concepts are interrelated, how they are relate to other

Table 12.1 Four Primary Mixed-Methods Designs and Uses

Design	Purpose and Uses	Primary Data	Advantages
Triangulation: Two types of data are integrated and compared for convergence or divergence.	*Convergent findings provide stronger conclusions. *Divergent findings necessitate more extensive extrapolation and interpretation.	*Quantitative and qualitative data are equally prioritized.	*Allows for a deeper and/or alternative examination. *Data can be collected simultaneously.
Embedded: Embedded design relies on one type of data, either quantitative or qualitative.	*Supplemental data provide added insight to primary data.	*One type of data is primary (either quantitative or qualitative).	*Secondary data can provide additional concreteness, insight, or understanding. *Data can be collected simultaneously.
Explanatory: Quantitative data are collected and analyzed as a basis for collecting qualitative data.	*Quantitative data analyses provide direction for a second phase of data collection (qualitative) and analyses.	*Typically, quantitative data are prioritized.	*Follow-up qualitative data can provide meaning and/or participants' voice and interpretation of initial quantitative data.
Exploratory: Qualitative data are collected and analyzed as a basis for collecting quantitative data.	*Qualitative data analyses provide direction for a second phase of data collection (quantitative) and analyses.	*Typically, qualitative data are prioritized.	*Initial qualitative data guide the selection and development of quantitative measures. *Follow-up quantitative data provide information about the widespread nature of initial qualitative findings.

Source: Based on Creswell and Plano Clark (2007).

words, and how they are hierarchically organized (Wheeldon, 2010). This approach to data analysis enables researchers to visualize participants' understandings of concepts and to use abductive reasoning to move between data and theory and then back to data again (Wheeldon, 2010). Concept maps are commonly used in the field of education to assess and reinforce students' learning (Novak, 1981), and clearly, organizational communication researchers could use variations of them. For example, Huffman (2012) created a visual display to analyze data that depicted the motivation of volunteers to help at a homeless youth organization.

Researchers who intend to use triangulation designs should consider the following recommendations. First, Glaser, Zamanou, and Hacker (1987) argue that "triangulation in organizational research has been advocated more than employed" (p. 175). Some investigators claim to use triangulation, but without fully interpreting and integrating the data. This practice goes against the true purpose of the design (Greene et al., 1989). Drawing on both types of data equally is difficult, because many researchers rely too heavily on data that best fits their commonly used perspectives. This practice makes the other data less relevant. Alternatively, researchers may rely on one type of data more than on the other, because they lack expertise in both methodologies (Fielding, 2012). These issues can be managed by conducting research with a team whose members have different skill sets.

A second concern emerges when the data do not tell the same story; that is, they do not triangulate. Although this issue can point to validity problems, divergent data can lead to thorough investigations when researchers are forced to reconsider their interpretations of the data and the phenomenon (Greene, 2007). Reevaluation, then, can lead to a more complex understanding of the phenomenon. Alternatively, this process introduces new questions and the necessity of conducting additional research before concluding the study. Finally, critics contend that true triangulation is never possible; in effect, it is impossible to measure precisely the same thing twice (Denzin, 2010; Fielding & Fielding, 1986; Richardson, 1994). Phenomena and the world around them are constantly changing, and these changes influence the human response to what is being studied (Fielding, 2012).

Despite these concerns, triangulation designs offer two important benefits that make them worthwhile. First, when the two types of data converge and support each other, the researchers' claims are stronger than when only one method is used (Creswell, 2003). In addition, convergence of data may incorporate more than one ontological perspective, which makes the claims of a study credible for a range of audiences. A second and very practical advantage of a triangulation design is that quantitative and qualitative data can be collected simultaneously, hence, making it time efficient for the researcher (Creswell & Plano-Clark, 2007).

To illustrate, Bullis and Bach (1989) used a *triangulation mixed-methods design* in their investigation of organizational identification and socialization turning points. Their objectives were to determine whether organizational socialization involved definable turning points and whether those turning points influenced organizational identification. Bullis and Bach's study, which involved 28 new communication graduate students, included several research questions focused on whether the students' organizational socialization was affected by identifiable turning points. They interviewed the students at four months and eight months following entry, first defining turning points and then asking about turning points they had experienced in the previous four months. The qualitative data included 15 turning point types. As the participants talked about turning points, they were asked to plot their identification levels as a percentage from 0% to 100% for each of the four preceding months. Rather than rely on their participants' descriptions about events that may have affected their identification, Bullis and Bach triangulated the qualitative data from interviews with a quantitative assessment. They asked students to complete a short questionnaire. With the plotted levels of organizational identification, they were able to link the types of turning points with positive or negative changes in identification. The quantitative identification data enabled the researchers to assess and triangulate with the interview data whether the students' levels of identification had increased or decreased between four and eight months of membership. As an example of mixed-methods research in organizational communication, this study reveals the usefulness of identifying turning points with interview data and assessing the effect (mostly valence) of each type of turning point with a basic quantitative plotting system. In addition, Bullis and Bach were able to examine the effect of turning-point experiences on another construct, organizational identification, using quantitative measurement. This triangulated the effect of each of the turning point types on the students' identification with their department.

Embedded Design

The second mixed-methods approach in this typology is the *embedded* design, in which one type of data supports and plays a secondary role to the other (Creswell & Plano-Clark, 2007). Embedded designs are useful when the researcher is primarily interested in the results of one type of data, and the other type of data serves as a baseline for the second phase of the study. In the second phase, investigators use the first stage to select or group participants to receive variant interventions or questionnaires (Greene et al., 1989). For example, the researcher could collect preliminary observations to identify interaction patterns among organizational members. These initial data may play a secondary but useful role in interpreting questionnaires, for instance, ones designed to analyze worker-supervisor relationship data.

Another use for an embedded design is to include open response questions as qualitative data within a quantitative survey to ascertain how or why relationships exist. For example, Strijbos, Martens, Jochems, and Broers (2004) used an experimental embedded design to examine whether assigned functional roles affected group learning, performance, and efficiency. Although they primarily relied on quantitative measures, they also drew on analysis of e-mail communication between members to assess the effects of their intervention on communicative collaboration.

Creswell and Plano-Clark (2007) cite several advantages to embedded designs; namely, they are efficient because minimal time is needed to collect and analyze secondary data, and they do not require extensive expertise to analyze the secondary data. In addition, funding agencies often prefer quantitative data but appreciate the added depth that qualitative data provide. The disadvantages to embedded designs are few. However, when time and space are limited, the secondary data set is sometimes set aside to focus on the primary one, which defeats the purpose of mixed-methods research.

To illustrate, Levine, Muenchen, and Brooks' (2010) example of an *embedded mixed-method design* examines whether charismatic leadership is assessed in items included in widely used leadership instruments. The authors argued that although no precise definition of charismatic leadership exists, charismatic leaders were thought to be inspirational visionaries (Hoyt & Ciulla, 2004) who could influence people to follow their vision and who could solve organizational crises (Avolio & Yammarino, 1990; Conger, 1989). They also pointed out that although charisma was included in most definitions of leadership (Bass, 1985; House, 1977; Yammarino, Spangler, & Bass, 1993; Yukl, 1999), including transformational leadership (Burns, 1978), items that measure charisma or charismatic behaviors appear to be missing from leadership measurement instruments.

In their embedded study, the authors used four leadership survey instruments (n = 422) to collect quantitative data (Bass, 1985; Conger & Kanungo, 1998; Kelley, 1992; Meindl & Ehrlich, 1988) and two open-ended questions that asked participants to define charisma and to describe its communicative behaviors. First, they employed Pearson's correlations to examine the relationships between the four leadership measures. Although the relationships were statistically significant due to their large sample size, the correlations were relatively low. To assess the relationships between existing leadership instruments and charismatic behaviors, the researchers next transformed the qualitative data drawn from the definitions of charismatic leadership into quantitative data by identifying and counting the frequencies of root words and phrases and developing a singular value decomposition (SVD) that they described as similar to factor analysis. They found five factors and used canonical correlation analysis between the two sets of measures—ones on the four leadership scores and ones on the five SVD scores. Overall, the study showed no relationship between the standard leadership scales and SVD factors, nor did they find statistical significance between the established leadership scales and the behaviors of charismatic leadership.

Levine and colleagues' (2010) study is an excellent example of research that effectively transforms embedded qualitative data for comparison with simultaneously collected quantitative data. Exploratory qualitative data were needed in this case to understand how participants defined charisma and to compare these definitions to the quantitative data derived from existing leadership instruments. The researchers clearly privileged the quantitative data but used the qualitative data to develop a new leadership dimension with items linked to charisma and charismatic behaviors. Drawing from the qualitative responses, the authors also had the data to develop these instruments.

Explanatory Design

The third major mixed-method design is *explanatory,* in which qualitative data are collected to explain the initial quantitative results. Explanatory designs address the *how* or *why* questions that result from quantitative findings or provide data when the researcher needs to categorize participants for purposive sampling or for follow-up interviews (Hesse-Biber, 2009). The intended purpose of the explanatory design shapes variations of the design. When researchers begin with quantitative data and then conduct qualitative research to understand the data, the quantitative data remain the primary focus of the study. However, when the purpose of the quantitative data is to define characteristics of the representative population for qualitative investigation, then the qualitative data become primary in interpreting the results and implications. Because the explanatory design draws on initial quantitative findings to guide the qualitative design, the study is conducted in two phases of data collection, analysis and interpretation. A thorough interpretation of the overall findings, however, should incorporate both types of data in drawing conclusions from the study.

A specialized type of approach, *crossover analysis,* combines quantitative and qualitative data analysis to develop quantitative instruments (Onwuegbuzie & Combs, 2009). Because it begins with quantitative data collection and then develops procedures for qualitative collection, it can broadly be defined as an explanatory design. However, crossover analysis, often called a *mixed analysis* technique, calls for nine phases and iterations between quantitative and qualitative data analysis techniques (Onwuegbuzie, Collins, & Leech, 2010). The steps involve reducing the two types of data by either using quantitative data analysis to specify the dimensions of qualitative data or using qualitative data analysis techniques to explore quantitative data. In their introduction to the method, Onwuegbuzie and Combs (2009) specify the nine phases of collection and analysis that have the potential to offer strong meta-inferences; these steps include

- *integrated data reduction* (reducing complexity of qualitative data and/or findings with quantitative data analysis or describing quantitative data using qualitative analysis techniques),
- *integrated data display* (representing both quantitative and qualitative data within one display),
- *data transformation* (converting quantitative data into data that can be qualitatively analyzed and/or qualitative data into quantitative data for quantitative analysis),
- *data correlation* (correlating quantitative with qualitative data),
- *data consolidation* (combining data sets to create new data sets, codes, or variables),
- *data comparison* (comparing quantitative and qualitative data and findings),
- *data integration* (interrelating quantitative and qualitative data sets into one informed whole or into two separate data sets that meaningfully draw from both sets of data),

- *warranted assertion analysis* (reviewing and carefully considering both quantitative and qualitative data to make meta-interferences), and
- *data importation* (using follow-up qualitative data to inform initial quantitative findings or follow-up quantitative data to inform initial qualitative data).

Researchers, however, can combine techniques that they deem suitable for their particular needs.

For example, investigators can employ types of thematic analysis commonly used in qualitative data analysis to compare themes derived from exploratory factor analysis (Greene et al., 1989). Alternatively, to further construct validity, Onwuegbuzie (2003) used exploratory factor analysis to interrogate the structures depicted in qualitative data. As this example demonstrates, using two distinctly different methods in a concurrent mixed-analysis design yields further integration of the two data sets (Onwuegbuzie, Bustamante, & Nelson, 2010). Because crossover analysis requires researchers to make several gestalt switches between quantitative and qualitative data (Kuhn, 1962), it enables investigators to extract optimal insights from the data, to develop a quantitative instrument, and to test for construct validity.

The explanatory design offers several advantages. First, on the one hand, it is straightforward to implement and is especially appealing for quantitative researchers who aim to emphasize quantitative findings. Reports can be written nearly chronologically by explaining the phases of the study as they occur. On the other hand, researchers may find it difficult to obtain human subjects approval for this type of procedure, because they cannot specify all the questions or types of participants for the second phase until they have the results of the first phase (Creswell & Plano-Clark, 2007). Researchers faced with this challenge may need to apply for human subjects' approval in two phases. A second disadvantage is that the two phases of research require more time to complete, sometimes substantially so, and this factor may make the explanatory design unfeasible for mixed-methods researchers who have short time horizons.

Research by Miller and Koesten (2008) provides an example of an *explanatory mixed-methods design*. The investigators examined emotional labor and emotion work among financial planners (i.e., emotions that result from interaction in the course of doing a job that has been associated with stress and burnout). They invited 5,000 randomly selected planners to participate in the web-based survey and received 299 respondents. The quantitative measures enabled Miller and Koesten to test several hypotheses related to emotional labor, emotion work, job satisfaction, and burnout (Miller, Stiff, & Ellis, 1988). In the second phase, the researchers conducted semistructured telephone interviews with 14 participants to gain an understanding of the communication patterns and emotions that characterized the financial planners' work. They found that emotion contagion did not predict several outcome variables but that communicative responsiveness was a strong predictor of reduced personal accomplishment (a burnout factor). In interviews, respondents explained that the communicative relationship with clients was the most attractive aspect of their work. They described their satisfaction in working with clients, making a difference in their clients' lives and in the lives of their children, but they also talked about the burnout that they experienced when they shared in their clients' disappointments. The quantitative data were the central focus of the study, but the qualitative data contextualized and provided added understanding about the results of the survey.

Exploratory Design

The fourth mixed-methods design is *exploratory*. As with the explanatory design, the research is conducted in two phases, but unlike the explanatory design, qualitative data are collected initially and followed by a quantitative phase. An exploratory mixed-method design is useful when quantitative measures of a phenomenon are nonexistent and when the phenomenon is relatively unexplored. Through qualitative examination, researchers can explore and develop definitions and dimensions of a phenomenon that can be operationalized in survey items. For these reasons, this method is often employed when the primary purpose of a study is to develop a measurement instrument (e.g., Larkey, 1996; Myers & Oetzel, 2003). The exploratory mixed-method design is useful when researchers want to ascertain the validity of qualitative findings by surveying a larger sample.

The exploratory method shares many of the same advantages (i.e., straightforward to conduct and report) and disadvantages (i.e., time consuming, difficult to sequence issues) of explanatory designs (Creswell & Plano-Clark, 2007). However, unlike the explanatory design, exploratory mixed methods emphasize qualitative findings and use them in a follow-up quantitative phase (Hesse-Biber, 2010). Similar to the explanatory design, two phases of research might be impractical for scholars who have tight time constraints.

An *exploratory mixed-methods design* is often used to develop items for quantitative instruments. Xu (2011) employed this approach to develop an instrument to assess academic leadership in Chinese universities. He asserted that leadership is strongly influenced by national culture; hence, characteristics of effective leadership vary from context to context and principles of Confucianism guide leader-member exchange among Chinese nobility and leaders. To conduct his study, he interviewed five deans and 12 faculty members in three Chinese universities about the behaviors that they liked or disliked in a dean. He then coded and grouped this data into seven factors drawn from Confucian principles of leadership and used them to create 41 survey items that were administered to faculty members in universities across China. The results of the quantitative analysis of 304 responses yielded a five-factor model in confirmatory factor analysis that focused on morality, nurturing, communicating/relating, fairness, and administrative competence. In this exploratory design, Xu placed a strong emphasis on the quantitative portion of the study, but the qualitative data laid the foundation for creating items that were previously excluded from empirical studies.

Guidelines for Selecting a Design

Organizational researchers should consider several issues in choosing a mixed-methods design. First, what is the purpose of the study? If the research questions can be answered with one type of data, but they could be enriched with using another type, then an embedded design is optimal. If the phenomenon is relatively unexplored and generalizability is also needed, then an exploratory design should be considered. If the phenomenon has received sufficient attention in previous research and an instrument is available to assess it, then an explanatory mixed-methods design could be useful to provide additional insights. Alternatively, if the phenomenon could be better understood through more than one vantage point, then triangulation should be selected.

Second, researchers need to consider their available skills and expertise. As previously mentioned, the field of organizational communication has welcomed multiple methodologies that are germane to mixed-methods designs. Solo researchers may select designs that favor their own skill sets; however, collaboration with others who have different methodological expertise may enable investigators to select the most suitable design. Third, researchers must be mindful of time constraints. Studies that involve two phases of research, in which the first phase must be analyzed and interpreted before implementing the second one, may require additional budgetary and temporal resources.

Occasionally, mixed-methods studies combine or modify elements of these four design types. Specifically, Leonardi and Bailey's (2008) examination of knowledge use and work practices in offshore engineering facilities used three phases of research. In the first phase, they observed and interviewed performance engineers and managers in three countries to understand how knowledge was transferred among sites. They then analyzed this qualitative data to develop a survey that they administered in the second phase to determine the scope of the findings from Phase One. In the final phase, they examined project logs to confirm survey findings. The three-phase sequence enabled the researchers to develop survey items ground in a unique context, and the examination of project logs extended the interpretations beyond the survey data.

Another example of combining features of the four designs occurs in Campbell and Russo's (2003) modified embedded design study of a social network that developed from cell phone use. The researchers asked student participants to identify someone with whom they regularly interacted. Then, they surveyed the students and their communication partners about purposes and use of mobile phones. In the second phase, Campbell and Russo interviewed participants to understand usage patterns and perceptions of mobile phones. Their study confirmed that mobile phone use was socially constructed within social networks.

Finally, Brummans et al.'s (2008) study of intractable multiparty conflict employed a different type of customized embedded design. Initially, the researchers collected archival data (e.g., media articles, meeting and court records, memos, and technical reports) that provided background information on the conflicts and participants. The primary data were collected from interviews gathered from 153 representatives from the various stakeholder groups. These data were analyzed using a variety of methods, including constant comparative for the interview data and content analysis of themes to generate quantitative data. From the quantitative data, the researchers found that disputants clustered into four groups, distinguished by how they framed the conflict, how they believed it should be managed, how societal decisions about conflicts should be made, and who held the power in the situations. The authors argued that using a variety of quantitative and qualitative data allowed them to analyze the interview data for deep-level interpretations, add validity to their claims, and potentially improve transferability of the findings.

Future Use of Mixed-Methods Designs

Despite the advantages of these designs, the number of mixed-methods studies published in organizational communication remains relatively low. In this section, I speculate about the reasons for the lack of mixed methods use in organizational communication and suggest three opportunities for future research.

The Absence of Mixed-Methods Designs

As discussed, mixed-methods research offers many opportunities for organizational communication scholars: So why are so few researchers using it? Several issues may curtail their use. First, although organizational communication scholars are receptive to a variety of metatheoretical, theoretical, and methodological approaches, many researchers rely on their usual perspectives to conceptualize research (Greene & Caracelli, 2003). The types of questions they formulate and the research designs they select, in turn, result in *either* using quantitative *or* qualitative methods.

A second reason that even researchers who are attracted to mixed methods may choose not to use them is that this type of research entails uncertainty. Mixed-methods designs often depend on what the data reveal and thus emerge in the study itself. To embrace a pragmatic approach requires the researcher to move back and forth between the data and the design, and often back and forth again, to interrogate the phenomenon fully. Although the end result can be powerful, researchers must be patient and must exert considerable analytical and interpretative energy.

In the National Communication Association Preconference (Ashcraft et al., 2012), participants often favored the use of mixed methods but were disinclined to use them because of pressures to complete projects in a timely manner. Professors expressed concern about getting their studies into publication quickly to support tenure and merit reviews. Students also lacked time to conduct meaningful mixed-methods research, given the need to complete theses and dissertations. These types of pressures suggest that research conducted with the use of mixed-methods designs may not appear in publication as mixed-method studies. Phases of data collection and analysis may be split into separate manuscripts. This practice is especially likely when the researcher completes one phase of the study before the other, when one phase can be analyzed quickly (Bryman, 2007) or when a scholar feels that separating the phases into multiple publications is rewarding. Alternatively, researchers may choose to publish only one portion of the study, either the quantitative or the qualitative findings (Greene & Caracelli, 1997).

A third reason may be expertise. Mixed-methods designs require both statistical analysis and working with qualitative data, which can be messy in both analysis and interpretation (Feilzer, 2010). Scholars may have expertise in particular types of data collection and analysis, which may make them more comfortable with one method over the other. Some investigators are unaware of or do not understand which methods could enhance their research designs, or they may shy away from them because they lack training in a necessary method (Morgan, 2007).

Fourth, researchers may believe that audiences for quantitative and qualitative research are quite different or that journals prefer one method over the other. These scholars may be reluctant to cast their studies as *mixed method,* because it might lead to higher expectations and different critical evaluations by readers and reviewers.

In these situations, researchers can benefit from using collaborative research teams, especially in exploring unfamiliar designs and in assisting to learn about and implement alternative data collection and analysis. Also, team members can divide the workload, contributing differentially to reviewing extant literature, collecting data, conducting data analysis, and writing the report. Division of labor can improve the quality of the study and make mixed-methods designs feasible and more pleasurable. Collaboration, however, does not necessarily shorten the time to publication.

Prospects for Mixed-Methods Research

Mixed-methods research can advance the field of organizational communication by probing sensitive organizational issues, replicating and expanding previous studies, and increasing the visibility of the field.

Sensitive Issues. For cases in which issues are sensitive and difficult to discuss (e.g., conflict, deceit, personal health issues), mixed-methods designs decrease employees' reluctance to disclose information (Jehn & Jonsen, 2010). In particular, as Jehn and Jonsen state,

> Observation and multiple interviews build rapport with the employees. This eliminates, or at least reduces, response sets, reactivity, lying, and misinterpretation, which are all characteristics of field studies in general but which increase when sensitive issues are the topic under study. (p. 332)

When scholars invest time in the field to collect data in multiple ways, organizational members believe that the scholar understands the context and nature of their experiences. "Surveys and structured interviews add to the richness of observation and archival data, while allowing for rigorous comparisons" (Jehn & Jonsen, 2010, p. 332). By approaching sensitive topics from multiple angles, researchers can ascertain their accuracy and completeness, even when participants feel uncomfortable discussing a topic. These approaches may require additional time investment, but the results may prove valuable.

Replicating and Expanding Knowledge. Researchers can also use mixed-method studies to replicate original research *and* to extend knowledge of studies based on one perspective. For example, the Eisenberg et al. (1984) post-positive investigation could be replicated as an explanatory study to unpack the employees' and supervisors' patterns of initiating communication. Follow-up interviews with workers and supervisors could reveal how the perceptions of co-orientation patterns, performance evaluations, and worker satisfaction affected interpersonal relationships.

Among the three dominant paradigms in organizational communication, mixed methods is least commonly used in critical research. However, Mertens (2011) argues that this approach can enhance critical scholarship. First, although interviews and observation give voice to marginalized members, survey methods may identify relationships among constructs that are important sources of power and domination. Second, using more than one method of data collection may help researchers gather data that aid in appreciating and respecting diversity by hearing and seeing power relationships *in situ*. Developing extensive contact with organizational members may translate to higher levels of trust between participants and researchers that could lead to undisclosed issues (Mertens, 2011). To illustrate, Riley's (1983) examination of the internal politics in two organizations revealed that the ways that groups structure tasks produce subcultures. Qualitative research (e.g., a replicating mixed-method study) could examine how task-created environments produce different political subcultures while a quantitative follow-up through surveys could assess their pervasiveness. Similarly, Murphy's (1998) study of flight attendants identified ways that they communicate resistance to management and customers. Had she extended this study through the use of a survey, she might show how widespread this phenomenon is, for what types of employees, and how resistance relates to stress and burnout.

Increasing Visibility of the Field. In the field of strategic management, mixed-methods studies have received proportionally higher citation statistics. Specifically, Molina-Azorin (2011) examined citation data of 1,330 articles that appeared in *Strategic Management Journal, Journal of Business Venturing, Entrepreneurship Theory and Practice*, and *Entrepreneurship & Regional Development.* He found that 11.4% of these articles employed mixed-methods designs. Drawing on data from the Social Science Citation Index and Google Scholar, he assessed the total number of citations for the mixed-methods articles. The mean citation count was 37.16 as compared to 23.71 for the non-mixed-methods studies; hence, as judged by these statistics, mixed-method publications are more influential than those that employ single methods (Molina-Azorin, 2011), perhaps because they are more convincing to audiences who read them and cite them in making their own claims than are other investigations.

Conclusion

Benoit and Holbert (2008) advocate that communication researchers should pursue interrelated, programmatic research—either across articles or within publications. They claim,

> research that relates to other research—reinforcing, integrating, elaborating—can provide greater breadth and depth to our understanding. Furthermore, programmatic research, which systematically investigates an aspect of communication with a series of related studies conducted across contexts *or*

> *with multiple methods*, has been particularly valuable in our efforts to understand communication. (p. 615; emphasis added)

Despite these calls (Faules, 1982; Myers, 2011), mixed-methods investigations are rare in communication studies, in general, and organizational communication, in particular. Overall, mixed-methods research breaks from the methodological confines of traditional perspectives and overcomes shortcomings of single methods. Using this hybrid approach requires researchers to suspend biases, consider new goals and objectives, and potentially extend their knowledge of methodology that they rarely use. Selecting mixed-methods designs aids in probing issues and developing a complex view of organizational phenomena. For these reasons, mixed-methods research can increase the value, usefulness, and visibility of organizational communication scholarship in organizational studies and the social sciences generally.

References

Alvesson, M., & Deetz, S. (1996). Critical theory and postmodernism approaches to organizational studies. In S. R. Clegg, C. Hardy, & W. R. Nord (Eds.), *Handbook of organization studies* (pp. 191–217). Thousand Oaks, CA: SAGE.

Alvesson, M., & Willmott, H. (1995). *Making sense of management: A critical analysis.* London, England: SAGE.

Anderson, J. (1987). *Communication research: Issues and methods.* New York, NY: McGraw-Hill.

Arnault, D. S., & Fetters, M. D. (2011). RO1 funding for mixed methods research: Lessons learned from the "mixed-method analysis of Japanese depression" project. *Journal of Mixed Methods Research, 5*(4), 309–329.

Ashcraft, K. L. (2005). Resistance through consent: Occupational identity, organizational form, and the maintenance of masculinity among commercial airline pilots. *Management Communication Quarterly, 19*(1), 67–90.

Ashcraft, K. L., Barge, J. K., Cunliffe, A., Fairhurst, G. T., Ganesh, S., Miller, K., . . . Poole, M. S. (2012, November). *Moving Methodology.* Presentation given at the preconference at the meeting of the National Communication Association conference, Orlando, FL.

Avolio, B. J., & Yammarino, F. J. (1990). Operationalizing charismatic leadership using a levels-of-analysis framework. *Leadership Quarterly, 1*(3), 193–208.

Babbie, E. R. (2009). *The practice of social research* (12th ed.). Belmont, CA: Wadsworth.

Bansal, P., & Corley, K. (2011). The coming of age for qualitative research: Embracing the diversity of qualitative methods. *Academy of Management Journal, 54*(2), 233–237.

Barker, J. R. (1993). Tightening the iron cage: Concertive control in a self-managing team. *Administrative Science Quarterly, 38*(3), 408–437.

Bass, B. M. (1985). *Leadership and performance beyond expectations.* New York, NY: Free Press.

Bazeley, P., & Kemp, L. (2012). Mosaics, triangles, and DNA: Metaphors for integrated analysis in mixed methods research. *Journal of Mixed Methods Research, 6*(1), 55–72.

Beck, S. J., & Keyton, J. (2009). Perceiving strategic meeting interaction. *Small Group Research, 40*(2), 223–246.

Benoit, W. L., & Holbert, L. (2008). Empirical intersections in communication research: Replication, multiple quantitative methods, and bridging the quantitative-qualitative divide. *Journal of Communication, 58*(4), 615–628.

Bergman, M. M. (2011). The politics, fashions, and conventions of research methods. *Journal of Mixed Methods Research, 5*(2), 99–102.

Blair, C., Brown, J. R., & Baxter, L. A. (1994). Disciplining the feminine. *Quarterly Journal of Speech, 80*(4), 383–409.

Brewer, J., & Hunter, A. (2006). *Foundations of multimethod research: Synthesizing styles.* Thousand Oaks, CA: SAGE.

Brown, M. H. (1985). That reminds me of a story: Speech action in organizational socialization. *Western Journal of Speech Communication, 49*(1), 27–42.

Brummans, B. H. J. M., Putnam, L. L., Gray, B., Hanke, R., Lewicki, R. J., & Wiethoff, C. (2008). Making sense of intractable multiparty conflict: A study of framing in four environmental disputes. *Communication Monographs, 75*(1), 25–51.

Bryman, A. (1988). *Quantity and quality in social research.* London, England: Unwin Hyman.

Bryman, A. (2007). Barriers to integrating quantitative and qualitative research. *Journal of Mixed Methods Research, 1*(1), 8–22.

Bullis, C., & Bach, B. W. (1989). Socialization turning points: An examination of change in organizational identification. *Western Journal of Speech Communication, 53*(3), 273–293.

Burns, J. M. (1978). *Leadership.* New York, NY: Harper & Row.

Buzzanell, P. M., & Lui, M. (2005). Struggling with maternity leave policies and practices: A feminist analysis of gendered organizing. *Journal of Applied Communication Research, 33*(1), 1–25.

Campbell, D., & Fiske, D. W. (1959). Convergent and discriminate validation by the multitrait-multimethod matrix. *Psychology Bulletin, 56*(2), 81–105.

Campbell, S., & Russo, T. C. (2003). The social construction of mobile telephony: An application of the social influence model to perceptions and uses of mobile phones within personal communication networks. *Communication Monographs, 70*(4), 317–334.

Cheney, G. (1995). Democracy in the workplace: Theory and practice from the perspective of communication. *Journal of Applied Communication Research, 23*(3), 167–200.

Conger, J. A. (1989). *The charismatic leader: Behind the mystique of exceptional leadership.* San Francisco, CA: Jossey-Bass.

Conger, J. A., & Kanungo, R. N. (1998). *Charismatic leadership in organizations.* Thousand Oaks, CA: SAGE.

Craig, R. T. (2007). Pragmatism in the field of communication theory. *Communication Theory, 17*(2), 125–145.

Craig, R. T., & Tracy, K. (1995). Grounded practical theory: The case of intellectual discussion. *Communication Theory, 5*(3), 248–272.

Creswell, J. W. (1994). *Research design: Qualitative and quantitative approaches.* Thousand Oaks, CA: SAGE.

Creswell, J. W. (2003). *Research design: Qualitative, quantitative, and mixed methods approaches.* Thousand Oaks, CA: SAGE.

Creswell, J. W., & Plano-Clark, V. L. (2007). *Designing and conducting mixed methods research.* Thousand Oaks, CA: SAGE.

Deetz, S. (1992). *Democracy in an age of corporate colonization: Developments in communication and the politics of everyday life.* Albany: State University of New York Press.

Deetz, S. (1996). Describing the differences in approaches to organization science: Rethinking Burrell and Morgan and their legacy. *Organization Science, 7*(2), 191–207.

Deetz, S. (2005). Critical theory. In S. May & D. K. Mumby (Eds.), *Engaging organizational communication theory & research: Multiple perspectives* (pp. 85–111). Thousand Oaks, CA: SAGE.

Deetz, S., & Kersten, A. (1983). Critical models of interpretive research. In L. Putnam & M. E. Pacanowsky (Eds.), *Communication and organizations* (pp. 147–172). Beverly Hills, CA: SAGE.

Denzin, N. K. (2010). *The qualitative manifesto: A call to arms.* Walnut Creek, CA: Left Coast Press.

Denzin, N. K. (2012). Triangulation 2.0. *Journal of Mixed Methods Research, 6*(2), 80–88.

Eisenberg, E. M., Monge, P. R., & Farace, R. V. (1984). Coorientation on communication rules in managerial dyads. *Human Communication Research, 11*(2), 261–271.

Erzberger, C., & Kelle, U. (2003). Making inferences in mixed methods: The rules of integration. In A. Tashakkori & C. Teddlie (Eds.), *Handbook of mixed methods in social and behavioral research* (pp. 457–488). Thousand Oaks, CA: SAGE.

Fairhurst, G. T., Green, S. G., & Snavely, B. K. (1984). Face support in controlling poor performance. *Human Communication Research, 11*(2), 272–295.

Faules, D. (1982). The use of multi-methods in the organizational setting. *Western Journal of Speech Communication, 46*(2), 150–161.

Feilzer, M. Y. (2007). Criminologists making news? Providing factual information on crime and criminal justice through a weekly newspaper column. *Crime, Media, Culture, 3*(3), 285–304.

Feilzer, M. Y. (2010). Doing mixed methods research pragmatically: Implications for the rediscovery of pragmatism as a research paradigm. *Journal of Mixed Methods Research, 4*(1), 6–16.

Festinger, L., Riecken, H. W., & Schachter, S. (1956). *When prophecy fails: A social psychological study of a modern group that predicted the destruction of the world.* Minneapolis: University of Minnesota Press.

Fielding, N. G. (2012). Triangulation and mixed methods designs: Data integration with new research technologies. *Journal of Mixed Methods Research, 6*(2), 124–136.

Fielding, N. G., & Fielding, J. (1986). *Linking data.* London, England: SAGE.

Flanagin, A. J. (2007). Commercial markets as communication markets: Uncertainty reduction through mediated information exchange in online auctions. *New Media & Society, 9*(3), 401–423.

Forester, J. (1989). *Planning in the face of power.* Berkeley: University of California Press.

Frandsen, S. (2012). Organizational image, identification, and cynical distance: Prestigious professionals in a low-prestige organization. *Management Communication Quarterly, 26*(3), 351–376.

Glaser, S. R., Zamanou, S., & Hacker, K. (1987). Measuring and interpreting organizational culture. *Management Communication Quarterly, 1*(2), 173–198.

Greene, J. C. (2007). *Mixed methods in social inquiry.* San Francisco, CA: Jossey-Bass.

Greene, J. C. (2008). Is mixed methods social inquiry a distinctive methodology? *Journal of Mixed Methods Research, 7*(2), 7–22.

Greene, J. C., & Caracelli, V. J. (2003). Making paradigmatic sense of mixed methods practice. In A. Tashakkori & C. Teddlie (Eds.), *Handbook of mixed methods in social and behavioral research* (pp. 91–110). Thousand Oaks, CA: SAGE.

Greene, J. C., Caracelli, V. J., & Graham, W. F. (1989). Toward a conceptual framework for mixed-method evaluation designs. *Educational Evaluation and Policy Analysis, 11*(3), 255–274.

Greene, J. C., & McClintock, C. (1985). Triangulation in evaluation: Design and analysis issues. *Evaluation Review, 9*(5), 523–545.

Hardt, H. (1992). *Critical communication studies: Communication, history, and theory in America.* New York, NY: Routledge.

Hess, J. A., Pollom, L. H., & Fannin, A. D. (2009). How much do we really know about equity's impact on relational communication? Issues in measuring equity in communication research. *Communication Methods and Measures, 3*(3), 173–194.

Hesse-Biber, S. N. (2009). Feminist approaches to mixed methods research: Linking theory and praxis. In A. Tashakkori & C. Teddlie (Eds.), *SAGE handbook of mixed methods in social & behavioral research* (pp. 169–192). Thousand Oaks, CA: SAGE.

Hesse-Biber, S. N. (2010b). *Mixed method research: Merging theory with practice.* New York, NY: Guilford Press.

Horkheimer, M., & Adorno, T. W. (1972). *Dialectic of enlightenment* (J. Cumming, Trans.). New York, NY: Seabury Press.

House, R. J. (1977). A 1976 theory of charismatic leadership. In J. G. Hunt & L. L. Larson (Eds.), *Leadership: The cutting edge* (pp. 189–207). Carbondale, IL: Southern Illinois University Press.

Hoyt, C. L., & Ciulla, J. (2004). *Using advanced gaming technology to teach leadership: A research-based perspective.* Foresight and Governance Project Working Papers. Available from the Woodrow Wilson International Center of Scholars, Washington, DC.

Huberman, A. M., & Miles, M. B. (2002). *The qualitative research companion.* Thousand Oaks, CA: SAGE.

Huffman, T. (2012, May). *Altruism, selfishness, and volunteer ecologies of social exchange.* Paper presented at the annual convention of the International Communication Association, Phoenix, AZ.

Infante, D. A., & Gordon, W. I. (1985). Superiors' argumentativeness and verbal aggressiveness as predictors of subordinates' satisfaction. *Human Communication Research, 12*(1), 117–125.

Jablin, F. M. (1980). Superiors' upward influence, satisfaction and openness in superior-subordinate communication: A reexamination of the "Pelz effect." *Human Communication Research, 6*(3), 210–220.

Jehn, K. A., & Jonsen, K. (2010). A multimethod approach to the study of sensitive organizational issues. *Journal of Mixed Methods Research, 4*(4), 313–341.

Johnson, R. B., & Onwuegbuzie, A. J. (2004). Mixed methods research: A research paradigm for whose time has come. *Educational Researcher, 33*(7), 14–26.

Johnson, R. B., Onwuegbuzie, A. J., & Turner, L. A. (2007). Toward a definition of mixed methods research. *Journal of Mixed Methods Research, 1*(2), 112–133.

Kelley, R. (1992). *The power of followership.* New York, NY: Doubleday.

Kuhn, T. S. (1962). *The structure of scientific revolutions* (1st ed.). Chicago, IL: University of Chicago Press.

Larkey, L., K. (1996). The development and validation of the workforce diversity questionnaire: An instrument to assess interactions in diverse workgroups. *Management Communication Quarterly, 9*(3), 296–337.

Leonardi, P. M., & Bailey, D. E. (2008). Transformational technologies and the creation of new work practices: Making implicit knowledge explicit in task-based offshoring. *MIS Quarterly, 32*(2), 411–436.

Levine, K. J., Muenchen, R. A., & Brooks, A. M. (2010). Measuring transformational and charismatic leadership: Why isn't charisma measured? *Communication Monographs, 77*(4), 576–591.

Levine, T. R. (2011). Quantitative social science methods of inquiry. In M. L. Knapp & J. A. Daly (Eds.), *The SAGE handbook of interpersonal communication* (4th ed., pp. 59–86). Thousand Oaks, CA: SAGE.

Maxwell, J. A. (2010). Using numbers in qualitative research. *Qualitative Inquiry, 16*(6), 475–482.

McClintock, C., & Green, J. C. (1985). Triangulation in practice. *Evaluation and Program Planning, 8*(4), 351–357.

Meindl, J. R., & Ehrlich, S. B. (1988, May). *Developing a romance of leadership scale.* Silver Anniversary Proceedings, Eastern Academy of Management, Washington, DC.

Mertens, D. M. (2011). Mixed methods as tools for social change. *Journal of Mixed Methods Research, 5*(3), 195–197.

Miller, K. I. (2000). Common ground from the post-positivist perspective: From "straw person" argument to collaborative coexistence. In S. R. Corman & M. S. Poole (Eds.), *Perspectives on organizational communication: Finding common ground* (pp. 46–67). New York, NY: Guilford Press.

Miller, K. I., & Koesten, J. (2008). Financial feeling: An investigation of emotion and communication in the workplace. *Journal of Applied Communication Research, 36*(1), 8–32.

Miller, K. I., Stiff, J. B., & Ellis, B. H. (1988). Communication and empathy as precursors to burnout among human service workers. *Communication Monographs, 55*(3), 250–265.

Mills, C. W. (1959). *The sociological imagination.* New York, NY: Oxford University Press.

Molina-Azorin, J. F. (2011). The use and added value of mixed methods in management research. *Journal of Mixed Methods Research, 5*(1), 7–24.

Morgan, D. L. (2007). Paradigms and pragmatism regained: Methodological implications of combining qualitative and quantitative methods. *Journal of Mixed Methods Research, 1*(1), 48–76.

Morse, J. M. (1991). Approaches to qualitative-quantitative methodological triangulation. *Nursing Research, 40*(2), 120–123.

Murphy, A. G. (1998). Hidden transcripts of flight attendant resistance. *Management Communication Quarterly, 11*(4), 499–535.

Myers, K. K. (2011). Mixed methods. In V. Miller, M. S. Poole, D. R. Seibold, K. K. Myers, H. S. Park, P. Monge, . . . M. Shumate, Advancing research in organizational communication through quantitative methodology. *Management Communication Quarterly, 25*(1), 4–58.

Myers, K. K., & Oetzel, J. (2003). Exploring the dimensions of organizational assimilation: Creating and validating a communication measure. *Communication Quarterly, 51*(4), 436–455.

Nastasi, B. K., Hitchcock, J. H., & Brown, L. M. (2009). An inclusive framework for conceptualizing mixed methods design typologies: Moving toward fully integrated synergistic research models. In A. Tashakkori & C. Teddlie (Eds.), *SAGE handbook of mixed methods in social & behavioral research* (pp. 305–338). Thousand Oaks, CA: SAGE.

National Science Foundation. (2004). *Workshop on scientific foundations of qualitative research.* Retrieved from http://www.nsf.gov/pubs/2004/nsf04219/start.htm

Novak, J. D. (1981). Applying learning psychology and philosophy of science to biology teaching. *The American Biology Teacher, 43*(1), 12–20.

Onwuegbuzie, A. J. (2003). Effect sizes in qualitative research: A prolegomenon. *Quality & Quantity, 37*(4), 393–409.

Onwuegbuzie, A. J., Bustamante, R. M., & Nelson, J. A. (2010). Mixed methods as a tool for developing quantitative instruments. *Journal of Mixed Methods Research, 4*(1), 56–78.

Onwuegbuzie, A. J., Collins, K. M. T., & Leech, N. L. (2010). *Mixed research: A step-by-step guide.* New York, NY: Taylor & Francis.

Onwuegbuzie, A. J., & Combs, J. P. (2009). Emergent data analysis techniques in mixed methods research: A synthesis. In A. Tashakkori & C. Teddlie (Eds.), *SAGE handbook of mixed methods in social and behavioral research* (pp. 397–430). Thousand Oaks, CA: SAGE.

Putnam, L. L. (1982). Paradigms for organizational communication research: A synthesis. *Western Journal of Speech Communication, 46*(2), 192–206.

Putnam, L. L. (1983). The interpretive perspective: An alternative to functionalism. In L. L. Putnam & M. E. Pacanowski (Eds.), *Communication in organizations, an interpretive approach* (pp. 31–54). Beverly Hills, CA: SAGE.

Reinharz, S. (1992). *Feminist methods in social research.* New York, NY: Oxford University Press.

Richardson, L. (1994). Writing: A method of inquiry. In N. K. Denzin & Y. S. Lincoln (Eds.), *Handbook of qualitative research* (pp. 516–529). Thousand Oaks, CA: SAGE.

Riley, P. (1983). A structurationist account of political culture. *Administrative Science Quarterly, 28*(3), 414–437.

Rorty, R. (1999). *Philosophy and social hope.* London, England: Penguin.

Russill, C. *(2004). Toward a pragmatist theory of communication (Doctoral dissertation).* The Pennsylvania State University, University Park, PA.

Shih, F. J. (1998). Triangulation in nursing research. *Journal of Advanced Nursing, 28*(3), 631–641.

Smith, R. C., & Eisenberg, E. M. (1987). Conflict at Disneyland: A root-metaphor analysis. *Communication Monographs, 54*(4), 367–379.

Spiker, B. K., & Daniels, T. D. (1981). Information adequacy and communication relationships: An empirical examination of 18 organizations. *Western Journal of Speech Communication, 45*(4), 342–354.

Strauss, A., & Corbin, J. (1998). *Basics of qualitative research: Techniques and procedures for developing grounded theory* (2nd ed.). Thousand Oaks, CA: SAGE.

Strijbos, J. W., Martens, R. L., Jochems, W. M. G., & Broers, N. J. (2004). The effect of functional roles on group efficiency: Using multilevel modeling and content analysis to investigate computer-supported collaboration in small groups. *Small Group Research, 35*(2), 195–229.

Sypher, B. D., & Zorn, T. E. (1986). Communication-related abilities and upward mobility: A longitudinal investigation. *Human Communication Research, 12*(3), 420–431.

Tashakkori, A., & Creswell, J. W. (2007). The new era of mixed methods. *Journal of Mixed Methods Research, 1*(1), 3–7.

Tashakkori, A., & Teddlie, C. (1998). *Mixed methodology: Combining the qualitative and quantitative approaches.* Thousand Oaks, CA: SAGE.

Tashakkori, A., & Teddlie, C. (2003). *Handbook of mixed methods in social and behavioral research.* Thousand Oaks, CA: SAGE.

Teddlie, C., & Tashakkori, A. (2009). Overview of contemporary issues in mixed methods research. In A. Tashakkori & C. Teddlie (Eds.), *SAGE handbook of mixed methods in social & behavioral research* (pp. 1–41). Thousand Oaks, CA: SAGE.

Teddlie, C., & Yu, F. (2007). Mixed methods sampling: A typology with examples. *Journal of Mixed Methods Research, 1*(1), 77–100.

Tompkins, P. K. (1994). Principles of rigor for assessing evidence in "qualitative" communication research. *Western Journal of Communication, 58*(1), 44–50.

Tompkins, P. K., & Cheney, G. (1985). Communication and unobtrusive control in contemporary organizations. In R. D. McPhee & P. K. Tompkins (Eds.), *Organization communication: Traditional themes and new directions* (pp. 179–210). Newbury Park, CA: SAGE.

Tracy, S. J. (2000). Becoming a character for commerce: Emotional labor, self-subordination, and discursive construction of identity in a total institution. *Management Communication Quarterly, 14*(1), 90–128.

Tracy, S. J. (2010). Qualitative quality: Eight "big tent" criteria for excellent qualitative research. *Qualitative Inquiry, 16*(10), 837–851.

Tracy, S. J. (2013). *Qualitative research methods: Collecting evidence, crafting analysis, communicating impact.* Hoboken, NJ: Wiley-Blackwell Publishing.

Trethewey, A. (1999). Disciplined bodies: Women's embodied identities at work. *Organization Studies, 20*(3), 423–450.

Trujillo, N. (1992). Interpreting (the work and the talk of) baseball: Perspectives on ball park culture. *Western Journal of Communication, 56*(4), 350–371.

Van Maanen, M. (1990). *Researching lived experience: Human science for an action sensitive pedagogy.* Albany: State University of New York Press.

Van Ness, P. H., Fried, T. R., & Gill, T. M. (2011). Mixed methods for the interpretation of longitudinal gerontologic data insights from philosophical hermeneutics. *Journal of Mixed Methods Research, 5*(4), 293–308.

Vitale, D. C., Armenakis, A. A., & Field, H. S. (2008). Integrating qualitative and quantitative methods for organizational diagnosis: Possible priming effects? *Journal of Mixed Methods, Research, 2*(1), 87–105.

Wesely, P. M. (2010). Language learning motivation in early adolescents: Using mixed methods research to explore contradiction. *Journal of Mixed Methods Research, 4*(4), 295–312.

Wheeldon, J. (2010). Mapping mixed methods research: Methods, measures, and meaning. *Journal of Mixed Methods Research, 4*(2), 87–102.

Xu, K. (2011). An empirical study of Confucianism: Measuring Chinese academic leadership. *Management Communication Quarterly, 25*(4), 644–662.

Yammarino, F. J., Spangler, W. D., & Bass, B. M. (1993). Transformational leadership and performance: A longitudinal investigation. *Leadership Quarterly, 4*(1), 81–102.

Yukl, G. A. (1999). An evaluation of conceptual weaknesses in transformational and charismatic leadership theories. *Leadership Quarterly, 10*(2), 285–305.

SECTION III

Communication and Post-Bureaucratic Organizing

James R. Barker

This section brings into sharp relief the movement and maturation of organizational communication research and conceptualizing since publication of the previous two editions of the present *Handbook*. The title of this section, "Communication and Post-Bureaucratic Organizing," signals how scholars' views of the purpose and function of organizational communication has changed. Far from positioning our organizations as any less bound by formal and informal hierarchies and rules than they were before, the term *post-bureaucratic organizing* refers instead to a standpoint, a way of viewing the organization more in communication terms rather than sociological and psychological terms. Whether the organization is virtual, team based, networked, dispersed, or traditionally bureaucratic, our scholarship sees the organization as a communication construction in the first instance. Rather than being a function of structure and culture, from a *post-bureaucratic* standpoint, the organization *is* a function of communication. In this section, chapter authors are making claims about the essential function of communication in organizing with more vigor, authority, and confidence than they have done in the first two editions of the *Handbook*.

The conceptual ground for our stronger assertions about communication in organizations is developed in Section I. This section takes us into the specific conceptualizations—developed largely since the last edition of the *Handbook*—of how communication creates our organizations. Indeed, a quick review of the previous two editions of the *Handbook* vividly illustrates the degree to which our conceptual developments and articulations have moved over time. The reader would be hard-pressed to find specific connections to our contemporary concept areas of embedded teams, work-life, workplace relationships, leadership, and information-communication technologies in the first two volumes. While the 2001 edition of the *Handbook* had chapters on leadership, networks, and technology, and the initial edition has a chapter on information technology, these chapters are bound up in quite traditional (especially sociological and psychological) frameworks for understanding organizational activity. In the previous two editions, the connections to our present chapters lay in sections on "Structure and Patterns" and

"Processes," key topic areas that certainly framed our thinking of the time.

But organizational communication scholarship has moved on from the framing of the past. While our thinking is richly indebted to previous ways of conceptualizing how communication works in an organization, we now explicitly advocate concepts and constructs that explain how communication constructs organization. Each of the six chapters in the present section will help the reader move from past to present. Each chapter develops that degree of indebtedness we hold to formative concepts such as superior-subordinate communication, information technology, motivation, socialization, and climate. But the chapters then quickly move into the present and detail how our current understanding of core organizational communication concepts reflect a uniquely communicative perspective on organizations—a perspective that has released us from the tight strictures of having to engage the organization firstly as a function of its hierarchy and rules.

Seibold, Hollingshead, and Yoon (Chapter 13) open the section with a chapter on *embedded teams*—purposeful groupings of people who have a signified place within the social fabric of the organization. The reader may find such a direct move into the quite specific concept of embedded teams surprising. What of teams in general? Or virtual teams? Or even groups, for that matter? By focusing on embedded teams, the chapter directs our attention to how we understand the organization as a collective of humans communicating with each other. In the organization, we naturally construct formal and informal groupings of people who collaborate together to create the organization's value. In particular, their conceptualization of embedded teams here reflects the negotiations, boundary management, and identity construction that occur anytime groups of people work together as part of an organization.

Seibold, Hollingshead, and Yoon first develop the evolution of research on groups and teamwork in organizational communication thinking so that we can understand the necessity and power of embedded teams as a concept. They trace the movement of the term *team* in recent years as it becomes our primary mechanism for engaging group activity in organizations, and they explain the role communication plays in forming and shaping team interaction and work. They then develop a full understanding of embedded teams as the outcome of communication-focused research on groups and teams and articulate the concept in a way that facilitates our engagement with the concept in future work. The reader will find the model of embedded teams useful to anchor our understandings of the different ways we encounter teamwork in today's organizations and as a useful framing device for subsequent study.

In their chapter, "Communicating Work-Life Issues" (Chapter 14), Kirby and Buzzanell engage the growing literature on how communication shapes our work-life experience. While the reader will find the concept of work-life familiar today, the term is still relatively new. Earlier editions of the *Handbook*, engaged what we today call *work-life issues* under broader rubrics such as climate, power, and message exchanges. Kirby and Buzzanell capture the movement in our thinking about the consequences of communicative activity in the organization that have led us to seeing how work-life issues have a powerful effect on the organization's capability for creating its value.

Kirby and Buzzanell discuss the emergence of the term *work-life* as a significant means for studying and conceptualizing the consequences of organizational participation. They then position the term communicatively and enable the reader to understand how organizational communication theory and research engage work-life issues from a different standpoint than related fields, such as organizational behavior.

Kirby and Buzzanell next detail five key content areas that frame our knowledge of work-life issues:

1. *Policies governing work-life issues*. Kirby and Buzzanell discuss the role of communication

in the formation of work-life policy. They pay particular attention to the cross-cultural and cross-governmental issues related to work-life policy formation as their development here moves across both organizational policy and government policy boundaries.

2. *Norms of work-life.* Kirby and Buzzanell describe the effects of our everyday organizational communication practices as well as our everyday assumptions about communication on the emergence of behavior-shaping norms.

3. *Production and reproduction of "ideal" workers.* Organizational communication scholars are especially attuned to the critical role of context in our ability to make sense of everyday organizational life. Kirby and Buzzanell explore the communicative construction of work-life contexts, especially in regards to our assumptions about what is ideal and what we aspire toward regarding expectations of self and others.

4. *Identity construction.* Closely related to production of context is how that context then shapes both our identification with the organization and our subsequent actions as guided by that identity. Readers will notice here the discussion of how we perform identity work, with a particular focus on the constitutive role of communication therein.

5. *Practical action.* The focus of the chapter here is less how we ensure that work-life actions create value and more how we deal with all the many possible ways of acting today. Work-life issues involve much more than human interaction, and Kirby and Buzzanell address such highly contemporary issues as how we negotiate work-life around mobile technology and how we consider the joining of organizational work and domestic work.

In developing these five areas, Kirby and Buzzanell are careful to make connections to the foundational literatures that have shaped our understanding of work-life, such as organizational culture, climate, gender, and identity. The authors' concluding section on future research steers our attention to a number of emerging trends in work-life studies. Readers will particularly note Kirby and Buzzanell's concern for issues of intercultural communication in work-life issues, especially regarding how we negotiate the many differences that confront us when we begin to view work-life from a global perspective.

In Chapter 15, Sias presents us with a relatively new way of considering organizational communication. Granted, scholars in the field have been writing about workplace relationships for a long time, but typically from within frameworks such as organizational processes, message exchange, or superior-subordinate communication. But the movement beyond a managerial model of organizing means that the complexities of workplace relational dynamics demand their own focus. Sias's chapter addresses the explanatory power of a communication approach in exploring how organizing functions as a set of relationships.

In the first section of the chapter, Sias carefully charts the historical development of workplace relationship studies from its early roots in social psychology to our contemporary anchoring in organizational communication theory. As *workplace relationships* is an emergent term clearly building on a long research tradition, Sias takes a deliberate approach that distinctly indicates how previous research traditions influence our present thinking. In this section, Sias develops four workplace relationship categories engaged by contemporary literature: (1) superior-subordinate, (2) peer/coworker, (3) friendship, and (4) romantic. For each major category, Sias further sets out the specific attributes and findings that characterize the relationship type. The reader will find that Sias uses concepts such as leadership, information exchange, feedback, appraisal, and mentoring to add both detail and connection to these four broad relationship categories.

Next, Sias moves us toward seeing the complexity of workplace relationships by connecting our current knowledge to broad organizational concerns of power, control, and resistance. This move both situates her perspective on workplace relationships within organizational communication research traditions and serves to frame her development of a new research agenda. Sias addresses several of the most pressing concerns for workplace relationship scholars today (e.g., abusive relationships at work) while still keeping her conceptual work linked to fundamental concepts (e.g., structuration) that frame how we understand the critical ways human work in relationship with each other.

Sias's research agenda also keeps the reader well connected to those serious relationship issues that warrant our attention today. She explains how we can move forward our study of relationships to address concerns such as inclusion at work, generational differences, and sexual orientation. Sias closes with a call to shift our future considerations of workplace relationships more toward macro-level conceptualizations, with a focus on more broad-based communication theory constructions of work relationship formation and practice.

Fairhurst and Connaughton's chapter, "Leadership Communication" (Chapter 16), has a clear historical connection to the second edition of the *Handbook*, also written by Fairhurst. In this chapter, however, the authors demonstrate how organizational communication scholarship on leadership has changed (and is currently changing) a concept widely studied across several fields.

Leadership studies present an expansive and complicated body of literature. Fairhurst and Connaughton begin the task of showing how such a large body of knowledge connects to organizational communication studies by framing leadership research into two areas familiar to communication scholars: (1) a post-positivist view of leadership and (2) a social constructionist view of leadership. As the authors develop each of these categories, they link leadership knowledge to a set of common connection points that enable the reader to understand the primary way each category depicts leadership: The post-positivist view focuses on the transmissional view of communication, supervisor-subordinate communication, global leadership attributes, and change; the social constructionist perspective frames leadership in terms of the comanagement of meaning, aesthetics, influence, reflexivity, and ethics.

Fairhurst and Connaughton develop these two significant categories of leadership by connecting their explanations to both foundational organizational communication theorizing mechanisms (e.g., sensemaking and communication as constitutive of organization) and to other contemporary schools of thought that complement organizational communication research (e.g., social psychology, critical management studies, and ethnomethodology). They then articulate a six-part framework that guides and shapes how communication scholarship can effectively engage leadership going forward.

Fairhurst and Connaughton demonstrate how we can frame a complex organizational phenomenon—leadership—from a communication perspective. The authors enable the reader to view leadership not simply as individuals acting, but as a complex process that is fundamentally communicative. Indeed, current organizational communication research depicts leadership as a socially constructed phenomenon that only exists through the complex communication dynamics and sensemaking practices of organization members.

The penultimate chapter in this section presents the field of study most connected to the first two *Handbooks*, as well as the field that has been the most dynamic over the last 25 years. The original *Handbook* included a single chapter on information technology. The second edition expanded the engagement with information into three chapters: networks, "wired" meetings, and technology. But this field has grown exponentially over the last decade, making the task of shaping our present chapter on information and communication technology (ICT) all the more difficult but all the more pressing.

In their chapter, "Information and Communication Technologies in Organizations," Rice and Leonardi begin by explicating two primary perspectives on ICT: a structural perspective and a communication perspective. They first detail the dynamics of the two perspectives and the advantages offered by merging the two standpoints. Then they propose a framework for such a merger—a way to understand the structural and communicative dynamics of ICT together. Rice and Leonardi develop their framework around three elements. The first element concerns the practices that *influence* ICT adoption, use, and outcomes and includes sections on how forces such as the organization's purpose, organizational culture, emotion, power dynamics, and institutional pressures influence how we understand and use ICT to achieve organizational objectives. The second element in their framework considers the *processes* of ICT use and how these processes create forces for change in the organization. Rice and Leonardi detail these processes at the individual, organizational, and social levels. The third element concerns the *outcomes* of ICT adoption and use. Here, Rice and Leonardi frame outcomes both in the familiar context of technological adoption and assimilation and in a number of less familiar (in previous ICT discussions) but still very influential and meaningful contexts, such as conflict, structure, knowledge management, and power.

Next, Rice and Leonardi bring their cross-disciplinary focus to the fore by detailing how different scholarly domains approach ICT. The authors first describe the key themes that mark differing disciplinary engagement. Then they discuss how different disciplines approach theorizing ICT practices and the differing methods that shape the discipline's theorizing.

Rice and Leonardi conclude the chapter by advocating three directions for future research that emerge from their cross-disciplinary framework. While the study of ICT emergence, the authors' first research direction, is a fruitful venue for organizational communication scholarship with its focus on communication practice, Rice and Leonardi caution against an overconcentration on the communicative element of ICT and recommend attention to the information side of ICT and such growing concerns as information management systems. The authors identify content and relations as the second focus for future research, noting a connection between ways of understanding ICT content and relations and current organizational communication theoretical trends such as communication as constitutive of organization. Knowledge management and sharing forms the third new research direction, which Rice and Leonardi demonstrate as an area that is already generating dynamic organizational communication research.

Rice and Leonardi conclude by returning to the challenges presented to researchers by the expansiveness and cross-disciplinarity of ICT theorizing. However, readers will find that the framework here offers them a well-grounded and communication-oriented mechanism for engaging ICTs and for moving their research in this demanding area forward.

Our final chapter concerns communication networks, one of the most long-standing sectors of organizational communication in our history and arguably the most rapidly evolving field of study. Shumate and Contractor's chapter on "Emergence of Multidimensional Social Networks" represents a fitting way to end a section on post-bureaucratic ways of understanding organizational communication, given the central role of social networks in reenvisioning organizational life.

Shumate and Contractor open by acknowledging the central role that communication network studies have played in previous editions of the *Handbook*. Early in their chapter, Shumate and Contractor develop a new concept for understanding the power of networks, particularly social networks: multidimensional networks. This enables the authors to identify and distinguish a new form in the rapidly evolving field of communication networks. Next, they identify ambient multidimensional networks extant today and describe the communicative relationships arising from them. Shumate and Contractor organize this section by distinguishing communication networks (e.g., networks that enable the construction of shared meaning) and infrastructure networks (e.g., networks that enable shared interaction) and assess current research within those two frames of reference.

The authors conclude by discussing the implications of a multidimensional understanding of communication networks for research going forward. Shumate and Contractor acknowledge the potential that multidimensional concepts of communication networks hold for our ability to articulate a communicative theory of organizing—a theory that has been steadily developed with each iteration of the *Handbook*. Ultimately, Shumate and Contractor's chapter brings us full circle: Network research is a field of study, deeply grounded in our intellectual history, that is marked by an emerging focus—multidimensionality—that takes seriously the constitutive role of communication in our ability to theorize organizing.

This introduction began with the consideration of exactly what is meant by the term *post-bureaucratic*. I proposed that the concept is best understood as a standpoint from which to see core organizational practices as ideally suited for organizational communication theorizing. Our ways of knowing organizations are shifting; organizational communication scholars are now less burdened by sociological and psychological traditions and more guided by our own theories and ways of knowing. This section highlights six exemplars of communication-focused ways of understanding organizing processes and for generating knowledge of organization practices. Each is tempered by our indebtedness to our conceptual history, but all are forward looking. Each chapter demonstrates how we can take organizational communication forward into the global environment of contemporary organizational life and generate new and ever-advancing knowledge that improves both the practice and experience of organization.

CHAPTER 13

Embedded Teams and Embedding Organizations

David R. Seibold, Andrea B. Hollingshead, and Kay Yoon

The study of teams in organizations and their rapidly changing forms and functions has received considerable scholarly attention in the past decade, particularly with the advent of globalization and the changing nature of work (Cheney, Christensen, Zorn, & Ganesh, 2011; Hollenbeck, Beersma, & Schouten, 2012; Kozlowski & Ilgen, 2006; Mathieu, Maynard, Rapp, & Gilson, 2008; O'Toole & Lawler, 2006; Poole, 1998; Seibold & Shea, 2001). The institutional and environmental forces shaping these changes have also proliferated and include such workplace changes as the pressures for employee participation and workplace democratization and the opportunities for collaboration across time and space through advances in information and communication technologies. Some of the most significant contributors to the growth and pervasiveness of teams in organizations are the diversity of organizational forms, the expanding range of organizational contexts, and the organizational shift to an information-intensive culture and service economy in a postindustrial age (Seibold, Kang, Gailliard, & Jahn, 2009).

Less well understood are the ways in which teams inhere in organizations: that is, how the embedded nature of organizational groups simultaneously alters group processes and how embedded teams constitute and transform the structure and processes of organizational systems. Relatedly (and especially important, since embedded teams are constituted in members' symbolic meanings and transformed in their interactions), organizational communication scholarship can advance our understanding of organizationally embedded teams (DeSanctis & Poole, 1997; Poole & Zhang, 2005).

Toward these ends, we undertake four tasks in this chapter, each of which is the focus of successive sections. First, we explicate the nature of embedded teams, including their characteristics, their recursive relationships in organizations, and the central and vital role of communication in this process. Second, we briefly discuss prominent reviews of research on teams and organizations. We identify not only what those summaries offer for our understanding of embedded teams, but what questions are left unanswered. Third, we report results of our own survey of scholarly works published between 2000 and 2012 on communication and embedded teams, ones not covered in the previous handbook edition (Jablin & Putnam, 2001). Fourth, we conclude with an assessment of the current state of research on communication and organizationally embedded teams, its contributions, and an agenda for future research.

Teams Embedded in Organizations

Embedded teams are nested in and embedded with organizations in multiple ways and at multiple levels. Before explicating this concept, we note that examples of traditional embedded teams include project teams, cross-functional teams, task forces, top management teams, semiautonomous and self-managing work teams, sales forces, standing and *ad hoc* committees, customer service teams, firefighter units, health care teams, flight crews, military and paramilitary squads, emergency response teams, and work collaborations.

Our conception of embedded teams draws on earlier definitions of work groups and teams offered by Deutsch (1973), Putnam (1987, 1989), Hoegl and Gemuenden (2001), McGrath and Argote (2001), Hackman (2004), and Seibold and Meyers (2012) as well as by Putnam and Stohl (1990) and Putnam, Stohl, and Baker (2012). However, we contend that aspects of past conceptions should be relaxed or altered to account for the changing nature of post-bureaucratic organizational units that have formed as a result of advances in cyberinfrastructure and the Internet.

Consider, for example, the open innovation platform, Innocentive.com, which calls itself "the world's largest problem solving marketplace" (Innocentive, 2013). Launched in 2005, Innocentive links companies that need solutions with a large, diverse, and skilled set of problem solvers. Company sponsors pay to post their challenges on the site, and problem solvers (who choose to work individually or in teams) generate ideas. The sponsors then select the solution(s) that best meet the criteria. Successful solvers can earn monetary prizes up to $1 million, although most prizes are considerably smaller. Innocentive also helps find teammates who have complementary skills. A variety of organizations routinely post challenges on Innocentive.com, including Fortune 500 companies, medical research centers, and governmental organizations.

Innocentive demonstrates how dramatically the nature of work, teams, and technology use in organizations has changed over the last decade since Jablin and Putnam (2001) published the second edition of this handbook. Innocentive is a virtual organization whose members and resources are dispersed geographically, but it functions as a coherent unit through the use of cyberinfrastructure. Innocentive solvers are, to some extent, members of multiple embedding organizations (including Innocentive, the corporate sponsor of the challenge, and other multiple organizations in which solvers work or consult in their daily lives). Solvers may collaborate with different teams on multiple Innocentive projects. Teams can be self-organized, assembled by the matchmaking service at Innocentive, or some combination of the two. Some teams may be temporary, working together for only one project, while others may be ongoing and collaborate on many projects over many years. Teams may be collocated or remote and use a range of communication technologies to interact and collaborate. Thus Innocentive supports a large variety of work group forms, many of which do not fit the traditional conceptions of *work group* or *virtual team*. This example also underscores the potential for teams to be embedded in multiple rather than single organizations.

The view of embedded teams in this chapter aims to capture this complexity and novelty. In the three subsections below, we (1) highlight the characteristics of embedded teams, including the novelty and complexity associated with their rapidly changing nature; (2) address important ways in which they relate with other groups in the organization; and (3) focus on *communication* in team and organizational relationships.

Dimensions of Embedded Teams

Embedded teams typically include a relatively small number of members who collaborate in pursuit of a goal or completion of a task. There must be a *compelling direction*, that is, at least one overarching common goal or interest that ostensibly unifies members and for which they collectively are accountable (Hackman, 2004). However, other individual and subgroup aspirations, some of which may be hidden from other members, may also typify embedded teams (Wittenbaum, Hollingshead, & Botero, 2004). Beyond real goals and hidden ones, embedded teams will vary in the degree to which they maintain discretion and control over the means to attain their ends (Hackman, 1990). Embedded teams characterized by high teamwork quality also evidence equitable effort and balance of members' contributions, coordination of activities, open and frequent communication, discretionary control over paths to group ends, cohesiveness, and mutual support (Hoegl & Gemuenden, 2001; Seibold & Meyers, 2012).

Members of embedded teams perceive themselves as a group and are viewed as one by others. However, embedded teams have permeable boundaries that may not always be stable, since individual membership can be fluid and dynamic (Putnam & Stohl, 1990). Boundaries may be created and perpetuated by one or more embedding organizations or through members' communication inside and outside the team (e.g., with other teams). Members can belong to multiple teams, which may influence their commitments to each group and to one another (Putnam, 1989). Embedded teams may be interdependent with multiple teams and even with multiple organizations. Individual members of embedded teams, depending on functional roles, may be interdependent with different external teams and different organizations.

Embedded teams create structures through their interactions by appropriating the norms, processes, procedures, and rules of the organization(s) in which they are embedded (Seibold, Meyers, & Shoham, 2010). Furthermore, the structure of embedded teams may vary in formality even as other structures, such as role differentiation, status hierarchies, and power distributions, emerge through team members' interactions.

Embedded teams may either be temporary or of lengthy duration. If in existence over protracted periods of time, embedded teams develop a history that affords additional rules and resources to aid their functioning (Arrow, McGrath, & Berdahl, 2000). Members derive some positive value from continuing their association with the team, and if sufficient numbers of members see value in the team, its existence is sustained.

Crucially important, embedded teams are constituted in communication among members. Team members process information, develop shared meanings, coordinate their actions, manage conflict and consensus, express emotions, and offer interpersonal support. Through their communication, members also exert influence on one another, albeit asymmetrical influence, due to differences in formal and informal power.

Embedded teams use a range of media to connect, to communicate, and to collaborate. Virtual teams are groups of individuals who work together across time, space, and organizational boundaries through the use of communication technology (Kirkman, Rosen, Tesluk, & Gibson, 2004). However, face-to-face teams often use virtual communication such as texting, e-mail, and mobile devices during meetings. Moreover, virtual teams can be visually connected through videoconferencing, which has gotten easier and less expensive in recent years. Although project teams may meet face-to-face on a regular basis, many of their daily interactions and collaborations take place online or over the telephone.

In sum, organizationally embedded teams are constituted in their interactions over time relative to task assignment, interdependence, goal achievement, and member satisfaction. While enabled (and constrained) by the conditions of the organization(s) in which they are embedded, team structures are constituted in members' communication. Specifically, formal structures and team sustainability become evident as members work together for lengthy periods of time.

Embedded teams typically have fewer than 20 intrateam members who collaborate to varying degrees. Even though membership and boundaries may vary in permeability and stability, they identify themselves as a team and they are identifiable as a team. Members' interactions may range across multiple interpersonal and electronic channels of communication as team members develop norms and practices regarding their linkages and topical foci.

In effect, the *groupness* of embedded teams, as reflected in team boundaries, identities, histories, practices, and norms, are constructed in and emerge through the ways that members manage (1) the permeability of team boundaries (i.e., dynamics surrounding multiple memberships and affiliations, representative and emergent roles, and turnover) and (2) the group's interdependence with its immediate context (i.e., processes involving coordination within and across teams; intragroup and intergroup communication; negotiating autonomy, governance, and jurisdiction; and collaborative sensemaking; Putnam & Stohl, 1990). Putnam et al. (2012) remind us that "group permeability and interdependence with context are articulated, interdependent, and interwoven processes that create, sustain, and dissolve group life" (p. 214).

Embedded Teams–Embedding Organization(s) Relationships

The characteristics of embedded teams noted above range from relatively static to highly dynamic. Although this set of features addresses attributes *in* embedded teams, it excludes other key characteristics that flow from the complex layering of team *relationships* within the organizations in which teams are embedded. Traditional research notes that organizational structures, supportive resources, and organizational context influence team processes and performance (Hackman, 2004; Sundstrom, De Meuse, & Futrell, 1990), but this work rarely focuses on the nature of embeddedness. Concerning organizational structure and resources, Hackman (1990, 2004) found that teams need clear goals from management; a balance between managerial and team authority; and structures that enable success, such as a motivating task, effective member composition, and metrics to track performance and alignment with organizational objectives. Teams also need an organizational system that supports teamwork,—namely, a reward system that reinforces collective performance, a training system, an information system that provides open access to managers, material resources to execute tasks (such as equipment, budget, staff support), and effective leadership.

With regard to context, the embedding organization (or multiple organizations) provides the social, political, spatial, and temporal context in which teams operate. The organization(s) enables and constrains teams through organizational climate, power, physical layout (Shockley-Zalabak, 2002), and temporal factors, such as pace, urgency, and horizons (Ballard & Seibold, 2004). Of course, these contextual effects are not unidirectional. Through their successes and failures, for example, embedded teams influence the organization.

In addition, the characteristics of embedded teams, delineated in the previous section, often fail to acknowledge the complexities of team-organization relationships. In nearly all organizations, and especially those that are team based (Mohrman, Cohen, & Mohrman, 1995), lateral interactions among teams are crucial. Organizational standards and rules, procedures and protocols, managerial planning and control, and information technology as well as other coordinative mechanisms promote or require interteam integration (Ancona, 1990; Karzanjian, Drazin, & Glynn, 2000). Furthermore, the most innovative and agile single organizations typically are characterized by dual structures in which traditional management-driven hierarchies and processes form a primary operating system that handles organizational needs and a complementary strategy network that is composed of a guiding coalition and subgroups of change agents

(Kotter, 2012). Not only are embedded teams central to these dual operating structures, but any teams are likely linked to and affected by both systems.

Complexities of Embedded and Embedding Relationships. Contemporary organizations range from traditional hierarchical designs to market-based and socio-politically driven collaborations. At one end of the continuum are authority-based organizations, in which hierarchies enable and constrain authority relationships for embedded teams. At the other end of the continuum, economic, technological, and socio-political forces invite collaborations among multiparty teams whose relationships are fluid, highly interactive, and negotiation oriented (e.g., see the Innocentive.com example above as well as numerous collective action movements that have become institutionalized). Between these poles are numerous organizational forms described as *adhocracy*, *technocracy*, *shamrock*, *post-bureaucratic*, *virtual*, and *networked*. They represent a shift from the traditional hierarchical organization to a more flexible, cooperative, stakeholder-responsive organizational design.

Although embedded teams exist in degrees along this continuum, the nature and effects of embeddedness varies for the teams and the organization. For example, as DeSanctis and Poole (1997) note in discussing the network organization (which the authors locate in the middle of the continuum), teams are the core structural units. Members are organized in teams that exist in relationships to other embedded teams, ones that are clearly defined. These teams, however, are more loosely coupled and more disaggregated than ones in traditional hierarchical organizations. Specifically, reporting relationships are more flat and work arrangements are more cooperative across formal organizational boundaries than are teams in traditional organizations. Further, authority relations are more multidirectional and less defined in network organizations than in the vertical ones that are the hallmark of traditional hierarchical organizations. As core units in network organizations, embedded teams are the coordination mechanisms; that is, they enable stakeholder involvement in information flows and responses to problems; they provide knowledge transfer through collaborating on tasks; and they can be created when needed and for as long as required.

Theoretical Perspectives on Embeddedness. Given this variation in organization types (i.e., from traditional hierarchies to team-based organizations to loosely coupled teams in network organizations to *ad hoc* teams in market-driven arrangements), Putnam's (1989) review of the theoretical perspectives on embeddedness as a unique feature of groups in organizations is instructive. Team embeddedness in organizational forms composed of multiple embedded teams can be characterized in at least three senses. First, *methodological* or *procedural embeddedness* refers to the relationships among embedded teams. A team may be dependent on another one and have no control over its fate; it may be interdependent with other teams who are mutually attached to it; or it may be autonomous and thus independent of other groups in the organization.

Second, *sociological embeddedness* refers to the degree of connectedness between any given team and the entire embedding organization. Those positional relationships vary along vertical and horizontal axes (e.g., their formal place in the organizational hierarchy versus their informal status and ties in the system). A team's sociological embeddedness also plays out in the functions that differentiate it from other teams (e.g., specialized tasks) and that integrate it with teams in the embedding organization (and other organizations to which it may be coupled).

Third, embedded teams also can be characterized in terms of the relationships that their members have with other groups and organizations, known as the team's *psychological embeddedness*. Psychological embeddedness typifies the multiple-group memberships that embedded team members have, ones that enable integration but also may lead to divided loyalties and problems with inclusion and marginalization. Psychological embeddedness also is manifested in how members' organizational roles interpenetrate with group roles (e.g., in how organizational status and titles affect group dynamics and performance).

To summarize, beyond the characteristics of embedded teams themselves, it is important to assay embedded team and embedding organization(s) relationships in terms of (1) the degree of *autonomy/dependence* in teams' relationships with other organizational groups, (2) the extent to which organizational teams are connected *formally/informally* as well as the *differentiating/integrating* functions they perform in relation to other teams, and (3) the *multiple memberships* that embedded team members have with other organizational teams to which they are linked as well as the impacts of their *multiple organizational roles* on key team processes and outcomes. Figure 13.1 summarizes this embedded teams and embedding organization(s) framework, the characteristics of embedded teams, and the salient features of embedding organizations.

Embedded Teams and Organizational Communication

Embedded teams offer organizational communication scholars a vital area of investigation. They are at once outcomes of interactions and bases of organizational structure and processes. Thus embedded teams and their embedding organizations represent a nexus of what organization communication scholarship emphasizes, that is, how such entities are constituted in members' symbolic meanings and transformed in their interactions.

As Putnam (1989) posits, interactions among members of long-standing embedded groups are likely to consist of messages that enable information exchange and verification (i.e., provision of information, clarification, and response). Furthermore, high interaction frequency is likely between embedded teams with diverse means to accomplish divergent goals (or even common means to those diverse ends), while low frequency of interaction is likely between teams characterized by common goals and common methods of achieving them. Such interactions would likely yield redundant and less novel information. Finally, just as the quality of relationships within embedded teams can have a spillover effect on relationships with other teams (Labianca, Brass, & Gray, 1998), interteam coordination can affect intrateam collaboration (Hoegl, Weinkauf, & Gemuenden, 2004).

In contrast, teams embedded in network organizations with multiparty and cooperative relationships across spatial and structural boundaries are likely to be characterized by flexible yet dense communication patterns. As DeSanctis and Poole (1997) observe, this pattern occurs because network organizations (as opposed to traditional ones) afford (1) an increase in communication linkages and information sharing among organizational members and likely a greater volume of intrateam and interteam communication, (2) an increase in interpersonal contact with potentially greater affiliation and support, and (3) an increase in collaboration with additional media used to support that work. The likely joint effect of these increases is faster organizational response times and increased adaptability, which are hallmarks of nontraditional, nonhierarchical organizations.

Interteam interaction among interdependent embedded teams contributes both to integration, as teams must coordinate their efforts, and to differentiation, as members cling to their own team identities while interacting with other teams (Lawrence & Lorsch, 1967). For these reasons, as Hoegl et al. (2004) observe, communication issues become central within teams (e.g., group identity and work commitment), between teams (e.g., coordination, cooperation, and negotiation), and for the embedding organization (e.g., emphasizing superordinate goals and fostering organizational identification).

Figure 13.1 Embedded Teams and Embedding Organization(s) Framework

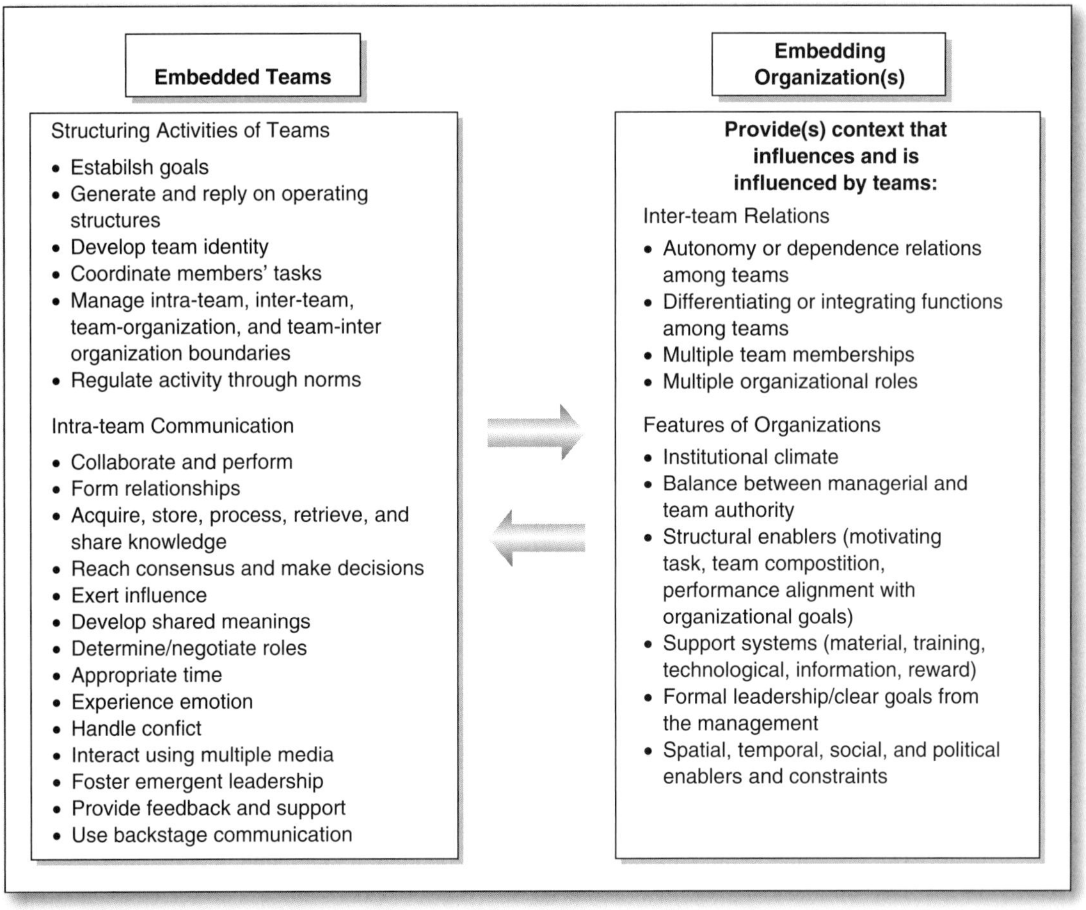

These brief sketches illustrate the importance and benefits of examining the relationships of embedded teams to their embedding organizations and the communication processes that constitute them and their relationships. The next major section examines recent reviews of groups and teams that have either direct or indirect ties to organizations. This synthesis establishes the ground for a survey of the literature published from 2000 to 2012 on embedded teams. It aims (1) to highlight findings on embedded teams and organizations germane to this chapter but not on communication and (2) to draw attention to relevant communication reviews of teams and groups that speak less directly to the *organizational* embeddedness of teams.

Review Articles and Implications for Embedded Teams

Reviews in the Communication Discipline

Several chapters in the second edition of this *Handbook* (Jablin & Putnam, 2001) touched on embedded teams (see Fulk & Collins-Jarvis, 2001; McPhee & Poole, 2001; Rice & Gattiker, 2001; Seibold & Shea, 2001), but no chapter was dedicated to this topic. Specifically, Seibold and Shea (2001) examined research on decision making in organizations, which included studies of self-directed work teams and quality circles as well as other organization-level participatory systems. Their review revealed that the effectiveness of both team-level and organization-level systems was directly related to the amount of participation in decision processes afforded to members. However, research in this area focused either on the team or the organizational structures and not their interrelationships.

In another chapter, Fulk and Collins-Jarvis (2001) examined the theory and research on *wired meetings*, that is, technology-supported synchronous interactions such as teleconferencing, computer conferencing, and group support systems. Even though the studies failed to address embedded teams directly, the authors raised important questions about the recursive effects of mediated meetings and changes in organizational forms. For example, while decentralized organizations relied on semiautonomous teams to replace vertical control structures, organizations could implement technologies that would perform the original control functions. Hence, Fulk and Collins-Jarvis (2001) called for studies to examine how multimedia collaborations enabled horizontal coordination and how dispersed multimedia systems affected connections among linked teams and organizations.

Since the Jablin and Putnam (2001) version of the *Handbook*, communication scholars have conducted reviews of particular types of organizational groups. For example, Zorn and Thompson (2002) examined communication in top management teams. Noting that new organizational forms have made top management teams the most influential groups in organizations and increasingly more important than individual leaders, they identified the unique characteristics of these teams. Those features illuminate the organizational influences of embedded top management teams, namely, strategic decision making, the complexity of decisions processes, the relative power of top management teams, and the heavily politicized environment in which they operate compared with other teams (including those embedded in the same organization). While mainly agenda setting in nature, their analyses illustrate how top management teams function as embedded teams in an embedding organizational relationship.

Poole and Zhang (2005) examined virtual teams whose members were dispersed, had limited face-to-face contact, and had interactions mediated by ICTs. Relevant to team embeddedness and the influences of the embedding organization, the authors overviewed the characteristics of group structure that facilitated virtual team effectiveness, organizational factors that affected virtual team processes and outcomes, the influence of goals and tasks on virtual team processes, and organizational reward structures designed for virtual teams. Later, Gibbs, Nekrassova, Grushina, and Abdul Wahab (2008), in their review and critique of research on virtual teams, argued that much of the research on virtual teams treats communication as a static variable rather than as a process that unfolds over time. The researchers advocate a constitutive approach to understanding communication in virtual teams by focusing on the development and enacting of team norms for forming relationships, sharing knowledge, negotiating identities, resolving conflict, and completing tasks.

Oetzel, Burtis, Sanchez, and Perez (2001) conducted a narrative review of research that examined communication in culturally diverse teams. They organized the review around three perspectives: (1) communication as affected by cultural and contextual factors, (2) communication affecting group outcomes, and (3) communication as a constitutive element of group culture. The researchers concluded that cultural, situational, and contextual factors interact to affect group communication. Like Gibbs et al. (2008), they advocate using a constitutive approach to understanding culture and communication in diverse teams that focuses on the development and enactment of norms and practices that emerge through communication in future research.

Recent Reviews Outside of Communication

Several major reviews of groups from other disciplines address issues related to embedded teams and embedding organizations, ones that focus on topics such as team effectiveness and teamwork behaviors that are germane to this chapter. While the authors may not have examined communication, their findings have implications for organizationally embedded teams.

For example, Guzzo and Dickson (1996) focus on the factors that contribute to the effectiveness of teams in organizations. They surveyed research on a wide range of organizationally embedded natural groups and discussed interconnections between teams and organizations, especially under conditions of planned and unplanned organizational change. Their review called for research concerning the potential roles of diversity, member familiarity, and team boundaries on team effectiveness as well as contextual factors such as organizational reward structures, information systems, and extra-organizational forces on team performance.

Rousseau, Aubé, and Savoie (2006) provided a review and integration of frameworks on teamwork behaviors. They distinguished two behavioral dimensions in teamwork. Regulation of team performance behaviors includes preparation for work accomplishment (e.g., team monitoring and system monitoring) and team adjustment behaviors (e.g., backing up behaviors, intrateam coaching, collaborative problem solving, and team practice innovations). Management of team maintenance includes teamwork behaviors (related to mission analysis, goal specification, planning), task-related collaborative behaviors (e.g., information exchange, coordination, and cooperation), and work assessment behaviors (e.g., performance psychological support and integrative conflict management). The authors also concluded that these subcategories have a temporal character that may have implications for embedded teams in that these behaviors may stem from cyclical phases of activity that lead to a team's task accomplishment.

In a particularly ambitious undertaking, Kozlowski and Ilgen (2006) sifted through over 50 years of psychological research in their effort to understand processes related to team effectiveness. The authors first reviewed theoretically based empirical research in three major areas—cognitive, motivational/affective, and behavioral team processes—that they identified as instrumental for members' combining their task-related resources and, therefore, for being effective. Kozlowski and Ilgen then specified three additional *levers*—team leadership selection and training, team design, and team training—with the intervention potential to align team process and thus to improve team effectiveness. These levers, then, may incorporate features that directly affect organizational embedding practices on team effectiveness.

Mathieu et al. (2008) reviewed literature on team effectiveness that appeared between 1997 and 2007—building from the prior, widely cited major review of work teams in the *Journal of Management* by Cohen and Bailey in 1997. Mathieu and his coauthors modified the input-process-output framework employed in many reviews. Since team research has evolved considerably beyond that orientation, they proposed an input-mediators-outcomes time-sensitive approach to capture the increased complexity in research on team effectiveness. Of particular relevance to embedded teams, the authors cautioned that contextual influences made teams more highly differentiated than their taxonomical type would imply. To gauge work-team effectiveness, Mathieu and colleagues concluded that research is needed on performance metrics of team-organization outcomes and on the development of numerous mediating processes over time (especially interpersonal processes and transition processes).

Wittenbaum and Moreland (2008) examined small-group research in social psychology from 1975 to 2006. They found that most studies focused on social identity and intergroup relations. Investigations of intragroup influences and processes (such as group composition, structure, and performance) and of context were much less commonly investigated. In fact, they concluded that context—including social, temporal, and physical aspects—was investigated in only 5% of the studies, and very little work examined communication among group members. Although a number of studies focused on intergroup relations, an area that should have important implications for interteam relationships in embedding organizations, relatively few studies examined groups in organizations or interteam interactions.

In summary, whether published in communication or in other disciplines, the foregoing major reviews offer important conclusions concerning intrateam processes in organizationally embedded work groups in general and in specific types of teams (e.g., virtual teams and top management teams). Considered together these reviews yield insights into organizational features that may impinge on team embeddedness, namely, leadership, decision making, technology, change, social identity, team composition, teamwork behaviors, temporality, team design, and performance. These reviews also illuminate many communication dynamics in embedded teams including information exchange, interaction, feedback, meetings, conflict management, appropriation of communication support technologies, and multimedia use. While less focused on the embedding organizational dynamics, these reviews provide useful knowledge claims related to organizational features that encourage and enable interteam coordination and mitigate vertical control, interteam dynamics during planned versus unplanned organizational change, intergroup relations, and organization-driven initiatives to improve teamwork.

However, these reviews do not speak to key interteam and embedding organization dimensions, specifically, autonomy/dependence in interteam relationships, formal/informal connectedness among teams, differentiating/integrating functions of intrateam and interteam relationships, multiple team memberships in the embedding organization, and impacts of members' multiple organizational roles on key team processes and outcomes. Instead, given the dearth of research on embedded teams and embedding organizational relationships, especially communication related to these concerns, these reviews typically call for research on technologies for linking collaborating teams, the effects of boundary management on team performance, and clearer specification of team-organization outcomes.

We turn next to our survey of recent studies of communication and embedded teams to analyze how these investigations advance our understanding of organizationally embedded teams and teamwork. In the conclusion, we assess the current state of research on communication and organizationally embedded teams, the contributions of this recent literature, and an agenda for future research on embedded teams and embedding organizations.

Studies From 2000 to 2012 on Embedded Teams

Scope of Review

To fill the lacunae of broad-based yet communication-focused reviews of workgroups and teams since Jablin and Putnam (2001), we conducted a major survey of scholarly works on embedded teams and communication published from January 2000 until September 2012. We selected only articles that explicitly addressed communication processes. The communication focus was an important criterion to establish a clear distinction between the current handbook chapter and other team-related review pieces outside the discipline (e.g., Kozlowski & Ilgen, 2006; Mathieu et al., 2008; Rousseau et al., 2006).

In addition, we conducted a keyword search of relevant studies that used *teams* and *groups* in the title, and we identified studies that focused on teams of 3–20 members. Our target publication venues included only communication journals (*Journal of Communication*, *Human Communication Research*, *Communication Research*, *Management Communication Quarterly*, *Communication Monographs*, *Journal of Applied Communication*

Research, Communication Studies, Western Journal of Communication, Communication Research Reports, Communication Quarterly, and *Communication Yearbook*).

Our search resulted in 92 articles that fit our initial criteria. We coded each publication based on the type of article (theoretical, empirical, review, other), nature of research method (experiment, survey, interview, ethnography, observation), type of participants (university students, organizational employees, etc.), and list of key variables.

From the 92 articles, we included only those that studied *embedded* teams. We were generous with how we classified research that met this criterion. We required that the article explore team-related phenomena and/or explicitly address the implications of the research for teams. However, we did not require that the embedded team be the unit of analysis. So articles that explored team contexts (such as meetings), investigated only specific team roles (such as leaders), or included data of individuals reporting on communication in their teams were included in the review.

We excluded 55 studies that sampled participants other than embedded team members or conducted laboratory studies removed from the team's organizational context. We also omitted review articles that did not introduce a new theoretical perspective. This yielded 37 investigations of teams, ranging from municipal firefighter crews to swift action teams to troupes of actors in a community theater, and organizations across multiple sectors and industries, including health, aerospace, legal, professional services, government, public/community, and military. Next, we reviewed the 37 articles. Those that were reviewed are listed with an asterisk (*) in the references section at the end of this chapter.

Results of Current Review and Embedded Team Findings

Of the 37 articles, 33 were empirical. Three were theoretical and one was a computer simulation. The empirical studies were about evenly divided between qualitative (15 studies) and quantitative (18 studies) methodologies. Qualitative studies tended to be ethnographic, whereas most quantitative studies investigated participants' perceptions of communication processes. There was not a consistent or programmatic theme across the set of articles, although the work of individual researchers and their collaborators was, in many cases, programmatic. The results, summarized below, fall into seven insights about embedded teams distilled from this literature. Most of these insights affirm and extend earlier work.

1. *The communication required by team members' multiple memberships can be a barrier to team performance, depending on the embedding context.*

This insight relates to the multiple-membership aspect of embedded teams. Multiple memberships can impose additional communication constraints and demands on team members, which can negatively affect their performance, especially when the team is temporary and/or of short duration. Strategies such as an added focus on intrateam communication or prioritizing multiple memberships may be necessary to achieve important team goals.

For example, Kramer (2005b) examined a temporary group whose members were dedicated to raising money for a nonprofit organization by participating in a marathon. He found that external as well as internal communication and maintaining multiple group memberships were positively associated with energizing members, finishing the marathon, and raising money. Being in the marathon group did not damage members' relationships with other groups, but demands from other groups negatively affected participation in the marathon group. Although team members were rarely together, e-mail updates about training, fundraising, and team events created team identity, even though not everyone attended team events. Similarly, Susskind, Odom-Reed, and Viccari (2011) examined 11 intact interuniversity research project teams that were part of a short-term alliance. Team leaders who worked more closely within their teams had better team outcomes than those that developed alliances with other team projects.

Constraints that arise from multiple memberships often create tensions. In particular, Kramer (2004) identified four main themes of dialectical tensions in community theater groups: commitment to the theater group versus commitment to other life activities, ordered versus emergent activities, inclusion and exclusion, and group norms for acceptable and unacceptable behaviors. To manage commitment to the theater group, members expected others to use one of three strategies: (1) audition first and then commit to the group only if the member could minimize the tensions, (2) delay or segment other life activities to reduce the tensions, or (3) negotiate conflicts with other groups prior to joining the theater group. Kramer (2002) found that most cast members worked out possible multiple membership conflicts and committed themselves to the theater in advance of their auditions. Inexperienced cast members did not always prioritize well; however, experienced members often cut them some slack. Members' own strong commitment to the group was associated with their expectations that other members share their commitment.

2. *Peer support is a very powerful motivator in embedded teams.*

Peer support in many forms has been identified as a positive influence on individual and group outcomes across many contexts. The studies in this review examine peer support from inside rather than outside the team and involve many practices, including offering relationally oriented communication, engaging in shared activities, spending time together, and laughing together.

In an ethnographic study of volunteer members of two community theater groups, Kramer (2005a) found that peer support and opportunity for social interaction, along with positive audience response, were the best predictors of group members' positive reactions to their experiences, commitment to the show, and loyalty to the community theater company.

Peer support was also critical in an interdisciplinary academic research team. Thompson (2009) discovered that communication practices such as spending time together, practicing trust, discussing language differences, sharing laughter, and engaging in team tasks were central for building and maintaining a sense of collective communication competence in research teams. Demonstrating presence, being open to new experiences, engaging in backstage communication, developing reflexive tasks, and sharing humor served as the foundations for collective communication competence. She also discovered processes that challenged collective communication competence, which included negative humor and sarcasm, communicating boredom, debating expertise, and jockeying for power.

This insight also applies to other countries. Bakar, Dilbeck, and McCroskey (2010) found that positive relationship communication, upward openness communication, and job-relevant communication accounted for much of the variance in team commitment in a Malaysian organization that managed airport services.

3. *Roles in teams are negotiated communicatively. They influence and are influenced by the embedding context.*

This insight informs the consensus/conflict and formal/informal dimensions of embedded teams. Even when leadership and other roles are formally assigned to members, they are often modified and changed through a negotiation process among team members. This negotiation process is shaped by the needs of the organization and, in turn, either meets or changes those organizational needs. Kramer (2009) presented a two-part process model of role negotiations in a study of an educational theater production. First, members negotiated the organizational role they would perform, and then, they negotiated the performance of that role once it was assumed. The conditions under which individuals became team members affected their abilities to negotiate their roles. For example, members who were recruited were more active in defining their roles than were those who auditioned. In a study of quality improvement teams, Garner and Poole (2009) identified and explicated the role of a foil (i.e., a difficult or contentious group member) in establishing and endorsing leadership. Leaders gained endorsement from other group members by counteracting the foil, moving the team forward on its task, and by emphasizing key team values.

In another study of role negotiation, Kramer (2006) examined how secondary leaders and cast members relied on communication and affective responses to put on a successful theatrical performance when the primary director was ineffective. Secondary leaders stepped in at various points of the production to provide task direction or social and relational focus to the group. Shared leadership emerged in similar ways in zero history leaderless groups. For example, passive people were not recognized as leaders. Those who demonstrated conscientiousness or provided direction were more likely to be viewed as leaders.

In contrast to responding to poor leadership, Galanes (2009) examined the factors that influenced the leadership of effective teams. She found, through interviews, that effective leaders tended to frame their actions in response to three dialectical tensions: group control by leader/by members, the leader's focus on task-related versus non-task-related issues, and the leader's focus on group process/outcome. Leaders consciously adjusted their communication strategies to manage the tensions, which enabled them to achieve multiple and often-conflicting goals.

4. *Individual participation and deliberation in civic and community group decision making can be a self-reinforcing process.*

This insight refers to the conflict and consensus aspect of embedded teams. Deliberation involves careful consideration and evaluation of different decision options as well as the information and opinions about them. The purpose of civic and community deliberations is to discuss and often make decisions on issues relevant to people who live in the same geographical area. These deliberations are often *ad hoc*, democratic, of short duration, and involve a public forum.

For example, Burkhalter, Gastil, and Kelshaw (2002) proposed a self-reinforcing theoretical model of democratic or public deliberation in small face-to-face groups that had relatively tight spatial and temporal constraints. The general hypothesis that underlies the model is that the effects of past deliberation will substantially increase the probability that participants will deliberate in the future. It uses structuration as a basis for the model and proposes that deliberation is more likely to occur when participants have a broad understanding of how the deliberation process works and positive reinforcement of deliberative habits. Gastil, Black, Dees, and Leighter (2008) provided a partial test of the model by examining the relation between jury service and civic engagement in two large panel studies. Jurors who rated their group communication as respectful and deliberative were more satisfied with the deliberations and the verdict. In addition, jurors expressing a positive view of their deliberations and decisions also reported more positive civic attitudes.

Also in the context of jury decision making, Sunwolf (2006) proposed *decisional regret theory,* which is the "production, sharing, and reconstruction of predecisional imaginary narratives that allow alternative decisional outcomes to be anticipated" (p. 122). The theory accounts for communicative behaviors in situations in which people experience anxiety and anticipate choice regret in considering decision alternatives. More specifically, it predicts that counterfactual storytelling, which describes "what if" shared narratives, will likely occur when members anticipate making a meaningful group decision and strive to reduce anxiety from the anticipated regret of unwanted outcomes.

Ryfe (2006) conducted a videotape analysis of five National Issues forums and discovered that deliberative talk in these public forums mostly took the form of storytelling. He argued that storytelling served individual and collective functions in deliberation without much explicit conflict or argument, such as helping participants overcome a lack of knowledge about issues and allowing groups to build a sense of moral community around issues. Renz (2006) observed a cohousing community decision about surfacing a parking area. The community's use of consensus decision making allowed the residents to balance three goals: making an appropriate decision, meeting members' needs, and maintaining the community's well-being. However, reaching agreement was complicated by members' value differences and discontinuity in their participation.

5. *High-reliability teams adapt their communication strategies to the immediate demands of the environment.*

This insight speaks to the tradeoffs inherent in the autonomy/dependence and the formal/informal dimensions of embedded teams. High-reliability environments are those in which teams must work with extremely high accuracy and diligence to avoid accidents or injury. They often rely heavily on protocols and procedures for doing their work. However, there are times when high-reliability teams need to demonstrate agility in their communication.

McKinney, Barker, Davis, and Smith (2005) observed airline flight deck crews and the factors that made these "swift starting action teams" effective in crisis situations. Swift-action teams were composed of highly trained strangers within one organization who worked together for a relatively short time. The researchers developed a descriptive proposition-based model and hypothesized that swift-action teams that stressed communication values early in their interactions would perform more effectively than those who did not. When a crisis occurred, teams with a metacapacity to engage in new interactions that departed from protocols would be more successful in their team response. This metacapacity can be gained from the organizational culture and training environment.

Myers and McPhee (2006) investigated the development, maintenance, and assimilation of highly interdependent workgroups in a municipal fire department. Firefighters responded to questions that reflected their own membership experiences and how their crew would assess the crew's performance. Members' involvement and trust were predictors of their commitment and acceptance. Perceived crew performance was positively associated with members' level of commitment through their tenure, proactivity, involvement, and acculturation.

Also demonstrating communication adaptation, Apker, Propp, and Ford (2005) investigated the evolving role of nurses in health care teams by exploring the interplay of competing forces or dialectical tensions associated with hierarchy, status, and personal identity and the communicative strategies they adapted to deal with these tensions. The researchers found that the use of interdependent teams and a flatter organizational structure promoted a more participative, equalitarian model of decision making, and yet often fell short, given the deeply ingrained medical hierarchy. Ellingson (2003) examined the backstage communication processes of an interdisciplinary health care team for geriatric oncology patients. *Backstage communication* is informal communication among members that takes place outside of team meetings in areas of the hospital that are off-limits to patients. Ellingson uncovered seven communication processes that took place backstage: information sharing about patients, checking clinic progress, relationship building among health care team members, space management, handling interruptions, training students, and formal reporting. She found that backstage communication affected team members' front stage communication with patients and their care in both positive and negative ways.

6. *Acquiring, sharing, and retrieving knowledge in embedded teams are social processes.*

This insight informs the differentiating/integrating functions of teams. Knowledge is a commodity in organizations, and its value shapes and is shaped by social processes invoked through communication. If there is uncertainty or conflict in the environment, it will be manifested in the knowledge-sharing patterns of embedded teams.

Using social network analysis, Palazzolo (2005) identified patterns of information retrieval at multiple levels in 12 work teams. Team members were likely to retrieve information from others who they perceived as experts on a particular topic. Some members were more central than others with regard to the flow of information in the teams, but members did not have a specific expert in mind when they needed information on a particular topic. In a computer simulation of generative mechanisms that influenced the development of transactive memory systems and the role of communication in that process, Palazzolo, Serb, She, Su, and Contractor (2006) demonstrated that teams starting with a small number of nonexperts who accurately perceived what others knew had the best chance of emerging into well-developed transactive memory systems.

De Vries, van den Hoof, and de Ridder (2006) discovered that team members' eagerness and willingness to share information was positively associated with information-sharing behavior. Members who were agreeable and/or extraverted also shared more information with their teams. In turn, knowledge sharing was positively associated with job satisfaction and self-rated performance.

Similarly, Grice, Gallois, Jones, Paulsen, and Callan (2006) used an intergroup perspective to examine information sharing and ratings of work-team communication in a public hospital. They operationalized in-group and out-group members based on occupation similarity. Interdisciplinary team members reported sending about the same amount of information to members with similar and different occupations in their work team. In contrast, they reported receiving less information from members with different occupations and rated that information as less effective than from team members with similar occupations.

Lyon (2005) studied an e-learning company after the former CEO announced his departure. Members' uncertain environment produced tensions between organizational members about the perceived value of expertise. The perceived value of knowledge in the organization was dependent on the socially constructed context to determine its value. Participants engaged in communicative activities that shaped the recognized value of their own knowledge in favorable ways.

7. *The relations among technology use, communication, and time in embedded teams are dynamic and recursive.*

This insight speaks to all dimensions of embedded teams developed in this chapter. The increasing integration of technology into organizations is making new forms and structures of embedded teams possible, as indicated in the Innocentive example described earlier in the chapter. Technology use shapes team communication, which in turn alters the norms and practices of embedded teams and their embedding organizations.

Team members who are distributed across diverse locations may have a more difficult time internalizing an organization's mission than those who are collocated. Shockley-Zalabak (2002) examined communication processes in a virtual customer support team in a major high-technology company composed of members from multiple countries. She found that the metaphor of the protean place, with its characteristics of shape-shifting, simultaneity, and sociality, was applicable to the changing nature of the team. Team members provided a description of a system that was not stable but rather was continually shaped by environmental pressures and needs. Team members lacked a sense of place within the team and larger organization. Despite external evaluations of success, the team became increasingly dissatisfied. Whitford and Moss (2009) showed that when leaders and followers worked at different locations, visionary leadership was positively associated with work attitudes when it centered on hopes and aspirations rather than on duties and obligations. When leaders and followers worked at the same location, personal recognition was positively associated with work engagement. In addition, when visionary leadership focused on duties and obligations, work engagement increased.

Features of the virtual team structure predicted embedded teams' use of communication technology. Timmerman and Scott (2006) found in a study of 98 virtual teams that team structures such as the number of remote locations was positively associated with teams' use of e-mail and video conferencing.

In turn, teams' use of communication technologies shaped task communication practices in embedded teams. Jackson and Poole (2003) used a group decision support system to investigate the idea-generation process in union-management quality improvement groups from a governmental agency. The quantity of ideas seemed less important than the normative function of idea generation in the group. For example, brainstorming was used to signal transitions to a new phase of the task. Groups rarely revisited ideas on their lists. Groups that used only the group decision support system generated fewer ideas overall than those that used paper or flipcharts.

And finally, embedded teams' communication practices rather than their use of communication technology predicted team communication-based outcomes. Timmerman and Scott (2006) discovered that virtual teams stressing communication competencies such as being thorough and responsive had higher levels of identification, communication satisfaction, cohesion, and trust. The researchers found no association between virtual teams' technology use and outcomes.

A number of studies examined the antecedents and consequences of using a shared repository or intranet for knowledge acquisition, storage, and retrieval in embedded teams across a range of organizational contexts, including military, aerospace, consulting, hospitality, and legal. Child and Shumate (2007) found that members' perceptions about whether their team had accurate who-knows-what knowledge rather than relying on a shared-information repository was positively related to perceived team effectiveness. In addition, remote work was negatively associated with perceived team effectiveness but was not correlated with use of shared repositories.

Yuan et al. (2005) investigated the joint impacts of social influence and technology competence on team members' use of intranets. Individuals' perceived Internet usage was predicted by their teammates' perceived usage. Technology competence was strongly related to both information contribution and retrieval with intranets. Building on this study, Yuan, Fulk, and Monge (2007) found that perceived usage of organizational information repositories by team members significantly influenced their actual usage. Moving to a multilevel analysis, Yuan, Fulk, Monge, and Contractor (2010) examined the influences of these repositories on individual expertise exchange at both the individual and team levels. Individual knowledge sharing occurred frequently in teams that had well-developed team-level expertise directories, higher communication-tie strength, and shared task interdependence. Su (2012) discovered that accuracy in expertise recognition was positively influenced by a member's degree centrality in the communication network and negatively influenced by the extent to which this person's work was done remotely.

Barley, Leonardi, and Bailey (2012) found that individuals used technology strategically to create boundary objects, such as graphs, tables, and mock-ups, to influence group meaning in cross-boundary collaborations. In a case study of automotive design engineers, they identified two different strategies used to achieve different goals. The first was *ambiguity*, designed to create multiple meanings so that members could attach their own meanings to the object. The second was *clarity*, meant to force collaborators to accept a particular outcome. Engineers preferred using ambiguity, which they believed maintained long-term relationships with coworkers, and used clarity only when they expected resistance to their ideas.

Ballard and Seibold (2004) examined relations

among communication-related structures that guided members' work and experiences of time among work teams of a university subcontractor that provided housing and residential services. The type of task interdependence, technologies used, and feedback cycles in teams affected their experiences of time. For example, sequentially interdependent teams and teams that used more constraining tasks reported using time in a more linear and less flexible way than did those who relied on pooled interdependence. Work-group members who used less constraining technologies had a more present-oriented or future focus. Teams with low variability and shorter task completion worked at a slower pace and were less likely to experience urgency, scarcity of time, and work delays.

The proliferation of mobile devices has changed team norms and practices in meetings. Social influence has a major impact on what individuals observe others doing, and perceptions of electronic multitasking affects individuals' multitasking behaviors in meetings. Stephens and Davis (2009) examined *electronic multitasking*, defined as using one or more devices during a face-to-face or mixed-mode meeting. They found considerable variance in how individuals used devices during meetings; organizational norms and concerns about self-presentation accounted for much of this variance. Stephens (2012) redefined multitasking in meetings as *multicommunication*, that is, communication technology practices involved in engaging in multiple, nearly simultaneous conversations. She developed a model of multicommunication that consisted of informing, influencing, supporting others, participating in parallel meetings, and being available.

Conclusions

Central to this chapter is the thesis that structures and processes in organizationally embedded teams are constituted in their interactions over time. The theoretical propositions and empirical findings discussed throughout this chapter led to the framework depicted in Figure 13.1. As we showed in this chapter, there is much in prior research and in previous reviews that highlights communication dynamics in embedded teams, including information exchange, interaction, feedback, centrality of meetings, management of conflict, appropriation of communication support technologies, and multimedia use. The post-2000 publications revealed other intrateam communication findings, such as the negotiation of roles; communication support among members; the sociality of knowledge acquisition, storage, and retrieval; the complementary influence of teams' internal and external communication; the prevalence and functions of backstage communication; and the appropriation of technology.

In our survey, we were surprised to find so few of the 2000–2012 journal articles that examined the communication processes of team member, embedded team, and embedding organizational relationships at multiple levels of analysis. Research typically focused on either the team or the organizational structures and not how their interrelationships were created, sustained, and modified communicatively. Most of the studies examined how the embedding context influenced intrateam communication rather than how the intrateam communication influenced its embedding context. There were only a few studies that examined interteam relationships within and across organizations. Clearly, we need to know more about both levels and about the communication processes through which relationships are manifested, managed, and changed.

Organizational (Miller et al., 2011) and group (Poole, Keyton, & Frey, 1999) communication scholars have called for examining the effects of individual, group, and organizational (multiple) levels of analysis, given the interdependence among them. Few of the post-2000 studies that we reviewed assessed embedded team processes at multiple levels. Notable exceptions were Myers and McPhee (2006), who used team interaction variables to predict individual membership and crew-level assimilation, and Yuan et al. (2010), who used team variables to predict individual outcomes. Specifically, Yuan and colleagues proposed that individual-level effects cumulated at the group level so that teams whose members had greater team-level tie strength exhibited higher individual levels of task exchange than did ones with less tie strength. They found support for this cross-level contextual influence from the team to the member. To understand embedded team and embedding organization relationships, much more research is needed on the embedding context and on both levels of analysis.

Based on this review, we offer a few additional observations on the current state of embedded team research. Many organizational communication scholars are collaborating with scholars in other disciplines and publishing excellent research outside of communication. *Organization Science* is a major outlet for this work. This practice could be both positive and negative for developing organizational communication scholarship. On the positive side, the work may reach a broad audience and help bridge the communication–management scholarship divide. On the negative side, that excellent work is not as visible to communication scholars as if it were published in the field.

We also noticed several cases in which multiple articles were based on the same data set but examined different variables, processes, or subsets of teams. So the total number of teams examined across the set of studies was considerably smaller than it appeared on the surface. In most of those cases, the researcher(s) did not describe or cite the earlier publications based on the same data set. In one notable exception, Yuan et al. (2007) elaborated in the method section on the similarities and differences in the data set they used in that study and the one used in Yuan et al. (2005). Researchers who are publishing multiple articles from a single data set should follow the example set by Yuan et al. (2007).

Finally, few articles linked communication processes to important outcomes, such as team and organizational performance. This linkage is important to gain the attention of scholars outside of communication and to make the research relevant for managers, administrators, and other practitioners who care about outcomes and the bottom line.

We conclude with a description of the most relevant and ambitious investigation in the past decade that focused on the relationships, linkages, and functions among organizationally embedded teams. The article was published in a management journal, which is why it was not included in our review. We hope it will inspire organizational communication scholars. Hoegl et al. (2004) studied the effects of interteam processes in a large-scale, multiteam innovation project. They employed a longitudinal (i.e., year-end points in time over three years), multi-informant design that involved team members, team leaders, and project managers to investigate 39 simultaneous engineering teams of a new product development project in the European automotive industry.

Hoegl and colleagues found, first, a positive relation between interteam coordination and team overall performance. The effect was largely attributable to interactions among teams about adherence to schedules. Although the quality of *intragroup* teamwork was most important in the early stages of the embedded teams, the team stage of development was not significantly associated with *interteam* coordination or with the team's quality of work." This finding was due primarily to the fact that the exchange of important technical data was of continuing importance to the majority of teams at all stages of their development. The recurrent and unanticipated changes as specific teams sought to implement their concepts and to design their modules in the larger project fostered additional information exchange, especially for the high-task interdependent teams. Finally, the intragroup teamwork quality was positively associated with project commitment and interteam coordination. They interpreted this observation as consistent with research demonstrating that collaboration within teams may effect interteam collaboration and vice versa (e.g., Williams, 2001).

Additional Research Directions

The future is bright for embedded team research. Software for capturing audio and video is becoming less expensive, more powerful, and easier to use. Rapidly improving automated object and text recognition software is making real time content coding of video possible. It has become so much easier that a growing number of team researchers outside of communication are studying team interaction and performance over time in complex simulated-task environments that are constantly changing (Cooke, Gorman, Myers, & Duran, 2012). These projects have received considerable external grant support for their work from the National Science Foundation, National Institutes of Health, and the U.S. military.

Embedded team scholarship in organizational communication needs to move beyond the traditional organization and examine team communication processes in new forms of organizations, such as Innocentive. It also needs to investigate new forms of communication, such as enterprise social media. Rather than focusing on how the embedding context affects embedded teams differently, researchers should focus on integrating findings across researchers and methodologies and on looking for similarities across contexts. This process will be important for future theory building.

References

Ancona, D. G. (1990). Outward bound: Strategies for team survival in an organization. *Academy of Management Journal, 33*(2), 334–365.

*Apker, J., Propp, K. M., & Ford, W. S. Z. (2005). Negotiating status and identity tensions in health care team interactions: An exploration of nurse role dialectics. *Journal of Applied Communication Research, 33*(2), 93–115.

Arrow, H., McGrath, J. E., & Berdahl, J. L. (2000). *Small groups as complex systems: Formation, coordination, development, and adaptation*. Thousand Oaks, CA: SAGE.

*Bakar, H. A., Dilbeck, K. E., & McCroskey, J. C. (2010). Mediating role of supervisory communication practices on relations between leader-member exchange and perceived employee commitment to workgroup. *Communication Monographs, 77*(4), 637–656.

*Ballard, D. I., & Seibold, D. R. (2004). Communication-related organizational structures and work group temporal experiences: The effects of coordination method, technology type, and feedback cycle on members' construals and enactments of time. *Communication Monographs, 71*(1), 1–27.

*Barley, W. C., Leonardi, P. M., & Bailey, D. E. (2012). Engineering objects for collaboration: Strategies of ambiguity and clarity at knowledge boundaries. *Human Communication Research, 38*(3), 280–308.

*Burkhalter, S., Gastil, J., & Kelshaw, T. (2002). A conceptual definition and theoretical model of public deliberation in small face-to-face groups. *Communication Theory, 12*(4), 398–422.

Cheney, G., Christensen, L. T., Zorn, T. E., Jr., & Ganesh, S. (2011). *Organizational communication in an age of globalization: Issues, reflections, practices* (2nd ed.). Prospect Heights, IL: Waveland Press.

*Child, J. T., & Shumate, M. (2007). The impact of communal knowledge repositories and people-based knowledge management on perceptions of team effectiveness. *Management Communication Quarterly, 21*(1), 29–54.

Cohen, S. G., & Bailey, D. E. (1997). What makes teams work: Group effectiveness research from shop floor to the executive suite. *Journal of Management, 23*(3), 239–290.

Cooke, N. J., Gorman, J. C., Myers, C. W., & Duran, J. L. (2012). Interactive team cognition. *Cognitive Science, 37*(2), 255–285.

*de Vries, R. E., van den Hoof, B., & de Ridder, J. A. (2006). Explaining knowledge sharing: The role of team communication styles, job satisfaction, and performance beliefs. *Communication Research, 33*(2), 115–135.

DeSanctis, G., & Poole, M. S. (1997). Transitions in teamwork in new organizational forms. *Advances in Group Processes, 14*, 157–176.

Deutsch, M. (1973). *The resolution of conflict: Constructive and destructive processes.* New Haven, CT: Yale University Press.

*Ellingson, L. L. (2003). Interdisciplinary health care teamwork in the clinic backstage. *Journal of Applied Communication Research, 31*(2), 93–117.

Fulk, J., & Collins-Jarvis, L. (2001). Wired meetings: Technological mediation of organizational gatherings. In F. M. Jablin & L. L. Putnam (Eds.), *Handbook of organizational communication: Advances in theory, research, and methods* (pp. 624–663). Thousand Oaks, CA: SAGE.

*Galanes, G. J. (2009). Dialectical tensions of small group leadership. *Communication Studies, 60*(5), 409–425.

*Garner, J. T., & Poole, M. S. (2009). Opposites attract: Leadership endorsement as a function of interaction between a leader and a foil. *Western Journal of Communication, 73*(3), 227–247.

*Gastil, J., Black, L. W., Dees, E. P., & Leighter, J. (2008). From group member to democratic citizen: How deliberating with fellow jurors reshapes civic attitudes. *Human Communication Research, 34*(1), 137–169.

Gibbs, J. L., Nekrassova, D., Grushina, S. V., & Abdul Wahab, S. (2008). Reconceptualizing virtual teaming from a constitutive perspective: Review, redirection, and research agenda. In C. S. Beck (Ed.), *Communication yearbook* (vol. 32, pp. 191–229). New York, NY: Routledge.

*Grice, T. A., Gallois, C., Jones, E., Paulsen, N., & Callan, V. J. (2006). "We do it, but they don't": Multiple categorizations and work team communication. *Journal of Applied Communication Research, 34*(4), 331–348.

Guzzo, R. A., & Dickson, M. W. (1996). Teams in organizations: Recent research on performance and effectiveness. *Annual Review of Psychology, 47*, 307–338.

Hackman, J. R. (1990). *Groups that work (and those that don't): Creating conditions for effective teamwork.* San Francisco, CA: Jossey-Bass.

Hackman, J. R. (2004, June). What makes for a great team? *APA Science Briefs, 18*(6). Retrieved from http://www.apa.org/science/about/psa/2004/06/hackman.aspx

Hoegl, M., & Gemuenden, H. G. (2001). Team quality and the success of innovative projects: A theoretical concept and empirical evidence. *Organization Science, 12*(4), 435–449.

Hoegl, M., Weinkauf, K., & Gemuenden, H. G. (2004). Interteam coordination, project commitment, and team work in multiteam R&D projects: A longitudinal study. *Organization Science, 15*(1), 38–55.

Hollenbeck, J. R., Beersma, B., & Schouten, M. E. (2012). Beyond team types and taxonomies: A dimensional scaling conceptualization for team description. *Academy of Management Review, 37*(1), 82–106.

Innocentive. (2013). *Frequently asked questions* [Website]. Retrieved from http://www.innocentive.com/faq/Seeker

Jablin, F. M., & Putnam, L. L. (Eds.). (2001). *The new handbook of organizational communication: Advances in theory, research, and methods.* Thousand Oaks, CA: SAGE.

*Jackson, M. H., & Poole, M. S. (2003). Idea-generation in naturally occurring contexts. *Human Communication Research, 29*(4), 560–591.

Karzanjian, R. K., Drazin, R., & Glynn, M. A. (2000). Creativity and technological learning: The roles of organization architecture and crisis in large-scale projects. *Journal of Engineering and Technology Management, 17*(3/4), 273–298.

Kirkman, B. L., Rosen, B., Tesluk, P. E., & Gibson, C. B. (2004). The impact of team empowerment on virtual team performance: The moderating role of face-to-face interaction. *Academy of Management Journal, 47*(2), 175–192.

Kotter, J. P. (2012, November). Accelerate! *Harvard Business Review*, 46–58.

Kozlowski, S. W. J., & Ilgen, D. R. (2006). Enhancing the effectiveness of work groups and teams. *Psychological Science in the Public Interest, 7*(3), 77–124.

*Kramer, M. W. (2002). Communication in a community theater group: Managing multiple group roles. *Communication Studies, 53*(2), 151–170.

*Kramer, M. W. (2004). Toward a communication theory of group dialectics: An ethnographic study of a community theater group. *Communication Monographs, 71*(3), 311–332.

*Kramer, M. W. (2005a). Communication and social exchange processes in community theater groups. *Journal of Applied Communication Research, 33*(2), 159–182.

*Kramer, M. W. (2005b). Communication in a fundraising marathon group. *Journal of Communication, 55*(2), 257–276.

*Kramer, M. W. (2006). Shared leadership in a community theater group: Filling the leadership role. *Journal of Applied Communication Research, 34*(2), 141–162.

*Kramer, M. W. (2009). Role negotiations in a temporary organization: Making sense during role development in an educational theater production. *Management Communication Quarterly, 23*(2), 188–217.

Labianca, G., Brass, D. J., & Gray, B. (1998). Social networks and perceptions of intergroup conflict: The role of negative relationships and third parties. *Academy of Management Journal, 41*(1), 55–67.

Lawrence, P. R., & Lorsch, J. W. (1967). Differentiation and integration in complex organizations. *Administrative Science Quarterly, 12*(1), 1–47.

*Lyon, A. (2005). Intellectual capital and struggles over the perceived value of members' expert knowledge in a knowledge-intensive organization. *Western Journal of Communication, 69*(3), 251–271.

Mathieu, J., Maynard, M. T., Rapp, T., & Gilson. L. (2008). Team effectiveness 1997–2007: A review of recent advancements and a glimpse into the future. *Journal of Management, 34*(3), 410–476.

McGrath, J. E., & Argote, L. (2001). Group processes in organizational contexts. In M. A. Hogg & R. S. Tindale (Eds.), *Blackwell handbook of social psychology: Group processes* (pp. 603–627). Malden, MA: Blackwell.

*McKinney, E. H., Barker, J. R., Davis, K. J., & Smith, D. (2005). How swift starting action teams get off the ground: What United Flight 232 and airline flight crews can tell us about team communication. *Management Communication Quarterly, 19*(2), 198–237.

McPhee, R. D., & Poole, M. S. (2001). Organizational structures and configurations. In F. M. Jablin & L. L. Putnam (Eds.), *Handbook of organizational communication: Advances in theory, research, and methods* (pp. 503–543). Thousand Oaks, CA: SAGE.

Miller, V. D., Poole, M. S., Seibold, D. R., Myers, K. K., Park, H. S., Monge, P., . . . Shumate, M. (2011). Advancing research in organizational communication through quantitative methodology. *Management Communication Quarterly, 25*(1), 4–58.

Mohrman, S. A., Cohen, S. G., & Mohrman, A. M. (1995). *Designing team-based organizations: New forms for knowledge work.* San Francisco, CA: Jossey-Bass.

*Myers, K. K., & McPhee, R. D. (2006). Influences on member assimilation in workgroups in high reliability organizations: A multilevel analysis. *Human Communication Research, 32*(4), 440–468.

Oetzel, J. G., Burtis, T. E., Sanchez, M. I. C., & Perez, F. G. (2001). Investigating the role of communication in culturally diverse work group: A review and synthesis. In W. B. Gundykunst, *Communication yearbook* (vol. 25, pp. 237–269). New York, NY: Psychology Press.

O'Toole, J., & Lawler, E. E., III. (2006). *The new American workplace.* New York, NY: Palgrave.

*Palazzolo, E. T. (2005). Organizing for information retrieval in transactive memory systems. *Communication Research, 32*(6), 726–761.

*Palazzolo, E. T., Serb, D. A., She, Y., Su, C., & Contractor, N. S. (2006). Coevolution of communication and knowledge networks in transactive memory systems: Using computational models for theoretical development. *Communication Theory, 16*(2), 223–250.

Poole, M. S. (1998). The small group should be the fundamental unit of communication research. In J. S. Trent (Ed.), *Communication: Views from the helm for the 21* (pp. 94–97). Boston, MA: Allyn & Bacon.

Poole, M. S., Keyton, J., & Frey, L. R. (1999). Group communication methodology: Issues and considerations. In L. R. Frey, D. S. Gouran, & M. S. Poole (Eds.), *The handbook of group communication theory and research* (pp. 92–112). Thousand Oaks, CA: SAGE.

Poole, M. S., & Zhang, H. (2005). Virtual teams. In S. A. Wheelan (Ed.), *The handbook of group research and practice* (pp. 363–384). Thousand Oaks, CA: SAGE.

Putnam, L. L. (1987). Understanding the unique characteristics of groups within organizations. In R. S. Cathcart & L. A. Samovar (Eds.), *Small group communication: A reader* (5th ed., pp. 76–85). Dubuque, IA: Wm C. Brown.

Putnam, L. L. (1989). Perspectives on research on group embeddedness in organizations. In S. S. King (Ed.), *Human communication as a field of study: Selected contemporary views* (pp. 163–181). Albany: University Press, State University of New York.

Putnam, L. L., & Stohl, C. (1990). Bona fide groups: A reconceptualization of groups in context. *Communication Studies, 41*(3), 248–265.

Putnam, L. L., Stohl, C., & Baker, J. S. (2012). Bona fide groups: A discourse perspective. In A. B. Hollingshead & M. S. Poole (Eds.), *Research methods for studying groups and teams: A behind-the-scenes guide to approaches, tools, and technologies* (pp. 211–234). New York, NY: Routledge.

Renz, M. A. (2006). Paving consensus: Enacting, challenging, and revising the consensus process in a cohousing community. *Journal of Applied Communication Research, 34*(2), 163–190.

Rice, R. E., & Gattiker, U. E. (2001). New media and organizational structuring. In F. M. Jablin & L. L. Putnam (Eds.), *Handbook of organizational communication: Advances in theory, research, and methods* (pp. 544–581). Thousand Oaks, CA: SAGE.

Rousseau, V., Aubé, C., & Savoie, A. (2006). Teamwork behaviors: A review and an integration of frameworks. *Small Group Research, 37*(5), 540–570.

*Ryfe, D. M. (2006). Narrative and deliberation in small group forums. *Journal of Applied Communication Research, 34*(1), 72–93.

Seibold, D. R., Kang, P., Gailliard, B. M., & Jahn, J. (2009). Communication that damages teamwork: The dark side of teams. In P. Lutgen-Sandvik & B. Davenport Sypher (Eds.), *Destructive organizational communication: Processes, consequences, and constructive ways of organizing* (pp. 267–289). New York, NY: Routledge/Taylor & Francis.

Seibold, D. R., & Meyers, R. A. (2012). Interventions in groups: Methods for facilitating team development. In A. B. Hollingshead & M. S. Poole (Eds.), *Research methods for studying groups and teams: A behind-the-scenes guide to approaches, tools, and technologies* (pp. 418–441). New York, NY: Routledge.

Seibold, D. R., Meyers, R. A., & Shoham, M. D. (2010). Social influence in groups and organizations. In C. R. Berger, M. E. Roloff, & D. Roskos-Ewolsen (Eds.), *Handbook of communication science* (2nd ed., pp. 237–253). Thousand Oaks, CA: SAGE.

Seibold, D. R., & Shea, C. (2001). Participation and decision making. In F. M. Jablin & L. L. Putnam (Eds.), *Handbook of organizational communication: Advances in theory, research, and methods* (pp. 664–703). Thousand Oaks, CA: SAGE.

*Shockley-Zalabak, P. (2002). Protean places: Teams across time and space. *Journal of Applied Communication Research, 30*(3), 231–250.

*Stephens, K. K. (2012). Multiple conversations during organizational meetings: Development of the multi-communicating scale. *Management Communication Quarterly, 26*(2), 195–223.

*Stephens, K. K., & Davis, J. (2009). The social influences on electronic multitasking in organizational meetings. *Management Communication Quarterly, 23*(1), 63–83.

*Su, C. (2012). Who knows who knows what in the group? The effects of communication network centralities, use of digital knowledge repositories, and work remoteness on organizational members' accuracy in expertise recognition. *Communication Research, 39*(5), 614–640.

Sundstrom, E., De Meuse, K. P., & Futrell, D. (1990). Work teams: Applications and effectiveness. *American Psychologist, 45*(2), 120–133.

*Sunwolf. (2006). Decisional regret theory: Reducing the anxiety about uncertain outcomes during group decision making through shared counterfactual storytelling. *Communication Studies, 57*(2), 107–134.

*Susskind, A. M., Odom-Reed, P. R., & Viccari, A. E. (2011). Team leaders and team members in interorganizational networks: An examination of structural holes and performance. *Communication Research, 38*(5), 613–633.

*Thompson, J. L. (2009). Building collective communication competence in interdisciplinary research teams. *Journal of Applied Communication Research, 37*(3), 278–297.

*Timmerman, T. E., & Scott, C. R. (2006). Virtually working: Communicative and structural predictors of media use and key outcomes in virtual work teams. *Communication Monographs, 73*(1), 108–136.

*Whitford, T., & Moss, S. A. (2009). Transformational leadership in distributed work groups: The moderating role of follower regulatory focus and goal orientation. *Communication Research, 36*(6), 810–837.

Williams, M. (2001). In whom we trust: Group membership as an affective context for trust development. *Academy of Management Review, 26*(3), 377–396.

Wittenbaum, G. M., Hollingshead, A. B., & Botero, I. (2004). From cooperative to motivated information sharing in groups: Going beyond the hidden profile paradigm. *Communication Monographs, 71*(3), 286–310.

Wittenbaum, G. M., & Moreland, R. L. (2008). Small group research trends in social psychology: Topics and trends over time. *Social and Personality Psychology Compass, 2*(1), 183–203.

*Yuan, Y., Fulk, J., & Monge, P. R. (2007). Access to information in connective and communal transactive memory systems. *Communication Research, 34*(2), 131–155.

*Yuan, Y., Fulk, J., Monge, P. R., & Contractor, N. (2010). Expertise directory development, shared task interdependence, and strength of communication network ties as multilevel predictors of expertise exchange in transactive memory work groups. *Communication Research, 37*(1), 20–47.

*Yuan, Y., Fulk, J., Shumate, M., Monge, P. R., Bryant, J. A., & Matsaganis, M. (2005). Individual participation in organizational information commons: The impact of team-level influence and technology-specific competence. *Human Communication Research, 31*(2), 212–240.

Zorn, T. E., Jr., & Thompson, G. E. (2002). Communication in top management teams. In L. R. Frey (Ed.), *New directions in group communication* (pp. 253–272). Thousand Oaks, CA: SAGE.

CHAPTER 14

Communicating Work-Life Issues

Erika L. Kirby and Patrice M. Buzzanell

Work-life issues surrounding the everyday enactments and intersections of work and personal life affect both women and men around the globe. Researchers from varying disciplines have provided insight into these work-life issues across such fields as sociology, psychology, management, political science, and family studies. Organizational communication scholars, however, provide a unique point of difference by focusing on *how* communication constitutes work-life phenomena. Communication shapes and is shaped by the contours of everyday life. In ongoing constitutive processes, communication underlies the work-life decision-making processes of individuals and collectivities.

Examining communication in work-life contexts means that research endeavors to understand how sensemaking takes place, for what reasons, in whose interests, and with what consequences. Anchoring work-life scholarship in the constitutive process of communication not only offers powerful insights into work-life phenomena—organizational communication scholarship also has the potential to shift the ways people see and talk about their worlds in order to positively transform the well-being of women and men. As Medved (2010) notes, "communication holds promise for enriching conversations about *work-life related social change* given that consciousness raising and social change are in part communicative processes" (para. 8, emphasis added).

We recognize that our emphasis on organizational communication still requires examining the intersections of organizations with different communication contexts and levels, and we incorporate theoretical overviews as necessary to understand organizational communication frameworks for work-life inquiry. Since work-life scholarship in the area of organizational communication has only emerged since 2000, with some exceptions (e.g., Ashcraft, 1999; Peterson & Albrecht, 1999), we review primarily articles from the last dozen years in communication and interdisciplinary journals that publish organizational communication scholarship. In our chapter, we first situate the emergence of work-life interests and scholarship in communication as responding to demographic, economic, and moral discourses. We then organize our review around five underlying themes in communicative processes (as conceptualized across scholars) that enable us to highlight the distinctive contributions of a communicative perspective, including pragmatic implications when possible. Finally, these five communicative processes ground our suggestions for future directions in work-life scholarship.

The Emergence of Work-Life Communication Scholarship

Conversations about work-life did not begin in earnest until there were demographic, economic, and moral reasons to attend to societal and global changes. These reasons consolidate shifts in thinking and talking about work-life that underlie not only research but also people's everyday actions. In other words, these reasons are invoked as rationales for why and how things are done the way that they are. Changes in workforce demography heralded a shift in organizational selection, retention, and promotion practices, as well as national laws and policies, to support women's increasing and sustained labor force participation (Cook, 2004; Esping-Andersen, 1999; Medved, 2007; U.S. Department of Labor, 2012; Work and Family Researchers Network, 2012).

Besides demographic changes and accompanying legal and policy shifts, economic factors have driven interest in work-life scholarship. These factors range from individuals' and families' expressed requirements for more than one wage earner to welfare-to-work policy requirements, lower wage increases that are unable to buffer accelerated costs of living, consequences of local and global unemployment, and differential economic patterns based on class, gender, race and ethnicity, national culture, and other forms of difference (e.g., Buzzanell, 2000). Furthermore, work-life scholarship has been affected by and affects the need for particular kinds of labor force talent (Kisselburgh, Berkelaar, & Buzzanell, 2009). Work-life issues also emerge because of the intensity of educational and promotion requirements for women and men during peak caregiving years (Association for Women in Science [AWIS], 2011; Townsley & Broadfoot, 2008). These issues surface structurally in highly competitive industries and pay for performance and billable hour systems and career and family trajectories oriented toward work, advancement, extreme jobs, and multiple work shifts (e.g., Blair-Loy, 2009; Hewlett & Luce, 2006).

Finally, the moral argument for interest in and research on work-life issues centers on quality of life. For individuals, scholars propose that fulfillment and dignity are shaped by access, agency, and opportunities to implement work-life choices (Buzzanell & Lucas, 2013). For organizations and nations, the moral argument centers on institutional and societal obligations to ensure that citizens are able, through laws and policies, to develop the human, social, cultural, and other forms of capital associated with a good life. However, good intentions and logical interventions do not always yield strategies designed for managing work-life complexities. Indeed, the force of neoliberal political-economic ideologies promotes meritocracy, competitive individualism, ideal workers, and managerialist rationalities (Buzzanell, 1994; Carter & Silva, 2011; Drago, 2007).

Work-life scholarship has incorporated these demographic, economic, and moral rationales, assumptions, and goals. Although other disciplines have drawn attention to and invoked such aspects, communication scholarship makes visible how these interests and their effects are constituted in ordinary interactions as well as policies and institutional structures. Specifically, organizational communication researchers' entry points into work-life processes come from diverse interdisciplinary contexts and key communication problematics of identity, rationality, boundary, and voice (Kirby, Golden, Medved, Jorgenson, & Buzzanell, 2003). Moreover, alongside growing recognition for engaged communication scholarship grounded in everyday politics and problem-focused inquiry (e.g., Frey & Cissna, 2009; Putnam, 2009), work-life scholarship that can inform everyday enactments as well as national and organizational policies has increased (e.g., Montoya & Trethewey, 2009; Riforgiate & Alberts, 2009; Rivera & Tracy, 2009).

Since the first mention of "work-family" communication research in *Communication Abstracts* with the publication of a special issue of the *Electronic Journal of Communication (EJC)* in 2000 (Golden, 2000a), communication researchers have steadily produced work-life scholarship. Indeed, the Organizational Communication Division's Article of the Year in 2003 was a foundational review of "work-life" communication in *Communication Yearbook*; this was considered a more comprehensive label (Kirby et al., 2003; see also Golden, Kirby, & Jorgenson, 2006, for another *Communication Yearbook* review). Other broad contributions include a special issue on work-life communication for *EJC* (Kirby, 2006b), the first (and second) handbook chapters on work-life conflict communication in *The SAGE Handbook of Conflict Communication* (Kirby, Wieland, & McBride, 2006, 2013), a special issue on mothering and academe for *Women's Studies in Communication* (Townsley & Broadfoot, 2008), an encyclopedia entry for the Work-Family Research Network highlighting communication and work-life scholarship (Medved, 2010), and the present chapter.

Work-life scholarship has begun to heed the call issued by Kirby and colleagues (2003) to examine the nuances and intersectionalities of difference in particular communication contexts. Some recent examples examine (a) family entrepreneurships (Helmle, Seibold, & Afifi, 2011), (b) family reconnection after military deployments (Wilson et al., 2011), (c) families and organizations as mutually enacted environments (Golden, 2009), and (d) influences of work and family on individuals' volunteer activities and identifications (Kramer, 2011). Such research utilizes and combines varied metatheoretical traditions and theories in communication, such as post-positivist, interpretive, critical, and postmodern, (for an overview, see May & Mumby, 2005) and different quantitative, qualitative, rhetorical, and mixed-methods approaches. Although organizational communication research on work-life issues is still emerging, it already spans diverse communication contexts, theories, topics, and methodologies. Given this context, we now review the state of the subdiscipline of work-life communication.

Five Processes for Framing Work-Life Communication Research

Our review of work-life communication is framed around five constitutive communicative processes: (1) *policy-ing* work-life in organizations, (2) *norm-ing* (or not) issues of work-life in organizations, (3) (re)producing "ideal" workers and the primacy of work, (4) constructing (gendered) (working) identities, and (5) acting practically and routinizing work and (personal) life.

Policy-ing Work-Life in Organizations

Conversations about work-life issues differ across nation-states, in part based on cultural values and attitudes, economic systems, history, gender ideologies, governmental policy (e.g., welfare and health), and state support regarding work-life assistance (Kirby et al., 2013). State support often reflects welfare-regime types and what Esping-Anderson (1999) refers to as *familiazation*: the degree to which either welfare state or market provisions ease the burdens of families' caring responsibilities. Work-life literature has primarily concentrated on comparing countries in social-democratic welfare state regimes (e.g., Scandinavian nations) and in market regimes (e.g., the U.K., the U.S.). In Scandinavia, equality among citizens and full employment for men and women is promoted through a substantial public childcare system and a broad range of leave arrangements, including paternity leave and specific "daddy" quotas within parental leave systems (den Dulk, Peters, Poutsma, & Ligthart, 2010).

In contrast, in the U.S. national regulations are limited and the development of work-life arrangements is left to market forces (den Dulk et al., 2010; Kossek & Distelberg, 2009). Indeed, Drago (2007) notes an *individualism* norm, that the government should not help those needing care; care is not typically seen as a common, collective good (see Tracy, 2008). Thus U.S. *organizations* have become increasingly involved in helping employees in their personal lives (Kirby, 2006a). Given that U.S. employers have latitude to determine work and family policy with few requirements to even offer policy support (Kossek & Distelberg, 2009), organizations imply a value for "balance" in choosing to implement initiatives. Cook (2004) notes four frameworks for conceptualizing why organizations implement work-life initiatives: (1) to be considered legitimate (*institutional theory*; DiMaggio & Powell, 1983), (2) to obtain needed human resources in recruitment and retention (*resource dependence theory*; Pfeffer & Salancik, 1978), (3) to follow key management figures' interpretations of work-life policies as important (*managerial interpretation theory*; Milliken, Martins, & Morgan, 1998), and (4) to (attempt to) align with changing environments (*organizational adaptation theory*; Daft & Weick, 1984).

In their report surveying 600 U.S. organizations about their work-life programs and benefits, the Society of Human Resource Management (SHRM) categorized initiatives as family-friendly, leave, and flexible working benefits. However, other issues such as working hours, wages, and health care can also impact work-life possibilities for individuals and, indeed, societies (Kirby et al., 2013). Family-friendly benefits were available to 59% of full-time and 36% of part-time employees in the organizations surveyed; some example categories of benefits included dependent care flexible spending accounts, domestic partner benefits, childcare centers, referrals and backup care (for children and elders), and adoption assistance (SHRM, 2011).

The only standardization for leave policies is the Family and Medical Leave Act (FMLA) of 1993. In 2011, 84% of full-time and 41% of part-time employees in the U.S. organizations surveyed had the option to receive leave benefits *beyond* what is provided by FMLA. Sample categories of such leave included paid family leave, paid time off for volunteering, paid parental leave, sabbatical programs, and donation programs for paid time off and/or sick leave (SHRM, 2011). Yet the existence of a policy says nothing about its content: Peterson and Albrecht's (1999) critique of one hospital's maternity leave policy illustrated that the language supported detrimental gendered assumptions based on pregnancy and maternity leave being framed as *voluntary choices*, *disabilities*, *abnormal*, and *private*. Furthermore, even when leave policies exist, organizations may treat their utilization as "burdens and nonroutine events" (Buzzanell & Liu, 2005, p. 11).

Noteworthy from a communication-centered perspective is the offering of *flexibility*. Cowan and Hoffman (2007) illustrated that employees identified *flexibility* and *permeability* as key concepts in work-life balance and constructed *flexibility* in terms of interdependent issues of time, space, evaluation, and compensation. Flexible working benefits, such as flextime, telecommuting, and compressed workweeks were an option for 76% of full-time and 46% of part-time employees in the organizations surveyed (SHRM, 2011). Yet formal measurements of flexibility do not always capture the possibilities of flexibility: It may be less, as some policies are only available to certain employee classes, or it may be more, as supervisors may, at times, permit more flexibility than is formally allowed (Eaton, 2003; Kirby, 2000; Kossek & Distelberg, 2009). Myers, Gailliard, and Putnam (2012) argue that organizations should think beyond flexibility to *adaptability*: a stance that "transforms workers' needs and the organization's objectives into a system of worker autonomy that incorporates fluidity in achieving both personal and organizational goals" (p. 194).

As a form of flexibility, telework has received attention in its capacity to change individual boundary transitions and organizational routines and relationships (Shumate & Fulk, 2004; see also Ballard & Gossett, 2007; Edley, Hylmö, &

Newsom, 2004; Fonner & Roloff, 2012; Fonner & Stache, 2012; Long, Kuang, & Buzzanell, 2013). Workers telecommuting more than 50% of the time have higher job satisfaction than those who work primarily on-site due to increased flexibility and respite from office politics (Fonner & Roloff, 2010). Whereas telecommuters may view the organization as "life friendly" in meeting their needs, they also perceive that the *legitimacy* of their work has been reduced as a result of the alternative work arrangement, meaning that they feel a need to legitimize their personal decisions to work in a preferred location (Hylmö, 2006; see also Hylmö & Buzzanell, 2002, for how discourses surrounding telecommuting create divisions between promotable and non-promotable employees). This research highlights the need to understand the meaning being invested in alternative working arrangements and consequences for those who take advantage of flexibility.

Researchers note that work-life initiatives are often added on and marginalized rather than mainstreamed into organizational systems (cf. Kirby, 2000; Kirby & Krone, 2002; Kossek, Lewis, & Hammer, 2010). Consequently, scholars have emphasized the need for continuous communication about work-life policies after their implementation (e.g., Kirby & Krone, 2002). Yet in a survey of 1,100 employers, Galinsky, Bond, Sakai, Kim, and Giuntoli (2008) found that only 21% reported it was "very true" that the organization makes a real and ongoing effort to inform employees of available work-life benefits. Importantly, providing information alone may not be enough, as "constructing policy knowledge is far from a simple process of information dissemination and it involves much more than information sharing" (Canary, 2010, p. 201). Supervisory and societal cultures regarding ideal workers continue to be barriers to policy use and create gender differences in policy experiences (see Kossek & Distelberg, 2009, as well as the work of Buzzanell and colleagues—Buzzanell, 2003; Buzzanell & Liu, 2005, 2007; Liu & Buzzanell, 2004, 2006). Furthermore, policies themselves can perpetuate stereotypes of ideal workers and increase work intensification, because employees work harder out of gratitude for the flexibility they have been granted (Drago, 2007).

Given that policy knowledge is a form of organizational knowledge constructed via policy language, forms, and technology, simply distributing work-life policies and assuming they will take hold does not necessarily work (Canary & McPhee, 2009). As Tracy and Rivera (2010) found, when male executives were asked about work-life policy, they repeatedly answered by talking about their *personal beliefs* and private family preferences (e.g., not wanting their own wives to work), resulting in the privatization of work-life policy. This becomes an organizational issue if and when such men generalize their personal preferences to all employees. Therefore, Tracy and Rivera emphasize a need for public recognition that women work "not simply as a privileged choice" but also "for financial support of themselves and their families, and as personal fulfillment" (p. 35).

Thinking about practical actions related to *policy-ing*, Medved (2010) convincingly argues that an analysis of policy texts, congressional discussions, policy debates, and organizational interpretations of federal statutes would significantly add to knowledge of this process. In light of the diversity of stakeholders in work-life initiatives, Drago (2007) recommends that workplace constituencies (including employees, supervisors, managers, and unions) should be involved in the (re)design of work-life benefit programs and career paths to fit ethnic, family, and life-course diversity. Finally, Hoffman and Cowan (2008) offer some resistance to *policy-ing*; they argue that work-life policies may actually disempower individuals by undermining their sense of agency and ability to make different choices about how to best integrate paid work and the rest of life.

Norm-ing (or Not) Issues of Work-Life in Organizations

Beyond the policy level, numerous scholars are concerned with daily practices surrounding whether work-life policies can really be used (what Eaton, 2003, calls *perceived usability*). A tension in U.S. policies is that while they are typically created at the organizational/human resources level, they are interpreted and implemented by supervisors, and their use is influenced by coworkers and the culture related to work-life—including if there are perceived career repercussions (cf. Eaton, 2003; Hoffman & Cowan, 2010; Kirby, 2000; Kirby & Krone, 2002). As Townsley and Broadfoot (2008) note regarding initiatives in institutions of higher learning, "even when coherent benefit policies, onsite child care, health coverage, tenure clock stops, and generous parental leave policies exist, cultural expectations about what is considered 'appropriate work' remain deeply entrenched" (p. 137).

The Role of Workplace Relationships. Organizational communication research on work-life acknowledges the role of supervisors in creating (or not) supportive work-life cultures. Supervisors are gatekeepers to effective implementation, since they often have final approval about employees' policy utilization, they influence whether employees are cross-trained and able to back each other during absences or periods of heavy workload, they affect whether policies are publicized and well understood, and they lead in the creation of norms supporting use of policies (Kossek & Distelberg, 2009). Indeed, supervisor flexibility in accommodating employee work-life issues is a powerful predictor of employee well-being (Lauzun, Morganson, Major, & Green, 2010). Supervisors' informal actions can have greater influence on employees than formal practices (Kirby, 2000).

However, managers face a dilemma: There are costs to granting a work-life accommodation, as it may disrupt how work is conducted. But the cost of not granting the request could lower employee productivity and create resentment for policies that cannot be used (den Dulk & de Riujter, 2008; see also Kirby & Krone, 2002). Lauzun et al. (2010) surveyed 425 supervisors from a Fortune 500 company regarding their responses to employees' requests for work-life accommodations. They discovered the biggest requests (n = 1,150) were for schedule changes/flexibility, which were accommodated 58% of the time. Further, when supervisors failed to accommodate requests, it was most often because they lacked the authority or necessary resources to make the accommodation or that they were prevented by organizational policies or norms. Kirby (2000) found that supervisors can (intentionally or not) send mixed messages about work and life and policy use. Such messages can emerge in direct verbal and written forms (e.g., emphasizing deadlines but encouraging family time) and indirect forms (e.g., sending e-mails in the middle of the night) and result in employee uncertainty as to whether it is acceptable to utilize work-life programs.

Despite the influence of supervisors, Galinsky et al.'s (2008) survey of 1,100 employers found that (only) 50% train supervisors in responding to employees' work-life needs. Briscoe and Kellogg (2011) therefore suggest that organizations should assign potential work-life program users to powerful supervisors. Rivera and Tracy (2009) offer additional practical strategies for supervisory work-life support, including (1) making changes (themselves) at home, (2) leading by example/role modeling, (3) not letting parental leave turn into an off-ramp from paid work, (4) putting policy onto paper, (5) creating strong cultures of work-life harmony, and (6) having the courage to embrace new ideas.

Communication scholars also explore the norms and practices of coworkers as related to work-life. Coworkers can be an important source of social support in negotiating working and personal life as employees seek affirmation and assurance, advice, and instrumental support (Krouse & Afifi, 2007). Farley-Lucas (2000) investigated women's motherhood talk in the workplace and found that employees valued highly talking with coworkers about children. Indeed, individuals who talk with coworkers about personal life have greater work satisfaction (Clark, 2002). Yet individuals may also protect themselves in terms of how open they are about personal life; Jorgenson (2000) illustrates how women engineers edited out family involvements in conversations so as not to invite questioning of commitment and professionalism.

This leads to another theme in the literature—that coworker talk about working and personal life also influences employee use (or nonuse) of existing work-life policies (Kirby & Krone, 2002). Kirby and Krone (2002) found that employees frequently communicated a perception that work-life policies granted preferential treatment based on whether employees had children, were male or female, and had part-time or full-time status. Organizational members who could not utilize benefits felt (unfairly) burdened and communicated feelings of resentment that in turn fostered environments where coworkers created informal rules evaluating policy use versus abuse that contributed to systems of peer pressure not to utilize available benefits (for more on coworker backlash, see Hayden, 2010; Warner, Slim-Jerusalim, & Korabik, 2009). In light of potential coworker backlash, Drago (2007) recommends that work groups should be involved (together) in the redesign of tasks and the implementation of flexible and alternative working-time arrangements. Kirby and Krone (2002) further suggest that supervisors should set up an open communication environment where employees feel free to share their perceptions of inequity so these perceptions do not fester in small groups.

The Role of Organizational Culture. Thompson, Beauvais, and Lyness (1999) defined *work-life culture* as "the shared assumptions, beliefs, and values regarding the extent to which an organization supports and values the integration of employees' work and (family) [personal] lives" (p. 394). Their elements of work-life culture include *organizational time demands* (regarding schedule rigidity, work hours, face time, etc.; see Cowan & Hoffman, 2007; Kuhn, 2006; Lucas, Liu, & Buzzanell, 2006), *perceived career consequences* for using work-life benefits (see Cowan & Hoffman, 2007; Hylmö & Buzzanell, 2002; Kirby & Krone, 2002), and *formal and informal managerial support* regarding work-life (see Kirby, 2000).

Andreassi and Thompson (2004) outline additional facets of work-life culture, including (1) the degree of (in)tangible instrumental, informational, and emotional support; (2) a work climate for sharing concerns that encourages employees to discuss personal life concerns with supervisors and coworkers; (3) a climate for boundary separation that represents the degree to which (in)formal norms support the integration or segmentation of work and personal life (see Ashforth, Kreiner, & Fugate, 2000); and (4) the degree to which an organization values the nonwork roles and activities of workers (see Golden, 2009, for an account of how a global high-tech organization and its employees' families enact one another as environments).

Thus *life-friendly* organizational cultures/climates (Pitt-Catsouphes, 2002) are those in which employees perceive that their nonwork life is respected, that they are not required to prioritize work above family/personal life or manage long hours or unrealistic schedules to achieve desired career consequences, that there are no negative career consequences associated with using work-life benefits, and that their managers and coworkers will listen to and support them (Andreassi & Thomson, 2004; Kirby & Krone, 2002; Thompson et al., 1999). Important enactments (or not) of organizational life-friendliness emerge when individuals attempt to utilize available policies or negotiate leaves (cf. Ashcraft, 1999).

In an in-depth project, Buzzanell and colleagues (Buzzanell, 2003, 2006; Buzzanell & Liu, 2005, 2007; Buzzanell, Waymer, Tagle, & Liu, 2007; Liu & Buzzanell, 2004, 2006; Meisenbach, Remke, Buzzanell, & Liu, 2008) studied women's maternity leave negotiations, examining how women talk about, enact, and respond to workplace pregnancy and maternity leave processes in both positive and negative ways. Buzzanell and Liu (2005) locate the presence of "multiple, competing, and shifting discourses that simultaneously resist and reinscribe dominant meanings of organizing and gender" during maternity leaves in the workplace (p. 18). One key finding is that maternity leaves are occasions for the (re)production of gender, especially in defining women as less-than-ideal workers. Cowan and Bochantin's (2009) study reinforced these findings: Female police officers argued that pregnancy put their careers at risk because their colleagues did not know what to do with them and therefore enacted the pregnancy as a crime (i.e., sent them home) or as an illness (i.e., mandated to light duty; see also Bochantin & Cowan, 2010).

A second conclusion is that although standardization is implied when maternity leave is part of benefits packages, it is enacted as a burden (Buzzanell & Liu, 2005). While Miller, Jablin, Casey, Lamphear-Van Horn, and Ethington (1996) theorized maternity leaves as role negotiation processes, Meisenbach et al. (2008) argue that *the organization* is really the meta-actor in these processes: "[I]f the decision making power is articulated as residing in fixed and inanimate policies and rules, then any discussion, let alone negotiation, becomes difficult" (p. 14).

Furthermore, Liu and Buzzanell (2004) argue that different parties in maternity leave discussions (i.e., women and their bosses) used disparate ethical discourses. Male and female bosses who denied requests for (pregnancy-related) accommodations made explicit and implicit references to feminine stereotypes and to equal treatment standards (*justice ethics*) that rendered the women powerless in their negotiations to change conditions to meet their individual needs (*care ethics*). When accommodations were granted, many of the women felt guilty, because coworkers had to handle their workload in addition to their own (cf. Wood & Dow, 2010). The findings imply a practical recommendation that training and dialogue about differential superior-subordinate expectations, rights, responsibilities, and ethical stances might assist people in creating mutually beneficial situations and avoiding potential litigation.

Expanding from maternity leave, Hoffman and Cowan (2010) analyzed 96 employee requests for accommodation to explore the rules and resources that govern work-life issues negotiations. They identified rules regarding what *types* of requests should be made: These rules stated that employees should weigh risks of requests carefully, acknowledge that family requests are easiest to make, and only make requests that will be granted. Rules also emerged as to *how* employees should ask for accommodations: They should emphasize organizational interests, frame requests as private and individual concerns, and find alternate routes to fulfill work-life needs if necessary. Finally, they noted three primary *resources* in asking for work-life accommodation: a societal or organizational value of family, employees' own competence, and organizational knowledge. Their work serves as both knowledge about, and practical recommendations for, making work-life requests.

(Re)Producing Ideal Workers and the Primacy of Work

Work-life communication scholars have also been concerned with how ideologies of success and ideal workers are (re)produced in organizations and the broader culture. Lucas et al. (2006) elucidate themes of U.S. and Chinese career discourses as embodied in the myth of the American Dream, including notions of meritocracy, hierarchy, and materiality. The discourse that one can never do enough—termed a *discourse of excess* (Wieland, 2011) and *no limits careerism* (Lucas et al., 2006)—is influential in shaping the ways people work and live. Such discourses result in extreme career models accompanied by ideal worker models that have destructive consequences for all (Wieland, Bauer, & Deetz, 2009). Drago (2007) illustrates how, historically, workers began working longer (and longer) hours and given corresponding wage increases. Eventually, a subset of workers internalized (and viewed as normal) the high demands and high incomes associated with the ideal-worker norm. Indeed, workers sometimes express preferences for spending time at work rather than at home (Hochschild, 1997). Cheney, Zorn, Planalp, and Lair (2008) further illustrate that when work is a primary source of self-esteem, this will likely make continually more intrusive claims on the worker and impede work-life balance. Thus constructions of the ideal worker intersect with work-life issues.

Such ideologies are produced in everyday discourse, including encouragements to have "a real job" (Clair, 1996), achieve "success" (Lucas et al., 2006), and "be professional" (Cheney & Ashcraft, 2007). Individuals are socialized into these ideologies through numerous sources tracing back to childhood. Children's career aspirations and occupational socialization into intergenerational and appropriate forms of work can be shaped by work, family, community, national, and mediated messages that are perceived as direct, indirect, and ambient (e.g., Buzzanell, Berkelaar, & Kisselburgh, 2011, 2012; Myers, Jahn, Gailliard, & Stoltzfus, 2011; Paugh, 2005).

In socializing children into work and family, parents and caregivers provide the resources and encouragement to enable children to locate their career choices in more individualistic cultures or to test into higher educational opportunities that will bring better lifestyles and honor to themselves and their communities (Buzzanell et al., 2011, 2012; Medved, Brogan, McClanahan, Morris, & Shepherd, 2006). Families apprentice children into discourses and ideologies of work through parents' dinnertime conversations (Paugh, 2005) and stories about family fortune and misfortune, incorporating tropes of the American dream, the Protestant work ethic, and bootstrapping (Langellier & Peterson, 2006). Medved et al. (2006) described how individuals report gendered parental messages about the ways that they can make choices about work and family issues, including exiting the workforce for women.

Popular culture also influences ideologies of work (and life). Sotirin, Buzzanell, and Turner (2007) analyze three different texts that embed managerialism into popular prescriptions for family management. Carlone (2001) explores Steven Covey's *seven habits*, including how the movement emphasizes self-improvement for the sake of one's (paid) work, and Dempsey and Sanders (2010) analyze how popular autobiographies of social entrepreneurs can reproduce ideal workers. These ideologies are also (re)produced in organizational discourses. Certainly, the reviewed work of Buzzanell and colleagues reveals a multiplicity of ways that maternity leave gives rise to communication that implicitly or explicitly draws forth discourses of the ideal worker. Tracy and Rivera (2010) illustrate the continued existence of *aversive sexism* (i.e., covert or unconscious discriminatory beliefs that guide action and policy) in male executives—and, consequently, in their ideologies of ideal workers. While the men espoused gender equity, when asked about specific hopes for their children's futures, most male executives discussed their daughters' future lives in general, often focusing on what her family life would be like. In contrast, for their sons, they envisioned a good job with a flexible environment, a wonderful wife, and *specific* careers. These male executives framed women's employment (but not men's) as a choice, and their "tacit hesitancy about women's participation in organizational life is closely connected to preferred gender relationships in the private sphere" (p. 3).

Mescher, Benschop, and Doorewaard (2009) analyzed company rhetoric regarding work-life on 24 websites of 10 different companies and found these sites reproduced the traditional cultural norms of an ideal worker (i.e., available full-time, allows work to prevail over private life, and willing to go the extra mile). Hoffman and Cowan (2008) performed a cluster analysis to reveal a *corporate ideology of work-life* within the websites of *Fortune*'s 2004 list of "100 Best Companies to Work For." This ideology had four tenets: (1) work is the most important element of life (e.g., always placing *work* before *life*), (2) *life* really means *family*, (3) individual employees are responsible for work-life balance (and the organization will help), and (4) organizations control work-life programs. Ultimately, Hoffman and Cowan conclude that by "defining balance as the goal" and "identifying (somewhat) those things that merit balancing" and "providing some form of assistance, organizations maintain control over how employees view their worlds and the proper relationship between paid work and the rest of life" (p. 238).

Thinking about practical actions related to (re) producing ideal workers, we agree with Kossek et al. (2010) that work-life initiatives need to be framed as part of the core employment system and not just as a strategy to support disadvantaged, nonideal workers. Based on individuals' potential to overwork themselves on the quest to be ideal, Montoya and Trethewey (2009) offer several practical suggestions for helping employees develop sustainable selves. They include (1) creating and communicating goals, (2) making health a priority by "recogniz[ing] that a sustainable/good employee is a well-rested, well-fueled, un-injured employee who is not burnt out" (p. 13), (3) supporting others and accepting social support, (4) knowing one's limitations, (5) cultivating all employees, and (6) thinking about what should be modeled for future generations.

Constructing (Gendered) (Working) Identities

As Medved (2010) argues, "The social construction of identities, particularly gendered identities, is the most frequent foci of communication work-life scholarship" (para. 13; see also Kirby et al., 2013). This work seeks to understand the complex intersectionalities of difference that come into play as women and men negotiate their caregiving and worker identities. Such research examines the role of (multiple forms of) communication in the (re)creation of selves but is particularly focused on how contemporary constructions of the self often surround paid work. Scholars' analyses range from parenthood, particularly motherhood in academe (see Townsley & Broadfoot's [2008] special issue of *Women's Studies in Communication*) to research on family leave policies and practices, particularly maternity leave, and caregivers' discourses about work-life concerns using interviews, focus groups, websites, and texts to do interpretive, critical, post-structuralist, feminist, rhetorical, and case study analyses (e.g., see Kirby, 2006b).

Self-identities regarding paid work emerge out of the interplay of *identity work* (individuals' efforts to portray a positive and distinctive identity) and *identity regulation* (the ways that organizational and social practices shape the process of identity construction; Alvesson & Willmott, 2002; see also Kuhn, 2006; Wieland, 2010). Questions such as "And what do you do?" pervade the modern social landscape, and the answers are consequential (Medved & Kirby, 2005). Thinking about work-life identities, processes of identity construction involve conscious reflection and ongoing practices and broaden the field to "not only on one's position as worker but also as family member, citizen, and consumer, among others, and as such involves a negotiation of the demands of work and other parts of life" (Wieland, 2010, p. 505).

Certainly, macro contexts of Western culture, ideal workers, and gender shape processes of identity construction and what is considered acceptable or desirable. Expectations of how women and men (should) do gender (West & Zimmerman, 1987) as related to working and personal life and the myth of separate worlds of work and family (Kanter, 1977) are prominent in this research. While the separation of men in the public (occupational) sphere and women in the private (family/domestic) sphere is no longer a given, the public/private distinction remains influential. Gendered discourses socialize women (and men) into "appropriate" forms of careers, and such gendering of occupations and careers both excludes women as potential contributors and also maintains gendered wage inequities (Drago, 2007; Kuhn et al. 2008).

Consistent with the myth of separate worlds, work-life problems are often considered "women's issues" (e.g., Tracy & Rivera, 2010). Drago

(2007) articulates a *motherhood norm* in the U.S.: a society-wide belief that women should be mothers and perform unpaid family care and low-paid care for others in need. Consequently, studies of working mothers show the surrounding identity tensions in navigating the expectations of being (ideal) workers and caregivers. For example, Buzzanell and colleagues (2005) found women managers returning to paid work following maternity leave (re)constructed the good mother image into the "good *working* mother" identity. In this construction of motherhood, good working mothers arrange quality child care, are (un)equal partners, and feel pleasure in their working mother role. In a similar vein, the in-home day care providers studied by Butler and Modaff (2008) also drew on mothering ideologies to strengthen their own identities—and framed work-life issues as belonging to women—in their negative judgments of the working mothers (but not fathers) who brought their children to be cared for.

Wieland (2010) articulates *identity construction* as a normative activity through which socially acceptable ideals of who one should be are woven into an individual's understanding of who he or she is, and thus "ideal selves" act as resources. In the Swedish organization she studied, these ideal selves were deliverers (committed, productive workers) and those who practiced well-being (having a balance of a meaningful job and a meaningful private life by not working more than 40 hours a week). When these ideals were in tension (i.e., the work could not be delivered in 40 hours a week), organizational members leveraged the value of moderation (*lagom*) to construct identities that achieved both ideals (Wieland, 2010, 2011). In the U.S., employees' time commitments to the organization are also influenced by identity work and identity regulation as related to organizational location and practices—while one company may demand a *demented work ethic*, another may be a *lifestyle firm* (Kuhn, 2006).

In performing identity work, women sometimes hide or justify caregiving to offset societal notions that they cannot be both caregiver and ideal worker (Buzzanell & D'Enbeau, 2009; D'Enbeau & Buzzanell, 2010; Jorgenson, 2000). Drago (2007) outlines bias-avoidance behaviors that may result: *Productive bias avoidance* suggests women who seek workplace success often delay marriage and childbearing and limit the number of children they have. Once women have children, they (blatantly) prioritize work, which can lead to *unproductive bias avoidance* behaviors such as skipping children's events and not requesting reduced work time or parental leave time when needed. This identity work to manage gendered expectations regarding work (and ideal worker norms) and caregiving (and intensive mothering norms) may be particularly salient in nontraditional occupations (such as in engineering; see Jorgenson, 2000, 2002) and when gender roles are questioned, such as with female breadwinners (Medved, 2009a; Meisenbach, 2010), commuter wives (Bergen, Kirby, & McBride, 2007), and stay-at-home fathers (Petroski & Edley, 2006; Vavrus, 2002). Buzzanell (2003) offers a counter to this notion in her study of Julianna, a person with a wheelchair who therefore was only actually noticed in her pregnancy: otherwise her coworkers saw her as her wheelchair.

Thinking about nontraditional occupations and roles, Jorgenson (2002) shows how women engineers were reluctant to acknowledge gender relations as consequential for their careers and indeed sought to distance themselves from women engineering organizations. In her study of female breadwinners, Meisenbach (2010) notes that essential to their experiences was having at least an opportunity for enacting financial and decision-making control (even if it was not necessarily wanted) and valuing career progress. Since these women are operating in a motherhood-normative culture, these "essential" parts of their experience can create tensions such that it is more likely that female breadwinners will articulate guilt and resentment than their male counterparts. Medved (2009a) illustrates three forms of (identity) justification breadwinning mothers (with primarily at-home partners) therefore use.

The first is *moral positioning*, where mothers construct a *good* or *right* mothering identity through the language of parental care as best and essential. *Personal positioning* is when mothers utilize their (personal) skills, characteristics, or personality traits as a rationale for working. Finally, *P/political positioning* is when mothers treat female breadwinning as a political act framed around feminist goals (Politics) as well as "daily micro-political acts framed more narrowly in relation to local, personal circumstances (politics with a lowercase p)" (p. 150); this situates breadwinning as part of an activist agenda and as role modeling for future generations. But as Medved (2010) illustrates, along with identity struggles, there are also moments of identity empowerment such as the ways that female breadwinning mothers enjoy having a greater sense of control in their marriage (see Meisenbach, 2010).

Men also are subject to gendered identity expectations and face tensions surrounding norms of masculinity, fathering, and breadwinning (cf. Ashcraft & Mumby, 2004)—especially for at-home fathers (Petroski & Edley, 2006). For example, Vavrus (2002) analyzed television news stories about stay-at-home fathers and found the ways in which they were represented reinforced hegemonic masculinity. Medved and Rawlins (2011) certainly illustrate the tensions felt by at-home fathers and breadwinning mothers as they unpack five different *stances* or *narratives* (that embody identity construction, role eligibility, and task responsibility) in viewing (who does) homemaking versus (who does) money making: *reversing*, *conflicting*, *collaborating*, *improvising*, and *sharing*.

Golden (2007) studied employed fathers of preschoolers and analyzed their communicative strategies for constructing their own performances of childrearing to advance a masculine concept of caregiving, where childrearing is seen as work in the expression of agency, in the experience of constraint, and as expression of pure relationship. Similarly, when fathers constructed work-family balance and their fatherhood roles, they elevated family as first by linking family to their meanings of work (i.e., organizing family around work, reframing family first, and revising fatherhood ideologies; Duckworth & Buzzanell, 2009). These (re)conceptualizations of fatherhood and masculinities may indicate that there are ideological changes in nature of fatherhood but that these are constrained by feminine definitions of care labor.

Work-life scholars have focused on identity construction during transitions associated with job loss (e.g., Buzzanell & Turner, 2003) and surrounding pregnancy (Buzzanell, 2003; Buzzanell & Liu, 2005, 2007; Liu & Buzzanell, 2004, 2006). Medved and Kirby (2005) examine identity construction for women who step out of paid work to be stay-at-home mothers and found that they drew upon professionalized discourses to construct corporate-like (mothering) identities using terms such as *Family CEO* and implicating subject positions of themselves as professionals, managers, productive citizens, and irreplaceable workers. The implication of (new) parenthood is that it operates as an occasion for worker-parents to develop their identities both individually and through spousal collaboration (Golden, 2000b, 2001, 2002).

Thinking about practical actions related to constructing (gendered) (working) identities, Kirby et al. (2013), note that much of this scholarship "presumes the possibility and desirability of developing a coherent self that incorporates all aspects of one's identity" (p. 394). Separating from this conception, Tracy and Trethewey (2005; also see Trethewey, Tracy, & Alberts, 2006) suggest viewing the self as *crystallized*—having multiple facets that potentially conflict with one another—as a theoretical and practical approach that illustrates the challenges in managing multiple, potentially conflicting identities (such as worker and mother; for an application of this framework, see Gill's [2006] study of women entrepreneurs).

Acting Practically and Routinizing Work and (Personal) Life

As the final area of scholarship for review, several scholars have explored the everyday routines of enacting work and personal life via communication and relational and domestic work. Clark (2002) offers the concept of *across the border* communication in thinking about how individuals communicate with family and friends about (paid) working life and with coworkers about personal life (see also Nippert-Eng, 1996). She asserts that in these conversations, home/work is framed as an *obligation*, *center of activities*, and an *understood, meaningful experience*. Ashforth et al. (2000) examine how individuals engage in daily role transitions (boundary-crossing activities where one exits and enters roles) and explain that these enactments range from being highly segmented (i.e., rigid boundaries) to having almost no boundaries and being highly integrated. Shuler (2006) explores these routines when working from home as a total institution for individuals who *live with* their coworkers and how they strive to create (not always successfully) some separation between their working and private lives.

Work-life communication research has also explored how mobile communication technologies fit into these everyday routines in constructing (or not) boundaries between home and work; technology "has been variously construed as empowering, exploitative, or dilemmatic" (Golden & Geisler, 2006, para. 1). Golden and Geisler (2007) found the users of personal digital assistants positioned the technology as a means to *contain work* by segregating work-life and personal-life, *integrate the self* by integrating work-life and personal-life, *transition work* by enabling the completion of work from home and in transit, and *protect the private* by calendaring life events and not allowing the organization to view private material contained in the device. Indeed, Edley's (2001) study of entrepreneurial mothers suggests the potential for corporate colonization of family life through technology when and if organizational needs are put before personal needs. Extending this colonization even further, Gregg (2011) has described *presence bleed* as the blurring of work-life boundaries through the compulsion to work and have a presence everywhere and at any time. Enabled by technologies, work becomes both a site of intimacy's colonization and a source of pleasure and meaning. Thus for some individuals, everyday routines of work and personal life are not only impacted by technology but intertwined with their most intimate performances of selfhood.

Medved (2004) illustrates how everyday (inter) actions illuminate the practices that constitute work-life balance (or conflict). She summarizes three practical action clusters: *routinizing practical actions* that are part of carrying out daily or reoccurring (routine) household, paid work, and childcare duties; *improvising practical actions* that are temporary ways of doing daily routines when perceived short-term interruptions occur; and *(re)structuring practical actions* that are triggered by perceived permanent changes related to children or the work situations and lead to a new set of routinizing behaviors. A further contribution is her notion that relational work in the everyday routine is a form of practical action—that "[d]*oing* work and family must also be explained as *doing* relationships, not just taken-for-granted as a function of time management or organizational policies" (p. 140).

An emerging area of work-life communication scholarship over the past five years focuses on issues of (routine) domestic and family labor—the "discursive and material (often inequitable) connections between how we arrange our private sphere relationships and tasks such as household work and care labor and their interrelations to our public and organizational lives" (Medved, 2010, para. 29; see Medved 2007, 2009b, for comprehensive reviews). While Clair and Thompson's (1996) early contribution connected discourses and material practices of housework to labor force pay discrimination, recent research examines how divisions of household labor influence paid work, relationship conflict, and even health (Riforgiate & Alberts, 2009). Certainly, these divisions of labor are often gendered (Alberts, Tracy, & Trethewey, 2011; Medved, 2007, 2009b; Riforgiate & Alberts, 2009).

As an example, Bergen et al. (2007) explore domestic (and relational) labor issues for commuter wives who live away from their spouses during the workweek. These women received messages from members of their social network that portrayed men as *incapable* of family labor and expressed traditional gendered expectations for them (as the wife) to perform caregiving. Indeed, Meisenbach (2010) interprets female breadwinners' ongoing claims to be the ones who see household messes and needs as a way to retain claims to an element of a traditional feminine identity. And as noted, Medved and Rawlins (2011) add to knowledge of gender and domestic work via their stances of how couples manage homemaking and moneymaking.

In response to these inequities in gendered divisions of domestic labor, Riforgiate and Alberts (2009) offer some practical actions. They note that couples often do not openly discuss (inequitable) divisions of labor but instead rely upon assumptions of "who should perform a task, how often the task needs to be performed as well as *how* a task should be performed" (p. 2), which results in women taking on an inequitable burden of domestic labor. They therefore suggest four practices couples can use to more fairly distribute domestic tasks: (1) explicitly allocating tasks, (2) switching tasks, (3) delaying task performance by overperformers, and (4) performing tasks on a schedule for underperformers.

Future Directions for Work-Life Communication Scholarship

Our review highlights five constitutive processes in which communication informs/is informed by work-life enactments and considerations, and thinking in terms of these processes also prompts a series of future directions for research.

In terms of *policy-ing work-life in organizations*, greater attention is required to understand the ways discourses and materialities intersect within work-life considerations and national and institutional policy and associated practices. Communication scholarship can have profound economic and policy consequences, particularly when driving multidisciplinary projects (e.g., see Pitt-Catsouphes, Kossek, & Sweet, 2006). Further multilevel and multimethodological communication scholarship is needed on the intersections of work-life communication and workforce diversity, health care, visa restrictions, economics, cultural assumptions about choice in work-life, and technological employment criteria (e.g., particularly social networking expertise and information and computer technologies) as well as understudied contexts. In other disciplines, research also has delved into secondary database analyses whereby national and global trends have been noted. To take part in policy and societal discussions, communication needs to publish large-scale research that represents the distinctive qualities of our discipline (e.g., see Carbaugh & Buzzanell, 2010). Despite the variety of topics and analytic tools, work-life communication scholarship has not moved into such macro studies. Given the rapid emergence of and interest in work-life communication scholarship, we envision increased attention to this area within our discipline.

In considering *how ideal workers and the primacy of work are (re)produced*, we see a need to pay greater attention to negotiating the body as a site of (re)production (cf. Ashcraft & Mumby, 2004). As Putnam and Bochantin (2009) state, "[V]ery few studies focus on negotiating about the body at work, but research on pregnancy and maternity leave shows how the body enters into the micro practices of negotiation" (p. 60; for exceptions, see Nadesan & Trethewey, 2000; Trethewey, 1999, 2001). They argue that issues such as menopause need to be named and negotiated, particularly labeling scenarios as rights-based issues. Moving beyond women's bodies, Kirby (2006c) illustrates how one organization "colonized" the bodies of its members by mandating that the management team (attempt to) climb Colorado's Mount Elbert—which in turn forced them to work out on their personal time to prepare for this work responsibility. While most wellness programs are less drastic, they are work-life concerns when organizations pressure individuals to rein in their bodies and/or personal lives for the benefit of their working lives (see Kirby, 2006a). Exploring how the body is (not) invoked in work-life conversations therefore seems fruitful.

Examining the *construction of identities* leads fairly naturally to investigating intersections of work-life and meaningful work (e.g., Cheney et al., 2008; Dempsey & Sanders, 2010; Kuhn et al., 2008). How does finding work that contributes to a personally significant purpose impact the work-life relationship and communication about it? Cheney et al. (2008) offer an "important question" as "to how life priorities influence the meaning of both work and home relationships and vice versa. . . . Do people work to live (including to support their personal relationships) or live to work?" (p. 160). The centralities of work and family/personal life exhibit different processes and consequences (e.g., Bagger & Li, 2012) and unfold over the course of lifetimes in considerably different ways (see work-life entangled strands; Lee, Kossek, Hall, & Litrico, 2011). Researchers still do not know how different cultural groups interpret choice, mobility, status, progress, and meaningful work and quality of life experiences; how work and life are communicatively constituted has yet to be explored fully (see Putnam & Nicotera, 2009).

A (re)consideration of *acting practically and routinizing work and (personal) life* suggests that scholars should attend to particular contexts in which work-life communication has distinctive qualities to provide greater understandings of difference in practical actions. As organizational and family communication have expanded beyond managerialist and nuclear family considerations, so too have some researchers begun to engage with the exigencies that impact and prompt different considerations of everyday work and personal life intersections. For instance, family members' negotiations of contradictions surrounding military deployments over time displays individuals' and families' efforts to manage difficult times (Wilson et al., 2011). Lucas and Buzzanell (2012) explore how *resilience* is constructed on an ongoing basis in families. Routinized family talk and material practices of (1) preparing for anticipated tough economic times, (2) sidelining or gaining employment through well-developed alternative skill sets, (3) tightening the belt, and (4) talking about numbers (i.e., income, budgets) served to develop a *dual-layer* of resilience as families alternated between dealing with immediate financial crises and developing values to withstand future difficulties. Thus considering the role of difference upon everyday routines is useful, if "routine" is even possible for some groups.

Finally, discussions of *norm-ing* (or not) issues of work-life in organizations intersect with issues of power. We encourage more critical scholarship on work-life issues focused on power dynamics in society in order to (re)imagine how some work-life interrelationships and norms could be different through communication (see *parallel call* in Kirby et al., 2013; see also Medved, 2010). Work-life communication scholarship can provide pathways for (re)negotiating divisions of labor (e.g., Alberts et al., 2011; Riforgiate & Alberts, 2009), for questioning a corporate ideology of work-life (e.g., Hoffman & Cowan, 2008), for negotiating workplace accommodations (e.g., Hoffman & Cowan, 2010; Kirby & Krone, 2002), and for revealing unethical (if not illegal) modes of communication in such negotiations (see Buzzanell, 2003; Buzzanell & Liu, 2005, 2007; Liu & Buzzanell, 2004, 2006). This scholarship can advance our understandings of how work and personal life arenas are politicized broadly (e.g., where and how they are gendered, raced, classed, religiously oriented, and locally culturally bound). Since Kirby et al. (2003) articulated a need to go beyond the voices of the privileged in work-life research, there is work beginning to overcome classist and professionalized assumptions as to who is studied (e.g., Buzzanell, 2003; D'Enbeau, Buzzanell, & Duckworth, 2010; Lucas & Buzzanell, 2004; Simpson & Kirby, 2006). For example, Cowan and Bochantin (2011) examine the work-life metaphors of blue-collar employees, namely custodians. And yet there is always more to be done as we strive to understand difference in experiences of work-life communication (Mumby, 2011).

In closing, there has been much interdisciplinary research and popular interest in issues of work-life. Whereas different disciplines have focused attention on the management of, sociological changes in, policy making for, and antecedents and consequences of work-life endeavors for individuals and collectivities, communication offers a constitutive approach to work-life. We start with the assumption that communication constitutes work and life enactments and is recursively constituted by these same enactments. Moreover, we acknowledge that the constitutive approach can potentially transform work-life understandings and their consequences. We find that the constitutive perspective asks questions about sensemaking and social construction. Specifically, questions that we ask would include the following: How do people make sense of their everyday work-life experiences? How do they explain their choices and decisions to other women and men? How are the material conditions of everyday life—embodiment, sites, artifacts, technologies—implicated in and constituted by communication about and within work-life? In following up on the five different constitutive processes we have identified as both current communication trends and future directions for work-life communication scholarship—(1) *policy-ing* work-life in organizations, (2) *norm-ing* (or not) issues of work-life in organizations, (3) (re)producing ideal workers and the primacy of work, (4) constructing (gendered) (working) identities, and (5) acting practically and routinizing work and (personal) life—we argue that these are both sites for sense-making and for transformation of everyday lives.

References

Alberts, J. K., Tracy, S. J., & Trethewey, A. (2011). An integrative theory of the division of domestic labor: Threshold level, social organizing and sense making. *Journal of Family Communication, 11*(1), 21–38.

Alvesson, M., & Willmott, H. (2002). Identity regulation as organization control: Producing the appropriate individual. *Journal of Management Studies, 39*(5), 619–644.

Andreassi, J., & Thompson, C. (2004, February). Work-family culture. In E. Kossek & M. Pitt-Catsouphes (Eds.), *Work and family encyclopedia.* Chestnut Hill, MA: Sloan Work and Family Research Network. Retrieved from https://workfamily.sas.upenn.edu/wfrn-repo/object/qq5vi45wj86xo1pg

Ashcraft, K. L. (1999). Managing maternity leave: A qualitative analysis of temporary executive succession. *Administrative Science Quarterly, 44*(2), 240–280.

Ashcraft, K. L., & Mumby, D. K. (2004). *Reworking gender: A feminist communicology of organization.* Thousand Oaks, CA: SAGE.

Ashforth, B. E., Kreiner, G. E., & Fugate, M. (2000). All in a day's work: Boundaries and micro role transitions. *Academy of Management Review, 25*(3), 472–491.

Association for Women in Science (AWIS). (2011). *Work-life balance executive summary.* Retrieved from http://www.awis.org/associations/9417/files/AWIS_Work_Life_Balance_Executive_Summary.pdf

Bagger, J., & Li, A. (2012). Being important matters: The impact of work and family centralities on the family-to-work conflict-satisfaction relationship. *Human Relations, 65*(4), 473–500.

Ballard, D. I., & Gossett, L. M. (2007). Alternative times: The temporal perceptions, processes, and practices defining the non-standard work arrangement. In C. S. Beck (Ed.), *Communication yearbook* (vol. 31, pp. 269–316). New York, NY: Routledge.

Bergen, K. M., Kirby, E. L., & McBride, M. C. (2007). "How do you get two houses cleaned?" Accomplishing family caregiving in commuter marriages. *Journal of Family Communication, 7*(4), 287–307.

Blair-Loy, M. (2009). Work without end? Scheduling flexibility and work-to-family conflict among stockbrokers. *Work and Occupations, 36*(4), 279–317.

Bochantin, J. E., & Cowan, R. L. (2010). "I'm not an invalid because I have a baby . . .": A cluster analysis of female police officers experiences as mothers on the job. *Human Communication, 13*(4), 319–335.

Briscoe, F., & Kellogg, K. (2011). The initial assignment effect: Local employer practices and positive career outcomes for work-family program users. *American Sociological Review, 76*(2), 291–319.

Butler, J. A., & Modaff, D. P. (2008). When work is home: Agency, structure and contradictions. *Management Communication Quarterly, 22*(2), 232–257.

Buzzanell, P. M. (1994). Gaining a voice: Feminist organizational communication theorizing. *Management Communication Quarterly, 7*(4), 339–383.

Buzzanell, P. M. (2000). The promise and practice of the new career and social contract: Illusions exposed and suggestions for reform. In P. M. Buzzanell (Ed.), *Rethinking organizational and managerial communication from feminist perspectives* (pp. 209–235). Thousand Oaks, CA: SAGE.

Buzzanell, P. M. (2003). A feminist standpoint analysis of maternity and maternity leave for women with disabilities. *Women & Language, 26*(2), 53–65.

Buzzanell, P. M. (2006). Pondering diverse work-life issues and developments over the lifespan. *The Electronic Journal of Communication, 16*(3–4). Retrieved from http://www.cios.org/EJCPUBLIC/016/3/01637.HTML

Buzzanell, P. M., Berkelaar, B., & Kisselburgh, L. (2011). From the mouths of babes: Exploring families' career socialization of young children in China, Lebanon, Belgium, and the United States. *Journal of Family Communication, 11*(2), 148–164.

Buzzanell, P. M., Berkelaar, B., & Kisselburgh, L. (2012). Expanding understandings of mediated and human socialization agents: Chinese children talk about desirable work and careers. *China Media Research, 8*(1), 1–14.

Buzzanell, P. M., & D'Enbeau, S. (2009). Stories of caregiving: Intersections of academic research and women's everyday experiences. *Qualitative Inquiry, 15*(7), 1199–1224.

Buzzanell, P. M., & Liu, M. (2005). Struggling with maternity leave policies and practices: A poststructuralist feminist analysis of gendered organizing. *Journal of Applied Communication Research, 33*(1), 1–25.

Buzzanell, P. M., & Liu, M. (2007). It's "give and take": Maternity leave as a conflict management process. *Human Relations, 60*(3), 463–495.

Buzzanell, P. M., & Lucas, K. (2013). Constrained and constructed choice in career: An examination of communication pathways to dignity. In E. L. Cohen (Ed.), *Communication yearbook* (vol. 37, pp. 3–31). New York, NY: Routledge.

Buzzanell, P. M., Meisenbach, R., Remke, R., Bowers, V., Liu, M., & Conn, C. (2005). The good *working* mother: Managerial women's sensemaking and feelings about work-family issues. *Communication Studies, 56*(3), 261–285.

Buzzanell, P. M., & Turner, L. H. (2003). Emotion work revealed by job loss discourse: Backgrounding-foregrounding of feelings, construction of normalcy, and (re)instituting of traditional masculinities. *Journal of Applied Communication Research, 31*(1), 27–57.

Buzzanell, P. M., Waymer, D., Tagle, M. P., & Liu, M. (2007). Different transitions into working motherhood: Discourses of Asian, Hispanic, and African American women. *Journal of Family Communication, 7*(3), 195–220.

Canary, H. E. (2010). Constructing policy knowledge: Contradictions, communication, and knowledge frames. *Communication Monographs, 77*(2), 181–206.

Canary, H. E., & McPhee, R. D. (2009). The mediation of policy knowledge: An interpretive analysis of intersecting activity systems. *Management Communication Quarterly, 23*(2), 147–187.

Carbaugh, D., & Buzzanell, P. M. (Eds.). (2010). *Distinctive qualities in communication research.* New York, NY: Routledge.

Carlone, D. (2001). Enablement, constraint, and *The 7 habits of highly effective people. Management Communication Quarterly, 14*(3), 491–497.

Carter, N., & Silva, C. (2011). *The myth of the ideal worker: Does doing all the right things really get women ahead?* New York, NY: Catalyst.

Cheney, G., & Ashcraft, K. L. (2007). Considering "the professional" in communication studies: Implications for theory and research within and beyond the boundaries of organizational communication. *Communication Theory, 17*(2), 146–175.

Cheney, G., Zorn, T. E., Jr., Planalp, S., & Lair, D. J. (2008). Meaningful work and personal/social well-being: Organizational communication engages the meanings of work. In C. S. Beck (Ed.), *Communication yearbook* (vol. 32, pp. 137–186). New York, NY: Routledge.

Clair, R. P. (1996). The political nature of the colloquialism, "A real job": Implications for organizational socialization. *Communication Monographs, 63*(3), 249–267.

Clair, R. P., & Thompson, K. (1996). Pay discrimination as a discursive and material practice: A case concerning extended housework. *Journal of Applied Communication Research, 24*(1), 1–20.

Clark, S. C. (2002). Communicating across the work/home border. *Community, Work, & Family, 5*(1), 23–48.

Cook, A. (2004). Corporate decision-making process: How organizations decide to adopt work/life initiatives. In E. Kossek & M. Pitt-Catsouphes (Eds.), *Work and family encyclopedia.* Chestnut Hill, MA: Sloan Work and Family Research Network. Retrieved from http://repo.library.upenn.edu/storage/content/2/kl3lc5nn0sx8b7hp/1/Corporate_Decision-Makin_Process.pdf

Cowan, R. L., & Bochantin, J. E. (2009). Pregnancy and motherhood on the thin blue line: Female police officers' perspectives on motherhood in a highly masculinized work environment. *Women and Language, 32*(1), 22–30.

Cowan, R. L., & Bochantin, J. E. (2011). Blue-collar employees' work/life metaphors: Tough similarities, imbalance, separation, and opposition. *Qualitative Research Reports in Communication, 12*(1), 19–26.

Cowan, R. L., & Hoffman, M. F. (2007). The flexible organization: How contemporary employees construct the work/life border. *Qualitative Research Reports in Communication, 8*(1), 37–44.

Daft, R. L., & Weick, K. E. (1984). Toward a model of organizations as interpretation systems. *Academy of Management Review, 9*(2), 284–295.

D'Enbeau, S., & Buzzanell, P. M. (2010). Caregiving and female embodiment: Scrutinizing (professional) female bodies in media, academe, and the neighborhood bar. *Women & Language, 33*(1), 29–52.

D'Enbeau, S., Buzzanell, P. M., & Duckworth, J. (2010). Problematizing classed identities in fatherhood: Development of integrative case studies for analysis and praxis. *Qualitative Inquiry, 16*(9), 709–720.

Dempsey, S. E., & Sanders, M. L. (2010). Meaningful work? Nonprofit marketization and work/life imbalance in popular autobiographies of social entrepreneurship. *Organization, 17*(4), 437–459.

den Dulk, L., & de Riujter, J. (2008). Managing work-life policies: Disruptive versus dependency arguments explaining managerial attitudes toward employee utilization of work-life policies. *International Journal of Human Resource Management, 19*(7), 1224–1238.

den Dulk, L., Peters, P., Poutsma, E., & Ligthart, P. E. M. (2010). The extended business case for childcare and leave arrangements in Western and Eastern Europe. *Baltic Journal of Management, 5*(2), 156–184.

DiMaggio, P., & Powell, W. (1983). The iron cage revisited: Institutional isomorphism and collective rationality in organizational fields. *American Sociological Review, 48*(2), 147–160.

Drago, R. W. (2007). *Striking a balance: Work, family, and life.* Boston, MA: Dollars & Sense.

Duckworth, J. D., & Buzzanell, P. M. (2009). Constructing work-life balance and fatherhood: Men's framing of the meanings of both work and family. *Communication Studies, 60*(5), 558–573.

Eaton, S. C. (2003). If you can use them: Flexibility policies, organizational commitment, and perceived performance. *Industrial Relations, 42*(2), 145–167.

Edley, P. P. (2001). Technology, employed mothers, and corporate colonization of the lifeworld: A gendered paradox of work and family balance. *Women & Language, 24*(2), 28–35.

Edley, P. P., Hylmö, A., & Newsom, V. A. (2004). Alternative organizing communities: Collectivist organizing, telework, home-based internet businesses, and online communities. In P. J. Kalbfleisch (Ed.), *Communication yearbook* (vol. 28, pp. 87–127). New York, NY: Routledge.

Esping-Andersen, G. (1999). *Social foundations of postindustrial economies.* Oxford, UK: Oxford University Press.

Farley-Lucas, B. (2000). Communicating the (in)visibility of motherhood: Family talk and the ties to motherhood with/in the workplace. *The Electronic Journal of Communication, 10*(3–4). Retrieved from http://www.cios.org/EJCPUBLIC/010/3/010317.html

Fonner, K. L., & Roloff, M. E. (2010). Why teleworkers are more satisfied with their jobs than are office-based workers: When less contact is beneficial. *Journal of Applied Communication Research, 38*(4), 336–361.

Fonner, K. L., & Roloff, M. E. (2012). Testing the connectivity paradox: Linking teleworkers' communication media use to social presence, stress from interruptions, and organizational identification. *Communication Monographs, 79*(2), 205–231.

Fonner, K. L., & Stache, L. (2012). Teleworkers' boundary management: Temporal, spatial and expectation-setting strategies. In S. Long (Ed.), *Virtual work and human interaction research* (pp. 31–58). Hershey, PA: IGI Global.

Frey, L., & Cissna, K. (Eds.). (2009). *Routledge handbook of applied communication research.* New York, NY: Routledge.

Galinsky, E., Bond, T., Sakai, K., Kim, S., & Giuntoli, N. (2008). *The 2008 National Study of Employers.* New York, NY: Families and Work Institute.

Gill, R. (2006). The work-life relationship for "people with choices:" Women entrepreneurs as crystallized selves? *The Electronic Journal of Communication, 16*(3–4). Retrieved from http://www.cios.org/EJCPUBLIC/016/3/01635.HTML

Golden, A. G. (Ed.). (2000a). Special issue on "communication perspectives on work and family." *The Electronic Journal of Communication, 10*(3–4). Retrieved from http://www.cios.org/www/ejc/v10n3400.htm

Golden, A. G. (2000b). What we talk about when we talk about work and family: A discourse analysis of parental accounts. *The Electronic Journal of Communication, 10*(3-4). Retrieved from http://www.cios.org/EJCPUBLIC/010/3/010315.html

Golden, A. G. (2001). Modernity and the communicative management of multiple role-identities: The case of the worker-parent. *The Journal of Family Communication, 1*(4), 233–264.

Golden, A. G. (2002). Speaking of work and family: Spousal collaboration on defining role-identities and developing shared meanings. *Southern Communication Journal, 67*(2), 122–141.

Golden, A. G. (2007). Fathers' frames for childrearing: Evidence toward a "masculine concept of caregiving." *Journal of Family Communication, 7*(4), 265–285.

Golden, A. G. (2009). Employee families and organizations as mutually enacted environments: A sensemaking approach to work-life interrelationships. *Management Communication Quarterly, 22*(3), 385–415.

Golden, A. G., & Geisler, C. (2006). Flexible work, time, and technology: Ideological dilemmas of managing work-life interrelationships using personal digital assistants. *The Electronic Journal of Communication, 16*(3–4). Retrieved from http://www.cios.org/EJCPUBLIC/016/3/01633.HTML

Golden, A. G., & Geisler, C. (2007). Work-life boundary management and the personal digital assistant. *Human Relations, 60*(3), 519–551.

Golden, A. G., Kirby, E. L., & Jorgenson, J. (2006). Work-life research from both sides now: An integrative perspective for organizational and family communication. In C. S. Beck (Ed.), *Communication yearbook* (vol. 30, pp. 143–195). New York, NY: Routledge.

Gregg, M. (2011). *Work's intimacy.* Hoboken, NJ: Wiley.

Hayden, S. (2010). Lessons from the baby boon: "Family-friendly" policies and the ethics of justice and care. *Women's Studies in Communication, 33*(2), 119–137.

Helmle, J. R., Seibold, D. R., & Afifi, T. D. (2011). Work and family in copreneurial family businesses. In C. T. Salmon (Ed.), *Communication yearbook* (vol. 35, pp. 51–91). New York, NY: Routledge.

Hewlett, S. A., & Luce, C. B. (2006). Extreme jobs: The dangerous allure of the 70-hour workweek. *Harvard Business Review, 84* (12), 49–58.

Hochschild, A. R. (1997). *The time bind: When work becomes home and home becomes work.* New York, NY: Metropolitan.

Hoffman, M. F., & Cowan, R. L. (2008). The meaning of work/life: A corporate ideology of work/life balance. *Communication Quarterly, 56*(3), 227–246.

Hoffman, M. F., & Cowan, R. L. (2010). Be careful what you ask for: Structuration theory and work/life accommodation. *Communication Studies, 61*(2), 205–223.

Hylmö, A. (2006). Telecommuting and the contestability of choice: Employee strategies to legitimize personal decisions to work in a preferred location. *Management Communication Quarterly, 19*(4), 541–569.

Hylmö, A., & Buzzanell, P. M. (2002). Telecommuting as viewed through cultural lenses: An empirical investigation of discourses of utopia, identity, and mystery. *Communication Monographs, 69*(4), 329–356.

Jorgenson, J. (2000). Interpreting the intersections of work and family: Frame conflicts in women's work. *The Electronic Journal of Communication, 10*(3–4). Retrieved from http://www.cios.org/EJCPUBLIC/010/3/010314.html

Jorgenson, J. (2002). Engineering selves: Negotiating gender and identity in technical work. *Management Communication Quarterly, 15*(3), 350–380.

Kanter, R. M. (1977). *Work and family in the U.S.: A critical review and agenda for research and policy*. Beverly Hills, CA: SAGE.

Kirby, E. L. (2000). Should I do as you say, or do as you do? Mixed messages about work and family. *The Electronic Journal of Communication, 10*(3–4). Retrieved from http://www.cios.org/EJCPUBLIC/010/3/010313.html

Kirby, E. L. (2006a). "Helping you make room in your life for your needs": When organizations appropriate family roles. *Communication Monographs, 73*(4), 474–480.

Kirby, E. L. (Ed.). (2006b). Special issue on "communication and the accomplishment of personal and professional life." *The Electronic Journal of Communication, 16*(3–4). Retrieved from http://www.cios.org/EJCPUBLIC/016/3/01631.HTML

Kirby, E. L. (2006c). Your attitude determines your altitude: Reflecting on a company-sponsored mountain climb. In J. Keyton & P. Shockley-Zalabak (Eds.), *Organizational communication: Understanding communication processes* (2nd ed., pp. 99–108). Los Angeles, CA: Roxbury.

Kirby, E. L., Golden, A. G., Medved, C. E., Jorgenson, J., & Buzzanell, P. M. (2003). An organizational communication challenge to the discourse of work and family research: From problematic to empowerment. In P. J. Kalbfleisch (Ed.), *Communication yearbook* (vol. 27, pp. 1–43). New York, NY: Routledge.

Kirby, E. L., & Krone, K. J. (2002). "The policy exists but you can't really use it": Communication and the structuration of work-family policies. *Journal of Applied Communication Research, 30*(1), 50–77.

Kirby, E. L., Wieland, S. M. B., & McBride, M. C. (2006). Work-life conflict. In J. G. Oetzel & S. Ting-Toomey (Eds.), *The SAGE handbook of conflict communication: Integrating theory, research, and practice* (pp. 327–357). Thousand Oaks, CA: SAGE.

Kirby, E. L., Wieland, S. M. B., & McBride, M. C. (2013). Work-life conflict. In J. G. Oetzel & S. Ting-Toomey (Eds.), *The SAGE handbook of conflict communication: Integrating theory, research, and practice* (2nd ed., pp. 377–402). Thousand Oaks, CA: SAGE.

Kisselburgh, L. G., Berkelaar, B., & Buzzanell, P. M. (2009). Discourse, gender, and the meanings of work: Rearticulating science, technology, and engineering careers through communicative lenses. In C. S. Beck (Ed.), *Communication yearbook* (vol. 33, pp. 258–299). New York, NY: Routledge.

Kossek, E. E., & Distelberg, B. (2009). Work and family employment policy for a transformed work force: Trends and themes. In A. C. Crouter & A. Booth (Eds.), *Work-life policies that make a real difference for individuals, families and organizations* (pp. 3–51). Washington, DC: Urban Institute Press.

Kossek, E. E., Lewis, S. L., & Hammer, L. B. (2010). Work-life initiatives and organizational change: Overcoming mixed messages to move from the margin to the mainstream. *Human Relations, 63*(1), 3–19.

Kramer, M. W. (2011). Toward a communication model for the socialization of voluntary members. *Communication Monographs, 78*(2), 233–255.

Krouse, S. S., & Afifi, T. D. (2007). Family-to-work spillover stress: Coping communicatively in the workplace. *Journal of Family Communication, 7*(2), 85–122.

Kuhn, T. (2006). A "demented work ethic" and a "lifestyle firm": Discourse, identity, and workplace time commitments. *Organization Studies, 27*(9), 1339–1358.

Kuhn, T., Golden, A. G., Jorgenson, J., Buzzanell, P. M., Berkelarr, B. L., Kisselburgh, . . . Cruz, D. (2008). Cultural discourses and discursive resources for meaning/ful work: Constructing and disrupting identities in contemporary capitalism. *Management Communication Quarterly, 22*(1), 162–171.

Langellier, K. M., & Peterson, E. E. (2006). "Somebody's got to pick eggs": Family storytelling about work. *Communication Monographs, 73*(4), 468–473.

Lauzun, H. M., Morganson, V. J., Major, D. A., & Green, A. P. (2010). Seeking work-life balance: Employees' requests, supervisors' responses, and organizational barriers. *The Psychologist-Manager Journal, 13*(3), 184–205.

Lee, M. D., Kossek, E. E., Hall, D. T., & Litrico, J-B. (2011). Entangled strands: A process perspective on the evolution of careers in the context of personal, family, work, and community life. *Human Relations, 64*(12), 1531–1553.

Liu, M., & Buzzanell, P. M. (2004). Negotiating maternity leave expectations: Perceived tensions between ethics of justice and care. *Journal of Business Communication, 41*(4), 323–349.

Liu, M., & Buzzanell, P. M. (2006). When workplace pregnancy highlights difference: Openings for detrimental gender and supervisory relations. In J. H. Fritz & B. L. Omdahl (Eds.), *Problematic relationships in the workplace* (pp. 47–67). New York, NY: Peter Lang.

Long, Z., Kuang, K., & Buzzanell, P. M. (2013). Legitimizing and elevating telework: Chinese constructions of a nonstandard work arrangement. *Journal of Business and Technical Communication, 27*(3), 243–262.

Lucas, K., & Buzzanell, P. M. (2004). Blue-collar work, career and success: Occupational narratives of *Sisu*. *Journal of Applied Communication Research, 32*(4), 273–292.

Lucas, K., & Buzzanell, P. M. (2012). Memorable messages of hard times: Constructing short- and long-term resiliencies through family communication. *Journal of Family Communication, 12*(3), 189–208.

Lucas, K., Liu, M., & Buzzanell, P. M. (2006). No limits careers: A critical examination of career discourse in the U.S. and China. *International and Intercultural Communication Annual, 28*, 217–242.

May, S., & Mumby, D. K. (Eds.). (2005). *Engaging organizational communication theory and research: Multiple perspectives*. Thousand Oaks, CA: SAGE.

Medved, C. E. (2004). The everyday accomplishment of work and family: Exploring practical actions in daily routines. *Communication Studies, 55*(1), 128–145.

Medved, C. E. (2007). Investigating family labor in communication studies: Threading across historical and contemporary discourses. *Journal of Family Communication, 7*(4), 225–243.

Medved, C. E. (2009a). Constructing breadwinning mother identities: Moral, personal, and political positioning. *Women's Studies Quarterly, 37*(3/4), 140–156.

Medved, C. E. (2009b). Crossing and transforming occupational and household divisions of labor: Reviewing literatures and deconstructing divisions. In C. S. Beck (Ed.), *Communication yearbook* (vol. 33, pp. 457–484). New York, NY: Routledge.

Medved, C. E. (2010). Communication work-life research. In S. Sweet & J. Casey (Eds.), *Work and family encyclopedia*. Chestnut Hill, MA: Sloan Work and Family Research Network. Retrieved from http://repo.library.upenn.edu/storage/content/2/3kb6k5cb4ft7918c/1/Communication_Work-Life_Research.pdf

Medved, C. E., Brogan, S. M., McClanahan, A. M., Morris, J. F., & Shepherd, G. J. (2006). Family and work socializing communication: Messages, gender, and ideological implications. *Journal of Family Communication, 6*(3), 161–180.

Medved, C. E., & Kirby, E. L. (2005). Family CEOs: A feminist analysis of corporate mothering discourses. *Management Communication Quarterly, 18*(4), 435–478.

Medved, C. E., & Rawlins, W. K. (2011). At-home fathers and breadwinning mothers: Variations in constructing work and family lives. *Women & Language, 34*(2), 9–39.

Meisenbach, R. J. (2010). The female breadwinner: Phenomenological experience and gendered identity in work/family spaces. *Sex Roles, 62*(1/2), 2–19.

Meisenbach, R. J., Remke, R. V., Buzzanell, P. M., & Liu, M. (2008). "They allowed": Pentadic mapping of women's maternity leave discourse as organizational rhetoric. *Communication Monographs, 75*(1), 1–24.

Mescher, S., Benschop, Y., & Doorewaard, H. (2009). Representations of work-life balance support. *Human Relations, 63*(1), 21–39.

Miller, V. D., Jablin, F. M., Casey, M. K., Lamphear-Van Horn, M., & Ethington, C. (1996). The maternity leave as a role negotiation process. *Journal of Managerial Issues, 8*(3), 286–308.

Milliken, F. J., Martins, L. L., & Morgan, H. (1998). Explaining organizational responsiveness to work-family issues: The role of human resource executives as issue interpreters. *Academy of Management Journal, 41*(5), 580–592.

Montoya, Y. J., & Trethewey, A. (2009). *Rethinking good work: Developing sustainable employees and workplaces*. Report presented for The Project for Wellness and Work-Life at Arizona State University, Phoenix, AZ. Retrieved from http://humancommunication.clas.asu.edu/content/pwwl-white-papers-and-other-resources

Mumby, D. K. (Ed.). (2011). *Reframing difference in organizational communication studies: Research, pedagogy, and practice*. Thousand Oaks, CA: SAGE.

Myers, K. K., Gailliard, B., & Putnam, L. L. (2012). Reconsidering the concept of workplace flexibility: Is adaptability a better solution? In E. L. Cohen (Ed.), *Communication yearbook* (vol. 36, pp. 194–230). New York, NY: Routledge.

Myers, K. K., Jahn, J., Gailliard, B., & Stoltzfus, K. (2011). Vocational Anticipatory Socialization (VAS): A communicative model of adolescents' interests in STEM. *Management Communication Quarterly, 25*(1), 87–120.

Nadesan, M. H., & Trethewey, A. (2000). Performing the enterprising subject: Gendered strategies for success (?). *Text & Performance Quarterly, 20*(3), 223–250.

Nippert-Eng, C. (1996). *Home and work: Negotiating the boundaries of everyday life*. Chicago, IL: Chicago University Press.

Paugh, A. L. (2005). Learning about work at dinnertime: Language socialization in dual-earner American families. *Discourse & Society, 16*(1), 55–78.

Peterson, L. W., & Albrecht, T. L. (1999). Where gender/power/politics collide: Deconstructing organizational maternity leave policy. *Journal of Management Inquiry, 8*(2), 168–181.

Petroski, D. J., & Edley, P. P. (2006). Stay-at-home-fathers: Masculinity, family, work, and gender stereotypes. *The Electronic Journal of Communication, 16*(3–4). Retrieved from http://www.cios.org/EJCPUBLIC/016/3/01634.HTML

Pfeffer, J., & Salancik, G. R. (1978). *The external control of organizations*. New York, NY: Harper and Row.

Pitt-Catsouphes, M. (2002). Family-friendly workplace. In E. Kossek & M. Pitt-Catsouphes (Eds.), *Work and family encyclopedia*. Chestnut Hill, MA: Sloan Work and Family Research Network. Retrieved from https://workfamily.sas.upenn.edu/wfrn-repo/object/0ob6wj5967320w87

Pitt-Catsouphes, M., Kossek, E. E., & Sweet, S. (2006). Charting new territory: Advancing multi-disciplinary perspectives, methods, and approaches in the study of work and family. In M. Pitt-Catsouphes, E. E. Kossek, & S. Sweet (Eds.), *The work and family handbook: Multi-disciplinary perspectives, methods, and approaches* (pp. 1–15). Mahwah, NJ: LEA.

Putnam, L. L. (2009, August). *The multiple faces of engaged scholarship*. Keynote presentation to the 7th Aspen Conference on Engaged Communication Scholarship, Aspen, CO.

Putnam, L. L., & Bochantin, J. (2009). Gendered bodies: Negotiating normalcy and support. *Negotiation and Conflict Management Research, 2*(1), 57–73.

Putnam, L. L., & Nicotera, A. M. (Eds.). (2009). *Building theories of organization: The constitutive role of communication*. New York, NY: Routledge.

Riforgiate, S. E., & Alberts, J. K. (2009). *Who's doing the dishes? Negotiating household tasks and improving relationships*. Report presented for The Project for Wellness and Work-Life at Arizona State University, Phoenix, AZ.

Rivera, K. D., & Tracy, S. J. (2009). *Work hard, live hard: Six things smart executives do to promote work-life harmony and improve their bottom line*. Report presented for The Project for Wellness and Work-Life at Arizona State University, Phoenix, AZ.

Shuler, S. (2006). Working at home as total institution: Maintaining and undermining the public/private dichotomy. *The Electronic Journal of Communication, 16*(3–4). Retrieved from http://www.cios.org/EJCPUBLIC/016/3/01632.HTML

Shumate, M., & Fulk, J. (2004). Boundaries and role conflict when work and family are colocated: A communication network and symbolic interaction approach. *Human Relations, 57*(1), 55–74.

Simpson, J. L., & Kirby, E. L. (2006). "Choices" for whom? A White privilege/social class communicative response to *the opt-out revolution*. *The Electronic Journal of Communication, 16*(3–4). Retrieved from http://www.cios.org/EJCPUBLIC/016/3/016315.HTML

Society of Human Resource Management (SHRM). (2011). *2011 Employee benefits report: Examining employee benefits amidst uncertainty*. Alexandria, VA: Author.

Sotirin, P., Buzzanell, P. M., & Turner, L. H. (2007). Colonizing family: A feminist critique of family management texts. *Journal of Family Communication, 7*(4), 245–263.

Thompson, C. A., Beauvais, L. L., & Lyness, K. S. (1999). When work-family benefits are not enough: The influence of work-family culture on benefit utilization, organizational attachment, and work-family conflict. *Journal of Vocational Behavior, 54*(3), 392–415.

Townsley, N. C., & Broadfoot, K. J. (Eds.). (2008). Care, career, and academe: Heeding the calls of a new professoriate. *Women's Studies in Communication, 31*(2), 133–142.

Tracy, S. J. (2008). Care as a common good. *Women's Studies in Communication, 31*(2), 166–174.

Tracy, S. J., & Rivera, K. D. (2010). Endorsing equity and applauding stay-at-home moms: How male voices on work-life reveal aversive sexism and flickers of transformation. *Management Communication Quarterly, 24*(1), 3–43.

Tracy, S. J., & Trethewey, A. (2005). Fracturing the real↔self–fake-self dichotomy: Moving toward "crystallized" organizational discourses and identities. *Communication Theory, 15*(2), 168–195.

Trethewey, A. (1999). Disciplined bodies: Women's embodied identities at work. *Organization Studies, 20*(3), 423–450.

Trethewey, A. (2001). Reproducing and resisting the master narrative of decline: Midlife professional women's experiences of aging. *Management Communication Quarterly, 15*(2), 183–226.

Trethewey, A., Tracy, S. J., & Alberts, J. K. (2006). Crystallizing frames for work life. *The Electronic Journal of Communication, 16*(3–4). Retrieved from http://www.cios.org/EJCPUBLIC/016/3/01636.HTML

U.S. Department of Labor. (2012, April 26). *Economic characteristics of families summary*. Retrieved from http://www.bls.gov/news.release/famee.nr0.htm

Vavrus, M. D. (2002). Domesticating patriarchy: Hegemonic masculinity and television's "Mr. Mom." *Critical Studies in Media Communication, 19*(3), 352–375.

Warner, M., Slim-Jerusalim, R., & Korabik, K. (2009). Co-worker backlash and support: Responses to work and family policies and practices. In S. Sweet & J. Casey (Eds.), *Work and Family Encyclopedia.* Chestnut Hill, MA: Sloan Work and Family Research Network. Retrieved from https://workfamily.sas.upenn.edu/wfrn-repo/object/yf8v30cm00li6o2m

West, C., & Zimmerman, D. H. (1987). Doing gender. *Gender & Society, 1*(2), 125–151.

Wieland, S. M. B. (2010). Ideal selves as resources for the situated practice of identity. *Management Communication Quarterly, 24*(4), 503–528.

Wieland, S. M. B. (2011). Struggling to manage work as a part of everyday life: Complicating resistance and contextualizing work/life studies. *Communication Monographs, 78*(2), 162–184.

Wieland, S. M. B., Bauer, J. C., & Deetz, S. (2009). Excessive careerism and destructive life stresses: The role of entrepreneurialism in colonizing identities. In P. Lutgen-Sandvik & B. D. Sypher (Eds.), *Destructive organizational communication: Processes, consequences, and constructive ways of organizing* (pp. 99–120). New York, NY: Routledge.

Wilson, S. R., Wilkum, K., Chernichky, S. M., MacDermid Wadsworth, S. M., & Broniarczyk, K. M. (2011). Passport toward success: Description and evaluation of a program designed to help children and families reconnect after a military deployment. *Journal of Applied Communication Research, 39*(3), 223–249.

Wood, J. T., & Dow, B. J. (2010). The invisible politics of "choice" in the workplace: Naming the informal parenting support system. In S. Hayden & L. O'Brien Hallstein (Eds.), *Contemplating maternity in the era of choice: Explorations into discourses of reproduction* (pp. 203–205). Lanham, MD: Lexington Press.

Work and Family Researchers Network. (2012). *Home page* [Website]. Retrieved from http://workfamily.sas.upenn.edu/

CHAPTER 15

Workplace Relationships

Patricia M. Sias

Organizations are essentially systems of relationships (Wheatley, 1994). Organizational activities such as motivating, information sharing, decision making, mentoring, and conflict (to name just a few) all occur in the context of interpersonal relationships. The quality of an organization is, therefore, virtually inextricable from the quality of the relationships among the organizational members. Unlike acquaintances marked by a single or occasional interaction, interpersonal relationships are ongoing entities defined by patterned interaction that occurs over time (Sias, Krone, & Jablin, 2002). Thus communication is central to workplace relationship dynamics.

This chapter describes the body of knowledge regarding workplace relationships, highlighting the contributions of organizational communication research to the study of these important entities. Specifically, I discuss organizational communication scholars' insights into the forms and communicative functions of workplace relationships and how theoretically conceptualizing workplace relationships as constitutive entities substantively influences our understanding of the nature and interpersonal dynamics of workplace relationships.

I begin with a brief overview of organizational communication contributions to the workplace relationship literature. That overview sets the foundation for the following sections that discuss research with respect to the forms and functions of workplace relationships, relational dynamics and processes, and workplace relationships as sites of power, control, and resistance. I conclude with a discussion of the limitations of workplace relationship research and a research agenda for the future.

A note about boundaries is important at this point. First, workplace relationship research is quite broad, as it focuses both on the characteristics of these entities and on organizational activities and functions (e.g., leadership, socialization, support, power and control, etc.) that occur in the context of workplace relationships, many of which are addressed in detail in other chapters in this volume. Thus rather than provide an exhaustive review of the literature, I provide an overview of the general topics and body of knowledge generated by workplace relationship research. Second, this chapter centers on *dyadic* interpersonal relationships, not teams or networks, which are, of course, comprised of interpersonal relationships. Networks and teams are addressed in Chapters 13

(Seibold, Hollingshead, & Yoon) and 18 (Shumate & Contractor), respectively, of this volume, and readers should consult those chapters for detailed discussions of that research.

Communication Contributions to the Study of Workplace Relationships

Like other organizational research, workplace relationship research has been, and continues to be, largely grounded in a functionalist approach. Post-positive/social-psychological theory guides this research as scholars attempt to identify effective organizational practices to improve organizational functioning (Sias, 2009). As the following sections demonstrate, such studies provide important knowledge and insights. They are constrained, however, by important theoretical assumptions. For example, the post-positive perspective is grounded in a naturalist principle that conceptualizes human beings as physical, observable objects who behave and occupy space in a physical world (Corman, 2005). This principle grounds a conceptualization of organizations, and workplace relationships, as containers in which people interact and exist (Sias, 2009; Smith & Turner, 1995). As Sias (2009) noted, "while the naturalist principle unites the social and physical world, it also bifurcates the two by placing people (the social world) *inside* physical locations such as organizations (the physical world)" (p. 9, emphasis in original). Because of this and other post-positive assumptions (see Corman, 2005, for a detailed discussion), early and much current research in workplace relationships seeks predictive links between workplace relationships and factors such as personality, context, and outcomes. Organizational communication research in this tradition examines links between workplace relationships and a variety of communication practices and functions such as information exchange, social support, and the like.

While communication scholars have contributed to the field throughout its inception, one of their most important contributions is the conceptualization of organizations, and relationships, as communicatively constituted (Taylor & Van Every, 2000). This development was spurred largely by the organizational communication discipline's *interpretive turn* in the 1980s (Putnam & Pacanowsky, 1983). This move transformed our understanding of social reality and directed attention to how realities are socially constructed and maintained in formal and informal communication (Deetz, 2001). In contrast to functionalist approaches, the interpretive approach is meaning centered and examines how meaning and individual experiences arise from social interaction and sensemaking (Putnam & Pacanowsky, 1983). This move turned scholarly attention away from identifying the functions of, and causal relationships between, workplace relationships and other organizational factors and outcomes and toward understanding the nature and experience of the workplace relationship itself. Moreover, the interpretive turn rejected the naturalist principle and enabled scholars to conceptualize and study workplace relationships not as isolated entities that exist *inside* organizations but instead as multidimensional and interdependent entities that comprise the organization itself (e.g., Bridge & Baxter, 1992; Sias, 1996).

Conceptualizing organizational phenomena as constituted in social practices also opened important avenues of research into the study of workplace relationships as dynamic, not static, entities drawing scholarly attention to relational *processes*. Organizational communication research specifically examined the communication processes through which employees socially construct their workplace relationships (e.g., Fairhurst, 1993; Sias & Cahill, 1998).

Finally, the constitutive conceptualization of workplace relationships enabled a more sophisticated understanding of workplace relationships as sites of power, control, and resistance. Early theory and research, grounded in a distinctly functionalist perspective, conceptualized power as residing with the supervisor who had legitimate power and as a unidirectional process by which supervisors gave orders to subordinate employees who were vulnerable to discipline if they failed to obey (Fayol, 1949). Others addressed the subordinate's role as a participant in the power and control processes and examined upward-influence tactics subordinates use to gain influence with their supervisors (e.g., rational arguments, assertiveness, coalitions, ingratiation) and impression management tactics used by subordinates and supervisors to influence one another (Ferris & Judge, 1991). The organizational communication field's embrace of critical theory in the 1980s brought theoretical complexity to the study of power, control, and resistance in workplace relationships, conceptualizing these processes as constituted in member interaction and discourse (Mumby, 1988).

In sum, organizational communication scholars have made important contributions to workplace relationship theory and research by examining the communicative functions of such relationships and revealing the communicative processes that constitute relationships as dynamic, not static, entities. Such understanding also enriched the examination of power, resistance, and control that underlie workplace relationships. With this overview in place, the following sections discuss the state of the art of workplace relationship research.

Workplace Relationship Forms and Functions

Much research centers on identifying and understanding the forms and functions of workplace relationships (Sias, 2009). This section reviews that literature. Specifically, this section discusses research with respect to supervisor-subordinate, peer, friendship, and romantic relationships.

Supervisor-Subordinate Relationships

W. Charles Redding, considered to be one of the founders of the organizational communication discipline, noted that the field emerged in the 1940s out of a broad concern with organizing large amounts of people efficiently and effectively (Redding, 1985). Chief among these concerns was improving communication between who were referred to at the time as *superiors* (i.e., managers, supervisors) and their lower-level reports. The study of supervisor-subordinate relationships began with organizational communication research centered on the communicative functions of supervisor-subordinate relationships, including leadership, information exchange, feedback and appraisal, and mentoring.

Leadership. Consistent with the field's concern with the formal aspects of organizing, early leadership research (see Fairhurst & Connaughton, Chapter 16, for a detailed discussion of leadership research) centered on the supervisor in the supervisor-subordinate relationship, placing subordinate employees, at least implicitly, in a passive role (Sias et al., 2002). For example, leadership research was initially grounded in a trait perspective, assuming that great leaders possess unique traits—such as charisma and intelligence—and those traits enable them to successfully lead anyone in any situation (e.g., Ghiselli, 1963). The specific subordinate was largely irrelevant and simply a receptive follower. A more nuanced understanding of leadership was introduced by theories focused on the *behaviors*—not traits—of leaders, conceptualizing leadership as a trainable skill. Employees retained a passive role in such theories however, because they assumed that leaders could learn and perform leadership skills that would be effective with any employee (e.g., Blake & Mouton, 1964). Later theories such as path-goal theory (House, 1971) and Situational Leadership Theory (Hersey & Blanchard, 1982) acknowledged the individual employee's role in the supervisor-subordinate relationship, assuming that specific leader behaviors would only be effective with specific types of employees (e.g., directive leadership works well with less-mature and less-skilled employees, while confident employees respond well to a delegating style). Employees played a somewhat more active role in the supervisor-subordinate relationship in these theories, although the supervisor was still positioned as the dominant partner.

Vertical Dyad Linkage theory (Graen & Cashman, 1975) was the first to acknowledge the *interactional* and *relational* nature of the supervisor-subordinate relationship. This theory highlighted the dyadic nature of leadership and of this relationship and conceptualized the employee or *member* as active and central to the relational development and maintenance. Later renamed Leader Member Exchange (LMX) theory, the theory has become the primary foundational theory for the vast majority of supervisor-subordinate relationship research.

LMX theory (Graen & Scandura, 1987) was an important turning point in workplace relationship research because it introduced complexity into our thinking about the nature of the supervisor-subordinate relationship and about how such relationships develop. Previous research was grounded in the average leadership style (ALS) paradigm, which assumed (at least implicitly) that leaders (supervisors) use a particular communication or leadership style consistently across situations and employees (e.g., Blake & Mouton, 1964). LMX theory introduced a new and, at the time, somewhat revolutionary assumption—the assumption that supervisors treat their various employees differently. Moreover, LMX theory acknowledged the supervisor-subordinate dyad as an *exchange* relationship in which the partners *mutually* exchange abilities, resources, and the like to form or *negotiate* a unique supervisor-subordinate relationship (Graen & Scandura, 1987). Thus LMX theory explicitly conceptualized the employee as an active, not passive, relationship partner. Studies consistently identify two primary types of supervisor-subordinate relationships: (1) *Leadership exchange* (or *high-quality exchange*) relationships are characterized by mutual trust, support, open communication, self-disclosure, and negotiating latitude, and (2) *supervisory exchange* (or *low-quality exchange*) relationships are characterized by low levels of trust, support, and self-disclosure, less open communication, and more direct supervision (Graen & Uhl-Bien, 1995).

Scholars then turned their attention to examining the consequences and outcomes associated with the different types of relationships and consistently demonstrated a number of advantages for both employees and supervisors who engage in high-quality LMX relationships. Specifically, employees who enjoy high-quality or leadership exchange relationships with their supervisor receive more, and higher quality, information from their supervisors (Sias, 2005), are more satisfied with supervisor-subordinate relationships (Gagnon & Michael, 2004; Graen, Liden, & Hoel, 1982), are more satisfied with their jobs (Turban, Jones, & Rozelle, 1990), and in general, perform better at their jobs (Brandes, Dharwadkar, & Wheatley, 2004; Michael, Leschinsky, & Gagnon, 2006) than those with supervisory exchange relationships.

Communication scholars, especially Fairhurst and her colleagues, made an important theoretical move by conceptualizing LMX relationships as communicatively constituted. Grounding their work in a constitutive perspective, their research took a discursive turn and examined how various LMX relationships were distinguished communicatively. Beyond simply noting different communication patterns enacted in high-quality versus low-quality relationships, the authors argued that the interaction patterns defined and constituted the relationship itself (e.g., Fairhurst & Chandler, 1989). Supervisors and subordinates do not communicate *in* a relationship; their communication *constitutes* the relationship. This marked a move toward a more dynamic (i.e., communicative) and mutual conceptualization of the supervisor-subordinate relationship in which both supervisor and subordinate (re)produce the relationship. Specifically, Fairhurst and Chandler (1989) found that communication between supervisors and subordinates in low-quality LMX relationships emphasizes power distance through performance monitoring, face-threatening acts (i.e., messages that present a threat to the hearer's positive self-image) and conflict. In contrast, interaction between those in high-quality relationships minimizes power distance with insider talk, value convergence, and nonroutine problem solving.

More recently, Yrle, Hartman, and Galle (2003) found that high- and low-quality LMX relationships are distinguished by two primary communication patterns. *Coordination* refers to interaction in which supervisors and subordinates mutually, rather than unidirectionally, coordinate activities. *Participation* refers to interaction patterns in which supervisors invite and enable employees to participate in decision making. Fix and Sias (2006) found similar patterns in their study, which found that employees reported higher-quality LMX relationships when they perceived their supervisor as using person-centered communication (e.g., communication that encourages employees to reflect on the complexities of a situation, define him/herself as an autonomous agent, and develop and engage in creative problem solving). In contrast, employees reported lower-quality LMX relationships when they perceived that their supervisor used position-centered communication (e.g., communication characterized by authority and direct supervision).

To review, leadership research has evolved from a focus on supervisors over subordinates in relationships in which supervisors were assumed to use a specific style and subordinates were passive recipients of leadership to the LMX conceptualization of the supervisor-subordinate relationship as a mutual, dyadic entity in which leaders develop different types of relationships with their various subordinates. Communication scholars developed LMX by providing a constitutive conceptualization of the leader-member relationships through which the leader and member together (re)produce leadership and their unique relationship via communication.

Information Exchange. Organizational communication scholars have played a central role in examining the supervisor-subordinate relationship as an important site of information exchange. This work centers on identifying the types of information shared between supervisors and subordinates and the processes used to accomplish such exchange. This research has primarily focused on new employees who rely on supervisors for information as they attempt to manage uncertainty about tasks, their ability to accomplish tasks, and the social relationships in the organization (see Chapter 21 for a detailed discussion of organizational socialization research). Supervisors are key information sources for new employees during their entry period, particularly with respect to information about the organization, department, and the newcomer's tasks, assignments, goals, and role in the organization (Jablin, 2001). New hires use several strategies to obtain information from their supervisors. These vary from obtrusive and overt strategies, such as asking direct questions, to more unobtrusive strategies, such as hinting, asking indirect questions, or simply observing and monitoring organizational goings-on (Miller & Jablin, 1991). New hires tend to use direct questioning more frequently during the early period of their new job but turn to more indirect tactics after their initial "honeymoon" period, largely due to concerns that asking questions may make them appear incompetent or unconfident (Morrison, 1993; Teboul, 1994).

Research has also addressed information exchange between supervisors and *veteran* employees. Although no longer new, veteran employees also experience uncertainty throughout their tenure in an organization. Budget woes, for example, create uncertainty for employees regarding the viability of the organization and the security of their positions (Bordia, Hobman, Jones, Gallois, & Callan, 2004; Casey, Miller, & Johnson, 1997). Veteran employees also experience uncertainty whenever a new employee joins the organization, including uncertainty about the nature of the new employee's position, the newcomer's ability and motivation to do the job, and how the newcomer may change organizational process, impact the veteran's own tasks, and the new employee's role in the social milieu of the unit and organization (Gallagher & Sias, 2009). Like new hires, veterans rely on several direct and indirect strategies to obtain information from their supervisor about newcomers. They may ask direct questions (e.g., "What is the new employee's job?" or "What shift is she working?"), rely on indirect tactics such as hinting, or they may simply observe the new hire's behavior and performance. Regardless of the tactics, studies indicate that information exchanged within the supervisor-subordinate relationship is crucial to effective uncertainty management for both new hires and veteran employees.

Research also indicates the important role the *subordinate* plays in information exchange in the supervisor-subordinate relationship. Supervisors rely on their direct reports for information about the unit and organization; in essence, subordinate employees function as extra sets of eyes and ears for the supervisor, helping the latter be better informed (e.g., Ramaswami, Srinivasan, & Gorton, 1997). Such information exchange requires trust between supervisors and employees; however, trust does not characterize all supervisor-subordinate relationships. Studies of upward distortion (i.e., the propensity of employees to distort or withhold information from their supervisor) indicate supervisors who are prey to upward distortion from their employees are at a serious disadvantage, because they make decisions based on faulty or incomplete information (Jablin, 1979). The quality of supervisor-subordinate relationships, therefore, is strongly associated with the quality of information exchanged within the dyad. As Sias (2005) found, employees and supervisors who perceived they were engaged in a high-quality relationship (i.e., characterized by trust, support, self-disclosure, and recognition) reported receiving significantly higher-quality information (i.e., information they perceived as accurate, timely, and useful) from one another than did those in lower-quality relationships.

Feedback and Appraisal. Another important communicative function of the supervisor-subordinate relationship is performance feedback and appraisal (Ashford, 1993; Fedor, 1991). As noted above, both new and veteran employees experience uncertainty about how well they are performing their jobs. This particularly stressful type of uncertainty is difficult to manage because of the face concerns that accompany interaction regarding one's abilities or lack of abilities. Because of these concerns, employees tend to avoid asking for feedback directly, and supervisors tend to avoid providing performance feedback to employees, particularly negative feedback (Benedict & Levine, 1988). This is unfortunate because effective, constructive feedback is necessary for employee development and success (Fedor, 1991). Research indicates, however, that the quality of supervisor-subordinate *relationships* is linked to functional and effective feedback and appraisal. Employees are more likely to listen to and accept negative feedback from supervisors they trust and like, and supervisors who perceive high-quality relationships with their employees are more likely to provide constructive feedback in a considerate and thoughtful fashion (Steelman & Rutowski, 2004). Although such studies do not establish the causal direction of this relationship, it is likely reciprocal; that is, providing considerate, constructive, and thoughtful feedback likely helps develop and maintain the respect and trust required of high-quality supervisor-subordinate relationships, and the trust and respect that characterize high-quality relationships likely provide an environment for the provision of considerate, constructive, and thoughtful feedback.

Mentoring. Although information exchange is an important aspect of mentoring, mentoring goes beyond that function. As Sias (2009) explained, "Mentoring refers to a specific type of relationship in which the mentor functions as a type of 'guide' for the development and career advancement of the protégé/mentee" (p. 29). In particular, mentoring relationships are unique in that they are, in general, unidirectional rather than reciprocal—information tends to flow in one way from mentor to protégé. Moreover, mentoring communication focuses on the mentee's career advancement and development, rather than the mentor's, and the explicit goal of mentoring is mentee development rather than improved organizational productivity and functioning (Sias, 2009).

Mentoring relationships can be formal and assigned by the organization or informal and naturally emerge between the mentor and mentee. Regardless of the formal or informal nature of the relationship, employees who receive mentoring obtain greater understanding of organizational issues and report higher levels of satisfaction than those who lack mentors (Jablin, 2001). Supervisors are often the initial, and sometimes only, mentor assigned to an employee, likely because of their formal authority status. However, supervisors are also likely candidates as informal mentors because of their frequent, regular interaction with employees—factors shown to increase the likelihood that an informal mentoring relationship will emerge (Jablin, 2001). Thus the supervisor-subordinate relationship is a primary site for the important mentoring function.

In sum, research has centered on examining various functions of the supervisor-subordinate relationship, including leadership, information exchange, feedback and appraisal, and mentoring. As the following section shows, peer/coworker relationship research shows a similar approach.

Peer/Coworker Relationships

The field's substantial focus on supervisor-subordinate relationships has been accompanied by a relative dearth of attention to peer/coworker relationships (i.e., those between coworkers at the same hierarchical level who have no formal authority over one another). This is likely due to the formal nature of the supervisor-subordinate relationship and the field's early focus on formal aspects of organizations and organizational processes. Peer relationships were addressed tangentially in research on organizational or communication climate, which typically included peer communication as a component of organizational climate rather than as a substantive area of research (e.g., Downs & Hazen, 1977).

Given their ubiquity, the relative lack of research attention to peer relationships is unfortunate. Individuals typically have one supervisor and several coworkers. We spend much of our time at work, and much of our time in general, with our peer/coworkers. Peer relationships, therefore, have an enormous impact on organizational processes and individual experiences. Peer relationship research largely centers on the functions of such relationships, including mentoring, information exchange, and social support.

Mentoring. Peer relationships first appeared as a substantive area of research in Kram and Isabella's (1985) study of mentoring, which focused on identifying alternatives to the traditional mentoring relationships between supervisors and subordinate employees. The primary alternative they found was peer relationships. Specifically, they identified three types of peer relationships in the workplace, distinguished largely by their *communication* characteristics. *Information peers* comprise the bulk of workplace relationships (Odden & Sias, 1997). These relationships are characterized by relatively superficial communication regarding work and the organization and by low levels of self-disclosure and trust. *Collegial peers* are characterized by communication regarding both work and personal issues and by moderate levels of trust, self-disclosure, emotional support, and friendship. *Special peers* are the most rare coworker relationship. Similar to best friends, or at least best friends at work (Sias & Cahill, 1998), these relationships are characterized by communication regarding a wide variety of topics and high levels of emotional support, personal feedback, trust, self-disclosure, and close friendship. Mentoring is, therefore, a central function and defining characteristic of collegial and special peer relationships. Such peers rely on one another for candid and honest job feedback and career advice and share information to enable improved performance and career strategizing.

Information Exchange. Peers are important sources of information for one another. In fact, employees rely more on their peer coworkers for information than any other source (Comer, 1991). This is logical when one considers the types of information to which coworkers are privy. An individual's coworkers most likely perform the same or similar tasks; thus they are qualified sources of task-related information. An individual's coworkers are usually best placed to observe the individual's task performance; thus they are credible sources of performance-related or appraisal-related information. And an individual's coworkers are members of the social network, often in more substantive roles than a supervisor; thus they are well-qualified to provide relational information.

Similar to supervisor-subordinate research, much research with respect to peer relationships has centered on the experience of the new employee being socialized into their new organizational role. This research consistently shows the important role coworkers play in this socialization process. While supervisors provide task assignments and direction, coworkers are the ones who show the ropes to the newcomer, teach him or her the unwritten rules, and provide insights into the unit's and the organization's unique cultural jargon, structures, and behavioral patterns (Miller & Jablin, 1991). Also similar to supervisor-subordinate information exchange, newcomers rely primarily on direct questioning to obtain information from their coworkers, but increasingly turn to indirect tactics over time to avoid the possibility of appearing incompetent or insecure (Miller & Jablin, 1991).

Certainly, employees do not rely on their coworkers for information only when they are newly hired. Coworkers share important information throughout their organizational tenure. In fact, a primary characteristic that differentiates information, collegial, and special peer relationships is the type and nature of information such peers share with one another. Information peers share superficial information primarily related to work, while collegial and special peers share information at increasing levels of intimacy and beyond the boundaries and requirements of their formal organizational roles. Along these lines, Sias (2005) found links between peer relationship type and information quality (i.e., perceived accuracy, timeliness, and usefulness). Specifically, individuals with relatively higher proportions of information peer relationships reported receiving lower-quality information than those reporting relatively higher proportions of collegial peer relationships. Thus individuals with high proportions of collegial peers enjoy a large informational advantage over those who lack such relationships.

Social Support. Peers play a uniquely important role for one another with respect to social support in the form of instrumental (e.g., tangible help), informational (e.g., providing information to reduce uncertainty), and emotional support (e.g., lending an ear or listening to a coworker vent; Miller, Ellis, Zook, & Lyles, 1990). When an individual experiences work-related stress (e.g., work overload, role ambiguity, etc.), peers can provide support that others (e.g., family and external friends) cannot because of their unique understanding of the work situation (Ray, 1993). Accordingly, when faced with work-related stress, employees tend to turn to their peer coworkers first for support (Cahill & Sias, 1997). Organizational communication research consistently demonstrates that peer social support is largely communicative in nature (e.g., Miller et al., 1990; Ray, 1993).

Peer relationships are crucial sites of mutual support, collaboration, confirmation, and emotional support (Persoff & Siegel, 1998). Thus the quality of one's peer relationships is linked to the quality of social support available to that individual. In fact, as with information exchange, social support is another factor that distinguishes various types of peer relationships. Information peer relationships, for example, are an important site of informational and instrumental support, but information peers do not provide substantive emotional support to one another, certainly not at the level of collegial and special peers. This is another way in which employees who lack the more intimate peer relationships are at a disadvantage in the workplace.

LMX and Peer Relationships. LMX theory's introduction of the concept of differential treatment opened up avenues of research examining the consequences of such treatment. In addition, the organizational communication field's interpretive turn enabled the conceptualization of workplace relationships as constitutive of the larger organizational social system. Together, these developments drew attention to the *interdependent* nature of various types of workplace relationships. Sias and Jablin (1995) and Sias (1996), for example, examined links between peer relationships and supervisor-subordinate relationships. Grounded in systems (Bertalanffy, 1962), LMX (Graen & Scandura, 1987), and social construction theory (Berger & Luckmann, 1966), these studies examined how the relationships a supervisor has with his or her various subordinate employees is linked to the peer relationships those employees have with one another. Specifically, they conceptualized LMX relationships as sites of differential treatment (i.e., supervisor treats employees differently and forms different relationships with them) that operate not in isolation but within a larger system of social relationships. This differential treatment creates uncertainty for the employees who evaluate the fairness of the treatment via conversations with one another. Their findings indicated, for example, that employees who are perceived by their coworkers to unfairly receive favorable differential treatment from the supervisors (i.e., the "boss's pet") tend to be excluded from the social friendship network, while those who unfairly receive unfavorable treatment (i.e., the "boss's victim") are drawn into the network by the others who develop an "us against the boss" mentality. These studies, therefore, linked one type of workplace relationship to another and identified coworker communication as a key site of sensemaking and the social construction of fairness perceptions and peer relationships.

More recently, Bowler, Halbesleben, and Paul (2010) also found that a particular LMX relationship is linked to others in the workplace. Specifically, they found that employees tended to interpret a coworker's organizational citizenship behavior (e.g., going above and beyond one's job requirements) as brownnosing and self-serving, while the supervisor and employee in the LMX relationship interpret such behavior as positive and other-serving. In a similar vein, Hooper and Martin (2008) found that employees who perceived differential treatment in their work teams reported lower levels of job satisfaction and well-being.

Supervisor-subordinate and peer relationships are considered to be formal relationships, assigned to members by management and by membership in a particular department or unit. The following sections address more informal and voluntary workplace relationships characterized by emotional and affective bonds—workplace friendships and romantic relationships.

Workplace Friendships

Workplace friendships differ from other workplace relationships in that they are voluntary and personalistic (Rawlins, 1992; Sias, 2009). While other workplace relationships are assigned (e.g., you typically do not choose your supervisor or coworkers), workplace friendships are voluntary (i.e., you do choose which of those coworkers to befriend). Workplace friendships also have a personalistic focus lacking in non-friendship relationships—friends come to know one another and interact with each other as whole persons, not simply role occupants (Sias, 2009). Thus workplace friendships are characterized by emotional and affective bonds lacking in other workplace relationships, and these bonds are associated with important outcomes, including increased employee commitment and decreased turnover (Feeley, Hwang, & Barnett, 2008), enhanced organizational learning and knowledge creation (Floyd & Woolridge, 1999), and enhanced performance and career progression (Brandes, Dharwadkar, & Wheatley, 2004). Friendships flourish in all types of organizations, within and across all levels of hierarchies, and between all types of employees (Sias, 2009). Their influence in organizations is, therefore, substantial. Workplace friendship research focuses largely on understanding their functions in organizational processes, including information exchange and social support.

Information Exchange. Lincoln and Miller (1979) were among the first to empirically examine workplace friendship. They identified the central role of informal friendship ties in organizational processes and concluded, "Friendship networks in organizations are not merely sets of linked friends. They are systems for making decisions, mobilizing resources, concealing or transmitting information, and performing other functions closely allied with work behavior and interaction" (p. 196). Thus information exchange is central to workplace friendship.

Sias and Cahill (1998) found that as friends grow closer, they share more, and more intimate, information with one another. As noted earlier, Sias (2005) found that employees reported receiving higher-quality information (i.e., more accurate, timely, and useful) from their collegial and special peers (both of which are characterized by friendship) than from their information peers. Employees also reported receiving higher-quality information from their supervisors when they were engaged in high-quality relationships characterized by friendship than those in lower-quality supervisory exchange relationships.

Workplace friendships are particularly important sites of *gossip*, or "informal and evaluative talk in an organization, usually among no more than a few individuals, about another member of that organization who is not present" (Kurland & Pelled, 2000, p. 429). As Sias (2009) noted, "Although gossip can, and often is, exchanged among acquaintances, it finds particular currency among friends" (p. 94). The exchange of gossip likely contributes to the friendship's personalistic focus—as coworkers exchange gossip, they come to know and interact as whole persons beyond the formal requirements of their organizational roles (Sias, 2009). Taken together, it is clear that employees who enjoy friendships with their colleagues enjoy a distinct information advantage over those who lack such relationships.

Social Support. As noted earlier, supervisor-subordinate and peer/coworker relationships are important sites of social support. When such relationships are characterized by friendship (i.e., high-quality LMX relationships, collegial, and special peer relationships), social support takes an even more substantive role. Several studies indicate that workplace friends have an understanding of one another and of the workplace context that enables them to provide support to one another with respect to work-related and personal issues and concerns (Cahill & Sias, 1997; Ray, 1993). Workplace friends are particularly important elements of what Kahn (2001) terms "holding environments," or "interpersonal or group-based relationships that enable self-reliant workers to manage situations that trigger potentially debilitating anxiety" (p. 260).

Workplace Friendships as Blended Relationships. As noted earlier, the interpretive turn brought scholarly attention to how individuals experience and interpret or make sense of organizational life (Putnam & Pacanowsky, 1983). Workplace friendship research gained important complexity when Bridge and Baxter (1992) conceptualized workplace friendships as *blended relationships* drawing scholarly attention to the challenges employees experience in these multidimensional relationships and how they communicatively manage those challenges. Workplace friendships emerge among employees within and across hierarchical levels and departments and functional units. LMX relationships, as well as collegial and special peer relationships, are characterized by friendship. These relationships *blend* two important types of interpersonal relationships—the friend relationship and the coworker relationship. As Bridge and Baxter (1992) note, each of these relationship types carries certain expectations that may, at times, conflict with one another.

To address the complexity of the blended relationship, Bridge and Baxter (1992) grounded their study in dialectical theory (Baxter, 1988) and identified five primary dialectical tensions that result from the blending of the two roles and present inherent challenges to workplace friendships. The *impartiality-favoritism* tension results from blending organizational expectations of objectivity inherent in the coworker role and expectations of support and favoritism among friends. The *equality-inequality* tension refers to assumptions of equality among friends in tension with workplace constraints such as hierarchy, rank, and authority. The *judgment-acceptance* tension results from blending friendship expectations of affirmation and acceptance with organizational requirements of evaluation and appraisal. These three tensions can be particularly challenging to friendships between supervisors and their subordinate employees (Sias, Heath, Perry, Silva, & Fix, 2004). The *openness-closedness* tension refers to conflicting communicative expectations—the expectation of open and frank information sharing among friends and workplace expectations of confidentiality. The *autonomy-connection* tension refers to the possibility that ongoing daily contact may impede individual autonomy, "jeopardizing their friendship through excessive connection" (Bridge & Baxter, 1992, p. 204). This theoretical move introduced a substantive examination of important complexities inherent to relationships and directed attention to deeper and more critical studies of supervisor-subordinate, peer, and workplace friendship relationships. Particularly noteworthy is the fact that this study conceptualized and examined the workplace friendship as a *dyadic* entity in which both partners socially construct and experience the tensions that underlie the relationship.

Romantic Workplace Relationships

Workplace relationship research took an important turn in the late 1970s, when researchers began studying romantic relationships in the workplace. The move was spurred largely by feminist movements that resulted in a substantial increase of women into the U.S. workforce. As organizations became increasingly populated by men and women, they became increasingly populated by romantic workplace relationships. Research on this topic evolved somewhat differently than that of supervisor-subordinate, peer, and friendship relationships, focusing on identifying types/categories and consequences of romantic relationships rather than specific communicative functions. In addition, relative to other types of workplace relationships, romantic relationships have received less attention from organizational *communication* scholars. Nonetheless, they are an important aspect of the workplace. This section addresses romantic workplace relationship research, noting the contributions of communication scholars where appropriate.

Types of Relationships. As with any type of relationship, all romantic workplace relationships are not alike. Researchers have identified a variety of romantic relationship types distinguished by the partners' varying motives for engaging in the relationship. Quinn (1977) identified three primary motives for participating in a romantic workplace relationship. The *job motive* refers to instances in which individuals engage in a romantic relationship for purposes of job advancement and security, financial rewards such as promotions and bonuses, increased power, and easier or more efficient tasks. Individuals who form romantic relationships for job motives engage in a *utilitarian* relationship. *Ego motives* reflect the desire for excitement, adventure, and ego gratification. Relationships driven by ego motives are referred to as *fling* relationships. *Love motives* reflect sincere affection, love, respect, and companionship. Employees motivated by love seek a long-term commitment from the romance. Such motives lead to the development of *companionate love* relationships.

Consequences of Workplace Romance. Research has identified several consequences of romantic relationships for the relationship partners and the larger organization. Generally, scholars and practitioners assumed workplace romance was harmful to the organization. This likely stemmed from the classical management school of thought that held large sway at the time and that held as a central tenet that emotion has no useful place in organizational processes (e.g., Weber, 1946).

Most research in this area has focused not on the individuals involved in the relationships, but on their coworkers. These studies examine how coworkers interpret and make attributions about the romantic relationships of other employees. These attributions are constructed largely through talk or gossip among coworkers (Michelson & Mouly, 2000; Quinn, 1977), highlighting the important role of *communication* in romantic relationship workplace dynamics. Communication research indicates that the nature of the gossip is, to some extent, associated with what the coworkers perceive to be the motives of the participants in the romance. In general, romantic relationships presumed to be motivated by love motives generate positive gossip, while those presumed to be motivated by job motives tend to generate negative gossip (Dillard, 1987).

Research also demonstrates that romantic relationships affect coworkers' attitudes and performance. Some studies indicate a workplace romance can improve workgroup morale by providing an uplifting and happier work environment and creating an exciting sexual electricity (Horn & Horn, 1982; Smith, 1988). Romance can also negatively impact coworker morale, especially those between a supervisor and a subordinate, fueling coworker jealousy and suspicions of favoritism (Pierce, Byrne, & Aguinis, 1996).

Engaging in a workplace romance also impacts the relationship partners in several ways. Studies show, for example, that engaging in a romance at work is linked to higher job satisfaction and motivation (Dillard & Broetzmann, 1980). As Pierce and Aguinis (2003) noted, this is likely due to an increased desire to be at work and near the romantic partner as well as a desire to prove to coworkers that the romance will not harm productivity. On the other hand, being the subject of gossip can take its toll on the partners. Accordingly, coworker attitudes and perceptions of the romance mediate these links. Research on how engaging in a romance impacts the partners' job performance has resulted in mixed findings. Quinn (1977), for example, found that engaging in a workplace romance can increase or decrease the partners' productivity. Subsequent research indicates the link between romance and performance is moderated by the type of relationship. Relationships between supervisors and subordinate employees tend to negatively impact productivity (Devine & Markiewicz, 1990). Research also suggests that productivity tends to increase for individuals motivated to engage in a romance for love rather than those motivated by job or ego motives (Dillard, 1987).

Studies indicate that coworkers perceive romantic relationships between supervisors and employees as sites of differential treatment. The coworkers tend to perceive such treatment as unfair and develop negative attitudes and relationships with the coworker engaging in the relationship (Pierce et al., 1996; Werbel & Hames, 1996).

Relationship Dynamics

Both LMX theory and the constitutive conceptualization of organizations as socially constructed contributed to an understanding of workplace relationships as dynamic rather than static entities. This directed scholarly attention toward relationship *processes.*

Supervisor-Subordinate Relational Processes

As noted above, LMX theory conceptualized the supervisor-subordinate relationship as a site of differential treatment—differential treatment that has consequences for the relationship partners and others in the work environment. Given the (dis)advantageous nature of (low) high-quality LMX relationships, scholars have studied the developmental factors and processes that distinguish leadership exchange relationships from supervisory exchange relationships. Much of this work is grounded in a functionalist approach and indicates several factors that influence LMX relationship development. For example, several studies link *employee competence* to LMX quality. Specifically, the more competent the employee, the more likely he or she is to develop a high-quality LMX relationship (Bauer & Green, 1996; Deluga & Perry, 1994; Wayne & Ferris, 1990). This is likely because high-quality LMX relationships require a great deal of trust in the employee's abilities to provide the autonomy and latitude characteristic of such relationships. At the same time, research demonstrates the importance of *supervisor competence*, especially competence in training and assisting employees (Cogliser & Schriesheim, 2000). Such abilities likely encourage the supervisor to decrease direct supervision and provide the employee with greater autonomy and control over his or her role.

Relatedly, studies indicate links between employees' and supervisors' *personality traits* and LMX relationship quality. Given the member autonomy and latitude that characterize high-quality LMX relationships, it is not surprising that employees with an internal locus of control are more likely to enjoy such relationships (Kinicki & Vecchio, 1994). In addition, the more authoritarian the employee, the less likely he or she will develop a high-quality LMX. This is because employees with authoritarian personalities are less likely to engage in extra-role activities such as socializing with the supervisor and are less open to role change (Finkelstein, Protolipac, & Kulas, 2000). An LMX relationship is a dyadic entity, of course, and a supervisor's personality is also linked to LMX quality. Smith and Canger (2004) found employees were more satisfied with supervisors who are agreeable, emotionally stable, and extroverted—all qualities that likely enhance LMX quality.

Various types of *similarity* are also linked to LMX relationship development. Supervisors and employees who share *cognitive similarity*, or similar beliefs and schemas regarding effective leadership and employee prototypes, are more likely to develop high-quality LMX relationships (Allinson, Armstrong, & Hayes, 2001; Engle & Lord, 1997). Studies also indicate the role of demographic similarity in LMX dynamics. Specifically, these studies consistently show that higher-quality LMX relationships are more likely to develop between supervisors of the same sex and race (Foley, Linnehan, Greenhaus, & Weer, 2006; Pelled & Xin, 2000).

Communication scholars have made several important contributions to the literature by examining how communication technologies and the distributed work they enable (e.g., telecommuting, virtual workplace) influence workplace relationships (Gregg, 2011). Huws, Korte, and Robinson (1990) found that telecommuting can hinder the development and maintenance of coworker relationships. Reinsch (1997) found similar patterns for LMX relationships, particularly for LMX relationships that had lasted a year or longer at the time of their study. More recently, however, Timmermann and Scott (2006) found that virtual communication does not necessarily harm relationships. What matters is an employee's competence (e.g., being responsive and thorough) in using that technology.

In one of the few studies of intercultural workplace relationships, Sergeant and Frankel (1998) identified cultural differences that impacted LMX relationship development between expatriate managers and their subordinate employees in Chinese subsidiaries. In particular, the high power distance (e.g., respect for hierarchy and authority) characteristic of Chinese culture proved to be a barrier to open and frank discussion, employee autonomy, and role negotiation required for development of a leadership exchange relationship.

Communication scholars have also examined the processes by which individuals work to *maintain* their LMX relationships. In general, those in high-quality exchanges tend to use personal and direct communication to maintain their relationships, while those in low-quality relationships use more regulative strategies, such as superficial talk and avoidance of discussion of problems (Lee & Jablin, 1995; Waldron, 1991). These differences reflect the higher levels of trust and openness that characterize high-quality LMX relationships.

Peer and Friendship Relational Processes

Much organizational communication research attention has been given to relational dynamics in peer relationships and workplace friendships. Odden and Sias (1997), for example, found that collegial peer relationships are more likely to develop in organizations characterized by cohesive climates. Studies also indicate that women are more likely than men to develop collegial peer relationships, and men tend to report higher proportions of information peer relationships than do women (Fritz, 1997; Odden & Sias, 1997). A later study, however, found that the sex composition of the peer dyad (i.e., same sex, opposite sex), not the sex of the individual partners, is what matters to peer relationship development. Specifically, employees are more likely to develop special peer relationships with coworkers of the same sex than with those of the opposite sex, and friendship development is more likely to be influenced by external factors such as life events and extra-organizational socializing for same-sex dyads (Sias, Smith, & Avdeyeva, 2003). Thus opposite-sex coworkers appear to keep their friendships more within the boundaries of the workplace than do same-sex coworkers. This is likely due to concerns that others in the workplace might mistakenly assume the relationship is romantic, not platonic.

Sias and Cahill's (1998) study of *workplace friendship development* identified three developmental stages: acquaintance-to-friend, friend-to-close friend, and close-to-very close/best friend. They found that two primary types of factors are important in a relationship moving through the various stages. *Individual* factors derive from the individuals involved in the relationship and include personality and perceived similarity. *Contextual* factors derive from the context (both internal and external to the organization) in which the relationship exists. Internal factors include physical proximity, shared tasks and projects, and work-related problems. External factors include important life events and socializing away from the workplace. Research indicates that the relative importance of these factors varies across relationship stages. Personality, similarity, and proximity were most important in moving a relationship from acquaintance to friend. Shared tasks, work-related problems, and life events played bigger roles in the later transitions from friend-to-close friend and close-to-very close/best friends.

Conceptualizing friendships as communicatively constituted, Sias and Cahill (1998) also examined the role of communication in the workplace-friendship development process. They found that friendship development was communicatively accomplished via more frequent and more intimate interaction, increased and more intimate discussion of nonwork topics, increased discussion of work-related problems, and a general decrease in cautious communication. These communication patterns enabled the partners to construct the voluntary nature and personalistic focus that characterize workplace friendships.

More recently, Sias, Pedersen, Gallagher, and Kopaneva (2012) examined peer workplace friendship dynamics in the contemporary electronically connected organization. Noting that prior work was conducted largely before a host of information and communication technologies (ICTs) were widely accessible to employees (e.g., social networking, Skype, etc.), they found that the importance of physical proximity to friendship initiation decreased significantly since the 1998 and 2003 studies. In fact, their respondents reported physical proximity (having workspaces physically near each other) was the *least* important factor in initiating a workplace friendship. Instead, shared tasks, personality, and perceived similarity were prime motivators. These findings held for people who work full-time in the same location as well as those who telecommuted (i.e., accomplished tasks from off-site locales) some or all of the time, indicating that ICTs remove the need to work in close proximity.

With respect to intercultural coworker relationships, Stage (1999) examined how expatriate and host employees in American subsidiaries in Thailand negotiated their cultural differences. Her analysis indicated that cultural differences regarding approaches to interpersonal relationships hindered coworker communication and relationship development. Similar to Sergeant and Frankel's (1998) study, power distance impeded relationship development between employees and expatriate managers. In addition, Thai employees tended to take a long-term view of relationships, which lengthened the development process, while they perceived that U.S. employees took a more short-term view, which hindered peer relationship development.

As noted earlier, workplace friendships are challenged by a number of tensions (Bridge & Baxter, 1992). When the partners are unable to manage those tensions, the friendship can deteriorate or even terminate. Research on *workplace friendship deterioration* indicates several causes of deterioration (Sias et al., 2004; Sias & Perry, 2004). Coworker friends often have *conflicting expectations* of the relationship, and when those expectations surface (e.g., an employee doesn't support his friend's proposal in a unit meeting), the friendship can suffer. *Betrayal* (e.g., sharing information that a friend provided in confidence, lying, etc.) can harm a workplace friendship, because it destroys the trust that characterizes friendship. *Personality* can lead to friendship deterioration when one partner comes to find a personality trait of the other to be annoying or intolerable. Friendships can suffer due to *distracting life events*, or situations in which one partner's important life event (e.g., wedding, marital problems, etc.) becomes such a distraction that the employee fails to maintain his or her job performance level and the friend has to pick up the slack. Finally, workplace friendships often deteriorate or even end when one of the partners is *promoted* to a position of authority over the other. This is due to the substantial tensions that are introduced when a peer friendship transforms into a supervisor-subordinate relationship (Sias et al., 2004).

Grounded in the social construction perspective, these studies also examined how coworkers communicatively transform their relationships. Specifically, Sias et al. (2004) and Sias and Perry (2004) found that individuals disengage from a workplace friendship using three primary communication tactics. With *cost escalation*, an individual intentionally communicates in a negative or rude way with the partner (e.g., snide, condescending tone of voice; interruptions). With *depersonalization*, individuals intentionally avoid interaction regarding personal issues with the coworker and avoid socializing with that coworker outside of work. As the authors note, depersonalization communicatively constructs a clear boundary between the work and personal spheres. In contrast, *withdrawal* involves an individual cutting off all interaction with the partner, even interaction required to do their jobs. Finally, *direct communication* or *state-of-the-relationship talk* involves explicit discussion of the relational deterioration. Overall, research indicates that employees rely primarily on the depersonalization tactic, which removes the personalistic focus characteristic of workplace friendship while still allowing the coworkers to communicate about work-related issues.

In contrast to peer relationship development and deterioration, peer relationship *maintenance* has been largely ignored by scholarly research. Sias, Gallagher, Kopaneva, and Pedersen (2012) examined the communication tactics by which peer coworkers maintain their friendships with one another. Specifically, they examined relationship maintenance in situations in which the stability of the relationship is threatened by one partner either attempting to increase the closeness of the relationship (escalating situations) or decrease the closeness of the relationship (deteriorating situations). Their study indicated a preference for the use of maintenance tactics perceived to be polite and face-saving. In escalating situations, such tactics include indirect conversational refocus (e.g., redirecting conversation away from personal topics when such topics are introduced by the partner) and general avoidance. Individuals were much less likely to use more face-threatening methods such as openness (e.g., stating a desire to not become closer friends) and direct conversational refocus (e.g., specifically stating to a coworker that you do not want to discuss personal issues). Respondents also preferred polite tactics to maintain friendships in deteriorating situations. These include circumspection (avoiding negative or uncomfortable topics) and creating closeness (e.g., attempts to maintain personal ties by recalling past joint experiences, etc.).

Romantic Relational Processes

Studies indicate several factors are associated with the initiation of a romance between coworkers. Similar to friendships, proximity enhances the emergence of a romantic relationship (Pierce & Aguinis, 2003; Quinn, 1977). Quinn (1977) identified three types of proximity linked to workplace romance: (1) *geographical proximity* (i.e., have workspaces physically near one another), (2) *ongoing work-requirement proximity* (e.g., working on joint projects, workshops, business trips), and (3) *occasional contact* (e.g., occasional contact but not regular, patterned proximity). *Attitude similarity* is another attractor for coworkers that helps to develop the liking and affection that leads to romance (Pierce & Aguinis, 2003). Studies also indicate that job autonomy enhances the likelihood of developing a workplace romance, because the freedom enables employees to create proximity and connections that enhance relational development (Haavio-Mannila, Kauppinen-Toropainen, & Kandolin, 1988; Pierce & Aguinis, 2003).

Research indicates that the organizational culture and climate can impact romantic relationship development. Mainiero (1989), for example, compared romantic relationships in *conservative* (e.g., slow-paced, conventional, and traditional) and *liberal* (e.g., fast-paced, action-oriented, dynamic) workplaces and found that workplace romances were less likely to flourish in conservative organizations, which discouraged such relationships through formal and informal policies, than in liberal environments, which are characterized by a high level of pressure and activity. Mano and Gabriel (2006) found similar patterns distinguished as *hot* and *cold* organizational climates. Specifically, hot climates "involve an aestheticization of labour that employees on display with respect to their physical appearance" (p. 10), while cold climates employ bureaucratic structures and principles to maintain an unemotional environment.

A few studies have assumed a social construction perspective, at least implicitly, and examined the role of communication in constituting romantic workplace relationships. Yelvington (1996) and Henningsen (2004) focused on the use of flirting in romantic relationships. *Flirting* refers to "indirect behavior designed to communicate a possible sexual interest in another individual, as well as to inquire through this indirection as to the other's possible interest" (Yelvington, 1996, p. 314). Thus flirting is typically the first step toward transforming a workplace relationship into a workplace romantic relationship. Hovick, Meyers, and Timmerman (2003) examined the role of face-to-face and e-mail communication in romantic workplace relationships. Results indicated that employees relied on e-mail communication primarily in ongoing relationships and only rarely to initiate a romance. Thus face-to-face interaction and flirting are important to the initial construction of a romantic relationship.

In summary, much research attention has been given to relational dynamics and processes. In particular, studies have addressed relationship development in supervisor-subordinate relationships, peer relationships and friendships, and romantic relationships. Studies of relational deterioration and maintenance are few, however, especially with respect to supervisor-subordinate and romantic relationships.

Relationships as Sites of Power, Control, and Resistance

The constitutive conceptualization of workplace relationships enabled rich critical examination of *power and control* dynamics. Early work conceptualized power as residing with the supervisor, who had legitimate power, and as a unidirectional process by which supervisors gave orders to subordinate employees who were vulnerable to discipline if they failed to obey (Fayol, 1949). Others addressed the subordinate's role as a participant in the power and control processes and examined upward-influence tactics subordinates use to gain influence with their supervisors, such as using rational arguments, assertiveness, coalitions, ingratiation and self-promotion, and impression management tactics used by subordinates and supervisors to influence one another (Ferris & Judge, 1991).

Critical theory, especially as appropriated by communication scholars, conceptualizes organizations and workplace relationships as socially constructed sites of power, control, dominance, and abuse (e.g., Mumby, 1988). Such a conceptualization directed scholarly attention away from functional, unidirectional, and generally overt control processes and toward more unobtrusive communicative forms of domination, control, and oppression.

Studies, for example, identify workplace relationships as primary sites of workplace abuse and, in particular, abusive workplace interactions (e.g., intimidation, public put-downs, name-calling, etc.; Keashly, Trott, & MacLean, 1994). This work reveals how such interaction enables relational dominance and oppression. Along these lines, scholars have recently directed attention to workplace bullying and mobbing. Bullying is a dyadic communicative phenomenon in which one coworker continually and repeatedly harasses and abuses another specific coworker. Bullying behaviors include verbal abuse, offensive verbal and nonverbal threatening behaviors, humiliation, intimidation, and work interference or sabotage (Lutgen-Sandvik, Namie, & Namie, 2009). The bullying constitutes an abusive dominant-power relationship. Mobbing is a group version of bullying in which a group of coworkers target a specific coworker, in essence constructing a set of abusive coworker relationships. Fritz (2002) similarly identified bullies as a troublesome type of peer who creates stress and anxiety for coworkers.

Sexual harassment is another form of workplace abuse. Distinct from romantic communication, sexual harassment refers to behavior that is unwelcomed by the target, is severe and repetitive, and, as a consequence, creates a hostile work environment (Robinson, Franklin, Tinney, Crow, & Hartman, 2005). Such behaviors can range from unwelcome comments, flirting, and jokes to the more overt quid pro quo requests for sexual favors in exchange for job security or job enhancement. Sexual harassment is a communicative phenomenon and, as such, communicatively constitutes an abusive power relationship (Dougherty, 1999). Although such relationships often occur between supervisors and subordinates, peer relationships are also sites of sexual harassment.

Scholars have also addressed how individuals respond to or resist such communication. Grounding her study in critical and structuration theory (Giddens, 1984), Lutgen-Sandvik (2006) identified several ways bullying/mobbing victims enact resistance. Some choose to leave the organization and the abusive environment or threaten to do so. Others construct a collective voice by talking with other coworkers and socially constructing the bully as cruel, unfair, and/or crazy. Employees may also create a *reverse discourse*, or communication through which victims' appropriate control by producing alternative meanings for labels (e.g., labeling one's self as a *troublemaker* to emphasize the willingness to fight back). Victims also pursue resolution by filing formal or informal grievances, documenting the abuse, and/or seeking help from influential organizational members or experts such as HR, lawyers, and the like.

Research has identified responses to sexual harassment ranging from passive avoidance of the topic to formally reporting the incidents to management to informally complaining to management and/or others to directly confronting the harasser (Bingham, 1994; Clair, 1994). As Dougherty (2009) noted, the move toward a discursive conceptualization of sexual harassment was important, because it led scholars "to see sexual harassment as a socially complex phenomenon" (p. 205).

Communication scholars have also used a social construction and discursive lens to examine how coworkers communicatively coproduce control and power structures in the organization. Kunda (1992), for example, revealed how coworkers' everyday conversations were important sites of meaning management and organizational power, highlighting workplace relationships as important sites of discursive control and influence. Barker's (1993) study of concertive control in self-managing teams also exemplifies this approach. His study revealed how a self-managing team communicatively developed normative rules that exerted powerful control over member behavior. In particular, the study showed how such rules were developed and formalized over time. As Barker (1993) explained,

> Workers achieve concertive control by reaching a negotiated consensus on how to shape their behavior according to a set of core values found in a corporate vision statement . . . concertive control reflects the adoption of a new substantive rationality, a new set of consensual values, by the organization and its members. (p. 411)

Of particular note here, such negotiation and construction of a substantive rationality occurred in the context of coworker relationships.

In sum, adopting a constitutive and critical theoretical lens enabled scholars to examine deep structures of power inherent in workplace relationships and produce rich and substantive insights into the complexities of control and resistance in workplace relationships.

Looking Forward

Reflecting on research in a specific area is useful not only for obtaining perspective on how the field has developed over time but also for drawing attention to what we have overlooked. I conclude this chapter by looking forward and outlining a brief agenda for future research.

Inclusion, Diversity, and Workplace Relationships

Despite substantial progress in research over the past decades, the above review indicates a strong bias toward conceptualizing and examining workplace relationships in traditional settings. Along these lines, our understanding of links between diversity and workplace relationships is underdeveloped and, in particular, our conceptualization of diversity is relatively simplistic and constrained by traditional categories such as race, ethnicity, and gender.

Generational Cohorts. Society and organizations are changing demographically, and workplace relationship research must do the same. For example, for the first time in U.S. history, organizations are often comprised of up to six generational cohorts (D'Aprix, 2010). The typical workplace now includes employees from generations as varied as Millennials and Generation X—generally considered to be under the age of 40—along with older cohorts labeled young or "echo" baby boomers and older baby boomers (Carlson, 2008; New Politics Institute, 2008). Consequently, employees are increasingly working and interacting with coworkers from different generational cohorts, some separated by several generations. Yet we know little about how generational differences impact workplace relationships. Recall, for example, that demographic similarity is an important factor for the initiation of a workplace friendship. In addition, studies indicate generational differences with respect to communication and communication technology preferences; specifically, those from younger cohorts have more positive attitudes toward and more frequently use Internet-based ICTs such as social networking and Skype (Pew Research Center, 2010). These differences likely influence workplace relationship dynamics. The presence of multiple generations also means that in many cases, employees from younger generations are supervising those from older generations. Research has not examined the challenges that employees face in such situations, and such studies are critical for understanding and enhancing employee experiences and organizational functioning.

Sexual Orientation. Current research has also largely ignored the relational experiences of gay and lesbian employees. Romantic relationship research, for example, has centered almost entirely on heterosexual relationships. In addition, links between sexual orientation and supervisor-subordinate, peer, and friendship dynamics remains largely unexamined. Gay and lesbian employees face a number of challenges managing their identity in the workplace and great anxiety deciding whether to *come out* or *pass* at work (Embrick, Walter, & Wickens, 2007; Lewis, 2009). Such decisions likely influence coworker relationships. As Lewis (2009) explains, "LGBT employees most likely find it difficult to develop trust-based relationships if, in every interaction, they are preoccupied with deciphering peers' attitudes and monitoring what they say" (p. 195). While the legal rights and privileges of homosexual individuals have widened (e.g., the recent repeal of the U.S. military's "Don't Ask, Don't Tell" [DADT] policy, increasing number of states legalizing same-sex marriage or civil unions), such anxieties remain. In one of the few studies in this area, Rumens (2010) examined the social support role of friendship for gay men in the workplace. His analysis identified workplace friendships as one of the most important sources of support for gay men at work. The support provided by friends is particularly important in helping gay men negotiate and affirm their sense of self in organizational environments that can be difficult. Future research must address sexual orientation and workplace relationships of all types. Scholars should examine how the repeal of DADT is influencing coworker relationships in military organizations, homosexual romantic relationships dynamics, and the like. Moreover, because *coming out* and *passing* are communicative acts, communication scholars are well suited for conducting research on those processes.

Communication and Romantic Workplace Relationships

As this chapter revealed, relative to other types of workplace relationships, organizational communication scholars have paid scant attention to romantic relationships, and the communication research that has focused on these relationships is quite dated. Romantic relationships continue to flourish in organizations and constitute the workplace in substantive ways. Yet we know little about how romantic relationships are constituted in interaction, how employees socially construct such relationships, and the role of communication in romantic relationship development, maintenance, and deterioration. Such areas are important topics for future organizational communication research.

Macro-Level Research

With few exceptions, workplace relationship research has centered on micro-level issues and examined relationships in relative isolation from the larger organization and society. An important area for future research is examining macro-level issues. Structuration theory (Giddens, 1979, 1984), for example, explains how structures (i.e., rules and resources that enable action) develop via interaction over and across time and space. These structures are both enabling (i.e., they provide knowledge and resources to help individuals understand how to behave in a particular situation) and constraining (i.e., they also help individuals understand how *not* to behave). The theory explains how certain structures (e.g., respect for authority) become systemically institutionalized. This theory would be very useful for developing macro-level understanding of workplace relationships. For example, studies indicate that employees and supervisors who share similar cognitive prototypes for the supervisor and employee roles are more likely to develop high-quality relationships (Allinson et al., 2001). Research grounded in structuration theory would provide valuable insights into how those prototypes have been developed and institutionalized over time. Recall also that opposite-sex friendships are less likely to develop into close friendships, because they are constrained by assumptions that such relationships may actually be romantic relationships; that is, men and women cannot be "just friends" (Sias et al., 2004). Structuration theory could usefully inform research that examines the origin of such assumptions and how they are reproduced via coworker interaction. In sum, research grounded in structuration theory would help develop our understanding of macro-level issues and processes and help move workplace relationship research forward in important ways.

References

Allinson, C. W., Armstrong, S. J., & Hayes, J. (2001). The effects of cognitive style on leader-member exchange: A study of manager-subordinate dyads. *Journal of Occupational and Organizational Psychology, 74*(2), 201–220.

Ashford, S. J. (1993). The feedback environment: An exploratory study of cue use. *Journal of Organizational Behavior, 14*(3), 201–225.

Barker, J. R. (1993). Tightening the iron cage: Concertive control in self-managing teams. *Administrative Science Quarterly, 38*(3), 408–437.

Bauer, T. N., & Green, S. G. (1996). Development of leader-member exchange: A longitudinal test. *Academy of Management Journal, 39*(6), 1538–1567.

Baxter, L. (1988). A dialectical perspective on communication strategies in relationship development. In S. Duck (Ed.), *Handbook of personal relationships* (pp. 257–273). New York, NY: John Wiley & Sons.

Benedict, M. E., & Levine, E. L. (1988). Delay and distortion: Tacit influence on performance appraisal effectiveness. *Journal of Applied Psychology, 73*(3), 507–514.

Berger, P. L., & Luckmann, T. (1966). *The social construction of reality: A treatise in the sociology of knowledge.* New York, NY: Doubleday and Company.

Bertalanffy, L. von (1962). General systems theory. *General Systems, 7*, 1–12.

Bingham, S. G. (1994). Introduction: Framing sexual harassment: Defining a discursive focus of study. In S. G. Bingham (Ed.), *Conceptualizing sexual harassment as discursive practice* (pp. 17–30). Westport, CT: Praeger.

Blake, R., & Mouton, J. (1964). *The managerial grid.* Houston, TX: Gulf.

Bordia, P., Hobman, E., Jones, E., Gallois, C., & Callan, V. J. (2004). Uncertainty during organizational change: Types, consequences, and management strategies. *Journal of Business and Psychology, 18*(4), 507–532.

Bowler, W. M., Halbesleben, J. R. B., & Paul, J. R. B. (2010). "If you're close with the leader, you must be a brownnose:" The role of leader-member relationships in follower, leader, and coworker attributions of organizational citizenship behavior motives. *Human Resource Management Review, 20*(4), 309–316.

Brandes, P., Dharwadkar, R., & Wheatley, K. (2004). Social exchanges within organizations and work outcomes: The importance of local and global relationships. *Group & Organization Management, 29*(3), 276–301.

Bridge, K., & Baxter, L. A. (1992). Blended relationships: Friends as work associates. *Western Journal of Communication, 56*(3), 200–225.

Cahill, D. J., & Sias, P. M. (1997). The perceived social costs and importance of seeking emotional support in the workplace: Gender differences and similarities. *Communication Research Reports, 14*(2), 231–240.

Carlson, E. (2008). *The lucky few: Between the greatest generation and the baby boom.* New York, NY: Springer.

Casey, M., Miller, V. D., & Johnson, J. R. (1997). Survivors' information seeking following a reduction in force. *Communication Research, 24*(6), 755–782.

Clair, R. C. (1994). Hegemony and harassment: A discursive practice. In S. G. Bingham (Ed.), *Conceptualizing sexual harassment as discursive practice* (pp. 59–70). Westport, CT: Praeger.

Cogliser, C. C., & Schriesheim, C. A. (2000). Exploring work unit context and leader-member exchange: A multi-level perspective. *Journal of Organizational Behavior 21*(5), 487–511.

Comer, D. R. (1991). Organizational newcomers' acquisition of information from peers. *Management Communication Quarterly, 5*(1), 64–89.

Corman, S. R. (2005). Postpositivism. In S. May & D. K. Mumby (Eds.), *Engaging organizational communication theory and research: Multiple perspectives* (pp. 15–34). Thousand Oaks, CA: SAGE.

D'Aprix, R. (2010). Leadership in a multi-generational workplace. *Strategic Communication Management, 14*(2), 13.

Deetz, S. D. (2001). Conceptual foundations. In F. M. Jablin & L. L. Putnam (Eds.), *The new handbook of organizational communication: Advances in theory, research, and methods* (pp. 3–46). Thousand Oaks, CA: SAGE.

Deluga, R. P., & Perry, J. T. (1994). The role of subordinate performance and ingratiation in leader-member exchanges. *Group & Organization Studies, 19*(1), 67–87.

Devine, I., & Markiewicz, D. (1990). Cross-sex relationships at work and the impact of gender stereotypes. *Journal of Business Ethics, 9*(4/5), 333–338.

Dillard, J. P. (1987). Close relationships at work: Perceptions of the motives and performance of relational participants. *Journal of Social and Personal Relationships, 4*(2), 179–193.

Dillard, J. P., & Broetzmann, S. M. (1980). Romantic relationships at work: Perceived changes in job-related behaviors as a function of participants' motive, partners' motive, and gender. *Journal of Applied Social Psychology, 19*(2), 93–110.

Dougherty, D. S. (1999). Dialogue through standpoint: Understanding women's and men's standpoints of sexual harassment. *Management Communication Quarterly, 12*(3), 436–468.

Dougherty, D. S. (2009). Sexual harassment as destructive organizational process. In P. Lutgen-Sandvik & B. D. Sypher (Eds.), *Destructive organizational communication: Processes, consequences, and constructive ways of organizing* (pp. 203–226). New York, NY: Routledge.

Downs, C. W., & Hazen, M. D. (1977). A factor analytic study of communication satisfaction. *Journal of Business Communication, 14*(3), 63–73.

Embrick, D. G., Walther, C. S., & Wickens, C. M. (2007). Working class masculinity: Keeping gay men and lesbians out of the workplace. *Sex Roles, 56*(11/12), 757–766.

Engle, E. M., & Lord, R. G. (1997). Implicit theories, self-schemas, and leader-member exchange. *Academy of Management Journal, 40*(4), 988–1011.

Fairhurst, G. T. (1993). The leader-member exchange patterns of women leaders in industry: A discourse analysis. *Communication Monographs, 60*(4), 321–351.

Fairhurst, G. T., & Chandler, T. A. (1989). Social structure in leader-member interaction. *Communication Monographs, 56*(3), 215–239.

Fayol, H. (1949). *General and industrial management* (C. Storrs, Trans.). London, England: Pitman.

Fedor, D. B. (1991). Recipient responses to performance feedback: A proposed model and its implications. In G. R. Ferris & K. M. Rowland (Eds.), *Research in personnel and human resources management* (vol. 9, pp. 73–120).Greenwich, CT: JAI.

Feeley, T. H., Hwang, J., & Barnett, G. A. (2008). Predicting employee turnover from friendship networks. *Journal of Applied Communication Research, 36*(1), 56–73.

Ferris, G. R., & Judge, T. A. (1991). Personnel/human resources management: A political influence perspective. *Journal of Management, 17*(2), 447–488.

Finkelstein, L. M., Protolipac, D. S., & Kulas, J. T. (2000). The role of subordinate authoritarianism in cross-level extra-role relationship. *The Journal of Psychology, 134*(4), 435–442.

Fix, B., & Sias, P. M. (2006). Person-centered communication, leader-member exchange, and job satisfaction. *Communication Research Reports, 23*(1), 35–44.

Floyd, S. W., & Woolridge, B. (1999). Knowledge creation and social networks in corporate entrepreneurship: The renewal of organizational capability. *Entrepreneurship Theory and Practice, 23*(3), 123–143.

Foley, S., Linnehan, F., Greenhaus, J. H., & Weer, C. H. (2006). The impact of gender similarity, racial similarity, and work culture on family supportive supervision. *Group & Organization Management, 31*(4), 420–441.

Fritz, J. H. (1997). Men's and women's organizational peer relationships: A comparison. *Journal of Business Communication, 34*(1), 27–46.

Fritz, J. H. (2002). How do I dislike thee? Let me count the ways. *Management Communication Quarterly, 15*(3), 410–438.

Gagnon, M. A., & Michael, J. H. (2004). Outcomes of perceived supervisor support for wood production employees. *Forest Products Journal, 54*(12), 172–177.

Gallagher, E., & Sias, P. M. (2009). Newcomers as a source of uncertainty: Veteran information seeking about new hires. *Western Journal of Communication, 73*(1), 23–46.

Ghiselli, E. E. (1963). Intelligence and managerial success. *Psychological Reports, 12*(3), 898.

Giddens, A. (1979). *Central problems in social theory.* London, England: Macmillan.

Giddens, A. (1984). *The constitution of society.* Berkeley: University of California Press.

Graen, G., & Cashman, J. F. (1975). A role-making model of leadership in formal organizations: A developmental approach. In J. G. Hunt & L. L. Hunt (Eds.), *Leadership frontiers* (pp. 143–165). Kent, OH: Kent State University Press.

Graen, G. B., Liden, R., & Hoel, W. (1982). Role of leadership in the employee withdrawal process. *Journal of Applied Psychology, 67*(6), 868–872.

Graen, G. B., & Scandura, T. (1987). Toward a psychology of dyadic organizing. In B. Staw & L. L. Cummings (Eds.), *Research in organizational behavior* (vol. 9, pp. 175–208). Greenwich, CT: JAI.

Graen, G. B., & Uhl-Bien, M. (1995). Relationship-based approach to leadership: Development of a leader-member exchange (LMX) theory of leadership over 25 years—Applying a multi-level multi-domain perspective. *Leadership Quarterly, 6*(2), 219–247.

Gregg, M. (2011). *Work's intimacy.* Cambridge, UK: Polity Press.

Haavio-Mannila, E., Kauppinen-Toropainen, K., & Kandolin, I. (1988). The effect of sex composition of the workplace on friendship, romance, and sex at work. In B. Gutek, A. H. Stromberg, & L. Larwood (Eds.), *Women and work* (vol. 3, pp. 123–137). Newbury Park, CA: SAGE.

Henningsen, D. D. (2004). Flirting with meaning: An examination of miscommunication in flirting interactions. *Sex Roles, 50*(7/8), 481–489.

Hersey, P., & Blanchard, K. H. (1982). *Management of organizational behavior* (4th ed.). Englewood Cliffs, NJ: Prentice Hall.

Hooper, D. T., & Martin, R. (2008). Beyond personal leader-member exchange (LMX) quality: The effects of perceived LMX variability on employee reactions. *Leadership Quarterly, 19*(1), 20–30.

Horn, P., & Horn, J. (1982). *Sex in the office.* Reading, MA: Addison-Wesley.

House, R. J. (1971). Path-goal theory of leader effectiveness. *Leadership Quarterly, 7*(3), 323–352.

Hovick, S. R. A., Meyers, R. A., & Timmerman, C. E. (2003). E-mail communication in workplace romantic relationships. *Communication Studies, 54*(4), 468–482.

Huws, U., Korte, W., & Robinson, S. (1990). *Telecommuting: Towards the elusive office.* Chichester, UK: Wiley.

Jablin, F. M. (1979). Superior-subordinate communication: The state of the art. *Psychological Bulletin, 86*(6), 1201–1222.

Jablin, F. M. (2001). Organizational entry, assimilation, and disengagement/exit. In F. M. Jablin & L. L. Putnam (Eds.), *The new handbook of organizational communication: Advances in theory, research, and methods* (pp. 732–818). Thousand Oaks, CA: SAGE.

Kahn, W. A. (2001). Holding environments at work. *Journal of Applied Behavioral Science, 37*(3), 260–279.

Keashly, L., Trott, V., & MacLean, L. M. (1994). Abusive behavior in the workplace: A preliminary investigation. *Violence and Victims, 9*(4), 341–357.

Kinicki, A. J., & Vecchio, R. P. (1994). Influences on the quality of supervisor-subordinate relations: The role of time pressure, organizational commitment, and locus of control: Summary. *Journal of Organizational Behavior, 15*(1), 75–83.

Kram, K. E., & Isabella, L. A. (1985). Mentoring alternatives: The role of peer relationships in career development. *Academy of Management Journal, 28*(1), 110–132.

Kunda, G. (1992). *Engineering culture: Control and commitment in a high-tech corporation.* Philadelphia, PA: Temple University Press.

Kurland, N. B., & Pelled, L. H. (2000). Passing the word: Toward a model of gossip and power in the workplace. *Academy of Management Review, 25*(2), 428–438.

Lee, J., & Jablin, F. M. (1995). Maintenance communication in superior-subordinate work relationships. *Human Communication Research, 22*(2), 220–257.

Lewis, A. P. (2009). Destructive organizational communication and LGBT workers' experiences. In P. Lutgen-Sandvik & B. Davenport-Sypher (Eds.), *Destructive organizational communication: Processes, consequences, and constructive ways of organizing* (pp. 184–202). New York, NY: Routledge.

Lincoln, J. R., & Miller, J. (1979). Work and friendship ties in organizations: A comparative analysis of relational networks. *Administrative Science Quarterly, 24*(2), 181–199.

Lutgen-Sandvik, P. (2006). Take this job and . . . : Quitting and other forms of resistance to workplace bullying. *Communication Monographs, 73*(4), 406–433.

Lutgen-Sandvik, P., Namie, G., & Namie, R. (2009). Workplace bullying: Causes, consequences, and corrections. In P. Lutgen-Sandvik & B. D. Sypher (Eds.), *Destructive organizational communication: Processes, consequences, and constructive ways of organizing* (pp. 27–52). New York, NY: Routledge.

Mainiero, L. A. (1989). *Office romance: Love, power, and sex in the workplace.* New York, NY: Rawson Associates.

Mano, R., & Gabriel, Y. (2006). Workplace romances in cold and hot organizational climates: The experience of Israel and Taiwan. *Human Relations, 59*(1), 7–35.

Michael, J. H., Leschinsky, R., & Gagnon, M. A. (2006). Production employee performance at a furniture manufacturer: The importance of supportive supervisors. *Forest Products Journal, 56*(6), 19–24.

Michelson, G., & Mouly, S. (2000). Rumour and gossip in organisations: A conceptual study. *Management Decision, 38*(5), 339–346.

Miller, K. I., Ellis, B. H., Zook, E. G., & Lyles, J. S. (1990). An integrated model of communication, stress, and burnout in the workplace. *Communication Research, 17*(3), 300–326.

Miller, V. D., & Jablin, F. M. (1991). Information seeking during organizational entry: Influences, tactics, and a model of the process. *Academy of Management Review, 16*(1), 92–120.

Morrison, E. W. (1993). Longitudinal study of the effects of information seeking on newcomer socialization. *Journal of Applied Psychology, 78*(2), 173–183.

Mumby, D. K. (1988). *Communication and power in organizations: Discourse, ideology, and domination.* Norwood, NJ: Ablex.

New Politics Institute. (2006). *Politics of the millennial generation.* Retrieved from http://ndn-newpol.civicactions.net/sites/ndn-newpol.civicactions.net/files/MillenialGenerationPolitics.pdf

Odden, C. M., & Sias, P. M. (1997). Peer communication relationships and psychological climate. *Communication Quarterly, 45*(3), 153–166.

Pelled, L. H., & Xin, K. R. (2000). Relational demography and relationship quality in two cultures. *Organization Studies, 21*(6), 1077–1094.

Persoff, I. L., & Siegel, P. H. (1998, June). Tax professionals, peer relationships, and CPA firm restructuring: A grounded theory approach. *Mid-Atlantic Journal of Business, 24*, 125–140.

Pew Research Center. (2010). *Pew generations online 2010.* Retrieved from http://www.pewinternet.org/Reports/2010/Generations-2010/Overview.aspx

Pierce, C. A., Byrne, D., & Aguinis, H. (1996). Attraction in organizations: A model of workplace romance. *Journal of Organizational Behavior, 17*(1), 5–33.

Pierce, C. A., & Aguinis, H. (2003). Romantic relationships in organizations: A test of a model of formation and impact factors. *Management Research, 1*(2), 161–169.

Putnam, L. L., & Pacanowsky, M. E. (Eds.). (1983). *Communication and organizations: An interpretive approach.* Beverly Hills, CA: SAGE.

Quinn, R. E. (1977). Coping with Cupid: The formation, impact, and management of romantic relationships in organizations. *Administrative Science Quarterly, 22*(1), 30–45.

Ramaswami, S. N., Srinivasan, S., & Gorton, S. A. (1997). Information asymmetry between salesperson and supervisor: Postulates from agency and social exchange theories. *Journal of Personal Selling and Sales Management, 17*(3), 29–51.

Rawlins, W. K. (1992). *Friendship matters: Communication, dialectics, and the life course.* New York, NY: Aldine de Gruyter.

Ray, E. B. (1993). When links become chains: Considering dysfunctions of supportive communication in the workplace. *Communication Monographs, 60*(1), 106–111.

Redding, C. W. (1985). Stumbling toward an identity: The emergence of organizational communication: Past and present tenses. In R. D. McPhee & P. K. Tompkins (Eds.), *Organizational communication: Traditional themes and new directions* (pp. 15–54). Newbury Park, CA: SAGE.

Reinsch, N. L., Jr. (1997). Relationships between telecommuting workers and their managers: An exploratory study. *Journal of Business Communication, 34*(4), 343–369.

Robinson, R. K., Franklin, G. M., Tinney, C. H., Crow, S. M., & Hartman, S. J. (2005). Sexual harassment in the workplace: Guidelines for educating healthcare managers. *Journal of Health and Human Services Administration, 27*(4), 501–530.

Rumens, N. (2010). Firm friends: Exploring the supportive components in gay men's workplace friendships. *Sociological Review, 58*(1), 135–155.

Sergeant, S., & Frankel, A. (1998). Managing people in China: Perceptions of expatriate managers. *Journal of World Business, 33*(1), 17–34.

Sias, P. M. (1996). Constructing perceptions of differential treatment: An analysis of coworker discourse. *Communication Monographs, 63*(2), 171–187.

Sias, P. M. (2005). Workplace relationship quality and employee information experiences. *Communication Studies, 56*(4), 375–395.

Sias, P. M. (2009). *Organizing relationships: Traditional and emerging perspectives on workplace relationships.* Thousand Oaks, CA: SAGE.

Sias, P. M., & Cahill, D. J. (1998). From coworkers to friends: The development of peer friendships in the workplace. *Western Journal of Communication, 62*(3), 273–299.

Sias, P. M., Gallagher, E. M., Kopaneva, I., & Pedersen, H. (2012). Peer workplace friendship maintenance: Impact of task interdependence, attachment style, and gender. *Communication Research, 39*(2), 239–268.

Sias, P. M., Heath, R. G., Perry, T., Silva, D., & Fix, B. (2004). Narratives of workplace friendship deterioration. *Journal of Social and Personal Relationships, 21*(3), 321–340.

Sias, P. M., & Jablin, F. M. (1995). Differential superior-subordinate relations, perceptions of fairness, and coworker communication. *Human Communication Research, 22*(1), 5–38.

Sias, P. M., Krone, K. J., & Jablin, F. M. (2002). An ecological systems perspective on workplace relationships. In M. L. Knapp & J. Daly (Eds.), *Handbook of interpersonal communication* (3rd ed., pp. 615–642). Thousand Oaks, CA: SAGE.

Sias, P. M., Pedersen, H. C., Gallagher, E. B., & Kopaneva, I. (2012). Workplace friendship in the electronically connected organization. *Human Communication Research, 38*(3), 253–279.

Sias, P. M., & Perry, T. (2004). Disengaging from workplace relationships: A research note. *Human Communication Research, 30*(4), 589–602.

Sias, P. M., Smith, G., & Avdeyeva, T. (2003). Sex and sex-composition differences and similarities in peer workplace friendship development. *Communication Studies, 54*(3), 322–340.

Smith, H. I. (1988). Singles in the workplace: Myths and advantages. *Personnel Administrator, 33*(2), 76–81.

Smith, M. A., & Canger, J. M. (2004). Effects of supervisor "big five" personality on subordinate attitudes. *Journal of Business and Psychology, 18*(4), 465–481.

Smith, R. C., & Turner, P. K. (1995). A social constructionist reconfiguration of metaphor analysis: An application of "SCMA" to organizational socialization theorizing. *Communication Monographs, 62*(2), 151–181.

Stage, C. W. (1999). Negotiating organizational communication cultures in American subsidiaries doing business in Thailand. *Management Communication Quarterly, 13*(2), 245–280.

Steelman, L. A., & Rutowski, K. A. (2004). Moderators of employee reactions to negative feedback. *Journal of Managerial Psychology, 19*(1), 6–18.

Taylor, J. R., & Van Every, J. (2000). *The emergent organization: Communication at its site and surface.* Mahwah, NJ: Lawrence Erlbaum.

Teboul, J. C. B. (1994). Facing and coping with uncertainty during organizational encounters.

Management Communication Quarterly, 8(2), 190–224.

Timmermann, C. E., & Scott, C. R. (2006). Virtually working: Communicative and structural predictors of media use and key outcomes in virtual work teams. *Communication Monographs, 73*(1), 108–136.

Turban, D. B., Jones, A. P., & Rozelle, R. M. (1990). Influences of supervisor liking of a subordinate and the reward context on the treatment and evaluation of that subordinate. *Motivation and Emotion, 14*(3), 215–233.

Waldron, V. R. (1991). Achieving communication goals in superior-subordinate relationships: The multi-functionality of upward maintenance tactics. *Communication Monographs, 58*(3), 289–306.

Wayne, S. J., & Ferris, G. R. (1990). Influence tactics, affect, and exchange quality in supervisor-subordinate interactions: A laboratory experiment and field study. *Journal of Applied Psychology, 75*(5), 487–500.

Weber, M. (1946). *From Max Weber: Essays in sociology* (H. H. Girth & C. W. Mills, Trans., Eds.). New York, NY: Free Press.

Werbel, J. D., & Hames, D. S. (1996). Anti-nepotism reconsidered. *Group & Organization Management, 21*(3), 365–379.

Wheatley, M. J. (1994). *Leadership and the new science: Learning about organization from an orderly universe.* San Francisco, CA: Berrett-Koehler Publishing.

Yelvington, K. A. (1996). Flirting in the factory. *Journal of the Royal Anthropological Institute, 2*(2), 313–324.

Yrle, A. C., Hartman, S. J., & Galle, W. P. (2003). Examining communication style and leader-member exchange: Considerations and concerns for managers. *International Journal of Management, 20*(1), 92–101.

CHAPTER 16

Leadership Communication

Gail T. Fairhurst and Stacey L. Connaughton

In the first *Handbook of Organizational Communication,* the chapter on leadership was written by two leadership psychologists (Dansereau & Markham, 1987). Some 14 years later, a communication scholar authored the next *Handbook* chapter, although it was largely derivative of leadership psychology; the communication implications of individualist and cognitive leadership theories were the primary focus (Fairhurst, 2001). Both of these chapters reflected the times: Organizational communication was still coming into its own as a discipline (Mumby, 2007), and psychology had long dominated leadership study (Bass, 1981; House & Aditya, 1997). It made sense then to equate *leadership* with leaders whose strong inner motors explained how they transformed the world (for better or worse), while communication played a contributory, albeit subsidiary, role.

However, since the last *Handbook* review, communication has played an increasingly central role in leadership studies due in no small measure to the emergence of a social and cultural lens—focusing on how culture and social interaction impact leadership—appearing alongside (the strong inner motor of) an individual and cognitive lens (Fairhurst, 2007a). As a result, organizational communication scholars are conceiving of leadership communication more complexly, for example, as an act of transmission *and* negotiated meaning. This, in turn, is moving communication scholars toward a more dialectical view of leadership: to see it as an individually informed yet relational phenomenon between people and even objects, to see leadership as a medium by which collectives mobilize to act but also as a highly desired (attributional) outcome of this interaction, and finally, to see *leadership* as definitionally unstable—across time, between people, and even among scholars—and yet oddly enduring. Turn to any recorded history to find that leadership is a concept for the ages. Unsurprisingly, with this new research complexity, the focus isn't just on leaders, but all actors (formal or informal leaders, followers, or other stakeholders) who can be transformative agents—and, as we will see, receptors of meaning and disciplined products of a leadership culture.

We begin the chapter with post-positivist approaches to leadership study, which are more individual and cognitive in focus while adopting a transmissional view of human communication. We then move on to an emerging narrative of more socially constructed views of leadership, which are more social and cultural in focus while emphasizing a meaning-centered view of communication. We conclude the chapter with a discussion of the net gains of the research of the past decade and the contributions of a communicative lens. Before proceeding, however, please note that this literature review makes no attempt to be comprehensive, only representative of the field. As such, we proffer no universal definition of *leadership*. Following Wittgenstein (1953), we adhere to the belief that leadership is one of those *blurred concepts* and, following Gallie (1956), an essentially contested one. Better to view leadership as a family resemblance among power and influence-oriented language games whose character we now seek to describe (Kelly, 2008; Wittgenstein, 1953).

The Post-Positivist Approach to Studying Leadership

The history of post-positivist approaches to leadership study is an impressive one. A perusal of this vast literature over several decades includes the study of leader traits (Antonakis, 2011), leader behavior styles (Stogdill & Coons, 1957), leader behavior contingencies (Fiedler, 1978), leader-member relationship theories (Graen & Uhl-Bien, 1995), charismatic and transformational leadership (Bass, 1985; House, 1977), implicit leadership theories (Lord, Foti, & Phillips, 1982), and information processing about leadership (Lord & Emrich, 2001) and leadership attributions (Calder, 1977), including romantic ones (Meindl, Ehrlich, & Dukerich, 1985)—not to mention a host of new topics we sample below.

Definitions of leadership have also varied over time, for example, viewing *leadership* from the perspective of those holding positions of authority (where the terms *leader* and *manager* can be used interchangeably) to its more current status as synonymous with *change* (while *managing* is about implementation; Kotter, 1990). Definitions notwithstanding, post-positivist (leadership) approaches view the functions of theory as prediction, explanation, and control, while the research is usually survey based or experimental. These are variable-analytic approaches that adopt a transmissional view of communication, such as we see in Shannon and Weaver's (1949) familiar Sender→Message→Receiver model, especially when concerned with predicting and understanding leader effectiveness.

After discussing the entailments of a transmissional view of communication, in the discussion below, we show how organizational communication scholars still contribute to research using post-positive approaches, particularly in the areas of supervisor-subordinate communication, global leadership, and leading change.

Transmissional Views of Communication

Historically, a transmissional view of communication dominated the organizational sciences due to roots in industrial and organizational psychology and (post-)positivistic science. When the primary lens is individual and cognitive and the preferred methods of choice are survey research or experimental design, the tendency is to view communication as a transmission, a process variable, or behavioral outcome. Accordingly, transmission views of communication see the world in terms of inputs, processes, and outputs. Communication is thus most advantageously treated as a conduit when the focus is on transmission and channel effects: message directionality, frequency, and fidelity; blockages that interfere with transmission; and perceptual filters that hinder message reception (Axley, 1984; Putnam, 1983).

For example, Neufeld, Wan, and Fang (2010) were interested in examining the relationship between perceived leader performance and physical distance, leader-follower communication effectiveness, and leadership style. In their study of 138 remote employees and 41 leaders, the authors conceive of *communication effectiveness* as the overall quality of interactions between leaders and followers as perceived by the followers. Because they view communication holistically and do not problematize issues of meaning, the default view of communication here is transmissional. As such, these analysts found that communication effectiveness was positively related to perceived leadership performance, but physical distance had no influence on communication effectiveness or perceived leader performance.

Underscoring the relational nature of leadership, Connaughton and Daly (2004a, 2004b, 2005) examined leadership in virtual teams. Interviews with positional leaders in a multinational technology organization revealed several aspects of (transmissional) communication crucial to virtual team functioning, including information adequacy, information equity, and communication frequency (at key moments), among others. The authors also report how these aspects of communication are related to trust, perceptions of isolation, and other process issues and outcomes. Similarly, in an experimental study, Marks, Zaccaro, and Mathieu (2000) contend that the quality of communication processes among team members is just as critical to team performance as the quantity of interactions. Moreover, Morgeson, DeRue, and Karam (2010) advance a team leadership model that presents several leadership functions. Here too, communication is identified as leadership (transmissional) behavior needed for teams to be effective. As these and other studies indicate, researchers interested in team leadership are shifting their focus from individual leaders to leadership processes needed for team effectiveness.

For some researchers who adopt a transmissional view, communication is conceived of as a behavioral outcome. For example, in two models of leadership trust, Shockley-Zalabak, Morreale, and Hackman (2010) and Burke and colleagues (Burke, Sims, Lazzara, & Salas, 2007) view communication not only as an input to trust in leadership, but they also see upward communication as a proximal behavioral outcome of trust in leadership. Notice how the language of the transmission view is evident when Burke et al. write:

> Taken together, by creating a sense of trust towards the team leader, communication lines will be opened up to transmit needed information to lead to innovation, error remediation/prevention, and an ever growing and reciprocated sense of trust between the team leader and the subordinate. (p. 623)

A transmissional view of communication also finds its way into studies that examine transformational leadership and communication. For example, Purvanova and Bono's (2009) experimental study tested whether transformational leadership behaviors are more strongly associated with team effectiveness in virtual teams as opposed to face-to-face ones. Their results suggest that transformational leadership behaviors impacted virtual teams' performance more than face-to-face teams. Balthazard, Waldman, and Warren (2009) shed light on the traits as well as behaviors of emerging transformational leaders, in both colocated and virtual teams, focusing on the influences of personality characteristics, activity level (timing and frequency of participation), and what they term *communication/expression quality* (idea density and grammatical complexity) on perceptions of transformational leadership. This study had all team members rate other team members along several emergent leadership lines and used language sample analysis to assess the relevant aspects of communication.

Relatedly, research continues to examine the effectiveness with which vision is communicated. In their field study in an Israeli telecommunication organization, Berson and Avolio (2004) studied the relationship between transformational leadership and the articulation of strategic organizational goals. Utilizing both quantitative and qualitative data, they noted whether those reporting to transformational leaders articulate goals in alignment with them and whether transformational leaders are considered more effective communicators (being open, being a careful listener, being a careful transmitter). Researchers have also focused on variables related to vision formation (Shipman, Byrne, & Mumford, 2010) and vision communication (Stam, Van Knippenberg, & Wisse, 2010).

While issues of meaning are narrowly problematized (if at all) in the foregoing research utilizing a transmissional view of communication, recall that the goal has often been to understand leadership communication amidst other relational and cognitive dynamics. A transmissional view best facilitates such a stance.

Supervisor-Subordinate Relationships

Post-positivist work on leadership has examined facets of supervisor-subordinate communication—for example, communication style (Sager, 2008), impression management strategies/social influence (Sosik & Jung, 2003), and contingencies impacting style such as found in Situational Leadership Theory (Thompson & Vecchio, 2009). In her literature review of this area, Sias (2009) goes a step further by arguing that post-positivist leadership research has been able to examine a variety of supervisor-subordinate communication functions (e.g., information exchange and performance feedback and appraisal, including upward and downward feedback) along with relationship development processes and outcomes (see Sias, Chapter 15).

Research on Leader Member Exchange (LMX) serves as a case in point (Graen & Uhl-Bien, 1995). It is among the most prevalent theoretical and empirical perspectives on the relational nature of leadership (Sparrowe, Soetjipto, & Kramer, 2006), often drawing communication scholars to add to its research base. For example, Kramer (1995) drew on LMX and assimilation research to find that the quality of the supervisor relationship significantly influenced the perceptions and job satisfaction of those transferring jobs. Lee (2001) examined the relationships among members' perceptions of fairness and LMX quality as well as cooperative communication. He found that members who perceived less distributive and procedural justice also tended to demonstrate less cooperative communication with other members. Members also reported fewer interactions and shared fewer ideas and resources as well as less information with each other. Olufowote, Miller, and Wilson (2005) found that the quality of LMX moderated the relationship between the magnitude of role change and rationality, one of four upward-influence tactics examined. Finally, Jian (2012) found a curvilinear relationship between LMX and two key role stressors, role conflict and role overload, suggesting that there may be deleterious consequences associated with the challenging tasks with great visibility that high-quality LMX members often enjoy.

Further developments in LMX have included examining relationships other than leader-member and have pointed to the potential influences that other dyadic relationships, in conjunction with LMX, may have on various outcomes (Sluss, Klimchak, & Holmes, 2008; Tangirala, Green, & Ramanujam, 2007). In addition, the conceptual space in which LMX is examined continues to broaden with work by Graen (2012), who recasts LMX in terms of strategic interpersonal alliances.

Other post-positivist relational leadership work focuses not only on the individual leader (or member) but also on other dyadic relationships, teams, and organizations. In doing so, researchers increasingly use analytic methods that get at multiple levels of analysis. For example, Bakar and Connaughton (2010) used WABA I and II analytic techniques to examine supervisory communication, as informed by LMX theory, and its relationship with workgroup commitment.[1] Network studies of leadership in teams and organizations get at communication relationships among leaders and members and their influences on various outcomes (Dionne, Sayama, Hao, & Bush, 2010). Huffaker (2010), for instance, investigated how online leaders (or *influencers*) communicate, finding that those who influence others communicate more often, are deemed more credible and central in the network, and exhibit assertiveness and linguistic diversity in their messages. Over a two-year period, Huffaker analyzed an impressive 632,000 messages from over 34,000 participants in 16 online discussion groups and utilized automated text analysis, social network analysis, and hierarchical linear modeling as analytic techniques.

Huffaker's (2010) study and the aforementioned Berson and Avolio (2004) and Balthazard et al. (2009) studies reflect a growing trend toward mixed methods. They demonstrate postpositivist tendencies with social constructionist sensibilities, in part because they are utilizing communication as data and/or turning to discursive methods, a point we address below.

Global Leader Effectiveness

Another body of leadership research examines leader effectiveness in the context of global organizations. Global/international leadership research grew out of the rise of the multinational corporation and scholars' quest to understand what makes (positional) leaders effective in these contexts. Two general themes can be observed in this body of work. For one, scholars have been interested in conceptualizing and measuring what global leadership is. In doing so, researchers have sought to explain the relationships between leadership and culture (Triandis, 1993) and how those relationships relate to performance. This work has prompted a scholarly conversation as to whether some universal attributes of leadership can be discerned across cultures and/or whether some features of leadership are culturally contingent. The large-scale data studies of the Global Leadership and Organizational Behavior Effectiveness or "GLOBE" project (Den Hartog, House, Hanges, Ruiz-Quintanilla, & Dorfman, 1999) empirically examined these issues and have contributed to scale development on cultural dimensions and to theory development (Scandura & Dorfman, 2004). Regarding GLOBE project findings, Den Hartog and colleagues (1999) note that communication skills were seen by participants across national cultures as contributing to perceptions of transformational/charismatic leadership; however, perceptions of effective communication differ across national cultures (Trompenaars, 1993).

In addition, research has sought to pinpoint what makes leaders effective in global contexts. Drawing from Hofstede (1980), Triandis (1993) proffered that leadership processes deemed effective would be different based on whether an individual was from a collectivist or an individualist culture. A concern with effective leadership can also be found in Adler, Brody, and Osland (2001), who focus on women and global leadership. In their study of Latin American expatriates, Osland, De Franco, and Osland (1999) underscore the importance of expatriates' understanding of nine cultural contingencies, some of which are communicative (e.g., humor and joy) or have implications for communication (i.e., in-group/out-group, trust). And, in their model of cultural sensemaking, Osland and Bird (2000) encourage practitioners to embrace cultural paradoxes and consider context to help detangle them and work effectively around the world. As a whole, this research historically is often focused on positional leaders, is comparative in nature, is focused on the relationship between national culture and leadership, and utilizes quantitative and qualitative methods.

Within this body of work, organizational communication researchers are also making their mark. Research on leadership in a global context has focused on diverse ways of understanding leadership in various national cultures, noting leadership's communicative constitution. These studies foreground different conceptualizations of leadership, oftentimes rooted in entrenched cultural beliefs, as compared to the majority of the leadership literature with its Western bias. For instance, Lin and Clair (2007) developed an instrument to test, and find evidence to support, the influences of what they term *Mao Zedong thought* in organizations in contemporary China, while Brummans and Hwang (2010) investigate the influence of Buddhist philosophy on organizing practices in a Taiwanese nonprofit voluntary organization. Xu (2011) contributes to our understandings of leadership in the Chinese context by developing an instrument to measure the leadership of Chinese academic leaders. In doing so, the author found that Confucian values still permeate Chinese understandings of leadership. In a study of LMX relationships and power distance in the U.S. and Colombia and their influence on voice, Botero and Van Dyne (2009) find that LMX and power distance relate to voice in different ways.

Moreover, recent organizational communication research interrogates how notions of leadership in various parts of the world are tied into larger structures and/or sets of values. For instance, Hall (2010) foregrounds Jamaica's postcolonial context, which informs Jamaican managers' notions of leading. Broader national cultural values of Malaysian society are highlighted as essential in understanding the supervisory communication examined in Bakar and Connaughton's (2010) work. Relatedly, contemporary organizational communication research has been concerned with non-Western sites in which to study leadership. Shi and Wilson (2010) examine upward-influence processes in China. Bakar and Connaughton (2010) investigate supervisor-subordinate relationships in Malaysia, and Hall (2010) highlights sensemaking narratives of managers in Jamaica. Relatively few of these studies are comparative across countries or cultures, although the aforementioned Botero and Van Dyne (2009) study is an exception.

To recap, leadership researchers, including many in organizational communication, are increasingly interested in understanding leadership through a non-Western lens and in non-Western organizational contexts—an organizational trend that is likely to continue with increased globalization.

Leading Change

One strand of leadership and change research contributes a communicative perspective to change implementation. In this body of work, change implementers are primarily leaders. For example, Hearn and Ninan (2003) underscore how leading change is communicative in the sense that it is about managing meaning. As Lewis's (2011) program of research has shown over the past several years, planned change implementation is most certainly a communicative endeavor (Lewis, 2000, 2007). Lewis writes: "Communication represents not only the primary mechanism of change in organizations, but for many types of change may constitute the outcome as well (e.g., management programs which are evidenced in styles of supervision)" (Lewis, 2000, p. 46). Lewis and colleagues unearth reasons why change implementers communicatively attend to some stakeholders more so than others (Lewis, Richardson, & Hamel, 2003) and present a testable model of change implementation communication (see Lewis, Chapter 20, for more discussion of organizational change).

As can be seen from the above literature review, current research reflecting a more post-positivist approach to leadership continues to utilize a transmissional view of communication. Post-positivist survey methods also continue to dominate, although there are signs that mixed-method studies are growing with the treatment of communication as data. Finally, an individualist and cognitive lens continues, although there is increased sensitivity to multiple levels and units of analysis, especially in the move to studies of leadership in teams and networks.

Social Constructionist Views of Leadership

As the introduction suggests, since the last *Handbook* review, another narrative is challenging that of post-positivist leadership study. In this emerging narrative, communication is not just one of many variables of interest; rather, communication is central, defining, and constitutive of leadership. As such, several organizational communication and management scholars who favor social constructionism (Berger & Luckman, 1966) are now casting leadership as a co-constructed product of socio-historical and collective meaning making (Barge, 2007; Barge & Fairhurst, 2008; Fairhurst,

2007a; Parker, 2005). They characterize this social and cultural lens in terms of three themes.

First, emphasis is given to a meaning-centered view of communication, which stresses authorship (i.e., leaders are neither the only nor the primary symbolizing agents), the formative power of language (i.e., the ability to categorize and label that which may only be vaguely sensed; Shotter, 1993), contested meaning (i.e., sometimes called *discursive struggle* because of a lack of agreement on matters ranging from world views to definitions of the *situation here and now*; Grint, 2000), and the role of socio-historical systems of thought (i.e., *discourses*) in sourcing not only ways of thinking, but ways of talking (Foucault, 1972).

Second, by emphasizing the centrality of communication to leadership, the constructionist processes that give rise to leadership attributions are key concerns. As such, there is a resistance to essentializing theory in which leadership is to be found in a leader's personal qualities (e.g., trait theory), situations they might face (e.g., Hersey and Blanchard's Situational Leadership Theory), or some combination thereof (e.g., contingency theories, such as when a strong leader and crisis coincides; Grint, 2000, 2005). Leadership is, instead, in the eye of the beholder (Calder, 1977) because "what counts as a 'situation' and what counts as the 'appropriate' way of leading in that situation are interpretive and contestable issues, not issues that can be decided by objective criteria" (Grint, 2000, p. 3). Constructionist leadership scholars thus problematize the variability and inconsistency in actors' accounts and/or analysts' findings and address how conflicting leadership truth claims might have been produced and even coexist (Fairhurst & Grant, 2010).

Third, the treatment of power in constructionist leadership approaches is much more encompassing than in post-positivist approaches (Fairhurst, 2007a). Constructionist approaches often integrate various forms of power and influence and conceive of them in both positive and negative terms (Collinson, 2006). As such, Foucault (1995) is a particular influence here, given his focus on discourse as constituting power and knowledge systems and its influence on subjectivity. By contrast, post-positivist leadership research typically treats *power* as a negative and repressive property, while positive influence is often tantamount to a definition of *leadership* (Collinson, 2006).

Together, these three influences have spawned a new research agenda involving leadership as (a) the comanagement of meaning; (b) influential acts of human and material organizing; (c) a site of power and influence; and (d) alive with the potential for moral accountability, reflexivity, and change. We sample from each of these areas in the discussion below.

Leadership as the Comanagement of Meaning

In the 1980s, charismatic and transformational leadership theories (Bass, 1985; Conger & Kanungo, 1987; House, 1977) initially appeared to challenge a transmissional view of communication by casting leaders as managers of meaning (Smircich & Morgan, 1982); however, leaders were often the primary (read: *only*) symbolizing agents (Fairhurst, 2001). Since the last review, however, leadership research is increasingly about the *comanagement* of meaning, in which followers or other leadership actors also manage meaning in such areas as sensemaking, framing, identity work, and leadership aesthetics.

Sensemaking, Framing, and Identity Work. A meaning-centered view of communication is a prerequisite to leadership actors' sensemaking accounts. As Drazin, Glynn, and Kazanjian (1999) explain, "Meaning—or sense—develops about the situation, which allows the individual to act in some rational fashion; thus meaning—or sensemaking—is a primary generator of individual action" (p. 293).

The meanings applied to situations have been called *frames* (Bateson, 1972; Goffman, 1974), *enactments* (Weick, 1979), *schemas* (Lord & Hall, 2003), and *cognitive maps* (Drazin et al., 1999). If *frame* represents a cognitive meaning structure, the process of communicating those structures has been called *framing* (Fairhurst, 2011) or *sensegiving* in a leadership context (Gioia & Chittipeddi, 1991). Moreover, if leadership actors or collectives develop a cause-map of the world as a result of their sensemaking efforts, inevitably, they situate themselves in this map (Drazin et al., 1999). Thus we are likely to find individual and collective identity work in their sensemaking accounts in the form of categorizing and framing linguistic activity in response to questions such as "Who am I (in this context)?" and "Who are we?"

For example, several studies examine the identity work of middle managers in their sensemaking of top managements' change initiatives (Balogun & Johnson, 2004, 2005; Stensaker & Falkenberg, 2007), while Lewis (2011) writes extensively about sensemaking and stakeholder identities in strategic change. Martin (2004) examines how female middle managers use humor to negotiate their identities to deal with paradoxical circumstances, while other studies feature the sensemaking and identity work of employees who resist management (Laine & Vaara, 2007; Sonenshein, 2010; Tourish & Robson, 2006). Moreover, Alvesson and Spicer (2011) explore the metaphorical basis (e.g., leaders as *saints*, *gardeners*, and *bullies*) of leader sensemaking and identity work. Notably, recent work adopting a sensemaking perspective moves beyond examining positional leaders and instead shifts attention to how interim or temporary leaders make sense of their roles and actions (Browning & McNamee, 2012).

Framing becomes a central focus in the work of Fairhurst (2011), whose goal is to capture how leadership actors reflexively use language and actions to create meaning and construct the realities to which they must then respond. Work by H. Liu (2010) and Craig and Amernic (2004) examine the *failure framing* strategies of leaders such as Al Dunlap and John Berardino, respectively. The latter deployed a mind-numbing panoply of accounting details in testimony before Congress to deflect responsibility for Arthur Anderson's role in the Enron debacle. Finally, work by Foldy, Goldman, and Ospina (2008); Sheep, Fairhurst, Khanzanchi, and Slay (2010); and Carroll and Simpson (2012) focus on framing strategies associated with problem and solution formulations highlighting cognitive shifts in collective identity or organizational change.

Leadership Aesthetics. An emerging area of meaning-centered leadership research involves aesthetics. Riley (1988) captured it as, "The notion of charisma, vision, and culture all share a sense of the aesthetic—the art form of leadership. . . . This requires forms of analysis . . . sensitive to style, to the creation of meaning, and to the dramatic edge of leadership" (p. 82). Working from a constructionist stance, Grint (2000) cast leadership as a series of art forms: philosophical, fine, martial, and performing. Eisenberg (2007) focuses on the ambiguity, contingency, and aesthetics of meaning in many leadership situations, while Harter, Leeman, Norander, Young, and Rawlins (2008) examine the tensions between aesthetic sensibilities and instrumental rationalities in the collaborative management of an arts organization.

A growing number of studies embrace aesthetics while decrying the "disembodied" leader in the mainstream literature. For example, Cunliffe (2002) and Shotter and Cunliffe (2003) speak of a (managerial) *social poetics* involving a "precognitive understanding in which poetic images and gestures provoke a response as we feel the rhythm, resonance, and reverberation of speech and sound" (Cunliffe, 2002, p. 134). Hansen, Ropo, and Sauer (2007) argue that *aesthetics* focuses on felt meaning, tacit knowing, and emotions integral to leading and following. Ladkin (2008) argues that "leading beautifully" requires mastery of the context, coherent (authentic) message congruence between speech and actions, and a sense of purpose that brings forth one's ethical commitments. Finally, Sinclair

(2005) examines the body performances of leaders, calling for more studies that "hold bodies, in their fleshy version, prominent, and to focus on bodies as possibilities," for example, in the ways they may interrupt systemic power (p. 388). Too often, she argues, "bodies disappear under the weight of theorizing" (p. 387).

To recap, understanding actors' sensemaking, identity work, framing strategies, and aesthetics requires a meaning-centered view of communication. With this view, what some have argued to be a richer one (Ashcraft, Kuhn, & Cooren, 2009), we are able to see rationalities-in-the-making, identities in flux, and bodies that now matter. We now turn our attention to communication scholars who build upon a meaning-centered view of communication as they try to put "abstract [leadership] structures into live motion" (Ashcraft et al., 2009, p. 4).

Leadership as Influential Acts of (Human-Material) Organizing

This category of research focuses on the ways that leadership emerges in the management of the tension between agency and structure. Giddens's (1979, 1984) *duality of structure* (i.e., structure, in the form of rules and resources, is the medium and outcome of action) has become a popular way to address this theme. In short, *influential acts of organizing* (e.g., communication surrounding a unit's mission, vision, or values; Hosking, 1988) are made possible by extant structures, which leadership actors draw upon to navigate *the situation here and now* while reproducing or renegotiating these structures with each deployment. After reviewing structurationist leadership studies, several studies by the Montréal School of organizational communication extend this discussion with human-material acts of organizing.

Structurationist Leadership Research. Two themes in Ashcraft et al.'s (2009) recent review of structurationist research are leadership related: (1) the relationship between structuration and discursive struggle and (2) a structurational rendition of communicative constitution of organizations (CCO) theory. The former is based on Giddens's (1984) view that all systems are marked by an *antagonism of opposites* as well as the dialectic of control in which the less powerful (e.g., employees) always maintain a measure of control over their leaders. While the dialectic of control is often used in studies of leading social or organizational change (Papa, Auwal, & Singhal, 1995; Putnam, 2003), others use Giddens's insight about the antagonism of opposites as a touchstone to identify tensions, contradictions, and paradoxes and their management by leadership actors (Jian, 2007; Real & Putnam, 2005; Seo, Putnam, & Bartunek, 2004; Sherblom, Keranen, & Withers, 2002; Sillince, 2007). For example, Tracy (2004) studied employee reactions to organizational tensions in a prison setting, while Fairhurst, Cooren, and Cahill (2002) examined leadership-induced tensions, tension management strategies, and their unintended consequences in successive downsizings. The implications for leading systems such as these lie in understanding and even embracing counter-rational thought in order to find creative ways to manage oppositional tensions (Sheep et al., 2010).

A second strain of studies focuses on McPhee and Zaug's (2000; Putnam, Nicotera, & McPhee, 2009; see McPhee, Poole, & Iverson, Chapter 3) structurational rendering of CCO theory in which four interrelated processes constitute organizations: (1) membership negotiation, (2) organizational self-structuring, (3) activity coordination, and (4) institutional positioning. For example, work by McPhee and Iverson (2009) in a Mexican community organization show how the "organization is a medium of agency by its designing managers" (p. 74). They demonstrate *reflexive self-structuring* through surveillance and performance monitoring at one site that reverberates throughout the system to sustain management interests, even while less powerful stakeholders reflexively monitor and rationalize ongoing conditions. In another study, Browning, Greene, Sitkin, Sutcliffe, and Obstfeld (2009) demonstrate *activity coordination* and *institutional positioning* in the dance between U.S. Air Force technicians and the civilian review boards charged with their oversight.

The Montréal School. The Montréal School of organizational communication and its scholars (Brummans, 2006; Cooren, 2000, 2004; Robichaud, 2003; Taylor & Van Every, 2000, 2011; see Brummans, Cooren, Robichaud, & Taylor, Chapter 7) see Giddens's agency-structure dialectic as overly narrow and oppositional. Drawing heavily from actor-network theory (Latour, 1994), their view of organizations is filled with a plenum of agencies that can be textual, mechanical, architectural, natural, and human (Cooren, 2006). When paired together, human and nonhuman agents create *hybrid agency* and *networks* with their own structuring affordances activated through interaction (Cooren, Brummans, & Charrieras, 2008). As such, structure is not the driver of action, but something to be explained (Latour, 2002).

Work in leadership with the Montréal School of organizational communication has demonstrated the distributed nature of leadership in a high-reliability organization, its episodic structuring, and the manner in which *command presence* emerges in the sequentiality of unfolding crises (Cooren & Fairhurst, 2004; Fairhurst & Cooren, 2004). Similar work with Cooren's (2007) analyses of a corporate board meeting charged with leadership succession demonstrates how leadership attributions, in general, cohere as a sequence (Fairhurst, 2007b).

Other studies from the Montréal School focus on the role of nonhuman agency in leadership. For example, Fairhurst's (2007a) analysis of New York Mayor Rudy Giuliani during 9/11 reveals that the mayor's charismatic leadership at the time emerged as a distributed network of human and nonhuman agents, including emotion-laden objects, texts, and spaces. Fairhurst and Cooren (2009) examined leadership presence through human and nonhuman agency in former Governor Kathleen Blanco's management of Hurricane Katrina in 2005 and former Governor Arnold Schwarzenegger's management of the 2007 California wildfires. Both leadership presence and successful crisis management appeared dependent on frequent hybridizing and networking with nonhuman agents—large or small—that were locally entrenched and responsive to conditions on the ground. Cooren, Fairhurst, and Huet (2012) examine nonhuman agency in a building manager's job and the manner in which such agency boldly asserts itself in construction matters yet falls silent with a topic change.

The Montréal School studies give credence to Grint's (1997) wry observation that "naked, friendless, money-less, and technology-less leaders are unlikely to prove persuasive" (p. 17). The role of nonhuman agency and its structuring potential with human hybrids in leadership situations is crucial in this genre. Like the Montréal School, structurationist research also examines the structure-in-action of leadership. However, it eschews nonhuman agency in favor of the structuring potential of rules and resources, which also enables less powerful leadership actors a measure of control based on access. Interestingly, neither theoretical framework is about leadership *per se*, but they easily adapt to better understand agency-structure tensions in the leadership relationship.

Leadership as a Site of Power and Influence

Post-positivist leadership research is often based on a Western conception of the self as autonomous from society. More constructionist approaches adopt a post-structuralist view in which the self and society are inseparable (Collinson, 2006), supplying yet another reason for a social and cultural lens on leadership (Fairhurst, 2007a). Here, leadership actors are looked upon as cultural products; they are receptors of socio-historical meanings, for example, about what constitutes leadership/management within a given historical era (du Gay, Salaman, & Rees, 1996; Western, 2008). As mentioned earlier, Foucault's (1990) more encompassing view of power is a key influence here; however, orientations toward power in this area vary in terms of how much they foreground power processes. As will be explained in the paragraphs that follow, more general constructionist approaches leave open the opportunity for power and politics while acting as the starting premise for critical management studies (CMS).

Constructionist Approaches. The approaches in this genre view leadership as attributional (Calder, 1977), grounded in social constructionist processes (Berger & Luckman, 1966) such as language games (Wittgenstein, 1953), and context-dependent (Fairhurst, 2009). Leaders must persuade themselves and others of their leadership, leaving open the possibility of contestation and conflict when multiple actors or observers are present. Contestation or discursive struggle implies power dynamics, as some views weigh more heavily than others by virtue of skill or position in the hierarchy (Smircich & Morgan, 1982); however, power concerns are not always foregrounded.

For example, Grint's (2000, 2005) constructionist leadership project not only recasts leadership as a series of art forms, as mentioned previously, but highlights the role of persuasion in creating believable leadership performances. His work on problem-centered leadership focuses on *wicked* and *tame problems* (Rittel & Webber, 1973), but also *crises* (Grint, 2005, 2010). *Wicked problems* require (collaborative) leadership, because no one person has the answer; *tame problems* require managerial solutions based on established processes; *crises* require commanders who do not waste time. Lest we form an addiction to elegant frameworks such as these, Grint reminds us that leaders often cast problems in one of these three ways to simply rationalize their preferred decision-making style.

Kelly (2008; Kelly, White, Martin, & Rouncefield, 2006) and colleagues use Wittgenstein (1953) to suggest that leadership should be seen as a family resemblance among language games understood best by those who use the term *leadership* and its derivatives. Ethnomethodological methods are needed in order to focus on the local logics and labeling that organize situated applications of the term, including that of analysts (Kelly et al., 2006). Reminiscent of Grint (2005), Kelly and colleagues (2006) cast leadership as a *design problem* in which actors must figure out what leadership is in the context of what they do and persuade themselves and others that they are doing it.

Critical Management Studies. Following Cunliffe (2009), CMS can be divided into three perspectives, all focusing on power and the politics of meaning. The first, Marxist and neo-Marxist perspectives, has little use for leadership study *per se*, preferring instead to focus upon forms of control that privilege elites such as shareholders, owners, and managers (Deetz, 1992). The second is postcolonial studies, which critique Western views of leadership and management in a global business society (Hall, 2010; Said, 1993), a topic addressed earlier. Finally, post-structuralist studies have been a prime generator of leadership research in recent years in the areas of denaturalization and dialectics and resistance.

In denaturalization studies, that which appears *the way things are* or *natural* are rendered problematic (Fournier & Grey, 2000). Here, post-structuralist studies center on discursive practices involving language systems, texts, ways of talking and thinking and nondiscursive practices such as institutionalized structures, social practices, and, particularly, techniques regulating what is normal or appears natural (Cunliffe, 2009, p. 25). For example, Fairhurst (2007a; Fairhurst, Church, Hagen, & Levi, 2011) and colleagues examine *discursive leadership* at the intersection of "little *d*" discourse or language-in-use practices, such as sequentiality, membership categorization, and narrative, with "big *D*" Discourses that, following Foucault (1990, 1995), are more enduring systems of thought sourcing communicating actors with linguistic repertoires. They pay particular attention to executive coaching Discourses and the manner in which Foucault's (1990) confessional and examination technologies operate within them but also how they work to *other* female leaders and normalize alpha males as senior leaders, even while disciplining them.

In her critical feminist study of African American women executives, Parker (2005) writes about race neutrality in leadership studies and the way it *dominates* African American women leaders through unquestioned assumptions about superiority and inferiority, *excludes* them from the site or sources of knowledge production, and *contains* them by silencing those who would speak out. Gordon's (2010) analysis of a police organization likewise demonstrates how certain historical practices (read: *discourses*) are accepted as the natural order of things, reinforce hierarchy, and undermine efforts to facilitate empowerment and disperse leadership. Several other studies focus on the power of discourse to influence the subjectivities of leadership actors who discipline themselves to its ways, including Sewell, Barker, and Nyberg's (2012) study of management training employees as "piggies-in-the-middle"; Ziegler's (2007) study of organizational lists and discourses portraying firefighters as benevolent leaders, heroic saviors, self-aware servants, obedient rule followers, or critical-thinking team members; and Medved and Kirby's (2005) analysis of corporate mothering discourses, which create subject positions for stay-at-home mothers as professionals, managers, productive citizens, and irreplaceable workers. Likewise, Western (2008) examines four leadership discourses—controller, therapist, messiah, and eco-leader—and demonstrates the ways in which they privilege certain views of the world, impact leadership practices and organizational culture accordingly, and may have emancipatory potential.

Finally, work by Alvesson and Sveningsson (2003a) takes the leadership literature to task for portraying leadership as something special when it often loses itself amidst the everyday aspects of work. They proclaim a need for leadership agnosticism as a result, thus following some CMS scholars' suspicion of leadership (cultural discourses) as a mechanism of domination (Hardy & Clegg, 1996) or as overly reductionist (Cunliffe, 2009). In another study, Alvesson and Sveningsson (2003b) argue that the mundane job of managing is socially shaped by *highly responsive subjects* (i.e., managers) willing to buy into managerialist attempts to inflate the job of managing. More recent work critiques Alvesson and Sveningsson's view of leadership as a disappearing act (Kelly, 2008) or suggests a rapprochement between critical theory and leadership studies (Alvesson & Spicer, 2012; Zoller & Fairhurst, 2007).

The second CMS area involves leadership dialectics and resistance. Increasingly, poststructuralist CMS scholars are speaking out against views of power and control as a simple binary that privileges one or the other in order to capture resistance (or dissent) and control in more complex terms (Banks, 2008; Fleming & Spicer, 2008; Mumby, 2005). Collinson (2005) argues that the very nature of leadership is "discursive, dialectical, contested, and contradictory" as he explores three dialectics—control/resistance, dissent/consent, and men/women—and how they operate in the leadership relationship (p. 1427). Zoller and Fairhurst (2007) add several additional dialectics to understand dissent leadership, including fixed/fluid meaning potentials, overt/covert behavior, and reason/emotion, to suggest how position in the hierarchy matters little regarding who emerges as leader when these dialectics are managed well. On the rise, however, are a growing number of discursive dialectical analyses that examine tension, contradiction, and paradox in leadership/management contexts more generally (Martin, 2004; Real & Putnam, 2005; Tracy, 2004; Trethewey & Ashcraft, 2004).

To recap, in viewing leadership as inherently power based and a site of contestation, we are compelled to see leadership actors more complexly in two ways. First, who can become a leader is less a function of position in the hierarchy and more a function of the ability to manage key dialectical tensions. Second, leadership actors are not just managers of meaning, they are also receptors of meaning based on the cultural discourses about leadership to which they are subject (Fairhurst, 2007a).

Leadership and the Potential for Reflexivity, Moral Accountability, and Change

The studies in this genre concern themselves with social constructionist praxis and are the product of four influences according to Fairhurst and Grant (2010). The first is a concern for ethics, heightened by a seemingly endless string of corporate scandals that bring attention to the dark side of leadership (Anderson & Englehardt, 2001; Christensen, Morsing, & Cheney, 2008; Johnson, 2009; Tourish, 2013). The second involves communication scholars' turn toward practical theory (Barge, 2001; Barge & Craig, 2009), which has roots in action science (Argyris & Schon, 1996; Schon, 1983) and the theorizing of Dewey (1938). The third influence in this genre is critical management education that, along with its emphasis on the operations of power, takes seriously the emancipatory goal of critical theory (Perriton & Reynolds, 2004). The final influence is the turn toward discourse, which Marshak and Grant (2008) describe as an interest in narrative, text, and conversation and the ways they shape and are shaped by organizational processes and change, the ways they reinforce mindsets, and the way that power structures require change via the story lines that instantiated them.

All four of these influences shape an emerging grammar of applied social constructionism that includes the following pairs of terms: (1) meaning and framing, (2) reflexivity and moral accountability (ethics), and (3) relationality and dialogue (Fairhurst & Grant, 2010). For example, the concern for *meaning* and *framing* counters the tendency of some (managerial) leadership actors to view communication as a simple transmission and to heighten sensitivity to language use as a basis for reflexive reality construction (Eisenberg, 2007; Fairhurst, 2005, 2011). As mentioned earlier, leadership aesthetics (Hansen et al., 2007) and social poetics (Shotter & Cunliffe, 2003) follow naturally from this work—as does research in the area of leadership narratives (Barge, 2004a; Boje, Alvarez, & Schooling, 2001) and appreciative inquiry in which the power of language is used to construct more positive, life-affirming ways to lead organizations (Barge & Oliver, 2003).

Reflexivity/moral accountability is another key pairing predicated on the role of introspection in promoting more ethical behavior (Anderson & Englehardt, 2001; Gardner, 2007). The work of Barge and colleagues (2004a, 2004b, 2004c, 2007; Barge & Fairhurst, 2008; Barge & Little, 2002) and Cunliffe and colleagues (2004, 2009; Cunliffe & Jun, 2005) is of interest here because of the ways in which they see opportunities for reflexivity and change in present moments, which they try to re-story to affect more ethically and relationally responsive leadership action. Such work is consistent with more general treatments of leadership ethics in the literature (Christensen et al., 2008; Johnson, 2009) as well as case analyses of ethical breakdowns by organizational leaders (Seeger & Ulmer, 2003; Tourish & Vatcha, 2005). Work by McKenna and Rooney (2008), which recasts *reflexivity* as *ontological acuity* to stress leaders' need to understand the cognitive *and* discursive basis of their knowledge foundations, is particularly interesting in this regard.

A final pairing involves *relationality* and *dialogue* among leadership actors (Forester, 1999; Isaacs, 1999). The view of relationality here is one of relational responsiveness (Cunliffe, 2002; Cunliffe & Eriksen, 2011; Shotter & Cunliffe, 2003) and sensitivity to systems dynamics (Barge, 2007; Barge & Fairhurst, 2008). Such views mesh nicely with a dialogic view, expressed by Gergen, Gergen, and Barrett (2004) as an "intersubjective connection or synchrony . . . (that may) serve many different purposes, both negative and positive" (pp. 42–44). Dialogue is increasingly a foundation for leadership praxis from a communication perspective (Barge, 2007; Barge & Little, 2002; Deetz, 2006).

In constructionist leadership, actors shape and are shaped by the realities, relationalities, and identities they jointly create. Ethnographic and discursive methods tend to be favored with this more social and cultural lens, which privileges a meaning-centered view of communication. In turn, leadership actors are encouraged to become reflexive practitioners and develop a heightened sensitivity to language and the meanings they cocreate in order to promote more ethical organizations and relationally responsive leadership.

Conclusion

We have been arguing that since the last *Handbook* review, there have been significant strides in the development of a communicative lens by which to study leadership. Based on the above literature review, we can conclude the following six points about the nature of this lens:

1. *Leadership communication is transmissional and meaning centered.* Analysts are fruitfully using both definitions to ask very different questions about leadership, such as those involving leadership outcomes and effectiveness for transmissional views and the (embodied) experience of leadership for meaning-centered views. This variety, including their combined use in future research agendas, should only enrich the study of leadership communication going forward.

2. *Leadership (communication) is relational, neither leader centric nor follower centric.* As we have seen, definitions of *relational* tend to vary in terms of post-positivist versus constructionist approaches (Uhl-Bien, Maslyn, & Ospina, 2011), where the former is mostly marked by theories of leadership relationships and its qualities (e.g., LMX) and a consideration of multiple levels and units of analysis (Connaughton & Daly, 2005). In the latter, constructionist approaches focus on leadership as codefined (and thus contestable), dialogic (versus monologic), and a self-conscious way of being in relation to others (Barge & Fairhurst, 2008; Cunliffe & Eriksen, 2011). Interestingly, management scholars are increasingly joining communication scholars in making the case for a relationality grounded in social constructionism, initiating sometimes-difficult conversations over the past dominance of scientific methods in leadership study (Fairhurst & Uhl-Bien, 2012; Uhl-Bien & Ospina, 2012).

3. *Influential acts of human-material organizing are the medium and outcome of leadership communication.* This claim not only takes seriously that leadership is interactionally produced (Fairhurst & Cooren, 2004; Wodak, Kwon, & Clarke, 2011) but emphasizes the study of leadership communicative *practices* embodied in talk, action, and other symbolic media increasingly associated with a material world (Cooren et al., 2012; Fairhurst & Cooren, 2009). We are only at the forefront of studies in this area, but the promise here is not just to "put abstract structures into live motion" (Ashcraft et al., 2009, p. 4), as interactional leadership scholars have been doing for some time now (Courtright, Fairhurst, & Rogers, 1989; Gronn, 1983), but the elucidation of leadership concepts (e.g., presence) once thought too abstract to understand in only the most general of terms.

4. *Leadership (communication) is inherently power based, a site of contestation about the nature of leadership.* This claim turns the view of leaders as transformative agents on its head, first, by recognizing that the agents are also receptors of meaning and disciplined products of culture based on the discourses about leadership to which they are subject (Fairhurst, 2007a). Second, based on the tensions, contradictions, and paradoxes of complex organizational life, who can become a leader appears less a function of position in the hierarchy and more a function of recognizing and managing these tensions. As such, there is much to learn through future

research regarding leadership actors' sensemaking, problem-setting, and tension-management strategies. This is because the discovery of counter-rational forms of thinking—most likely, within collaborative structures, because no one person can have all of the answers in complex environments—may hold the keys to navigating contemporary organizational life and the qualities leadership must assume in the 21st century (Grint, 2010; Sheep et al., 2010).

5. *Leadership (communication) is a diverse, global phenomenon.* If ever there was a need for post-positivist and constructionist views of leadership to work in tandem, it lies in understanding the cultural bases of leadership (L. Liu, 2010), especially in intercultural and postcolonial contexts. Post-positivist approaches to leadership study can be especially useful in noting central tendencies across cultures and cross-cultural comparisons, while constructionist leadership approaches help us to understand the unique power dynamics and meaning potentials wrought by multiple and competing (cultural) discourses. Just as important are the broader issues of space, distance, and time as they interlace with the affordances of new technologies and leading in multicultural environments (Connaughton & Daly, 2005).

6. *Leadership communication is alive with the potential for reflexivity, moral accountability, and change.* Work by Lewis (2011) reflects the kind of cross-paradigmatic and mixed-method commitment that many post-positivist leadership communication scholars are making to understand organizational change. However, at this juncture, the promise of more ethical leadership is perhaps best realized in constructionist leadership scholars' projects on reflexivity, moral accountability, dialogue, and inclusion (Barge, 2004c, 2007; Deetz, 2006; Parker, 2005). Unfortunately, the urgency of continuing to develop ethical leadership has never been greater.

Although organizational communication scholars have not been alone in establishing this communicative lens on leadership, they are certainly making their mark—and, arguably, are uniquely positioned to continue to do so. Communication scholars have benefited enormously from the linguistic turn in philosophy in which language no longer mirrors or represents reality but constitutes it (Rorty, 1967). They have many tools by which to understand the negotiation of meaning and communication's unending variety and detail. They are also used to a healthy eclecticism and cross-paradigm work, as the humanists and social scientists occupying their departments long ago learned to talk to one another. Given rhetoric's strong presence in the communication discipline, analysts are also used to managing the tension between representation and critique, a key feature of a critical perspective. At the same time, organizational communication leadership scholars are as likely to describe or critique the discursive construction of leadership as they are to demonstrate how such constructions predicatively relate to various other processes and outcomes. It is an appreciation of this overall diversity that will best serve the field of organizational communication as it looks further into 21st century leadership.

References

Adler, N. J., Brody, L. W., & Osland, J. S. (2001). Going beyond twentieth century leadership: A CEO develops his company's global competitiveness. *Cross Cultural Management, 8*(3/4), 11–34.

Alvesson, M., & Spicer, A. (2011). *Metaphors we lead by: Understanding leadership in the real world.* London, England: Routledge.

Alvesson, M., & Spicer, A. (2012). Critical leadership studies: The case for critical performativity. *Human Relations, 65*(3), 367–390.

Alvesson, M., & Sveningsson, S. (2003a). The great disappearing act: Difficulties in doing "leadership." *Leadership Quarterly, 14*(3), 359–381.

Alvesson, M., & Sveningsson, S. (2003b). Managers doing leadership: The extra-organization of the mundane. *Human Relations, 56*(12), 1435–1459.

Anderson, J. A., & Englehardt, E. E. (2001). *The organizational self and ethical conduct: Sunlit virtue and shadowed resistance*. Fort Worth, TX: Harcourt.

Antonakis, J. (2011). Predictors of leadership: The usual suspects and the suspect traits. In A. Bryman, D. Collinson, K. Grint, B. Jackson, & M. Uhl-Bien (Eds.), *The SAGE handbook of leadership* (pp. 269–285). London, England: SAGE.

Argyris, C., & Schon, D. A. (1996). *Organizational learning II: Theory, method and practice*. Reading, MA: Addison-Wesley.

Ashcraft, K. L., Kuhn, T., & Cooren, F. (2009). Constitutional amendments: "Materializing" organizational communication. *The Academy of Management Annals, 3*(1), 1–64.

Axley, S. R. (1984). Managerial and organizational communication in terms of the conduit metaphor. *Academy of Management Review, 9*(3), 428–437.

Bakar, H. A., & Connaughton, S. L. (2010). Relationships between supervisory communication and commitment to workgroup: A multilevel analysis approach. *International Journal of Strategic Communication, 4*(1), 39–57.

Balogun, J., & Johnson, G. (2004). Organizational restructuring and middle manager sensemaking. *Academy of Management Journal, 47*(4), 523–549.

Balogun, J., & Johnson, G. (2005). From intended strategies to unintended outcomes: The impact of change in recipient sensemaking. *Organization Studies, 26*(11), 1573–1601.

Balthazard, P. A., Waldman, D. A., & Warren, J. E. (2009). Predictions of the emergence of transformational leadership in virtual decision teams. *Leadership Quarterly, 20*(3), 651–663.

Banks, S. (Ed.). (2008). *Dissent and the failure of leadership*. Northampton, MA: Edward Elgar.

Barge, J. K. (2001). Practical theory as mapping, engaged reflection, and transformative practice. *Communication Theory, 11*(1), 5–13.

Barge, J. K. (2004a). Antenarrative and managerial practice. *Communication Studies, 55*(1), 106–127.

Barge, J. K. (2004b). Articulating CMM as a practical theory. *Human Systems: The Journal of Systemic Consultation & Management, 15*(3), 13–32.

Barge, J. K. (2004c). Reflexivity and managerial practice. *Communication Monographs, 71*(1), 70–96.

Barge, J. K. (2007). The practice of systemic leadership. *OD Practitioner, 39*(1), 10–14.

Barge, J. K., & Craig, R. T. (2009). Practical theory. In L. R. Frey & K. N. Cissna (Eds.), *Handbook of applied communication* (pp. 55–78). Mahwah, NJ: Lawrence Erlbaum.

Barge, J. K., & Fairhurst, G. T. (2008). Living leadership: A systemic, constructionist approach. *Leadership, 4*(3), 227–251.

Barge, J. K., & Little, M. (2002). Dialogical wisdom, communicative practice, and organizational life. *Communication Theory, 12*(4), 375–397.

Barge, J. K., & Oliver, C. (2003). Working with appreciation in managerial practice. *Academy of Management Review, 28*(1), 124–142.

Bass, B. M. (1981). *Stogdill's handbook of leadership*. New York, NY: Free Press.

Bass, B. M. (1985). *Leader and performance: Beyond expectations*. New York, NY: Free Press.

Bateson, G. (1972). *Steps to an ecology of the mind*. New York, NY: Ballantine.

Berger, P., & Luckman, T. L. (1966). *The social construction of knowledge: A treatise on the sociology of knowledge*. Garden City, NY: Doubleday.

Berson, Y., & Avolio, B. (2004). Transformational leadership and the dissemination of organizational goals: A case of a telecommunication firm. *Leadership Quarterly, 15*(5), 625–646.

Boje, D., Alvarez, R. C., & Schooling, B. (2001). Reclaiming story in organization: Narratologies and action sciences. In R. Westwood & S. Linstead (Eds.), *The language of organization* (pp. 132–175). London, England: SAGE.

Botero, I. C., & Van Dyne, L. (2009). Employee voice behavior: Interactive effects of LMX and power distance in the United States and Colombia. *Management Communication Quarterly, 23*(1), 84–104.

Browning, B. W., & McNamee, L. G. (2012). Considering the temporary leader in temporary work arrangements: Sensemaking processes of internal interim leaders. *Human Relations, 65*(6), 729–752.

Browning, L. D., Greene, R. W., Sitkin, S. B., Sutcliffe, K. M., & Obstfeld, D. (2009). Constitutive complexity: Military entrepreneurs and the synthetic character of communication flows. In L. L. Putnam & A. M. Nicotera (Eds.), *Building theories of organization: The constitutive role of communication* (pp. 89–116). New York, NY: Routledge.

Brummans, B. H. J. M. (2006). The Montréal School and the question of agency. In F. Cooren, J. R. Taylor, & E. Van Every (Eds.), *Communication as organizing:*

Empirical and theoretical explorations in the dynamic of text and conversation (pp. 197–227). Mahwah, NJ: LEA.

Brummans, B. H. J. M., & Hwang, J. M. (2010). Tzu Chi's organizing for a compassionate world: Insights into the communicative praxis of a Buddhist organization. *Journal of International and Intercultural Communication, 3*(2), 136–163.

Burke, C. S., Sims, D. E., Lazzara, E. H., & Salas, E. (2007). Trust in leadership: A multi-level review and integration. *Leadership Quarterly, 18*(6), 606–632.

Calder, B. J. (1977). An attribution theory of leadership. In B. M. Staw & G. R. Salancik (Eds.), *New directions in organizational behavior* (pp. 179–202). Chicago, IL: St. Clair Press.

Carroll, B., & Simpson, B. (2012). Moving between frames: Building sociality in leadership development. *Human Relations, 65*(10), 1283–1309.

Christensen, L. T., Morsing, M., & Cheney, C. (2008). *Corporate communications: Convention, complexity, and critique*. Los Angeles, CA: SAGE.

Collinson, D. L. (2005). Dialectics of leadership. *Human Relations, 58*(11), 1419–1442.

Collinson, D. L. (2006). Rethinking followership: A post-structuralist analysis of follower identities. *Leadership Quarterly, 17*(2), 179–189.

Conger, J. A., & Kanungo, R. M. (1987). Toward a behavioral theory of charismatic leadership in organizational settings. *Academy of Management Review, 12*(4), 637–647.

Connaughton, S. L., & Daly, J. (2004a). Leading from afar: Strategies for effectively leading virtual teams. In S. Godar & S. P. Ferris (Eds.), *Virtual & collaborative teams: Process, technologies & practice* (pp. 49–75). Hershey, PA: Idea Group, Inc.

Connaughton, S. L., & Daly, J. (2004b). Leading in geographically dispersed organizations: An empirical study of long distance leadership from the perspective of individuals being led from afar. *Corporate Communication: An International Journal, 9*(2), 89–103.

Connaughton, S. L., & Daly, J. (2005). Leadership in the new millennium: Communication beyond temporal, spatial, and geographical boundaries. In P. Kalbfleisch (Ed.). *Communication yearbook* (vol. 29, pp. 187–213). Mahwah, NJ: Lawrence Erlbaum.

Cooren, F. (2000). *The organizing property of communication*. Amsterdam, the Netherlands: John Benjamins.

Cooren, F. (2004). Textual agency: How texts do things in organizational settings. *Organization, 11*(3), 373–393.

Cooren, F. (2006). The organizational world as a plenum of agencies. In F. Cooren, J. R. Taylor, & E. J. Van Every (Eds.), *Communication as organizing: Empirical and theoretical explorations in the dynamic of text and conversation* (pp. 81–100). Mahwah, NJ: Lawrence Erlbaum.

Cooren, F. (Ed.). (2007). *Interacting and organizing: Analyses of a board meeting*. Mahwah, NJ: Lawrence Erlbaum.

Cooren, F., Brummans, B., & Charrieras, D. (2008). The coproduction of organizational presence: A study of Médecins sans Frontières in the Democratic Republic of Congo in action. *Human Relations, 61*(10), 1339–1370.

Cooren, F., & Fairhurst, G. (2004). Speech timing and spacing: The phenomenon of organizational closure. *Organization, 11*(6), 797–828.

Cooren, F., Fairhurst, G. T., & Huet, R. (2012). Why matter always matters in organizational communication. In B. Nardi, P. M. Leonardi, & J. Kallinikos (Eds.), *Materiality in organizations* (pp. 296–314). Ann Arbor: University of Michigan Press.

Courtright, J. A., Fairhurst, G. T., & Rogers, L. E. (1989). Interaction patterns in organic and mechanistic systems. *Academy of Management Journal, 32*(4), 773–802.

Craig, R. J., & Amernic, J. H. (2004). Enron discourse: The rhetoric of a resilient capitalism. *Critical Perspective on Accounting, 15*(6/7), 813–851.

Cunliffe, A. L. (2002). Social poetics as management inquiry: A dialogical approach. *Journal of Management Inquiry, 11*(2), 128–146.

Cunliffe, A. L. (2004). On becoming a critically reflexive practitioner. *Journal of Management Education, 28*(4), 407–426.

Cunliffe, A. L. (2009). *A very short, fairly interesting and reasonably cheap book about management*. Thousand Oaks, CA: SAGE.

Cunliffe, A. L., & Eriksen, M. (2011). Relational leadership. *Human Relations, 64*(11), 1425–1450.

Cunliffe, A. L., & Jun, J. S. (2005). The need for reflexivity in public administration. *Administration & Society, 37*(2), 225–242.

Dansereau, F., Alutto, J. A., & Yammarino, F. J. (1984). *Theory testing in organizational behavior: The variant approach*. Englewood Cliffs, NJ: Prentice Hall.

Dansereau, F. M., & Markham, S. E. (1987). Superior-subordinate communication: Multiple levels of analysis. In F. M. Jablin, L. L. Putnam, K. H. Roberts, & L. W. Porter (Eds.), *The handbook of organizational communication* (pp. 343–388). Newbury Park, CA: SAGE.

Deetz, S. A. (1992). *Democracy in an age of corporate colonization: Developments in communication and the politics of everyday life*. New York: State University of New York Press.

Deetz, S. A. (2006). Dialogue, communication theory, and the hope of making quality decisions together. *Management Communication Quarterly, 19*(3), 368–375.

Den Hartog, D. N., House, R. J., Hanges, P. J., Ruiz-Quintanilla, S. A., & Dorfman, P. W. (1999). Culture specific and cross-culturally generalizable implicit leadership theories: Are attributes of charismatic/transformational leadership universally endorsed? *Leadership Quarterly, 10*(2), 219–256.

Dewey, J. (1938). *Logic: The theory of inquiry*. New York, NY: Basic Books.

Dionne, S. D., Sayama, H., Hao, C., & Bush, B. J. (2010). The role of leadership in shared mental model convergence and team performance improvement: An agent-based computational model. *Leadership Quarterly, 21*(6), 1035–1049.

Drazin, R., Glynn, M. A., & Kazanjian, R. K. (1999). Multilevel theorizing about creativity in organizations: A sensemaking perspective. *Academy of Management Review, 24*(2), 286–307.

du Gay, P., Salaman, G., & Rees, B. (1996). The conduct of management and the management of conduct: Contemporary managerial discourse and the constitution of the "competent manager." *Journal of Management Studies, 33*(3), 263–282.

Eisenberg, E. (2007). *Strategic ambiguities: Essays on communication, organization, and identity*. Thousand Oaks, CA: SAGE.

Fairhurst, G. T. (2001). Dualisms in leadership research. In F. M. Jablin & L. L. Putnam (Eds.), *The new handbook of organizational communication* (pp. 379–439). Thousand Oaks, CA: SAGE.

Fairhurst, G. T. (2005). Reframing the art of framing: Problems and prospects for leadership. *Leadership, 1*(2), 165–185.

Fairhurst, G. T. (2007a). *Discursive leadership: In conversation with leadership psychology*. Thousand Oaks, CA: SAGE.

Fairhurst, G. T. (2007b). Liberating leadership in corporation after Mr. Sam: A response. In F. Cooren (Ed.), *Interacting and organizing: Analyses of a board meeting* (pp. 53–71). Mahwah, NJ: Lawrence Erlbaum.

Fairhurst, G. T. (2009). Considering context in discursive leadership research. *Human Relations, 62*(11), 1607–1633.

Fairhurst, G. T. (2011). *The power of framing: Creating the language of leadership*. San Francisco, CA: Jossey-Bass.

Fairhurst, G. T., Church, M., Hagen, D. E., & Levi, J. T. (2011). Whither female leaders? Executive coaching and the alpha male syndrome. In D. Mumby (Ed.), *Discourses of difference*. Thousand Oaks, CA: SAGE.

Fairhurst, G. T., & Cooren, F. (2004). Organizational language in use: Interaction analysis, conversation analysis, and speech act schematics. In D. Grant, C. Hardy, C. Oswick, & L. Putnam (Eds.), *The SAGE handbook of organizational discourse* (pp. 131–152). London, England: SAGE.

Fairhurst, G. T., & Cooren, F. (2009). Leadership as the hybrid production of presence(s). *Leadership, 5*(4), 1–22.

Fairhurst, G. T., Cooren, F., & Cahill, D. (2002). Discursiveness, contradiction, and unintended consequences in successive downsizings. *Management Communication Quarterly, 15*(4), 501–540.

Fairhurst, G. T., & Grant, D. (2010). The social construction of leadership: A sailing guide. *Management Communication Quarterly, 24*(2), 171–210.

Fairhurst, G. T., & Uhl-Bien, M. (2012). Organizational Discourse Analysis (ODA): Examining leadership as a relational process. *Leadership Quarterly, 23*(6), 1043–1062.

Fiedler, F. E. (1978). The contingency model and the dynamics of leadership process. In L. Berkowitz (Ed.), *Advances in experimental social psychology* (pp. 60–112). New York, NY: Academic Press.

Fleming, P., & Spicer, A. (2008). Beyond power and resistance: New approaches to organizational politics. *Management Communication Quarterly, 21*(3), 301–309.

Foldy, E. G., Goldman, L., & Ospina, S. (2008). Sensegiving and the role of cognitive shifts in the work of leadership. *Leadership Quarterly, 19*(5), 514–529.

Forester, J. (1999). *The deliberative practitioner*. Cambridge, MA: MIT Press.

Foucault, M. (1972). *The archeology of knowledge and the discourse on language*. London, England: Tavistock Publications.

Foucault, M. (1990). *The history of sexuality* (vol. 1). New York, NY: Vintage/Random House.

Foucault, M. (1995). *Discipline and punish*. New York, NY: Vintage/Random House.

Fournier, V., & Grey, C. (2000). At the critical moment: Conditions and prospects for critical management studies. *Human Relations, 53*(1), 7–32.

Gallie, W. B. (1956). Essentially contested concepts. *Proceedings of the Aristotelian Society. New series, 56 (1955–1956)*, 167–198.

Gardner, H. (2007, March). The ethical mind: A conversation with psychologist Howard Gardner. *Harvard Business Review, 85*(3), 51–56.

Gergen, K. J., Gergen, M. M., & Barrett, F. J. (2004). Dialogue: Life and death of the organization. In D. Grant, C. Hardy, C. Owick, N. Phillips, & L. L. Putnam (Eds.), *SAGE handbook of organizational discourse* (pp. 39–60). London, England: SAGE.

Giddens, A. (1979). *Central problems in social theory*. Berkeley: University of California Press.

Giddens, A. (1984). *The constitution of society*. Berkeley: University of California Press.

Gioia, D. A., & Chittipeddi, K. (1991). Sensemaking and sensegiving in strategic change initiation. *Strategic Management Journal, 12*(6), 433–448.

Goffman, E. (1974). *Frame analysis*. Philadelphia: University of Pennsylvania Press.

Gordon, R. D. (2010). Dispersed leadership: Exploring the impact of antecedent forms of power using a communicative framework. *Management Communication Quarterly, 24*(2), 260–287.

Graen, G. B. (2012). The new LMX theory: The missing link of interpersonal strategic alliances. In M. G. Rumsey (Ed.), *The many sides of leadership*. London, England: Oxford University Press.

Graen, G. B., & Uhl-Bien, M. (1995). Relationship-based approach to leadership: Development of a leader-member exchange (LMX) theory of leadership over 25 years—Applying a multi-level multi-domain perspective. *Leadership Quarterly, 6*(2), 219–247.

Grint, K. (1997). *Leadership: Classical, contemporary, and critical approaches*. Oxford, UK: Oxford University Press.

Grint, K. (2000). *The arts of leadership*. Oxford, UK: Oxford University Press.

Grint, K. (2005). Problems, problems, problems: The social construction of "leadership". *Human Relations, 58*(11), 1467–1494.

Grint, K. (2010). *Leadership: A very short introduction*. Oxford, UK: Oxford University Press.

Gronn, P. (1983). Talk as the work: The accomplishment of school administration. *Administrative Science Quarterly, 28*(1), 1–21.

Hall, M. (2010). Constructions of leadership at the intersection of discourse, power, and culture: Jamaican managers' narratives of leading in a postcolonial cultural context. *Management Communication Quarterly, 20*(4), 1–32.

Hansen, H., Ropo, A., & Sauer, E. (2007). Aesthetic leadership. *Leadership Quarterly, 18*(6), 544–560.

Hardy, C., & Clegg, S. R. (1996). Some dare call it power. In S. R. Clegg, C. Hardy, & W. R. Nord (Eds.), *Handbook of organization studies* (pp. 622–641). London, England: SAGE.

Harter, L. M., Leeman, M., Norander, S., Young, S. L., & Rawlins, W. K. (2008). The intermingling of aesthetic sensibilities and instrumental rationalities in a collaborative arts studio. *Management Communication Quarterly, 21*(4), 423–453.

Hearn, G., & Ninan, A. (2003). Managing change is managing meaning. *Management Communication Quarterly, 16*(4), 440–445.

Hofstede, G. (1980). *Culture's consequences: International differences in work-related values*. Beverly Hills, CA: SAGE.

Hosking, D. M. (1988). Organizing, leadership and skillful process. *Journal of Management Studies, 25*(2), 147–166.

House, R. J. (1977). A 1976 theory of charismatic leadership. In J. G. Hunt & L. L. Larson (Eds.), *Leadership: The cutting edge* (pp. 189–207). Carbondale: Southern Illinois University Press.

House, R. J., & Aditya, R. N. (1997). The social scientific study of leadership: Quo vadis? *Journal of Management, 23*(3), 409–473.

Huffaker, D. (2010). Dimensions of leadership and social influence in online communities. *Human Communication Research, 36*(4), 593–617.

Isaacs, W. (1999). *Dialogue: And the art of thinking together*. New York, NY: Currency.

Jian, G. (2007). Unpacking unintended consequences in planned organizational change: A process model. *Management Communication Quarterly, 21*(1), 5–28.

Jian, G. (2012). Revisiting the association of LMX quality with perceived role stressors: Evidence for inverted U relationships among immigrant employees. *Communication Research,* 0093650 211432468, first published on January 3, 2012.

Johnson, C. (2009). *Meeting the ethical challenges of leadership: Casting light or shadow.* Thousand Oaks, CA: SAGE.

Kelly, S. (2008). Leadership: A categorical mistake? *Human Relations, 61*(6), 763–782.

Kelly, S., White, M. I., Martin, D., & Rouncefield, M. (2006). Leadership refrains: Patterns of leadership. *Leadership, 2*(2), 181–201.

Kotter, J. P. (1990). *A force for change: How leadership differs from management.* New York, NY: Free Press.

Kramer, M. W. (1995). A longitudinal study of superior-subordinate communication during job transfers. *Human Communication Research, 22*(1), 39–64.

Ladkin, D. (2008). Leading beautifully: How mastery, congruence and purpose create the aesthetic of embodied leadership practice. *Leadership Quarterly, 19*(1), 31–41.

Laine, P-M., & Vaara, E. (2007). Struggling over subjectivity: A discursive analysis of strategic development in an engineering group. *Human Relations, 60*(1), 29–58.

Latour, B. (1994). On technical mediation: Philosophy, sociology, genealogy. *Common Knowledge, 3*(2), 29–64.

Latour, B. (2002). Gabriel Tarde and the end of the social. In P. Joyce (Ed.), *The social in question: New bearings in history and the social sciences* (pp. 117–133). London, England: Routledge.

Lee, J. (2001). Leader-member exchange, perceived organizational justice, and cooperative communication. *Management Communication Quarterly, 14*(4), 574–589.

Lewis, L. K. (2000). "Blindsided by that one" and "I saw that one coming": The relative anticipation and occurrence of communication problems and other problems in implementers' hindsight. *Journal of Applied Communication Research, 28*(1), 44–67.

Lewis, L. K. (2007). An organizational stakeholder model of change implementation communication. *Communication Theory, 17*(2), 176–204.

Lewis, L. K. (2011). *Organizational change: Creating change through strategic communication.* New York, NY: Wiley-Blackwell.

Lewis, L. K., Richardson, B. K., & Hamel, S. A. (2003). When the "stakes" are communicative: The lamb's and the lion's share during nonprofit planned change. *Human Communication Research, 29*(3), 400–430.

Lin, C., & Clair, R. P. (2007). Measuring Mao Zedong thought and interpreting organizational communication in China. *Management Communication Quarterly, 20*(4), 395–429.

Liu, H. (2010). When leaders fail: A typology of failures and framing strategies. *Management Communication Quarterly, 24*(2), 232–259.

Liu, L. (2010). *Conversations on leadership: Wisdom from global management gurus.* Hoboken, NJ: John Wiley & Sons.

Lord, R. G., & Emrich, C. G. (2001). Thinking outside the box by looking inside the box: Extending the cognitive revolution in leadership research. *Leadership Quarterly, 11*(4), 551–579.

Lord, R. G., Foti, R. J., & Phillips, J. S. (1982). A theory of leadership categorization. In J. G. Hunt, U. Sekaran, & C. A. Schriesheim (Eds.), *Leadership: Beyond establishment views* (pp. 104–121). Carbondale: Southern Illinois University Press.

Lord, R. G., & Hall, R. (2003). Identity, leader categorization, and leadership schema. In D. van Knippenberg & M. A. Hogg (Eds.), *Leadership and power: Identity processes in groups and organizations* (pp. 48–64). London, England: SAGE.

Marks, M. A., Zaccaro, S. J., & Mathieu, J. E. (2000). Performance implications of leader briefings and team-interaction training for team adaptation to novel environments. *Journal of Applied Psychology, 85*(6), 971–986.

Marshak, R. J., & Grant, D. (2008). Organizational discourse and new organization development practices. *British Journal of Management, 19*(1), S7–S19

Martin, D. M. (2004). Humor in middle management: Women negotiating the paradoxes of organizational life. *Journal of Applied Communication, 32*(2), 147–170.

McKenna, B., & Rooney, D. (2008). Wise leadership and the capacity for ontological acuity. *Management Communication Quarterly, 21*(4), 537–546.

McPhee, R. D., & Iverson, J. (2009). Agents of constitution in Communidad: Constitutive processes of communication in organizations. In L. L. Putnam & A. M. Nicotera (Eds.), *Building theories of organization: The constitutive role of communication* (pp. 49–88). New York, NY: Routledge.

McPhee, R. D., & Zaug, P. (2000). The communicative constitution of organizations: A framework for explanation. *The Electronic Journal of Communication, 10*(1/2), 1–16.

Medved, C. E., & Kirby, E. (2005). Family CEOs: A feminist analysis of corporate mothering discourses. *Management Communication Quarterly, 18*(4), 435–478.

Meindl, J. R., Ehrlich, S. B., & Dukerich, J. M. (1985). The romance of leadership. *Administrative Science Quarterly, 30*(1), 78–102.

Morgeson, F. P., DeRue, D. S., & Karam, E. P. (2010). Leadership in teams: A functional approach to understanding leadership structures and processes. *Journal of Management, 36*(1), 5–39.

Mumby, D. K. (2005). Theorizing resistance in organization studies: A dialectical approach. *Management Communication Quarterly, 19*(1), 19–44.

Mumby, D. K. (2007). Organizational communication. In G. Ritzer (Ed.), *The encyclopedia of sociology* (pp. 3290–3299). London, England: Blackwell.

Neufeld, D. J., Wan, Z., & Fang, Y. (2010). Remote leadership, communication effectiveness, and leader performance. *Group Decision and Negotiation, 19*(2), 227–246.

Olufowote, J. O., Miller, V. D., & Wilson, S. R. (2005). The interactive effects of role change goals and relational exchanges on employee upward influence tactics. *Management Communication Quarterly, 18*(3), 385–403.

Osland, J. S., & Bird, A. (2000). Beyond sophisticated stereotyping: Cultural sensemaking in context. *Academy of Management Perspectives, 14*(1), 65–79.

Osland, J. S., De Franco, S., & Osland, A. (1999). Organizational implications of Latin American culture: Lessons for the expatriate manager. *Journal of Management Inquiry, 8*(2), 219–237.

Papa, M. J., Auwal, M. A., & Singhal, A. (1995). Dialectic of control and emancipation in organizing for social change: A multitheoretic study of the Grameen Bank in Bangladesh. *Communication Theory, 5*(3), 189–223.

Parker, P. S. (2005). *Race, gender, and leadership.* Mahwah, NJ: Lawrence Erlbaum.

Perriton, L., & Reynolds, M. (2004). Critical management education: From pedagogy of possibility to pedagogy of refusal? *Management Learning, 35*(1), 61–77.

Purvanova, R. K., & Bono, J. E. (2009). Transformational leadership in context: Face-to-face and virtual teams. *Leadership Quarterly, 20*(3), 343–357.

Putnam, L. L. (1983). Organizational communication: Toward a research agenda. In L. L. Putnam & M. E. Pacanowsky (Eds.), *Communication and organizations: An interpretive approach* (pp. 31–54). Beverly Hills, CA: SAGE.

Putnam, L. L. (2003). Dialectical tensions and rhetorical tropes in negotiations. *Organization Studies, 25*(1), 35–53.

Putnam, L. L., Nicotera, A. M., & McPhee, R. D. (2009). Introduction: Communication constitutes organization. In L. L. Putnam & A. M. Nicotera (Eds.), *Building theories of organizations: The constitutive role of communication* (pp. 1–19). New York, NY: Routledge.

Real, K., & Putnam, L. L. (2005). Ironies in the discursive struggle of pilots defending the profession. *Management Communication Quarterly, 19*(1), 91–119.

Riley, P. (1988). The merger of macro and micro levels of leadership. In J. G. Hunt, B. R. Baglia, H. P. Dachler, & C. A. Schriesheim (Eds.), *Emerging leadership vistas* (pp. 80–83). Lexington, MA: Lexington Books.

Rittel, H., & Webber, M. (1973). Dilemmas in a general theory of planning. *Policy Sciences, 4*(2), 155–169.

Robichaud, D. (2003). Narrative institutions we organize by: The case of a municipal administration. In B. Czarniawska & P. Gagliardi (Eds.), *Narratives we organize by* (pp. 37–53). Amsterdam, the Netherlands: John Benjamins.

Rorty, R. (Ed.). (1967). *The linguistic turn: Recent essays in philosophical method.* Chicago, IL: University of Chicago Press.

Sager, K. L. (2008). An exploratory study of the relationships between Theory X/Y assumptions and superior communication style. *Management Communication Quarterly, 22*(2), 288–312.

Said, E. W. (1993). *Culture and imperialism.* New York, NY: Knopf.

Scandura, T. A., & Dorfman, P. W. (2004). Leadership research in an international and cross-cultural context. *Leadership Quarterly, 15*(2), 277–307.

Schon, D. A. (1983). *The reflective practitioner: How professionals think in action.* New York, NY: Basic Books.

Seeger, M., & Ulmer, R. (2003). Explaining Enron: Communication and responsible leadership. *Management Communication Quarterly, 17*(1), 58–84.

Seo, M., Putnam, L. L., & Bartunek, J. M. (2004). Contradictions and tensions of planned organizational change. In M. S. Poole & A. H. Van de Ven (Eds.), *Handbook of organizational change and innovation* (pp. 73–107). New York, NY: Oxford University Press.

Sewell, G., Barker, J. R., & Nyberg, D. (2012). Working under intensive surveillance: When does "measuring everything that moves" become intolerable? *Human Relations, 65*(2), 189–215.

Shannon, C., & Weaver, W. (1949). *The mathematical theory of communication*. Urbana: University of Illinois Press.

Sheep, M. L., Fairhurst, G. T., Khanzanchi, S., & Slay, H. (2010). *Knots, wickedness, and spiral death: Making sense of creativity tensions following an acquisition*. Montreal, Canada: Academy of Management.

Sherblom, J. C., Keranen, L., & Withers, L. A. (2002). Tradition, tension, and transformation: A structuration analysis of a game warden service in transition. *Journal of Applied Communication, 30*(2), 143–162.

Shi, X., & Wilson, S. R. (2010). Upward influence in contemporary Chinese organizations: Explicating the effects of influence goal type and multiple goal importance on message reasoning and politeness. *Management Communication Quarterly, 24*(4), 579–606.

Shipman, A. S., Byrne, C. L., & Mumford, M. M. (2010). Leader vision formation and forecasting: The effects of forecasting extent, resources, and timeframe. *Leadership Quarterly, 21*(3), 439–456.

Shockley-Zalabak, P., Morreale, S., & Hackman, M. (2010). *Building the high-trust organization: Strategies for supporting five key dimensions of trust*. San Francisco, CA: Jossey-Bass.

Shotter, J. (1993). *Conversational realities: Constructing life through language*. London, England: SAGE.

Shotter, J., & Cunliffe, A. L. (2003). Managers as practical authors: Everyday conversations for action. In D. Holman & R. Thorpe (Eds.), *Management and language* (pp. 1–37). London, England: SAGE.

Sias, P. M. (2009). *Organizing relationships: Traditional and emerging perspectives on work relationships*. Thousand Oaks, CA: SAGE.

Sillince, J. A. A. (2007). Organizational context and the discursive construction of organizing. *Management Communication Quarterly, 20*(4), 363–394.

Sinclair, A. (2005). Body possibilities in leadership. *Leadership, 1*(4), 387–406.

Sluss, D. M., Klimchak, M., & Holmes, J. J. (2008). Perceived organizational support as a mediator between relational exchange and organizational identification. *Journal of Vocational Behavior, 73*(3), 457–464.

Smircich, L., & Morgan, G. (1982). Leadership: The management of meaning. *Journal of Applied Behavioral Science, 18*(3), 257–273.

Sonenshein, S. (2010). We're changing—Or are we? Untangling the role of progressive, regressive, and stability narratives during strategic change implementation. *Academy of Management Journal, 53*(3), 477–512.

Sosik, J. J., & Jung, D. I. (2003). Impression management strategies and performance in information technology consulting: The role of self-other rating and agreement on charismatic leadership. *Management Communication Quarterly, 17*(2), 233–268.

Sparrowe, R. T., Soetjipto, B. W., & Kramer, M. L. (2006). Do leaders' influence tactics relate to members' helping behavior? It depends on the quality of the relationship. *Academy of Management Journal, 49*(6), 1194–1208.

Stam, D., Van Knippenberg, D., & Wisse, B. (2010). Focusing on followers: The role of regulatory focus and possible selves in visionary leadership. *Leadership Quarterly, 21*(3), 457–468.

Stensaker, I., & Falkenberg, J. (2007). Making sense of different responses to corporate change. *Human Relations, 60*(1), 137–177.

Stogdill, R. M., & Coons, A. E. (1957). *Leader behavior: Its description and measurement*. Columbus: Ohio State University Press for Bureau of Business Research.

Tangirala, S., Green, S. G., & Ramanujam, R. (2007). In the shadow of the supervisor's boss: How supervisors' relationships with their bosses influence frontline employees. *Journal of Applied Psychology, 92*(2), 309–320.

Taylor, J. R., & Van Every, E. (2000). *The emergent organization: Communication at its site and surface*. Mahwah, NJ: Lawrence Erlbaum.

Taylor, J. R., & Van Every, E. (2011). *The situated organization: Case studies in the pragmatics of communication research*. New York, NY: Routledge.

Thompson, G., & Vecchio, R. P. (2009). Situational leadership theory: A test of three versions. *Leadership Quarterly, 20*(5), 837–848.

Tourish, D. (2013). *The dark side of transformational leadership: A critical perspective.* London, England: Routledge.

Tourish, D., & Robson, P. (2006). Sensemaking and the distortion of critical upward communication in organizations. *Journal of Management Studies, 43*(4), 711–730.

Tourish, D., & Vatcha, N. (2005). Charismatic leadership and corporate cultism at Enron: The elimination of dissent, the promotion of conformity and organizational collapse. *Leadership, 1*(4), 455–480.

Tracy, S. J. (2004). Dialectic, contradiction, or double bind? Analyzing and theorizing employee reactions to organizational tensions. *Journal of Applied Communication Research, 32*(2), 119–146.

Trethewey, A., & Ashcraft, K. L. (2004). Practicing disorganization: The development of applied perspectives on living with tension. *Journal of Applied Communication, 32*(2), 81–88.

Triandis, H. C. (1993). *The contingency model in cross-cultural perspectives.* San Diego, CA: Academic Press.

Trompenaars, F. (1993). *Riding the waves of culture: Understanding cultural diversity in business.* London, England: Nicholas Brealey.

Uhl-Bien, M., Maslyn, J., & Ospina, S. (2011). The nature of relational leadership: A multi-theoretical lens on leadership relationships and processes. In D. Day & J. Antonakis (Eds.), *The nature of leadership* (2nd ed., pp. 289–330). London, England: SAGE.

Uhl-Bien, M., & Ospina, S. (Eds.). (2012). *Advancing relational leadership research: A dialogue among perspectives.* Charlotte, NC: Information Age.

Weick, K. (1979). *The social psychology of organizing* (2nd ed.). Reading, MA: Addison-Wesley.

Western, S. (2008). *Leadership: A critical text.* London, England: SAGE.

Wittgenstein, L. (1953). *Philosophical investigations.* Oxford, UK: Blackwell.

Wodak, R., Kwon, W., & Clarke, I. (2011). 'Getting people on board': Discursive leadership for consensus building in team meetings. *Discourse & Society, 22*(5), 592–616.

Xu, K. (2011). An empirical study of Confucianism: Measuring Chinese academic leadership. *Management Communication Quarterly, 25*(4), 644–662.

Ziegler, J. A. (2007). The story behind an organizational list: A genealogy of wildland firefighters' 10 standard fire orders. *Communication Monographs, 74*(4), 415–442.

Zoller, H. M., & Fairhurst, G. T. (2007). Resistance as leadership: A critical, discursive perspective. *Human Relations, 60*(9), 1331–1360.

Note

1. *WABA* stands for "within and between (group) analysis" (Dansereau, Alutto, & Yammarino, 1984).

CHAPTER 17

Information and Communication Technologies in Organizations

Ronald E. Rice and Paul M. Leonardi

Organizational researchers first began to study technology use seriously in organizations in the late 1950s and early 1960s. Since that time, two dominant streams of research have emerged. The first has focused on the relationship between technology use and an organization's formal and informal structure. The second has focused on how use of a newly implemented information and communication technology (ICT) shapes the way people communicate with one another within and across organizations. Over the years, the directions of both streams have flowed back and forth like a pendulum.

Technology and Organizational Structure

The pendulum of research on technology use and organizational structure has swung between the opposing philosophical poles of technological determinism and social constructivism. *Technological determinism* is the belief that the introduction of certain types of technologies (typically manufacturing or operational systems) directly causes certain kinds of outcomes, such as the centralization of an organization's decision making or the widening of its span of control. Early examples include Thompson and Bates's (1957) essays on the role of technology in the mechanization of work, Woodward's (1958) research into manufacturing and production organizations, and Perrow's (1967) examination of the administrative structure of U.S. hospitals.

By the 1980s, scholars who studied the relationship between technological and organizational change largely eschewed notions of technological determinism in favor of the philosophical stance of social construction. Social construction holds that both the meanings of and outcomes involving technology are shaped or mediated by the social contexts and interactions into which the new technology is implemented. For example, Johnson and Rice's (1987) study of the implementation of stand-alone word processing revealed that managers' initial agendas about, and the extent to which supervisors proactively shaped the uses and reinvention of, the systems lead to significantly different structuring and outcomes of word processing. More sociological approaches included structurational analyses of organizational information technology (IT), such as Barley's (1986) detailed study of how uses and meanings of hospital CT scanners were adapted by technicians and shaped organizational roles.

Since the early 2000s, the pendulum seems to oscillate somewhere in the middle. A new stream of research, somewhat similar to the earlier position of socio-technical systems analysis (Hirschheim, 1986), focuses on the *materiality* of technologies. This approach argues that although organizational users can exercise considerable discretion in choosing how the technology will affect their work, the artifact's functional properties do place some constraints on and offer particular opportunities for social action (Leonardi, 2009; Orlikowski, 2007).

Technology and Communication

During this same time period, research on the relationship between ICT use and communication occurring within and across organizations also followed pendulum-like swings. From the 1960s to the mid-1980s, numerous studies suggested technologically deterministic views about the relationship between technology use and effective communication. These studies suggested that certain types of information and communicative needs required particular kinds of media if they were to be effective (Daft & Lengel, 1986; Short, Williams, & Christie, 1976). By the late 1980s and early 1990s, the pendulum swung toward the constructivist pole, as studies showed how choices about what technologies to use for which communication activities were often the products of social negotiations and influence and subject to socially defined rubrics (DeSanctis & Poole, 1994; Fulk, Schmitz, & Steinfield, 1990; Rice, 1999; Rice & Aydin, 1991). Since the early 2000s, the pendulum characterizing the movement of this research stream has also been oscillating around a middle position. During the last decade, many researchers have shown that different communication technologies provide different capabilities for communication and that the value of these capabilities as they relate to communication effectiveness is a social construct (Leonardi, 2007; Rice & Gattiker, 2001).

Merging the Two Theoretical Visions

As these two research programs have begun to find a balance between the extreme perspectives that forged their histories, they have also come to take on many similarities. For example, one similarity is that both programs largely focus on the influences, implementation, use, and outcomes associated with ICT. *Information and communication(s) technologies* most generally refers to the devices, applications, media, and associated hardware and software that receive and distribute, process and store, and retrieve and analyze digital information between people and machines (as information) or among people (as communication). In the organizational context, ICT refers to a broad range of computer-based digital systems from transaction and information processing to wired and wireless communication media, connected through internal intranet or external Internet and wireless networks.

It no longer makes sense to treat these two research programs (on structure and on communication) separately. Additionally, organizational researchers have begun to rely on metatheoretical stances, such as structuration theory (Giddens, 1984), critical realism (Archer, 1995), actor-network theory (Latour, 2005), and theories of the communicative constitution of organizing (Ashcraft, Kuhn, & Cooren, 2009). Such approaches underscore how organizing is a process that is produced and sustained through people's routine communication with each other. Thus separating studies of ICTs' effects on organizing from their role in facilitating organizational communication seems unproductive. In other words, the communicative events that occur through organizational ICT use are also the building blocks of an organization's formal and informal structure (Rice & Gattiker, 2001).

Given these insights, our review of studies on ICT use in organizations over the last decade addresses four questions about ICTs and organizations: (1) What are the influences on ICT adoption, use, and outcomes? (2) Through what contexts and processes do ICTs' occasions change at various levels of analysis? (3) What outcomes are associated with ICT adoption and use? We then ask another question: (4) How do the three social science disciplines of communication, information systems, and management compare in their treatment of these questions?

We begin by summarizing the method by which we identified the major themes and general phases represented in our sample of articles. The subsequent section synthesizes empirical findings from these disciplines to show how they have answered the first three questions. The following section examines the fourth question by describing differences and similarities among the three disciplines in themes, theories, and method. The final section considers the intersection of these three fields to ask what researchers in general (and communication scholars in particular) might begin to explore about ICT use in organizations.

Analysis and Framework for Understanding ICT Use in Organizations

We chose major journals in the three disciplines that had the greatest research attention to ICTs: communication studies, information systems, and management.[1] We searched the online reference databases and publishers' sites for the years 2000 through August 2011, using broad search terms (*organize* and *tech*). From an initial 444 articles, we selected those that had (1) a focus on organizations and communication and (2) a focus on ICT use (thus not including financial investment strategies in technology, manufacturing, e-commerce, information systems security issues, or references to technology firms in general) but (3) were neither specifically methodological nor pedagogical, (4) were not focused specifically on systems design and evaluation issues, or (5) were not industry-level studies where organizations were merely represented as variables. This process narrowed the set to 202 relevant articles: 38 from communication, 101 from information systems, and 63 from management. Next, we iteratively read, discussed, and grouped the titles, abstracts, and articles based on their empirical findings, theoretical directions, and research approaches. That is, we did not apply a preexisting typology of research topics.

Thirteen general themes emerged from this process. *Influences* range from intentions and attitudes to emotions, norms, and power. *Technology* encompasses the various forms of ICT. *Levels* include *individual* (employee, role), *group* (team, network), *organizational*, and *societal* (community, organizational environment). *Structure* concerns issues of boundary, space, and time. *Process* covers design, implementation, adoption, and changes. *Interaction* emphasizes communicative processes, such as collaboration, discourse, and social relations. *Problems* vary from resistance to disruptions. *Knowledge* represents topics such as expertise and learning. *Outcomes* incorporate adoption, use, and adaptation of ICT and associated changes. *Research* is the method used (quantitative, qualitative) or type of article (review, theory). Table 17.1 lists the most frequent words from article titles that reflect each of these themes. Each article included one or more themes; for example, six articles had only one theme, 32 articles had six themes, and two articles had 11 themes.

We then iteratively discussed how these 13 themes might relate to each other. We did so within a general framework consisting of the influences on ICT use, the contexts and processes in which people use them, and the outcomes with which they are associated. Figure 17.1 portrays these three phases, how we felt the

Table 17.1 Research Themes in Article Titles and Most Frequent Words Associated With Each Theme

Influence: attitude; belief*; culture*; emotion; frame; gender; habit; influence**; intention*; norm; power*; support
Interaction: collaboration*; communication**; connectivity; control*; coordination*; discourse; face; feedback; interaction*; relation; shared; social**; talking*
Knowledge: cognitive; expertise; knowledge**; learning**; memory *; transactive; understanding*
Level—individual: customer; employee; individual*; member; peer; professional; role**; self; user**
Level—group: distributed*; group**; network**; team
Level—organizational: business; corporation; firm*; management*; organization**; workplace
Level—social: commons; community; environment; global; human; public; sector; world
Outcomes: acceptance**; adaptation; assimilation; behavior; capability; effect*; impact*; outcome; overload; perceived; performance*; reuse; satisfaction; usage
Problems: challenge; conflict*; disruptive; problem; resistance
Process: acquiring; action*; activity; adopt**; agency; change**; choice; construction; contribute; design; dynamic*; evolution; formation; implementation*; innovation**; managing*; organizing*; practice**; process*; task*; work**
Research: analysis*; approach; building; capturing; case*; commentary; concept*; determinant; dimension; empirical*; exploration*; extension; field; investigation; issue; longitudinal; model**; narrative; perspective**; predictor; research**; review; study**; test; theory**
Structure: boundary**; form; level; space; structure*; time**; virtual*
Technology: application; computer**; database; digital*; electronic; e-mail; groupware; ICT**; information**; interactive; internet**; machines; media*; mediated; mobile; nomadic; online*; software; system**; technical; technology**

Note: no asterisk = 2 to 4 occurrences; * = between 5 and 10; ** = more than 10.

themes were positioned within and across them, and the percentage representation of themes overall and by the three disciplines (C=communication, I=information systems, and M=management). The arrangement of each theme's box in the figure implies, based on the vertical dotted lines, how they overlap in phases. For example, analyses of social interaction occurred primarily within the contexts/processes phase, while issues involving levels occurred in all three phases. This initial framework also suggests that the level, structure, and process themes may moderate or mediate relationships among the three phases. For example, the relationship between the kind of technology and knowledge sharing may vary based on the level of communication. Thus the framework represents a general model of causal relationships among the themes across the phases within the analyzed articles.

Figure 17.1 General Framework Representing Relationships Among Themes and Phases Represented in Articles on Organizations and ICTs

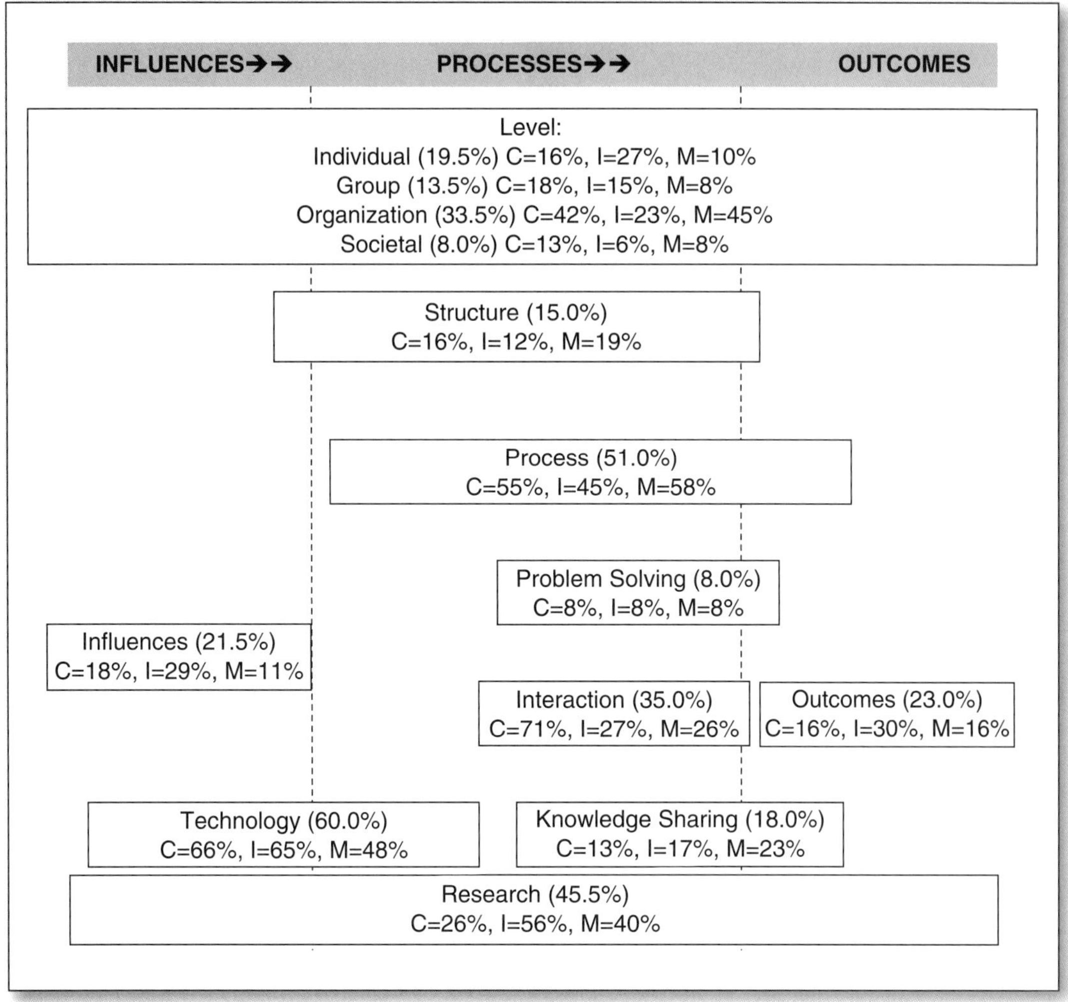

Note: The location of each theme portrays the relationships among the themes, indicating how the various themes might array along the general causal framework. Note that some themes overlap across phases. Percentages are of each theme occurring in all article titles (in parentheses) and in discipline-specific article titles (C = communication, I = information systems, M = management).

Research on Influences, Processes, and Outcomes Across Disciplines

This section explores answers to our three main research questions. First, we discuss what factors influence the adoption, use, and subsequent outcomes associated with the introduction of new ICTs in organizations. Our analysis highlights various phenomena that shape people's reactions to a new technology. We then turn our focus toward an explanation of the contexts in and processes through which ICTs occasion organizational change. These processes may vary depending upon the level at which social action takes place. The third section highlights types of outcomes associated with the adoption and use of ICTs within organizations.

Influences: What Factors Shape ICT Adoption, Use, and Outcomes?

A major research tradition of ICT is *adoption*, particularly exploring the evolution of the technology acceptance model (TAM; Venkatesh, Davis, & Morris, 2007). This model incorporates four influences (performance expectancy, effort expectancy, social influence, and facilitating conditions) on behavioral intentions, which then affect technology use. Moreover, these relationships are moderated by gender, age, experience, and voluntariness of use and have demonstrated strong validity, reliability, and predictive power.

Another central theoretical approach to influences on ICT adoption is examining it as a *socially situated process*. That is, the adoption and use of organizational ICTs are not solely individual decisions nor determined necessarily by objective or even perceived characteristics. Influences may come from individual (e.g., innovativeness and self-efficacy), social (e.g., influence), and institutional (e.g., top management commitment) contexts (Lewis, Agarwal, & Sambamurthy, 2003) via central or peripheral cognitive processing routes (Bhattacherjee & Sanford, 2006).

Intraorganizational Norms and Agendas. Social influence and norms may come from a variety of sources, may be supportive or resistant, and may have both intended and unintended consequences. In the case of one organization's IT planning, three influences played a major role: the company's business process reengineering, the consultant, and the organization's business environment. These three converged in the development of new rules and norms about crucial aspects and relevant stakeholders that limited the consideration of alternatives because of detrimental results (Tillquist, 2002). Opinion seekers may have greater influence on one's attitudes about an ICT than opinion leaders because of the implied status conferral (Vishwanath, 2006). Moreover, the influence of the number of opinion seekers on attitudes may be moderated by the degree of cohesiveness of the group—indicating internalization of attitudes rather than compliance with the group norm. One department's positive rationales for adoption of an ICT (or technology concept) may be rejected by other departments within the same organization, what Leonardi (2011a) calls *innovation blindness*. But both this rejection and the diffusion of technology across organizational boundaries may reflect a reciprocal influence process that takes place over time. Ongoing usage is also likely to alter one's beliefs and attitudes and affect the nature of subsequent use (Bhattacherjee & Premkumar, 2004).

Johnson and Rice (1987) analyzed how initial *agenda setting* (framing of the problem and potential solutions) in an organizations' adoption process influenced the failure or successful integration of stand-alone word processing. Messages about a potential ICT, which are particularly influential during early stages of adoption, can reframe salient attributes of a technology, thereby helping to constrain and organize the innovation's meaning. Vishwanath's (2009) experiment revealed how social influence frames affected how important particular attributes and expectations about an ICT were, which in turn affected adoption decisions. Positive framing, then, can generate unrealistic expectations and lead to rejection or later disadoption. The strongest effect occurred when the frame presented negative social information about the innovation. Similar to agenda setting and framing, influences may also consist of *metaphors* about the hazards or success of technologies (such as silver bullets or the inherent uniqueness of every innovation and its context; Ramiller, 2001; see also Hiemstra, 1983).

Emotions. The influence of emotions on adoption, use, and outcomes are underanalyzed. TAM could be extended to include emotional and psychological aspects of use and users (such as temporal dissociation, focused immersion, heightened enjoyment, control, curiosity, playfulness, and innovativeness) as factors that affect perceived ease of use and usefulness (Ahuja & Thatcher, 2005), thus increasing the likelihood of adopting an ICT. Ortiz de Guinea and Markus (2009) believe that emotion, consensus, and automatic behavior may be more important than traditional concepts in explaining ongoing use. Other influential emotions include challenge, achievement, loss and deterrence (Beaudry & Pinsonneault, 2010), or cognitive absorption (consisting of temporal dissociation, focused immersion, heightened enjoyment, control, and curiosity; Agarwal & Karahanna, 2000).

Power. Power affects communication, meaning, and decisions about the use of new ICTs (Avgerou & McGrath, 2007), whether at the governmental, organizational, managerial, vendor, IT culture, or user level. Jasperson et al.'s review (2002, especially Table 6) concluded that analyses that focus on technology or focus on power and the interactions between these two lenses differentially emphasize the development, deployment, management, use, and impact of organizational ICTs. Ball and Wilson's (2000) analysis of interpretive repertoires revealed that both individual and institutional discourses about a computer-based performance monitoring system engaged power in different but interlinked ways.

Organizational Culture. An organization's culture is both a direct and moderating influence on ICT adoption and implementation (Harrington & Guimaraes, 2005). The term *culture* generally refers to "specific norms, values, assumptions, and social structures that shape members' beliefs and behaviors within these organizations" (Gallivan & Srite, 2005, p. 299). One cultural characteristic specifically related to new ICTs (and much studied) is *absorptive capacity*, the "organization's ability to recognize the value of new information, assimilate it, and apply it to commercial ends" (p. 39).

Understanding cultural influences is especially salient with increased corporate mergers, globalization, and standardization of business practices. Organizational culture research needs to be integrated into ICT research, which Gallivan and Srite (2005) attempt to do through social identity theory. This theory argues that individuals have both personal identities and social identities. Indeed, they may have membership in multiple social identities, including organizational and national cultures. These identities are associated with categorization, identification with certain groups, and social comparison (of in-groups and out-groups) processes. Each of these identities can influence attitudes toward and ways of adopting and using ICTs (e.g., relevant regulations, mediated trust, support for reinvention, gender roles). For example, cultures with high respect for authority are likely to adopt an ICT more readily but with less reinvention (Al-Shohaib, Frederick, Jamal Al-Kandari, & Dorsher, 2010). Leidner and Kayworth (2006) integrate IT and cross-cultural research to develop a *theory of IT-culture conflict* at organizational and national levels. This theory highlights the importance of fit between value orientations of the potential users and values embedded in the IT. Developing a match between organizational and national culture and IT values reduces conflict and thus increases adoption and use of new technology.

Institutional Forces. Organizations may also be influenced by *other organizations*, especially if the focal organizations perceive themselves as leaders, scan the environment, and emulate other leaders (Teo, Wei, & Benbasat, 2003; Zorn, Flanagin, & Shoham, 2011). Organizations may also learn about an ICT concept through consultants, the press and industry discourse, other firms, industrial infrastructure, and so on (Wang, 2009).

Materiality. The physical and digital properties of ICTs may also influence the way people adopt and use them. *Materiality* refers to the arrangement of an artifact's physical and/or digital materials into particular forms that endure across differences in place. Use of the adjective *material* is chosen to remind readers that there are some aspects of the technology that are intrinsic to it and not part of the social context in which the technology was used.

Orlikowski (2000), for example, wrote that software for groupware embodies "particular symbol and material properties," such as features contained in a program's menus (p. 406). Leonardi (2007) documented use of a help-desk queuing software by IT technicians and argued that its "material features" made possible activities such as assigning jobs or documenting what one did to solve a particular use problem (p. 816). Thus the materiality of an ICT, by virtue of providing capabilities to do some things and by making others difficult, can shape the way that people decide to adopt and use it (Jonsson, Holmström, & Lyytinen, 2009; Wagner, Newell, & Piccoli, 2010).

In turn, other scholars argue that the materiality of a technology is so thoroughly shaped by social processes, and is always interpreted and used in the context of social interaction, that it makes most sense to describe people's organizational activities with a new ICT as *socio-material* (Orlikowski, 2007). Within this emerging perspective, scholars have set forth two arguments for how to study the relationship between the social and the material. The first suggests that researchers should refrain from treating activities of technology development and use as *special cases* of the organizing process and instead should examine what the material characteristics of a technology do once they have become *constitutively entangled* in organizational life. Thus Orlikowski and Scott (2008) urge researchers to move away from studying development, implementation, and initial use and instead study technologies already incorporated in people's routine practices. The second argument takes a different approach by insisting that such activities mark a time when an existing socio-material fabric is disturbed, offering researchers an opportunity to see more clearly how the social and the material become constitutively entangled (Leonardi & Barley, 2008, 2010). This claim means that, in addition to studying social processes, researchers should attend to what a technology lets developers, implementers, and users do; what it does not let them do; and how people work around these constraints (Rice & Cooper, 2010; Rice & Schneider, 2006).

Processes: How Do ICTs Occasion Change at Different Levels of Analysis?

Technology and organization researchers have explored ICT adoption, implementation, and use in a variety of contexts and processes. As indicated in Figure 17.1, we identify nine major processes of organizational ICTs: four primary levels of analysis (*individual*, *group*, *organizational*, and *societal*), *organizational structure* (Leonardi & Bailey, 2008), *process* (Sykes, Venkatesh, & Gosain, 2009), *problems* (Flanagin, 2000; Rice & Cooper, 2010; Rice & Schneider, 2006), *social interaction* (Sherif & Menon, 2004), and *knowledge* (Vaast & Walsham, 2005).

Individual Level. Individuals' decisions to use ICTs are shaped by many personal factors, such as competence at using the technology's features (Vaast, 2007), familiarity with professional and organizational communication genres (Rains & Young, 2006), impression management goals (Leonardi, Treem, & Jackson, 2010), need for productivity (Fulk, Heino, Flanagin, Monge, & Bar, 2004), and internal motivation (Woiceshyn, 2000).

Most research implicitly assumes that individuals use only one ICT when communicating with others, but Stephens (2007) and her colleagues show that people use *ICTs in sequence* when they are preparing for meetings, performing daily tasks, or following up to persuade (Stephens, Sørnes, Rice, Browning, & Sætre, 2008). When people need to follow up on initial communication episodes, the overall groupings of ICTs represent two underlying attributes: degree of connection with others and extent of synchronicity. These ICT sequences can expand cues and channels and provide error-reducing redundancy for equivocal and uncertain tasks.

Researchers also focus on *emotions* surrounding the use of a new ICT. McGrath (2006), for example, found that strong emotional reactions to a new technology often led to innovations in use. Indeed, people's emotions may be stronger predictors of continued ICT use in organizations than most rational-oriented models of planned behavior and reasoned action would propose (Ortiz de Guinea & Markus, 2009). Rennecker and Godwin (2005) showed that ICTs that disrupted and interrupted people's work often resulted in delays, which caused users to become frustrated with and often abandon their new tools. Ragu-Nathan, Tarafdar, Ragu-Nathan, and Tu (2008) introduced the concept of *technostress*—stress experienced by end users of technologies in organizations, which was associated with decreased job satisfaction and organizational commitment. Beaudry and Pinsonneault (2010) found that users choose different coping strategies when adjusting to a newly implemented technology, based on whether they feel they have control over their situation or not.

Individual *perceptions and motivations* obviously affect ICT adoption and use. One's perception of perceived switching costs (time, effort, and uncertainty associated with changing to a new ICT), generated from one's own experimentation with the ICT, also helps explain continued use or rejection (Kim & Kankanhalli, 2009). Gender may influence what an individual focuses on when they perceive or assess a new ICT. For example, men's technology decisions were more strongly influenced by their perceptions of its usefulness (Venkatesh & Morris, 2000), while women were more strongly influenced by perceptions of ease of use and subjective norms circulating in an organization. Research in the 1990s focused heavily on the extent to which *social influence* from one's peers influenced adoption (e.g., Fulk, Schmitz, & Steinfield, 1990; Kraut, Rice, Cool, & Fish, 1998; Rice & Aydin, 1991). Although social influence remains important, in the last decade, scholars have begun to explore the impact of organizational environment on an individual's perceptions of a new ICT's usefulness. Jeyaraj and Sabherwal (2008) noted that when individuals developed perceptions of an ICT's usefulness by matching their perceptions of the technology's capabilities to the needs of the organization, writ large, they were more likely to adopt the innovation fully than when they let themselves be influenced by the opinions of their coworkers. Similarly, Leonardi (2009) showed that individuals spent a good deal of time alone with the newly implemented ICT, testing its features and matching emerging perceptions of utility to information about the ICT provided by the organization. Alignment between their perceptions and the information explained continued system use or abandonment.

Group Level. Newly implemented ICTs may bring individuals into contact with other employees who do not normally interact with one another, such as organizational units that obtain and provide different kinds of information (Aydin & Rice, 1992). Virtual teams are common contexts for *new interactions* of this type (Jones, Ravid, & Rafaeli, 2004; Kirkman, Rosen, Tesluk, & Gibson, 2004; Maznevski & Chudoba, 2000; Timmerman & Scott, 2006), as are colocated, cross-functional, or multidivisional teams (Butler, 2001; Black, Carlile, & Repenning, 2004). Studies by Bechky (2003); Boland, Lyytinen, and Yoo (2007); and Carlile (2004) concluded that the design and use of new ICTs were occasions in which new groups were formed from members of different occupational communities. The groups relied on the visual representations *of* the technologies or *produced by* the technologies to help them learn to speak a common language. Other studies have shown that new technologies can reduce task conflict, although team leaders may also mitigate task conflict by performing coordinator activities (Wakefield, Leidner, & Garrison, 2008).

These potential and actual group interactions, however, can also generate *obstacles to adoption* and use. In these new interaction contexts, group members often build shared meaning and translate knowledge across boundaries. Membership in multiple organizational social groups created tensions for potential adopters of data-conferencing technology in a large distributed organization (Mark & Poltrock, 2004). To function effectively, all team members must adopt the ICT and use it in similar ways. Some members may face resistance from other professional, occupational, and social worlds to which they belong (Aydin & Rice, 1992). Moreover, problems of coordinating cultural differences can proliferate when new technologies bring groups of scientists together (Walsh & Maloney, 2007). In one study, when scientists and engineers came together to collaborate on the design of a new rocket thruster, the team initially experienced significant misalignments among the organizational environment, group, and technology structures (Majchrzak, Rice, Malhotra, King, & Ba, 2000). To resolve these misalignments and effectively share information and knowledge, the team had to modify team structure, the organizational environment, and the technology itself.

Other studies have focused on the role that particular *members play in shaping a group's use of an ICT* over time. Edmondson, Bohmer, and Pisano (2001) noted that successful implementers of a new technology underwent a qualitatively different team-learning process than those who were unsuccessful. Successful implementers were team leaders who used enrollment to motivate the team, designed preparatory practice sessions and early trials to create psychological safety and encourage new behaviors, and promoted shared meaning and process improvement through reflective practices. A team's existing informal communication network can moderate the effects that technologies have on information sharing and knowledge transfer. Generally, people in a group use a new ICT to share knowledge with each other when they perceive that it enhances their professional reputations, when they have experience to share, and when they are structurally embedded in a network. Surprisingly, though, contributions often occur without expectations of reciprocal knowledge sharing from others (Heinz & Rice, 2009; Jian & Jeffres, 2006; Wasko & Faraj, 2005).

In a series of studies, Yuan and colleagues (Yuan et al., 2005; Yuan, Fulk, Monge, & Contractor, 2010) showed that perceived *team member behavior and technology-specific competence* were positively related to an individual's use of intranets for knowledge sharing. These findings supported a socialized model of motivation to participate in organizational information sharing through the use of collective repositories. This model suggested that management could boost levels of intranet usage through group-level social influence and technology-specific training. In addition, although the relationship between directory development (who knows what in the group) and expertise exchange was mediated by communication tie strength and moderated by shared task interdependence, team-level variables were also significantly related to individual-level outcomes.

Organizational Level. The topics of *organizational learning* and *knowledge management* have received considerable treatment in the literature, including how ICTs may enhance both (Alavi & Leidner, 2001). Organizational variables can affect the rate and extent of organizational learning after the implementation of a new ICT (García-Morales, Matías-Reche, & Verdú-Jover, 2011). For example, prior organizational learning moderates the effects of newly implemented ICTs on organizational effectiveness (Harwood, 2011). Studies by Kane and Alavi (2007) and Nan (2011) found that ICT-based learning mechanisms enable capabilities that have a distinct effect on the exploration (finding out new knowledge) and exploitation (applying known knowledge) dynamics in the organization. Further, this effect is dependent on organizational and environmental conditions as well as on the interaction effects between technological mechanisms when used in combination with one another. The use of an ICT platform can produce online profiles of new and experimental work practices and help diffuse them within a user community (Kang, 2006).

A second related major theme at the organizational level is *organizational decision making*. Decision making is typically defined as the organization's ability to leverage past learning to make rational and, sometimes, optimal decisions. Harrington and Guimaraes (2005) found that an organization's *absorptive capacity*—its ability to absorb and make sense of new information given past areas of expertise—influenced the use of ICTs to improve organizational decision making. Zorn, Flanagin, and Shoham (2011) noted that nonprofit organizations that adopted and used technologies tended to be self-perceived industry leaders or ones that scanned the environment and emulated other leaders. They also tended to be spurred by institutional forces if they were characterized by self-perceived leadership and appropriate organizational resources. Such institutional forces influenced the kinds of decisions that organizations made based on use of ICTs.

Societal Level. At the societal level, research has addressed the relationship between *popular discourse about ICTs* that has circulated in history or popular culture and strategies that organizational actors take to control their work when they use new tools. For example, nongovernmental organizations often appropriate technology discourse that is popular in society (Ganesh, 2003). However, because of limited conceptualizations of what technology is and can do, such organizations often define their rural constituents as a passive market. In addition, Leonardi (2008) observes that managers often draw on technologically deterministic discourses circulated in Western societies to promote certain organizational changes. Further, they blame organizational changes on stereotypic notions of technological progress and remove themselves from being seen as agents of change. Wang (2009, 2010) showed that the popularity of an ICT innovation in tech culture and in popular press responds to the broad climate of business. Firms whose names were associated with ICT fashions in the press did not have higher performance, but they had better reputations and higher executive compensations. Companies who invested in ICTs that were currently in fashion also had higher reputations and executive pay than did those who did not, but they also had lower performance in the short term and improved performance in the long term. Thus, following fashion can legitimate organizations and their leaders, regardless of performance improvement in the short term.

Organizations may have *identities with inertial tendencies,* because they are well known in society at large and their identities are reinforced by outsiders and the press (Munir & Phillips, 2005). For example, Tripsas (2009) found that in firms of this type, capitalizing on identity-challenging technologies is difficult for two reasons. First, identity serves as a filter, such that organizational members notice and interpret external stimuli in a manner consistent with the existing identity (similar to framing and agenda setting). Second, because identity becomes intertwined with routines, procedures, and beliefs of both organizational and external constituents, explicit efforts to accommodate to the identity-challenging technology are difficult.

Outcomes: What Follows From ICT Adoption and Use?

Research considers a wide variety of outcomes (i.e., consequences, implications, effects) associated with ICT adoption and use. From the more proximate to the more distal, or the more individual to the more organizational, we group them into seven types of outcomes: adoption/acceptance/adaptation, organizational assimilation, conflict, knowledge management, structure, organizational environment, and performance.

Adoption, Acceptance, and Adaptation. The primary outcomes of influences and processes are adoption and use of the ICT. The *adoption* process includes more than just adopting or rejecting the technology (Rice, 2009; Rogers, 2003). Research also examines rejection, discontinuance, acceptance, and adaptation/reinvention.

Indeed, Barki, Titah, and Boffo (2007) conceptualize user-related activity of information systems as including adoption, acceptance, and adaptation.

Acceptance includes concepts such as user satisfaction, responses, attitudes, and beliefs and whether the ICT is integrated with or routinized into other work processes. Acceptance does not necessarily follow from initial adoption or system use but depends on user satisfaction. Scholars are expanding research on end-user satisfaction through exploring different theoretical explanations. Au, Ngai, and Cheng (2008) apply expectation, needs, and equity theories to argue that the ratio of inputs to needs (equitable needs fulfillment) varies across individuals; thus the technical aspects of a new ICT alone cannot explain end-user satisfaction. This work suggests that research would benefit from integrating user satisfaction (beliefs and attitudes about using the system) with ICT acceptance (beliefs and attitudes about the system; Wixom & Todd, 2005). Managerial frames (e.g., benefits, threats, and adjustments) may interact with organizational capabilities (technological opportunism and sophistication) to affect the use of technologies, such as business-to-business electronic markets (Mishra & Agarwal, 2010). Overall, assimilating technologies into organizational practice, as opposed to simply using them, seems necessary for integration and for sharing fragmented organizational knowledge (Purvis, Sambamurthy, & Zmud, 2001). Institutional forces play both a constraining and facilitating role in such assimilation (see also Rice & Gattiker, 2001).

Adaptation or *reinvention* is the process whereby individuals, groups, and organizations modify, reinvent, appropriate, or adapt particular features or uses of a new ICT (Johnson & Rice, 1987). This is a subtle and complex process that takes place over time and may be heavily constrained by preexisting social and organizational norms, managerial agendas, individual needs and abilities, work networks, training, and technology features. Feedback about the use of technologies includes such responses as maintaining current practices, supplementing channels, expanding or learning new uses, or discontinuing use (Waldeck, Seibold, & Flanagin, 2004). The research model developed by Jasperson, Carter, and Zmud (2005) sets forth factors that influence continued acceptance and adaptation, including organizational interventions (internal and external experts, managerial support, incentives), individual learning interventions (e.g., training, experimentation with features, peers), and individual cognitions (e.g., innovation attributes, expectancies, behavioral control, media characteristics, social influences) and differences (demographics, cognitive style, use voluntariness, organizational position).

Software reuse and *knowledge reuse* are two appropriate arenas for studying ICT adaptation. For example, Sherif and Menon (2004) show, through four case studies of software reuse, that actors at various organizational levels change strategy, process, and culture to enable innovative applications of the software. Further, these changes become new routines that increase an organization's absorptive capacity, thereby improving its ability to implement future innovations. Unfortunately, discrepant or misaligned events may stimulate unexpected and dysfunctional adaptations (Rice & Cooper, 2010). Specifically, Leonardi's (2007) study revealed that such events led technicians to appropriate certain features of an ICT service management tool, which resulted in generating new information and knowledge management potentials, fostering different advice networks, and changing an organization's social structure.

Organizational Assimilation. A few studies assess how ICTs affect an individual's *organizational assimilation* (or *socialization*), that is, the extent to which newcomers learn about and adjust to the culture, values, and norms of an organization. In Waldeck, Seibold, and Flanagin's (2004) study, advanced technologies were second in importance only to face-to-face communication in fostering the socialization of new employees. Use of workplace technologies can also shape organizational members' construals and enactments of time (such as pace, urgency, or future perspective) as elements of organizational culture (Ballard & Seibold, 2004).

Conflict. Several studies analyze how new technologies contribute to conflict or are used to manage it. These conflicts may arise from the acceptance and adaptation processes of ICTs or the unexpected and undesirable problems that occur in technology use. Conflict is especially likely to arise if an ICT disrupts existing organizational structures and work processes. In the context of software reuse, managerial interventions, such as coordination mechanisms and organizational learning practices, often reduce conflict (Sherif, Zmud, & Browne, 2006). Virtual teams may also generate conflicts due to geographical, cultural, professional, and temporal differences and dispersion (Majchrzak et al., 2000; Wakefield et al., 2008). Hence, virtual team leaders must use ICTs to occupy various roles for different kinds of conflict.

Knowledge Management. ICTs may affect or restructure organizational knowledge management by changing encoding, storage, retrieval, coordination, and reuse processes (Heinz & Rice, 2009). These changes in turn can improve knowledge sharing and use as well as team performance (Choi, Lee, & Yoo, 2010). Nonetheless, there is considerable doubt about the effectiveness of knowledge management systems, partially because of the crucial role of *tacit knowledge* (experiential understanding not easily transferable) that is difficult to manage through technologies. More generally, Ruey-Lin, Tsai, and Ching-Fang (2006) showed that interactions among the technical, social, and innovative contexts in a semiconductor-fabrication equipment company explained problems in knowledge transfer, coordination, and reuse. Closely related, communicative structures such as advice networks may be reshaped when users appropriate an ICT in response to discrepant events. In Leonardi's (2007) study of technicians in a large IT organization, appropriations generated new and different types of information. This new information became the basis for seeking and finding advice in different ways and through different organizational member networks.

Structure. ICTs may provide the occasion for changes in organizational structure at different levels and in either content (e.g., discourse) or relationships (communicative or transactional; Rice & Gattiker, 2001). Organizational-level studies have explored the validity of a number of popular hypotheses about technology's effects on organization form and function. For example, new technologies do not always bring about the demise of hierarchy or the fixtures of authority that historically dominate organizations (Schwarz, 2002). Hierarchy may be reshaped or reinforced, depending on management's implementation approach and nonmanagement's responses. Although ICTs may facilitate organizational downsizing, technologies do not deterministically cause it. Adverse environmental conditions can trigger downsizing, and the role that technologies play in organizational downsizing may vary according to the change strategy (Pinsonneault & Kraemer, 2002).

Organizational Environment. Two societal-level structural outcomes include the organization's *market environment* and its *public communication space.* In the market context, ICTs can influence managerial decisions to engage in new structural relationships with other organizations (e.g., a CEO considering entering the fiber-optics product market) and levels of organizational factors (e.g., orientation toward emerging or existing technology; Eggers & Kaplan, 2009). In public online Usenet groups, levels of interaction and information overload shape both the content and relational structure of message as well as response complexity and participation duration (Jones et al., 2004). Straub and Watson's review (2001) focuses on the network-enabled relationships of businesses with consumers and identifies four primary research issues: strategy, organizational design, metrics, and managing ICTs.

Performance. Finally, a primary motivation for implementing ICTs is to improve performance, whether at the individual, group, organizational, or societal level. At the individual level, IT "road warriors" suffer from family-work conflicts, overload, lack of reward fairness, and job autonomy. These factors can lead to exhaustion and turnover, which negatively affect performance (Ahuja, Chudoba, Kacmar, McKnight, & George, 2007). Thus technology management strategies need to consider sources of stress for this type of worker. At the group level, ICT managers may coordinate activities among their employees to improve user performance, but organizational climate (especially attitudes about the ICT organizational function) significantly moderates that relationship (Li, Jiang, & Klein, 2003). At the organizational level, a different kind of ICT-related performance is web-based search success. In this case, web sites that provide a sense of context (i.e., cues about the organization of and one's location within the information space) reduce the use of search and improve retrieval performance (Webster & Ahuja, 2006).

Disciplinary Differences in the Study of ICTs in Organizations

This section explores differences in the ways that the fields of communication, information systems, and management address the three research questions examined in the literature published between 2000 and 2011. We begin by assessing different ways they approach influences, contexts and processes, and outcomes. Next, we compare the theoretical approaches they use to conceptualize organizational action within each of these phases. Finally, we highlight similarities and differences in the foci these disciplines make in their research on ICT use in organizations.

Themes

The percentages in Figure 17.1 indicate the most frequent themes overall and the degree to which each discipline examines them. Overall, technology, process, and level themes occurred in more than half of the articles, followed by research, interaction, outcomes, influences, and problems.

Influences. Researchers in the field of information systems focus the most on the factors that influence ICT adoption, use, and outcomes in organizational settings, while those in management are the least interested in this question. Additionally, scholars in communication and information systems spend the most time documenting and describing the ICT artifacts and systems that they study, while management researchers focus on these features in fewer than half of their articles (for a similar account, see Orlikowski & Scott, 2008).

Contexts and Processes. Information systems researchers place most of their focus on the individual-level of analysis, while scholars in management attend to the organizational level. Communication researchers focus mostly on the organizational level of analysis but also have the highest percentage of attention on the group and societal levels.

Questions of structure and process are treated nearly equally across disciplines. However, research in management tends to combine both structure and process more than the other two disciplines do. For example, many studies discuss how processes enacted by organizational members produce or constitute the organizational structures in which they work (Doolin, 2003; Leonardi, 2011b; Orlikowski, 2007). It is surprising that organizational communication researchers have done less integration of structure and process, insofar as communication studies dominate the percentage of articles that focus on people's interactions about new ICTs (with much lower percentages in information systems and management). This finding may be due in part to the long tradition of constitutive models of communication within the field, which hold that communication constitutes organizational structures, and to a focus on relationships, network analysis, and interactions.

Outcomes. Information systems researchers have spent more time considering the outcomes associated with ICT use in organizations than have the other two disciplines. However, when interaction is considered an outcome, communication researchers often specify how ICTs affect organizational relationships. Management researchers have turned their attention to outcomes, especially change in organizational knowledge.

Theories

As articles in each discipline often use the same set of theories, the following subsections identify the theories that appear in at least two articles in any of three phases. Overall, the most frequent theories that communication scholars emphasize are social interaction (social influence, social network theory, and social constructivism) and diffusion processes and attributes (diffusion of innovations, structuration and adaptive structuration, and media richness).

By far the most frequent information systems theory was the TAM or its extension, the Unified Theory of Acceptance and Use of Technology (UTAUT; Venkatesh, Morris, Davis, & Davis, 2003), followed by the related theories of reasoned action, social cognitive theory, and theory of planned behavior, as well as expectation disconfirmation theory and information processing theory. The use of these theories indicates a strong emphasis on individual adoption and use of ICTs, as was noted under the individual-level section. The use of activity, practice, and social network theories characterize the work on group and organizational levels. Theories also address ICT and organizational characteristics, such as materiality, task-technology fit, and absorptive capacity. Finally, organization-level theories include institutional theory, social shaping of technology, and structuration theory.

In management articles, structuration is the most frequently applied theory, followed by institutional theory. All other theories occurring more than once in management focus on the firm (knowledge-based theory of the firm, transaction cost economics), innovation processes (organizational learning, exploration/exploitation), emergent processes (collective action), or metatheoretical approaches (e.g., critical realist perspective, actor-network theory). As noted, organizational level and process are the only two themes in which there were proportionally more management articles.

Interestingly, the majority of the most frequently used theories in each discipline are unique to that discipline. The only common theoretical concerns across the disciplines—i.e., theories that appear in at least two articles in at least two disciplines—include structuration theory, institutional theory, diffusion of innovations theory, and social network theory (including actor-network theory).

Methods

Table 17.2 summarizes the extent to which articles in each of the disciplines employed qualitative, quantitative, or mixed-method analyses or were theory or review articles. Overall, qualitative and quantitative analysis methods were used about equally. Still, clear differences existed by discipline. Management articles used qualitative methods more frequently than other disciplines, while communication articles used them the least frequently. Communication and information systems differed in their use of qualitative methods but were equally likely to use quantitative methods. In general, information systems researchers were the most explicit in discussing research methods and approaches for studying the relationship between technologies and organization. Only communication articles used mixed methods in any notable amount.

A number of studies, however, were adopting new approaches. For example, in response to calls for methodological diversity (e.g., Orlikowski & Barley, 2001), studies of technologies and

Table 17.2 Frequency and Percentage of Type of Research Within and Across Disciplines

Research Type	Communication	Information Systems	Management	Total
Qualitative	7 (19%)	30 (30%)	35 (56%)	72 (36%)
Quantitative	15 (40%)	39 (38%)	10 (16%)	64 (32%)
Mixed Method	10 (27%)	4 (4%)	1 (1%)	15 (7%)
Theory	4 (11%)	22 (22%)	13 (21%)	40 (20%)
Review	1 (3%)	6 (6%)	4 (6%)	11 (5%)

N = 202

organizations have employed narrative analysis (e.g., Doolin, 2003; Pentland & Feldman, 2007), interpretive analysis (e.g., Jian, 2007; Mutch, 2010), longitudinal designs (e.g., Boudreau & Robey, 2005; Leonardi, 2011b), and comparative case-based designs (e.g., Boczkowski, 2004; Edmondson et al., 2001). Some of them used agent-based simulation models (e.g., Black et al., 2004; Nan, 2011) and network analysis (e.g., Leonardi, 2007; Sykes et al., 2009; Yuan et al., 2010) to develop and test theories about ICTs in organizational settings.

Information systems and management articles were equally likely to be about theory or to provide reviews; both information systems and management had twice as many articles on these topics as communication. However, review articles on ICTs in organizations appear infrequently in all three disciplines during this time period. Banker and Kauffman's (2004) review of the information systems literature resembles this chapter's focus on managerial problems, organizational levels, group communication, knowledge management, and ICT acceptance and diffusion.

Directions for Future Research at Disciplinary Intersections

The final section of this chapter considers how organizational communication researchers might use ideas and concepts within the field to advance their own ICT research and to illuminate puzzles faced in other disciplines.

Emerging ICTs

Most articles published by communication researchers in the last decade have continued the general trend of examining influences, processes, uses, and outcomes of organizational ICTs, ones that enable members to communicate and share meanings with one another. Consequently, organizational communication researchers are drawn to technologies that represent the *C* rather than ones that represent the *I* aspect in *ICTs*. Studies of communication media, such as e-mail, teleconferencing, instant messaging, intranets, the Internet, and mobile devices are common. This focus is certainly an appropriate interest, given that communication messages and processes underlie the intellectual history of the field. However, students of ICT use in organizations would do well to consider the role that new knowledge management systems (Heinz & Rice, 2009) and social media tools, such as social networking sites, blogs, wikis, and microblogs (Treem & Leonardi, 2012), play in organizational members' communication patterns and practices. We suggest that scholars study these types of ICTs for two reasons.

First, organizations are widely adopting *knowledge management* and *social media tools* (for discussion, see Treem & Leonardi, 2012). Indeed, one information systems review highlights the shift away from hierarchical and centralized information control to examining underexplored practices and arrangements (Zammuto, Griffith, Majchrzak, Dougherty, & Faraj, 2007). One new context, in particular, is the rise of mass collaboration—that is, technology-enabled large-group problem solving, social networking; crowdsourcing and prosumers; decentralized control over digital content; and public relations/activist campaigns by nonorganizational members—all of which challenge and extend the nature of organizations. The popular press is filled with descriptions of dramatic and revolutionary changes that such technologies will bring to the workplace.

Organizational communication researchers should level a steady critique at such utopian and often technologically deterministic views through the use of rigorous conceptual and empirical analyses of how organizational practices shape, enmesh, and affect these new ICTs. Specifically, *nomadic information environments* are facilitated by *cloud computing,* where data and even applications are accessed and shared through distributed servers outside a person's or an organization's building or ownership. These environments enable physically and socially mobile communication services among intra- and interorganizational users—ones that require both service and infrastructure development. They involve and raise issues of social and technological interdependencies and the crucial phases of design, use, adoption, and outcomes of ICTs that form a rich interdisciplinary area of research and practice (Lyytinen & Yoo, 2002).

Second, many of these new knowledge management and social media technologies allow users to draw on the technology's materiality in ways that enact affordances that are useful in achieving group, organizational, and public communication and that were previously impossible, or at least difficult, to achieve. For example, unlike dyadic telephone calls or e-mail messages, communication that occurs in knowledge management and social media tools can be public and visible by (many) third parties who may not be involved in the initial communication. If someone posts a question to a coworker on a social networking site or ICT discussion forum, other organizational members who are not directly involved or aware that the two people are communicating can learn about their interactions as well as contribute to them.

Content and Relationships

This increased visibility of other people's communication could have important implications for interaction in the workplace. It might affect critical processes such as knowledge sharing, discourse and framing, impression management, the development of expertise directories, organizational learning, socialization processes, the formation of subgroups, and ICT adaptation. For these reasons, we suggest that organizational communication researchers attend to new ICTs that are entering the workplace by distinguishing what capabilities they provide that may reinforce, constrain, and restructure organizational communication in both content (including discourse about it) and relationships (including network structures; Rice & Gattiker, 2001). If organizational communication researchers take seriously the notion that communication is constitutive of organizing (Putnam & Nicotera, 2010), new ICTs in the workplace should become an important research area.

Adding research about how new technologies might alter the dynamics of organizing would make it easier for communication scholars to focus on ICTs that are more *I* than they are *C* without losing sight of important communicative phenomena. For example, Aydin and Rice's (1992) over-time analysis showed how a new health information system required new kinds and formats of information that fostered increased understanding of other work units. Boland et al. (2007) described how engineers, contractors, and architects who used new 3-D simulation technologies shifted patterns of information sharing and innovation across professions. Carlile (2004) analyzed how different engineering occupations changed their communication and decision-making patterns after they began using complex computational fluid dynamic tools to create design specifications. None of these studies focused on the communication that occurred through a newly implemented organizational ICT. Instead, they examined how the ICT created information that was not previously available to its users and how this information spilled over into communication patterns that occurred around the ICT in ways that changed the organization of work (Leonardi, 2011b). Rice and Gattiker (2001; Rice, 1987) also emphasized that ICTs can be both the channel as well as the content of organizational innovation.

Such an approach could also make room for organizational communication scholars who do not consider themselves students of technological change *per se* to engage in meaningful discussions of technologies and organizations. By removing the requirement to study only communication occurring *through* ICTs and adding the option to study communication occurring *around* ICTs, scholars who are interested in popular organizational communication topics (such as socialization, power, resistance, information processing, decision making, discourse, culture, knowledge sharing, networks, self-presentation, etc.) would be emboldened to incorporate an understanding of technologies into the explanation of their phenomena of interest. Research of this type could add to the perspectives on sociomateriality that are emerging in information systems and management (Leonardi & Barley, 2008; Orlikowski & Scott, 2008).

Knowledge Management and Sharing

A final topic area that organizational communication researchers need to examine is organizational knowledge and knowing. As this review demonstrates, the topic of knowledge is of interest to all three disciplines. But organizational communication scholars who focus on ICTs have not devoted extensive empirical analysis or theoretical development to the ways that technologies produce, maintain, and change knowledge. Given recent interest in this topic, especially as a capability enacted through interactions about one's work (e.g., Heinz & Rice, 2009; Kuhn, Chapter 19; Kuhn & Jackson, 2008), communication researchers have much to offer this line of work.

Conclusion

Research on ICTs and organizations in the first decade of the 21st century is broad, diverse, and interrelated within and across disciplines. This review sets forth 13 main themes in this research: influence, interaction, knowledge, level of analysis (individual, group, organization, societal), problems, process, research, structure, technology, and outcomes. These themes and their relationships within and across phases respond to central questions about the three phases of influences, contexts and processes, and outcomes. This review also notes similarities and differences in themes and research emphases across the disciplines of communication, information systems, and management. Finally, we suggest some areas that are particularly appropriate for organizational communication researchers to consider as they continue to unravel the complex and important relationships among influences, contexts and processes, and outcomes of ICTs in organizations.

References

Agarwal, R., & Karahanna, E. (2000). Time flies when you're having fun: Cognitive absorption and beliefs about information technology usage. *MIS Quarterly, 24*(4), 665–694.

Ahuja, M. K., Chudoba, K. M., Kacmar, C. J., McKnight, D. H., & George, J. F. (2007). IT road warriors: Balancing work-family conflict, job autonomy, and work overload to mitigate turnover intentions. *MIS Quarterly, 31*(1), 1–17.

Ahuja, M. K., & Thatcher, J. B. (2005). Moving beyond intentions and toward the theory of trying: Effects of work environment and gender on post-adoption information technology use. *MIS Quarterly, 29*(3), 427–459.

Alavi, M., & Leidner, D. E. (2001). Review: Knowledge management and knowledge management systems: Conceptual foundations and research issues. *MIS Quarterly, 25*(1), 107–136.

Al-Shohaib, K., Frederick, E., Jamal Al-Kandari, A. A., & Dorsher, M. D. (2010). Factors influencing the adoption of the internet by public relations professionals in the private and public sectors of Saudi Arabia. *Management Communication Quarterly, 24*(1), 104–121.

Archer, M. (1995). *Realist social theory: The morphogenetic approach.* New York: Cambridge University Press.

Ashcraft, K. L., Kuhn, T. R., & Cooren, F. (2009). Constitutional amendments: "Materializing" organizational communication. *Academy of Management Annals, 3*(1), 1–64.

Au, N., Ngai, E. W. T., & Cheng, T. C. E. (2008). Extending the understanding of end user information systems satisfaction formation: An equitable needs fulfillment model approach. *MIS Quarterly, 32*(1), 43–66.

Avgerou, C., & McGrath, K. (2007). Power, rationality, and the art of living through socio-technical change. *MIS Quarterly, 31*(2), 295–315.

Aydin, C., & Rice, R. E. (1992). Bringing social worlds together: Computers as catalysts for new interactions in health care organizations. *Journal of Health and Social Behavior, 33*(2), 168–185.

Ball, K., & Wilson, D. C. (2000). Power, control and computer-based performance monitoring: Repertoires, resistance and subjectivities. *Organization Studies, 21*(3), 539–565.

Ballard, D. I., & Seibold, D. R. (2004). Communication-related organizational structures and work group temporal experiences: The effects of coordination method, technology type, and feedback cycle on members' construals and enactments of time. *Communication Monographs, 71*(1), 1–27.

Banker, R. D., & Kauffman, R. J. (2004). The evolution of research on information systems: A fiftieth-year survey of the literature in "management science." *Management Science, 50*(3), 281–298.

Barki, H., Titah, R., & Boffo, C. (2007). Information system use-related activity: An expanded behavioral conceptualization of individual-level information system use. *Information Systems Research, 18*(2), 173–192.

Barley, S. R. (1986). Technology as an occasion for structuring: Evidence from observations of CT scanners and the social order of radiology departments. *Administrative Science Quarterly, 31*(1), 78–108.

Beaudry, A., & Pinsonneault, A. (2010). The other side of acceptance: Studying the direct and indirect effects of emotions on information technology use. *MIS Quarterly, 34*(4), 689–710.

Bechky, B. (2003). Sharing meaning across occupational communities: The transformation of understanding on the production floor. *Organization Science, 14*(3), 312–330.

Bhattacherjee, A., & Premkumar, G. (2004). Understanding changes in belief and attitude toward information technology usage: A theoretical model and longitudinal test. *MIS Quarterly, 28*(2), 229–254.

Bhattacherjee, A., & Sanford, C. (2006). Influence processes for information technology acceptance: An elaboration likelihood model. *MIS Quarterly, 30*(4), 805–825.

Black, L. J., Carlile, P. R., & Repenning, N. P. (2004). A dynamic theory of expertise and occupational boundaries in new technology implementation: Building on Barley's study of CT scanning. *Administrative Science Quarterly, 49*(4), 572–607.

Boczkowski, P. J. (2004). The processes of adopting multimedia and interactivity in three online newsrooms. *Journal of Communication, 54*(2), 197–213.

Boland, J. R. J., Lyytinen, K., & Yoo, Y. (2007). Wakes of innovation in project networks: The case of digital 3-D representations in architecture, engineering, and construction. *Organization Science, 18*(4), 631–647.

Boudreau, M-C., & Robey, D. (2005). Enacting integrated information technology: A human agency perspective. *Organization Science, 16*(1), 3–18.

Butler, B. S. (2001). Membership size, communication activity, and sustainability: A resource-based model of online social structures. *Information Systems Research, 12*(4), 346–362.

Carlile, P. R. (2004). Transferring, translating, and transforming: An integrative framework for managing knowledge across boundaries. *Organization Science, 15*(5), 555–568.

Choi, S-Y., Lee, H., & Yoo, Y. (2010). The impact of information technology and transactive memory systems on knowledge sharing, application, and team performance: A field study. *MIS Quarterly, 34*(4), 855–870.

Daft, R. L., & Lengel, R. H. (1986). Organizational information requirements, media richness and structural design. *Management Science, 32*(5), 554–571.

DeSanctis, G., & Poole, M. (1994). Capturing the complexity in advanced technology use: Adaptive structuration theory. *Organization Science, 5*(2), 121–147.

Doolin, B. (2003). Narratives of change: Discourse, technology and organization. *Organization, 10*(4), 751–770.

Edmondson, A. C., Bohmer, R. M., & Pisano, G. P. (2001). Disrupted routines: Team learning and new technology implementation in hospitals. *Administrative Science Quarterly, 46*(4), 685–716.

Eggers, J. P., & Kaplan, S. (2009). Cognition and renewal: Comparing CEO and organizational effects on incumbent adaptation to technical change. *Organization Science, 20*(2), 461–477.

Flanagin, J. (2000). Social pressures on organizational website adoption. *Human Communication Research, 26*(4), 618–646.

Fulk, J., Heino, R., Flanagin, A. J., Monge, P. R., & Bar, F. (2004). A test of the individual action model for organizational information commons. *Organization Science, 15*(5), 569–585.

Fulk, J., Schmitz, J., & Steinfield, C. (1990). A social influence model of technology use. In J. Fulk & C. Steinfield (Eds.), *Organizations and communication technology* (pp. 117–140). Newbury Park, CA: SAGE.

Gallivan, M., & Srite, M. (2005). Information technology and culture: Identifying fragmentary and holistic perspectives of culture. *Information and Organization, 15*(4), 295–338.

Ganesh, S. (2003). Organizational narcissism. *Management Communication Quarterly, 16*(4), 558–594.

García-Morales, V. J., Matías-Reche, F., & Verdú-Jover, A. J. (2011). Influence of internal communication on technological proactivity, organizational learning, and organizational innovation in the pharmaceutical sector. *Journal of Communication, 61*(1), 150–177.

Giddens, A. (1984). *The constitution of society.* Berkeley: University of California Press.

Harrington, S. J., & Guimaraes, T. (2005). Corporate culture, absorptive capacity and IT success. *Information and Organization, 15*(1), 39–63.

Harwood, S. A. (2011). The domestication of online technologies by smaller businesses and the 'busy day.' *Information and Organization, 21*(2), 84–106.

Heinz, M., & Rice, R. E. (2009). An integrated model of knowledge sharing in contemporary communication environments. In C. Beck (Ed.), *Communication yearbook* (vol. 33, pp. 172–195). London, England: Routledge.

Hiemstra, G. (1983). You say you want a revolution? "Information technology" in organizations. In R. N. Bostrom & B. H. Westley (Eds.), *Communication yearbook* (vol. 7, pp. 802–827). New York, NY: Routledge.

Hirschheim, R. (1986). *Office automation: A social and organizational perspective.* New York, NY: Wiley.

Jasperson, J. T., Carte, T. A., Saunders, C. S., Butler, B. S., Croes, H. J. P., & Zheng, W. (2002). Review: Power and information technology research: A metatriangulation review. *MIS Quarterly, 26*(4), 397–459.

Jasperson, J. T, Carter, P. E., & Zmud, R. W. (2005). A comprehensive conceptualization of post-adoptive behaviors associated with information technology enabled work systems. *MIS Quarterly, 29*(3), 525–557.

Jeyaraj, A., & Sabherwal, R. (2008). Adoption of information systems innovations by individuals: A study of processes involving contextual, adopter, and influencer actions. *Information and Organization, 18*(3), 205–234.

Jian, G. (2007). "Omega is a four-letter word": Toward a tension-centered model of resistance to information and communication technologies. *Communication Monographs, 74*(4), 517–540.

Jian, G., & Jeffres, L. W. (2006). Understanding employees' willingness to contribute to shared electronic databases. *Communication Research, 33*(4), 242–261.

Johnson, B., & Rice, R. E. (1987). *Managing organizational innovation: The evolution from word processing to office information systems.* New York, NY: Columbia University Press.

Jones, Q., Ravid, G., & Rafaeli, S. (2004). Information overload and the message dynamics of online interaction spaces: A theoretical model and empirical exploration. *Information Systems Research, 15*(2), 194–210.

Jonsson, K., Holmström, J., & Lyytinen, K. (2009). Turn to the material: Remote diagnostics systems and new forms of boundary-spanning. *Information and Organization, 19*(4), 233–252.

Kane, G. C., & Alavi, M. (2007). Information technology and organizational learning: An investigation of exploration and exploitation processes. *Organization Science, 18*(5), 796–812.

Kang, D. (2006). The workflow application as an unintended medium for organizational learning: A longitudinal field study. *Information and Organization, 16*(2), 169–190.

Kim, H-W., & Kankanhalli, A. (2009). Investigating user resistance to information systems implementation: A status quo bias perspective. *MIS Quarterly, 33*(3), 567–582.

Kirkman, B. L., Rosen, B., Tesluk, P. E., & Gibson, C. B. (2004). The impact of team empowerment on virtual team performance: The moderating role of face-to-face interaction. *Academy of Management Journal, 47*(2), 175–192.

Kraut, R. E., Rice, R. E., Cool, C., & Fish, R. S. (1998). Varieties of social influence: The role of utility and norms in the success of a new communication medium. *Organization Science, 9*(4), 437–453.

Kuhn, T., & Jackson, M. H. (2008). Accomplishing knowledge: A framework for investigating knowing in organizations. *Management Communication Quarterly, 21*(4), 454–485.

Latour, B. (2005). *Reassembling the social: An introduction to actor-network-theory*. Oxford, UK: Oxford University Press.

Leidner, D. E., & Kayworth, T. (2006). Review: A review of culture in information systems research: Toward a theory of information technology culture conflict. *MIS Quarterly, 30*(2), 357–399.

Leonardi, P. M. (2007). Activating the informational capabilities of information technology for organizational change. *Organization Science, 18*(5), 813–831.

Leonardi, P. M. (2008). Indeterminacy and the discourse of inevitability in international technology management. *Academy of Management Review, 33*(4), 975–984.

Leonardi, P. M. (2009). Why do people reject new technologies and stymie organizational changes of which they are in favor? Exploring misalignments between social interactions and materiality. *Human Communication Research, 35*(3), 407–441.

Leonardi, P. M. (2011a). Innovation blindness: Culture, frames, and cross-boundary problem construction in the development of new technology concepts. *Organization Science, 22*(2), 347–369.

Leonardi, P. M. (2011b). When flexible routines meet flexible technologies: Affordance, constraint, and the imbrication of human and material agencies. *MIS Quarterly, 35*(1), 147–167.

Leonardi, P. M., & Bailey, D. E. (2008). Transformational technologies and the creation of new work practices: Making implicit knowledge explicit in task-based offshoring. *MIS Quarterly, 32*(2), 411–436.

Leonardi, P. M., & Barley, S. R. (2008). Materiality and change: Challenges to building better theory about technology and organizing. *Information and Organization, 18*(3), 159–176.

Leonardi, P. M., & Barley, S. R. (2010). What's under construction here? Social action, materiality, and power in constructivist studies of technology and organizing. *Academy of Management Annals, 4*(1), 1–51.

Leonardi, P. M., Treem, J. W., & Jackson, M. H. (2010). The connectivity paradox: Using technology to both decrease and increase perceptions of distance in distributed work arrangements. *Journal of Applied Communication Research, 38*(1), 85–105.

Lewis, W., Agarwal, R., & Sambamurthy, V. (2003). Sources of influence on beliefs about information technology use: An empirical study of knowledge workers. *MIS Quarterly, 27*(4), 657–678.

Li, E. Y., Jiang, J. J., & Klein, G. (2003). The impact of organizational coordination and climate on marketing executives' satisfaction with information systems services. *Journal of the Association for Information Systems, 4*(1), 99–115.

Lyytinen, K., & Yoo, Y. (2002). Research commentary: The next wave of nomadic computing. *Information Systems Research, 13*(4), 377–388.

Majchrzak, A., Rice, R. E., Malhotra, A., King, N., & Ba, S. (2000). Technology adaptation: The case of a computer-supported inter-organizational virtual team. *MIS Quarterly, 24*(4), 569–600.

Mark, G., & Poltrock, S. (2004). Groupware adoption in a distributed organization: Transporting and transforming technology through social worlds. *Information and Organization,14*(4), 297–327.

Maznevski, M. L., & Chudoba, K. M. (2000). Bridging space over time: Global virtual team dynamics and effectiveness. *Organization Science, 11*(5), 473–492.

McGrath, K. (2006). Affection not affliction: The role of emotions in information systems and organizational change. *Information and Organization, 16*(4), 277–303.

Mishra, A. N., & Agarwal, R. (2010). Technological frames, organizational capabilities, and IT use: An empirical investigation of electronic procurement. *Information Systems Research, 21*(2), 249–270.

Munir, K. A., & Phillips, N. (2005). The birth of the "Kodak moment": Institutional entrepreneurship and the adoption of new technologies. *Organization Studies, 26*(11), 1665–1687.

Mutch, A. (2010). Technology, organization, and structure: A morphogenetic approach. *Organization Science, 21*(2), 507–520.

Nan, N. (2011). Capturing bottom-up information technology use processes: A complex adaptive systems model. *MIS Quarterly, 35*(2), 505–532.

Orlikowski, W. J. (2000). Using technology and constituting structures: A practice lens for studying technology in organizations. *Organization Science, 11*(4), 404–428.

Orlikowski, W. J. (2007). Sociomaterial practices: Exploring technology at work. *Organization Studies, 28*(9), 1435–1448.

Orlikowski, W. J., & Barley, S. R. (2001). Technology and institutions: What information systems research and organization studies can learn from each other. *MIS Quarterly, 25*(2), 145–165.

Orlikowski, W. J., & Scott, S. V. (2008). Sociomateriality: Challenging the separation of technology, work and organization. *The Academy of Management Annals, 2*(1), 433–474.

Ortiz de Guinea, A., & Markus, M. L. (2009). Why break the habit of a lifetime? Rethinking the roles of intention, habit, and emotion in continuing information technology use. *MIS Quarterly, 33*(3), 433–444.

Pentland, B. T., & Feldman, M. S. (2007). Narrative networks: Patterns of technology and organization. *Organization Science, 18*(5), 781–795.

Perrow, C. (1967). A framework for the comparative analysis of organizations. *American Sociological Review, 32*(2), 194–208.

Pinsonneault, A., & Kraemer, K. L. (2002). Exploring the role of information technology in organizational downsizing: A tale of two American cities. *Organization Science, 13*(2), 191–208.

Purvis, R. L., Sambamurthy, V., & Zmud, R. W. (2001). The assimilation of knowledge platforms in organizations: An empirical investigation. *Organization Science, 12*(2), 117–135.

Putnam, L. L., & Nicotera, A. M. (2010). Communicative constitution of organization is a question: Critical issues for addressing it. *Management Communication Quarterly, 24*(1), 158–165.

Ragu-Nathan, T. S., Tarafdar, M., Ragu-Nathan, B. S., & Tu, Q. (2008). The consequences of technostress for end users in organizations: Conceptual development and empirical validation. *Information Systems Research, 19*(4), 417–433.

Rains, S. A., & Young, A. M. (2006). A sign of the times: An analysis of organizational members' email signatures. *Journal of Computer-Mediated Communication, 11*(4), 1046–1061.

Ramiller, N. C. (2001). The 'textual attitude' and new technology. *Information and Organization, 11*(2), 129–156.

Rennecker, J., & Godwin, L. (2005). Delays and interruptions: A self-perpetuating paradox of communication technology use. *Information and Organization, 15*(3), 247–266.

Rice, R. E. (1987). Computer-mediated communication systems and organizational innovation. *Journal of Communication, 37*(4), 65–94.

Rice, R. E. (1999). Artifacts and paradoxes in new media. *New Media and Society, 1*(1), 24–32.

Rice, R. E. (2009). Diffusion of innovations: Theoretical extensions. In R. Nabi & M. B. Oliver (Eds.), *Handbook of media effects* (pp. 489–503). Thousand Oaks, CA: SAGE.

Rice, R. E., & Aydin, C. (1991). Attitudes towards new organizational technology: Network proximity as a mechanism for social information processing. *Administrative Science Quarterly, 36*(2), 219–244.

Rice, R. E., & Cooper, S. (2010). *Organizations and unusual routines: A systems analysis of dysfunctional feedback processes*. Cambridge, UK: Cambridge University Press.

Rice, R. E., & Gattiker, U. (2001). New media and organizational structuring. In F. Jablin & L. Putnam (Eds.), *New handbook of organizational communication* (pp. 544–581). Thousand Oaks, CA: SAGE.

Rice, R. E., & Schneider, S. (2006). Information technology: Analyzing paper and electronic desktop artifacts. In C. Lin & D. Atkin (Eds.), *Communication technology and social change: Theory, effects, and applications* (pp. 101–121). Mahwah, NJ: Lawrence Erlbaum.

Rogers, E. M. (2003). *Diffusion of innovations* (5th ed.). New York, NY: Free Press.

Ruey-Lin, H., Tsai, S. D-H., & Ching-Fang, L. (2006). The problems of embeddedness: Knowledge transfer, coordination and reuse in information systems. *Organization Studies, 27*(9), 1289–1317.

Schwarz, G. M. (2002). Organizational hierarchy adaptation and information technology. *Information and Organization, 12*(3), 153–182.

Sherif, K., & Menon, N. M. (2004). Managing technology and administration innovations: Four case studies on software reuse. *Journal of the Association for Information Systems, 5*(7), 247–281.

Sherif, K., Zmud, R. W., & Browne, G. J. (2006). Managing peer-to-peer conflicts in disruptive information technology innovations: The case of software reuse. *MIS Quarterly, 30*(2), 339–356.

Short, J., Williams, E., & Christie, B. (1976). *The social psychology of telecommunications.* London, England: Wiley.

Stephens, K. K. (2007). The successive use of information and communication technologies at work. *Communication Theory, 17*(4), 486–507.

Stephens, K. K., Sørnes, J. O., Rice, R. E., Browning, L. D., & Sætre, A. S. (2008). Discrete, sequential, and follow-up use of information and communication technology by experienced ICT users. *Management Communication Quarterly, 22*(2), 197–231.

Straub, D. W., & Watson, R. T. (2001). Research commentary: Transformational issues in researching IS and net-enabled organizations. *Information Systems Research, 12*(4), 337–345.

Sykes, T. A., Venkatesh, V., & Gosain, S. (2009). Model of acceptance with peer support: A social network perspective to understand employees' system use. *MIS Quarterly, 33*(2), 371–393.

Teo, H. H., Wei, K. K., & Benbasat, I. (2003). Predicting intention to adopt interorganizational linkages: An institutional perspective. *MIS Quarterly, 27*(1), 19–49.

Thompson, J. D., & Bates, F. L. (1957). Technology, organization, and administration. *Administrative Science Quarterly, 2*(3), 325–343.

Tillquist, J. (2002). Rules of the game: Constructing norms of influence, subordination and constraint in IT planning. *Information and Organization, 12*(1), 39–70.

Timmerman, C. E., & Scott, C. R. (2006). Virtually working: Communicative and structural predictors of media use and key outcomes in virtual work teams 1. *Communication Monographs, 73*(1), 108–136.

Treem, J. W., & Leonardi, P. M. (2012). Social media use in organizations: Exploring the affordances of visibility, editability, persistence, and association. In C. T. Salmon (Ed.), *Communication yearbook* (vol. 36, pp. 143–189). New York, NY: Routledge.

Tripsas, M. (2009). Technology, identity, and inertia through the lens of "the digital photography company." *Organization Science, 20*(2), 441–460.

Vaast, E. (2007). What goes online comes offline: Knowledge management system use in a soft bureaucracy. *Organization Studies, 28*(3), 282–306.

Vaast, E., & Walsham, G. (2005). Representations and actions: The transformation of work practices with IT use. *Information and Organization,15*(1), 65–89.

Venkatesh, V., Davis, F. D., & Morris, M. G. (2007). Dead or alive? The development, trajectory and future of technology adoption research. *Journal of the Association for Information Systems, 8*(4), 268–286.

Venkatesh, V., & Morris, M. G. (2000). Why don't men ever stop to ask for directions? Gender, social influence, and their role in technology acceptance and usage behavior. *MIS Quarterly, 24*(1), 115–139.

Venkatesh, V., Morris, M. G., Davis, G. B., & Davis, F. D. (2003). User acceptance of information technology: Toward a unified view. *MIS Quarterly, 27*(3), 425–478.

Vishwanath, A. (2006). The effect of the number of opinion seekers and leaders on technology attitudes and choices. *Human Communication Research, 32*(3), 322–350.

Vishwanath, A. (2009). From belief-importance to intention: The impact of framing on technology adoption. *Communication Monographs, 76*(2), 177–206.

Wagner, E. L., Newell, S., & Piccoli, G. (2010). Understanding project survival in an ES environment: A sociomaterial practice perspective. *Journal of the Association for Information Systems, 11*(5), 276–297.

Wakefield, R. L., Leidner, D. E., & Garrison, G. (2008). A model of conflict, leadership, and performance in virtual teams. *Information Systems Research, 19*(4), 434–455.

Waldeck, J. H., Seibold, D. R., & Flanagin, A. J. (2004). Organizational assimilation and communication technology use. *Communication Monographs, 71*(2), 161–183.

Walsh, J. P., & Maloney, N. G. (2007). Collaboration structure, communication media, and problems in scientific work teams. *Journal of Computer-Mediated Communication, 12*(2), 712–732.

Wang, P. (2009). Popular concepts beyond organizations: Exploring new dimensions of information technology innovations. *Journal of the Association for Information Systems, 10*(1), 1–30.

Wang, P. (2010). Chasing the hottest IT: Effects of information technology fashion on organizations. *MIS Quarterly, 34*(1), 63–85.

Wasko, M. M., & Faraj, S. (2005). Why should I share? Examining social capital and knowledge contribution in electronic networks of practice. *MIS Quarterly, 29*(1), 35–57.

Webster, J., & Ahuja, J. S. (2006). Enhancing the design of web navigation systems: The influence of user disorientation on engagement and performance. *MIS Quarterly, 30*(3), 661–678.

Wixom, B. H., & Todd, P. A. (2005). A theoretical integration of user satisfaction and technology acceptance. *Information Systems Research, 16*(1), 85–102.

Woiceshyn, J. (2000). Technology adoption: Organizational learning in oil firms. *Organization Studies, 21*(6), 1095–1118.

Woodward, J. (1958). *Management and technology.* London, England: HSMO.

Yuan, Y. C., Fulk, J., Monge, P. R., & Contractor, N. (2010). Expertise directory development, shared task interdependence, and strength of communication network ties as multilevel predictors of expertise exchange in transactive memory work groups. *Communication Research, 37*(1), 20–47.

Yuan, Y. C., Fulk, J., Shumate, M., Monge, P. R., Bryant, J. A., & Matsaganis, M. (2005). Individual participation in organizational information commons. *Human Communication Research, 31*(2), 212–240.

Zammuto, R. F., Griffith, T. L., Majchrzak, A., Dougherty, D. J., & Faraj, S. (2007). Information technology and the changing fabric of organization. *Organization Science, 18*(5), 749–762.

Zorn, T. E., Flanagin, A. J., & Shoham, M. D. (2011). Institutional and noninstitutional influences on information and communication technology adoption and use among nonprofit organizations. *Human Communication Research, 37*(1), 1–33.

Note

1. By discipline, the included journals were communication (*Communication Monographs*; *Communication Research*; *Human Communication Research*; *Journal of Applied Communication Research*; *Journal of Communication*; *Journal of Computer-Mediated Communication*; and *Management Communication Quarterly*), information systems (*Information and Organization*; *Information Systems Research*; *Journal of the Association for Information Systems*; and *MIS Quarterly*) and management (*Academy of Management Journal*; *Academy of Management Review*; *Administrative Science Quarterly*; *Management Science*; *Organization*; *Organization Science*; and *Organization Studies*). Please see http://www.comm.ucsb.edu/faculty/rrice/c71RiceLeonardi2013ArticlesTheories.pdf for the full list of analyzed articles and a list of the theories appearing in those articles by discipline and phase.

CHAPTER 18

Emergence of Multidimensional Social Networks

Michelle Shumate and Noshir S. Contractor

Each edition of the *Handbook of Organizational Communication* has contained a chapter on communication networks. In the first edition, Monge and Eisenberg (1987) reviewed literature on the antecedents and outcomes of communication networks. In the second edition, Monge and Contractor (2001) reviewed ten families of theories that explained the emergence of communication networks. The third edition of the *Handbook of Organizational Communication* reenvisions the study of communication networks, beginning with its definition. In the second edition, Monge and Contractor (2001) define *communication networks* as "the patterns of contact between communication partners that are created by transmitting and exchanging messages through time and space" (p. 440). Although patterns of contact are a type of communication network, the current chapter expands the scope of this definition. In particular, we define *communication networks* as *relations among various types of actors that illustrate the ways in which messages are transmitted, exchanged, or interpreted.* This definition extends the previous one in three important ways. First, it includes multidimensional networks (Contractor, 2009; Contractor, Monge, & Leonardi, 2011) that are composed of a variety of types of actors including, but not limited to, individuals, groups, organizations, artifacts, concepts, and technologies. Second, the definition highlights that communication networks are multiplex, meaning that it is useful to simultaneously consider multiple types of relations. Finally, it suggests that networks capture communication processes that are more complex than message exchange.

This chapter focuses on the various types of relations that constitute multidimensional communication networks. As such, it provides an important alternative to other ways in which the literature has been reviewed (Borgatti & Foster, 2003; Krackhardt & Bass, 1994; Monge & Contractor, 2001; Monge & Eisenberg, 1987). We begin with an overview of multidimensional networks and their importance for organizational communication research. The core of the chapter then focuses on the various types of communication relations that constitute or support communication networks. These relations include flow, affinity, representation, semantic, technological, physical, and affiliation. We review both the theoretical frameworks that scholars utilize and the key empirical findings for each type of relation. The section concludes with a discussion of *multiplexity*, or the various ways in which these relations may interact with one another and the implications of these interactions for the study of multidimensional networks. The chapter ends with a discussion of four trends that suggest now is an opportune moment to theorize the emergence of multidimensional networks.

Multidimensional Networks

Multidimensional networks consist of different types of nodes and relations that are embedded in the same network (Contractor, 2009; Contractor et al., 2011). They are an extension of two previously studied types of social networks, multimodal networks and multiplex networks. Multimodal networks include more than one type of node. For example, a network in which individuals are members of multiple voluntary organizations is a multimodal network. In this example, there are two types of nodes: individuals and voluntary organizations. Multiplex networks are single modal, meaning they have only one type of node but have multiple types of relations. For example, individuals who dislike one another but communicate with each other about work can be modeled as a multiplex network. Multidimensional networks contain a variety of different types of actors as nodes (e.g., individuals, documents, organizations) and different types of relations among them, making them both multimodal and multiplex.

Multidimensional networks are therefore better suited to capture the complexities inherent in organizational life. The network perspective has been criticized for failing to take into account the context and content of communication. Multidimensional networks embrace the challenge of this critique by bringing the context and content into focus; that is, communication context elements can become nodes in the network. Various concepts or networks formed by discourse, in which the nodes are words, can also be included.

Such a move has the important benefit of enabling researchers to explain the interdependencies across multidimensional nodes and relations. As illustrated by Contractor et al. (2011), the emergence of multidimensional networks can be explained by extending the multitheoretical, multilevel model approach (MTML; for an overview, see Contractor, Wasserman, & Faust, 2006; Monge & Contractor, 2003). Including different types of nodes creates theoretical contingencies; for example, unlike individuals, words do not engage in social exchange with one another, making that mechanism irrelevant to the emergence of links between words. Further, mechanisms such as reciprocity or transitivity can apply across multiplex relations. For example, one organization may provide financial resources to another organization and, in return, receive public affirmation; here, multiplex reciprocity would have occurred based on exchange theory mechanisms. Finally, multidimensional networks allow communication researchers to explore the dynamics of networks and, indeed, specific relational events within these systems. Longitudinal analysis of these dynamics, especially given the affordances that technology allows for in data collection, is within reach.

To understand the various types of relations among different types of actors that compose multidimensional networks, this chapter extends the work done by Contractor and colleagues (2011) on an MTML model for multidimensional networks. In particular, this chapter introduces a new taxonomy for classifying various relation types. We then use the taxonomy to review the current research in organizational communication and draw conclusions about the theoretical families that are used to study particular relation types. These patterns provide the groundwork for advancing an MTML approach to multiplex relations in multidimensional networks.

Network Relations

Network relations describe the ways in which actors of various types are connected to one another. Relations that appear in the organizational communication literature include communication mediated via technology (Cho, Trier, & Kim, 2005), collaboration among organizations (Doerfel & Taylor, 2004; Taylor & Doerfel, 2003), and hyperlinks (Shumate & Dewitt, 2008; Shumate & Lipp, 2008), to name a few. We contend that the relation among actors is the primary mechanism for organizing sets of findings in organizational communication network research. This claim is motivated by two studies. First, Faust and Skvoretz (2002) note that the vast majority of social network research can be characterized as case studies of individual communities. They suggest that these case studies can and should be compared to one another. In doing so, researchers might address the question as to whether networks are structured in similar ways, despite their surface differences on dimensions, such as type of actor, size, time and space of observation, and type of relation. To illustrate, they compare the structural characteristics of 42 social networks that vary considerably on these dimensions. These types include advice networks among managers, licking behaviors of cows, communication among monastic novices, and grooming patterns among chimpanzees. They found that types of relations better explained similar patterns in networks than types of actors. This study offers two intriguing possibilities that lie at the core of this chapter: (1) that organizational communication network research can collectively generalize findings across individual case studies and (2) that models based on similar types of relations may offer more generalizable explanations than models that focus on levels of analysis (e.g., individual, group, organization).

Second, Leskovec, Kleinberg, and Faloutsos (2007) provide additional insight into the nuanced ways in which relations may influence the emergence of networks. They report evidence of positive link growth rates (i.e., the relationship between the rate in which links and nodes are added to a network) across 12 networks of seven types. However, the relationship between the addition of nodes and the addition of relations was much stronger for the citation networks than for the communication networks (e.g., communication via e-mail). Monge, Heiss, and Margolin (2008) suggest that Leskovec and colleagues' (2007) findings indicate that various type of relations have different carrying capacities or limitations. To push this idea further, communication relations based on message exchange among human actors differ fundamentally from relations such as citations networks. This chapter explores this possibility by highlighting the different types of network relations that compose multidimensional networks. Each of these relational types has certain logical limits because of the nature of the communication linkage. In addition, patterns of theoretical investigation and empirical research become evident when they are organized by type of relation.

This section explores four types of communication and three types of infrastructure relations (see Table 18.1). The following sections describe the different types of communication relations and the theoretical perspectives used to study them.

Flow relations depict the exchange or transmission of information or resources among nodes. Flow can occur among different types of nodes, including individuals, technologies, or other artifacts. For example, flow occurs when individuals exchange messages or a person retrieves information from a website.

In contrast, *affinity relations* refer to socially constructed relationships that may have either a positive or negative valence. Although one might assume that these relations imply flow, they do not explicitly focus on the exchange or transmission of, say, information among actors.

Examples of affinity relations include friendship, collaboration, and alliances. Affinity relations can occur between individuals and other types of nonhuman actors, but in these cases, the networks are constructed in the minds of actors that exert agency (i.e., human actors can form positive attachments to computer systems, but the computer systems do not form positive attachments to the human actors). In cases where multiple actors have agency, the affinity relation can be mutual or perceived only by one party.

Representational relations involve messages about an association among actors communicated to a third party or to the public. Specifically, these relations focus on messages about one node's affiliation with other nodes that are communicated to others. Examples of representational ties include hyperlink networks[1] (e.g., Tateo, 2005) and bibliometric networks[2] (e.g., So, 1998). These relations differ from flow relations because no messages are exchanged between nodes. Additionally, they differ from affinity relations because they do not necessarily entail enduring relationships among actors. Consider, for example, the contrast between conversing with a friend (a flow relation), having a friend (an affinity relation), and name-dropping (a representational relation). In the representational relation, the person whose name is dropped does not necessarily receive a message. Additionally, the person whose name is dropped may not even have an enduring relationship with the person who is dropping his or her name.

Semantic relations focus on shared meaning or symbol use. Researchers examine semantic relations on two levels: (1) the shared meanings that result from the patterns of word usage in text or discourse and (2) individuals' cognitive maps of shared meanings. In the first type of semantic network, researchers examine word frequencies and patterns of usage. In the second type, individuals are asked about their interpretation of, say, an issue (Monge & Eisenberg, 1987). The degree to which individuals share an interpretation forms the relation.

Infrastructure Networks

Scholarship from the perspective of communicative constitution of organizations (see Putnam & Nicotera, 2008, for a review) argues that we cannot ignore materiality in explaining symbolically constructed relationships and structures of an organization. We note three types of infrastructure networks that enable and constrain the configuration of various types of communication networks. These include technological networks, physical networks, and affiliation networks.

Technological networks describe the supporting path along which flows, affiliations, or representational networks are manifested. If a technology only permits messages to be exchanged among certain users, then the infrastructure networks would only link actors who use that technology. For example, in Cooper and Shumate's (2012) study, the lack of infrastructure to support communication and collaboration among nongovernmental organizations (NGOs) concerned with gender-based violence in Lusaka, Zambia, significantly hindered the development of both the communication and affinity networks among these organizations. Lack of consistent telephone service, spotty Internet service, and disruptions in power made such network connections difficult.

Physical networks describe the proximity of actors to one another. Research on flow and affinity networks has consistently shown that physical proximity plays an important role in network structuring. For example, Van den Bulte and Moenaert (1998) demonstrated that changing the physical network, or the distance between individuals, resulted in a reconfiguration of the communication flow network. At a macro level, analyzing the evolution of the global network of intergovernmental organizations since 1820, Beckfield (2010) found the network to be increasingly influenced by regional proximity.

Affiliation networks are two-mode networks (i.e., networks in which connections are only permitted among actors of two different types), in which actors are affiliated with entities, such as organizations, social movements, online communities, events, documents, or technologies. Affiliation networks describe how individuals identify with various entities and may provide a supporting condition for flow and affinity relations among individuals. An example is interlocking boards of directors, in which individuals are affiliated with the various boards in which they serve (e.g., Haunschild & Beckman, 1998). Researchers then study how messages flow across companies through the cross-affiliation of individuals on common boards.

These seven types of relations constitute the taxonomy for discerning patterns of network research—an important element in the development of a MTML approach to multidimensional networks. In the next sections, we examine these four types of communication networks in more detail. In particular, we identify families of theoretical mechanisms that are often used to explain the emergence and outcomes of each of the four types of relations. To decipher the prevalent theories and types of research for each communication relation, we conducted an exhaustive review of empirical social network research using organizational communication concepts from the 1990s to 2012. We searched communication, sociology, and management journals to find articles that examined at least one of the four types of communication networks. We included articles that utilized network analytic techniques to empirically analyze organizational communication phenomena. This search excluded articles that presented only new theories or articles that offered rich metaphorical descriptions of networks but did not operationalize them. This review yielded

Table 18.1 A Taxonomy of Relation Types for Communication Networks

Relation Type	Definition	Examples
Communication Networks		
Flow	The transmission or exchange of messages among actors	E-mail messages sent among a group of college students (Postmes, Spears, & Lea, 2000), communication to retrieve and allocate information among experts (Palazzolo, 2005)
Affinity	A socially constructed relationship that has either a positive or negative valence	Joint ventures among companies (Ahuja, 2000), collaboration among NGOs (Taylor & Doerfel, 2003), generic friendship relations (Pollock, Whitebred, & Contractor, 2000)
Representational	A message about an association among actors communicated to a third party or the public	Hyperlinks among organizational actor websites (Tateo, 2005), public communication of the relationship between a NGO and corporation (Shumate & O'Connor, 2010a)
Semantic	Co-occurrence of words in text or shared meaning that individuals give to concepts or organizational fields	Shared meaning surrounding employee participation (Stohl, 1993), common usage of words in organizational websites (Shumate, 2012)

(Continued)

Table 18.1 (Continued)

Relation Type	Definition	Examples
Infrastructure Networks		
Technological	The supporting path for messages to flow among technologies	Connections among distributed database systems, telephone networks, Internet connectivity
Physical	Proximity of agents in time and space	Physical distance between employees' offices (Corman, 1990)
Affiliation	Relation between agents and organizational entities	Organizational identification with multiple organizational targets (Scott, 1997), nation-states that belong to intergovernmental organizations (Beckfield, 2010)

214 articles that we categorized by type of relation(s) and node(s), family of theoretical mechanisms, whether the communication network was an independent or dependent variable, source of data, and analytic method. The patterns of theory development and testing described in the subsequent sections stem from this classification. For the complete list of articles and their classification, including simulation-based studies not reviewed in this chapter, please visit http://www.michelleshumate.com/resources.

Theories to Explain the Outcomes of Communication Network Relations

This chapter focuses on the types of relations that compose multidimensional networks. However, we would be remiss if we ignored findings on the outcomes of the types of relations. There is only a modicum of organizational communication research that focuses on the outcomes of representational or semantic networks. As such, this section exclusively reviews the research on flow and affinity relations.

Most research that utilizes flow relations as an explanatory variable invokes theories of self-interest, contagion theories, cognitive/semantic theories, and theories of exchange and dependency. At the core of each of these theories is a similar logic; that is, information or messages that flow through a network give some actors advantages because of their network roles. The most popular version of this explanation derives from the family of theories of self-interest. Theories of self-interest posit that individuals and organizations rationally decide to enter into network relationships to maximize their gains and minimize their losses (Monge & Contractor, 2001). Social capital theory (Burt, 1982) and transaction costs economics (Williamson, 1975) are both theories of self-interest. When applied to flow relationships, the core argument of this research is that actors seek to gain advantages through their position in the message flow (e.g., occupying a structural hole or being highly central in the network). For example, Cross and Cummings (2004) find that the higher an employee's centrality in their information and awareness networks, the more positively they are rated in their performance.

Mechanisms based on the family of contagion theories are also used to explain outcomes of flow relations. Contagion theories suggest that exposure to messages from the network lead to attitude or behavior changes. These theories include social information processing theory (Fulk, Steinfield, Schmitz, & Power, 1987; Salancik & Pfeffer, 1978), institutional theory (DiMaggio & Powell, 1983), and the diffusion of innovation theory (Rogers, 1995). Flow relations, in this view, are the channels for attitude and behavior changes. For example, Yuan, Cosley, Welser, Ling, and Gay (2009) reported that interpersonal exposure, tie homophily, and network cohesion increased the likelihood of adoption of SuggestBot, a software that recommends contributions one can make to Wikipedia.

Cognitive/semantic and exchange/dependency theories are also utilized to explain the outcome of flow relations. Research from the cognitive/semantic family focuses on the outcomes of knowledge-sharing networks. Such research reports that centrality in knowledge networks is related to productivity with new technology (Papa, 1990) and work group performance (Cummings, 2004). Research from the exchange/dependency perspective utilizes flow networks as explanations for trust. Specifically, individuals who are central in communication networks (Prell, 2003), who have advocates with dense communication networks (Wong & Boh, 2010), and who are embedded in reciprocal relationships (Molm, Collett, & Schaefer, 2007) are treated as trustworthy.

Across these theories, flow relations are the mechanism through which information is shared. They provide explanations for actor differences based on their positions in the social network. Actors with advantageous positions reap benefits, such as better performance, higher productivity, greater innovativeness, and high levels of trustworthiness.

Despite differences between affinity and flow relations, they use similar families of theories to explain the outcomes of communication networks. In particular, contagion, exchange/dependency, and self-interest theories are the most prevalent frameworks for research about affinity networks. The one difference is that cognitive/semantic theories are not frequently utilized to understand these networks.

Research utilizing contagion and self-interest theories to explain outcomes based on implicit information exchange is assumed to take place in affinity relations. The vast majority of studies that use this relation type focus on alliances. Although alliances create opportunities for collaboration and information sharing, communication researchers recognize that alliances do not necessarily result in either of these processes (Heath & Sias, 1999). However, alliances may provide opportunities for organizations to monitor their partners in ways not available to them without an alliance. For example, Pek-Hooi, Mahmood, and Mitchell (2004) demonstrate that firms are aware of the product awards that their partners receive. The number of these awards has an inverted-U relationship with subsequent research and development (R&D) investment.

Research that utilizes exchange/dependency theories appear better suited for affinity than flow relations. Much of this research seeks to explain trust. For example, Shane and Cable (2002) demonstrate that affinity relations increase the likelihood that investors will fund ventures. In this case, affinity relations (namely friendship and social relations) provide a better explanation for trust than flow relations. In particular, affinity relations create a structure in which violating agreements creates significant costs, and the loss of information flow does not necessarily lead to a similar disruption in one's social world.

Theories to Explain the Emergence of Communication Network Relations

Although, as discussed above, research investigating the influence of communication networks on outcomes is important, this chapter primarily focuses on research that seeks to explain the emergence of multidimensional networks. Our review indicates that there are systematic patterns in the families of theories that scholars use to explain the emergence of flow, affinity, representational, and semantic networks. In examining these families, this section lays the groundwork for applying different theories to the various types of relations embedded in multidimensional networks.

Flow

Flow relations depict the patterns of message exchange or transmission among nodes. In this section, we classify them based on two factors: whether the network is observed or perceived and whether the actors are engaged in joint or individual goal-oriented activities. We categorize studies based on their theoretical families into a two-by-two table (Table 18.2).

Whether a communication is observed or perceived is one of the most significant differences in flow relations (Faust & Skvoretz, 2002). Indeed, communication researchers have long been aware that observed and self-reported networks are fundamentally different and often bear little to no relationship to one another (Bernard & Killworth, 1977; Corman, 1990). Scholars suggest that rather than seeing this as a problem, communication researchers should consider perceived communication networks as objects worthy of study in their own right (Corman, 1990; Richards, 1985). In many cognitive theories, individuals' perceptions of flows are more relevant than some objective measure of flow. It therefore follows that different patterns of relations may occur in these two types of flow networks.

Further, flow relations differ based on the type of collective activity in which the actors are involved (see Poole & Contractor, 2011, for a more nuanced typology). We categorize the existing literature into two groups: (1) networks in which the goals of an individual actor dominate communication flow and (2) networks in which joint goals characterize communication patterns.

Observed Flow Networks

Perhaps because digital trace data are more prevalent in cases in which individual goals dominate, only one study examines observed communication networks in the context of joint goals. Oh and Jeon (2007) have investigated two open source communities, Linux and Hypermail, using both empirical and simulation data to identify the factors that influence average participation. In general, they find that as outside influence increases, average participation declines. In comparison, research on observed flow networks when individual goals predominate is more common. This research is derived from three of the 10 theoretical families: homophily, cognitive/semantic theories, and theories of self-interest. As appropriate for an examination of individual-goal networks, these theories emphasize psychological processes and individual choice in the emergence of flow networks.

Homophily-based research on observed flow generally focuses on e-mail networks and the ways in which similarity leads to high rates of exchange. For example, Kossinets and Watts (2009) examine the dynamic interaction of choice homophily and induced homophily. *Choice homophily* refers to the selection of others derived from individual psychological preference, while *induced homophily* depicts the selection of others based on similarity of opportunities, or triadic closure in this case. They find that both types of homophily operate together over time and create a network in which highly similar others exchange messages.

Research drawing on the cognitive/semantic family of theoretical mechanisms focuses largely on patent citations[3] as indicators of knowledge flow among inventors and organizations. Research reports that interfirm mobility of inventors (Almeida & Kogut, 1999; Rosenkopf & Almeida, 2003), interfirm alliances (Rosenkopf & Almeida, 2003), geographic localization (Almeida & Kogut, 1999; Singh, 2005), and relations among inventors (Singh, 2005) influence the flow of knowledge. In short, research from

Table 18.2 Types of Flow Networks and Theoretical Families

	Joint Goals Predominate	Individual Goals Predominate
Observed	Contagion (Oh & Jeon, 2007)	Homophily (Kleinbaum, Stuart, & Tushman, 2011; Kossinets & Watts, 2009) Cognitive/Semantic theories (Almeida & Kogut, 1999; Rosenkopf & Almeida, 2003; Singh, 2005) Theories of self-interest (Burt, 2011a, 2011b)
Perceived	Homophily (Klein, Beng-Chong, Saltz, & Mayer, 2004; Salk & Brannen, 2000; Yuan & Gay, 2006) Cognitive/Semantic theories (Borgatti & Cross, 2003; Casciaro & Lobo, 2008; Klein et al., 2004; Palazzolo, 2005; Yuan, Fulk, Monge, & Contractor, 2010) Exchange and dependency theories (Klein et al., 2004; Sosa, Eppinger, & Rowles, 2004) Theories of mutual self-interest and collective action (Baldassarri & Diani, 2007; Stevenson & Greenberg, 2000; Taylor & Doerfel, 2003) Theories of physical and electronic proximity (Van den Bulte & Moenaert, 1998) MTML (Contractor et al., 2006)	Homophily (Ibarra, 1995) Theories of self-interest (McDonald, Khanna, & Westphal, 2008; Mehra, Kilduff, & Brass, 2001; Shah, 1998)

the cognitive/semantic perspective examines how geographic localization restricts knowledge flow and how multiplex relations among firms enable it.

Burt's (2011a, 2011b) research has applied his social capital theory to the online gaming and virtual world contexts. He finds that individuals tend to build the same types of networks across the games that they play. However, it is their network *role*, not network *personality*, which determines their ultimate success. Consistent with findings in offline networks, Burt finds that brokers accrue significant benefits.

In sum, research on observed flow networks suggests that actors' attributes, network roles, and multiplex network embeddedness influence the patterns of communication. The MTML perspective indicates that theories in each of these areas might complement one another, providing a richer explanation in combination than in isolation. Moreover, case studies in each of these areas might be fruitfully combined through the use of meta-analysis to examine the degree to which systematic differences exist across networks. Faust and Skvoretz's (2002) work suggests that many of the apparent differences across these networks are minimal in comparison to studies that examine perceived flow, which is discussed next.

Perceived Flow Networks

Research on perceived flow networks is more prevalent than research on observed flow networks. Such research tends to focus on circumstances in which *joint goals* predominate. This research draws from five families of theories—homophily, cognitive/semantic, exchange/dependency, theories of mutual self-interest/collective action, and theories of physical/electronic proximity—and generally falls into two logics: (1) the impact of endogenous factors and attributes on the pattern of networks relations and (2) the impact of exogenous factors on the network itself.

Endogenous network factors and attributes are explained on the basis of homophily and cognitive/semantic theories. This research investigates the psychological inducements that lead to particular configurations in perceived communication networks, specifically, the network environment and individual perception of others in it. For example, Salk and Brannen's (2000) research, based in social identity theory, focuses on the differences in network formations among Japanese and German managers. Drawing from homophily theory, they suggest that managers from the same country utilize similar logics in developing their self-reported, task-related, advice-related, and private communication patterns. Yuan and Gay (2006) similarly examine instrumental and expressive communication among student teams and report that gender-based and race-based homophily has no impact on perceived flow patterns in these groups. Instead, location and previous collaboration explains the majority of variance in these relationships. Research from cognitive/semantic theory also studies the conditions in which self-reported information exchange, task communication, or advice occur. This research indicates that individuals are more likely to seek information from experts (Borgatti & Cross, 2003; Palazzolo, 2005), especially when the costs for seeking information are low (Borgatti & Cross, 2003) and when team level task interdependence and communication density are high (Yuan et al., 2010). However, Casciaro and Lobo (2008) observe that personal affect overrides the impact of expert or competence-related information seeking on network patterns. In short, if a person is liked, despite their level of competence, they are sought out for task-related information.

The impact of exogenous network factors on perceived flows is explained on the basis of exchange/dependency, mutual self-interest/collective action, and physical/electronic proximity. This research addresses how various types of exchange, either across subgroups, network regions, or teams, influence the ways that groups work together and the outcomes of their coordination. For example, Baldassarri and Diani (2007) focus on the different roles that social bonds and transaction relations play in collective action. They demonstrate how social bonds shape solidarity and unite organizations that are pursuing the same type of actions. Transactional relations, however, coordinate subgroups of actors who have less interest similarity. Drawing from exchange/dependence and electronic/physical proximity theories, Van den Bulte and Moenaert (1998) focus on the types of relations that connect actors across subgroups. They note circumstances that induce subgroups to form relationships, specifically, colocation to the same physical space. In short, research on perceived flows when joint goals predominate suggests that both endogenous network factors (e.g., homophily, perceived attractiveness) and exogenous factors (e.g., multiplex network relations) influence network configurations. The MTML approach goes further and suggests that these two sets of factors should be used in combination to predict the configuration of these networks.

Research that examines perceived flow networks in conditions when *individual goals* predominate utilizes homophily and self-interest theories. The research in this cell focuses on how individuals seek information in order to advance their careers. For instance, Shah (1998) investigates how employees use referents in job-related information seeking. She reports that employees monitor structurally equivalent actors and use them for social comparison, but they seek out organizational information from cohesive relations (e.g., those with whom they share a personal relationship). Further, to enhance opportunities for advancement over time, high self-monitoring employees strategically maneuver themselves into the central locations of a firm's networks (Mehra, Kilduff, & Brass, 2001).

In summary, two conclusions emerge from an examination of Table 18.2. First, researchers study perceived communication networks in the same ways that they examine networks of observed flow. This conclusion is somewhat troubling, since organizational communication researchers have long known that these two networks barely correlate with one another (Bernard & Killworth, 1977; Corman, 1990). Communication researchers have yet to take seriously the call to theorize about perceived communication networks in a way that is different from observed communication networks (Richards, 1985).

Second, although homophily and cognitive/semantic theories are prevalent across both perceived and observed communication networks, there are clear theoretical distinctions between joint and individual goal-oriented networks. Studies of joint goal-oriented networks rely on theories of mutual self-interest/collective action and exchange/dependency. Research on individual goal-oriented networks draws from the self-interest family, primarily social capital theories. As such, researchers can now draw conclusions about the typical patterns expected across network case studies, ones that could aid in developing a contingency-based MTML theory for the emergence of flow networks. Such a theory could also consider expected patterns in affinity networks as researchers embrace the study of multidimensional networks.

Affinity Relations

The study of affinity relations focuses on socially constructed relationships among actors that may have either a positive or negative valence. As illustrated by the perspective on the communicative constitution of organization (Putnam & Nicotera, 2008), researchers must rely on individual or organizational reports to determine whether socially constructed relationships, such as friendship or collaborations, exist among parties. As such, affinity relations are perceived communication networks. However, researchers can apply a more stringent criterion to affinity relations. Instead of relying on a single report as evidence of the relation, each party can confirm the relational connections. The reviewed studies, however, do not treat perceived and confirmed affinity relations differently. Instead, the research typically falls into two categories: studies of forming alliances and studies of developing interpersonal relationships.

The research on individual goal-oriented affinity relations typically examines patterns of alliances or collaborative relationships across organizations that are included in a sector. The primary explanation for alliance formation or collaborative relations among organizations derives from exchange/dependency theories. This work shows that alliance relationships are more prevalent among organizations that are embedded in multiplex relationships (Gimeno, 2004; Rosenkopf, Mentiu, & George, 2001; Stuart, 1998), are both high-status or unconstrained incumbents (Jensen, 2008), are central in the network (Gulati & Gargiulo, 1999), have previously had a relationship (although that decreases with each subsequent partner), and have common mutual partners (Atouba & Shumate, 2010; Gulati, 1995b; Gulati & Gargiulo, 1999). In addition, research that focuses on alliances investigates their evolution over time

(Lavie & Rosenkopf, 2006; Powell, White, Koput, & Owen-Smith, 2005; Shumate, Fulk, & Monge, 2005), their contractual nature (Gulati, 1995a), how patterns differ by region (Owen-Smith, Riccaboni, Pammolli, & Powell, 2002), and alliance withdrawal (Greve, Baum, Mitsuhashi, & Rowley, 2010).

The remaining studies of affinity relations generally focus on interpersonal cooperative relationships and friendships. Almost half of these studies investigate the circumstances in which individual goals predominate, including academic collaboration on papers (Hughes, Peeler, & Hogenesch, 2010), friendship networks in schools (Conti & Doreian, 2010; Moody, 2001), work collaborations (Bacharach, Bamberger, & Vashdi, 2005), cooperative relations among entrepreneurs (Vissa, 2011), and friendships based on coappearances on Facebook[4] photos (Wimmer & Lewis, 2010). In contrast, studies of networks when joint goals predominate focus on workgroups (Balkundi, Kilduff, Barsness, & Michael, 2007; Milton & Westphal, 2005). A theme that appears across these studies is greater contact among different individuals can override homophily-based influences on individual affinity relationships. Although individuals tend to form affinity relations with others like them, they can be influenced to form heterogeneous relationships through contact with diverse others, including through workgroup formations (Balkundi et al., 2007) or school integration (Moody, 2001). In short, diverse interactions can induce birds of a feather not to flock together.

The reviews of the research on flow and affinity relations point to two interesting implications. The first is that studies of perceived flow and those on affinity relations may have more in common than do investigations of perceived and observed flow. The research based in homophily theory provides a compelling case. Research that examines observed communication networks finds homophily-based effects (Kleinbaum et al., 2011; Kossinets & Watts, 2009). In contrast, research on perceived communication networks (Yuan & Gay, 2006) and affinity networks (Balkundi et al., 2007) find little support for homophily-based explanations and instead point to the role of colocation and previous collaboration on networks. One possible explanation for this finding is that an individual's communication behavior is driven by homophily and that the recognition of such behavior causes dissonance for participants; hence, individuals may socially construct communication networks that embrace diversity. Alternatively, individuals may think about their social worlds based on those with whom they are colocated and are in similar social and/or task groups, but they have a broader set of communication contacts that are relatively homogenous.

Second, although cognitive/semantic theories and homophily theory account for both affinity and flow relations, some theoretical families provide more dominant explanations for one type of relation than others. Theories of mutual self-interest/collective action explain flow relations; evolutionary theory accounts for affinity networks. Cognitive/semantic theoretical explanations are prevalent in flow networks, while exchange/dependency explanations appear in studies of affinity networks. Such patterns suggest that different families of theories may explain some types of relations in multidimensional networks better than others.

Representational Relations

Representational relations describe messages about affiliations among a set of actors that are communicated to a third party; hence, they are by definition self-reported communication relations. The properties of flow versus the characteristics of representational communication networks are logically different. For the receiver, the cost of receiving flow relations increases with each link, assuming that message is received and processed. Receiving too many flow links can result in information overload and therefore present a practical cap on indegree centrality (i.e., the number of links coming to an actor). In contrast, receiving additional representational communication links has no corresponding costs. As such, the structure of networks composed of representational relations and flow relations are likely to differ. Networks composed of representational relations often contain a few actors with relatively high indegree centrality in comparison to other actors in their network. Networks possessing this pattern are said to follow a scale-free indegree distribution (Barabási, Albert, & Jeong, 2000). In contrast, because of the cost of receiving a multitude of flow relations, the degree centrality of actors in flow networks is likely to be constrained, making the differences between the degree centrality of actors in these networks smaller than between actors in networks composed of representational relations. The study of representational networks is new to organizational communication. Even though other types of representational relations exist, organizational communication research has focused on two types: hyperlink networks and the public communication of corporate-NGO relations.

Hyperlink Networks. As Shumate and Lipp (2008) and Lusher and Ackland (2010) note, hyperlinks are connections based on public affiliation or representation instead of flow. Indeed, electronic communication can hyperlink to websites without the author(s) of that website becoming aware of the link. Through representational communication, hyperlinks seek to socially construct the relationship among actors for third parties. For organizational communication researchers, hyperlinks among websites provide insights into the varied relationships among government, for-profit, and nonprofit institutions. However, the majority of studies focus on nonprofit organizations, NGOs, and social movement websites.

In general, interorganizational hyperlink research focuses on three related but distinct issues. The first is to decipher the pattern of hyperlink relations based on the overall network structure. Shumate and Dewitt (2008) and Shumate and Lipp (2008) describe particular patterns that are prevalent in these hyperlink networks, including reciprocal relations, relations to two unlinked other websites, relations from two unlinked websites, and transitive relations. A second, more prominent focus has been on organizational attributes that influence the prevalence of relations. The most prominent theoretical explanation in this work is homophily, whereby various types of similarities influence the likelihood of a hyperlink among organizational actors; these similarities include same goals (Bae & Choi, 2000), same global region (Shumate & Dewitt, 2008), and same political party and committee affiliation (Park & Kluver, 2009). However, a second explanation, based on resource dependence theory, also receives attention. Gonzalez-Bailon (2009a, 2009b) observes that groups with greater economic resources are significantly more likely to receive hyperlinks than groups with fewer economic resources.

A third focus centers on the ways that hyperlinks intersect with other relations. Pilny and Shumate (2011) suggest that NGO hyperlinks are an extension of offline instrumental collective action behaviors. They report that offline relations, including financial relations, membership relations, and collaborative relations, influence hyperlinking. However, the relation that has received the most interest is issue networks, particularly the ways that they align with hyperlink networks. Issue networks depict political entities (Kim, Barnett, & Park, 2010) or NGOs (Rogers & Ben-David, 2008) who are engaged in similar policy discourses; such networks link together the politicians or NGOs who address the same social issues. Researchers have found that issue networks correlate with hyperlink networks (Kim et al., 2010; Menczer, 2004; Shumate, 2012).

Relationships Between Corporations and NGOs. A second example of representational communication comes from research associated with the Symbiotic Sustainability Model (Shumate & O'Connor, 2010b). The Symbiotic Sustainability Model focuses on the public communication of relationships between corporations and NGOs.

It asserts that such relations are part of the institutional positioning of communication (McPhee & Zaug, 2000). Such representational relations are the constitutive elements through which organizations mobilize capital and convince stakeholders of their legitimacy and character. Shumate and O'Connor (2010a) examine the portfolio of NGO partners identified by corporations. Practically, the research reports the types and numbers of social issues that are likely to be salient in corporate-funded communication.

In effect, research on representational relations is relatively scarce in the organizational communication literature. These studies rely on theoretical families such as homophily (Bae & Choi, 2000), resource dependency (Gonzalez-Bailon, 2009a), collective action (Pilny & Shumate, 2011), and evolutionary theory (Shumate & O'Connor, 2010a). Clearly, more work is needed before conclusions can be drawn. In particular, more attention needs to be paid to the ways that impression management (Schlenker, 1980) influences these relations, especially since they stem from messages communicated to third parties in a public venue. Moreover, because representational networks have a few actors that receive significantly more links than others in their network (Barabási et al., 2000), the formation of links is likely driven by social influence. Hence, both social influence and impression management theories may provide robust explanations of the patterns that depict representational relations.

Semantic Relations

Communication scholars were among the first researchers to conduct semantic network analysis (Danowski, 1988; Monge & Eisenberg, 1987). In their early book, Rogers and Kincaid (1981) suggest, "We need to combine the research method of content analysis of communication messages with the technique of network analysis to better understand how individuals give meaning to information that is exchanged through communication processes" (p. 77). However, since 1990, our survey of organizational communication network research reveals only one article that conducted a semantic network analysis of individuals (Stohl, 1993). Based on a content analysis of unstructured interviews, Stohl derived a network of the extent to which 60 managers shared their interpretations of the term *participation*. Overall, her study supports the use of Hofstede's (1980) cultural dimensions, using data that were not subject to common methods bias or quantitative reduction through survey-based items. Stohl's study illustrates Rogers and Kincaid's (1981) claim regarding the potential of combining social network analysis and content analysis methods.

However, the lack of studies that use this combined approach may stem from the need for theories to guide semantic network researchers. Stohl (1993) notes some difficulty in interpreting the meaning of measures, such as centrality, in semantic networks. Carley and Kaufer (1993), in perhaps the only theoretical work on semantic networks, suggest that the concepts of conductivity and consensus provide helpful interpretations or directions for research. *Conductivity* is a concept's ability to trigger other concepts or its ability to act as a gateway to other concepts. In contrast, *consensus* describes the degree to which people agree on the structure of the semantic network. Carley and Kaufer draw researchers' attention to two important elements of semantic network analysis: (a) understanding the relationships between words or concepts within the network and (b) understanding the ways in which individuals' cognitive maps of semantic networks vary. Both elements are ripe areas for future research, especially with access to digital texts.

Even though other types of communication network relations may exist, the four presented in this chapter account for most of organizational communication network research to date. *Flow networks* focus on the exchange of messages among actors while *affinity networks* describe the socially constructed relations among actors that may imply flows but are conceptually distinct from flows. *Representational networks* signal actors' affiliations to third parties. *Semantic networks* describe shared meanings among people and concepts.

Foundations of Multiplexity in Multidimensional Networks

The explanatory power of multidimensional networks lies in their ability to capture both the variety of nodes that make organizing possible (e.g., individuals, organizations, concepts, technologies) and the relations that constitute organizing. The above sections highlight the theoretical families that are frequently used to examine these types of communication networks. In this section, we draw this work together and discuss seven issues undergirding the foundations of a MTML approach to multidimensional networks.

First, by creating a taxonomy for classifying relations among types of networks, we address a first hurdle in the MTML approach to multidimensional networks. Communication relations such as information seeking, sharing information on various topics, and receiving unsolicited information fall within the same category. As such, these networks should be explained by the same set of theoretical families. For example, perceived relations when individual goals predominate are most commonly, and perhaps best, explained by theories of self-interest. In contrast, different types of relations (i.e., confirmed friendship and observed communication about a topic) are guided by different theories. Specifically, when individual goals predominate, theories of homophily, exchange/dependency, and physical proximity apply to the confirmed affinity relation, and theories of self-interest guide studies of observed flow relations.

Second, certain logical patterns arise in particular relation types. Observed flow relations have a logical ceiling on the expected degree centrality, because time constrains the number of individuals with whom one can communicate. In contrast, representational relations bear no direct cost to the recipient. As such, the indegree centrality of these relations is likely to be relatively unconstrained, perhaps explaining preferential attachment to a few nodes in such networks. Further, since affinity networks describe the social construction of enduring relationships, cognitive consistency is likely to drive the creation of triangles in positively valenced networks, a pattern explained by balance theory (see Monge & Contractor, 2003). Although more work is needed to empirically validate these logical patterns, this taxonomy underscores the importance of incorporating differences into a MTML approach to multidimensional networks.

Third, this review provides additional insights into data collection methods that influence the object of studies. As explicated by Corman (1990), perceived communication networks are not simply the results of relying on self-reported data; they are a fundamentally different object of study than observed communication networks. Perceived flow relations may bear more resemblance to unconfirmed affinity relations than to observed communication relations. As such, this finding calls into question organizational communication researchers' decisions to use the same theoretical families to explicate perceived and observed communication relations.

Fourth, in multidimensional networks that include nonhuman nodes, particular patterns of relations are logically not possible (i.e., friendship with a repository); however, unconfirmed positive affinity relations are plausible (e.g., the positive relationship that many people have with Siri on their iPhone). Researchers should explore differences between such unconfirmed and the confirmed affinity relations.

Fifth, affinity and communication relations do not necessarily implicate each other. That is, even though individuals report a friendship, they do not necessarily communicate with each other more often via e-mail or as observed in server logs. In short, multiplexity in multidimensional networks is likely to be more complicated than simple replication of relations within the same network; instead, relation types may suppress, facilitate, or trigger complex compound interactions (i.e., where a relation of one type among actors explains relations of other types among other actors). For example, in the nonprofit-corporate partnership domain, representational linkages between corporations and nonprofits may influence both affinity relations among nonprofits in the network and the ways that semantic networks framing the social issue are construed by the community of organizations.

Sixth, our taxonomy underscores the importance of specifying the boundary of the network—an important precondition for understanding multidimensional networks. *Network boundary specification* refers to the researcher's decision about what actors and relations to include in a network and what to exclude. Researchers set up a network boundary in two ways: an open boundary approach and a positional network approach (see Wasserman & Faust, 1994, for differences from a methodological perspective). In the open boundary approach, the researcher selects nodes based on the accessibility of the data. Studies that use snowball sampling based upon interpersonal contacts rely on an open boundary approach. In contrast, positional network approaches make purposive choices about actors in the network based upon some understood grouping, often based upon a common goal or membership (i.e., all of the employees of an organization). The choice between the two influences the types of theories that should be used in a study. In open boundary networks, individual goals predominate and, as such, theories of self-interest play a larger role. In contrast, in the positional approach, joint goals predominate and theories of mutual self-interest/collective action play a large role. In the positional approach, the actors' common goal orientation and the resources they use fall within the network's boundaries.

Seventh, and finally, the taxonomy points to gaps in theorizing multidimensional networks; that is, there are relatively few theories about the emergence of representational or semantic networks. Although homophily, resource dependency, collective action theory, or evolutionary theories explain some representational relations, future research needs to explicate the conditions under which these theories apply. Similarly, although Carley and Kaufer (1993) provide two important theoretic concepts for understanding semantic networks, empirical research in organizational communication has yet to demonstrate the heuristic value of this work. Both theory development and empirical exploration are needed to develop an MTML model for the emergence of multidimensional networks.

Theorizing the Emergence of Multidimensional Networks: The Perfect Storm

This chapter has advocated for a MTML explanation for the emergence of multidimensional networks. It would be fair to ask if and why this is the right time to be advancing this research agenda. In this section, we argue that there are four factors that put us on the brink of a positive "perfect storm" to witness the ascendance of this intellectual enterprise: novel undertheorized network forms of organizing, a data deluge, advances in analytics, and the exponential growth in computational capabilities (Contractor, 2013).

Novel Undertheorized Network Forms of Organizing

The advent of new technologies has ushered in a new generation of creative thinking around novel modalities for organizing (Shirky, 2009). These new inherently network forms of organizing represent a disruptive change from the less technologically enabled forms of network organizing described just over a decade ago by Powell (1990). One overarching feature of these models of organizing is the ability to facilitate spontaneous mobilization of globally distributed individuals and resources to generate innovative solutions to problems, contribute to real-time data collection and creation, or engage in collective action. Here are just a few examples. Innocentive.com solicits external solvers for problems confronting large R&D intensive corporations (Jeppesen & Lakhani, 2010). Individuals contribute to real-time collection and curation of knowledge, such as mapping mobility patterns in the event of a disaster (Bengtsson, Lu, Thorson, Garfield, & von Schreeb, 2011). Editors team up to compose a breaking news story on Wikipedia (Keegan, Gergle, & Contractor, 2013). Programmers collaboratively develop software on GitHub.com (Dabbish, Stuart, Tsay, & Herbsleb, 2012). Publics contribute to the funding of a start-up, product, or scientific study on kickstarter.com or rockethub.com (Wheat, Wang, Byrnes, & Ranganathan, 2012).

These phenomena are not just quantitatively but also qualitatively different from conventional modes of organizing. As a result, there is a pressing need to develop new theories, or at the very least, extend existing theories, to understand and enable these novel forms of organizing. Recent theoretical contributions on collective intelligence (Malone, Laubacher, & Dellarocas, 2009; Woolley, Chabris, Pentland, Hashmi, & Malone, 2010), social movements (Castells, 2012), collective leadership (Contractor, DeChurch, Carson, Carter, & Keegan, 2012), and the emergence and equifinality of group behavior (Hackman, 2012) allude to the importance of networks in explaining these phenomena and hence pave the way for the development of a more explicitly network-based explanation.

Data Deluge: From Big Data to Broad Data

While the development of new information technologies has ushered in novel undertheorized forms of organizing, they have also opened the fire hose of data associated with these models of organizing. This has heralded the advent of computational social science (Lazer et al., 2009) as yet another arrow in the quiver of methodologies used by social network researchers alongside field studies, experiments, and ethnography.

The emergence of digital trace data as a method of data collection has important implications for the study of some of the types of social network relations highlighted in the previous section. *Digital trace data* refers specifically to the logs of actions, interactions, and transactions that were created in digital spaces. Examples include e-mail interactions (Kossinets & Watts, 2009), hyperlinks between webpages (Lusher & Ackland, 2010), and activities in Wikipedia (Yuan et al., 2009). Digital trace data is distinct from archival data, which refers to the use of any secondary data that was previously recorded such as archival patent citation data (Singh, 2005). Research using digital trace data is relatively new, and only 17 of the 241 studies examined in this review use it. In contrast, archival data is the most commonly used data source in our review, with almost 35% of studies using it (n = 84).

Digital trace data can be used to gather observed flow, semantic, and representational communication relations. However, the study of observed flow relations may be the most important of these types. Research on observed flow relations has been scant, and much of the recent research in our review relies on digital trace data. Because we know that observed and perceived flow relations differ significantly (Bernard & Killworth, 1977; Corman, 1990), the emergence of big data is a revolutionary opportunity to understand a type of communication network we know relatively little about. Further, the "mashing" of traditional data sources with one or more digital traces moves us from utilizing *big data* to constructing *broad data* (Hendler, 2012). Broad data holds the greatest promise for developing novel research that examines multidimensional networks that contains observed flow relations and many other types of relations described in the typology.

Advances in Network Analytics

Although developing new theories and accessing large tracts of data are necessary, they are insufficient to advance our understanding of new forms of organizing without substantial advances in the development of network methodologies. In particular, we point to three methodological developments in the past decade that make analysis of such data both more effective and efficient: the creation of semantic networks from texts, inferential social network analysis methods, and methods to analyze longitudinal networks. We will briefly discuss each of these in turn.

First, recent methodological developments make future research on semantic networks both easier and more rigorous. Tools such as Automap, an assemblage of text analysis techniques (Carley, Columbus, Bigrigg, & Kunkle, 2011), provide a number of utility techniques (e.g., stemming words so that *cat* and *cats* are not treated as separate concepts) that streamline the analysis. Further, tools such as Crawdad (Corman & Dooley, 2006) implement a technique called *centering resonance analysis* that allows for the automatic creation of semantic networks from texts (Corman, Kuhn, McPhee, & Dooley, 2002). It indexes noun phrases that have the most discursive importance in texts and links them based on their co-occurrence. Along with techniques for topic modeling (Griffiths, Steyvers, & Tenenbaum, 2007), syntax analysis (Pennebaker, 2011), and sentiment analysis (Thelwall, Buckley, & Paltoglou, 2012), they have the potential for fulfilling the unrealized potential of investigating semantic networks.

Second, the move from descriptive to inferential approaches in networks research necessitated the development of new methodologies; p* or exponential family of random graph models (ERGMs) are one of the most influential inferential approaches that have emerged in the last two decades to test theoretically interesting network hypotheses. The potential of these statistical models have prompted their adoption by a small but growing number of scholars interested in empirically testing hypotheses. Twelve of the 214 publications reviewed for this chapter used p*/ERGMs. Lusher, Koskinen, and Robins (2013) offer excellent methodological and empirical examples for the use of p*/ERGMs in a variety of contexts. p*/ERGMs are also being extended to the analysis of multidimensional networks where nodes could be of more than one type. For instance, Keegan, Gergle, and Contractor (2012) used bipartite p*/ERGMs to test hypotheses about the extent to which attributes of editors on Wikipedia (experienced or novices) and attributes of the entries on Wikipedia (breaking news or average news articles) would pattern the assembly of editors working on a specific article.

Third, there have been a number of techniques recently developed for the study of longitudinal networks. To examine changes in networks from one time period to another, the most dominant model for the study of network dynamics has been the stochastic actor-oriented models (Snijders, Van de Bunt, & Steglich, 2010). These models, implemented in a software called SIENA (Simulation Investigation for Empirical Network Analysis), capture the coevolution or the mutual influence of the attributes of actors in a network (such as their attitudes and behaviors) on their relations (such as friendship and advice) and vice versa. There have been recent efforts to extend stochastic actor-oriented models to study multidimensional networks. Snijders, Lomi, and Torló (2012) test hypotheses about the extent to which friendship and advice relations among students (the first set of nodes) coevolved dynamically with their preferences for employment by a set of organizations (the second set of nodes).

However, the advent of digital trace or digitally annotated data has forced network researchers to reconsider their conceptualizations of longitudinal network data (Mathur, Poole, Peña-Mora, Hasegawa-Johnson, & Contractor, 2012). Traditional longitudinal models such as the aforementioned stochastic actor-oriented models utilize the network as it appears at one slice in time to explain the structure of the network at subsequent slices in time. However, digital trace data is often logged as the occurrence of a relational event from actor A to actor B at a particular point in time that is often recorded up to the second. For instance, a relational event would be the exact moment where an individual A began to follow the Twitter feed of an individual B. In this case, collapsing the networks into slices of time is an unnecessary aggregation resulting in loss of the richness associated with the unfolding dynamics of each relational event. The greater prevalence of relational event data captured from digital traces is motivating the development of new relational event network models that eschew the need for slices of networks at time intervals. Instead, they model the rate and weight associated with the occurrence of each relational event as a function of all prior relational events weighted by their recentness (Brandes, Lerner, & Snijders, 2009; Butts, 2008). Leenders, DeChurch, and Contractor (in press) provide a theoretical overview and an exemplar for the study of relational events in multiteam systems.

Exponential Growth in Computational Capabilities

The preceding subsections have outlined three reasons for the ascendance of a research agenda dedicated to multidimensional networks: undertheorized novel forms of organizing, a deluge of data, and advances in analytics. The final element is the exponential growth in computational capabilities. As has been immortalized in Moore's (1965) law, growth in computational capabilities has doubled every 18–24 months over the past five decades. Today, petascale computing enables us to test theoretical models using sophisticated techniques on large data sets in hours or days, rather than the months or years it would have taken a decade ago. Williams et al. (2011) describe how communication researchers can productively collaborate with computer scientists to leverage supercomputing infrastructure to analyze terabytes of network data from teams involved in online combat and quest activities within a massive multiplayer online game. A more technical discussion of those issues is beyond the scope of this chapter.

In summary, multidimensional networks are important objects of study for organizational communication researchers. They represent the complexity of organizational life and address the context and content of communication. This chapter has classified the types of communication and infrastructure relations that comprise these networks; and in doing so, it presents opportunities for both empirical and theoretical work. This chapter has also argued that the emergence of novel forms of organizing, the deluge of data, advances in analytics, and growth in computational capabilities make it a particularly opportune moment for theorizing the emergence of multidimensional networks. Hence, although it has been 25 years since a chapter in the first edition of the *Handbook of Organizational Communication* summarized social network research in the field, in many ways, the area is just entering its adolescence, with new and exciting research possibilities.

References

Ahuja, G. (2000). Collaboration networks, structural holes, and innovation: A longitudinal study. *Administrative Science Quarterly, 45*(3), 425–455. doi: 10.2307/2667105

Almeida, P., & Kogut, B. (1999). Localization of knowledge and the mobility of engineers in regional networks. *Management Science, 45*(7), 905–917. doi: 10.1287/mnsc.45.7.905

Atouba, Y., & Shumate, M. (2010). Interorganizational networking patterns among development organizations. *Journal of Communication, 60*(2), 293–317. doi: 10.1111/j.1460-2466.2010.01483.x

Bacharach, S. B., Bamberger, P. A., & Vashdi, D. (2005). Diversity and homophily at work: Supportive relations among White and African-American peers. *Academy of Management Journal, 48*(4), 619–644. doi: 10.5465/amj.2005.17843942

Bae, S., & Choi, J. (2000). *Cyberlinks between human rights NGOs: A network analysis.* Paper presented at the 58th annual national meeting of the Midwest Political Science Association, Chicago, IL.

Baldassarri, D., & Diani, M. (2007). The integrative power of civic networks. *American Journal of Sociology, 113*(3), 735–780. doi: 10.1086/521839

Balkundi, P., Kilduff, M., Barsness, Z. I., & Michael, J. H. (2007). Demographic antecedents and performance consequences of structural holes in work teams. *Journal of Organizational Behavior, 28*(2), 241–260. doi: 10.1002/job.428

Barabási, A-L., Albert, R., & Jeong, H. (2000). Scale-free characteristics of random networks: The topology of the world-wide web. *Physica A: Statistical Mechanics and Its Applications, 281*(1–4), 69–77.

Beckfield, J. (2010). The social structure of the world polity. *American Journal of Sociology, 115*(4), 1018–1068.

Bengtsson, L., Lu, X., Thorson, A., Garfield, R., & von Schreeb, J. (2011). Improved response to disasters and outbreaks by tracking population movements with mobile phone network data: A post-earthquake geospatial study in Haiti. *PLOS Medicine, 8*(8), e1001083. doi:10.1371/journal.pmed.1001083

Bernard, H. R., & Killworth, P. D. (1977). Informant accuracy in social network data II. *Human Communication Research, 4*(1), 3–18. doi: 10.1111/j.1468-2958.1977.tb00591.x

Borgatti, S. P., & Cross, R. (2003). A relational view of information seeking and learning in social networks. *Management Science, 49*(4), 432–445. doi: 10.1287/mnsc.49.4.432.14428

Borgatti, S. P., & Foster, P. C. (2003). The network paradigm in organizational research: A review and typology. *Journal of Management, 29*(6), 991–1013. doi: 10.1016/s0149-2063_03_00087-4

Brandes, U., Lerner, J., & Snijders, T. A. B. (2009). *Networks evolving step by step: Statistical analysis of dyadic event data* (pp. 200–205). Presented at the International Conference on Advances in Social Network Analysis and Mining, Athens, Greece. doi: 10.1109/ASONAM.2009.28

Burt, R. S. (1982). *Toward a structural theory of action: Network models of social structure, perception, and action*. New York, NY: Academic Press.

Burt, R. S. (2011a). *Network-related personality and the agency question: Multi-role evidence from a virtual world* [Working paper]. University of Chicago, IL. Retrieved from http://stiet.cms.si.umich.edu/sites/stiet.cms.si.umich.edu/files/Network%20Related%20Personality%20and%20the%20Agency%20Question.pdf

Burt, R. S. (2011b). *Structural holes in virtual worlds* [Working paper]. University of Chicago, IL. Retrieved from http://faculty.chicagobooth.edu/ronald.burt/research/files/SHVW.pdf

Butts, C. T. (2008). A relational event framework for social action. *Sociological Methodology, 38*(1), 155–200. doi:10.1111/j.1467-9531.2008.00203.x

Carley, K. M., Columbus, D., Bigrigg, M., & Kunkle, F. (2011). *Automap user's guide 2011*. Pittsburgh, PA: Carnegie Mellon University, School of Computer Science, Institute for Software Research.

Carley, K. M., & Kaufer, D. S. (1993). Semantic connectivity: An approach for analyzing symbols in semantic networks. *Communication Theory, 3*(3), 183–213. doi: 10.1111/j.1468-2885.1993.tb00070.x

Casciaro, T., & Lobo, M. S. (2008). When competence is irrelevant: The role of interpersonal affect in task-related ties. *Administrative Science Quarterly, 53*(4), 655–684.

Castells, M. (2012). *Networks of outrage and hope: Social movements in the Internet age*. Hoboken, NJ: Wiley.

Cho, H-K., Trier, M., & Kim, E. (2005). The use of instant messaging in working relationship development: A case study. *Journal of Computer-Mediated Communication, 10*, article 17. Retrieved from http://jcmc.indiana.edu/vol10/issue14/cho.html. doi: 10.1111/j.1083-6101.2005.tb00280.x

Conti, N., & Doreian, P. (2010). Social network engineering and race in a police academy: A longitudinal analysis. *Social Networks, 32*(1), 30–43. doi: 10.1016/j.socnet.2009.08.001

Contractor, N. S. (2009). The emergence of multidimensional networks. *Journal of Computer-Mediated Communication, 14*(3), 743–747. doi: 10.1111/j.1083-6101.2009.01465.x

Contractor, N. S. (2013). Some assembly required: Leveraging web science to understand and enable team assembly. *Philosophical Transactions of the Royal Society, A*, 1–15. doi:10.1098/rsta.2012.0385&domain=pdf&date_stamp

Contractor, N. S., DeChurch, L. A., Carson, J. B., Carter, D., & Keegan, B. (2012). The topology of collective leadership. *The Leadership Quarterly, 23*(6), 994–1011.

Contractor, N. S., Monge, P. R., & Leonardi, P. M. (2011). Multidimensional networks and the dynamics of socimateriality: Bringing technology inside the network. *International Journal of Communication, 5*, 1–20.

Contractor, N. S., Wasserman, S., & Faust, K. (2006). Testing multitheoretical, multilevel hypotheses about organizational networks: An analytic framework and empirical example. *Academy of Management Review, 31*(3), 681–703.

Cooper, K., & Shumate, M. (2012). Interorganizational collaboration explored through the bona fide network perspective. *Management Communication Quarterly, 26*(4), 623–654.

Corman, S. R. (1990). A model of perceived communication in collective networks. *Human Communication Research, 16*(4), 582–602. doi: 10.1111/j.1468-2958.1990.tb00223.x

Corman, S. R., & Dooley, K. J. (2006). *Crawdad text analysis system 2.0.* Chandler, AZ: Crawdad Technologies, LLC.

Corman, S. R., Kuhn, T., McPhee, R. D., & Dooley, K. J. (2002). Studying complex discursive systems: Centering resonance analysis of communication. *Human Communication Research, 28*(2), 157–206. doi: 10.1111/j.1468-2958.2002.tb00802.x

Cross, R., & Cummings, J. N. (2004). Tie and network correlates of individual performance in knowledge-intensive work. *Academy of Management Journal, 47*(6), 928–937. doi: 10.2307/20159632

Cummings, J. N. (2004). Work groups, structural diversity, and knowledge sharing in a global organization. *Management Science, 50*(3), 352–364. doi: 10.1287/mnsc.1030.0134

Dabbish, L., Stuart, C., Tsay, J., & Herbsleb, J. (2012, February). *Social coding in GitHub: Transparency and collaboration in an open software repository* (pp. 1277–1286). Proceedings of the ACM 2012 conference on Computer Supported Cooperative Work Seattle, WA.

Danowski, J. (1988). Organizational infographics and automated auditing: Using computers to unobtrusively gather as well as analyze communication. In G. M. Goldhaber & G. A. Barnett (Eds.), *Hanbook of organizational communication* (pp. 385–434). Norwood, NJ:Ablex.

DiMaggio, P. J., & Powell, W. W. (1983). The iron cage revisited—Institutional isomorphism and collective rationality in organizational fields. *American Sociological Review, 48*(2), 147–160.

Doerfel, M., & Taylor, M. (2004). Network dynamics of interorganizational cooperation: The Croatian civil society movement. *Communication Monographs, 71*(4), 373–394. doi: 10.1080/0363452042000307470

Faust, K., & Skvoretz, J. (2002). Comparing networks across space and time, size and species. *Sociological Methodology, 32*(1), 267–299. doi: 10.1111/1467-9531.00118

Fulk, J., Steinfield, C. W., Schmitz, J., & Power, J. G. (1987). A social information processing model of media use in organizations. *Communication Research, 14*(5), 529–552.

Gimeno, J. (2004). Competition within and between networks: The contingent effect of competitive embeddedness on alliance formation. *Academy of Management Journal, 47*(6), 820–842. doi: 10.2307/20159625

Gonzalez-Bailon, S. (2009a). Opening the black box of link formation: Social factors underlying the structure of the web. *Social Networks, 31*(4), 271–280. doi: 10.1016/j.socnet.2009.07.003

Gonzalez-Bailon, S. (2009b). Traps on the web. *Information, Communication & Society, 12*(8), 1149–1173. doi: 10.1080/13691180902767265

Greve, H. R., Baum, J. A. C., Mitsuhashi, H., & Rowley, T. J. (2010). Built to last but falling apart: Cohesion, friction, and withdrawal from interfirm alliances. *Academy of Management Journal, 53*(2), 302–322.

Griffiths, T. L., Steyvers, M., & Tenenbaum, J. B. (2007). Topics in semantic representation. *Psychological Review, 114*(2), 211–244.

Gulati, R. (1995a). Does familiarity breed trust? The implications of repeated ties for contractual choice in alliances. *The Academy of Management Journal, 38*(1), 85–112.

Gulati, R. (1995b). Social structure and alliance formation patterns: A longitudinal analysis. *Administrative Science Quarterly, 40*(4), 619–652. doi: 10.2307/2393756

Gulati, R., & Gargiulo, M. (1999). Where do interorganizational networks come from? *American Journal of Sociology, 104*(5), 1439–1493. doi: 10.1086/210179

Hackman, J. R. (2012). From causes to conditions in group research. *Journal of Organizational Behavior, 33*(3), 428–444. doi:10.1002/job.1774

Haunschild, P. R., & Beckman, C. M. (1998). When do interlocks matter? Alternate sources of information and interlock influence. *Administrative Science Quarterly, 43*(4), 815–844. doi: 10.2307/2393617

Heath, R. G., & Sias, P. M. (1999). Communicating spirit in a collaborative alliance. *Journal of Applied Communication Research, 27*(4), 356–376.

Hendler, J. (2012). Increasing access to the web of "broad data" (pp. 1–2, article 31). Proceedings of the International Cross-Disciplinary Conference on Web Accessibility, Lyon, France. doi:10.1145/2207016.2207041

Hofstede, G. (1980). *Culture's consequences: International differences in work-related values* (vol. 5). Thousand Oaks, CA: SAGE.

Hughes, M. E., Peeler, J., & Hogenesch, J. B. (2010). Network dynamics to evaluate performance of an academic institution. *Science Translational Medicine, 2*(53), 53. doi: 10.1126/scitranslmed.3001580

Ibarra, H. (1995). Race, opportunity, and diversity of social circles in managerial networks. *The Academy of Management Journal, 38*(3), 673–703.

Jensen, M. (2008). The use of relational discrimination to manage market entry: When do social status and structural holes work against you? *Academy of Management Journal, 51*(4), 723–743. doi: 10.5465/amj.2008.33665259

Jeppesen, L. B., & Lakhani, K. R. (2010). Marginality and problem-solving effectiveness in broadcast search. *Organization Science, 21*(5), 1016–1033. doi:10.1287/orsc.1090.0491

Keegan, B., Gergle, D., & Contractor, N. (2012). Do editors or articles drive collaboration? Multilevel statistical network analysis of Wikipedia coauthorship. In S. Poltrack & C. Simone (Eds.), *Proceedings of the CSCW '12 Computer Supported Cooperative Work. Seattle, WA* (pp. 427–436). New York, NY: ACM. doi:10.1145/2145204.2145271

Keegan, B., Gergle, D., & Contractor, N. (2013). Hot off the wiki: Structures and dynamics of Wikipedia's coverage of breaking news events. *American Behavioral Scientist, 57*(5), 595–622. doi: 10.1177/0002764212469367

Kim, J. H., Barnett, G. A., & Park, H. W. (2010). A hyperlink and issue network analysis of the United States Senate: A rediscovery of the web as a relational and topical medium. *Journal of the American Society for Information Science and Technology, 61*(8), 1598–1611. doi: 10.1002/asi.21357

Klein, K. J., Beng-Chong, L., Saltz, J. L., & Mayer, D. M. (2004). How do they get there? An examination of the antecedents of centrality in team networks. *Academy of Management Journal, 47*(6), 952–963. doi: 10.2307/20159634

Kleinbaum, A. M., Stuart, T., & Tushman, M. (2011). *Discretion within the constraints of opportunity: Gender homophily and structure in a formal organization* [Working paper 12-050]. Harvard Business School, Allston, MA. Retrieved from http://www.hbs.edu/faculty/Publication%20Files/12-050.pdf

Kossinets, G., & Watts, D. J. (2009). Origins of homophily in an evolving social network. *American Journal of Sociology, 115*(2), 405–450.

Krackhardt, D., & Bass, D. J. (1994). Interorganizational networks: The micro side. In S. Wasserman & J. Galaskiewicz (Eds.), *Advances in social network analysis: Research in the social and behavioral sciences* (pp. 207–253). Thousand Oaks, CA: SAGE.

Lavie, D., & Rosenkopf, L. (2006). Balancing exploration and exploitation in alliance formation. *Academy of Management Journal, 49*(4), 797–818. doi: 10.5465/amj.2006.22083085

Lazer, D., Pentland, A., Adamic, L., Aral, S., Barabási, A-L., Brewer, D., . . . Van Alstyne, M. (2009). Computational social science. *Science, 323*(5915), 721–723. doi: 10.1126/science.1167742

Leenders, R., DeChurch, L., & Contractor, N. (in press). Once upon a time: Understanding team dynamics as relational event networks. *Organizational Psychology Review.*

Leskovec, J., Kleinberg, J., & Faloutsos, C. (2007). Laws of graph evolution: Densification and shrinking diameters. *ACM Transactions on Knowledge Discovery from Data, 1*(1), article 2.

Lusher, D., & Ackland, R. (2010). A relational hyperlink analysis of an online social movement. *Journal of Social Structure, 11.* Retrieved from http://www.cmu.edu/joss/content/articles/volume11/Lusher/

Lusher, D., Koskinen, J., & Robins, G. (Eds.). (2013). *Exponential random graph models for social networks: Theory, methods, and applications.* New York, NY: Cambridge University Press.

Malone, T. W., Laubacher, R., & Dellarocas, C. (2009). *Harnessing crowds: Mapping the genome of collective intelligence.* Cambridge, MA: MIT.

Mathur, S., Poole, M. S., Peña-Mora, F., Hasegawa-Johnson, M., & Contractor, N. (2012). Detecting interaction links in a collaborating group using manually annotated data. *Social Networks, 34*(4), 515–526. doi:10.1016/j.socnet.2012.04.002

McDonald, M. L., Khanna, P., & Westphal, J. D. (2008). Getting them to think outside the circle: Corporate governance, CEOs' external advice networks, and firm performance. *Academy of Management Journal, 51*(3), 453–475. doi: 10.5465/amj.2008.32625969

McPhee, R. D., & Zaug, P. (2000). The communicative constitution of organizations: A framework for explanation. *The Electronic Journal of Communication, 10*(1), 1–17. Retrieved from http://www.cios.org/EJCPUBLIC/010/1/01017.html

Mehra, A., Kilduff, M., & Brass, D. J. (2001). The social networks of high and low self-monitors: Implications for workplace performance. *Administrative Science Quarterly, 46*(1), 121–146.

Menczer, F. (2004). Lexical and semantic clustering by web links. *Journal of the American Society for Information Science and Technology, 55*(14), 1261–1269. doi: 10.1002/asi.20081

Milton, L. P., & Westphal, J. D. (2005). Identity confirmation networks and cooperation in work groups. *Academy of Management Journal, 48*(2), 191–212. doi: 10.5465/amj.2005.16928393

Molm, L. D., Collett, J. L., & Schaefer, D. R. (2007). Building solidarity through generalized exchange: A theory of reciprocity. *American Journal of Sociology, 113*(1), 205–242. doi: 10.1086/517900

Monge, P. R., & Contractor, N. S. (2001). Emergence of communication networks. In F. M. Jablin & L. L. Putnam (Eds.), *The new handbook of organizational communication* (pp. 440–502). Thousand Oaks, CA: SAGE.

Monge, P. R., & Contractor, N. S. (2003). *Theories of communication networks*. Oxford, UK: Oxford University Press.

Monge, P. R., & Eisenberg, E. M. (1987). Emergent communication networks. In F. M. Jablin, L. L. Putnam, K. H. Roberts, & L. W. Porter (Eds.), *Handbook of organizational communication: An interdisciplinary perspective* (pp. 304–342). Newbury Park, CA: SAGE.

Monge, P. R., Heiss, B. M., & Margolin, D. (2008). Communication network evolution in organizational communities. *Communication Theory, 18*(4), 449–477. doi: 10.1111/j.1468-2885.2008.00330.x

Moody, J. (2001). Race, school integration, and friendship segregation in America. *American Journal of Sociology, 107*(3), 679–716. doi: 10.1086/338954

Moore, G. E. (1965). Cramming more components onto integrated circuits. *Electronics, 38*(8), 1–4.

Oh, W., & Jeon, S. (2007). Membership herding and network stability in the open source community: The ising perspective. *Management Science, 53*(7), 1086–1101. doi: 10.1287/mnsc.1060.0623

Owen-Smith, J., Riccaboni, M., Pammolli, F., & Powell, W. W. (2002). A comparison of US and European university-industry relations in the life sciences. *Management Science, 48*(1), 24–43. doi: 10.1287/mnsc.48.1.24.14275

Palazzolo, E. T. (2005). Organizing for information retrieval in transactive memory systems. *Communication Research, 32*(6), 726–761.

Papa, M. J. (1990). Communication network patterns and employee performance with new technology. *Communication Research, 17*(3), 344–368. doi: 10.1177/009365090017003004

Park, H. W., & Kluver, R. (2009). Trends in online networking among South Korean politicians—A mixed-method approach. *Government Information Quarterly, 26*(3), 505–515. doi: 10.1016/j.giq.2009.02.008

Pek-Hooi, S., Mahmood, I. P., & Mitchell, W. (2004). Dynamic inducements in R&D investment: Market signals and network locations. *Academy of Management Journal, 47*(6), 907–917. doi: 10.2307/20159630

Pennebaker, J. W. (2011). *The secret life of pronouns: What our words say about us* (1st ed.). New York, NY: Bloomsbury Press.

Pilny, A., & Shumate, M. (2011). Hyperlinks as extensions of offline instrumental collective action. *Information, Communication & Society, 15*(2), 260–286. doi: 10.1080/1369118x.2011.606328

Pollock, T. C., Whitebred, R. C., & Contractor, N. S. (2000). Social information processing and job characteristics: A simultaneous test of two theories with implications for job satisfaction. *Human Communication Research, 26*(2), 292–310.

Poole, M. S., & Contractor, N. S. (2011). Conceptualizing the multiteam system as an ecosystem of networked groups. In S. J. Zaccaro, M. A. Marks, & L. A. DeChurch (Eds.), *Multiteam systems: An organization form for dyanamic and complex environments* (pp. 193–224). New York, NY: Routledge Academic.

Postmes, T., Spears, R., & Lea, M. (2000). The formation of group norms in computer-mediated communication. *Human Communication Research, 26*(3), 341–371. doi: 10.1111/j.1468-2958.2000.tb00761.x

Powell, W. W. (1990). Neither market nor hierarchy: Network forms of organization. *Research in Organizational Behavior, 12*, 105–124.

Powell, W. W., White, D. R., Koput, K. W., & Owen-Smith, J. (2005). Network dynamics and field evolution: The growth of interorganizational collaboration in the life sciences. *American Journal of Sociology, 110*(4), 1132–1205. doi: 10.1086/421508

Prell, C. L. (2003). Community networking and social capital: Early investigations. *Journal of Computer-Mediated Communication, 8*(3), 1–22. Retrieved from http://jcmc.indiana.edu/vol8/issue3/prell.html. doi: 10.1111/j.1083-6101.2003.tb00214.x

Putnam, L. L., & Nicotera, A. M. (Eds.). (2008). *Building theories of organization: The constitutive role of communication*. New York, NY: Routledge.

Richards, W. D. (1985). Data, models and assumptions in network analysis. In R. D. McPhee & P. K. Tomkins (Eds.), *Organizational communication: Traditional themes and new directions*. Beverly Hills, CA: SAGE.

Rogers, E. M. (1995). *Diffusion of innovations*. New York, NY: Free Press.

Rogers, E. M., & Kincaid, D. L. (1981). *Communication networks: Toward a new paradigm for research*. New York, NY: Free Press.

Rogers, R., & Ben-David, A. (2008). The Palestinian–Israeli peace process and transnational issue networks: The complicated place of the Israeli NGO. *New Media & Society, 10*(3), 497–528. doi: 10.1177/1461444807085321

Rosenkopf, L., & Almeida, P. (2003). Overcoming local search through alliances and mobility. *Management Science, 49*(6), 751–766. doi: 10.1287/mnsc.49.6.751.16026

Rosenkopf, L., Metiu, A., & George, V. P. (2001). From the bottom up? Technical committee activity and alliance formation. *Administrative Science Quarterly, 46*(4), 748–772. doi: 10.2307/3094830

Salancik, G., & Pfeffer, J. (1978). A social information processing approach to job attitudes and task design. *Administrative Science Quarterly, 23*(2), 224–253.

Salk, J. E., & Brannen, M. Y. (2000). Research notes. National culture, networks, and individual influence in a multinational management team. *Academy of Management Journal, 43*(2), 191–202. doi: 10.2307/1556376

Schlenker, B. R. (1980). *Impression management: The self-concept, social identity, and interpersonal relations*. Monterey, CA: Brooks/Cole.

Scott, C. R. (1997). Identification with multiple targets in a geographically dispersed organization. *Management Communication Quarterly, 10*(4), 491–522.

Shah, P. P. (1998). Who are employees' social referents? Using a network perspective to determine referent others. *The Academy of Management Journal, 41*(3), 249–268.

Shane, S., & Cable, D. (2002). Network ties, reputation, and the financing of new ventures. *Management Science, 48*(3), 364–381. doi: 10.1287/mnsc.48.3.364.7731

Shirky, C. (2009). *Here comes everybody: The power of organizing without organizations*. New York, NY: Penguin Group.

Shumate, M. (2012). The evolution of the HIV/AIDS NGO hyperlink network. *Journal of Computer-Mediated Communication, 17*(2), 120–134. doi: 10.1111/j.1083-6101.2011.01569.x

Shumate, M., & Dewitt, L. (2008). The north/south divide in NGO hyperlink networks. *Journal of Computer-Mediated Communication, 13*(2), 405–428. doi: 10.1111/j.1083-6101.2008.00402.x

Shumate, M., Fulk, J., & Monge, P. R. (2005). Predictors of the international HIV/AIDS INGO network over time. *Human Communication Research, 31*(4), 482–510. doi: 10.1111/j.1468-2958.2005.tb00880.x

Shumate, M., & Lipp, J. (2008). Connective collective action online: An examination of the hyperlink network structure of an NGO issue network. *Journal of Computer-Mediated Communication, 14*(1), 178–201. doi: 10.1111/j.1083-6101.2008.01436.x

Shumate, M., & O'Connor, A. (2010a). Corporate reporting of cross-sector alliances: The portfolio of NGO partners communicated on corporate websites. *Communication Monographs, 77*(2), 238–261. doi: 10.1080/03637751003758201

Shumate, M., & O'Connor, A. (2010b). The symbiotic sustainability model: Conceptualizing NGO-corporate alliance communication. *Journal of Communication, 60*(3), 577–609. doi: 10.1111/j.1460-2466.2010.01498.x

Singh, J. (2005). Collaborative networks as determinants of knowledge diffusion patterns. *Management Science, 51*(5), 756–770. doi: 10.1287/mnsc.1040.0349

Snijders, T. A. B., Lomi, A., & Torló, V. J. (2012). A model for the multiplex dynamics of two-mode and one-mode networks, with an application to employment preference, friendship, and advice. *Social Networks, 35*(2), 265–276. doi: http://dx.doi.org/10.1016/j.socnet.2012.05.005

Snijders, T. A. B., Van de Bunt, G. G., & Steglich, C. E. G. (2010). Introduction to stochastic actor-based models for network dynamics. *Social Networks, 32*(1), 44–60. doi:10.1016/j.socnet.2009.02.004

So, C. Y. K. (1998). Citation ranking versus expert judgment in evaluating communication scholars: Effects of research specialty size and individual prominence. *Scientometrics, 41*(3), 325–333. doi: 10.1007/bf02459049

Sosa, M. E., Eppinger, S. D., & Rowles, C. M. (2004). The misalignment of product architecture and organizational structure in complex product development. *Management Science, 50*(12), 1674–1689. doi: 10.1287/mnsc.1040.0289

Stevenson, W. B., & Greenberg, D. (2000). Agency and social networks: Strategies of action in a social structure of position, opposition, and opportunity. *Administrative Science Quarterly, 45*(4), 651–678. doi: 10.2307/2667015

Stohl, C. (1993). European managers' interpretations of participation: "A semantic network analysis." *Human Communication Research, 20*(1), 97–117.

Stuart, T. E. (1998). Network positions and propensities to collaborate: An investigation of strategic alliance formation in a high-technology industry. *Administrative Science Quarterly, 43*(3), 668–698. doi: 10.2307/2393679

Tateo, L. (2005). The Italian extreme right on-line network: An exploratory study using an integrated social network analysis and content analysis approach. *Journal of Computer-Mediated Communication, 10*, article 10. Retrieved from http://jcmc.indiana.edu/vol10/issue12/tateo.html. doi: 10.1111/j.1083-6101.2005.tb00247.x

Taylor, M., & Doerfel, M. L. (2003). Building interorganizational relationships that build nations. *Human Communication Research, 29*(2), 153–181.

Thelwall, M., Buckley, K., & Paltoglou, G. (2012). Sentiment strength detection for the social web. *Journal of the American Society for Information Science and Technology, 63*(1), 163–173.

Van den Bulte, C., & Moenaert, R. K. (1998). The effects of R&D team co-location on communication patterns among R&D, marketing, and manufacturing. *Management Science, 44*(11), S1–S18. doi: 10.1287/mnsc.44.11.S1

Vissa, B. (2011). A matching theory of entrepreneurs' tie formation intentions and initiation of economic exchange. *Academy of Management Journal, 54*(1), 137–158. doi: 10.5465/amj.2011.59215084

Wasserman, S., & Faust, K. (1994). *Social network analysis: Methods and applications* (vol. 8). Cambridge, UK: Cambridge University Press.

Wheat, R. E., Wang, Y., Byrnes, J. E., & Ranganathan, J. (2012). Raising money for scientific research through crowdfunding. *Trends in Ecology & Evolution, 28*(2), 71–72.

Williams, D., Contractor, N., Poole, M. S., Srivastava, J., & Cai, D. (2011). The virtual worlds exploratorium: Using large-scale data and computational techniques for communication research. *Communication Methods and Measures, 5*(2), 163–180. doi:10.1080/19312458.2011.568373

Williamson, O. (1975). *Markets and hierarchies.* New York, NY: Free Press.

Wimmer, A., & Lewis, K. (2010). Beyond and below racial homophily: ERG models of a friendship network documented on Facebook. *American Journal of Sociology, 116*(2), 583–642. doi: 10.1086/653658

Wong, S-S., & Boh, W. F. (2010). Leveraging the ties of others to build a reputation for trustworthiness among peers. *Academy of Management Journal, 53*(1), 129–148. doi: 10.5465/amj.2010.48037265

Woolley, A. W., Chabris, C. F., Pentland, A., Hashmi, N., & Malone, T. W. (2010). Evidence for a collective intelligence factor in the performance of human groups. *Science, 330*(6004), 686–688. doi:10.1126/science.1193147

Yuan, Y. C., Cosley, D., Welser, H. T., Ling, X., & Gay, G. (2009). The diffusion of a task recommendation system to facilitate contributions to an online community. *Journal of Computer-Mediated Communication, 15*(1), 32–59. doi: 10.1111/j.1083-6101.2009.01491.x

Yuan, Y. C., Fulk, J., Monge, P. R., & Contractor, N. S. (2010). Expertise directory development, shared task interdependence, and strength of communication network ties as multilevel predictors of expertise exchange in transactive memory work groups. *Communication Research, 37*(1), 20–47. doi: 10.1177/0093650209351469

Yuan, Y. C., & Gay, G. (2006). Homophily of network ties and bonding and bridging social capital in computer-mediated distributed teams. *Journal of Computer-Mediated Communication, 11*(4), 1062–1084. doi: 10.1111/j.1083-6101.2006.00308.x

Notes

1. *Hyperlink networks* describe the hypertext relationships that exist between websites.

2. *Bibliometric networks* describe the citation and authorship relationships that exist, often in academic papers.

3. Patent citations are created by three parties: the applicant, the patent lawyer, and the patent office. The goal of patent citations is to accurately account for all prior knowledge upon which the current patent builds. As such, it is a measure of knowledge flow.

4. In the case of copresence in photos, as argued by Wimmer and Lewis (2010), there exists documentation of an offline relationship and time spent together. As such, these relations are better classified as affinity.

Acknowledgments

The authors would like to thank Curie Chang, Andrew Pilny, and Yannick Atouba for their help with collecting, coding, and organizing the articles reviewed in this chapter. This work was supported by grants from the National Science Foundation (SES-1264417; CNS-1010904; BCS-0940851; OCI-0904356), Army Research Institute (W5J9CQ-12-C-0017), and Army Research Laboratory under Cooperative Agreement Number (W911NF-09-2-0053).

SECTION IV

Organizing Knowledge, Meaning, and Change

Kathleen J. Krone

Section IV features the contributions of organizational communication scholars to research on the subjects of knowledge and knowing, organizational change, organizational socialization, organizational culture, and organizational emotions. Each chapter locates the subject area within a larger historical context and within larger bodies of interdisciplinary work. Each contributor also highlights influential theoretical perspectives and major themes in the research before proposing promising directions for future communication research. Two of the chapters (organizational culture and organizational socialization) build upon agenda-setting chapters appearing in earlier editions of the *Handbook of Organizational Communication* (Jablin & Putnam, 2001; Jablin, Putnam, Roberts, & Porter, 1987), while the remaining three chapters (knowledge and knowing, organizational change, emotion) address subjects of more recent interest to organizational communication scholars. Whether addressing a classic or emerging research area, each chapter makes clear the centrality of communication to these processes. Taken together, this set of chapters illustrates what it means to continue moving beyond simpler understandings of communication as contained by organizations toward the development of communication-centered understandings of organizing. Developing that view further, the chapters also illustrate what it means to take information-centered or meaning-centered approaches to studying organizational communication (Deetz, 1994; Poole, 2011) and even ways in which the use of one approach might complement the use of the other. As a set, these chapters also illustrate the field's commitment to developing understandings of organizational communication as both ordering and tension filled. This section of the handbook, then, represents a microcosm of the field's theoretical and methodological breadth and depth and its ongoing story of development.

Knowledge and Knowing in Organizational Communication

Kuhn begins by situating the subject of knowledge and knowing in organizational communication within the larger interdisciplinary field of organizational studies and a broader interest in understanding and managing knowledge-intensive organizations. At the same time, because of the centrality of communication to processes of constructing and deploying knowledge, he sees potential for this work to contribute to the development of communication-centered understandings of organizations, an argument he returns to throughout the chapter. Kuhn helps lay the foundation for this argument by distinguishing between a cognitive view and a practice-based model of knowledge, detailing the consequences of each for organizational communication theory and research. Briefly, the cognitive view promotes information transfer models of communication in that it assumes that knowledge can be extracted from the knower and transferred, while the practice model positions communication as a potentially complex, tension-filled process of socially constructing and deploying knowledge.

Kuhn then presents an overview of organizational communication research on knowledge and knowing, organized around the themes of knowledge management (KM) systems, communication networks and knowledge, and communities of practice (CoPs) and the production of power. For Kuhn, the communication contribution to understandings of KM systems rests largely in framing groups as complex information-processing and problem-solving transactive memory systems, disrupting deterministic understandings of information and communication technologies (ICTs), and articulating alternative conversation design logics in the development of knowledge. The communication contribution to understandings of networks and knowledge rests in identifying the consequences of various communication patterns on the organizational creation, transfer, and adoption of knowledge at several levels of analysis and in detailing processes of knowledge emergence within and among organizations. The contribution of communication research to understandings of CoPs and power rests in the ways in which studies problematize and reframe expertise, boundary spanning, and power in organizing and organizations. For Kuhn, projects such as this illustrate the potential of practice-based understandings of knowledge and models of CoPs to describe organizing processes.

Kuhn concludes the chapter by developing an agenda for knowledge and knowing research in organizational communication. He begins by recapping how organizational communication scholars already have used concepts related to knowledge and knowing to explain important organizing phenomena. Grounded in this work, he goes on to sketch the contours of an agenda for future research. Specifically, Kuhn offers suggestions to guide studies that will continue to address dualisms evident in earlier research, including the subject-object dualism and the division between cognitive and practice approaches. He also notes the Western bias in the research and calls for work grounded in non-Western understandings of knowledge and knowing. And last, while noting the current research emphasis on materiality in knowledge and knowing, he calls for extensions of this work. Kuhn draws the chapter to a close by reframing knowledge and knowing not just as topics of inquiry but as ways to develop distinctly communicative modes of explaining organizations and organizing.

Organizational Change and Innovation

In Chapter 20, Lewis showcases the communication contribution to the interdisciplinary research area of organizational change and innovation. Lewis begins by highlighting central themes in organizational change research and contrasting these with important questions yet to be addressed in the literature. She goes on to review a range of ways to conceptualize organizational change along with classic and alternative models of change, all of which help to lay the groundwork for the remainder of the chapter and its more specific focus on the role of communication in organizational change processes. Noting the centrality of communication to a variety of organizational change processes, Lewis devotes the rest of the chapter to a discussion of research organized around a broad range of communicative themes including communication-related triggers and diffusion of change, communication processes related to implementing change, the social construction of change, discourses in change, and dialectical processes of change.

Lewis details how organizational communication with and among a variety of important internal and external stakeholders creates pressure for change and also influences change implementation. Importantly, the diversity embedded in this set of forces adds complexity to the change process, drawing further attention to the importance of communication in framing the need for organizational change. In discussing the role of communication in implementing change, Lewis highlights the interdisciplinary nature of the research and its grounding in a managerial perspective. The attempt to produce knowledge useful to managers as they attempt to guide and control organizational change processes operates as a central theme in this expansive body of research. Lewis organizes her discussion of this research around the more specific communicative themes of information sharing and knowledge creation, soliciting input, stakeholders' attitudes, dispositions and reactions to change, and managing negative reactions to organizational change.

Lewis then turns to a discussion of social constructionist approaches to studying organizational change. Here, research focuses on how stakeholders interact and make sense of organizational change and innovation. Through this lens, organizational change becomes a fluid process of interpretation that shapes stakeholders' orientation to change in expected and unexpected ways. Lewis advocates the use of this approach to develop theoretical explanations of how and why stakeholders' interpretations remain in flux over time. Next, Lewis highlights the contribution and potential of research designed to explore discourse and organizational change. In particular, she features the contribution of research on processes of framing and storytelling related to organizational change. With respect to framing, one area of interest involves exploring framing and reframing of organizational change among managers and employees and the ways in which politics can figure in to these processes. With respect to the role of stories and storytelling, Lewis highlights the ways in which explorations of these processes provide insight into the nature of the everyday experience of organizational change, including identity work, sensemaking, social support, and the negotiation of stakeholder interests over time.

Last, Lewis turns her attention to a discussion of a dialectical approach to organizational change and research devoted to conceptualizing and researching change as a tensional process. Here, research examines the nature of tensions and contradictions arising from such changes as organizational downsizing and the implementation of new technology and a range of communicative responses to those tensions. As Lewis concludes the chapter, she identifies a number of opportunities for future communication research in these areas, many of which involve moving beyond or further contextualizing a managerial perspective on organizational change. Specifically, she invites scholars to adopt a multistakeholder perspective and design projects that take into account the views and experiences of a wider range of stakeholders. She also invites scholars to reframe employee resistance to change in a number of creative ways that move beyond positioning employee resistance as an obstacle to overcome. And third, while noting the challenges of doing so, she calls for research that explores interaction processes related to planned and unplanned change over time.

Socialization and Assimilation: Theories, Processes, and Outcomes

Kramer and Miller highlight developments in communication and organizational socialization research subsequent to Jablin's characterizations appearing in the first and second editions of the *Handbook of Organizational Communication.* Kramer and Miller locate communication research within a larger body of interdisciplinary research that includes significant contributions from management and organizational behavior scholars. At the same time, they note the increased tendency among communication scholars to conceptualize socialization as an interactive process and to include a variety of occupations, social classes, and organizational types in their work.

Kramer and Miller go on to provide an overview of the major theoretical perspectives drawn upon to explore communication and organizational socialization, including uncertainty management, sensemaking, social exchange, and social identity theory. They then identify five major lines of research taken up by organizational communication scholars. First, communication scholars continue to study and build upon the earlier work on newcomer experiences of organizational socialization. Here, they identify socialization tactics, unmet expectations, message content, and information seeking as continuing foci of interest in recent years. Communication scholars also continue to explore socialization as a process of learning organizational culture and the role of supervisor-subordinate and peer workplace relationships in organizational socialization. The last two themes emerging from their assessment of the research consist of efforts to develop more complex conceptualizations and measures of successful organizational socialization and explorations of communication processes related to voluntary and involuntary organizational exit.

Kramer and Miller conclude by calling for additional longitudinal studies of communication and organizational socialization as well as studies capable of taking into account multilevel influences on communication and organizational socialization. They also provide several methodological options for meeting the challenges associated with such research. And last, they invite organizational communication scholars to continue exploring communication and organizational socialization processes among groups currently underrepresented in the research.

Organizational Culture: Creating Meaning and Influence

Keyton begins by locating the study of organizational culture within a larger historical and interdisciplinary context. Given the centrality of communication to the study of organizational culture, however, the contribution of communication scholars stands out, particularly as it relates to the development of meaning-centered conceptualizations of communication and organizations. In this chapter, Keyton sets out to build upon previous *Handbook* chapters on this subject and to illustrate the field's more recent theoretical and methodological contributions.

Keyton goes on to review a range of communication-centered definitions of organizational culture that, taken together, highlight the nature of both culture and organization as social and symbolic constructions. She traces the roots of organizational culture to the human-relations approach to organizations and these early attempts to illustrate the importance of a variety of social factors to employee well-being in organizations. She details the earliest attempts to distinguish organizational culture from organizational structure and additional attempts to distinguish between manifest and latent organizational culture. As the focus shifted over time to attempts to develop more theoretically sophisticated accounts of organizational culture and communication, such developments emerged in parallel with popular appropriations of the idea of culture as something that could and should be managed. As communication scholars broadened their focus to include interpretive and critical studies of organizational communication, they provided leadership for additional developments in the study of organizational culture.

Next, Keyton identifies current frameworks for the study of communication and organizational culture and examples of research that illustrate each. The first of these highlights the role of discourse in organizational culture, while the other proposes a set of lenses that can be used in a variety of ways to guide studies of organizational culture. A discourse approach to studying organizational culture positions the relationship between organizational culture and discourse in one of three ways: organizational culture precedes discourse, discourse precedes organizational culture, or culture and discourse arise together. Keyton then proposes and illustrates the use of multiple lenses to guide studies of organizational culture, including symbolic performance, narrative reproduction, textual reproduction, power and politics, and technology. Before concluding the chapter, Keyton presents a discussion of engagements between communication scholars and the three theoretical perspectives on organizational culture proposed by Martin.

Keyton concludes the chapter by revisiting the contribution of communication scholars to organizational culture research and beginning to sketch the contours of a communication perspective on organizational culture. For Keyton, such a perspective emphasizes ways in which all organizational members influence culture, sensemaking, and the interactive production of social and symbolic realities and how culture is produced, enacted, and communicated in organizations. But she also identifies a set of questions that, once addressed, will further develop a communication perspective on organizational culture. Primarily, she calls for the use of multiresearcher and multilayered methodological approaches capable of building generalizable models and theories of how cultural meanings evolve over time.

Organizational Emotions and Compassion at Work

Miller begins by detailing the history of organizational communication scholars' research on emotion, noting how interest grew along with an interdisciplinary movement toward conceptualizing organizations more expansively and away from the nearly exclusive emphasis on rationality, logic, and the pursuit of instrumental outcomes. Miller identifies three turning points as central to the development of communication research on organizational emotion. The first of these arose from the creative use of post-structuralist critique to reframe the theory of bounded rationality in organizational life as bounded emotionality. A second turning point involved a shift toward the study of nonprofit and human service organizations for which profit either is not an outcome or is only one of many other desired outcomes. And third, and more recently, there has been emergence of positive organizational studies (e.g., the study of organizational compassion) that also downplay an exclusively rational view of the workplace. Miller also credits Hochschild's 1983 book, *The Managed Heart*, and her groundbreaking work on emotional control in service-sector jobs as central turning points in the growth of this research. Thus over the past two decades, a communication emphasis on emotion research in organizations has emerged that involves downplaying psychological explanations of emotion in favor of framing emotion as an interactive, negotiated process.

Miller reviews organizational communication research on emotion around two themes: emotion as part of the work role and emotion as part of work life. Research on emotion as part of the work role largely investigates individuals occupying service roles, including, for example, flight attendants, emergency call-center employees, and medical technicians. Miller draws a distinction between the concepts of emotional labor and emotional work as a part of the work role. She then goes on to clarify the conceptual origins and developments in emotional labor research, followed by a discussion of emotional work with particular emphasis on the importance of empathy in human service roles. For research in this area to move forward, Miller suggests drawing upon a variety of theoretical approaches to explore the complex relationships between emotion and identity at work. Second, Miller urges researchers to move beyond strictly cataloguing specific contexts of emotional labor and to explore how contextual features transform the experience and communication of emotion. And third, she encourages researchers to explore the agency of various organizational actors to resist attempts at emotional control and creatively cope with problems arising from emotional labor and emotional work.

In her discussion of research on emotion as part of work life, Miller features organizational communication scholarship highlighting workplace relationships as rich sites for emotional communication. She discusses research on the process of enacting emotion in workplace relationships, including work exploring the more and less skillful use of emotional communication in organizations, and questions regarding the rules guiding the communication of emotion in the workplace. To build upon this research, Miller advocates exploring embodied expressions of emotion in the workplace and going further in considering the ways in which various contextual features may be figuring in to emotional communication and workplace relationships.

Miller expands upon this recommendation further in her subsequent discussion of compassion in the workplace. Here, she emphasizes the contribution of communication scholars to conceptualizing compassion as a relational, interactive process and highlights the ways in which research examines compassion as part of the work role and as part of workplace relationships. She goes on to discuss ways collectives create contexts that make possible the coordination and enactment of compassion. Notably, this work identifies a set of core mechanisms necessary to make compassion more central to the organizing process.

Conclusion

The chapters in this section illustrate that organizational communication scholars are well positioned to continue making meaningful contributions to the interdisciplinary study of knowledge and knowing, organizational change, organizational socialization, organizational culture, and emotion. The various processes addressed in this section are revealed as complex and as unfolding over time in expected and unexpected ways. Interesting and important work in each of these areas remains to be accomplished. For organizational communication scholars, these chapters provide important signposts to help guide the way.

References

Deetz, S. A. (1994). Future of the discipline: The challenges, the research, and the social contribution. In S. A. Deetz (Ed.), *Communication yearbook* (vol. 17, pp. 565–600). Thousand Oaks, CA: SAGE.

Jablin, F. M., & Putnam, L. L. (2001). (Eds.). *The new handbook of organizational communication: Advances in theory, research, and methods.* Thousand Oaks, CA: SAGE.

Jablin, F. M., Putnam, L. L., Roberts, K. H., & Porter, L. W. (1987). (Eds.). *Handbook of organizational communication: An interdisciplinary perspective.* Newbury Park, CA: SAGE.

Poole, M. S. (2011). Communication. In S. Zedeck (Ed.), *APA handbook of industrial and organizational psychology* (vol. 3, pp. 249–270). Washington, DC: APA.

CHAPTER 19

Knowledge and Knowing in Organizational Communication

Timothy R. Kuhn

Across the interdisciplinary field of organization studies, knowledge and knowledge management (KM) have become hot topics in recent decades, attracting increasing interest from scholars and practitioners alike (Contu, Grey, & Örtenblad, 2003). As with any growth area, some see the explosion of research on knowledge as a fad that will quickly fade (e.g., Ponzi & Koenig, 2002; Scarbrough & Swan, 2001). This is an unlikely trajectory in this case for two reasons. First, explicitly or implicitly, built into all organization theories are conceptions of knowledge. Whether framing organizations as systems that process information and make decisions, sets of distinctive production capabilities, negotiated cultural orders, or textual coorientation systems, theorists ground their conceptions of organization in both agents' knowledgeability and the processes of activity coordination in which those agents participate. Second, in the contemporary socio-economic context known as the *knowledge economy* (Thrift, 2005)—where, at least in the postindustrial West, personal lives and organizational actions require less of the hands and more of the head—knowledge has become seen as a crucial component of individual and organizational performance. Organizational communication scholars, in particular, have become interested in knowledge not only for these reasons but also because communication is axial to the constitution and deployment of knowledge, an understanding that suggests opportunities for the development of distinctly communicative visions of organization.

In this chapter, I attempt to make sense of scholarship on organizational knowledge and knowing. To do so, I first distinguish two common visions of knowledge (and, thereby, communication) employed in organization studies, based on the belief that metatheoretical assumptions have "practical consequences for the way we do research in terms of our topic, focus of study, what we see as 'data,' how we collect and analyze the data, how we theorize, and how we write up our research accounts" (Cunliffe, 2011, p. 651). From there, I review three main bodies of work on knowledge in organizational communication—KM systems, networks and knowledge, and CoPs—to uncover contrasting assumptions about communication and knowledge in these literatures. Finally, I address several broad issues that form an agenda for the future development of knowledge and knowing research.

Conceptualizing Knowledge and Knowing

Those who study knowledge and knowing in organization studies frequently begin by distinguishing among data, information, and knowledge. *Data* are framed as objective facts regarding events (such as the record of a financial transaction); *information* is data linked together in a message engineered by a sender to alter a receiver's thinking (such as a statement comparing the number of transactions in a site over some span of time); and *knowledge* refers to information made meaningful and valuable with respect to evaluation and action (such as the insight that the number of transactions in a given site are likely to change because of what one has ascertained about a competitor's actions). Defining knowledge as fundamentally about meaning and action suggests its inherent complexity and irreducibility to data or information. Knowledge becomes "a fluid mix of framed experience, values, contextual information, and expert insights that provides a framework for evaluating and incorporating new experiences and information" (Davenport & Prusak, 1998, p. 5). It is the ability to make meaningful distinctions in a given context (Nonaka & Takeuchi, 1995; Tsoukas & Vladimirou, 2001), connecting data and information while providing a frame for action. This broad vision has developed in two distinct directions in the organization studies literature.

First is a *cognitive* view, where knowledge is portrayed as an identifiable entity, a commodity stored (i.e., located) *in* brains or bodies. In organization studies, knowledge is not merely individual, however: Those who assert that knowledge can be held by collectives find analogies of brains and bodies at the level of the organization, such as Walsh and Ungson's (1991) suggestion that organizational cultures, production processes, structures, and physical settings can be storehouses for knowledge. In this cognitive view, a common assumption is that organizations are systems produced by information processing and decision making; knowledge, consequently, is that which becomes encoded in routines and repositories in development of distinctive and rare production capabilities (Grant, 1996; Spender, 1996).

Marking the cognitive view is an assumption that organizational productivity is a function of intellectual capital. Organization and management theories built on a cognitive foundation call for knowledge to be extracted from its locations, transferred to others, purchased from suppliers, inserted into new contexts, measured, and evaluated. Knowledge is consequently rendered as a sharable commodity, while contexts, practices, and persons (as well as organizations) are seen as containers for knowledge exchange. In this currently dominant approach, knowledge is cognitive in the sense that it is a possession of the (individual or collective) knower gained through experience, training, or some other form of procurement—its existence is ontologically distinct from those events (Maier, Prange, & von Rosenstiel, 2001). Because it is rendered as a commodity, knowledge may be accumulated across those events, and more extensive collections of knowledge, if managed well, lead the knower to exploit new opportunities and to make better choices. Knowledge, moreover, is private (and must be guarded, according to Szulanski, 2003)—but it is made meaningful and shareable because it is coded by a preexisting and objective public realm (i.e., the organization or organizational field) into signs that have relatively stable meanings. Communication, in this perspective, becomes the means of freeing knowledge from the knower, a transfer and processing function that enables the identification, sharing, accumulation, and protection of the commodity.

The alternative view generally does not deny that knowledge can have a cognitive location but asserts that cognitive views ignore substantial communicative complexity in their efforts to show how knowledge contributes to organizational effectiveness. This second view, a *practice* model, argues that *to know* implies competent participation in a complex web of relationships among people, artifacts, discourses, and (often-conflicting) streams of action (Blackler, 1995; Cook & Brown, 1999; Gherardi, 2000; Orlikowski, 2002). The unit of analysis shifts from the individual knower to activity processes, because the perspective holds that the doing of conjoint action is the primary site of social/organizational reality. As such, the practice view prefers the term *knowing* (over knowledge) to highlight the performative, provisional, dynamic, ongoing, and often mundane production of a social practice. Knowing is portrayed as situated in contexts and communities; it is oriented toward addressing problems that threaten preferred trajectories of action. Processes of knowing are deeply material in the sense that both knowledge and artifacts are intimately bound up with—and thus mutually determinative of—language and discursive practices, but there is a recognition that nonhuman actors can exert power that exceeds human agency (Law, 2002; Rennstam, 2012). Moving beyond a cognitive vision, practice-based conceptions also acknowledge emotional and aesthetic factors in the development and deployment of knowledge (Gherardi, 2003; Strati, 2003). Knowing is a practical accomplishment, and solutions to problematic situations encountered in organizing are always interactively realized, even when the response is scripted (Kuhn & Jackson, 2008). At the organizational level, a practice perspective argues that the cognitive view's effort to tie organizational success to the capacity to mobilize personal knowledge produces coherent action but marginalizes doubt and, in turn, reduces the possibility of innovation-producing disruptions (Alvesson & Spicer, 2012; Kuhn, 2012).

Communication in the practice model takes on a rather different cast than in the cognitive perspective. Here, communication is indexical, polysemous, processual, and situated in broader discursive/cultural contexts. Language, along with the distinctions it carries, constructs power relations and the criteria for what counts as knowledge (Contu & Willmott, 2003). Intersubjectivity is not the product of information transmission but rather "is the emergent product of interactions among subjects located in a constantly rearticulated system of intersubjective relations and meanings" (Grossberg, 1982, p. 221). That system, moreover, is medium and outcome of interaction; the context exists only insofar as it is communicatively reaffirmed (and, of course, modified). Communication, then, is seen as potentially complex and tension ridden; communities are seen as potentially fragmented; and reifying any element of communication (not to mention organization and knowledge) is avoided.

If the cognitive-oriented and practice-oriented conceptions of knowledge sound familiar, it is not because knowledge and communication naturally possess such characteristics. Rather, scholars' renderings are usually cast in the images proffered by existing models of organization. Theories of organization (as well as broader social theories) generally encode one or the other vision of knowledge/knowing in their portrayal of organizational reality, as I show in the next section.

Three Themes in Organizational Communication Scholarship on Knowledge and Knowing

In this section, I review developments in scholarship on knowledge and knowing that operate at the individual, group, organization, and interorganizational levels of analysis. Although there are overlapping themes and conceptions of knowledge across these three topical areas, I present them as distinct to highlight the areas in which streams of communicative thinking have made the most significant contributions.

Knowledge Management Systems

A first, and perhaps dominant, line of scholarship is that investigating the growing organizational use of systems and technologies to manage knowledge. KM is a practice that involves coordinating and controlling the generation, codification, and application of knowledge in organizational practice; it has become organizationally widespread (Jackson & Williamson, 2011). Companies increasingly see KM as key to organizational strategy (and those lacking KM systems are perceived as managerially suspect), and KM products and services are offered by most management consultancies. Much of this work draws its inspiration and justification from cognitively based theories of knowledge and organization, where cultivating, protecting, harvesting, and transferring individual and collective intellectual capital are imperative, because they contribute to competitive advantage (Bontis, 1999). With that in mind, this section addresses three of those shared interests and the insights generated by communication-based studies of KM.

Transactive Memory and Knowledge Management. A first subset of this stream of research on KM systems is work on transactive memory systems. Originally articulated by psychologist Daniel Wegner (1987), transactive memory (TM) addresses how participants in a joint endeavor work together to encode, process, store, and retrieve information. The theory assumes that memory is both an individual, internal characteristic and an external, shared process in which communication plays a central role. A TM system is a property of a group that emerges as members develop knowledge of the *other* members and their domains of expertise as well as of locations for knowledge ("who knows what"). In smooth-functioning TM systems, members have also developed communication processes, such as verbal and nonverbal cueing, to locate and deploy knowledge in response to a given problem (Hollingshead, 1998). When such a system is in place, the cognitive load for individuals is reduced, and the capacity of the group to marshal knowledge is accentuated. Communication scholars have shown that information about tasks, expertise, and people is stored in persons, in networks, and in repositories; these scholars tend to frame communication as the process required to access and transmit knowledge across locations (Brandon & Hollingshead, 2004; Palazzolo, Serb, She, Su, & Contractor, 2006). The role of communication in this work is both for processing (coding, storing, and retrieving) information and for creating the connections between elements in the TM system.

Organizational communication scholars have employed the TM concept in understanding work teams and larger groupings within organizations and in developing explanations for how knowledge-sharing errors and shortcomings occur as well as for how workgroups might improve storage and retrieval processes. Findings indicate that workgroups often lack a shared mental model and fail to develop understandings of "who knows what" and that a common reason is that members fail to take responsibility for their areas of expertise (Garner, 2006). Some have shown that shared training can overcome that lack (Liang, Moreland, & Argote, 1995) and that the accuracy of members' perceptions of "who knows what" leads to increases in perceived team effectiveness (Child & Shumate, 2007). When it comes to KM tools such as knowledge directories and expertise exchanges, members' levels of technological competence with these tools, along with their perceptions of others' use of them, can be instrumental in TM systems' development (Palazzolo, 2005; Yuan, Fulk, Monge, & Contractor, 2010). Thus TM systems research suggests that the development of information processing systems can overcome informational errors and magnify groups' capacities to engage in intelligent problem solving.

Technological Systems for KM. Transactive memory names a cognitive and communicative system for the encoding and retrieval of knowledge among members of a team. It therefore can be seen as a form of KM, but contemporary KM literature extends beyond group-based work to address interventions to improve organization-wide operations, boundary spanning, and governance. KM activities are often manifest in *information audits* (formal assessments of what information organizations have and what they need), *knowledge mapping* (representations of relevant knowledge in a setting), *knowledge bases* (repositories of codified best practices or lessons learned), *groupware* (using computerized collaboration, decision, and documentation tools to support group-level knowledge development and codification), *advanced search capabilities* (using computerized tools to scour large information areas, including the Internet, to locate and classify relevant texts), and *simulations* (scenarios and environments to train members in managing challenging and important situations).

As this list of activities suggests, KM is frequently equated with computational tools. For organizational communication scholars, however, the ICTs employed in KM are useful points of entry for understanding the organizing properties of communication and knowledge. For instance, Flanagin (2002) noted that many organizations take a "stockpile" approach, developing technological repositories that "artificially reduce knowledge complexity . . . to increase the capacity to process it efficiently" (p. 244). In the language introduced above, the point is that the desire to use ICTs as KM tools requires a cognitive reduction. To address this simplification, Flanagin and Bator (2011) argue for the value that emergent web-based technologies hold for KM. The key difference offered by newer generations of these technologies is that they do not rely on a central repository or single point of contact (e.g., an intranet); instead, they provide local and customized points of contact in connecting users who are engaged in collaborative activity, capitalize on large sets of distributed expertise, and reduce the costs of communication and coordination.

As another illustration of the use of ICTs in KM, Leonardi (2011; Leonardi & Bailey, 2008) studied automotive engineering processes distributed across a large automaker's facilities around the world. Particularly interested in the "offshoring" of tasks to a site in India from several locations, Leonardi noted that the digital artifacts created in the work were transmitted as if they were objective, decontextualized, and straightforward bits of engineering knowledge. As might be expected, considerable implicit knowledge was embedded in the artifacts; and Indian engineers engaged in a good deal of interpretation, and generated novel practices, to make sense of it. Leonardi showed that engineers' reliance on technology, belief in the possibility of simple knowledge transmission, and lack of insight into cultural differences regarding the location of knowledge combined to create coordination problems. But, interestingly, management responded by investing *more* money in the firm's already-advanced technological system. Reducing knowledge to a conveyable entity and communication to a mode of conveyance may provide a justification for the investment in the technological elements of KM systems, but analyses such as Leonardi's display the problems such choices create.

Conversational Design for KM. Beyond studying the effects of KM technologies on group-level outcomes, some scholars advocate alternative system design logics. Wagner (2006), for instance, holds that existing ICTs are inadequate for acquiring members' (cognitively held) knowledge because they are too slow, lack complexity, are inaccurate, and require ongoing maintenance. In response, he advocates configuring organizations to resemble the development of wikis (e.g., Wikipedia) or open-source software communities, as these designs revolve around conversations that "facilitate back-up, clarity, and shared understanding" (p. 73). Here, conversations, rather than ICTs, are central to the very notion of knowledge. Von Krogh and Roos (1996) argue for the organizational need to create an organizational *lexicon*, a shared understanding of concepts, phrases, and their meanings, both for the coordination it affords and the possibility that introducing new phrases can induce innovation. Still others, such as Barge and Little (2002) and Tsoukas (2009), argue that the practice of genuine dialogue can generate shared responsibility, distancing from narrow self-interest, and conceptual change that, taken together, form the basis of new knowledge.

Reasoning in a similar fashion, Aakhus (2007) argues that organizations can help individual experts develop their specialist knowledge by encouraging transformations and transitions in their expertise. He developed a model for inquiry based on *conversations for reflection*, interactions that surface actors' (implicit) theories of practice along with those theories' consequences. Designing conversations using this model requires a dialectic of opposition by another participant and accounting by the professional regarding an event; the text produced through such a conversation can then become available for appropriation by others. Conversational designs such as this (and the others mentioned here) shift the scholarly focus, showing how interaction, rather than technology, can be the cornerstone of KM efforts.

Summary. KM has become a key concern in both research and practice. Communication scholars have contributed to KM thinking by framing groups as complex information processing and problem-solving TM systems, disrupting deterministic visions of ICTs in KM, and articulating alternative conversation design logics in knowledge development. Cutting across these themes is an interest in articulating the processes by which communication and knowledge are connected in organizing. The literature in the next section takes a slightly different tack on the explanatory power of communication, seeking to understand the effects of communication networks on knowledge and action as well as the ways communication networks can themselves become forms of knowledge.

Communication Networks and Knowledge

The study of communication networks has long played a central role in organizational communication thinking (see Shumate & Contractor, Chapter 18). This section reviews research on the ways network structures and processes affect knowledge in organizing as well as literature on how connections between actors can foster the emergence of a collective-level resource.

Network Effects on Knowledge. A central concern of network-based studies of knowledge in organizational communication is understanding the effects connected actors have upon one another. Usually operating from the assumption that knowledge is a possession of the units comprising a system, network approaches typically examine how social structures influence cognitive structures (e.g., Carley, 1986). What actors know, what they value, and the meanings they attach to objects and experiences are products of social influence processes and, as such, are always communicative. Interaction is frequently seen as creating shared information that leads members' knowledge to become integrated, or converge, due to participation in a network (e.g., Contractor & Grant, 1996; Rice & Aydin, 1991). By way of illustration, Burkhardt (1994), studying the implementation of a new computer system, reported that changes in communication partners were related to changes in individuals' attitudes and beliefs, suggesting that a contagion mechanism was at work. Similarly, Isabella's (1990) examination of managers' interpretations of events advanced a four-stage change process, showing "distinct similarities across function and level in the manner by which managers construe their world" (p. 31).

Not all communication network research assumes convergence, however. A good deal of work has found that *divergences* between individuals and/or subgroups can form on the substrate of network connections. Bastien's (1992) and Howard and Geist's (1995) investigations of mergers showed that structurally connected members used a variety of communicative strategies to cope with events; these strategies produced considerable diversity in members' knowledge regarding the mergers. Participation in activities with others who are different from oneself can create *deeper* knowledge divisions without dissolving the communication link, especially if the activity is organizationally mandated (Bovasso, 1996; Levesque, Wilson, & Wholey, 2001). Pursuing this insight, Kuhn and Corman (2003), in a study of a municipal government unit's planned change process, found a simultaneous movement toward homogeneity *and* heterogeneity across members' knowledge over time; they explained the complex movement by making reference to the structural positions and interpretive schemes of both individuals and workgroups. Communication networks, in other words, generate effects on knowledge that are neither simple nor straightforward, suggesting that an important area of inquiry is the network conditions and configurations leading to particular outcomes.

Examinations drawing upon network concepts have deepened our understandings of the characteristics and dynamics of knowledge, particularly when investigating features of a broader system. Networks of affinity and trust have been found to enhance knowledge sharing, because they create a context in which contributing to public goods, such as KM repositories, is valued. Yuan et al. (2005) investigated participation in an "information commons" among members of work teams. They found that usage of the knowledge repository was predicted by members' perceptions of other team members' usage—evidence that communication networks shape actors' motivations for sharing with, and drawing from, KM resources (Fulk, Flanagin, Kalman, Monge, & Ryan, 1996).

One of the advantages of the network approach is that it does not limit itself to conceiving of systems of interacting persons. Instead, network nodes can also be nonhuman entities (such as KM systems or knowledge repositories), teams, or entire organizations. From there, one can examine the consequences of, for instance, a KM system's centrality in a broader network, the modes by which network elements are linked together, and the role brokers and boundary-spanners play in connecting a network with other sources of information. Network concepts can then be employed to determine the suitability of the inclusion of any given node in terms of the network's task performance and evolving task requirements (Hollingshead, Fulk, & Monge, 2002). Network principles can also be used heuristically to develop computational models of propositions about how elements come together under particular circumstances, structural configurations, interaction media, system dynamics, or pragmatic goals (Deng & Poole, 2011; Monge & Contractor, 2003).

Networks as Knowledge. Following the move to examine the system level, a second network-based approach theorizes knowledge as a collective capacity. Seeing communication networks themselves as forms of collective knowledge requires an attention to the process of emergence, as a group-level construct produced from the interactions of network nodes. Knowledge from this perspective is not merely located in an individual member of the network (though it is undeniably there, too); rather, "knowledge networks are distributed repositories of knowledge elements from a larger knowledge domain that are tied together by knowledge linkages within and among organizations" (Monge & Contractor, 2003, p. 300). For instance, Kogut (2000) suggested that interorganizational networks develop structures and rules that can produce differential value for participating firms, depending on the forms of coordination operating in the network. Using the case of the Toyota production system as an illustration, Kogut showed that repeated interactions between supplier firms generated innovations and the acquisition of relationship-specific skills, largely because of emergent rules regarding suppliers' knowledge demonstration, codification, and sharing. He concludes that the capabilities of the system

> did not reside in any given firm, but were created by the knowledge of how to coordinate among firms with a history of cooperation. . . . [T]o remove a firm from this network would be to deprive it of important capabilities it could not immediately recreate. (p. 422)

Thus the knowledge network created effects at both the individual firm and production system level, indicating the emergence of an informational resource key to the performance of both the network and the organizations comprising it.

Pursuing a similar line of argument about the generation of collective knowledge, Shumate and Lipp (2008) showed how hyperlinks—connections to other organizations found on a given organization's website—in a nongovernmental organization (NGO) issue network demonstrated evidence of the network's ability to determine the location of knowledge throughout the system. Their analysis suggested that the set of hyperlinks emerged as a public good for members of the network and illustrated the importance of generalist organizations alongside the specialist NGOs. Further, O'Hair, Kelley, and Williams (2011; see also Koschmann, Kuhn, & Pfarrer, 2012) argued that designing particular forms of cross-sector stakeholder collaboration can create information infrastructures that are essential in managing risk and crises in civil society, as illustrated by Doerfel and colleagues' (Doerfel, Lai, & Chewning, 2010; Taylor & Doerfel, 2011) work on the communicative generation of social capital in interorganizational networks following severe disruptions, such as New Orleans after Hurricane Katrina and in post-war Croatia.

In studies such as these, interest lies less in understanding knowledge transfer between actors and more with the factors leading to the emergence of structures and information sources that can be considered *collective knowledge*. Here, *knowledge* is defined as the capacity to identify expertise and its locations, the skill to collaborate with others, and the links between nodes that become instrumentally important when activated in subsequent situations.

Summary. Networks provide a powerful conceptual and empirical tool to examine the consequences of various communication patterns and connections on the organizational creation, transfer, and adoption of knowledge at several levels of analysis. This work also supplies much-needed specificity to the notion of knowledge *emergence*, a frequently invoked term that is left ambiguous in much organizational theorizing (Goldstein, 1999). In its emphasis on structure and cognition, as well as its frequent interest in organizational effectiveness, the network perspective provides a useful contrast with the final body of knowledge scholarship, presented next.

Communities of Practice and the Production of Power

The perspective most closely associated with a practice-oriented conception of knowledge in organizational communication is found in the communities of practice (CoP) literature.[1] Its adoption in organization studies is usually traced to Lave and Wenger's (1991) claim that developing and deploying knowledge is rarely an isolated cognitive endeavor. Rather, learning almost always occurs in the context of others—most specifically, in CoPs. Moreover, learning is often most obvious at boundaries, such as when individuals or organizations are peripheral to a given community and seek fuller membership or when they occupy liminal positions with respect to two or more communities (Tempest & Starkey, 2004). CoPs are not, however, reducible to workgroups; the *community* term is meant to suggest not merely a joint enterprise but also the development of a sense of collectivity, a shared repertoire for action, a site for belonging and identity, the construction and enforcement of boundaries, the negotiation of meaning, and the importance of interpersonal trust in the ongoing production of knowledge (Adler, 2001; Iverson, 2011; Iverson & McPhee, 2002; Kuhn, 2002; Taylor, 2011; Wenger, 1998; Zorn & Taylor, 2004). In this section, I overview three themes in the organizational communication literature emanating from a perspective informed by CoP thinking: problematizing expertise, boundary spanning, and power.

Problematizing Expertise. A core concern of the literature on knowledge in organizing is the generation and utilization of expertise. The dominant assumption about expertise is that it is to be found embodied in an individual expert, that a person's accumulated knowledge and experience constitutes the person's expertise and is often manifested intuitively. When foregrounding practice, however, scholars find that experts are often unable to make their intuition explicit:

> When an expert attempts to say what he [or she] knows—when he tries to put his know*ing* into the form of know*ledge*—his formulations of principles, theories, maxims, and rules of thumb are often incongruent with the understanding and know-how implicit in his pattern of practice. (Schön, 1992, p. 60, emphasis in original)

One route to challenging the orthodox conception of expertise within organizational communication scholarship has been to direct attention to *individual actors' efforts to construct images of knowledgeability.* Alvesson (1994), in a study of an advertising agency, noted that the culturally formed habitus of advertising professionals led them to assert personal expertise through a range of symbolic means not necessarily tied to the content of the work. The upshot of this argument is that many forms of knowledge-intensive work are based on inherent ambiguity in the product and process of the work, making the *perception* of quality and the identity of the practitioner the operative concerns—and those perceptions are contingent upon the rhetorical skill of knowledge workers. The key capacity, then, is an ability to manage ambiguity in one's own interest.

Orr (1996) showed how experts constructed images of knowledgeability in his study of photocopier repair technicians engaging in storytelling. Their stories not only generated responses to problems that escaped codification in repair manuals but also constructed conceptions of expertise among them. Similarly, Treem's (2012) study of work at two public-relations firms noted that expertise was the product of attributions made by others about actors' performances. And in science studies, Collins and Evans (2007) highlight the value of scientists' exchanges with participants and publics in the production of what becomes labeled as "scientific" knowledge. In this vision, expertise becomes connected with communication (and, specifically, interactive ability) but retains the individual actor as the knowing subject. In conceptions such as these, experts are seen to be deeply relationally embedded in CoPs, but the units of analysis tend to be the individual expert's decisions or attributions about an individual made by others.

A second view of expertise begins by framing problem solving as a joint communicative endeavor. Here, concern is less involved in labeling a person (or her actions) as possessing expertise and more in understanding the ways responses to complex problems are interactive accomplishments not reducible to any individual. Framing *expertise as collaborative* implies that solutions frequently emerge from, are recognized in, and are justified through communication processes. For example, Kuhn and Jackson (2008) found evidence of multiparty improvisation as a route to constructing—and often stumbling upon—solutions to ambiguous and intractable problems. In deeply indeterminate situations, simply transmitting knowledge (or information) does not work, and possessing a vision of "who knows what" is inadequate for grasping the character of the problem or the requirements of a solution. Organizational participants—even those labeled experts by those around them—jointly construct seemingly reasonable responses until one of them sticks by appearing ameliorative; thus negotiating meanings for what sorts of solutions are taken to be ameliorative in a given setting becomes a crucial communicative task that depends on the community. In this way, the assumption that expertise is located *in* a person is loosened, and attention is directed toward the joint accomplishment of a practice.

In this line of thinking, Engeström (1992) argued for seeing expertise as an interactive accomplishment situated in socially distributed activity systems. Collaborative expertise becomes particularly interesting when there exist *discoordinations* or disturbances of interaction in a system, when there are ruptures of understanding, and when members are strongly interdependent, because it is then that actors engage in informal, interactive processing of information. Although one might counter such an assertion by arguing that this (along with the preceding example) is a description of what one might call *collaboration* or *teamwork* rather than *expertise*, Engeström suggests that *interactions in the system* are the necessary unit of analysis. To ground that claim, he shows how everyday attributions of expertise to individuals require system-based allocations of authority. In studies of judges in a court of law (Engeström, 1992) and a team of primary school teachers (Engeström, 1994), he displayed that all knowing occurs via system-situated interaction, and thus knowledge is stored in (and emerges from) the system itself. It is that same system that reinforces judges' and teachers' claims to expertise (and authority) by refraining from challenging the logics upon which their claims to expertise are based. When systems experience disjunctures, however, processes of claiming jurisdiction and disabling agency take center stage—uncovering how communication is central to the production, maintenance, and change of expertise systems.

A third conception of collaborative expertise is in studies of *distributed cognition and collective mind*. An important first step in this literature is to suggest that *mind* is simply that which processes ideas, a move that separates mind from the human brain and allows one to reason by analogy to the group or organization without endowing the collective construction with "mysterious, superorganic" characteristics (Douglas, 1986, p. 14). When applied to task-related activity, the activity can be framed as *distributed cognition* (or *intelligence*), a concept that directs our attention to both the manner in which *mind* is formed and to ways in which the group coordinates activity. Weick and Roberts (1993) argue that *collective mind* emerges in practices of social interrelating (contributing, representing, and subordinating). When these processes are conducted "heedfully"—when people are acting carefully and consistently and when they have developed intersubjective meanings or "mutually shared fields" (p. 365)—something called *mind* may emerge, located within the practice of the activity system.

The notion of collective mind has received relatively little attention from organizational communication scholars (see, however, McKinney, Barker, Davis, & Smith, 2005; Myers & McPhee, 2006), but Cooren's (2004) study of a board meeting in a drug rehabilitation center represents a distinctly communicative involvement with the concept. Cooren examined contribution, representation, and subordination occurring in talk among five members of the board. He showed how these actors created a joint situation and how they expanded it by drawing upon absent individuals and departments (as well as past interactions), thereby linking their in-the-moment organizing (the "here and now") with the past and future (the "there and then"). McPhee, Myers, and Trethewey (2006) responded to Cooren by arguing for the need to go beyond conversational data to the larger interactional system. They asserted that group qualities such as heedfulness or collective mind depend upon institutional conditions for their emergence and continuation and studying only situated talk limits an understanding of collective mind's constitution.

This view, in conjunction with those discussed above, suggests that expertise and intelligence can be fruitfully seen as interactive achievements situated in CoPs that are, in turn, positioned in an array of other forces. Communication scholars are accustomed to studying local talk as embedded in context, and pursuing such perspectives can display situational contingency, community shaping, and *ad hoc* quality of expertise. Consequently, there is great potential for organizational communication scholarship to further problematize, and intervene in, the practice of expertise.

Spanning Community Boundaries. A second theme in the organizational communication literature influenced by CoP thinking is work on spanning boundaries. If organizations are comprised of multiple CoPs, and if many practices extend beyond traditional organizational and occupational groupings (Brown & Duguid, 1991, 2001), and if cross-unit cooperation is required for collective activity, then it stands to reason that coordination across communities' boundaries is necessary to produce coherent action, innovation, and learning. In the study of science, Star and Griesemer (1989) state the issue well:

> The creation of new scientific knowledge depends on communication as well as on creating new findings. But because these new objects and methods mean different things in different worlds, actors are faced with the task of reconciling these meanings if they wish to cooperate. This reconciliation requires substantial labour on everyone's part. Scientists and other actors contributing to science translate, negotiate, debate, triangulate and simplify in order to work together. (pp. 388–389)

Understanding how boundaries are constructed, how knowing occurs across boundaries, and the challenges encountered in cross-boundary collaboration have thus occupied a central position in studies of knowledge and knowing.

One of the key contributions to understanding boundary-spanning focuses on artifacts called *boundary objects*. Boundary objects provide a common representation that enables the bridging of differences; they allow actors to selectively enlist and reinterpret the concerns of others while remaining resistant to a single dominant interpretation. One development of this notion is to reframe the site of boundary spanning as a *trading zone* (Kellogg, Orlikowski, & Yates, 2006), where groups of experts—characterized by distinct knowledge, logics, and codes—collaborate through the vehicle of objects and other practices that represent, store, and retrieve knowledge to facilitate learning across groups. As experts display their work by making it available through some medium, represent it in a shared code, and assemble (i.e., integrate) it with the work of others, intergroup boundaries can be traversed (Bechky, 2003; Carlile, 2002; Hinds & Kiesler, 1995).

These conceptions of boundary spanning display the complexity of cross-community practice but tend to leave its communicative accomplishment relatively unexamined. A more thoroughly communicative view of boundary spanning would begin by acknowledging that knowledge is not merely a cognitive entity or a characteristic of an individual, but has other important manifestations, including a presence inherently *in* social practice. It would also include an interrogation of boundaries, understanding communities (and their boundaries) not merely as preexisting differences in worldview, language, or action but instead as constantly communicatively (re)negotiated sites that mark the limits of local resources for identification, accountability, and legitimacy (Kuhn & Jackson, 2008). Such a view would replace the assertion that boundaries are simply fuzzy with an attempt to understand the reasons for, and consequences of, their apparent slipperiness.

A communicative view of boundary spanning would examine the intended and unintended consequences for subsequent communicative accomplishments that are generated by the object, person, text, or practice participating in the spanning activity. It would examine how and when communities allocate responsibilities to generate differential practices that enable boundary crossing. And, finally, a communicative view would resist the unidirectional assumption present in the boundary objects literature, where communities' use of artifacts is portrayed as claiming order out of a preceding (or potential) disorder. If, as mentioned above, communication creates meaning convergence and divergence simultaneously, communicative thinking should complicate our understandings of the processes and products of boundary spanning, along with the material employed to accomplish it.

Communication scholars who advance such an understanding of boundary spanning encourage a shift in attention from knowledge, knowledge transfer, and technological artifacts to the ongoing reconstruction of a situated practice (Cooren, 2010; Leonardi & Barley, 2010; Taylor, Groleau, Heaton, & Van Every, 2001). They show how levels, locales, and interests recursively shape one another and encourage consideration of the communicative effort involved in establishing a context in which boundary spanning is perceived as a possibility (and one that objects might facilitate). In this way, communication scholarship highlights knowing as a discursive/material process that not only complicates existing object-based conceptions of boundary spanning but also provides conceptual resources for the messy task of the negotiation of interests in organizing, a theme I turn to next.

Examining Power and Politics in Knowing. Practice-based and CoP perspectives appear to offer unique insights into the communicative accomplishment of power but have generally relegated such issues to a secondary position (Roberts, 2006). In foregrounding the sharing of meanings, connecting disparate groups across boundaries, and generating collaborative competencies, the practice-based literature often "glosses over a fractured, dynamic process of formation and reproduction in which there are often schisms and precarious alignments that are held together and papered over by nonreflexive invocations of hegemonic notions including 'community,' 'family,' 'team,' and 'partnership'" (Contu & Willmott, 2003, p. 287). Yet there is a growing body of literature that connects knowledge with struggles over power and meaning in organizing. There are two streams here: a conception of situated knowing as a site in which power and politics play out and another framing knowledge work as amenable to novel forms of control.

Theories of social practice are, for many authors, inherently *critical* theories (Nicolini, 2012), and scholars who see practices of organizing as political have made important contributions to our understanding of *struggles over what counts as knowledge*, the first stream of power and politics scholarship. At the base of this move is an interrogation of *epistemological politics*, or how knowledge and expertise come to be recognized and valued as such in a given practice. By paying particular attention to *articulation* as a representational practice—the process of making manifest a particular object (or person, artifact, symbol, idea, etc.) and connecting it in a conceptual system with other objects—organizational communication scholars display how particular portrayals of knowledge are privileged and others are suppressed. That which becomes defined as knowledge is the result of sedimented historical processes, seen as individual and collective actors pursue their interests, as groups develop favored interpretations regarding the world with respect to varied audiences, and in organizational practices such as classification, accounting, and calculation (Covaleski, Dirsmith, Heian, & Samuel, 1998; Nadesan, 1997; Power, 1997).

Organizational communication scholars have engaged this theme most explicitly by examining the establishment and enforcement of organizational (and professional) norms, both at a managerial and micro level. Deetz (1992), for instance, provided a vocabulary for studying types of *discursive closure*, moves intended to discontinue discussion and enforce a particular conception of knowledge. Leonardi and Jackson (2004) drew upon this notion to show how the use of *technological determinism* enforced an entrenched interest, and a particular version of knowledge, in organizational change. Likewise, Lyon (2004, 2005), in a case study of an e-learning organization's KM system, showed how organizing develops conceptions of intellectual, social, and symbolic capital that materially benefit some interests over others. And Murphy and Eisenberg (2011) studied the political character of knowledge during physician transitions in hospital emergency departments, finding communicative outlets that both enforced conceptions of identity and knowledge and, simultaneously, enabled dialogue, idea generation, and voice.

A second theme in the power and politics literature is framing *knowledge work and knowledge-intensive organizations as particularly interesting sites of struggle*. Because most knowledge-intensive work operates on the basis of an individual's expertise or creativity, direct and bureaucratic forms of control tend to be less effective than the autonomy and self-management typically associated with normative control (Alvesson, 2001). The ambiguity characterizing knowledge work makes it necessary for participants to construct group-level meanings regarding the standards for both quality of work and appropriate levels of effort (Barker, 1993) and for clients to frequently become intimately involved in production processes, which alters both the location of control and the need for the presentation of expertise (Kärreman & Rylander, 2008).

Of course, any effort at control is likely to be met with resistance, resulting in complex relations, and practices, of power. Studies examining struggles over meaning in knowledge-intensive work thus tend to foreground organizational and occupational identity, and there are many examples in the literature. In a study of a nuclear fusion laboratory, Kinsella (1999) showed how symbolic constructions disseminated through myriad discourses framed results as scientific fact, forming the basis of knowledge claims that produced individual and collective identities. Kuhn (2009) studied the subject positions of junior attorneys at a large corporate law firm, finding that the discursive resources they employed to display knowledge about their profession, as well as about the firm, both enabled and constrained capacities for ethical engagement in their work. And, finally, McClellan's (2011) study of a planned change at an art and design college showed how conflict suppression during change-oriented conversations protected some knowledge from interrogation and prevented some proposals from gaining traction, ultimately leading to the change's failure.

Summary. Organizational communication scholars seek to understand and explain communicatively complex forms of organizing. In the knowledge-intensive organizations associated with the "knowledge economy," traditional mechanisms of coordination and control tend to be of limited utility. Scholars have thus increasingly turned to practice-based conceptions of knowledge and models of CoPs to describe organizing processes in communicatively richer terms. As a result, they reframe expertise, boundary spanning, and power in organizing and organizations, providing a powerful alternative to cognitively based views.

Conclusion: An Agenda for Knowledge and Knowing in Organizational Communication Research

What becomes clear from this review is that organizational communication scholars are interested in using concepts related to knowledge and knowing to explain important organizing phenomena. They study knowledge and knowing, in other words, to pursue novel insights on the problems of organization. It thus becomes important to call attention to three issues characterizing contemporary appropriations of knowledge and knowing in an effort to sketch an agenda for future organizational communication inquiry.

A first issue with which organizational communication scholars might grapple is the subject-object dualism inherent in much of the scholarship reviewed here (as well as in my cognitive-practice division). In the cognitive view, knowledge is held by actors (or by any node in the network) and is considered a resource upon which they draw when pursuing their private aims through social action. Important questions about the degree to which actors' knowledge corresponds with an external reality (i.e., whether it is a "justified true belief"), whether managers can extract and transfer it accurately, and whether researchers can adequately capture knowledge *in* a unit of analysis betray a clear split between an assumed interior and exterior world. The practice-oriented view challenges such distinctions but does not interrogate the sources of the concepts orienting this alternative perspective, such that it generally fails to follow the practice-based theorizing to a thoroughly distinctive vision of organization (see, e.g., Orlikowski, 2002). Even the claim that knowledge is a form of power, found in different forms in both perspectives seen here—a claim, incidentally, that can be traced back at least to Francis Bacon but is dramatically reworked by post-structuralists such as Foucault—typically assumes that knowing involves being able to access something intrinsic to a concept or an object and that the ability to access it (or ignore it, or resist it) produces meaningful effects in the world.

Efforts to dissolve the subject-object dualism would begin by acknowledging the importance of language, both in making distinctions and in constituting the world (as well as organizations) in which those distinctions are rendered valuable (Rorty, 1999). From there, investigating the ways in which persons, organizations, and interests are positioned in language would become a standard part of communicative analyses. Knowledge and beliefs would then be seen as rules for action rather than representations of an external world. And, because almost all beliefs can find *some* form of justification, merely exposing the forces that enable justifications is inadequate. Instead, important tasks for inquiry would become understanding (a) how conflicts between knowledge claims proceed, how they shape organizational trajectories, and the consequences the trajectories create for communities (Canary & McPhee, 2009); (b) how elements that are linguistically constructed as material entities *participate* in practices of knowing (Ashcraft, Kuhn, & Cooren, 2009; Barad, 2003); (c) how identity fragmentation can produce alternative forms of—and approaches to studying—knowledge and knowing (Kuhn & Porter, 2011); and (d) how to trace the mutations in the knowledge society that enforce new forms of knowledge and new conceptions of value, such as financialization, to situated organizing practices (Ho, 2009; Neff, 2012). Such moves, moreover, need not be associated with any particular knowledge perspective or epistemological paradigm but should encourage scholars to show communication, and its constitutive power, as capable of creating not merely that which we take to be knowledge but also as creating groups, organizations, and knowledgeable performances themselves.

A second, and related, issue is the Western bias in knowledge and knowing research. That organization studies as a field is deeply entrenched in worldviews reflecting its primary geographical locations—North America, Northern and Western Europe, and Australia-New Zealand—is unsurprising and understandable. But the important question is what might be gained from broadening our collective conceptual gaze, beyond seeking a closer correspondence with (as an attempt to mirror) a heterogeneous world. Ul-Haq and Westwood (2012) argue that engaging with Islam not only would enable insight into the experience of a large but underrepresented (and oft-distorted) group but would provide novel perspectives on the organizing practices of groups constructed as the *other* as well as showing how branding and consumption practices can become melded with spiritually derived rules and standards (see also Lundry & Cheong, 2011). Likewise, the Chinese concept of *guanxi*, a form of personal networking that combines knowledge, favors, and feelings (Hardy & Jian, 2011), could alter the conceptions of knowledge networks mentioned above. The studies of this notion display the complexities of a concept akin to social capital; understanding *guanxi* might encourage network scholars to expand network ties to simultaneously include reputation, face, and the (often unintended) benefits of extending a favor, all of which are involved in a continuous process of development beyond observable (or reportable) interaction. Thus even beyond challenging divisions between subject and object, non-Western scholarship on knowledge and knowing can point to assumptive occlusions in studies of justifications, networks, and organizational authority.

Finally, to expand upon a point mentioned in the preceding discussion of the subject-object split, literature on knowledge and knowing could profit from a more sustained engagement with materiality. To be sure, studies of knowledge by no means *ignore* materiality: From studies of ICT use in KM to explanations of how tacit knowledge (that which is held within a person and is difficult to express discursively) becomes written on a body to investigations of how buildings shape community knowing, the research cited above frequently makes the material an important category of the social. At the same time, however, calls for (organizational) communication to confront the material world and redress the field's emphasis on the symbolic features of organizational life are increasingly prevalent (Aakhus et al., 2011; Ashcraft et al., 2009; Barad, 2003; Lilley, Lightfoot, & Amaral, 2004). Such claims usually touch upon the desire to avoid the aforementioned dualistic visions of the social world (i.e., the ontological distinction between symbolic and material, mirroring the distinction between agency and structure), but the important question for scholars of knowledge and knowing is less about finding a way to conceive of duality or to strike the right balance between conceptual poles; it is more about the desire to see how pursuing creative engagements with the socio-material might prove heuristic for our conceptions of communication, organization, and agency (Kuhn, 2011).

The issues, then, are what such an engagement might look like and how it might alter investigations of knowledge and knowing. Following Ashcraft et al.'s (2009) division of materiality into objects, sites, and bodies, three possible routes emerge. First, transactive memory theorizing might develop more thoroughly *communicative* approaches to objects and artifacts in its explanations of system constitution and action. The TM perspective clearly considers objects important in the coding, storing, and retrieval of information but generally does not render problematic their impact on collective self-determination or actors' capacity to reflect on alternatives. To do so would involve a recognition that KM tools are, in fact, not best understood as entities employed in action that is already organizational (because it occurs in settings prelabeled as organizations or interorganizational relationships); rather, KM tools could be seen as active participants in the ongoing accomplishment of organization.

Second, the CoP literature would benefit from a more sustained engagement with sites. Knowing, in the CoP view, is very much situated in given contexts, including virtual or electronically mediated settings. But the literature's consideration of sites, whether geographical/spatial settings or virtual, tends to portray the sites primarily as containers within which communities form, as presenting challenges to coordination, or as supplying site-specific discursive resources to organizing. If CoP scholars become interested in how the (dynamic) configurations of material/symbolic features shape the achievement of distributed work practices, they would likely see that sites are imbued with a surplus of potential meanings. Those meanings come from the communicative appropriation of the physical components of the scene as well as the myriad of interests actors represent in organizing (Dale & Burrell, 2008; Halford, 2008; Kuhn, 2006). And, because these sites increasingly involve persons and objects not physically copresent, a central analytical concern should be how sites affect both representational and decisional practices (Vásquez & Cooren, 2013). An attention to the socio-materiality of sites in CoP theorizing might then lead analysts to examine how particular meanings become preferred in situated organizing, perhaps even extending the interest in meaning negotiation to broader networks of practice and cross-site innovation practices.

A third contribution that an emphasis on materiality could make to scholarship on knowledge would be to make the body a focus of practice-based research. Physical bodies, both human and nonhuman, are always bound up in, and are productive of, social practice. But focusing on the effects different bodies produce in work, how forms of work prefer a given body type, or how bodies interact with other material factors in work runs the risk of reproducing the symbolic-material dualism. Scholarship on knowledge work encounters the same problem when it associates knowledge with the content of the mind and divorces it from the body. Within the line of research seeing knowing as a struggle over meaning, one corrective is to show how communication processes are, at base, *embodied,* because they draw upon (and generate) attributions about the appropriateness for particular bodies at work—acknowledging that this can occur even when work is virtual. Organizing, in turn, is seen as often requiring a disciplining of the body to align with professional or occupational codes, particularly those revolving around gender. Instead of assuming a causal force whereby the codes exert the pressure to which bodies respond, communication studies frequently highlight the contingent, precarious, and polysemous performances that accomplish both subjectivity and knowledge in the conduct of work (Ashcraft, 1999; Tracy & Scott, 2006). Building on this, future scholarship on knowing might move beyond the claim that bodies' engagement in self-presentation and self-discipline evince certain types of knowledge that produce benefit for particular performers to attend to how communities are constituted by configuring practices of knowing around physical bodies. Communication, then, would be seen as the site upon which those practices and struggles over meaning occur. From there, the task would be to demonstrate that such forms of emergent and embodied knowledge shape organizing practices in other communities in the organizational constellation of communities (Brown & Duguid, 2001), across a distributed occupation, or throughout some other institutionalized organizing practice.

In the end, organizational communication is well positioned to make important contributions to the development of scholarship on knowledge and knowing. Not only could a communication perspective encourage a broadening of knowledge work beyond the confines of technical activity and highly educated workers but it could also problematize the cognition-practice dualism employed here by developing a vision of communication that moves past the transmission/constitutive division common in the field to suggest novel conceptions of persons, practices, materiality, and intersubjectivity. Beyond this, however, lies another possibility. Communication scholars regularly argue that communication theory holds the potential to alter conceptions of organizations dominant across the social sciences and, in making that case, they position communication as the organization's very foundation and mode of existence (see Brummans, Cooren, Robichaud, & Taylor, Chapter 7). Substantiating this claim requires an engagement with, and a fundamental challenging of, existing organization orthodoxies. Organization theories employed by those who study knowledge and knowing could provide avenues for communication scholars to connect interests in knowledge with unique answers to broadly held questions about organizational existence, boundaries, and action (Deetz & Putnam, 2001; Kuhn, 2008, 2012). Knowledge and knowing, then, could be seen as much more than topics of inquiry. They can serve as conceptual vehicles for the development of distinctly communicative modes of organizational explanation.

References

Aakhus, M. (2007). Conversations for reflection: Augmenting transitions and transformations in expertise. In C. McInerney & R. Day (Eds.), *Rethinking knowledge management: From knowledge objects to knowledge processes* (pp. 1–20). New York, NY: Springer.

Aakhus, M., Ballard, D., Flanagin, A. J., Kuhn, T., Leonardi, P., & Mease, J. (2011). Communication and materiality: A conversation from the CM Café. *Communication Monographs, 78*(4), 557–568.

Adler, P. S. (2001). Market, hierarchy, and trust: The knowledge economy and the future of capitalism. *Organization Science, 12*(2), 215–223.

Alvesson, M. (1994). Talking in organizations: Managing identity and impressions in an advertising agency. *Organization Studies, 15*(4), 535–563.

Alvesson, M. (2001). Knowledge work: Ambiguity, image, and identity. *Human Relations, 54*(7), 863–886.

Alvesson, M., & Spicer, A. (2012). A stupidity-based theory of organization. *Journal of Management Studies, 49*(7), 1194–1220.

Ashcraft, K. L. (1999). Managing maternity leave: A qualitative analysis of temporary executive succession. *Administrative Science Quarterly, 44*(2), 240–280.

Ashcraft, K. L., Kuhn, T., & Cooren, F. (2009). Constitutional amendments: "Materializing" organizational communication. In A. Brief & J. Walsh (Eds.), *The Academy of Management Annals* (vol. 3, pp. 1–64). New York, NY: Routledge.

Barad, K. (2003). Posthuman performativity: Toward an understanding of how matter comes to matter. *Signs, 28*(3), 801–831.

Barge, J. K., & Little, M. (2002). Dialogical wisdom, communicative practice, and organizational life. *Communication Theory, 12*(4), 375–397.

Barker, J. R. (1993). Tightening the iron cage: Concertive control in self-managing teams. *Administrative Science Quarterly, 38*(3), 408–437.

Bastien, D. T. (1992). Change in organizational culture: The use of linguistic methods in a corporate acquisition. *Management Communication Quarterly, 5*(4), 403–442.

Bechky, B. A. (2003). Object lessons: Workplace artifacts as representations of occupational jurisdiction. *American Journal of Sociology, 109*(3), 720–752.

Blackler, F. (1995). Knowledge, knowledge work and organizations: An overview and interpretation. *Organization Studies, 16*(6), 1021–1046.

Bontis, N. (1999). Managing organizational knowledge by diagnosing intellectual capital: Framing and advancing the state of the field. *International Journal of Technology Management, 18*(5–8), 433–462.

Bovasso, G. (1996). A network analysis of social contagion processes in an organizational intervention. *Human Relations, 49*(11), 1419–1435.

Brandon, D. P., & Hollingshead, A. B. (2004). Transactive memory systems in organizations: Matching tasks, expertise, and people. *Organization Science, 15*(6), 633–644.

Brown, J. S., & Duguid, P. (1991). Organizational learning and communities-of-practice: Toward a unified view of working, learning, and innovation. *Organization Science, 2*(1), 40–57.

Brown, J. S., & Duguid, P. (2001). Knowledge and organization: A social-practice perspective. *Organization Science, 12*(2), 198–213.

Burkhardt, M. E. (1994). Social interaction following a technological change: A longitudinal investigation. *Academy of Management Review, 37*(4), 869–898.

Canary, H. E., & McPhee, R. D. (2009). The mediation of policy knowledge: An interpretive analysis of intersecting activity systems. *Management Communication Quarterly, 23*(2), 147–187.

Carley, K. (1986). An approach for relating social structure to cognitive structure. *Journal of Mathematical Sociology, 12*(2), 137–189.

Carlile, P. (2002). A pragmatic view of knowledge and boundaries: Boundary objects in new product development. *Organization Science, 13*(4), 442–455.

Child, J. T., & Shumate, M. (2007). The impact of communal knowledge repositories and people-based knowledge management on perceptions of team effectiveness. *Management Communication Quarterly, 21*(1), 29–54.

Collins, H. M., & Evans, R. (2007). *Rethinking expertise.* Chicago, IL: University of Chicago Press.

Contractor, N. S., & Grant, S. (1996). The emergence of shared interpretations in organizations. In J. Watt & A. VanLear (Eds.), *Dynamic patterns in communication processes* (pp. 215–230). Thousand Oaks, CA: SAGE.

Contu, A., Grey, C., & Örtenblad, A. (2003). Against learning. *Human Relations, 56*(8), 931–952.

Contu, A., & Willmott, H. (2003). Re-embedding situatedness: The importance of power relations in learning theory. *Organization Science, 14*(3), 283–296.

Cook, S. D. N., & Brown, J. S. (1999). Bridging epistemologies: The generative dance between organizational knowledge and organizational knowing. *Organization Science, 10*(4), 381–400.

Cooren, F. (2004). The communicative achievement of collective minding: Analysis of board meeting excerpts. *Management Communication Quarterly, 17*(4), 517–551.

Cooren, F. (2010). *Action and agency in dialogue: Passion, incarnation and ventriloquism.* Philadelphia, PA: John Benjamins.

Covaleski, M. A., Dirsmith, M. W., Heian, J. B., & Samuel, S. (1998). The calculated and the avowed: Techniques of discipline and struggles over identity in big six public accounting firms. *Administrative Science Quarterly, 43*(2), 293–327.

Cunliffe, A. (2011). Crafting qualitative research: Morgan and Smircich 30 years on. *Organizational Research Methods, 14*(4), 647–673.

Dale, K., & Burrell, G. (2008). *Spaces of organization and the organization of space: Power, identity and materiality at work.* London, England: Palgrave Macmillan.

Davenport, T. H., & Prusak, L. (1998). *Working knowledge: How organizations manage what they know.* Boston, MA: Harvard Business School Press.

Deetz, S. A. (1992). *Democracy in an age of corporate colonization: Developments in communication and the politics of everyday life.* Albany: State University of New York Press.

Deetz, S. A., & Putnam, L. L. (2001). Thinking about the future of communication studies. In W. Gudykunst (Ed.), *Communication yearbook* (vol. 24, pp. 1–14). Thousand Oaks, CA: SAGE.

Deng, L., & Poole, M. S. (2011). Knowledge utilization in electronic networks of practice. In H. E. Canary & R. D. McPhee (Eds.), *Communication and organizational knowledge: Contemporary issues for theory and practice* (pp. 209–220). New York, NY: Routledge.

Doerfel, M. L., Lai, C-H., & Chewning, L. V. (2010). The evolutionary role of interorganizational communication: Modeling social capital in disaster contexts. *Human Communication Research, 36*(2), 125–162.

Douglas, M. (1986). *How institutions think.* Syracuse, NY: Syracuse University Press.

Engeström, Y. (1992). *Interactive expertise: Studies in distributed working intelligence, research bulletin 83.* Helsinki, Finland: University of Helsinki Department of Education.

Engeström, Y. (1994). *Training for change: New approach to instruction and learning in working life.* Geneva, Switzerland: ILO.

Flanagin, A. J. (2002). The elusive benefits of the technological support of knowledge management. *Management Communication Quarterly, 16*(2), 242–248.

Flanagin, A. J., & Bator, M. (2011). The utility of information and communication technologies in organizational knowledge management. In H. E. Canary & R. D. McPhee (Eds.), *Communication and organizational knowledge: Contemporary issues for theory and practice* (pp. 173–190). New York, NY: Routledge.

Fulk, J., Flanagin, A. J., Kalman, M. E., Monge, P., & Ryan, T. (1996). Connective and communal public goods in interactive communication systems. *Communication Theory, 6*(1), 60–87.

Garner, J. T. (2006). It's not what you know: A transactive memory analysis of knowledge networks at NASA. *Journal of Technical Writing and Communication, 36*(4), 329–351.

Gherardi, S. (2000). Practice-based theorizing on learning and knowing in organizations. *Organization, 7*(2), 211–223.

Gherardi, S. (2003). Knowing as desiring: Mythic knowledge and the knowledge journey in communities of practitioners. *Journal of Workplace Learning, 15*(7/8), 352–358.

Gherardi, S. (2008). Situated knowledge and situated action. In D. Barry & H. Hansen (Eds.), *The SAGE handbook of new approaches in management and organization* (pp. 516–525). Thousand Oaks, CA: SAGE.

Goldstein, J. (1999). Emergence as a construct: History and issues. *Emergence, 1*(1), 49–72.

Grant, R. M. (1996). Toward a knowledge-based theory of the firm [Special issue]. *Strategic Management Journal, 17,* 109–122.

Grossberg, L. (1982). Intersubjectivity and the conceptualization of communication. *Human Studies, 5*(1), 213–235.

Halford, S. (2008). Sociologies of space, work, and organisation: From fragments to spatial theory. *Sociology Compass, 2*(3), 925–943.

Hardy, M., & Jian, G. (2011). Materializing *guanxi*: Practice of *liao tian* in Chinese business settings. In T. Kuhn (Ed.), *Matters of communication: Political, cultural, and technological challenges* (pp. 167–196). New York, NY: Hampton.

Hinds, P., & Kiesler, S. (1995). Communication across boundaries: Work, structure, and use of communication technologies in a large organization. *Organization Science, 6*(4), 373–393.

Ho, K. (2009). *Liquidated: An ethnography of Wall Street*. Durham, NC: Duke University Press.

Hollingshead, A. B. (1998). Communication, learning, and retrieval in transactive memory systems. *Journal of Experimental Social Psychology, 34*(5), 423–442.

Hollingshead, A. B., Fulk, J., & Monge, P. (2002). Fostering intranet knowledge sharing: An integration of transactive memory and public goods approaches. In P. J. Hinds & S. Kiesler (Eds.), *Distributed work* (pp. 335–356). Cambridge, MA: MIT Press.

Howard, L. A., & Geist, P. G. (1995). Ideological positioning in organizational change: The dialectic of control in a merging organization. *Communication Monographs, 62*(2), 110–131.

Isabella, L. A. (1990). Evolving interpretations as a change unfolds: How managers construe key organizational events. *Academy of Management Journal, 33*(1), 7–41.

Iverson, J. O. (2011). Knowledge, belonging, and communities of practice. In H. E. Canary & R. D. McPhee (Eds.), *Communication and organizational knowledge: Contemporary issues for theory and practice* (pp. 35–52). New York, NY: Routledge.

Iverson, J. O., & McPhee, R. D. (2002). Knowledge management in communities of practice: Being true to the communicative character of knowledge. *Management Communication Quarterly, 16*(2), 259–266.

Jackson, M. H., & Williamson, J. (2011). Challenges of implementing systems for knowledge management: Static systems and dynamic practices. In H. E. Canary & R. D. McPhee (Eds.), *Communication and organizational knowledge: Contemporary issues for theory and practice* (pp. 53–68). New York, NY: Routledge.

Kärreman, D., & Rylander, A. (2008). Managing meaning through branding: The case of a consulting firm. *Organization Studies, 29*(1), 103–125.

Kellogg, K. C., Orlikowski, W. J., & Yates, J. (2006). Life in the trading zone: Structuring coordination across boundaries in postbureaucratic organizations. *Organization Science, 17*(1), 22–44.

Kinsella, W. J. (1999). Discourse, power, and knowledge in the management of 'big science': The production of consensus in a nuclear fusion laboratory. *Management Communication Quarterly, 13*(2), 171–208.

Kogut, B. (2000). The network as knowledge: Generative rules and the emergence of structure. *Strategic Management Journal, 21*(3), 405–425.

Koschmann, M., Kuhn, T. R., & Pfarrer, M. P. (2012). A communicative framework of value in cross-sector partnerships. *Academy of Management Review, 37*(3), 332–354.

Kuhn, T. (2002). Negotiating boundaries between scholars and practitioners: Knowledge, networks, and communities of practice. *Management Communication Quarterly, 16*(1), 106–112.

Kuhn, T. (2006). A "demented work ethic" and a "lifestyle firm": Discourse, identity, and workplace time commitments. *Organization Studies, 27*(9), 1339–1358.

Kuhn, T. (2008). A communicative theory of the firm: Developing an alternative perspective on intra-organizational power and stakeholder relationships. *Organization Studies, 29*(8/9), 1227–1254.

Kuhn, T. (2009). Positioning lawyers: Discursive resources, professional ethics, and identification. *Organization, 16*(5), 681–704.

Kuhn, T. (2011). Engaging materiality, communication, and social problems. In T. Kuhn (Ed.), *Matters of communication: Political, cultural, and technological challenges* (pp. 1–10). New York, NY: Hampton.

Kuhn, T. (2012). Negotiating the micro-macro divide: Communicative thought leadership for theorizing organization. *Management Communication Quarterly, 26*(4), 543–584.

Kuhn, T., & Corman, S. R. (2003). The emergence of homogeneity and heterogeneity in knowledge structures during a planned organizational change. *Communication Monographs, 70*(3), 198–229.

Kuhn, T., & Jackson, M. (2008). Accomplishing knowledge: A framework for investigating knowing in organizations. *Management Communication Quarterly, 21*(4), 454–485.

Kuhn, T., & Porter, A. J. (2011). Heterogeneity in knowledge and knowing: A social practice perspective. In H. Canary & R. D. McPhee (Eds.), *Communication and organizational knowledge:*

Contemporary issues for theory and practice (pp. 17–34). New York, NY: Routledge.

Lave, J., & Wenger, E. (1991). *Situated learning: Legitimate peripheral participation*. New York, NY: Cambridge University Press.

Law, J. (2002). Objects and spaces. *Theory, Culture and Society, 19*(5), 91–105.

Leonardi, P. M. (2011). Information, technology, and knowledge sharing in global organizations: Cultural differences in perceptions of where knowledge lies. In H. E. Canary & R. D. McPhee (Eds.), *Communication and organizational knowledge: Contemporary issues for theory and practice* (pp. 89–112). New York, NY: Routledge.

Leonardi, P. M., & Bailey, D. (2008). Transformational technologies and the creation of new work practices: Making implicit knowledge explicit in task-based offshoring. *MIS Quarterly, 32*(2), 411–436.

Leonardi, P. M., & Barley, S. R. (2010). What's under construction here? Social action, materiality, and power in constructivist studies of technology and organizing. In J. Walsh & A. Brief (Eds.), *The Academy of Management Annals* (vol. 4, pp. 1–51). Philadelphia, PA: Taylor & Francis.

Leonardi, P. M., & Jackson, M. (2004). Technological determinism and discursive closure in organizational mergers. *Journal of Organizational Change Management, 17*(6), 615–631.

Levesque, L. L., Wilson, J. M., & Wholey, D. R. (2001). Cognitive divergence and shared mental models in software development project teams. *Journal of Organizational Behavior, 22*(2), 135–144.

Liang, D. W., Moreland, R. L., & Argote, L. (1995). Group versus individual training and group performance: The mediating role of transactive memory. *Personality and Social Psychology Bulletin, 21*(4), 384–393.

Lilley, S., Lightfoot, G., & Amaral, P. (2004). *Representing organization: Knowledge, management, and the information age*. Oxford, UK: Oxford University Press.

Lundry, C., & Cheong, P. H. (2011). Rumors and strategic communication: The gendered construction and transmediation of a terrorist life story. In T. Kuhn (Ed.), *Matters of communication: Political, cultural, and technological challenges* (pp. 145–166). New York, NY: Hampton.

Lyon, A. (2004). Participants' use of cultural knowledge as cultural capital in a dot-com start-up organization. *Management Communication Quarterly, 18*(2), 175–203.

Lyon, A. (2005). "Intellectual capital" and struggles over the perceived value of members' expert knowledge in a knowledge-intensive organization. *Western Journal of Communication, 69*(3), 251–271.

Maier, G. W., Prange, C., & von Rosenstiel, L. (2001). Psychological perspectives of organizational learning. In M. Dierkes, A. Berthoin-Antal, J. Child, & I. Nonaka (Eds.), *Handbook of organizational learning and knowledge* (pp. 14–34). Oxford, UK: Oxford University Press.

McClellan, J. (2011). Reconsidering communication and the discursive politics of organizational change. *Journal of Change Management, 11*(4), 465–480.

McKinney, E. H., Barker, J. R., Davis, K. J., & Smith, D. R. (2005). How swift starting action teams get off the ground: What United flight 232 and airline flight crews can tell us about team communication. *Management Communication Quarterly, 19*(2), 198–237.

McPhee, R. D., Myers, K. K., & Trethewey, A. (2006). On collective mind and conversational analysis: Response to Cooren. *Management Communication Quarterly, 19*(3), 311–326.

Monge, P., & Contractor, N. S. (2003). *Theories of communication networks*. New York, NY: Oxford University Press.

Murphy, A. G., & Eisenberg, E. M. (2011). Coaching to the craft: Understanding knowledge in health care organizations. In H. E. Canary & R. D. McPhee (Eds.), *Communication and organizational knowledge: Contemporary issues for theory and practice* (pp. 264–284). New York, NY: Routledge.

Myers, K. K., & McPhee, R. D. (2006). Influences on member assimilation in workgroups in high-reliability organizations: A multilevel analysis. *Human Communication Research, 32*(4), 440–468.

Nadesan, M. H. (1997). Constructing paper dolls: The discourse of personality testing in organizational practice. *Communication Theory, 7*(3), 189–218.

Neff, G. (2012). *Venture labor: Work and the burden of risk in innovative industries*. Cambridge, MA: MIT Press.

Nicolini, D. (2012). *Practice theory, work, and organization: An introduction*. Oxford, UK: Oxford University Press.

Nonaka, I., & Takeuchi, H. (1995). *The knowledge-creating company: How Japanese companies create the dynamics of innovation*. New York, NY: Oxford University Press.

O'Hair, H. D., Kelley, K. M., & Williams, K. L. (2011). Managing community risks through a community-communication infrastructure approach. In H. E. Canary & R. D. McPhee (Eds.), *Communication and organizational knowledge: Contemporary issues for theory and practice* (pp. 223–243). New York, NY: Routledge.

Orlikowski, W. J. (2002). Knowing in practice: Enacting a collective capability in distributed organizing. *Organization Science, 13*(3), 249–273.

Orr, J. E. (1996). *Talking about machines: An ethnography of a modern job*. Ithaca, NY: ILR Press.

Palazzolo, E. T. (2005). Organizing for information retrieval in transactive memory systems. *Communication Research, 32*(6), 726–761.

Palazzolo, E. T., Serb, D. A., She, Y., Su, C., & Contractor, N. S. (2006). Coevolution of communication and knowledge networks in transactive memory systems: Using computational models for theoretical development. *Communication Theory, 16*(2), 223–250.

Ponzi, L. J., & Koenig, M. (2002). Knowledge management: Another management fad? *Information Research, 8*(1), paper no. 145. Retrieved from http://informationr.net/ir/8-1/paper145.html

Power, M. (1997). *The audit society: Rituals of verification*. Oxford, UK: Oxford University Press.

Rennstam, J. (2012). Object-control: A study of technologically dense knowledge work. *Organization Studies, 33*(8), 1071–1090.

Rice, R. E., & Aydin, C. (1991). Attitudes toward new organizational technology: Network proximity as a mechanism for social information processing. *Administrative Science Quarterly, 36*(2), 219–244.

Roberts, J. (2006). Limits to communities of practice. *Journal of Management Studies, 43*(3), 623–639.

Rorty, R. (1999). *Philosophy and social hope*. New York, NY: Penguin.

Scarbrough, H., & Swan, J. (2001). Explaining the diffusion of knowledge management: The role of fashion. *British Journal of Management, 12*(1), 3–12.

Schön, D. (1992). The crisis of professional knowledge and the pursuit of an epistemology of practice. *Journal of Interprofessional Care, 6*(1), 49–63.

Shumate, M., & Lipp, J. (2008). Connective collective action online: An examination of the hyperlink network structure of an NGO issue network. *Journal of Computer Mediated Communication, 14*(1), 178–201.

Spender, J-C. (1996). Making knowledge the basis of a dynamic theory of the firm [Special issue]. *Strategic Management Journal, 17*, 45–62.

Star, S. L., & Griesemer, J. R. (1989). Institutional ecology, "translations," and boundary objects: Amateurs and professionals in Berkeley's Museum of Vertebrate Zoology, 1907–39. *Social Studies of Science, 19*(3), 387–420.

Strati, A. (2003). Knowing in practice: Aesthetic understanding and tacit knowledge. In D. Nicolini, S. Gherardi, & D. Yanow (Eds.), *Knowing in organizations* (pp. 53–75). Armonk, NY: M. E. Sharpe.

Szulanski, G. (2003). *Sticky knowledge: Barriers to knowing in the firm*. Thousand Oaks, CA: SAGE.

Taylor, J. R. (2011). Organization as an (imbricated) configuring of transactions. *Organization Studies, 32*(9), 1273–1294.

Taylor, J. R., Groleau, C., Heaton, L., & Van Every, E. (2001). *The computerization of work: A communication perspective*. Thousand Oaks, CA: SAGE.

Taylor, M., & Doerfel, M. L. (2011). Evolving network roles in international aid efforts: Evidence from Croatia's post war transition. *Voluntas, 22*(2), 311–334.

Tempest, S., & Starkey, K. (2004). The effects of liminality on individual and organizational learning. *Organization Studies, 25*(4), 507–527.

Thrift, N. (2005). *Knowing capitalism*. London, England: SAGE.

Tracy, S. J., & Scott, C. (2006). Sexuality, masculinity, and taint management among firefighters and correctional officers. *Management Communication Quarterly, 20*(1), 6–38.

Treem, J. W. (2012). Communicating expertise: Knowledge performances in professional-service firms. *Communication Monographs, 79*(1), 23–47.

Tsoukas, H. (2009). A dialogical approach to the creation of new knowledge in organizations. *Organization Science, 20*(6), 941–957.

Tsoukas, H., & Vladimirou, E. (2001). What is organizational knowledge? *Journal of Management Studies, 38*(7), 973–993.

Ul-Haq, S., & Westwood, R. (2012). The politics of knowledge, epistemological occlusion, and

Islamic management and organization knowledge. *Organization, 19*(2), 229–257.

Vásquez, C., & Cooren, F. (2013). Spacing practices: The communicative configuration of organizing through space-times. *Communication Theory, 23*(1), 25–47.

von Krogh, G., & Roos, J. (1996). Conversation management for knowledge development. In G. von Krogh & J. Roos (Eds.), *Managing knowledge: Perspectives on cooperation and comptetition* (pp. 218–225). London, England: SAGE.

Wagner, C. (2006). Breaking the knowledge acquisition bottleneck through conversational knowledge management. *Information Resources Management Journal, 19*(1), 70–83.

Walsh, J. P., & Ungson, G. R. (1991). Organizational memory. *Academy of Management Review, 16*(1), 57–91.

Wegner, D. M. (1987). Transactive memory: A contemporary analysis of the group mind. In B. Mullen & G. R. Goethals (Eds.), *Theories of group behavior* (pp. 185–208). New York, NY: Springer-Verlag.

Weick, K. E., & Roberts, K. H. (1993). Collective mind in organization: Heedful interrelating on flight decks. *Administrative Science Quarterly, 38*(3), 357–381.

Wenger, E. (1998). *Communities of practice: Learning, meaning, and identity.* Cambridge, UK: Cambridge University Press.

Yuan, Y., Fulk, J., Monge, P. R., & Contractor, N. (2010). Expertise directory development, shared task interdependence, and strength of communication network ties as multilevel predictors of expertise exchange in transactive memory work groups. *Communication Research, 37*(1), 20–47.

Yuan, Y., Fulk, J., Shumate, M., Monge, P. R., Bryant, J. A., & Matsaganis, M. (2005). Individual participation in organizational information commons: The impact of team level social influence and technology-specific competence. *Human Communication Research, 31*(2), 212–240.

Zorn, T. E., & Taylor, J. R. (2004). Knowledge management and/as organizational communication. In D. Tourish & O. Hargie (Eds.), *Key issues in organizational communication* (pp. 96–112). London, England: Routledge.

Note

1. Gherardi (2008), however, usefully distinguishes lineages of practice-based work that result in (at least) five contemporary perspectives. The CoP view is but one of these, and I foreground it here to both highlight a prominent communication manifestation of practice-based work and to provide contrast with the preceding sections.

CHAPTER 20

Organizational Change and Innovation

Laurie K. Lewis

> Only the wisest and the stupidest of men never change.
>
> —Confucius

> If you don't change direction, you'll end up where you're headed.
>
> —Chinese proverb

Change is a prominent feature of organizational, civic, and personal life and a frequent topic of scholarly and popular discourse. Change can serve as means to address many important challenges, such as those related to distribution of rights and resources; challenges of efficiency, effectiveness, and competitiveness; and challenges hinged on shared values, understanding, and cooperation. Change can also be wrongheaded, faddish, unnecessary, and a waste of resources.

The topics of innovation and change have received considerable attention in a vast range of disciplines, including those that examine these ideas and processes as technique, management practice, social process, and psychological orientation. The key terms are also heavily invested with cultural meaning—typically embraced as *god terms*, expressed as desirable, modern, progressive, and improvement. On the presumption of these taken-for-granted goods, a good deal of research and theory has been devoted to explaining how we can change faster, more often, and more fundamentally. The popular business notion of *continuous improvement* is a prime example of this cultural value. The trend is so strong and the assumption that innovation and change are undeniably good that there is only a tiny pocket of literature examining organizations that deliberately do not innovate (cf. Keupp, Palmie, & Gassmann, 2011). There is also scant research on what has been referred to as *negative* or *malevolent* creativity (Cropley, Kaufman, & Cropley, 2008), which might range from creative ways of stealing from one's organization or avoiding unpleasant work at the expense of others to creativity endeavors intended to do harm (e.g., during terrorism, war, and crime).

In the many decades of research and theorizing about innovation and change (see previous reviews by Crossan & Apaydin, 2010; Keupp et al., 2011; Lewis & Seibold, 1998; Poole

& Van de Ven, 2004; Rogers, 1983, 1995), the questions have tended to revolve around how to get innovation and change going rather than if a particular innovation or change—or changing at all—is a good idea. Further, much research and theory assumes that the champions of change, typically those in power in organizations, are the target audience for this topic. Thus the research on organizational change often focuses on helping leaders foster innovation and bring about desired outcomes and on managing people through the change process. Far less has been researched or theorized about the strategies of other stakeholders who ignite, resist, reinvent change, or live with its repercussions. The outcomes for stakeholders aside from the target organization are rarely considered in assessing success.

This chapter reviews the threads of communication-centered research and theory about organizational change, with a focus on planned change scholarship. One goal of this chapter is to problematize key assumptions and to ask how scholars' questions and research might be different if we frame change within broader sets of perspectives. This chapter (1) discusses definitional issues surrounding innovation and change, (2) introduces major approaches to change processes, (3) examines major roles that communication plays in change, and finally, (4) discusses limitations to current approaches and future directions for change research.

What Is Change?

The change literature applies key terminology in sometimes loose and varied ways. For example, *innovation* has been used both as a verb (to create something new) and a noun (a new thing). *Adoption* has been used to describe the initial decision to bring a new idea into an organization as well as the concluding outcome of a change process whereby a new idea becomes ordinary accepted practice.

Further, *creativity* is often used interchangeably with *innovation,* and some scholars treat *creativity* as the precursor to *innovation* and equate it with *implementation.* Three terms that are useful for understanding the scope of innovation-related and change-related processes are *innovation*, *planned change*, and *unplanned change*. Crossan and Apaydin's (2010) review of the innovation literature note that definitions of *innovation* abound and emphasize different aspects of the term. Their own definition of the term highlights both process and outcome that results in "valued-added novelty" (p. 1155). Zorn, Christiansen, and Cheney (1999) define *planned change* as referring "to any alteration or modification of organizational structures or processes" (p. 10). In contrast, *unplanned changes* are those brought into the organization due to environmental or uncontrollable forces (e.g., fire burns down plant, governmental shutdown of production) or emergent processes and interactions in the organization (e.g., drift in practices, erosion of skills).

The language of early models of change process often implies that organizations are at one moment stable and at another in flux. Even though stakeholders may experience organizations as more familiar and stable at some points and as more disrupted and in flux at other points, organizing activity is made up of processes and, as such, is always in motion and always changing (Lewis, 2011). This difference is described in terms of *episodic* and *continuous* change. Weick and Quinn (1999) define *episodic change* as "infrequent, discontinuous and intentional" (p. 365) and *continuous change* as "ongoing, evolving and cumulative" (p. 375). Scholars often refer to this distinction as *planned* versus *unplanned* change. Poole (2004) draws attention to the false separation of these two modes of change when he notes "all planned change occurs in the context of the ambient change processes that occur naturally in organizations" (p. 4).

Organizational sociologists have devoted a good deal of scholarship to examining unplanned change. For example, some scholars (Hannan & Freeman, 1977, 1989) focus on the level of whole communities or niches of organizations and examine the ways in which these systems evolve over time. For some theorists, change is conceptualized as occurring gradually as an inherent part of organizing (Miller & Friesen, 1982, 1984). Life-cycle theories specify standard stages of organizational development, such as birth, growth, decline, and death. Other scholars specify the sequential development of organizations through the variation, selection, and retention of organizational and environmental characteristics.

Classic and Alternative Models of Change

Classic models of organizational innovation and change tend to highlight a linear path from problem formation to introduction of novelty to restabilization (Graetz & Smith, 2010). Rogers (1995) arrayed the critical terms as *agenda-setting*, *matching*, *redefining/restructuring* (*reinvention*), *clarifying*, and *routinizing*. The first two of these phases he considers *initiating stages*, in which new ideas are compared against perceived problems, and the last three stages are treated as part of *implementation*, in which the changes are brought into use and fit into existing practices. The decision to adopt divides the phases of the process. Lewin (1951) suggested the phases of unfreezing, changing, and refreezing. In his conceptualization, organizations exist as stable processes with broken episodes of change activity that disrupt routines temporarily until settling into stability again. The breaks in routine might be attributable to innovation that sparks change or sometimes to other causes. As these two models illustrate, the language of change and innovation is, by nature, a language of contrasts. Change is contrasted with continuity, and innovation is contrasted with the familiar.

Van de Ven and Poole (1995) describe four different motors of change: life cycle, teleological, dialectical, and evolutionary. The life cycle motor depicts change processes as progressing through a necessary sequence of stages or phases that are proscribed through institutional, natural, or logical causes. The teleological model, in which change is accomplished through intentional goal formation and implementation and modification of behaviors, is closest to the notion of planned change, which dominates the management literature. The dialectical motor of change emerges through the development of conflicts between entities that espouse opposing theses. A cycle of dialectical progression of confrontation and conflict between opposing entities generates change. The evolutionary model of development and change consists of repetitive sequences of variation, selection, and retention events among entities. Evolutionary change is driven by competition for scarce resources. Poole (2004) argues that these four theories of change are distinguishable in terms of two key dimensions: the degree to which change is premised on the actions of a single or of multiple entities and whether the change events are *a priori* or emerging as the change process unfolds. Poole (2004) explains the advantage of examining motors for change through the use of two dimensions—unit and mode of change:

> They differ from other dimensions such as incremental and radical change and competence-enhancing and competence-destroying change which classify organizational changes based on their consequences or outcomes rather than by their starting or process conditions. One advantage of the typology is that it is possible to identify the motor(s) of a change process before it has concluded. (p. 8)

The Role of Communication in Change Processes

Communication plays a central role in organizational change processes, including triggers and diffusion, change implementation, social construction, discourses in change, and dialectical change.

Triggers and Diffusion

Communication plays a central role in both surfacing and suppressing triggers for change. However, the focus on interaction and communication of these change processes has been spotty and inconsistent, with no prominent sustained research since Rogers's (1983) seminal work on diffusion of innovations. The classic models of change depict a linear path rooted in individual ingenuity that leads to organizational change and ultimately spreads to the environment (see Figure 20.1). In this model, organizational changes are generated through accidental or intentional innovation processes used by organizations to create new ways of doing things or new things to do. *Diffusion* then follows when new ideas are shared to the point that they catch on in the environment (e.g., industry, profession).

Although the rational depiction of invention-selection-diffusion is prevalent in some of the change literature, there is increasing acknowledgement that oftentimes change is thrust upon an organization rather than selected for potential "innovativeness." For example, in the case of regulatory change, organizations are compelled to adopt new practices and processes. Further, even change that is developed within organizations is not always borne of mere creative processes. Zorn et al. (1999) make the case that "change for change's sake" (p. 4) has been glorified to the extent that it has become managerial fashion for stakeholders to constantly change their organizations. These scholars argue that cultural and market pressures demand constant organizational change, despite evidence that innovation may not be necessary for competitive advantage (Keupp et al., 2011). This constant change can lead to disastrous outcomes, including ill-considered timing of change, dysfunctional human resource management practices, exhaustion from repetitive cycles of change, and loss of benefits that stem from stability and consistency.

In addition to faddish and regulatory required change, organizations must adapt to dire or rapidly changing environments merely to survive rather than to improve. Dwindling supplies of a needed resource (raw materials, labor, technology); increases in competition; major economic or social upheaval in the immediate environment; political change in local, state, or national government; and changes in demands for products, services, or mode of delivery are all examples of triggers for change and innovation that are not necessarily rooted in creative processes and intentional selection.

Triggers of change often stem from social pressures exerted through communicative relationships. In a study of the adoption of websites, Flanagin (2000) found evidence that nonprofit organizations' self-perceptions of their status and leadership position in their field were positively correlated with adoption decisions. They ascribed this pattern in part to the felt pressures to stay on the leading edge. As more and more organizations in a local area or within an industry adopt a specific innovation, the pressure mounts for those who do not have that innovation to mimic the adopters. In contrast, if powerful stakeholders eschew an idea or find they desire other alternatives, pressure to drop or discontinue a new idea may mount. In two case studies of nonprofit organizations in New Zealand, Zorn, Grant, and Henderson (2012) also found evidence that talk within professional networks influenced the ways in which new technologies were viewed and the initial enthusiasm for their use and adoption.

Figure 20.1 General Diffusion Model

Invention → Organization Selection → Other Organizations Adopt → Widespread Use

However, they also found that organizational resource issues (e.g., time, money, infrastructure) played a critical role in determining use, especially the dual pressures and enticements of internal and external environments.

Thus triggers for change often stem from communication among key stakeholders who notice features of the internal or external environment that lead them to make a case for a change and/or to develop an innovative response. For example, decision makers often work through the adoption of a change communication by comparing their understandings and sense of "what is going on" with that of competitors, regulators, customers, industry partners, and internal stakeholders, such as employees, volunteers, and affiliated national organizations. The ways in which implementers and other stakeholders talk about a given change forms the basis of what the change becomes for that organization.

As illustrated in Figure 20.2, change processes in organizations have a reciprocal impact with processes of environmental diffusion and innovation. What is often missed in the classic presentation of the diffusion process is the simultaneous and mutually influential internal and environmental sensemaking processes. That is, a given organization's decision to adopt, its implementation process, and its success in implementing a change are related to the diffusion of the change in the environment. Any judgment of success may increase the chances of it diffusing further in the environment. So organizations that are judged successful with an

Figure 20.2 Relationships Between Innovation, Diffusion, Adoption, and Implementation

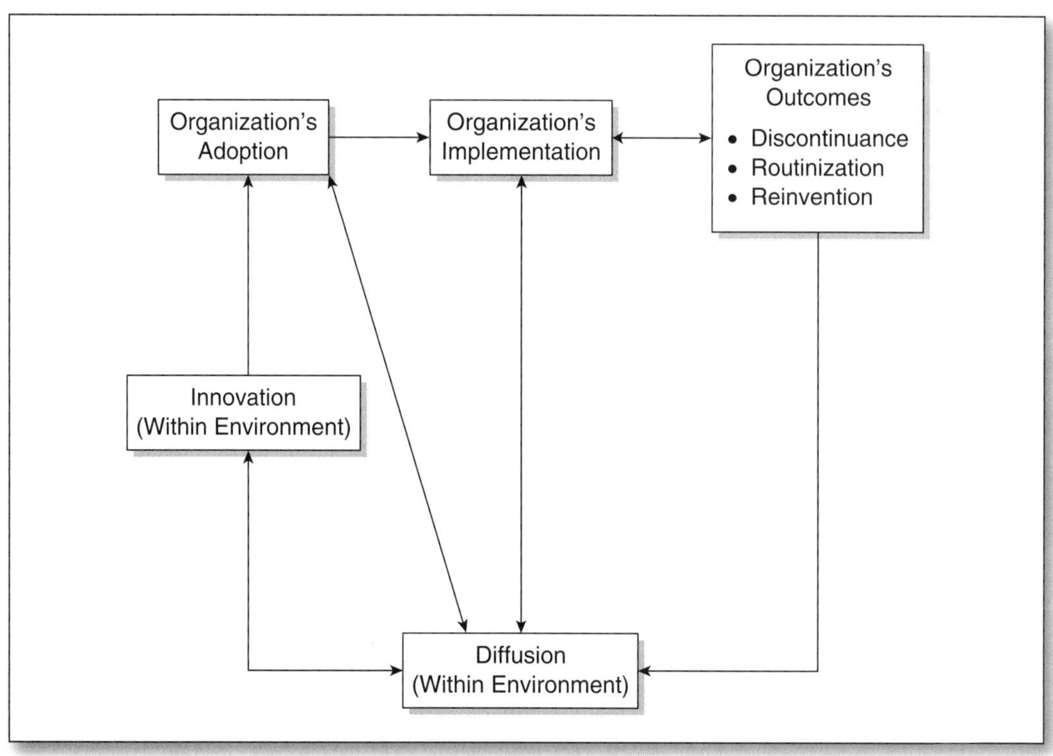

Source: Lewis (2011).

innovation are likely to be noticed and mimicked by other organizations. This explanation calls attention to the multiple locations of social interaction and sensemaking that play roles in organizational *routinization* (continued use in everyday practice), *discontinuance* (the ending of a change effort and/or use of an innovation), and/or *reinvention* (alteration of the change through practice) as well as environmental diffusion.

In a recent empirical investigation of the power of institutional forces, Zorn, Flanagin, and Shoham (2011) make the case that the adoption of information and communication technologies (ICTs) was due to a combination of institutional pressures (from the environment) that supported or prescribed the use of ICTs and to organizational characteristics (e.g., information technology [IT] knowledge, IT support) that encouraged adoption. They state, "Organizations most likely to adopt and use ICTs were those who scanned their peer organizations for emerging technologies and technology-related practices and had the expertise to make sense of and use them" (p. 19). They note that this observation is reminiscent of the social influences of literature on technology adoption (cf. Fulk, 1993: Fulk, Schmitz, & Steinfield, 1990). However, their data extend this perspective in illustrating that these processes "also operate at the *inter*organizational level" (Zorn et al., 2011, p. 19, emphasis in original).

Each of these examples calls into question the assumption of a rational process of invention-selection-diffusion as the dominant case. In fact, the triggers for change are likely quite diverse and it may be that change in any given organization arises from a complex set of independent but interrelated triggers (e.g., an idea is created in response to regulatory pressure in an environment, in which competitors are developing their own responses that have more or less traction in those industries/fields and where internal stakeholders have more or less buy-in to both the supposed problem and proposed solution). Doubtlessly, as renewed research in this area of change scholarship demonstrates, communication plays an important role for creating social pressure, framing opportunities and crises, and spreading opinions and attitudes about the need for change.

Change Implementation

Tornatzky and Johnson (1982) define *implementation* as "the translation of any tool or technique, process, or method of doing, from knowledge to practice" (p. 193). Implementers often see a need to convince stakeholders to alter practices, processes, procedures, work arrangements, and values as well. Knowledgeable experts often help to install the necessary technology, train personnel, explain changes to clients and customers, and redesign work processes around the changes. As Lewis (2011) argues "in change implementation, communication is a means by which stakeholders describe, persuade, define, instruct, support, resist, and evaluate the new and old practices" (p. 31). This process is typically viewed as activity planned and executed by managers of the change; however, the communicative activity of stakeholders plays a central role in accounting for the implementation process and outcomes.

A growing body of literature in multiple disciplines addresses how communication influences the implementation processes during change. For example, in a line of research dating back to the 1990s (Lewis, 1999, 2000, 2006; Lewis, Hamel, & Richardson, 2001; Lewis, Richardson, & Hamel, 2003; Lewis & Russ, 2012), Lewis and colleagues have charted the communication strategies of implementers, their rationales for communication approaches, and the reactions of stakeholders to these approaches. As this chapter suggests, the questions, models, and theories focus on explanations that help managers control the change processes in their organizations. Much of the change literature that has the most relevance to communication focuses on how to get "good ideas" to move from formulation to routine practice. In broad strokes, this literature examines (1) information sharing and knowledge creation; (2) soliciting input; (3) stakeholders' attitudes, dispositions, and reactions; and (4) management of negative reactions.

Information Sharing and Knowledge Creation. In a majority of approaches to change implementation, the delivery of information to stakeholders (typically employees) is considered a critically important activity for managers. Some scholars assert that information sharing supports the adoption of innovations in organizations. For example, Kanter (1983) suggests that organizations that overly control information (as well as actions and decisions) are less innovative. Angle (1989) also points to the importance of information flows in an organization as an enabling factor for innovation. Sharing information is typically viewed as an uncertainty reduction activity. As Bordia, Hobman, Jones, Gallois, and Callan (2004) describe, uncertainty during change typically involves strategic, structural, and job-related questions. Further, Lewis (2011) argues that

> implementers are depicted [in the change literature] as the possessors of information and their tasks as (1) appropriate dissemination of information about a change, (2) discovery of inaccurate interpretations or misunderstandings of information they disseminate, and (3) clarification of misconstrued information. (p. 57)

This approach to information during change aligns with a traditional transmission model of information sharing and communication. In that perspective, information is a commodity that moves between nodes in a system (individuals, departments, organizations).

An important initial activity in information sharing during change involves the announcement of change and decision making about what sort of information should be shared with stakeholders about the upcoming change. Smeltzer and Zener (1992, 1994, 1995; Smeltzer, 1991) have published a number of articles on effective planned-change announcements. Based on interviews with implementers of changes in 43 large organizations, Smeltzer (1991) provides a list of commonly perceived failures of change announcements, including lack of a communication strategy, circulation of rumors, poor channel selection, failure to adapt to different audiences, use of euphemisms, and overly positive announcements.

In general, in the change literature, stakeholders prefer that implementers be honest and open, and research suggests that these characteristics produce subsequent cooperativeness and enhanced ability of stakeholders to cope with change. For example, in Schweiger and DeNisi's (1991) field experiment, extensive realistic previews in the case of the implementation of a merger were examined. Early previews of the details of the merger and its process in the experimental plant significantly lowered uncertainty and increased job satisfaction, commitment, perceived trustworthiness, honesty, and caring as well as self-reported performance. These effects endured over time as the merger progressed. Laster's (2008) study of a merger that was followed by multiple additional changes found that forewarning stakeholders of the complexity of change helped employees cope. In her study, the ways in which implementers talked about the change at the outset influenced how employees made sense of the size and scope of the change. In many cases, the initial announcements had a significant impact on what employees were expecting at the outset of change and set them up for surprises, additional stress, and sometimes disappointment. A study by Griffith and Northcraft (1996) found that messages that balanced positive and negative previews of a new technology significantly affected performance of new users in a positive direction. Miller and Monge's (1985) study found that employees so valued information during change that they found even negative information more helpful than providing no information at all. Other research has established the important function of information sharing in the reduction of stress, uncertainty, and negative attitudes about change (Bird,

2007; Covin & Kilmann, 1990; Robinson & Griffiths, 2005; Schweiger & DeNisi, 1991).

Lewis, Laster, and Kulkarni's (2013) recent investigation of change announcements used an experimental design to examine the extent to which acknowledging potentially negative aspects of change heightened perceptions of honesty and trustworthiness and improved stakeholders' favorability toward the change. Further, the study examined stakeholders' communication purposes and subsequent targets as a result of receiving different versions of the announcement of change. Their findings demonstrated that previews of possible negatives did not increase initial favorability or judgments of credibility of implementers. This study also found that high-risk change created a challenging context for implementers to announce change.

Research and theory also suggests that uncertainty is managed in other ways than merely information accumulation (Brummans & Miller, 2004). For example, Kramer, Dougherty, and Pierce (2004) examined uncertainty in the context of an airline acquisition. Kramer et al.'s (2004) study found that individuals differed in the degrees to which they sought out information. Those who were less active in seeking information managed uncertainty internally and discounted the available information that they could have sought out as likely to be inaccurate, misleading, or unavailable and therefore not worth the effort to gather. They also found that a majority of the pilots sought information to create comfort, share rumors (even if they were thought to be false), and seek mutual support.

Soliciting Input. Solicitation of input is another key communicative activity that implementers need to execute during change. Accumulating evidence supports soliciting input as a way to lower resistance to change, increase the satisfaction of participants, and increase stakeholders' feelings of control (cf. Bordia et al., 2004; Sagie, Elizur, & Koslowsky, 2001; Sagie & Koslowsky, 1994). Innovation scholars point to participative processes and structures as key as well. Among the characteristics of organizational environments that have been found to encourage creativity and innovation are providing information and feedback, giving encouragement, stimulating risk taking, and creating a fun and trusting environment (Klijn & Tomic, 2010). Kanter's (1988) work argues that innovation is most likely to occur in organizations marked by highly integrative structures, diversity, multiple internal and external linkages, and emphases on teamwork and collaboration. Angle (1989) found in his research (part of the Minnesota Innovation Survey) that the frequencies of interactions among individuals with different frames of reference were more likely to generate new and creative ideas. In the realm of public-sector innovation, Nyhan (2000) and Page (2003) maintain that public entrepreneurs should encourage collaboration, participation, and inclusive decision-making processes that engender trust in their work settings.

However, research also reveals that organizations emphasize downward dissemination of information over soliciting stakeholder input (Doyle, Claydon, & Buchanan, 2000; Lewis, 1999, 2006; Lewis et al., 2003). When input is sought, the opportunities for voice are rarely equal (Lewis et al., 2003; Lewis & Russ, 2012) and determining whom to invite to the conversation is often difficult (Barge, Lee, Maddux, Nabring, & Townsend, 2008). Even if a given stakeholder finds himself/herself invited to the table, his or her input may not always be used to affect the path or shape of the change effort. Neumann (1989) argued that employees' participation in change efforts typically exhibits no direct influence over the primary organizational decision-making process. Further, Graetz and Smith (2010) note that a typical response to stakeholders who are not implementers "is not to listen to, but to silence, dissident voices" (p. 137).

In a recent study, Lewis and Russ (2012) interviewed human resource professionals who were charged with change implementation in a variety of organizations. Subjects were asked to report strategies for collecting and using stakeholder input. Informants reported that stakeholders who questioned a change or objected to it tended to be characterized by implementers as completely self-motivated and/or emotionally opposed to the idea of change. However, implementers welcomed the input of stakeholders who were perceived as embracing the change and as offering ways to promote it or tweak it to make it work better. From their data, Lewis and Russ developed four models of or approaches to soliciting and using input (open, restricted, political, and advisory). None of these models embraced what Lewis (2011) calls *widespread empowerment*, where solicitation of input involves stakeholders in important decision making, permits reciprocity in expression, sets aside authority relations, opens consideration of stakeholders wants and interests, and provides open, transparent processes. Rather, the dominant approach in their data was the *restricted model*, in which input was solicited from a narrow, specific pool of stakeholders and was sought to gain support for the original change vision. At best, the advisory approach entailed use of input to forestall negative reactions but was used occasionally to alter the strategy of the change. Even in this approach, implementers sought to avoid "complainers."

Stakeholders' Attitudes, Dispositions, and Reactions. A key thread of the change literature is concerned with attitudes and reactions toward change (in general or specific changes). Employees' (and other stakeholders') attitudes toward the idea of changing and toward specific changes that are implemented are often viewed as core explanations of *success* (achievement of management's goals) and examined to determine rates of resistance. Bouckenooghe (2010) summarizes this literature as focusing on readiness, resistance, cynicism, commitment, openness, acceptance, coping, and adjustment—with little clarity about distinctions among these terms.

Readiness is rooted in health literature focusing on how to get individuals to be "ready" to engage in healthy life-habit changes (Choi, 2011). Armenakis and colleagues, in a research program spanning over 30 years, have accomplished the most extensive development of this concept. They have explored "what change recipients consider when making their decision to embrace and support a change effort or reject and resist it" (Armenakis & Harris, 2009, p. 128). They define *readiness* as "organizational members' beliefs, attitudes and intentions regarding the extent to which changes are needed and the organization's capacity to successfully make those changes" (Armenakis, Harris, & Mossholder, 1993, p. 681). They conclude from an extensive body of research into these processes that focusing on "creating readiness for change rather than waiting to reduce resistance" (Armenakis & Harris, 2009, p. 129) is the most beneficial practice for implementers.

Armenakis and colleagues' research identified five specific beliefs that are key in the change assessment made by stakeholders (especially the assessments made by employees): *discrepancy* (change is necessary), *appropriateness* (this change is the correct one for the situation), *efficacy* (organization is capable to execute this change), *principal support* (high-level decision makers are committed to this change), and *valence* (this change is good for the individual). They argue that with these five beliefs, an individual is ready for change. Further, they suggest these beliefs can be achieved in part through early communication and participation with stakeholders. Other ways in which stakeholders may come to hold these beliefs is through "sharing with other stakeholders who already hold them; exposure to the evidence that led decision-makers to these beliefs; and independent assessment of evidence gathered outside of the organization" (Lewis, 2011, p. 228).

Openness is a similar concept to *readiness*. Miller, Johnson, and Grau (1994) defined openness to change as willingness to support a change coupled with positive affect toward the likely outcomes of it. Miller et al. (1994) examined how the information environment affects this outcome. They found that when employees are well informed about their role and the organization in general and when they feel more included in the social network, they are more likely to be open to change.

Some approaches to attitudes about change and specific changes focus on cognition and rational assessments of cost-benefits as well as responses to felt pressure to follow other employee's opinions and persuasive attempts (Bouckenooghe, 2010). The work on commitment to change may be categorized in this general set of approaches. For example, Herscovitch and Meyer (2002) define commitment to change as "a force (mind-set) that binds an individual to a course of action deemed necessary for the successful implementation of a change initiative" (p. 475). They include exploration of *affective* (sense of benefit of change), *normative* (sense of obligation), and *continuance* commitment (fear of consequences of failure).

Research on coping is more focused on behavior and behavioral intentions than other work on stakeholder reactions. *Coping* is defined by Folkman, Lazarus, Gruen, and DeLongis (1986) as "a person's cognitive and intentional/behavioural efforts to manage (reduce, minimize or tolerate) the internal and external demands" (p. 572). Lewis and Seibold (1996) defined *coping tactics* as "relatively specific behaviors [stakeholders] engage in to achieve specific goals" (p. 136). Lewis (1997) arrayed coping tactics on a typology of three dimensions: *valence* (positivity or negativity of the tactic), *decidedness* (reflection of a firm decision about the change), and *focus* (orientation toward others or self). One version of the concept of *coping* used in the change literature concerns the role of social support (Ashford, 1988; Bird, 2007; Napier, Simmons, & Stratton, 1989). For example, Robinson and Griffiths (2005) studied the various roles of stressors and social-support coping mechanisms, including the effects of *instrumental social support* (seeking advice or assistance from others), *informational support* (seeking information from others), and *emotional social support* (moral support, sympathy, and opportunities to vent).

The most common attitude discussed in the empirical literature (as well as the popular press literature) concerns *resistance*. Scholars often consider anything apart from enthusiastic endorsement and participation in change as a form of resistance. Piderit's (2000) review of the resistance literature identifies three manifestations of resistance: cognitive, emotional, and behavioral. Resistance can also be arrayed from subtler forms to more forceful forms, including ambivalence, peer complaints, upward dissent, sabotage, and refusal to comply (Lewis, 2011). Piderit (2000) points out that an individual's emotional, cognitive, and behavioral responses to change may contradict one another. A stakeholder may have both negative feelings and cooperative behavior simultaneously.

Resistance is often characterized as an emotional reaction to the mere idea of changing (Dent & Goldberg, 1989). Oreg (2003, 2006) and colleagues have devoted a line of research to exploring *dispositional resistance*, that is, "an individual's tendency to resist or avoid making changes, to devalue change generally, and to find change aversive across diverse contexts and types of change" (Oreg, 2003, p. 680). Although Oreg's scale for dispositional resistance has shown validity and has been predictive of affective reactions (e.g., worry, concern, distraction) to imposed workplace changes, it has not been used to predict behavioral resistance in terms of expressed cynicism, dissent, or sabotage.

Cynicism is a construct that is similar to *resistance* in that it also emphasizes a fairly enduring attitude (if not personality trait) of change stakeholders. Cole, Bruch, and Vogel (2006) define *cynicism* as "an evaluative judgment that stems from an individual's employment experiences" (p. 463). It is comprised of (1) a belief that the organization lacks integrity, (2) a negative affect toward the organization, and (3) tendencies to use disparaging and critical behaviors toward the organization. In the context of organizational change, cynicism is related to pessimism about future change, particularly in blaming management for one's pessimism or lack of success (Reichers, Wanous, & Austin, 1997; Wanous, Reichers, & Austin, 2000).

Each of these approaches to stakeholder attitudes about change and about specific changes provide tremendous opportunity for communication scholars to investigate the role of communication in attitude formation, expression, and the influence of others on the development of attitudes.

Management of Negative Reactions. A common approach to the management of negative reactions to change is to examine perceptions of justice and fairness. Rousseau (1996) describes psychological contracts as the good-faith relationships between stakeholders and organizations that clarify what is expected of each party. Organizational change often alters these expectations and psychological contracts can be broken, resulting in perceptions of unfairness. For example, stakeholders may feel they were cheated or misled or that what they were promised has been unfairly withdrawn.

Recent empirical work on the perceptions of procedural justice (i.e., perceived fairness of the procedures used in decision making) and interactional justice (i.e., perceptions that one is treated with respect and dignity in communicative interactions surrounding change) relates directly to change outcomes (Karriker, 2007; Kernan & Hanges, 2002; Michel, Stegmaier, & Sonntag, 2010; Paterson & Cary, 2002). In a study of broken promises in the context of radical organizational change, Kickul, Lester, and Finkl (2002) found that procedural interactional fairness mitigated the negative results of psychological contract breaches. Further, Korsgaard, Sapienza, and Schweiger's (2002) longitudinal study examined how planning of an organizational change in two U.S. plants impacted perceptions of procedural justice. The findings supported the authors' proposition that reactions to planned change depend on perceptions of procedural justice.

Social Construction

A common assumption in the innovation and change literatures concerns the immutability of any given change. Change scholars have long tended to treat change or innovation as if it has a fixed set of inherent qualities (cf. Lewin, 1951). This assumption ignores the social construction of the change itself. In this way, change is treated as a static and fixed object in the context of ongoing organizational activity, similar to placing a rock in a stream. In contrast, Lewis (2011) argues,

> Organizations are socially constructed largely through the communicative interactions of internal and external stakeholders. Stakeholders enact the organization as the embodiment of their own purposes, their sense of how activities are related; how people are known; how outcomes arise and how processes unfold. (p. 6)

Clearly, changes/innovations are socially constructed, as are organizations and organizational environments. Weick (1979) describes *enactment*: "[M]anagers [and others] construct, rearrange, single out, and demolish many objective features of their surroundings" (p. 164). In this process, stakeholders *enact* or *construct* their environment through a process of social interaction and sensemaking. As people encounter their worlds, they have biases about the truth of the situations that they encounter and are influenced heavily by the enacted realities of those around them (Weick, 1995). Through communication, individuals share their theories of "what is going on" and purposefully and incidentally influence other organizational members' enactment of reality. Individuals may simply forget some facts, reconstruct some to better fit the theory of reality they prefer, and look for supportive evidence to bolster preferred positions.

Weick (1995) suggests that sensemaking is as much about authoring as it is about interpretation. Thus what a given change *is* depends on how it is being enacted by those who are living the change in organizational life. Is it *innovative* or *modest improvement*? Is it a good thing or a bad thing? Is it a technique or a philosophy?

These issues are decided through social enactment processes. For example, any theory of reality (e.g., the organization needs to change; change is a bad idea; everyone is changing) can be supported and refuted through different ways of looking at evidence, different ways of framing evidence, and constructing evidence through managing meanings that other employees attach to their observations. Other theories of reality can reconstitute observations, history, and the narrative around "facts." Moreover, sensemaking during innovation and change is not accomplished within an impenetrable bubble. Organizations and their stakeholders are sensitive to various environments and the sensemaking within numerous spheres.

Leonardi's (2009) study of the implementation of a new technology in an auto manufacturing plant is an excellent example of how enactment processes make a change regarding what the technology "is." Leonardi argued that stakeholders develop interpretations of what a technology can do through both material interactions (that is, actually using a new technology) and social interactions and talking about the new technology. He found that "users of the new technology developed one interpretation of the change that so informed these stakeholders' expectations and interpretations that it seriously shaped their material interactions with it" (Lewis, 2011, p. 254). In that case, the users shaped the change in ways that led to a negative understanding of the technology.

Many of the challenges in the terminology applied in the change literature—for example, the order of *phases* or *stages*, such as *create*, *innovate*, *adopt*, *implement*, and *emanate* from the social construction of change in organizations in real time. Thus a change may be judged *creative* or *innovative* or *new* only after it has been in use for some time and compared against some standard that becomes created in interaction (see Weick's 1979 notion of *retrospective sensemaking*). For example, a modest adjustment to existing practice might, after being awarded as "innovation of the year" by industry, be quickly reconstructed by some stakeholders as *creative change*. Whether organizations are *developing*, *adopting*, *reconsidering*, or *discontinuing use* of a change or innovation is also socially constructed and reconstructed differently through time for and by different stakeholders. Scholars should consider situating their models, labels, and theorizing in the context of this ongoing social construction of organizational change, the processes being experienced or executed, and the meanings that the change has for stakeholders over time.

Discourses in Change

Scholars often overlook or misconstrue the informal communication among nonimplementers (i.e., those not tasked with responsibilities for installing the change) in their theory and research. Stakeholders discuss changes among themselves. They sometimes question purpose, vision, and goals; express fear and uncertainty concerns; ponder implications and ripple effects of change; request clarification; seek opinions of others; provide opinions to others; lobby for alternatives; offer and receive support; and promote the proposed change among myriad other expressions. These stakeholder interactions, to the extent that they are examined, tend to be viewed from the lens of *resistance* or considered as rumor communication typically characterized in the management literature as *dysfunctional* (Lewis, 2011). However, research that examines dissent in organizational contexts has shown that these expressions serve as sensemaking tools, social support-seeking functions, or a form of advocacy against organizational actions or strategy (Garner, 2009a). Further, some scholars have argued for the potential benefits of change resistance (Lewis, 2011; Maurer, 1996; Piderit, 2000).

Social sensemaking is a dynamic process of enacting meaning in ongoing interaction. It oftentimes includes the formation of powerful coalitions and rivalries among stakeholders as they come together to understand how and what is changing. Scholars often ignore the social aspects of sensemaking in favor of examining cognitive sensemaking of stakeholders as they individually receive and decode messages from implementers and managers. Although the formal communication of implementers certainly plays a critical role as an ongoing assertion of information, social construction, persuasion, and so on, it is likely less influential than the subsequent interactions among stakeholders surrounding a change effort. As Sonenshein (2010) argues, "[A]lthough less politically dominant groups lack formal power, they nonetheless shape change implementation through their alteration of its meaning" (p. 478).

Frames. A significant example of change discourse focuses on how stakeholders (typically employees) understand managers' and others' communication about change. This process has often identified a change in either positive or negative terms but has, at times, focused on various framing of changes. Framing involves bracketing off stimulus, experience, observation, and messages to contextualize them against a specific reference point (e.g., in the context of *failure* or *success*; in the context of a *fight*). Dewulf et al. (2009) distinguish between cognitive frames that live in our heads and interactional frames that are dynamic processes of enacting and shaping meaning in ongoing interaction. "Cognitive frames capture chunks of what people believe is external reality. From an interactional perspective, frames are co-constructions created by making sense of events in the external world. Framing thus constructs the meaning of the situations it addresses" (p. 164).

Cherim (2006) describes how employees appropriate managerial frames. An appropriation constitutes acceptance of the frame and what it implies, including the internalization of the values, goals, and means to achieving it. Cherim argues that employees respond to managerial frames for change through three types of appropriation: willing, reluctant, or partial appropriations. In a study of a technology change at an Australian subsidiary of a North American carmaker, Cooney and Sewell (2008) illustrate the reframing effort of shop stewards. They show how employees framed managers as having selfish political motives in the ways they implemented the change.

Sonenshein (2010) argues that much of the scholarship in this vein builds from Lewin's (1951) classic work, "arguing that the change process involves managers first breaking down employees' existing meaning constructions (unfreezing), then establishing new meanings (moving), and finally solidifying those new meanings (refreezing)" (p. 477). He further critiques the current work on narratives and change as overly focused on the single dimension of positivity or negativity toward the change being implemented. In his investigation of a Fortune 500 retailer, he concluded that mangers tended to tell strategically ambiguous narratives that implied change and stability simultaneously by balancing needs to promote change and minimize uncertainty. He found that employees embellished these managerial narratives as efforts to resist, champion, and accept the change.

Stories. A recent wave of research on change discourses is found in the narrative literature. Narrative scholars have examined the nature and function of stories in general (Boudens, 2005; Boudes & Laroche, 2009; Boyce, 1995; Gabriel, 2000) and in the context of organizational change (Balogun & Johnson, 2005; Bartunek, 1984; Bird, 2007; Brown, 1998; Bryant & Cox, 2004; Gallivan, 2001; Sonenshein, 2010) for several years. Boje (1991) defines a *storytelling organization* as a "collective storytelling system in which the performance of stories is a key part of members' sensemaking and a means to allow them to supplement individual memories with institutional memory" (p. 106). Thus stories serve individuals in both sensemaking (helping to enact reality) as well as in sensegiving (giving that sense to others).

Stories chronicle and capture the *in situ* experiences of change as well as influence and construct the after-the-change accounts of what happened (Lewis & Laster, 2011). Brown, Gabriel, and Gheradi (2009) propose, "In a world of change, . . . stories and other narratives then help us make sense of change, explain it, domesticate it and, at times, celebrate it" (p. 328). Research into stories told during change has provided insights into types of stories, interpretive frames built from stories, and sensemaking represented in stories that have important implications for power and control in organizations (Bean & Hamilton, 2006; Brown & Humphreys, 2003; Cherim, 2006; Cooney & Sewell, 2008; Whittle, Mueller, & Mangan, 2009); identity and reputation creation and maintenance (Bean & Hamilton, 2006; Beech, MacPhail, & Coupland, 2009; Bird, 2007; Brown & Humphreys, 2003; Whittle et al., 2009); levels of stress associated with different types of rumor stories during change (Bordia, Jones, Gallois, Callan, & Difonzo, 2006); the effect of stress reduction and social support through sharing stories about change (Bird, 2007); negotiation and transformation of stakeholder interests (Whittle, Suhomlinova, & Mueller, 2010); the variation of different stakeholder groups' interpretations of change program goals and outcomes (Cherim, 2006; Gallivan, 2001; Heracleous & Barrett, 2001); and forms of story presentation that hold the most meaning for listeners (Sims, Huxham, & Beech, 2009). This work represents an emerging trend in the change literature, one that focuses on the experience and narratives of stakeholders of change.

Stories have the potential to be very powerful in organizations in the sense that "they express the dominant concerns of employees (description), vent anxiety but also create stress (energy control), and garner support for collective action for or against organizational goals (system maintenance)" (Bordia et al., 2006, p. 616). Bird (2007) found in her study of a women's community of practice that sharing stories was a means of dealing with the stress of change: "Stories told by network members verified their access to resources, career development advice, and support for solving specific work problems" (p. 324). Similarly, Brown and Humphreys (2003) found in their study of *epic* and *tragic* stories during change that shared narratives among subordinate groups assisted in their efforts to resist the worldviews of superiors.

In general, this research has focused on categorizing stakeholders' stories according to the elements and themes within the stories themselves as reported in interviews after the change efforts. That is, this approach aims to make sense of the residual of a change from the accounts given of "what was going on" at a particular point in time. Whittle et al. (2009) suggest methodological limitations of this approach. In their own work, they found a stark contrast between the nature of the storytelling that occurred in their research interviews and the contestation and negotiation of story making that they observed in their fieldwork. Consequently, they concluded, "The storytelling that occurs during research interviews may not be representative of the storytelling that occurs in other naturally-occurring work conversations" (Whittle et al. 2009, p. 429).

Dialectical Change

In this approach to change, scholars embrace Poole and Van de Ven's (2004) dialectical motor for change. Stemming from the need to balance a sense of stability and certainty, organizations often experience a dialectic of change and stability (Howard & Geist, 1995). Scholars working in this vein of theory and research focus on paradox, tension, contradiction, and conflict during organizational change. A common concern for communication scholars who adopt this perspective is examining organizational members' interpretations and responses to change expressed in their discourse (Howard & Geist, 1995; Kellet, 1999).

Tension concerns the clash of ideas, principles, and actions and the associated feelings of discomfort (Stohl & Cheney, 2001). *Contradictions* are defined as opposing ideas, principles, and actions that exert tensions within a process (Stohl

& Cheney, 2001). These contradictions exist in bipolar pairs. As Fairhurst, Cooren, and Cahill (2002) note, "One inference from work on paradox and contradiction in organizations suggests that highly effective organizations perform in contradictory ways because they must satisfy contradictory expectations" (p. 504). In some cases, contradictions lead to *paradox,* characterized by simultaneous presence of contradictory and mutually exclusive elements (Putnam, 1986; Stohl & Cheney, 2001).

The study of dialectical tensions and paradox represents a growing research trend in examining an organizational change process. For example, Fairhurst et al. (2002) examined contradictions in the context of multiple downsizings in a single organization. They found evidence in actors' discourse to identify the contradictions, which not only included a set of contradictions based on the organizational mission but also one based on a collision of cultures. Further, they discerned a wide range of strategies for managing contradictions. In addition, Jian's (2007) study of the adoption of and resistance to ICTs explored how the employees' interpretations of technologies in oppositional ways resulted in various forms of resistance behaviors.

In examining paradox during organizational change, Beech, Burns, Caestecker, MacIntosh, and MacLean (2004) argue,

> Paradoxes, as intrinsic features in organizational life, cannot always be resolved through cognitive processes. What may be possible, however, is that such paradoxes are transformed, or 'moved on' through action and as a result the overall change effort need not be stalled by the existence of embedded paradoxes. (p. 1313)

In their study of a project in the U.K.'s National Health Service, they found that a paradoxical situation was moved on through the use of emotional expression and personal contact rather than through purely rational arguments. They illustrated "how rules were challenged and recast, introducing some instability and maintaining the fluidity of an interactive 'game'" (p. 1327). This project and other studies of dialectics in organizations reveal the communication dynamics of negotiating conflicts that are frequently present during major organizational change.

Limitations to Current Approaches and Future Directions

As this review suggests, scholarship about organizational change and innovation has thus far produced interesting results. After years of important theoretical development and rich empirical investigation, there remain limitations to our approaches and opportunities for future research.

One striking observation is how much the change scholarship tends to be defined by management-centric models. Approaches to these topics are nearly always grounded in a perspective of managers and owners of organizations and the ways in which *success* is defined for them. Innovation is often assumed as a good, because it is likely to increase bottom-line value for managers and owners. Change is a chance worth taking for the same reason. The costs incurred by other stakeholders (e.g., employees, clients, community, end-users) from innovation or change are rarely even raised as more than a potential obstacle. This observation easily leads to questioning the consequences, especially the negative ones, for individuals and organizations to constantly be innovative and creative. Is there something at the individual level akin to "emotional labor" when every idea has to be novel, new, and radical? Do individuals have to craft a persona of being innovative or creative? When, if ever, is it okay to be stable or a member of the old-guard? At an organizational level, what costs are associated with always having to change? How much of this positive stereotyping of innovation and change is empty rhetoric and how much actually improves the delivery of products/services and the survivability of organizations? Scholars should embrace a more critical perspective to raise these questions in future research. To the extent that critical theory has been applied to the study of organizational change, it may have focused too much on resistance and paid too little attention to the core issues of less empowered stakeholders.

Consideration of the perspectives of a wider array of stakeholders during change would not only expand scholars' understandings of the consequences of a hegemony of innovation and change in the organizational landscape but would also help researchers to better understand the potential that interaction among and with nonmanagerial stakeholders would have for beneficial change processes. So, even when an innovation and change are considered valuable for numerous stakeholders, the process of development and implementation of ideas would benefit from a multistakeholder perspective. This is quite rare, if not nearly absent, in the current literature.

Scholarship in the field has often focused too much on the diagnosis of resistance and resistors from a lens of personality dysfunction. Researchers often ask the questions that imply that resistant stakeholders are somehow flawed. The communication scholar's focus then becomes overcoming or overpowering those flaws. Often overlooked in the search for a personality-rooted explanation for resistance is a focus on the principled perspectives of stakeholders who value their organizations stakes. If scholars consider the key components of *principled dissent* offered by Graham (1986)—expression of dissatisfaction for reasons of justice, honesty, or organizational benefit—they could reconstitute resistant expression as bringing potential benefit to organizations, stakeholders, and to change initiatives. For example, scholarship by Kassing (2002, 2005, 2006, 2009) and Garner (2009a, 2009b; Garner & Wargo, 2009) has investigated trigger events, types of strategies, frequency of use and characteristics of dissenters, and contexts for dissent. Explorations of dissent expression within the context of organizational change could aid in building theory about how processes unfold in contested and dialectic spaces. In doing so, researchers can attend to nonimplementer stakeholders rather than simply treat them as audiences for managers' messages. Further, if scholars examine resistance as a force for many ends, including improvement of change efforts, they might reflect less of a managerial approach to study of this critical organizational activity.

Another key weakness in the innovation and change literature is the lack of focus on actual messages and ongoing interaction. Much of the research has focused on attitudes and self-reports of actions that are taken in support of or in opposition to change. Rarely have researchers examined interaction among stakeholders in real time to uncover how communication plays various roles throughout a change process. Rather, researchers seem attuned to retrospective evaluations of changes at a given point in time. Although collecting real-time interaction data raises some serious methodological challenges, the only way that researchers can discover and describe how interaction works in these processes is to capture communication data in the moment.

A myriad of topics of organizational process and interaction are possible to examine within the context of organizational change, and many organizational communication scholars find the context of change to be a rich one for study. Issues of attitude formation, influence, and message design and effects; cultural clash and cultural change; learning and knowledge creation; formal and informal leadership; social justice and democratic workplace structures; identification, organizational history, and the merits of stability are only a handful of possible foci for research. Broadly construed, organizational change is metaphorically the water of process through which all organizations swim. Organizations always are moving and thus always are changing. In some cases, change is packaged as a purposeful activity designed to meet someone's goal(s); in other cases, it is experienced as evolutionary drift towards something new and different; and in some cases, change is revolutionary and potentially transformational. Researchers have focused primarily on the first of these three cases, but there is no reason that communication scholars cannot focus on the other two. The field could learn a great deal from understanding how organizational stakeholders conceive of change in organizations and how they experience it over the lifespan of a job or even of a career.

Certainly, there are many directions research and theory building on innovation and change can take. Communication scholars have much to add to the understanding of how, in what ways, and with what consequences organizations change or don't change. Hopefully, communication scholars will focus on asking some of the important, and thus far unanswered, questions and pursuing the less traveled paths.

References

Angle, H. L. (1989). Psychology and organizational innovation. In A. H. Van de Ven, H. L. Angle, & M. S. Poole (Eds.), *Research on the management of innovation: The Minnesota studies* (pp. 135–170). New York, NY: Harper & Row.

Armenakis, A. A., & Harris, S. G. (2009). Reflections: Our journey in organizational change research and practice. *Journal of Change Management, 9*(2), 127–142.

Armenakis, A. A., Harris, S. G., & Mossholder, K. (1993). Creating readiness for organizational change. *Human Relations, 46*(6), 681–703.

Ashford, S. J (1988). Individual strategies for coping with stress during organizational transitions. *Journal of Applied Behavioral Science, 24*(1), 19–36.

Balogun, J., & Johnson, G. (2005). From intended strategies to unintended outcomes: The impact of change recipient sensemaking. *Organization Studies, 26*(11), 1573–1601.

Barge, J. K., Lee, M., Maddux, K., Nabring, R., & Townsend, B. (2008). Managing dualities in planned change initiatives. *Journal of Applied Communication Research, 36*(4), 364–390.

Bartunek, J. (1984). Changing interpretive schemes and organizational restructuring: The example of a religious order. *Administrative Science Quarterly, 29*(3), 355–372.

Bean, C. J., & Hamilton, F. E. (2006). Leader framing and follower sensemaking: Response to downsizing in the brave new workplace. *Human Relations, 59*(2), 321–349.

Beech, N., Burns, H., Caestecker, L., MacIntosh, R., & MacLean, D. (2004). Paradox as invitation to act in problematic change situations. *Human Relations, 57*(10), 1313–1332.

Beech, N., MacPhail, S. A., & Coupland, C. (2009). Anti-dialogic positioning in change stories: Bank robbers, saviours, and peons. *Organization, 16*(3), 335–352.

Bird, S. (2007). Sensemaking and identity: The interconnection of storytelling and networking in a women's group of a large corporation. *Journal of Business Communication, 44*(4), 311–339.

Boje, D. M. (1991). The storytelling organization: A study of story performance in an office-supply firm. *Administrative Science Quarterly, 36*(1), 106–126.

Bordia, P., Hobman, E., Jones, E., Gallois, C., & Callan, V. (2004). Uncertainty during organizational change: Types, consequences, and management strategies. *Journal of Business and Psychology, 18*(4), 507–532.

Bordia, P., Jones, E., Gallois, C., Callan, V. J., & Difonzo, N. (2006). Management are aliens! Rumors and stress during organizational change. *Group & Organization Management, 31*(5), 601–621.

Boudens, C. J. (2005). The story of work: A narrative analysis of workplace emotion. *Organization Studies, 26*(9), 1285–1306.

Boudes, T., & Laroche, H. (2009). Taking off the heat: Narrative sensemaking in post-crisis inquiry reports. *Organization Studies, 30*(4), 377–396.

Bouckenooghe, D. (2010). Positioning change recipients' attitudes toward change in the organizational change literature. *Journal of Applied Behavioral Science, 46*(4), 500–531.

Boyce, M. E. (1995). Collective centering and collective sense-making in the stories and storytelling of one organization. *Organization Studies, 16*(1), 107–137.

Brown, A. D. (1998). Narrative, politics and legitimacy in an IT implementation. *Journal of Management Studies, 35*(1), 35–58.

Brown, A. D., Gabriel, Y., & Gheradi, S. (2009). Storytelling and change: An unfolding story. *Organization, 16*(3), 323–333.

Brown, A. D., & Humphreys, M. (2003). Epic and tragic tales: Making sense of change. *Journal of Applied Behavioral Science, 39*(2), 121–144.

Brummans, B., & Miller, K. I. (2004). The effect of ambiguity on the implementation of a social change initiative. *Communication Research Reports, 21*(1), 1–10.

Bryant, M., & Cox, J. W. (2004). Conversion stories as shifting narratives of organizational change. *Journal of Organizational Change Management, 17*(6), 578–592.

Cherim, S. (2006). Managerial frames and institutional discourses of change: Employee appropriation and resistance. *Organization Studies, 27*(9), 1261–1287.

Choi, M. (2011). Employees' attitudes towards organizational change: A literature review. *Human Resource Management, 50*(4), 479–500.

Cole, M. S., Bruch, H., & Vogel, B. (2006). Emotion as mediators of the relations between perceived supervisor support and psychological hardiness on employee cynicism. *Journal of Organizational Behavior, 27*(4), 463–484.

Cooney, R., & Sewell, G. (2008). Shaping the other: Maintaining expert managerial status in a complex change management program. *Group & Organization Management, 33*(6), 685–711.

Covin, T. J., & Kilmann, R. H. (1990). Participant perceptions of positive and negative influences on large-scale change. *Group & Organization Studies, 15*(2), 233–248.

Cropley, D. H., Kaufman, J. C., & Cropley, A. J. (2008). Malevolent creativity: A functional model of creativity in terrorism and crime. *Creativity Research Journal, 20*(2), 105–115.

Crossan, M. M., & Apaydin, M. (2010). A multidimensional framework of organizational innovation: A systematic review of the literature. *Journal of Management Studies, 47*(6), 1154–1191.

Dent, E. B., & Goldberg, S. G. (1989). Challenging "resistance to change." *Journal of Applied Behavioral Science, 35*(1), 25–41.

Dewulf, A., Gray, B., Putnam, L. L., Lewicki, R., Aarts, N., Bouwen, R., & van Woekum, C. (2009). Disentangling approaches to framing in conflict and negotiation research: A meta-analytic perspective. *Human Relations, 62*(2), 155–193.

Doyle, M., Claydon, T., & Buchanan, D. (2000). Mixed results, lousy process: The management experience of organizational change. *British Journal of Management, 11*(S1), S59–S80.

Fairhurst, G. T., Cooren, F., & Cahill, D. J. (2002). Discursiveness, contradiction, and unintended consequences in successive downsizings. *Management Communication Quarterly, 15*(4), 501–540.

Flanagin, A. (2000). Social pressures on organizational website adoption. *Human Communication Research, 26*(4), 618–646.

Folkman, S., Lazarus, R. S., Gruen R. J., & DeLongis, A. (1986). Appraisal, coping, health status, and psychological symptoms. *Journal of Personality and Social Psychology, 50*(3), 571–579.

Fulk, J. (1993). Social construction of communication technology. *Academy of Management Journal, 36*(5), 921–950.

Fulk, J., Schmitz, J., & Steinfield, C. W. (1990). A social influence model of technology use. In J. Fulk & C.W. Steinfield (Eds.), *Organizations and communication technology* (pp. 117–140). Newbury Park, CA: SAGE.

Gabriel, Y. (2000). *Storytelling in organizations: Acts, fictions, and fantasies.* New York, NY: Oxford University Press.

Gallivan, M. J. (2001). Meaning to change: How diverse stakeholders interpret organizational communication about change initiatives. *IEEE Transactions on Professional Communication, 44*(4), 243–266.

Garner, J. T. (2009a). Strategic dissent: Expressions of organizational dissent motivated by influence goals. *International Journal of Strategic Communication, 3*(1), 34–51.

Garner, J. T. (2009b). When things go wrong at work: An exploration of organizational dissent messages. *Communication Studies, 60*(2), 197–218.

Garner, J. T., & Wargo, M. R. (2009). Feedback from the pew: A dual-perspective exploration of organizational dissent in churches. *Journal of Communication and Religion, 32*(2), 375–400.

Graetz, F., & Smith, A. C. T. (2010). Managing organizational change: A philosophies of change approach. *Journal of Change Management, 10*(2), 135–154.

Graham, J. W. (1986). Principled organizational dissent: A theoretical essay. In B. M. Staw & L. L. Cummings (Eds.), *Research in organizational behavior* (vol. 8, pp. 1–52). Greenwich, CT: JAI.

Griffith, T. L., & Northcraft, G. B. (1996). Cognitive elements in the implementation of new technology: Can less information provide more benefits? *MIS Quarterly, 20*(1), 99–109.

Hannan, M. T., & Freeman, J. (1977). The population ecology of organizations. *American Journal of Sociology, 82*(5), 929–964.

Hannan, M. T., & Freeman, J. (1989). *Organizational ecology*. Cambridge, MA: Harvard University Press.

Heracleous, L., & Barrett, M. (2001). Organizational change as discourse: Communicative actions and deep structures in the context of information technology implementation. *Academy of Management Journal, 44*(4), 755–778.

Herscovitch, L., & Meyer, J. P. (2002). Commitment to organizational change: Extension of a three-component model. *Journal of Applied Psychology, 87*(3), 474–487.

Howard, L. A., & Geist, P. (1995). Ideological positioning in organizational change: The dialectic of control in a merging organization. *Communication Monographs, 62*(2), 110–131.

Jian, G. (2007). "Omega is a four-letter word": Toward a tension-centered model of resistance to information and communication technologies. *Communication Monographs, 74*(4), 517–540.

Kanter, R. M. (1983). *The change masters: Innovation for productivity in the American corporation.* New York, NY: Simon & Schuster.

Kanter, R. M. (1988). When a thousand flowers bloom: Structural, collective and social conditions for innovation in organizations. In B. M. Staw & L. L. Cummings (Eds.), *Research in organizational behavior* (vol. 10, pp. 123–167). Greenwich, CT: JAI Press.

Karriker, J. (2007). Justice as strategy: The role of procedural justice in an organizational realignment. *Journal of Change Management, 7*(3/4), 329–342.

Kassing, J. W. (2002). Speaking up: Identifying employees' upward dissent strategies. *Management Communication Quarterly, 16*(2), 187–209.

Kassing J. W. (2005). Speaking up competently: A comparison of perceived competence in upward dissent strategies. *Communication Research Reports, 22*(3), 227–234.

Kassing, J. W. (2006). Employees' expressions of upward dissent as a function of current and past work experiences. *Communication Reports, 19*(2), 79–88.

Kassing, J. W. (2009). "In case you didn't hear me the first time": An examination of repetitious upward dissent. *Management Communication Quarterly, 22*(3), 416–436.

Kellet, P. (1999). Dialogue and dialectics in managing organizational change: The case of a mission-based transformation. *Southern Communication Journal, 64*(3), 211–231.

Kernan, M. C., & Hanges, P. J. (2002). Survivor reactions to reorganization: Antecedents and consequences of procedural, interpersonal, and informational justice. *Journal of Applied Psychology, 87*(5), 916–928.

Keupp, M. M., Palmie, M., & Gassmann, O. (2011). The strategic management of innovation: A systematic review and paths of future research. *International Journal of Management Reviews, 14*(4), 367–390. doi: 10.1111/j.1468-2370.2011.00321.x

Kickul, J., Lester, S. W., & Finkl, J. (2002). Promise breaking during radical organizational change: Do justice interventions make a difference? *Journal of Organizational Behavior, 23*(4), 469–488.

Klijn, M., & Tomic, W. (2010). A review of creativity within organizations from a psychology perspective. *Journal of Management Development, 29*(4), 322–343.

Korsgaard, M. A., Sapienza, H. J., & Schweiger, D. M. (2002). Beaten before begun: The role of procedural justice in planning change. *Journal of Management, 28*(4), 497–516.

Kramer, M., Dougherty, D. S., & Pierce, T. A. (2004). Managing uncertainty during a corporate acquisition: A longitudinal study of communication during an airline acquisition. *Human Communication Research, 30*(1), 71–101.

Laster, N. (2008). *Communicating multiple change: Understanding the impact of change messages on stakeholder perceptions.* (UMI No. AAT 3342339). Ann Arbor, MI: Dissertation Abstracts International.

Leonardi, P. (2009). Why do people reject new technologies and stymie organizational changes of which they are in favor? Exploring misalignments between social interactions and materiality. *Human Communication Research, 35*(3), 407–441.

Lewin, K. (1951). *Field theory in social science.* New York, NY: Harper.

Lewis, L. K. (1997). Users' individual communicative responses to intraorganizationally implemented innovations and other planned changes. *Management Communication Quarterly, 10*(4), 455–490.

Lewis, L. K. (1999). Disseminating information and soliciting input during planned organizational change: Implementers' targets, sources, and channels for communicating. *Management Communication Quarterly, 13*(1), 43–75.

Lewis, L. K. (2000). "Blindsided by that one" and "I saw that one coming": The relative anticipation and occurrence of communication problems and other problems in implementers' hindsight. *Journal of Applied Communication Research, 28*(1), 44–67.

Lewis, L. K. (2006). Employee perspectives on implementation communication as predictors of perceptions of success and resistance. *Western Journal of Communication, 70*(1), 23–46.

Lewis, L. K. (2011). *Organizational change: Creating change through strategic communication.* Chichester, UK: Wiley-Blackwell.

Lewis, L. K., Hamel, S., & Richardson, B. K. (2001). Communicating change to nonprofit stakeholders: Models and predictors of implementers' approaches. *Management Communication Quarterly, 15*(1), 5–41.

Lewis, L. K., & Laster, N. (2011). *Changing stories.* NCA Conference Paper, Organizational Communication Division, New Orleans, LA.

Lewis, L. K., Laster, N., & Kulkarni, V. (2013). Telling 'em how it will be: Previewing pain of risky change in initial announcements. *Journal of Business Communication, 50*(3), 278–308.

Lewis, L. K., Richardson, B. K., & Hamel, S. (2003). When the stakes are communicative: The lamb's and the lion's share during nonprofit planned change. *Human Communication Research, 29*(3), 400–430.

Lewis, L. K., & Russ, T. (2012). Soliciting and using input during organizational change initiatives: What are practitioners doing? *Management Communication Quarterly, 26*(2), 267–294.

Lewis, L. K., & Seibold, D. R. (1996). Communication during intraorganizational innovation adoption: Predicting users' behavioral coping responses to innovations in organizations. *Communication Monographs, 63*(2), 131–157.

Lewis, L. K., & Seibold, D. R. (1998). Reconceptualizing organizational change implementation as a communication problem: A review of literature and research agenda. In M. Roloff (Ed.), *Communication yearbook* (vol. 21, pp. 93–151). Thousand Oaks, CA: SAGE.

Maurer, R. (1996). *Beyond the wall of resistance.* Austin, TX: Bard Books.

Michel, A., Stegmaier, R., & Sonntag, K. (2010). I scratch your back—You scratch mine. Do procedural justice and organizational identification matter for employees' cooperation during change? *Journal of Change Management, 10*(1), 41–59.

Miller, D., & Friesen, P. H. (1982). Innovation in conservative and entrepreneurial firms: Two models of strategic momentum. *Strategic Management Journal, 3*(1), 1–25.

Miller, D., & Friesen, P. H. (1984). *Organizations: A quantum view.* Englewood Cliffs, NJ: Prentice Hall.

Miller, J. D., Johnson, J. R., & Grau, J. (1994). Antecedents to willingness to participate in a planned organizational change. *Journal of Applied Communication Research, 22*(1), 59–80.

Miller, K. I., & Monge, P. R. (1985). Social information and employee anxiety about organizational change. *Human Communication Research, 11*(3), 365–386.

Napier, N. K., Simmons, G., & Stratton, K. (1989). Communication during a merger: The experience of two banks. *Human Resource Planning, 12*(2), 105–122.

Neumann, J. E. (1989). Why people don't participate in organizational change? In R. W. Woodman & W. A. Pasmore (Eds.), *Research in organizational change and development* (vol. 3, pp. 181–212). Greenwich, CT: JAI Press.

Nyhan, R. (2000). Changing the paradigm: Trust and its role in public sector organizations. *American Review of Public Administration, 30*(1), 87–109.

Oreg, S. (2003). Resistance to change: Developing an individual differences measure. *Journal of Applied Psychology, 88*(4), 680–693.

Oreg, S. (2006). Personality, context, and resistance to organizational change. *European Journal of Work and Organizational Psychology, 15*(1), 73–101.

Page, S. (2003). Entrepreneurial strategies for managing inter-agency collaboration. *Journal of Public Administration Research and Theory, 13*(3), 311–340.

Paterson, J. M., & Cary, J. (2002). Organizational justice, change anxiety, and acceptance of downsizing: Preliminary tests of an AET-based model. *Motivation and Emotion, 26*(1), 83–103.

Piderit, S. K. (2000). Rethinking resistance and recognizing ambivalence: A multidimensional view of attitudes toward an organizational change. *Academy of Management Review, 24*(4), 783–794.

Poole, M. S. (2004). Central issues in the study of change and innovation. In M.S. Poole & A. H. Van de Ven (Eds.), *Handbook of organizational change and innovation* (pp. 3–31). Oxford, UK: Oxford University Press.

Poole, M. S., & Van de Ven, A. H. (2004). *Handbook of organizational change and innovation.* Oxford, UK: Oxford University Press.

Putnam, L. L. (1986). Contradictions and paradoxes in organizations. In L. Thayer (Ed.), *Organization-communication: Emerging perspectives I* (pp. 151–167). Norwood, NJ: Ablex.

Reichers, A. E., Wanous, J. P., & Austin, J. T. (1997). Understanding and managing cynicism about organizational change. *Academy of Management Executive, 11*(1), 48–58.

Robinson, O., & Griffiths, A. (2005). Coping with the stress of transformational change in a government department. *Journal of Applied Behavioral Science, 41*(2), 204–221.

Rogers. E. M. (1983). *Diffusion of innovations* (3rd ed.). New York, NY: Free Press.

Rogers, E. M. (1995). *Diffusion of innovations* (4th ed.). New York, NY: Free Press.

Rousseau, D. M. (1996). Changing the deal while keeping the people. *Academy of Management Executive, 10*(1), 50–59.

Sagie, A., Elizur, D., & Koslowsky, M. (2001). Effect of participation in strategic and tactical decisions on acceptance of planned change. *Journal of Social Psychology, 13*(4), 459–465.

Sagie, A., & Koslowsky, M. (1994). Organizational attitudes and behaviors as a function of participation in strategic and tactical change decisions: An application of path-goal theory. *Journal of Organizational Behavior, 15*(1), 37–47.

Schweiger, D. M., & DeNisi, A. S. (1991). Communication with employees following a merger: A longitudinal field experiment. *Academy of Management Journal, 34*(1), 110–135.

Sims, D., Huxham, C., & Beech, N. (2009). On telling stories but hearing snippets: Sense-taking from presentations of practice. *Organization, 16*(3), 371–398.

Smeltzer, L. R. (1991). An analysis of strategies for announcing organization-wide change. *Group & Organization Studies, 16*(1), 5–24.

Smeltzer, L. R., & Zener, M. F. (1992). Development of a model for announcing major layoffs. *Group & Organization Management, 17*(4), 445–472.

Smeltzer, L. R., & Zener, M. F. (1994). Minimizing the negative effect of employee layoffs through effective announcements. *Employee Counseling Today, 6*(4), 3–9.

Smeltzer, L. R., & Zener, M. F. (1995). Organization-wide change: Planning for an effective announcement. *Journal of General Management, 20*(3), 31–43.

Sonenshein, S. (2010). We're changing—Or are we? Untangling the role of progressive, regressive, and stability narratives during strategic change implementation. *Academy of Management Journal, 53*(3), 477–512.

Stohl, C., & Cheney, G. (2001). Participatory processes/paradoxical practices: Communication and the dilemmas of organizational democracy. *Management Communication Quarterly, 14*(3), 349–407.

Tornatzky, L. G., & Johnson, E. C. (1982). Research on implementation: Implications for evaluation practice and evaluation policy. *Evaluation and Program Planning, 5*(3), 193–198.

Van de Ven, A. H., & Poole, M. S. (1995). Explaining development and change in organizations. *Academy of Management Review, 20*(3), 510–540.

Wanous, J. P., Reichers, A. E., & Austin, J. T. (2000). Cynicism about organizational change: Measurement, antecedents, and correlates. *Group & Organization Management, 25*(2), 132–153.

Weick, K. E. (1979). *The social psychology of organizing.* Reading, MA: Addison-Wesley.

Weick, K. E. (1995). *Sensemaking in organizations.* Thousand Oaks, CA: SAGE.

Weick, K., & Quinn, R. E. (1999). Organizational change and development. *Annual Review of Psychology, 50*, 361–386.

Whittle, A., Mueller, F., & Mangan, A. (2009). Storytelling and 'character': Victims, villains, and heroes in a case of technological change. *Organizing*, 16(3), 425–442.

Whittle, A., Suhomlinova, O., & Mueller, F. (2010). Funnel of interests: The discursive translation of organizational change. *Journal of Applied Behavioral Science, 46*(1), 16–37.

Zorn, T. E., Christensen, L. T., & Cheney, G. (1999). *Constant change and flexibility: Do we really want constant change?* San Francisco, CA: Berrett-Koehler.

Zorn, T. E., Flanagin, A. J., & Shoham, M. D. (2011). Institutional and noninstitutional influences on information and communication technology adoption and use among nonprofit organizations. *Human Communication Research, 37*(1), 1–33.

Zorn, T. E., Grant, S., & Henderson, A. (2012). Developing the social media competencies and voluntary organizations in New Zealand. *Voluntas.* doi: 10.1007/s11266-012-9265-1

CHAPTER 21

Socialization and Assimilation

Theories, Processes, and Outcomes

Michael W. Kramer and Vernon D. Miller

The study of the socialization process of individuals joining, participating in, and leaving organizations has become increasingly critical to organizational communication over the last few decades as the pattern of lifetime employment with one company has been replaced with individuals having multiple jobs and careers (Sullivan, 1999). As a result of these changes, individuals experience multiple organizational entry experiences throughout their lifetimes, where they interact as newcomers with incumbents in a context overlaid with uncertainty, sensemaking, and identity development. Among other actions, incumbents welcome, inform, train, and facilitate the work of newcomers as they learn new jargon, procedures, and norms; develop expertise; and build relationships. Alone or together, these experiences impact the organization's viability and shape newcomers' subsequent contributions to the organization regardless of the following: its size, the nature of member responsibilities, ownership, mission, and full- or part-time member involvement (Kristof, 1996; Van Maanen & Schein, 1979).

Understanding, then, the role of communication during socialization has both intellectual and practical value. The socialization context influences the communication messages that are constituted and shared between individuals; concurrently, communication shapes individuals' interpretation of context and organizational processes (Poole, 2011). Accordingly, first, we consider several research traditions and the questions that socialization scholars sought to answer. Next, we overview the major theoretical perspectives used to explore the central role of communication in the socialization process. We then present major lines of research in this area, emphasizing their contributions to understanding communication during socialization. We conclude by identifying gaps in our knowledge and offering directions for future research.

The vibrancy of the study of communication throughout the socialization process is apparent in the number of summaries written over the last few decades (Ashforth, Sluss, & Harrison, 2007; Jablin, 1984, 1987, 2001; Kramer, 2010; Waldeck & Myers, 2008). Because such high-quality summaries exist, this essay focuses on identifying the major topics and current concerns relating to communication messages, acts, and processes within the body of research instead of on summarizing its breadth. Readers unfamiliar with the literature are encouraged to consult previous summaries.

Historic Roots and Development

Although its roots go back farther in fields such as sociology, the study of socialization began to take hold in the fields of management and organizational behavior in the late 1960s and 1970s. Scholars such as Schein (1968) and Feldman (1981) developed early concepts and models to explore the socialization process of organizational outsiders becoming participating and effective members or insiders. Van Maanen and Schein (1979) wrote a seminal article that began explicating many issues that are still being studied today, such as the strategies used to socialize newcomers (e.g., individual versus group), the issue of boundary passages (functional, hierarchical, or inclusionary), and concern over focusing on general trends or individual experiences during the process.

In the 1980s, Jablin (1984) brought the study of socialization into the burgeoning field of organizational communication and focused on how communication was the means by which individuals navigated the assimilation process. His elegant but simple model of assimilation suggested four phases: (1) *anticipatory socialization*, individuals' experiences prior to joining organizations; (2) *encounter*, newcomers' experiences during the first days, weeks, or months of membership; (3) *metamorphosis*, the time when individuals no longer feel like newcomers but like established organizational members; and (4) *exit*, the process by which individuals leave organizations (Jablin, 1987). Jablin created some ambiguity about the model by sometimes referring to *encounter* and *metamorphosis* as one phase—*assimilation*—and discussing them separately and at other times referring to the entire process as assimilation. A careful reading of his work indicates that he saw the model's phases as fluid and overlapping rather than as a set of linear, distinct phases (Jablin, 2001).

Since the 1980s, the fields of organizational communication and management have followed somewhat parallel research lines on this phenomenon. Various summaries have been published in management (e.g., Bauer & Erdogan, 2011; Bauer, Morrison, & Callister, 1998) in addition to those in organizational communication. Some scholars have published in both fields. Research in both disciplines has tended to focus on newcomer experiences, perhaps out of practical concerns of wanting to assist newcomers to learn the ropes more quickly. However, some scholars in both areas have focused on other parts of the broader process, such as employees who experience individual transitions (e.g., job transfers in Brett, 1982; Kramer, 1993) and organizations that undergo mergers and acquisitions (e.g., Kramer, Dougherty, & Pierce, 2004; Napier, Simmons, & Stratton, 1989) or reductions in work force (e.g., Brockner, Grover, O'Malley, Reed, & Glynn, 1993; Casey, Miller, & Johnson, 1997), which can be viewed as part of the ongoing metamorphosis phase (Kramer, 2010).

Due to parallel but often-separate research lines, terminology and definitions are sometimes inconsistent. For example, Jablin preferred *assimilation* for describing the overall process and divided it into *socialization*, the efforts of organizations and their members to change newcomers to meet their needs, and *individualization*, the efforts of individuals to negotiate changes in the organization to meet personal needs (Jablin, 1984). Most scholars outside of communication use *socialization* as the broad term and use different terms to describe the tension between organization and individual needs. In the most contrary set of definitions, Moreland and Levine (2001) view *socialization* as the overall process (Jablin's *assimilation*) and *assimilation* as the process of altering individuals to meet group needs (Jablin's *socialization*). It is within this multidisciplinary domain, with its inconsistent terminology, that we examine the issues involved in the study of socialization.

Despite the similarities across the two fields, the communication focus has contributed to the socialization literature in important ways. For example, prior to Jablin's (1984) delineation of the difference between socialization and individualization, there was little recognition of the two-way influences during the process. The focus was almost entirely on how individuals were influenced by the organization and its established members, with little recognition that individuals joining an organization also influence and change it. Now, scholars examine the ways that newcomers are proactive during the process (Ashford & Black, 1996) and how they negotiate changes in their roles (Kramer, 2009; Miller, Jablin, Casey, Lamphear-Van Horn, & Ethington, 1996; Scott & Myers, 2010). Although there is still more focus on how newcomers are influenced, scholars at least acknowledge that the process is interactive.

The use of multiple paradigmatic approaches has also broadened the understanding of the socialization process (Krone, Kramer, & Sias, 2010). For example, scholars who embrace a critical perspective examine how the public devalues certain types of occupations, such as self-employment, part-time jobs, or seasonal work and treat them as falling short of "a real job" (Clair, 1996). Researchers have recognized the need to include volunteers as organizational members (Kramer, 2011) rather than excluding them from consideration (e.g., Jablin, 2001). Scholars have also embraced feminist standpoint theory to show how newcomers of particular minority groups, race, or gender have strikingly different socialization experiences than do members of majority groups (e.g., Allen, 2000; Bullis & Stout, 2000).

The assimilation perspective also broadened the field beyond the focus on newcomers. It now includes an examination of how communication during anticipatory socialization influences the entire process. For example, parental messages encourage children to reproduce their parent's occupation or to seek upward mobility (Lucas, 2011), and parents pass on insider information that makes the adjustment process easier when children enter the same occupations (Gibson & Papa, 2000). At the other end of the process, the assimilation perspective recognizes communication during organizational exit as part of the ongoing socialization process. Communication during the preannouncement decision to leave, announcement and exit, and post-exit time period influences not only how individuals leave (Jablin, 2001) but also the communication of those who remain as they adjust to their changed work setting (Kramer, 1989).

Theoretical Perspectives

Occasionally, researchers refer to this area of study as *assimilation theory* or *socialization theory*. Although Feldman (1981) calls his socialization model a theory, the models are actually descriptive frameworks in which sometimes atheoretical, variable-analytic studies are conducted. Various scholars have used specific theories to study the process. Waldeck and Myers (2008) and Kramer (2010) identify four primary theories that have been used: uncertainty management theory (UMT), sensemaking theory, social exchange theory (SET), and an emerging use of social identity theory (SIT). Each is examined briefly, along with references to complementary theoretical perspectives.

Uncertainty Management Theory

Based on the interpersonal theory, uncertainty reduction theory (URT; Berger & Calabrese, 1975), UMT provides a theoretical lens for exploring how individuals communicate to reduce or otherwise manage the unfamiliar throughout the socialization process. For example, newcomers experience uncertainty about many things—the nature of their jobs and how to perform them, the norms and culture of the organization, and their relationships to coworkers and supervisors (Morrison, 1995). Uncertainty changes over time, but even established members experience uncertainty, for example, when newcomers join the organization (Gallagher & Sias, 2009) or during mergers and acquisitions (Kramer et al., 2004).

As originally conceptualized in URT, uncertainty in a situation produced motivation to seek information to reduce uncertainty (Berger & Calabrese, 1975). UMT recognizes that sometimes individuals prefer to maintain uncertainty rather than to gain certainty, such as when they choose to remain hopeful by avoiding potentially negative but certain information (Brashers, Goldsmith, & Hsieh, 2002). In other instances, individuals manage uncertainty by seeking information to increase their uncertainty to create hope in a negative but certain situation (Brashers, 2001). For example, amid rumors of potential layoffs, employees may avoid seeking information that would confirm the rumors to remain uncertain but optimistic. Alternatively, after receiving information substantiating layoffs, an employee may seek disconfirming information to increase uncertainty and remain hopeful. UMT also recognizes that individuals may manage uncertainty through cognitive processes without seeking information, such as when they rely on previous experiences rather than seeking information. They may also fail to seek information when faced with uncertainty because other competing motives, such as appearing knowledgeable, are stronger (Kramer, 2004).

UMT has been used to explore many aspects of the socialization process. For example, it has been used to explore the information-seeking strategies of newcomers (e.g., direct inquiry or observations; Miller & Jablin, 1991) and their sources of information (e.g., peers and family; Teboul, 1994). As such, information management or information processing theory (Afifi & Weiner, 2004) may be considered a subset of UMT rather than a completely separate theoretical lens. Similarly, those who focus on newcomers' proactive information-seeking behaviors during socialization explore another aspect of UMT (Ashford & Black, 1996). UMT has been valuable in examining how newcomers, transferees (Kramer, 1993), and established organizational members (Gallagher & Sias, 2009) communicate to adapt to their changing work settings. It can be used to explain how communication in interviews during anticipatory socialization reduces newcomers' uncertainty as well as how communication from supervisors assists layoff survivors (Casey et al., 1997). As such, UMT provides a strong theoretical lens for testing hypotheses relating to communication and socialization.

Sensemaking Theory

Although some scholars posit that sensemaking and uncertainty management may be similar and complimentary theoretical explanations, since both explain how individuals assign meaning to experiences (Kramer, 2011), the two theories have separate bodies of research. As developed by Weick (1995), sensemaking examines how individuals retrospectively assign meaning to experiences rather than the process of proactively seeking information to manage uncertainty. In her seminal work, Louis (1980) explicates examples of sensemaking of three types of newcomers' experiences: (1) differences that can be objectively anticipated by both newcomers and others, such as new locations and job titles; (2) differences that are subjectively experienced by a newcomer, such as discovering that a new supervisor is less flexible than a previous one; and (3) unanticipated differences or surprises that result in strong emotional reactions, such as discovering that working in a cubicle is intolerable compared to the privacy of an office.

The process of assigning meaning to these experiences, *sensemaking*, includes a number of characteristics (Weick, 1995). Sensemaking is an intersubjective process of reaching agreement on meaning with others through communication; an individual cannot subjectively assign any meaning to a situation. Sensemaking is driven by plausibility rather than accuracy; a group can incorrectly agree on a situation's meaning if the meaning possibly makes sense. Finally, sensemaking involves creating an identity, because communicating a particular interpretation of experiences creates a commitment to a particular identity (Weick, 2001).

Sensemaking has been used to examine aspects of the entire socialization process. Newcomers take leave of their old roles and make sense of the differences between their old and new positions (Louis, 1980). Transferees, who make sense of their unmet support and community expectations through their communication, experience greater ease in adapting to their new settings (Jablin & Kramer, 1998). During exit, individuals voluntarily leaving their positions make sense of their decisions by developing accounts that communicate their reasons for leaving to others (Klatzke, 2008). As such, sensemaking provides a framework for examining how people create meaning throughout the socialization process.

Social Exchange Theory

SET is a generalized name for scholarship that focuses on how individuals weigh the costs and benefits of entering, maintaining, and ending social relationships. Although criticized as an overly rational model of human motivation based on maximizing returns, SET provides valuable understanding of decisions to join and leave organizations.

According to SET, individuals participate in economic exchanges in which exact rates of exchange are known (for example, hourly compensation) and in social exchanges in which costs and benefits are more ambiguous (such as doing a favor for someone without discussing how or when it will be reciprocated; Roloff, 1981). Organizational membership involves a combination of economic and social exchanges as individuals exchange money, goods, services, information, affect (friendship), and status (Foa & Foa, 1980). The decision to continue the relationship is based on two calculations (Thibaut & Kelley, 1959): (1) the *comparison level,* or an examination of the relationship's costs and benefits; and (2) the *comparison level of alternatives,* or comparing options to alternative relationships. Accordingly, individuals consider not only what financial and social benefits they receive for the efforts they expend but also whether the exchange rate is better than if they joined another organization.

During anticipatory socialization, individuals compare the costs and benefits of selecting alternative careers and organizations. The person-organization or person-job fit literature implicitly uses SET to evaluate whether individuals will remain in a job long enough to benefit the organization in comparison to the costs of hiring and training new members (Adkins, Russell, & Werbel, 1994). During involuntary exit, supervisors discuss costs and benefits of retaining employees rather than dismissing them (Cox & Kramer, 1995; Fairhurst, Green, & Snavely, 1984). Peers and supervisors use various communication strategies to assess the cost-benefit ratios of keeping poorly performing employees as opposed to urging them to leave on their own (Cox, 1999). Employees use the comparison level of alternatives to make decisions about voluntarily changing jobs and careers or retiring. Although research using SET would benefit from greater focus on how individuals communicate as they make decisions, SET provides a useful theory for exploring communication during such decisions, especially whether to remain in current positions or change jobs.

Social Identity Theory

SIT is an emerging approach for the study of socialization. Although identification is sometimes considered a component of or synonymous with organizational commitment (e.g., Postmes, Tanis, & de Wit, 2001), other scholars consider it distinct (Ashforth & Mael, 1989) and assert that identity is central to organizational membership. For example, Cheney (1991) discussed how individuals manage multiple identities, because they are typically members of multiple organizations. Weick (2001) includes identity as a component of sensemaking, since adopting a particular meaning for organizational membership simultaneously creates an identity. Given identity's association with organizational membership, scholars have called for examining socialization with SIT (Forward & Scheerhord, 1996).

According to SIT, individuals have both personal identities, including physical, psychological and personality characteristics, and social identities, based on how they and others perceive them as group or organizational members (Ashforth & Mael, 1989). It is likely that these two identities overlap, given the way the two interact and influence each other (Alvesson, Ashcraft, & Thomas, 2008). Individuals' identities are based both on participation in particular organizations and disassociation from other institutions (Scott, 2007).

Research suggests that SIT is useful in understanding socialization. Minimal levels of identification are probably necessary for individuals to consider joining organizations. During recruiting, training, and ongoing education, organizations exert efforts to influence and regulate employees' identities (Alvesson et al., 2008). Moreover, members may develop different levels of identification with the multiple targets, such as personal, group, organization, or occupations (Scott, Corman, & Cheney, 1998). These different identification levels are important factors in decisions to remain or leave an organization (Scott et al., 1999).

These four theories—uncertainty management, sensemaking, social exchange, and social identity—are useful for exploring the entire socialization process, but further theoretical developments should also be pursued. For example, it may be possible to extend some of the micro theories that have been used to explore only one aspect of socialization to broader issues. The use of additional theories, such as structuration theory (Scott & Myers, 2010), may be insightful. A combination of building on the foundational work based on these four theories and exploration of additional theoretical perspectives will likely produce the broadest increase in our understanding of socialization processes.

Major Lines of Research

For a thorough review of the theory and research spanning the entire socialization process, readers should consult major literature reviews. What follows are highlights of the most common lines of research and brief critiques of their contributions to understanding communication during socialization. The primary focus in the literature has been on the newcomer's experiences during the encounter phase. Other important lines of research center on the outcomes of socialization and the leaving process.

Newcomer Experiences

The primary focus of socialization research on newcomers' experiences is probably due to its inherit interest and practicality. Everyone has been an organizational newcomer, and most organizations want to be more successful in moving outsiders to insiders who remain in the organization. Within the newcomer focus, five areas have received extensive attention.

Socialization Tactics. The seminal article by Van Maanen and Schein (1979) set forth six pairs of tactics that organizations may intentionally or unintentionally choose from in socializing newcomers: group versus individual; formal versus informal; sequential versus random; fixed versus variable; serial versus disjunctive; and divestiture versus investiture. They proposed that certain tactics lead newcomers to adopt more custodial roles whereby they adopt organizational values and norms, while others lead to more innovative roles in which they bring changes into the organization (Schein, 1968). Empirical studies since Jones (1986) have divided the tactics into *institutional tactics* that encourage newcomers to adapt to the organization and *individual tactics* that encourage newcomers to be innovative and creative. Results generally indicate that institutional tactics lead to more custodial roles, while individual tactics lead to more innovation (Ashforth & Saks, 1996; Jones, 1986).

Research on socialization tactics provides critical insights into incumbents as potential information sources, role models, and emotional links for newcomers. As Saks, Uggerslev, and Fassina's (2007) meta-analysis of these tactics concludes, the "social or interpersonal aspects of socialization [from serial and investiture tactics] are most important for newcomers' adjustment" (p. 440). The socialization tactic approach provides a broad understanding of the context (e.g., singularly or in a cohort; supportive or debasing) newcomers enter while providing little insight into the actual communication (Kramer, 2010). For instance, investiture tactics reveal the extent to which newcomers perceive receiving positive affect messages and formal tactics reveal perceptions that incumbents prepared specific materials for newcomers, but the actual content and form of these messages is, at best, inferred (Jablin, 2001). As a result, researchers can only generalize about the context and say very little regarding messages that are received, their specific sources, or their respective value. So while serial tactics indicate the presence of potential role models, it is unclear if newcomers receive valued information from incumbents or model incumbent behaviors.

This research also assumes a false dichotomy in which newcomers experience either one or the other of the paired tactics (Kramer, 2010). Newcomers often experience both tactics simultaneously or sequentially, such as when initial group orientations to the organization are followed by individual training for specific jobs. In addition, newcomers experience socialization in contexts beyond management's control, such as stories from incumbents, informal initiations and rituals, social and recreational activities, and trial-by-fire tactics (Hart & Miller, 2005). Since, with few exceptions (e.g., Hart & Miller, 2005), researchers neglect to examine the communication content within socialization tactics, research can explore the influence of the communication in conjunction with a tactic, such as when a mentor repeatedly remarks that "we follow the book around here," which encourages custodial rather than innovative roles. Finally, research needs to explore the influence of newcomers' hierarchical position when considering their response to tactics; newcomers may be less likely to be innovative in entry-level than in advanced positions.

Unmet Expectations. Newcomers inevitably experience differences between their expectations and experiences. Although newcomers' experiences may exceed expectations, research has focused primarily on unmet expectations related to the recruitment process. Differences occur because newcomers have unrealistic expectations in general (e.g., expecting rapid promotion) or because promises made or implied were not met (Jablin, 2001).

Research has demonstrated that recruiters' messages can reduce initial expectations and have long-term influences on employee actions. Summaries of findings (Wanous, Poland, Premack, & Davis, 1992) and theoretical explanations indicated that initial reductions in expectations reduce "reality shock" and thereby reduce voluntary turnover (Wanous, 1992). One important meta-analysis (Phillips, 1998) indicated that realistic job previews (RJPs) significantly lowered ($r = -.18$) the job expectations of new hires. Results also found small but significant relationships between RJPs and lower attrition rates and higher job performance. More recent research exploring the means and consequences of expectation-lowering procedures (ELPs) suggests that ELPs or a combination of RJPs and ELPs are associated with reduced turnover compared to no preview or RJP-only conditions (e.g., Buckley et al., 2002). Overall, information sharing during recruitment and entry is linked to reduced employee turnover and other positive outcomes, including increased trust in the organization (Phillips, 1998).

From a communication perspective, research in this area suffers from message design and testing issues. For example, it is unclear to what extent recruiters actually share realistic previews, especially if they fear discouraging valued recruits from accepting positions (Baker, Miller, & Gardner, 2004). It is unlikely that recruiters across the large organizations typically sampled shared consistent messages, since the realistic content and information communicated often varied across recruiters, particularly in field versus laboratory settings (Breaugh & Billings, 1988). In addition, rather than simple sets of facts, realistic preview content may be complex and difficult to convey and accept (Meglino, Denisi, & Ravlin, 1993). Moreover, RJPs are often conceptualized as scripted, one-way messages although previews are more likely conveyed as a natural "by-product of discourse processes (e.g., question, answer, statements sequences)" (Jablin, 2001, p. 748). Consequently, research needs to examine message construction and effects systematically. Aside from Meglino et al. (1993), there is little pretesting of message effectiveness prior to lab or field experiments.

Research is needed on how communication from ambient sources, such as the education system, and discrete sources, such as organizational recruiters, contributes to unrealistic expectations during anticipatory socialization and on whether the sources, channels, or timing of communication of RJPs influence outcomes. Investigations should consider how organizational and other web pages, word-of-mouth, social networks, and other organizational sources, such as current employees met at second or on-site interviews (Miller & Buzzanell, 1996) and corporate trainers (Kristof, 1996), influence realistic perceptions of work and organizations. Researchers should move from samples of college graduates entering the workforce to include more job and career changers, who may have more nuanced interpretations of organizational preview messages or less inflated expectations. Finally, researchers should clarify message effects of RJPs and ELPs as researchers are increasingly challenging the importance of preview messages on newcomer adjustment in favor of training programs. Rather than changing newcomers expectations, some advocate "validating their initial perceptions of organization values" (Cooper-Thomas, van Vianen, & Anderson, 2004, p. 69) as members' perceptions of fit are likely to grow more congruent with the passage of time.

Message Content. During socialization, coworkers are remarkably valuable and are usually informal information sources, whose tips and informal advice can greatly aid newcomer adaptation and performance (e.g., Louis, Posner, & Powell, 1983). Two primary approaches exist to exploring the nature of messages received by newcomers and their subsequent influence: memorable messages and socialization content.

Memorable messages are communication events, perhaps words of wisdom or practical advice, that significantly impact newcomers (Stohl, 1986). The memorable message approach implies that newcomers' gradual, incremental learning is marked by dramatic moments or significant changes due to receiving certain messages. These messages typically occur in informal settings with more senior organizational members who newcomers generally perceive as attempting to assist them (Barge & Schlueter, 2004). Often, these messages take the form of stories that represent organizational values and culture (Brown, 1985). Memorable messages can have a positive or negative impact on newcomers. For example, new female faculty responded negatively to messages that reinforced negative gender or marital status stereotypes (Dallimore, 2003). Depending on their valence, memorable messages may influence newcomers to develop more distant or closer personal relationships and lead to weaker or stronger organizational identification (Bullis & Bach, 1989).

Chao, O'Leary-Kelly, Wolf, Klein, and Gardner (1994) began examining the multiple dimensions of information provided to newcomers by examining accounting students' reported knowledge in six areas: (1) *history*, the knowledge of organizational traditions, customs, and background; (2) *language*, the mastery of specialized slang/jargon; (3) *politics*, the knowledge of the influential members and how things "really work;" (4) *people*, the work group acceptance; (5) *organizational goals and values*, the knowledge and supporting of organizational objectives and standards; and (6) *performance proficiency*, the mastery of required tasks and skills. Subsequent studies either modified Chao et al.'s scale or used similar multiple-dimension frameworks. For instance, Hart and Miller (2005) reworded items so that participants reported the extent to which they received messages about each content area since entering the organization. Cooper-Thomas and Anderson (2002) conceive of dimensions of information received into social, role, interpersonal resources, and organizational areas.

Other studies explored newcomers' exposure to specific types of information. In a series of studies (e.g., Saks, 1996), Saks addressed the extent, length, and helpfulness of information received in eight training areas. Cawyer and Friedrich (1998) measured university orientation sessions at department and institutional levels (e.g., expectation for research, tenure process). Chow (2002) measures perceived organizational support from messages received in career information, coaching and mentoring, job/organization information, and career planning. George and Bettenhausen (1990) assess the extent to which organizations emphasize certain values (e.g., customer service) to newcomers.

Investigations into the message content contribute to our understanding of socialization in three ways. In the last two decades, researchers have more precisely explicated the types of information received during entry and explored their relationship to newcomer adjustment and advancement. Investigations also identified circumstances when specific types of information are especially helpful to newcomers. Finally, inquiries into memorable messages suggest that some information received may be more salient or certainly remembered more than others. Assessments of message content help discover the antecedents that shape newcomers' role expectations and identification with organizations and their positions (Jablin, 2001).

Perhaps due to the complexity of measuring messages, this research is beset with various difficulties. One particularly vexing problem associated with memorable messages is the unreliability of individuals' memory when individuals recall messages from months or years earlier (Stafford & Daly, 1984). Snowball and convenience samples diminish the generalizability of findings. By sampling one organization's newcomers, investigators might better determine the circumstances when messages are particularly helpful or memorable, if the message was purposefully sent, or even how frequently certain information was conveyed.

Another challenge in assessing messages imparted to newcomers is the degree to which newcomers receive new information during entry as opposed to during pre-entry, including employment interviews. Several studies (e.g., Chao et al., 1994; Taormina & Law, 2000) asked newcomers to report the sum of their knowledge gained to date, including information gained outside organization-initiated socialization activities (e.g., information from teachers, peers, news) confounding efforts to assess messages received during entry.

Research opportunities exist regarding the helpfulness of information content received on newcomer adjustment. With few exceptions (e.g., Chow, 2002; Haueter, Macan, & Winter, 2003; Ostroff & Kozlowski, 1992), investigations rarely compared socialization messages received from management and supervisors with those from coworkers and mentors. Conflicting advice and support can dramatically change employees' perspectives or assist them in their adjusting or "getting ahead" (Kram & Isabella, 1985; Noe, 1988). In addition, research lags behind in understanding newcomers' role-readiness to receive and apply information. The link between messages received and why the messages are particularly meaningful or helpful is an important step in understanding agents' influence on newcomers' role-taking and sensemaking (Brim, 1966; Jablin, 2001). Kammeyer-Mueller and Wanberg's (2003) longitudinal analysis linking organizational, supervisory, and coworker influence to seven learning outcomes may be particularly exemplary. Researchers rarely assess the degree of message acceptance or perceived value among newcomers, in essence, overlooking opportunities to test linkages between messages received and the development of subsequent values, attitudes, or behaviors (Brim, 1966).

Information Seeking. Systematic examination of newcomers' information-seeking behaviors as they attempt to manage uncertainty or make sense of their situations began in the mid-1980s. Newcomers are often unclear concerning expectations of them due either to information overload when briefed or incomplete briefings (e.g., incumbents forgetting what it is like to be a newcomer; Miller & Jablin, 1991). One focus has been on the type of information newcomers seek. Kramer's (2010) summary of this material suggests four main categories: *task-related information,* including what to do, how to do it, and how it will be evaluated; *relational information,* including work-related and social relationships within the workgroup and beyond; *organizational information,* including its history, norms, and culture; and *political or power information,* concerning who is influential and how to influence others.

A second focus investigates newcomers' information sources. Although most studies use a limited list of sources, a comprehensive list suggests multiple sources: peers/coworkers, supervisors, subordinates, other organizational personnel, customers/clients, written materials and manuals, friends or family members, and the task itself (Miller & Jablin, 1991; Teboul, 1994). Implicit under written materials, internal and external electronic sources are increasingly important information sources to consider in future studies.

A third focus examines newcomers' information-seeking strategies. Although scholars use alternative terms (e.g., Kramer, 1993; Morrison, 1995), the Miller and Jablin (1991) typology represents the strategies most commonly identified: *overt questions, indirect questions*, and *disguising* represent interactive strategies of seeking information from a source of uncertainty; *third-party inquiries* represent an active strategy of seeking information from someone other than the source of uncertainty; *observing* and *surveillance* represent passive strategies of waiting for information; and finally *testing*, the least used strategy, involves breaking organizational norms and evaluating responses. UMT (Kramer, 2004) and motivated information management (Afifi & Weiner, 2004) suggest additional strategies newcomers use to manage information, including cognitively reducing uncertainty by accessing past experiences, reappraising information needs, and actively or passively avoiding information that may create unpleasant certainty.

A major contribution of information-seeking research to understanding socialization is recognizing that newcomers are proactive and not passive; they take the initiative to figure out their roles or satiate their curiosity. Researchers conclude that a key indicator of newcomer adjustment is the frequency of information seeking. That is, newcomers who inquire more of their supervisors and coworkers have greater role clarity and higher levels of performance and commitment than those seeking less information (Jablin, 2001; Morrison, 2002). Research also points to the value of observation tactics depending upon work conditions and social dynamics (Ashforth et al., 2007). Future research should continue focusing on the complex interplay of the types, sources, and information-management strategies, including factors as such newcomer networking proclivity (Morrison, 2002), organizational tenure (Bauer & Green, 1994), and work-unit dynamics (Kozlowski & Bell, 2003).

Future research needs to explore newcomers' differences in language use and information-gathering skills. Measurements of information seeking may not adequately represent the frequency or intensity of newcomers' discursive behaviors. A couple of well-stated questions by one newcomer may be equivalent or superior to another's poorly constructed dozen. A potential confound is the work unit's information-sharing environment. For example, unsolicited information volunteered to newcomers has been shown to be more valuable than solicited information (Kramer, 1993; Morrison, 1993). Bauer and Green's (1994) longitudinal study suggests that newcomer information seeking adds little when communication-minded managers clarify assignments and are supportive.

Learning Organizational Culture. To move from outsider to insider, newcomers must learn the organizational culture. Culture is a broad construct that has been reviewed elsewhere extensively (see Keyton, Chapter 22). For purposes here, an organization's culture is the stated and unstated values and beliefs represented in an organization's artifacts, individuals, stories, language, norms, and rituals (Pacanowsky & O'Donnell-Trujillo, 1983). Although an organization's culture includes an integrated or unified culture across the organization, subcultures can easily differ between or within units or work group, especially where ambiguity and change are common (Martin, 1992). The complexity of an organization's culture was evident in a study of new bank tellers who needed to make sense of the dominant, unified culture taught during orientation and the unique, sometimes contrary, ways things were done in local branches and instances in which the culture was so ambiguous that they were unable to determine how to function (DiSanza, 1995).

The importance of learning the culture during the socialization process is evident from early work on pivotal, relevant, and peripheral norms (Schein, 1968) to more recent studies on firefighters learning norms for managing emotion when interacting with the public versus the privacy of fire stations (Scott & Myers, 2005). Research exploring linkages between communication and learning organizational culture generally follows two approaches. The narrative and story approach (e.g., Brown, 1990) examines the constitution of language and its use in announcements, stories, and dialogue by which newcomers socially construct the values held by the organization or unit members. The critical incidents approach (e.g., Gundry & Rousseau, 1994) examines meanings derived from events as well as how those meanings influence perceptions of organizations and work units and subsequent organizational adjustment. In addition, individuals learn about an organization's culture prior to entry. For example, parents communicate organizational values to children who assume positions in the same company (Gibson & Papa, 2000). Knowledge and acceptance of the organizational culture is often considered evidence of successful socialization.

Research on learning organizational culture through communication provides explanations of how sensemaking processes function, emphasizes how language creates meanings that influence newcomers' attitudes and actions, and demonstrates how seemingly small events develop into mythical and lasting status for organizational members (Martin, Feldman, Hatch, & Sitkin, 1983). In addition to capturing the emotions, energy, and stresses associated with communication during entry, research on learning organizational culture showcases consistencies and inconsistencies between organizations and units.

In the larger scheme, research considering how newcomers learn culture needs to address issues of person-organization fit. Much like unmet expectations research, scholars investigating culture must answer questions raised by those who posit that newcomers exiting the organization due to lack of fit are part of the natural cycle of selection, attraction, and attrition (Schneider, 1987). This perspective holds that newcomers fit or do not fit the organization based on their underlying values and personalities, and socialization experiences through training or unit induction only accomplish so much (Kristof-Brown, Zimmerman, & Johnson, 2005).

Relationships

The development of relationships with organizational members is a particularly important part of the entire socialization process. Although relationships with other organizational members such as mentors (e.g., Ragins & Cotton, 1999) or customers and clients (Sias, 2009) have been examined, researchers have focused on two primary relationships: supervisor-subordinate and peer relationships.

Supervisor-Subordinate Relationships. Until the mid-1970s, research on supervisor-subordinate communication assumed that supervisors used an average leadership style with their subordinates, treating all subordinates equally. Studies found that subordinates were more satisfied with supervisors who were more open and communication minded (Jablin, 1979). Research developed since then by Graen and his associates, Leader Member Exchange (LMX), indicates that supervisors develop differential relationships with subordinates (see Graen, 2003; Graen & Uhl-Bien, 1995). Partnership and insider relationships are characterized by mutual influence and trust and subordinates who are allowed to interrupt, whereas overseer, outsider relationships are characterized by brief interactions in which subordinates comply with supervisors' requests and suggestions (Fairhurst & Chandler, 1989). Findings consistent with both approaches have important implications for the socialization process, since supervisors determine newcomers' roles, serve as role models, and have authority to reward or sanction actions (Miller & Jablin, 1991).

Research consistently shows that newcomers who develop positive supervisor relationships and receive more information from them experience more positive outcomes, particularly if that information comes early in the organizational experience (Jablin, 2001). For newcomers, supervisors are the most satisfying source of information, in part due to their influential role compared to peers (Jablin, 1984). Newcomers in partnership relationships likely experience a greater latitude in negotiating and individualizing their roles (Sias, Krone, & Jablin, 2002). Supervisor relationships influence a wide range of outcomes including job satisfaction, organizational commitment, performance, and turnover (Sias, 2009).

The exploration of information-exchange patterns in newcomers' relationship development with their supervisors has contributed substantially to understanding organizational entry and newcomer adjustment. Although it is not surprising that newcomers develop stronger or weaker information ties to their supervisors, Jablin's (1984) finding that supervisors initiated most of the interactions with newcomers initially but that more mutual initiation of interactions occurred after two months, suggests that both supervisors and newcomers face challenges as the supervisors try to make sure newcomers are on track and newcomers attempt to satisfy supervisors' performance expectations. Additional research on supervisor-newcomer interaction patterns *over time* can increase understanding of how relationship closeness or distance emerges, how patterns of interactions develop, and how role expectations evolve (Anand, Hu, Liden, & Vidyarthi, 2011; Scott & Myers, 2005). Too few investigations explore how discursive patterns (Fairhurst, 2011) facilitate newcomers' understanding of roles and relationship development or consider the viewpoints of both supervisors and subordinates (Anand et al., 2011).

Peer Relationships. Peer relationships are newcomers' most common and available information sources (Louis et al., 1983). As a result, peers provide much of the information newcomers need to adapt to an organization and learn its culture, along with social support and mentoring

(Myers, 2005; Sias, 2009). Similar to the relationship range with supervisors, newcomers potentially develop acquaintance, friend, or close-friend relationships (Sias & Cahill, 1998) or information, collegial, or special relationships (Kram & Isabella, 1985). Developing closer relationships with peers who share information with the newcomers influences a range of outcomes such as satisfaction, performance, and retention (Jablin, 2001; Morrison, 1993; Sias, 2009).

Peer relationships also interact with supervisor-subordinate relationships. Peers are aware of coworkers' LMX relationships. When a coworker's insider relationship seems deserved because an individual is hardworking and competent, peers view the individual as a conduit for influencing their supervisor. When the insider relationship is viewed as undeserved, resulting from favoritism and brownnosing, peers ostracize and avoid the individual. In contrast, when the coworker's outsider relationship is viewed as deserved due to poor work habits, peers avoid the individual. Yet when the outsider relationship is viewed as undeserved and resulting from supervisor bias, then peers empathize with and support the individual (Sias & Jablin, 1995).

The notion that friends anchor newcomers cognitively, attitudinally, and emotionally to a work unit has long been known (Kozlowski & Bell, 2003; Zurcher, 1983). More recent investigations of peer relationships reinforce the importance of peer interactions on newcomers' attitudes and productivity. In extending this research, investigations should examine peer interactions in team settings, where individuals may be highly interdependent versus settings where they act relatively autonomously (Kozlowski & Bell, 2003). In highly interactive teams, the repercussions of constructive versus divisive peer relationships may be more pronounced.

The previous sections focused on the potential positive aspects of supervisor and peer relations without considering the impact of negative work relationships. Since the impact of negative relationships is discussed extensively elsewhere in this volume (see Kassing & Waldron, Chapter 26), suffice it to say that supervisor and peer relations potentially have negative rather than positive effects. The effort expended on managing negative relationships reduces individual and work-unit productivity and leads to stress, dissatisfaction, and turnover (e.g., Harden Fritz, 2006).

Overall, workplace relationships are a critical component of socialization. Through supervisor and peer interactions, newcomers gain the information and support they need to move from outsiders to insiders. Further research needs to explore the influence of communication involving positive and negative relationships throughout the entire socialization process. In particular, investigations could explore how newcomers change the unit norms in positive or negative ways (Moreland & Levine, 2001) and how negative actions threatened the psychological safety of individuals and teams (Edmondson, 1999). How newcomers and incumbents respond to changes in personnel and negative events likely impacts how units operate and demonstrates the extent to which they value individuals' well-being.

Defining Successful Socialization

Although learning the organizational culture and developing relationships are important indications of newcomer adjustment, they do not fully embody the meaning of *successful* socialization. Researchers have used a wide variety of cognitive, attitudinal, and behavior measures as criterion variables to assess socialization outcomes, including role ambiguity, job satisfaction, organizational commitment, identification, and job survival (Ashforth et al., 2007).

In the last two decades, researchers have developed more comprehensive measures for successful socialization. Chao et al. (1994) considered successful socialization to include performance proficiency, knowledge of organizational history and culture, understanding of organizational politics, knowing people and developing positive relationships, and understanding of the organization's unique language. Kammeyer-Mueller and

Wanberg (2003) measure newcomer adaptation as learning the ropes, demonstrating appropriate behaviors, knowledge of how the organization works and what is important to learn, adapting to the work environment, and following appropriate attitudes and norms. In turn, Myers and colleagues (Gailliard, Myers, & Seibold, 2010; Myers & Oetzel, 2003) measured job competency, familiarity with coworkers, familiarity with supervisors, acculturation, recognition, involvement, job competency, and role negotiation. These multidimensional measures reflect a broad range of threshold competencies necessary for organizational and unit integration and early role success in four broad areas: task learning and performance, relationship development, organizational knowledge, and positive affect.

Taken together, these studies suggest that socialization outcomes are more complex than simply satisfaction or job survival. A critical outcome that has continued to be measured is newcomers' role clarity (i.e., role ambiguity and role conflict), which derives from both incumbents' information giving and newcomers' information seeking and most likely reflects the overall communication climate into which newcomers entered (Jablin, 2001). The measurements of developing relationships, learning the workplace's informal rules, and acquiring the unit and organizational jargon offer insights into the extent to which newcomers have established core competencies necessary for success in their new environments (Zurcher, 1983).

One major limitation to these measurements is their reliance on self-reports for behavioral aspects such as newcomer performance or integration into the unit, which can be measured by incumbents (e.g., Chen, 2005). Although challenging, actual behavior measures and cognitive tests would be valuable in evaluating newcomers' success in moving from outsiders to insiders. Additional conceptual and empirical development is needed into what constitutes successful socialization. For example, most conceptualizations of newcomer acclimation assume a set of communication behavioral and knowledge competencies, but research has yet to explore the communication competencies newcomers possess upon entry or other important communication outcomes, such as knowledge of the communication climate, integration into emergent networks, or how newcomers move to full competency (Jablin & Krone, 1994; Jablin & Sias, 2001). Research has also not explored changes in the meanings of *fit* and *commitment* for newcomers (Schaubroeck & Green, 1989). For example, a newcomer's concept of commitment after two weeks likely develops into a more complex and multifaceted gestalt over time (Barge & Schlueter, 2004). Yet the role of communication in contributing to changes in the meaning of newcomers' commitment is unclear.

Organizational Exit

Although numerous studies have attempted to determine predictors of voluntary turnover and have resulted in a number of meta-analyses (e.g., Griffeth, Hom, & Gaertner, 2000), Jablin (2001) noted that communication during the actual exit process is relatively understudied compared to the encounter and metamorphosis phases. The groundwork for more extensive research in this area exists for both voluntary and involuntary exit processes.

For involuntary exit, research has explored the process of documenting problems and dismissing problematic employees (Cox & Kramer, 1995; Fairhurst et al., 1984). Researchers have also explored how peers and supervisors encourage turnover that appears to be voluntary through a variety of communication and behavioral strategies, from relatively benign actions such as mentioning employment opportunities elsewhere to active efforts such as sabotaging work efforts (Cox, 1999). Research on layoffs provided insight into how individuals respond to others involuntarily exiting and the importance of communication from managers to mitigate the negative impact on those who remain (Casey et al., 1997).

For voluntary exit, the study of job transfers suggests a gradual loosening of communication ties as individuals prepare to leave for new locations within the same organization (Kramer, 1989). More generally, as employees consider voluntarily exit, individuals strategically communicate different messages to diverse audiences prior to exiting in order to maintain current positions and relationships and, afterward, to avoid burning bridges for possible future needs (Klatzke, 2008). Similarly, during voluntary downward career moves, individuals gather information to make the decision and gain support, announce the decision strategically, and then communicate to bolster the identity of their new occupation (Tan & Kramer, 2011).

Research suggests that Jablin's (2001) three-phase model of pre-announcement, announcement and exit, and post-exit may be applicable to both voluntary and involuntary exits. In both cases, information gathering leads to a decision, that decision is communicated and an individual leaves the organization, and then those affected by the exit communicate to support their perspective and adapt to the voluntary or involuntary exit. So, while the research is limited in comparison to newcomer research, it provides ample grounds for further study of communication during organizational exit.

Gaps and Future Research

The understanding of the role of communication within socialization has advanced considerably over the years, but explorations into gaps in current research should lead to additional important insights. Reviews by Jablin (2001), Ashforth et al. (2007), and others make compelling cases for directions for future research. Other scholars have suggested the need to develop additional theoretical perspectives to explore socialization, such as structuration theory (Scott & Myers, 2010). In previous sections, we identified weaknesses within specific research lines. Here, we address three pressing gaps that extend across lines of research.

Multiple Time Frames

A common criticism of socialization research is that many scholars examine it in static rather than dynamic relationships. Studies that measure newcomers' entry experiences and corresponding attitudes or knowledge at the same time give only a snapshot of newcomers' experiences and have two shortcomings. First, measuring the independent variable at only one point in time can miss the growing or waning influence of supervisors, coworkers, and events over time. For instance, gathering data on predictor variables only during orientation events, dominated by human resource professionals, misses the potentially stronger influences of supervisors or work units that occur in the weeks following. Second, researchers may assess newcomers' entry experiences during the formal training period, but work-unit members' may not disclose long-standing rules of thumb, rituals, standards of work, and interpretations of daily experiences until weeks or months later, when newcomers have been socially accepted (Zurcher, 1983). For communication scholars, the timing of when received messages have their greatest influence on newcomers is critical. Relying on a single source or time period runs counter to what is preferable in the socialization literature (Ashforth et al., 2007; Brim, 1966; Jablin, 2001).

The remedy for these issues is relatively straightforward. More sophisticated studies can examine newcomers' experiences at one point in time and their attitudes or knowledge at a later time (e.g., Ashforth & Saks, 1996; Kammeyer-Mueller & Wanberg, 2003). Longitudinal studies and panel studies provide insights into the enduring influence of socialization events or messages (Saks & Ashforth, 1997) and address common method-variance analysis issues (Miller et al., 2011). Similarly, adopting the panel-like study formats used in medical and education fields, where independent variables are measured more than once, would provide additional insight into socialization. Though not without data gathering and analytic challenges (Miller et al., 2011),

Monge (1990) and Poole, Van de Ven, Dooley, and Holmes (2000) set forth frameworks that consider how a single construct varies across time and can influence a criterion variable. To gain insights into the temporary or growing influence of communicative acts, scholars must cease assuming that socialization events in newcomers' first month are not mitigated by other influences. The starting point for investigating process is assessing the constancy of an independent variable's influence. In short, "knowledge about how variables behave independently over time provides a basis for better understanding how they relate to each other over time" (Monge, 1990, p. 409).

Unit-Level Influence

With few exceptions (e.g., Gibson & Papa, 2000), socialization studies focus on individual-level influences and omit unit-level influences. With individual influences, researchers theorize the association of one individual's attribute with another individual's outcome (Klein, Dansereau, & Hall, 1994) as in, for example, the direct influence of a supervisor's openness on the newcomer's satisfaction. In contrast, at the unit-level, Klein et al. (1994) conceptualize that the group or unit influences via either homogeneity (similarity of messages), independence (individual-level influences), or heterogeneity (individual messages moderated by the group context). For example, if supervisory and coworker messages are consistent, group influence is homogeneous. Yet if an informal group leader provides contrary messages, the influence may be direct (independent) or influenced by context, including other work group messages and the timing of the messages in relation to each other (heterogeneity).

It is very appropriate to conceptualize socialization as primarily occurring at the unit level, since, as Jablin (1987) notes, "Research consistently supports the notion that newcomers' daily interactions with coworkers/peers are one of the most important factors affecting their socialization" (p. 701). Work-unit members have a vested interest in speaking forthrightly to newcomers who may jeopardize unit productivity or social norms (Collinson, 1992). Newcomers have great interest in learning workgroup norms and values, as adjustment and friendships occur at the unit level (Louis et al., 1983; Ostroff & Kozlowski, 1992). In addition, socializing messages by workgroup members may differ from those espoused by top management or orientation programs due to units' task environments, occupational cultures, personnel, and unit histories.

The measure of unit-level communication requires a shift in research designs by creating measures targeting unit influence as well as data aggregation and analytic practices. First, models of group socialization (Moreland & Levine, 2001) do not adequately consider the influence of communication behaviors and messages operating in a homogeneous, independent, or heterogeneous manner, or they may skim over the importance of work-unit contexts and developing relationships in socialization outcomes. Second, since differences between norms abound across work units (e.g., Chen, 2005), there is little reason to assume that newcomers entering different organizational units experience similar communicative behaviors or that they result in similar outcomes. Analyses at the unit level in a single organization sample could shed light on the extent to which different units share similar socialization practices and equally facilitate newcomer adjustment. Third, instruments that provide insight into the ease, consistency, and helpfulness of unit members' information sharing are needed in addition to extant measures of newcomer information receiving or seeking proclivities. For example, in the memorable-message research (e.g., Barge & Schlueter, 2004; Stohl, 1986), little is known about how the messages newcomers receive relate to unit norms or how workgroups create memorable messages to communicate their expectations. Fourth, data analyses typically focus solely on newcomers' self-reports of socialization influences and related outcomes; incumbent members could provide valuable insights into their own as well as newcomers' behaviors, especially in regard to newcomers' interaction patterns, observance of norms, and performance.

Wide-Ranging Sample Populations

An important contribution of communication scholars to the study of organizations has been its interest in newcomers from divergent samples and its focus on specific contexts instead of the rather generic white-collar jobs most frequently studied in management and psychology. Settings range from firefighters (Myers, 2005) to blue-collar factory workers and miners (Gibson & Papa, 2000; Lucas, 2011; Lucas & Buzzanell, 2004) and medical specialists (Apker, 2001). More scholarship needs to focus on larger sample of specific groups such as minorities (Allen, 2000), women (Bullis & Stout, 2000; Dallimore, 2003), and other marginalized groups to understand how their experiences are similar to and different from the dominant group.

Relatively unexplored are the experiences on nonentry-level newcomers, particularly newcomers in supervisory or management positions, or even CEOs. While much remains to be explored among recent college graduates, increasing numbers of individuals change jobs and careers frequently. Others reenter the workforce after leaves of absence (Miller et al., 1996), raising children, or prolonged layoffs. Hence, many newcomers bring with them vast work experiences that shape and inform their entry behaviors (Jablin, 2001). Understanding the similarities and unique aspects of experienced newcomers would lead to a more nuanced understanding of the socialization process.

Researchers should also explore the transition experiences as part of the ongoing socialization process. As noted, preliminary findings exist on individual transitions, such as job transfers (Brett, 1982; Kramer, 1993) and job promotions (Kramer & Noland, 1999), and organizational transitions, such reductions in force (Casey et al., 1997) and mergers and acquisitions (Bastien, 1992; Kramer et al., 2004). Investigations into other individual transitions where individuals' careers have limits in ascension or duration such as career plateaus (e.g., Rotondo & Perrewé, 2000) or reorganization under Title 11 bankruptcy seem especially relevant in times of a stagnant economy.

Explorations of the communication behaviors and experiences of volunteers entering nonprofit organizations have much to offer to the traditional socialization literature. Given a volunteer organization's need to balance newcomers' motivations to contribute in a volunteer setting and the organization's interest in training, orderly processes, and reliable participation, those who seek to understand the constitution of an engaged workforce would benefit from explorations of socialization processes for volunteers (Kramer, 2011). Alternatively, since most nonprofit organizations are made up of paid and volunteer employees, the interaction of these two groups during socialization presents a range of paradoxes and challenges. In addition, there are multiple types of voluntary associations, from volunteering in a local community service organization to coaching recreational teams to joining career-oriented associations. Examining the similarities and differences across these experiences can contribute to understanding the socialization processes in non-volunteer settings.

Concluding Thoughts

We began this review by pointing to a number of summary articles as evidence of the vibrancy of study of communication in the socialization process. Our conclusion is much the same. The study of communication during socialization has examined many important issues already. Research has extensively examined socialization tactics, information seeking, social support, peer relationship development, and the learning of the organizational culture. More work can explore the communication linkage to developing unmet expectations, the communication content within the socialization tactics, and the role negotiation process with supervisors. Additional insights will also be gained by exploring more diverse samples (including volunteers), further developing the understanding of communication outcomes, and exploring socialization at multiple levels of analysis over time. This suggests that socialization research can continue to grow in the coming years.

References

Adkins, C. L., Russell, C. J., & Werbel, J. D. (1994). Judgments of fit in the selection process: The role of work value congruence. *Personnel Psychology, 47*(3), 605–623.

Afifi, W. A., & Weiner, J. L. (2004). Toward a theory of motivated information management. *Communication Theory, 14*(2), 167–190.

Allen, B. J. (2000). "Learning the ropes": A Black feminist standpoint analysis. In P. M. Buzzanell (Ed.), *Rethinking organizational & managerial communication from feminist perspectives* (pp. 177–208). Thousand Oaks, CA: SAGE.

Alvesson, M., Ashcraft, K. L., & Thomas, R. (2008). Identity matters: Reflections on the construction of identity scholarship in organization studies. *Organization, 15*(1), 5–28.

Anand, S., Hu, J., Liden, R. C., & Vidyarthi, P. R. (2011). Leader-member exchange: Recent research findings and prospects for the future. In A. Bryman, D. Collinson, K. Grint, B. Jackson, & M. Uhl-Bien (Eds.), *The SAGE handbook of leadership* (pp. 311–325). Thousand Oaks, CA: SAGE.

Apker, J. (2001). Role development in the managed care era: A case of hospital-based nursing. *Journal of Applied Communication Research, 29*(2), 117–136.

Ashford, S. J., & Black, J. S. (1996). Proactivity during organizational entry: The role of desire for control. *Journal of Applied Psychology, 81*(2), 199–214.

Ashforth, B. E., & Mael, F. (1989). Social identity theory and the organization. *The Academy of Management Review, 14*(1), 20–39.

Ashforth, B. E., & Saks, A. M. (1996). Socialization tactics: Longitudinal effects on newcomer adjustment. *Academy of Management Journal, 39*(1), 149–178.

Ashforth, B. E., Sluss, D. M., & Harrison, S. H. (2007). Socialization in organizational contexts. In G. P. Hodgkinson & J. K. Ford (Eds.), *International review of industrial and organizational psychology* (vol. 22, pp. 1–70). Sussex, England: Wiley.

Baker, C. R., Miller, V. D., & Gardner, P. D. (2004). *Unmet expectations: Reconsidering recruiters' realistic and traditional information sharing in employment screening interviews.* Paper presented at the National Communication Association, New Orleans, LA.

Barge, J. K., & Schlueter, D. W. (2004). Memorable messages and newcomer socialization. *Western Journal of Communication, 68*(3), 233–256.

Bastien, D. T. (1992). Change in organizational culture. *Management Communication Quarterly, 5*(4), 403–442.

Bauer, T. N., & Erdogan, B. (2011). Organizational socialization: The effective onboarding of new employees. In S. Zedeck (Ed.), *APA handbook of industrial and organizational psychology* (vol. 3, pp. 51–64). Washington, DC: APA.

Bauer, T. N., & Green, S. G. (1994). Effect of newcomer involvement in work-related activities: A longitudinal study of socialization. *Journal of Applied Psychology, 79*(2), 211–223.

Bauer, T. N., Morrison, E. W., & Callister, R. R. (1998). Organizational socialization: A review and directions for future research. In G. R. Ferris & K. M. Rowland (Eds.), *Research in personnel and human resource management* (vol. 16, pp. 149–214). Greenwich, CT: JAI Press.

Berger, C. R., & Calabrese, R. J. (1975). Some explorations in initial interaction and beyond: Toward a developmental theory of interpersonal communication. *Human Communication Research, 1*(2), 99–112.

Brashers, D. E. (2001). Communication and uncertainty management. *Journal of Communication, 51*(3), 477–497.

Brashers, D. E., Goldsmith, D. J., & Hsieh, E. (2002). Information seeking and avoiding in health contexts. *Human Communication Research, 28*(2), 258–271.

Breaugh, J. A., & Billings, R. S. (1988). The realistic job preview: Five key elements and their importance for research and practice. *Journal of Business and Psychology, 2*(4), 291–305.

Brett, J. M. (1982). Job transfer and well-being. *Journal of Applied Psychology, 67*(4), 450–463.

Brim, O. G., Jr. (1966). Socialization through the life cycle. In O. G. Brim, Jr. & S. Wheeler (Eds.), *Socialization after childhood: Two essays* (pp. 1–49). New York, NY: Wiley.

Brockner, J., Grover, S., O'Malley, M. N., Reed, T. F., & Glynn, M. A. (1993). Threat of future layoffs, self-esteem, and survivors' reactions: Evidence from the laboratory and the field. *Strategic Management Journal, 14*(S1), 153–166.

Brown, M. H. (1985). That reminds me of a story: Speech action in organizational socialization. *Western Journal of Speech Communication, 49*(1), 27–42.

Brown, M. H. (1990). "Reading"; an organization's culture: An examination of stories in nursing homes. *Journal of Applied Communication Research, 18*(1), 64–75.

Buckley, M. R., Mobbs, T. A., Mendoza, J. L., Novicevic, M. M., Carraher, S. M., & Beu, D. S. (2002). Implementing realistic job previews and expectation-lowering procedures: A field experiment. *Journal of Vocational Behavior, 61*(2), 263–278.

Bullis, C., & Bach, B. W. (1989). Are mentor relationships helping organizations? An exploration of developing mentee-mentor-organizational identifications using turning point analysis. *Communication Quarterly, 37*(3), 199–213.

Bullis, C., & Stout, K. R. (2000). Organizational socialization: A feminist standpoint approach. In P. M. Buzzanell (Ed.), *Rethinking organizational & managerial communication from feminist perspectives* (pp. 47–75). Thousand Oaks, CA: SAGE.

Casey, M. K., Miller, V. D., & Johnson, J. R. (1997). Survivors' information seeking following a reduction in workforce. *Communication Research, 24*(6), 755–781.

Cawyer, C. S., & Friedrich, G. W. (1998). Organizational socialization: Processes for new communication faculty. *Communication Education, 47*(3), 234–245.

Chao, G. T., O'Leary-Kelly, A. M., Wolf, S., Klein, H. J., & Gardner, P. D. (1994). Organizational socialization: Its content and consequences. *Journal of Applied Psychology, 79*(5), 730–743.

Chen, G. (2005). Newcomer adaptation in teams: Multilevel antecedents and outcomes. *Academy of Management Journal, 48*(1), 101–116.

Cheney, G. (1991). *Rhetoric in an organizational society: Managing multiple identities.* Columbia: University of South Carolina Press.

Chow, I. H-S. (2002). Organizational socialization and career success of Asian managers. *International Journal of Human Resource Management, 13*(4), 720–737.

Clair, R. P. (1996). The political nature of the colloquialism, "a real job": Implications for organizational socialization. *Communication Monographs, 63*(3), 249–267.

Collinson, D. L. (1992). *Managing the shopfloor: Subjectivity, masculinity, and workplace culture.* Berlin, Germany: Walter de Gruyter.

Cooper-Thomas, H. D., & Anderson, N. (2002). Newcomer adjustment: The relationship between organizational socialization tactics, information acquisition and attitudes. *Journal of Occupational and Organizational Psychology, 75*(4), 423–437.

Cooper-Thomas, H. D., van Vianen, A., & Anderson, N. (2004). Changes in person-organization fit: The impact of socialization tactics on perceived and actual P-O fit. *European Journal of Work & Organizational Psychology, 13*(1), 52–78.

Cox, S. A. (1999). Group communication and employee turnover: How coworkers encourage peers to voluntarily exit. *Southern Communication Journal, 64*(3), 181–192.

Cox, S. A., & Kramer, M. W. (1995). Communication during employee dismissals. *Management Communication Quarterly, 9*(2), 156–190.

Dallimore, E. J. (2003). Memorable messages as discursive formations: The gendered socialization of new university faculty. *Women's Studies in Communication, 26*(2), 214–265.

DiSanza, J. R. (1995). Bank teller organizational assimilation in a system of contradictory practices. *Management Communication Quarterly, 9*(2), 191–218.

Edmondson, A. (1999). Psychological safety and learning behavior in work teams. *Administrative Science Quarterly, 44*(2), 350–383.

Fairhurst, G. T. (2011). Discursive approaches to leadership. In A. Bryman, D. Collinson, K. Grint, B. Jackson, & M. Uhl-Bien (Eds.), *The SAGE handbook of leadership* (pp. 495–507). Thousand Oaks, CA: SAGE.

Fairhurst, G. T., & Chandler, T. A. (1989). Social structure in leader-member interaction. *Communication Monographs, 56*(3), 215–239.

Fairhurst, G. T., Green, S. G., & Snavely, B. K. (1984). Managerial control and discipline: Whips and chains. In R. N. Bostrom & B. H. Westley (Eds.), *Communication yearbook* (vol. 8, pp. 558–593). Beverly Hills, CA: SAGE.

Feldman, D. C. (1981). The multiple socialization of organization members. *Academy of Management Review, 6*(2), 309–318.

Foa, U. G., & Foa, E. B. (1980). Resource theory: Interpersonal behavior as exchange. In K. J. Gergen, M. S. Greenberg, & R. H. Willis (Eds.), *Social exchange: Advances in theory and research* (pp. 77–94). New York, NY: Plenum.

Forward, G. L., & Scheerhord, D. (1996). Identities and the assimilation process in the modern organization. In H. B. Mokros (Ed.), *Interaction & identity* (vol. 5, pp. 371-391). New Brunswick, NJ: Transaction.

Gailliard, B. M., Myers, K. K., & Seibold, D. R. (2010). Organizational assimilation: A multidimensional reconceptualization and measure. *Management Communication Quarterly, 24*(4), 552–578.

Gallagher, E. B., & Sias, P. M. (2009). The new employee as a source of uncertainty: Veteran employee information seeking about new hires. *Western Journal of Communication, 73*(1), 23–46.

George, J. M., & Bettenhausen, K. (1990). Understanding prosocial behavior, sales performance, and turnover: A group-level analysis in a service context. *Journal of Applied Psychology, 75*(6), 698–709.

Gibson, M. K., & Papa, M. J. (2000). The mud, the blood, and the beer guys: Organizational osmosis in blue-collar work groups. *Journal of Applied Communication Research, 28*(1), 68–88.

Graen, G. B. (2003). Interpersonal workplace theory at the crossroads. In G. B. Graen (Ed.), *Dealing with diversity: LMX leadership: The series* (vol. 1, pp. 145–182). Greenwich, CT: Information Age.

Graen, G. B., & Uhl-Bien, M. (1995). Relationship-based approach to leadership: Development of a leader-member exchange (LMX) theory of leadership over 25 years—Applying a multi-level multi-domain perspective. *Leadership Quarterly, 6*(2), 219–247.

Griffeth, R. W., Hom, P. W., & Gaertner, S. (2000). A meta-analysis of antecedents and correlates of employee turnover: Update, moderator tests, and research implications for the next millennium. *Journal of Management, 26*(3), 463–488.

Gundry, L. K., & Rousseau, D. M. (1994). Critical incidents in communicating culture to newcomers: The meaning is the message. *Human Relations, 47*(9), 1063–1088.

Harden Fritz, J. M. (2006). Typology of troublesome others at work: A follow-up study. In J. M. Harden Fritz & B. L. Omdahl (Eds.), *Problematic relationships in the workplace* (pp. 21–46). New York, NY: Peter Lang.

Hart, Z. P., & Miller, V. D. (2005). Context and message content during organizational socialization. *Human Communication Research, 31*(2), 295–309.

Haueter, J. A., Macan, T. H., & Winter, J. (2003). Measurement of newcomer socialization: Construct validation of a multidimensional scale. *Journal of Vocational Behavior, 63*(1), 20–39.

Jablin, F. M. (1979). Superior-subordinate communication: The state of the art. *Psychological Bulletin, 86*(6), 1201–1222.

Jablin, F. M. (1984). Organizational communication: An assimilation approach. In R. N. Bostrom (Ed.), *Communication yearbook* (vol. 8, pp. 594–626). Beverly Hills, CA: SAGE.

Jablin, F. M. (1987). Organizational entry, assimilation, and exit. In F. M. Jablin, L. L. Putnam, K. H. Roberts, & L. W. Porter (Eds.), *Handbook of organizational communication: An interdisciplinary perspective.* (pp. 679–740). Thousand Oaks, CA: SAGE.

Jablin, F. M. (2001). Organizational entry, assimilation, and disengagement/exit In F. M. Jablin & L. L. Putnam (Eds.), *The new handbook of organizational communication: Advances in theory, research, and methods* (pp. 732–818). Thousand Oaks, CA: SAGE.

Jablin, F. M., & Kramer, M. W. (1998). Communication-related sense-making and adjustment during job transfers. *Management Communication Quarterly, 12*(2), 155–182.

Jablin, F. M., & Krone, K. (1994). Task/work relationships: A life-span perspective. In M. L. Knapp & G. R. Miller (Eds.), *Handbook of interpersonal communication* (2nd ed., pp. 621–675). Thousand Oaks, CA: SAGE.

Jablin, F. M., & Sias, P. M. (2001). Communication competence. In F. M. Jablin & L. L. Putnam (Ed.), *The new handbook of organizational communication: Advances in theory, research, and methods* (pp. 819–864). Thousand Oaks, CA: SAGE.

Jones, G. R. (1986). Socialization tactics, self-efficacy, and newcomers' adjustments to organizations. *Academy of Management Journal, 29*(2), 262–279.

Kammeyer-Mueller, J. D., & Wanberg, C. R. (2003). Unwrapping the organizational entry process: Disentangling multiple antecedents and their pathways to adjustment. *Journal of Applied Psychology, 88*(5), 779–794.

Klatzke, S. R. (2008). *Communication and sensemaking during the exit phase of socialization* (Unpublished dissertation). University of Missouri, Columbia, MO.

Klein, K. J., Dansereau, F., & Hall, R. I. (1994). Levels issues in theory development, data collection, and analysis *Academy of Management Review, 19*(2), 195–229.

Kozlowski, S. W. J., & Bell, B. S. (2003). Work groups and teams in organizations. In W. C. Borman, D. R. Ilgen, & R. J. Klimoski (Eds.), *Handbook of psychology* (pp. 333–375). Hoboken, NJ: Wiley.

Kram, K. E., & Isabella, L. A. (1985). Mentoring alternatives: The role of peer relationships in career development. *Academy of Management Journal, 28*(1), 110–132.

Kramer, M. W. (1989). Communication during intra-organization job transfers. *Management Communication Quarterly, 3*(2), 219–248.

Kramer, M. W. (1993). Communication after job transfers: Social exchange processes in learning new roles. *Human Communication Research, 20*(2), 147–174.

Kramer, M. W. (2004). *Managing uncertainty in organizational communication.* Mahwah, NJ: Lawrence Erlbaum.

Kramer, M. W. (2009). Role negotiations in a temporary organization: Making sense during role development in an educational theater production. *Management Communication Quarterly, 23*(2), 188–217.

Kramer, M. W. (2010). *Organziational socialization: Joining and leaving organizations.* Cambridge, UK: Polity.

Kramer, M. W. (2011). A study of voluntary organizational membership: The assimilation process in a community choir. *Western Journal of Communication, 75*(1), 52–74.

Kramer, M. W., Dougherty, D. S., & Pierce, T. A. (2004). Managing uncertainty during a corporate acquisition. *Human Communication Research, 30*(1), 71–101.

Kramer, M. W., & Noland, T. L. (1999). Communication during job promotions: A case of ongoing assimilation. *Journal of Applied Communication Research, 27*(4), 335–355.

Kristof, A. L. (1996). Person-organization fit: An integrative review of its conceptualizations, measurement, and implications. *Personnel Psychology, 49*(1), 1–49.

Kristof-Brown, A. L., Zimmerman, R. D., & Johnson, E. C. (2005). Consequences of individuals' fit at work: A meta-analysis of person-job, person-organization, person-group, and person-supervisor fit. *Personnel Psychology, 58*(2), 281–342.

Krone, K., Kramer, M. W., & Sias, P. M. (2010). Theoretical developments in organizational communication research. In C. R. Berger, M. E. Roloff, & D. R. Roskos-Ewoldsen (Eds.), *The handbook of communication science* (2nd ed., pp. 165–182). Thousand Oaks, CA: SAGE.

Louis, M. R. (1980). Surprise and sense making: What newcomers experience in entering unfamiliar organizational settings. *Administrative Science Quarterly, 25*(2), 226–251.

Louis, M. R., Posner, B. Z., & Powell, G. N. (1983). The availabilty and helpfulness of socialization practices. *Personnel Psychology, 36*(4), 857–866.

Lucas, K. (2011). Socializing messages in blue-collar families: Communicative pathways to social mobility and reproduction. *Western Journal of Communication, 75*(1), 95–121.

Lucas, K., & Buzzanell, P. M. (2004). Blue-collar work, career, and success: Occupational narratives of Sisu. *Journal of Applied Communication Research, 32*(4), 273–292.

Martin, J. (1992). *Cultures in organizations: Three perspectives.* New York, NY: Oxford University Press.

Martin, J., Feldman, M. S., Hatch, M. J., & Sitkin, S. B. (1983). The uniqueness paradox in organizational stories. *Administrative Science Quarterly, 28*(3), 438–453.

Meglino, B. M., DeNisi, A. S., & Ravlin, E. C. (1993). Effects of previous job exposure and subsequent job status on the functioning of a realistic job preview. *Personnel Psychology, 46*(4), 803–822.

Miller, V. D., & Buzzanell, P. M. (1996). Toward a research agenda for the second employment interview. *Journal of Applied Communication Research, 24*(3), 165–180.

Miller, V. D., & Jablin, F. M. (1991). Information seeking during organizational entry: Influences, tactics, and a model of the process. *Academy of Management Review, 16*(1), 92–120.

Miller, V. D., Jablin, F. M., Casey, M. K., Lamphear-Van Horn, M., & Ethington, C. (1996). The maternity leave as a role negotiation process. *Journal of Managerial Issues, 8*(3), 286–309.

Miller, V. D., Poole, M. S., Seibold, D. R., Myers, K. K., Park, H. S., Monge, P., . . . Shumate, M. (2011). Advancing research in organizational communication through quantitative methodology. *Management Communication Quarterly, 25*(1), 4–58.

Monge, P. R. (1990). Theoretical and analytical issues in studying organizational processes. *Organization Science, 1*(4), 406–430.

Moreland, R. L., & Levine, J. M. (2001). Socialization in organizations and work groups. In M. E. Turner (Ed.), *Groups at work: Theory and research* (pp. 69–112). Mahwah, NJ: Lawrence Erlbaum.

Morrison, E. W. (1993). Longitudinal study of the effects of information seeking on newcomer socialization. *Journal of Applied Psychology, 78*(2), 173–183.

Morrison, E. W. (1995). Information usefulness and acquisition during organizational encounter. *Management Communication Quarterly, 9*(2), 131–155.

Morrison, E. W. (2002). Information seeking within organizations. *Human Communication Research, 28*(2), 229–242.

Myers, K. K. (2005). A burning desire. *Management Communication Quarterly, 18*(3), 344–384.

Myers, K. K., & Oetzel, J. G. (2003). Exploring the dimensions of organizational assimilation: Creating and validating a measure. *Communication Quarterly, 51*(4), 438–457.

Napier, N. K., Simmons, G., & Stratton, K. (1989). Communication during a merger: The experience of two banks. *Human Resource Planning, 12*(2), 105–122.

Noe, R. A. (1988). An investigation of the determinants of successful assigned mentoring relationships. *Personnel Psychology, 41*(3), 457–479.

Ostroff, C., & Kozlowski, S. W. J. (1992). Organizational socialization as a learning process: The role of information acquisition. *Personnel Psychology, 45*(4), 849–874.

Pacanowsky, M. E., & O'Donnell-Trujillo, N. (1983). Organizational communication as cultural performance. *Communication Monographs, 50*(2), 126–147.

Phillips, J. M. (1998). Effects of realistic job previews on multiple organizational outcomes: A meta-analysis. *Academy of Management Journal, 41*(6), 673–690.

Poole, M. S. (2011). Communication. In S. Zedeck (Ed.), *APA handbook of industrial and organizational psychology* (vol. 3, pp. 249–270). Washington, DC: APA.

Poole, M. S., Van de Ven, A. H., Dooley, K., & Holmes, M. E. (2000). *Organizational change and innovation processes: Theory and methods for research.* New York, NY: Oxford University Press.

Postmes, T., Tanis, M., & de Wit, B. (2001). Communication and commitment in organizations: A social identity approach. *Group Processes & Intergroup Relations, 4*(3), 227–246.

Ragins, B. R., & Cotton, J. L. (1999). Mentor functions and outcomes: A comparison of men and women in formal and informal mentoring relationships. *Journal of Applied Psychology, 84*(4), 529–550.

Roloff, M. E. (1981). *Social exchange: Key concepts.* Beverly Hills, CA: SAGE.

Rotondo, D. M., & Perrewé, P. L. (2000). Coping with a career plateau: An empirical examination of what works and what doesn't. *Journal of Applied Social Psychology, 30*(12), 2622–2646.

Saks, A. M. (1996). The relationship between the amount and helpfulness of entry training and work outcomes. *Human Relations, 49*(4), 429–451.

Saks, A. M., & Ashforth, B. E. (1997). Organizational socialization: Making sense of the past and present as a prologue for the future. *Journal of Vocational Behavior, 51*(2), 234–279.

Saks, A. M., Uggerslev, K. L., & Fassina, N. E. (2007). Socialization tactics and newcomer adjustment: A meta-analytic review and test of a model. *Journal of Vocational Behavior, 70*(3), 413–446.

Schaubroeck, J., & Green, S. G. (1989). Confirmatory factor analysis procedures for assessing change during organizational entry. *Journal of Applied Psychology, 74*(6), 892–900.

Schein, E. H. (1968). Organizational socialization and the profession of management. *Industrial Management Review, 9*(2), 1–16.

Schneider, B. (1987). The people make the place. *Personnel Psychology, 40*(3), 437–453.

Scott, C., & Myers, K. K. (2005). The socialization of emotion: Learning emotion management at the fire station. *Journal of Applied Communication Research, 33*(1), 67–92.

Scott, C., & Myers, K. (2010). Toward an integrative theoretical perspective on organizational membership negotiations: Socialization, assimilation, and the duality of structure. *Communication Theory, 20*(1), 79–105.

Scott, C. R. (2007). Communication and social identity theory: Existing and potential connections in organizational identification research. *Communication Studies, 58*(2), 123–138.

Scott, C. R., Connaughton, S. L., Diaz-Saenz, H. R., Maguire, K., Ramirez, R., Richardson, B., . . . Morgan, D. (1999). The impacts of communication and multiple identifications on intent to leave. *Management Communication Quarterly, 12*(3), 400–435.

Scott, C. R., Corman, S. R., & Cheney, G. (1998). Development of a structurational model of identification in the organization. *Communication Theory, 8*(3), 298–336.

Sias, P. M. (2009). *Organizing relationships: Tradition and emerging perspectives on workplace relationships.* Thousand Oaks, CA: SAGE.

Sias, P. M., & Cahill, D. J. (1998). From coworkers to friends: The development of peer friendships in the workplace. *Western Journal of Communication, 62*(3), 273–299.

Sias, P. M., & Jablin, F. M. (1995). Differential superior-subordinate relations, perceptions of fairness, and coworker communication. *Human Communication Research, 22*(1), 5–38.

Sias, P. M., Krone, K., & Jablin, F. M. (2002). An ecological systems perspective on workplace relationships. In M. L. Knapp & G. R. Miller (Eds.), *Handbook of interpersonal communication* (3rd ed., pp. 615–642). Thousand Oaks, CA: SAGE.

Stafford, L., & Daly, J. A. (1984). Conversation memory. *Human Communication Research, 10*(3), 379–402.

Stohl, C. (1986). The role of memorable messages in the process of organizational socialization. *Communication Quarterly, 34*(3), 231–249.

Sullivan, S. E. (1999). The changing nature of careers: A review and research agenda. *Journal of Management, 25*(3), 457–484.

Tan, C. L., & Kramer, M. W. (2011). Communication and voluntary downward career changes. *Journal of Applied Communication Research, 40*(1), 87–106.

Taormina, R. J., & Law, C. M. (2000). Approaches to preventing burnout: The effects of personal stress management and organizational socialization. *Journal of Nursing Management, 8*(2), 89–99.

Teboul, J. B. (1994). Facing and coping with uncertainty during organizational encounter. *Management Communication Quarterly, 8*(2), 190–224.

Thibaut, J. W., & Kelley, H. H. (1959). *The social psychology of groups.* New York, NY: Wiley.

Van Maanen, J., & Schein, E. G. (1979). Toward a theory of organizational socialization. In B. M. Staw (Ed.), *Research in organizational behavior* (pp. 209–264). Greenwich, CT: JAI Press.

Waldeck, J. H., & Myers, K. (2008). Organizational assimilation theory, research, and implications for multiple areas of the discipline: A state of the art review. In C. S. Beck (Ed.), *Communication yearbook* (vol. 31, pp. 322–367). New York, NY: Lawrence Erlbaum.

Wanous, J. P. (1992). *Organizational entry: Recruitment, selection, orientation, and socialization of newcomers.* Reading, MA: Addison-Wesley.

Wanous, J. P., Poland, T. D., Premack, S. L., & Davis, K. S. (1992). The effects of met expectations on newcomer attitudes and behaviors: A review and meta-analysis. *Journal of Applied Psychology, 77*(3), 288–297.

Weick, K. E. (1995). *Sensemaking in organizations.* Thousand Oaks, CA: SAGE.

Weick, K. E. (2001). *Making sense of the organization.* Malden, MA: Blackwell.

Zurcher, A. L. (1983). *Social roles: Conformity, conflict and creativity.* Beverly Hills, CA: SAGE.

CHAPTER 22

Organizational Culture

Creating Meaning and Influence

Joann Keyton

The study of organizational culture continues to generate scholarly interest in communication, management, and psychology disciplines but also in sociology, anthropology, political science, and public administration. With more direct ways of communicating to the public and customers, some organizations are well known for marketing their cultures in addition to the products and services that they sell (e.g., Zappos, Apple, and Google); thus organizational culture is often mentioned in the business press. Additionally, individuals who are entering the work force are encouraged to ask questions of their potential employers that implicitly reveal the organizational culture that they might enter. Indeed, the frequently asked question, "What's it like to work at . . . ?" suggests that the construct of organizational culture is embedded in everyday talk about organizational life.

Beyond its popularity, the study of organizational culture through a communication lens has contributed to and highlighted a meaning-centered approach to the study of organizational communication. Moving beyond a focus on information transmission, organizational culture scholars have examined how meaning is socially produced by members at all levels of an organization. What people think about an organization's culture or what they do in an organization's culture is important. But the unique role of a communication approach to organizational culture is to identify, analyze, and theorize how people create and negotiate meaning through interaction (see Deetz, 1994; Putnam, 1983).

This chapter aims to build on Eisenberg and Riley's (2001) handbook chapter by considering recent theoretical and methodological developments in the study of organizational culture, the contributions of communication scholars to this area of research, limitations and gap in organizational culture research, and directions for future scholarship. This review focuses on organizational culture scholarship (1) written by communication scholars, (2) based on a communicative perspective, (3) dealing directly with communication phenomena, (4) using methodologies generally accepted by communication scholars, (5) published in communication and closely related journals, and/or (6) cited in communication scholarship. Finally, preference for inclusion was given to articles that studied organizational members within one organization rather than employees across different organizations. The objective of this review is to identify the communication discipline's contributions to the study and understanding of organizational culture. To do this, this chapter is organized into four sections: defining organizational culture, history of organizational culture, the emergence of a communicative focus on organizational culture, and frameworks for studying communication and organizational culture.

Defining Organizational Culture

As Eisenberg and Riley (2001) so astutely note, the organizational culture construct is itself a cultural artifact—one created by us to explore our relationships and communicative behaviors with one another in work settings. Whether work is performed voluntarily or for pay in profit and nonprofit organizations, many people are concerned about their lived cultural experiences in organizations as well as the ways in which they interact with an organization's culture as customers and clients. Clearly, people make choices about staying and leaving organizations based on *what it feels like to be there.* Culture has become so dominant that organizational artifacts, values, and assumptions spill over into interactions with internal organizational stakeholders as well as with customers and clients.

Conceptually, organizational culture is "the set(s) of artifacts, values, and assumptions that emerges from the interactions of organizational members" (Keyton, 2011, p. 28). This definition provides a communicative focus to conceptions of organizational culture. For example, anthropologists offer early definitions of *culture* that focus on shared symbols and patterns of meaning transmitted from person to person within societies, regions, or countries. This conceptualization was adopted in the 1980s and 1990s by communication, organizational behavior, and sociology scholars and extended to refer to the day-to-day work environments in organizational settings. Relatedly, Keyton (2011) identified several key features common to definitions of organizational culture that scholars currently adopt. First, organizational culture is a multilevel system of artifacts, values, and assumptions; an organization's culture cannot be defined by any one feature in isolation. Second, some organizational members or groups of them must share interpretations of the cultural elements found in organizational life; yet it is highly unlikely that all organizational members share all or even most interpretations.

While definitions of organizational culture remain contested, communication scholars generally agree that culture is manifested through communication as artifacts, values, and assumptions. Artifacts are visible and tangible. Common artifacts found in organizations include norms, standards, customs, social conventions, logos, and mission statements. Values are ideals or beliefs about what an organization should pursue (e.g., innovation) or how an organization and its members should behave (e.g., with honesty). Presented in a positive form (e.g., always *honesty*, never *dishonesty*), values are difficult to identify until they are manifested in the behaviors of organizational members—often as workplace practices, vocabulary, metaphors, stories, and rites and rituals (Pacanowsky & O'Donnell-Trujillo, 1983). Assumptions are taken-for-granted or deeply entrenched beliefs that are difficult for organizational members to discuss explicitly. Similar to artifacts and values, organizational members do not talk about assumptions directly. Rather, organizational members reveal them in their work conversations with others and in talking about their work experiences.

Scholars in other disciplines have focused on organizational culture as "a pattern of shared basic assumptions" (Schein, 2004, p. 17) or as "patterns of interpretation composed of the meanings associated with various cultural manifestations" (Martin, 2002, p. 330). While informative, communication scholars have generally adopted a view of organizational culture in which culture and organization fold into one another (Parker, 2000); in other words, an organization does not *have* a culture, it *is* culture (Smircich, 1983). This conceptualization uses culture as a root metaphor for organization. Rather than talking about an organization in economic or physical terms, this view promotes the notion of an organization as a social phenomenon created by human symbolic expression.

History of Organizational Culture

The beginnings of the construct of organizational culture date back to three sources: (1) Mayo's (1934) human relations studies in the early 1900s, (2) Jacques's (1951) book, *The Changing Culture of a Factory: A Study of Authority and Participation in an Industrial Setting*, and (3) Becker and Geer's (1960) article on the distinctions between structure and culture published in *Administrative Science Quarterly*.

Mayo's (1934) observations in a textile mill found that workers in one unit with extremely high turnover were doing dangerous and solitary work. But more stressful than the working conditions was the low opinion they held of themselves and their work, coupled with their high opinion of the factory president. Mayo initiated rest periods and incentives for these employees, which resulted in higher employee satisfaction. These improvements in their working conditions were abandoned and then eventually reinstated. Across these changes, however, employee morale improved. Mayo attributed this gain to the factory president, who allowed the workers to control who would rest and when, thereby creating a social unit where none had existed previously. This study and others that Mayo conducted revealed that teamwork and social cooperation were values that employees responded to and, when allowed to be developed, made employees' work lives more satisfying.

Similarly, Jacques's (1951) data collection in a metal factory focused on the relationships within and between groups during a time when the organization was making significant changes to work performance. The research team uncovered deeply rooted conflicts in the communication between upper- and middle-level managers. Additional stress was occurring in employees' abilities to enact the roles that they were expected to perform. Thus this ethnographic-type examination identified the values and assumptions that were pivotal to how employees behaved and felt about their work environments and the organization.

While early studies focused on values and work environments, Becker and Geer (1960) directly identified the term *culture* and distinguished it from the structure of an organization. By *structure*, they meant "an orderly arrangement of social relations, a continuing arrangement of kinds of people (named and defined), governed by a concept of proper behavior for them in their relations with one another" (p. 305). Therefore, culture consisted of "the conventional understandings shared by the participants" (p. 305) in the organization. Furthermore, cultures developed in response to problems that groups faced. As the group found or created ways to resolve its common problems, members created assumptions and values. Following closely the ideas of sociologist Gouldner, Becker and Geer further distinguished latent and manifest roles and identities as features of organizational culture. Latent identities, which were often informal, were evident when people brought identity issues from a social group (e.g., social class, ethnicity, regionalism) to an organizational group. Latent identities could be contrasted to manifest identity, which was the organizational culture created in response to a common problem.

Although the focus of these early scholars was on improved effectiveness and efficiency of the workplace, Becker and Geer (1960) acknowledged that manifest culture was not necessarily sanctioned by the organization and might even be in opposition to it. Identifying people who developed a common response to a shared problem was the basis by which subcultures organized and become known. Importantly, these scholars recognized that communication among members of a latent culture could influence an organization's manifest culture.

Within two decades, the focus of organizational culture as an academic topic of research changed. Weick (1979) drew scholarly attention to discovering systems or patterns of interpretations. During the same time period, Pettigrew (1979) emphasized the study of symbols, rituals, ideology, language, and myths as ways of understanding longitudinal organizational processes. But management scholar Schein (1985) likely had the most lasting influence on contemporary views of organizational culture with his model that placed fundamental assumptions as the core from which values, norms, patterns of behaviors, artifacts, and symbols developed. His model created relationships among the components of organizational culture in which artifacts appeared on the surface level as direct reflections of deeply held values and assumptions.

Also influential, and at about the same time, Trice and Beyer (1984) distinguished the network of meanings linked to assumptions, norms, and values from the forms or practices of organizational culture. That is, the former is where meaning resides and the latter is where meanings are communicated and expressed. These scholars believed that researchers should focus on the forms of expression—or the organizational rites and ceremonies. This approach was well received by organizational communication scholars because "in performing the activities of a rite or ceremonial, people make use of other cultural forms—certain customary language, gestures, ritualized behaviors, artifacts, other symbols, and settings—to heighten the expression of shared meanings" (p. 654). Later, Trice and Beyer's 1993 book, *The Cultures of Work Organizations*, introduced the *cultural approach* and further developed the concept by drawing from theoretical and empirical literature across disciplines.

Also in the 1970s and 1980s, communication scholars, especially Bormann (1982, 1983, 1985) and Tompkins (Bullis & Tompkins, 1989; Tompkins, Fisher, Infante, & Tompkins, 1975), were examining organizational issues using rhetorical analysis and symbolic interaction. The work of these scholars coincided with the use of systems theory as the dominant approach to understanding communication in organizations, and communicating was equated with organizing (e.g., Farace, Monge, & Russell, 1977). Within a few years, the interpretive turn (e.g., Putnam & Pacanowsky, 1983) described how employees created messages and symbols, how they interpreted them, and what these messages revealed about organizational culture. This approach aimed to promote communication scholars and their ideas to other disciplines. Then, as now, the study of organizational culture was explored by communication scholars who used humanistic methods, quantitative research, and qualitative social science approaches.

Just as the academic study of organizational culture was gaining theoretical and methodological steam, popular press books highlighted organizational culture in case studies (Deal & Kennedy, 1982; Peters & Waterman, 1982). These books further energized the popular acceptance of organizational culture as a construct, because they offered prescriptive advice to those at the top of organizations. With this type of managerial bias, *corporate culture* was the preferred term and became popular with practitioners and consultants. This popular stream envisioned *organizational culture* (aka *corporate culture*) as a singular culture that senior level management believed they created. As a result, the corporate focus on culture aimed at enhancing productivity and organizational effectiveness.

Emergence of a Communicative Focus on Organizational Culture

In the 1980s and 1990s, communication scholars continued their exploration of organizational culture under the label of the *cultural approach.* Pacanowsky and O'Donnell-Trujillo (1982) were among the first to identify a communicative approach to the study of organizational culture and embrace the assumption that communication constituted organizational life. As a result, these authors moved the study of organizational communication from a managerial perspective to one inclusive of all levels of organizational employees. Thus the organizational culture perspective in communication was based on two questions: "What are the key communication activities and indicators, the unfolding of which are occasions when sensemaking is accomplished?, and What is the sense members of any particular organization have made of their experiences?" (p. 124).

At the same time, the study of organizational communication was taking an *interpretive turn,* which also embraced a social rather than an economic view of organizations (Putnam, 1983). Interpretive studies sought to explore the social reality of work by examining the day-to-day talk of organizational members. Thus the interpretive approach to the study of organizational communication further facilitated communicative studies of organizational culture. At this point, the view that organizational culture could be controlled by management-approved formal messages was replaced with the view that organizational culture was created by all organizational members as they produced and reproduced the daily reality of organizational life.

Although functional and post-positivist studies of organizational culture existed, most studies began to use an *interpretive approach* (see Putnam, 1983), which supported both naturalistic and critical examinations. Naturalistic studies were characterized by (1) description and interpretation of organizational messages and meanings, (2) reflection of an organization's social reality as recognized by its members, and (3) informative outcomes for those outside the organization (Bantz, 1993). Critical studies were characterized by (1) the ability to uncover practices that constrain communication and (2) the development of findings that contribute to free and open communication in which social, organizational, and individual interests could be mutually accomplished (Deetz & Kersten, 1983). Both types of studies treated organizations as social constructions with the processes of organizing and communicating being inextricably intertwined.

Frameworks for Studying Communication and Organizational Culture

To date, no comprehensive theory of communication and organizational culture has been developed. Communication scholars often turn to Schein's (2004) theory in which organizational culture is derived from a combination of artifacts, values, and assumptions that create the basis of some level of shared social experience for organizational members.

The Role of Discourse in Organizational Culture

A more recent and communication-centered approach for theorizing about organizational culture is based on the premise that organizations emerge from communication (Taylor & Van Every, 2000). Fairhurst and Putnam (2004) ground the organizing process in talk; and Bisel, Messersmith, and Keyton (2010) extend their three positions to explain the relationship between organizational discourse and organizational culture. In the *object orientation,* the researcher (or research design) assumes that organizational culture comes before discourse. In other words, organizational culture can be changed to influence the discourse of organizational members. This discourse-organizational culture relationship aligns with normative or functional approaches, as "research conducted from this orientation assumes (1) culture is measurable, (2) culture produces discourse, (3) cultures can be managed, and (4) changes to the culture will result in changes to communicative activities in the organization" (Bisel et al., 2010, p. 349). To illustrate this type of discourse-culture relationship, Bisel et al. point to Pepper and Larson's (2006) examination of the cultural tensions that resulted when one company merged with another. Both the merged organization and the acquiring one routinely sent messages designed to create uniformity and conformity across the two companies. While the acquiring firm valued a unified corporate identity, members of the acquired firm preferred to retain their unique identity rather than being assimilated wholly. This study also explained why other discourse-culture relationships were needed: "Although blaming culture for an acquisition's struggles is not wrong, it also is inadequate. Culture is too large a concept" (Pepper & Larson, 2006, p. 62). As described by these authors, in instances when culture influences communication, the controlling features of culture are emphasized at the expense of recognizing its multifaceted phenomenon (Bisel et al., 2010).

In the *becoming orientation*, the relationship is reversed, with discourse among organizational members constituting the organization's culture. The dominant question is, "How is discourse culturing?" (Bisel et al., 2010, p. 353). This question positions organizational culture in a state of becoming; that is, an organization's culture is never fixed. An example of research that seeks to uncover properties of discourse and linguistic forms that create, sustain, or challenge culturing is Fairhurst and Cooren's (2004) analysis of dialogue between a dispatcher and a police officer. The officer, who has been shot four times, calls the dispatcher and when asked if she is hurt, responds, "That's affirmative." By changing her discourse from unintelligible screaming to calmer slower talk, the officer returns to the values of resilience and the use of procedures consistent with her police training. Their interaction is an example of the way that discourse may be considered similar to culturing as the officer and dispatcher communicatively construct assumptions "about what the problem was as well as the cultural value of an appropriate solution" (Bisel et al., 2010, p. 354).

The *grounded-in-action orientation* privileges neither discourse nor culture. Rather, this orientation views organizational discourse and organizational culture as mutually constitutive, with each simultaneously influencing the other. Thus the question is changed to "How are the constancies of organizational culture fixed in the dynamic flow of discourse?" (Bisel et al., 2010, p. 356). Fairhurst and Putnam (2004) caution that the grounded-in-action orientation is not simply a combination of the object and becoming orientations. Rather, the grounded-in-action orientation "treats action and structure as mutually constitutive. Thus the organization never assumes the form of an identifiable entity because it is anchored at the level of social practices and discursive forms" (p. 16). As Bisel et al. (2010) further explain,

> the culture's ontology is found at the level of everyday interaction as enabled and constrained by past interactions. Therefore, researchers seeking to uncover how constancies of organizational life are fixed in everyday talk will investigate how actors appropriate the rules and resources gained from previous interactions in their present conversations. (p. 356)

Because this orientation examines the communication-culture flow, it is positioned to provide the most comprehensive understanding of organizational culture. For example, Bisel et al. (2010) argue that Dougherty and Smythe's (2004) case study of sexual harassment in an academic department reflects the characteristics of the grounded-in-action approach, especially in demonstrating how communication is both enabled and constrained by organizational culture and how organizational culture is reflected in the department's present and past communication. During a visit to the department, a donor sexually harasses three women in the department. The department informally and formally uses talk to make sense of what has occurred. These conversations and storytelling both reflect and affirm an existing value of group cohesion and challenge the assumption regarding the need for this donor's financial gift. The authors conclude that the sensemaking that occurred in informal and formal conversations allowed departmental members to create culture around a shared experience (see Weick, 1995). Using case study data, the authors address how the constancies of organizational culture become fixed in the dynamic flow of discourse.

However promising a discourse-oriented approach to organizational culture appears, one limitation of such an approach is that it is devoid of the material aspects of organizational culture. Dougherty (2011) has forcefully argued that an important dimension of reality is lost when material conditions that shape day-to-day life are forfeited for a focus on discourse. Even in knowledge and service work, the material and physical aspects of work life are present. Dougherty is not the first to draw our attention to material aspects of organizational culture. Earlier, Alvesson (2004) reminded us that "a cultural approach to organizations would be language-sensitive, but not necessarily language-focused" (p. 317). Most artifacts of organizational life are material or physical; for example, an employee's name badge not only identifies him or her for security reasons but also tracks movement from one part of the building to another. This type of artifact holds (likely different) symbolic meaning for employees and managers, ones that are not directly communicated. Alvesson suggests such an artifact of organizational life calls "for reading between and behind the lines" (p. 317). This practice positions organizational culture, as Alvesson reminds us, not inside people's heads, but "somewhere 'between' the heads of a group of people where symbols and meanings are publicly expressed . . . but also in material objects" (p. 318).

To illustrate, Zoller's (2003) study of the work environment at an automobile production plant demonstrates how the materiality of the workplace influences associates' acceptance of organizational values. Employees manifested the *good associate* value by consenting to work in hazardous conditions. In fact, associates emphasized that their level of personal fitness (in part, due to the benefit of having an on-site gym) allowed them to manage the increased pace instead of acknowledging that it would be potentially hazardous. Thus management's cultural value of fast-paced work is reinforced by the assumption that associates need to match the pace of the production line (an artifact). Not only do employees embrace these values, they identify them as their own, particularly as they accept responsibility for being physically fit enough to work the line. Employees also refrained from reporting injuries as OSHA (Occupational Safety and Health Administration) incidents or violations. Likewise, associates told stories about health problems that arose directly from their work but spoke positively about the company and especially about their jobs. In these ways, employees both adopted and accepted management's values, even though doing so created an unsafe working environment and potentially long-term negative physical effects.

Lenses for Studying Organizational Culture

In their *Handbook* chapter, Eisenberg and Riley (2001) captured the communicative perspective of organizational culture as a thematic framework of (1) *communicative processes*—culture as symbolism and performance, culture as text, culture as critique, culture as identity, and culture as cognition—and (2) *communicative goals*—culture as climate and effectiveness.

Later, Keyton (2011) expanded on these themes and reconceptualized them as lenses for the study of organizational culture: symbolic performance, narrative reproduction, textual reproduction, management, power and politics, technology, and globalization. A *lens* is a particular orientation that sharpens, or brings into focus, some specific aspect of organizational culture. Since any lens by itself is incomplete, Keyton argued that treating analytical strategies as lenses allows each to have both merit and limitations. As a result, multiple lenses can be used in combination to reveal different cultural elements and interpretations. Moreover, multiple lenses acknowledge the complexity of organizational life. This next section explores the research contributions since 2001 of communication scholars who embrace these lenses. The section concludes with an updated critique of each lens as a way of examining organizational culture.

Lens of Symbolic Performance. As Eisenberg and Riley (2001) described, research from a symbolic-performance lens examines both routine and unique communication—specifically, any communication responsible for the creation, maintenance, and transformation of organizational reality. Using the symbolic-performance lens allows the researcher to examine how culture is brought into being. According to Pacanowsky and O'Donnell-Trujillo (1982), symbolic performance is characterized in four ways. First, organizational performances are created through the interactions of organizational members, as role enactments acknowledge the role(s) of others. Second, organizational performances are contextual, as they occur within a larger set of organizational events. This characteristic highlights the temporal embeddedness of organizational performances and allows for localized meanings to be created. Third, organizational performances are episodic and differentiated from one another by a beginning and end. Fourth, organizational performances are improvisational in that an organization's culture has some structure, but a performance is never fully scripted. Organizational member interactions, structured through routines, procedures, or policies, always vary based on the unique needs of the individuals who are communicating.

In addition to these four characteristics, Pacanowsky and O'Donnell-Trujillo (1982) identified five types of performances. One type of symbolic performance is a *ritual*, or personal, task, social action, or behavior that occurs regularly to punctuate work experiences. How members of a department start their work day by talking about how to meet the day's sales goal exemplifies a ritual. *Social codes* or behaviors can be found in talk in which courtesies and pleasantries of greeting or leaving are exchanged. The symbolic performance of *politics* is evident when employees recruit allies or negotiate with one another. In doing so, employees create political performances of power and control. *Enculturation* refers to the interactions through which organizational members acquire knowledge and skills to be considered competent in their work roles. Learning how to negotiate the organizational reality beyond their jobs is a symbolic performance. The final type of symbolic performance, *passion*, or the heightened description of common workplace activities, is well described in Carmack's (2008) study of ice cream store employees who were required to demonstrate their passion for their product and the organization through singing and dancing while selling their products. Their physical performances were symbolic expressions to their customers and also to themselves. Some employees were enthusiastic in these symbolic displays, while others admitted to faking the passion that they displayed. Carmack's study underscores the point that "performances can be more than symbolic [and] performances can be corporeal as well" (p. 124).

Lens of Narrative Reproduction. The importance of storytelling in organizations has a long history. Storytelling is a device for employees to make sense of their organization; and stories become artifacts laden with an organization's values, norms, and beliefs (Bruner, 1991; Meyer, 1995). Whereas stories are generated from one person's point of view, they become part of the culture as well as convey the organization's culture when stories are told and retold. As a result, the past influences the future (Linde, 2009). Stories are powerful cultural vehicles, because storytelling is never neutral. Why? Because stories relay more information than do factual forms of explanation (Taylor & Van Every, 2000), and they often express the interests of dominant groups (Putnam & Fairhurst, 2001). In other words, stories indicate which values are accepted and which ones are rejected in an organization (Coopman & Meidlinger, 2000). Stories also are used as explanations for how things are done when conflicts or problems arise (Jameson, 2001).

McCarthy (2008) explored the role of employees' stories, or *narratives*, in a multinational shipping company that had offices in Norway, Sweden, the U.S., and Australia. Stories around two critical organizational events (i.e., a company plane crash that killed key organizational members and the organization's merger) and the more general topics of leadership and working environment were captured through open-ended interviews and then coded for story type, value reference, story strength, story tone, and modeling behavior. As expected, McCarthy found that members with longer tenure told more stories that were positive about the organization and in alignment with the organization's espoused values. These findings affirm that organizational members reproduce organizational values and assumptions by "draw[ing] lessons from a deep reservoir of stories" (p. 184).

Lens of Textual Reproduction. Organizational texts that exist in written or digital form provide a fixed view or record of organizational culture (Eisenberg & Riley, 2001). Texts such as mission statements and organizational websites are formal and permanent types of artifacts; organizational texts can also be informal and exist in fleeting forms (e.g., e-mail exchanges). Formal texts are controlled by management and are more likely to focus on espoused values than on enacted values. Policies and procedures describe what should happen, and promotional materials explain the culture from a managerial perspective. Informal organizational texts are more likely to express the enacted culture or what actually happens. Because of the informality and speed associated with e-mails, this textual form can give employees an efficient way to express consent or dissent with organizational values. For example, the Enron e-mail corpus, prior to and during the organization's collapse, revealed that employees used this upward communication medium to first uphold Enron's corporate values and praise its leader, Ken Lay, and then to crucify him. By examining the e-mails across time, Turnage and Keyton (2013) discovered that subcultures of employees bifurcated on their trust in and support for their leader. Despite the impending organizational crisis, some employees maintained their loyalty to the leader and the company's values while others expressed their dissent to Lay by turning the organization's values around to negatively evaluate his behavior.

Lens of Power and Politics. Commonly, the critical perspective is the philosophical foundation for examining organizational culture as the site of power and politics. Chapters 4 (Mumby) and 24 (Zoller) in this volume provide an extensive overview of the theory and review of the literature in this area. Here, I draw upon a critical-research orientation as a way of discovering and investigating organizational culture; this lens embraces "a broad, interdisciplinary body of theory and research that conceives of organizations as dynamic sites of control and resistance" (Mumby, 2008, p. 3427). Specifically, the critical-research orientation examines "the communicative practices through which control and resistance are produced, reproduced, and transformed in the process of organizing" (Mumby, 2008, p. 3427) and "exploration of alternative communication practices that allow greater democracy and more creative and productive cooperation among stakeholders" (Deetz, 2005, p. 85).

Organizations are sites of hierarchy, dominance, and power; and organizational members having varying degrees of power and status as well as varying degrees of control over message creation and meaning. Normative practices are created when the more powerful organizational members get the less powerful ones to accept their views about reality and their values of working. In many cases, the views of the more powerful are not favorable to those who have less power. As a result, the quality of work life (and life more generally) of employees can be negatively affected. A critical-research orientation also uncovers how organizational members understand and contest artifacts, values, and assumptions that they must accept as a condition of employment. In this way, the power over others, the resulting struggle, and even resistance to the power reveal information about an organization's culture.

For example, Fleming's (2005) examination of a call center demonstrates how pushing organizational values on employees can result in a harmful psychological work environment. In this center, management acknowledged that work could be mundane, monotonous, and alienating. As a means of covering up these features, management tried to create a fun and playful environment and promoted it with the slogan, "Remember the 3Fs: Focus, Fun, Fulfillment." Fleming labeled this culture as paternalistic, because the leader and management team promoted themselves as keeping employees' best interests at heart and guiding them with a firm hand. The paternalistic assumptions of management and the promoted value of paternalism were further reinforced as employees were encouraged to dress up as cartoon figures and sing songs designed for and marketed to children. Even the workplace was painted in primary colors, much like a classroom and decorated with cartoon figures. By placing employees as children in a parent-child relationship, the parent (i.e., the CEO or the organization) was always right and always in control. Some employees appeared to enjoy these activities and embraced the paternalistic relationship. Other employees were cynical and sarcastic and viewed the paternalistic values as patronizing. These employees resisted the culture by asserting their adult identities with dignity and maturity and by co-opting the 3F slogan into a vulgar parody.

Issues of gender and race are also associated with the power and politics lens of organizational culture. Because organizational culture is imbued with assumptions and norms drawn from societal culture, organizational culture privileges gender and racial stereotypes of the dominant White culture. For example, Dougherty (2001) examined sexual behaviors in a health care center through feminist standpoint theory. Her analysis revealed that male employees presumed that sexual communication and touching behaviors were not sexual harassment. Since men engaged in these behaviors to cope with stress caused by the work environment, the communication and behaviors could not be sexual harassment, even if they were sexual. Female employees viewed the males' sexual behaviors as normative but neither appropriate nor functional. Thus sexual behavior was functional for one gender group and dysfunctional for the other. Most importantly, with respect to organizational culture, Dougherty's analysis revealed how the power to name certain acts as *good* or *bad* and to determine value judgments for them belonged primarily to the dominant gender group.

Lens of Technology. In organizational life, *technology* refers to any tool used to complete work, from fully mechanical tools such as pencils to fully digital and automated ones such as cloud computing. When an organization's image, identity, and market are dependent upon the production or selling of technology, its vision and values will likely be associated with this technology. As Leonardi and Jackson (2009) explain, technology is viewed as a "practice that entwines itself with other work and communication practices to constitute a culture" (p. 396). These scholars propose the concept of *technological grounding* to distinguish an organization whose image is dependent upon "the functionality of the technology it produces, services, or sells" (p. 397) from an organization in which technology is used but is less central to the company's viability. In a merger of two telecommunications companies, Leonardi and Jackson (2009) discovered that employees in each organization had identities and values associated with the technologies that they produced prior to a merger. The technical superiority of one company's product over the other's translated into organizational superiority, leading the dominant organization to absorb the culture of the other company. Similar to other discursive practices in organizations, technology "cannot be abstracted or extracted from the culture that helps create its function and need" (Leonardi & Jackson, 2009, p. 412). Even when technology is not central to an organization's business model, the adoption of technology changes how employees view work. Specifically, Hylmö (2006) found that telecommuting created differentiated beliefs and values. Employees who telecommuted believed that the work was the same whether done in the office or in remote locations, while employees working in the traditional office setting held negative views of telecommuting. Moreover, those who telecommuted believed that their office colleagues understood the practice of telecommuting, whereas employees working in the office reported having "no idea what telecommuting is" (p. 552). Thus subcultures were created as the organization supported differing views of what constituted an appropriate work environment. To some employees, these views were conflicting:

> On the one hand, employees embraced messages supporting telecommuting by arguing for its positive benefits on mental health. On the other hand, they challenged the consequences of each other's choices of work arrangement by questioning impacts on productivity and work processes facilitated through colleague interactions. (p. 556)

In this case, technology was central (or not) to *how* employees performed their work, and employees adopted organizational messages that supported their choice to telecommute or not.

A study of employees who managed and wrote for an entertainment website (Hendrickson, 2009) is particularly illustrative of the way in which instant messaging (IM) organized and shaped the organizational culture. Hendrickson argued that "even within the realm of virtual teamwork, individuals cultivate internalized knowledge that is then contrasted with data in their environment" (p. 5). In this case, the website was staffed by a managing editor and five editors, each working in their own unique workspace; employees only communicated online via IM. The study revealed that team members' norms for communicating were cultivated by the managing editor and challenged by others on the editorial team. Thus the organization operated in the virtual sphere. The choice to work virtually was made by the managing editor in an effort to tightly control organizational decisions and to increase productivity. Editors, however, reported using IM for relational and nonwork-related messages—a view that stood in contrast to the managing editor, who positioned the nonwork-related use of IM for periods at the end of the day when she believed ("knew") that the work was completed. Hendrickson argued that the workplace culture was a direct result of the organization's use and the managing editor's control of IM as the communication channel. Despite the managing editor's control and the value she placed on nonwork messages, the other editors found ways to circumvent this norm. In this case, technology could have potentially leveled hierarchical differences between the managing editor and the editorial staff. However, the managing editor's norms and values about how IM was to be used increased rather than decreased those differences. IM could have been used for collective communication among everyone, but the managing editor's desire to control workflow ultimately resulted in a spoke-and-wheel communication flow. As a result, to create collegiality, the editorial team bypassed the espoused value and used IM for nonwork messages.

Commentary on the Lenses. A hidden aspect of organizational culture research is that in most instances, researchers do not begin a project or enter the organization to examine organizational culture *per se*. Rather, scholars have an opportunity for organizational entry, often to study some other organizational communication phenomenon, and then discover while there that the explanation for that phenomenon is the organization's culture. (See Smith & Keyton, 2001, and Zoller, 2003, as to how these researchers entered the field and then began to examine organizational culture.) Thus this review of the lenses for examining organizational culture is restricted to those lenses that scholars identify as particular perspectives. The lenses presented here are not exhaustive. Other areas of organizational communication that offer perspectives for studying organizational culture include globalization, temporality, networks, and teams.

Accepting and Rejecting Other Traditions

Perhaps in lieu of theory development, communication scholars have turned to the work of management scholar Martin (1992, 2002) in her book, *Organizational Culture: Mapping the Terrain*. She argues that organizational culture research represents three theoretical perspectives: integration, differentiation, and fragmentation. First, I present Martin's views and describe how communication scholars have used this work, and then I comment on Martin's model.

Integration "focuses on those manifestations of a culture that have mutually consistent interpretations" (Martin, 2002, p. 94). Although not all organizational members need to be in agreement, an organization's culture from this perspective is consistent, clear, and consensual. When an aspect of an organization's culture deviates from the norm, it is characterized as a "regrettable shortfalls from an integrated ideal" (p. 99) rather than as a change or opportunity worth pursuing. Differentiation, in contrast, focuses "on cultural manifestations that have inconsistent interpretations" (p. 101). Cultural inconsistencies, for example, can occur when executives verbally promote one set of organizational values, and frontline management promotes another. When cultural inconsistencies occur, subcultures are likely to develop. Typically, artifacts, values, and assumptions are consistent within a subculture, but subcultures, then, are differentiated from one another. Often, this type of differentiation leads to conflict, but not always. Subcultures can also exist in harmony or be independent from one another. When subcultures exist, ambiguity occurs "in the interstices among subcultural 'islands' of consistency, consensus, and clarity" (pp. 103–104). Finally, fragmentation focuses on ambiguity, which can arise from a lack of clarity, confusion, or ignorance. As Martin (2002) describes it, fragmentation "also encompasses the complications that the clear oppositions of dichotomous thinking omit" (p. 104). These complications emerge as ironies, paradoxes, or contradictions that make it impossible to use clarity as an analytical device for identifying subcultures. As a result, ambiguity can become a normal aspect of organizational life.

Martin describes each metatheory as a worldview that emphasizes some features of organizational culture and obscures or hides others. Further, the three perspectives are incommensurate to the degree that only by using all three can a researcher construct a comprehensive representation of an organization's culture.

> A particular culture is not more, or less, accurately represented by [any] one of these perspectives. There is no such [thing] as an 'integrated culture' or a 'fragmented culture.' There can, however, be a culture viewed from the integration perspective and such a view is incomplete until that culture is examined from the differentiation and fragmentation perspectives. (Martin, 2002, p. 156)

Martin's model of organizational culture has influenced communication scholars, since it (1) resonates with a communicative approach to the study of organizations and organizational communication, (2) is useful as a heuristic device, and (3) provides clear, distinct labels through which to communicate the complexity of organizational culture to scholars and practitioners.

Martin's ideas, however, have been challenged by Taylor and his colleagues (Taylor, Irvin, & Wieland, 2006), who identified advantages, problems, and implications for communication scholars. Taylor et al.'s review of the communication scholarship on organizational culture revealed five benefits of Martin's metatheory of organizational culture. First, by using the epistemological metaphor of *worldviews*, communication scholars are "able to develop sophisticated and heuristic representations of organizational culture" (p. 308). For example, Eisenberg, Murphy, and Andrews (1998) use integration, differentiation, and fragmentation to create a multivocal approach to the study of organizational culture. These authors discuss their findings in this way:

> Each perspective appears as a very different version of the same event [a search for a university provost]. From an integration perspective, the search process was a sensible progression of events based on clearly articulated criteria and shared meanings. From a differentiation perspective, the process revealed cultures within cultures, people and groups divided with inconsistent meanings and goals. Finally, the fragmentation narrative exposed the search process as rife with confusion and ambiguity. (pp. 16–17)

Secondly, Martin's metatheory advances the "decentering and dereification by communication scholars of 'the organization' as an objective phenomenon" (p. 308). Communication scholars Hylmö and Buzzanell (2002) describe this characteristic as a benefit, because multiple perspectives are necessary to represent the plurality and simultaneity of organizational realities. Specifically, "Martin's three cultural lenses provided different analyses that individually supplied fresh insights into telecommuting practices and processes, but that collectively displayed the interwoven nature of telecommuting realities" (p. 346). Third, communication scholars' use of Martin's theory reveals that each perspective yields useful cultural interpretations that confirm "that communication and culture are not discrete attributes of an organization" (Taylor et al., 2006, p. 309). Rather, "communication is the key process through which the cultural nexus is performed" (Eisenberg et al., 1998, p. 17).

Fourth, Martin's metatheory "facilitates the development of diverse explanations of organizational communication" (Taylor et al., 2006, p. 309). As Eisenberg et al. (1998) detailed:

> As interviewers, we witnessed numerous instances of people constituting the meaning of events. The tales they told were to us in context. In light of this, we found Martin's (1992) three perspectives (integration, differentiation, and fragmentation) to best be thought of as rhetorical resources that organizational actors use to communicate with an audience. From a rhetorical view, different participants choose a perspective because it works at a given time for a given audience. They shift their accounts when the perceived audience changes and when they have different communication demands. (p. 21)

Finally, Martin's metatheory fosters a position "consistent with postmodernist calls for researchers to reflect on their claims as constructed fictions and on 'the rhetorical, political, and practical consequences of selecting one interpretation over another'" (Taylor et al., 2006, p. 309). As a result, Martin's metatheory has facilitated interpretive and critical studies of organizational culture (Taylor et al., 2006).

Despite the popularity of Martin's model, criticisms exist. Taylor et al. (2006) draw upon two reviews of Martin's book by communication scholars (i.e., Brummans & Putnam, 2003; Mumby, 1994) to identify three problems with its use. First, the metatheory conflates "ontological and epistemological claims within—and between—paradigms" (Taylor et al., 2006, p. 310). As Taylor et al. (2006) explain, Martin's "claims about organizational culture research become confounded with claims about the nature of organizational culture [itself]" (p. 314). That is, the model can lead researchers to use the integration, differentiation, and fragmentation perspectives as *a priori* conceptual devices without excavating an organizational culture for what naturally exists and is occurring. Also problematic is Martin's claim that organizational members' communicative practices are fragmented, integrated, or ambiguous. In this case, the behaviors of organizational members are one and the same thing with the researcher's conceptualization of these behaviors. "No longer are organizational members acting in an empirical manner that supports the validity of a particular construct as a resource for explaining that social action: Instead, they are 'doing' the construct" (Taylor et al., 2006, p. 315).

A second criticism is that "Martin's metatheory is characterized by residual objectivism" (Taylor et al., 2006, p. 310). That is, the structure of Martin's presentation of the metatheory as selective and partial undermines the theoretical and the conceptual contributions of it (Mumby, 1994). A third concern is that "Martin's metatheory mistakenly encourages its users to view communicative practices as the manifestation of preexisting meanings, rather than as the means of their creation, reproduction, and transformation" (p. 311). In other words, Martin's metatheory does not emphasize or explain how culture arises from talk or text—a hallmark of organizational communication studies. Undoubtedly, these problems arise, in part, because communication scholars who embrace this typology have adopted a theoretical framework from another discipline. Still, it is incumbent upon communication scholars to move organizational culture from a cognitive phenomenon to a communicative one.

Ultimately, Taylor et al. identify several sets of implications for using Martin's organizational culture metatheory. The first set centers around how organizational culture phenomena are conceptualized; that is, integration, differentiation, and fragmentation cannot be simultaneously discourses that constitute organizational culture, preexisting objective phenomena, and "incommensurable-yet-heuristic discourses generated by analysts that bear no corresponding relationship to the reality of organizational culture" (2006, p. 317). Too frequently, Martin's ideas about integration, differentiation, and fragmentation are adopted in communicative studies of organizational culture without asking these questions: What are integration, differentiation, and fragmentation? Where, how, and when do these phenomena exist? How are they associated with, reflective of, or related to communication? (Taylor et al., 2006). In other words, adopting the theories of other scholars, especially ones from other disciplines, can only be done well when researchers acknowledge their reasons for the adoption and their commitments to (or revisions of) the underlying assumptions of the theories.

The second set of implications focuses on reconciling claims that arise from the use of integration, differentiation, and fragmentation perspectives. Taylor et al. (2006) provide two suggestions for communication scholars. First, the authors offer Parker's (2000) more consistent ontological and epistemological position:

> Organizational culture is a process which is locally produced by people, but . . . can also be usefully talked about as a thing with particular effects on people. In other words, . . . [organizational culture] is both a verb and a noun. (p. 83)

This view is consistent with Fairhurst and Putnam's (2004) becoming-realism perspective on organizational discourse and places *discourse* and *interaction* as the primary objects of organizational culture studies. Taylor et al. (2006) also identify Eisenberg et al.'s (1998) use of Martin's metatheory as an exemplar for how communication scholars can adopt theory from another discipline and retain the assumptions that "communication constitutes the social reality of organization, that this reality is plural, and that it is constructed locally and socially" (p. 320).

The second suggestion that Taylor et al. (2006) propose is to adopt Fairhurst and Putnam's (2004) grounded-in-action position from organizational discourse analysis. Here, discourse and organization are mutually constitutive. In such a case, the researcher would ask, "How is organizational culture grounded in the flow of discourse practices of organizational members?" Moving research questions about organizational culture to these types of issues would allow communication scholars to "engage integration, differentiation, and fragmentation as heuristic classifications of ontologically hybrid phenomena that are not reducible to cognitive perspectives" (p. 324).

Discussion and Conclusions

Very purposely, this chapter has focused on ways that communication scholars examine organizational culture. Certainly, we have drawn upon definitions, concepts, and theories from other disciplines, but we have also developed a communicative focus of organizational culture that is distinct from other disciplines. With a communicative perspective, scholars have moved from a focus on how managers or leaders influence organizational members to one that includes organizational members at all levels. In doing so, we have a better understanding of not only organizational culture as an emerging and organizing phenomenon but also how informal communication in organizations contributes to and influences organizational culture. That is, a communication perspective on organizational culture demonstrates that out-of-role and informal communication are as much a part of organizational culture as formal communication practices and messages.

Most predominantly, what underscores a communicative focus is employees' sensemaking of their social and symbolic realities created from their interactions (Keyton, 2011). Communication scholars have developed this unique focus by accepting that artifacts, values, and assumptions comprise organizational culture. Thus the descriptive device for theory building appears firm. Indeed, a strength of organizational culture scholarship is that it has moved beyond making distinctions between the artifact-values-assumptions framework to examining ways in which culture is produced, enacted, and communicated in organizations.

Over time, the contributions of communication scholars have become clear. Eisenberg and Riley (2001) point to five of these contributions. First, a communication perspective highlights the symbolic nature of day-to-day conversations and routines practices. Communication researchers emphasizes that culture is present in all acts of communicative behavior. Their position supports the existence and identification of other lenses. Second, a communication perspective emphasizes both action and interpretation. That is, communicative actions (e.g., verbal or written messages, an informal conversation among colleagues) become organizational culture as members interpret and comment on these actions. Third, a communication perspective acknowledges the role of societal patterns and norms in facilitating or constraining individuals within organizational culture. Clearly, internal organizational influences are central to organizational culture, but regional, national, and other societal dynamics permeate day-to-day interactions in organizations.

Fourth, a communication perspective honors a wide range of researcher-organization relationships from intimate to more distant. While previously, some organizational culture research was based on traditional hypothetical-deductive reasoning or survey studies, scholars have demonstrated that qualitative, interpretive research may be better suited for identifying an organization's cultural tendencies. Still, there is a range of how embedded the researcher is (or can be) in the organization. Some organizational culture research is conducted through studying organizational artifacts at a distance, while other organizational culture research is conducted through prolonged direct observation (and sometimes participation). Fifth, a communication perspective on organizational culture legitimates motives for its study. In other words, motives for studies can be found in the practical concerns of management or employees or in the desire to inform and empower multiple organizational stakeholders. Smircich (1983) adds a sixth contribution of communication scholars; that is, organizational culture provides a conceptual bridge between the micro and macro levels of organizations. Aspects of organizational culture exist at many levels of analysis. An employee's communication can be observed and then interpreted against the background of his or her peers. The interactions and negotiated meanings of employees in one division can be compared with those of employees in another division. Across these levels of analysis, organizational culture scholars connect the everyday experiences of members to the whole of the organization.

Less clear, but becoming clearer, are the lenses through which to study organizational culture. A lens, which crystalizes and focuses researchers' attention on a specific organizational communication phenomenon, could be an explanatory device for how organizational culture is developed, maintained, or challenged. Unfortunately, too few scholars clearly articulate which, if any, lens they use in their analyses. Thus scholars have not determined the scope of possible lenses. However, implicit use of some lenses (e.g., symbolic performance, narrative reproduction, textual reproduction, power and politics) by communication scholars suggests that these approaches are uncontested. Clearly, organizational communication scholarship has shifted away from the management lens. The lenses of technology and globalization are more recent additions. A few studies have used the technology lens; even fewer have published organizational culture research from a globalization lens. These are areas in which communication scholars could contribute to theory development in organizational culture. A criticism of this area of scholarship is that the concept of organizational culture is often used in a casual way. That is, the concept appears as a keyword in an article, but the scope of the analytical project or the design of the research project does not place primary emphasis on organizational culture. As a result, discoveries about culture are a byproduct of the central object of a study (see, for example, Cotter & Marschall, 2006; Elson, 2007; Myers, 2005). We learn about the culture of the organization studied, but organizational culture *per se* is addressed only peripherally. Likewise, organizational culture is often positioned as a vehicle through which to study other organizational phenomena (e.g., organizational spirituality; Sass, 2000). While these studies provide insights about organizational culture, they fail to explore the cultural aspects of organizational communication fully.

Conversations with other scholars and close readings of method sections reveal the secondary ways in which communication scholars locate organizations to study cultures. Scholars do not enter an organization to explore the entirety of its communication practices and processes; rather, they enter it to examine some aspect of communication. When scholars have extended access to organizational life, members' residual communication, such as identity and change, become more obvious and reveal features of organizational culture. It is for this reason that many of the same topical interests of the general organizational communication literature are reflected in the organizational culture literature.

Overwhelmingly, communication scholars are relying on philosophical perspectives and methodologies that require time in the field to capture the richness and depth of organizational discourse from which to make judgments about organizational culture. While this type of scholarship has the benefit of producing rich and detailed accounts of organizational culture that are both theory-generative and theory-contextualizing, it all but precludes the opportunity for theory testing. This limitation is not a problem in communication scholarship *per se*, but it limits the applications that scholars can generate and deliver to practitioners, management, and employees as well as the teachable advice for students.

A recommendation for scholars who conduct organizational culture research is to consider carefully what a comprehensive model of communication and organizational culture might include. With the lens approach, our studies are partial, leaving other aspects of organizational culture hidden. This partial examination most likely results from the difficulty of gaining organizational entry and time restrictions for fieldwork (both necessary and practical concerns for researchers). One way to overcome this challenge might be to use a multiresearcher and multilayered methodological approach. It is here that a multiple-lens approach could be beneficial, theoretically and practically. How, for example, are the power and politics in an organization influenced by members' use and understanding of technology? Could using the technology lens to explore organizational culture reveal differential meanings derived from organizational texts?

Earlier, Deetz (1988) argued that the goals of organizational culture studies should be to understand how employees create meanings at a particular time and location and to demonstrate how making sense of work lives provides basic information about cultural processes. Organizational culture scholarship has accomplished the first part of this goal. The next step is to create models and theories with greater generalizability as to *how* those processes occur. Asking "How are the spaces among artifacts, values, and assumptions negotiated by organizational members?" and "What meanings do organizational members derive from those negotiated spaces?" may lead to understanding the processes by which organizational culture emerges, changes, and declines. If culture-creating communication processes and practices are specific to an organization or location, we need to identify these features directly in research reports. Certainly, communication scholars need to be vigilant about the specifics *and* the generalities that capture organizational culture. Communication scholars can make these contributions by asking, "What does this study tell us about organizational culture specifically and in general?" and "Generally, what does this study of organizational culture tell us about organizational communication?" Authors of organizational culture research should also ask, "What theoretical, methodological, or practical considerations (or advances) are made with this study?" The communicative study of organizational culture could be the frame through which organizational power and politics, the use of technology, and globalization, for example, could be further explored, especially if scholars were to reverse the research frame. Rather than entering an organization to study one aspect or domain of its culture (e.g., its power and politics), scholars could study an organization's culture to better understand its power and politics. Taking this approach closely aligns with the grounded-in-action orientation (Bisel et al., 2010). Focusing on meaning negotiation in the interstices of organizational communication could drive the contributions of organizational culture research.

References

Alvesson, M. (2004). Organizational culture and discourse. In D. Grant, C. Hardy, C. Oswick, & L. Putnam (Eds.), *The SAGE handbook of organizational discourse* (pp. 317–333). Thousand Oaks, CA: SAGE.

Bantz, C. R. (1993). *Understanding organizations: Interpreting organizational communication cultures.* Columbia: University of South Carolina Press.

Becker, H. S., & Geer, B. (1960). Latent culture: A note on the theory of latent social roles. *Administrative Science Quarterly, 5*(2), 304–313.

Bisel, R. B., Messersmith, A. S., & Keyton, J. (2010). Understanding organizational culture and communication through a gyroscope metaphor. *Journal of Management Education, 34*(3), 342–366. doi:10.1177/1052562909340879

Bormann, E. G. (1982). Fantasy and rhetorical vision. Ten years later. *Quarterly Journal of Speech, 68*(3), 283–305.

Bormann, E. G. (1983). Symbolic convergence: Organizational communication and culture. In L. L. Putnam & M. Pacanowsky (Eds.), *Communication and organizations: An interpretive approach.* (pp. 99–122). Beverly Hills, CA: SAGE.

Bormann, E. G. (1985). Symbolic convergence theory: A communication formulation. *Journal of Communication, 35*(4), 128–138. doi:10.1111/j.1460-2466.1985.tb02977.x

Brummans, B. H., & Putnam, L. L. (2003). Review of the book *Organizational culture: Mapping the terrain* and the book *Understanding organizational culture. Organization, 10*(3), 640–644.

Bruner, J. (1991, Autumn). The narrative construction of reality. *Critical Inquiry, 18*(1), 1–21.

Bullis, C. A., & Tompkins, P. K. (1989). The forest ranger revisited: A study of control practices and identification. *Communication Monographs, 56*(4), 287–306. doi:10.1080/03637758909390266

Carmack, H. J. (2008). "The ultimate ice cream experience": Performing passion as expression of organizational culture. *Ohio Communication Journal, 46,* 109–129.

Coopman, S. J., & Meidlinger, K. B. (2000). Power, hierarchy, and change: The stories of a Catholic parish staff. *Management Communication Quarterly, 13*(4), 567–625. doi:10.1177/0893318900134002

Cotter, C., & Marschall, D. (2006). The persistence of workplace ideology and identity across communication contexts. *Journal of Applied Linguistics, 3*(1), 1–24.

Deal, T. E., & Kennedy, A. A. (1982). *Corporate cultures: The rites and rituals of corporate life.* Reading, MA: Addison-Wesley.

Deetz, S. A. (1988). Cultural studies: Studying meaning and action in organizations. In J. A. Anderson (Ed.), *Communication yearbook* (vol. 11, pp. 335–345). Newbury Park, CA: SAGE.

Deetz, S. A. (1994). Future of the discipline: The challenges, the research, and the social contribution. In S. A. Deetz (Ed.), *Communication yearbook* (vol. 17, pp. 565–600). Thousand Oaks, CA: SAGE.

Deetz, S. A. (2005). Critical theory. In S. May & D. K. Mumby (Eds.), *Engaging organizational communication theory & research* (pp. 85–111). Thousand Oaks, CA: SAGE.

Deetz, S. A., & Kersten, A. (1983). Critical models of interpretive research. In L. L. Putnam & M. E. Pacanowsky (Eds.), *Communication and organizations: An interpretive approach* (pp. 147–171). Beverly Hills, CA: SAGE.

Dougherty, D. S. (2001). Sexual harassment as [dys] functional process: A feminist standpoint analysis. *Journal of Applied Communication Research, 29*(4), 372–402. doi:10.1080/00909880128116

Dougherty, D. S. (2011). *The reluctant farmer: An exploration of work, social class & the production of food.* Leicester, UK: Troubador.

Dougherty, D. S., & Smythe, M. J. (2004). Sensemaking, organizational culture, and sexual harassment. *Journal of Applied Communication Research, 32*(4), 293–317. doi:10.1080/0090988042000275998

Eisenberg, E. M., Murphy, A., & Andrews, L. (1998). Openness and decision making in the search for a university provost. *Communication Monographs, 65*(1), 1–23. doi:10.1080/03637759809376432

Eisenberg, E. M., & Riley, P. (2001). Organizational culture. In F. M. Jablin & L. L. Putnam (Eds.), *The new handbook of organizational communication: Advances in theory, research, and methods* (pp. 291–322). Thousand Oaks, CA: SAGE.

Elson, O. T. (2007). Gender-agency as communicated in the intra-interorganizational structures of the Spiritual Baptists of Barbados: A postcolonial account of cultural resistance. *The Howard Journal of Communication, 18*(1), 15–37. doi:10.1080/10646170601147440

Fairhurst, G. T., & Cooren, F. (2004). Organizational language in use: Interaction analysis, conversation analysis and speech act semantics. In D. Grant, C. Hardy, C. Oswick, & L. Putnam (Eds.), *SAGE handbook of organizational discourse* (pp. 131–152). London, England: SAGE.

Fairhurst, G. T., & Putnam, L. (2004). Organizations as discursive constructions. *Communication Theory, 14*(1), 5–26. doi:10.1111/j.1468-2885.2004.tb00301.x

Farace, R., Monge, P., & Russell, H. (1977). *Communicating and organizing.* Reading, MA: Addison-Wesley.

Fleming, P. (2005). Metaphors of resistance. *Management Communication Quarterly, 19*(1), 45–66. doi:10.1177/0893318905276559

Hendrickson, E. (2009). Good for business? Instant messaging at a virtual newsroom. *Journal of Magazine and New Media Research, 11*(1), 1–20. Retrieved from http://aejmcmagazine.arizona.edu/Journal/Fall2009/Hendrickson_IM.pdf

Hylmö, A. (2006). Telecommuting and the contestability of choice: Employee strategies to legitimize personal decisions to work in a preferred location. *Management Communication Quarterly, 19*(4), 541–569. doi:10.1177/0893318905284762

Hylmö, A., & Buzzanell, P. M. (2002). Telecommuting as viewed through cultural lenses: An empirical investigation of the discourses of utopia, identity, and mystery. *Communication Monographs, 69*(4), 329–356. doi:10.1080/03637750216547

Jacques, E. (1951). *The changing culture of a factory: A study of authority and participation in an industrial setting.* London, England: Tavistock.

Jameson, D. A. (2001). Narrative discourse and management action. *Journal of Business Communication, 38*(4), 476–511. doi:10.1177/002194360103800404

Keyton, J. (2011). *Communication and organizational culture: A key to understanding work experiences* (2nd ed.). Thousand Oaks, CA: SAGE.

Leonardi, P. M., & Jackson, M. H. (2009). Technological grounding: Enrolling technology as a discursive resource to justify cultural change in organizations. *Science, Technology, & Human Values, 34*(3), 393–418. doi:10.1177/0162243908328771

Linde, C. (2009). *Working the past: Narrative and institutional memory*. New York, NY: Harper & Row.

Martin, J. (1992). *Culture in organizations: Three perspectives.* New York, NY: Oxford University Press.

Martin, J. (2002). *Organizational culture: Mapping the terrain.* Thousand Oaks, CA: SAGE.

Mayo, E. (1934). Revery and industrial fatigue. *Journal of Personnel Research, 3*(8), 273–281.

McCarthy, J. F. (2008). Short stories at work: Storytelling as an indicator of organizational commitment. *Group & Organization Management, 33*(2), 163–193. doi:10.1177/1059601108314582

Meyer, J. C. (1995). Tell me a story: Eliciting organizational values from narratives. *Communication Quarterly, 43*(2), 210–224. doi:10.1080/01463379509369970

Mumby, D. K. (1994). Review of the book, *Cultures in organizations. Academy of Management Review, 19*(1), 156–159.

Mumby, D. K. (2008). Organizational communication: Critical approaches. In W. Donsbach (Ed.), *International Encyclopedia of Communication* (vol. VIII, pp. 3427–3433). Oxford, England: Blackwell. doi: 10.1111/b.9781405131995.2008.x Retrieved from http://www.communicationencyclopedia.com/public/

Myers, K. K. (2005). A burning desire: Assimilation into a fire department. *Management Communication Quarterly, 18*(3), 344–384. doi:10.1177/0893318904270742

Pacanowsky, M. E., & O'Donnell-Trujillo, N. (1982). Communication and organizational cultures. *Western Journal of Speech Communication, 46*(2), 115–130.

Pacanowsky, M. E., & O'Donnell-Trujillo, N. (1983). Organizational communication as cultural performance. *Communication Monographs, 50*(2), 126–147. doi:10.1080/03637758309390158

Parker, M. (2000). *Organizational culture and identity: Unity and division at work.* Thousand Oaks, CA: SAGE.

Pepper, G. L., & Larson, G. S. (2006). Cultural identity tensions in a post-acquisition organization. *Journal of Applied Communication Research, 34*(1), 49–71. doi:10.1080/00909880500420267

Peters, T. J., & Waterman, R. J. (1982). *In search of excellence.* New York, NY: Harper & Row.

Pettigrew, A. M. (1979). On studying organizational cultures. *Administrative Science Quarterly, 24*(4), 570–581.

Putnam, L. L. (1983). The interpretive perspective: An alternative to functionalism. In L. L. Putnam & M. E. Pacanowsky (Eds.), *Communication and organizations: An interpretive approach* (pp. 31–54). Beverly Hills, CA: SAGE.

Putnam, L. L., & Fairhurst, G. T. (2001). Discourse analysis in organizations. In F. M. Jablin & L. L. Putnam (Eds.), *The new handbook of organizational communication: Advances in theory, research, and methods* (pp. 78–150). Thousand Oaks, CA: SAGE.

Putnam, L. L., & Pacanowsky, M. E. (Eds.). (1983). *Communication and organizations: An interpretive approach.* Beverly Hills, CA. SAGE.

Sass, J. S. (2000). Characterizing organizational spirituality: An organizational communication culture approach. *Communication Studies, 51*(3), 195–217.

Schein, E. H. (1985). *Organizational culture and leadership: A dynamic view.* San Francisco, CA: Jossey-Bass.

Schein, E. H. (2004). *Organizational culture and leadership* (3rd ed.). San Francisco, CA: Jossey-Bass.

Smircich, L. (1983). Concepts of culture and organizational analysis. *Administrative Science Quarterly, 28*(3), 339–358.

Smith, F., & Keyton, J. (2001). Organizational storytelling: Metaphors for relational power and identity struggles. *Management Communication Quarterly, 15*(2), 149–182. doi:10.1177/0893318901152001

Taylor, B. C., Irvin, L. R., & Wieland, S. M. (2006). Checking the map: Critiquing Joanne Martin's metatheory of organizational culture and its uses in communication research. *Communication Theory, 16*(3), 304–332. doi:10.1111/j.1468-2885.2006.00272.x

Taylor, J. R., & Van Every, E. J. (2000). *The emergent organization: Communication as its site and surface.* Mahwah, NJ: Lawrence Erlbaum.

Tompkins, P. K., Fisher, J. Y., Infante, D. A., & Tompkins, E. L. (1975). Kenneth Burke and the inherent characteristics of formal organizations: A field study. *Speech Monographs, 42*(2), 135–142. doi:10.1080/03637757509375887

Trice, H. M., & Beyer, J. M. (1984). Studying organizational cultures through rites and ceremonials. *Academy of Management Review, 9*(4), 653–669. doi:10.5465/AMR.1984.4277391

Trice, H. M., & Beyer, J. M. (1993). *The cultures of work organizations.* Englewood Cliffs, NJ: Prentice Hall.

Turnage, A., & Keyton, J. (2013). Ethical contradictions and e-mail communication at Enron Corporation. In S. May (Ed.), *Case studies in organizational communication: Ethical perspectives and practices* (2nd ed., pp. 87–97). Thousand Oaks, CA: SAGE.

Weick, K. E. (1979). *The social psychology of organizing* (2nd ed.). Reading, MA: Addison-Wesley.

Weick, K. E. (1995). *Sensemaking in organizations.* Thousand Oaks, CA: SAGE.

Zoller, H. M. (2003). Health on the line: Identity and disciplinary control in employee occupational health and safety discourse. *Journal of Applied Communication Research, 31*(2), 118–139. doi:10.1080/0090988032000064588

CHAPTER 23

Organizational Emotions and Compassion at Work

Katherine Miller

A reader perusing scholarship in organizational communication (or related fields such as management, organization studies, and industrial/organizational psychology) in the mid to late period of the 20th century would notice several patterns. Until the last two decades of that century, scholarship was marked by a clear and consistent privileging of particular kinds of processes, outcomes, and settings. First, in terms of processes, work in organizational studies and organizational communication favored rationality and logic. Research emphasized processes such as decision making, conflict resolution, information flow, leadership, and the orderly socialization of new organizational members. Second, research during this time period emphasized the importance of instrumental outcomes. The dependent variables of choice in scholarship involved individual and organizational effectiveness and efficiency and concepts that could in some way contribute to the bottom line of organizational success. Third, in terms of research setting, scholarly interest was largely vested in for-profit businesses—organizations for which these bottom-line instrumental values held particular sway. During these years, when emotions were mentioned, they were framed in instrumental terms as affective outcomes that might influence effectiveness, efficiency, and profitability. Researchers considered *satisfaction with work* because it might enhance an employee's productivity and investigated stress in the workplace in large part because stressed-out workers were less effective and more likely to leave the organization. The hegemonic influence of profit, rationality, and instrumental outcomes continues to exert its force today in much of academia and popular culture. Trends ranging from knowledge management and learning organizations to "moneyball" strategies in baseball (Lewis, 2003) all emphasize the importance of cool heads and logical thinking in the pursuit of organizational effectiveness and profit.

During the last several decades, however, there has been a marked movement away from this emphasis on rationality and instrumentality. This shift can be seen in a variety of specific turning points and trends. One important theoretical shift with reverberations throughout organization studies was instigated by communication scholars Mumby and Putnam. In the early 1990s, these scholars focused a critical and feminist lens on the dominance of rational and instrumental frameworks in conceptualizations of organizational life (Mumby & Putnam, 1992; Putnam & Mumby, 1993). In their post-structuralist critique, Mumby and Putnam (1992) argue that traditional scholarship in organizational studies, such as Simon's concept of *bounded rationality* (Simon, 1976), draws on a cognitive metaphor in which "mental processes are valorized, whereas physical and emotional experiences are marginalized" (Mumby & Putnam, 1992, p. 470). These scholars deconstruct the concept of *bounded rationality* and propose the value of theorizing *bounded emotionality* instead—an "alternative mode of organizing in which nurturance, caring, community, supportiveness, and interrelatedness are fused with individual responsibility to shape organizational experiences" (Mumby & Putnam, 1992, p. 474).

This theoretical move was accompanied by other shifts in the study of organizational processes. For example, since the late 1980s, communication scholars (and other organizational researchers) have increasingly turned their attention toward nonprofit and human service organizations in which the instrumental pursuit of profit is replaced by goals such as the provision of health services, social welfare, and care provision (see Miller & Considine, 2009, for review). In the late 1990s, the positive-psychology movement began (Seligman & Csikszentmihalyi, 2000) and soon spawned widespread interest in positive organizational studies that emphasize "dynamics that are typically described by words such as excellence, thriving, flourishing, abundance, resilience, and virtuousness" (Cameron, Dutton, & Quinn, 2003, p. 4). This kind of work represents another move away from a strictly rational view of the workplace in embracing "an expanded perspective that includes instrumental concerns but puts an increased emphasis on ideas of 'goodness' and human potential" (Cameron et al., 2003, p. 4). And, in the popular management press, purveyors of the concept of *emotional intelligence* (e.g., Goleman, 1995) argued that some people are better at understanding and managing emotions in the workplace. Though proponents of emotional intelligence were clearly advocating an understanding of emotion as a tool for enhancing instrumental organizational outcomes (Dougherty & Krone, 2002; Fineman, 2000), the popularity of the concept pointed to a growing dissatisfaction with a purely rational and logical view of organizational life.

To a greater or lesser extent, all of these movements toward the consideration of emotion in the workplace trace their lineage back to a common influential work—*The Managed Heart* by Hochschild (1979, 1983). Hochschild's classic work was based on a study of flight attendants and bill collectors (the "toe and heel of capitalism"—Hochschild, 1983, p. 16) and pointed to the importance of emotional control in service sector jobs. Hochschild argued that employees in such jobs are governed by *feeling rules* that dictate the appropriate emotion in various work situations. In interacting with customers and clients, employees are governed by display rules about the ways to "induce or suppress feeling in order to sustain the outward countenance that produces the proper state of mind in others" (Hochschild, 1983, p. 7). Further, because the displays of emotion are prescribed by the organization, they are commodities—emotion labor performed to enhance organizational profits. Though scholars studying emotion in the workplace often disagree with some of Hochschild's ideas and many have taken very different directions in research, it is hard to find contemporary work in this area that does not either rely explicitly on many of Hochschild's concepts or at least provide an homage citing of her work. Thus *The Managed Heart* could be seen as a *paradigm study* (Kuhn, 1962) that continues to shape scholarship investigating emotion in organizational settings.

This chapter will consider a wide array of scholarship considering emotion and organizing that has grown from these roots and flourished in recent decades. Interestingly, researchers studying workplace emotion rarely consider the foundational question of what emotion is—the key point for many scholars is that they are studying processes that are distinct from the rational ones considered in traditional organizational scholarship. Psychological considerations of emotion often describe a process model in which some kind of antecedent event leads to conscious or unconscious appraisal and "triggers a cascade of response tendencies that manifest across loosely coupled component systems, such as subjective experience, facial expression, and physiological changes" (Fredrickson, 2003, p. 164). Organizational scholars studying emotion would probably be uncomfortable with this very specific definition, however, and also want to include related concepts such as *mood* or general affective traits. As Sandelands and Boudens (2000) note, "psychology . . . thinks feeling is a moment's appraisal of opportunity or threat on the way to approach or avoidance, yet we live among powerful and enduring moods that lack a clear evaluation or motive" (p. 46). Those interested in communication in the workplace would also emphasize the importance of context and of situating emotion within interaction. Sandelands and Boudens (2000) continue, "[A]nd psychology thinks feeling is an individual affair, yet at the office water cooler, or in the tavern or therapist's office, we hear stories of feeling tangled in webs of personal and group relationships" (p. 46). Exemplifying these positions, Tracy (2008) draws on Waldron (1994) and describes a communicative approach to emotion and organizations as "an interactive, negotiated process that is continuously experienced across work groups and relationships" (p. 1) and that involves both display and the social construction of feelings. As Tracy (2008) notes, "[T]hrough interaction and storytelling, employees negotiate cultural expectations of emotion, interpret the emotional displays of others, recreate and make sense of past emotional events, and elicit emotion in others" (p. 1).

The remainder of this chapter will be divided into three major sections. In the first section, I will consider ways in which emotion has been studied as part of the work role by considering the processes of emotion labor and emotion work and the ways in which emotion is an integral part of a wide range of work roles, especially in service occupations. In the second section of the chapter, I will consider the ways in which emotion is played out in organizational life apart from specific role requirements. This section will describe processes in which emotion is experienced and expressed in the midst of workplace relationships, the extent to which communicating about emotion is a specific competency in the workplace, and the rules that guide emotional communication in organizations. In the final section of the chapter, I will look at the special case of compassion in the workplace. This section will cross the boundaries of the first two sections by considering the role of compassion in both the work role (especially in human service occupations) and in workplace life.

Emotion as Part of the Work Role

The concept of *work role* has been central to theorizing in organizational studies for many years. For example, Katz and Kahn (1978) in their classic book, *The Social Psychology of Organizations,* defined the organization as a "system of roles" (p. 78). Though clearly there is much to know about organizational communication processes beyond interaction specified by roles (defined by Zurcher, 1983, p. 11, as "the behavior expected of individuals who occupy particular social categories"), *role behavior* is a critical aspect of organizational life; and communication processes are implicated both in the role-development process (e.g., the leader-member exchange process; see Graen & Scandura, 1987) and in the actual enactment of many roles. Further, though emotion can be a part of any organizational role, it is most strongly implicated in roles that involve interaction with others—especially others in corresponding roles such as customers, clients, patients, and students. Thus it is not surprising that the majority of research investigating emotion as part of the work role has considered individuals employed in some kind of service occupation. A sampling of such occupations investigated by scholars in the communication discipline include flight attendants (Murphy, 1998), workers in emergency call centers (Shuler & Sypher, 2000; Tracy & Tracy, 1998), cruise ship employees (Tracy, 2000), correctional officers (Tracy, 2005), financial advisors (Miller & Koesten, 2008), judges (Scarduzio, 2011), medical technicians and physicians (Morgan & Krone, 2001), college instructors (Miller, 2002), and firefighters (Scott & Myers, 2005).

Emotion can be implicated in role-related communication processes in several ways. For example, Miller, Considine, and Garner (2007) differentiate between *emotional labor* and *emotional work*. Following Hochschild (1979, 1983) and many others, they define *emotional labor* as "the display of largely inauthentic emotions, emotions that are used by management as a commodity that can be controlled, trained, and prescribed in employee handbooks" (Miller et al., 2007, p. 233). Emotional labor, then, could involve emotional communication of a variety of types—smiles and friendliness from a waiter or anger and toughness from a corrections officer—with the commonality that the expression is in the service of occupational goals, is often not genuine, and, at least for some of these roles, is prescribed by management. In contrast, *emotional work* involves largely authentic emotions and is often associated with human service workers (e.g., physicians, nurses, social workers). Clearly, however, these categories are not mutually exclusive, and there are many work roles that involve both kinds of emotional communication—either simultaneously or as different aspects of the work role.

Emotional Labor—Conceptual Origins

Considerations of emotion as part of the work role draw directly on Hochschild's (1979, 1983) early development of the emotional labor concept. Hochschild introduced the notion of *feeling rules* that guide appropriate emotion in social interaction. These feeling rules are sometimes easy to follow but can also involve effort that Hochschild calls *emotion management* or *emotion work*. For example, there are widespread societal expectations that we feel joy at weddings and sorrow at funerals. Though it is often easy to comply with these feeling rules, there also could be situations in which feeling these emotions—and displaying these emotions in interaction—requires effort. Hochschild takes these ideas into the workplace context by arguing that organizations often prescribe specific feelings—or at least the display of those feelings—as part of the work role. It is at this point that emotion management becomes *emotional labor* and integral to a prescribed work performance that contributes to organizational effectiveness and, perhaps, profits. As Mumby and Putnam (1992) describe, emotional labor occurs "when feelings are treated as organizational commodities, when intimate and private feelings are appropriated to public domains, when the mind-body split is amplified, and when cultures are managed through the inculcation of values" (p. 472).

Hochschild (1983) argues that the display of these organizationally sanctioned emotions occurs through several distinct processes. One process, *surface acting*, involves displaying the emotion in interaction (through words, facial expression, or bodily displays) without actually feeing the emotion. As Hochschild explains, "[I]n surface acting we deceive others about what we really feel, but we do not deceive ourselves" (1983, p. 33). In contrast, following the *method acting* ideas of Stanislavski (1965), *deep acting* involves an effort to actually feel the prescribed emotions in order to produce an appropriate display. The contrast here, then, is between the flight attendant pasting on a smile or the flight attendant reminding himself that the irate passenger in 14E may have had a very difficult day and deserves kindness in the air. In either surface acting or deep acting, there is the presumption that the displayed emotion is in some way inauthentic—not a representation of the actor's true feelings. Because of this schism between real and displayed emotion, Hochschild (1983) argues that emotional labor can lead to stress through emotional dissonance (in the case of surface acting) or estrangement from self (in the case of deep acting).

Emotional Labor—Conceptual Development

Since Hochschild's early work, a number of scholars have worked to develop the theoretical implications of emotion as part of the work role. Two efforts by management scholars attempted systematic accounts of the ways in which emotion is part of the work role. Rafaeli and Sutton (1987) proposed a model in which the work context and emotional transactions function as a source of role expectations and in which emotions conveyed in the workplace lead to both organizational and individual outcomes. Similarly, Morris and Feldman (1996) presented a detailed propositional model in which aspects of emotional labor are a function of antecedent variables including gender, task variety, and job autonomy and lead to consequences including job satisfaction and emotional exhaustion. These models served to connect the work of Hochschild and others to larger concerns in the management discipline such as instrumental outcomes, and these authors also questioned the received wisdom at that time, that outcomes of emotional labor were predominantly negative. For example, Rafaeli and Sutton point to positive outcomes of emotional labor, such as financial gain and the physiological benefits of smiling, and comment directly on the occupation that was the focus of Hochschild's research: "[F]light attendants whom the present authors have spoken with take pride in their ability to cope with airborne emergencies by hiding their own fears and offering calm faces to passengers" (Rafaeli & Sutton, 1987, p. 31).

In recent years, scholars have continued to develop and refine theoretical issues and enhance empirical understanding of emotion as part of the work role, particularly emotional labor processes involving inauthentic emotion. For example, Kruml and Geddes (2000) built on the modeling work discussed above, proposing a dimensional model of emotional labor that includes the distinct processes of emotive effort and emotive dissonance (and develops measures for these concepts). Communication scholars have explored the performative and discursive aspects of emotional labor. For example, Tracy's (auto)ethnographic analysis of her work on a large cruise ship (Tracy, 2000) highlighted the ways in which ongoing performances of emotion labor in a total institution (Goffman, 1961) are intertwined with power, self-subordination, and identity. Other scholars have continued this interest in emotional performances, considering the ways in which health care workers improvise or bend the rules of emotional display (Morgan & Krone, 2001) and judges draw on and enhance their power when they deviate from the expectation of emotional neutrality (Scarduzio, 2011).

One important strain of research on emotional labor has considered issues of identity and authenticity. This scholarship is grounded in a central theme of Hochschild's foundational work—that emotional labor can lead to negative outcomes such as stress and burnout because there is a clash between an individual's true feelings and the display of organizationally required emotions (through either deep or surface acting). This fundamental premise suggests the importance of accounting for a worker's identity and identification with the work role. Ashforth and Humphrey (1993) developed a theoretical framework for this work by drawing on social identity theory (Ashforth & Mael, 1989; Tajfel & Turner, 1985) and arguing that the effects of emotional labor are moderated by social and personal identities and an individual's connection to the work role. Following this framework, Ashforth and Tomiuk (2000) argue for a distinction between *surface authenticity* (when an emotional display matches current feelings) and *deep authenticity* (when an emotional display is consistent with an internalized identity regardless of current feelings). Relatedly, Rafaeli and Sutton (1989) suggest a distinction between employees who *fake in good faith* (those who believe that the prescribed emotions should be part of the job) and employees who *fake in bad faith* (those who deny the legitimacy of the organizational demand for emotion). These conceptual developments have been useful in describing the nuanced ways in which identity might be implicated in understanding emotional labor processes. However, these approaches also rely on an essentialist view of the self in which there is a clear distinction between the *fake self* and the *real self* that creates dissonance or estrangement from an authentic identity. Tracy and Trethewey (2005) present an important critique of this distinction and argue for a crystallized view of organizational identity that appreciates the ways in which identity is socially created through interaction and is therefore embedded in many personal, organizational, and institutional discourses that might be contradictory. For example, Haman and Putnam (2008) describe the ways in which emotional labor is embedded within systems of peer interaction and pressure, and Tracy (2005) draws on this problematized view of identity in a post-structuralist examination of correctional officers that "highlights how the ease of emotion work is intricately connected to discourses of power and organizational structures that enable and constrain the construction of identity" (p. 278).

Communication scholars have extended understandings of emotional labor in additional ways as well. For example, Scott and Myers (2005) explored the ways in which firefighters learned about emotion management through processes such as observational information seeking and retrospective surveillance. They also found evidence for the positive outcomes of emotion management (see also Conrad & Witte, 1994), arguing that "emotion labor is in many cases practically beneficial to members, providing emotional equilibrium in trying circumstances" (Scott & Myers, 2005, p. 85). Similarly, Shuler and Sypher (2000) concluded that workers in a 911 call center often sought emotional labor because it enhanced their enjoyment of the work setting. Murphy (1998) provided an alternative to received views of emotional labor by documenting the ways in which flight attendants resisted managerial calls for emotion work through the "hidden transcripts" of backstage interaction. These communication scholars emphasize both the complex nature of emotional labor in the workplace as well as the agency that workers bring to performing their roles in ways that can resist managerial control and provide positive experiences in organizational life.

Emotional Work—Empathy in Human Service Roles

Most scholarship regarding emotion as part of the work role has considered *emotional labor*—that is, emotion that workers would typically describe as inauthentic. Of course, as is clear from the previous discussion, the notion of *authenticity* has been productively problematized in the literature (e.g., Tracy & Trethewey, 2005) and many work roles involve the expression of emotion that involves varying levels of deep acting, surface acting, and "real" feeling. However, there is clearly a difference between the role of emotion for a frontline service worker (e.g., retail clerk, waiter, flight attendant) and a worker in a human service occupation such as health care, social work, teaching, or the ministry (see Miller & Considine, 2009). Scholars considering human service workers have argued that the negative effects (such as stress and burnout) of emotion in these roles are different from those in frontline service roles (Brotheridge & Grandey, 2002; Meyerson, 1998). That is, burnout in direct service roles is described as an outgrowth of the emotional dissonance created by faking emotion in interaction. In contrast, burnout in human service organizations can be seen as arising from the ideological grounding of caring professions (Meyerson, 1994) and from the challenges of caring for others in need.

In communication, a consideration of emotional work in human service occupations can be seen in scholarship conducted by Miller and her colleagues (Miller, Stiff, & Ellis, 1988) investigating the ways in which empathy and communicative responsiveness can lead to both more effective caregiving and to stress and burnout. Miller et al. (1988) originally proposed a model that illustrated the distinct effects of two types of empathy in emotional work. Specifically, empathic concern (or feeling "for" the client) enhances communicative responsiveness, while emotional contagion (a parallel experience of feeling "with" the client) detracts from responsiveness. In turn, workers who are less responsive to clients (in part because of their high levels of emotional contagion) are more likely to feel the stress and burnout associated with emotional work in the human services. Maslach (1982), a leading scholar on burnout, explains that

> emotional [contagion] is really a sort of weakness or vulnerability rather than a strength. The person whose feelings are easily aroused (but not necessarily easily controlled) is going to have far more difficulty in dealing with emotionally stressful situations than the person who is less excitable and more psychologically detached. (p. 70)

The model originally tested with psychiatric hospital staff by Miller et al. (1988) has been supported by research considering workers who provide services for homeless clients (Miller, Birkholt, Scott, & Stage, 1995), nurses (Omdahl & O'Donnell, 1999), and financial planners (Miller & Koesten, 2008). The takeaway from these studies is that when emotional communication in the workplace could be characterized as more *genuine,* without the involvement of deep or surface acting, stress is more likely to result from the pain of overinvolvement rather than the dissonance of *faking it* with clients. As a result, human service professionals have traditionally been advised to take a stance of *detached concern* (Lief & Fox, 1963) in which workers practice a simultaneous distance from and sensitivity toward their clients. Recently, however, one of the scholars who coined the term *detached concern* has suggested that in many settings, a more appropriate stance is increased attention to felt emotion in the form of "noticing how you feel" (Fox, 2006).

Emotion as Part of the Work Role—Moving Forward

The last decade of the 20th century and first decade of the 21st century were marked by extensive research exploring and explicating the ways in which emotion is deployed and displayed as part of work roles. This scholarship often owed a large debt to the work of Hochschild and was productive in developing the concept of emotional labor and demonstrating both its complexity and its integral place in organizational life. Notably, much of this research has been conducted by communication scholars. Moving forward from this work, however, it is important that researchers avoid the trap of cookie-cutter research. That is, there is a seductive pull toward research that simply documents the existence and operation of emotional labor and emotional work in a new occupation or context. At this point, we should not be surprised that emotional processes are implicated in a very wide range of work roles, so documenting those processes in yet another occupational group opens scholars to the questions of "So what?" and "Didn't we already know that?" Avoiding these dismissive questions requires that scholars seek to answer important questions that are still outstanding regarding emotion and communication as part of the work role. Several avenues hold particular promise in this regard.

First, as noted above, some of the most productive conceptual work in the area of emotional labor has involved the concepts of identity and identification. This is not surprising, given the origins of the emotional labor concept in Hochschild's (1983) notions of authenticity, deep and surface acting, and estrangement from self. However, although scholars of emotion in work roles have introduced interesting contrasts such as deep versus surface authenticity (Ashforth & Tomiuk, 2000) and faking in good faith versus faking in bad faith (Rafaeli & Sutton, 1989), there have been few efforts to theoretically probe the complex intersections of emotion and identity at work. Scholars continually call for such work. For example, Tracy (2005), in her study of correctional officers, reached complex conclusions about identity and emotion: that "emotion labor is easier when it confirms a preferred identity," that "high identification does not always ease emotion work" (p. 279), and that the status of individuals being served and the framing of the emotion can substantially influence the experience of emotion in the work role. These findings highlight the importance of problematizing relationships among work, identity, and emotion. Further understanding of these relationships can be most productively advanced by connecting *in situ* research findings to theoretical approaches to identity and identification (Hatch & Schultz, 2002), including those that are critical (Alvesson & Willmott, 2002), structurational (Scott, Corman, & Cheney, 1998), narrative (Czarniawska-Joerges, 1994), and post-structuralist (Tracy & Trethewey, 2005).

Second, future research can usefully explore the nuances of specific organizational contexts in which emotion is deployed as part of the work role. This work will be most productive if it moves beyond the descriptive level of *finding* emotional labor and emotional labor in yet another context to exploring the ways in which aspects of the context transform the experience and communication of emotion. For example, McGuire (2010) has discussed the special case of *spiritual labor* in an essay that explores how the religious organizational context introduces the dynamics of morality and hypocrisy into extant understandings of emotional labor. Miller (2002) considers how concepts of community and liminality may be critical to an understanding of emotion during organizational tragedy. Meyerson (1994) demonstrates the strong influence of organizational culture and institutional ideology in the experience and impact of emotional work for social workers. Other contextual issues seem ripe for the consideration in advancing our understanding of emotional labor and emotional work. For example, changing organizational forms such as dispersed organizations and telework are likely to shift the emotional experience of work (see, e.g., Marsh & Musson, 2008), and our increasingly global workplace changes the emotional landscape of customer service relationships (e.g., Parameswaran, 2008). In short, it is critical that we enhance our understanding of emotional communication in work roles by interrogating the nature of the organizational, institutional, and cultural contexts in which those work roles are embedded.

Third, scholars should continue efforts to understand the ways in which organizational actors exercise agency to resist organizational control in emotional labor processes and to cope with the problems that might arise from both emotional labor and emotional work. For example, as noted earlier, Murphy (1998) described the ways in which flight attendants deployed "hidden transcripts" of resistance through interaction and behavioral choices including dress. Morgan and Krone (2001) considered a similar theme in their description of how "backstage" communication at a cardiac care center allowed caregivers to drop their professional demeanor and vent about the stress of emotional work, though this imposed its own emotion rules regarding open expression (see also Sutton, 1991, for consistent findings regarding bill collectors and emotional labor). Future work should continue to investigate the ways in which workers in a variety of roles resist the constraints of emotional labor or mitigate the stresses of emotional work through interaction with others in the workplace. Research on these issues would provide an important link to the scholarship considered in the next section of this chapter, which considers the emotional communication that is woven throughout interactions with coworkers in organizational settings.

Emotion as Part of Work Life

As discussed in the previous section, a great deal of scholarly work has explored the ways in which emotion is experienced, deployed, and often commodified as part of work roles—especially roles involving direct customer service and human service relationships. However, emotion is clearly a critical feature of work life in all occupations—not just those that involve a relationship with a client, patient, or customer. Further, even in roles that involve emotional labor and/or emotional work, there is a rich tapestry of emotional communication with others in the workplace. Indeed, Waldron (2000) contends that "it is the nature of work relationships, not the nature of the task itself that creates the highest potential for intense emotional experience" (p. 66). There is, of course, a wide array of relationships that contribute to emotional experience in organizations. Further, scholarly attention to these various relationships and interaction processes often consider questions in which issues of emotion are implicated but are not the central concern. In this section, I will concentrate on scholarship that has specifically highlighted the ways in which emotional communication—of a variety of types—is woven into relationships with others in the workplace. I will first consider the characteristics of work relationships in which emotion becomes especially salient and then consider the ways in which emotion is enacted in the workplace.

Emotion and Workplace Relationships

Waldron (1994, 2000, 2012) has been instrumental in emphasizing the importance of considering workplace relationships as a focal point for understanding emotion at work. In an early study, Waldron and Krone (1991) highlighted the variety of emotional experiences and emotional messages described by workers in a state department of corrections and rehabilitation. Through subsequent work investigating reports from a variety of organizational settings, Waldron (2000) came to describe features of work relationships that make them a breeding ground for emotional experience. First, work relationships require the balancing of public and private concerns, and that tension can lead to emotional reactions, especially when there are power differentials at play. Second, because work relationships are interdependent and situated within larger systems, there are often strong reverberations in which emotional events can be magnified "across relational connections that are activated and reactivated through the buzz of daily interaction" (Waldron, 2000, p. 68). Third, conflicting loyalties within organizational relationships can lead to issues of loyalty and betrayal. Waldron describes these emotional experiences as particularly devastating and notes that they "are typically related using language that is both colourful and bitter" (Waldron, 2000, p. 70). Finally, workplace relationships bring with them beliefs about organizational justice and fairness (Bies, 1987), and "[w]orkers frequently get emotional about violations of unspoken relational obligations and values" (Waldron, 2000, p. 71).

Other scholarship has described the emotion that is associated with specific workplace relationships and interactions. For example, Kassing (2007) has explored some of the emotional experiences that surround processes of upward dissent, and Metts, Cupach, and Lippert (2006) consider the emotions associated with forgiveness in the workplace. A number of studies have highlighted the complex emotions associated with workplace romance (see Dillard & Miller, 1988, for review), and Gayle and Preiss (1998) observe that the emotional intensity of workplace conflict is especially lasting when the conflict is unresolved or protracted. Scholars examining published narratives of workplace experience (Bowe, Bowe, Streeter, Murphy, & Kernochan, 2000; Terkel, 1972) have identified the clusters of emotions associated with specific workplace events (Boudens, 2005) and have pointed to the importance of specific emotions such as respect in supervisory relationships and support in coworker relationships (Miller et al., 2007). Krone and Morgan (2000), in their study of managers in Chinese organizations, remind readers of the importance of including cultural difference in understanding emotional experience. In contrast to the typical Western pattern of containing and segmenting emotion, Chinese managers embraced a homeostatic metaphor in which "it is as if emotion surrounds them, as reflected by one manager who said 'never forget one's responsibility and places that can be improved in work, even in the *middle* of such good moods'" (Krone & Morgan, 2000, p. 93). These studies all point to the complexity of emotional experiences that occur as part of ongoing organizational relationships.

Enacting Emotion in Workplace Relationships

Waldron (2012) summarizes research regarding the wide array of emotions experienced in the workplace, the various levels at which these emotions are felt and expressed, and the processes through emotions are enacted. For example, he notes the ubiquity of nonverbal cues related to feeling and emotion (see also Planalp, 1999) and the challenges of interpreting these cues in the workplace context: "Some non-verbal cues are quite ambiguous, so the employee must interpret them in terms of organizational and relational norms" (Waldron, 2012, p. 43). Workplace emotion is also, of course, communicated through language, including emotion words (e.g., angry, trilled, irritated, nervous), slogans and catchphrases, and metaphors (see Waldron, 2012, pp. 45–48). Further, these nonverbal and verbal behaviors are organized into larger communication events that can hold great emotional meaning. These include the tactical use of emotion (see, e.g., Waldron, 2009); interaction sequences that can serve to reflect, sharpen, and uncover emotions; narratives that (re)create the emotional fabric of a workplace; and rituals that help workers share and reinforce emotional experiences (see Waldron, 2012, pp. 49–60). Further, Coupland, Brown, Daniels, and Humphreys (2008) found that coworkers help to shape the interpretation of emotions through interaction through the "upgrading" or "downgrading" of emotional expressions. It is little wonder that Waldron concludes that "[t]he communication of feeling is a high-stakes activity" and that "[t]he misreading of emotional cues, the jarring emotional message, or the failure to appreciate the emotional needs of key audiences can all be costly mistakes" (Waldron, 2012, p. 60). Thus it is important to consider the extent to which individuals might be particularly skilled in the practice of emotional communication and the rules that employees believe shape the enactment of emotion in the workplace.

Several strands of scholarship address the idea that some individuals might be particularly adept at emotional communication in the workplace. The most well-known concept in this area is the notion of *emotional intelligence*, initially proposed in the popular management press by Goleman (1995, 1998). Emotional intelligence has been defined as "the ability to monitor one's own and others' emotions, to discriminate among them, and to use the information to guide one's thinking and actions" (Salovey & Mayer, 1990, p. 189) and is discussed in terms of two dimensions—awareness versus management of emotions and the self versus others as the target. Though there has been widespread research and discussion regarding the emotional intelligence construct, it has been critiqued on several fronts. First, there seems to be little support for an empirical link between emotional intelligence and positive organizational outcomes. After a thorough review of the literature, Zeidner, Matthews, and Roberts (2004) conclude that

> [m]any of the popular claims presented in the literature regarding the role of [emotional intelligence] in determining work success and well-being are rather misleading in

that they seem to present scientific studies supporting their claims, while in fact failing to do so. (p. 393)

Further, the emotional intelligence concept has been critiqued for failing to appreciate the communicative dimensions of emotion (Dougherty & Krone, 2002) and as a commodification of emotional experience for corporate profit (Fineman, 2000). Communication scholars considering issues of interactive skill in interpersonal communication have provided evidence, however, that competence in emotional communication can be valuable in social life. For example, Spitzberg and Cupach (2002) have pointed to key emotional components in communication competence, including sensitivity to emotion and expressive skills. Thus emotional communication in the workplace is characterized by a wide array of micro behaviors, relational sequences, and group processes, and it is likely that individual competence in this emotional communication may vary among employees.

Scholars have also considered the related question of rules that guide the communication of emotion in organizational settings. Kramer and Hess (2002), drawing on models of emotional communication based on both the concepts of display rules (e.g., Hochschild, 1983) and expectations (e.g., Fiebig & Kramer, 1998; Omdahl, 1995), conducted research that led to a typology of rules that employees reported about emotional communication in the workplace. The most common rule reported was the principle that employees should express emotions professionally (see also Cheney & Ashcraft, 2007, for a discussion of professionalism in the workplace). Other rules included the dictate that emotion should be expressed to improve situations and to help individuals. Further, rules were reported about the need to carefully consider the target of emotional expression and that emotional communication should not be used for self-promotion. Kramer and Hess (2002) noted that few respondents reported rules about masking negative emotions, and these scholars concluded that such norms were probably seen as general rules of civility that are part of organizational life. Subsequent research (Domagalski & Steelman, 2007) has supported this general norm of repressing negative emotion in interaction but also found that there are exceptions based on status and gender (i.e., lower-status males were more likely to express upward-negative emotion).

Emotion and Workplace Relationships—Moving Forward

The work described in this section provides a rich description of the ways in which organizational relationships shape and are shaped by emotional communication. Relationships among coworkers and between supervisors and subordinates provide fertile ground for emotional interaction and experience. Further, scholars have made progress in describing the nature of emotional communication in the workplace and the communicative competencies and rules that shape that interaction. Most of this research has been based on retrospective accounts of emotional experiences with coworkers or on survey research that has sought to systematize the nature of emotional rules and experiences. The nature of this work suggests several important avenues for extending our understanding of emotion and workplace relationships.

First, it is important that we move our understanding of emotion and workplace relationships (and emotion in the work role as well) beyond accounts, both qualitative and quantitative. These statistics, descriptions, and narratives can be informative and evocative, of course. But it is critical to remember that emotional communication—probably more than its "rational" counterpart—is felt and displayed. Nervousness can mean sweating hands and a queasy stomach. Joy is often accompanied by giggles and light-headed euphoria. Anger raises our blood pressure and can redden our faces. In short, our appreciation for emotion in the workplace could be noticeably enhanced by considerations of the way in which emotion is embodied in organizational settings. Trethewey (1999, 2001) has been a leading advocate for the consideration of embodiment in organizational communication studies (Trethewey, Scott, & LeGreco, 2006), arguing from a feminist perspective for increased attention to the way that bodies are disciplined and commodified in organizational settings. An approach embracing the concept of embodiment could similarly enhance our appreciation for emotional experiences in the workplace. As Sturdy (2003) explains,

> [E]motional displays ('body vocabularies'), feelings and understandings of them might be explored in more depth and linked to immediate and broader contexts and dynamics. For example, how might the . . . discourse of emotional intelligence be embodied? . . . [H]ow is the process of learning/unlearning the feeling rules of organizations and paid employment experienced? What are the 'physical' insults, injuries and embellishments of capitalist and other organizations? (p. 91)

Second, and similar to the recommendations for future work in the area of emotion in the work role, it is important to pay careful attention to the context in which emotion at work occurs. Accounts and experiences of emotion are intimately bound to and create the *culture* and the *climate* of the workplace (to use two well-worn but still valuable terms). There are undoubtedly workplaces with destructive work climates and cultures (see Lutgen-Sandvik & Davenport-Sypher, 2009, for examples) and those where more positive values and norms are encouraged. There have, of course, been some studies that emphasized the ways in which organizational culture influences emotional workplace experiences, such as Martin, Knopoff, and Beckman's (2000) discussion of bounded emotionality at The Body Shop. However, it is important for researchers to continue to emphasize the organizational ecology in which particular kinds of emotional interaction can and do flourish. One specific area of scholarship that has taken up this call is work on compassion in organizations, and it is to this area of research that I now turn.

Compassion in the Workplace

One specific emotion that has received a great deal of attention from organizational scholars is compassion. Frost (1999) initially issued a call for the study of compassion, arguing (following the Buddha) that "suffering is optional but an inevitable part of the human condition" (Frost, 1999, p. 128) and that we have a moral obligation to respond to this aspect of the human condition that can be triggered by grief, physical and mental illness, other personal life events, workplace incivility, public tragedies, and the stresses inherent in many jobs (see Driver, 2007). Lilius, Kanov, Dutton, Worline, and Maitlis (2011) further note that "[t]his is not only a moral concern, but also a financial one" (p. 274), citing the high costs of employee grief, job stress, and burnout, among other forms of suffering. Frost's initial call has been met with years of scholarship investigating the ways in which compassion—which Kornfield (1993, p. 326) calls "the heart's response to the sorrow" (p. 326) and Kahn (1993, p. 546) defines as "an emotional presence by displaying warmth, affection, and kindness"—plays an integral part in workplace communication and behavior.

A conceptual starting point for much of the work on compassion in the workplace is a model of compassion proposed by Kanov et al. (2004). This model describes a three-part process that begins with *noticing* suffering—a necessary but not sufficient precondition for compassion (Frost, 2003). The second step of this model is the empathic *feeling* regarding "another's hurt, anguish, or worry" (Kanov et al., 2004, p. 813). The model concludes with *responding*, described as "actions or displays that occur in response to others' suffering with the aim of lessening, alleviating, or making it more bearable" (Lilius, Kanov et al., 2011, p. 275). Communication scholars have taken up this model but have also developed it in ways that reflect the interactive nature of compassionate communication. For example, Miller (2007) recast the *feeling* step of the model as *connecting* and noted that the connection found in compassion could be both cognitive in the form of perspective taking (Stiff, Dillard, Somera, Kim, & Sleight, 1988) and affective in the form of empathic concern. More recently, Way and Tracy (2012) drew on ethnographic work to propose an embodied understanding of compassion in the workplace as *recognizing, relating,* and *(re)acting,* with (re)acting posited as the core or the heart of compassion. Though these models point to different nuances in the enactment of compassion in the workplace, they are similar in seeing compassion as a complex process that includes the acknowledgement of suffering, seeing the importance of connections through relationships, and seeing the centrality of communicative behavior. As both Miller (2007, p. 233) and Way and Tracy (2012, p. 310) argue, "[I]t is not compassion without a response."

Research on compassion in the workplace has followed the paths of other work considering emotion in organizational settings. Considerations of compassion as part of the work role (emotional work) have looked at the ways in which workers in human service roles experience and enact compassion in dealing with clients and patients. For example, Miller's (2007) study of workers in a wide range of human service occupations pointed to classic ideas from communication theory such as *audience analysis* (noticing both the need for compassion and details of clients' lives that could lead to more effective communication) and the importance of both nonverbal cues (i.e., immediacy and environmental structuring) and verbal strategies (i.e., balancing information and emotion in communication) in responding to those in distress. Way and Tracy's (2012) ethnographic study of hospice workers led to a more holistic, nuanced, and embodied view of compassion that emphasized timing, context, interpretation, and silence. Further, both of these studies highlighted the rewards that can accrue in compassionate work. Indeed, Way and Tracy (2012) found that "employees' acts of compassion were accompanied by feelings of self-worth and appreciation for their work" (p. 311).

The work of Frost and colleagues encompasses a second important strand of compassion research that corresponds with the second major section of this chapter—emotion as part of workplace relationships. Frost et al. (2006, p. 847) describe this scholarship as conceptualizing "compassion [as] a form of everyday talk that takes place in organizations." In one exemplary study (Lilius et al., 2008), this group of scholars found that compassion in the workplace took the forms of giving emotional support in the guise of both gestures and conversation, giving time or flexibility to allow for recovery, and giving material goods such as money or food. Further, this study described the positive outcomes of these compassionate relationships and interactions. Individuals who had been on the receiving end of compassion reported a more positive sense of self, positive beliefs about the character and trustworthiness of those around them, and positive conclusions about the desirability of organizational membership. Frost et al. (2006) argue that there can be large consequences for even small acts of compassion among coworkers—the "human moments" at work (Hallowell, 1999).

> Even seemingly simple things, such as taking a few minutes to visit someone who is suffering or offering a card with a few words of comfort to someone who has experienced a loss can renew a sense of hope in the recipient. (Frost et al., 2006, p. 850)

However, these scholars also caution that "this view facilitates seeing that the work of compassion, like other forms of relational work, is often gendered through its association with the work of women in the private sphere" (Frost et al., 2006, p. 850) and hence may be devalued or "disappeared" (Fletcher, 1999). The importance of compassion as a relational leadership process has also been highlighted (Dutton, Frost, Worline, Lilius, & Kanov, 2002). As Dutton et al. (2002) suggest, "[T]here is always grief somewhere in the room. . . . You can't eliminate such suffering, nor can you ask people to check their emotions at the door. But you can use your leadership to begin the healing process" (p. 61).

Finally, this group of scholars has investigated the ways in which collectives create contexts in which compassion can be socially coordinated and enacted. Dutton, Worline, Frost, and Lilius (2006) use an extended case analysis to elaborate on five core mechanisms that explain the pattern of compassion organizing. First, they highlight the importance of *pain triggers* to set off compassion organizing. Second, they argue that emotions must be generated and spread as a way to prompt, accelerate, and guide the compassion process. Third, trust and legitimacy must exist during the ongoing compassionate response. Fourth, "organizational members [draw] on their particular knowledge, position, and relationship with persons in pain to improvise roles and routines that further [shape] the organizing process" (Dutton et al., 2006, p. 86). Fifth, following the ideas regarding relational compassion noted above, leadership was key in creating meaning and evoking emotion in compassion organizing. Thus these scholars see "compassion organizing as a joint product of structures of the organization (the social architecture), the agency of individuals who get engaged in the process (activation and mobilization), and emergent features (structural and symbolic) that are unique to the situation" (Dutton et al., 2006, p. 84). In more recent work, Lilius, Worline, Dutton, Kanov, and Maitlis (2011) discuss the idea of a collective capacity for compassion at the unit level. They argue that compassion capability is conditioned (1) by relational practices (e.g., acknowledgement, play, celebrating, collective decision making) that encourage high-quality connections and (2) by a "dynamic boundary-permeability norm" that "enables compassion capability by making it more likely that people can discuss their suffering with those who will empathize and be best equipped to respond effectively" (Lilius, Worline et al., 2011, p. 891).

Scholarship on compassion, then, provides a window into the complexity of research considering emotion in the workplace. This scholarship is notable in several regards. First, it responds to important organizational and societal needs for coping with suffering on a number of levels. Second, it comports with important current trends in social research such as the move toward positive organizational scholarship (Cameron et al., 2003; Lutgen-Sandvik, Riforgiate, & Fletcher, 2011) and the study of gratitude in relationships (Wood, Froh, & Geraghty, 2010) and has engaged in the critical task of theory development in concert with engaged empirical work. Finally, it illustrates the often interdependent ways in which emotion is displayed and deployed in organizational settings (as part of the work role and as part of ongoing organizational relationships) and has also taken the important step of considering contextual factors that contribute to a particular emotional ecology in organizations—one of compassion.

Conclusion

This chapter opened with a consideration of organizational communication scholarship from the 1960s through the 1980s. This scholarship was largely concerned with rational processes, with instrumental outcomes, and with profit-making businesses. As this chapter illustrates, however, the decades since then have marked a departure from these norms; as scholars now see emotion as integrally woven into work roles and work relationships, attention has shifted to service and human service organizations in which emotion is prevalent, and considerations have shifted from the bottom line. This chapter has considered the related areas of emotion as part of the work role and emotion as part of relationships in organizations. The scholarship described is dynamic and rich and has contributed to increased understanding about the complexities of organizational life and about critical theoretical concepts such as identity and control and important practical outcomes such as stress and burnout. The specific emotion of compassion served as illustration of how research on emotion in the workplace could be elaborated in enhancing our understanding of how organizational actors and systems can respond to suffering. Communication scholars have been active participants in this ongoing stream of research, and their work is especially important in terms of describing and understanding the interactive nature of emotion in various contexts, in explicating the importance of relationships (both with coworkers and with actors such as customers, clients, and patients) in understanding emotion, and in teasing out emerging theoretical complexity in the study of identity and emotion. Throughout this review, however, several directions for future research were noted if we are to continue productive scholarship beyond cookie-cutter considerations of emotion in the workplace. Specifically, the next moves should be to carefully consider issues of context (be it relational, organizational, or cultural); to engage in work that can reveal more about the embodied and enacted experience of workplace emotion; to use our enhanced understanding of emotion to elaborate theoretical understandings of issues such as workplace identity, dissent, and empowerment; to follow the lead of researchers considering compassion; and to connect our research to critical needs in organizational life.

References

Alvesson, M., & Willmott, H. (2002). Identity regulation as organizational control: Producing the appropriate individual. *Journal of Management Studies, 39*(5), 619–644.

Ashforth, B. E., & Humphrey, R. H. (1993). Emotional labor in service roles: The influence of identity. *Academy of Management Review, 18*(1), 88–115.

Ashforth, B. E., & Mael, F. (1989). Social identity theory and the organization. *Academy of Management Review, 14*(1), 20–39.

Ashforth, B. E., & Tomiuk, M. A. (2000). Emotional labour and authenticity: Views from service agents. In S. Fineman (Ed.), *Emotion in organizations* (2nd ed., pp. 184–203). London, England: SAGE.

Bies, R. J. (1987). The predicament of injustice: The management of moral outrage. In L. L. Cummings & B. M. Staw (Eds.), *Research in organizational behavior* (vol. 9, pp. 289–319). Greenwich, CT: JAI Press.

Boudens, C. J. (2005). The story of work: A narrative analysis of workplace emotion. *Organization Studies, 26*(9), 1285–1306.

Bowe, J., Bowe, M., Streeter, S., Murphy, D., & Kernochan, R. (Eds.). (2000). *Gig: Americans talk about their jobs at the turn of the millennium.* New York, NY: Crown.

Brotheridge, C. M., & Grandey, A. A. (2002). Emotional labor and burnout: Comparing two perspectives of "people work." *Journal of Vocational Behavior, 60*(1), 17–39.

Cameron, K. S., Dutton, J. E., & Quinn, R. E. (2003). Foundations of positive organizational scholarship. In K. S. Cameron, J. E. Dutton, & R. E. Quinn (Eds.), *Positive organizational scholarship: Foundations of a new discipline* (pp. 3–13). San Francisco, CA: Berrett-Koehler.

Cheney, G., & Ashcraft, K. L. (2007). Considering "the professional" in communication studies: Implications for theory and research within and beyond the boundaries of organizational communication. *Communication Theory, 17*(2), 146–175.

Conrad, C., & Witte, K. (1994). Is emotional expression repression oppression? Myths of organizational affective regulation. In S. A. Deetz (Ed.), *Communication yearbook* (vol. 17, pp. 417–428). Thousand Oaks, CA: SAGE.

Coupland, C., Brown, A. D., Daniels, K., & Humphreys, M. (2008). Saying it with feeling: Analysing speakable emotions. *Human Relations, 61*(3), 327–353.

Czarniawska-Joerges, B. (1994). Narratives of individual and organizational identities. In S. A. Deetz (Ed.), *Communication yearbook* (vol. 17, pp. 193–221). Thousand Oaks, CA: SAGE.

Dillard, J. P., & Miller, K. I. (1988). Intimate relationships in task environments. In S. Duck (Ed.),

Handbook of personal relationships (pp. 449–465). New York, NY: Wiley.

Domagalski, T. A., & Steelman, L. A. (2007). The impact of gender and organizational status on workplace anger expression. *Management Communication Quarterly, 20*(3), 297–315.

Dougherty, D. S., & Krone, K. J. (2002). Emotional intelligence as organizational communication: An examination of the construct. In W. B. Gudykunst (Ed.), *Communication yearbook* (vol. 26, pp. 202–229). Mahwah, NJ: Lawrence Erlbaum.

Driver, M. (2007). Meaning and suffering in organizations. *Journal of Organizational Change Management, 20*(5), 611–632.

Dutton, J. E., Frost, P. J., Worline, M. C., Lilius, J. M., & Kanov, J. M. (2002, January). Leading in times of trauma. *Harvard Business Review*, 54–61.

Dutton, J. E., Worline, M. C., Frost, P. F., & Lilius, J. (2006). Explaining compassion organizing. *Administrative Science Quarterly, 51*(1), 59–96.

Fiebig, G. V., & Kramer, M. W. (1998). A framework for the study of emotions in organizational contexts. *Management Communication Quarterly, 11*(4), 536–572.

Fineman, S. (2000). Commodifying the emotionally intelligent. In S. Fineman (Ed.), *Emotion in organizations* (2nd ed., pp. 101–114). London, England: SAGE.

Fox, J. (2006). "Notice how you feel": An alternative to detached concern among hospice volunteers. *Qualitative Health Research, 16*(7), 944–961.

Fletcher, J. K. (1999). *Disappearing acts: Gender, power and relational practices at work.* Cambridge, MA: MIT Press.

Fredrickson, B. L. (2003). Positive emotions and upward spirals in organizations. In K. S. Cameron, J. E. Dutton, & R. E. Quinn (Eds.), *Positive organizational scholarship: Foundations of a new discipline* (pp. 163–175). San Francisco, CA: Berrett-Koehler.

Frost, P. J. (1999). Why compassion counts! *Journal of Management Inquiry, 8*(2), 127–133.

Frost, P. J. (2003). *Toxic emotions at work: How compassionate managers handle pain and conflict.* Boston, MA: Harvard Business School Press.

Frost, P. J., Dutton, J. E., Maitlis, S., Lilius, J. M., Kanov, J. M., & Worline, M. C. (2006). Seeing organizations differently: Three lenses on compassion. In S. R. Clegg, C. Hardy, T. B. Lawrence, & W. R. Nord (Eds.), *The SAGE handbook of organization studies* (2nd ed., pp. 843–866). London, England: SAGE.

Gayle, B. M., & Preiss, R. W. (1998). Assessing emotionality in organizational conflicts. *Management Communication Quarterly, 12*(2), 280–302.

Goffman, E. (1961). *Asylums.* New York, NY: Anchor.

Goleman, D. P. (1995). *Emotional intelligence.* New York, NY: Bantam Books.

Goleman, D. P. (1998). *Working with emotional intelligence.* New York, NY: Bantam Books.

Graen, G. B., & Scandura, T. A. (1987). Toward a psychology of dyadic organizing. In B. Staw & L. L. Cummings (Eds.), *Research in organizational behavior* (vol. 9, pp. 175–208). Greenwich, CT: JAI.

Hallowell, E. M. (1999). The human moment at work. *Harvard Business Review, 77*(1), 58–66.

Haman, M., & Putnam, L. L. (2008). In the gym: Peer pressure and emotional management among coworkers. In S. Fineman (Ed.), *The emotional organization: Passions and power* (pp. 61–73). Malden, MA: Blackwell.

Hatch, M. J., & Schultz, M. (2002). The dynamics of organizational identity. *Human Relations, 55*(8), 989–1018.

Hochschild, A. R. (1979). Emotion work, feeling rules, and social structure. *American Journal of Sociology, 85*(3), 551–575.

Hochschild, A. R. (1983). *The managed heart: Commercialization of human feeling.* Berkeley: University of California Press.

Kahn, W. A. (1993). Caring for the caregivers: Patterns of organizational caregiving. *Administrative Science Quarterly, 38*(4), 539–563.

Kanov, J. M., Maitlis, S., Worline, M. C., Dutton, J. E., Frost, P. J., & Lilius, J. M. (2004). Compassion in organizational life. *American Behavioral Scientist, 47*(6), 808–827.

Kassing, J. W. (2007). Going around the boss: Exploring the consequences of circumvention. *Management Communication Quarterly, 21*(1), 55–74.

Katz, D., & Kahn, R. L. (1978). *The social psychology of organizations* (2nd ed.). New York, NY: Wiley.

Kornfield, J. (1993). *A path with heart.* New York, NY: Bantam Books.

Kramer, M. W., & Hess, J. A. (2002). Communication rules for the display of emotions in organizational settings. *Management Communication Quarterly, 16*(1), 66–80.

Krone, K. L., & Morgan, J. M. (2000). Emotion metaphors in management: The Chinese experience. In S. Fineman (Ed.), *Emotion in organizations* (2nd ed., pp. 83–100). London, England: SAGE.

Kruml, S. M., & Geddes, D. (2000). Exploring the dimensions of emotional labor: The heart of Hochschild's work. *Management Communication Quarterly, 14*(1), 8–49.

Kuhn, T. S. (1962). *The structure of scientific revolutions.* Chicago, IL: University of Chicago Press.

Lewis, M. (2003). *Moneyball: The art of winning an unfair game.* New York, NY: W. W. Norton.

Lief, H. I., & Fox, R.C. (1963). Training for "detached concern" in medical students. In H. I. Lief, V. F. Lief, & N. R. Lief (Eds.), *The Psychological Basis of Medical Practice* (pp. 12–35). New York, NY: Harper & Row.

Lilius, J. M., Kanov, J., Dutton, J. E., Worline, M. C., & Maitlis, S. (2011). Compassion revealed: What we know about compassion at work (and where we need to know more). In K. S. Cameron & G. M. Spreitzer (Eds.), *The Oxford handbook of positive organizational scholarship* (pp. 273–287). New York, NY: Oxford University Press.

Lilius, J. M., Worline, M. C., Dutton, J. E., Kanov, J. M., & Maitlis, S. (2011). Understanding compassion capability. *Human Relations, 64*(7), 873–899.

Lilius, J. M., Worline, M. C., Maitlis, S., Kanov, J., Dutton, J. E., & Frost, P. (2008). The contours and consequences of compassion at work. *Journal of Organizational Behavior, 29*(2), 193–218.

Lutgen-Sandvik, P., & Davenport Sypher, B. (Eds.). (2009). *Destructive organizational communication: Processes, consequences, and constructive ways of organizing.* New York, NY: Routledge.

Lutgen-Sandvik, P., Riforgiate, S., & Fletcher, C. (2011). Work as a source of positive emotional experiences and the discourses informing positive assessment, *Western Journal of Communication, 75*(1), 2–27.

Marsh, K., & Musson, G. (2008). Men at work and at home: Managing emotion in telework. *Gender, Work, & Organization, 15*(1), 31–48.

Martin, J., Knopoff, K., & Beckman, C. (2000). Bounded emotionality at the body shop. In S. Fineman (Ed.), *Emotion in organizations* (2nd ed., pp. 64–82). London, England: SAGE.

Maslach, C. (1982). *Burnout: The cost of caring.* New York, NY: Prentice Hall.

McGuire, T. (2010). From emotions to spirituality: "Spiritual labor" as the commodification, codification, and regulation of organizational members' spirituality. *Management Communication Quarterly, 24*(1), 74–103.

Metts, S., Cupach, W. R., & Lippert, L. (2006). Forgiveness in the workplace. In J. M. Harden-Fritz & B. L. Omdahl (Eds.), *Problematic relationships in the workplace* (pp. 249–278). New York, NY: Peter Lang.

Meyerson, D. E. (1994). Interpretations of stress in institutions: The cultural production of ambiguity and burnout. *Administrative Science Quarterly, 39*(4), 628–653.

Meyerson, D. E. (1998). Feeling stressed and burned out: A feminist reading and re-visioning of stress-based emotions within medicine and organization science. *Organization Science, 9*(1), 103–118.

Miller, K. I. (2002). The experience of emotion in the workplace: Professing in the midst of tragedy. *Management Communication Quarterly, 15*(4), 571–600.

Miller, K. I. (2007). Compassionate communication in the workplace: Exploring processes of noticing, connecting, and responding. *Journal of Applied Communication Research, 35*(3), 223–245.

Miller, K. I., Birkholt, M., Scott, C., & Stage, C. (1995). Empathy and burnout in human service work: An extension of a communication model. *Communication Research, 22*(2), 123–147.

Miller, K. I., & Considine, J. (2009). Communication in the helping professions. In L. Frey & K. Cissna (Eds.), *Handbook of applied communication research* (pp. 405–428). Mahwah, NJ: Erlbaum.

Miller, K. I., Considine, J., & Garner, J. (2007). "Let me tell you about my job": Exploring the terrain of emotion in the workplace. *Management Communication Quarterly, 20*(3), 231–260.

Miller, K. I., & Koesten, J. (2008). Financial feeling: An investigation of emotion and communication in the workplace. *Journal of Applied Communication Research, 36*(1), 8–32.

Miller, K. I., Stiff, J. B., & Ellis, B. H. (1988). Communication and empathy as precursors to burnout among human service workers. *Communication Monographs, 55*(3), 250–265.

Morgan, J. M., & Krone, K. J. (2001). Bending the rules of "professional" display: Emotional improvisation in caregiver performances. *Journal of Applied Communication Research, 29*(4), 317–340.

Morris, J. A., & Feldman, D. C. (1996). The dimensions, antecedents, and consequences of emotional labor. *Academy of Management Review, 21*(4), 986–1010.

Mumby, D. K., & Putnam, L. L. (1992). The politics of emotion: A feminist reading of bounded rationality. *Academy of Management Review, 17*(3), 465–486.

Murphy, A. G. (1998). Hidden transcripts of flight attendant resistance. *Management Communication Quarterly, 11*(4), 499–535.

Omdahl, B. L. (1995). *Cognitive appraisal, emotion, and empathy.* Mahwah, NJ: Lawrence Erlbaum.

Omdahl, B. L., & O'Donnell, C. (1999). Emotional contagion, empathic concern and communicative responsiveness as variables affecting nurses' stress and occupational commitment. *Journal of Advanced Nursing, 29*(6), 1351–1359.

Parameswaran, R. (2008). The other sides of globalization: Communication, culture, and postcolonial critique. *Communication, Culture, & Critique, 1*(1), 116–125.

Planalp, S. (1999). *Communicating emotion: Social, moral, and political processes.* Cambridge, UK: Cambridge University Press.

Putnam, L. L., & Mumby, D. K. (1993). Organizations, emotion, and the myth of rationality. In S. Fineman (Ed.), *Emotion in organizations* (pp. 36–57). London, England: SAGE.

Rafaeli, A., & Sutton, R. I. (1987). Expression of emotion as part of the work role. *Academy of Management Review, 12*(1), 23–37.

Rafaeli, A., & Sutton, R. I. (1989). The expression of emotion in organizational life. In L. L. Cummings & B. M. Staw (Eds.), *Research in organizational behavior* (vol. 11, pp. 1–42). Greenwich, CT: JAI Press.

Salovey, P., & Mayer, J. D. (1990). Emotional intelligence. *Imagination, Cognition and Personality, 9*(3), 185–211.

Sandelands, L. E., & Boudens, C. J. (2000). Feeling at work. In S. Fineman (Ed.), *Emotion in organizations* (2nd ed., pp. 46–63). London, England: SAGE.

Scarduzio, J. A. (2011). Maintaining order through deviance? The emotional deviance, power, and professional work of municipal court judges. *Management Communication Quarterly, 25*(2), 283–310.

Scott, C., & Myers, K. K. (2005). The socialization of emotion: Learning emotion management at the fire station. *Journal of Applied Communication Research, 33*(1), 67–92.

Scott, C. R., Corman, S. R., & Cheney, G. (1998). Development of a structurational model of identification in the organization. *Communication Theory, 8*(3), 298–336.

Seligman, M. E. P., & Csikszentmihalyi, M. (2000). Positive psychology: An introduction. *American Psychologist, 55*(1), 5–14.

Shuler, S., & Sypher, B. D. (2000). Seeking emotional labor: When managing the heart enhances the work experience. *Management Communication Quarterly, 14*(1), 50–89.

Simon, H. (1976). *Administrative behavior* (3rd ed.). New York, NY: Free Press.

Spitzberg, B. H., & Cupach, W. R. (2002). Interpersonal skills. In M. L. Knapp & J. A. Dally (Eds.), *Handbook of interpersonal communication* (3rd ed., pp. 564–611). Thousand Oaks, CA: SAGE.

Stanislavski, C. (1965). *An actor prepares* (Elizabeth Reynolds, Trans.). New York, NY: Theatre Arts Books.

Stiff, J. B., Dillard, J. P., Somera, L., Kim, H., & Sleight, C. (1988). Empathy, communication, and prosocial behavior. *Communication Monographs, 55*(2), 198–213.

Sturdy, A. (2003). Knowing the unknowable? A discussion of methodological and theoretical issues in emotion research and organizational studies. *Organization, 10*(1), 81–105.

Sutton, R. I. (1991). Maintaining norms about expressed emotions: The case of bill collectors. *Administrative Science Quarterly, 36*(2), 245–268.

Tajfel, H., & Turner, J. C. (1985). The social identity theory of intergroup behavior. In S. Worchel & W. G. Austin (Eds.), *Psychology of intergroup relations* (2nd ed., pp. 7–24). Chicago, IL: Nelson-Hall.

Terkel, S. (1972). *Working.* New York, NY: The New Press.

Tracy, S. J. (2000). Becoming a character for commerce: Emotion labor, self-subordination, and discursive construction of identity in a total institution. *Management Communication Quarterly, 14*(1), 90–128.

Tracy, S. J. (2005). Locking up emotion: Moving beyond dissonance for understanding emotion labor discomfort. *Communication Monographs, 72*(3), 261–283.

Tracy, S. J. (2008). Emotion and communication in organizations. In W. Donsbach (Ed.), *International encyclopedia of communication* (vol. IV, pp. 1513–1519). Oxford, England: Blackwell.

Tracy, S. J., & Tracy, K. (1998). Emotion labor at 911: A case study and theoretical critique. *Journal of Applied Communication Research, 26*(4), 390–411.

Tracy, S. J., & Trethewey, A. (2005). Fracturing the real-self←→fake-self dichotomy: Moving toward crystallized organizational identities. *Communication Theory, 15*(2), 168–195.

Trethewey, A. (1999). Disciplined bodies. *Organization Studies, 20*(3), 423–450.

Trethewey, A. (2001). Reproducing and resisting the master narrative of decline: Midlife professional women's experience of aging. *Management Communication Quarterly, 15*(2), 183–226.

Trethewey, A., Scott, C., & LeGreco, M. (2006). Constructing embodied organizational identities: Commodifying, securing, and servicing professional bodies. In B. J. Dow & J. T. Wood (Eds.), *The SAGE handbook of gender and communication* (pp. 123–142). Thousand Oaks, CA: SAGE.

Waldron, V. R. (1994). Once more, with feeling: Reconsidering the role of emotion in work. In S. A. Deetz (Ed.), *Communication yearbook* (vol. 17, pp. 388–416). Thousand Oaks, CA: SAGE.

Waldron, V. R. (2000). Relational experiences and emotion at work. In S. Fineman (Ed.), *Emotion in organizations* (2nd ed., pp. 64–82). London, England: SAGE.

Waldron, V. R. (2009). Emotional tyranny at work: Suppressing the moral emotions. In P. Lutgen-Sandvik & B. Davenport-Sypher (Eds.), *Destructive organizational communication: Processes, consequences, and constructive ways of organizing* (pp. 9–26). New York, NY: Routledge.

Waldron, V. R. (2012). *Communicating emotion at work.* Cambridge, UK: Polity Press.

Waldron, V. R., & Krone, K. J. (1991). The experience and expression of emotion in the workplace: A study of a corrections organization. *Management Communication Quarterly, 4*(3), 287–309.

Way, D., & Tracy, S. J. (2012). Conceptualizing compassion as recognizing, relating and (re)acting: A qualitative study of compassionate communication at hospice. *Communication Monographs, 79*(3), 292–315.

Wood, A. M., Froh, J. J., & Geraghty, A. W. A. (2010). Gratitude and well-being: A review and theoretical integration. *Clinical Psychology Review, 30*(7), 890–905.

Zeidner, M., Matthews, G., & Roberts, R. D. (2004). Emotional intelligence in the workplace: A critical review. *Applied Psychology: An International Review, 53*(3), 371–399.

Zurcher, L. (1983). *Social roles: Conformity, conflict, and creativity.* Beverly Hills, CA: SAGE.

SECTION V

Organizations, Stakeholders, and Conflict

Steven K. May

This section makes clear the significant shifts that have occurred in organizational communication in the last 25 years. Only one of the topics—power—was covered in any depth in the first edition of the *Handbook of Organizational Communication* and most were not addressed in the second edition, either. The title of this section, "Organizations, Stakeholders, and Conflict," shows us, in vivid relief, how much has changed in our theoretical influences, our modes of inquiry, and our attention to new, emerging phenomena, even in the last decade. To the editors' credit, the chapters in this section stake a new claim on the relevance of today's complex and contradictory practices of organizing in a rapidly changing global economy. They suggest, I think, that we need to take seriously the contention that "organizing matters" because, as the chapters show, (1) power/knowledge constitutes our ways of being and knowing in organizations, (2) race, class, and gender structure our organizations, (3) destructive workplace behavior impacts our personal and organizational well-being, and, finally, (4) our communities need us to engage their challenges and bring our research to bear on today's social, political, economic, and ecological problems. As the chapter authors focus on these important topics, they are mindful of our tradition, but they are also cognizant that the instrumental legacy of the past must now transition to a stronger sense of social justice in organizational life.

In each of the chapters, this shift is most evident in the centrality of communication, less as a variable in past *Handbooks* and more as a constitutive function of power, difference, destructive behavior, and engagement. This section is evidence that scholars have responded to calls for more communication-centered research since the publication of the last *Handbook*. Conceptions of power, for example, have transitioned from early explanations of power as the exercise of political influence in organizations to power as a substantive and constitutive feature of organizational life. We see a shift from perspectives on power that depend on sociological and political explanations (e.g., strategies and games) to scholarship that demonstrates the mutually constitutive role of communication, power, and organizing. Conflict, which had a prominent place in the first edition, recedes in this edition and is largely subsumed in the discussion of power and resistance, for example. It is additionally repositioned from a focus on interpersonal, intergroup, and interorganizational conflict to an emphasis on the divergent interests of diverse stakeholders. Conflict is now viewed less from the perspective of the dyad and more from the orientation of dispersed, diffuse technologies of power. As such, the purpose of such research has moved from an impulse to manage conflict to a desire to confront inequities that give rise to or, in some cases, sublimate conflict.

The significance of the shift in organizational communication is even more apparent when we consider that the theories and concepts related to difference, destructive workplace behavior, and engagement—the final three chapters of this section—were largely absent from the first two editions of the *Handbook*. When difference was acknowledged, it was primarily in terms of gender and in a form that is hardly recognizable in today's research. In past editions, gender was viewed primarily through the prism of other features of organizations, such as communication competence, roles, leadership, hierarchy, and networks. Only in the chapter on power and politics in the second edition was substantive attention devoted to feminist theory, for example. Similarly, class was mentioned in passing, as a brief aside to an explanation of critical theory in organizational communication. In past editions, race was largely ignored, as was ethnicity, sexual orientation, and disability. In this edition, however, feminist and postcolonial theories are covered in great depth in Section I and are also interspersed throughout the *Handbook*. As such, questions of difference have become increasingly central to our understanding of, and research about, organizations.

These emphases on power and difference in the current edition are made explicit in a chapter on destructive workplace behavior in organizations found in this section. This "dark side" of organizational life had been acknowledged, to some extent, through discussions of critical scholarship in organizational communication, but rather than treating it as an abstraction of economic conditions, today's scholars have begun to explore the "real" conditions of existence in organizations. The manifestations of hierarchy, structure, power, and difference are enacted through communicative behaviors such as bullying and, as a result, the dark side is now studied in all of its complexity, with specific attention paid to the strategies and outcomes of discourse. Past editions of the *Handbook* alluded to such difficult communication via supervisor-subordinate communication or leadership but rarely, if ever, did scholars confront abusive organizational behavior in such a direct manner. The most direct consideration of abusive communication came in the second edition, which briefly accounted for why employees might exit an organization.

The chapters in this section also reflect the growing theoretical and topical diversity of organizational communication research in general. While our current scholarship is deeply indebted to functionalist and interpretive traditions, we now explicitly study theories and concepts that explain how communication constructs organization from what is now a well-established critical perspective. This trend is perhaps most evident in engaged scholarship in organizational communication, which takes seriously the admonition to "make a difference" in organizations. In recent years, we have begun to directly take into account those whom we study as legitimate stakeholders who have an important interest not only in organizing processes but also in how we conduct our research.

Overall, in this section, readers will find chapters that respond to calls for meaning-centered critical research that seeks to more fully understand the distinct, day-to-day lived experiences of organizational members. Readers will also discover that each of the chapter authors explores what I consider to be more nuanced theorizing, particularly in the ways in which they acknowledge the tensions, contradictions, and paradoxes of organizing. As such, these chapters are likely to help us become more self-reflexive about our research as they challenge us to rethink our naturalized assumptions regarding power, difference, conflict, and communication. In addition, the chapters indicate how our research has begun to connect micro, meso, and macro levels of research, taking into account, for example, how power and difference are simultaneously instantiated in everyday talk, institutional practices, and cultural structures. Finally, the chapters give us a sense of how truly interdisciplinary organizational communication has become, particularly since the first edition, given the focus on feminist, race, and postcolonial theories, among others, that are discussed in the chapters. The chapters also make clear, though, that we are not borrowing from those other disciplines as much as we are building on those foundations and, in turn, building our own theories that, increasingly, approach communication as a constitutive force of organizing more so than a functional variable.

Zoller begins the section with a chapter on "Power and Resistance in Organizational Communication" (Chapter 24). Chapters on "Power, Politics, and Influence" (by Peter Frost) and "Power and Politics" (by Dennis Mumby) were present in earlier editions of the *Handbook*, respectively, but Zoller extends this past research to more extensively explore recent trends in research on power and resistance. For example, Frost focused on power as a political phenomenon that entailed the exercise of influence based on personal attributes, resources, and strategies that were evident in surface and deep-structure games. In this instrumental approach to power, communication is viewed as both medium and meaning but primarily as an avenue for altering organizational behavior via structure, channels, networks, and rules. By contrast, Mumby provided an extensive history of the intellectual traditions that serve as a foundation for the study of power in/through organizations, including systems rationality, interpretive, critical, postmodern, and feminist approaches to power. In doing so, he explicated how communication, power, and organizing are interdependent and co-constructed phenomena. His central premise was that organizations are intersubjective systems of meaning that are produced, maintained, and transformed through communicative processes, albeit mediated by power as an inherent practice in organizations.

Using this assumption as a starting point for her chapter, Zoller explores not only several diverse theoretical perspectives on power but also a range of methodological and topical approaches to the study of power and politics. In terms of theoretical developments, Zoller updates readers on the current state of research from interpretive, critical, postmodern, and feminist perspectives while offering insights into the emergence of discursive and postcolonial approaches since the most recent *Handbook*. She notes, for example, that a discursive perspective focuses on how organizational actions are a contested terrain in the effort to construct and manage meaning. From this point of view, Zoller explains, discourse is linked intimately to power in that it lays down the "conditions of possibility" that determine what can be said, by whom, and when via the construction and application of knowledge.

Further, Zoller explores recent postcolonial research in organizational communication, with its emancipatory agenda that investigates marginalization resulting from projects of colonization and decolonization. More specifically, she explains that postcolonial theorizing complicates our understanding of national and geographic borders as well the intersection of communicating and organizing with race, class, gender, and ethnicity. As such, global conditions of labor and geopolitics, in general, come to the fore for scholars interested in studying power and organizational communication.

Finally, Zoller offers a constructive discussion of the key theoretical debates common to research on organizational power and resistance that not only includes helpful definitions of power but also a useful discussion of substantive dialectical tensions common in the research. In that section of the chapter, she explores how scholars have promoted understanding the links between *micro* (interpersonal, intraorganizational) levels and *macro* (interorganizational, cultural, institutional, and policy) levels of communication as they relate to power. An additional tension that Zoller explores is the debate around power as material or symbolic. Similarly, she recounts some of the recent studies that have sought to consider the agency-determinism dialectic in understanding organizational power. Inevitably, this discussion leads to a closer look at conceptions of resistance that have emerged since the last edition of the *Handbook*. Here again, Zoller draws on dialectical tensions to examine how scholars have sought to negotiate between overt/covert and individual/collective forms of resistance. All the while, she takes into account how important it is to consider context, multiple potential meanings, and various intended and unintended outcomes of resistance that have been largely ignored until recently.

In her chapter, "Difference and Organizing" (Chapter 25), Parker engages the growing literature on communication and difference that has emerged as a prominent area of study in our discipline (and organizational communication, specifically), offering the potential for sustained critique and transformation. Although the focus on difference has begun to play a prominent role in organizational communication, it has, nevertheless, been a fairly recent focus, at least in the context of the *Handbook*. Studies of race in the workplace, for example, were entirely absent from earlier volumes. As such, this chapter represents an important contribution to the future direction of organizational communication.

In the chapter, Parker argues that early research on difference in organizations can be broadly described as "additive and piecemeal," moving from simpler, causal forms of power inequities to an emphasis on gender differences at work to an interest in categories of identity such as race, class, and ability. Similar to other authors in the section, Parker suggests that more complex theorizing about difference—drawing on feminist, critical race, postcolonial, and transnational theories—enables scholars to more appropriately locate difference as a communicative, constitutive feature of organizing. This important conceptual shift, she explains, moves difference from being viewed as an essential property of individuals, groups, and organizations to a multifaceted set of structures, practices, and systems of meaning that organize the economy of work in ways that simultaneously enable and constrain how we both see and do difference.

In the chapter, Parker identifies four central themes that are common to these theoretical perspectives. First, she explores how these theories of difference complicate binaries (e.g., object/subject, agency/structure) and their impact on knowledge and identity as a means to empower, if not emancipate, marginalized groups. Second, she cites a range of studies that expose, critique, and dismantle discursively reproduced racial projects that normalize and protect White supremacy. Third, she explicates research that focuses on alternative histories and self-representations of indigenous peoples in a range of global contexts in order to deconstruct and reconfigure the material impact of neo-liberal/neo-conservative capitalist practices. Finally, she identifies research that complicates difference across space, place, and identity as a means to illuminate strategies of macro and micro resistance that cut across and bring together multiple axes of socio-spatial difference.

By exploring frameworks that take up questions related to intersectionality, essentialism, binary thinking, and group identity politics, Parker complicates our understanding of how we organize difference. In doing so, she points to future opportunities to examine concepts of place, space, and identity, among others, which problematize our assumptions regarding how we approach, understand, and experience difference in organizational life. Future research on difference, in this respect, will further examine it as a social construct, with scholars seeking to confront the ways in which power coalesces to produce persistent political, economic, and social conditions that mark differences that matter in/through organizations.

In Chapter 26, Kassing and Waldron provide readers with a relatively new way of considering organizational communication through their discussion of "Incivility, Destructive Workplace Behavior, and Bullying." Although inappropriate and untoward behavior is not new to organizations, Kassing and Waldron bring it to our attention as a problem to theorize and, ultimately, to confront. They explain that, even though organizations benefit us in a myriad of ways, they are also fraught with destructive behavior in which people are harmed, collaboration declines, and trust recedes.

Kassing and Waldron review a range of destructive organizational processes, beginning with a brief overview of the historical trends and theoretical strands that have emerged from this important area of research and practice. They note, for example, that scholars from management and organization studies have addressed related topics, including abusive supervision, destructive leadership, petty tyranny, rudeness, sexual harassment, workplace aggression, and workplace violence, among others. They suggest that this earlier work in cognate disciplines has been largely descriptive and has focused on identifying the types of abusive behavior, their frequency, the characteristics of the perpetrators and victims of abusive behavior, and contexts in which this behavior occurred. Often, they suggest, such research is grounded in trait, relational, and identity theories.

By contrast, Kassing and Waldron note that research by communication scholars is increasingly grounded in the discourse practices that enact and resist destructive organizational behavior. Yet, they note, a significant amount of the empirical work in the discipline tends to use the individual as the exclusive unit of analysis. Macro-level cultural and organizational forces that create the conditions for destructive behavior tend to merit less attention in the discipline and, by extension, the organizational communication literature reflects these gaps.

After the authors have laid the groundwork for the broad literature of abusive behavior, they then explore the notion of *incivility*, a term that describes a variety of destructive behaviors in organizations. After noting the range of negative effects of incivility on both members and their organizations, they discuss, in greater depth, emotional manipulation and bullying as two areas that have received greater scholarly attention in recent years. In the case of bullying, for example, Kassing and Waldron indicate that it is typically marked by intensity, repetition, duration, and power disparity. After defining bullying and explaining why employees have difficulty recognizing and acknowledging it, they provide a detailed and informative explication of the causes and effects of bullying that should be required reading for any scholar or manager. Weaving theory and practice throughout this section, they also offer an insightful look at the myriad of ways that employees try to cope with bullying.

They conclude the chapter with a broader focus on ethics, addressing how destructive behavior in organizations undermines not only the social contract between coworkers but also the moral culture of organizations. Perhaps most importantly, Kassing and Waldron then turn to a discussion of communicative practices that have the potential to restore personal and organizational well-being in the aftermath of destructive communication. To their credit, they acknowledge that restorative systems and practices in the aftermath of destructive behavior require individual, group, organizational, and cultural efforts in combination rather than in isolation. In particular, they note that further research on specific intervention strategies is needed to better understand and implement changes that are most likely to promote personal and organizational well-being.

Dempsey and Barge's chapter on "Engaged Scholarship and Democracy" (Chapter 27) represents one of the new, emerging areas of organizational communication scholarship. For readers familiar with the significant growth of engaged scholarship, its noticeable absence from earlier editions of the *Handbook* would come as no surprise. Engagement is rarely, if ever, acknowledged, aside from the occasional reference to applied organizational communication research in previous volumes. As such, Dempsey and Barge offer us the first comprehensive review of engaged scholarship in the field of organizational communication to date. They do note the long legacy of applied research—beginning in the 1930s and 1940s—within organizational communication, especially as scholars with a pragmatic focus sought to bring research to bear on everyday problems and practices of organizing. Yet they also explain that today's iteration of engagement is unique and, increasingly, self-reflexive. More specifically, they argue that today's engaged research reflects a growing commitment of scholars to directly confront substantive social, political, economic, and ecological problems. As an example of this new inflection of engagement, Dempsey and Barge note that some engaged scholars have reconsidered the possibilities of community-based economies while others strive for dialogue and deliberation aimed at improving governance at the local level.

Regardless of the specific strand of engaged scholarship, however, they argue that all engaged scholarship (1) is committed to using the resources of scholarly research to address practical concerns and useful ends; (2) serves as a mode of inquiry whereby recursive practices integrate the interests of the academy and communities; and (3) brings to focus the communicative dimensions that structure the research process, seeking to democratize the coproduction of knowledge via dialogue and collaboration with those most directly impacted by the research. From this set of assumptions as a starting point, they summarize the *four faces* of engagement: (1) applied communication research, (2) collaborative learning, (3) activism and social justice, and (4) practical theory.

Later in the chapter, Dempsey and Barge draw upon research on participatory dialogue, democracy, and governance to argue that the full promise of engaged scholarship lies in its ability to enact new forms of governance grounded in a democratic model of communication, particularly with regard to the engagement of diverse stakeholders, some of whom have been denied voice and decision-making abilities in the past. They suggest that engaged scholarship, when understood as participatory democracy, creates alternative practices of research, teaching, and practice that are more reflexive, responsive, and, ultimately, responsible. One of the unique contributions of this chapter, then, is to stimulate future scholarship in organizational communication that enables ethically and socially responsible research, both in process and outcome.

As is clear from this introduction, each of these chapters reflects, at the least, substantive extensions of contributions found in the previous editions of the *Handbook* and, more likely, constructive new contributions that have emerged in the last decade. All but the chapter on power and resistance represent new additions to the editions and, as such, indicate a growing body of important research that takes up questions of fairness, equity, and justice not only within organizations but also across and around them. These chapters suggest that organizational communication scholars are less encumbered by traditional conceptions of organizational politics, identification, supervisor-subordinate communication, dyadic conflict, feedback, and decision making evident in the first edition or even more recent iterations of power, identity, structure, participation, and socio-political environments found in the most recent edition. Each chapter undoubtedly owes a certain scholarly debt to the decades of organizational communication research that preceded them. Yet none seems limited by those assumptions, theories, concepts, and methods. Instead, the chapters offer interesting and important scholarship that is generative in the best sense of the word. In that regard, these chapters remind us that not only do the outcomes of our research matter but that the ways in which we conduct our work make a difference, too. In that sense, the chapters in this section challenge past models of organizational communication while also offering new ways to articulate transformative organizational practices.

CHAPTER 24

Power and Resistance in Organizational Communication

Heather M. Zoller

Power remains a central concern of organizational studies writ large, and elucidating relationships among communication, organizing, and power is a significant element of organizational communication research. The communicative construction of political relationships of influence is key to understanding the organizing process, the everyday experience of organizational life, and institutional policy choices. In the second edition of this *Handbook*, Mumby (2001) provided a detailed history of the intellectual traditions undergirding the study of power and organizations. He also highlighted the significance of understanding resistance as central to organizational politics. Thus this chapter places more emphasis on research developments since that time. Any review of such a large body of literature is necessarily limited and subject to the author's biases, but I attempt to represent a diversity of theoretical, methodological, and topical approaches to the study of power and politics.

The chapter begins by describing some of the predominant theoretical approaches to studying power and resistance in organizational communication. The subsequent section elucidates major theoretical debates in the field, with an emphasis on research that was published over the last decade. The conclusion discusses potential avenues for future research.

Theoretical Perspectives on the Study of Power

Organizational communication employs multiple theoretical perspectives to study questions of power and politics. Though they often overlap, each can be understood as a discourse that emphasizes different elements of the communication-power relationship. Many of the perspectives and methodologies that I address are covered in more depth in other chapters. Here, I briefly describe how interpretive, rhetorical, critical, postmodern, discursive, feminist, and postcolonial perspectives conceptualize and investigate relationships among communication, organizing, power, and resistance.

First, the interpretive approach focuses on the role of everyday language use and social interaction in socially constructing reality. Methodologically, interpretive research rejects the concept of objectivity in favor of intersubjectivity and reflexivity, focusing on the human being as research instrument. This tradition emphasizes ethnographic and other forms of qualitative research that focus on questions of meaning in social contexts. In organizational communication, interpretive work addresses the relationships among intersubjective meanings, culture, and power (Ellingson, 2005; Harter, Deardorff, Kenniston, Carmack, & Rattine-Flaherty, 2008; Scott & Trethewey, 2008). Generally, this work focuses on the achievement of consensus versus conflict and takes a descriptive rather than prescriptive stance (Deetz, 2001). For instance, Lucas's (2011) study of contradictions between the *working-class promise* and *the American dream* addresses how these two working-class discourses reify class differences and privileges. Although the study bears similarity to Willis's (1977) Marxist ethnography of working-class school dropouts ("the lads"), it focuses more on describing how these cultural discourses contribute to working-class ambivalence about class mobility than it does locating those discourses within structural contradictions of capitalism.

Rhetorical perspectives share commonalities with interpretive and discursive approaches, although scholars in this tradition may hold varied philosophical assumptions. Arguably, rhetorical studies' historical Greek tradition uniquely emphasizes issues of influence and persuasion. According to Conrad (2011), "rhetoric is a complex process through which people develop and refine their beliefs, values, and views of reality by communicating with others" (pp. 2–3), and is therefore closely linked with power and social control. Rhetorical criticism in organizational communication focuses on the "description, interpretation, analysis, and critique of organized persuasion—and by extension, identification" (Cheney & Lair, 2005, p. 60). By conceptualizing organizations as rhetorical entities, researchers investigate questions of motivation, persuasion, hierarchy, and categorization in the organizing process (Cheney & Lair, 2005; McMillan, 2007). The perspective addresses *internal* political issues (Cloud, 2005; Morgan & Krone, 2001) but also examines the rhetorical representation of organizations as influence agents, advancing understanding of the political role of organizations in society (Aune, 2001; Conrad, 2011).

Critical perspectives encompass multiple theoretical approaches, including critical modernism, postmodernism, feminism, and postcolonial theorizing (Ganesh, 2009a). Major influences in the critical tradition include scholars as varied as Marx, Gramsci, and Frankfurt School theorists including Adorno, Horkheimer, and Habermas. Mumby (1997) characterized the critical lens as a discourse of suspicion, focused on uncovering structural inequalities. Critical perspectives investigate issues of power, domination, and control, with the goals of understanding, critique, emancipation, and social change. This approach built on the interpretive turn in organizational communication, helping us to understand how certain meanings become dominant in the organizing process and whose interests are served by those meaning constructions (Deetz, 1992a).

Critical studies "see organizations in general as social historical creations accomplished in conditions of struggle and power relations" (Deetz, 2001, p. 25). More specifically, "organizations are conceived as political sites where various organizational actors and groups struggle to 'fix' meaning in ways that will serve their particular interests" (Mumby, 2004, p. 237). Critical research may entail ideology critique, investigating questions of reification and hegemony, or communicative action, drawing from Habermas (1984) to theorize and investigate forms of systematically distorted communication (Deetz, 1992a; Thackaberry, 2004). Generally, critical research critiques domination and asymmetry with the goals of reformation toward social justice. Historically, critical perspectives were concerned with obedience, acquiescence to oppression, rewards, and punishments but over time, developed concerns with questions of concertive control, identity, and forms of open communication.

Mumby (1997) contrasted the discourse of suspicion with a postmodern *discourse of vulnerability*, which questions foundational concepts and master narratives such as objective truth, knowledge, and the unitary self. Postmodernism tends to emphasize contradiction and paradox (Ganesh, 2009b). Often associated with the work of Lyotard, Derrida, Foucault, Lacan, and others, it is important to note that *postmodernism* is a contested term, and theorists described using this label defy boundaries (Jones, 2009). Deetz's (2001) use of the label *dialogic* helps to avoid confusion regarding the difference between postmodernism as a historical era and various strains of intellectual thought. The term is also more inclusive of anti-essentialist traditions such as American pragmatism (Dewey, 1993; James, 1890) and dialogic theorists such as Bakhtin (Holquist, 1990). Deetz suggested that the perspective foregrounds the constructed nature of language and discourse, the fragmentation of identities, and local and contextualized epistemologies while sharing a critical concern with dissensus and conflict. Although critical and postmodern research intersects and informs one another, theorists in the latter tradition are more likely to treat power as shifting, diffuse, and disciplinary and emphasize the productive role of power, particularly as it relates to questions of identity (Tracy, 2000).

A burgeoning literature investigates organizational power and resistance through a discursive lens. In a 2005 special issue of *Management Communication Quarterly*, Putnam, Grant, Michelson, and Cutcher (2005) delineated discourse as "the practices of talking and writing; the collection of texts that are produced, disseminated, and consumed; and the larger discursive context embodied in these texts" (p. 7), whereas Mumby (2005) described a discursive frame of analysis as "focusing on the ways that organizational behavior is subject to competing efforts to shape and fix its meaning" (p. 22).

Foucault (1979, 1980a, 1980b) is a significant influence on discourse perspectives on power (as he is on critical and postmodern perspectives). Hardy and Phillips (2004) draw from Foucault to describe *discursive formations* as "bodies of knowledge that 'systematically form the object of which they speak'" (Foucault, 1979, p. 492). Discourse is linked intimately to power in that it "lays down the 'conditions of possibility' that determine what can be said, by whom, and when" (Hardy & Phillips, 2004, p. 30). Critical discourse analysis involves "articulation, disarticulation and rearticulation of elements in a discourse" (Fairclough, 1995, p. 93) as it relates to power and domination. There is some question about the degree to which discourse represents a unique perspective on organizational experience because of the already shared concerns in communication with the social and political construction of knowledge, meaning, and identity. Putnam et al. (2005) suggested that discursive approaches are unique in emphasizing the construction of knowledge as it relates to power and resistance but did not say how specifically.

Feminist research provides another lens for understanding power, foregrounding gender and sexuality as constitutive of organizing and relations of domination, often with attention to the ways that ethnicity, class, nationality, and other points of distinction work together to create inequalities (Allen, 1995; Ashcraft & Allen, 2003; Buzzanell, 1994; Buzzanell & Liu, 2005; Dempsey, 2011). Feminist perspectives tend to share an emancipatory goal of emphasizing communication practice and the creation of spaces for marginalized voices. For instance, Trethewey's (2001) investigation of women's narratives about aging and work suggested that "to at once critique and possibly begin to transform a patriarchal capitalist system that denigrates older working women, we need to first hear from those women and learn from their experience" (p. 185). Feminist research questions binary distinctions such as subject/object, masculinity/femininity, public/private, and emotionality/rationality, thereby developing a rich critique of taken-for-granted patriarchal assumptions embedded in dominant approaches to organizing (Ashcraft, 2009; Mumby & Ashcraft, 2004).

Finally, postcolonial research represents an emancipatory agenda that investigates marginalization resulting from projects of colonization and decolonization (Guha, 1983; Shome, 2002; Spivak, 1988). Postcolonial theorizing brings our attention to border crossing and the interplay of race, class, gender, ethnicity, and language, and it questions the neocolonial assumptions of European management styles exported to the global south (Broadfoot & Munshi, 2007). Subaltern studies focus "on rewriting history from below, based on the argument that dominant narratives of colonial histories have systematically represented the interests of the colonizers and the national elite" (Dutta & Pal, 2010, p. 364). Economic marginalization is bound up intrinsically with exclusion from the public sphere and the production of and definition of what counts as knowledge. Hall (2010) observed in his investigation of Jamaican managers in a multinational bank that

> the impact of national culture on organizing in Jamaica calls for a theoretical vocabulary that more explicitly addresses issues of colonial power, history, geopolitical power, and national culture than is generally available in the managerial, organizational, and organizational communication literature. (p. 4)

Theoretical Issues and Debates: Power, Resistance, and Organizing

Having described some of the major approaches to theorizing organizational power and communication, this section discusses developments in organizational research by examining some significant theoretical debates in the field. These debates include differences in the way we define power, the levels at which we investigate political issues, and the degree to which we should construe power in material and symbolic terms. Scholars also disagree about how we should theorize relationships between power and resistance. Finally, debates emerge regarding avenues for social change.

Defining Power in Organizational Communication

Fundamental to research about organizational politics is the question of how to conceptualize power. Organizational communication scholarship draws from multiple conceptions of power, and debate focuses on how to best emphasize the constitutive role of communication in power relationships. Theorizing has evolved from one-dimensional, pluralist models of power, such as Dahl's (1957) emphasis on a person's or group's direct influence over the behavior of others, to two-dimensional models, such as Bachrach and Baratz's (1962) model that elucidates how elite groups mobilize bias in ways that suppress the open discussion of issues that would threaten their preferences, to Lukes's (1974) three-dimensional model that describes how power operates not only through conflict and decision making but through the absence of conflict and explicit decision points resulting from the ability to shape and articulate the very wants of others.

Structural explanations tend to describe power as a commodity, focusing on intentional and observable acts. For instance, French and Raven (1959) detailed the bases of social power, including reward, coercive, legitimate, referent, and expert power. Pfeffer and Salancik's (1978) coalitional model of power viewed organizations as sites of conflict that can be explained by comparing the relative power of different groups in the organization. Indicative of much of this early research, Pfeffer (1981) viewed communication as reproducing and legitimizing already existent relations of power, but not as playing a constitutive role in organizational power. Mumby (2001) observed that organizational research from resource-dependency perspectives often used a transmission model of communication, measuring power in terms of network centrality, access to resources, and control. The research did not interrogate how relations of power were formed or enacted communicatively.

Organizational communication scholars advocated for understanding power as a communicative phenomenon, building on the three-dimensional model of power. The work of Deetz and Mumby integrated critical theories, hermeneutics, and social constructionist epistemologies, highlighting how struggles over meaning (including ideology, hegemony, and distorted communication) are constitutive of organizational life (Deetz, 1992a; Mumby, 1993). Communication-centered approaches also highlighted the construction of subjectivity as a central component of relations of power (Holmer-Nadesan, 1996). The following definitions illustrate this tradition:

- The most effective use of power occurs when those with power are able to get those without power to interpret the world from the former's point of view. Power is exercised through a set of interpretive frames that each worker incorporates as part of his or her organizational identity. (Mumby & Clair, 1997, p. 184)
- "The production and reproduction of, resistance, to, or transformation of relatively fixed (sedimented) structures of communication and meaning that support the interests (symbolic, political, and economic) of some organizational members or groups over others. (Mumby, 2001, p. 587)
- Hardy and Phillips (2004) suggested that individuals and groups exercise power by "articulating meaning in ways that legitimate their particular views as 'natural' and 'inevitable,' link the actions and preferences of other actors to the achievement of their interests, and make particular socially constructed structures take on a neutral and objective appearance. (p. 304)

These definitions of power provide a useful foundation for communication studies, because they focus attention on the play between the centripetal and centrifugal forces of symbolism and meaning making. Stohl and Cheney (2001) created a more inclusive definition: "Power is associated with influence, the allocation and mobilization of resources, the ability to manipulate situations, the capacity to affect interpretive processes, the fulfillment of needs, the attainment of goals, and the overcoming of resistance" (p. 384), but this definition may separate the role of meaning from the other functions listed.

A significant trend over the last 20 years emphasizes power's dialectical relationship with resistance (Mumby, 2005; Mumby & Ashcraft, 2004). For instance, Mumby (2004) defined power "as a dialectical phenomenon characterized by interdependent processes of struggle, resistance, and control" (pp. 240–241). The dialectical perspective emphasizes mutual struggles over meaning among individuals and groups within shifting relations of power, thus challenging domination views of power (Fleming & Spicer, 2007). Berger's (2005) public relations research, which can be understood as a branch of organizational communication, reflects the dialectical approach by theorizing *power over* in terms of dominance, *power with* in terms of empowering and dialogic relationships, and *power to* as a form of resistance that counters dominance.

Conrad and McIntush (2003) theorized the *punctuated equilibria model*, which arguably reflects a dialectical approach by describing power as a struggle involving outflanking and counter-outflanking between economic/political elites and nonelites (see also Mann, 1986). Significantly, the theory represents a counterpoint to the community-power debates that is more macro level than those discussed earlier. Focused on policy creation, Conrad (2004a) argued that business elites have knowledge, resources, and connections to maintain policy monopolies, but that

> lengthy periods of policy quiescence are broken by intense periods of change when three conditions occur simultaneously: (1) long-standing sociopolitical conditions become visible to the public and are defined as *"problems"* of sufficient import to demand action by policymakers, (2) potential *solutions* are made available to policymakers, and (3) *political pressures* are sufficiently intense to overcome the dominance by political and economic elites that characterize quiescent periods. (p. 312, emphasis in original)

This approach represents a third option between elite theories that focus on policy domination by powerful groups and pluralist models that emphasize equality of competition among social groups.

The existence of multiple conceptions of power represents an opportunity to understand organizational dynamics in complex ways. Moving forward, though, it is critical that researchers continue to clearly define their assumptions about power and its relationship to communication. At times, scholarship (even postmodern and post-structuralist) continues to draw from French and Raven and resource dependency (Pierce & Dougherty, 2003; Scarduzio, 2011; Tracy, 2005). As organizational communication scholars extend the idea that organizing is a communicative process (Mumby, 1993), we should theorize communication-power relationships as central to that process. For instance, the communicative constitution of organization (CCO) perspective brings attention to micro-level organizing processes, but has been criticized for treating workers and managers as equally capable of discursively constructing the organization (Cloud, 2005) and for a tendency to "delimit the examination of power in communication to issues such as: the competencies of individual actors; the effects of organizational structure on actors; or the concentration of power in authority figures" (Kwon, Clarke, & Wodak, 2009). Similarly, Kuhn (2008) critiqued governance theories of the firm for treating power as an objective element of organizational hierarchy rather than as linguistically constructed and criticized resource theories for missing tension and conflict.

Investigating Power at Micro and Macro Levels

Researchers responding to calls for contextualized organizational research have brought greater attention to the micro levels of organizational power. Recently, scholars have promoted understanding the links between micro (interpersonal, intraorganizational) levels and macro (interorganizational, cultural, institutional, and policy) levels of interaction (Alvesson & Karreman, 2000; Conrad, 2004b; Kuhn, 2008; LeGreco & Tracy, 2009).

Qualitative research, including organizational ethnographies and interviews, highlights the lived experience of organizational politics, adding greater complexity to theorizing through contextualized methods that address sensemaking and interaction, particularly in everyday interaction (Ashcraft, 2005; Barker, 1993; Bisel, Ford, & Keyton, 2007; Dempsey, 2010; Harter et al., 2008; Larson & Tompkins, 2005; Lynch, 2009; Murphy, 1998). One set of examples comes from research that builds on early critiques of rational models of organizational behavior (Crozier, 1964; March & Simon, 1958; Putnam & Mumby, 1993) by investigating the everyday experience of emotionality and sexuality. Morgan and Krone (2001) described the *emotional social order* in a hospital as a form of social control. Using a rhetorical, dramaturgical perspective, they concluded that "actors work to negotiate the emotional order through improvised performances that directly oppose or otherwise depart from the scripted organizational emotion rules" (p. 318). Similarly, Scarduzio

(2011) reported that judges express *privileged deviance* because of their ability to alter established emotional norms in the courtroom, with material consequences for defendants. Tracy (2000) shed light on the disciplinary identity work through which emotional norms are constituted on a cruise ship from the perspective of her own experience as an employee. Although much of this research is ethnographic, it is important to note that quantitative research in areas such as dissent also addresses issues of power at the micro level (Kassing & Armstrong, 2002).

Perhaps as a result of this turn toward the everyday, micro level, scholars have called for more attention to the connection between interpersonal/intraorganizational politics and macro-level power issues (Alvesson & Karreman, 2000; Conrad, 2004b; Kuhn, 2008; LeGreco & Tracy, 2009). Discourse theorists propose that scholars address multiple levels from discourse in interaction to systematic grand Discourses (Alvesson & Karreman, 2000). One way to do so is to investigate how macro-level social issues (such as gender and economic ideologies) influence organizations (Norton, 2009). Such work connects intraorganizational politics with broader social structures (Carlone & Larson, 2006; Dempsey, 2007a; Ganesh, 2007). For example, Harter (2004) extended Stohl and Cheney's (2001) paradoxes of organizational participation by examining how masculine and individualist ideologies in the U.S. cultural context undercut participative solidarity in an agrarian cooperative. Gillespie (2001) investigated how bureaucratic discourses of rationalization and efficiency influenced Medicaid's adoption of managed care principles, creating disciplinary standards that reinforced discourses of individual responsibility and overlooked the material barriers to compliance for low-income asthma patients.

Another way to connect micro and macro levels is to examine the political role organizations play in society (Norton, 2009). Conrad (2004a) argued that critical research has focused on the micro processes through which managerial power is established communicatively but has failed to address relationships between managerialism and public policy, evidencing "almost no effort to examine the communicative processes through which managers use the power of the state to further their interests or maintain their dominance" (p. 331). Deetz's (1992b) early work is an exception that provided a foundation for understanding the growing influence of corporate/managerial logics at the level of everyday politics and public policy. Today, a growing number of researchers are examining the political influence of organizational discourse on social structures (Knight, 2007; Stohl, Stohl, & Townsley, 2007; Weaver, 2010), such as corporate efforts to shape public opinion and public policy. They also consider the possibility of transforming corporations as sites of decision making (Deetz, 2007). For example, Ritz (2007) detailed the discursive construction of corporate personhood through legal decision making and political influence and discussed its implications for democracy. Conrad (2004a) described the issue management strategy of containment used by elites during financial reform debates in the wake of the Enron scandal to delay action until public anger receded. This critical research locates public relations as a macro-level site of contestation, negotiation, and resistance. Motion and Weaver (2005) identified public relations practitioners as central cultural figures who work to establish Foucauldian regimes of truth in a critical study of the Life Sciences Network, which encouraged the public to overlook potential risks to accept genetically modified food. Other research examines the role of public relations in promoting acceptance of corporate self-regulation in areas such as environmental risk (Zoller & Tener, 2010). Such work uncovers potential vulnerabilities and opportunities for public participation in political decision making and resistance to corporate influence. Broadening this focus, Nadesan (2008) employed Foucault's concept of governmentality to examine the confluence of biopolitical discourses in neo-liberal economics, neo-conservative military/security approaches, and social conservatism.

Conceptualizing Power as Material and Symbolic

Accompanying the development of communicative theories of power has been debate about the degree to which power should be understood in material or symbolic terms. Although much of this debate dichotomizes material and symbolic approaches, from a communication perspective, it is more useful to think about the relative emphasis of symbolism and materialism in any given work. Below, I briefly describe these debates in terms of contemporary social trends.

Cloud (2005) called for greater attention to materiality in organizational communication research. Her study of a union newsletter during the lockout at Staley Manufacturing theorized the "limits of symbolic agency" (p. 511). She argued that the union's rhetorical skill (symbolic power) was not sufficient to overcome management's material advantages (coercive power). This is an important observation; however, this position fails to account for the partly symbolic means through which management attains, defends, and legitimizes their access to coercive resources. Ganesh, Zoller, and Cheney (2005) promoted a complex view of material-symbolic relationships, suggesting that a return to Gramsci's (1971) dual focus on processes of coercion and consent may help us to move beyond a dichotomous approach.

Debates about materiality often center on the degree to which research on identity politics addresses class conflicts and material forms of inequality. Organizational researchers have identified subjectification as a key disciplinary process through which employees take on subject positions consistent with managerial imperatives (e.g., Fleming & Spicer, 2007; Thomas, 2009). A significant line of research views the normative control of the self as a powerful means of managerial hegemony (Alvesson & Willmott, 2002; Collinson, 1992; Kunda, 1992), with more recent studies theorizing conflict through the active constitution of identity by both managers and employees. Postmodern and post-structuralist perspectives treat the self as an effect of power and therefore often view resistance as a form of identity work (Carlone & Larson, 2006; Fleming & Sewell, 2002; Knights & McCabe, 2000; Mumby, 2005).

Whereas postmodern scholars see emancipatory potential in the way identity politics can deconstruct dominant relations of power (Ashcraft, 2005; Fleming, 2007), others view the focus on identity struggle as a way to avoid the political commitments central to a critique of capitalism (Contu, 2008). For instance, Cloud (2001) accused cultural studies and organizational communication of having a misplaced faith in the transgressive potential of identity politics and the deconstruction of the self.

These questions of identity and materiality are central to debates regarding power and new forms of management. A significant line of research argues that a shift toward a *new/information/liquid* economy and post-Fordist flexible workplaces signifies the demise of traditional class politics. In this view, the transition from manufacturing to knowledge-based work marks identity politics as a primary nexus of control (Bauman, 2007; Hardt & Negri, 2000; Lash & Urry, 1994). Scholars suggest that manufacturing work, which has become more participative, flexible, and knowledge intensive, is also becoming a less relevant mode of economic production in the face of outsourcing, downsizing, and information technologies. This new system is characterized by immaterial, precarious, and contingent labor (McRobbie, 2010).

Cloud (2001) challenged the argument that a *new* economy makes class analyses irrelevant, countering that manufacturing, class antagonism, and capitalist relationships remain fundamental to the economy. Scholars suggest that the new economic thesis overlooks the materiality of contemporary production, including the worker and environmental impact of technology in the information economy (Cheney & Cloud, 2006; Rodino-Colocino, 2008), observations that are borne out by recent suicides highlighting sweatshop conditions at the Chinese Foxconn plant that makes iPads and other communication technologies (Barboza, 2010). Additionally, researchers question whether contemporary organizing should be characterized as post-Fordist rather than a neo-Taylorist extension of managerial control strategies (Crowley, Tope, Chamberlain, & Hodson, 2010). These contradictory views of economic change are tied to the philosophical tendency to view power relationships as relatively enduring and stable versus shifting and unstable.

There is a clear need to connect organizational theories with the physical manifestations of organizing in the 21st century such as job insecurity, poverty, occupational illness and injury, and environmental impact, but these issues are themselves linked to discourse and identity in complex ways (Gillespie, 2001; Kuhn, 2006; Nadesan, 2008; Rodino-Colocino, 2011; Zoller, 2009b). For instance, Zoller (2003) investigated how managerial ideologies, class-based assumptions about risk, and masculine identity norms encouraged employee consent to workplace health hazards. Constructions of gender and race have material consequences for work-life policy implementation (Kirby, Golden, Medved, Jorgenson, & Buzzanell, 2003; Kirby & Krone, 2002; Wieland, 2011) and the precarious status of a growing number of temporary employees (Townsley & Stohl, 2003) and technology workers (Rodino-Colocino, 2011).

Moving forward, research should consider how materiality and symbolism along with multiple forms of difference, inequity, and marginalization work together and with what consequences (McRobbie, 2010; Mumby & Ashcraft, 2004). Intersectionality, which views identity as a crystallization of multiple discourses of race, class, age, gender, and other forms of difference, is one means of doing so (e.g., Dougherty, 2011). Fraser (2009) offers a theoretical path for connecting identity, materiality, and social change by seeking to reconcile the politics of redistribution, recognition, and representation. She reminds us that marketization, resistance in the form of seeking protection from the market, and emancipation in the form of struggling against protection, may interrelate in unpredictable ways. For example, markets can disrupt other relations of domination in society, and movements of emancipation can sometimes reinforce neo-liberalism. Organizational communication research is well-suited to address these complexities by virtue of its focus on the intersection of the symbolic and the material.

Investigating the Organizational Self by Theorizing Agency and Determinism

Closely related to this discussion of materiality and identity are continued questions about the relationships among communication, power, and agency. To what degree is the self *constructed* versus *real,* and how do we theorize human agency versus determinism?

A significant body of research, often post-modern and post-structuralist, challenges the real-self/fake-self dichotomy invoked when theorists depict power as an external force that restrains or influences the self (Tracy & Trethewey, 2005). For instance, Fleming (2005) argued that concepts such as *resistance through distance* (Collinson, 1994) and *psychological distancing* (of front-stage roles and backstage selves) in theories of employee cynicism metaphorically treat the self as stable and given *a priori.* Fleming promoted the alternative metaphor of production that highlights how cynicism enables and constructs identity. Tracy (2000) drew from Foucault to describe how arbitrary and contingent emotional rules on a cruise ship helped to produce what we think of as the self, noting that the relations of power inscribed in those rules are unstable and contingent. Her study of prison guards (Tracy, 2005) also demonstrated how selves are constituted, constrained, and interpreted through discourses of power in multiple and fragmented discourses. Researchers investigate how disciplinary workplace discourses implicate employee *and* management identities, with the purpose of understanding the production of self, particularly in terms of entrepreneurial and self-governing subjects under "new" forms of concertive control (Holmer-Nadesan, 1996; Kondo, 1990; Kunda, 1992).

Theorizing agency remains a central point of debate. For instance, Mumby (2004) argued that the ideology critique tradition (Althusser, 1971; Burawoy, 1979) lacked a theory of agency because it construed power as pervasive and relatively immune from resistance. Neo-Marxist perspectives investigating corporate colonization, manufacturing consent, and designing selves have been criticized for depicting managers as powerful agents versus relatively powerless and reactive workers (Mumby, 2005). Today, writers frequently critique postmodernism, and Foucault in particular, for failing to adequately theorize agency. For example, Conrad (2004b) argued that the idea of organizations as constituted through discourse can be taken too far, to the point that "there is no agency and there are no oppressors" (p. 429).

Multiple authors have proposed ways of theorizing agency from the perspective of a socially constructed self, often by focusing on the multiplicity of power discourses. For instance, Zoller and Fairhurst (2007) described *agency* as follows:

> Our own reading of Foucault locates agency in the act of choosing among multiple Discourses, while recognizing that one is never outside of Discourse; we simply move from one discursive network to another (Calás & Smircich, 1999). Nevertheless, resistance to a Discourse is achievable, suggesting possibilities for simultaneous control and change where behavior can be reproductive at one level and resistant at another because of the space of action that multiple Discourses make available (Daudi, 1986). (p. 1336)

Postmodernists continue to emphasize that agency itself does not stand outside relations of power. Mumby (2005) suggested that discursive perspectives avoid the power and resistance dichotomy so that "social actors are neither romanticized nor viewed as unwitting dupes but rather are seen as engaging in a locally produced, discursive process of self-formation that is always ongoing, always tension filled" (p. 38). Critical and feminist research also encourages theorists to avoid dichotomizing between passive and active, victim and agent (Trethewey, 2001). Hall (2010) treated the question of agency as an empirical one by investigating the degree to which Jamaican managers mimicked Western discourses or recognized themselves as agents able to resist dominant Western discourses (see also Kuhn, 2006). This empirical approach regarding the performance of agency and its implications is a promising path for organizational communication researchers.

Investigating the Pervasiveness and Productivity of Power

As the preceding discussion suggests, theorists disagree about the pervasiveness of power and the degree to which it enables or constrains. Studies of resistance are central to our understanding of power, dominance, the self, and social change. Although few authors explicitly define the term, *resistance* is generally associated with contesting, nonconforming, or negotiating dominant relationships of power.

A number of researchers continue to indict organization studies for understanding power in terms of domination (Larson & Tompkins, 2005). For example, Pierce and Dougherty (2003) argued that a domination view of power prevails in functionalist, materialist, and postmodern scholarship. Yet Foucault-inspired interest in power as both productive and repressive, and the growing characterization of resistance as a form of communicative struggle, contradicts these claims.

Certainly, researchers continue to explore the ways in which communication promotes hegemonic relationships and forms of discursive closure. For instance, Thackaberry's (2004) investigation of a U.S. Fire Service self-study showed how potential discursive openings for transforming outdated assumptions about fire safety practices fell victim to discursive closure as technical and bureaucratic solutions superseded cultural changes (see also Lyon & Mirivel, 2011). However, much of this research also emphasizes potential openings for change and therefore rarely depicts power as totalizing. Ainsworth, Hardy, and Harley (2005) investigated how a World Bank development program attempted to co-opt and control development debates but also how an independent initiative by nongovernmental organizations (NGOs) and grassroots groups resisted the World Bank's approach and created opportunities for participation in the program.

The emphasis on communicative struggles of power and resistance has undermined totalizing views of power. It is therefore surprising that a number of contemporary studies continue to offer as a major finding the observation that power is not totalizing. Such work often contrasts this finding with functionalist studies from the 1970s and 1980s or early research concerned with the development of concertive and cultural control in workplaces rather than engaging with more contemporary research.

The continued indictment that organization studies employ totalizing and dominating views of power ignores the rise of dialectical and complex views of organizational power. Inherent in many of the definitions of power at the start of the chapter was a focus on how power can be simultaneously constraining and enabling, productive and repressive. For instance, Scott and Trethewey's (2008) ethnography of a fire department suggested that "the relations among discourse, identity, and ontological security are significant because of their capacity to shape interpretive repertoires with the practical, secondary effect of enabling and constraining particular risk management strategies" (p. 301). Knight and Greenberg (2002) described how Nike's promotionalism, while often deflecting public political concerns about factory conditions in their supply chain (which can therefore be understood as a form of domination), also made it a target for subpolitics from social activists focused on counterbranding through the use of reflexivity.

Mumby (2005) proposed the dialectical view of power to overcome dichotomies associated with privileging either control or resistance rather than understanding their interrelations. He suggested that those who privilege control tend to see resistance as ineffectual (reproductive of power relationships), while those who privilege resistance may romanticize the concept. By contrast, "a dialectical approach examines the inherent tensions and contradictions between agency and structure, between the interpretive possibilities that exist in every discourse situation and institutional efforts to impose or fix meaning" (Mumby & Ashcraft, 2004, p. 53). Ashcraft (2005) described dialectics from a discourse perspective, indicating that "such conceptual developments imply that everyone who participates in discursive activity engages in control and resistance, sometimes simultaneously, and that participants derive their differential capacities to do so from their fluctuating positions vis-à-vis multiple discourses" (p. 72).

Dialectical perspectives emphasize the simultaneity of control and resistance, domination and subordination. For instance, Lynch (2009) conceptualized humor in dialectical terms. He observed that humor can reinforce existing power relations when those in authority use it to mask or normalize their power and when employees use humor to let off steam in ways that reinforce the status quo. But workers also use humor to attenuate managerial encroachment on their work and to enforce health and safety standards. Similarly, Fleming (2007) theorized sexuality as both an object of control and site of resistance and empowerment in a high-commitment culture, and Carlone and Larson (2006) investigated self-help groups as sites of control and resistance in identity formation in a knowledge-intensive firm.

Dialectical theorists highlight linkages between domination and subordination by accounting for shifting relations of power. Larson and Tompkins (2005) revisited unobtrusive control through a dialectical lens that treats managerial identity and employee relations as more tenuous and vulnerable than previous studies, recognizing that individuals may move from subordinate to dominant status over time or may simultaneously occupy different positions of control. Real and Putnam (2005) observed that, although unions are often positioned as fighting for the marginalized, they also are systems of power and hierarchy in themselves. This observation underlines the need to specify the contextualized relations of power that researchers choose to foreground. For instance, Ashcraft (2005) employed the concept of *resistance through consent* to describe airline pilots who consented to a new team-based leadership program that threatened their status and authority. The pilots accommodated the program into their existing professional framework by viewing it instrumentally as a mechanism to achieve better control among the crew or as legitimating their roles as fathers who encourage sons to take some control. She argued that pilots resisted a loss of control through this redescription. Reconceptualizing this process as "resistance *and* consent" may more clearly situate pilots (similar to managers) as both employees and supervisors who seek to maintain authority over subordinates while complying with demands from superiors.

Norton (2009) promoted a diachronic view of resistance as he described how relations of power and what counts as transformation changed during the course of an extended controversy over land-use decision making. In a somewhat similar vein, Lutgen-Sandvik (2006) argued that existing bullying research dichotomizes the powerful and powerless in defining bullying, whereas a dialectic view of power reveals how resistance and abuse can escalate as employees cycle through individual and collective, overt and covert forms of resistance.

Mumby (2005) critiqued taxonomies of resistant behaviors for reifying the concept and overlooking context, multiple potential meanings, and various intended and unintended outcomes. The dialectical perspective highlights the partiality and often-unanticipated consequences of resistance. For instance, bullied employees may exit the organization as sign of defiance, but the departure may be the outcome desired by the bully (Lutgen-Sandvik, 2006). Real and Putnam (2005) found that when a group of airline pilots chose to critique union leaders instead of the company, the resulting policy created unintended consequences as Eagle and AA pilots became somewhat interchangeable. Gill and Ganesh (2007) conceptualized *bounded empowerment* among female entrepreneurs, finding that although participants framed entrepreneurialism as a form of empowerment, empowerment was marked by tension and contradiction, as it resulted from negotiating constraints such as individuality and current capitalist conditions. Dempsey (2007a) complicated the relationship between accountability and empowered practice in a study of an international environmental justice NGO. NGOs face competing pressures for accountability from potential funders as well as clients, yet increasing calls for NGO accountability to stakeholders may reify those groups or impede local autonomy. She argued that reducing voice can sometimes have empowering effects in terms of protecting vulnerable members, making more room for marginalized voices, and addressing local participants' limited time and energy.

Moving forward, researchers should clarify what is being resisted (for instance, preventing a loss of control may entail very different communication processes than seeking to gain control). We need to carefully stipulate and support our description of the often-layered relations of power in question and how they may change over time and across contexts, thus influencing how we decide what to conceptualize as *resistance*.

Additionally, returning to the question of agency, we should avoid associating agency and resistance with *any* behavior that either does not conform to what are presumed dominant discourses or that indicates the slightest level of choice making. For instance, showing creativity in a bureaucratic structure (Coopman & Burnett Meidlinger, 2000) is not necessarily resistance, particularly when it is not apparent that these choices reflect awareness of relations of power, let alone an attempt to alter them. As Larson and Tompkins (2005) observed, what appears to be resistance may reflect employee sensitivity to managerial ambivalence about preferred decisions. Fleming and Spicer (2003) noted that although reactions such as employee cynicism are treated as resistance to cultural directives, cynicism can be the vehicle through which consent is achieved at the level of *behavior*, because it encourages employees to view themselves as liberal, choosing subjects. Fleming and Spicer's observation about consent at the level of behavior challenges some conceptions of resistance. For example, Jordan (2003) examined career advice authors who encouraged temporary workers to perform compliance with managerial expectations for professional work. Jordan interprets this *performed compliance* as a form of resistance, because it prompts temporary workers to view work as less central to their identity. This interpretation ignores significant power issues by overlooking the ways in which management gains behaviorally compliant workers without providing supportive working environments, job security, or long-term benefits.

Seeking Social Change: Resistance as Overt-Covert and Individual-Collective

Even within the dialectical perspective, scholars still tend to differ in the degree to which they investigate forms of resistance that are relatively overt (public and visible) or covert (hidden and indirect), and individual or collective (Putnam et al., 2005). Although these choices should not be understood as binaries, significant theoretical debates about these issues have implications for our understanding of power and social change.

Over the last 20 years, scholars have investigated everyday forms of resistance that are relatively covert, in part as a reaction to the perception that early organizational research dismissed small acts of resistance as incapable of disrupting capitalism (Zoller & Fairhurst, 2007). Scott's (1990) *hidden transcripts* have been examined as employee nonconformist discourse—such as humor and bitching—that occurs outside the purview of management (Murphy, 1998; Tracy, 2000). In addition, employee irony and cynicism are investigated as relatively private ways to resist managerial influence (Fleming & Spicer, 2003), along with ambivalence (Gabriel, 1999), foot-dragging, disengagement (Prasad & Prasad, 2000), sabotage, theft, and noncooperation (Morrill, Zald, & Rao, 2003). The focus on "below the radar" or "guerilla" resistance calls attention to forms of communication that make visible hidden forms of conflict and establish some measure of agency and autonomy by withdrawing compliance from what are often unobtrusive forms of control aimed at worker subjectivity (Fleming, 2005; Trethewey, 1997).

Of course, there are no hard and fast distinctions between covert and overt forms of resistance. Given that what counts as resistance is context based, subtle attempts to defy dominant meanings through humorous plays on managerial slogans or the expression of cynicism may be performed for powerful organizational members, as resisters rely on ambiguity to avoid sanction (Mumby, 2009). Nonetheless, recent scholarship has called into question whether the focus on subtle, everyday forms of resistance in the workplace is building adequate understanding of the broad range of communicative processes by which relatively hidden forms of resistance link to more self-consciously confrontational efforts to challenge power relationships in a variety of settings. Central to these debates are different assumptions about communication and social change.

Scholars who emphasize the theoretical goals of emancipation (often critical modernist or affirmative postmodern in orientation) argue that much extant resistance research has little to say about the potential for material and social changes in relations of power in achieving social justice (Contu, 2008; Ganesh et al., 2005). Contu (2008) critiqued researchers for sidestepping Marxist concerns with anticapitalist relationships, juxtaposing *decaf resistance* concerned with cynicism and misbehavior with *real resistance*, defined as an effort that may involve existential risks and material losses in its aim for transformation. Researchers with a constructionist rather than realist ontology (Ganesh et al., 2005; Mumby, 2005) also observe that studies of covert and everyday resistance may capitulate to managerialist and capitalist interests.

Questions of change and the degree of risk involved in communicating resistance are important ways to distinguish among different, contextualized forms of power struggle. Many researchers investigate the significance of covert forms of resistance in reclaiming and articulating conflicting interests but also recognize their limits in achieving change. For instance, Wieland (2011) characterized a Swedish system for managing work-life balance as resistant not because it successfully altered work expectations but because the system kept conflict apparent. Tracy (2000) observed that hidden transcripts of bitching gave employees the impression of control but largely left disciplinary expectations in place, including those that may lead to harassment and burnout. Significantly, Lynch (2009) distinguished between humor's role as a safety valve that allowed employees to express dissatisfaction while leaving systems of power and control in place and its role in protecting workers' preferred identities and resisting external control of the labor process: "Humor's power as a form of resistance lies in this unsanctionable quality that workers can safely use resistance humor to express grievance, resist, and challenge unfair and/or burdensome managerial constraints to effectively change organizational practices" (p. 459). Lynch thus draws attention to the relative safety of humor versus riskier approaches to seeking change.

Additionally, Ganesh et al. (2005) argued that studies of resistance in organizational communication have largely been theorized as the individual ability to see through dominant ideological systems (such as cynical reactions), in part because Foucauldian theories can lead us to view forms of group action as disciplinary. This tendency resulted in overlooking the development of more collective forms of resistance and new forms of organizing represented by such efforts. Ganesh et al. (2005) called for work that explicitly theorizes or documents pathways between relatively individual and more coordinated forms of collective resistance. Research that explores these connections includes Gossett and Kilker's (2006) analysis of the website "radioshacksucks." Although the website facilitates anonymous complaint outside the workplace, the hidden transcripts of this site fomented overt and collective resistance by airing complaints that were visible to management and encouraging members to participate in an ongoing lawsuit against the company. Zoller and Fairhurst (2007) theorized how discursive leadership can connect hidden transcripts of resistance with the development of social movements and other collective forms of resistance.

Ganesh et al. (2005) called for renewed attention to forms of resistance that entail conscious efforts at transforming dominant meaning systems and power relationships: "We see transformation as a term that highlights attempts to effect large-scale, collective changes in the domains of state policy, corporate practice, social structure, cultural norms, and daily lived experience" (p. 177; see also Trethewey, 1997). They encouraged attention to protest and activism as forms of transformative resistance and a return to Gramsci's (1971) counter-hegemony as a collective practice. At the same time, they noted that understanding what counts as transformative in terms of goals or outcomes must be understood contextually and over time.

Activism and social movements represent one avenue of organizing social change (Clemens & Minkoff, 2004). Cloud's (2005) study of Staley's union strike encourages attention to the need for confrontational economic strategies versus a discourse of victimhood and moralizing. Social movement and activism research sheds light on struggles among grassroots organizing, more formal social movement organizations, union campaigns, and corporate issue management (Kendall, Gill, & Cheney, 2007; Knight & Wells, 2007; Rodino-Colocino, 2012; Weaver, 2010; Zoller, 2009a). For instance, Kim and Dutta (2009) investigated the Common Ground Collective as a force of solidarity and struggle against neo-liberal forms of crisis management that seized on post-Katrina New Orleans as a site for austerity and privatization. Research into networked forms of resistance to neo-liberal institutions, including New Zealand activists (Ganesh & Stohl, 2010) and the transnational Zapatista model (Dutta & Pal, 2010), highlight tensions between the democratic potential of open access and "leaderless" participation and the challenges of participant commitment and decision making. Researchers bring attention to activists' strategic use of communication to challenge dominant assumptions about corporations and the corresponding tactics used to promote change among groups in the corporate accountability movement (Bendell, 2004; Bendell & Bendell, 2007). Additional research can lend insight into the development of new organizational forms and decision-making processes that emerge through activism (Rao, Morrill, & Zald, 2000), as well as creative efforts to avoid traditional win-lose frames for activist goals. At the same time, the dialectical perspective reminds us to attend to the ways in which such efforts to fix meaning themselves become nascent forms of hegemony or discipline. For example, Dempsey's (2007b) research into transnational advocacy networks cautions us to address potential tensions and inequalities that develop within advocacy groups and among such groups and the communities with which they work (see also Papa, Singhal, & Papa, 2006).

Researchers also investigate alternative, participative, and democratic organizing models as methods of social change (Cheney, 1998; Harter, 2004; Koschmann & Laster, 2011; Medved et al., 2001; Stohl & Cheney, 2001). Employee cooperatives, local exchange trading systems (wherein local communities develop democratic alternatives to dominant forms of currency), and local farming efforts (Dougherty, 2011; LeGreco & Leonard, 2011) represent a potential material and discursive challenge to corporate hegemony.

Scholarship that questions dominant, taken-for-granted cultural meanings (though not necessarily explicitly deconstructionist) represents another avenue for social change by highlighting the potential for cultural change in areas such as employment and career discourse (Roper, Ganesh, & Inkson, 2010; Trethewey, 2001), market fundamentalism (McMillan & Cheney, 1996), and managerial control (Deetz, 1992a). Deetz (2007) promotes the institutionalization of deep democracy through programs such as stakeholder participation models that educate the public about collaborative methods of decision making and governance. One goal is to overcome liberal models of decision making and information-oriented conceptions of communication in order to allow emergent solutions to develop from the ground up rather than constitute groups that merely reinforce existing positions. More research is needed to help us understand how such efforts scale up to create significant cultural changes and evaluate the potential of alternative and democratic organizing to confront dominant discourses and the material and social inequalities they support.

The tensions among the different research trajectories—subjectivity, culture, and social movements as sources of change—are productive to the degree that they pursue the interconnections of individual and collective efforts, the need to resist the reproduction of existing relations of power, and articulate potential alternatives to the status quo. We should encourage scholars to develop more communication theories *for* social change as well as theories *about* social change. These efforts may entail designing participation methods and partnering with organizations and social movements in ways that challenge traditional understandings of scholarship. Participatory action research represents a significant model for this kind of work (Harter, Hamel-Lambert, & Millesen, 2011; Parker, Oceguera, & Sanchez, 2011), although we must take seriously the implications of managing multiple forms of privilege and inequality in the process (Dempsey, 2010).

Conclusion

Reflecting the edition as a whole, this chapter demonstrates the theoretical and topical diversity of organizational communication research. A key challenge is to maintain dialogue across perspectives so that we continue to build organizational communication theory and praxis rather than retreat to intellectual silos. A potential weakness of this chapter's focus on theoretical debates is the risk of reinforcing differences as binaries. My hope is that discussion of these debates helps us to focus on useful tensions and highlight ways to move beyond tensions that impede developments in theory and practice. This conclusion considers directions for future research.

Since the publication of the last *Handbook* in 2001, scholars have responded to calls for more communication-centered research. Scholarship has highlighted the mutually constitutive role of communication, power, and organizing, signaling the centrality of power and politics to organizational communication research as a whole. We should continue to develop communication-based explanations of power, treating communication as constitutive of power rather than merely an effect or expression of power. We also need to ensure that critical developments regarding power in organizational life and the politics of scholarly representation inform incipient research areas such as new media, CCO, and positive organizing. The concept of *positive* organizing (Cameron, Dutton, & Quinn, 2003), for instance, would benefit from thinking about how framing research as positive eschews a dialectical approach to understanding how power is both enabling and constraining. Positive research should also engage with questions of power and reflexivity by asking what counts as positive organizational experiences and outcomes and for whom.

Research also has responded to calls for ethnographic and meaning-centered research that uncovers the everyday lived experience of organization members. This body of research has contributed to more nuanced theorizing and more recognition of tensions, contradictions, and paradoxes in organizational life. This micro-level focus has engendered new calls for connecting micro-level with meso-level and macro-level research. As we consider these connections, we should also encourage multimethod approaches involving varied forms of qualitative research (such as ethnography, interviewing, case comparisons, histories, textual analysis) and quantitative research (surveys, experiments, network modeling) to expand our theoretical reach.

Since the publication of the last *Handbook*, research has given increased attention to organizing and globalization (and related questions of localization), including transnational business, economic institutions, NGOs, and activist networks. Organizational communication scholars have begun to account for how the Western setting of so much of our research influences our theories of power and resistance. More work remains to be done to address the connections among the symbolic and material aspects of globalization and organizational politics, including neocolonial relationships and the dynamic interplay of cultural and ethnic hegemony and resistance, new patterns of outsourcing work and their relation to constructions of gender and ethnicity, and changing configurations of power relations among nation-states, transnational corporations, and transnational NGOs.

At one time, scholars accused organizational communication of being largely atheoretical and practitioner focused. This edition is evidence of the theoretical and conceptual development of communication-centered explanations of organizational experience. There is some danger that organizational communication theories redescribe the same phenomenon in new terms based on emerging theoretical fads (systems, cultures, discourses). This observation does not discount the need to develop new vocabulary—from a pragmatist approach, theory development as description and redescription is significant in developing new ways of thinking (Rorty, 1989). However, in order to maintain relevance, we need to articulate clearly the implications of different descriptions for the practice of organizational communication. For example, we should consider how insights regarding power as both enabling and constraining and its intertwined relationship with resistance can be garnered to not only explain organizational life and critique existing practices but also develop potential models for challenging dominant relations of power and articulating transformative organizational practices.

As we build explanatory theories that address ontological and epistemological debates (e.g., What is human agency? What is the nature of power and organization?), we should articulate how these insights inform praxis in multiple contexts. Fortunately, organizational communication researchers have challenged managerial biases that evaluated communication almost entirely in terms of effective outcomes as defined by organizational leaders, providing space for us to think about how theories of organizational power and politics can speak directly to major contemporary political challenges. For example, how can organizational communication inform efforts to contest dominant constructions of the economy to promote ecologically sustainable and democratically equitable organizing in the face of climate change, peak oil, and population demands? Can unions reassert their role as advocates for the working class through cooperative and innovative strategies, and what other models exist for organizing working class and impoverished people? How do organizational communication theories translate into recommendations for meaningful change in racist and/or patriarchal work experiences in practice? How can the public participate in policy and electoral politics in the face of corporate influence (such as the Citizens United vs. U.S. Supreme Court decision and global trade pacts)? How do we recommend that northern-based NGOs and activists partner with communities in the global south in ways that avoid reproducing relations of dominance and dependence as they work to achieve social justice goals? In many ways, our research responds to these issues, but the challenge remains to move from the journal/book page to public engagement and back again (see Keashly & Neuman, 2009; Rodino-Colocino, 2012).

Much debate is likely to occur regarding what constitutes relevance and utility in engaged research. As this chapter demonstrates, debates will be compounded by conflicting views about the degree and nature of social change that is possible as well as what constitutes an improvement in organizational life, a model of social justice, or a method of empowered organizing. There are no universalistic articulations of values from which to base claims or a suspension of power relations toward which to aim. These conversations, though, are central to improving the social relevance of organizational communication theory when they inform and are informed by various models of practice and build dialogue across communication research perspectives.

References

Ainsworth, S., Hardy, C., & Harley, B. (2005). Online consultation. *Management Communication Quarterly, 19*(1), 120–145.

Allen, B. J. (1995). "Diversity" in organizations. *Journal of Applied Communication Research, 23*(2), 143–155.

Althusser, L. (1971). *Lenin and philosophy*. New York, NY: Monthly Review Press.

Alvesson, M., & Karreman, D. (2000). Varieties of discourse: On the study of organizations through discourse analysis. *Human Relations, 53*(9), 1125–1149.

Alvesson, M., & Willmott, H. (2002). Identity regulation as organizational control: Producing the appropriate individual. *Journal of Management Studies, 39*(5), 619–644.

Ashcraft, K. L. (2005). Resistance through consent? Occupational identity, organizational form, and the maintenance of masculinity among commercial airline pilots. *Management Communication Quarterly, 19*(1), 67–90.

Ashcraft, K. L. (2009). Gender and diversity: Other ways to "make a difference." In M. Alvesson, T. Bridgman, & H. Willmott (Eds.), *The Oxford handbook of critical management studies* (pp. 304–327). Oxford, UK: OxfordUniversity Press.

Ashcraft, K. L., & Allen, B. J. (2003). The racial foundation of organizational communication. *Communication Theory, 13*(1), 5–38.

Aune, J. (2001). *Selling the free market*. New York, NY: Guilford Press.

Bachrach, P., & Baratz, M. (1962). Two faces of power. *American Political Science Review, 56*(4), 947–952.

Barboza, D. (2010, June 7). After suicides, scrutiny of China's grim factories. *The New York Times,* p. A1. Retrieved from http://www.nytimes.com/2010/06/07/business/global/07suicide.html?pagewanted=all

Barker, J. (1993). Tightening the iron cage: Concertive control in self-managing teams. *Administrative Science Quarterly, 38*(3), 408–437.

Bauman, Z. (2007). *Liquid times: Living in an age of uncertainty*. Cambridge, UK: Polity Press.

Bendell, J. (2004). *Barricades and boardrooms: A contemporary history of the corporate accountability movement*. Geneva, Switzerland: United Nations Research Institute for Social Development.

Bendell, J., & Bendell, M. (2007). Facing corporate power. In S. May, G. Cheney, & J. Roper (Eds.), *Debates over corporate social responsibility* (pp. 59–73). Oxford, UK: Oxford University Press.

Berger, B. K. (2005). Power over, power with, and power to relations: Critical reflections on public relations, the dominant coalition, and activism. *Journal of Public Relations Research, 17*(1), 5–28.

Bisel, R. S., Ford, D. J., & Keyton, J. (2007). Unobtrusive control in a leadership organization: Integrating control and resistance. *Western Journal of Communication, 71*(2), 136–158.

Broadfoot, K. J., & Munshi, D. (2007). Diverse voices and alternative rationalities: Imagining forms of postcolonial organizational communication. *Management Communication Quarterly, 21*(2), 249–267.

Burawoy, M. (1979). *Manufacturing consent: Changes in the labor process under monopoly capitalism*. Chicago, IL: University of Chicago Press.

Buzzanell, P. (1994). Gaining a voice: Feminist organizational communication theorizing. *Management Communication Quarterly, 7*(4), 339–383.

Buzzanell, P., & Liu, M. (2005). Struggling with maternity leave policies and practices: A poststructuralist feminist analysis of gendered organizing. *Journal of Applied Communication Research, 33*(1), 1–25.

Calas, M., & Smirchich, L. (1999). Post modernism: Reflections and tentative directions. *Academy of Management Review, 24,* 649–671.

Cameron, K. S., Dutton, J. E., & Quinn, R. E. (2003). *Positive organizational scholarship*. San Francisco, CA: Berrett-Koehler.

Carlone, D., & Larson, G. S. (2006). Locating possibilities for control and resistance in a self-help program.*Western Journal of Communication, 70*(4), 270–291.

Cheney, G. (1998). *Values at work: Employee participation meets market pressure at Mondragon*. Ithica, NY: Cornell University Press.

Cheney, G., & Cloud, D. (2006). Doing democracy, engaging the material: Employee participation and labor activity in an age of market globalization. *Management Communication Quarterly, 19*(4), 1–40.

Cheney, G., & Lair, D. (2005). Theorizing about rhetoric and organizations: Classical, interpretive, and critical aspects. In S. May & D. K. Mumby (Eds.), *Engaging organizational communication theory and research* (pp. 55–84). Thousand Oaks, CA: SAGE.

Clemens, E., & Minkoff, D. (2004). Beyond the iron law: Rethinking the place of organizations in social movement research. In S. Soule & H. Kriesi (Eds.), *The Blackwell companion to social movements* (pp. 155–170). Malden, MA: Blackwell Publishing.

Cloud, D. L. (2001). Laboring under the sign of the new: Cultural studies, organizational communication, and the fallacy of the new economy. *Management Communication Quarterly, 15*(2), 268–278.

Cloud, D. L. (2005). Fighting words: Labor and the limits of communication at Staley, 1993 to 1996. *Management Communication Quarterly, 18*(4), 543–592.

Collinson, D. (1992). *Managing the shopfloor: Subjectivity, masculinity and workplace culture.* New York, NY: Walter de Gruyter.

Collinson, D. (1994). Strategies of resistance: Power, knowledge and resistance in the workplace. In J. M. Jermier, D. Knights, & W. M. Nord (Eds.), *Resistance and power in organizations* (pp. 25–68). London, England: Routledge.

Conrad, C. (2004a). The illusion of reform: Corporate discourse and agenda denial in the 2002 "corporate meltdown." *Rhetoric & Public Affairs, 7*(3), 311–338.

Conrad, C. (2004b). Organizational discourse analysis: Avoiding the determinism-voluntarism trap. *Organization, 11*(3), 427–439.

Conrad, C. (2011). *Organizational rhetoric: Strategies of resistance and domination.* Cambridge, UK: Polity.

Conrad, C., & McIntush, H. G. (2003). Organizational rhetoric and healthcare policymaking. In T. L. Thompson, A. M. Dorsey, K. I. Miller, & R. Parrott (Eds.), *Handbook of health communication* (pp. 403–422). Mahwah, NJ: Lawrence Erlbaum.

Contu, A. (2008). Decaf resistance: On misbehavior, cynicism, and desire in liberal workplaces. *Management Communication Quarterly, 21*(3), 364–379.

Coopman, S. J., & Burnett Meidlinger, K. (2000). Power, hierarchy, and change: The stories of a Catholic parish staff. *Management Communication Quarterly, 13*(4), 567–626.

Crowley, M., Tope, D., Chamberlain, L. J., & Hodson, R. (2010). Neo-Taylorism at work: Occupational change in the post-Fordist era. *Social Problems, 57*(3), 421–447.

Crozier, M. (1964). *The bureaucratic phenomenon.* London, England: Tavistock.

Dahl, R. (1957). The concept of power. *Behavioral Science, 2*(3), 201–215.

Daudi, P. (1986). *Power in the organization: The discourse of power in managerial praxis.* Oxford, UK: Basil Blackwell.

Deetz, S. (1992a). *Democracy in an age of corporate colonization: Developments in communication and the politics of everyday life.* New York: State University of New York Press.

Deetz, S. (1992b). Disciplinary power in the modern corporation. In M. Alvesson & H. Willmott (Eds.), *Critical management studies* (pp. 21–45). Newbury Park, CA: SAGE.

Deetz, S. (2001). Conceptual foundations. In F. M. Jablin & L. L. Putnam (Eds.), *The new handbook of organizational communication* (pp. 3–47). Thousand Oaks, CA: SAGE.

Deetz, S. (2007). Corporate governance, corporate social responsibility, and communication. In S. May, G. Cheney, & J. Roper (Eds.), *The debate over corporate social responsibility* (pp. 267–278). Oxford, UK: Oxford University Press.

Dempsey, S. (2007a). Negotiating accountability within international contexts: The role of bounded voice. *Communication Monographs, 74*(3), 311–332.

Dempsey, S. (2007b). Towards a critical organizational approach to civil society contexts: A case study of the difficulties of transnational advocacy. In B. J. Allen, L. A. Flores, & M. P. Orbe (Eds.), *The international and intercultural communication annual* (pp. 317–339). Washington, DC: National Communication Association.

Dempsey, S. (2010). Critiquing community engagement. *Management Communication Quarterly, 24*(3), 359–390.

Dempsey, S. (2011). Theorizing difference from transnational feminisms. In D. K. Mumby (Ed.), *Reframing difference in organizational communication studies* (pp. 55–76). Thousand Oaks, CA: SAGE.

Dewey, J. (1993). The problem of truth. In D. Morris & I. Shapiro (Eds.), *John Dewey:The political writings.* Indianapolis, IN: Hackett Publishing Co.

Dougherty, D. (2011). *The reluctant farmer: An exploration of work, social class, and the production of food.* Leicester, UK: Troubador Publishing.

Dutta, M., & Pal, M. (2010). Dialog theory in marginalized settings: A subaltern studies approach. *Communication Theory, 20*(4), 363–386.

Ellingson, L. (2005). *Communicating in the clinic: Negotiating frontstage and backstage teamwork.* Cresskill, NJ: Hampton Press.

Fairclough, N. (1995). *Critical discourse analysis: The critical study of language.* London, England: Longman.

Fleming, P. (2005). Metaphors of resistance. *Management Communication Quarterly, 19*(1), 45–66.

Fleming, P. (2007). Sexuality, power and resistance in the workplace. *Organization Studies, 28*(2), 239–256.

Fleming, P., & Sewell, G. (2002). Looking for the good soldier, Svejk: Alternative modalities of resistance in the contemporary workplace. *Sociology, 36*(4), 857–874.

Fleming, P., & Spicer, A. (2003). Working at a cynical distance: Implications for power, subjectivity and resistance. *Organization, 10*(1), 157–179.

Fleming, P., & Spicer, A. (2007). *Contesting the corporation: Struggle, power and resistance in organizations*. Cambridge, UK: Cambridge University Press.

Foucault, M. (1979). *Discipline and punish: The birth of the prison* (A. Sheridan, Trans.). New York, NY: Vintage.

Foucault, M. (1980a). *The history of sexuality: An introduction* (R. Hurley, Trans., vol. 1). New York, NY: Vintage.

Foucault, M. (1980b). *Power/knowledge: Selected interviews and other writings 1972–1977* (C. Gordon, L. Marshall, J. Mepham, & K. Soper, Trans.). New York, NY: Pantheon.

Fraser, N. (2009). *Scales of justice: Reimagining political space in a globalizing world*. New York, NY: Columbia University Press.

French, J., & Raven, B. (1959). The bases of social power. In D. Cartwright (Ed.), *Studies in social power*. Ann Arbor: University of Michigan Press.

Ganesh, S. (2007). Outsourcing as symptomatic: Class visibility and ethnic scapegoating in the US IT sector. *Journal of Communication Management, 11*(1), 71–83.

Ganesh, S. (2009a). Critical organizational communication. In S. W. Littlejohn & K. A. Foss (Eds.), *Encyclopedia of communication theory* (pp. 226–231). Thousand Oaks, CA: SAGE.

Ganesh, S. (2009b). Organizational communication: Postmodern approaches. In S. W. Littlejohn & K. A. Foss (Eds.), *Encyclopedia of communication theory* (pp. 1–5). Thousand Oaks, CA: SAGE.

Ganesh, S., & Stohl, C. (2010). Qualifying engagement: A study of information and communication technology and the global social justice movement in Aotearoa New Zealand. *Communication Monographs, 77*(1), 51–74.

Ganesh, S., Zoller, H. M., & Cheney, G. (2005). Transforming resistance: Critical organizational communication meets globalization from below. *Communication Monographs, 72*(2), 169–191.

Gill, R., & Ganesh, S. (2007). Empowerment, constraint, and the entrepreneurial self: A study of White women entrepreneurs. *Journal of Applied Communication Research, 35*(3), 268–293.

Gillespie, S. R. (2001). The politics of breathing: Asthmatic Medicaid patients under managed care. *Journal of Applied Communication Research, 29*(2), 97–116.

Gossett, L., & Kilker, J. (2006). My job sucks: Examining counterinstitutional web sites as locations for organizational member voice, dissent, and resistance. *Management Communication Quarterly, 20*(1), 63–90.

Gramsci, A. (1971). *Selections from the prison notebooks* (Q. Hoare & G. N. Smith, Trans.). New York, NY: International Publishers.

Guha, R. (1983). *Elementary aspects of peasant insurgency in colonial India*. Delhi, India: Oxford University Press.

Habermas, J. (1984). *The theory of communicative action: Reason and the rationalization of society* (T. McCarthy, Trans., vol. 1). Boston, MA: Beacon Press.

Hall, M. L. (2010). Constructions of leadership at the intersection of discourse, power, and culture: Jamaican managers' narratives of leading in a postcolonial cultural context. *Management Communication Quarterly, 25*(4), 612–643.

Hardt, M., & Negri, A. (2000). *Empire*. Cambridge, MA: Harvard University Press.

Hardy, C., & Phillips, N. (2004). Discourse and power. In D. Grant, C. Hardy, C. Oswick, & L. L. Putnam (Eds.), *The SAGE handbook of organizational discourse* (pp. 299–316). London, England: SAGE.

Harter, L. (2004). Masculinities, the agrarian frontier myth, and cooperative ways of organizing: Contradictions and tensions in the experience and enactment of democracy. *Journal of Applied Communication Research, 32*(2), 89–118.

Harter, L., Deardorff, K., Kenniston, P., Carmack, H., & Rattine-Flaherty, E. (2008). Changing lanes and changing lives: The shifting scenes and continuity of care of a mobile health clinic. In H. M. Zoller & M. Dutta (Eds.), *Emerging perspectives in health communication* (pp. 313–334). New York, NY: Routledge.

Harter, L., Hamel-Lambert, J., & Millesen, J. (2011). *Participatory partnerships for social action and research*. Dubuque, IA: Kendall Hunt.

Holmer-Nadesan, M. (1996). Organizational identity and space of action. *Organization Studies, 17*(1), 49–81.

Holquist, M. (1990). *Dialogism: Bakhtin and his world*. London, England: Routledge.

James, W. (1890). *The principles of psychology*. Cambridge, MA: Harvard University Press.

Jones, C. (2009). Poststructuralism in critical management studies. In M. Alvesson, T. Bridgman, & H. Willmott (Eds.), *The Oxford handbook of critical management studies* (pp. 76–98). Oxford, UK: Oxford University Press.

Jordan, J. W. (2003). Sabotage or performed compliance: Rhetorics of resistance in temp worker discourse. *Quarterly Journal of Speech, 89*(1), 19–40.

Kassing, J. W., & Armstrong, T. (2002). Someone's going to hear about this. *Management Communication Quarterly, 16*(1), 39–65.

Keashly, L., & Neuman, J. H. (2009). Building a constructive communication climate. In P. Lutgen-Sandvik & B. Davenport Sypher (Eds.), *Destructive organizational communication* (pp. 339–362). New York, NY: Routledge.

Kendall, B., Gill, R., & Cheney, G. (2007). Consumer activism and corporate social responsibility. In S. May, G. Cheney, & J. Roper (Eds.), *The debate over corporate social responsibility* (pp. 241–266). Oxford, UK: Oxford University Press.

Kim, I., & Dutta, M. J. (2009). Studying crisis communication from the subaltern studies framework: Grassroots activism in the wake of Hurricane Katrina. *Journal of Public Relations Research, 21*(2), 142–164.

Kirby, E. L., Golden, A. G., Medved, C. E., Jorgenson, J., & Buzzanell, P. (2003). An organizational communication challenge to the discourse of work and family research: From problematics to empowerment. In P. J. Kalbfleisch (Ed.), *Communication yearbook* (vol. 27, pp. 1–43). Mahwah, NJ: Lawrence Erlbaum.

Kirby, E. L., & Krone, K. (2002). "The policy exists, but you can't use it": Negotiating tensions inwork-family policy. *Journal of Applied Communication Research, 30*(1), 50–77.

Knight, G. (2007). Activism, risk, and communicational politics: Nike and the sweatshop problem. In S. May, G. Cheney, & J. Roper (Eds.), *The debate over corporate social responsibility* (pp. 305–318). Oxford, UK: Oxford University Press.

Knight, G., & Greenberg, J. (2002). Promotionalism and its subpolitics: Nike and its labor critics. *Management Communication Quarterly, 15*(4), 571–600.

Knight, G., & Wells, D. (2007). Bringing the local back in: Trajectories of contention and the union struggle at Kukdong/Mexmode. *Social Movement Studies, 6*(1), 83–103.

Knights, D., & McCabe, D. (2000). Ain't misbehavin'? Opportunities for resistance under new forms of 'quality' management. *Sociology, 34*(3), 421–436.

Kondo, D. (1990). *Crafting selves: Power, discourse and identity in a Japanese factory*. Chicago, IL: University of Chicago Press.

Koschmann, M., & Laster, N. M. (2011). Communicative tensions of community organizing: The case of a local neighborhood association. *Western Journal of Communication, 75*(1), 28–51.

Kuhn, T. (2006). A "demented work ethic" and a "lifestyle firm": Discourse, identity, and workplace time commitments. *Organization Studies, 27*(9), 1339–1358.

Kuhn, T. (2008). A communicative theory of the firm: Developing an alternative perspective on intra-organizational power and stakeholder relationships. *Organization Studies, 29*(8/9), 1227–1254.

Kunda, G. (1992). *Engineering culture: Control and commitment in a high-tech corporation*. Philadelphia, PA: Temple University Press.

Kwon, W., Clarke, I., & Wodak, R. (2009). Organizational decision-making, discourse, and power: Integrating across contexts and scales. *Discourse & Communication, 3*(3), 273–302.

Larson, G., & Tompkins, P. (2005). Ambivalence and resistance: A study of management in a concertive control system. *Communication Monographs, 72*(1), 1–21.

Lash, S., & Urry, J. (1994). *Economies of signs and space*. London, England: SAGE.

LeGreco, M., & Leonard, D. (2011). Building sustainable community-based food programs: Cautionary tales from "The Garden." *Environmental Communication: A Journal of Nature and Culture, 5*(3), 356–362.

LeGreco, M., & Tracy, S. (2009). Discourse tracing as qualitative practice. *Qualitative Inquiry, 15*(9), 1516–1543.

Lucas, K. (2011). The working class promise: A communicative account of mobility-based ambivalence. *Communication Monographs, 78*(3), 347–369.

Lukes, S. (1974). *Power: A radical view*. London, England: MacMillan.

Lutgen-Sandvik. (2006). Take this job and . . . : Quitting and other forms of resistance to workplace bullying. *Communication Monographs, 73*(4), 406–433.

Lynch, O. H. (2009). Kitchen antics: The importance of humor and maintaining professionalism at work. *Journal of Applied Communication Research, 37*(4), 444–464.

Lyon, A., & Mirivel, J. C. (2011). Reconstructing Merck's practical theory of communication: The ethics of pharmaceutical sales representative-physician encounters. *Communication Monographs, 78*(1), 53–72.

Mann, M. (1986). *The sources of social power* (vol. 1). New York, NY: Cambridge University Press.

March, J. G., & Simon, H. (1958). *Organizations*. New York, NY: Wiley.

McMillan, J. J. (2007). Why corporate social responsibility? Why now? How? In S. May, G. Cheney, & J. Roper (Eds.), *The debate over corporate social responsibility* (pp. 15–29). Oxford, UK: Oxford University Press.

McMillan, J. J., & Cheney, G. (1996). The student as consumer: The implications and limitations of a metaphor. *Communication Education, 45*(1), 1–15.

McRobbie, A. (2010, Summer). Reflections on feminism, immaterial labour and the post-Fordist regime. *New Formations, 70*, 60–76.

Medved, C. E., Morrison, K., Dearing, J. W., Larson, R. S., Cline, G., & Brummans, B. (2001). Tensions in community health improvement initiatives: Communication and collaboration in a managed care environment. *Journal of Applied Communication Research, 29*(2), 137–152.

Morgan, J., & Krone, K. (2001). Bending the rules of "professional" display: Emotional improvisation in caregiver performances. *Journal of Applied Communication Research, 29*(4), 317–340.

Morrill, C., Zald, M., & Rao, H. (2003). Covert political conflict in organizations: Challenges from below. *Annual Review of Sociology, 29*, 391–415.

Motion, J., & Weaver, C. K. (2005). A discourse perspective for critical public relations research: Life Sciences Network and the battle for truth. *Journal of Public Relations Research, 17*(1), 49–67.

Mumby, D. K. (Ed.). (1993). *Narrative and social control: Critical perspectives*. Newbury Park, CA: SAGE.

Mumby, D. K. (1997). Modernism, postmodernism, and communication studies: A rereading of an ongoing debate. *Communication Theory*, 7(1), 1–28.

Mumby, D. K. (2001). Power and politics. In F. Jablin & L. L. Putnam (Eds.), *The new handbook of organizational communication* (pp. 585–623). Thousand Oaks, CA: SAGE.

Mumby, D. K. (2004). Discourse, power and ideology: Unpacking the critical approach. In D. Grant, C. Hardy, C. Oswick, & L. L. Putnam (Eds.), *The SAGE handbook of organizational discourse* (pp. 237–258). London, England: SAGE.

Mumby, D. K. (2005). Theorizing resistance in organizational studies: A dialectical approach. *Management Communication Quarterly, 19*(1), 19–44.

Mumby, D. K. (2009). The strange case of the farting professor: Humor and the deconstruction of destructive communication. In P. Lutgen-Sandvik & B. Davenport Sypher (Eds.), *Destructive organizational communication* (pp. 316–338). New York, NY: Routledge.

Mumby, D. K., & Ashcraft, K. L. (2004). *Reworking gender: A feminist communicology of organization*. Thousand Oaks, CA: SAGE.

Mumby, D. K., & Clair, R. P. (1997). Organizational discourse. In T. A. van Dijk (Ed.), *Discourse studies, volume 2: Discourse as social interaction* (pp. 181–205). London, England: SAGE.

Murphy, A. G. (1998). Hidden transcripts of flight attendant resistance. *Management Communication Quarterly, 11*(4), 499–535.

Nadesan, M. (2008). *Governmentality, biopower, and everyday life*. London, England: Routledge.

Norton, T. (2009). Situating organizations in politics: A diachronic view of control-resistance dialectics. *Management Communication Quarterly, 22*(4), 525–554.

Papa, M., Singhal, A., & Papa, W. (2006). *Organizing for social change: A dialectic journey of theory and praxis*. Thousand Oaks, CA: SAGE.

Parker, P., Oceguera, E., & Sanchez, J. (2011). Intersecting differences: Organizing [ourselves] for social justice research with people in vulnerable communities. In D. K. Mumby (Ed.), *Reframing difference in organizational communication studies* (pp. 219–244). Thousand Oaks, CA: SAGE.

Pfeffer, J. (1981). *Power in organizations*. Cambridge, MA: Ballinger Publishing.

Pfeffer, J., & Salancik, G. (1978). *The external control of organizations: A resource dependence perspective*. New York, NY: Harper & Row.

Pierce, T., & Dougherty, D. (2003). The construction, enactment, and maintenance of power-as-domination through an acquisition: The case of

TWA and Ozark Airlines. *Management Communication Quarterly, 16*(2), 129–164.

Prasad, A., & Prasad, P. (2000). *Organizational research methods: The coming of age of interpretive organization research*. Thousand Oaks, CA: SAGE.

Putnam, L. L., Grant, D., Michelson, G., & Cutcher, L. (2005). Discourse and resistance: Targets, practices, and consequences. *Management Communication Quarterly, 19*(1), 5–18.

Putnam, L. L., & Mumby, D. K. (1993). Organizations, emotion, and the myth of rationality. In S. Fineman (Ed.), *Emotion in organizations* (pp. 36–57). London, England: SAGE.

Rao, H., Morrill, C., & Zald, M. N. (2000). Power plays: How social movements and collective action create new organizational forms. *Organizational Behaviour, 22*, 239–282.

Real, K., & Putnam, L. L. (2005). Ironies in the discursive struggle of pilots defending the profession. *Management Communication Quarterly, 19*(1), 91–119.

Ritz, D. (2007). Can corporate personhood be socially responsible? In S. May, G. Cheney, & J. Roper (Eds.), *The debate over corporate social responsibility* (pp. 190–204). Oxford, UK: Oxford University Press.

Rodino-Colocino, M. (2008). Technomadic work: From promotional vision to WashTech's opposition. *Work Organization, Labour and Globalization, 2*(1), 104–116.

Rodino-Colocino, M. (2011). Geek Jeremiads: Speaking the crisis of job loss by opposing offshored and H-1B labor. *Communication and Critical/Cultural Studies, 9*(1), 22–46.

Rodino-Colocino, M. (2012). Participant activism: Exploring a methodology for scholar-activists through lessons learned as a precarious labor organizer. *Communication, Culture & Critique, 5*(4), 541–562.

Roper, J., Ganesh, S., & Inkson, K. (2010). Neoliberalism and knowledge interests in boundaryless careers discourse. *Work, employment and society, 24*(4), 661–679.

Rorty, R. (1989). *Contingency, irony, and solidarity*. Cambridge, UK: Cambridge University Press.

Scarduzio, J. (2011). Maintaining order through deviance? The emotional deviance, power, and professional work of municipal court judges. *Management Communication Quarterly, 25*(2), 283–310.

Scott, C. W., & Trethewey, A. (2008). Organizational discourse and the appraisal of occupational hazards: Interpretive repertoires, heedful interrelating, and identity at work. *Journal of Applied Communication Research, 36*(3), 298–317.

Scott, J. C. (1990). *Domination and the arts of resistance: Hidden transcripts*. New Haven, CT: Yale University Press.

Shome, R. (2002). Postcolonial approaches to communication: Charting the terrain, engaging the intersections. *Communication Theory, 12*(3), 249–270.

Spivak, G. C. (1988). Can the subaltern speak? In L. Grossberg, C. Nelson, & P. Treichler (Eds.), *Marxism and the interpretation of culture* (pp. 271–313). Urbana: University of Illinois Press.

Stohl, C., & Cheney, G. (2001). Participatory processes/paradoxical practices. *Management Communication Quarterly, 14*(3), 349–407.

Stohl, M., Stohl, C., & Townsley, N. (2007). A new generation of corporate social responsibility. In S. May, G. Cheney, & J. Roper (Eds.), *The debate over corporate social responsibility* (pp. 30–44). Oxford, UK: Oxford University Press.

Thackaberry, J. A. (2004). "Discursive opening" and closing in organisational self-study. *Management Communication Quarterly, 17*(3), 319–359.

Thomas, R. (2009). Critical management studies on identity: Mapping the terrain. In M. Alvesson, T. Bridgman, & H. Willmott (Eds.), *The Oxford handbook of critical management studies* (pp. 166–185). Oxford, UK: Oxford University Press.

Townsley, N., & Stohl, C. (2003). Contracting corporate social responsibility: Swedish expansions in global temporary agency work. *Management Communication Quarterly, 16*(4), 599–605.

Tracy, S. J. (2000). Becoming a character for commerce: Emotion labor, self-subordination, and discursive construction of identity in a total institution. *Management Communication Quarterly, 14*(1), 90–128.

Tracy, S. J. (2005). Locking up emotion: Moving beyond dissonance for understanding emotion labor discomfort. *Communication Monographs, 72*(3), 261–283.

Tracy, S. J., & Trethewey, A. (2005). Fracturing the real-self↔fake-self dichotomy: Moving toward "crystallized" organizational discourses and identities. *Communication Theory, 15*(2), 168–195.

Trethewey, A. (1997). Resistance, identity, and empowerment: A postmodern feminist analysis of clients in a human service organization. *Communication Monographs, 64*(4), 281–301.

Trethewey, A. (2001). Reproducing and resisting the master narrative of decline. *Management Communication Quarterly, 15*(2), 183–226.

Weaver, C. K. (2010). Carnivalesque activism as a public relations genre: A case study of the New Zealand group Mothers Against Genetic Engineering. *Public Relations Review, 36*(1), 35–41.

Wieland, S. (2011). Struggling to manage work as a part of everyday life: Complicating control, rethinking resistance, and contextualizing work/life studies. *Communication Monographs, 78*(2), 162–184.

Willis, P. (1977). *Learning to labor: How working class kids get working class jobs.* New York, NY: Columbia University Press.

Zoller, H. M. (2003). Health on the line: Identity and disciplinary control in employee occupational health and safety discourse. *Journal of Applied Communication Research, 31*(2), 118–139.

Zoller, H. M. (2009a). Narratives of corporate change: Public participation through environmental health activism, stakeholder dialogue, and regulation. In M. Dutta & L. Harter (Eds.), *Communicating for social impact: Engaging theory, research, and pedagogy* (pp. 91–114). Cresskill, NJ: Hampton Press.

Zoller, H. M. (2009b). The social construction of occupational and environmental health: Barriers and resources for coalitional organizing. *New Solutions: A Journal of Occupational and Environmental Health Policy, 19*(3), 293–318.

Zoller, H. M., & Fairhurst, G. T. (2007). Resistance leadership: The overlooked potential in critical and leadership studies. *Human Relations, 60*(9), 1331–1360.

Zoller, H. M., & Tener, M. (2010). Corporate proactivity as a discursive fiction: Managing environmental health activism and regulation. *Management Communication Quarterly, 24*(3), 391–418.

CHAPTER 25

Difference and Organizing

Patricia S. Parker

> [S]tudying difference in all its complexities is damn hard. . . . Maybe it's time for a different approach to difference. (Mumby, 2011, pp. viii–ix)

This chapter traces current trends in difference studies in organizational communication and proposes a map for the future. The above quotation signals the challenge of this effort, while the persistence of researchers doing difference scholarship suggests its importance. Difference has emerged as a prominent area of study in the discipline, particularly for critical organizational communication scholars interested in advancing frameworks that challenge the status quo and reveal pathways for sustained critique, transformation, and equality. Past approaches to difference in organization studies can be broadly characterized as "additive and piecemeal," progressing from viewing power in a generic sense to focusing on gender differences to considering additional social identity categories such as race, social class, and ability (Mumby, 2011, p. ix). However, there are frameworks that enable us to theorize complexities of difference more comprehensively, and these are the focus of the chapter.

Specifically, this chapter highlights critical/postmodern feminisms, critical theories of race, postcolonial theories, and transnational perspectives as useful lenses for difference studies in organizational communication. While feminist perspectives have long provided prescient theoretical and practical pathways for organization studies and continue to do so, critical race, postcolonial, and transnational perspectives are particularly important in this chapter because of their relative absence in our field. These perspectives have enjoyed a rather robust application in a range of other disciplines since the 1980s, including cultural studies, anthropology, sociology, literary studies, ethnic studies, and gender studies (see Essed & Goldberg, 2002). However, they have not gained a strong foothold in organizational communication studies. For example, the 2001 edition of this *Handbook* does not include *postcolonial* or *race* in its index. Although *racial issues* is indexed, the reference is not to a critical treatment of those issues; rather, it references a cursory discussion of *diversity* in a chapter on qualitative research and a variable analytic treatment of the problem of *cultural adjustment* within multinational corporations in a chapter on global organizational communication. There is no mention of transnational communication in the context of a critical, decolonizing tradition.

Critical/postmodern feminisms, critical theories of race, postcolonial theories, and transnational perspectives each have the capacity for situating difference as a communicative, constitutive feature of organizing, providing conceptual and practical routes through the entanglements and indeterminacies that difference produces. These frameworks are consistent with Ashcraft's (2011) call to shift conceptions of difference from being an essentializing property of individuals, groups, and organizations to viewing difference as "the cultural organization of work via difference," such that difference is seen as "an organizing principle of the meaning, structure, practice, and economy of work" (p. 4). Furthermore, the frameworks organizing this chapter provide a lens for imagining what Grimes and I refer to as "organizational communication as a decolonizing project," which takes into account the cultural organization of the discipline via difference, that is, how difference organizes choice points in research, publishing, and management practice (Grimes & Parker, 2008). Both of these call for difference as a constitutive and potentially decolonizing force point to an expansive, plural, and communicational conception of work. Ashcraft (2008, 2011) lays out such a view of work that occurs not only as the *concrete practices* associated with traditional institutional systems but also as an *ongoing historical formation* and as a *discourse formation* that involves many sites of cultural activity such as "formal organizations, . . . families, educational institutions, popular and trade discourse, legal and regulatory agencies, labor and professional associations, and where ever else we encounter representations, negotiations, and enactments of (who does what) work" (2011, p. 15). This view of difference, work, and organization as mutually constitutive can be summed up as, paraphrasing Ashcraft (2011), "Where and how does (or has) [the communication of difference] organize(d) work [writ large]?" (p. 15). Such a view can only be pursued from the perspectives of frameworks emerging after the discursive turn in organization studies.

Doing Difference After the Discursive Turn

Feminist, critical race, postcolonial, and transnational perspectives are all useful frameworks for theorizing and exploring difference because, collectively, they attend to the most important contemporary debates, conceptual developments, and conflicts in difference studies. Emerging from the discursive turn in critical social theory, these frameworks take up the critical, postmodern, and post-structuralist concerns with *essentialism*, *intersectionality*, *binary thinking*, *group identity politics,* and *representation*. These are central problematics in contemporary studies of difference and organization, because they point to the interrelated questions of subjectivity (*intersectional* or *essentialist* concerns about whose experiences and voices can/should matter, when they matter, and how they are expressed), performativity (What *binary* categories do we [de]construct and how do we use them to [re]constitute meaningful social arrangements?), politics (When and how are *group identity* politics relevant? How/can truth claims and relations of power be established/maintained/resisted/disrupted?), and language (*representational* concerns about what is [un]nameable, [un]seeable, [un]doable, [un]speakable, and [un]writeable and how these trouble or establish everyday thought and practice).

As will be shown, the frameworks organizing this chapter both illuminate and complicate possibilities for working in/through/around these problematics. This is partly because of their fluctuating connections to critical, postmodern, and post-structuralist approaches. Gannon and Davies (2012) note the slipperiness of the labels *critical, postmodern*, and *post-structuralist* as they are taken up by feminist researchers, but I think their observations are relevant to the researchers of critical race, postcolonialism, and transnational difference as well:

> [Critical, postmodern, and post-structuralist] frameworks are . . . hard to pin down, not the least because they are, in some times

> and some places, used as if they were interchangeable. At other times and in other places, one will be used to clarify what the other is not. There is no orderly, agreed upon, and internally consistent set of ideas that sits obediently under each of these headings. (p. 65)

Complicating matters for organizational scholars is the protean character of the term *postmodernism* in organization studies, which is sometimes used to describe "a historical period filled with major social and organizational changes" (signaling the flawed assumption that modernity, with its emphasis on validating reason, logic, and universal truth as the foundation for action in the social world, is over) *and* as an "umbrella term" for critical theory, post-structuralist theory, postmodern theories, and post-Fordist theories *and* as "a set of philosophical approaches" that distinguish the postmodern from the critical, linking it more so to the "deconstruction" move in post-structuralist thought (Alvesson & Deetz, 2000, p. 13). Furthermore, postmodernism is sometimes synonymous with a kind of neo-liberalism, "an aggressive, entrepreneurial capitalism," emphasizing neo-liberal approaches to management that capitalize on the flexibility of workforces and workplaces that, when presented uncritically, becomes at odds with the paradigmatic shift ushered in by critical social theory (Bertens & Natoli, 2002, p. xv). To create some conceptual boundaries for this slippery label, I follow the lead of many authors who now use *post-structuralist* as a reference to both postmodern and post-structuralist thought (or use them interchangeably). More specifically, in this chapter, postmodernism and post-structuralist will be used in terms of their links with the deconstruction projects of post-structuralist philosophies.

Perhaps it is this layering and entanglement of perspectives that reveal difference studies as "damn hard," as Mumby notes. Nevertheless, paraphrasing Gannon and Davies (2012), I believe that critical, postmodern, and post-structuralist perspectives, "each of one of them, along with the disputed ground between them, has produced new ideas that have helped [difference scholars] break loose from previously taken-for-granted assumptions about issues such as subjectivity, performativity, politics, and language" (p. 65).

The sections that follow attend to these four frameworks and their associated projects in difference studies: (a) critical and post-structuralist feminisms: (de)constructing binary categories; (b) critical theories of race: exposing, critiquing, and dismantling racial projects; (c) postcolonial theories: engaging and centering indigenous histories and self-representations; and (d) transnational perspectives: complicating difference across space, place, and identity.

Though not intended as a grand narrative for doing difference in organizational communication, I explicate these frameworks as ways of knowing, illuminating (the complicated) choice points for researching, theorizing, and practicing difference. Authors' epistemologies-in-use often are not explicitly acknowledged (Parker, Oceguera, & Sanchez, 2011). Thus this chapter is intended as a resource for scholars seeking diverse entry points in difference studies. The following questions guide the analysis: *What conceptual logics do scholars draw on when theorizing, speaking of, and doing difference in organizing and communicating? What questions, issues, and experiences do various logics address as worthy of consideration? What possibilities do logics open not only for critiquing social ordering that include some and marginalize others, but also for doing the transformative work of difference?*

Feminisms and Difference: (De) Constructing Binary Categories

There are both interconnections and points of departure among feminisms that use critical, postmodern, and post-structuralist theories.[1] Importantly, what unites these perspectives is their concern for theorizing and researching difference, with "an emphasis on including the 'other' in the process of research" (Hesse-Biber, 2012, p. 11). Each of these perspectives sees discourse as the means through which particular, situated versions of the world are accounted for and reject what Haraway (1988) refers to as the positivistic "god trick" in social science that purportedly offers an objective "value-free" vision "that is from everywhere and nowhere, equally and fully" (p. 584). Also, these perspectives view relations of power as established and maintained through discourse and through positions taken up and made possible within particular discourses. Discourse is seen as both representational and productive: It silences, it serves different interests, and it produces meaningful social arrangements that result in different kinds of material socio-cultural effects.

However, for feminist scholars, some important distinctions among critical, postmodern, and post-structuralist perspectives on difference relate to how *power, emancipation, empowerment, freedom*, and *(subjective) agency* are treated as organizing logics. As will be shown in the following sections, these and other commitments attached to critical, postmodern, and post-structuralist perspectives shape logics of difference as revealed in radical feminisms, standpoint theories/intersectional analyses, and postmodern/post-structural feminisms.

Critical Feminisms: Social/Radical/isms, Standpoints, Intersectionality

Critical feminisms are grounded in critical social theory, which focuses on the empowerment of individuals and operates from the belief that certain groups in any society are privileged over others. As Kincheloe, McLaren, and Steinberg (2011) assert,

> Inquiry that aspires to the name 'critical' must be connected to an attempt to confront the injustices of a particular society or public sphere within the society. Research becomes a transformative endeavor unembarrassed by the label 'political' and unafraid to consummate a relationship with emancipatory consciousness. (p. 164)

Imbued, then, with an emancipatory consciousness, critical feminisms commit to a hierarchical conception of power in which subjects are (becoming) empowered with sufficient agency to potentially overturn those hierarchical relations of power (Benhabib 1995; Fraser, 1995). This view sees difference in terms of the binaries of *dominator/oppressed* and the associated subcategories of privileged/vulnerable, worker/manager, men/women, heterosexual/homosexual, public/private, parent/child, and so on. Critical feminists taking up these binaries seek to empower people within subordinated categories, with the understanding that this happens within the context of "concurrent struggles among different classes, racial and gender groups, and sectors of capital" (Kincheloe & McLaren, 2005, p. 310). Not only is there a commitment to emancipation but there is also an emphasis on neo-Marxist and praxis-oriented social research (Smith, 1974, 1987). The critical feminist's project, paraphrasing Marx, is not only to interpret social life but also to transform it.

Socialist and radical feminisms, standpoint theories, and intersectional analyses are three frameworks that adhere to the traditions of the critical perspective, which I want to highlight as important to difference studies in organizational communication. Within these three strands of critical feminisms, we see logics of inquiry that take as a starting point the everyday lived experiences of women. We also see the emergence of debates about anti-essentialism, the continued significance of group-identity politics, and commitments to social, political, and economic transformation. From the perspectives of these critical feminisms, difference as a constitutive feature of organizing might begin with the following question: *How can/does/should women's situated experiences organize work?*

Socialist/Radical Feminisms. Socialist (new left, neo-Marxist) and radical feminisms are traced to the social and political changes of the 1950s through the 1970s and the emergence of women's activism around the world. For example, during this time, women in Latin America were organizing protests and action against the state's economic and physical aggression (Radcliffe & Westwood, 1993, as cited in Brisolara & Seigart, 2012); and in the United States, Black[2] feminist and human rights activists, such as Pauli Maurry and Ella Baker, were helping to ignite the Civil Rights Movement and were inspiring young women (White and Black) to step into their activists identities (Holsaert et al., 2010). Meanwhile, class-based struggles aligned with Marxist and socialist movements were fueling women's protests and collective organizing in Great Britain, while the mainly White, middle-class U.S. women's movement emerged as the women's liberation movement in the 1970s and the later focus on reproductive rights.

These feminisms focus on critiquing the capitalist, patriarchal state that creates women's oppression as workers within totalizing capitalist systems and as unpaid reproductive laborers (socialist feminism) and reject theories and methodologies that are not women centered, relying solely on women's experiences (radical feminisms). There are contrasts as well as overlaps between and among socialist and radical feminisms, and I urge readers to consult the excellent comprehensive reviews on these and other forms of feminisms (Hesse-Biber, 2012; Shaw & Lee, 2009). However, in summarizing them here, I focus on the areas of overlap that inform difference and organizing. The aim of both socialist and radical approaches is to do the transformative work to improve the material (oppressive) conditions of women's lives—conditions ushered in by modernity (Benhabib, 1995; MacKinnon, 1982). As is often noted, in taking up the Enlightenment ideal of emancipation, socialist and radical feminisms operate to a certain extent from within the modernist project while at the same time critiquing its always already hegemonic masculine subject (Ashcraft & Mumby, 2004; Hekman, 1990).

This approach seals a commitment to the dominator/oppressor binary, where the project is always focused on (and here is where the trajectories vary): eliminating, resisting, or exposing as deficient patriarchal ideologies and male-dominated institutions, practices, and norms. The mantra, *the personal is political*, declared women as experts on women's own lives. Women's experience of oppression is the starting point for critique, liberation, and social justice. For difference scholars, this provides an important focus on the material conditions of women as a class. Fruitful inquiry might begin with the question: *How are gender, class, and capitalist practices interrelated?*

Standpoint Theory. Still working in the binary spaces of dominator/oppression, standpoint feminisms provide methods of inquiry—*feminist epistemologies*—that use women's everyday lived experience as a starting point for producing new modes of knowledge, representations, and rhetoric (Collins, 1986, 1991; Harding, 1998; Smith, 1990). Indeed, as Harding (2012) asserts, standpoint logics are recognized "in every other social justice movement's knowledge production process" (p. 46). Among the various trajectories of standpoint approaches, I highlight *standpoint logic as critique of Western science as universal* and *standpoints as political achievements*, two frameworks that provide currency for difference studies. Lorde's (1984) influential essay, "The Masters Tools Will Never Dismantle the Master's House," points to the limiting uses of Western science for women's liberation and raises the question of what other ways of thinking and modes of representation feminist researchers might employ. Sociologist and pioneering standpoint theorist, Dorothy Smith (1990), provides us with one such tool with her institutional ethnography approach, which has an emphasis on narrative and storytelling. Smith (1990) argues that feminists should trace the *conceptual practices of power* mediated through the texts—job descriptions, time cards, mission statements, and so on—that become data bases, strategic plans, policies, and so forth that employ media portrayals, official versions of events, and other conceptual framings. These conceptual practices of power discursively produce and reproduce institutional arrangements (such as transnational corporations, welfare systems, the Supreme Court, Ivy League schools, and so on) that become the "ruling relations" that reach into people's daily lives. Institutional ethnography, then, necessarily begins with a standpoint, exposing local experience as *problematic*, because institutional ideologies fragment "what's actually happening" for the person. A key tool becomes distinguishing between *primary narratives* told by an embodied narrator from her experience (e.g., of sexual violence) and various *institutional narratives* (which might be reproduced from the "raw materials" of primary narratives but become "worked up" to an official, institutional, oppressive, and distorted account).

Standpoint-as-political-achievement shifts the locus of authority from personal experience to subject positions tied to political (group) oppression. Furthermore, standpoint epistemology rests on the premise that an oppressed group must become a group "for itself" and not based on how others observe that group. As Harding (2012) observes,

> Women have always been an identifiable category . . . conceptualized from the perspective of men. It took women's movements for women to recognize their shared interests and transform themselves into groups 'for women'—defining themselves, their lives, their needs, and desires for themselves. (p. 51)

However, the emphasis on group identity politics raises a number of critiques and questions and presents a conundrum for researching and doing difference: If oppression is ultimately the subject of and catalyst for feminist research, organizing, and liberation, how is group to be defined, without "othering" some other group of women (inside and outside of the group)? Who is authorized to speak and for whom (see Roof, 2012, p. 532)? These were the questions emerging in the early 1970s from African American women, often already involved in the ongoing Civil Rights Movement and acutely aware of the effects of racism and the difficulties they faced, which were different from those of their more privileged White sisters (Bambara, 1970; Davis, 1971). Throughout the 1980s, Black feminist and womanist (hooks, 1984; Walker, 1983) critiques of the assumptions of universal womanhood emerging from the second-wave feminist movement were joined by the critiques and standpoint accounts of lesbian feminists (Rich, 1980), Chicana feminists (Anzaldua, 1987), and postcolonial feminists (Mohanty, 2003; Spivak, 1988). These simultaneous critiques of, *and* solidarity through, group identity politics were creating the ontological space to theoretically and practically deal with the fact of multiple-group positioning. Intersectional analyses provided the ontology and epistemic tools for doing so.

Intersectionality. Intersectional analyses represent both a critique of a universalizing view of women and an approach to difference that crystalizes the multiple, sometimes contradictory, social positions and experiences that situate people's lives. Crenshaw (1989) coined the term *intersectionality* to conceptualize women's social reality as a nexus of intersecting forms of social oppressions, where embodied experiences of gender, class, race, sexuality, and other categories of difference are defined as major markers and controllers of oppression. Intersectionality "does not question difference; rather it assumes that differential experiences of common events are to be expected" (Dill & Kohlman, 2012, p. 154). Importantly, intersectional scholarship has been applied across a wide range of disciplines, using a multiplicity of methodological approaches and producing insights about difference as constitutive of the academy, the labor market, law, and public policy (Dill & Kohlman, 2012). Also, an intersectional approach emphasizing multiple dimensions of identity and their relationship to systems of power has been an important part of sexuality and queer studies

(Johnson & Henderson, 2005) and transnationalism (Sandoval, 2004). The intersections of multiplicative social categories (Wing, 1997) raises this question for difference scholars: *Which comparisons and interrelationships should be foregrounded while at the same time not negating or undermining the complexities and particular character of an individual, group, system of oppression, or culture?*

There are different approaches to imagining how *intersections* constitute *difference*, and these imaginaries have important implications for researching, theorizing, and doing difference. For example, Collins (1991) introduced the *matrix of domination* to emphasize the interlocking systems of oppressions, replacing the *additive* models that characterized the earliest challenges to the universalizing tendency of feminist theorizing. Collins argues that, "people experience and resist oppression . . . [at] the level of personal biography; the group or community level of cultural context created by race, class, and gender; and the systemic level of social institutions" (p. 227). Highlighting interlocking systems creates the conceptual space for understanding how context provides discursive resources for understanding difference. Depending on the context, an individual may be "an oppressor, a member of an oppressed group, or simultaneously oppressor and oppressed" (Collins 1991, p. 225; also see Allen, 2004). In more recent work, Ken (2008) exposed the somewhat limiting images of *intersections* and *interlocking systems of inequality*, proposing instead that intersectional analyses address how race, class, gender, and other oppressions are produced in the first place, what people and institutions do with them, and how people experience them. In each of these views, intersectional analyses focus on mutually constituting processes of identity and structures of inequality. Race, class, gender, and other axes of inequality are always intertwined, co-constructed, and simultaneous (Weber in Dill & Kohlman, 2012, p. 162).

Summary: Doing Difference in Critical Feminisms. Difference studies emerging from within the binary spaces of critical feminisms and maintaining a commitment to emancipatory political action can be subjected to post-structuralist critiques charging essentialism (i.e., characterizing individuals and groups in terms of essences) or that difference (as individual and group agents acting to empower themselves) ultimately is being imagined as something outside of discourse—with a false presumption of freedom from discursive constitution and regulation (Davies, 2000). However, critical feminists can do difference studies in ways that benefit from postmodern ideas about discourse *and* maintain a commitment to emancipatory goals, if there is attention to the constitutive properties of language and the rejection of abstract universal reason (Fraser, 1995).

For example, both institutional ethnography (as standpoint epistemology) and contemporary approaches to intersectional analyses maintain a central focus on discourse, emphasizing partial understandings of interconnected difference and producing a shifting network of material and virtual sites. Both these approaches hold promise as productive frameworks for difference as constitutive. Thus for organizational scholars wishing to adhere to the logics of critical feminisms (and the commitment to an emancipatory consciousness), doing difference as a discursive, constitutive process requires a dialectical frame, deploying as necessary, text, context, and the careful attention to "the ongoing, interactive process," where difference becomes "an accomplishment rather than a set of traits, schemas, or categories that reside in individuals or reference groups (Putnam, Jahn, & Baker, 2011, p. 36).

This dialectal move gets beyond static binaries, but it is also consistent with the notion of *strategic essentialism*, where potential emancipatory projects happen through the temporary bracketing of difference-as-accomplishment (Prasad, 2012; Spivak, 1993). For example, my research with Black women executive leaders within dominant-culture (Western, White, masculine) organizations employs standpoint epistemology to illustrate how difference emerged and was negotiated as these particular women and their colleagues deconstructed the historically situated oppositional binaries "Black woman/executive leader" to socially construct new meanings that served as counter narratives to the controlling dominant cultural meanings (Parker, 2005).[3] Deployed through a dialectical frame and other social constructionist lenses, critical feminist approaches to difference—institutional ethnography as standpoint epistemology, intersectionality, and strategic essentialism as temporary tactical strategy—provide lenses to investigate the following questions: *How do theories of organizing and related constructs help to perpetuate dominant ideologies? What everyday social practices do organizational members enact to make, maintain, and modify meanings of constructions of difference? Who benefits from prevailing constructions? Who tends to be disadvantaged? How have constructions of difference varied across socio-historical contexts of organizing? How have individuals and groups contested oppressive ideologies and constructed more equitable contexts?*

Postmodern/ Post-structuralist Feminisms

In this section, I use *post-structuralist* as an umbrella term for both postmodern and post-structuralist feminisms that view discourse as the primary site for analysis and that trouble the individualism of critical humanism (Gannon & Davies, 2012). As distinct from critical feminisms' focus on confronting oppressive power structures and practices and emancipating people within subordinated categories, post-structuralist feminisms search for ways to *disrupt* the grip of binaries on thought and identity by deconstructing taken-for-granted practices (Martin, 1990) and attending more centrally to the constitutive, historically contingent, but still productive, power of discourse (Foucault, 1997). Post-structuralism rejects definitions of power as being *held* in hierarchical and institutional arrangements by certain groups and individuals; rather, power is seen as "capillary," proceeding in every direction at once and reaching "into the very grain of individuals, discourses, and everyday lives" (Foucault, 1982, p. 20).

Influenced by feminists Luce Irigaray and Hélène Cixous, and theorists Judith Butler, Jean Baudrillard, Jacques Derrida, Gilles Deleuze, Michel Foucault, and Jean-Francois Lyotard, post-structuralist feminists do not assume, nor believe it is possible to attain, freedom of the individual from social worlds, for the individual subject is implicated *with* social worlds, which are actively spoken into existence by individuals and collectives (Davies, 2000). The subject is always already within discourse, so central to post-structuralist analyses is *text*—cultural objects such as film and literary texts but also texts read as lived cultural experiences (Olsen, 2011, p. 133). As a feminist project researching difference, a starting point for post-structuralism is discourse studies as a way of denaturalizing what seems natural, interrupting binaries, and conceptualizing power, agency, and difference as contingent webs of meaning (historically, socially, culturally, and materially constituted). This approach rejects binaries (dominator/oppressed, man/woman, etc.) and focuses instead on the infinite discursive practices that situate the range of possible ways of thinking and doing.

The post-structuralist focus on discourse does not preclude attention to the material conditions of difference. Rather, an important aspect of the post-structuralist project is to illuminate material consequences of difference processes so as to denaturalize and disrupt them and allow us to think differently. Foucault (1984, 1997) provides a tool box of strategies for doing so: *technologies of the self* (focusing on the conditions of possibility through which disciplinary knowledge is formed and becomes sedimented), *archeology* (tracing how knowledge has come to define a particular domain and to underpin its associated "regimes of truth"), and *genealogy* (interrogating knowledge and power relations, particularly as they operate at the level of the body). The Foucauldian concept of biopower is an especially useful entry point for understanding how discourse produces difference materially, as it focuses on how the body is "the inscribed surface of events," the object of the operations and technologies of power (Foucault, 1984, p. 83).

Post-structuralist feminist studies of organizing, communication, and difference analyze how power is materialized in desires, bodies, social relations, and institutional structures. Of particular interest are the ways that power relations and dominant discourses are (re)produced in everyday interactions and larger social structures within specific socio-historical, political, economic, and cultural contexts (Buzzanell & Liu, 2005). For example, Buzzanell and Liu analyzed workplace pregnancy and maternity leaves to illustrate how discourse evokes certain subjectivities and meanings. They concluded that discursive power struggles might deter women, family members, and supervisors or coworkers from constructing preferable identities and positive material conditions. Post-structuralist feminist studies of organizational communication often examine relations between macro- and micro-level discourses while also appraising material practices and consequences. Thompson (2010) employed a post-structuralist feminist reading of a Food and Drug Administration (FDA) approval hearing for a vaccine to prohibit a virus that can lead to cervical cancer to interrogate and deconstruct "discursive barriers that inhibit a full involvement of males as reproductive beings in matters of health communication, research, public debate, and implementation of public health policies" (p. 120). She excavated deeply embedded ideologies and fossilized conceptions of gender, sexuality, and reproductive health. Her study demonstrated the historically contingent nature of power relations evident not only in discourse but also in material practices.

A group of scholars applied post-structuralist feminist theory to analyze six years of public discourse about the U.S. YWCA's decision to reverse its 150-year-old single-sex membership mandate (Harter, Kirby, & Gerbensky-Kerber, 2010). They highlighted discursive and material aspects of YWCA women's struggles to assess their feminist agendas, concluding that "discursive practices (e.g., definitions of organizational membership) have material consequences (e.g., fundraising options) and serve material interests in the world even as material practices and environmental conditions (e.g., United Way policies) intermingle with and shape symbolic interactions" (p. 24). Gerbensky-Kerber (2011) applied post-structuralist feminist theory to investigate discourse surrounding a mandated health care initiative in Arkansas. Her analysis illustrated the policy's differential impacts based on class and gender differences.

Buzzanell, Dohrman, and D'Enbeau (2011) analyzed popular and academic discourses about work-life balance and caregiving related to two primary political economies in the United States: neo-liberal and social welfare. They described ways that differing constructions of difference related to women's issues privilege some political interests and marginalize others. They explored ways that difference is "deeply embedded in policy language and structures and participation of stakeholders in policymaking processes and uses" (p. 247). They offered recommendations for theory and policy as well as "pragmatic suggestions for discursive and material change" (p. 259).

Summary: Doing Difference in Post-Structuralist Feminisms. While critical feminists have critiqued the deconstructive move as rendering *oppressive* categories unusable for the work of emancipation and shifting attention away from the potential for real social and political change (see Benhabib, 1995), the exemplars above have shown that this is not so. Indeed, Gannon and Davies (2012) argue that change agendas are not absent from postmodern and post-structuralist feminisms although, following Butler (1997), the commitment is to a "radically conditioned" form of agency (p. 15). In this view,

> the social subject is a site of ambivalence where power acts to constitute these subjects . . . in certain limiting ways but where, at the same time and through the same effects of power, possibilities to act (albeit constrained and limited) also emerge. (Gannon & Davies, 2012, p. 69)

Thus post-structuralists see agency,

> not as imagining a world external to being and setting out as an individual to bring that imagined possibility into existence, but in seeing that thought is already happening in the world, evolutionary and creative thought, that can be mobilized and pushed further in a continual unfolding of difference or differentiation. (Gannon & Davies, 2012, p. 73)

Post-structuralist analyses focus on the processes through which the subject is produced and the dislodging of fixed notions of the subject as a mode of agency. Social change becomes possible as an "ongoing and continuous process of self and societal critique and engagement" (Gannon & Davies, 2012, p. 81).

Postmodern feminists and post-structuralist feminists who study communication, organizing, and difference explore the following questions: *What are historical, cultural, social, and discursive patterns through which organizational divisions, inequities, traditions, and practices are held in place? What subjugated knowledges exist in historical archives and discursive formations? How does power manifest through discourses that socialize individuals to enact subjectivity? What are the discursive regimes through which people become gendered subjects? What forms of power-knowledge relations do dominant discourses (re)create, and what are their material consequences? How does power operate unobtrusively and blatantly during mundane micro practice? What ironies and paradoxes are evident in organizing practices? Whose needs do organizational discourses address or neglect?*

Critical Theories of Race: Exposing, Critiquing, and Dismantling Racial Projects

Critical perspectives on race encompass interdisciplinary writings in critical, post-structuralist, and intersectional analyses of race gender, nation, citizenship, and immigration. While it is well understood that race has no biological basis, it persists as a social construct through which various codes and manifestations of power (sometimes hidden, sometimes evident) coalesce to produce persistent "political, economic, and social conditions that mark [differences in] opportunities and access, patterns of income and wealth, privilege and relative power" (Essed & Goldberg, 2002, p. 4). In organization studies, more than 20 years after Nkomo's (1992) groundbreaking call for a rewriting of race in organizations, the issue of organization and management as racialized still has not been adequately addressed (Ashcraft & Allen, 2003). Silences and concealment surrounding Whiteness and White privilege persist in organization studies writ large (Parker & Grimes, 2009).

As frameworks for analysis of *race*, Essed and Goldberg (2002) distinguish between what they term *race critical theory* and the popular conception of *critical race theory* (CRT). CRT is identified particularly with an aspect of law in the U.S. and is restricted primarily to legal issues within that context. CRT looks at issues such as the contradiction between egalitarian and democratic ideals of the United States and its racist history and present (Bell, 1992) and the history of and legal justification for legal and material advantages that accrue to Whiteness (Lipsitz, 1998). In contrast to CRT, *race critical theories* address a wider history of racial theorizing in the critical tradition. This broader view of theorizing race emphasizes that no singular national space or theoretical orientation should dominate thinking about race and its material consequences (Essed & Goldberg, 2002). Also, this broader view of race intersects with postcolonial and transnational perspectives in its placement within global flows of power. Each of these perspectives is addressed in the following sections.

Critical Race Theory

Linking theory, policy, and social justice advocacy is a primary focus of CRT, and the primary agenda for difference scholars using this theory "must be in creating and discovering previously unlooked-for analyses and histories" (Dill & Kohlman, 2012, p. 165). Arguments underlying CRT point to ways of conceptualizing difference projects (see Parker & Grimes, 2009): (a) challenging legal justifications that operate through *race neutrality* to sustain White supremacy, (b) exposing claims of *normal racism* as it is structured through the legal system and other socio-political structures, and (c) giving voice to experiences and realities of the oppressed to expose consequences of White supremacist norms. Engaged scholars, such as the Prison Communication, Activism, Research, and Education (PCARE) group, provide one CRT exemplar that intersects each of the above projects. In challenging the Prison Industrial Complex in the United States, PCARE (2007) uses Debord's (1967) description of the United States as a "society of the spectacle" to illustrate how the U.S. government and major corporations who lobby the government often divert attention to a heightened sense of criminality, which keeps their sense of power largely unseen and invisible to the masses (Debord, 1967, as cited in PCARE, 2007, p. 407). What is also accomplished is the erasure of the racial caste system, which has produced increased incarceration rates while "the prisoners' lives, the conditions of prisons, the fate of prisoners' families, and the actual workings of the prison industrial complex remain largely invisible" (PCARE, 2007, p. 407).

Much of the CRT scholarship, legal advocacy, and social action has been advanced through the intersectional work of four identity groups, comprised mostly of law professors and students: The African American Policy Forum (AAPF), which pursues race and gender equality both globally and domestically; Latina & Latino Critical Legal Theory, Inc. (LatCrit), an intersection of scholars who align with various "out groups" including people of color, sexual minorities, and others in the United States and globally (OutCrit); and Asian Pacific American CRT (APACrit; Dill & Kohlman, 2012; Valdes, 2002). The work of these groups provides insights for difference scholars interested in writing, researching, and advocating through an anti-essentialist, intersectional lens. For example LatCrit seeks consciously to present Latino/a identity as a multifaceted, intersectional construction, traversing many different identities, including Black, White, Asian, gay, and straight, speaking many different languages, and having many different nationalities. Incorporating issues of identity, hybridity, anti-essentialism, and liberation into the analysis of law, legal institutions, and processes, LatCrit scholars attempt to "break apart the global category 'Latina/o' into its many important differences [and] hold the shared experiences and the factors that divide and differentiate in productive tension" (Dill & Kohlman, 2012, p. 165).

Important questions emerging from CRT include the following: *What are legal justifications for sustaining White supremacist norms in organizational processes, practices, and divisions of labor? What are racialized knowledge claims linked to discourses, images, and other representational practices that sustain White supremacist norms? In what ways can we expose and critique "colorblind" racism and claims of race neutrality in organizational contexts? What are the necessary conditions, potentialities for democratization, and possible complications in centering the voices, experiences, and realities of groups marginalized by White supremacist practices?*

Race Critical Perspectives

Placing race at the center of analysis within a global context is a key contribution of race critical perspectives for understanding difference in organizational communication studies. Grounded in critical and post-structuralist theories, these perspectives point to the embeddedness of racialized transnational histories, ideologies, and discursive formations manifested as organization structures and processes that normalize hierarchical difference.

This is what Omi and Winant (1994) refer to as a *racial project*—articulating how racialized social arrangements (e.g., hierarchies based on White privilege) are formed, transformed, destroyed, and reformed through structural, institutional, and discursive means. Understanding work as a *racial project* would be a robust area of inquiry for difference scholars in organizational communication.

However, even as organizational communication scholars helped to lead the critical/discursive turn in the 1970s and 1980s (Alvesson & Deetz, 2000), they did not study *race* as an important, socio-historical critical construction, as one might expect. Parker and Grimes (2009) reviewed the literature on race and management studies and concluded that the literature generally has not treated race as a social construct and has rarely considered the historic foundation and systemic character of contemporary racial oppression (Feagin, 2006). Nevertheless, organizational communication scholars are starting to build a body of literature, drawing upon the conceptual logics mentioned earlier. The overarching theme in this research is exposing and critiquing *racial projects* that normalize and protect White privilege in organizational communication theory and practices. Racial projects perpetuate oppressive forces that materialize in the lives of indigenous people throughout the world and rearticulate tensions across socially constructed lines of difference.

Ashcraft and Allen (2003) provided a foundational framing for the work of exposing/critiquing/dismantling racial projects in organizational communication scholarship and practice. They used a critical race framework to expose the ways in which Whiteness is normalized in the field of organizational communication by considering its foundational textbooks. They observed how "the normative power of organized whiteness" is preserved, even as these foundational texts purportedly attend to issues of race (p. 5). This is accomplished, for example, by treating race as a discrete variable that becomes relevant only in certain circumstances and essentializing race by conflating it with *cultural* or *international differences*. Equating race with national cultures makes race doubly invisible, because it also assumes national cultures have no diversity within them and leaves the impression of a homogenous, race-neutral American culture.

In my own work (Parker, 2002, 2003, 2005) following Allen (2000), I have used a Black feminist standpoint approach to demonstrate how mainstream leadership theories advance idealized images of White feminine and masculine models of leadership as the universal, race-neutral way of viewing leadership. These models discursively erase the racialized and colonizing histories that connect them to White middle-class norms, values, and experiences, casting others as deficient, devalued, or nonexistent leaders. Specifically, my research with Black women executive leaders within dominant-culture (Western, White, masculine) organizations centered on the voices and experiences of the women and the racialized histories that situated them—and their colleagues—to deconstruct and redefine two raced, gendered, and supposedly diametrically opposed notions of leadership—collaboration and instrumentality—common in the management literature.

Employing intersectionality, Richardson and Taylor (2009) analyzed experiences of African American and Hispanic women to investigate intersecting implications of gender and race for how these women made sense of and responded to sexual harassment. They presented a four-stage model detailing complexities of the women's experiences based on macro (societal) and micro (specific organizational cultures) constructions of race and gender. For instance, an African American woman might remain silent for fear that others will perceive her as "the angry Black woman" while also being afraid that accusing a Black male perpetrator would make her seem a traitor to her race and lead to negative consequences for that colleague. Richardson and

Taylor shared implications of their findings for organizational and legal policies, which often neglect to consider that women of color may simultaneously experience racial and sexual discrimination. These and related studies seem to respond to calls for research about intersections of multiple forms of identity and interlocking systems of oppression (Allen, 2011; Dempsey, 2011; Putnam, Jahn, & Baker, 2011). However, the need persists to focus on multiple, interrelated constructions of difference.

In concert with other communication scholarship that investigates Whiteness as a socially constructed, political aspect of identity (see, e.g., Nakayama & Martin, 1999), Grimes (2002) argued for a need to study Whiteness and organizing. Based on the premise that discourse designed to challenge the racial status quo might perpetuate it, she analyzed diversity management literature to identify subtle ways that discourse constructs assumptions about race. In turn, this led her to excavate hidden power issues related to organizational communication by illustrating the subtle ways that discourse portrays Whiteness and either supports or challenges White privilege. She concluded that interrogating Whiteness holds powerful potential for analyzing and transforming organizational issues such as group dynamics, leadership, and change management. She used the perspective to critique management discourses, including managing diversity discourses that *mask* and/or *re-center* Whiteness.

Central questions for scholars doing difference using racial project epistemologies include the following: *What emerging global organizational forces (e.g., new technologies, new media, global networks, financial market flows) are signaling emerging racial projects? How are current and emerging racial projects defining difference in the context of global organization and 21st-century organizational life? What are the possibilities for creating less racialized and more egalitarian/democratized organizational arrangements?*

Postcolonial Theory: Engaging and Centering Indigenous Histories and Self-Representations

Postcolonial theory in organizational communication studies highlights the enduring material effects of colonialism in 21st-century organizational life and in the theories and practices we create to rearticulate those effects (Broadfoot & Munshi, 2007). Postcolonial researchers posit that discourses of myth, fantasy, ambivalence, and the West's paranoiac desire for supremacy in the colonial encounter rearticulate East and West divisions into categories of colonizer/colonized, us/them, and self/other (Fanon, 1967; Mohanty, 2003; Said, 1978; Spivak, 1988). The concepts of *hybridity* and *subalternity* provide important conceptual frames and also reveal how postcolonial concerns intersect with narrative epistemologies. *Hybridity* (Bhabha, 1990)—and the associated tropes of liminality, border cultures, diaspora, and immigration (see Hall, 2007)—describes the instances where "experience, discourse, and self-understandings collide with larger cultural assumptions concerning race ethnicity, nationality, gender, class, and age" (Denzin & Lincoln, 2005, p. xvi). Relatedly, subalternity refers to the hidden and silenced voices of indigenous experience (the *colonized*; see Beverly, 2005, pp. 551–552). Important considerations for postcolonialists (and more specifically, organizational communication scholars researching difference) are conditions and desirability of subaltern experiences serving as a counter, parallel, and potentially transforming narrative in relation to dominant voices.

The deployment of *voice* (e.g., making one's self visible and heard) as a counter-narrative strategy has many complicated layers (Bhavnani & Talcott, 2012, p. 136). For example, Hammonds (1995) notes, in discussing Black female queer sexualities, that making one's self visible does not necessarily challenge the structure of power and domination that diminishes one's visibility and agency. Similarly, Rose (1997) discusses how difference is sometimes erased under the *myth of community*, which often denies the existence of difference. Following Rose (1997), Bhavnani and Talcott (2012) call for a politics of voice *and* translation as dual epistemological strategies, emphasizing the need to simultaneously research visibility and how voices and lives are represented in practice.

Knowledge production in the global context is itself a colonizing project that continues to recreate and advance the West's reliance on a subordinated *Other* (Prasad, 2003; Smith, 1999, 2005). The charge for organizational scholars, then, is to levy challenges to these colonizing processes, and several management and organizational communication scholars have begun to do so (Broadfoot & Munshi, 2007; Grimes & Parker, 2008; Kwek, 2003; Prasad, 2003; Tilbury & Colic-Peisker, 2006). One exemplar of this kind of work is Kwek's (2003) postcolonial critique of the cross-cultural management literature, which reveals the underlying logics of representation that impose Western cultural dimensions upon the very reality they seek to describe. Kwek argued that cross-cultural studies "become Western tools for colonization . . . preemptively preventing other cultures from having a voice in their own representation" (p. 122). Kwek's work points to several ideas for work in this area, including critiquing and revealing racialized representations in organization and management theory and practice (Tilbury & Colic-Peisker, 2006), giving voice to alternative histories of the *other* (Kwek, 2003, p. 131), "offering [and, I would add, not silencing/disciplining] analytical categories and representational approaches for subordinated groups to represent themselves in 'their own terms'" (Calás & Smircich, 1996, p. 250), and "acknowledging the pervasiveness of the dominant discourse in its ability to marginalize and silence" (Kwek, 2003, p. 130).

Important questions about postcolonial frameworks for theorizing and practicing difference can be gleaned from reviews by Parker and Grimes (2009) and the series of articles in *Management Communication Quarterly* inspired by Broadfoot and Munshi's (2007) call for imagining forms of postcolonial organizational communication (Grimes & Parker, 2008; Mumby & Stohl, 2007). While these essays reveal both the dearth of organizational communication scholarship in this area and the ongoing debates about the character of postcolonial approaches in the field, they also provide beginning points for taking seriously postcolonial concerns in addressing issues, questions, and problematics beyond those we currently engage. Broadfoot and Munshi (2007) begin the dialogue with this overarching question that seems foundational to a postcolonial framework for understanding difference: *How do we recover alternative rationalities, worldviews, and voices on the processes of organizing in diverse contexts?* In response, Mumby and Stohl (2007) provide eight key questions that are excellent starting points, which are summarized here: *How do postcolonial concepts (voice and difference in conversation with post-structuralism, feminism, and queer theory; an explicit political agenda) intersect, illuminate, challenge, and help us rethink, extant notions of difference as discursive, fragmented/multiple, and the effects of power?* (Questions 1–4 & 7) and *How does postcolonial theory enable us to rethink the relationships among and between communication, democracy, and ethics?* (Questions 5, 6, & 8). Grimes and Parker take these questions a step further: *What are possibilities for reframing the postcolonial project in organizational communication as a decolonizing project that identifies and brackets colonizing practices (e.g., the "race-ing" of organizational structures) and replaces those practices and structures with new, equitable ones?* (Grimes & Parker, 2008; Parker & Grimes, 2009).

Transnational Perspectives: Complicating Difference Across Space, Place, and Identity

A critical transnational perspective incorporates ideas from race critical theories and postcolonial concepts but with an emphasis on the intersections of space, place and identity (Dempsey, Parker, & Krone, 2011; Hall, 2007; Mohanty, 2003). Space and spatial references provide a framework in which we understand *space* as being filled with "all kinds of social, cultural, epistemic, and affective attributes" that become *place*, "a particular space on which senses of belonging, property rights, and authority can be projected" (Blommaert, 2005, p. 222). As Blommaert explains, "Individuals can traverse among diverse identities as they access different 'places'" (p. 222). Concepts of place, space, and identity, when connected with the postcolonial logics of hybridity, liminality, border cultures, nationality, and so on, complicate the very notion of organizing difference, especially the assumptions that we can know difference and how difference is experienced.

A critical transnational perspective highlights the necessity of conceptual frameworks that engage multiplicity and simultaneity in organizing and mobilizing across difference. Intersectional analyses of multiple forms of differences—a concept mentioned earlier as central to feminist/social constructionist perspectives—provides an important conceptual frame for doing difference in transnational spaces. Intersectional analyses reveal cultural differences as relational, illustrating, for example, that some women's economic empowerment is often derived at the relative expense of other women's. Thus intersectional analyses provide a *starting point* for engaging difference transnationally, for it gives the vantage point of seeing how identities and experiences of inequality and colonizing forces differ from place to place.

Recent analyses by organizational communication scholars explicate the importance of using an intersectional framework in transnational contexts (Dempsey et al., 2011; Ganesh, Zoller, & Cheney, 2005; Hall, 2011). These scholars are building upon work in the development literature generally and postcolonial/feminist studies particularly (Cole & Norander, 2011; Mohanty, 2003). Responding to Ganesh et al.'s (2005) call for analyses exploring transnational and feminist forms of organizing and collective action, Dempsey and her colleagues (2011) analyzed seven transnational feminist and women's networks (TFNs), foregrounding intersectional analyses as a central feature of women's transnational activism for economic development. Their central argument is that TFNs make socio-spatial differences meaningful in part through their constructions of regional, international, and *translocal imaginaries*; and they construct resistant feminist *counter-spaces* through dialogue and strategies aimed at destabilizing dominant structures, cautioning that the viability of these counter-spaces is highly contextual and often temporary. They concluded that the tension-filled process of organizing across socio-spatial differences remains undertheorized and unexplained as a transformative practice, and they encouraged scholars to "continue grappling with the many ways in which politicized histories of nation-state relationships and post/coloniality continue to organize the experience and expression of alliance-building" (Dempsey et al., 2011, p. 217).

Cole and Norander's (2011) analysis of two organizations that work to empower women in post-conflict societies provides an exemplar of Dempsey et al.'s concerns about wrestling with tensions across socio-spatial differences. Cole and Norander explored how transnational feminist practices and theories can offer new insights into peace-building processes, transform gender relations in post-conflict societies, and reconfigure global-local relationships. They reported on their fieldwork with two international organizations working in different post-conflict contexts. The first, Fambul Tok International (Family Talk), is a nongovernmental organization (NGO) with corporate headquarters in the United States and global program headquarters in Sierra Leone. The other is Kvinna till Kvinna (Woman to Woman), a Swedish NGO that partners with women's organizations in post-conflict areas to provide long-term support for peace-building initiatives; its work began in 1993 in the former Yugoslavia and has since expanded to the South

Caucasus, Middle East region, and Kenya. Both organizations focus on forging connections across lines of difference in the interest of peace building and development, but in different ways. Fambul Tok attends to local understandings of gender relations and uses them to evolve organizational practices. In contrast, Kvinna till Kvinna emphasizes including diverse others by reaching out to women (and sometimes men) whose needs and interests are often overlooked by traditional humanitarian aid efforts. In both cases, the authors revealed that challenges remain about "how to practice reflexivity and emergent design amid growth and pressures from external funding agencies to produce tangible outcomes of their work" (p. 46). In both cases, local organizations and communities are using the post-conflict context as a place to create spaces in which men and women can articulate new understandings of themselves, one another, and their relations. Both transform extant understandings of gender, gender roles, and gender relations by offering the opportunity for women to take the lead in activities of their own choosing. However, this does not mean that such activities are easy or unproblematic. Although they can be transformative, they also reflect the enactment of strategic essentialism in order for women to create strategic and emancipatory spaces for women (Pollock, 2007). Also, the authors noted that both organizations are relatively small within the peace-building community and underscored that ability of these organizations to impact policies is overshadowed by UN-affiliated and large, state-supported organizations. Despite these limitations, these exemplars of local-global spaces of differences point to transnational processes that deserve attention from organizational scholars.

From a critical transnational perspective, the following questions are important for organizational communication scholars: *What are conditions and potentialities of intersectional alliance-building across lines of discursively and spatially produced power? What are potentially disempowering aspects of such alliances? What are challenges and potentialities of resistance, contestation, and agency in transnational/post/colonial organizational contexts?*

Conclusion: Mapping the (Im)possibilities of Doing Difference

This chapter has traced trends in difference studies in organizational communication, drawing on critical and post-structuralist feminisms, critical theories of race, postcolonial theories, and transnational perspectives as useful lenses for future difference studies in organizational communication. Each of the above sections provides conceptual and practical insights for situating difference as a communicative, constitutive feature of organizing, a necessary move given the entanglements and indeterminacies that difference produces. Critical and post-structuralist feminisms raise questions about (de)constructing binary categories and exploring the (im)possibilities for emancipating people within subordinated categories and/or disrupting the grip that binaries have on thought and identity. Critical theories of race enable scholars to pursue projects exposing, critiquing, and dismantling discursively reproduced racial projects that normalize and protect White supremacy. Postcolonial theories provide frames for engaging and centering alternative histories and self-representations of indigenous peoples throughout the world as a way to expose and counter the deleterious material consequences of neo-liberal/neo-conservative capitalist practices and power flows. Transnational approaches help to complicate difference across space, place, and identity, illuminating a contentious and crucial process of grassroots alliance-building across multiple axes of socio-spatial difference. In each of these perspectives, difference can be seen as a *cultural heuristic,* generating new knowledge about the meaning, structure, practice, and economy of work.

An important advantage of explicating distinct entry points and logics for approaching difference is that it provides researchers with tools for working across these various perspectives. Drawing on the strengths of one perspective to shore up gaps in another enables a problem-focused and more comprehensive approach to difference studies. For example, critical feminists, critical race theorists, and some transnational and postcolonial theorists, concerned with emancipation and agency, see the deconstructive work of destroying categories of difference as diminishing the advocacy power for subordinated groups (Benhabib, 1995). These critiques view post-structuralist approaches to difference as being nihilistic, excessively relativist, amoral, or apolitical (Davies, 2010). On the other hand, post-structuralist critiques of critical theories point to the binary thinking and essentialism that characterize those perspectives. Given the challenges of doing difference (alluded to in the introduction) and given the questions raised in each of the previous sections, what do we gain from bringing, for example, the deconstructive stances toward language and the social world in post-structuralist perspectives together with the action-orientation of critical feminisms, critical race theorists, and transnational and postcolonial theorists? Also, what do combining these frameworks map for the future of difference studies?

Several authors point to ways forward, emerging from the connections between and among these approaches that signal spaces of commensurability among them. For example, Kincheloe and McLaren (2005) assert that "a critical theory reconceptualized by post-structural feminism promotes a politics of difference that refuses [pathologies or exoticism in reference to] the 'Other'" (p. 314). In one example of integrating critical humanism and post-structuralist influence, Dixon's (2007) essay exploring accountability for reporting sexual harassment, hazing, embezzlement, and other forms of abuse in organizational contexts questions a narrow reading of Foucauldian power as conflictual, antagonistic, and based on fear and calls for an interpretation of power that reveals empathy and protective love as relational choices.

Prasad (2012) provides another example for connecting critical humanism and post-structuralist frameworks by calling for movement beyond binary analytical categories, in this instance, sexuality, at work. He argues for a reclaiming of strategic essentialism (Spivak, 1988), which places his project firmly within the critical humanist call for emancipatory politics, but he utilizes post-structuralist thought to do so:

> [S]trategic essentialism can realize two mutually enabling objectives: i) it can serve as a salient tool in the poststructuralist endeavour to transgress from delimiting essentialisms; and, ii) it can appropriate and cautiously deconstruct the discourse of the essentialist. In this way, I move against the current of what is now Lorde's (1984) famous line: 'The master's tools can never dismantle the master's house'. Indeed, following from Spivak, I believe that a strategic engagement with the discourse of essentialism, which would provocatively expose the inherent fallacies of essentialism, is precisely what is necessary to dislocate the locus of essentialism's oppressive power that functions as the means by which to maintain contemporary injustices within organizations. (Prasad, 2012, p. 570)

Putnam et al.'s (2011) dialectical approach to studying difference as a form of resistance to prevailing binary conceptions (e.g., female/male, femininity/masculinity) offers a means for studying difference as discursive practices that encompass interdependent relationships between presumed opposites. They assert that studying dialectical tensions can reveal difference as a process embedded in the way that actors socially construct opposites: as a medium where difference "surfaces through the interplay of trying to hold *both* poles together" and as an outcome where difference "surfaces in dialectics through unfolding contradictions that shift, evolve, and change though the interplay between tensions" (p. 39, emphasis in original). As an example, they refer to Hopson and Orbe's (2007) study of Black masculinity and organizing. This study details five dialectical tensions that characterize African American men's experiences in predominantly White institutions, as portrayed in three literary texts that span the eras of enslavement of Africans in the United States, the subsequent Jim Crow era of legal segregation, and a more contemporary timeframe involving White, male-dominated cultural corporate settings. Differences emanated from the tensions African American men experienced between, on the one hand, choices about inclusion and exclusion in White, male-dominated institutions and, on the other hand, interpreting derogatory statements in particular ways. Difference emerged "from discursively managing the dialectical tensions in ways that favored one pole—the one privileged by White, middle-class patriarchal culture" (Putnam et al., 2011, p. 40). Importantly, Hopson and Orbe (2007) emphasize that these negotiated tensions reflect "playing the game," which "take[s] different forms and reflect[s] generations of experience" and where "players in the game include both dominant and non-dominant group members who recognize that power is manipulated within organizational structures" and where "victory is constantly negotiated and never definitive" (p. 83). This kind of nuanced reading of the open-ended, ongoing negotiated process of organizational power plays is foundational to conceptualizing a complex understanding of difference.

There are implications for practice associated with the frameworks presented in this chapter. First they provide organizational communication scholar activists interested in difference with tools for praxis—"transformative social practice" that puts theory into action (Ganesh, 2009, p. 228; also see Cole, Quinlan, & Hayward, 2009). For example, these frameworks provide pathways for scholars to more fully embrace their roles as public intellectuals, moving beyond description to develop actionable interventions (Frey & Carragee, 2012). Also, with these frameworks, scholar-practitioners can expand their repertoire of inquiry practices to include strategies that focus on the creativity, resources, capacities, imagination, and resilience of organizational members. Several options are available, including critical pedagogy and popular education approaches (Boal, 2002; Freire, 1993; hooks, 1994), and human methods for engaging whole systems (Holman, Devane, & Cady, 2007). Finally, these frameworks provide pathways for scholars to continue to expand the contexts where they conduct their scholarship. These include domestic and global grassroots and not-for-profit organizations that are proliferating in size and scope to address atrocities such as the aftermath of ethnic cleansing, human rights violations, and human trafficking. In addition, we should turn lenses inward to critique and transform our own disciplinary practices. We might consult work from scholars who have narrated their personal and professional experiences as members of non-dominant groups within our discipline and/or identified gaps and presented ideas for transforming theory and practice (e.g., Allen, 1995, 2000; Broadfoot & Munshi, 2007; Parker et al., 2011). Turning a critical eye on ourselves might inform theory and practice related to difference and organizing. Moreover, reflexive analyses might also help us to engage in more inclusive pedagogical practices and to diversify our field.

Looking Forward: Toward a Creative [R]evolution

Difference remains an important area of study in the discipline, and the frameworks presented in this chapter enable us to build on the work that has been done in the past and look toward researching and theorizing the complexities of difference more comprehensively in the future. As a path forward, I advocate that the above frameworks be used as a starting point for conceptualizing and engaging the pressing issues that are the *predicaments of difference*, which flow through organizational and institutional arrangements that embed human suffering, inequality, and a general propensity to suppress joy and creativity. Paraphrasing, Bergson

(1998), I end this chapter with a call for a *creative (r)evolution* in critical organizational studies, where we imagine and do difference as a generative—rather than destructive—project. This is entirely possible if we take seriously the constitutive force of discourse to normalize and naturalize particular versions of difference and work to transform how we think, making what seemed self-evident, persistent, and unquestionably part of the status quo no longer thinkable.

References

Allen, B. J. (1995). "Diversity" and organizational communication. *Journal of Applied Communication Research, 23*(2), 143–155.

Allen, B. J. (2000). "Learning the ropes": A Black feminist critique. In P. Buzzanell (Ed.), *Rethinking organizational & managerial communication from feminist perspectives* (pp. 177–208). Thousand Oaks, CA: SAGE.

Allen, B. J. (2004). *Difference matters: Communicating social identity*. Prospect Heights, IL: Waveland Press.

Allen, B. J. (2011). Critical communication pedagogy as a framework for teaching difference and organizing. In D. K. Mumby (Ed.), *Reframing difference in organizational communication studies: Research, pedagogy, practice* (pp. 103–126). Thousand Oaks, CA: SAGE.

Alvesson, M., & Deetz, S. (2000). *Doing critical management research*. Thousand Oaks, CA: SAGE.

Anzaldua, G. (1987). *Borderlands: The new mestizo=La frontera*. San Francisco, CA: Aunt Lute Books.

Ashcraft, K. L. (2008). *Bringing the body back to work, whatever and wherever that is: Occupational evolution, segregation, and identity*. Paper presented at the National Communication Association conference, San Diego, CA.

Ashcraft, K. L. (2011). Knowing work through the communication of difference. In D. K. Mumby (Ed.), *Reframing difference in organizational communication studies: Research, pedagogy, practice* (pp. 3–29). Thousand Oaks, CA: SAGE.

Ashcraft, K. L., & Allen, B. J. (2003). The racial foundation of organizational communication. *Communication Theory, 13*(1), 5–38.

Ashcraft, K. L., & Mumby, D. K. (2004). *Reworking gender: A feminist communicology of organization*. Thousand Oaks, CA: SAGE.

Bambara, T. C. (1970). *The Black woman*. New York, NY: Penguin.

Bell, D. (1992). *Faces at the bottom of the well: The permanence of racism*. New York, NY: Basic Books.

Benhabib, S. (1995). Feminism and postmodernism. In S. Benhabib, J. Butler, D. Cornell, & N. Fraser (Eds.), *Feminist contentions: A philosophical exchange* (pp. 17–34). New York, NY: Routledge.

Bergson, H. (1998). *Creative evolution* (A. Mitchell, Trans.). Mineola, NY: Dover Publications, Inc. (Original work published 1911)

Bertens, H., & Natoli, J. (Eds.). (2002). *Postmodernism: The key figures*. Martens, MA: Blackwell.

Beverly, J. (2005). Testimonio, subalternity, and narrative authority. In N. K. Denzin & Y. L. Lincoln (Eds.), *SAGE handbook of qualitative research* (pp. 547–559). Thousand Oaks, CA: SAGE.

Bhabha, H. (1990). *Nation and narration*. New York, NY: Routledge.

Bhavnani, K., & Talcott, M. (2012). Interconnections and configurations: Toward a global feminist ethnography. In S. N. Hesse-Biber (Ed.), *The handbook of feminist research: Theory and praxis* (2nd ed., pp. 135–153). Thousand Oaks, CA: SAGE.

Blommaert, J. (2005). *Discourse: A critical introduction*. Cambridge, UK: Cambridge University Press.

Boal, A. (2002). *Games for actors and non-actors*. New York, NY: Routledge.

Brisolara, S., & Seigart, D. (2012). Feminist evaluation research. In S. N. Hesse-Biber (Ed.), *The handbook of feminist research: Theory and praxis* (2nd ed., pp. 290–312). Thousand Oaks, CA: SAGE.

Broadfoot, K. J., & Munshi, D. (2007). Diverse voices and alternative rationalities: Imagining forms of postcolonial organizational communication. *Management Communication Quarterly, 21*(1), 249–267.

Butler, J. (1997). Performative acts and gender constitution. In K. Conboy, N. Medina, & S. Stanbury (Eds.), *Writing on the body: Female embodiment and feminist theory* (pp. 401–417). New York, NY: Columbia University Press.

Buzzanell, P. M., Dohrman, R., & D'Enbeau, S. (2011). Problematizing political economy differences and their respective work-life policy constructions. In D. K. Mumby (Ed.), *Reframing difference in organizational communication studies: Research, pedagogy, practice* (pp. 245–266). Thousand Oaks, CA: SAGE.

Buzzanell, P. M., & Liu, M. (2005). Struggling with maternity leave policies and practices: A post-structuralist feminist analysis of gendered organizing. *Journal of Applied Communication Research, 33*(1), 1–25.

Calás, M. B., & Smircich, L. (1996). From "the woman's" point of view: Feminist approaches to organization studies. In S. Clegg, C. Hardy, & W. Nord (Eds.), *Handbook of organization studies* (pp. 218–257). London, England: SAGE.

Cheney, G., Christensen, L., Zorn, T., & Ganesh, S. (2011). *Organizational communication in an age of globalization: Issues, reflections, practices* (2nd ed.). Long Grove, IL: Waveland Press.

Cole, C. E., & Norander, S. (2011). From Sierra Leone to Kosovo: Exploring the possibilities for gendered peacebuilding. *Women and Language, 34*(1), 29–49.

Cole, C. E., Quinlan, M. M., & Hayward, C. (2009). In L. M. Harter, M. J. Dutta, & C. E. Cole (Eds.), *Communicating for social impact: Engaging theory, research, and pedagogy* (pp. 79–90). Cresskill, NJ: Hampton Press.

Collins, P. H. (1986). Learning from the outsider within: The sociological significance of Black feminist thought. *Social Problems, 33*(6), 14–32.

Collins, P. H. (1991). *Black feminist thought: Knowledge, consciousness, and the politics of empowerment.* New York, NY: Routledge.

Crenshaw, K. (1989). Demarginalizing the intersection of race and sex: A Black feminist critique of antidiscrimination doctrine, feminist theory, and antiracist politics. In K. Bartlett & R. Kennedy, *Feminism in the law: Theory, practice, and criticism* (pp. 139–167). Chicago, IL: University of Chicago Law School.

Davies, B. (2000). *(In)scribing body/landscape relations*. Walnut Creek, CA: AltaMira Press.

Davis, A. Y. (1971). *A letter from Angela to Ericka*. New York, NY: New York Committee to Free Angela Davis.

Davies, B. (2010). The struggle between the individualized subject of phenomenology and the multiplicities of the poststructuralist subject: The problem of agency. *Reconceptualizing Educational Research Methodology, 1*(1), 54–68.

Dempsey, S. (2011). Theorizing difference from transnational feminisms. In D. K. Mumby (Ed.), *Reframing difference in organizational communication studies: Research, pedagogy, practice* (pp. 55–76). Thousand Oaks, CA: SAGE.

Dempsey, S., Parker, P. S., & Krone, K. (2011). Navigating socio-spatial difference, constructing counter-space: Insights from transnational feminist praxis. *Journal of International & Intercultural Communication, 4*(3), 201–220.

Denzin, N. K., & Lincoln, Y. L. (Eds.). (2005). *SAGE handbook of qualitative research*. Thousand Oaks, CA: SAGE.

Dill, B. T., & Kohlman, M. H. (2012). Intersectionality: A transformative paradigm in feminist theory and social justice. In S. N. Hesse-Biber (Ed.), *The handbook of feminist research: Theory and praxis* (2nd ed., pp. 154–175). Thousand Oaks, CA: SAGE.

Dixon, M. A. (2007). Transforming power: Rethinking our inheritance of Michel Foucault in organizational communication. *Management Communication Quarterly, 20*(3), 283–290.

Essed, P., & Goldberg, D. T. (2002). *Race critical theories: Text and context.* Malden, MA: Blackwell Publishers.

Fanon, F. (1967). *The wretched of the earth* (C. Farrington, Trans). Harmondsworth, UK: Penguin.

Feagin, J. R. (2006). *Systemic racism: A theory of oppression*. New York, NY: Routledge.

Foucault, M. (1982). The subject and power. *Critical Inquiry, 8*(4), 777–795.

Foucault, M. (1984). Nietzsche, genealogy, history. In P. Rabinow (Ed.), *The Foucault reader* (pp. 76–120). New York, NY: Pantheon.

Foucault, M. (1997). On technologies of the self. In P. Rabinow (Ed.), *Essential works of Foucault 1954–1984* (vol. 1, pp. 223–252). London, England: Penguin.

Fraser, N. (1995). Pragmatism, feminism, and the linguistic turn. In S. Benhabib, J. Butler, D. Cornell, & N. Fraser (Eds.), *Feminist contentions: A philosophical exchange* (pp. 157–172). New York, NY: Routledge.

Freire, P. (1993). *Pedagogy of the oppressed.* New York, NY: Continuum. (Original work published in 1970)

Frey, L. R., & Carragee, K. M. (2012). Introduction: Communication activism for social justice scholarship. In L. R. Frey & K. M. Carragee (Eds.), *Communication activism volume 3: Struggling for social justice amidst difference* (pp. 1–68). New York, NY: Hampton Press.

Ganesh, S. (2009). Critical organizational communication. In S. W. Littlejohn & K. A. Foss (Eds.), *Encyclopedia of communication theory* (pp. 226–231). Thousand Oaks, CA: SAGE.

Ganesh, S., Zoller, H. M., & Cheney, G. (2005). Transforming resistance, broadening our boundaries: Critical organizational communication meets globalization from below. *Communication Monographs, 72*(2), 169–191.

Gannon, S., & Davies, B. (2012). Postmodern, poststructural, and critical theories. In S. N. Hesse-Biber (Ed.), *The handbook of feminist research: Theory and praxis* (2nd ed., pp. 46–64). Thousand Oaks, CA: SAGE.

Gerbensky-Kerber A. (2011). Grading the "good" body: A poststructural feminist analysis of body mass index initiatives. *Health Communication, 23*(4), 354–365.

Grimes, D. (2002). Challenging the status quo? Whiteness in the diversity management literature. *Management Communication Quarterly, 15*(3), 381–409.

Grimes, D., & Parker, P. S. (2008). Imagining organizational communication as a decolonizing project: In conversation with Broadfoot, Munshi, Mumby, and Stohl. *Management Communication Quarterly, 22*(3), 502–511.

Hall, M. (2007). The postcolonial Caribbean as a liminal space: Authoring other modes of contestation and affirmation. *The Howard Journal of Communications, 18*(1), 1–13.

Hall, M. (2011). Constructions of leadership at the intersection of discourse, power, and culture: Jamaican managers' narratives of leading in a postcolonial cultural context. *Management Communication Quarterly, 25*(4), 612–643.

Hammonds, E. (1995). Black (w)holes and the geometry of Black female sexuality. *Differences, 6*(2/3), 126–145.

Haraway, D. (1988). Situated knowledges: The science question in feminism and the privilege of partial perspective. *Feminist Studies, 14*(3), 575–600.

Harding, S. (1998). *Is science multicultural? Postcolonialism, feminism, and epistemologies.* Bloomington: Indiana University Press.

Harding (2012). Feminist standpoints. In S. N. Hess-Biber (Ed.), *The handbook of feminist research: Theory and praxis* (pp. 46–64). Thousand Oaks, CA: SAGE.

Harter, L., Kirby, E., & Gerbensky-Kerber, A. (2010). Enacting and disrupting the single-sex mandate of the YWCA: A poststructural feminist analysis of separatism as an organizing strategy. *Women & Language, 33*(1), 9–28.

Hekman, S. J. (1990). *Gender and knowledge: Elements of a postmodern feminism.* Boston, MA: Northeastern University Press.

Hesse-Biber, S. N. (2012). Feminist research: Exploring, interrogating, and transforming the interconnections of epistemology, methodology, and method. In S. N. Hesse-Biber (Ed.), *The handbook of feminist research: Theory and praxis* (pp. 2–26). Thousand Oaks, CA: SAGE.

Holman, P., Devane, T., & Cady, S. (2007). *The change handbook: The definitive resource on today's best methods for engaging whole systems.* San Francisco, CA: Berrett-Koehler.

Holsaert, F., Prescod, M., Richardson, J., Robinson, J., Young, J., & Zellner, D. (2010). *Hands on the freedom plow: Personal accounts by women in SNCC.* Urbana: University of Illinois Press.

hooks, b. (1984). *Feminist theory: From margin to center.* Boston, MA: South End Press.

hooks, b. (1994). *Teaching to transgress: Education as the practice for freedom.* New York, NY: Routledge.

Hopson, M. C., & Orbe, M. P. (2007). Playing the game: Recalling dialectics and group communication. *Howard Journal of Communication*, 18, 69–86.

Johnson, E. P., & Henderson, M. (2005). *Black queer studies: A critical anthology.* Durham, NC: Duke University Press.

Ken, I. (2008). Race-class-gender theory: An image(ry) problem. *Gender Issues, 24*(2), 1–20.

Kincheloe, J., & McLaren, P. (2005). Rethinking critical theory and qualitative research. In N. K. Denzin & Y. S. Lincoln (Eds.), *The SAGE handbook of qualitative research* (3rd ed., pp. 303–342). Thousand Oaks, CA: SAGE.

Kincheloe, J., McLaren, P., & Steinberg, S. R. (2011). Critical pedagogy and qualitative research: Moving to the bricolage. In N. K. Denzin & Y. Lincoln (Eds.), *The SAGE handbook of qualitative research* (4th ed., pp. 163–177). Los Angeles, CA: SAGE.

Kwek, D. (2003). Decolonizing and re-presenting culture's consequences: A postcolonial critique of cross-cultural studies in management. In A. Prasad (Ed.), *Postcolonial theory and organizational analysis: A critical engagement* (121–146). New York, NY: Palgrave.

Lipsitz, G. (1998). *The possessive investment in Whiteness: How White people profit from identity politics*. Philadelphia, PA: Temple University Press.

Lorde, A. (1984). *Sister outsider*. Freedom, CA: The Crossing Press.

MacKinnon, C. (1982). Feminism, Marxism, method, and the state: An agenda for theory. *Signs: Journal of Women in Culture and Society, 7*(3), 515–544.

Martin, J. (1990). Deconstructing organizational taboos: The suppression of gender conflict in organizations. *Organization Science, 1*(4), 339–359.

Mohanty, C. T. (2003). *Feminism without borders: Decolonizing theory, practicing solidarity*. Durham, NC: Duke University Press.

Mumby, D. K. (2011). *Reframing difference in organizational communication studies: Research, pedagogy, practice*. Thousand Oaks, CA: SAGE.

Mumby, D. K., & Stohl, C. (2007). (Re)disciplining organizational communication studies: A response to Broadfoot and Munshi. *Management Communication Quarterly, 21*(2), 268–280.

Nakayama, T. K., & Martin, J. N. (1999). Thinking dialectically about culture and communication. *Communication Theory, 9*(1), 1–25.

Nkomo, S. M. (1992). The emperor has no clothes: Rewriting race in organizations. *Academy of Management Review, 17*(3), 487–513.

Olsen, V. (2011). Feminist qualitative research in the millennium's first decade: Developments, challenges, prospects. In N. K. Denzin & Y. Lincoln (Eds.), *The SAGE handbook of qualitative research* (4th ed., pp. 129–146). Thousand Oaks, CA: SAGE.

Omi, M., & Winant, H. (1994*). Racial formation in the United States: From the 1960s to the 1980s*. New York, NY: Routledge.

Parker, P. S. (2001). African American women executives within dominant culture organizations: (Re) conceptualizing notions of instrumentality and collaboration. *Management Communication Quarterly, 15*(1), 42–82.

Parker, P. S. (2002). Negotiating identity in raced and gendered workplace interactions: The use of strategic communication by African American women senior executives within dominant culture organizations. *Communication Quarterly, 50*(3/4), 251–268.

Parker, P. S. (2003). Control, resistance, and empowerment in raced, gendered, and classed work contexts: The case of African American Women. In P. J. Kalbfleisch (Ed.), *Communication yearbook* (vol. 27, pp. 257–291). New York, NY: Routledge.

Parker, P. S. (2005). *Race, gender, and leadership: Reconceptualizing organizational leadership from the perspectives of African American women executives*. Mahwah, NJ: Lawrence Erlbaum.

Parker, P. S., & Grimes, D. S. (2009). "Race" and management discourse. In F. Bargiela-Chiappini (Ed.), *The handbook of business discourse* (pp. 292–304). Edinburgh, UK: Edinburgh University Press.

Parker, P. S., Oceguera, E., & Sanchez, J., Jr. (2011). Intersecting differences: Organizing (ourselves) for social justice work with people in vulnerable communities. In D. K. Mumby (Ed.) *Reframing difference in organizational communication studies: Research, pedagogy, practice* (pp. 219–244*)*. Thousand Oaks, CA: SAGE.

PCARE. (2007). Fighting the prison industrial complex: A call to communication and cultural studies scholars to change the world. *Communication and Critical/Cultural Studies, 4*(4), 402–420.

Pollock, J. (2007). (En)gendering peace: Female agency, civil society, and peacebuilding in Liberia. *Undercurrents, 4*(1), 1–15.

Prasad, A. (2003). *Postcolonial theory and organizational analysis: A critical engagement*. New York, NY: Palgrave.

Prasad, A. (2012). Beyond analytical dichotomies. *Human Relations, 65*(5), 567–595.

Putnam, L. L., Jahn, J., & Baker, J. S. (2011). Intersecting difference: A dialectical perspective. In D. Mumby (Ed.), *Reframing difference in organizational communication studies: Research, pedagogy, practice* (pp. 31–54). Thousand Oaks, CA: SAGE.

Rich, A. (1980). Compulsory heterosexuality and the lesbian existence. *Signs, 5*(4), 631–660.

Richardson, B. K, & Taylor, J. (2009). Sexual harassment at the intersection of race and gender. A theoretical model of the sexual harassment experiences of women of color. *Western Journal of Communication, 73*(3), 248–272.

Roof, J. (2012). Authority and representation in feminist research. In In S. N. Hesse-Biber (Ed.), *The handbook of feminist research: Theory and praxis* (2nd ed., pp. 520–543). Thousand Oaks, CA: SAGE.

Rose, G. (1997). Performing inoperative community: The space and the resistance of some community arts projects. In S. Pile & M. Keith (Eds.), *Geographies of resistance* (pp. 184–202). London, UK: Routledge.

Sandoval, C. (2004). U.S. third world feminism: The theory and method of oppositional consciousness in the postmodern world. *Genders, 10*, 1–24.

Said, E. (1978). *Orientalism*. New York, NY: Vintage Books.

Shaw, S., & Lee, J. (Eds.). (2009). *Women's voices, feminist visions: Classic and contemporary readings* (4th ed.). Boston, MA: McGraw-Hill.

Smith, D. (1974). Women's perspective as a radical critique of sociology. *Sociological Inquiry, 44*(1), 7–13.

Smith, D. (1987). *The everyday world as problematic: A feminist sociology*. Boston, MA: Northeastern University Press.

Smith, D. (1990). *The conceptual practices of power. A feminist sociology of knowledge*. Boston, MA: Northeastern University Press.

Smith, L. T. (1999). *Decolonizing methodologies: Research and indigenous peoples*. London: Zed Books.

Smith, L. T. (2005). On tricky ground: Researching the native in the age of uncertainty. In N. K. Denzin & Y. L. Lincoln (Eds.), SAGE handbook of qualitative research (pp. 85–108). Los Angeles, CA: SAGE.

Spivak, G. C. (1988). Can the subaltern speak? In C. Nelson & L. Grossberg (Eds.), *Marxism and the interpretation of culture* (pp. 271–313). London, UK: Macmillan.

Spivak, G. (1993). *Outside in the teaching machine*. New York, NY: Routledge.

Thompson, M. (2010). Who's guarding what? A post-structural feminist analysis of gardasil discourses. *Health Communication, 25*(2), 119–130.

Tilbury, F., & Colic-Peisker, V. (2006). Deflecting responsibility in employer talk about race discrimination. *Discourse and Society, 17*(5), 651–676.

Valdes, F. (2002). Outsider scholars, critical race theory, and "OutCrit" perspectivity: Post-subordination vision as jurisprudential method. In F. Valdes, J. M. Culp, & A. P. Harris (Eds.), *Crossroads, directions, and a new critical race theory* (pp. 399–410). Philadelphia, PA: Temple University Press.

Walker, A. (1983). *In search of our mothers' gardens*. New York, NY: Harcourt, Brace, Jovanovich.

Wing, A. K. (1997). Brief reflections toward a multiplicative theory and praxis of being. In A. K. Wing (Ed.), *Critical race feminism: A reader* (pp. 27–34). New York, NY: New York University Press.

Notes

1. The writing of this section was influenced by Gannon and Davies (2012), who provide an excellent comprehensive review of the emergence of postmodern, post-structural, and critical theories and how these theories have been taken up in feminist research.

2. Shifting racialization processes complicate the use of labels, such as *Black, White*, and *African American*. In this chapter, I use such labels as they are invoked by authors in the original texts; in other instances, I use *African American* when it is clear that the reference is to descendants of enslaved Africans in the U.S. and not a collective *Black* imaginary in the African Diaspora. In still other instances, I use the labels *Black* and *African American* interchangeably to flow with the slipperiness of these labels.

3. Though not intended as such, this research is sometimes characterized as a universal view of "African American women's Leadership Styles" (see Cheney, Christensen, Zorn, & Ganesh, 2011). However, contrary to this view (and consistent with a discursive approach) there is a clear focus throughout the book on the historical discourses that situate racial, gendered, and classed meanings of *leader, executive, women*, and *Black women*, which produced everyday contradictions and tensions that the women and their colleagues negotiated.

CHAPTER 26

Incivility, Destructive Workplace Behavior, and Bullying

Jeffrey Kassing and Vincent R. Waldron

Our organizational lives are strongly tied to our identities (Scott, 2007), providing us with the opportunity to seek and achieve a sense of accomplishment as well as the opportunity to form lasting relationships. But these benefits can come at a cost that, at times, threatens our sense of well-being. Thus even as organizations benefit us professionally, personally, and relationally, they can also function as breeding grounds for "destructive interactions at work, in which people are harmed, workgroup communication deteriorates, and trust and cooperation decline" (Lutgen-Sandvik & Sypher, 2009, p. 1).

In examining these destructive organizational processes, this chapter begins with a brief overview of the historical trends and theoretical strands found within the rapidly growing research literature. It then considers the notion of *incivility*, a term that describes a great variety of destructive behaviors. We move quickly to a consideration of how incivility is detrimental to members and organizations, focusing particularly on the undermining of the agreements that make working life not only comfortable but *good* in the moral sense of the word. Next, we consider in detail two particularly potent forms of destructive communication (emotional manipulation and, most extensively, bullying) that have received increasing attention in the research literature. We close the chapter by introducing two areas of emerging interest and possible development. The first concerns the ways in which destructive practices both emerge from and potentially undermine the moral character of workgroups and organizations. The second involves the practices that might restore personal and organizational well-being in the aftermath of destructive communication.

Before proceeding, we note that scholars of organizations, mostly from management and organization studies, have addressed topics that intersect with our own. Our review will focus on communicative processes, but we point the reader toward exemplary studies of these related phenomena. For example, spurred by Tepper's (2000) seminal work, research on abusive supervision has stimulated considerable research. The focus on managerial relationships makes this strand of research a special case in the broader class of bullying studies addressed below. Later, this work expanded to include various forms of destructive leadership (Tierney & Tepper, 2007), including corruption and other moral lapses—topics that exist outside the boundaries of this essay. Studies of petty tyranny (Ashforth, 1994) and rudeness (Porath & Erez, 2007) connect to our discussion of incivility, and readers may find them worth revisiting. Workplace aggression has been considered in some detail (Corney, 2008). Finally, violence at work is an extreme case of destructive organizational behavior, one that is addressed in a growing literature (e.g., Howard & Wech, 2012); and, of course, a sizeable body of work already exists on the destructive nature of sexual harassment (Dougherty, 2009).

Historical Themes and Theoretical Strands

Research on destructive organizational communication practices is not new (Rayner & Hoel, 1997), but it has exploded in the last decade. Earlier work tended to be descriptive, identifying its prevalence, the characteristics of those who initiated abusive behavior and those who were targets, types of abusive behavior, and contexts in which it occurred (e.g., Lewis, 2006; Lutgen-Sandvik, Tracy, & Alberts, 2007; Salin, 2003; Tepper, 2000). The work took a more communicative turn in the late 2000s, driven in large part by the vibrant program of research initiated by Lutgen-Sandvik and her colleagues (see below and Lutgen-Sandvik & McDermott, 2011; Lutgen-Sandvik, Namie, & Namie, 2009). This work focused squarely on communicative dimensions of bullying and the ways in which targets responded through narrative, metaphors, and identity-managing discourses. All of this work continues, but the literature has matured to the point that communication scholars have begun to distill practical lessons about the practices that might transform abuse in organizations (Lutgen-Sandvik & Tracy, 2012).

Scholars have approached the topic from a variety of theoretical perspectives. Trait theorists trace destructive behavior to the personality characteristics of individual employees. Boddy (2011) takes this approach, suggesting that corporate psychopaths are the source of a disproportionate amount of bullying behavior. More commonly, relational theories are invoked. For example, Leader Member Exchange (LMX) quality has been established as a mediator in the relationship between destructive supervision and employee citizenship behavior (Hu, Huang, Lam, & Miao, 2012). These authors also draw on another theme familiar in this literature: interactional justice. Bullying and other types of abuse are often perceived by victims as acts of relational immorality (Waldron, 2012), which leads to feelings of indignation, vengefulness, and a desire to even the scales through retaliation or reduced work contributions.

Identity is a prominent theoretical concept in this literature. Incivility has been characterized as a *face-threat* (Gill & Sypher, 2009). Targets of bullying are said to face the task of repairing damaged identities, sometimes by recrafting personal narratives to make sense of the abusive experience and its role in the target's past and future (Lutgen-Sandvik, 2008). This emphasis on discourse is mirrored in other conceptual projects, including explorations of the metaphors and sensemaking devices used to describe workplace bullying and responses to it (Lutgen-Sandvik & McDermott, 2011; Tracy, Lutgen-Sandvik, & Alberts, 2006). For example, the need to stand up to a bully is sometimes invoked by targets and observers of this destructive form of behavior.

The research by communication scholars is increasingly grounded in the discourse practices that enact and resist destructive organizational behavior. At the same time, a good deal of the empirical work in the discipline and elsewhere focuses on the individual as the unit of analysis. The macro-organizational, cultural, and institutional forces that create the conditions for destructive behavior tend to receive less attention. In response, Waldron and Kassing (2011) applied their multilevel risk-management model in the context of bullying. They suggest that organizational policies that ignore bullying reduce the risk to bullies and those that encourage their behavior (also see D'Cruz & Noronha, 2010). In addition, economic conditions may limit options for organizational exit, leaving employees more vulnerable to the destructive practices of their organizations. Indeed, the degree to which employees are locked in power-dependent relationships with their organizations may increase the likelihood that they will tolerate abusive practices (Tepper et al., 2009). Additional theorizing about the role these and other macro processes play should prove useful.

Incivility

To be civil is to exhibit respect for others and the mutual obligations that bind people together in community. In contrast, incivility is expressed through "communication behaviors that demean, demoralize, and degrade others" (Gill & Sypher, 2009, p. 55). In this sense, civility can be linked to Goffman's (1955) now-classic discussion of *face-work*—civil communication is that which facilitates self-presentation by multiple parties within the constraints of a given work situation. Scholars have debated the nuances of incivility for quite some time (for an excellent review, see Sypher, 2004), arguing, for example, about whether the term refers to mere rudeness or includes more aggressive, intentionally harmful forms of behavior. Following Sypher, we agree that incivility varies in intensity, ranging from low-level, passive-aggressive face-threats to more blatant and acutely harmful attacks. Gill and Sypher (2009) make a strong case that insidious but low-intensity forms of incivility undermine organizational trust perhaps even more than the occasional act of naked aggression. Indeed, even "unintended" incivility can fray the bonds of mutual respect that make communal life functional and sometimes rewarding.

Here, we focus on behavior that falls toward the intentional and intense ends of the incivility spectrum. Those are what we refer to as *destructive behavior* in the remainder of this essay. In particular, we are concerned with destructive behavior that undermines the moral commitments that make an organization not only comfortable but good. Rather than delineate all of these behaviors, we focus on two that have received attention of late—emotional manipulation and bullying—the former of which has recently been labeled *emotional tyranny* (Waldron, 2009).

Emotional Tyranny

Emotional tyranny is the "use of emotion by powerful organization members in a manner that is considered to be destructive, controlling, unjust, or even cruel" (Waldron, 2009, p. 9). Drawing from Sypher's (2004) analysis, the term covers a broad range of manipulative behaviors that span moderate to high levels of intensity. Emotional manipulation can be the work of an individual, as when a supervisor crafts a threatening message designed to intimidate a member who merely questions a managerial practice. Emotional tyranny can also be practiced collectively. Team members might conspire to create feelings of intense embarrassment or shame in a coworker, perhaps to encourage quitting or to discourage a high-performing team member from working "too hard" (and thus making other members look unproductive by comparison). Whether initiated as an individual or collective act, emotional tyranny is often enacted communicatively. For example, emotion can be exploited as a communicative *resource* in the construction of messages. The coworker who displays glee at the misfortune of a peer and the manager who predictably "flies off the handle" in fits of rage are examples. In these cases, the source of destructive communication draws on emotion to create messages that are potent and often hurtful.

The complex and hierarchical arrangements that characterize many organizations are particularly conducive to emotion-eliciting communication. For example, embarrassment, in its milder forms, can be an important emotional experience when people are joined in complex and cooperative communities (Keltner, 2009). Teasing, as a form of communication that elicits embarrassment, may create a sense of solidarity among coworkers, although it subtly reminds the target that he or she is engaging in behavior that in some way stands out against a backdrop of expected identities and behaviors. By looking embarrassed, the recipient may signal a certain understanding of these expectations and even a willingness to defer to them. In this way, teasing may relieve tensions that arise among organization members.

However, unwanted or distressing emotions can be elicited in others by abusers of power, who sometimes prove masterful at evoking feelings of guilt, fear, embarrassment, remorse, and distress. For example, extreme embarrassment is among the most reported of unpleasant emotional work experiences (Waldron, 2012). Work settings often include audiences of peers or powerful others, a condition that magnifies embarrassment and sometimes transforms it into humiliation. Indeed, work identity is a central part of self-perception for many members, and support for that aspect of face may be a defining feature of workplace civility (Gill & Sypher, 2009). Unwarranted or hurtful communication in highly visible work interactions are face-threats that may have ripple effects as coworkers share what they have witnessed, a practice that may prolong the embarrassment as the victim is subjected to repeated inquiries about the incident. Thus it is not surprising that the experience of public embarrassment by a supervisor is viewed as a particularly impactful form of destructive behavior. The line between teasing and tyranny is rarely a fine one, but the latter is typically perceived by recipient and audience as intended to hurt rather than support the recipient.

Waldron (2012) observed emotional elicitation in a variety of destructive forms, only some of which can be mentioned here. *Grinding* is an intentional effort to wear down the target emotionally, often through sustained attempts to elicit feelings of distress, fear, or guilt. *Ridiculing* leaves the target feeling humiliated, ashamed, and unworthy. *Vanquishing* tactics extinguish an employee's positive feelings, replacing them with those preferred by the abuser. Statements such as "I don't think you should feel proud about that" (in reaction to a peer's justified sense of accomplishment) or "Wipe that smile off of your face" are examples of vanishing statements. *Guilting* is a tactic familiar to many employees. It involves effort to manipulate performance norms or tap an employee's proclivity to feel highly responsible. A tyrant might elicit guilt by suggesting that a hardworking member is letting down the team if he or she doesn't work late (again) or by expressing "disappointment" when a promising employee passes up a choice assignment in order to meet family obligations.

These forms of emotional manipulation figure greatly in the literature on destructive communication. For example, public humiliation has been identified as a feature of abusive supervision (Tepper, 2000), and aggressive emotional displays of anger have been linked to destructive leadership (Lu, Ling, Wu, & Liu, 2012). But it is organizational bullies that seem most adept at these forms of emotional weaponry. This most-investigated form of destructive organizational communication will receive the bulk of our attention.

Workplace Bullying

While definitions of workplace bullying vary, they generally center on several key features (Lutgen-Sandvik et al., 2007; Moayed, Daraiseh, Shell, & Salem, 2006). Fundamentally, bullying is marked by intensity, repetition, duration, and power disparity (Lutgen-Sandvik et al., 2007). Different types of attacks bring about intensity, and how often they occur becomes a matter of frequency. Additionally, bullying attacks transpire repeatedly over time. Some degree of power disparity, either apparent initially through rank or status in the organization or developed over time as the bullying plays out, is also apparent. This power disparity leaves the target feeling unable to prevent or stop the continued abuse.

Although there are clear-cut cases of workplace bullying that occur along distinct lines of difference such as race, ethnicity, and disability (Salin, 2003; Vickers, 2006a), employees generally continue to believe that bullying is something that belongs on the childhood playground, not something that manifests robustly across all sorts of workplaces and professions. As such, employees have difficulty recognizing and admitting that it does occur and that they or others in the workplace are suffering as a result of it (Tracy et al., 2006). In fact, victims do not always realize they are being bullied, even when they experience feelings of shame, inadequacy, self-blame, and low self-esteem (Corney, 2008). This is due in part to discourses that discredit workplace bullying as something psychologically rooted in people's inability to tolerate modest levels of harassment and discourses that position employee mistreatment as tolerable and expected in the service of competition and productivity (Lutgen-Sandvik & Tracy, 2012).

Bullying occurs in a matter of degrees, ranging on a continuum from unpleasant and insulting to more serious and debilitating (Lutgen-Sandvik et al., 2007). Waldron and Kassing (2011) compiled a categorical list comprised of five distinct types of bullying tactics. General aggressive behavior and physical aggression are overt tactics that include shoving, the invasion of someone's personal space, acts of physical intimidation, and verbal abuse/shouting. These acts leverage physical and aggressive behavior to be effective. In contrast, self-esteem/confidence attacks involve spreading rumors, making belittling remarks, persistent criticism, stigmatizing, highlighting mistakes, humiliation, ridicule, and positioning the victim as a scapegoat. These are primarily psychological and relational in nature and do not rely on physical acts. Similarly, the manipulation of work/capacity to perform tactic is comparatively subtle and more psychological in nature. Setting unrealistic targets, providing excessive workloads, removing responsibilities, and assigning meaningless tasks all work to disrupt one's capacity to perform. Another bullying technique involves ostracizing/isolating employees by ignoring, excluding, and differentiating them through social practices such as practical jokes. Finally, threats, which can surface as personal, professional, or physical, are powerful forms of bullying that rely upon the capacity to enforce the outcomes associated with other forms of bullying.

Bullying tends to be studied in peer-to-peer relationships or in downward relationships (Lutgen-Sandvik & McDermott, 2011) but also can occur when staff members bully managers (Branch, Ramsay, & Barker, 2007). Workplace bullying is often construed as a one-to-one (i.e., perpetrator and victim) offense; more recent work, however, has documented the communal nature of bullying (Namie & Lutgen-Sandvik, 2010). Duffy and Sperry (2007) define *mobbing* as "the nonsexual harassment of a coworker by a group of other workers of an organization designed to secure the removal from the organization of the one who is targeted" (p. 398). The term derives from the practice of animals singling out and ganging up on a specifically targeted animal with the intention of removing it from the herd or flock. Mobbing can be subtle and subversive (Hubert & Veldhoven, 2001; Zapf, Knorz, & Kulla, 1996), intended to make the coworker being attacked look as if he or she is the person at fault (Invernizzi, 2000).

In an effort to enlarge the conceptualization of workplace bullying and to clarify the differentiation between bullying and mobbing, Namie and Lutgen-Sandvik (2010) examined the communal nature of workplace bullying across a large sample of employees. Their work challenges the commonly held notion that victims of bullying simply fail to stand up to and confront a single individual bully. By uncovering the complicit role that others play in bullying, they illustrate how bullying is (more often than not) enacted collectively. And by moving beyond the concept of *mobbing,* which includes active participants, they drew attention to covert and passive accomplishes as well. They found convincing evidence that the majority of cases involved multiple employees. Indeed, 70% of reported cases of bullying involved other perpetrators or the support of other organizational members. Their data revealed that, while group bullying/mobbing took place with some degree of regularity, in more instances, individual bullies perpetrated abusive behavior with the endorsement and approval of others. Bullies received support from various organizational audiences, including upper managers, human resources (HR) staff, bullies' peers, and even the peers of targets. They concluded that bullying should be understood as a "social process embedded in workgroup and organizational communication networks" rather than as the act of a specific bully operating independently (p. 356).

Effects of Bullying. The effects of workplace bullying are well and widely documented (Brotheridge & Lee, 2010; Corney, 2008; Meglich-Sespico, Faley, & Knapp, 2007; Moayed et al., 2006). They range from emotional imbalance experienced as confusion, restlessness, and sadness (Brotheridge & Lee, 2010) to workplace disruption seen in absenteeism, employee turnover, and reductions in efficiency, work quality, and job satisfaction (Moayed et al., 2006). Bullying also takes a toll on victims' psychological well-being, as targets can end up feeling ashamed and inadequate and suffer through bouts of low self-esteem and self-blame (Corney, 2008). And physical ailments that stem from bullying-induced employee stress can lead to health related issues, too (Moayed et al., 2006). In fact, Djurkovic, McCormack and Casimir (2006) were able to demonstrate support for a psychosomatic explanation for the physical symptomology that accompanies workplace bullying. They found that bullying acted independent of disposition in accounting for negative affect and concluded "that the disposition of the victim does not influence emotional reactions to bullying" (p. 83). Thus victims experience psychosomatic symptoms of bullying regardless of their psychological makeup and/or predisposition to experience negative affect.

In an attempt to give some shape to the varied and extensive effects of bullying, Meglich-Sespico et al. (2007) classified them into three broad areas: psychological/emotional, physical, and work related. Psychological/emotional outcomes include mental health problems such as depression, post-traumatic stress disorder, hypersensitivity, anxiety, irritability, nervousness, self-hate, concentration difficulties, suicidal thoughts, social withdrawal, and lower confidence levels. Physical outcomes range in nature from increased alcohol use to increased risk of cardiovascular and chronic diseases. Insomnia and chronic fatigue are additional physical symptoms. Work-related outcomes can manifest as long-term sick leaves, layoffs, transfers, reassignments, and termination—either forced or voluntary.

Beyond the effects bullying poses for targets, there are consequences for organizations and fellow workgroup members. Organizations that fail to adequately address workplace bullying jeopardize financial stability, general productivity, and corporate reputation (Harvey, Heames, Richey, & Leonard, 2006). In particular, organizations stand to suffer from lost work days due to absenteeism, increased health insurance and workers' compensation costs associated with chronic health and stress issues, lower-quality work and less productivity due to reduced employee satisfaction and motivation, and increased training and recruiting costs that result from turnover (Moayed et al., 2006). Additional expenses surface with litigation and compensation when employees file grievances and pursue legal action (Harvey et al., 2006) and when an organization's reputation diminishes and attracting and keeping talented employees proves difficult (Heames & Harvey, 2006).

Workplace bullying also can affect performance (Harvey et al., 2006). Operations are disrupted when bullied employees can no longer functionally complete their daily tasks. Employees working in an environment that tolerates and permits bullying become less likely to contribute in ways that benefit the organization or workgroup. Similarly, employees are less likely to bring innovative ideas forward for fear of being bullied for doing so. And finally, the organization suffers holistically as bullying acts as an "organizational cancer" (p. 3) that attacks the well-being of employees and the organization as a whole.

Moreover, people who observe bullying also seem to experience negative impacts. For example, Lutgen-Sandvik et al. (2007) reported that non-bullied coworkers witnessing abusive and aggressive acts experienced increased levels of stress and negativity and reduced job satisfaction. Such spillover effects are considerable (Heames & Harvey, 2006). The relationships victims have with other coworkers, for example, can become strained as the individual difficulties they confront easily bleed into interactions with coworkers and taint interpersonal work relationships. At the same time, the negativity introduced by a bully may deter others from confronting the bully for fear of being victimized and can disrupt group processes when interaction patterns become dysfunctional. Thus the costs of failing to deal with workplace bullying impact organizations as well as individuals.

The negative consequences of bullying can have a ripple effect that extends outside the organization. In these instances, the difficulty of dealing with bullying undermines previously healthy and socially supportive relationships with friends and family. Lewis and Orford (2005) found that as workplace stress linked to bullying increased, people found it more difficult to maintain supportive relationships outside of work. Relational partners grew weary of needing to provide support to friends and loved ones who seemingly failed to take any or enough action to correct and address the situation. These detrimental relational effects stem from the aforementioned assumptions and entrenched discourses that convince people that bullying is child's play, unserious, and easily corrected (Lutgen-Sandvik & Tracy, 2012). The way in which we talk about and conceptualize bullying is one of many causes associated with it.

Causes of Bullying. There are multiple factors to consider when assessing the causes of bullying, and these link together in powerful and complex ways, allowing for bullying to proceed as "a self-reinforcing or spiraling process" (Salin, 2003, p. 1217). Harvey et al. (2006) categorized these as key characteristics related to the environment, the perpetrator, and the victim. With regard to victims, targets of bullying tend to be employees who are socially isolated and those who are viewed as particularly vulnerable. And the vulnerability of targets amplifies when already isolated employees become further physically and socially disconnected from their workplace counterparts (Harvey et al., 2006). At the same time, targets can be people who possess considerable influence in the organization and pose a perceived threat to the bully (Salin, 2003).

Environmental characteristics range from the physical makeup of the workspace to the attitudes of employees (Baillien, Neyens, De Witte, & De Cuyper, 2009; Harvey et al., 2006; Harvey, Treadway, Heames, & Duke, 2008; Salin, 2003). An organization's tolerance for bullying is shaped by organizational climates that maintain a degree of civility, possess clear norms of behavior and rules of conduct, and adhere to standard operating procedures. Organizational systems that embrace internal competition, that rank and compare employees, and that reward based on performance tied to competitive measures end up being fertile ground for bullying (Salin, 2003). Moreover, stress resulting from heavy workloads, hectic work environments, and time pressures can contribute to bullying behavior (Salin, 2003). Intrapersonal frustrations can lead to displaced aggression and harassment (as can interpersonal conflict) and intergroup behavior marked by backbiting, mockery, and gossip (Baillien et al., 2009).

Sound supervision plays an important role in preventing workplace bullying and gives rise to susceptibility in its absence (Harvey et al., 2006; Mathisen, Einarsen, & Mykletun, 2010). Poor oversight and training can contribute to supervisors' inability to see and address bullying, and this is compounded by downsizing, which has resulted in decreases in middle management personnel and increased spans of control for those who remain in supervisory roles (Harvey et al., 2006). Moreover, sloppy and careless supervisors (as well as anxious and vulnerable ones) seem to allow for more bullying to take place in their respective staffs (Mathisen et al., 2010). Bullying can surface, then, when supervisors fail to address it appropriately either because they are incapable of doing so, reticent, or apathetic. Finally, bullying becomes more likely when supervisors treat their staff poorly, leading employees to become accustomed to substandard treatment and more likely to tolerate and practice bullying behavior in their ranks (Harvey et al., 2006).

Along with the social and psychological attributes that characterize organizations, scholars have considered the physical makeup and situatedness of workplaces (Harvey et al., 2006; Harvey et al., 2008). For example, workspaces that are poorly lit and physically separated can prove problematic as both put employees in vulnerable positions (Harvey et al., 2006). And some thought should be directed toward the larger corporate global environment in which organizations function. Globalization, for instance, is a factor that has an impact on organizational structures and processes and, as such, can affect workplace bullying. Harvey et al. (2008) located several causes of bullying that could derive from globalization. First, greater workforce diversity and the cultural novelty of employees working in nonnative cultures could present particular challenges. Second, the remote and asynchronous nature of foreign assignments could give rise to numerous and differentiated subcultures within an organization that will vary with regard to tolerance for and detection of bullying. And third, legal protections against bullying behavior fluctuate across the globe—meaning that employees in certain places could be more vulnerable and less able to take action against it.

As perpetrators, bullies are socially and politically skilled, able to avoid being sanctioned while continuously engaging in bullying behavior (Harvey et al., 2006). They often have aggressive personalities and, in some cases, would even be classified as corporate psychopaths (Boddy, 2011; Harvey et al., 2006). According to Boddy (2011) psychopaths "have no conscience, few emotions, and an inability to have any feelings or empathy for other people" (p. 368). They deploy bullying to intimidate those who may criticize or scrutinize their behavior, to humiliate and hurt others who threaten them, and to distract attention away from their own behavior. The presence of corporate psychopaths seems to increase the prevalence of workplace bullying considerably, even though they represent a small proportion of the workforce. According to Boddy (2011), only 1% of the supervisory population can be classified as corporate psychopaths, yet these individuals were implicated in more than a quarter (26%) of bullying incidents. Those predisposed to bullying are enabled by low perceived costs associated with bullying. These include the absence or irregular enforcement of formal policies sanctioning bullies, the abdication of enforcement to lower-level managers, and the normalization of bullying behavior as part of an organization's culture (Salin, 2003).

Coping With Bullying. People appear to cope with bullying in a variety of ways, depending on the extent and nature of it (D'Cruz & Noronha, 2010; Djurkovic et al., 2005; Lewis, 2006). Targets of bullying can leave the organization, avoid the situation, assert themselves and contest the bully, or seek formal assistance. Avoidance behaviors seem to be more common among victims than either assertive or help-seeking behaviors, and these behaviors were exercised in response to all forms of bullying except the assignment of too much work (Djurkovic et al., 2005). Conversely, seeking formal help was used predominantly in response to violence, indicating that only the most extreme and demonstrable cases of bullying were associated with seeking formal help. Exiting the organization proved to be an effective adaptive and constructive response to workplace bullying for some (D'Cruz & Noronha, 2010). While this coping strategy does not resolve the bullying situation, it does help to restore hope and a sense of control for victims. But feelings of defeat, victimization, powerlessness, and defenselessness can persist even after organizational exit. For others, coping manifested in medical ailments (Lewis, 2006). Becoming physically ill and remaining unwell helped explain the physically and mentally disruptive symptoms that plagued victims of bullying. Health explanations allowed victims to individualize the affront instead of dealing with the rupture it created in the social fabric of one's organization.

One apparent and key turning point for victims is identifying the pattern of abusive behavior they experience as bullying (Lewis, 2006; Lutgen-Sandvik, 2008). This realization marks an important moment for victims and brings into relief the need to understand coping as a process rather than a simple response. Several scholars have considered the processual nature of coping with workplace bullying (Lewis, 2006; Lutgen-Sandvik, 2006, 2008). Lewis (2006) found that in the early phases of bullying, people tended to minimize interpersonal differences, overlooking patterned acts of abuse and their seriousness as a result. When bullying behavior became more apparent, targets shifted to acts of self-preservation. They avoided calling abusive behavior into question while they sought to address the issue via a host of proactive strategies. When these efforts failed to curtail bullying, they questioned their commitment to professional and organizational values. In the end, employees were forced to reassess their relationships with management and the power dynamics within their respective organizations. They often felt as if they no longer fit within the given profession or their specific organization.

Lutgen-Sandvik (2008) produced one of the most extensive and communicatively focused treatments of coping to date. This entailed analyzing the bullying process as involving several distinct phases in order to determine the sense-making processes apparent in each. In particular, she found that employees were preoccupied with making sense of abusive behavior in the pre-bullying phase. During this phase, they wrestled with their own uncertainty regarding whether or not they were being targeted. Employees reached out to coworkers for confirmation of abusive acts, hoping to receive some feedback that either legitimized or helped dismiss their concerns. When successful, employees were able to "reduce discomfort, increase predictability and reclaim the relatively uneventful nature of day-to-day worklife" (p. 106).

Any doubts about being bullied evaporated in the bullying phase as it became patently clear to employees that the abusive acts, which transpired regularly and across time, constituted bullying. Abusive acts in this phase lasted from six months to an astonishing eight years (Lutgen-Sandvik, 2008), forcing employees to reconcile their self-narratives, since understanding that one was being victimized contradicted notions of being able to stand up for oneself. Reconciling helped victims regain a sense of equilibrium that was lost when bullying became pronounced and reduced the dissonance felt when their identities were threatened. Targets also took action to recoup their damaged professional reputations by demonstrating the extent of the abuse for others and by impugning the bully. Targets had to adjust in this phase to the realization that commonly held beliefs—that people do the right thing, organizations protect their employees, and hard work is rewarded—were not necessarily viable. For targets, "regaining equilibrium, coming to grips with injustice and rebuilding identity narratives with a set of altered beliefs" (Lutgen-Sandvik, 2008, p. 110) was necessary and fundamental in the bullying phase.

Those who suffered from bullying eventually confronted the need to reposition themselves in the story of abuse. This entailed "re-storying one's damaged self-identity and weaving the experience into a long-term aspect of one's biography" (Lutgen-Sandvik, 2008, p. 110). The post-bullying phase then involved grieving and eventually accepting the loss of professional reputation, organizational identity, self-confidence, and core beliefs in justice and fairness. Grieving victims were able to craft revised self-narratives that helped explain their victimization. Restructuring enabled victims to see bullying as a learning experience that transformed them and confirmed their self-confidence.

Other exemplary studies that focus on coping with bullying consider the discourse, metaphors, and sensemaking processes people use (Lutgen-Sandvik & McDermott, 2011; Tracy et al., 2006). Tracy et al.'s (2006) analysis of metaphor use found that bullying was compared to a game or battle in which targets vividly described being wounded or hurt in a game that was "fixed or unfairly weighted in the bully's favor" (p. 160). Yet contesting bullies was routinely framed as justifiable and righteous. Those who grew weary of the fight often viewed bullying as an ongoing nightmare, which helped them explain and understand the surreal and inexplicable nature of what they were experiencing. The enduring nature of bullying was captured by metaphors that likened it to torture—that is, metaphors captured the relentless patterns and wearing-down processes of bullying. Still others likened bullying to a noxious substance forced upon victims against their will, something that they needed to physically rid themselves of once they began a process of recovery.

Targets of bullying engaged several metaphors for speaking about perpetrators. Bullies who clearly saw themselves as more important than others were characterized as *dictators* or *royalty*, whereas those who were skilled at acting differently in various social settings (i.e., as a bully in one setting and as a helpful colleague in another) were described as *two-faced actors*. This sort of social adeptness ran counter to and challenged targets' testimony and made it particularly difficult for victims to lodge credible allegations against bullies. Finally, the notion of *evil demons* was used to describe bullies who possessed demon-like qualities and who exhibited devilish spurts of anger and emotion.

Their analysis also considered the metaphors used to describe and discuss targets of bullying. These included the *slave* metaphor, whereby people felt they were expected to be subservient and remain indentured to the bully, and the *prisoner* metaphor, whereby people felt isolated from others and inescapably captive to the whims of the bully. The *child* metaphor was deployed by those who felt that bullying positioned them in a child-like state of existence, while the *heartbroken lover* metaphor helped victims explain the loss of a beloved job or career as a result of being bullied.

In a related work, Lutgen-Sandvik and McDermott (2011) discovered that employees used several different sensemaking lenses to explain bullying. For example, the *actor-focused lens* positioned the bully's personality as the root cause of bullying. This resulted from a close inspection of the characteristics, beliefs, and values that lead some people to be abusive or from recognition that bullies were incapable of handling frustration well and resorted to blaming others for their mistakes.

An *organizational-focused* lens suggested that bullying resulted from employee-abusive cultures that failed to address and, at times, enabled bullying. Alternatively, it could be explained as a HR function that embraced bullying as a mechanism to drive out selected employees for the purpose of increasing productivity. This lens proved helpful, too, for explaining how bullying persisted over time. Employees believed that management failed to intervene because it feared the emotional fallout that taking a stance might incur and because there was some hidden protection extended to the bully. In other cases, people simply felt that supervisors bullied because they did not possess the appropriate skills to manage effectively. Bullying related to supervisor incompetence has surfaced in work that examines tyrannical bosses and the circumvention of managers (Bies & Trip, 1998; Kassing, 2009).

Targets also used sensemaking frames to situate themselves relative to the act of bullying. In these cases, they explained bullying by taking some accountability for the abuse, recognizing past action or lack thereof as a contributing factor. "Standing Up metaphors marked this type of sensemaking: standing up to actors, failing to stand up, or standing up too late" (Lutgen-Sandvik & McDermott, 2011, p. 358). Similarly, people viewed their own personal attributes as catalysts for abuse (e.g., difference markers, beliefs/values, social/occupational capital, or simple dislike). Finally, there were instances in which targets believed specific situations (e.g., family or health issues) contributed. Interestingly, the fact that other means for explaining abuse were available did not automatically relieve targets from feeling accountable.

Finally, employees looked to their work group and society at large for explanations. *Work group-focused* sensemaking implicated other coworkers as complicit because they either remained silent or sided with the bully, serving as "spies, infiltrators, or agents" (Lutgen-Sandvik & McDermott, 2011, p. 360). *Society-focused* sensemaking entailed recognizing the lack of protections afforded targets and the priority placed on achievement and success in the workplace.

Moving beyond coping research, Lutgen-Sandvik (2006) explored the forms of resistance people use to combat workplace bullying. She discovered that people craft and use "multiple communicative tactics to (re)create a workplace environment marked by respect, dignity, and justice" (p. 422). This occurred via several tactics: exodus, collective voice, reverse discourse, subversive (dis)obedience, and confrontation.

A combination of exit and avoidance behaviors coalesced to form the *exodus* tactic, which involved "quitting, intentions/threats to quit, transfers/requests for transfers, and aiding others' exit" (p. 415). Accordingly, those who used this tactic talked with one another about quitting, exchanged information about alternative job opportunities, and shared and revisited stories about how previous victims had escaped. It also entailed quitting on one's own terms and clearly sharing one's disgust, resentment, and anger with former employers.

A second form of resistance, *collective voice*, appeared when employees banded together to confront bullying behavior. Those using collective voice clearly benefitted from the social support and comfort it provided, but they remained strategically focused on being action oriented. This was achieved through the realization of mutual advocacy and contagious voice. Crafting shared action plans, protecting one another, and connecting via struggle and survivorship worked as agents of mutual advocacy; speaking out in concert with other victims or concerned organizational members signified contagious voice.

Reverse discourse stood as another powerful means for combating bullying. In these instances, employees embraced pejorative labels such as *troublemaker* and accessed influential allies such as union representatives, trusted managers, and attorneys. Employees located alternative sources to depict bullying (e.g., news and popular reports) to help those being victimized recognize patterns of abusive behavior. Filing formal and informal grievances against bullies and documenting interactions with them functioned as additional means of resisting bullying. These actions worked to empower targets and victims of bullying—and helped them reconstitute relationships with bullies and repair their professional standing.

Subversive (dis)obedience involved manipulating labor efforts, working-to-rule, and avoiding or withholding information (Lutgen-Sandvik, 2006). Here, targets intentionally altered their interaction with the bully. Subversive (dis)obedience also occurred when targets openly shared hostile gossip about the bully with coworkers and directed character assassinations at the perpetrator in front of other employees. While candid and proactive, these strategies did not address the bully directly. *Confrontation*, in contrast, entailed confronting the bully in face-to-face conversations or challenging the bully in public interactions. This practice was deployed early in the bullying process and often resulted in additional abuse. The study of resistance to bullying offers an important bridge between potential victimization and proactive neutralization of bullying behavior. The next section discusses other means of addressing workplace bullying.

Organizational Responses to Bullying. At the organizational level, bullying can be addressed through policy development and enforcement, through training, and through promoting civil organizational cultures. Having policies in place that forbid workplace bullying is important but problematic at times (Bryant, Buttigieg, & Hanley, 2009; Cowan, 2011). Unfortunately, policies are often absent or wanting with regard to enforcement and not necessarily well understood by personnel charged with enforcing them (Bryant et al., 2009). Cowan (2011) found that while many HR professionals felt they had policies in place, those policies did not specifically identify bullying or even use the term. Moreover, there was divergence in what the HR professionals believed the policies connoted and what they actually stipulated. Another study concluded that most companies did not have policies in place, and those that did poorly enforced their stated goal of no tolerance (Bryant et al., 2009). Moreover, anti-bullying policies can prove paradoxical, as they provide an outlet for victims to report concerns but require them to risk alienation, ostracism, career disruption, and possibly unemployment (Vickers, 2006b).

Effective training seems to be a potential deterrent of workplace bullying (Mikkelsen, Hogh, & Puggaard, 2011; Pate & Beaumont, 2010). Research indicates that employees benefit from training and that it can reduce incidents of bullying (Mikkelsen et al., 2011). In one particular case, an organization that was suffering from widespread workplace bullying showed dramatic improvement after a new CEO instituted a program entitled Dignity at Work. Besides pursuing clear-cut cases of bullying, which resulted in the dismissal of employees at all levels, a compulsory training program that underscored the company's code of behavior was instituted. Three years later, the company had cut in half the perception that bullying was a problem among employees—and this change was evident across all sectors of the organization (Pate & Beaumont, 2010).

The enforcement of formal policies and the development of effective training are only part of the equation, though, as organizations should strive to create cultures that promote civility. Bryant et al. (2009) argued, "Organizations need to develop a proactive stance and establish codes of civil workplace conduct alongside anti-bullying policies and procedures" (p. 58). Cultures of civility need to emanate from the highest levels of an organization (Bryant et al., 2009), because "once institutionalized, bullying is an organizing discourse that could close down discussion of what is and is not a legitimate exercise of power in organizations" (Liefooghe & MacKenzie Davey, 2010, p. 74).

In a comprehensive effort to address workplace bullying via multiple levels, Lutgen-Sandvik and Tracy (2012) offered several prescriptions. At the macro level, they recognized the importance of addressing bullying by considering the macro discourses that contribute to and define bullying. This should involve interrogating discourse that marks and identifies difference along the lines of race, gender, disability, and ethnicity; examining discourse that associates bullying with childhood; making bullying inappropriate and easily dismissible in the workplace; and scrutinizing discourse that enables employee mistreatment through the prioritization of competition. The fact that employees "have naturalized bullying as a normal part of the job" (p. 854) and that they often see being subjected to bullying as a sign of weakness and passivity demonstrates the potency of these discourses (Lutgen-Sandvik et al., 2007). However, discourses can be inverted or reversed (Lutgen-Sandvik, 2008), serving as tools for intervening against bullying behavior. As Liefooghe and MacKenzie Davey (2010) state,

> While institutionalization allows organizations to take the nature of bullying for granted as unsanctioned, interpersonal, or individual abuse of power, discourse can also be used to highlight the precariousness of these processes and the ways they may be ambushed by other organization members to resist and protest unfair work practices. (p. 87)

At the meso level, Lutgen-Sandvik and Tracy (2012) suggested that researchers attend to how bullying mutes organizational members' voices, particularly when enacted by managers and other influential organizational members. And they argued for examining how workplace bullying can become complicit and communal when other employees participate directly or when they condone bullying indirectly by remaining silent about its occurrence (Namie & Lutgen-Sandvik, 2010). Finally, Lutgen-Sandvik and Tracy (2012) contended that, at the micro level, "workplace bullying is a communicative phenomenon that is talked into being" (p. 18). It is at the micro level that employees become aware and make sense of bullying through conversations and interaction with fellow organizational members (Lutgen-Sandvik & McDermott, 2011; Tracy et al., 2006).

Emerging Trends and New Thinking

From the recent work on incivility, emotional tyranny, and bullying, we see two emerging trends. The first is that destructive communication is most alarming when the harmful acts of individuals are tolerated by the organization and implicitly encouraged by the indifferent response of the work group. Thus we argue that researchers should examine the role of destructive interactions in undermining the moral understandings that might ordinarily discourage abusive behavior. Second, the literature has recently taken a prescriptive turn, with increasing interest in the means by which the damage done by bullies and other destructive communicators might be remedied and the well-being of targets restored. In the next section, we also explore potentially restorative practices.

Destructive Communication and Organizational Morality

As we have documented, destructive organizational communication can have potent negative effects on individual employees and work groups. People feel distressed, relationships are frayed, careers are disrupted, and employees sometimes choose to quit. But intense forms of incivility have indirect effects as well; these are manifested in the ways employees come to perceive and react to behaviors that might normally be considered wrong or immoral. In his study of motivation and "moral emotions," Weiner (2006) examines how feelings of anger and sympathy shape reactions to perceived injustice. For Weiner, anger is a kind of emotional accusation that arises from a belief that another should have (and could have) acted differently. As a moral emotion, anger motivates organizational members to restore what they perceive to be proper moral codes. They might do so by correcting a team member who engages in inappropriate conduct or exhorting slacking peers to work harder. As Waldron (1994) observed in a study of factory workers, an increasingly indignant workforce may be motivated to resist the abusive tendencies of managers who become too enthralled with their own power. In that case, workers conspired to embarrass their leader by subjecting him to a series of practical jokes and work slowdowns.

Weiner sees moral emotions as closely aligned with attributions about the controllability of apparently destructive behaviors. If a manager's irritable behavior is attributed to family stresses, workers may feel sympathy rather than anger. In this case, they may choose patient waiting over corrective action. If a peer is performing poorly due to external factors (e.g., disrupted childcare arrangements are causing her or him to be chronically late), they may also respond sympathetically. Sympathy could motivate them to act on the larger, systemic sources of the norm-violating behavior. Perhaps they would offer suggestions for better childcare providers or ask the HR department to assist the coworker. Of course, if one's own behavior is at variance with prevailing work norms, feelings of guilt or shame may motivate self-correction (especially if these feelings are reinforced by the comments of valued others). In each of these examples, emotion serves a kind of signal function, indicating that values and conventions are threatened and motivating a corrective response.

It is this connection between feeling and moral response that is disrupted by incivility and destructive behavior, particularly when it becomes repetitive and normalized. The rupture emerges at one of several points in the attribution-emotion-response cycle. First, the moral infractions that might normally elicit moral emotions may be redefined by the destructive actions of powerful organizational members. For example, ridicule and deception may become just two examples of the many tactics endorsed by a leader who celebrates competitiveness and degrades employees who raise moral objections. Over time, principled employees will leave the organization, shelve their objections, or come to accept that such behavior is just part of doing business. In essence, the abusive leader succeeds in redefining the moral codes, so that feelings of guilt, shame, or fear (of being caught) are not only extinguished but perhaps replaced with the kind of fearless swagger that we have come to associate with the worst corporate pirates.

Destructive communication behavior can degrade the motivational potency of moral emotions. Employees who are made to feel guilty too often—those who are worn down by continual feelings of alarm or fear—may become emotionally detached as a kind of survival strategy. In essence, they learn to stop caring or simply can't muster the considerable energy required to mount an effective protest. Finally, even when moral violations are perceived and emotions are intensely experienced, employees often choose not to express their feelings or do so in ways that are likely to be ineffective. Having observed previous destructive responses from peers or supervisors, concerned employees are likely to use what Kassing (1997) labeled *displaced dissent*. Seeing no constructive avenues for communication within the organization, they share their concerns with family members and other supporters. In this way, the pattern of morally questionable behavior goes unchallenged.

This line of thinking spawns a variety of new queries about destructive communication. What kinds of moral interpretations do organizations and workers associate with bullying and other destructive patterns of behavior? How and why and to whom do they communicate (or not) when these kinds of acts are committed? Are there connections between the expression or suppression of moral emotions in an organization and the prevalence of destructive practices? To what extent do (should) organizations enact codes of relational conduct that define destructive communication practices as morally unacceptable?

Restorative Practices and Employee Well-Being

We assume that nearly all destructive behavior threatens the well-being of individual employees and the larger organization. Thus far, scholars have examined ways to cope with or mitigate bullying, but few have considered the more daunting challenge of restoring the well-being of individuals, relationships, and organizations that have been harmed. Our thinking is influenced by evolving models of employee well-being (e.g., Keys, 2002; Page & Vella-Brodrick, 2009), which emphasize not just the absence of stress and negative feeling but the presence of both positive feelings and positive functioning. The notion of well-being is multifaceted (see Ryff, 1989), including at least these dimensions: (1) positive relations with others, (2) environmental mastery, (3) personal growth, (4) autonomy, (5) purpose in life, and (6) self-acceptance.

It is obvious that bullying and other destructive practices have deleterious effects on one or more of these indicators of well-being. For example, an employee who has been ostracized will experience reduced opportunities to interact positively with coworkers. A bullied low-power employee may perceive limited options for self-defense (reduced autonomy). Violations of civility may be confusing and disorienting, leaving the employee feeling little control over the workplace environment. Employees who experience abuse at work may cope by disengaging, at the cost of losing the sense of purpose and opportunities for growth that many people receive from their work. This disengagement effect was evident in a recent review of the literature, which indicated that lowered levels of employee well-being are associated with negative outcomes such as absenteeism and poor performance (Page & Vella-Brodrick, 2009). Interestingly, well-being was found in some studies to be more important than simple job satisfaction in predicting such outcomes as intention to stay or leave the organization.

As we envision them, restorative practices acknowledge the loss of well-being even as they create possibilities for rebuilding and reimagining working lives that have been damaged. Moreover, destructive behavior can undermine employee confidence in organizational justice. Thus any process of restoration must begin with accountability for harmful and wrongful conduct as a first step in rebuilding this confidence. Restorative processes must not subject abused employees to revictimization.

Individual-Level Efforts. As Lutgen-Sandvik et al. (2009) argue convincingly, destructive behavior should be corrected by systemic interventions rather than the efforts of individual victims. Nevertheless, workers must often tend to their own well-being as they wait, sometimes in vain, for organizational change. To increase what theorists have labeled *environmental mastery* (Ryff, 1989), employees may take steps to educate themselves about the nature of the abuse and common reactions to it. This insight can come from the many publications and websites that have emerged in recent years with the purpose of translating relevant research for use by the general public. Part of this process may involve educating oneself about the nature and prominence of bullying by visiting relevant websites. The Project for Wellness and Work-life hosted by Arizona State University is one such source, with resources and articles such as "How to Bust the Office Bully" (Tracy, Alberts, & Rivera, 2007). Stories shared on these sites can help the victim recognize common forms of abusive behavior and possible forms of remediation. Therapists familiar with workplace stress can be important sources of insight as well. Additional research is needed to assess the relative effectiveness of these resources in enhancing the well-being of abused workers.

Victims of unjust behavior often describe enduring patterns of negative rumination, a repetitive process of mentally reviewing the hurtful circumstances and sometime rehearsing strategies for revenge (Thomsen, 2006). Rumination leaves an employee fixated on the past, leaving little time for future-oriented thinking. The result is a reduction in purposeful, future-oriented thought (one of the dimensions of well-being). One technique for managing rumination involves verbalizing the negative thoughts both orally and in writing. The written recording may be burned as a way to symbolically bring closure to the event. Engaging in mindful dialogue about promising aspects of the future may restore a sense of hope and purpose.

For many people, self-concept is influenced by work identity. Destructive behavior may threaten that identity, particularly if it persists over time, if the employee feels alienated, or if the employee chooses to disengage from the work role for a period of time (see Lutgen-Sandvik, 2008). The effects on well-being can be significant in such cases. For these employees, identity expansion may facilitate well-being. This may involve assumption of extra-organizational roles via volunteer commitments, involvement in faith communities, or development of interests and skills unrelated to work. In rethinking the notion of burnout, Tracy (2009) develops a similar idea by observing that employees sometimes calibrate their engagement in work as a means of managing stress. By selectively investing in alternative identities, members may limit their exposure to destructive workplace practices. Empirical studies are needed to further assess this possibility.

This last point speaks to the role of resilience in responses to disruptive organizational circumstances. Although resilience has long interested developmental psychologists, it has recently drawn attention from management theorists (Sutcliffe & Vogus, 2003) and organizational communication scholars (Buzzanell, Shenoy, Remke, & Lucas, 2009). Resilience can be conceptualized as an individual's or system's capacity to recover from a disruptive event and reintegrate in response to changed circumstances. But Buzzanell and colleagues argue that it is also a process, in part, a communicative one: "As organizational members deal with trauma, doubts, and challenges, they actively search for and give meanings to their worlds" (p. 299). It is in negotiating these meanings in conversations with coworkers, family, and friends that workers may come to frame difficult situations in ways that help them bounce back from adversity, retain a sense of stability in turbulent times, and live with new workplace realities, at least until things change for the better. In this way, workers facing hostile supervisors "talk into being" (p. 302) a feeling of pride (for refusing to reciprocate the destructive behavior), a belief that "this too shall pass," and a metaphorical understanding of the tormentor ("a locomotive that will eventually run off the tracks"). These understandings may foster a sense of confidence in the self, flexibility rather than rigidity, and hope for the future.

Restorative Systems and Practices. Employees at all levels are more likely to experience destructive behavior when organizational norms are silent about its unacceptability and the organization fails to promote fair and just ways of resolving differences. One apparently successful effort to institute constructive practices at the level of the workgroup was described by Keashly and Neuman (2009), who worked with the U.S. Veteran's Administration on a multisite effort to alter the workplace conditions that give rise to stress and aggression. The program was grounded in the assumption that "the prevention of workplace aggression requires a change in the nature of the conversations and interactions between people in work settings" (p. 352). With cooperation from management and union leaders, the authors used a collaborative action inquiry framework to help employees identify local practices that caused stress and consternation. A safe space was created for employees to articulate their perceptions of noxious practices (such as inequitable treatment of employees by supervisors), to examine the evidence, and to develop just solutions.

Cultivating perceptions (and experiences) of fairness was a central theme of the program. Doing so required all parties to commit to a process that was (1) consistent, (2) responsive to the interests of all parties and not just self-interest, (3) grounded in evidence, and (4) guided by moral commitments. Participants were trained in the art of advocacy: taking positions, assertiveness, and politically skillful discussion. But they were also taught the skills of inquiry: asking questions, seeking dialogue, and collecting information through interviews with differing parties. The process was guided by the assumption that these tools would increase the capacity to approach apparent workplace injustice with civility, which in turn might increase feelings of mutual respect. The desired outcome was a reduction in workplace aggression and other destructive behaviors.

Using a quasi-experimental design, Keashly and Neuman (2009) compared 11 intervention sites with carefully matched nonparticipating sites over the course of the multiyear intervention. Results were promising. Test sites showed post-test reductions in more than half of the 62 forms of perceived aggression measured in the study. These included intentional exclusion and other forms of passive aggression, verbal expressions of hostility, intentional unfairness, and physical expressions of violence. The comparison sites also showed improvements on some measures, but these primarily involved acts of aggression by external sources, such as clients or members of the public rather than coworkers. The authors attributed those results to another organization-wide customer service initiative that had been implemented during the study period.

In short, by involving workers in a structured communication process, the research team appeared to restore perceptions of fairness and rehumanized a workplace plagued by destructive behavior. Although the losses incurred by workers subjected to past abuses are not addressed by interventions of this kind, these interventions may create healthier working conditions and reduce the chances workers will be victimized again. They increase the odds that constructive communication practices will prevail when stress and conflict arise, as they inevitably will. The result may be increased well-being for the members and the organization. Intervention studies of this type are rare. The field experiment is a particularly promising way to gauge the effectiveness of interventions under realistic organizational conditions.

Forgiveness and Reconciliation. As a potentially constructive response to acts of wrongdoing and harm, forgiveness has recently drawn the attention of organizational scholars and practitioners (Aquino, Grover, Goldman, & Folger, 2003; Butler & Mullis, 2001; Cameron & Caza, 2002; Eaton & Struthers, 2006; Waldron & Kloeber, 2012). The workplace is rife with relational incidents that cause hurt, harm, moral outrage, and lingering bitterness (Metts, Cupach, & Lippert, 2006). In addition, task-related events sometimes require the forgiveness of coworkers (Eaton & Struthers, 2006). Inability to perform a task correctly, slowing team performance, and failing to meet work commitments are examples of consequences of unforgiveness. Forgiveness is an alternative to other less-positive responses to workplace transgressions, such as revenge, grudge holding, and verbal aggression. Organizational researchers, such as Aquino et al. (2003), define *forgiveness* as a psychological process involving the recognition of a serious transgression and a decision to lessen hostility toward the offending employee or organization. The definition offered by Waldron and Kelley (2008) emphasized its processual nature:

> Forgiveness is a relational process whereby harmful conduct is acknowledged by one or both partners, the harmed partner extends undeserved mercy to the perceived transgressor, one or both partners experience a transformation from negative to positive psychological states, and the meaning of the relationship is renegotiated, with the possibility of reconciliation. (p. 5)

Contrary to popular perception, forgiveness and justice are compatible. For forgiveness to proceed, according to most authorities, wrongdoing must be acknowledged and the perpetrator must be held accountable. Forgiveness is the voluntary "letting go" of a legitimate claim on continued hostility and recrimination. *Reconciliation*, the resumption of a relationship between the parties, is a possible outcome of the process but not always a desirable one, especially for low-power employees. Abusers are often able to manipulate forgiveness processes, and the victim should not be compelled to forgive or reconcile. Indeed, forgiveness processes should be voluntary; "compelled" forgiveness can be a kind of revictimization. Because forgiveness is called for only after serious incidents of destructive behavior—those that require more than forbearance or simple understanding—the process typically takes considerable time (Waldron & Kelley, 2008).

Waldron and Kelley (2008) observed that many forgiveness episodes include moral undercurrents, with the parties voicing values that were presumed to be shared, expressing disappointments, and seeking assurances about improved future conduct. Table 26.1 from Waldron and Kloeber (2012) presents some of the moral functions served by forgiveness dialogues at work. Skillfully facilitated forgiveness processes in organizations may serve the purpose of (re)negotiating formal and informal standards of conduct (see Butler & Mullis, 2001) and restoring a sense of organizational justice. They allow emotional tensions to surface and apologies to be made and accepted. Working relationships may not be restored to previous levels of closeness or collegiality, but they are often improved (Rusbult, Hannon, Stocker, & Finkel, 2005). Recent reviews of the research suggest that forgiveness is associated with feelings of improved well-being (Waldron & Kelley, 2008). If the process is handled well, victims may feel a renewed sense of self-esteem, and more aggressive forms of conflict resolution will be eschewed. Few organizations have implemented forgiveness-based responses to destructive behavior, but guidelines for doing so have begun to be developed (Waldron & Kloeber, 2012). Studies of forgiveness-based interventions are needed.

Table 26.1 Moral Function of Forgiveness Discourse (adapted from Waldron & Kloeber, 2012)

Moral Function	**Characteristics/Example(s)**
Defining moral standards	Requesting equitable treatment; identifying disrespectful behavior
Establishing accountability	Accepting responsibility for incivility; monitoring compliance with moral codes
Engaging moral tensions	Balancing mercy versus justice; balancing personal and organizational values
Restoring relational justice	Offering a public apology to team members; seeking restitution
Reimagining a moral future	Offering a path to redemption; promising more civil behavior in the future
Honoring the self	Claiming respect from coworkers; recognizing the dignity of individual employees
Redirecting hostility	Safely venting moral indignation; foregoing aggression
Increasing safety and concern	Creating formal processes of forgiveness; protecting victims from retribution
Finding closure	Halting negative rumination; restoring a focus on tasks rather than relationships; letting go of grudges
Possible reconciliation	Instituting new relational boundaries; conforming to revised communication rules

Source: Adapted from Waldron & Kloeber (2012).

Conclusion

We end this review impressed by the quality of research that has been conducted recently on destructive organizational communication practices. Indeed, communication scholars have made laudable contributions, and that is particularly evident in the area of bullying. The prevalence, nature, and consequences of bullying have been well studied. A notable feature of this literature is its focus on communicative acts—as sources of abuse, sensemaking tools, and coping mechanisms. The literature has evolved to the point that researchers have felt confident enough to offer prescriptions and create resources. Even so, scholars make clear that destructive practices persist due in part to systemic and cultural factors. Mounting individual resistance to bullying is daunting, and it may often be futile. Organization-level intervention is needed.

We have invited organizational scholars to consider two emerging areas of thinking, one having to do with organizational morality and the other with restorative practices. In concluding, we offer several other directions of new research. First, relatively little work has been conducted thus far on cultural differences in destructive organizational practices. An exception would be recent work in China, documenting prevailing forms of destructive leadership (Lu et al., 2012). On a related note, we chose not to address the literature on the role of class, gender, ethnicity, or sexual orientation in conflict. These are widespread and serious problems that deserve the attention of researchers and organizational leaders. We simply couldn't do the topics justice, given the space limitations. A second area deserves further inquiry. Although the literature makes clear that group- and organizational-level intervention is required if destructive patterns of behavior are to be curtailed, few intervention studies have been reported. We applaud the field experiment reported by Keashly and Neuman (2009) and encourage more studies of communication-based interventions. Finally, in surveying this literature, we noted that similar phenomena have been studied under different labels. For example, the abusive supervision practices studied by management researchers (e.g., Tepper, 2000) are defined in a manner similar to the supervisory bullying studied by prominent organizational communication scholars (Lutgen-Sandvik & McDermott, 2011). Given this trend, we would simply encourage scholars to seek synergies across disciplines as research progresses.

Most of us spend considerable amounts of time in and around organizations. As a consequence, we benefit and we suffer. The push and pull of organizational life will remain, but ideally, over time, it will become less oppressive and more uplifting as a growing group of scholars collaborates to address the problems of incivility and destructive behavior in the workplace (Lutgen-Sandvik & Sypher, 2009). This work confronts individual and organizational practices that undermine the psychological safety and basic humanity of the workplace. Few areas of research ring with more importance. As destructive communication and incivility are brought to life communicatively, so too are the restorative practices that can address them. Thus our work in this area, while unfinished, will continue to be consequential.

References

Aquino, K., Grover, S., Goldman, B., & Folger, R. (2003). When push doesn't come to shove: Interpersonal forgiveness in workplace relationships. *Journal of Management Inquiry, 12*(3), 209–216.

Ashforth, B. (1994). Petty tyranny in organizations. *Human Relations, 47*(7), 755–778.

Baillien, E., Neyens, I., De Witte, H., & De Cuyper, N. (2009). A qualitative study on the development of workplace bullying: Towards a three way model. *Journal of Community & Applied Social Psychology, 19*(1), 1–16.

Bies, R. J., & Trip, T. M. (1998). Two faces of the powerless: Coping with tyranny in organizations. In R. M. Kramer & M. A. Neale (Eds.), *Power and influence in organizations* (pp. 203–219). Thousand Oaks, CA, SAGE.

Boddy, C. R. (2011). Corporate psychopaths, bullying and unfair supervision in the workplace. *Journal of Business Ethics, 100*(3), 367–379.

Branch, S., Ramsay, S., & Barker, M. (2007). Managers in the firing line: Contributing factors to workplace bullying by staff—An interview study. *Journal of Management & Organization, 13*(3), 264–281.

Brotheridge, C. M., & Lee, R. T. (2010). Restless and confused: Emotional responses to workplace bullying in men and women. *Career Development International, 15*(7), 687–707.

Bryant, M., Buttigieg, D., & Hanley, G. (2009). Poor bullying prevention and employee health: Some implications. *International Journal of Workplace Health Management, 2*(1), 48–62.

Butler, D. S., & Mullis, F. (2001). Forgiveness: A conflict resolution strategy in the workplace. *The Journal of Individual Psychology, 57*(3), 259–272.

Buzzanell, P. M., Shenoy, S., Remke, R. V., & Lucas, K. (2009). Responses to destructive organizational contexts: Intersubjectively creating resilience to foster human dignity and hope. In P. Lutgen-Sandvik & B. D. Sypher (Eds.), *The destructive side of organizational communication* (pp. 339–362). New York, NY: Routledge.

Cameron, K. S., & Caza, A. (2002). Organizational and leadership virtues and the role of forgiveness. *Journal of Leadership and Organizational Studies, 9*(1), 33–48.

Corney, B. (2008). Aggression in the workplace: A study of horizontal violence utilizing Heideggerian hermeneutic phenomenology. *Journal of Health Organization and Management, 22*(2), 164–177.

Cowan, R. L. (2011). "Yes, we have an anti-bullying policy, but . . . ": HR professionals' understandings and experiences with workplace bullying policy. *Communication Studies, 62*(3), 307–327.

D'Cruz, P., & Noronha, E. (2010). The exit coping response to workplace bullying: The contribution of inclusivist and exclusivist HRM strategies. *Employee Relations, 32*(2), 102–120.

Djurkovic, N., McCormack, D., & Casimir, G. (2005). The behavioral reactions of victims to different types of workplace bullying. *International Journal of Organization Theory and Behavior, 8*(4), 439–460.

Djurkovic, N., McCormack, D., & Casimir, G. (2006). Neuroticism and the psychosomatic model of workplace bullying. *Journal of Managerial Psychology, 21*(1), 73–88.

Dougherty, D. S. (2009). Sexual harassment as destructive organizational process. In P. Lutgen-Sandvik & B. D. Sypher (Eds.), *The destructive side of organizational communication* (pp. 203–226). New York, NY: Routledge.

Duffy, M., & Sperry, L. (2007). Workplace mobbing: Individual and family health consequences. *The Family Journal: Counseling and Therapy for Couples and Families, 15*(4), 398–404.

Eaton, J., & Struthers, C. W. (2006). The reduction of psychological aggression across varied interpersonal contexts through repentance and forgiveness. *Aggressive Behavior, 32*(3), 195–206.

Gill, M. J., & Sypher, B. D. (2009). Workplace incivility and organizational trust. In P. Lutgen-Sandvik & B. D. Sypher (Eds.), *The destructive side of organizational communication* (pp. 53–73). New York, NY: Routledge.

Goffman, E. (1955). On face-work: Analysis of ritual elements of social interaction. *Psychiatry, 18*(3), 213–231.

Harvey, M. G., Heames, J. T., Richey, R. G., & Leonard, N. (2006). Bullying: From the playground to the boardroom. *Journal of Leadership and Organizational Studies, 12*(4), 1–11.

Harvey, M. G., Treadway, D., Heames, T. J., & Duke, A. (2008). Bullying in the 21st century global organization: An ethical perspective. *Journal of Business Ethics, 85*(1), 27–40.

Heames, J., & Harvey, M. (2006). Workplace bullying: A cross-level assessment. *Management Decision, 44*(9), 1214–1230.

Howard, J. L., & Wech, B. A. (2012). A model of organizational and job environment influences on workplace violence. *Employee Rights and Responsibilities Journal, 24*(2), 111–127.

Hu, E., Huang, X., Lam, C. K., & Miao, Q. (2012). Abusive supervision and work behaviors: The mediating role of LMX. *Journal of Organizational Behavior, 33*(4), 531–543.

Hubert, A. B., & Veldhoven, M. V. (2001). Risk sectors for undesirable behaviours and mobbing. *European Journal of Work and Organizational Psychology, 10*(4), 415–425.

Invernizzi, G. (2000). New concepts on the workplace relationships: The so called "mobbing." *New Trends in Experimental & Clinical Psychiatry, 16*(1–4), 5–6.

Kassing, J. W. (1997). Articulating, antagonizing, and displacing: A model of employee dissent. *Communication Studies, 48*(4), 311–312.

Kassing, J. W. (2009). Breaking the chain of command: Making sense of employee circumvention. *Journal of Business Communication, 46*(3), 311–334.

Keashly, L., & Neuman, J. H. (2009). Building a constructive communication climate: The workplace stress and aggression project. In P. Lutgen-Sandvik & B. D. Sypher (Eds.), *The destructive side of organizational communication* (pp. 339–362). New York, NY: Routledge.

Keltner, D. (2009). *Born to be good.* New York, NY: W.W. Norton & Company.

Keys, C. L. M. (2002). The mental health continuum: From languishing to flourishing in life. *Journal of Health and Social Behavior, 43*(2), 207–222.

Lewis, S. E. (2006). Recognition of workplace bullying: A qualitative study of women targets in the public section. *Journal of Community & Applied Social Psychology, 16*(2), 119–135.

Lewis, S. E., & Orford, J. (2005). Women's experiences of workplace bullying: Changes in social relationships. *Journal of Community and Applied Social Psychology, 15*(1), 29–47.

Liefooghe, A., & MacKenzie Davey, M. (2010). The language and organization of bullying at work. *Administrative Theory & Praxis, 32*(1), 71–95.

Lu, H., Ling, W., Wu, V., & Liu, Y. (2012). A Chinese perspective on the content and structure of destructive leadership. *Chinese Management Studies, 6*(2), 271–283.

Lutgen-Sandvik, P. (2006). Take this job and . . . : Quitting and other forms of resistance to workplace bullying. *Communication Monographs, 73*(4), 406–433.

Lutgen-Sandvik, P. (2008). Intensive remedial identity work: Responses to workplace bullying trauma and stigmatization. *Organization, 15*(1), 97–119.

Lutgen-Sandvik, P., & Sypher, B. D. (Eds.). (2009). *Destructive organizational communication: Processes, consequences, and constructive ways of organizing.* London, England: Routledge.

Lutgen-Sandvik, P., & McDermott, V. (2011). Making sense of supervisory bullying: Perceived powerlessness, empowered possibilities. *Southern Communication Journal, 76*(4), 342–368.

Lutgen-Sandvik, P., Namie, G., & Namie, R. (2009). Workplace bullying: Causes, consequences, and corrections. In P. Lutgen-Sandvik & B. D. Sypher (Eds.), *Destructive organizational communication: Processes, consequences, and constructive ways of organizing* (pp. 27–52). London, England: Routledge.

Lutgen-Sandvik, P., & Tracy, S. J. (2012). Answering five key questions about workplace bullying: How communication scholarship provides thought leadership for transforming abuse at work. *Management Communication Quarterly, 26*(1), 3–47.

Lutgen-Sandvik, P., Tracy, S. J., & Alberts, J. K. (2007). Burned by bullying in the American workplace: Prevalence, perception, degree and impact. *Journal of Management Studies, 44*(6), 837–862.

Mathisen, G. E., Einarsen, S., & Mykletun, R. (2010). The relationship between supervisor personality, supervisors' perceived stress, and workplace bullying. *Journal of Business Ethics, 99*(4), 637–651.

Meglich-Sespico, P., Faley, R. H., & Knapp, D. E. (2007). Relief and redress for targets of workplace bullying. *Employee Responsibilities & Rights Journal, 19*(1), 31–43.

Metts, S., Cupach, W. R., & Lippert, L. (2006). Forgiveness in the workplace. In J. M. H. Fritz & B. L. Omdahl (Eds.), *Problematic relationships in the workplace* (pp. 249–278). New York, NY: Peter Lang.

Mikkelsen, E. G., Hogh, A., & Puggaard, L. B. (2011). Prevention of bullying and conflicts at work: Process factors influencing the implementation and effects of interventions. *International Journal of Workplace Health Management, 4*(1), 84–100.

Moayed, F. A., Daraiseh, N., Shell, R., & Salem, S. (2006). Workplace bullying: A systematic review of risk factors and outcomes. *Theoretical Issues in Ergonomics Science, 7*(3), 311–327.

Namie, G., & Lutgen-Sandvik, P. E. (2010). Active and passive accomplices: The communal character of workplace bullying. *International Journal of Communication, 4,* 343–373.

Page, K. M., & Vella-Brodrick, D. A. (2009). The "what," "why" and "how" of employee well-being: A new model. *Social Indicators Research, 90*(3), 441–458.

Pate, J., & Beaumont, P. (2010). Bullying and harassment: A case of success? *Employee Relations, 32*(2), 171–183.

Porath, C. L., & Erez, A. (2007). Does rudeness really matter? The effects of rudeness on task performance and helpfulness. *Academy of Management Journal, 50*(5), 1181–1197.

Rayner, C., & Hoel, H. (1997). A summary review of literature relating to workplace bullying. *Journal of Community and Applied Social Psychology, 7*(3), 181–191.

Rusbult, C. E., Hannon, P. A., Stocker, S. L., & Finkel, E. J. (2005). Forgiveness and relational repair. In E. L. Worthington Jr. (Ed.), *Handbook of forgiveness* (pp. 185–205). New York, NY: Routledge.

Ryff, C. D. (1989). Happiness is everything, or is it? Explorations on the meaning of psychological well-being. *Journal of Personality and Social Psychology, 57*(6), 1069–1081.

Salin, D. (2003). Ways of explaining workplace bullying: A review of enabling, motivating and precipitating structures and processes in the work environment. *Human Relations, 56*(10), 1213–1232.

Scott, C. R. (2007). Communication and social identity theory: Existing and potential connections in organizational identification research. *Communication Studies, 58*(2), 123–138.

Sutcliffe, K. M., & Vogus, T. J. (2003). Organizing for resilience. In K. S. Cameron, J. S. Dutton, & R. E. Quinn (Eds.), *Positive organizational scholarship* (pp. 94–110). San Francisco, CA: Berret-Kohler.

Sypher, B. D. (2004). Reclaiming civil discourse in the workplace. *Southern Communication Journal, 69*(3), 257–269.

Tepper, B. J. (2000). Consequences of abusive supervision. *Academy of Management Journal, 43*(2), 178–190.

Tepper, B. J., Carr, J. C., Breaux, D. M., Geider, S., Hu, C., & Hua, W. (2009). Abusive supervision, intentions to quit, and employees' workplace deviance: A power-dependence analysis. *Organizational Behavior and Human Decision Processes, 109*(2), 156–167.

Thomsen, D. K. (2006). The association between rumination and negative affect: A review. *Cognition and Emotion, 20*(8), 1216–1235.

Tierney, P., & Tepper, B. J. (2007). Destructive leadership [Special issue]. *The Leadership Quarterly, 18*(3), 171–173.

Tracy, S. (2009). Managing burnout and moving toward employee engagement: A critical literature review and communicative approach toward reinvigorating the study of stress at work. In P. Lutgen-Sandvik & B. D. Sypher (Eds.), The *destructive side of organizational communication: Processes, consequences and constructive ways of organizing* (pp. 77–98). London, England: Routledge.

Tracy, S., Alberts, J., & Rivera, K. D. (2007). How to bust the office bully. *Arizona State University*. Retrieved from http://humancommunication.clas.asu.edu/files/HowtoBusttheOfficeBully.pdf

Tracy, S. J., Lutgen-Sandvik, P., & Alberts, J. (2006). Nightmares, demons, slaves: Exploring the painful metaphors of workplace bullying. *Management Communication Quarterly, 20*(2), 148–185.

Vickers, M. H. (2006a). Bullying, disability and work: A case study of workplace bullying. *Qualitative Research in Organizations and Management: An International Journal, 4*(3), 255–272.

Vickers, M. H. (2006b). Towards employee wellness: Rethinking bullying paradoxes and masks. *Employee Responsibilities & Rights Journal, 18*(4), 267–281.

Waldron, V. R. (1994). Once more, with feeling: Reconsidering the role of emotion in work. In S. A Deetz (Ed.), *Communication yearbook* (vol. 17, pp. 388–416). Thousand Oaks, CA: SAGE.

Waldron, V. R. (2009). Emotional tyranny and managerial power. In P. Lutgen-Sandvik & B. D. Sypher (Eds.). *The destructive side of organizational communication* (pp. 7–26). New York, NY: Routledge.

Waldron, V. R. (2012). *Emotional communication at work*. San Francisco, CA: Polity Press.

Waldron, V. R., & Kassing. J. W. (2011). *Managing risk in communication encounters: Strategies for the workplace*. Thousand Oaks, CA: SAGE.

Waldron, V. R., & Kelley, D. L. (2008). *Communicating forgiveness*. Thousand Oaks, CA: SAGE.

Waldron, V. R., & Kloeber, D. (2012). Communicating forgiveness in work relationships. In J. M. H. Fritz & B. L. Omdahl (Eds.), *Problematic relationships in the workplace* (2nd ed., pp. 267–289). New York, NY: Peter Lang.

Weiner, B. (2006). *Social motivation, justice, and the moral emotions: An attributional approach*. Mahwah, NJ: Lawrence Erlbaum.

Zapf, D., Knorz, C., & Kulla, M. (1996). On the relationship between mobbing factors, and job content, social work environment, and health outcomes. *European Journal of Work and Organizational Psychology, 5*(2), 215–237.

CHAPTER 27

Engaged Scholarship and Democracy

Sarah E. Dempsey and J. Kevin Barge

Increasing interest in engaged scholarship reflects a growing concern that academic scholarship address pressing social, political, economic, and ecological problems. Some scholars work from an engaged position to rethink the possibilities of community-based economies (Gibson-Graham, 2006), while others enact models of community dialogue and deliberation aimed at improving governance (Pearce, 2002; Pearce & Pearce, 2001; Pearce, Spano, & Pearce, 2009). The growth of engaged scholarship also reflects the increasing pressure for public universities to demonstrate greater accountability to their diverse constituents. Our chapter sheds light on how the contested meanings and practices of engaged scholarship have emerged over the course of this area's development within organizational communication.

Questions about relevance are far from new within organizational communication and its allied fields. Since its emergence in the late 1930s and 1940s, organizational communication has reflected a robust sense of engagement, including a pragmatic interest in how research can be usefully brought to bear on everyday problems and practices of organizing (Tompkins & Wanca-Thibault, 2001). The 1940s ushered in a triple alliance among academe, the military, and industry, all aimed at providing communication training to workers. The War Manpower Commission's Training Within Industry program focused on improving workers' oral and written skills. These measures aimed at boosting productivity, performance, and efficiency (Redding, 1985). The interest in the applicability of research to the practical problems of organizing extended beyond training and educational contexts to theory building and research. For example, diffusion of organizational innovation theory and research in the late 1950s began with a focus on equipping farmers with new agricultural methods (Rogers, 2003). This practical focus is not surprising, given that many organizational scholars were associated with land grant institutions whose missions centered on utilizing academic knowledge to increase economic productivity, particularly within agriculture and mining industries.

Research from the 1960s through the 1980s solidified a commitment to producing actionable forms of knowledge. For example, the "Redding tradition" of organizational research at Purdue University was grounded in the notion that workplace practices might be modified and improved through the conduct of rigorous social scientific research that explored message-exchange processes (Buzzanell & Stohl, 1999; Stohl & Redding, 1987). A number of researchers have further developed the Redding tradition, including Tompkins' work (1993; Tompkins & Tompkins, 2004) on the space program and Ziegler's (2007) research addressing occupational cultures of firefighters. Similarly, researchers at Michigan State University pioneered network approaches to organizational communication with applicability for managing message flows and diffusing innovations (Susskind, Schwartz, Richards, & Johnson, 2005). The organizational communication division of the International Communication Association (ICA) also contributed to the practicality of organizational communication research as evidenced by its development of the ICA Audit in the 1970s (DeWine & James, 1988; Goldhaber & Krivonos, 1997; Scott, Shaw, Timmerman, Frank, & Quinn, 1999).

The critical turn of the 1970s and 1980s brought a massive shift in thinking about the politics of engagement, including a focus on how teaching and research could be utilized in the service of social change. Freire's (1970, 1973) theory of dialogic pedagogy that contained a critique of a *banking*, or *transmission*, model of education became particularly influential. Feminist, Marxist, and post-structuralist theories offered compelling accounts of power, coupled with a commitment to fostering emancipation and greater equality (Buzzanell, 1994; Deetz & Mumby, 1985; Mumby, 1987, 1988, 2001; Tompkins & Cheney, 1985). The subsequent politicization of teaching and research practice meant that knowledge production increasingly became seen as having social and political effects.

The adoption of critical perspectives challenged normative models of academic practice as disinterested and neutral, opening up new modes of engagement centered on social justice. Participatory action methods became increasingly popular, particularly for researchers working within the field of development communication (McAnany, 2012; Servaes, Jacobsen, & White, 1996). Engaging in critical praxis with local communities gained legitimacy as a form of political action. Organizational communication is currently experiencing a resurgence of critical applied work through a reengagement with Marxist and feminist forms of praxis stemming from Paulo Freire, bell hooks, and others. Growing interest in postcolonial theories and practices has simultaneously brought new insights (Broadfoot & Munshi, 2007; Grimes & Parker, 2009; Hall, 2011; Norander & Harter, 2012; Prasad, 2003). The (re)turn to praxis brings an explicitly political focus and intent to engaged scholarship in organizational communication.

After reviewing the rich traditions of practically focused scholarship within the field, we explore the implications of viewing engaged scholarship as a democratic conversation. Our approach is informed by Deetz's (2010) framework of politically attentive relational constructionism (PARC), which sees "knowledge, facts, and social order as outcomes of communicative processes rather than existing independently to be represented" (p. 40). Such a framework departs from a model of communication as expression by autonomous individuals of already formed positions and identities. Instead, we place meaning construction and contestation at the center of engaged scholarship. Generative, democratic forms of engagement are characterized by collaborative forms of talk aimed at both preserving and inviting meaningful differences into conversation (Deetz, in press). We see this framework of democratic conversation as a particularly promising future direction for engaged scholarship in organizational communication.

While the practical contributions of engaged scholarship to groups seen as external to the university has received much attention, the relationships between engaged scholarship and democratic practice and ethically and socially responsible research remain ripe for further extension. We develop Boyer's (1997) vision of the scholarship of engagement, building on insights from research addressing issues of participatory dialogue, democracy, and governance (Beech, MacIntosh, & MacLean, 2010; Deetz, 1995, 2008; Heath, 2007; Heath & Frey, 2004; Pearce & Pearce, 2001; Stohl & Cheney, 2001; Weaver, 2007) to argue that the full promise of engaged scholarship lies in its ability to enact new forms of governance grounded in a democratic model of communication, including the development of responsive and sustainable models of democratic conversation among diverse stakeholders. Viewing engaged scholarship as participatory democratic practice in this double sense opens creative avenues for scholarship and pedagogy, including productive new connections to management and organization studies, as well as politically responsive participatory action traditions.

Articulating Engaged Scholarship

Engaged scholarship has grown dramatically since the publication of Boyer's (1997) landmark *Scholarship Reconsidered: Priorities of the Professorate*. More recently, the Aspen Conference on Engaging Communication has created a vital space for discussion, reflection, and action around the possibilities of engagement, including the publication of an edited book on the theory, research, and pedagogy of engaged scholarship (Simpson & Shockley-Zalabak, 2005) as well as a forum section in the 2008 *Journal of Applied Communication Research* (*JACR*). In organizational communication as well as organization and management studies, scholars have focused on addressing three important questions: (1) What counts as engaged scholarship? (2) What are the historical antecedents of engaged scholarship? and (3) What are the tensions or challenges associated with conducting engaged scholarship?

Defining Engaged Scholarship

Defining what counts as engaged scholarship has always been a vexing concern, whether linked to questions of the good life or tethered to questions of the academy's relevance. The engaged scholarship movement is best described as a diffuse field of logics, practices, and projects brought together by a concern with fostering participative modes of scholarly inquiry that meaningfully address practical concerns. Across modes and projects, engaged scholarship can be distinguished by its fidelity to three interlinked qualities (Boyer, 1997; Doberneck, Glass, & Schweitzer, 2010; Simpson & Seibold, 2008; Van de Ven, 2007; Van de Ven & Johnson, 2006).

First, engaged scholarship is committed to utilizing the resources of academic inquiry for practical concerns and useful ends. As Boyer (1996) argues, the scholarship of engagement is a mode of inquiry "connecting the rich resources of the university to our most pressing social, civil, civic and ethical problems" (p. 21). Here, meaningful scholarship is motivated by, and provides a response to, important social problems. For Boyer, engaged scholarship demands a reenvisioning of the university enterprise to include a "larger purpose, mission, and clarity in the life of the nation" (p. 21). His insights productively challenge researchers to transform traditional forms of academic scholarship at the level of its conception, design, enactment, and circulation.

A second quality of engaged scholarship is that it functions as a mode of scholarly inquiry. Engaged scholarship adheres to the standards of academic knowledge production by posing new questions, employing systematic and rigorous methods for investigating those questions, and creating new insights into those concerns and questions. What makes engaged scholarship more than the sum of research or practice alone are those "recursive and reflexive practices that build a bridge between the pursuits of the academy and those of practitioner communities" (Simpson & Seibold, 2008, p. 270). The outcomes of engaged scholarship as a mode of inquiry allow richness in theory building that would not be possible without this integration. At the same time, the goals for this research remain tethered to a concern about how the knowledge that is produced informs and directly impacts practical problems and concerns.

Third, engaged scholarship brings sustained focus to the relational, communicational dynamics that define the research process, seeking to democratize knowledge production (Van de Ven, 2007). Informed by participatory action research traditions (Reason & Bradbury, 2008), engaged scholarship enacts a collaborative form of inquiry. Engaged scholarship shares many characteristics with action research, including the goal of engaging "with people in collaborative relationships, opening up new 'communicative spaces' in which dialogue and development can flourish calls for engagement" as well as the incorporation of diverse ways of knowing (Reason & Bradbury, 2008, p. 3). Engaged scholarship emphasizes the coproduction and co-ownership of the research process. Ideally, "academics and practitioners leverage their different perspectives and competence in co-producing knowledge about complex problems" (Van de Ven & Johnson, 2006, p. 803). The call for coproduction and co-ownership challenges visions of academics as the sole knowledge producers and drivers of academic inquiry. A continuum of participative practices exist across stages of the research, including the initial posing of research questions and themes, the design and enactment of the research process itself, data analysis and interpretation, and the publication and application of results.

Traditions of Engagement

The historical antecedents of engaged scholarship draw on different motivations, aims, and research procedures. However, they each are motivated in large part by practical concerns, adhere to the conventions of scholarly research, and tend to involve some level of participatory processes involving researchers and practitioners, community-based groups, and policymakers. Each places different emphases on these distinctive qualities as well as their reliance on coproduction. Deetz (personal communication, 2012) locates diverse practices of engagement along a continuum spanning from disengaged to relevant, applied, cooperative, and collaborative (see Table 27.1). Each stance brings different implications for the selection of research topics, the role of the researcher and external community member roles, and the intended audience. Putnam's (2009) review of existing work in organizational communication identified four "faces" of engagement: (1) applied communication research, (2) collaborative learning, (3) activism and social justice, and (4) practical theory. We highlight connections to these distinctive qualities of engaged scholarship as motivated by practical concerns, rigorous inquiry using theory and research, and the coproduction of knowledge.

Applied Communication Research. Applied communication research is characterized by the systematic investigation into practical concerns, with an emphasis on the immediate implications of the research for practice (Frey & Cissna, 2009). Its institutionalization as a distinct tradition is reflected in the 1981 founding of the *JACR*. In addition to providing an outlet for the publication of applied research, the journal's forum sections have fostered reflexive debate about public intellectuals (2007), engaged scholarship (2008), and the extent to which communication research has had an impact in addressing practical concerns (2009).

Seibold, Lemus, Ballard, & Myers (2009) identify four substantive applied research threads regarding organizational communication research: (1) organizational socialization/assimilation, (2) organizational culture, (3) diffusion of organizational innovations, and (4) communication and planned organizational change. Organizational socialization has focused on practical issues related to the way communication may be used to negotiate one's sense of identity and relationship with the organization during the pre-entry, entry, and

Table 27.1 Stanley Deetz's Continuum of Engagement in the Areas of Research, Teaching, and Service

Disengaged	Relevant	Applied	Cooperative	Collaborative
Topic-driven, abstracted, empiricist studies *of* the world, with questions and conceptions coming mostly from the researcher's disciplinary community.	Issue-driven, inductive studies *of* the world, mostly focusing on representing concepts and practices as present in external (non-researcher) communities.	External, community-developed, problem-directed studies *in* the world, taken on in applied and administrative studies aimed at collecting data (mostly planning and assessment) and reaching conclusions for the external community.	External, community-developed, problem-directed studies *in* the world, taken on by action research projects, where researchers reframe and reconfigure external community understandings and actively aim at reforms based on values such as social justice.	Cooperatively developed, problem-directed studies *in* the world, taken on generally by participatory action research projects and cogenerative theorizing.
Value neutrality is embraced and proclaimed. Intrinsic values of the researcher's discipline, methods, and conceptions are trivialized, denied, and rarely explored.	Personal values and perspectives regarding topics are permitted (mostly to account for their effects) but intrinsic values of researcher methods and conceptions are not explored.	Values are presumed by the external community and may enter into selection of projects and problems by the researcher.	Personal values are explicit in project selection and research process, but intrinsic values may not be seen on the surface.	Active transformation of conceptions, language, and research methods around new and emerging goals arises from the active inclusion of multiple stakeholders and surfacing of intrinsic values.
Minimal engagement with nonacademic communities.	Sustained individual interest-based engagement.	Often *ad hoc* but sustained by individual relationships.	Often long term and sustained by team relationships.	Long term and often institutionalized through centers and institutes.

(Continued)

Table 27.1 (Continued)

Disengaged	Relevant	Applied	Cooperative	Collaborative
Faculty driven, input-centered instruction, guided by disciplinary topics and subject divisions.	Driven by relevancy to students, input-centered instruction, organized around disciplinary topics and subject divisions using extended examples and case studies.	External, community-driven, outcome-based instruction, often focused on professional training, application to real-world problems, and internships.	Multiple communities interactively arrived at problem-centered, outcome-based instruction, including in-class projects and simulations extending to external service-learning activities.	Project based on on-site educational activities with active, faculty involvement and genuine reciprocity with external communities.
Value neutrality is embraced and proclaimed.	Personal values and perspectives regarding topics permitted.	External community values may be uncritically accepted and academic and wider community values ridiculed.	Student values and interests are of focus and mostly uncritically accepted.	Active value discussion and emergent goals based in interaction among multiple stakeholders.
Minimal engagement with nonacademic communities.	Sustained individual, interest-based engagement.	Often *ad hoc* but sustained by individual relationships.	Often long term and sustained by team relationships.	Long term and often institutionalized through centers and institutes.
Private service, based on personal interests and values often linked to university and disciplinary service needs.	Private service, knowledge distribution, and presentation related to professional expertise.	Expertise-based consulting linked to external community needs, with web-based courses and knowledge systems designed for external audiences. Insider/outsider identities maintained.	University/external communities' cooperative projects producing shared products initiated for mutual gain around existing missions and group identities.	Active combination of research and instructional activities, producing shared communities with emergent identities, goals, and products.
Most service to external groups is unrelated to professional expertise.	Sustained individual interest-based engagement.	Often *ad hoc* but sustained by individual relationships.	Often long term and sustained by team relationships.	Long term and often institutionalized through centers and institutes.

Source: Stanley Deetz, personal communication (2012).

settling-in phases (Jablin, 1987, 2001), including the way organizations formally orient newcomers and how newcomers manage uncertainty through communicative activities such as information seeking (see Kramer & Miller, Chapter 21). Organizational culture research has focused on articulating the various ways that culture can be studied (Eisenberg & Reilly, 2001) as well as the way that particular kinds of cultures, such as those emphasizing high reliability in organizing, can be constituted through communication (Weick & Sutcliffe, 2001; see Keyton, Chapter 22). Diffusion of innovation research has informed an understanding of networked organizational forms (Rogers, 2003). In addition, organizational change and innovation studies have explored change as a multistakeholder process (Lewis, 2011).

Seibold (2008; Seibold et al., 2009) argues that applied communication adopts divergent models for managing the relationship between theory and practice: treating theory and practice as separate spheres, as the intersection of research with practice, or the integration of research and practice. Much of the research within the applied tradition keeps a separation between theory and practice and, as a result, has been less concerned with the transformation of the relationship between researchers and what are seen as the traditional subjects of research. The applied tradition often adopts a model of translational scholarship that deemphasizes the coproduction of knowledge between academics and stakeholders and foregrounds the dissemination of knowledge from academics to stakeholders.

Collaborative Learning Research. Collaborative management research (CMR) focuses on how academics and practitioners can leverage their respective expertise to generate actionable knowledge. Borjesson (2011) highlights key characteristics of CMR: (1) mutual exploration to create joint knowledge versus finding a solution to a problem, (2) close long-term relationships between academics and practitioners, (3) research problems are emergent and use abductive forms of theorizing, and (4) the creation of actionable scientific knowledge that can easily be translated into action. CMR is interested in fostering conversations among scholars and practitioners that generate learning to build theory and intervene into systems in localized contexts.

CMR draws on a number of theoretical tributaries and research methodologies such as action research (Reason & Bradbury, 2008), learning theory (Docherty & Shani, 2008), dialogue (Holmstrand, Harnsten, & Lowstedt, 2008), clinical inquiry research (Schein, 1999, 2008), action science (Argyris, Putnam, & Smith, 1985), reflective design theory (Boud, Cressey, & Docherty, 2006; Docherty, Kira, & Shani, 2008; Stebbins & Shani, 2009), and appreciative inquiry (Cooperrider & Whitney, 1999). Scholars working from a CMR perspective have tackled a number of important issues such as how organizations can foster innovation (Borjesson, 2011) and creativity (Cirella, Guerci, & Shani, 2012) as well as how organizations can be redesigned to become more effective (Beer, 2011).

Collaborative learning develops processes and practices that enable academics and practitioners to coproduce useful and actionable knowledge through rigorous research methods. CMR involves three processes: (1) *codetermination* or mutual problem setting that creates a joint focus for the research, (2) *co-evolution* or the emergent nature of the research through conversations between academics and practitioners, and (3) *co-interpretation* or the joint analysis of findings by academics and practitioners (Cirella, Guerci, & Shani, 2012). CMR research brings academics and practitioners together to conduct joint research projects (e.g., Boyatzis, Howard, Rapisarda, & Taylor, 2008); participate in learning forums such as seminars, roundtables, and self-studies (e.g., Bartunek, 2008; Mirvis, 2008); and investigate the kind of research leadership required to manage boundary spanning initiatives and research (Adler, Elmquist, & Norrgren, 2009).

Activism and Social Justice Research. A third stream of engaged scholarship is informed by traditions of activism and social justice research emerging from workers' movements, civil rights and antiracist movements, feminist and women's rights movements, and decolonization movements. The varied conceptual influences include the critical theories of Karl Marx, Max Weber, Emile Durkheim, Antonio Gramsci, Anthony Giddens, and Jürgen Habermas; post-structuralist and postmodernist thinking by Michel Foucault, Jean-François Lyotard, Hélène Cixous, and Gayatri Spivak; and feminist theory by Simone de Beauvoir, Adrienne Rich, and bell hooks. Together, these influences have laid the groundwork for understanding organizations and organizing processes as "social historical creations accomplished in conditions of struggle and domination" (Alvesson & Deetz, 2000, p. 83). From such a position, engagement adopts an explicitly political agenda focused on benefiting historically marginalized groups. A particularly rich example includes Ritchie's (2007) study, which sought to shift power relations between employees and management. Informed by Habermasian conceptions of communicative action and critical dialogic theories, Ritchie's (2007) study took the form of an organizational change process focused on developing meaningful employee voice within organizational decision making. The study illustrates central characteristics found within a social justice tradition: the focus on relations of power and domination coupled with a process of direct intervention into those unequal power relations.

Social justice traditions pursue direct forms of action aimed at promoting social change (Frey & Carragee, 2007). An activist orientation stems in part from Freire's (1970, 1973) critical pedagogy, which critiques the student-teacher hierarchy guiding classic models of education. Freire's critical pedagogy transforms hierarchies, recovers the power relations tied to education and knowledge creation, and focuses on the self-empowerment of the oppressed. Social justice and activist traditions of engagement attempt to enact each of these exemplary practices.

This tradition often involves getting research subjects directly involved in the research, including training them in research methods (e.g., Gaventa, 1982). Reflexivity about the engagement process and the nature of the researcher-(co)participant relationship and its impacts is a hallmark of activist and social justice projects. This reflexivity speaks to the continued influence of Freire's critical pedagogy as well as participatory action research traditions (Reason & Bradbury, 2008). Engaged scholarship grounded in social justice and activism regularly draws on reflexive accounts to inform conceptual understandings of engaged scholarship or to show how particular power dynamics constrain and enable social justice work. For example, Sukandar, Agustiana and Hale (2009) identify emotional challenges emerging from research projects centered on fostering rebuilding and social change in contexts of violence and conflict. Parker, Oceguera, and Sanchez (2011) reflect on their involvement with a community-based nonprofit organization committed to empowering leadership, the building of equitable partnerships, and providing social justice. The authors highlight the contours of a grounded, participatory process of organizing, including how that process is shaped by the particulars of the setting and community.

Within a social justice and activism approach, the application of research takes center stage. However, determining the extent to which the research project results in transformative change—either in the short or long term—is difficult. Scholars working within a *communicating for social impact* framework shift from an emphasis on individual-level or one-off projects to fostering broader structural changes (Harter, Dutta, & Cole, 2009). Here, researchers target structures seen as underlying the reproduction of social problems, such as public participation in environmental decision making (Zoller, 2009) or information communication capabilities in rural communities (Chib & Zhao, 2009). Similar to its allied traditions of applied communication and collaborative learning, the use of participative practices reflects different approaches. In some cases, researchers maintain an expert position, perhaps advocating on the behalf of marginalized groups based on their research findings. Researchers drawing on dialogic, Freireian, and action-research frameworks bring an explicit focus to the relational dynamics of the research.

Practical Theory Research. Practical theory adopts three distinctive approaches to address theory/practice divides: (1) mapping, (2) engaged reflection, and (3) transformative practice (Barge & Craig, 2009). First, practical theory may be viewed as a form of mapping. This approach emphasizes the importance of using and testing theory to create a conceptual map of a communicative activity or process. Once the conceptual map has been developed and deemed to be either accurate or rich in detail, then practical implications can be derived. For example, Fay and Kline (2011) mapped the set of relationships among forms of communication, communication satisfaction, and organizational commitment to explore the role of coworker relationships in buffering the effects of high-intensity telecommuting. Using a critical-interpretive approach, Harter (2004) mapped the dialectics constituting cooperative organizations to articulate the way members enacted cooperative life.

Second, practical theory emphasizes normative standards for evaluating and developing practice. For example, grounded practical theory (Craig, 1989; Craig & Tracy, 1995) focuses on creating a normative reconstruction of a practice by focusing attention on the problems that inform a practice, the technical moves that address these problems, and the set of philosophical norms that comprise the logic of what moves need to be used to respond to a problem and when. Researchers have focused on interactional problems across organizational contexts, including 911 call centers (Tracy & Tracy, 1998) and school board meetings (Tracy, 2010; Tracy & Durfy, 2007). Similarly, a *communication as design* approach (Aakhus, 2007; Aakhus & Jackson, 2005) identifies interactional problems to propose an ideal practice. Both approaches emphasize the development of good practice by theorizing the normative standards informing practice, identifying interactional challenges, or developing tools to manage the challenges.

Third, *practical theory as transformative practice* views theory as an intervention tool. Both Weick's (1995) model of sensemaking and the coordinated management of meaning theory (Pearce & Pearce, 2001) may be viewed as practical theories, as they provide a rich set of concepts, tools, and models for academics to engage with practitioners to understand, critique, and transform their practice.

All three approaches emphasize pressing problems and the importance of rigorous research methods. They vary in their emphasis on the coproduction of knowledge. *Practical theory as mapping* tends to privilege researcher-generated accounts of knowledge with the idea that good practice should flow from rigorous research. *Practical theory as engaged reflection* treats coproduction in terms of either textual or conversational reflexivity. Craig's approach to practical theory emphasizes *textual reflexivity* by placing academic discourses in conversation with practical discourses in order to produce a normative reconstruction of a practice. By *conversational reflexivity*, we refer to the process of engaging practitioners in conversations regarding how their practices can be transformed. *Communication as design* emphasizes both textual reflexivity and conversational reflexivity in the design of communication tools. *Practical theory as transformative practice* has the clearest focus on the coproduction of knowledge, as it privileges direct conversations with participants when co-creating and crafting interventions (Pearce & Pearce, 2001). Throughout, the coproduction of knowledge may or may not be emphasized and may take the shape of either textual or conversational reflexivity.

Tensions of Engaged Scholarship

Each of the above traditions shares a family resemblance based on the collaborative production of what is seen as actionable knowledge.

Across these traditions, engaged scholarship can also be understood as a tensional activity. *Tensions* refer to a clash of ideas, principles, or actions that requires individuals to manage the competing pulls and oppositions constituting the tension (Stohl & Cheney, 2001). Research suggests that engaged scholarship is marked by three important tensions: (1) distance-empathy, (2) representation-intervention, and (3) scholar-practitioner roles. This set of intertwined, nested tensions is neither exhaustive nor mutually exclusive. Nonetheless, this articulation provides an initial vocabulary for naming the challenges associated with conducting engaged scholarship.

Distance-Empathy Tensions. Tensions associated with distance-empathy center on competing pulls between a distancing stance involving the unencumbered pursuit of a researcher's scholarly agenda and an empathetic stance that minimizes critique and is centered on the goals and expectations of engaged partners (Cheney, 2008). This tension emerges during the negotiation of the focus and scope of the research project and the methods for knowledge production. Scholars may experience competing pulls between academic freedom and organizational politics. What gets included in a project, both in terms of the problem that drives the project and who is invited to participate, depends in part on multiple and potentially conflicting interests (Dempsey, 2010). Organizational partners may have specific problems and issues they wish researchers to address and, as a result, may be inclined to more narrowly define the scope of the project and its relevant participants. Scholars may wish to more broadly define the scope of the project in order to meet academic expectations and norms.

In addition, scholars are often invited to conduct research because they can provide a reflexive and potentially critical account of practice. However, a fully immersive, empathetic stance can make it difficult for researchers to challenge normative practices or engage in critical analysis of existing practices. Conquergood (1991) captures this tension nicely, distinguishing between researchers acting in ways that are complicit with the organization's interests and cultivating a position that challenges current configurations of power and privilege. Academic scholarship assumes a rigorous process that critically examines an issue to render an informed judgment. From within a distancing stance, quality scholarship does not predetermine the answers to research questions or hypotheses; rather, it poses research questions or articulates hypotheses and then develops a methodology for rigorously generating and analyzing data to develop knowledge that answers their research questions or tests their hypotheses. Yet researchers may feel compelled to frame the research and the knowledge generated in more sympathetic terms for those involved. This might take the form of minimizing unpalatable findings, selective uses of quotes, or putting a particular spin on results (Martin, 2010). Here, the challenge is to find ways of coproducing studies that are empathetic in that they are relevant and useful to partners, while also maintaining a critical distance that protects the integrity of the research process. Rich precedents for navigating this tension include work by Goodall (2000, 2006), Trujillo (2004), and Vande Berg & Trujillo (2008).

Representation-Intervention Tensions. Tensions associated with representation-intervention consist of competing pulls between descriptive and preparatory outcomes and more immediate, actionable interventions. Engaged scholarship can include basic research aimed at constructing a representation of the organization or community (Van de Ven, 2007). Yet engaged scholarship also takes the form of collaborative inquiry and action research devoted to producing immediate intervention and applications. The former may take the form of translational scholarship, which emphasizes the importance of conducting sound basic research to develop and empirically test theory that can be subsequently used to inform practice (e.g., Petronio, 1999). The latter is represented by more transformative approaches to theory-practice integration in the form of action research and practical theorizing (Barge, 2001; Barge & Craig, 2009).

Several factors may influence how researchers experience this tension. First, academic logics and practices such as institutional review boards (IRBs) sustain a model of research that privileges description over change. As Dempsey (2010) observes, "When IRBs require university-level reviews of research aims without a similar form of community reviews, they perpetuate a model of research as an extractive, rather than productive force for communities" (p. 374). IRBs may be much more comfortable with facilitating basic research and less likely to certify research that directly intervenes in communication practices. Academic reward structures such as tenure and promotion also tend to privilege forms of research practice that are more easily translated into academic publications.

Second, the pull to produce more immediate outcomes is made difficult by the complexities and politics of change efforts. The notion of coproduction implicitly carries with it expectations regarding mutuality, shared responsibility, and partnership. The ideal relationship between scholars and organizations is easily romanticized as being equal partners in the coproduction of research. However, the choice of who is or is not included in the research process directly influences the possibilities for intervention. Representation within engagement efforts is a contested issue. Who is invited to represent an organization or particular group of stakeholders not only influences how the research problem is constructed but also the resulting resources developed to produce change (Dempsey, 2010). If influential members or opinion leaders are not invited to participate, the likelihood that they will support attempts to intervene is lessened. Yet this move can also serve to further marginalize less-skilled, less-articulate, or less-powerful members. In addition, researchers may shift their identifications and resultant plans for intervention in response to their emerging understanding of existing power relations.

Ritchie (2007) documents a remarkable process whereby she shifts from taking a managerial perspective to adopting a more explicitly political, interventionist approach aimed at equalizing power relations for employees. Ritchie (2007) recounts her initial discomfort in contradicting management's functionalist imperative by advocating for low-status employees. At the same time, she identifies a particularly telling contradiction: While embracing a social justice mission, the design of the project as well as the engagement process itself was not fully participatory and collaborative in nature; employees had little say in the guiding theories used, the structure of the intervention, or in the writing up of the research. In this example, the move to adopt an explicitly interventionist stance evinced its own problems of participation.

Scholar-Practitioner Role Tensions. Engaged scholars often use the terms *scholar-practitioner* or *practitioner-scholar* to describe their practice. Wasserman and Kram (2009) quote Edgar Schein, who defines a *scholar-practitioner* as "someone who is dedicated to generating new knowledge that is useful to practitioners" (p. 12). On the other hand, Bartunek (2007) defines the *practitioner-scholar* as an individual who sees their primary contribution as a practitioner but is also attracted to academic scholarship. The use of the hyphen to link the roles of the scholar and practitioner is suggestive of competing pulls between two distinct but connected worlds: academia, with its emphasis on theory, and practice, which foregrounds action and activity. Such tension is also indicative of a longstanding interpretive-critical divide in engaged research.

In addition, scholars and the organizations they work with often have different time horizons and expectations for the pacing of the research (Simpson & Seibold, 2008). Scholars may be used to having longer periods of time to conduct their research and may be inclined to conduct it at a slower pace, while organizations need the research to occur at a faster pace because of the pressures they face to take action quickly to address pressing concerns. Scholar-practitioners also balance competing demands placed on their time by being colocated in the worlds of academics and practice while needing to be present in both (e.g., Martin, 2010). Academic colleagues may become concerned about how much time is spent off-campus and how this absence bears on the workload and overall departmental culture.

Scholar-practitioners also negotiate divergent expectations regarding what kind of knowledge should be produced through research. Academic knowledge is typically portrayed as being more theoretical, acontextual, and *knowing about* an activity, whereas the knowledge desired by practitioners is much more about *knowing how* a practice works in a local context and how this knowledge can be used to make judgments regarding what to do next (Bartunek, 2007; Van de Ven, 2007). Differences in desired outcomes result in a number of dilemmas for scholar-practitioners regarding the kind of knowledge they wish to generate (theoretical versus practical), the type of outcomes they wish to pursue (academic publications versus social and material change), and the venues in which they publish their work (academic versus lay).

Colleagues may view scholar-practitioners as pursuing less-rigorous forms of research. While concerns about applied work and consulting activities have lessened over the years, there has always been strong skepticism regarding the value of such activities (e.g., Ellis, 1982), in part because there is a dearth of strong models regarding what such research entails. Scholar-practitioners may not only face questions regarding the value and quality of their work by fellow academics, they may also lack legitimacy in the eyes of the people they work with and wish to support (Dempsey, 2010). Academics may face resistance, as members of those groups may question their ability to understand the problems they face and their commitment to staying with the process. This suggests that one of the challenges scholar-practitioners confront is how to negotiate power within the research relationship, including when to emphasize power inequalities, when to invite practitioners to take a one-up position, and when to emphasize mutual expertise. Democratically informed conceptions of engagement provide a particularly promising way forward.

Engaged Scholarship and the Recovery of Democratic Practice

The term *engagement* invokes a broad range of scholarly practices including cogenerative community partnerships, action research, community engagement, civic participation, applied research, translational research, and public scholarship. The range of practices variously attributed to engaged scholarship reflects its vibrant, emergent status. Yet such ill-defined boundaries raise vital questions about the extent to which engaged scholarship should function as a transformative practice, including the extent to which it includes cogenerative, democratic practices.

Early visions of engaged scholarship such as those informed by Dewey (1916) saw the coproduction of knowledge as a vitally important public good and connected research to the civic mission of higher education institutions. This perspective provides an explicit link to democratic communication practice. Here, the cultivation of democratic communication capacities—including speech and debate, critical judgment, and participative abilities critical to democratic processes—are seen as essential to building a vibrant democracy and enriched public life. Engaged scholarship can be used to facilitate a deeper understanding of the obligations and duties of democratic citizenship to a broader set of publics, particularly within the communication discipline, which has a long-standing tradition of fostering democratic forms of communication. For example, the lead article in the first issue of the National Communication Association's oldest journal, *The Quarterly Journal of Speech*, focused on the role of forums as an educative agency that develops the ability of persons to make logical judgments based on reliable facts and data that can be presented to others—a key skill associated with citizenship in a democracy (Lyman, 1915).

Conceived of in terms of democratic practice, engaged scholarship brings to light important differences among existing efforts aimed at engaging the university in practical concerns and problems. Broadly speaking, university-initiated engagement overwhelmingly takes the form of one-off, unilateral forms of outreach. A container metaphor informs this approach, where academics are seen as expanding beyond the walls of the university through outreach. For example, public intellectuals are typically conceived of as *ones who intervene* into social problems (Said, 1994). Public intellectuals typically pursue forms of translational research, where the emphasis is on disseminating ideas and writing for a variety of publics. A similar metaphor exists within volunteerist conceptions of service learning, which are characterized by a charitable mode of engagement in which the university gives back by providing services to the communities of which it is a part (Crabtree, 1998). Engaged scholarship as democratic practice involves shifting from a model of one-way outreach and a view of organizations and clients as data collection sites and funding sources to one that sees the process of scholarly inquiry as being fundamentally about the cogeneration of collaborative modes of governance. Particularly rich examples within organizational communication include work by Harter and her colleagues (Harter, Leeman, Norander, Young, & Rawlins, 2008; Novak & Harter, 2008; Singhal, Harter, Chitnis, & Sharma, 2007).

While the coproduction of knowledge is strongly foregrounded in the literature on engaged scholarship, an important theme that is often implicit is the way engaged scholarship democratizes the production of knowledge and how it influences the way organizations and other groups subsequently address challenges. Engaged scholarship is typically distinguished by its focus on social problems and often touches on issues of democratic practice by working with populations that are disadvantaged and under-resourced. However, such approaches may or may not adopt a democratic approach toward the coproduction of knowledge. Strangely, much of the discussion of engagement focuses on outcomes rather than its enactment within daily practice. Engaged scholarship as a mode of democratic practice remains ripe for further extension. To address this need, we pursue a democratic, process-based vision of engaged scholarship as a mode of (re)turn to the civic mission of higher education institutions. We outline the characteristics of an embodied organizing process of engagement characterized by democratic conversation, involving mutual influence between scholars and stakeholders in the coproduction of knowledge.

Engaged Scholarship as Democratic Conversation

Viewing engaged scholarship as democratic conversation recalibrates the hierarchical model of academic knowledge production to one emphasizing the mutual influence of academics and practitioners. Here, both research and practice can be viewed as systems of knowledge production, each with its own distinct rules and modes of inquiry. The challenge of engaged scholarship is to cultivate democratic practices able to reclaim conflict and address these potentially conflicting knowledge systems. Engaged scholarship as democratic conversation involves cogenerating knowledge about how communication creates forms of organizing and the consequences of these forms. A central goal of democratic conversation is the coproduction of insights that improve practice while also adding to the broader body of knowledge in the communication discipline.

Three guiding assumptions inform our development of democratic conversation. First, democratic conversation involves the recognition of difference and the attempt to connect insider-outsider perspectives, however broadly defined. From this perspective, insiders (organizational members, community-based partners, or practitioners) and outsiders (academic scholars) have different relationships, standpoints, and concerns relative to the problem being addressed. Given robust forums to facilitate coproduction and cogeneration, these differences produce unique insights (Bartunek, 2007; Coghlan & Shani, 2008; Deetz, 2010; Deetz & Irvin, 2008; Mirvis, 2008; Van de Ven, 2007). Thus this approach recognizes the need to attend to the built-in differences, conflicts, and inequalities that emerge within community engagement efforts.

Second, democratic conversations are inquiry-based, emphasizing cogenerative theorizing (Deetz, 2008). Rather than reproduce a communication model based on simple expression, a framework such as this attempts to reclaim a deeper political significance for communication based on the structuring of meaning and experience (Deetz, in press). Through the design of interactional forums and structures, conversations can be catalytic, providing new understandings of issues at hand with an eye toward generating learning and action (Baker, 2009).

Third, engaged scholarship as democratic conversation enlarges participants' capacity to manage difficult conversations in a productive manner. We take for granted that one of the primary goals of scholars is to produce knowledge addressed to academic readers; however, that notion is contested, given the ongoing debate regarding the kinds of knowledge that academics should be publishing as well as appropriate publication forums (Barge & Shockley-Zalabak, 2008). Democratic conversations both provide a means to conduct engaged scholarship as well as serve as a desired outcome of engaged scholarship. Treating engaged scholarship as democratic conversation not only focuses attention on the everyday organizing practices through which engagement efforts are enacted but also on cultivating participants' future abilities to engage in democratic conversation. Engaged scholarship as democratic conversation may be viewed as a specific type of action research. Hatchuel and David (2008, p. 146) describe action research as a model of enlightened and democratic action that focuses attention on the relational coordination among participants. Holmstrand et al. (2008, p. 184) suggest that action research's democratic impulse tends to be more normative than change oriented—making social inequality and injustice visible versus improving the democratic process by creating and sharing knowledge. The focus on a critical conception of democratic conversation both during and following the research emphasizes the importance of treating the coproduction of knowledge as an ongoing, contested process.

There are at least three practices associated with engaged scholarship as democratic conversation: (1) co-missioning, (2) co-design, (3) and co-enactment.

Co-missioning. Co-missioning refers to how the focus and scope of the research project is co-created between academics and those seen as external to the university. Research projects need to address the occasionally divergent needs of both academics and their partners. Co-missioning conversations can involve both texts and embodied conversations. Textual conversations place academic and practitioner texts in conversation with one another to explore how an issue or problem is constituted. For example, by conducting a systematic review of academic and practitioner literature on positive approaches to organization studies, we can place academic texts in a textual conversation with material on positive organization studies from popular press books or practitioner journals such as *The OD Practitioner* or *The AI Practitioner*. This approach highlights similarities and differences between discourses regarding a particular topic, allowing participants to articulate common interests and to identify how the differences between the two might be productively leveraged to meet the needs and interests of academics and practitioners.

Embodied conversations occur between academics and practitioners. Some conversations may take place between academics and practitioners who are associated with the general problem domain or context that is being studied but who are not directly involved in the problem being addressed. For example, if an academic is interested in studying the governance of nonprofit organizations, having informal or formal conversations with directors or board members of nonprofits may be useful to gain a sense of how they experience their organization; the kinds of challenges, problems, and tensions they must manage; and what they would view as useful research. Through embodied conversations, participants gain insight into the needs and interests of the range of participants in order to develop a more pluralist or inclusive framing of the problem being addressed. The goal of embodied conversations is to generate robust knowledge that elaborates theory formulations and enables richer action and practice. These conversations reflect a shift from a wholly researcher-driven focus to a cogenerative one. Co-missioning conversations may employ a variety of deliberation formats or structures that allow academics and practitioners to generate creative fresh problem formulations. Jovanovic's (2008; Jovanovic, Steger, Symonds, & Nelson, 2007) engaged research centered on reconciliation and community-based deliberative forums provide particularly rich examples.

Co-design. Engaged scholarship as democratic conversation calls for projects designed with both the interests of academics and their partners in mind. The design must be rigorous from the perspective of both parties while doable and understandable from the perspective of the parties involved. The notion of co-design has emerged over the last few years in a number of areas, including information technology (Sanders & Stappers, 2008), customer services (Steen, Manschot, & De Koning, 2011), strategic planning and change processes (Somerville & Nino, 2007), and as a way to invite multiple stakeholders into a deliberative conversation over the ways processes can be designed that meet their needs. Co-design is aimed at developing a sense of joint ownership regarding the specific project as various stakeholders have a voice in the process. Co-design involves the creation of a collaborative space that unfolds over time where stakeholders can create designs, try them out, and then alter their designs to better fit the diverse needs of participants. Designers need to keep in close contact with each other as the process unfolds, as the emerging design needs to be responsive to changing needs.

Researchers adopting a co-design perspective must be able to manage the tension between academic freedom and the need for organizations to keep information confidential or proprietary. Depending on the political environment of the organization or the need to keep proprietary information confidential, it may not be possible to freely interview everyone or create empirical material from outside the normal reporting process. Design work requires engaged scholars to navigate the tensions associated with having academic freedom and producing relevant knowledge. In addition, given the dynamism of organizing processes, improvisation, *bricolage*, and adaptation are also crucial skills.

Co-enactment. Co-enactment involves developing forums and tools to deliberate over the meaning, utility, and implications of the knowledge that is coproduced for future work across academic and practitioner contexts. Practitioners are more inclined to view research as useful when they are involved in discussing and interpreting the findings (Mohrman, Gibson, & Mohrman, 2001). The creation of conversational forums where participants can deliberate over the meaning of the empirical material they have generated and engage in sense making is vital. The notion of *shared interpretation* has been used in both organizational (Singh, Hawkins, & Whymark, 2009) and educational settings (Yukawa, 2006) to read empirical material in different ways, given participants' experience and background. For academic participants, this might include publishing white papers and blog postings, producing documentaries, and presenting the material in seminars, conventions, and workshops. For practitioners, this might involve designing forums where participants can engage in dialogue over the scholarship, make sense of the material, and create action steps. Docherty and Shani (2008) also highlight a number of mechanisms that can facilitate deliberation over research analyses, such as debriefing procedures (Lipshitz, Popper, & Friedman, 2002), democratic dialogues (Gustavsen, 2001), learning circles and learning cycles (Holmstrand et al., 2008; Mohrman, Mohrman, Cohen, & Winby, 2008), and the use of socio-technical systems theory (Trist & Murray, 1993) to facilitate the diffusion of learning and knowledge. Throughout, the knowledge that is produced needs to be jointly critiqued and determined by both the academics and practitioners.

In sum, engaged scholarship as democratic conversation involves the design of deliberative forums and conversational structures aimed at coproducing knowledge as well as critically assessing that knowledge. Deliberation within an organization or community starts once the inquiry begins. One's participation with co-missioning, co-designing, and co-enacting influences knowledge production, creating an evolving set of criteria for what counts as useful and actionable knowledge and setting the stage for subsequent conversations among and between participants and academics. If engaged scholars are inviting and attempting to model more democratic forms of conversation in these activities, participants build their capacity to create democratic futures.

Imagining Engaged Futures

While the notion of engagement has long been a heralded part of academic culture, the development of engaged scholarship and practice continues to unfold. We have emphasized the value of a model of engaged scholarship aimed at cultivating civically oriented, democratic praxis. Such an approach conceives of research as a democratic practice involving academics and practitioners deliberating and jointly determining the focus of the project, the way the project will be structured, how the data will be analyzed, and the procedures for its enactment. Central to this model of engaged scholarship is the cogeneration and coproduction of knowledge, including the embodied organizing practices of co-missioning, co-design, and co-enactment. Research drawing on postcolonial theory suggests additional possibilities for rethinking new futures of engaged scholarship within a framework of decolonization (Broadfoot et al., 2008; Broadfoot & Munshi, 2007; Norander & Harter, 2012). For instance, Broadfoot, Munshi, and Nelson-Marsh (2010) develop Shome's (1996) call for decolonization of academic research and practice. Their case study of a radically decentralized virtual academic conference illustrates how skillful use of participatory technologies can facilitate more-inclusive modes of working within and across the academy.

Additional possibilities lie in new forms of distributed knowledge production such as those seen in Occupy Research, an open, shared space centered on research addressing the Occupy movement. Occupy Research involves diverse participants "sharing ideas, research questions, research methods, tools, data sets, and working together to gather, analyze, discuss, write, code, and otherwise develop the theory and practice of occupy research together" (http://occupyresearch.wikispaces.com/). Within the framework of Occupy Research, principles of radical decentralization and the collectivization of knowledge present new opportunities for developing models of engaged scholarship that explode and dissolve researcher/participant roles.

As organizational communication continues to develop and extend engaged models of scholarship, there remains a need for sustained critical attention to the role of institutional practices in shaping these opportunities. In particular, there is a need to attend to their influence on a democratically informed model of engaged scholarship grounded in communication as constitutive of experiences, identities, knowledge, information, and values (Deetz, 2010). Developing richer modes of engagement requires ongoing reexamination and critique of existing academic practices, including pedagogy and the intertwined issues of tenure and promotion requirements and publishing conventions.

Currently, a gulf exists between achieving academic impact in terms of scholarly articles, books, and monographs and achieving community impact in terms of new programs, activities, or policies (Stanton, 2008). The pursuit of higher academic standing by universities continues to be associated with the scholarship of discovery, which defines scholarship and impact as publication in peer-reviewed academic journals (Braxton, Luckey, & Helland, 2002; DeWine, 2005; O'Meara, 2005). Not surprisingly, the tenure and promotion committees of most universities, particularly research-intensive universities, emphasize publishing in peer-reviewed journals and academic presses. Additional attention needs to be placed on restructuring the tenure and promotion process to reward and acknowledge diverse modes of engaged scholarship. Faculty would benefit from developing tenure and promotion dossiers able to demonstrate accountability to theory and practice. Gelmon and Agre-Kippenhan (2002) stress the need to show how faculty engagement relates to traditional theoretical and research streams, suggesting that faculty pay close attention to university and tenure-promotion committee norms regarding what counts as publication. However, such a strategy primarily assigns responsibility to individual faculty members to account for how their engagement fits within local research norms.

University administrations must revise tenure and promotion processes to reward and acknowledge engaged scholarship. Even if an academic is rhetorically skilled and can produce a compelling dossier, the tenure or promotion case will likely fail if the university community does not accept such work. A number of universities have undertaken initiatives to reconceptualize their tenure and promotion documents in ways that acknowledge engaged scholarship by blurring the lines between service and scholarship, reworking publication venues to include a broader range of academic journals as well as trade publications or local newspapers, embracing multidisciplinary work, inviting evaluations from community members or end-users of the research, and reshaping the content of tenure and promotion dossiers or portfolios (Ellison & Eatman, 2008; Seeger, 2009). For engaged scholarship to continue to develop, both individual-level and organizational-level strategies need to be identified that allow academics to make the case for engaged work and to create a supportive environment for such work.

Finally, we suggest new directions for developing innovative pedagogy regarding theory and methods designed to equip students with the needed skills to conduct engaged scholarship. The heart of engaged scholarship is the notion of coproduction. What counts as useful knowledge and the methods for generating such knowledge are contested. However, equipping students with increased understanding of the practices and politics of coproducing knowledge, including their participation in modes of governance and decision making, should accompany the continued development of engaged scholarship (see Heath, 2010, for a particularly rich example of such an effort).

Developing research skills that address the relational dynamics associated with coproducing knowledge would greatly enhance future practice. Several practices in particular deserve explicit attention. One of the key skills of the engaged scholar is conflict management (Van de Ven, 2007). Given that engaged scholarship works with the differences that academics and practitioners bring to the research project, there will often be conflict over the aims and purposes of the research, appropriate methods, and other issues that must be managed. Moreover, engaged scholars benefit from increased improvisational skills. Democratic engaged scholarship is dynamic, requiring responsive research focus and designs. Similar to Silverman's (2006) notion of the progressive focusing of the research question within an unfolding research project, the focus and shape of engagement may change over time. Engaged researchers must be responsive to their partners' changing goals and needs while also maintaining their research commitments. In this way, engaged scholars benefit from developing translation skills allowing them to move across academic and practical discourses. Increased familiarity with evaluation research (Atkins, 2010) can also help academics envision flexible forms of assessment. We believe that emphasizing conflict management, improvisation, translation, and evaluation calls for innovative methods sequences and curriculum.

Viewing engaged scholarship as a knowledge-based activity that emphasizes coproduction and democratic conversation is interventionist in nature. The more that organizational scholars are able to identify models of engagement, hone their skills for conducting such work, and develop the abilities to translate their work in meaningful and pragmatic ways, the more likely that this scholarship will make a tangible and lasting difference. Thus a fruitful area for future research includes the articulation of robust models and practices of engaged scholarship that enable academics and their partners to jointly pursue ideas and topics that are of mutual interest and benefit.

References

Aakhus, M. (2007). Communication as design. *Communication Monographs, 74*(1), 112–117.

Aakhus, M., & Jackson, S. (2005). Technology, interaction, and design. In K. Fitch & R. Sanders (Eds.), *Handbook of language and social interaction* (pp. 411–436). Mahwah, NJ: Lawrence Erlbaum.

Adler, N., Elmquist, M., & Norrgren, F. (2009). The challenge of managing boundary-spanning research activities: Experiences from the Swedish context. *Research Process, 38,* 1136–1149.

Alvesson, M., & Deetz, S. (2000). *Doing critical management research.* Thousand Oaks, CA: SAGE.

Argyris, C., Putnam, R., & Smith, D. (1985). *Action science.* San Francisco, CA: Jossey-Bass.

Atkins, C. (2010, November). Training the communication researcher of the future. *Spectra,* 16–19.

Baker, A. C. (2009). *Catalytic conversations: Organizational communication and innovation.* Armonk, NY: M.E. Sharpe.

Barge, J. K. (2001). Practical theory as mapping, engaged reflection, and transformative practice. *Communication Theory, 11*(1), 5–13.

Barge, J. K., & Craig, R. T. (2009). Practical theory in applied communication scholarship. In L. R. Frey & K. Cissna (Eds.), *The handbook of applied communication* (pp. 55–78). Thousand Oaks, CA: SAGE.

Barge, J. K., & Shockley-Zalabak, P. (2008). Engaged scholarship and the creation of useful organizational knowledge. *Journal of Applied Communication Research, 36*(3), 251–265.

Bartunek, J. (2007). Academic-practitioner collaboration need not require joint or relevant research: Toward a relational scholarship of integration. *Academy of Management Journal, 50*(6), 1323–1333.

Bartunek, J. M. (2008). Insider/outsider team research: The development of the approach and its meanings. In A. B. (Rami) Shani, S. A. Mohrman, W. A. Pasmore, B. Stymne, & N. Adler (Eds.), *Handbook of collaborative management research* (pp. 73–91). Thousand Oaks, CA: SAGE.

Beech, N., MacIntosh, R., & MacLean, D. (2010). Dialogues between academics and practitioners: The role of generative dialogic encounters. *Organization Studies, 31*(9/10), 1341–1367.

Beer, M. (2011). Developing an effective organization: Intervention method, empirical evidence, and theory. *Research in Organizational Change and Development, 19,* 1–5.

Borjesson, S. (2011). Collaborative research for sustainable learning: The case of developing innovation capabilities at Volvo cars. *Action Learning: Research and Practice, 8*(3), 187–209.

Boud, D., Cressey, P., & Docherty, P. (2006). *Productive reflection at work.* London, England: Routledge.

Boyatzis, R. E., Howard, A., Rapisarda, B., & Taylor, S. (2008). Coaching for sustainable change. In A. B. (Rami) Shani, S. A. Mohrman, W. A. Pasmore, B. Stymne, & N. Adler (Eds.), *Handbook of collaborative management research* (pp. 231–242). Thousand Oaks, CA: SAGE.

Boyer, E. (1996). The scholarship of engagement. *Journal of Public Service & Outreach, 1*(1), 11–20.

Boyer, E. (1997). *Scholarship reconsidered: Priorities of the professoriate.* Princeton, NJ: The Carnegie Foundation for the Advancement of Teaching.

Braxton, J. M., Luckey, W., & Helland, P. (2002). *Institutionalizing a broader view of scholarship through Boyer's four domains.* New York, NY: Jossey-Bass.

Broadfoot, K. J, Cockburn, T., Cockburn-Wootten, C., do Carmo Reis, M., Gautam, D., Malshe, A., . . . N. Srinivas (2008). A mosaic of visions, daydreams and memories: Diverse inlays of organizing and communicating from around the globe. *Management Communication Quarterly, 22*(2), 322–350.

Broadfoot, K. J., & Munshi, D. (2007). Diverse voices and alternative rationalities: Imagining forms of postcolonial organizational communication. *Management Communication Quarterly, 21*(1), 249–267.

Broadfoot, K. J., Munshi, D., & Nelson-Marsh, N. (2010). COMMUNEcation: A rhizomatic tale of participatory technology, postcoloniality and professional community. *New Media & Society, 12*(5), 797–812.

Buzzanell, P. M. (1994). Gaining a voice: Feminist organizational communication theorizing. *Management Communication Quarterly, 7*(4), 339–383.

Buzzanell, P. M., & Stohl, C. (1999). The Redding tradition of organizational communication scholarship: W. Charles Redding and his legacy. *Communication Studies, 50*(4), 324–336.

Cheney, G. (2008). Encountering the ethics of engaged scholarship. *Journal of Applied Communication Research, 36*(3), 281–288.

Chib, A., & Zhao, J. (2009). Sustainability of ICT interventions: Lessons from rural projects in China and India. In L. M. Harter, M. J. Dutta, & C. Cole (Eds.), *Communicating for social impact: Engaging communication theory, research, and pedagogy.* Cresskill, NJ: Hampton Press.

Cirella, S., Guerci, M., & Shani, A. B. (Rami). (2012). A process model of collaborative management research: The study of collective creativity in the luxury industry. *Systemic Practice and Action Research, 25*(3), 281–300.

Coghlan, D., & Shani, A. B. (Rami). (2008). Collaborative management research through communities of inquiry: Challenges and skills. In A. B. (Rami) Shani, S. A. Mohrman, W. A. Pasmore, B. Stymne, & N. Adler (Eds.), *Handbook of collaborative management research* (pp. 601-614). Thousand Oaks, CA: SAGE.

Conquergood, D. (1991). Rethinking ethnography: Towards a critical cultural politics. *Communication Monographs, 58*(2), 179–194.

Cooperrider, D. L., & Whitney, D. (1999). *Appreciative inquiry.* San Francisco, CA: Berrett-Koehler.

Crabtree, R. D. (1998). Mutual empowerment in cross-cultural participatory development and service learning: Lessons in communication and social justice from projects in El Salvador and Nicaragua. *Journal of Applied Communication, 26*(2), 182–209.

Craig, R. T. (1989). Communication as a practical discipline. In B. Dervin, L. Grossberg, B. J. O'Keefe, & E. Wartella (Eds.), *Rethinking communication: Vol. 1. Paradigm issues* (pp. 97–122). Newbury Park, CA: SAGE.

Craig, R. T., & Tracy, K. (1995). Grounded practical theory: The case of intellectual discussion. *Communication Theory,* 5(3), 248–272.

Deetz, S. (1995). *Transforming communication, transforming business: Building responsive and responsible workplaces.* Cresskill, NJ: Hampton Press.

Deetz, S. (2008). Engagement as co-generative theorizing. *Journal of Applied Communication Research, 36*(3), 289–297.

Deetz, S. (2010). Politically attentive relational constructivism (PARC): Making a difference in a pluralistic, interdependent world. In D. Carbaugh & P. M. Buzzanell (Eds.), *Distinctive qualities in communication research* (pp. 32–52). New York, NY: Routledge.

Deetz, S. (in press). Power and the possibility of generative community dialogue. In S. Littlejohn (Ed.), *The coordinated management of meaning: A festschrift in honor of W. Barnett Pearce.* Hackensack, NJ: Fairleigh Dickinson University Press.

Deetz, S., & Irvin, L. (2008). Governance, stakeholder involvement, and new communication models. In S. Odugbemi & T. L. Jaconsen (Eds.), *Governance reform under real-world conditions: Citizens, stakeholders, and voice* (pp. 163–179). Washington, DC: The World Bank.

Deetz, S., & Mumby, D. (1985). Metaphors, information, and power. In B. Ruben (Ed.), *Information and behavior* (vol. 1, pp. 369–385). New Brunswick, NJ: Transaction Press.

Dempsey, S. E. (2010). Critiquing community engagement. *Management Communication Quarterly, 24*(3), 359–390.

Dewey, J. (1916). *Democracy and education: An introduction to the philosophy of education.* New York, NY: The MacMillan Company.

DeWine, S. (2005). Contributions of engaged scholarship to the academic community. In J. L. Simpson & P. Shockley-Zalabak (Eds.), *Engaging communication, transforming organizations* (pp. 191–202). Cresskill, NJ: Hampton Press.

DeWine, S., & James, A. C. (1988). Examining the communication audit: Assessment and modification. *Management Communication Quarterly, 2*(2), 144–169.

Doberneck, D. M., Glass, C. R., & Schweitzer, J. (2010). From rhetoric to reality: A typology of publicly engaged scholarship. *Journal of Higher Education Outreach and Engagement, 14*(4), 5–35.

Docherty, P., Kira, M., & Shani, A. B. (Rami). (Eds.). (2008). *Creating sustainable work systems: Emerging perspectives and practice* (2nd ed.). London, England: Routledge.

Docherty, P., & Shani, A. B. (Rami). (2008). Learning mechanisms as means and ends in collaborative management research. In A. B. (Rami) Shani, S. A. Mohrman, W. A. Pasmore, B. Stymne, & N. Adler (Eds.), *Handbook of collaborative management research* (pp. 163–182). Thousand Oaks, CA: SAGE.

Eisenberg, E. M., & Riley, P. (2001). Organizational culture. In F. M. Jablin & L. L. Putnam (Eds.), *The new handbook of organizational communication* (pp. 291–322). Thousand Oaks, CA: SAGE.

Ellis, D. G. (1982, March). The shame of speech communication. *Spectra, 18*(3), pp. 1–2.

Ellison, J., & Eatman, T. K. (2008). *Scholarship in public: Knowledge creation and tenure policy in the engaged university.* Syracuse, NY: Syracuse University, Imagining America. Retrieved from http://imaginingamerica.org/wp-content/uploads/2011/05/TTI_FINAL.pdf

Fay, M. J., & Kline, S. L. (2011). Coworker relationships and informal communication in high-intensity telecommuting. *Journal of Applied Communication Research, 39*(2), 144–163.

Freire, P. (1970). *Pedagogy of the oppressed.* New York, NY: H & R Paperback Books.

Freire, P. (1973). *Education for critical consciousness.* New York, NY: Seabury Press.

Frey, L. R., & Carragee, K. M. (Eds.). (2007). *Communication activism* (vols. 1 & 2). Cresskill, NJ: Hampton Press.

Frey, L. R., & Cissna, K. N. (Eds.). (2009). *Routledge handbook of applied communication research.* New York, NY: Routledge.

Gaventa, J. (1982). *Power and powerlessness: Quiescence and rebellion in an Appalachian valley.* Chicago, IL: University of Illinois.

Gelmon, S., & Agre-Kippenhan, S. (2002, January). Promotion, tenure, and the engaged scholar: Keeping the scholarship of engagement in the review process. *AAHE Bulletin,* 7–11.

Gibson-Graham, J. K. (2006). *A postcapitalist politics.* Minneapolis: University of Minnesota Press.

Goldhaber, G. M., & Krivonos, P. D. (1977). The ICA communication audit: Process, status, critique. *Journal of Business Communication, 15*(1), 41–55.

Goodall, H. L., Jr. (2000). *Writing the new ethnography.* Walnut Creek: AltaMira.

Goodall, H. L., Jr. (2006). *A need to know: The clandestine history of a CIA family.* Walnut Creek: Left Coast.

Grimes, D., & Parker, P. (2009). Imagining organizational communication as a decolonizing project. In conversation with Broadfoot, Munshi, Mumby, and Stohl. *Management Communication Quarterly, 22*(3), 502–511.

Gustavsen, B. (2001). Theory and practice: The mediating discourse. In P. Reason & H. Bradbury (Eds.), *Handbook of action research: Participative inquiry and practice* (pp. 17–27). London, England: SAGE.

Hall, M. (2011). Constructions of leadership at the intersection of discourse, power, and culture. Jamaican managers' narratives of leading in a postcolonial cultural context. *Management Communication Quarterly, 25*(4), 612–643.

Harter, L. M. (2004). Masculinity(s), the agrarian frontier myth, and cooperative ways of organizing: Contradictions and tensions in the experience and enactment of democracy. *Journal of Applied Communication Research, 32*(2), 89–118.

Harter, L. M., Dutta, M. J., & Cole, C. (2009). *Communicating for social impact: Engaging communication theory, research, and pedagogy.* Cresskill, NJ: Hampton Press.

Harter, L. M., Leeman, M., Norander, S., Young, S., & Rawlins, W. K. (2008). The intermingling of aesthetic and instrumental rationalities in a collaborative art studio for individuals with developmental disabilities. *Management Communication Quarterly, 21*(4), 423–453.

Hatchuel, A., & David, A. (2008). Collaborating for management research: From action research to intervention research in management. In A. Shani, S. Mohrman, W. Pasmore, B. Stymne, & N. Adler (Eds.), Handbook of collaborative management research. (pp. 143–163). Thousand Oaks, CA: SAGE.

Heath, R. G. (2007). Rethinking community collaboration through a dialogic lens: Creativity, democracy, and diversity in community organizing. *Management Communication Quarterly, 21*(2), 145–171.

Heath, R. G. (2010). The community collaboration stakeholder project. *Communication Teacher, 24*(4), 215–220.

Heath, R. G., & Frey, L. R. (2004). Ideal collaboration: A conceptual framework of community collaboration. In P. Kalbfleisch (Ed.), *Communication yearbook* (vol. 28, pp. 189–231). Mahwah, NJ: Lawrence Erlbaum.

Holmstrand, L., Harnsten, G., & Lowstedt, J. (2008). The research circle approach: A democratic form for collaborative research in organizations. In A. B. (Rami) Shani, S. A. Mohrman, W. A. Pasmore, B. Stymne, & N. Adler (Eds.), *Handbook of collaborative management research* (pp. 183–200). Thousand Oaks, CA: SAGE.

Jablin, F. M. (1987). Organizational entry, assimilation, and exit. In F. M. Jablin, L. L. Putnam, K. H. Roberts, & L. W. Porter (Eds.), *Handbook of organizational communication: An interdisciplinary perspective* (pp. 679–740). Newbury Park, CA: SAGE.

Jablin, F. M. (2001). Organizational entry, assimilation, and disengagement/exit. In F. M. Jablin & L. L. Putnam (Eds.), *The new handbook of organizational communication: Advances in theory, research, and methods* (pp. 732–818), Thousand Oaks, CA: SAGE.

Jovanovic, S. (2008). Community as ethical expression: How discourse shapes a vision of hope. *Bridges: An Interdisciplinary Journal of Theology, Philosophy, History, and Sciences, 15*(1/2), 135–157.

Jovanovic, S., Steger, C., Symonds, S., & Nelson, D. (2007). Promoting deliberative democracy through dialogue: Communication contributions to a grassroots movement for truth, justice, and reconciliation. In L. R. Frey & K. M. Carragee (Eds.), *Communication activism* (vol. 1, pp. 53–94). Cresskill, NJ: Hampton.

Lewis, L. K. (2011). *Organizational change: Creating change through strategic communication.* Chichester, UK: Wiley-Blackwell.

Lipshitz, R., Popper, M., & Friedman, V. J. (2002). A multifacet model of organizational learning. *Journal of Applied Behavioral Science, 38*(1), 78–98.

Lyman, R. L. (1915). The forum as an educative agency. *The Quarterly Journal of Speech, 1*(1), 1–8.

Martin, S. (2010). Co-production of social research: Strategies for engaged scholarship. *Public Money & Management, 30*(4), 211–218.

McAnany, E. G. (2012). *Saving the world: A brief history of communication for development and social change.* Urbana: University of Illinois Press.

Mirvis, P. H. (2008). Academic-practitioner learning forums: A new model for interorganizational research. In A. B. (Rami) Shani, S. A. Mohrman, W. A., Pasmore, B. N. Stymne, & Adler, N. (Eds.), *Handbook of collaborative management research* (pp. 201–224). Thousand Oaks, CA: SAGE.

Mohrman, S. A., Gibson, C. B., & Mohrman, A. M., Jr. (2001). Doing research that is useful to practice: A model and empirical exploration. *Academy of Management Journal, 44*(2), 357–376.

Mohrman, S. A., Mohrman, A. M., Jr., Cohen, S. G., & Winby, S. (2008). The collaborative learning cycle: Advancing theory and building practical design frameworks through collaboration. In A. B. (Rami) Shani, S. A. Mohrman, W. A. Pasmore, B. Stymne, & N. Adler (Eds.), *Handbook of collaborative management research* (pp. 509–530). Thousand Oaks, CA: SAGE.

Mumby, D. K. (1987). The political function of narrative in organizations. *Communication Mono-graphs, 54*(2), 113–127.

Mumby, D. K. (1988). *Communication and power in organizations: Discourse, ideology, and domination.* Norwood, NJ: Ablex.

Mumby, D. K. (2001). Power and politics. In F. M. Jablin & L. L. Putnam (Ed.), *The new handbook of organizational communication: Advances in theory, research and methods.* (pp. 585–623). Thousand Oaks, CA: SAGE.

Norander, S., & Harter, L. M. (2012). Reflexivity in practice: Challenges and potentials of transnational organizing. *Management Communication Quarterly, 26*(1), 74–105.

Novak, D. K., & Harter, L. M. (2008). Flipping the scripts of poverty and panhandling: Organizing democracy by creating connections. *Journal of Applied Communication Research, 36*(4), 391–414.

O'Meara, K. A. (2005). Encouraging multiple forms of scholarship in faculty reward systems: Does it make a difference? *Research in Higher Education, 46*(5), 479–510.

Parker, P. S., Oceguera, E., & Sanchez, J. (2011). Intersecting differences: Organizing [ourselves] for social justice research with people in vulnerable communities. In D. K. Mumby (Ed.), *Reframing difference in organizational communication studies: Research, pedagogy, practice* (pp. 219–242). Thousand Oaks, CA: SAGE.

Pearce, K. A. (2002). *Making better social worlds: Engaging in and facilitating dialogic communication.* Redwood City, CA: Pearce Associates.

Pearce, K. A., & Pearce, W. B. (2001). The public dialogue consortium's school-wide dialogue process: A communication approach to develop citizenship skills and enhance school climate. *Communication Theory, 11*(1), 105–123.

Pearce, K. A., Spano, S., & Pearce, W. B. (2009). The multiple faces of the Public Dialogue Consortium. In L. R. Frey & K. N. Cissna (Eds.), *Routledge handbook of applied communication research* (pp. 611–632). New York, NY: Routledge.

Petronio, S. (1999). Translating scholarship into practice: An alternative metaphor. *Journal of Applied Communication Research, 27*(2), 87–91.

Prasad, A. (Ed.). (2003). *Postcolonial theory and organizational analysis.* New York, NY: Palgrave MacMillan.

Putnam, L. L. (2009). *The multiple faces of engaged scholarship.* Paper presented at the 7th Aspen Conference on Engaged Communication Scholarship Keynote Speech, Aspen, CO.

Reason, P., & Bradbury, H. (2008). *The SAGE handbook of action research: Participative inquiry and practice* (2nd ed.). Los Angeles, CA: SAGE.

Redding, W. C. (1985). Stumbling toward identity: The emergence of organizational communication as a field of study. In R. D. McPhee & P. K. Tompkins (Eds.), *Organizational communication: Traditional themes and new direction* (pp. 15–54). Beverly Hills, CA: SAGE.

Ritchie, L. (2007). The organizational consultant as activist. In L. R. Frey & K. M. Carragee (Eds.), *Communication activism* (vol. 1, pp. 411–440). Cresskill, NJ: Hampton Press.

Rogers, E. (2003). *Diffusion of innovations* (5th ed.). New York, NY: Free Press of Glencoe.

Said, E. W. (1994). *Representations of the intellectual: The 1993 Reith Lectures.* London, England: Vintage.

Sanders, E. B. N., & Stappers, P. J. (2008). Co-creation and the new landscapes of design. *CoDesign, 4*(1), 5–18.

Schein, E. H. (1999). *Process consultation revisited: Building the helping relationship.* Reading, MA: Addison-Wesley.

Schein, E. H. (2008). Clinical inquiry/research. In P. Reason & H. Bradbury (Eds.), *The SAGE handbook of action research: Participative inquiry and practice* (pp. 266–279). Thousand Oaks, CA: SAGE.

Scott, C. R., Shaw, S. P., Timmerman, C. E., Frank, V., & Quinn, L. (1999). Using communication audits to teach organizational communication to students and employees. *Business Communication Quarterly, 62*(4), 53–70.

Seeger, M. (2009). Does communication research make a difference? Reconsidering the impact of our work. *Communication Monographs, 76*(1), 12–19.

Seibold, D. R. (2008). Applied communication research. In W. Donsbach (Ed.), *The international encyclopedia of communication* (pp. 189–194). Malden, MA: Wiley Blackwell.

Seibold, D. R., Lemus, D. R., Ballard, D. I., & Myers, K. K. (2009). Organizational communication and applied communication research. In L. R. Frey & K. N. Cissna (Eds.), *Routledge handbook of applied communication research* (pp. 331–354). New York, NY: Routledge.

Servaes, J., Jacobson, T. L., & White, S. A. (Eds.). (1996). *Participatory communication for social change.* New Delhi, India: SAGE.

Shome, R. (1996). Postcolonial interventions into the rhetorical cannon: An "other" view. *Communication Theory, 6*(1), 40–59.

Silverman, D. (2006). *Interpreting qualitative data: Methods for analyzing talk, text, and interaction* (3rd ed.). London, England: SAGE.

Simpson, J. L., & Seibold, D. R. (2008). Practical engagements and co-created research. *Journal of Applied Communication Research, 36*(3), 266–280.

Simpson, J. L., & Shockley-Zalabak, P. (Eds.). (2005). *Engaging communication, transforming organizations: Scholarship of engagement in action.* Cresskill, NJ: Hampton Press.

Singh, G., Hawkins, L., & Whymark, G. (2009). Collaborative knowledge building process: An activity theory analysis. *The Journal of Information and Knowledge Management Systems, 39*(3), 223–241.

Singhal, A., Harter, L. M., Chitnis, K., & Sharma, D. (2007). Participatory photography as theory, method and praxis: Analyzing an entertainment-education project in India. *Critical Arts, 21*(1), 212–227.

Somerville, M. M., & Nino, M. (2007). Collaborative co-design: A user-centric approach for advancement of organizational learning. *Performance Measurement and Metrics, 8*(2), 180–188.

Stanton, T. K. (2008). Opportunities and challenges for civic engagement at research universities. *Education, Citizenship and Social Justice, 3*(1), 19–42.

Stebbins, M. W., & Shani, A. B. (Rami). (2009). Clinical inquiry and reflective design in a secrecy-based organization. *Journal of Applied Behavioral Science, 45*(1), 59–89.

Steen, M., Manschot, M., & De Koning, N. (2011). Benefits of co-design in service design projects. *International Journal of Design, 5*(2), 53–60.

Stohl, C., & Cheney, G. (2001). Participatory processes/paradoxical practices: Communication and the dilemmas of organizational democracy. *Management Communication Quarterly, 14*(3), 349–407.

Stohl, C., & Redding, W. C. (1987). Messages and message exchange processes. In F. M. Jablin, L. L. Putnam, K. H. Roberts, & L. W. Porter (Eds.), *Handbook of organizational communication* (pp. 451–502). Newbury Park, CA: SAGE.

Sukandar, R., Agustiana, E., & Hale, C. L. (2009). Researching post-violent conflict: The emotional challenges faced by researchers concerned with social change and community building. In L. M. Harter, M. J. Dutta, & C. Cole (Eds.), *Communicating for social impact engaging communication theory, research, and pedagogy.* Cresskill, NJ: Hampton Press.

Susskind, A. M., Schwartz, D. F., Richards, W. D., & Johnson, J. D. (2005). Evolution and diffusion of the Michigan State University tradition of organizational communication network research. *Communication Studies, 56*(4), 387–418.

Tompkins, P. K. (1993). *Organizational communication imperatives: Lessons of the space program.* New York, NY: Oxford University Press.

Tompkins, P. K., & Cheney, G. (1985). Communication and unobtrusive control in contemporary organizations. In R. D. McPhee & P. K. Tompkins (Eds.), *Organization communication: Traditional themes and new directions* (pp. 179–210). Beverly Hills, CA: SAGE.

Tompkins, P. K., & Tompkins, E. V. (2004). *Apollo, Challenger, Columbia: The decline of the space program: A study in organizational communication.* New York, NY: Oxford University Press.

Tompkins, P. K., & Wanca-Thibault, M. (2001). Organizational communication: Preludes and prospects. In F. M. Jablin & L. L. Putnam (Eds.), *The new handbook of organizational communication: Advances in theory, research, and methods* (pp. xvii–xxxi). Thousand Oaks, CA: SAGE.

Tracy, K. (2010). *Challenges of ordinary democracy: A case study in deliberation and dissent.* University Park: Pennsylvania State University Press.

Tracy, K., & Durfy, M. (2007). Speaking out in public: Citizen participation in contentious school board meetings. *Discourse and Communication, 1*(2), 223–249.

Tracy, K., & Tracy, S. J. (1998). Rudeness at 911: Reconceptualizing face and face attack. *Human Communication Research, 25*(2), 225–251.

Trist, E., & Murray, H. (Eds.). (1993). *The social engagement of social science: Vol. 1. The socio-technical perspective.* Philadelphia: University of Pennsylvania Press.

Trujillo, N. (2004). *In search of Naunny's grave: Age, class, gender, and ethnicity in an American family.* Walnut Creek, CA: AltaMira.

Van de Ven, A. H. (2007). *Engaged scholarship: A guide for organizational and social research.* New York, NY: Oxford University Press.

Van de Ven, A. H., & Johnson, P. E. (2006). Knowledge for theory and practice. *Academy of Management Review, 31*(4), 802–821.

Vande Berg, L., & Trujillo, N. (2008). *Cancer and death: A love story in two voices.* Cresskill, NJ: Hampton Press.

Wasserman, I. C., & Kram, K. E. (2009). Enacting the scholar-practitioner role: An exploration of narratives. *Journal of Applied Behavioral Science, 45*(1), 12–38.

Weaver, K. C. (2007). Reinventing the public intellectual through communication dialogue civic capacity building. *Management Communication Quarterly, 21*(1), 92–104.

Weick, K. E. (1995). *Sensemaking in organizations.* Thousand Oaks, CA: SAGE.

Weick, K. E., & Sutcliffe, K. M. (2001). *Managing the unexpected: Assuring high performance in an age of complexity.* San Francisco, CA: Jossey-Bass.

Yukawa, J. (2006). Co-reflection in online learning: Collaborative critical thinking as narrative. *Computer-Supported Collaborative Learning, 1*(2), 203–228.

Ziegler, J. A. (2007). The story behind an organizational list: A genealogy of wildland firefighters' 10 standard fire orders. *Communication Monographs, 74*(4), 415–442.

Zoller, H. (2009). Narratives of corporate change: Environmental health activism, stakeholder dialogue, and regulatory action. In L. M. Harter, M. J. Dutta, & C. Cole (Eds.), *Communicating for social impact: Engaging communication theory, research, and pedagogy.* Cresskill, NJ: Hampton Press.

SECTION VI

Communication and the Organization-Society Relationship

Janet Fulk

Early conceptions of organizations and of organizational communication largely extracted the organization from the larger social context (Barnard, 1938; March & Simon, 1958), preferring instead to focus on internal processes and communication structures. Research in this tradition examined issues such as grapevine, rumors, or distortion of communication and efficient communication within the bounded organization. As contingency theories of organizational design took hold in the management field in the 1960s, organizational communication in parallel focused on information processing across organizational borders and conceptualized design as ideally focused on minimizing communication costs internally but also on effectively linking with external constituencies (Galbraith, 1973; Thompson, 1967). In those early days, organizational theory and organizational communication were often intertwined. Indeed, the first *Handbook of Organizational Communication* was edited by two communication scholars, Linda Putnam and Fred Jablin, and two organization theory scholars, Karlene Roberts and Lyman Porter; the chapters included a mix of authors from both disciplines.

Over time, scholars such as the late Fred Jablin recast the management models to focus on communication processes. For example, leadership was recast to highlight the communicative nature of supervisor-subordinate interaction (Jablin, 1979), and socialization was theorized as essentially a communication process (Jablin, 1984). Other scholars highlighted the uniquely communicative aspects of organizations that had long been understudied by organizational scholars (e.g., Farace, Monge, & Russell, 1977; Putnam & Pacanowsky, 1983). Organizational communication scholarship has not only developed a separate identity apart from organization theory but has also conceptualized richer and more complex models of the communicative aspects of how organizations interact with the environments in which they are embedded. Yet despite the increasing distinctiveness of organizational communication scholarship, the synergy between the two disciplines remains today. Both fields grapple with the major changes and challenges that accompany the realization that organizational processes are intricately linked to the societal context in which they are embedded.

Looking back today from our very complex and globally organized world, it may seem difficult to imagine that anyone ever envisioned organizational communication as *in* the organization and largely uninfluenced by the broader environment and society. Yet time moves on, and as Stohl and Ganesh so well document, the world itself has changed dramatically since those early days. Organizational communication scholars have been at the forefront of understanding how those changes are reflected in discourse, processes, and relationships. In this section of the *Handbook,* we see just how much the concern with global society has permeated thinking about organizational communication.

The chapters offer a number of prisms on the organization-society relationship. In combination, they are by no means exhaustive; rather each illustrates the many points of communicative intersection between organizations and global society. Despite this diversity of content, two themes underlie all four chapters. One theme is the source and function of individual and organizational identity in the global society. Each chapter in some way addresses the new complexities for the core concept of identity as it is practiced in global society. A second theme is the plurality of sometimes contrasting conceptualizations of the organization-society relationship. These chapters address questions such as the following: What is the boundary between organization and society? What are an organization's obligations to society given these boundaries? What new forms of organization are made possible as organizations envision a new relation to society? How do organizations manage conflicting expectations about the organization-society relationship that emanate from different stakeholders? Although these two themes are not in themselves comprehensive, they do offer points of intersection across the chapters and thus serve as reference points in this introductory chapter. Since the two themes are related, I discuss them together in the paragraphs that follow.

Cheney, Christensen, and Dailey (Chapter 28) offer a foundation as they take us on a tour through the historical development of identity constructs and how identity shapes and is shaped by internal and external communication. Cheney et al. provide evidence of five changes in the ways communication scholars imagine identity and identification. First, identity can no longer be seen as *in* an organization. In lieu of the container metaphor, organizations are seen as porous in that identity narratives from the broader social context are inextricably intertwined with organizational identity construction. Second, contemporary employment takes a wide variety of different forms other than the traditional full-time employed worker. Temporary employment, part-time work, volunteer work, and virtual organizations are on the rise, raising interesting questions about just who *is* a member of an organization and even whether the concept of *member* as traditionally envisioned is appropriate in the current social and economic context. Third, as relationships are increasingly mediated by technologies, the technologies become implicated in the construction and communication of identity. The increased rise of technology-supported global networks challenges organizational communication scholars to understand how people develop identities in global virtual networks. Fourth, scholars are increasingly recognizing the "dark side" of identification and the potential for concertive control. Fifth, scholarship is needed to address the complex interplay of material and symbolic aspects of work in relation to creation and expression of identity.

These five changes offer many points of connection with the other chapters. One is the role of corporate social responsibility (CSR) in the strategies and discourses of organizations today. In their conclusion, Cheney et al. note that the process of constructing and communicating messages for external audiences "may help organizations explore the boundaries of their identities and the ideal roles they hope to play in the world" (p. 703). The articulation of organizational aspirations, for example, in the area of corporate social responsibility, may be essential for stimulating new insight and moving the organization toward better standards and practices (Christensen, Morsing, & Thyssen, 2011). This perspective connects to the chapter by May and Roper (Chapter 31), who make a similar argument in that although

> CSR initiatives are directed at external stakeholders . . . A range of discussions and decisions within the organization regarding, for example, CSR strategy and implementation, precede the external communication of a company's CSR activities . . . [and thus] the most interesting questions may be less related to differentiating between the types of communication and more to understanding the organizational processes of integrating internal and external communication to produce a seemingly coherent organizational identity. (p. 782)

Indeed, the increased role of CSR in organizations today is a core example of the interpenetration of the organizational and the societal. In their tour of approaches to CSR, May and Roper illustrate the contested theoretical terrain regarding organizations' appropriate relationship to society. *Shareholder value theory* argues that the organization's primary responsibility is to benefit financial shareholders. *Corporate social performance theory* recognizes the role of society in granting legitimacy and power to organizations and argues that part of this bargain is the need for the organization to uphold societal values. *Corporate citizenship theory* sees organizations as citizens of their communities in much the same way as individuals are citizens, and with citizenship comes the obligation to proactively act in the interests of society, even without evidence of a positive effect of such activities on the bottom line. *Stakeholder theory* argues that organizations should attend to the multiple and conflicting interests of a wide variety of stakeholders beyond financial shareholders.

These different theories generate different discourses about CSR that contain implicit assumptions about what is the right interconnection between organizational and societal realms. May and Roper conceptualize four discourse-based approaches. *Normative* research is premised on the view of organizations as objective entities that researchers can describe and whose actions they can predict and, in some cases, control. CSR, in this view, is an objectively identifiable program that organizations create to maintain competitive advantage in the global marketplace; research examines how communication is instrumental in crafting communications for various CSR stakeholders. *Interpretative* logic assumes that organizations are social constructions created and maintained by communication practices. Research in this tradition to date has largely examined managers' perceptions of CSR initiatives. *Critical* perspectives see organizations as locations for negotiating conflicting interests through the exercise of power, benefitting some groups over others. Research focuses on how corporate discourses that appear to benefit the social instead most benefit the economic interests of organizations. *Dialogic* perspectives focus on power issues in micro behaviors and highlight the different significations attached to any particular CSR concept.

These conflicting discourses are also reflected in Ganesh and Stohl's (Chapter 30) distinction of three possible ways to conceive of the relationship between organizations and communities. The first is that organizations are outsiders to the rest of society. This reflects and is consistent with much of the research in the normative and, to some degree, the critical perspective on CSR. As outsiders, organizations are seen to develop relationships with various parts of society. These relationships can take many forms, such as service provision, partnership, or advocacy. From an identity perspective, organizational identification is separate from identification with other aspects of society. The second type of relationship between organization and society is when the organization is conceptualized as constituting the community and exists for the benefit of the members of the community, similar to what Blau and Scott (1962) labeled *mutual benefit associations*. Examples of this type include professional associations, trade associations, and labor unions. Identity is a particularly important source of cohesion in such organizations and, as Cheney et al. note in Chapter 28, this identity can be an important counterpoint to identification in an employment situation, particularly when professional and organizational expectations and discourses conflict. This type of organization focuses less on benefitting society as a whole and more on benefitting its own members' professional and/or business interests. Ganesh and Stohl's third conceptualization of the relationship between organizations and communities is the organization as inside a larger collective that constitutes a community. Federated forms such as collectives of social justice groups exemplify this relationship. As Ganesh and Stohl note, identity may be anchored more in the larger goals of the set of organizations than in any particular organization. For example, individual identity as "global social justice activist" may transcend that of identity as a participant in the Human Rights Watch organization.

Just as Ganesh and Stohl's "Community Organizing, Social Movements, and Collective Action" (Chapter 30) describes alternative conceptualizations of the relationship between organizations and communities, Stohl and Ganesh's treatise on "Generating Globalization" (Chapter 29) provides a valuable historical lens on how perspectives of organization-society relationships evolved with the increasing globalization of political, economic, and social life. Their historical framework identifies three stages in the development of models of globalization in organizational communication. *First-generation* scholarship treated formal organizations as the locus of internationalization and the members of those organizations as the agents of internationalization. This generation challenged the acontextual view presented by classic scholars but treated global society as something "out there" to be assessed and harnessed by organizations. When Chester Barnard was writing, very few organizations had an international presence, much less the wide-ranging global systems that exist today. Over time, with developments in communication and transportation technologies, organizations developed enough interest to add *international* units to their organization charts. First-generation scholars studied internationalization processes in organizational communication, imagining a society divided into different cultures, about which organizations needed to be aware. Such scholarship was highly influential in identifying the Western bias in much organizational communication theory and research.

As organizations stopped walling off these expanded markets in separate international divisions and instead developed networked global structures (Monge, 1995), *second-generation* scholars developed sophisticated theories of the globally networked organization and even began to question the preeminence of the nation-state (e.g., Castells, 1998; Golden, 1993; Held, McGrew, Goldblatt, & Perraton, 1999). A network logic dominated in this age of interconnectedness, and the locus of influence could be any node in the network, not just the formal organization. Scholars focused on partnerships, interorganizational relationships, and linked clusters of organizations as sites of competition and cooperation. Much more than cultural differences were involved in the second-generation network view. Globalization could not be managed by an international division; it had to be addressed through all aspects of the organizational communication enterprise through structures and processes that reflected the interconnected nature of the all aspects of organizational life. Scholars studied links and partnerships as they exploded as a normative way to do business for all kinds of organizations—for-profit, nonprofit, and governmental.

Even as the significant reconceptualizations of the second generation were taking a significant hold, new ideas were bubbling to the surface. Were formal organizations losing their power as nodes in global networks? Could alternatives exist alongside formal organizations as a way to accomplish societal goals? *Third-generation* scholarship is only just emerging, and it is unclear how deeply it permeates the many different sectors of society. But the emerging picture is one that Chester Barnard may not even have imagined possible. According to Stohl and Ganesh, globalization has become taken for granted, a ubiquitous force that organizations consider a normal part of business. They also argue that civil society is increasingly prominent in globalization processes. Communication research is increasingly focusing on collective action and entrepreneurial activities outside the corporate realm. One trend they note is decreased need for formal organization of collective actions. Developments in technologies for connectivity have enhanced capabilities for communicating and organizing outside the bounds of formal structures. Stohl and Ganesh conclude,

> Boundaries between public and private are fuzzy and easily traversed, individual affiliations wax and wane, membership is relative and context dependent, and individuals come together and work apart in ways that transcend, complement, replace, and/or support organizational structures. This transformation applies to all forms of contemporary organizing, whether it be in the government, corporate, or civil sector. (p. 734)

The argument is bold in the context of large, powerful multinational firms that control significant parts of the global economy, but the premise is intriguing and suggests a very fruitful direction for organizational communication research. In a future with the transformations that Stohl and Ganesh envision, what will happen to organizational identification?

Cheney et al. (Chapter 28) also point to the changing meanings of organizational identity in the globalizing world. They note that,

> studies of reformulations of national identities have enormous implications for positioning corporate identities and vice versa. . . . A great deal remains to be explored regarding how organizational identities and identifications connect "upward" to broader institutional and cultural formations (as called for by Carlone & Taylor, 1998). (p. 710)

Like Cheney et al., Stohl and Ganesh point to new forms of organizing that challenge the context of traditional industrial organization as the site and locus of identity construction and reconstruction. They point to two relevant developments. The first is the radical growth in peer production (e.g., Benkler, 2006; Weber, 2010) that relies on distributed but networked nonmarket mechanisms. The second is entrepreneurial forms that are neither independent nor organizationally contracted employment, including Neff's (2012) concept of venture labor and Norander and Harter's (2012) study of a type of communicative entrepreneurialism focused on creating spaces in individual rather than institutional terms. Stohl and Ganesh argue that identities in these new forms take on more individual and personal elements compared to traditional forms and can disrupt identity performance not just in individual organizations but in entire industries as well.

In addition to themes regarding identity and the conflicting views of the organization-society relationship, a final theme across these chapters is interdisciplinarity. Even as organizational communication is striving to become a discipline in its own right, each of these chapters acknowledges its connection with other disciplines. Just as organizations can no longer wall off the global context, so our discipline cannot extract itself from the larger social and humanistic theories and discourses on organizations and society. Each of these chapters adeptly highlights communication scholarship while acknowledging roots, branches, and shooters to the larger academic enterprise that has been grappling with how to theorize, study, and practice the relationship between organizations and society. The story is far from over, and these chapters highlight changes and exciting new directions that early organizational theorists could never have imagined. Our challenge is to think broadly and creatively to conceptualize this shifting, fascinating landscape.

References

Barnard, C. (1938). *The functions of the executive.* Cambridge, MA: Harvard University Press.

Benkler, Y. (2006). *The wealth of networks: How social production transforms markets and freedom.* New Haven, CT: Yale University Press.

Blau, P. M., & Scott, W. R. (1962). *Formal organizations.* San Francisco, CA: Chandler.

Carlone, D., & Taylor, B. (1998). Organizational communication and cultural studies: A review essay. *Communication Theory, 8*(3), 337–367.

Castells, M. (1998). *The rise of the network society.* Malden, MA: Blackwell.

Christensen, L. T., Morsing, M., & Thyssen, O. (2011). The polyphony of corporate social responsibility: Deconstructing accountability and transparency in the context of identity and hypocrisy. In G. Cheney, S. May, & D. Munshi (Eds.), *Handbook of communication ethics* (pp. 457–474). New York, NY: Routledge.

Farace, R. V., Monge, P. R., & Russell, H. M. (1977). *Communicating and organizing.* Reading, MA: Addison-Wesley.

Galbraith, J. R. (1973). *Designing complex organizations.* Reading, MA: Addison-Wesley.

Golden, J. (1993, Summer). Economics and national strategy: Convergence, global networks, and cooperative competition. *The Washington Quarterly, 16*(3), 91–113.

Held, D., McGrew, A., Goldblatt, D., & Perraton, J. (1999). *Global transformations: Politics, economics, and culture.* Stanford, CA: Stanford University Press.

Jablin, F. M. (1979). Superior-subordinate communication: The state of the art. *Psychological Bulletin, 86*(6), 1201–1222. doi: 10.1037/0033-2909.86.6.1201

Jablin, F. M. (1984). Organizational entry, assimilation, and exit. In F. M. Jablin, L. L. Putnam, K. H. Roberts, & L. W. Porter (Eds.), *Handbook of organizational communication: An interdisciplinary perspective* (pp. 679–740). Beverly Hills, CA: SAGE.

March, J. G., & Simon, H. A. (1958). *Organizations.* New York, NY: Wiley.

Monge, P. (1995). Global network organizations. In R. Cesaria & P. Shockley-Zalabak (Eds.), *Organization means communication: Making the organizational communication concept relevant to practice* (pp. 135–151). Rome, Italy: Servizio Italiano Pubblicazioni Internationali Srl.

Neff, G. (2012). *Venture labor: Work and the burden of risk in innovative industries.* Cambridge, MA: Cambridge University Press.

Norander, S., & Harter, L. (2012). Organizing reflexivity in practice: Challenges and potentials of transnational organizing. *Management Communication Quarterly, 26*(1), 74–105.

Putnam, L. L., & Pacanowsky, M. E. (Eds.). (1983). *Communication and organization: An interpretive approach.* Beverly Hills, CA: SAGE.

Thompson, J. D. (1967). *Organizations in action.* New York, NY: McGraw-Hill.

Weber, M. (2010). *Media reinvented: The transformation of news in a networked society.* (Doctoral dissertation). University of Southern California, Los Angeles, CA.

CHAPTER 28

Communicating Identity and Identification In and Around Organizations[1]

George Cheney, Lars Thøger Christensen, and Stephanie L. Dailey

Introduction: The Interwoven Histories of Organizational Identity and Identification

Any reasonably comprehensive discussion of identity, identification, and organizational communication must consider at once (1) the grounds for and resources of identity construction and transformation in contemporary global society; (2) the articulation and promotion of corporate identities by institutions and organizations of all sorts; and (3) the individual linkages to and bonds with organizations, industries, professions, brands, and other features.

Theoretically, as well as practically, identity is a given for units from biological cells to international systems, and its establishment and maintenance involves a variety of forms and levels of communication. There is, in other words, a certain universal dimension to identity in the sense that it is a drive that characterizes all living systems (Morin, 1986; see also Luhmann, 1990). Yet it is impossible to appreciate contemporary manifestations of organizational identity and identification without an understanding of their historical and cultural contexts.

The *explicit* focus on identity, which is one of the defining preoccupations of the contemporary industrialized world, is a fairly recent phenomenon. For tribal or "traditional" societies, individual identity was not subject to constant repetition, performance, and negotiation (see Durkheim, 1933). Rather it was relatively fixed, ascribed by traditions and practices largely beyond the influence of the individual person. The rise of modernity, however, questioned such traditional practices and authorities and gradually eroded the institutions through which people had previously defined their roles and positions in society (Mongin, 1982; Nisbet, 1970). Consequently, identity emerged as a salient *issue*, pursued and contested at many different levels. For most large organizations today, identity is not only a key point of reference but also a practical building block for other objectives and projects; that is, organizations use their established identity programs and identity messages within networks of activities and projects, including mission statements, articulations of values and ethics, and marketing materials. Most organizational activities, in other words, are pervaded by identity concerns (Haslam, Postmes, & Ellemers, 2003).

Considering identity as a defining issue of the modern world, we can look to its changing treatments in key discourses. With its *uniqueness* emphasis ("I am myself distinct from you") in contrast to a stress on *sameness* ("I share identity with you"), the issue of identity emerged in the European Renaissance and then attained full expression in Enlightenment discourses and beyond (compare Foucault, 1984; Mackenzie, 1978). By the early 1800s, identity-as-possession-of-a-unique-self had made its way audibly into political debates in Britain and the United States. In his travels around the United States in the 1830s and 1840s, de Toqueville (1847) observed a stress on individuality and at the same time the formation of a distinctive national identity. A century later, Lasswell (1935) keenly observed parallels and linkages between national and cultural expressions and individual needs and desires for self-definition and security (cf. Tracy & Trethewey, 2005). Lasswell's analysis laid the foundation for a more communication-centered treatment of identity for organizations and institutions, especially in terms of how organizations answer questions about why they do things, albeit in often circular ways: "This action is right because of who we are [fill in the characteristics and values]."

Organizational identity formations and, ultimately, obsessions with identity grew up together in modern industrialized societies (Foucault, 1984). During the last 150 years especially, identity has become a focused and professionalized enterprise, adopted by organizations in all sectors through the successive development of advertising, public relations, and marketing. And, with applications from personal branding to international social movement identification, these disciplines have exerted a growing influence on individual identities and self-perceptions. Although the field of organizational communication has been rather slow in acknowledging the role external communication practices might play in shaping the identification of individuals with organizations (Cheney, 1983; Cheney & Christensen, 2001), the questions of organizational identity and membership identification have, in practice, been treated as one issue. As documented by Marchand (1998), many public relations campaigns from the early 20th century—often designed to improve public sentiments toward capitalist enterprises—were directed not only to external audiences but also to the corporations themselves and their members. By the 1940s, organizations often combined internal and external communication concerns in attempts to build public respectability while demonstrating what Marchand (1998, p. 15) calls a "compassionate concern" for their employees.

Despite persistent and increasingly professionalized attempts to invest individuals in various organizational resources of identity (compare Kuhn & McPartland, 1954; Whyte, 1956), this contextual backdrop has been disregarded in a number of ways since the mid-1980s due to the predominantly social-psychological treatments of individual identity and organizational identification. We argue that identity and identification cannot be divorced from historical and cultural contexts, including such macro trends as the saturation of the communication universe with itself (e.g., Baudrillard, 1988), the rupture in the social contract between many organizations and their members, and the global economic crisis. Although in-depth commentary on such trends is beyond the scope of this essay, we emphasize the necessary interplay between operationalizations of individual identifications with organizations, organizational formulations of identity, and the larger social landscape for identity formulation in the contemporary world.

Notably, one of the great advances in identity-related research in recent years has been the coalescence of disciplines around key questions, such as comparative cross-cultural assessments of identity (e.g., Allen, 2011; Hofstede, 1980; Munshi, 2006), along with the treatment of identity at multiple levels of society (e.g., Silva & Sias, 2010), including national, ethnic, linguistic, professional, organizational, and group levels (see Ashcraft, 2007). Organizational identity and identification as foci of studies in organizational communication and allied areas can now benefit from this theoretical richness, bringing together the studies of culture and identity in important ways (Kenny, Whittle, & Willmott, 2011).

In the remainder of this essay, we pursue three goals: (1) to revisit the ontology and epistemology of organizational identity and identification, (2) to organize recent research in the area according to key theoretical-practical themes, and (3) to suggest some future avenues of investigation.

The Ontology and Epistemology of Organizational Identity and Identification

In spite of decades of research—and although identity and identification play a central role in the modern experience—both terms are fraught with ambiguity (e.g., Kenny et al., 2011). The notion of identification, for example, assumes the existence of a more or less stable and discernible entity or identity. Since such existence is precarious and open to multiple interpretations, the ontological grounds for identification are uncertain and fragile. This section develops the definitional complexities of identity at the aggregate organizational level, followed by an account of research on individual-organizational bonds and the ways they shape identification and professional identities.

The Nature of Organizational Identity

A recurrent question in the literature on organizational identity centers on *ontological status*: that is, what is the reality or nature of an organization's identity, presuming an organization has one or ought to have one? Most answers to this question tend toward seeing organizational identity as *either* an essential or inherent property of an organization *or* seeing it as a social construction. Much talk about organizational identity, however, draws on both perspectives. This is clearly the case in managerially oriented writings where descriptions of organizational identity as *essence and continuity* often coexist with discussions of identity as managerial *projects of communication* (e.g., Kunde, 2000; Olins, 1989). A similar ambiguity, however, is found in the scholarly literature that frequently talks about organizational identity as something intrinsic, solid, and reliable that sets it apart from its surroundings while at the same time assuming that identities can be planned, shaped, and manufactured (e.g., van Riel & Balmer, 1997).

With their now-classical understanding of organizational identity as the central, distinct, and enduring dimensions of an organization, Albert and Whetten (1985) provide a theoretical backup to the largely essentialist perspective on organizational identity. They refer to *identity* as the inviolable core of an organization that shapes its choices and defines its integrity. This identity becomes a focal point in the organization's official communications, just as it is a key referent for individual members and other stakeholders (e.g., Balmer, 1995).

By contrast, Ashforth and Mael regard organizational identity as *changeable*. In line with the work of Nietzsche (1954), who conceived of identities as ongoing stories, Ashforth and Mael (1996) define organizational *identity* as "unfolding and stylized narratives about the 'soul' or essence of the organization" (p. 21). From this perspective, organizations enact their identities through the stories they tell, directly or indirectly, about themselves, their past, their ambitions, and their perceptions of the environment.

Scholars of communication as well as organizational studies are gradually assuming a more complex understanding of identity, which sees both qualified objectivity and intersubjectivity as playing important roles in the epistemology of individual-organizational relationships. Further, these relationships are seen in explicitly processual terms through the application of *narrativity*, where organizational identities are seen as volatile social constructions based in large part on the interpretive capabilities and preferences of their audiences (Christensen & Askegaard, 2001).

On the one hand, identity is permeated by otherness as well as shaped by narratives and interactions. According to Dunne (1996) and Rasmussen (1996), identity is *a storied self*, a self that unfolds in the stories that we tell ourselves and in the accounts we provide to others about our past and present behavior. *Narrativity*, in other words, is essential in the development and maintenance of identity. Narratives link the past with the future and provide a sense of continuity to our self-identity (see also, Ashforth & Mael, 1996; Browning & Morris, 2012). Important as the narrative-identity linkage is to understanding the deeply processual nature of identity formation and change, there has been relatively little longitudinal research on how stories told by individual members, leaders, and corporate voices are part and parcel of identity development in an organization (Grant, 2004). However, a recent ethnographic study shows how narratives from three interwoven levels (societal, organizational/family, and individual) come together to shape both individual and organizational identities (Watson & Watson, 2012).

On the other hand, organizational identities are often related to as immutable facts of life. In this sense, *identity* is usually counterposed to *image*, with the latter seen as a less stable or reliable projection but one that is nevertheless very important in public settings (e.g., Alvesson, 1990). This dialectical relationship is fortified in everyday as well as professional discourses, for example, about the need for organizations to come forth and express their *true selves*. The everyday focus on *real* identity reflects the experience of organizational audiences that organizations *have* identities with real effects and significance. As the neo-Weberian (Weber, 1978) position makes clear, organizational identities are *real* to the extent that people extend such cherished concepts to organizations; thus organizational identities become objects of study just as they are points of reference in everyday life. This is different, however, from asserting that we can discover the *true* identity of an organization. Facing identity as a relatively stable reference point in a constantly unfolding communication process inevitably reveals both the fluidity and solidity that preoccupies individuals and organizations (Cheney & Christensen, 2001; Chreim, 2005), fueling consultants' and others' efforts to name, grasp, and hold on to the organization's identity.

Often, when people talk about an organization's identity, they do not relate it to the organization as a whole but refer to specific organizational attributes that stand for the organization in question. In practice, an organization's identity corresponds to what is commonly used to *represent* the organization (Christensen & Askegaard, 2001). From a social psychological perspective, Haslam et al. (2003) refer to such representations as "stereotypic attributes . . . conferred upon [the organization] by those for whom the organization is relevant and meaningful" (p. 360). Such stereotypic attributes, although context dependent and thus potentially fluid, are widely shared and provide a basis for coordinated action, including organizational *identification*. The stereotypic attributes inform behavior and define individuals as members or nonmembers of a particular group or organization. Such complex understanding of organizational identity has only recently made its way into more processual notions of organizational identification.

The Individual-Organizational Bond

To date, research on organizational identification has been more influenced by psychological and motivation-centered perspectives than by any other tradition of research. This pattern makes sense from the focus on certain human needs and resources for identity as well as targets of attachment. Advancing what has become known as the *belongingness hypothesis*, Baumeister and Leary (1995) present a wide range of evidence to support the notion that "human beings have a pervasive drive to form and maintain at least a minimum quantity of lasting, positive, and significant interpersonal relationships" (p. 497). The authors, however, are not as concerned with explaining *how* individuals create and maintain such bonds; rather, they argue that the need to belong is a fundamental human motivation. While Baumeister and Leary discuss this psychological need in terms of interpersonal relationships, scholars—mainly those in organization studies and organizational psychology—have begun to apply this psychological perspective to the organizational context and to consider what it means for communication processes in organizations. In the context of this discussion, the stress on belonging highlights the *membership* or *solidarity* component of Patchen's (1970) formulation of identification, which considers *belongingness* to be a key underlying feature of organizational identification.

Other similar psychological characterizations of organizational identification (and relatedly, commitment) include the work of Mael and Ashforth (1992), who define *organizational identification* as the "*perception* of oneness with or belongingness to an organization" (p. 104, emphasis added). Likewise, Dutton, Dukerich, and Harquail (1994) describe identification as a "cognitive connection" (p. 239) between an individual and his or her organization. The concept of *dis*-identification or not identifying with an organization is also considered a "cognitive separation between one's identity and the organization's identity" (Elsbach & Bhattacharya, 2001, p. 393).

Since the early 20th century, theorists in psychology, sociology, political science, anthropology, and economics have approached identification as an *attachment* with an organization, exhibited through attitudinal or behavioral components. Freud's (1992) accounts of attachments at work are framed chiefly in terms of identification as a defense mechanism; thus, one might find transference of a role vis-à-vis a father figure to a "boss" in the workplace. Psychoanalysis placed a strong emphasis on the emotional side of identity formation and from a very different theoretical standpoint, as did the pragmatic psychology of James (1950). Inspired by Burke (1969) and Mead (1934), Goffman (1959) placed a strong emphasis on roles and role-related identifications, for example, with respect to front-stage and backstage performances. Similarly, Simon (1976) suggested that "a person identifies himself [or herself] with a group when, in making a decision, he [or she] evaluates the several alternatives of choice in terms of the consequences for the specified group" (p. 205, emphasis removed). In this formulation, the notion of role is operationalized in terms of specific contexts of and perceived parameters for decisions.

Scholars who take a more communicative approach to identification highlight how an individual's identity arises from and is shaped by interaction with an interest or reference group (or even an object). As Foote (1951) notes, "One has no identity apart from society; one has no individuality apart from identity" (p. 51; cf. Mills, 1940). Collectively, these works set the stage for language-centered investigations of identity, especially in the form of expressed accounts for one's connections, decisions, and behaviors (Chaput, Brummans, & Cooren, 2011; Harré & Secord, 1972; Tompkins & Cheney, 1983); the fluidity of identity formation; and the interplay of individuality and sociality.

Moreover, scholars of organizational communication and management have been influenced by *social identity theory* (Ashforth & Mael, 1989; Scott, 2007; Tajfel & Turner, 1986), a perspective that treats individuals as classifying themselves into social categories that define that individual. Because organizational membership can serve as a social identity, organizational identification is considered *a specific form* of social identification (Haslam et al., 2003). According to social identity theory, identification implies that the individual perceives him- or herself as psychologically entangled with the fate of the group (Ashforth

& Mael, 1989). In its extreme form, "identification does *not* require actual affiliation or a desire for future affiliation, nor admiration for or even knowledge of specific group members" (Mael & Ashforth, 1995, p. 313, emphasis in original). For instance, the *minimal group effect* shows that individuals implicitly favor and identify with a group, even if their categorization to that group is *ad hoc* and trivial (Tajfel & Turner, 1986). This finding suggests a different angle on *partial inclusion* in terms of the type and intensity of an attachment and how it is conveyed or expressed (Weick, 1979).

In spite of its heritage, much of the early work in organizational identification was limited, because it conceptualized and measured identification at a specific point in time (Cheney, 1983). While a growing number of studies have begun to examine identification as both a product and process (e.g., Kuhn & Nelson, 2002), research has traditionally "focused more on a static sense of *being* identified rather than *becoming* identified" (Glynn, 1998, p. 238, emphasis in original), thus reproducing the notion of organizational identity as an immutable dimension of organizational life. This static approach to operationalization and measurement was mirrored in public relations and marketing studies of organizational reputation, image, and identity (e.g., Fombrun, 1996). Notions of identity as an accomplishment, as a focal point, as a presentation, or as a package for wider consumption are all suggestive of the product- or outcome-oriented conceptions.

Bullis and Bach (1989) are among the earliest organizational communication scholars to examine an individual's change in organizational identification at different points in time. In addition, Scott, Corman, and Cheney's (1998) structurational model of organizational identification notes a duality between, on the one hand, identity as a set of resources (i.e., a pool of symbolic as well as material points of reference and supplies for identity construction for individuals, groups, and the organization as a whole), and on the other hand, the very process through which these resources are mobilized and their reference points invoked. This model is logically applicable to studying the construction and reproduction of identities at the organizational level, particularly in terms of how resources for identity both enable and constrain new formulations.

Another process-centered or developmental approach to organizational identification has emerged under the rubric of *consubstantialization*. Chaput et al. (2011) described how identification processes unfold through everyday interactions, which "play into the coproduction of the organization's substance" (p. 254). Their study of a Canadian nonprofit organization, Quebec Solidaire, demonstrated how identification occurred through the (re)negotiation of various mobilizing agents, including (1) a policy document; (2) the organization's name; and (3) its history, foundation, and basic principles, which, in turn, fed into the communicative constitution of this young political party.

Treating identification as a process that is constantly in the making points to the notion of identity as an organizational dimension that is realized over time (King, Clemens, & Fry, 2011). By examining the identity emergence of new charter schools, King and colleagues developed a theory of identity realization, described as "the process whereby organizations make concrete their organization-level identity" (p. 561). King et al.'s analysis of Arizona schools showed that there was a great deal of variance among organizational identities, because identity is realized in local and institutional contexts. Put together, these studies illustrate a recursive loop between organizational identity and identification. While identity constitutes the grounds for identification, it is these latter processes that shape and develop organizational identity.

In reviewing the past and current literatures on organizational identity and identification and in reflecting on future directions of this work, we have identified the following communication-sensitive themes that arise from our initial interrogation of these concepts: (1) traversing and transforming formal boundaries, (2) reconsidering organizational membership, (3) encountering identity and identification through technology, (4) challenging the desirability of identification and unitary expressions, and (5) grasping material-symbolic dialectics in identity formation and expression. Each theme can be rephrased usefully as an issue of importance for organizational communication scholars who conduct research on identity.

Traversing and Transforming Formal Boundaries

Although it is generally accepted that internal and external dimensions of an organization's communication are interrelated and difficult to distinguish from each other (e.g., Cheney & Christensen, 2001), much theorizing continues to think of an organization's communication as something that occurs *within* the organizational setting (Carlone & Taylor, 1998). The field thus is still largely shaped by what Axley (1984) calls a *container metaphor* of organizational communication. This metaphor assumes that organizational communication is encapsulated within the confines of a preestablished organization and views communication as messages, events, and episodes *within* organizations and, more specifically, within the bonds connecting individuals to those organizations. Organizations, in other words, *produce* communication not as their general way of being or existence but as something distinct and separate from other organizing practices. This containment of communication was for decades reinforced by the regulation of activities and associated media such as advertising, public relations, and marketing to domains entirely external to the organization.

Recently, work in organizational communication has taken a different perspective, one that considers *organizing as emergent in communication itself* (Taylor & Van Every, 2000). Inspired by phenomenology, speech-action theory, and conversational analysis and with a strong orientation toward sociolinguistics, Taylor and Van Every show how an organization comes into being through the ways its leaders and members speak about and account for its actions and activities. Communication and organization are, from this standpoint, *equivalent* terms (see also Cooren, 2000; Fairhurst & Putnam, 2004; Putnam & Nicotera, 2009). Obviously, this latter perspective, sometimes referred to as the *communicative constitution of organization* (CCO), owes much to Weick (1979), who initiated a dramatic shift in how scholars approach organizational communication by focusing on the power of talk to enact and thus constitute organizational reality, albeit often within the established boundaries of authority and decision making for an organization.

Yet much of the literature in the field continues to assume that organizing and identification occurs *in* organizations. Ashcraft (2007) speaks to the "lingering legacy" of the site-bound lens, as "many studies continue to treat organizational discourse/communication as phenomena *in* organizations or *within* their physical borders, no matter how much we interrogate the ontological status of such boundaries" (p. 11). Furthermore, when theory and research considers the *organizational* environment, it narrowly treats it as consisting of other institutions (Cheney & Ashcraft, 2007). Of course, none of this is to deny the concrete, ontological presence of specific organizations and sites, not to mention centers of power, authority, and membership, in individuals' experiences of work and other activities. Rather, the point to consider is the range of multiple influences that bear on identity formation and expression within any particular case and to recognize that professional identities are established both across and within sites (see Cheney & Ashcraft, 2007). There are several useful illustrations that bear mention here.

For example, Kuhn (2006) demonstrated how locales, identities, and organizational practices shape discursive resources and identity construction. Sociologists of work and occupations have long charted multiple levels of and influences on identity (e.g., Abbott, 1988; Larson, 1977; Macdonald, 1995), but recently, this research has been complemented by more attention to discourse. For example, in her study of *occupational* identities of airline pilots, Ashcraft (e.g., 2007) emphasized the importance of "dislocating" or decentering the organization and moving identity research in organizational communication toward considering broad professional fields (see also Cheney & Ashcraft, 2007). Gossett's work (2002, 2006) on identification in the temporary work industry likewise moved beyond the implied container metaphor by examining employees' attachment (or lack thereof) to their staffing agency and the clients that contract for their labors. This research illustrated how identification is not bound by the physical location or even abstract boundaries of the organization. Similarly, Stephens and Dailey (2012) showed how a new employee's prior experiences with an organization can influence his or her organizational identification, which also reinforces the notion that identity formation occurs in a variety of ways and places. Also, Richardson and McGlynn (2011) demonstrated how highly identified sports fans—that is, non-organizational members who were, formally speaking, outside of the sport organization—acted as agents of retaliation against collegiate whistle-blowers who took corrective action against the organization's tarnished identity. Pratt (2000) also explored the process of identification for Amway distributors, who are employees of an organization with "no central business location, and [whose] work occurs outside of a traditional organizational context" (p. 456). Furthermore, several scholars in organization studies and organizational communication have examined identification in geographically dispersed organizations and virtual organizations (Scott, 1997; Wiesenfeld, Raghuram, & Garud, 1999, 2001). Kraimer, Shaffer, Harrison, and Ren (2012), for example, who explored employees of multinational corporations who were returning from international assignments, found that returning employees often face identity strain between their roles, which can lead to turnover. Also, in professional and organizational cultures, Lair's (2011) study of the TV reality series *The Apprentice* and its spin-offs has shown how discourses about economy, career, and success are negotiated at several different levels, often within uncertain results for identity formation.

Organizational efforts to construct identities for themselves and their members are equally dependent on communication that crosses formal organizational boundaries. The concept of *auto-communication*, or self-communication, places communication about organizational identity within a broad systemic context and explains how externally directed messages may influence internal audiences. Born out of semiotics, anthropology, and biology, auto-communication was initially conceived as an act in which all cultures engaged. Lotman (1990), who coined the notion of auto-communication, was primarily interested in understanding what happens to an individual speaker when he or she addresses an audience but emphasized that all societies and social institutions communicate with themselves to a higher or lesser degree. Rituals, for example, confirm a culture's basic values and introduce members to the community and reinforce their feeling of belongingness (e.g., Geertz, 1973). Auto-communication thus helps cultures maintain, construct and develop themselves.

Applying auto-communication to the organizational context, Broms and Gahmberg (1983) showed how companies, through strategic planning documents and annual reports, are projecting their identities for the future. Extending this perspective to marketing, Christensen (1997, 2004) has emphasized the significant role an external medium may play in the process of auto-communication. External media grant status and authority to organizational messages and influence how members evaluate communication from their own workplace (Christensen, 2004). More than a century ago, large monopolistic corporations, such as AT&T, recognized that internal audiences could be reached more convincingly through external messages and thus began depicting their employees as essential nodes in a large neighborhood (Marchand, 1998). And today, organizations increasingly talk to themselves while pretending to talk to somebody else (that is, in external media) in order to confirm and reproduce their own cultures (Cheney & Christensen, 2001; Christensen, 1997).

Research has in various ways illustrated the inward effects of external communication on processes of identity and identification. In addition to Dutton and Dukerich's (1991) now-classic study of the New York Port Authority, Elsbach and Glynn (1996) demonstrated the effect of United Parcel Service employees being featured in an advertisement, resulting in an increase in their sense of identification with the company. In a similar manner, Gilly and Wolfinbarger's (1998) study of how organizational members perceive advertising campaigns from their own workplace confirms the idea that employees are generally involved in such messages and evaluate dimensions such as accuracy, value congruence, and effectiveness in advertising messages with far more interest and detail than external audiences usually do. Moreover, positive evaluations along these dimensions are crucial to maintain employee pride and loyalty. Likewise, Cheney's (1999) work with the Mondragón Cooperative Corporation in the Basque Country of Spain shows how "externally driven programs and messages are also serving to maintain a need to identify with ones' place of work" (Cheney & Christensen, 2001, p. 247). Along the same lines, Morsing (2006) argues that organizational members usually are more dedicated readers of corporate social responsibility (CSR) messages than other audiences and that "corporate CSR communication profoundly influences the willingness of managers and employees to identify with their workplaces" (p. 171). In this perspective, auto-communication is essential in building and maintaining an organization's identity and in stimulating organizational identification.

Focusing on potentially *dys*functional aspects of auto-communication, however, Christensen and Cheney (2000) argue that many organizational identity projects become highly self-centered undertakings, characterized by self-absorption and self-seduction. This finding has become even more applicable in the age of electronic organizational presence. While external audiences rarely care about the specifics of an organization's identity, members (and managers in particular) are often so deeply involved in the organization's expressions of identity that they lose touch with the issues of stakeholder relevance and interest. Hatch and Schultz (2002) take this point a step further and argue that such identities are pathological and narcissistic. They cite the example of Royal Dutch Shell and its decision to dump the oil platform Brent Spar in the North Sea, as an illustration of an organization that was so engaged in reflections about its own identity that it could not respond adequately to external stakeholder interests and demands. Hatch and Schultz emphasize that narcissism, if more than temporary, poses a real threat to the survival of the organization. In a similar manner, Ganesh (2003) applies Christensen's (1997) notion of marketing as self-referential to the discourse surrounding information and communication technology (ICT) and its relationship to the organizational identity of an Indian nongovernmental organization (NGO). Like Hatch and Schultz, Ganesh (2003) uses the term *organizational narcissism* to describe the organizational identity "that is so oriented toward improving itself and enhancing its legitimacy at the expense of some of its constituents that it sees itself as the only active agent in a larger process of social change" (p. 568).

While such dysfunctional aspects of organizational identity work are important to illuminate and critique, auto-communication may still be indispensable in processes of building identities and fostering identification. As Lotman (1977, 1990) pointed out, messages are not neutral; they potentially affect and shape the sender. Externally directed messages may help organizations explore the boundaries of their identities and the ideal roles they hope to play in the world. And the mere *possibility of expression* may be essential in stimulating participation and involvement (Pingree, 2007). The articulation of organizational aspirations (for example, in the area of

CSR) may be essential for stimulating new insight and moving the organization toward better standards and practices (Christensen, Morsing, & Thyssen, 2011).

Reconsidering Organizational Membership

The relevance of approaching organizational communication as less bounded is obvious when we address the intricacies of organizational membership, inclusion, and socialization. The concept of membership is usually treated as binary—either you are a member or you are not. Thus, most scholarship in organizational communication tends to approach membership as paid, full-time, and permanent employment (Ashcraft & Kedrowicz, 2002). Considering the development of the field, this makes sense. Traditionally, organizations served as identity resources for individuals because they were physically and temporally present in the organization. In contemporary organizations, however, one might have many other forms of attachment with an organization, and some of these are not well recognized in the research literature. In addition, economic shifts have resulted in so-called contingent employment as being a far bigger part of the economy than before, say, the 1980s (Bennett, 1991). Moreover, as we discuss in the subsequent section on technology, membership in many types of organizations is greatly complicated by the growth of technology.

Several broad societal trends have both enabled and constrained the capacity for membership and identification in organizations. First, temporary employment, which has grown in part due to the capacity to perform work at a distance, complicates traditional understandings of identification. Research demonstrates that the process of organizational identification is different for these nonstandard employees. Gossett (2001, 2002), for example, finds that temporary work may serve as a barrier to organizational identification, as contingent workers draw boundaries around their membership and maintain separate social identities. Similarly, Ashcraft and Kedrowicz (2002), who explored staff-volunteer relations at a domestic violence shelter, discuss how volunteers may experience conflicted identification because "they labor for the organization on leisure time, though not for livelihood" and often interact with the organization in different ways, as "many volunteers are present infrequently [and] some conduct the bulk of their work outside formal organizational space" (p. 91). As a result, volunteers may see their identities within the nonprofit as neither work nor leisure but rather as a "third membership contract."

Second, virtual work also makes the discussion of membership and identity more complex. Research on work performed via technology has shown that identifications can both wax and wane as a result of dispersion (Rock & Pratt, 2002). Because individuals can be physically and/or temporally removed from others, their membership and identities in the organization are nontraditional. Ballard and Gossett (2007) discuss how virtual workers' identities within their respective organizations fundamentally change as a result of their lack of physical connection to the organization. Whereas all employees manage their work and home identities and the various degrees to which those overlap, identity issues may be a more salient concern for virtual employees who often work from home (Ashforth, Kreiner, & Fugate, 2000).

Yet even as the notion of membership evolves and grows more complex, concepts of membership, inclusion, and socialization will continue to be intimately related to organizational identity and identification. Burke (1969) noted that organizational efforts to socialize newcomers are successful when the individual identifies with the organization. Identification and socialization are empirically, highly correlated processes (e.g., Klein & Weaver, 2000; Myers & Oetzel, 2003), and discursive resources (Kuhn, 2006), such as sensemaking and sensebreaking socialization practices, lead members to deidentify or disidentify, or experience ambivalent identification with the organization (Pratt, 2000). In addition, Scott and Myers (2010) propose *a membership negotiations perspective*, which acknowledges a mutually implicative relationship among the organization, incumbent members, and newcomers. In this perspective, identification is one medium of membership negotiation, "because it aids attempts to resolve tensions between individual needs for identity and collective organizational interests" (Scott & Myers, 2010, p. 95).

At a broader level, scholars might consider how organizations "socialize" each other by acknowledging the typical imbalance of power, a concept that does not usually appear in research on socialization and assimilation. Such mutual socialization occurs as organizations are constantly communicating messages to express themselves as special and unique. At the same time, however, they are looking over their shoulders at the expressed uniqueness of their competitors (e.g., Martin, Feldman, Hatch, & Sitkin, 1983).

Encountering Identity and Identification Through Technology

As organizational membership grows more complex with advances in computer-based technology and mobile applications, full-time members, nonstandard employees, virtual workers, and individuals outside of the organization may see the organization as an identity resource, even if in oppositional terms. So what implications does technology have for the creation and maintenance of individual and organizational identity?

On the one hand, technology enables or allows individuals with various types of membership to experience the organization as a resource for identity in ways that would otherwise have required physical (co)presence. However, group cohesion and identity may have different features and limits when interaction is online (Rock & Pratt, 2002; Thatcher & Zhu, 2006). The history of technology shows that its usage can help shape the very nature of work and the identified dimensions of it. Certainly, cases as diverse as oil drilling and micro computing testify to this, where the material presence of technology and its powers become important resources of identity. With the rise of the Internet, social media, and mobile applications, ICT use has become more ubiquitous and more interactive in the lives and work of individuals. Microblogging and social networking websites, in particular, have created space for individuals, who may not be physically or only temporally aligned with the organization, to learn about and feel part of it. For example, one recent study at IBM found that geographically distributed as opposed to colocated employees used the company's social media tool to integrate the organization's values into their identity (Thom-Santelli, Millen, & Gergle, 2011). As another example, NGO Amnesty International relies heavily on computer-mediated communication in its global network of information, advocacy, and action. Interactive information and communication technologies that facilitate two-way communicative exchanges have the potential to establish and maintain identification among parties, even if strictly supported by virtual means. Social networking sites open up new pathways of communication between individuals who would not otherwise connect because such sites contain socially relevant information (e.g., profile, picture, mutual friends) that "serves as a social lubricant, providing individuals with social information that is critical for exploiting the technical ability to connect provided by the site" (Ellison, Steinfield, & Lampe, 2011, p. 887, emphasis removed). Just as these sites strengthen connections, they are also likely to foster attachments. In just a decade, the possibility for organizational identification and various other forms of attachment have dramatically expanded. Technology even allows nonmembers to feel consistently connected to an organization. For example, Marine wives cultivate and share their identification with the Marines online, even though they may not be Marines themselves (O'Brien, 2010).

While technology provides temporary workers, virtual workers, and even nonmembers with flexibility to engage with organizations remotely, it may also remove individuals from elements that foster identification. Specifically, identification may be more difficult to sustain because values and norms, traditionally communicated through artifacts (dress codes, shared language, rituals, routines, buildings) and identifiers (such as logos and decorative material) are less readily available in a virtual context. When working from a distance, face-to-face interaction and behavioral cues are less readily available, which pose as a threat to organization-related identities (Scott, 2001; Thatcher & Zhu, 2006). Similarly, and echoing media richness theory, Pratt, Fuller, and Northcraft (2000) argue that "communication technologies vary in the extent to which they make it easier or harder to send rich messages, and this will affect identification by influencing the salience of different referent groups" (p. 241).

In exploring the relationship between technology and identification, various studies have examined if there are specific communication technologies that enhance identification. Overall, this body of research suggests many moderators of the relationship between ICT usage and identification. For example, Timmerman and Scott (2006) showed that communicative predictors (i.e., efforts to understand, responsiveness, thoroughness) moderate the relationships between electronic messaging (e.g., e-mail and instant messaging) and identification. Other moderators include social support (Wiesenfeld et al., 2001), amount of ICT use (Scott & Timmerman, 1999), and stress (Fonner & Roloff, 2012). Future research should collect longitudinal data of ICT use and identification, as it may be that over time, the relationship between these variables may change.

Several scholars have suggested how organizations can overcome the dispersion that technology creates. Rock and Pratt (2002), for example, assert that organizational symbols could be used to enhance identification among distributed individuals (e.g., business cards and laptops with corporate logos). Here, qualitative research may aid in understanding the meanings that members attach to these organizational technologies and how those materials impact identification.

Challenging the Desirability of Identification and Unitary Expressions of Identity

In the multidisciplinary literature, identification is typically deemed unequivocally desirable by both individuals and organizations. However, recent work has questioned this notion. Challenging the desirability of identification is an important endeavor, especially in the domains of politics and ethics. As history has clearly demonstrated, investment of the self in one resource, an organization, can easily slide into extremism. Examples are prevalent in politics, religion, economy, work, intergroup relations, and the family. Moreover, the ethics of identification raise questions about the loss of self or the drastic conditions that an individual undergoes to become part of an in-group. For example, divestiture socialization tactics (which involves stripping away certain personal characteristics)

> almost require a recruit to sever old friendships, undergo extensive harassment from experienced members, and engage for long periods of time in doing the "dirty work" of the trade typified by low pay, low status, low interest value, and low skill requirements. (Van Maanen & Schein, 1979, p. 64)

Questions about excessive identification rest to some extent on concepts of subjective (un) certainty and self-conceptual uncertainty reduction, which assume that individuals strive for certainty in the areas of life that are important to their self-concept. Subjective certainty is connected to group membership, as "things that we are certain about are linked to who we are via the prototypical features of social groups with which we identify and which form our self-concept"

(Hogg & Mullin, 1999, p. 254). While much of this work is conceptual in nature, a series of controlled laboratory studies show that in conditions of greater uncertainty about a task, higher group identification was fostered (Hogg & Mullin, 1999). From this perspective, the identification process allows individuals to reduce uncertainty by bonding with a collective and trying to banish uncertainty from her or his experience through a kind of total identification.

In addition, when individuals experience identity threats, they often use various tactics to increase the esteem of their social identities. For example, Ashforth and colleagues (Ashforth & Kreiner, 1999; Ashforth, Kreiner, Clark, & Fugate, 2007) show how employees who experience the stigma of "dirty work" may develop a strong work culture to reframe social comparisons for defense against negative identities. Frandsen (2012), for example, illustrates how finance professionals working in a low-prestige telecommunication corporation adopt a cynical distance to the tainted image of their workplace and instead secure a positive sense of self by identifying strongly with their professional work teams. Business students use similar tactics when their identities as MBA students are challenged by *Business Week* rankings (Corley & Gioia, 2004; Elsbach & Kramer, 1996). This research illustrates the comparative, relational, and relative nature of social identities vis-à-vis one another.

In sum, the desirability and degree of identification is context based. Considerable work shows that organizational identification is related to a number of beneficial work-related attitudes and behaviors, including cooperation, effort, motivation, participation, group decision making, tenure, and turnover (see Ashforth, Harrison, & Corley, 2008; Riketta, 2005). At a deeper level, however, identification may function as a source of thoroughgoing managerial, administrative, or political control. Many communication scholars have noted that team-based pressure for identification, referred to as *concertive* control, is more powerful than simple, technical, and bureaucratic control (Barker, 1993; Tompkins & Cheney, 1985). Extending this line of work, Alvesson and Willmott (2002) have analyzed the discursive and reflexive processes of identity constitution and regulation in contemporary work organizations. Rejecting the notion that management is omnipotent in determining employee identity, they nonetheless focus their analysis on identity regulation as a significant "modality of organizational control" (p. 621). Specifically, they suggest that the employee of today is an *identity worker*. While employee identities are not regulated exclusively by managerial sources, organizations intentionally provide a significant part of the discursive material through which individuals accomplish their life projects and recognize themselves as carriers of specific identities. However, the connection between power/control and identity needs to be fully explored in communication research, especially through multiple levels of analysis and new means of messaging that may not be classed as propaganda yet in practice function that way.

The "dark side" of identification has been explored through notions of *dis*identification, *de*identification, *ambivalent* identification, *under*identification, *over*disidentification, *schizo*-identification, and dual identities—all of which describe different forms of organizational attachment (Blazejewski, 2012; Dukerich, Kramer, & Parks, 1998; Elsbach & Bhattacharya, 2001; Pratt, 2000). Several potential negative consequences for individuals and organizations emanate from these alternative expressions of attachment, such as whistle-blowing, distrust, paranoia, and burnout (e.g., Dukerich et al., 1998; Pratt, 2000). In contrast, some research shows that *dis*identifications may be just as useful for enhancing positive social identities as identifications are (Elsbach & Bhattacharya, 2001), as is the case of productive dissent, for example (Kassing, 2007; Waldron & Kassing, 2011). One area that begs the question for further research is the connection between charismatic leadership and overidentification, something investigated extensively in the sociological and psychological literature on cults (Cook, 2010) but not examined in organizational communication.

Material-Symbolic Dialectics in Identity Formation and Expression

The interplay of materiality and symbolicity in workplace and professional identities has been given relatively scant attention in organizational communication in contrast to the sociology of work (Smith, 2000). Three distinct but interrelated issues are important in this work, namely, (1) the in-depth engagement of work activities, work contexts, conditions and activities (see, e.g., Evans, Kunda, & Barley, 2004; Kunda, Barley, & Evans, 2002); (2) the recognition that material as well as symbolic work contexts are wrapped up with identity both with respect to the embodiment of roles and experiences and their various other representations, including, for example, well-established public images of various types of work (Tietze & Musson, 2010; Turner, 2004); and (3) the fact that materiality, as with symbolicity, has multiple senses that have yet to be fully articulated and applied in organizational communication research (Ashcraft, Kuhn, & Cooren, 2009; Simpson, Cheney, & Weaver, in progress).

In organizational communication, scholars have been a bit slower to go back to work in examining detailed specific work activities and communication processes (for exceptions, see Ashcraft, 2007; Gossett, 2002). More research needs to focus on how organizational identity and identification shape the work that people do and how the complete context of work shapes identity (both directions of influence are illustrated beautifully in the 1999 film *Human Resources*). For example, scholars interested in investigating the meaning of work might ask about the ways in which people actually structure and use their time vis-à-vis their stated life and professional goals (Cheney, Zorn, Planalp, & Lair, 2008) or how they relate to official expressions of what their workplace stands for (Llewellyn & Harrison, 2006). Researchers could examine multiple roles and situations in terms of identity formation, transformation, and narratives of work and life aimed at various audiences across domains.

Three examples are important when considering the intersection of materiality and identity. First, the material and the symbolic both play an important role in the process of identity work. For instance, Alvesson and Willmott (2002) examine identity work as a medium and outcome of organizational control by showing how employees are encouraged to align their identities to managerially inspired discourses. Yet the authors note that "the role of discourse in targeting and moulding [sic] the human subject is balanced with other elements of life history" (p. 628).

Second, Ashforth et al. (2000) have conceptualized the shift between boundaries—home, work, and social—as *micro role transitions.* The authors note that *role identification* is a factor that is likely to affect the boundaries that one creates, maintains, and crosses. Tracy (2005) found, for example, that correctional officers who highly identified with their professional roles had more difficulties managing emotional labor. This form of identification occurs when "a role occupant *defines* himself or herself at least partly in terms of the role and its identity (e.g., 'I am a machinist, a bowler, a parent')" (Ashforth et al., 2000, p. 483, emphasis in original). While research has studied multiple targets and sources of identification on a large scale (e.g., during company transition; see Larson & Pepper, 2003), scholars have done little work on what Ashforth and colleagues call *micro role transitions* or ones between roles and other levels of identification.

Third, an interesting example of an organizational and social context especially appropriate for considering the interplay of body, place, symbolism, organization, and identity is that of retirement communities. As both landscapes (e.g., Laws, 1993, 1995) and organizations (Simpson & Cheney, 2007), retirement communities influence identities and expectations of residents and employees. Retirement villages are organizing landscapes and corporate bodies, where residents and employees respond to and enact physical and symbolic dimensions of aging identities as well as organize their work and relationships with each other. Retirement villages represent a division or a transition between work and retirement (Laws, 1995), one that signals a departure from and yet a reminder of the familiar work spaces. Following Laws, Simpson et al. (in progress) argue that the process of *emplacement* may help to navigate relationships between organizing work and organizing elders. Emplacement is a conceptual and practical means of conceiving of the complex relationships of material conditions/contexts and symbolic/discursive formulations that bear on the positioning and identity of retirement village residents (Simpson & Cheney, 2007).

Future studies need to investigate the material grounds, contexts, and resources for identity and work. In some ways, popular culture and everyday understandings of work, identity, and materiality are more advanced or at least more penetrating than the ways organizational scholars have examined material conditions. In this regard, the metaphor of *translation* has contributed greatly to understanding of how physical objects achieve a kind of agency as they enter streams of consciousness and discourse (Ashcraft et al., 2009; Latour, 1993). This perspective is clearly relevant to identity formation in work, professional life, and occupational contexts, especially regarding how such identities are formed and expressed (Ashcraft, 2007; Cheney & Ashcraft, 2007). At the same time, however, the *mythos* and attendant biases of organizational communication often lead scholars to overlook the powerful and sometimes overwhelming presence of the material. Thus an unintended empirical bias in research may make it difficult to account for the role of materiality in a complete way. Where identity and identification are concerned, even the context of virtuality has important material dimensions that scholars are only beginning to understand in their studies of physical, physiological, cognitive, emotional, and social factors.

Conclusion

In this chapter, we have brought together established and emerging lines of research, including diverse theories and methodologies that highlight the historical and cultural contexts of organizational identity and identification studies. Above all, though, we have argued for the simultaneous consideration of multiple levels of analysis and suggested theoretical and practical bridges as areas of investigation for organizational *identity* and *identification*. Our review has been multidisciplinary, with a focus on communication-oriented insights that have not yet realized their full potential in this long-standing arena of investigation.

We conclude this review with a call for specific types of research on organizational identity and identification that are

- culturally and historically informed by being sensitive to both synchronic and diachronic analysis;
- integrative in moving across levels of analysis from micro to macro and vice versa;
- multimethodological in bridging case-based investigations, critical reflections, and broad-based empirical data;
- engaged with assisting organizations not only in crafting identities but also in prodding them and their members to reflect on the meanings of them; and
- ethically aware in grappling with key practical and policy-related issues of identity, work, and institutions today.

The cultural situatedness of identities and identifications is, by now, well established; however, it is equally important to consider how economic, political, and social trends shape and are shaped by those identities and identifications. Spanning levels of analysis in research on organizational identity and identification is as important now as it was in the early 20th century not only because of interrelated developments at the levels of nation state, corporation, and community but also because studies of reformulations of national identities have enormous implications for positioning corporate identities and vice versa. Frequently, studies address both team and organizational identification (Barker & Tompkins, 1994). A great deal remains to be explored regarding how organizational identities and identifications connect "upward" to broader institutional and cultural formations (as called for by Carlone & Taylor, 1998).

Studies of organizational identities and identifications have used empirical, interpretive, and critical methodologies. To date, however, few investigations take full advantage of multiple strategies or methods that are in conversation with one another, for example, surveys that also include interpretive and/or critical reflection. In addition, we echo calls for major longitudinal case studies, voiced in 1981 at the Organizational Communication Conference in Alta, Utah (see Cheney, Grant, & Hedges, in press).

Engagement is a popular but ambiguous theme in the contemporary academy; we use it here to advocate critical reflection by producers and consumers of the key messages that represent organizations, especially with an eye toward agency and pragmatic implications of such messages. Finally, we highlight *ethics*, because it has not received much attention in the research on organizational identity and identification (Hedges, 2008). Intense and enduring loyalties or affiliations make a difference in the lives of individuals and groups, and abuses as well as noble achievements can occur in their names. This observation alone is an important reason for scholars to give more attention to the ethics of identification in work and organizational settings.

In closing, given the enormous volume of research on organizational identity and identification, the centrality of the concepts to contemporary social life, and the important insights that communication studies offer, we call for investigations of both wider scope and greater depth with the aim of contributing to the key issues and discussions of our simultaneously local and global world.

References

Abbott, A. (1988). *The system of professions: An essay on the division of expert labor*. Chicago, IL: The University of Chicago Press.

Albert, S., & Whetten, D. A. (1985). Organizational identity. *Research in Organizational Behavior, 7*, 263–295.

Allen, B. J. (2011). *Difference matters: Communicating social identity*. Long Grove, IL: Waveland Press.

Alvesson, M. (1990). On the popularity of organizational culture. *Acta Sociologica, 33*(1), 31–49.

Alvesson, M., & Willmott, H. (2002). Identity regulation as organizational control: Producing the appropriate individual. *Journal of Management Studies, 39*(5), 619–644.

Ashcraft, K. L. (2007). Appreciating the "work" of discourse: Occupational identity and difference as organizing mechanisms in the case of commercial airline pilots. *Discourse & Communication, 1*(1), 9–36.

Ashcraft, K. L., & Kedrowicz, A. (2002). Self-direction or social support? Nonprofit empowerment and the tacit employment contract of organizational communication studies. *Communication Monographs, 69*(1), 88–110.

Ashcraft, K. L., Kuhn, T., & Cooren, F. (2009). Constitutional amendments: "Materializing" organizational communication. *The Academy of Management Annals, 3*(1), 1–64.

Ashforth, B. E., Harrison, S. H., & Corley, K. G. (2008). Identification in organizations: An examination of four fundamental questions. *Journal of Management, 34*(3), 325–374.

Ashforth, B. E., & Kreiner, G. E. (1999). "How can you do it?" Dirty work and the challenge of constructing a positive identity. *The Academy of Management Review, 24*(3), 413–434.

Ashforth, B. E., Kreiner, G. E., Clark, M. A., & Fugate, M. (2007). Normalizing dirty work: Managerial tactics for countering occupational taint. *Academy of Management Journal, 50*(1), 149–174.

Ashforth, B. E., Kreiner, G. E., & Fugate, M. (2000). All in a day's work: Boundaries and micro role transitions. *Academy of Management Review, 25*(3), 472–491.

Ashforth, B. E., & Mael, F. (1989). Social identity theory and the organization. *Academy of Management Review, 14*(1), 20–39.

Ashforth, B. E., & Mael, F. (1996). Organizational identity and strategy as a context for the individual. In J. A. C. Baum & J. E. Dutton (Eds.), *Advances in strategic management* (vol. 13, pp. 17–62). Greenwich, CT: JAI.

Axley, S. (1984). Managerial and organizational communication metaphor. *Academy of Management Review, 9*(3), 428–437.

Ballard, D. I., & Gossett, L. M. (2007). Alternative times: Temporal perceptions, processes, and practices defining the nonstandard work relationship. In C. S. Beck (Ed.), *Communication yearbook* (vol. 31, pp. 276–320). New York, NY: Lawrence Erlbaum.

Balmer, J. M. T. (1995). Corporate branding and connoisseurship. *Journal of General Management, 21*(1), 24–46.

Barker, J. R. (1993). Tightening the iron cage: Concertive control in self-managing teams. *Administrative Science Quarterly, 38*(3), 408–437.

Barker, J. R., & Tompkins, P. K. (1994). Identification in the self-managing organization: Characteristics of target and tenure. *Human Communication Research, 21*(2), 223–240.

Baudrillard, J. (1988). *Simulacra and simulations.* In M. Poster (Ed.), *Jean Baudrillard: Selected writings* (pp. 166–184). Stanford, CA: Stanford University Press.

Baumeister, R. F., & Leary, M. R. (1995). The need to belong: Desire for interpersonal attachments as a fundamental human motivation. *Psychological Bulletin, 117*(3), 497–529.

Bennett, A. (1991). *The death of the organization man.* New York, NY: Simon & Schuster.

Blazejewski, S. (2012). Betwixt or beyond the lines of conflict? Biculturalism as situated identity in multinational corporations. *Critical Perspectives on International Business, 8*(2), 111–135.

Broms, H., & Gahmberg H. (1983). Communication to self in organizations and cultures. *Administrative Science Quarterly, 28*(3), 482–495.

Browning, L., & Morris, G. H. H. (2012). *Narrative theory and organizational life: Ideas and applications.* Hoboken, NJ: Taylor & Francis.

Bullis, C. A., & Bach, B. W. (1989). Socialization turning points: An examination of change in organizational identification. *Western Journal of Speech Communication, 53*(3), 273–293.

Burke, K. (1969). *A rhetoric of motives.* Berkeley: University of California Press.

Carlone, D., & Taylor, B. (1998). Organizational communication and cultural studies: A review essay. *Communication Theory, 8*(3), 337–367.

Chaput, M., Brummans, B. H. J. M., & Cooren, F. (2011). The role of organizational identification in the communicative constitution of an organization: A study of consubstantialization in a young political party. *Management Communication Quarterly, 25*(2), 252–282.

Cheney, G. (1983). The rhetoric of identification and the study of organizational communication. *Quarterly Journal of Speech, 69*(2), 143–158.

Cheney, G. (1999). *Values at work: Employee participation meets market pressure at Mondragón.* Ithaca, NY: Cornell University Press.

Cheney, G., & Ashcraft, K. L. (2007). Considering "the professional" in communication studies: Implications for theory and research within and beyond the boundaries of organizational communication. *Communication Theory, 17*(2), 146–175.

Cheney, G., & Christensen, L.T. (2001). Organizational identity. Linkages between 'internal' and 'external' organizational communication. In F. Jablin & L. L. Putnam (Eds.), *The new handbook of organizational communication* (pp. 231–269). Thousand Oaks: SAGE.

Cheney, G., Grant, S., & Hedges, J. (in press). Interpretation, culture and identity. In Marchiori, M. (Ed.), *The faces of culture, organization, and communication.* São Paula, Brazil: Difusao Editorial

Cheney, G., Zorn, T. E., Planalp, S., & Lair, D. J. (2008). Meaningful work and personal/social well-being: Organizational communication engages the meanings of work. In C. S. Beck (Ed.), *Communication yearbook* (vol. 32, pp. 137–186). New York, NY: Routledge.

Chreim, S. (2005). The continuity-change duality in narrative texts of organizational identity. *Journal of Management Studies, 42*(3), 567–593.

Christensen, L.T. (1997). Marketing as auto-communication. *Consumption, Markets & Culture, 1*(3). 197–227.

Christensen, L. T. (2004). Det forførende medie. Om autokommunikation i markedsføringen. *Mediekultur, 37,* 14–23.

Christensen, L. T., & Askegaard, S. (2001). Corporate identity and corporate image revisited. A semiotic perspective. *European Journal of Marketing, 35*(4), 292–315.

Christensen, L. T., & Cheney, G. (2000). Self-absorption and self-seduction in the corporate identity game. In M. Schultz, M. J. Hatch, & M. H. Larsen (Eds.), *The expressive organization* (pp. 246–270). Oxford, UK: Oxford University Press.

Christensen, L. T., Morsing M., & Thyssen, O. (2011). The polyphony of corporate social responsibility: Deconstructing accountability and transparency in the context of identity and hypocrisy. In G. Cheney, S. May, & D. Munshi (Eds.), *Handbook of communication ethics* (pp. 457–474). New York, NY: Routledge.

Cook, A. (2010, December). *Organizational identification: A case study of the Davis County Cooperative Society, The Latter Day Church of Christ, or The Kingston Order* (Doctoral dissertation). University of Utah, Salt Lake City, UT.

Cooren, F. (2000). *The organizing property of communication.* Amsterdam, the Netherlands: John Benjamins.

Corley, K. G., & Gioia, D. A. (2004). Identity ambiguity and change in the wake of a corporate spin-off. *Administrative Science Quarterly, 49*(2), 173–208.

de Toqueville, A. (1847). *Democracy in America.* New York, NY: Ban.

Dukerich, J. M., Kramer, R., & Parks, J. M. (1998). The dark side of organizational identification. In D. A. Whetten & P. C. Godfrey (Eds.), *Identity in organizations: Building theory through conversations* (pp. 245–256). Thousand Oaks, CA: SAGE.

Dunne, J. (1996). Beyond sovereignty and deconstruction: The storied self. In E. R. Kearney (Ed.), *Paul Ricoeur. The hermeneutics of action* (pp. 137–157). London, England: SAGE.

Durkheim, E. (1933). *The division of labor in society.* Glencoe, IL: Free Press.

Dutton, J. E., & Dukerich, J. M. (1991). Keeping an eye on the mirror: Image and identity in organizational adaptation. *Academy of Management Journal, 34*(3), 517–554.

Dutton, J. E., Dukerich, J. M., & Harquail, C. V. (1994). Organizational images and member identification. *Administrative Science Quarterly, 39*(2), 239–263.

Ellison, N. B., Steinfield, C., & Lampe, C. (2011). Connection strategies: Social capital implications of Facebook-enabled communication practices. *New Media & Society, 13*(6), 873–892.

Elsbach, K. D., & Bhattacharya, C. B. (2001). Defining who you are by what you're not: Organizational disidentification and the National Rifle Association. *Organization Science, 12*(4), 393–413.

Elsbach, K. D., & Glynn, M. A. (1996). Believing your own "PR": Embedding identification in strategic reputation. In J. A. C. Baun & J. E. Dutton (Eds.), *Advances in strategic management* (pp. 63–88). Greenwich, CT: JAI Press.

Elsbach, K. D., & Kramer, R. M. (1996). Members' responses to organizational identity threats: Encountering and countering *Business Week* rankings. *Administrative Science Quarterly, 41*(3), 442–476.

Evans, J., Kunda, G., & Barley, S. R. (2004). Beach time, bridge time, and billable hours: The temporal structure of technical contracting. *Administrative Science Quarterly, 49*(1), 1–38.

Fairhurst, G., & Putnam, L. (2004). Organizations as discursive constructions. *Communication Theory, 14*(1), 5–26.

Fombrun, C. J. (1996). *Reputation: Realizing value from the corporate image.* Boston, MA: Harvard Business Press.

Fonner, K. L., & Roloff, M. E. (2012). Testing the connectivity paradox: Linking teleworkers' communication media use to social presence, stress due to interruptions, and organizational identification. *Communication Monographs, 79*(2), 205–231.

Foote, N. N. (1951). Identification as the basis for a theory of motivation. *American Sociological Review, 16*, 14–21.

Foucault, M. (1984). *The Foucault reader* (P. Rabinow, Ed.). New York, NY: Penguin.

Frandsen, S. (2012). Organizational image, identification, and cynical distance: Prestigious professionals in a low-prestige organization. *Management Communication Quarterly, 26*(3), 351–376.

Freud, S. (1922). *Group psychology and the analysis of the ego.* London, England: The International Psychoanalytical Press.

Ganesh, S. (2003). Organizational narcissism: Technology, legitimacy and identity in an Indian NGO. *Management Communication Quarterly, 16*(4), 558–594.

Geertz, C. (1973). *The interpretation of cultures.* New York, NY: Basic Books.

Gilly, M. C., & Wolfinbarger, M. (1998, January). Advertising's internal audience. *Journal of Marketing, 62*, 69–88.

Glynn, M. A. (1998). Individuals' need for organizational identification (NOID): Speculations on individual differences in the propensity to identify. In D. Whetten & P. Godfrey (Eds.), *Identity in organizations: Building theory through conversations* (pp. 238–244). Thousand Oaks, CA: SAGE.

Goffman, E. (1959). *The presentation of self in everyday life.* New York, NY: Anchor.

Gossett, L. M. (2001). Short-term workers: The work life concerns posed by the growth of the contingent workforce. *Management Communication Quarterly, 15*(1), 115–120.

Gossett, L. M. (2002). Kept at arm's length: Questioning the organizational desirability of member identification. *Communication Monographs, 69*(4), 385–404.

Gossett, L. M. (2006). Falling between the cracks: Control and communication challenges of a temporary workforce. *Management Communication Quarterly, 19*(3), 376–415.

Grant, S. (2004). *Narrating The Body Shop: A story about corporate identity* (Unpublished doctoral dissertation). The University of Waikato, Hamilton, New Zealand.

Harré, R., & Secord, P. (1972). *The explanation of social behaviour.* Oxford, England: Blackwell.

Haslam, S. A., Postmes, T., & Ellemers, N. (2003). More than a metaphor: Organizational identity makes organizational life possible. *British Journal of Management, 14*(4), 357–369.

Hatch, M. J., & Schultz, M. S. (2002). The dynamics of organizational identity. *Human Relations, 55*(8), 989–1018.

Hedges, J. (2008). *The expressions and transformations of identity in Alcoholics Anonymous: A multi-method study of individual, group, and organization.* (Unpublished doctoral dissertation). University of Utah, Salt Lake City, UT.

Hofstede, G. (1980). *Culture's consequences.* Beverly Hills, CA: SAGE.

Hogg, M. A., & Mullin, B. A. (1999). Joining groups to reduce uncertainty: Subjective uncertainty reduction and group identification. In D. Abrams & M. A. Hogg (Eds.), *Social identity and social cognition* (pp. 249–279). Oxford, UK: Blackwell.

James, W. (1950). *The principles of psychology* (vol. 1). New York, NY: Dover.

Kassing, J. W. (2007). Going around the boss: Exploring the consequences of circumvention. *Management Communication Quarterly, 21*(1), 55–74.

Kenny, K., Whittle, A., & Willmott, H. (2011). *Understanding identity & organizations.* London, England: SAGE.

King, B. G., Clemens, E. S., & Fry, M. (2011). Identity realization and organizational forms: Differentiation and consolidation of identities among Arizona's charter schools. *Organization Science, 22*(3), 554–572.

Klein, H. J., & Weaver, N. A. (2000). The effectiveness of an organizational-level orientation training program in the socialization of new hires. *Personnel Psychology, 53*(1), 47–66.

Kraimer, M. L., Shaffer, M. A., Harrison, D. A., & Ren, H. (2012). No place like home? An identity strain perspective on repatriate turnover. *Academy of Management Journal, 55*(2), 399–420.

Kuhn, M. H., & McPartland, T. S. (1954). An empirical investigation of self-attitudes. *American Sociological Review, 19*(1), 68–76.

Kuhn, T. (2006). A 'demented work ethic' and a 'lifestyle firm': Discourse, identity, and workplace time commitments. *Organization Studies, 27*(9), 1339–1358.

Kuhn, T., & Nelson, N. (2002). Reengineering identity: A case study of multiplicity and duality in organizational identification. *Management Communication Quarterly, 16*(1), 5–38.

Kunda, G., Barley, S. R., & Evans, J. (2002). Why do contractors contract? The experience of highly skilled technical professionals in a contingent labor market. *Industrial and Labor Relations Review, 55*(2), 234–261.

Kunde, J. (2000). *Corporate religion. Building a strong company through personality and corporate soul.* London, England: Prentice Hall.

Lair, D. J. (2011). Surviving the corporate jungle: *The Apprentice* as equipment for living in the contemporary work world. *Western Journal of Communication, 75*(1), 75–94.

Larson, G. S., & Pepper, G. L. (2003). Strategies for managing multiple organizational identifications. *Management Communication Quarterly, 16*(4), 528–557.

Larson, M. S. (1977). *The rise of professionalism: A sociological analysis.* Berkeley: University of California Press.

Lasswell, H. (1935). *World politics and personal insecurity.* New York, NY: Free Press.

Latour, B. (1993). *We have never been modern.* New York, NY: Harvester Wheatsheaf.

Laws, G. (1993). The land of old age: Society's changing attitudes toward urban built environments for elderly people. *Annals of the Association of American Geographers, 83*(4), 672–693.

Laws, G. (1995). Embodiment and emplacement: Identities, representations and landscape in Sun City Retirement Communities. *International Journal of Aging and Human Development, 40*(4), 253–280.

Llewellyn, N., & Harrison, A. (2006). Resisting corporate communications: Insights into folk linguistics. *Human Relations, 59*(4), 567–596.

Lotman, J. M. (1977). Two models of communication. In D. P. Lucid (Ed.), *Soviet semiotics: An anthology* (pp. 99–101). London, England: Johns Hopkins University Press.

Lotman, Y. M. (1990). *Universe of the mind. A semiotic theory of culture.* London, England: I. B. Tauris.

Luhmann, N. (1990). *Essays of self-reference.* New York, NY: Columbia University Press.

Macdonald, K. M. (1995). *The sociology of the professions.* London, England: SAGE.

Mackenzie, W. J. M. (1978). *Political identity.* Manchester, UK: Manchester University Press.

Mael, F., & Ashforth, B. E. (1992). Alumni and their alma mater: A partial test of the reformulated model of organizational identification. *Journal of Organizational Behavior, 13*(2), 103–123.

Mael, F., & Ashforth, B. E. (1995). Loyal from day one: Biodata, organizational identification, and turnover among newcomers. *Personnel Psychology, 48*(2), 309–333.

Marchand, R. (1998). *Creating the corporate soul. The rise of public relations and corporate imagery in American big business.* Berkeley: University of California Press.

Martin, J., Feldman, M. S., Hatch, M. J., & Sitkin, S. B. (1983). The uniqueness paradox in organizational stories. *Administrative Science Quarterly, 28*(3), 438–453.

Mead, G. H. (1934). *Mind, self and society: From the standpoint of a social behaviorist.* Chicago, IL: University of Chicago Press.

Mills, C. W. (1940). Situated actions and vocabularies of motive. *American Sociological Review, 5*(6), 904–913.

Mongin, O. (1982, February). La democratie a corps perdu. *Esprit, 2*, 206–214.

Morin, E. (1986). *La metode III: La connaisance de la connaisance. Livre premier: Antropologie de la connaisance.* Paris, France: Editions du Seuil.

Morsing, M. (2006). Corporate social responsibility as strategic auto-communication: On the role of external stakeholders for member identification. *Business Ethics: A European Review, 15*(2), 171–182.

Munshi, D. (2006). Through the subject's eye: Situating the other in discourses of diversity. In G. Cheney & G. Barnett (Eds.), *International and multicultural organizational communication* (pp. 45–70). Cresskill, NJ: Hampton Press.

Myers, K. K., & Oetzel, J. G. (2003). Exploring the dimensions of organizational assimilation: Creating and validating a measure. *Communication Quarterly, 51*(4), 438–457.

Nietzsche, F. (1954). *The portable Nietzsche* (W. Kaufmann, Ed.). Harmondsworth, England: Penguin.

Nisbet, R. (1970). *The sociological tradition.* New York, NY: Basic Books.

O'Brien, B. (2010, July 12). Blog helps Marine wife cope with husband's death. *Morning Edition on NPR Podcast.* Podcast retrieved from http://www.npr.org/templates/story/story.php?storyId=128458153

Olins, W. (1989). *Corporate identity: Making business strategy visible through design.* Cambridge, MA: Harvard University Press.

Patchen, M. (1970). *Participation, achievement, and involvement on the job.* Englewood Cliffs, NJ: Prentice Hall.

Pingree, R. J. (2007). How messages affect their senders: A more general model of message effects and implications for deliberation. *Communication Theory, 17*(4), 439–461.

Pratt, M. G. (2000). The good, the bad, and the ambivalent: Managing identification among Amway distributors. *Administrative Science Quarterly, 45*(3), 456–493.

Pratt, M. G., Fuller, M., & Northcraft, G. B. (2000). Media selection and identification in distributed groups: The potential cost of 'rich' media. In T. L. Griffith, E. Mannix, & M. A. Neale (Eds.), *Research on managing groups and teams* (vol. 3, pp. 231–254). Stamford, CT: JAI Press.

Putnam, L. L., & Nicotera, A. M. (2009). *Building theories of organization: The constitutive role of communication.* London, England: Routledge.

Rasmussen, D. (1996). Rethinking subjectivity: Narrative identity and the self. In Richard Kearney (Ed.), *Paul Ricoeur. The hermeneutics of action* (pp. 159–172). London, England: SAGE.

Richardson, B. K., & McGlynn, J. (2011). Rabid fans, death threats, and dysfunctional stakeholders:

The influence of organizational and industry contexts on whistle-blowing cases. *Management Communication Quarterly, 25*(1), 121–150.

Riketta, M. (2005). Organizational identification: A meta-analysis. *Journal of Vocational Behavior, 66*(2), 358–384.

Rock, K. W., & Pratt, M. G. (2002). Where do we go from here? Predicting identification among dispersed employees. In B. Moingeon & G. Seonen (Eds.), *Corporate and organizational identities: Integrating strategy, marketing, communication, and organizational perspectives* (pp. 51–71). London, England: Routledge.

Scott, C., & Myers, K. (2010). Toward an integrative theoretical perspective on organizational membership negotiations: Socialization, assimilation, and the duality of structure. *Communication Theory, 20*(1), 79–105.

Scott, C. R. (1997). Identification with multiple targets in a geographically dispersed organization. *Management Communication Quarterly, 10*(4), 491–522.

Scott, C. R. (2001). Establishing and maintaining customer loyalty and employee identification in the new economy: A communicative response. *Management Communication Quarterly, 14*(4), 629–636.

Scott, C. R. (2007). Communication and social identity theory: Existing and potential connections in organizational identification research. *Communication Studies, 58*(2), 123–138.

Scott, C. R., Corman, S. R., & Cheney, G. (1998). Development of a structurational model of identification in the organization. *Communication Theory, 8*(3), 298–336.

Scott, C. R., & Timmerman, C. E. (1999). Communication technology use and multiple workplace identifications among organizational teleworkers with varied degrees of virtuality. *IEEE Transactions on Professional Communication, 42*(4), 240–260.

Silva, D., & Sias, P. M. (2010). Connection, balancing, and buffering: The role of groups in the individual-organizational relationship. *Journal of Applied Communication Research, 38*, 145–166.

Simon, H. A. (1976). *Administrative behavior* (3rd ed.). New York, NY: Free Press.

Simpson, M., & Cheney, G. (2007). Marketization, participation, and communication within New Zealand retirement villages: A critical-rhetorical and discursive analysis. *Discourse and Communication, 1*(2), 191–222.

Simpson, M., Cheney, G., & Weaver, C. K. (in progress). *Organizing landscapes and corporate bodies: Material and symbolic dimensions of worker and resident identities in retirement villages* (Unpublished paper). The University of Waikato, Hamilton, NZ.

Smith, V. (2000). *Crossing the great divide: Worker risk and opportunity in the new economy*. Ithaca, NY: Cornell University Press.

Stephens, K. K., & Dailey, S. L. (2012). Situated organizational identification in newcomers: Impacts of pre-entry organizational exposure. *Management Communication Quarterly, 26*(3), 404–422.

Tajfel, H., & Turner, J. C. (1986). The social identity theory of intergroup behavior. In S. Worchel & W. G. Austin (Eds.), *Psychology of intergroup relations* (2nd ed., pp. 7–24). Chicago, IL: Nelson-Hall.

Taylor, J. R., & Van Every, E. J. (2000). *The emergent organization: Communication as its site and surface.* Mahwah, NJ: Lawrence Erlbaum.

Thatcher, S. M. B., & Zhu, X. (2006). Changing identities in a changing workplace: Identification, identity enactment, self-verification, and telecommuting. *Academy of Management Review, 31*(4), 1076–1088.

Thom-Santelli, J., Millen, D. R., & Gergle, D. (2011). *Organizational acculturation and social networking*. Proceedings from Computer Supported Cooperative Work and Social Computing (CSCW) 2011, Hangzhou, China.

Tietze, S., & Musson, G. (2010). Identity, identity work and the experience of working from home. *Journal of Management Development, 29*(2), 148–156.

Timmerman, C. E., & Scott, C. R. (2006). Virtually working: Communicative and structural predictors of media use and key outcomes in virtual work teams. *Communication Monographs, 73*(1), 108–136.

Tompkins, P. K., & Cheney, G. (1983). Account analysis of organizations: Decision making and identification. In L. L. Putnam & M. E. Pacanowsky (Eds.), *Communication and organizations: An interpretive approach* (pp. 123–146). Beverly Hills, CA: SAGE.

Tompkins, P. K., & Cheney, G. (1985). Communication and unobtrusive control in contemporary organizations. In R. D. McPhee & P. K. Tompkins (Eds.), *Organizational communication: Traditional themes and new dimensions* (pp. 179–210). Newbury Park, CA: SAGE.

Tracy, S. J. (2005). Locking up emotion: Moving beyond dissonance for understanding emotion labor discomfort. *Communication Monographs, 72*(3), 261–283.

Tracy, S. J., & Trethewey, A. (2005). Fracturing the real-self↔fake-self dichotomy: Moving toward "crystallized" organizational discourses and identities. *Communication Theory, 15*(2), 168–195.

Turner, B. S. (2004). *The body in society* (2nd ed.). London, England: SAGE.

Van Maanen, J., & Schein, E. (1979). Toward a theory of organizational socialization. *Research in Organizational Behavior, 1*, 209–264.

van Riel, C. B. M., & Balmer, J. M. T. (1997). Corporate identity: The concept, its measurement and management. *European Journal of Marketing, 31*(5/6), 340–355.

Waldron, V. R., & Kassing, J. W. (2011). *Managing risk in communication encounters: Strategies for the workplace*. Thousand Oaks, CA: SAGE.

Watson, J., & Watson, D. H. (2012). Narratives in society, organizations and individual identities: An ethnographic study of pubs, identity work and the pursuit of "the real." *Human Relations, 65*(6), 683–704.

Weber, M. (1978). *Economy and society.* Berkeley: University of California Press.

Weick, K. E. (1979). *The social psychology of organizing* (2nd ed.). Reading, MA: Addison-Wesley.

Whyte, W. H. (1956). *The organization man.* New York, NY: Simon & Schuster.

Wiesenfeld, B. M., Raghuram, S., & Garud, R. (1999). Communication patterns as determinants of organizational identification in a virtual organization. *Organization Science, 10*(6), 777–790.

Wiesenfeld, B. M., Raghuram, S., & Garud, R. (2001). Organizational identification among virtual workers: The role of need for affiliation and perceived work-based social support. *Journal of Management, 27*(2), 213–229.

Note

1. The authors would like to thank Linda L. Putnam, Janet Fulk, Shawna Malvini Redden, Sarah Tracy, and Sanne Frandsen for their helpful comments on previous drafts of this essay.

CHAPTER 29

Generating Globalization

Cynthia Stohl and Shiv Ganesh

> Indeed, the entire subject matter of the social sciences can be considered to consist of explanations of aspects of social organization.
>
> (Blau & Scott, 1962, p. 1)

A longstanding question of social science is "What ways do humans come together to address individual and collective needs?" Whether referencing governmental organizations, large multinational corporations, small local companies, or nongovernmental and community organizations, scholars have always been concerned with the role of organizations in the structuring, maintenance and dissolution of societies. Thus it is not surprising that the rapid globalization of economic, political, and social life has had enormous impact not only on organizations themselves but on organizational studies in general and organizational communication in particular. This chapter focuses on the emergence of a global perspective in organizational communication research. Basing our review on the most commonly referenced issues inside our discipline, our account privileges work published by organizational communication scholars but acknowledges theoretical contributions from scholarship outside the field.

Organizational communication and globalization are intricately related. At its most basic level, *organizational communication* is the collective and interactive process of generating and interpreting messages, or what is called *connectedness in action* (Stohl, 1995). Globalization is "the widening, deepening, and speeding up of worldwide interconnectedness" (Held, McGrew, Goldblatt, & Perraton, 1999, p. 5). In both processes, networks of relationships and meaning are interactively created and these connections transcend spatio/temporal boundaries, organizational sectors, and routine social practices. According to Chanda (2007),

> the basic motivations that propelled humans to organize and connect with others—the urge to profit by trading, the drive to spread religious belief, the desire to exploit new lands . . . all had been assembled by 6000 BCE to start the process we now call globalization. (p. 11)

However, the word *globalization* did not even appear in Webster's dictionary until 1961, and in academic texts, *globalization* entered the vocabulary of social science and humanities around

1975 (Scholte, 2000). In 1993, Stohl argued that organizational communication needed to explore the "requisite [organizational] variety needed to address the intricate tapestry of globalization" (p. 377). There was also the publication of Kozminski and Cushman's (1993) *Organizational Communication and Management: A Global Perspective* and Monge's (1995) chapter, "Global network organizations," but overall, it was not until the late 1990s that the process terms *globalizing* and *globalization* began to appear regularly in the organizational communication literature. Monge's (1998) ICA presidential address highlighted the centrality of communication to the study of globalization, but after identifying a few global communication scholars, he noted, "Most of the rest of us in the communication discipline are just beginning to respond to the global imperative" (p. 143).

In the last 15 years, scholars have certainly responded! Globalization is now part of the everyday lexicon of organizational communication research and teaching, and the number of studies focused on globalization has grown exponentially. For example, three of the four organizational communication top papers at the 2012 International Communication Association conference dealt directly with globalization issues, ranging from the interorganizational networks of international health organizations (Shumate & Yannick, 2012) to agent-based modeling of technology use in virtual teams (Clark, Barley, & Leonardi, 2012) and the emotional experiences of travelers in international airports (Redden, 2012). Two of the best-selling textbooks in organizational communication, Conrad and Poole's (2012) *Strategic Organizational Communication in a Global Economy* and Cheney, Christensen, Zorn, and Ganesh's (2010) *Organizational Communication in an Age of Globalization,* specifically reference global processes in their titles. *The New Handbook of Organizational Communication* (Jablin & Putnam, 2001) added a chapter on globalization (Stohl, 2001), whereas the previous handbook (Jablin, Putnam, Roberts, & Porter, 1987) only had a chapter on cross-cultural perspectives (Triandis & Albert, 1987). We have traveled far as a subdiscipline, engaging in unfamiliar territory and gaining new perspectives on contemporary organizing.

In this chapter, we identify three generations of organizational communication research that focus specifically on globalization: (1) *the generation of uncertainty*, (2) *the generation of connectivity*, and (3) *the generation of ubiquity.* Each generation represents a unique perspective and set of assumptions about organizing, communicating, and globalizing. Taking a generational approach highlights the breadth of topics and the complexity of findings developed in this body of research as it has come of age over the last two decades. We do not, however, claim to uncover the actual mechanisms by which generations emerge. Rather, we focus on the features of the research that distinguish one generation from another.

Assessing differences in how globalization is conceptualized and communication is problematized across a large body of scholarship enables comparisons of research that emerged under rapidly changing social and technological conditions and generates avenues for further research in these times of flux. Consider that at the time this *Handbook* was conceptualized, it was inconceivable that a 29-minute video about a Ugandan warlord, Joseph Kony, posted on YouTube, produced by a very small nongovernmental organization (NGO), Invisible Children, would go so explosively viral. In just four days in March 2012, it was viewed by over 60 million people throughout the world, mentioned tens of thousands of times on Twitter, featured in thousands of media outlets, and debated by hundreds of organizational bloggers (Kron & Goodman, 2012). Clearly, the relations between organizations and society are transforming, and so is organizational communication scholarship.

Before we begin our generational analysis, however, two caveats are in order. First, although each generation of research grew out of a particular set of economic, political, historical, social, and technological circumstances, the generations are neither mutually exclusive nor temporally discrete. Rather, as in a family where generations reside together under the same roof, each generation is continually influenced by the others' perspectives; each succeeding generation contains traces of the past, and earlier generations adapt to and live alongside subsequent generations. Second, each research generation represents an archetype, and so specific studies are likely to contain some but not all the archetypal features of that generation. Just as *millennials* and *digital natives* are generational terms that describe a cohort who has grown up in the age of digitization and hence is considered to be more digitally literate than *Generation X* or *baby boomers,* there is great variation among them. Members of *Generation Y* may share many of the attitudes and assumptions of their cohorts, but some may embrace earlier generational perspectives and exhibit similar communication practices as their older siblings, parents, and grandparents. In the same sense, many scholars engage multiple generational perspectives.

Table 29.1 presents a summary of the three generations of globalization research in organizational communication. Looking downward, each column provides the rubric, that is, the defining attributes of globalization and communication embodied in a particular generation. Looking across the rows enables a comparison of the generations on a particular attribute. We first provide a brief overview of the two sets of attributes and then explore these attributes in the organizational communication research that exemplifies each generation. (For more details regarding specific theories and studies of globalization, we refer the reader to Stohl, 2005.) We conclude with suggestions for future research.

The Attributes of Globalization Research

> Despite the wealth of material written and analysis regarding globalization, the concept is still elusive. Each author, or school of thought, when attempting to give his or her own definition of the process . . . runs the risk of upsetting someone else's viewpoint or attributes describing globalization. (Katsiaoun, 2002, p. 3)

Across generations, there are two distinct types of attributes that distinguish the organizational communication literature. The first set of attributes reflect the *ontology* of globalization; that is, the archetypal beliefs about the nature of the phenomenon under investigation. The second set includes *communicative attributes*: the distinctive foundational assumptions about communication processes and competencies that guide research.

Ontological Attributes

The *problematic of globalization* identifies what each generation of research conceives as the reality and positioning of globalization phenomena in relation to organizational phenomena. Over time, there have been varying viewpoints regarding whether globalization means a radical departure from past practices or is merely a continuation and evolution of processes begun long ago. Emphases vary on whether globalization is situated within the internal dynamics of organizations (e.g., multicultural workforces), at the edges of an increasingly dense network (e.g., connections between and among organizational nodes), and/or in liminal spaces (e.g., interactions among individuals, groups, and organizations). *Agents of globalization* references the primary actors who constitute the rules, routines, and practices that accomplish globalization within each generation of scholarship. Agents may be (a) formal organizational representatives who reshape organizational culture, structure, and interaction through the management of difference, (b) individual boundary spanners who link organizations across time and space, or (c) entrepreneurial agents who leverage organizational identity and

Table 29.1 Three Generations of Globalization Research

	The Generation of Uncertainty	**The Generation of Connectivity**	**The Generation of Ubiquity**
Ontological Attributes of Globalization			
Problematic of Globalization	Is globalization a distinct and unique phenomenon of the time?	Globalization exists and is at the foreground of study. How do organizations respond to globalization dynamics?	Globalization exists and is in the background of study. What is the relationship between individual efficacy and organizational action?
Locus of Globalization	Formal organizations	Interorganizational linkages	Liminal or transnational public spheres
Agents of Globalization	Formal members of organizations	Interorganizational actors; boundary spanners	Entrepreneurial actors; community stakeholders
Foundational Debate: Organizational Form	Are there distinct organizational forms that can be called *global*?	What are the relationships among organizations in the global system?	Are formal organizations still relevant?
Communicative Attributes of Globalization			
Communication Logic	Intergroup logic	Networking logic	Deinstitutionalized logic
Communication Problem	Engaging intercultural differences	Creating new forms of partnerships	Collective action
Communication Skill: Global Communicative Competence	Cultural awareness and accommodation	Building extensive and effective stakeholder relations	Coherence management
Foundational Debate: Communication Ethics	Cultural relativity vs. universalism	Communitarianism vs. cosmopolitanism	Individual efficacy vs. expanded corporate interest

simultaneously create and sustain new groups and identities.

Finally, *the foundational ontological debate* in communication research underscores generational questions regarding the emergence, maintenance, and evolution of organizational forms in globalization. Raising questions about organizational forms enables scholars to see intricate connections between social structure and communication.

Communicative Attributes

Communication logics identify the central rationale informing normative material practices and symbolic constructions that constitute organizing. Building upon the idea of *institutional logics* (Friedland & Alford, 1991)—belief systems that sustain different types of social relations—*communication logics* provide fundamental principles that guide interaction. Each generation foregrounds a particular logic, although (as in all of social science literature) researchers rely upon and integrate insights and ideas from the past. An *intergroup logic* suggests that communication processes are grounded in the salience of social group identity rather than personal identity (Harwood & Giles, 2005). A *network logic* is predicated on the notion that communication is no longer bound by spatial proximity and temporality, and a *deinstitutionalized logic* of communication is rooted in individual agency and organizational efficacy.

The primary communication problem for each generation of globalization research is, at its most basic level, a problem of interdependence, coordination, control, and collaboration. Moreover, in each generation, problems are found at the nexus of the macro context (e.g., regulatory rules, institutional norms, national values, cultural variability) and the micro context of the organizing unit (e.g., worker values, group attitudes, organizational stereotypes, communication climate), but the entry point is different. The central problem may be seen as how to manage intercultural differences, create meaningful partnerships, and/or engage multiple sectors, stakeholders, and modes of action without formal authority and incentive systems.

The foundational communication debate across generations of research revolves around issues of communicative ethics. Communication inquiry is pragmatic as well as normative, identifying good, effective, and useful communication processes or, conversely, critiquing destructive and unjust practices. Ethics are at the heart of communication studies, and as with other areas of inquiry, scholars of globalization engage in vigorous ethical debates relating to issues of relativism versus universalism, cultural imperialism, and possibilities for voice and choice in volatile environments.

The Generation of Uncertainty

> We live in a world of transformations, affecting almost every aspect of what we do. For better or worse, we are being propelled into a global order that no one fully understands, but which is making its effects felt upon all of us. (Giddens, 1999)

The first generation of globalization research in communication focuses on globalization as a turbulent and uncertain multidimensional process that influences and is influenced by economic, political, cultural, technological, and organizational dynamics. Until the late 1990s, organizational communication studies narrowly explored intercultural differences across management or organizational styles. The research tended to be comparative, rooted in the cultural differences identified by social psychologists (e.g., Hofstede, 1984). In contrast, first-generation scholars address the ways in which organizations change as a result of globalization dynamics, including the ways in which macro mechanisms of convergence are entrenched in the micro processes of divergence and cultural variability (see Stohl, 2001).

Globalization references increasing extensity, intensity, velocity, and deepening of the impact of worldwide interconnectedness (Held et al., 1999). Rather than simply extending traditional topics into the global workplace, the first generation of communication globalization researchers took seriously the notion that emerging technology and "the rise of informationalism was the new material, the technological basis of economic activity and social organization" (Castells, 1996, p. 12). *The central problematic of this new generation was whether (and if so, how) globalization was a unique phenomenon that radically altered the relationship between communication and organization.* The three dynamics of globalization—the compression of time and space, disembeddedness of events, and global consciousness through processes of reflexivity (see Monge, 1998)—became the fundamental building blocks of scholarship. For example, Fulk (2001) explored the ways in which the integration of new communication technologies with computerization (what she describes as the move from connectivity to communality) "created a level of flexibility in organizational arrangements necessary for institutional reforms involving deregulation, privatization, and weakening the social contract between worker and employer" (p. 93).

Other first-generation communication researchers addressed issues of global restructuring and increasing flexibility by interrogating post-Fordist practices that shaped a new communication order. For some, flexibility and the emerging social contract were seen as empowering communicative processes. Gossett (2006), for example, found possibilities of a contingent workforce of temporary workers "organizing into a distinct work community to improve their own work conditions" (p. 116). For others, organizational restructuring and the flexibility that was embodied in neo-liberalism/globalization was seen as a new form of workplace control in which gendered and discriminatory work practices were still maintained and even strengthened (e.g., Nadesan, 2001). Significantly, regardless of organizational communication scholars' definitions and positions on globalization, first-generation researchers agreed that the locus of globalization was found in formal organizations across civil, governmental, and business sectors, and the agents of globalization were formal members, including managers and employees of these organizations. There may have been uncertainty about the unique features of globalization, but the centrality and power of formal organizations were affirmed.

Nonetheless, reflecting the volatile and uncertain global environment, debates about the very existence and meaning of globalization for organizations were common (see Held et al., 1999, for accounts of the debate among hyperglobalists, skeptics, and transformationalists). The beneficiaries of globalization (Cheney & Barnett, 2005), the oppositional tensions of global processes (Papa, Auwal, & Singhal, 1995; Stohl, 2001), and the nature, causes, timing, and effects of globalization were contested (Nadesan, 2001).

First-generation scholarship also reflects the uncertainty and intensification of consciousness that comes with increasing connectedness—what Robertson (1992) describes as *relativization*. That is, within the emerging global system, individuals and groups take shape relative to the others that surround them so that even when they see themselves as separate from the rest of the world, they establish their position in relation to the others. As one reads first-generation research, it is striking that no matter what globalization stance the scholarship takes, most author(s) explicitly describe their position relative to others. For example, Cloud (2001) argued that despite apparent socio-economic and cultural changes associated with globalization, the most fundamental feature of workplace social relations and communication (i.e., the powerful class antagonism between workers and employers) remained the same. In direct challenge to the hyperglobalist position of a radical disjuncture from the past, Cloud specified the critical difference between her skeptical position and others: "Cultural studies and critical organizational communication possess a common shortcoming, namely, misplaced faith in the idea that we are living in new times that require new politics" (p. 269).

As scholars were debating what globalization meant, organizational typologies were being developed that created radically different views of the movement from domestic to global organizing (see Stohl, 2001). Because organizations were seen as the building blocks of this uncertain world, the foundational organizational debate revolved around whether or not there were distinct global organizational forms. Relying on the work of institutional theorists (e.g., DiMaggio & Powell, 1991) many argued that globalization processes (e.g., the series of agreements to reduce international trade tariffs and open national markets to international corporate investment) coerced structural and interactive convergence in organizations and institutions across countries. As organizations competed in the uncertain and rapidly changing environment, they also became more similar insofar as they developed mimetic mechanisms to look to each other to see what to do. Some scholars argued that increased interactional and informational flows among educational, professional, and market-driven institutions created similar experience, socialization practices, and norms that resulted in similar organizing practices throughout the globe (see Stohl, 2001). Many first-generation scholars posited that global organizations needed to be networked, team oriented, nonhierarchical, culturally diverse, flexible, and highly responsive to volatile environmental conditions (Weick & Van Orden, 1990). For example, in a special forum on *Management Communication in the Age of Globalization*, Cesaria (2000) argued that global organizations "must blur internal and external communication, demand high levels of employee participation, develop simultaneously loose and tight couplings, and value the coordination of horizontal expertise" (p. 170).

But at the same time that some scholars identified the competitive and institutional pressures that were making organizations more similar, two related paradoxes of global organizational communication became evident. First, globalizing processes of convergence called forth localizing dynamics of divergence—that is, differences in organizing principles that were intersubjectively constructed and culturally saturated. The coterminous drives for (a) sustenance, development, and democracy and (b) maintenance of roots and distinctiveness (linguistic, geographic, religious, and historical) were vividly captured in two early metaphors of globalization: Friedman's (1999) *The Lexus and the Olive Tree* and Barber's (1992) *Jihad vs. McWorld*. This duality became part of organizational communication discourse. Deetz's 1997 ICA presidential address described the "character of the times" by referring to the tensions between the "fi" and "phe" (i.e., the profit and the prophet motives). Chen (2000) made a strong communicative case that integration into the global economy was only possible if organizations in the People's Republic of China were able to modernize and manage cultural and social change. She argued, "Chinese enterprises must negotiate their history of state and family owner ship—which value personal connections and relationships—with their future in a competitive market-driven economic environment" (p. 153).

The second global paradox emerging from the first generation of scholarship is that emerging global consciousness simultaneously gives rise to a strong sense of individual and group identity. For example, in an ethnographic study of intercultural communication in U.S.-owned *maquiladoras* in Mexico, Lindsley (1999) found that cultural group identities and intercultural group histories were the foundation of interpretive processes and problematic interaction. Observations and interviews with *maquiladora* owners, managers, and employees as well as analyses of documents and newspaper articles suggested that in-group/out-group perceptions of socio-structural inequalities, intergroup power relationships, and negative stereotypes were exacerbated in the context of increased global consciousness.

Overall, global uncertainty and tensions between convergence and divergence gave rise to a communicative *intergroup logic* in which communication processes are grounded in the salience of contextual social group identity rather than personal identity (Harwood & Giles, 2005). Further, social identities, normative expectations, and societal institutions are continually being negotiated in a context in which organizational boundaries no longer remain spatially or communicatively distinct (Jones, Watson, Gardner, & Gallois, 2004). Rather than conducting comparative analyses in which one culture is referenced in terms of another, an intergroup logic frames communication as a form of mutual negotiation and accommodation, often creating a new, global identity. Stage (1999), for example, studied how locals and expatriates in American subsidiaries in Thailand negotiated their common organizational culture.

Gomes, Cohen, and Mellahi's (2011) study of South African and Congolese managers illustrates the power of intergroup logic. In a highly conflict-ridden strategic alliance between Vodacom and

Congolese Wireless, they found that restructuring new management policies and procedures to reduce disparities in career opportunities between these groups was circumscribed "by the continued presence of perceived interactional injustice . . . the feeling of not being treated with respect and dignity during interactions with managers from the other partner in the alliance" (Gomes et al., 2011, p. 5). Resolving the conflicts required an intergroup understanding of the legacy of apartheid and multiple, iterative, and radical structural, personnel, and interactive changes that transcended traditional internal and micro-level solutions.

Following intergroup logic, the central communication problem in the first generation of research is engaging cultural difference, and the primary communication skill is global awareness and accommodation. Problems are shaped by differences found at the nexus of the macro and micro contexts of the organizing unit. By the late 1990s, research from an intergroup perspective demonstrated that, in the face of the high failure rate of global ventures, there was a need to better integrate and accommodate geographically dispersed operations. A culturally diverse workforce required a different set of skills for both managers and workers. The 1993 Corning (U.S.)–Vitro (Mexican) merger, for instance, was described as a "marriage made in hell" (DePalma, 1994, p. A16); not only did national economic policy influence the merger but cultural differences and non-accommodation related to hierarchy, temporal, and work/life issues were paramount.

But despite the millions of dollars corporations spent each year on traditional cross-cultural training (Wiseman, 2002), culture-specific knowledge and accommodation were insufficient. The problem was that an "Italian" company might have as many non-Italians as Italians, a quintessential American company could be operating in France, and the manager of a large German company was likely to have moved on within months of a new appointment. For first-generation scholars, a global mindset was needed.

To address these changing organizational demands, communication researchers (e.g., Kienzle & Husar, 2007) began to embrace the idea of *cultural intelligence* (Earley & Ang, 2003). Cultural intelligence is the ability to recognize which behaviors are specifically grounded in cultural, structural, or individual factors and which are not. Rather than focusing on specific cultural differences and how they impact organizational communication, cultural intelligence embodies the multidimensional nature of a global mindset in which knowledge of cultural differences is only a small part of the competent global organizational actor.

As first-generation globalization researchers investigated problems relating to cultural difference, accommodation, and global organizational forms, a myriad of ethical communication issues emerged. Chief among ethical dilemmas was a debate about *relativism* versus *universalism*: Would researchers and practitioners have to understand ethics in relative, emic terms that were specific to a particular cultural environment or would an emerging world order require the articulation of universal and global ethical organizational communication principles? Debates about the need for civility in organizational communication exemplify this continued debate. On one hand, scholars such as Kramer and Hess (2002) have called for the investigation of general rules for organizational civility that facilitate continued coexistence and coordination. On the other, Kisselberg and Dutta (2009) posit that the construct of organizational civility is infused by dominant, hegemonic, Western cultural norms that potentially position non-Western norms as uncivil. They argue for a postcolonial approach to organizational communication ethics that deconstructs dominant discourse on civility to make space for alternative and marginalized voices.

Debates about the merits of universalist and culture-general versus particularistic and culture-specific approaches to communication ethics have not abated. The enormous growth of communication studies in Asia, South America, and Africa over the past 15 years shows that these issues are still highly relevant. In a special issue of the *Asian Journal of Communication*, Wang and

Kuo (2010) identify several tensions among Eastern and Western communication ethics and suggest transcendence through the concept of cultural commensurability, emphasizing "similarity and equivalence, rather than commonality and uniformity" (p. 152). Collier (2009) emphasizes the importance of the emergence of new hybrid identifications by Israeli and Palestinian women in determining the success of an organizational peace-building initiative.

In summary, first-generation scholarship set the groundwork for the study of organizational communication as a process that is embedded in the micro and macro dynamics of the emerging global system. It continues to influence the thinking of following generations.

The Generation of Connectivity

> As an historical trend, dominant functions and processes in the Information Age are increasingly organized around networks. Networks constitute the new social morphology of our societies, and the diffusion of networking logic substantially modifies the operation and outcomes in processes of production, experience, power, and culture. (Castells, 1996, p. 500)

Concomitant with the network turn in both sciences and social sciences (Monge & Contractor, 2003), the second generation of globalization scholarship ushered in a concentrated focus on connectivity in organizational communication studies. Scholarly debates about the existence and uniqueness of contemporary globalization processes were virtually silenced by a general agreement that there were unique dynamics associated with increasing interdependence and the ease of transcending spatio-temporal boundaries.

Organizational communication studies continued to move away from comparative studies of organizational differences based primarily on location, and greater attention was given to the attributes and implications of global connectivity. For example, in comparing national fair trade organizations (TransFair in the United States and Fair Trade Foundation in the United Kingdom) Bennett, Foot, and Xenos (2011) studied the interorganizational network structure of the websites in each organization's network. Linking network properties such as centrality to different organizational narratives, their analyses suggest that structural and semantic connectivity not only define the strategic relationships among global organizations and individuals but they empirically demonstrate that forms of global activism and participation are constituted through interorganizational linkages.

Generally, second-generation globalization scholarship is less concerned with defining globalization and more interested in identifying and understanding the communicative constitution of the emerging world system. Castells (2001) persuasively argued that "new information technologies are integrating the world in global networks of instrumentality" (p. 21). An underlying assumption was now that issues of the environment, economy, workplace health and safety, human rights, and so on are so complex and interconnected that they require new approaches, hybrid structuring, and innovative solutions. Thus the central problematic moved from questioning what may be unique about globalization to examining how societies must organize to meet the demands and consequences of global interconnectedness.

This central problematic revolves around some of the most robust findings and propositions of earlier research. First, the demands of globalization require flexibility, responsiveness, speed, and efficient knowledge production, generation, and dissemination (Monge & Fulk, 1999). These organizing features are most likely to be found in nonhierarchical, emergent, inter- and intraorganizational networks (Stohl, 2005). Second, increasing global and local interconnectedness evokes organizational tensions and paradox. Third, the continuing evolution of communication technologies, widespread dispersion of organizational members across time and space, decreasing costs of communication, and increased electronic dependence magnify the communicative tensions, contradictions, challenges, and opportunities embedded in new forms of organizing (Poole & Van De Ven, 1989).

Second-generation studies of virtual software teams (Gibson & Gibbs, 2006) exemplify the integration of these propositions within a framework of interconnectedness. Gibbs (2006) identified three main tensions in global team interaction rooted in the need for global integration and local differentiation: autonomy/connectedness, inclusion/exclusion, and empowerment/disempowerment. In these studies, the constraining effects, challenges, and tensions of the global/virtual teams' network structure were mitigated by creating a local safe communication climate, bridging the local/global divide and transcending cultural differences (see Seibold, Hollingshead, & Yoon, Chapter 13, for discussion of research on virtual teams).

In second-generation scholarship, we find interconnectedness more firmly rooted in political, socio-economic, technological, and historical contexts of organizing than earlier studies. The organizational communication dimensions of topics addressing issues such as political crises (Taylor & Doerfel, 2003), human rights (Stohl & Stohl, 2005), market liberalization (Cheney & Cloud, 2006), and health epidemics (Shumate, Fulk, & Monge, 2005) are featured to a greater and greater extent. These studies take on the trans-spatial nomenclature of globalization theorists—including webs, scapes, networks, distanciation, and space of flows (e.g., Appadurai, 1997; Robertson, 1992)—treating them as remarkable but uncontested features of the organizational landscape. Note how Monge and Contractor (2003) describe organizational processes:

> Capital, material, labor, messages, and symbols circulate through suppliers, producers, customers, strategic partners, governing agencies, and affiliates to form what Hall (1990) calls the "global postmodern culture" (p. 29), one that is simultaneously global and local. Built on the basis of flexible, dynamic, ephemeral relations, these network flows constitute the bulk of organizational activity (Monge & Fulk, 1999). Thus, global organizations are processes, not places. (p. 4)

In the generation of connectivity, the locus of globalization moves from discrete organizations to interorganizational linkages and connections. Organizations remain the basic organizing feature of global systems, but the agents of globalization are the links themselves. Globalization is seen to be located on the edges—that is, the network connections among *organizational nodes*. From transnational advocacy networks to transnational feminist network (Dempsey, Parker, & Krone, 2011) and small world networks to wide area networks (Barnett, 2011), an alphabet soup of interorganizational linkages permeate second-generation literature. The principal debate within this literature revolves around what types of interorganizational relationships are most efficacious for various stakeholder groups.

At first blush, it may seem that because connectivity is the hallmark of this generation of scholarship, it is limited to studies utilizing network theory and formal structural analyses. However, while there is a strong legacy of network analyses within this generation, this is not the defining feature. Rather, the central assumption—globalization embodies communication no longer constrained by spatial proximity, temporality, and rigid organizational boundaries—transforms even the most traditional organizational constructs into multilevel relational phenomena. For example, organizational justice has typically been conceived as an internally derived construct, and research focused on employer-employee exchange and dissent within the narrow purview of an organization (Kassing, 2008). In contrast, typical of second-generation global organizational communication scholars, Whiteman (2009) focuses on organizational justice in the context of relations and connections between local indigenous peoples and multinational firms. She finds that cultural relations and indigenous beliefs permeate organizational boundaries and reinforce patterns of inclusion and exclusion producing unique notions of justice.

Discursive analyses of interorganizational dialogues between government and business also point to the centrality of connectivity in understanding globalization processes within this generation. Zoller (2004) persuasively demonstrates that a primary source of transnational power includes corporate access to economic and regulatory policy construction. Globalization dynamics are embodied in the linkages of the Transatlantic Business Dialogue, a corporate coalition between business and governments. Such studies not only emphasize the importance of connectivity in constructing transnational corporate power, they emphasize the causative role of globalization in the formation of activist resistance. Dutta (2012) argues that "just as globalization expands the geographic and material scopes of transnational corporations, it also opens up new spaces and methods for global organizing directed at social transformation" (p. 192). Dense connections between local and transnational organizers are central to such resistance: "Grassroots organizers are increasingly networking with transnational activists to effect changes in specific communities, thereby connecting the local and the global" (p. 193).

Thus in this generation, regardless of paradigm or method, organizational communication is conceptualized as global, multilevel linkages among three sectors of society. Each sector has its own set of actors with differing properties of relationships depending upon which sectors are interacting: (1) civil society, including nonprofit and NGOs; (2) the commercial sector, including small businesses, corporations, and industry groups; and (3) the public sector, comprised of states, intergovernmental organizations (IGOs), and parties to treaties and other international accords.

No longer is an intergroup logic dominating research agendas. Rather, we find a communication logic of networks. Predicated on the collapse of space and time in the global system, no longer bound by spatial proximity and temporality, a *network logic* assumes multilevel relational linkages as the building blocks of globalization. Organizational relations (e.g., trust), tasks (e.g., mobilization), and resource needs (e.g., informational goods) are construed in a context of connectivity. Complex and seamless connections among individuals, objects, events, and organizations inform the material practices, communicative routines, and symbolic constructions that constitute organizing principles.

As suggested above, some of the empirical work in this generation has been inspired by theoretical developments in community ecology and coevolutionary theory (Monge, Heise, & Margolin, 2008) and methodological developments in network theory (Monge & Contractor, 2003). For example, Shumate and her colleagues have developed an expansive program of research that explores properties and evolution of organizational networks across sectors (Atouba & Shumate, 2010). Using coevolutionary theory to predict patterns of alliances and collaborations within HIV-AIDS International NGOs, Shumate et al. (2005) found that although proximity and common ties with IGOs helped predict patterns of alliances, the best predictor of such alliances was past connectivity. Testing the propositions of their Symbiotic Sustainability Model, Shumate and O'Connor (2010) found that most corporations only develop alliances with a few NGOs and with one NGO in an issue industry.

Network relationships have also been explored in the quest to understand global dynamics of interorganizational cooperation and competition in the development of civil society. Two research exemplars are Doerfel and Taylor's (2004) study of the two-year political transformation of Croatia into a democratic nation and Stohl and Stohl's (2005) analyses of two interdependent historical cases—the creation of the Universal Declaration of Human Rights in 1948 and the Helsinki Final Declaration of 1975. Each adapts Burt's (1992) theory of structural holes to explore the social and political impact of linkages between NGOs and IGOs. The theory of structural holes, designed to explore the competitive advantage (greater information and control) of brokerage roles, is adapted for a cooperative system of increasingly globalized intensive and extensive connections.

In the generation of connectivity, links not only transmit information/control between network clusters, they also build relationships and close social distances, enabling interpretive diversity, relational support, representational participation, legitimacy, and institutionalization. Filling structural holes may strengthen a particular position within the global network but also may develop symbiotic rather than solely competitive relations (Stohl & Stohl, 2005). Globalization, for second-generation scholars, has wrought a radically new set of communicative contingencies and theoretical connections.

Also embedded within second-generation scholarship is the idea that the issues facing organizations are so interdependent and complex that (1) they cannot be addressed successfully by individuals or organizations acting alone and (2) information about these issues is no longer within the purview of any one region, individual, group, or organization. Digitized technology and mobile media also mean there is no longer a monopoly of information by any one elite group. Structured by these highly interdependent relations and interorganizational connections embedded in globalization, the central communication problem moves from how to engage multicultural differences to how to create new forms of partnerships that are viable and enable organizations to meet their goals.

These answers are communicatively complex. Competitive and cooperative strategies, consolidated and constrained alliances, convergent and divergent discourses, and individual and collective identities are linked in the global organizational landscape. The core-periphery interorganizational network structure Kim and Barnett (2000) found among international telecommunications organizations, for example, can be contrasted with the more recent work of scholars who found that "a trend toward regionalization and decentralization . . . is taking place even as the world telecommunications network has become denser" (Lee, Monge, Bar, & Matei, 2007, p. 416).

Clearly, organizational partnerships, mergers, and joint ventures as well as global configurations including offshoring and outsourcing were part of first-generational studies (e.g., Bastien, 1987; Søderberg & Varra, 2003). But intergroup logic meant that the emphasis was primarily on the search for cultural commonalities as actors attempted to build new organizational structures. As suggested above, in communication studies, the very high failure rate of mergers (most estimates are 50%–80%) was typically blamed on cultural conflicts at the interpersonal, group, organizational, and interorganizational levels (see Stohl, McCann, & Baku, 2013). What is new about the second generation focus on partnerships is the emphasis on the inevitability of connectivity and the necessity of collaboration to achieve global organizational goals. This is manifested in (1) the move to study linkages across sectors as well as organizations, (2) a focus on both formal and informal partnerships, and (3) highlighting the interdependence between technological materiality and every day social practices that constitute global partnership. In all three areas, the research is grounded within the socio-economic/political/cultural/environmental changes brought by globalization.

Cross-Sector Partnerships

The reasons for an amplified focus on cross-sector partnerships are rooted in the increased complexity and interdependencies of globalization. Advocacy and operational NGOs today are more tightly linked to the profit and government sectors (Yaziji & Doh, 2009). Brugmann and Prahalad (2007) describe a "new social compact" in which traditional adversarial relationships between business and civil society are transformed. The different competencies, infrastructures, network positions, and knowledge that each sector possesses are needed by the other. NGOs can pave "legitimate" paths to new markets and multinational corporations can provide new business models that enhance NGO legitimacy and their ability to survive. The growing expectations for corporations to act in socially responsible ways (see May & Roper, Chapter 31, on corporate social responsibility [CSR]) also are increasingly predicated upon novel types of partnerships among different types of organizations.

The generation of connectivity also highlights informal grassroots partnerships and stakeholder collaborations. Communities and organizations are increasingly enmeshed in expanding stakeholder groups. Social identities, normative expectations, and societal institutions must continually be negotiated as they can no longer remain spatially or communicatively distinct. Dempsey (2007), for example, explores how formal NGO linkages with funding agencies and institutional regulators and informal partnerships with diverse stakeholder groups complicate issues of voice and accountability. She unpacks the paradoxical practices of *bounded voice*, which enable those with less social, political, or economic power to speak.

The generation of connectivity also provides a nuanced view of technological, cultural, and interpretive processes across global partnerships and collaborations. Leonardi and Bailey (2008) persuasively argue that "transformational technologies," that is, those "technologies that allow the creation, modification and manipulation of digital artifacts . . . [are] dramatically reshaping the way offshoring occurs by permitting the global distribution of work within, rather than only across, functions" (p. 414). Using the logic of connectivity, they describe these global partnerships as *task-based offshoring*. Unlike earlier work in which propositions about global partnerships were developed in isolation from the constitutive tasks that embody the partnership, second-generation scholarship addresses the ways in which transformed and transformative interpretations of everyday work practices constitute global partnerships.

Moore's (2011) ethnographic study of a car assembly work group in a joint venture between German car manufacturer, BMW, and the British Morris Mini is a case in point. Her *holistic ethnography* focused on the ways that processes of integration were influenced by culturally divergent interpretations of specific tasks. In a study of performance engineers at centers in the U.S. and Mexico who offshored work to engineers in India, Leonardi (2012) found that different conceptualizations "about what knowledge is and where it lies stifled sharing, impeded learning, and led to general animosity among members of the organization who needed to work collaboratively to design and test vehicles" (p. 92).

The intensity and extensity of global partnerships requires communicative skills that go beyond the global mindset identified in first-generation scholarship. In communication terms, the critical global skill of the second generation is building extensive, inclusive and effective stakeholder relations and networks. New forms of cooperation require organizational ability to (1) understand changing stakeholder preferences and values, (2) utilize culturally determined notions of expertise, and (3) maintain trust and credibility through open communicative practices (Johansson & Stohl, 2012). To know whom to network with, what to network about, and how to develop and maintain the appropriate kinds of connections are foundational skills in a world of increasing connectivity. In the last 10 years, the *Harvard Business Review* has published more than 20 articles on networking as a critical global skill.

Another significant by-product of connectedness and new types of networking is the blurring of taken-for-granted distinctions between public and private experiences and obscuring boundaries among local, national, and global spheres of influence. "On the one hand, 'social' organizations now have to emulate the characteristics, norms and behaviors of the market. On the other hand, 'economic' organizations have begun to take on tasks once understood as public sector responsibilities" (Larner, 2002, p. 654).

Not surprisingly, a central ethical debate in the second generation revolves around the role of organizations in society. Is corporate social responsibility primarily grounded in what is good for an organization's stockholders or for all its stakeholders? Are relevant stakeholders only those who are directly involved or engaged with organizational missions, or does it extend to the entire community, whether that be local, national, or global? In her analysis of a CSR campaign carried out by Vattenfall, a Global 500 Swedish energy company, Trapp (2012) illustrated the dangers inherent in global boundary crossing. During the campaign, Vattenfall was portrayed as being a part of both the business and civil society sectors. Organizational credibility was weakened, she argued, by the inconsistent and discordant messaging regarding "Vattenfall being more intent on organizing a public, collective action to fight climate change than on securing company-related business interests" (p. 463).

Second-generation discussions of corporate social responsibility mirror long-held ethical debates within international relations about what has been described as the *cosmopolitan-communitarian divide* (Linklater, 1982). The cosmopolitan perspective contends that our shared sense of humanity renders distinctions between insiders and outsiders meaningless when it comes to ethical decisions. Ethical judgments transcend local communities, organizations, or sovereign states. Communitarianism, on the other hand, conceptualizes morality and ethical responsibility "as being socially constructed within a political community rather than being shared by humanity at large" (Rosamond, 2011, p. 67). This debate still has relevance (May, Cheney, & Roper, 2007). A content analysis of the Codes of Ethics of 157 corporations on the Global 500 and/or Fortune 500 lists, for example, found that ethical concerns were most often narrowly construed as related to profits/stockholders and behaviors mandated by law. Only corporations headquartered in the European Union contained within their Codes of Ethics a significant degree of concern for the larger global environment and community (Stohl, Stohl, & Popova, 2009).

In summary, the second generation accepts the reality of globalization. By interrogating the communicative, structural, and ethical arrangements deemed to be most suitable for this complex environment, the stage was set for a new generation to study collective spaces that were no longer bound by the limiting assumptions of the past.

The Generation of Ubiquity

The *Economist* (2009) posted a chart of the number of mentions of the word *globalization* in their magazine since 1979. Somewhat interestingly, it seems that *globalization* as a search term has been decreasing steadily from 2004–2009.

Just as the term *globalization* has begun to recede from public discourse, third-generation scholarship tends to gives less direct attention to the term. However, this does not mean that there is less concern for, or fewer studies of, the processes of globalization. Rather, globalization has become ubiquitous in the sense that it is taken for granted and therefore no longer remarkable. In a similar vein, Bimber, Flanagin, and Stohl (2012) describe the contemporary socio-technical infrastructure as ubiquitous. That is, regardless of individual ability to access digital technology, social life has become organized around easy and relatively inexpensive connectivity among global interactants.

Third-generation scholars, therefore, are less likely to explicitly label globalization dynamics. Instead, they are considered part of the ordinary, expected infrastructure of organizing. In writing about contemporary conceptions of work Ashcraft (2011), for example, evokes the permeable boundaries and interconnectedness of globalization explicitly addressed in earlier generations. But her discussion of the dislocated or relocated conception of work does not reference globalization *per se*. Ashcraft conceives of work "not only as a concrete practice occurring amid institutional systems . . . but also as a discourse formation that evolves across many sites of cultural activity" (Ashcraft, 2011, p. 15).

Castells (2008) points to the pervasive influence of globalization in all aspects of life: "Not everything or everyone is globalized, but the global networks that structure the planet affect everything and everyone" (p. 81). It is not just technology that has made globalization ubiquitous, but rather, as recent Occupy Movement and protests throughout the world suggest, it is the interpenetration and interdependence among national economies and all aspects of socio-cultural activity that make globalization inescapable.

In the generation of ubiquity, the communicative landscape is considered one of decentralized interconnectedness, enhanced flows of information sharing, and potentially combustible relations between social actors. But at the same time, the global power and influence of small clusters of economic actors are acknowledged. Unique to the third generation is the primary focus on the positioning and interaction amongst these powerful corporate actors *and* nontraditional, self-organizing agents. Globalization has produced new spaces for individual action that create opportunities for organizing that are challenging fundamental assumptions about organizations. The central problematic moves from how do organizations respond to globalization dynamics to how does organizing, whether for profit, social change, and/or other collective goals, occur when formal authority, membership, or incentive systems may be sufficient but are no longer necessary?

For third-generation scholarship, the locus of globalization is now found primarily in the liminal spaces betwixt and between individuals, groups, and organizations (i.e., an expanded and reconfigured public sphere). The relationships and links among organizational sectors (the locus in the second generation) continue to evolve as they are augmented by digitally enhanced, formally unaffiliated personal connections. Whereas in the generation of connectivity, the network logic referred primarily to connections among *organizationally focused* links (members, teams, flows, information, etc.), now the agents of globalization reference both organizations and entrepreneurial actors who leverage organizational identities and simultaneously create and sustain new groups and identities. Entrepreneurs may represent established organizations even as they construct newer, smaller, less formal organizing structures (Ganesh & Stohl, 2010).

Third-generation scholarship directly problematizes the nature of organizational forms and communication, raising provocative questions about the role and shape of organizations in the face of heightened individual efficacy. Some scholars such as Fisher, Stanley, Berman, and Neff (2005) are at the cusp of the transition from the *generation of connectivity* to the *generation of ubiquity*. In light of the transformative possibilities of social technologies, they raise the central question of the third-generation debate: Do organizations matter? Using survey data from participants at five global protests and disaggregating protesters by distance, they answered their question in the affirmative. Formal organizations extended the protesting population at the events beyond the local citizenry. Formal organizations, others concur, continue to be salient, because they serve to legitimate activism and give individual activists a coherent collective identity (Toft, 2011). However, several scholars (e.g., Bennett & Segerberg, 2012; Shirky, 2008) argue that informal and individualized communication brokerage processes now enable individuals to function in ways that previously required large-scale organizational infrastructure. Popular press accounts of the "Facebook revolution" and the power of Twitter also reinforce the notion that formal organizations are no longer necessary within the public sphere (Taylor, 2011).

Third-generation researchers often argue that individuals no longer need to establish trusting and rich relationships; relationships come and go without much cost, and they can experiment more easily because failure itself isn't costly. Benkler (2006) points out that decentralized "social production . . . [and] non-proprietary cooperative action carried out through radically distributed, nonmarket mechanisms" (p. 3) distinguishes the networked information from the industrial information economy in which formal organizations were central. Bimber et al. (2012) argue that organizations still matter, but rather than offering fixed and inflexible templates for involvement, organizations offer much broader opportunities for people to define their roles and to establish their own participatory styles.

The decentering of organizational activity occurs both in civil society and within the corporate, for-profit world. *Crowdsourcing*, a process by which organizations describe specific tasks or problems on a specialized digital platform so that nonaffiliated participants can solve them, is becoming commonplace in all sectors. The *New York Times* and *The Guardian* have crowdsourced the labeling, tagging, and archiving of over 24,000 e-mails from Sarah Palin; NGOs crowdsource translations of their mission statements; Procter and Gamble, Intel, Google, and Hewlett Packard are just a few of the Global 500 companies that are engaging skilled independent entrepreneurs to help solve problems associated with production errors, technical glitches, and/or research and development needs (Howe, 2006).

Weber (2012), in a study of the newspaper industry, highlights the ways in which individual and organizational spaces become enmeshed, thus altering the for-profit organizational landscape and institutional context in fundamental ways. Employing an evolutionary approach, he explores how participatory forms of news production (e.g., blogs and social networking) that developed outside the boundaries of the traditional news media organizations and specific geographic borders create competitive and separate resource spaces that disrupt traditional organizational routines. He then empirically demonstrates how new variations in routine practices (i.e., *speciated* forms) eventually developed linkages with the existing community, unsettling and then transforming organizing routines throughout the community.

A deinstitutionalized logic of communication is grounded in these decentered, turbulent, participatory processes. Although similar to the generation of connectivity's elevation of linkage as a primary mechanism of a globalized system, in the generation of ubiquity, the nature of those linkages is oftentimes rooted in individual agency rather than organizational efficacy. When the devices people have in their pockets can do what organizations typically have done (broker information and coordinate resources and activity across time and space), globalizing comes not only from concerted strategy but from participatory, unstable, and sometimes dissensus-seeking communicative processes (Deetz, 1992). The fundamental principles that guide interaction are no longer bound by the constraints embodied in relationships defined by organizational identity. Neff's (2012) insightful analysis of Silicon Valley's "venture labor" (where employees act as entrepreneurs and bear some of the risk of their companies without actually owning the company) is an exemplar of this new emerging logic. Without using the term *globalization* anywhere in her book, she references the socio-economic environment of the times and reflects upon the relationship between individual agency and corporate organizations:

> By the early 1990s many of the institutional and organizational arrangements for handling risk and uncertainty were being replaced to a large degree by individual level strategies and this I argue helped lead to the rise of entrepreneurialism on the part of individuals during the dot-com boom. (p. 34)

Similarly, although operating from a very different theoretical frame and organizational sector, Norander and Harter (2012) apply postcolonial theory to explore the complex relationship between institutions and individuals in transnational organizing. They unpack a communicative entrepreneurialism that operates within the liminal space of individuals and organizations. Focusing on an international women's

NGO, Kvinna till Kvinna, the study explored how marginalized members engage in *spatial politics*, crossing boundaries and creating new spaces on their own rather than on institutional terms. Jackson's (2007) study of mobility also embodies the deinstitutionalized logic of the generation of ubiquity but in a different manner. She notes how mobile devices "free communication from the constraints of place and space" (p. 409). When information is removed from its context and can be repackaged, reshaped, repurposed, and reconnected, communication becomes a *mash-up*: "the archetype in a fluid and promiscuous environment: It brings together disconnected and mutable information from multiple and disparate sources to maintain the form of a coherent, meaningful whole" (pp. 412–413).

This kind of deinstitutionalized logic turns a long-studied communication problem, *collective action,* on its head. Traditionally, collective action refers to the association of two or more people who share interests or identities and act together toward the establishment of some shared public good (Olson, 1965). Although always a part of the organizational communication research agenda, it is now complicated by the enhanced capabilities of individuals to accomplish communicative tasks that heretofore needed formal organizing structures (Flanagin, Stohl, & Bimber, 2006). New and powerful forms of engagement not only are reconfiguring what was traditionally studied under the rubric of collective action—what Bennett and Segerberg (2012) describe as *connective action*—but globalization has reshaped what has heretofore been considered the public sphere.

A firm's ability to harness the power of collective action for privatized ends encapsulates the influence of formal organizations in the logic of deinstitutionalization while problematizing traditional communication constructs. InnoCentive, a for-profit company that has crowdsourcing as its core business, for example, has shown that decentered global collaboration not only saves money, transforms research and development processes, and leverages skills and knowledge that transcend a corporation's own labor force, it has also created a new generation of entrepreneurial scientists who no longer work within traditional labor markets and the constraints of traditional labor contracts (Howe, 2006). Work processes and performances are thus separated from organizational membership, socialization, and identity, transforming core relationships found in first- and second-generation research.

New forms of venture capital investment operating in the spaces among formal organizations, individual entrepreneurship, and the public sphere are also transforming traditional communication processes. *Equity-based crowd funding,* represented by Internet-based companies such as Earlyshares.com, Kickstarter.com, and Idiegogo.com, gives the public new opportunities to invest in start-up companies and creative ventures across the globe in ways never before conceived. Not only does this create new forms of global financial capital that coexist alongside the very powerful and established global financial networks but it allows organizations to develop and engage customer bases and the general public in radically different ways. An elaborated and reconfigured public sphere arises from these new forms of public/private engagement.

In the third generation, problems of collective action therefore move from a focus on organizations and how to solve the *free-riding problem* (typically answered through some form of incentive offered by formal organizations) to questions regarding the nature of multistakeholder arrangements, or what Flyverbom (2011) describes as *hybrid forums*. These forums have emerged as a novel way of addressing global problems and opportunities and creating public goods. In an ethnographic study of *ordering*—the routine ways in which particular agents, practices, objects, and subjects are assembled in different locations—Flyverbom (2011) highlights the analytic power of studying multiple and layered attempts to act on the world, without an *a priori* distinction among organization, membership, individuals, and governance. He finds that "multistakeholder networks comprised of public and private actors working in and around the organizational apparatus of the United Nations make new political domains accessible and unsettle established ways of organizing transnational governance" (p. 34).

In summary, no longer can we think only of discrete entities within global systems; rather, third-generation researchers maintain that boundaries between public and private are fuzzy and easily traversed, individual affiliations wax and wane, membership is relative and context dependent, and individuals come together and work apart in ways that transcend, complement, replace, and/or support organizational structures. This transformation applies to all forms of contemporary organizing, whether it be in the government, corporate, or civil sector.

As organizational communication scholars turn more and more attention to contemporary organizing, it is not surprising that terrorist and other types of clandestine organizations are also becoming a topic of interest (Corman, 2006; Scott, 2013; Stohl & Stohl, 2007, 2011). From a third-generation perspective, the theoretical and empirical challenges to studying a global interactional field in which actors are simultaneously known and unknown, voice is deinstitutionalized, organizational membership is fuzzy, and identities are shifting and continually in flux are the very same challenges that apply to all organizations, not just clandestine ones. Secret agency, Stohl and Stohl (2011) argue, not only challenges theoretical assumptions regarding organizational transparency but the assumption of transparency results in undertheorizing two concepts central to understanding the communicative constitution of organizations, legitimacy, and voice (see Taylor, Cooren, Giroux, & Robichaud, 1996).

Given the complexity, unpredictability, and volatility of where one stands in relation to others in the global system, the major communication competence in the third-generation becomes a sort of *coherence management* in which individuals and organizations must be able to navigate through and negotiate among the multiple levels of interaction that comprise all forms of organizing. Third-generation scholars have begun to explore how contemporary actors must be able to work simultaneously within multiple discourses (Maguire & Hardy, 2009), manage to situate themselves within diffuse and dislocated environments (Shockley, Morreale, & Hackman, 2010), maintain and solidify fragmented social borders (Juris, 2008), engage post-colonial voices (e.g. Broadfoot & Munshi, 2007), and filter ever-increasing amounts of information while brokering critical informational flows (Shirky, 2008). Coherence management operates at the nexus of interpersonal/organizational communication, not only in the sense of areas of overlap and intersection but as a skill that enables actors simultaneously to communicate and manage individual agency and organizational representativeness. Third-generation scholarship recognizes that rather than offering fixed and inflexible templates for involvement and engagement, individuals have far broader opportunities to define their roles and establish their own participatory style. Issues of power and control are far more complicated within these liminal spaces.

An emerging ethical debate among third-generation scholars extends the second generation's focus on corporate social responsibility. It elaborates the debate to include questions of the efficacy of increasingly individualized, informal, and entrepreneurial organizing practices in the face of powerful and expanding corporate interests. Castells (2009) reflects this tension in his articulation of a dialectical cycle in which "the more corporations invest in expanding communication networks (benefiting from a hefty return), the more people build their own networks of mass self-communication, thus empowering themselves" (p 421).

From a communication ethics perspective, this suggests that the more corporations try to accumulate their own power, the more they end up empowering people. But at the same time, the greater the degree to which digital forms of empowerment become ubiquitous, the more likely individuals will enshrine the power of the global network makers (i.e., corporations). The ethical implications of this dialectic are far ranging. Some scholars maintain that individualized and technologically mediated action cannot sustain the energy required to build the community trust and resources required for transformative change (Baviskar, 2011). They have coined terms such as *clicktivism* and *slacktivism* to criticize what they see as the ultimately ineffectual and weak forms of digital participation and engagement with social problems such as corporate malfeasance to human rights (Gladwell, 2010; White, 2010). Others argue that such informal engagement increases the communicative possibilities for a range of grassroots and transnational activist groups, creating and sustaining an informal and emergent ethical power that contests the ubiquity and influence of corporate enterprise networks (Dutta, 2012; Ganesh, Zoller, & Cheney, 2005). For third-generation scholars, the ubiquity of globalization expands the ethical dimensions of all organizational communication practices.

Conclusions

In summary, the three generations of globalization research capture the fluid shapes and evolving relations of organizing in a volatile global environment. In *The New Handbook of Organizational Communication* (Jablin & Putnam, 2001), organizational communication scholars interested in globalization were challenged to "reconsider past practices and develop creative and collaborative solutions that reflect the dynamic and complex environment of contemporary organizations" (Stohl, 2001, p. 359). Theoretical, methodological, and pragmatic parochialism were identified as barriers to our field's development of a truly global perspective. Our theories were American-centric, our research designs and methods were too often culturally bound, and our research domain was narrowly conceived and decontextualized from larger societal conditions.

A little more than a decade later, it is clear that global organizational communication scholarship has evolved. Each generation has built upon theoretical developments across the social sciences and humanities; we have integrated postcolonial viewpoints and macro-level sensibilities and embraced new methodologies for studying organizational communication processes in a highly interdependent and connected world. Pragmatically, we have moved beyond the almost singular focus on for-profit organizations, and our research crosses disciplinary areas. We are clearly less parochial than we were.

But many challenges and opportunities lie ahead. The Internet, mobile technology, and ongoing digitalization of social information are a continuing source of unprecedented research opportunities. For the first time, we are now able to develop extraordinarily large data sets that contain within them detailed and often complete records of what is said or meant by individuals who converse and share meanings with others in their networked world of organizing.

Global processes bring informal and emergent organizing increasingly in contact with traditional organizational forms in ways that are transforming our economic models, changing industry patterns, altering professions, and complicating our notions of organizational communication. We certainly know more today about the ways in which organizations such as KIVA and Avaaz leverage the Internet and a worldwide network of institutions, individuals, and small groups to accomplish their goals. And we have a better understanding of how the restructuring of multinational global relationships and collaborative processes includes an expansive notion of member and stakeholder relations. But we know little about the implications and effects of these changes on organizational actors. When individuals are asked to become active in organizationally designated and designed activities while simultaneously encouraged to start their own initiatives, blog, and post photos or videos on You Tube, what does that mean for issues of organizational commitment? When corporations no longer move operations offshore for cheap labor but rather utilize unpaid global labor pools in cyberspace, what does this type of organizing do to communication theories of organizational control, socialization, membership negotiation, or organizational identity? How do communication systems such as iStockphoto, which grew out of a free image-sharing exchange, change the way people do and are rewarded for their jobs? Are members who decide to act on their own without the sanctioning of the organization still acting as members? How are organizations communicatively constituted, and where do these conversations take place? These are just some of the questions that organizational communication scholars will need to address in the future.

The last *Handbook* chapter on globalization ended with the following observation:

> Organizational communication scholars are well-positioned to study the dynamic structuring of globalization and the culturally saturated processes of organizing and sensemaking. As a field we are sensitized to the central problematics of voice and pluralistic understandings of what counts as rational, unified by a fundamental concern with messages, interpretations, symbols and discourse, and grounded by an integrative communication orientation that at its most basic level recognizes meaning as internally experienced, subjective, embedded within larger systems, and socially constructed. Our participation and contributions to the scholarly discourse of globalization is just beginning. (Stohl, 2001, pp. 366–367)

As a new generation of global communication research continues to grapple with the volatile role of organizations in our personal, social, economic, and cultural lives, we suggest that the most original ideas will be those that operate at the intersection of traditional and new forms of theoretical expression and conventional and innovative methodologies. Even as the word *globalization* itself continues to merge into the conceptual background of organizational communication theory and research, the blending and bending of organizational forms and sectors, the interpenetration of profit and nonprofit goals, and the tensions between entrepreneurial and institutional interaction will provide new and exciting avenues for the study of global organizational communication. This profound hybridity will be a hallmark of our research in years to come.

References

Appadurai, A. (1997). *Modernity at large: Cultural dimensions of globalization.* Minneapolis: University of Minnesota Press.

Ashcraft, K. (2011). Knowing work through the communication of difference. In D. Mumby (Ed.), *Reframing difference in organizational communication studies: Research, pedagogy and practice* (pp. 3–30). London, England: SAGE.

Atouba, Y., & Shumate, M. (2010). Interorganizational networking patterns among development organizations. *Journal of Communication, 60*(2), 293–317.

Barber, B. (1992, March). Jihad vs. McWorld. *The Atlantic Monthly,* 53–63.

Barnett, G. (2011). *Handbook of social networks.* Thousand Oaks, CA: SAGE.

Bastien, D. (1987). Common patterns of behavior and communication in corporate mergers and acquisitions. *Human Resource Management, 26*(1), 17–33.

Baviskar, A. (2011, September 6). A tale of two movements. *The Times of India.* Retrieved from http://timesofindia.indiatimes.com/home/opinion/edit-page/A-tale-of-two-movements/articleshow/9875905.cms

Benkler, Y. (2006). *The wealth of networks: How social production transforms markets and freedom.* New Haven, CT: Yale University Press.

Bennett, W. L., Foot, K., & Xenos, M. (2011). Narratives and network organization: A comparison of fair trade systems in two nations. *Journal of Communication, 61*(2), 219–245

Bennett, W. L., & Segerberg, A. (2012). The logic of connective action: Digital media and the personalization of contentious politics. *Information, Communication, & Society, 15*(5), 739–768.

Bimber, B., Flanagin, A., & Stohl, C. (2012). *Collective action in organizations: Interaction and engagement in an era of technological change.* Cambridge, UK: Cambridge University Press.

Blau, P., & Scott, W. (1962). *Formal organizations: A comparative approach.* San Francisco, CA: Chandler Publishing Company.

Broadfoot, K., & Munshi, D. (2007). Diverse voices and alternative rationalities: Imagining forms of postcolonial organizational communication. *Management Communication Quarterly, 21*(2), 249–267.

Brugmann, J., & Prahalad, C. (2007, February). Creating business's new social compact. *Harvard Business Review*, 80–90.

Burt, R. (1992). *Structural holes: The social structure of competition.* Cambridge, MA: Harvard University Press.

Castells, M. (1996). *The rise of the network society.* Oxford, UK: Blackwell.

Castells, M. (2001). *The Internet galaxy. Reflections on the Internet, business, and society.* Oxford, UK: Oxford University Press.

Castells, M. (2008). The new public sphere: Global civil society, communication networks, and global governance. *The Annals of the American Academy of Political and Social Science, 616*(1), 78–92.

Castells, M. (2009). *Communication power.* Oxford, UK: Oxford University Press.

Cesaria, R. (2000). Organizational communication issues in Italian multinational corporations. *Management Communication Quarterly, 14*(1), 161–172.

Chanda, N. (2007). *Bound together: How traders, preachers, adventurers, and warriors shaped globalization.* New Haven, CT: Yale University Press.

Chen, L. (2000). Connecting to the world economy: Issues confronting organizations in Chinese societies. *Management Communication Quarterly, 14*(1), 152–160.

Cheney, G., & Barnett, G. (Eds.). (2005). *Organization←→Communication: Emerging perspectives, Vol. 7: International and multicultural approaches.* Cresskill, NJ: Hampton Press.

Cheney, G., Christiansen, L., Zorn, T., & Ganesh, S. (2010). *Organizational communication in an age of globalization: Issues, reflections, practices* (2nd ed.). Prospect Heights, IL: Waveland.

Cheney, G., & Cloud, D. (2006). Doing democracy, engaging the material: Employee participation and labor activity in an age of market globalization. *Management Communication Quarterly, 19*(4), 1–40.

Clark, A., Barley, W., & Leonardi, P. (2012). *Transparency, and practice: Communicative and material factors contributing to convergence in technology use.* International Communication Association, Top Four Organizational Communication Division, Phoenix, AZ.

Cloud, D. L. (2001). Laboring under the sign of the new: Cultural studies, organizational communication, and the fallacy of the new economy. *Management Communication Quarterly, 15*(2), 268–278.

Collier, M. J. (2009). Contextual negotiation of cultural Identifications and relationships: Interview discourse with Palestinian, Israeli, and Palestinian/Israeli young women in a U.S. peace-building program. *Journal of International and Intercultural Communication, 2*(4), 344–368.

Conrad, C., & Poole, M. S. (2012). *Strategic organizational communication in a global economy.* London, England: Wiley-Blackwell.

Corman, S. (2006). Using activity focus networks to pressure terrorist organizations. *Computational Mathematical Organization Theory, 12*(1), 35–49.

Deetz, S. (1992). *Democracy in an age of corporate colonization.* Albany, NY: SUNY Press.

Deetz, S. (1997). Communication in the age of negotiation. *Journal of Communication, 47*(4), 118–134.

Dempsey, S. (2007). Negotiating accountability within international contexts: The role of bounded voice *Communication Monographs, 74*(3), 311–332.

Dempsey, S., Parker, P. S., & Krone, K. (2011). Navigating socio-spatial difference, constructing counter-space: Insights from transnational feminist praxis. *Journal of International and Intercultural Communication Research, 4*(3), 201–220.

DePalma, A. (1994, June 26). It takes more than a visa to do business in Mexico. *The New York Times,* pp. A16–A17.

DiMaggio, P., & Powell, W. (1991). *The new institutionalism in organizational analysis.* Chicago, IL: University of Chicago Press.

Doerfel, M., & Taylor, M. (2004). Network dynamics of inter-organizational cooperation: The Croatian civil society movement. *Communication Monographs, 71*(4), 373–394.

Dutta, M. (2012). *Voices of resistance: Communication and social change.* West Lafayette, IN: Purdue University Press.

Earley, P. C., & Ang, S. (2003). *Cultural intelligence.* Stanford, CA: Stanford University Press.

Fisher, D., Stanley, K., Berman, D., & Neff, G. (2005). How do organizations matter? Mobilization and support for participants at five globalization protests. *Social Problems, 52*(1), 102–121.

Flanagin, A. J., Stohl, C., & Bimber, B. (2006). Modeling the structure of collective action. *Communication Monographs, 73*(1), 29–54.

Flyverbom, M. (2011). *The power of networks: Organizing the global politics of the Internet.* Cheltenham, UK: Edward Elgar.

Friedland, R., & Alford, R. (1991). Bringing society back in: Symbols, practices and institutional contradictions. In W. Powell & P. DiMaggio (Eds.), *The new institutionalism in organizational analysis* (pp. 232–266). Chicago, IL: University of Chicago Press.

Friedman, T. (1999). *The Lexus and the olive tree: Understanding globalization.* New York, NY: Farrar, Strauss, & Giroux.

Fulk, J. (2001). Global network organizations: Emergence and future prospects. *Human Relations, 54*(1), 91–99.

Ganesh, S., & Stohl, C. (2010). Qualifying engagement: A study of information and communication technology and the global social justice movement in Aotearoa New Zealand. *Communication Monographs, 77*(1), 51–74.

Ganesh, S., Zoller, H. M., & Cheney, G. (2005). Transforming resistance, broadening our boundaries: Critical organizational communication studies meets globalization from below. *Communication Monographs, 72*(2), 169–191.

Gibbs, J. L. (2006). Decoupling and coupling in global teams: Implications for human resource management. In G. K. Stahl & I. Bjorkman (Eds.), *Handbook of research in international human resource management* (pp. 347–363). Northampton, MA: Edward Elgar Publishing.

Gibson, C. B., & Gibbs, J. L. (2006). Unpacking the concept of virtuality: The effects of geographic dispersion, electronic dependence, dynamic structure, and national diversity on team innovation. *Administrative Science Quarterly, 51*(3), 451–495.

Giddens, A. (1999, May 3). *Runaway world.* Retrieved from http://news.bbc.co.uk/hi/english/static/events/reith_99/default.htm

Gladwell, M. (2010, October 4). Small change: Why the revolution will not be tweeted. *The New Yorker.* Retrieved from http://www.newyorker.com/reporting/2010/10/04/101004fa_fact_gladwell

Gomes, E., Cohen, M., & Mellahi, K. (2011). When two African cultures collide: A study of interactions between managers in a strategic alliance between two African organizations. *Journal of World Business, 46*(1), 5–12.

Gossett, L. (2006). Falling between the cracks: Control and communication challenges of a temporary workforce. *Management Communication Quarterly, 19*(3), 376–415.

Harwood, J., & Giles, H. (Eds.). (2005). *Intergroup communication: Multiple perspectives.* New York, NY: Peter Lang.

Held, D., McGrew, A., Goldblatt, D., & Perraton, J. (1999). *Global transformations: Politics, economics, and culture.* Stanford, CA: Stanford University Press.

Hofstede, G. (1984). *Culture's consequences: International differences in work related values.* Beverly Hills, CA: SAGE.

Howe, J. (2006). The rise of crowdsourcing. *Wired Magazine, 14*(6), 21–25.

Jablin, F., & Putnam, L. (Eds.). (2001). *The new handbook of organizational communication.* Thousand Oaks, CA: SAGE.

Jablin, F., Putnam, L., Roberts, K., & Porter, L. (Eds.). (1987). *The handbook of organizational communication* (pp. 451–502). Beverly Hills, CA: SAGE.

Jackson, M. H. (2007). Fluidity, promiscuity and mash-ups: New concepts for the study of mobility and communication. *Communication Monographs, 74*(3), 408–413.

Johansson, C., & Stohl, C. (2012). Cultural competence and institutional contradictions: The hydropower referendum. *Journal of Applied Communication Research, 40*(4), 329–349.

Jones, E., Watson, B., Gardner, J., & Gallois, C. (2004). Organization communication: Challenges for the new century. *Journal of Communication, 54*(4), 722–750.

Juris, J. (2008). *Networking futures: The movements against corporate globalization.* Durham, NC: Duke University Press.

Kassing, J. (2008). Consider this: A comparison of factors contributing to expressions of employee dissent. *Communication Quarterly, 56*(3), 342–355.

Katsiaoun, O. (2002). *Globalization and the state: Some awkward corners.* Retrieved from http://unpan1.un.org/intradoc/groups/public/documents/un/unpan006229.pdf

Kienzle, N., & Husar, S. (2007). How can cultural awareness improve communication in the global workplace? *Journal of the Communication, Speech & Theatre Association of North Dakota, 20,* 81–85.

Kim, K., & Barnett, G. (2000). The structure of the international telecommunications regime in transition: A network analysis of international organizations. *International Interactions, 26*(1), 91–127.

Kisselberg, L., & Dutta, M. (2009). The construction of civility in multicultural organizations. In P. Shockley-Zalabak (Ed.), *Destructive organizational communication: Processes, consequences and constructive ways of organizing* (pp. 121–142). Oxford, UK: Routledge.

Kozminski, A., & Cushman, D. (1993). *Organizational communication and management: A global perspective.* Albany, NY: SUNY Press.

Kramer, M. W., & Hess, J. A. (2002). Communication rules for the display of emotions in organizational settings. *Management Communication Quarterly, 16*(1), 66–80.

Kron, D., & Goodman, J. (2012, March 8). Online, a distant conflict soars to topic No. 1. *The New York Times,* A1.

Larner, W. (2002). Globalization, governmentality, and expertise. *Review of International Political Economy, 9*(4), 650–674.

Lee, S., Monge, P. R., Bar, F., & Matei, S. (2007). The emergence of clusters in global telecommunications networks. *Journal of Communication, 57*(3), 415–434.

Leonardi, P. (2012). *Car crashes without cars: Lessons about simulation technology and organizational change from automotive design.* Cambridge, MA: MIT Press.

Leonardi, P., & Bailey, D. (2008). Transformational technologies and the creation of new work practices: Making implicit knowledge explicit in task-based offshoring. *MIS Quarterly, 32*(2), 411–436.

Lindsley, S. (1999). Communication and 'the Mexican way': Stability and trust as core symbols in maquiladoras. *Western Journal of Communication, 63*(1), 1–31.

Linklater, A. (1982). *Men and citizens in the theory of international relations.* London, England: Macmillan Press.

Maguire, S., & Hardy, C. (2009). Discourse and deinstitutionalization: The decline of DDT. *Academy of Management, 52*(1), 148–178.

May, S., Cheney, G., & Roper, J. (Eds.). (2007). *The debate over corporate social responsibility.* Oxford, UK: Oxford University Press.

Monge, P. (1995). Global network organizations. In R. Cesaria & P. Shockley-Zalabak (Eds.), *Organization means communication: Making the organizational communication concept relevant to practice* (pp. 135–151). Rome, Italy: Servizio Italiano Pubblicazioni Internationali Srl.

Monge, P. (1998). ICA presidential address: Communication structures and processes in globalization. *Journal of Communication, 48*(4), 142–153.

Monge, P., & Contractor, N. (2003). *Theories of communication networks.* Oxford, UK: Oxford University Press.

Monge, P., & Fulk, J. (1999). Communication technologies for global network organizations. In G. DeSanctis & J. Fulk (Eds.), *Communication technologies and organizational forms* (pp. 71–100). Thousand Oaks, CA: SAGE.

Monge, P., Heise, B., & Margolin, D. (2008). Communication network evolution in organizational communities. *Communication Theory, 18*(4), 449–477.

Moore, F. (2011). Holistic ethnography: Studying the impact of multiple national identities on post-acquisition organizations. *Journal of International Business Studies, 42*(5), 654–671.

Nadesan, M. (2001). Post-Fordism, political economy, and critical organizational communication studies. *Management Communication Quarterly, 15*(2), 259–267.

Neff, G. (2012). *Venture labor: Work and the burden of risk in innovative industries.* Cambridge, MA: Cambridge University Press.

Norander, S., & Harter, L. (2012). Reflexivity in practice: Challenges and potentials of transnational organizing. *Management Communication Quarterly, 26*(1), 74–105.

Olson, M. (1965). *The logic of collective action.* Cambridge, MA: Harvard University Press.

Papa, M., Auwal, M., & Singhal, A. (1995). Dialectic of control and emancipation in organizing for social change: A multitheoretic study of the Grameem Bank in Bangladesh. *Communication Theory, 5*(3), 189–223.

Poole, M. S., & Van De Ven, A. (1989). Using paradox to build management and organizational theories. *Academy of Management Review, 14*(4), 562–578.

Redden, S. (2012). *Exploring the emotional cueing of airport security queues: Implications of passenger emotional experience in airports.* International Communication Association, Top Four Organizational Communication Division, Phoenix, AZ.

Robertson, R. (1992). *Globalization: Social theory and global culture.* London, England: SAGE.

Rosamond, A. (2011). The cosmopolitan-communitarian divide and celebrity anti-war activism. In A. Huliaras, L. Tsaliki, & C. Frangonikolopoulos (Eds.), *Transnational celebrity activism in global politics* (pp. 63–82). Bristol, UK: Intellect Publishers.

Scholte, J. (2000). *Globalization: A critical introduction.* New York, NY: St. Martin's Press.

Scott, C. R. (2013). *Anonymous agencies, backstreet businesses, and covert collectives: Rethinking organizations in the 21st century.* Palo Alto, CA: Stanford University Press.

Shirky, C. (2008). *Here comes everybody: The power of organizing without organization.* New York, NY: Penguin Press.

Shockley, P., Morreale, S., & Hackman, M. (2010). *Building the high trust organization: Strategies for supporting five key dimensions of trust.* San Francisco, CA: Jossey-Bass.

Shumate, M., Fulk, J., & Monge, P. (2005). Predictors of the international HIV/AIDS NGO network overtime. *Human Communication Research, 31*(4), 482–510.

Shumate, M., & O'Connor, A. (2010). The symbiotic sustainability model: Conceptualizing NGO-corporate alliance communication. *Journal of Communication, 60*(3), 577–609.

Shumate, M., & Yannick, A. (2012, May). *The evolution of population networks: Multilevel mechanisms that influence selection and a research agenda.* Paper presented at the International Communication Association Conference, Phoenix, AZ.

Søderberg, A., & Varra, E. (Eds.). (2003). *Merging across borders. People, cultures and politics.* Copenhagen, Denmark: Copenhagen Business School Press.

Stage, C. (1999). Negotiating organizational communication cultures in American subsidiaries doing business in Thailand. *Management Communication Quarterly, 13*(2), 245–280.

Stohl, C. (1993). International organizing and organizational communication. *Journal of Applied Communication Research, 21*(4), 377–384.

Stohl, C. (1995). *Organizational communication: Connectedness in action.* Thousand Oaks, CA: SAGE.

Stohl, C. (2001). Globalizing organizational communication. In F. Jablin & L. Putnam (Eds.), *The new handbook of organizational communication* (pp. 323–375). Thousand Oaks, CA: SAGE.

Stohl, C. (2005). Globalization theory. In S. May & D. Mumby (Eds.), *Engaging organizational communication theory and research: Multiple perspectives* (pp. 223–262). Thousand Oaks, CA: SAGE.

Stohl, C., McCann, R., & Baku, H. (2013). Conflict in the global workplace. In J. Oetzel & S. Ting-Toomey (Eds.), *SAGE handbook of conflict.* Thousand Oaks, CA: SAGE.

Stohl, C., & Stohl, M. (2007). Terrorism networks: Theoretical assumptions and pragmatic consequences. *Communication Theory, 17*(2), 93–124.

Stohl, C., & Stohl, M. (2011). Secret agencies: The communicative constitution of a clandestine organization. *Organization Studies, 32*(9), 1197–1215.

Stohl, C., Stohl, M., & Popova, L. (2009). A new generation of corporate social responsibility. *Journal of Business Ethics, 90*(4), 607–622.

Stohl, M., & Stohl, C. (2005). Human rights, nation states, and NGOs: Structural holes and the emergence of global regimes. *Communication Monographs, 72*(4), 442–467.

Taylor, C. (2011, October 31). Why not call it a Facebook revolution? *CNN.com.* Retrieved from http://www.cnn.com/2011/TECH/social.media/02/24/facebook.revolution/index.html

Taylor, J. R., Cooren, F., Giroux, N., & Robichaud, D. (1996). The communicational basis of organization: Between the conversation and the text. *Communication Theory, 6*(1), 1–39.

Taylor, M., & Doerfel, M. (2002). Building interorganizational relationships that build nations. *Human Communication Research, 29*(2), 153–181.

The Economist (2009). Going Global. Retrieved from http://www.economist.com/node1481678

Toft, A. (2011). Contextualizing technology use: Communication practices in a local homeless movement. *Information, Communication, & Society, 14*(5), 1–22.

Trapp, N. L. (2012). Corporation as climate ambassador: Transcending business sector boundaries in a Swedish CSR campaign. *Public Relations Review, 38*(3), 458–465.

Triandis, H., & Albert, R. (1987). Cross-cultural perspectives. In F. Jablin, L. Putnam, K. Roberts, & L. Porter (Eds.), *Handbook of organizational communication: An interdisciplinary perspective* (pp. 264–296). Newbury Park, CA: SAGE.

Wang, G., & Kuo, E. (2010). The Asian communication debate: Culture-specificity, culture-generality, and beyond. *Asian Journal of Communication, 20*(2), 152–165.

Weber, M. (2012). Newspapers and the long term implications of hyperlinking. *Journal of Computer Mediated Communication, 17*(2), 187–201.

Weick, K., & Van Orden, P. (1990). Organizing on a global scale: A research and teaching agenda. *Human Resource Management, 29*(1), 49–61.

White, M. (2010, August 12). Clicktivism is ruining leftist activism. *The Guardian.* Retrieved from http://www.guardian.co.uk/commentisfree/2010/aug/12/clicktivism-ruining-leftist-activism

Whiteman, G. (2009). All my relations: Understanding perceptions of justice and conflict between companies and indigenous peoples, *Organization Studies, 30*(1), 101–120.

Wiseman, R. (2002). Intercultural communication competence. In W.B. Gudykunst & B. Mody (Eds.), *Handbook of international and intercultural communication* (2nd ed., pp. 207–224). Thousand Oaks, CA: SAGE.

Yaziji, M., & Doh, J. (2009). *NGOs and corporations: Conflict and collaboration.* Cambridge, UK: Cambridge University Press.

Zoller, H. (2004). Dialogue as global issue management: Legitimizing corporate influence in the Transatlantic Business Dialogue. *Management Communication Quarterly, 18*(2), 204–240.

CHAPTER 30

Community Organizing, Social Movements, and Collective Action

Shiv Ganesh and Cynthia Stohl

The emergence and crystallization (Redding, 1985) of organizational communication studies was guided by a relatively focused concern with communication in industrial and workplace contexts. It has only been in the last decade or so that organizational communication scholarship has truly ventured outside workplaces and engaged substantively with community groups (Medved et al., 2001; Zoller, 2000), activist organizing (Ganesh & Stohl, 2013), and social justice organizations (Toft, 2011; Tompkins, 2009) as worthy subjects of study. There are several reasons for this significant shift.

To begin, the period of ferment that characterized organizational communication research in the 1980s helped create the bedrock for this body of work. As Cheney (2007) has argued, emerging critiques of the managerial bias in early organizational communication studies led to a concern for aspects of organizational life that were not explicitly about productivity, leading to some early studies of civil society and social justice organizing (Cheney & Stohl, 1991; Goldzwig & Cheney, 1984). Likewise, the interpretive turn and theoretical expansion of organizational communication inquiry also saw scholars beginning to make new identity claims that significantly broadened organizational communication studies. As Ashcraft (2011) maintained, at least part of the reason Redding and Tompkins (1988) called for organizational communication inquiry to examine organizations whose coordinated activities were not considered *work* in a narrow sense was to distinguish the growing field from managerial, corporate, and business communication studies—a claim also echoed by Mumby and Stohl (1996).

Additionally, the emerging interest in civil society organizing has been fueled by prominent, visible, and impactful protests in various parts of the world during the same period as well as by creative ways in which communities around the world have begun to self-organize around important issues relating to justice and public interests. As we argue in Chapter 29, these phenomena are emblematic of a new generation of research that positions globalization as a background against which organizing efforts discursively identify and construct social problems and give rise to new modes of participation. As the repertoires, frames, strategies, and tools of contemporary civil society organizing evolve, they will continue to reshape and revitalize organizational communication research on social movements, collective action, and change. As such, they create new implications for our theoretical understanding of central concerns in organizational communication studies, including power and resistance, the communicative constitution of organizations, and technology and the shape of collective action itself.

Our objective in this chapter, then, is to consolidate this diverse and emerging investment in studies of community organizing, social movements, and collective action with reference to a key problematic in organizational communication research: that of the organization-society relationship. As Mumby and Stohl (1996) said, this research problematic pays attention to "the ways in which society, culture, organizations and communication are inextricably and reciprocally bound" (p. 65), attending to questions of how organizations are embedded in their environments and ways in which broader discourses, trends, and imperatives affect organizations. In the last decade, studies of community organizing, social movements, and collective action have shed significant light on this problematic by developing rich and multiple perspectives on the relationship between organizing practices and community, public, and social interests. Below, we offer a threefold framework of how such studies have conceived of these relationships.

Organizations, Publics, and Communities

We utilize the term *public* in Dewey's (1927) classical sense, in terms of a group of people who have a common interest in controlling the consequences of actions that affect them. Organizational communication scholars have understood the public dimensions and societal consequences of organizing efforts through a variety of lenses, sometimes explicitly using the construct *public* or *public interest* (e.g., Ganesh & Zoller, 2012). More often, however, they have used the concept of *community* to describe and analyze the organization-society relationship, casting the relationship between organizing and communities in a variety of ways.

Studies of community have a central place in communication scholarship (Depew & Peters, 2000), and for several organizational communication scholars, community operates as a root metaphor for organizational communication itself (Jenkins, 2012; Trujillo, 1992). Iverson and McPhee (2008), for example, followed Wenger (1998) and discussed communities of practice as constituted by mutual engagement, shared repertoires, and the negotiation of joint enterprise, describing foundational aspects of organizing and communicating in the process. Others have approached the notion of community as a form of organizational control (Gossett & Tompkins, 2000) or dialogue (Pearce & Pearce, 2000), while still others have examined the consequences of the rhetorical deployment of the term *community* itself (Della-Piana & Anderson, 1995). Our interest lies not with these theoretically diverse conceptualizations of community but in how studies have discursively constructed the relationship between organizing practices and community interests, drawing from different notions of community and articulating different conceptions of both participation and collective action issues. Mumby and Stohl's (1996) definition of the organization-society relationship implies that the relationship between organizations and communities is likely to be complex, multifaceted, and reciprocal. However, we observe that studies have historically embodied at least one of three perspectives, each of which conceives of communities and the role of organizations in distinct ways (see Table 30.1).

The first perspective treats the *organization as outsider*. Here, communities are understood

Table 30.1 Perspectives on Organizations and Communities

	Organization as Outsider	Organization as Constitutive	Organization as Insider
View of Organization	Organization is structurally distinct from the community	Organization positions members as representative of the community	Organization is a part of a larger community of practice
View of Community	Defined in terms of locality	Defined as an interest group	Defined as a population or public
Role of Organization	Locality development, social policy/planning, and social action	Formal and informal sites of community participation	Contentious and cooperative interorganizational community relations
Sample Studies	Ashcraft & Kedrowicz, 2002; Dempsey, 2010; Koschmann, 2012	Bimber, Flanagin, & Stohl, 2012; Cheney, 1999; Cloud, 2007	Knight & Greenberg, 2002; Shumate, Fulk, & Monge, 2005; Taylor & Doerfel, 2003

largely in terms of particular geographic locations. The organization is seen as structurally distinct from communities and their interests, even though the range of relationships between the organization and the community can vary widely, ranging from service delivery to partnerships to advocacy. For instance, Tompkins (2009) detailed the multiple kinds of actions that volunteers at a community-based organization performed for homeless communities in Denver, from providing material resources, including food and shelter, to advocating to the city on the community's behalf. A second perspective treats the *organization as constituting* the community. Here, communities are framed primarily as interest groups whose members may or may not be colocated. The organization itself plays a crucial role in positioning its own members as representative of the community or interest group. Studies of traditional interest groups, including large, formal professional associations and interest groups such as the American Association of Retired Persons (Bimber, Flanagin, & Stohl, 2012) or labor unions (Cloud, 2007), exemplify such organizations, but several studies of smaller, more local, and informal civil society organizing also fall into this category. A final perspective treats the *organization as insider*. Here, communities are cast as entire populations or publics, and the organization is considered one component of a larger community of action and practice. Many studies of social movement organizing illustrate this point of view. Ganesh and Stohl's (2010) study of a range of social movement organizations and social justice groups that together made up the global social justice community in Aotearoa New Zealand is a case in point.

These three perspectives thus cover a wide variety of organizational forms, levels of analysis, organizing contexts, and communicative practices, reflecting many of the organizational types found in Blau and Scott's (1962) influential "cui bono" typology of the prime beneficiaries of organizations: mutual benefit associations, business concerns, service organizations, and commonwealth organizations (p. 43). Studies of all types of community-based organizations have proliferated in the last 10 years (Lewis, 2005). At the same time, interest in the communicative mechanisms and constitution of social movement organizing has increased, ranging from such contexts as homelessness advocacy (Toft, 2011) and environmental health (Zoller,

2012) to transnational feminist networks (Dempsey, Parker, & Krone, 2011) and global social justice (Ewalt, 2012). Cutting across all of these foci are studies of collective action, which have a longer and more established history in the social sciences in general and organizational communication studies in particular. We focus on two communicative aspects of collective action (i.e., the kinds of participation involved in organizing *and* the ways in which public and community issues are discursively constructed and acted upon) that help position organizations as community outsiders, organizations as constitutive of community, and organizations as community insiders.

Relating Collective Action, Community Organizing, and Social Movements

Studies of collective action have been a vibrant part of the social science landscape for the last 60 years. Olson's (1965) classic formulation of collective action as oriented toward the establishment of a shared public good is one of the most widely cited ideas in social science research and has generated research on collective action in multiple disciplines, including economics, political science, psychology, sociology, social movement studies, and also communication studies. *The Logic of Collection Action* (Olson, 1965) provides a theoretical *rational* account of the choices faced by individuals to participate in collective efforts and rests upon two fundamental processes: (1) individuals confronting conscious and discrete decisions about free riding and (2) communication activities, including identifying people with common interests, communicating among or to them, and coordinating resources and individuals. Organizations and communication dynamics are fundamental to this account. Communication scholars have extended this work by drawing upon theoretical frames that complicate issues of rational choice and narrow self-interest in collective behavior (Monge & Contractor, 2004) as well as reconceptualizing collective action dynamics in the digital era (Bimber et al., 2012). However, in organizational communication, the term *collective action* also finds expression not only in work that draws from Olson's formulation but also in other theoretical traditions, including institutional perspectives (Lammers, 2011), critical and feminist approaches (Mumby, 1996), and the emerging communicative constitution of organization tradition (Taylor & Robichaud, 2004).

Across these perspectives, there are multiple meanings ascribed to the term that resonate with larger interdisciplinary ambiguity in what counts as collective action itself. We find an interesting tension between two major understandings of collective action. Some perspectives equate collective action with any kind of organizing effort, in contrast to others that, like us, understand it in terms of the production of shared benefits, public interests, or community outcomes.

Several scholars of collective action have *treated collective action as equivalent to any kind of social action*. Melucci's (1996) influential definition is a case in point:

> I will define collective action as a set of social practices (i) involving simultaneously a number of individuals or groups (ii) exhibiting similar morphological characteristics in contiguity of time and space (iii) implying a social field of relationships and (iv) the capacity of the people involved to make sense of what they are doing. (p. 20)

If this definition, which emphasizes processes of coordinated activity, collective sensemaking, and structural coherence, sounds similar to a description of what we might call *organizational communication*, that is surely no accident. The term *collective action* in organizational communication scholarship has often been used as an implicit and sometimes casual metaphor for organizational communication itself. Cheney's (1983) work, for example, understood organizational identification in terms of collective action, casting it as a communicative and cooperative response to social hierarchy and estrangement. Mumby and Stohl (1996) also listed collective action as a central concern of organizational communication, stating that the "central problematics [of organizational communication scholarship] emphasize a concern with *collective action*, agency, messages, symbols, and discourse" (p. 53, emphasis added). Other relatively broad references to the term include Kuhn and Ashcraft (2003) who, in their development of a communicative theory of the firm, described it as "a text-object which is necessary to enable and constrain collective action" (p. 42). Cooren and Taylor (1997) also cast organizations themselves in terms of collective action, saying that an "organization is an object in the absence of which collective action would cease to exist" (p. 254).

Collective Action and Public Outcomes

Equating collective action with organizational communication is a form of *equivalence* (Putnam, Philips, & Chapman, 1996; Smith, 1993), useful because it helps expand communicative conceptions of what counts as collective action. However, casting collective action as equivalent with all organizational communication processes and contexts also blunts the edge of the term itself, putting at risk its unique contributions. Thus, in this chapter, our view of collective action emphasizes ends and social outcomes of organizing, placing prominence on societal outcomes and *shared benefits*. This emphasis is evident in both Olson's (1965) arguments about the logic of collective action and Samuelson's (1954) theory, both of which understand collective action in terms of the production of public goods that are non-excludable and non-rival in that they are designed for the benefit of society at large or for marginalized subgroups. This perspective is also reiterated across multiple disciplines. Wright (2003), for example, posited a social-psychological definition of collective action as follows: "A group member engages in collective action any time she or he is acting as a representative of the group and the action is directed at improving the condition of the entire group" (p. 410).

This take on collective action has also been evident in organizational communication scholarship. Bimber et al. (2012), for instance, argued that "only through some form of collective action can people realize important individual and group goals and produce the myriad of shared benefits associated with social life" (p. 1). Likewise, Stohl (2011) defines collective action as the "association of two or more people who share interests or identities, and act together toward the establishment of some shared 'public good'" (p. 125). The most widely cited work on collective action and public goods in organizational communication studies is that of Fulk, Monge, and their colleagues (Fulk, Flanagin, Kalman, Monge, & Ryan, 1996; Monge et al., 1998) who identified two distinctively communicative public goods—connectivity and communality—produced by digital technology networks.

Studies of communicative public goods, such as the other studies cited above, explicitly draw our attention to the organization-society problematic (Mumby & Stohl, 1996) and the many ways in which organizations relate to institutions and communities around them. However, we wish to provide a perspective on collective action that focuses not only on the production of public goods by large, formal collective action organizations but on the multiple ways in which public and community interests are constructed and represented by a wide variety of social formations and civil society groups (Lewis, 2005). These include local communities and collectives as well as emergent, informal, and self-organizing movements and groups that proliferate in the contemporary digital environment. Accordingly, at the risk of oversimplification, in this chapter, we understand collective action to be *two or more people acting for the benefit of three or more people.* Even radical groups such as People for the Ethical Treatment of Animals (PETA), whose collective actions focus on the rights of animals rather than people, explicitly recognize the value and benefit of their collective action for humans. "Together," they write on their membership webpage, "we can make the world a better place for all beings" (PETA, 2013).

Communication and Collective Action

Within our simple definition of *collective action*, the verb *acting* references the full range of communicative interactions undertaken by social collectives. Specifically, a major interactional feature of collective efforts on behalf of others has to do with the kind of participation that they involve. Stohl and Cheney (2001) defined *participation* as "constituted by the discretionary interactions of individuals or groups resulting in cooperative linkages" (p. 356). The term is emblematic of interactive dimensions of communication and, considered in terms of collective action, often addresses modes of civic engagement such as volunteering or activism (Bennett, Wells, & Freelon, 2011; Ganesh & McAllum, 2009). Others have understood participation in terms of location, and how it is transformed when people interact across space and time with a range of others (Fulk & DeSanctis, 1995). Participation varies along multiple dimensions and can be more or less intense or more or less impersonal (Cheney et al., 1997). Importantly, participation is not restricted to communicative acts involving coordination and collaboration but can also include contestation and conflict (Cheney & Cloud, 2006).

Additionally, our definition emphasizes that there are always more people who stand to benefit from collective action efforts than there are those involved in those efforts, underscoring the inherently public character of collective action efforts and its attendant problematics of representation and issue construction. A major discursive feature of collective action involves the construction and definition of issues of public, collective, or community interest, around which collective action occurs.

Thus for our purposes, the word *issues* refers to the discursive mechanisms through which collectives understand and frame the objectives and goals of collective action efforts. It involves asking the following questions: How are social problems defined and constructed? Who are considered relevant stakeholders and audiences for collective action efforts? By what processes are they created? In the context of civil society organizing, this enables us to bring together research on multiple kinds of community organizations that hitherto may not have been considered in terms of collective action. These questions also highlight representation as a key problematic in research on civil society organizing. As Deetz and Simpson (2003) outlined, a "politically responsive constructionist theory of communication" (p. 143) needs to move beyond focusing on what individuals, communities, or stakeholders are saying about social problems to processes that "construct what is to be said" (p. 148).

In the next section, we explore ways in which specific studies reproduce one or sometimes more of the three perspectives and, in some cases, challenge them. As we do so, we consolidate what we currently know about major communicative dynamics involved in collective action, focusing on multiple forms of participation and a diverse range of issues evident in organizational communication scholarship.

Organization as Outsider

Since the turn of the millennium, organizational communication scholars have created a rich body of scholarship on community organizing, often drawing from a range of perspectives, including realist, interpretive, critical, and poststructural perspectives, and employing both qualitative and quantitative methods. A majority of these studies of community organizations have treated the organization as a distinct structural entity that has an identifiable relationship with a particular community but is not a part of it. In some instances, organizations can emerge from communities but eventually become *outsiders*. Peruzzo (2009) for example, talks about third-sector organizations in Brazil that emerged from community concerns but eventually formed a structurally distinct sector, with professional identities and formal structures. In other instances, organizations can be outsiders from the start, expanding their work and outreach into multiple locations, as is the case with large national and international organizations such as the Red Cross, Doctors without Borders, or Big Brothers and Big Sisters.

Thus the kinds of organizations researchers have studied have varied widely, ranging from small women's shelters (Ashcraft, 2001; Maguire & Mohtar, 1994) to large nonprofit organizations and nongovernmental organizations or NGOs (Ganesh, 2003). Equally varied are the forms of community under study, including local neighborhoods (Zoller, 2000), geographically dispersed vulnerable communities such as victims of gender violence (Cooper & Shumate, 2012), or people living with HIV/AIDS (Shumate, Fulk, & Monge, 2005). Of special relevance to us, however, are the multiple terms researchers have used to characterize relationships between community organizations and communities themselves, including *service, collaboration, partnership,* and *advocacy*.

Interestingly, these relationships are reminiscent of the classic three-fold catalogue of strategies for community intervention and development first identified by Rothman (1970): locality development, social policy/planning, and social action, each of which has distinct assumptions about community issues and needs, participation, and inequality. Approaches oriented toward *locality development* see communities as chaotic and vulnerable, in need of building, with a pressing urge for democratic and local participation in community issues. In turn, the organization is seen as a facilitator and supporter in service of local communities. A *social planning* approach sees community issues in terms of deficits and concrete, pre-identified problems such as health or housing. Community participation is often seen programmatically, sometimes in terms of compliance and sometimes as responsiveness to "clients" (e.g., Zorn, Flanagin, & Shoham, 2011), and the organization itself is often seen as a resource provider or a partner. Finally, a *social action* approach frames the community as oppressed and in need of justice. Community participation is understood in terms of mobilization, and the organization is seen as an advocate for the community. Each of these three forms are archetypal, and in practice, actual community interventions may draw from one or more approach; nonetheless, they shed light on how a wide variety of organizational communication studies position community organizations as being embedded in but remaining distinct from communities.

Locality Development

Several studies that see organizations as remaining separate from but influential in the community are located within a locality development framework. For example, Hale and James (2013) studied women's "builds" by Habitat for Humanity. While Habitat for Humanity is a large, international organization that works on the objective social problem of housing, Hale and James understood it as engaging locality development much more than social planning. Houses are constructed by teams, or *builds*, composed of volunteers drawn from local communities, and as Hale and James showed, the experience of working on a build has significant consequences for collective identity, civility, citizenship, and community relationships. Likewise, Harter, Leeman, Norander, Young, and Rawlins (2008) traced how Passion Works, a collaborative art studio, facilitated participative and aesthetic opportunities for artists with special developmental needs. Other examples include Medved et al.'s (2001) study of stakeholder participation in healthcare initiatives and Kirby's (2007) study of the Hmong Resource Coalition, a nonprofit collective designed to educate, conscientize (Freire, 1970), and empower Hmong refugees.

Locality development also informs several studies of development communication that are influenced by organizational communication studies. While early development communication studies tended to privilege the role of mass media technologies in driving community change processes in developing countries (Casimir, 1991), work by Rogers (1976) and his colleagues critiqued the ethnocentric "modernization" paradigm that informed such scholarship and began a shift from mass media studies toward analyses of participatory communication practice as a major means to achieve democratic change. This in turn resulted in a productive and ongoing engagement with organizational communication studies, and several studies in development communication have been informed by organizational communication perspectives. Jones and Bodtker (1998), for example, used a Weickean sensemaking framework to analyze how an international team, composed of a South African NGO, U.S. university educators, and a U.S. NGO, started peace education and community dialogue processes in vulnerable school districts in Gauteng province in South Africa. Similarly, Crabtree's (1998) study of participatory development projects in Nicaragua and El Salvador was based on participatory research methods, which traced how international student service learning projects based in those countries enabled mutual empowerment. Finally, organizational communication scholars such as Houston and Jackson (2003) have drawn from structuration theories of technology to highlight the importance of locality in determining technology design in processes of development.

Social Planning

Many other studies can be comfortably placed in a social planning framework (e.g., Ganesh, 2005). Several studies that examine interorganizational collaboration and networks appear to be oriented toward social planning approaches when they understand the objective of collective action in relatively local terms. Koschmann and colleagues' research (Koschmann, 2012; Koschmann & Isbell, 2009; Lewis, Isbell, & Koschmann, 2010), for instance, studied a group of nonprofit organizations that "work[ed] to improve social outcomes related to health, education, and economic sustainability by coordinating public, private, and individual actions and resources" (Koschmann, 2012, p. 9). The network originally began in 1981 as a collaborative endeavor between the local city council, county, mental health board, and the school district. Of particular interest was how members of the collaborative network developed an externalized and objectified image of the community using what members started calling a *community dashboard* metaphor, where the collaborative network itself was seen by members as a *dashboard* or a barometer of community health. Likewise, McComb (1995) studied how volunteers in a Travelers Aid Society were organized by a charismatic leader to provide service to distressed travelers at a major airport. Here, the travelers themselves are constructed as relatively passive recipients of services. Other studies have been critical of such passive constructions of the recipients of services. Trethewey (1997) studied how clients of a women's social service organization were positioned as passive recipients of services for low-income single parents but were still able to resist those constructions in a number of ways.

Social Action

A few studies have understood the relationship between organizations and communities in terms of social action, focusing on advocacy and community activism. Zoller and Tener (2010), for example, discussed the Ohio Citizens Action, an environmental activist group that developed the Good Neighbor Campaign, a template to mobilize members of local communities in Ohio to persuade a local chemical plant run by the Lanxess Corporation to reduce the level of toxicity in its emissions. They did so by creating an action group, composed of activists from Ohio Citizens Action and members of the local community, to lobby the corporation to reduce both the accident and the pollution rate. Harter, Berquist, Titsworth, Novak, and Brokaw (2005) also showed how an organization that worked for highly vulnerable homeless youth took on important advocacy functions by resisting debilitating dominant community discourses that stigmatized homelessness, such as NIMBYism.

Conceiving of organizations as structural outsiders regardless of the orientation toward locality development, social planning, or social action pays analytical dividends. For instance, the conceptual bifurcation of community organizations from the communities they serve can be of pragmatic use when assessing such practical communication issues as the level of participation, the quality of service delivery, or the effectiveness of dialogue processes with stakeholders. The bifurcation sets up community interests as an object of analysis distinct from the organization itself.

This bifurcation also leads to critique and assessment regarding the organization's ability to legitimately represent a community. Some critical studies have challenged the bifurcation of community organizations and communities, focusing on problems created as organizations attempt to represent communities. Dempsey (2010), for example, examined attempts in a university to collaborate with its local community, arguing that the notion of community engagement itself was shaped by material and discursive inequalities that determined how *community* participants in the collaboration effort represented it. More critically, the study showed how abstract organizational conceptions of community interests made it difficult to see highly porous boundaries between the campus and community and the back-and-forth movement of individuals across these boundaries. Similarly, Ganesh and Barber (2009) studied how a highly abstract and impersonal definition of community interests by a NGO served to ultimately silence community voices in the organization itself, resulting in a lack of attention to community needs.

Organizations as Constitutive of Community

Unlike the first perspective, where the organization is conceived as being structurally distinct from the community, in the second, the organization is considered to play a key role in articulating its members as *representing* a community, in whose interests they work. Archetypal groups studied include traditional interest groups such as professional and trade associations, labor unions, and cooperatives (Harter & Krone, 2001). Understanding organizations as constitutive of communities in some ways involves, as Fulk and DeSanctis (1995) said, a "shift in conception of community from an association of neighbors to an interest-oriented collective" (p. 342). Given this, the ways in which such research constructs both community participation and issues is often explicitly political. Consequently, this research has often focused on interest and lobby groups from the perspective of political communication and/or public relations. Karpf (2012), for example, coined the term *The MoveOn Effect* to talk about ways in which the new, fluid technological environment has led to the emergence of netroot (online grassroots) organizations that are transforming the organizational layer of American politics—the zone in which formal interest groups have traditionally operated.

Given the fewer number of studies, there has not yet emerged a comprehensive framework to consider various kinds of organizational communication research on such organizations. However, participation and issue definition vary in such studies in the degree to which the community or interest group is formalized; that is, how rules, systems of governance, and hierarchies are codified and proceduralized. While some studies of formal organizations have focused on the enabling features of participation, others have focused on the constraining effects of organizational structures and processes on participatory practices.

Formal Organizations

Bimber et al.'s (2012) study of three large, formal collective action organizations is a good example of research that examines how participation can enable and construct organizational practice. The authors argued that individual participation styles within formal organizations such as the AARP (formerly the American Association for Retired Persons) or the American Legion now interact with organizational structures and processes in hitherto unprecedented ways. While members of these communities continue to choose to articulate their interests and affect public life institutionally through their organizations, they have begun to affect and influence the formal structure of their organizations in new and powerful ways.

Cheney's (1999) study of the Mondragón cooperatives is the converse of Bimber et al.'s research inasmuch as, instead of looking at the transformative impact of participation on organizational structure, it traced the constraining impact that organizational structures and processes (in the form of marketization) had on participation in the cooperatives and, consequently, on workplace democracy. The need to respond to the pressures of globalization resulted in severe challenges to the workplace cooperatives that transformed the small Basque town of Mondragón immediately after the Spanish Civil War.

Some studies also examine both constraining and enabling aspects of participation on organizing outcomes. For example, Cloud's (2005) study of union organizing at the Staley Corporation focused on newsletters published over a two-year period by locked-out workers. Her analysis revealed that while initial constructions of workers as heroes fighting a worthy battle helped build a sense of confrontation and mobilized workers to participate in such tactics as picketing, their ultimate inability to materially and economically challenge the corporation through strikes and other kinds of industrial action was eventually reflected in their rhetorical recasting of themselves as victims and martyrs. Brimeyer, Eaker, and Clair (2004) also illustrate how management strategies constrain communicative possibilities for unions. Drawing from Bowers, Ochs, and Jensen's (1993) distinctions between rhetorics of agitation and control, they show how communication strategies crafted by a labor union were co-opted by management and transformed into a rhetoric of control.

Another series of studies, by Papa, Auwal, and Singhal (1995, 1997), of Bangladesh's Grameen Bank trace both the constraining and enabling effects of participation in membership-based collective action organizations. Notably, they found that while the micro loans offered by the bank and enabled by its two-million-strong membership had significant empowering effects resulting in tangible material benefits for participants, the system of concertive control produced by the collective system often had debilitating and punitive effects on its members in the form of overwork, large pressures to return loans, and the movement from a system of solidarity to one of self-surveillance. Likewise, Harter (2004) traced how members of a farmers' cooperative in Nebraska experienced significant participative tensions in experiencing democracy related to the enactment of efficiency versus the need for equity.

Informal and Self-Organizing Groups

Scholars have understood member participation in political terms not only in formal interest groups but also in more informal, self-organizing, and emergent contexts where small and ephemeral groups represent and construct community interests. Adelman and Frey (1996), for example, traced the multiple constructions of community by long-term residents of Bonaventure House, a halfway home for people living with HIV/AIDS. Their seven-year study outlines multiple ways in which members participated in and co-constructed community, including dealing with social life, bereavement, coping with and resisting the stigma and prejudice associated with HIV/AIDS, and advocating for the rights of people living with HIV/AIDS. Themes of such resistance are also evident in Howell, Brock, and Hauser's (1992) study of a bona fide or naturally emerging youth group that formed in Detroit in the wake of severe riots to rebuild a youth community, resist the culture of violence, and create a series of events that members characterized as a "radical, direct and imaginative response to injustice and dehumanization" (p. 88).

Simpson and Cheney's (2007) study of a New Zealand retirement community also highlighted the political dimensions of participation in interest-based communities as residents began to organize themselves around senior citizen rights. Their study of the affective dimensions of such emergent organizing, however, draws attention to not only political but also important aesthetic and consummatory aspects of participation processes in groups that express and construct community interests. Kramer's (2004, 2009, 2013) studies of community groups is another interesting example of such work. His analyses of voluntary community theater groups and community choirs composed of community members shed light on the multiple affective reasons that members participate in them, including finding joy, a sense of communion and creativity, and, ultimately, community identification. These studies illustrate important ways in which informal community groups ranging from churches to theatres serve to construct and create community interests. While the community interests and issues themselves may be ultimately political in multiple senses of the term, the participatory processes that construct them may not.

Most studies that fall under the rubric of organizations as constitutive have tended to focus exclusively on either formal or informal organizational structures. However, there are good reasons to look at how formal and informal kinds of organization might intermingle, interact, and affect each other. This is important in at least three respects. First, the very idea of *membership-based* organizations is changing in highly mediated environments. Many formal advocacy and interest-based groups have stopped making significant distinctions between dues-paying members and other kinds of supporters (Bimber et al., 2012). Therefore, we need to ask more questions about what counts as membership and support in a digital environment. What sort of support does "liking" a Facebook post by an organization constitute, for example? If definitions of organizational membership are expanding and diluting, do organizations have the same ethical responsibilities to their expanded constituencies as they do to those official members of the organization who expect their interests to be those primarily represented by the organization? As formal organizations become more and more embedded in the digital environment, their boundaries are likely to become more permeable, and they are likely to be affected by and take on the organizing dynamics of smaller and more transient digital groups. Much more work is needed on the specific dynamics of such processes.

Second, it is also important to study how small, voluntary, and self-organized community groups composed exclusively of community members may develop and evolve into more highly structured outsider organizations and acquire professional and paid staff and distinct organizational structures, in many ways recapitulating the emergence of the highly structured and professionalized nonprofit sector itself (Frumkin, 2002). Ganesh (2007), for example, studied how small community groups in Goa, India, which were originally organized around children's issues, were restructured over time. These transformations were evident during a yearlong statewide planning process on children's rights. As the articulation of children's interests became more and more influenced by postcolonial identity politics and international funding priorities, it changed the grassroots structure of these groups themselves, and money became available to tackle issues relating to sex trafficking.

Third and finally, just as self-organizing intracommunity groups can transform into structured nonprofits and NGOs, it is important to trace converse relationships and examine how issue advocacy by external organizations can lead to significant amounts of community self-organizing. Indeed, some research already shows that advocacy as a participative form, when well enacted, appears to engender community self-organizing. Zoller's accounts of Addyston's Good Neighbor Campaign (Ganesh & Zoller, 2012; Zoller, 2012; Zoller & Tener, 2010) illustrate how initial organizing by Ohio Citizen Action, a statewide group, resulted in the formation of a community-organized collective in Addyston called the Westside Action Group. This group itself became a central mechanism for several community members to represent the neighborhood, actively construct community interests as lying in tension with the Lanxess corporation, and effectively lobby for changes in their emission standards. Likewise, Toft's (2011) study of local community activism around homelessness in the Seattle area discusses the impact of inclusive and participatory organizing efforts by churches and nonprofits in the 1990s. Their incipient organizing fostered self-organized advocacy by homeless groups themselves a full decade later in the form of "no sweeps" and "no jail" campaigns after the city attempted to gentrify its image and passed aggressive laws that enabled police to effectively criminalize homelessness.

Organization as Insider

A third way in which organizational communication scholars have understood the relationship between organizations and community interests is by framing organizations as nodes or elements of a larger, diffuse community and movement. Often, community interests are expressed broadly, as public issues, including major social, economic, environmental, and political problems such as climate change or civil rights and liberties. Sometimes, community issues and interests are constructed, defined, and negotiated in transcendent terms by the organizations and groups involved. Global social justice groups, for instance, often describe themselves as part of a *movement of movements* or a *network of networks* (Ganesh & Stohl, 2010; Mertes, 2004). While in some ways, the distinction between the organization as outsider and organization as insider is one of level of analysis, organizations are seen as community insiders precisely because the community boundaries themselves are diffuse and hard to define, and issues are constructed in translocal terms.

How these public issues and interests are framed affects the construction of interorganizational relationships and dynamics of participation. Cheney and Cloud (2006), for example, discuss how framing contemporary social justice issues as "globalization from below" (Brecher, Costello, & Smith, 2000; Ganesh, Zoller, & Cheney, 2005) can affect the linking of organizational practices across time and space. They argue that such framing is "vital for linking micro-organizational practices, community-based networks, and broader social movements" (p. 513). Therefore, studies that employ an organization as insider frame are often explicitly interorganizational in focus, and the modes of participation that they describe are sometimes overtly *collaborative* and, at other times, overtly confrontational, focusing on *contention*, and in some cases, a hybrid of both (Ganesh & Zoller, 2012).

Contention

Several studies have focused on contention as a driving feature of community participation, understanding it in multiple ways. Knight and Greenberg (2002) for example, employ Beck's (1992) notion of subpolitics to describe anticorporate activism around human rights issues, notably anti-sweatshop campaigns against Nike. They characterize subpolitics in terms of interorganizational coalition politics, calling it "the politics of interest groups, social movements, activism, and advocacy groups whose interests radiate out beyond the sphere of institutional politics and whose targets include power centers other than the State" (p. 544). In describing the organizational features of these movement communities, they state that the organizing nodes of the anti-sweatshop movement "assume a looser, more mobile and flexible form than more bureaucratically structured organizations; they are typically organized in terms of network arrangements that lack a definite center with binding decision-making power" (p. 555).

This formulation echoes Castells's (1996) conceptualization of the network society and the contradictions of informational capitalism, where social and economic practices are heavily dependent on the digital circulation of information. Such *informationalism* gives rise to a networking logic, one that sees increased connectivity as both socially desirable and a source of economic value (Castells, 2004, 2009). These networking logics can take the form of informational domination; conversely, they can also be decentralized and subversive. Castells (1996) describes these subversive logics as involving a "networking, decentered form of organization and intervention, characteristic of the new social movements, mirroring, and counteracting the networking logic of domination in the information society" (p. 367). Bennett and his associates have done some groundbreaking work on the implications of informationalism and networking logics for collective action. Bennett and Segerberg (2012) in particular argue that in late modern societies, local group and community ties are being replaced by large-scale, fluid digital social networks. Traditional collective action is thus replaced by a more individualized *connective* action that is archetypally organizationless, highly personalized, and volatile. They identify two forms of networked contention as a result: self-organizing connective action that does not require any kind of organizational activity and results in such movements as Occupy and organizationally enabled networks of connective action that may involve some kind of organizational coordination but unlike traditional collective action, lack formal organizational sponsorship and branding.

The emphasis on networks and interorganizational relationships in collective action and community is also reflected in Norton's (2009) work on diachronic views of power and resistance in public controversies. Norton claims that it is inadequate for organizational communication scholars interested in social movement organizing to continue to study single organizations. Rather, understanding the long-term dynamics of power in ongoing disputes about justice involves paying close attention to "a glut of organizational entities including public bureaus, local governments, liberal and conservative social movement organizations, and local business and recreation groups" (p. 549).

Thus participation in social movement organizing is inevitably multileveled, involving not only the involvement of individuals but also extensive coordination, consensus, exchange, and debate between individuals and groups, between groups and organizations, and between and across factions. The overall frame of participation in social movement organizing, however, is typically conflictual and oriented toward addressing issues of justice and inequity (e.g., Norton & Paveglio, 2009). In social movement studies, Diani and McAdam (2003) have argued that the presence of conflict is a defining feature of social movement networks, distinguishing them from non-conflictual movements or forms of collective action that, while oriented toward the creation, negotiation, and maintenance of some form of community or public good, do not identify particular social actors as opponents. Here, frames for participation often tend to be collaborative rather than conflictual.

Coordination

Several organizational studies addressing interorganizational dynamics have been conducted using a coordination frame, focusing on relationships among collaboration, cooperation, and competition. The distinction between coordination-oriented studies and those oriented toward contention echoes a larger sociological and paradigmatic tension in organizational studies between theories of order and theories of conflict (Burrell & Morgan, 1979)—a tension that continues to flourish.

Monge, Fulk, and their associates' research in community ecology has been particularly useful in highlighting the longitudinal dynamics of collaboration and coordination in organizational populations. Community ecology theorists attend to ways in which communities of organizations coevolve (Shumate et al., 2005). Dimensions of cooperative relationships between coevolving organizations can be described along two dimensions: symbiosis and commensalism. *Symbiosis* describes cooperative relationships between organizations that do not compete for the same resources. Shumate and O'Connor (2010), for example, understand NGO-corporate alliances in terms of symbiosis, highlighting the communicative role of the public and representational network created by these alliances in co-constructing the alliance and the issue itself.

In this literature, *commensalism* refers to cooperative situations where organizations potentially compete for the same resources. Taylor and Doerfel's (2003, 2004) work is illuminating in this regard. Their 2003 study of a network of 17 civil society organizations in Croatia shows how they were highly instrumental in negotiating democratic elections and ensuring the emergence and construction of a civil society; moreover, it sheds light into the evolutionary dynamics of cooperation in collective action networks. Several years later, the cooperative relationships among these organizations had evolved into a form of *cooperative competition* (Doerfel & Taylor, 2004), with organizations beginning to focus on specific public interests including women's issues, human rights, and environmental crises and competition beginning to emerge as a result of cycles of resource seeking by various organizations. Their studies help confirm Flanagin, Monge, and Fulk's (2001) finding that foundational members in interorganizational alliances centered around the creation of public goods are more likely to reap long-term cooperative benefits because of their network centrality.

Doerfel's work also illustrates the key role that cooperative interorganizational relationships play in the process of rebuilding community in the wake of disasters (Doerfel, Lai, & Chewning, 2010). This study of collaborations between a range of community groups, businesses, nonprofits, and public organizations in the wake of the devastation wreaked by Hurricane Katrina on New Orleans used a qualitative approach to identify four post-disaster phases: a personal emergency phase, a professional emergency phase, a transitional phase, and a rebuilding phase. The key role of collaborative businesses in the rebuilding stage had significant implications for the reconstruction of civil society and social capital in the years immediately following the hurricane.

Other theoretical traditions in organizational communication have also focused on interorganizational collaboration in the context of community interests. Heath (2007), for example, used a dialogic frame to study collaborative interaction amongst members of Metro Collaboration, an inter-sectoral group formed to act on issues relating to children's education. Deetz's work on deliberative democracy, dialogue, and community collaboration is also significant, because it asks communication scholars to pay meticulous attention to specific models of communicative participation in action (Deetz, 2007; Deetz & Irwin, 2008). Deetz addresses how multiple community stakeholders can engage with each other in order to construct and craft joint dialogic outcomes on issues ranging from conflict and peace to land use and environmental stewardship.

Despite the distinct theoretical traditions that have grounded studies oriented toward collaboration and studies oriented toward contention, we posit that scholars need to turn their attention further, to ways in which both collaboration and conflict are intertwined in communicative processes that construct relationships between groups and organizations involved in collective action. Some organizational communication scholars and critics have already argued this. Deetz (2007), for example, highlighted the idea that disagreement is a necessary part of intersectoral dialogue and collaboration. Scholars of social movements are also increasingly questioning the assumption of internal equality within clusters of social movement organizations. For example, in an analysis of North-South relationships among NGOs working to protect the remaining Amazon rainforest, Dempsey (2007) established clear structural power differences between U.S.-based environmental activists and local networks of indigenous activists; she highlights how the former exerted much more influence in crafting issues around which collective action occurred. Ganesh and Zoller (2012) also pointed out flaws in the assumption that internal communication between various social movement factions should be primarily collaborative and consensus based. They argued that just as activist confrontation has important dialogic consequences for how collective action issues are eventually understood and framed, so too can internal movement-dissent work to help movements procure multiple goals.

Discussion

These three perspectives—organizations as outsiders, organizations as constitutive, and organizations as insiders—describe a wide variety of scholarship in organizational communication on the subject of community organizing, social movements, and collective action. We emphasize again that the distinctions we have drawn are illustrative rather than categorical, that studies can and do draw on more than one perspective on the organization-community relationship, and that some studies are manifestly hybrid. For example, Norton and Sadler's (2006) study of a planning process in Ruralton, a small U.S. town of less than 600 people, adopts such a hybrid approach. They show how the board, created by the town council, was in some ways an outside organization engaging in a social planning process inasmuch as it was driven not only by the local council but also by nearby city planners and state mandates, which were viewed by local community members as outsiders. The planning board came to take on important constitutive features, however, as it was composed of townspeople who used it as a forum for debate and to articulate their vision of the town's future, grounded in local tradition.

The three-fold discussion of organizations and community interests animates the two major communicative features of collective action drawn from our definition at the outset: two or more people acting for the benefit of three or more people. The collective action studies we have reviewed reinforce what we already know about participation: that it can be understood at multiple levels (Monge & Contractor, 2004) and that it is a deeply paradoxical process (Stohl & Cheney, 2001). At the same time, this body of work shows evidence of diverse and vibrant understandings of this critical interactive aspect of communication. Some studies cast participation problems in terms of outcomes, discussing democratic difficulties or deficits (Toft, 2011) or political mobilization as a critical feature of participation (Zoller, 2012). Several others highlight participation problems in terms of form and process, focusing on such difficulties as collaboration (Lewis, Isbell, & Koschmann, 2010) or on aesthetic and consummatory aspects of participation (Harter et al., 2008). Still others have understood participation largely as contestation (Norton, 2009), in contrast with others who see it largely in terms of coordination (Doerfel et al., 2010).

The studies we have reviewed also emphasize that the issues and benefits around which collective action efforts are organized are highly complex. While some studies have understood benefits in terms of social justice (Harter, 2004), others have understood it in terms of concrete public goods (Fulk et al., 1996). Some studies treat community issues in highly emergent terms (Howell et al., 1992), while others understand them in predetermined ways (Koschmann, 2012). Finally, how studies frame collective action issues have significant implications for how communities themselves are understood: When studies frame issues and interests purely in local terms, the notion of community is locally bounded (Zoller, 2000), but when issues are framed in terms of global or larger public significance, the notion of community itself expands and diffuses accordingly (Cooper & Shumate, 2012).

This review also shows that participation and issue construction are highly intertwined in various studies and that they can mutually construct each other. If, for example, health issues are understood in terms of disease prevention, then community participation is likely to be framed in terms of compliance. Conversely, if issues are framed in terms of social injustice, then participation is much more likely to be articulated in terms of empowerment or mobilization. Participation itself can also be viewed as the community issue. This is especially true of locality development and other approaches that attempt to increase community and stakeholder participation (Medved et al., 2001), framing their goals as "conscientization" (Freire, 1970) and empowerment (Crabtree, 1998).

Implications and Further Studies

In the last 15 years, organizational communication scholars have engaged issues of community organization and social movements as critical aspects of contemporary collective action. Such scholarly engagement will continue to grow and occupy a more central place in organizational communication studies in the decades to come. We have already offered specific suggestions for studies grounded in one orientation or the other toward community and public interests, but there is much more to be done to integrate the diverse approaches. While the range of research location, methods, and theoretical perspectives make it difficult to predict the overall direction of organizational communication research on civil society organizing, a few broad trends and implications can be drawn. We discuss three: locality, hybridity, and engagement.

Shepherd and Rothenbuhler's (2001) edited volume on communication and community indicated that scholarship about community in communication studies would continue to engage with locality as a key spatial and theoretical problematic. This prediction has been borne out in organizational communication studies in the last decade. We believe that organizational communication scholars will continue to grapple with issues involved in the translocalization of collective action. As networking logics of informational capitalism infuse movements and structures (Castells, 2009), as funding and coordination pressures require nonprofit organizations to collaborate (Lewis et al., 2010), and as logics of rationalization and professionalization transform civil society organizing (Ganesh & McAllum, 2012), forms of participation and collective action issues will continue to change. Therefore, as Lewis (2005) argued, organizational communication studies of civil society organizing need to interpret and understand communities and their interests in terms larger than immediate face-to-face or neighborhood contexts, even in studies of those contexts.

We traced this impact of globalization on organizational communication in much greater detail in Stohl and Ganesh (Chapter 29). Here, we also observe that as organizational communication studies continue to globalize, we anticipate that studies of collective action located outside the U.S. will continue to grow; indeed, scholars have already studied local contexts for community organizing and activism in a host of nations including Kenya (Murphy, 2013), India (Mudaliar, Donner, & Thies, 2012), and New Zealand (Ganesh & Stohl, 2010). The increasing locational diversity cannot but increase the cosmopolitan and hybrid sensibility of organizational communication studies in the coming decades. Additionally, we anticipate that questions of locality and community will assume greater significance in the context of large-scale collective action problems as we continue to understand the organizational implications of large ecological crises such as climate change. In this context, resilience is one core principle of effective and ethical community engagement that is likely to attract a lot of analysis (Chewning, Lai, & Doerfel, 2012; Ganesh & Zoller, 2013). As scholars examine how communities respond to and are reconstructed in the wake of crises and disasters (Doerfel et al., 2010), our understanding of the range of methods available to and invented by communities and coordinating networks will evolve significantly.

Second, as we outlined earlier, organizational hybridity is an important concern, and it is likely to be an explicit focus of studies of emerging forms and spaces of collective action. As Bimber et al. (2012) observe, technology is having an ecological impact on collective action in large formal organizations. As legacy organizations (Karpf, 2012) formed prior to digitization transform and adapt to the digital environment, the emergent structures and practices will likely be novel combinations of established and emergent forms of advocacy and organizing (Chadwick, 2007). Hybridity involves not only transformations in organizational structure and practice but also new patterns of organizational disembeddedness and reembeddedness as participation practices transform and collective action organizations are more able to connect with others in the digital environment and less able to connect with those outside it. Consequently, the current research emphasis on interorganizational relationships in collective action is likely to continue, even as studies continue to emerge of complicated and hybrid organizational forms as a result of changes in collective action.

Third, we note that scholars are likely to identify and construct new models of citizenship and civic engagement as a cumulative result of research on community organizing and social movements. The boundaries between these two bodies of work are increasingly blurred, as frameworks of civic engagement and participation appear to be shifting from a dutiful citizenship model to a more expressive form of actualizing citizenship that is less authoritative and more collaborative (Bennett et al., 2011). This is likely to have implications for how we understand such modes of engagement and participation as volunteering or activism themselves. Lewis (2013), for example, suggested that we are likely to see an increase in episodic volunteering outside of formal organizational contexts in the future. The contours of activism as a form of civic participation will also shift, as it continues to diffuse broadly as a result of digital technologies and as forms of issue engagement sometimes referred to as *clicktivism* or *slacktivism* become more prevalent (Earl & Kimport, 2011). Within this landscape, a core challenge for scholars of civic engagement in a network society is "to suggest conditions by which democratic institutions may evolve to integrate civic engagement and to provide meaningful and sustainable governance" (Booher, 2008, p. 130). We look forward to such transformative research.

Acknowledgments

Our sincere thanks to Dennis Mumby, Janet Fulk, George Cheney, Kirstie McAllum, and Heather Zoller for reading through earlier drafts of this chapter. Our participation on this project was enabled by a grant from the Royal Society of New Zealand's Marsden Foundation on contemporary organizational transformations in collective action.

References

Adelman, M., & Frey, L. (1996). *The fragile community.* New York, NY: Lawrence Erlbaum.

Ashcraft, K. (2001). Organized dissonance: Feminist bureaucracy as hybrid form. *Academy of Management Journal, 44*(6), 1301–1322.

Ashcraft, K. L. (2011). Knowing work through the communication of difference: A revised agenda for difference studies. In D. K. Mumby (Ed.), *Reframing difference in organizational communication studies: Research, pedagogy and practice* (pp. 3–30). Thousand Oaks, CA: SAGE.

Ashcraft, K. L., & Kedrowicz, A. (2002). Self-direction or social support? Nonprofit empowerment and the tacit employment contract of organizational communication studies. *Communication Monographs, 69*(1), 88–111.

Beck, U. (1992). *Risk society: Towards a new modernity.* Newbury Park, CA: SAGE.

Bennett, W. L., & Segerberg, A. (2012). The logic of connective action: Digital media and the personalization of contentious politics. *Information, Communication & Society, 15*(5), 739–768.

Bennett, W. L., Wells, C., & Freelon, D. (2011). Communicating civic engagement: Contrasting models of citizenship in the youth web sphere. *Journal of Communication, 61*(5), 835–856.

Bimber, B., Flanagin, A., & Stohl, C. (2012). *Collective action in organizations: Interaction and engagement in an era of technological change.* Cambridge, UK: Cambridge University Press.

Blau, P., & Scott, W. R. (1962). *Formal organizations: A comparative approach.* San Francisco, CA: Chandler.

Booher, D. E. (2008). Civic engagement as collaborative complex adaptive systems. In K. Yang & E. Bergrud (Eds.), *Civic engagement in a network society* (pp. 111–148). Charlotte, NC: IAP.

Bowers, J. W., Ochs, D. J., & Jensen, R. J. (1993). *The rhetoric of agitation and control.* Long Grove, IL: Waveland Press.

Brecher, J., Costello, T., & Smith, B. (2000). *Globalisation from below: The power of solidarity.* Cambridge, UK: South End Press.

Brimeyer, T., Eaker, A., & Clair, R. P. (2004). Rhetorical strategies in union organizing: A case of labor versus management. *Management Communication Quarterly, 18*(1), 45–75.

Burrell, G., & Morgan, G. (1979). *Sociological paradigms and organisational analysis.* London, England: Heinemann.

Casimir, F. L. (1991). *Communication in development.* Norwood, NJ: Ablex Publishing.

Castells, M. (1996). *The rise of the network society.* Oxford, UK: Blackwell Publishers Ltd.

Castells, M. (Ed.). (2004). *The network society: A cross-cultural perspective.* Cheltenham, UK: Edward Elgar.

Castells, M. (2009). *Communication power.* Oxford, UK: Oxford University Press.

Chadwick, A. (2007). Digital network repertoires and organizational hybridity. *Political Communication, 24*(3), 283–301.

Cheney, G. (1983). The rhetoric of identification and the study of organizational communication. *Quarterly Journal of Speech, 69*(2), 143–158.

Cheney, G. (1999). *Values at work: Employee participation meets market pressure at Mondragón.* Ithaca, NY: Cornell University Press.

Cheney, G. (2007). Organizational communication comes out. *Management Communication Quarterly, 21*(1), 80–91.

Cheney, G., & Cloud, D. (2006). Doing democracy, engaging the material: Employee participation and labor activity in an age of market globalization. *Management Communication Quarterly, 19*(4), 1–40.

Cheney, G., & Stohl, C. (1991). Communicating about human rights: An advocacy model. *Peace Research, 23*(2), 105–117.

Cheney, G., Straub, J., Speirs-Glebe, L., Stohl, C., Degooyer, D., & Whalen, S. (1997). Democracy, participation, and communication at work: A multidisciplinary review. In M. E. Roloff (Ed.), *Communication yearbook* (vol. 21, pp. 35–91). Thousand Oaks, CA: SAGE.

Chewning, L. V., Lai, C-H., & Doerfel, M. L. (2012). Organizational resilience and using information and communication technologies to rebuild communication structures. *Management Communication Quarterly, 27*(2), 1–27. doi: 10.1177/0893318912465815

Cloud, D. L. (2005). Fighting words: Labor and the limits of communication at Staley, 1993 to 1996. *Management Communication Quarterly, 18*(4), 509–542.

Cloud, D. (2007). Corporate social responsibility as oxymoron: Universalization and exploitation at Boeing. In S. May, G. Cheney, & J. Roper (Eds.), *The debate over corporate social responsibility* (pp. 219–231). Oxford, UK: Oxford University Press.

Cooper, K. R., & Shumate, M. (2012). Inter-organizational collaboration explored through the bona fide network perspective. *Management Communication Quarterly, 26*(4), 623–654.

Cooren, F., & Taylor, J. R. (1997). Organization as an effect of mediation: Redefining the link between organization and communication. *Communication Theory, 7*(3), 219–260.

Crabtree, R. (1998). Mutual empowerment in cross-cultural participatory development and service learning: Lessons in communication and social justice from projects in El Salvador and Nicaragua. *Journal of Applied Communication Research, 26*(2), 182–209.

Deetz, S. (2007). Corporate governance, corporate social responsibility, and communication. In S. May, G. Cheney, & J. Roper (Eds.), *The debate over corporate social responsibility* (pp. 267–279). Oxford, UK: Oxford University Press.

Deetz, S., & Irwin, L. (2008). Governance, stakeholder involvement, and new communication models. In S. Odugbemi & T. Jacobson (Eds.), *Governance reform under real world conditions: Citizens, stakeholders and voice* (pp. 163–179). Washington, DC: The World Bank.

Deetz, S., & Simpson, J. (2003). Critical organizational dialogue: Open formation and the demand of "otherness." In R. Anderson, L. Baxter, & K. Cissna (Eds.), *Dialogue: Theorizing difference in communication studies* (pp. 141–158). Thousand Oaks, CA: SAGE.

Della-Piana, C. K., & Anderson, J. A. (1995). Performing community: Community service as cultural conversation. *Communication Studies, 46*(3), 187–200.

Dempsey, S. E. (2007). Towards a critical organizational approach to civil society contexts: A case study of the difficulties of transnational advocacy. In B. J. Allen, L. A. Flores, & M. P. Orbe (Eds.), *The international and intercultural communication annual* (vol. 30, pp. 317–339). Washington, DC: National Communication Association.

Dempsey, S. E. (2010). Critiquing community engagement. *Management Communication Quarterly, 24*(3), 359–390.

Dempsey, S. E., Parker, P. S., & Krone, K. J. (2011). Navigating socio-spatial difference, constructing counter-space: Insights from transnational feminist praxis. *Journal of International and Intercultural Communication, 4*(3), 201–220.

Depew, D., & Peters, J. D. (2000). Communication and community: The conceptual background. In G. Shepherd & E. W. Rothenbuhler (Eds.), *Communication and Community* (pp. 3–20). Oxford, UK: Taylor and Francis.

Dewey, J. (1927). *The public and its problems.* New York, NY: Swallow Press.

Diani, M., & McAdam, D. (Eds.). (2003). *Social movements and networks: Relational approaches to collective action.* Oxford, UK: Oxford University Press.

Doerfel, M. L., Lai, C-H., & Chewning, L. V. (2010). The evolutionary role of inter-organizational communication: Modeling social capital in disaster contexts. *Human Communication Research, 36*(2), 125–162.

Doerfel, M. L., & Taylor, M. (2004). Network dynamics of inter-organizational cooperation: The Croatian civil society movement. *Communication Monographs, 71*(4), 373–394.

Earl, J., & Kimport, K. (2011). *Digitally enabled social change: Activism in the Internet age.* Boston, MA: MIT Press.

Ewalt, J. (2012, November 16). *An uncontrollable presence: The paradoxes of public memory and the globalization from below movement.* Paper presented at the National Communication Association Annual Convention, Orlando, FL.

Flanagin, A. J., Monge, P., & Fulk, J. (2001). The value of formative investment in organizational federations. *Human Communication Research, 27*(1), 69–93.

Freire, P. (1970). *Pedagogy of the oppressed* (M. Ramos, Trans.). New York, NY: Continuum.

Frumkin, P. (2002). *On being nonprofit.* Cambridge, UK: Harvard University Press.

Fulk, J., & DeSanctis, G. (1995). Electronic communication and changing organizational forms. *Organization Science, 6*(4), 337–349.

Fulk, J., Flanagin, A. L., Kalman, M. E., Monge, P. R., & Ryan, T. (1996). Connective and communal public goods in interactive communication systems. *Communication Theory, 6*(1), 60–87.

Ganesh, S. (2003). Organizational narcissism: Technology, legitimacy and identity in an Indian NGO. *Management Communication Quarterly, 16*(4), 558–594.

Ganesh, S. (2005). The myth of the non-governmental organization: Governmentality and transnationalism in an Indian NGO. In G. Cheney & G. Barnett (Eds.), *International and intercultural organizational communication* (vol. 7, pp. 193–219). Cresskill, NJ: Hampton Press.

Ganesh, S. (2007). Grassroots agendas and global discourses: Tracking a local planning process on children's issues. *International and Intercultural Communication Annual, 30*, 289–316.

Ganesh, S., & Barber, K. F. (2009). The silent community: Organizing zones in the digital divide. *Human Relations, 62*(6), 853–876.

Ganesh, S., & McAllum, K., L. (2009). Discourses of volunteerism. In C. Beck (Ed.), *Communication yearbook* (vol. 33, pp. 342–383). New York, NY: Routledge.

Ganesh, S., & McAllum, K. L. (2012). Volunteering and professionalization: Trends in tension? *Management Communication Quarterly, 26*(1), 152–158.

Ganesh, S., & Stohl, C. (2010). Qualifying engagement: A study of information and communication technology and the global social justice movement in Aotearoa New Zealand. *Communication Monographs, 77*(1), 51–75.

Ganesh, S., & Stohl, C. (2013). From Wall Street to Wellington: Protests in an era of digital ubiquity. *Communication Monographs, 80,* 1–27.

Ganesh, S., & Zoller, H. M. (2012). Dialogue, activism and democratic social change. *Communication Theory, 22*(1), 66–91.

Ganesh, S., & Zoller, H. M. (2013). Organizing transition: Eco-localism, resilience and democracy in the transition movement. In M. Parker, G. Cheney, V. Fournier, & C. Land (Eds.), *The Routledge companion to alternative organisation.* Oxford, UK: Routledge.

Ganesh, S., Zoller, H. M., & Cheney, G. (2005). Transforming resistance, broadening our boundaries: Critical organizational communication studies meets globalization from below. *Communication Monographs, 72*(2), 169–191.

Goldzwig, S., & Cheney, G. (1984). The U.S. Catholic bishops on nuclear arms: Corporate advocacy, role redefinition, and rhetorical adaptation. *Central States Speech Journal, 35*(1), 8–23.

Gossett, L., & Tompkins, P. K. (2000). Community as a means of organizational control. In G. J. Shepherd & E. W. Rothenbuhler (Eds.), *Communication and community* (pp. 111–133). London, England: Lawrence Erlbaum.

Hale, C., & James, A. (2013). The sisterhood of the hammer: Women organizing for community and self. In M. W. Kramer, L. K. Lewis, & L. M. Gossett (Eds.), *Communication and volunteering: Studies from multiple contexts* (pp. 133–152). New York, NY: Peter Lang.

Harter, L. M. (2004). Masculinity(s), the agrarian frontier myth, and cooperative ways of organizing: Contradictions and tensions in the experience and enactment of democracy. *Journal of Applied Communication Research, 32*(2), 89–118.

Harter, L. M., Berquist, C., Titsworth, B. S., Novak, D., & Brokaw, T. (2005). The structuring of invisibility among the hidden homeless: The politics of space, stigma, and identity construction. *Journal of Applied Communication Research, 33*(4), 305–327.

Harter, L. M., & Krone, K. J. (2001). The boundary-spanning role of a cooperative support organization: Managing the paradox of stability and change in non-traditional organizations. *Journal of Applied Communication Research, 29*(3), 248–277.

Harter, L. M., Leeman, M., Norander, S., Young, S. L., & Rawlins, W. K. (2008). The intermingling of aesthetic sensibilities and instrumental rationalities in a collaborative arts studio. *Management Communication Quarterly, 21*(4), 423–453.

Heath, R. W. (2007). Rethinking community collaboration through a dialogic lens: Creativity, democracy, and diversity in community organizing. *Management Communication Quarterly, 21*(2), 145–171.

Houston, R., & Jackson, M. H. (2003). Technology and context within research on international development programs: Positioning an integrationist perspective. *Communication Theory, 13*(1), 57–77.

Howell, S., Brock, B., & Hauser, E. (1992). A multicultural, intergenerational youth program: Creating and sustaining a youth community group. In L. Frey (Ed.), *Group communication in context: Studies of bona fide groups* (pp. 85–104). Mahwah, NJ: Lawrence Erlbaum.

Iverson, J., & McPhee, R. (2008). Communicating knowing through communities of practice: Exploring internal communication processes and differences amongst CoPs. *Journal of Applied Communication Research, 36*(2), 176–199.

Jenkins, J. J. (2012). *Community as metaphor: Dialectical tensions of a racially diverse organization.* Tampa: University of South Florida.

Jones, T. S., & Bodtker, A. (1998). A dialectical analysis of a social justice process: International collaboration in South Africa. *Journal of Applied Communication Research, 26*(4), 357–373.

Karpf, D. (2012). *The MoveOn Effect: The unexpected transformation of American political advocacy.* Oxford, UK: Oxford University Press.

Kirby, E. (2007). Organizing to "meet like real Americans": The case of a Hmong nonprofit organization. *International and Intercultural Communication Annual, 30*, 201–228.

Knight, G., & Greenberg, J. (2002). Promotionalism and subpolitics: Nike and its labor critics. *Management Communication Quarterly, 15*(4), 541–570.

Koschmann, M. A. (2012). The communicative constitution of collective identity in inter-organizational collaboration. *Management Communication Quarterly, 27*(1), 1–29.

Koschmann, M. A., & Isbell, M. (2009). Toward a communicative model of interorganizational collaboration: The case of the community action network. *Case Research Journal, 29*(1/2), 1–28.

Kramer, M. W. (2004). Toward a theory of dialectics in group communication: An ethnographic study of a community theater group. *Communication Monographs, 71*(3), 311–332.

Kramer, M. W. (2009). Role negotiation in a temporary organization: Making sense of role development in an educational theatre production. *Management Communication Quarterly, 23*(2), 188–217.

Kramer, M. W. (2013). The socialization of community choir members: A comparison of new and continuing volunteers. In M. W. Kramer, L. L. Lewis, & L. Gossett (Eds.), *Communication and volunteering: Studies from multiple contexts* (pp. 67–88). New York, NY: Peter Lang.

Kuhn, T., & Ashcraft, K. (2003). Corporate scandal and the theory of the firm: Formulating the contributions of organizational communication studies. *Management Communication Quarterly, 17*(1), 20–57.

Lammers, J. (2011). How institutions communicate: Institutional messages, institutional logics, and organizational communication. *Management Communication Quarterly, 25*(1), 154–182.

Lewis, L. K. (2005). The civil society sector: A review of critical issues and a research agenda for organizational communication scholars. *Management Communication Quarterly, 19*(2), 238–267.

Lewis, L. K. (2013). An introduction to volunteers. In M. W. Kramer, L. K. Lewis, & L. M. Gossett (Eds.), *Communication and volunteering: Studies from multiple contexts* (pp. 1–23). New York, NY: Peter Lang.

Lewis, L. K., Isbell, M. G., & Koschmann, M. (2010). Collaborative tensions: Practitioners' experiences of inter-organizational relationships. *Communication Monographs, 77*(4), 460–479.

Maguire, M., & Mohtar, L. F. (1994). Performance and the celebration of a subaltern counterpublic. *Text and Performance Quarterly, 14*(3), 238–252.

McComb, M. (1995). Becoming a travelers aid volunteer: Communication in socialization and training. *Communication Studies, 46*(3/4), 297–316.

Medved, C. E., Morrison, K., Dearing, J. W., Larson, R. S., Cline, G., & Brummans, B. H. J. M. (2001). Tensions in community health improvement initiatives: Communication and collaboration in a managed care environment. *Journal of Applied Communication Research, 29*(2), 137–152.

Melucci, A. (1996). *Challenging codes: Collective action in the information age*. Cambridge: University of Cambridge.

Mertes, T. (Ed.). (2004). *A movement of movements: Is another world really possible?* London, England: Verso.

Monge, P., & Contractor, N. (2004). *Theories of communication networks*. Oxford, UK: Oxford University Press.

Monge, P. R., Fulk, J., Kalman, M. E., Flanagin, A. J., Parnassa, C., & Rumsey, S. (1998). Production of collective action in alliance-based interorganizational communication and information systems. *Organization Science, 9*(3), 411–433.

Mudaliar, P., Donner, J., & Thies, W. (2012, March 13–15). *Emergent practices around CGNet Swara: A voice forum for citizen journalism in rural India*. Paper presented at the International Conference on Information and Communication Technologies and Development, Atlanta, GA.

Mumby, D. K. (1996). Feminism, postmodernism, and organizational communication studies: A critical reading. *Management Communication Quarterly, 9*(3), 259–295.

Mumby, D. K., & Stohl, C. (1996). Disciplining organizational communication studies. *Management Communication Quarterly, 10*(1), 50–72.

Murphy, A. (2013). Discursive frictions: Power, identity, and culture in an international working partnership. *Journal of International and Intercultural Communication, 6*(1), 1–20.

Norton, T. (2009). Situating organizations in politics: A diachronic view of control-resistance dialectics.

Management Communication Quarterly, 22(4), 525–554.

Norton, T., & Paveggio, T. (2009). Organizing Step It Up 2007: Social movement organizations as collective resistance. In D. Endres, L. Sprain, & T. R. Peterson (Eds.), *Social movement to address climate change: Local steps for global action* (pp. 155–177). Amherst, NY: Cambria Press.

Norton, T., & Sadler, C. (2006). Dialectical hegemony and the enactment of contradictory definitions in a rural community planning process. *Southern Communication Journal, 71*(4), 363–382.

Olson, M. (1965). *The logic of collective action: Public goods and the theory of groups.* Boston, MA: Harvard University Press.

Papa, M. J., Auwal, M. A., & Singhal, A. (1995). Dialectic of control and emancipation in organizing for social change: A multitheoretic study of the Grameen Bank in Bangladesh. *Communication Theory, 5*(3), 189–223.

Papa, M. J., Auwal, M. A., & Singhal, A. (1997). Organizing for social change within concertive control systems: Member identification, empowerment and the masking of discipline. *Communication Monographs, 64*(3), 219–249.

Pearce, B. W., & Pearce, K. A. (2000). Extending the theory of the coordinated management of meaning (CMM) through a community dialogue process. *Communication Theory, 10*(4), 405–424.

People for the Ethical Treatment of Animals. (2013). *About PETA: Our mission statement* [Website]. Retrieved from http://www.peta.org/about/default.aspx

Peruzzo, C. M. K. (2009). Organizational communication in the third sector: An alternative perspective. *Management Communication Quarterly, 22*(4), 663–670.

Putnam, L. L., Phillips, N., & Chapman, P. (1996). Metaphors of communication and organization. In S. R. Clegg, C. R. Hardy, & W. R. Nord (Eds.), *Handbook of organization studies* (pp. 375–408). London, England: SAGE.

Redding, W. C. (1985). Stumbling toward identity: The emergence of organizational communication as a field of study. In R. D. McPhee & P. K. Tompkins (Eds.), *Organizational communication: Traditional themes and new directions* (pp. 15–54). Beverly Hills, CA: SAGE.

Redding, W. C., & Tompkins, P. K. (1988). Organizational communication: Past and future tenses. In G. Goldhaber & G. Barnett (Eds.), *Handbook of organizational communication* (pp. 5–33). Norwood, NJ: Ablex.

Rogers, E. (1976). *Communication and development: Critical perspectives.* Beverly Hills, CA: SAGE.

Rothman, J. (1970). Three models of community organization practice. In F. Cox, J. L. Erlich, J. Rothman, & J. E. Tropman (Eds.), *Strategies of community intervention: A book of readings* (pp. 20–36). Itasca, NJ: Peacock.

Samuelson, P. A. (1954). The pure theory of public expenditure. *Review of Economics and Statistics, 36*(4), 387–389.

Shepherd, G., & Rothenbuhler, E. W. (Eds.). (2001). *Communication and community.* Oxford, UK: Taylor and Francis.

Shumate, M., Fulk, J., & Monge, P. (2005). Predictors of the international HIV-AIDS INGO network over time. *Human Communication Research, 31*(4), 482–510.

Shumate, M., & O'Connor, A. (2010). The symbiotic sustainability model: Conceptualizing NGO-corporate alliance communication. *Journal of Communication, 60*(3), 577–609.

Simpson, M., & Cheney, G. (2007). Marketization, participation, and communication within New Zealand retirement villages: A critical-rhetorical and discursive analysis. *Discourse and Communication, 1*(2), 191–222.

Smith, R. C. (1993). *Images of organizational communication: Root metaphors of the organization-communication relation.* Paper presented at the International Communication Association Annual Convention, Washington, DC.

Stohl, C. (2011). Paradoxes of connectivity: Boundary permeability, technological variability, and organisational durability. *Australian Journal of Communication, 38*(2), 123–139.

Stohl, C., & Cheney, G. (2001). Participatory processes/paradoxical practices: Communication and the dilemmas of organizational democracy. *Management Communication Quarterly, 14*(3), 349–407.

Taylor, M., & Doerfel, M. L. (2003). Building interorganizational relationships that build nations. *Human Communication Research, 29*(2), 153–181.

Taylor, J. R., & Robichaud, D. (2004). Finding the organization in the communication: Discourse as action and sensemaking. *Organization, 11*(3), 395–413.

Toft, A. (2011). Contextualizing technology use: Communication practices in a local homeless movement. *Information, Communication & Society, 14*(5), 704–725.

Tompkins, P. (2009). *Who is my neighbor? Communicating and organizing to end homelessness.* Boulder, CO: Paradigm.

Trethewey, A. (1997). Resistance, identity, and empowerment: A postmodern feminist analysis of clients in a human service organization. *Communication Monographs, 64*(4), 281–301.

Trujillo, N. (1992). Interpreting (the work and talk of) baseball: Perspectives on ballpark culture. *Western Journal of Communication, 56*(4), 350–371.

Wenger, E. (1998). *Communities of practice: Learning, meaning and identity.* Cambridge, UK: Cambridge University Press.

Wright, S. (2003). Strategic collective action: Social psychology and social change. In R. Brown & S. L. Gertner (Eds.), *Blackwell handbook of social psychology* (pp. 409–430). Oxford, UK: Blackwell.

Zoller, H. M. (2000). "A place you haven't visited before": Creating the conditions for community dialogue. *Southern Communication Journal, 65*(2/3), 191–207.

Zoller, H. M. (2012). Communicating health: Political risk narratives in an environmental health campaign. *Journal of Applied Communication Research, 40*(1), 20–43.

Zoller, H. M., & Tener, M. (2010). Corporate proactivity as a discursive fiction: Managing environmental health activism and regulation. *Management Communication Quarterly, 24*(3), 391–418.

Zorn, T. E., Flanagin, A. J., & Shoham, M. D. (2011). Institutional and noninstitutional influences on information and communication technology adoption and use among nonprofit organizations. *Human Communication Research, 37*(1), 1–33.

CHAPTER 31

Corporate Social Responsibility and Ethics

Steven K. May and Juliet Roper

Corporate social responsibility (CSR) has numerous definitions, many of which we discuss in this chapter, but none of which is definitive. In many respects, these definitions have evolved according to historical, cultural, and political contexts (see May, Cheney, & Roper, 2007, for an overview). Further, CSR is described under different terminologies, many of which follow trends—again formed by contexts and, from a critical standpoint, expediencies. For example, CSR in the United States is built upon a tradition of corporate philanthropy—a necessary tradition in a country where government provision for social welfare is not the norm, nor even necessarily seen as desirable. In such cases, business is required to fill that gap, especially in times when corporations' coffers were growing rapidly in times of industrial development. Added motive for corporate philanthropy stemmed from threats of U.S. government taxation on industries such as petroleum, whose "windfall" profits were seen to be excessive (Crable & Vibbert, 1983). European countries, on the other hand, which have tended to have stronger traditions of government-provided social welfare, have not had the same expectations of corporate giving. Thus philanthropy is not a strong feature of CSR in that region. This is particularly so in the Scandinavian countries. In other cases, such as in Mexico and other areas of South America, religion has been a key driver, with philanthropy seen primarily as a moral imperative driven by religious values (Sanborn, 2004).

Although philanthropy is one of the most widely recognized examples of CSR, many other sets of practices also fall within the definition of CSR, according to most scholars and practitioners (Bowen, 1953; Carroll, 1979). Some businesses, for example, have engaged in cause promotion as they seek to increase awareness and concern for causes such as literacy (e.g., Microsoft), poverty (e.g., World Cocoa Foundation), and clean water (e.g., Coca-Cola), among others. As an extension of cause promotion, some organizations have developed cause-related marketing campaigns, whereby consumers contribute to a cause via consumption of a product or service (e.g., Think Pink, GAP's red campaign). Yet other corporations have focused on corporate social marketing, which focuses on specific behavior-change initiatives that may interest the general public, such as vaccinations (e.g., Johnson &

Johnson), nutrition (e.g., Whole Foods), recycling (e.g., Patagonia), and environmental stewardship (e.g., Timberland). Finally, many organizations have established community volunteering programs, in which employees donate their time and skills in their local communities.

Regardless of the specific practice, from its inception, CSR has been used as a means to focus organizational efforts toward programs of corporate social stewardship, corporate social responsiveness, corporate/business ethics, and corporate global citizenship, among others (Cheney, Roper, & May, 2007; Frederick, 2006). The past 10 years has seen fluctuations in terminologies used by the business sector, reflecting some of the research approaches we discuss in this chapter. While no data are currently available on connections between research approaches and adoption of terms in practice, the links would be interesting to explore. Shifts have been noted in European practitioner usage, for example, from *corporate social responsibility* to *corporate responsibility*—perhaps suggesting a strategic drop of the *social*. More recently, CSR is seen to be in the process of being replaced in corporate reports by *sustainability*. In New Zealand, *business social responsibility* was briefly introduced in the early 1990s but was quickly replaced by *sustainability* and *sustainable development* (Allen, 2009).

The purpose of this chapter is to explore extant literature and the approaches taken by scholars on CSR in the field of organizational communication (for a broader discussion of communication ethics, see Cheney, May, & Munshi, 2011). Because CSR has only relatively recently emerged within the field as a topic of study, we necessarily first address CSR literature in other fields, primarily business and management, which have a longer research tradition in the area. We then turn to several theoretical discourses of organizational communication that provide a framework for the literature on CSR. We conclude the chapter with a discussion of scholarly tensions that are common in CSR scholarship and offer several directions for future research.

Theories of Corporate Social Responsibility: The Historical Legacy of Business and Management

To date, there have been many conceptualizations of CSR. In the late 1990s, Carroll (1999) noted over 20 ways that CSR has been defined in the academic literature. The theory and research on CSR has ranged from narrow views of specific CSR strategies and practices to broader approaches that explore theories of the firm or the role of business in society (see Windsor, 2006, for a summary). Such study of CSR has been increasingly widespread in a number of academic disciplines, such as business/management, economics, political science, sociology, environmental studies, and, more recently, communication studies. In the case of communication studies, the primary subareas that have taken up questions of CSR have been organizational communication (Kuhn & Deetz, 2008) and public relations (Marchand, 1998; Roper, 2005), although scholars in rhetoric (Aune, 2007) and environmental communication (Peterson & Norton, 2007) have also begun to explore the topic recently.

During the 1980s and 1990s, however, the debates circulating around CSR were largely dominated by business and management scholars (see, e.g., Crane, McWilliams, Matten, Moon, & Siegel, 2008, for a summary). Over the years, there have been several attempts to classify CSR theories. In a review article that has been widely used by CSR scholars in business and management, Mele (2008) distinguishes four strands of CSR research: (1) shareholder value theory, (2) corporate social performance, (3) corporate citizenship, and (4) stakeholder theory. Because these strands have been widely adopted by scholars in those disciplines, we address each one more specifically.

Shareholder value theory takes the view that the sole responsibility of businesses is to make a profit for their shareholders and thus is described by some scholars as *fiduciary capitalism*. From this theoretical perspective, CSR activities would only be appropriate if they contribute to the maximization of shareholder value or are required by law. This theory serves as a foundation for neoclassical economic theory and is focused on shareholder utility maximization. In a famous article in *The New York Times*, Friedman (1970) argued against the popular CSR practices of the day and noted that "the only one responsibility of business towards society is the maximization of profits to the shareholders, within the legal framework and the ethical custom of the country" (p. 32).

Other scholars have also argued for profit maximization, drawing on agency theory with its distinction between the responsibilities of owners and managers, albeit with managers seeking to align their economic interests with those of owners around a single objective (e.g., Jensen, 2002). In related iterations of this view, scholars have suggested that *enlightened value maximization* should focus on the long-term market value of the firm (Keim, 1978). As such, CSR research in business and management has focused on cause-related marketing (Smith & Higgins, 2000), corporate philanthropy (Porter & Kramer, 2006), and investments in the bottom of the economic pyramid (Prahalad, 2003) as means to balance social goods and economic value. A popular version of this perspective, *strategic CSR*, has gained considerable traction as an opportunity to engage in community-based policies and programs while still supporting core business activities (Logsdon & Wood, 2005). CSR research is deemed valuable as a mechanism to conduct cost-benefit analyses of CSR initiatives (for a critique, see May, 2008).

Shareholder value theory is rooted in several ethical assumptions, largely grounded in the writings of British philosopher John Locke. With Locke as a conceptual guide, CSR research from this approach assumes an atomistic view of society that includes "natural" liberties that are embedded in social contracts that enable social commerce with relatively limited government oversight. The organization—or firm—is seen as a *nexus of contracts* or principal-agent relations. Advocates of this theoretical perspective focus on human rights to life, liberty, and property and, as such, argue that investors are due their return for their financial commitments and any other use of profit for the social good is inappropriate or, worse, unjust. CSR, according to shareholder value theory, should only be pursued if and when corporate initiatives support the bottom line. Shell Oil, for example, engaged in a number of defensive CSR-oriented responses as a result of polluting the Niger Delta in Nigeria. Characterized as environmental racism by activists, Shell's actions on human rights and environmental justice seemed bound by its focus on utilitarian, expedient outcomes that served its shareholders (Jordan, 2001).

Corporate social performance (CSP), another common theoretical approach for scholars in business and management, is grounded in sociology and views business and society as interdependent (Sahlin-Andersson, 2006). From this perspective, businesses have simultaneous economic and social responsibilities. This theory suggests that, in addition to the creation of wealth for investors, businesses are responsible for any negative consequences that are produced as a result of their actions, beyond economic and legal expectations (Wartick & Cochran, 1985). Wood (1991) defined CSR as "a business organization's configuration of principles of social responsibility, processes of social responsiveness, and policies, programs and observable outcomes as they relate to the firm's societal relationships" (p. 693). Following Wood and others, authors from this point of view argue that firms should pay attention to societal expectations and, in particular, social needs at the time.

Business scholars such as Davis (1960, 1975), for example, noted that a business's wealth and power also creates additional responsibility. Scholars from this perspective suggest that companies run a risk if they do not meet the expectations of the people who constitute their broader social environment. Often referred to as a *corporate responsiveness model* (Ackerman & Bauer,

1976) of CSR, scholars began to distinguish among (1) *social obligations*, with a focus on legal and market constraints; (2) *social responsibility*, with an emphasis on social norms and expectations; and (3) *social responsiveness*, which may be adaptive, anticipatory, or preventive (Sethi, 1975). As a result, this approach also focused scholars' attention on proactive business initiatives (including issues management) as researchers have sought to understand the complex relationship between corporations and NGOs, activists, communities, and governments, among other interested stakeholders.

More recent scholarship on CSP has emphasized measurable outcomes in both economic and public realms, including social responsibility. In either variant, though, the focus has been to uncover the elusive link between social performance and financial performance. Although many studies have found a positive link (Orlitzky, Schmidt, & Rynes, 2003) between social responsibility and company profit, many others have pointed to mixed results depending on the type of measurements used (Margolis & Walsh, 2003). Thus, although academics continue to pursue studies that link corporate responsibility and financial performance, recent scholars in business and management have begun to acknowledge the inherent tension between economic and social goals (Vogel, 2006).

Research in CSP is grounded in a set of views based on ethical principles of human values and responsibility, social legitimacy, and a pragmatic related to the consequences of abuse of power. So, for example, scholars from this perspective have suggested that the ethical foundation of CSR is necessarily a power-responsibility equation tied to the general economic welfare of society first and to developing and preserving human values second. From this theoretical perspective, society necessarily grants legitimacy and power to businesses and, therefore, businesspersons must uphold those collective obligations. Couched as a *principle of public policy* by some (Preston & Post, 1975), business practices should reflect not only the literal interpretation of the law via regulations but also the broad direction of public opinion reflected in emerging issues. These might include studies of both external issues (e.g., regulatory environment, public-private partnerships, community impact) and internal issues (e.g., compliance, ethics codes) for the firm. Perhaps one of the most relevant examples of CSP is the case of Nike's evolution from exploiting cheap, global labor markets to collaborating with The Fair Labor Association to establish labor standards and policies. Driven by a decline in its market share in response to negative publicity of its plants in Indonesia, Nike has sought to ameliorate those concerns by appealing to the public's growing interest in both economic and social value.

Corporate citizenship is another theoretical perspective used by CSR scholars in business and management. It emerged out of political science and carries with it assumptions regarding what constitutes appropriate citizenship. Carroll (2004), for example, argues that "good corporate citizens" promote human welfare or goodwill in ways that "reflect global society's expectations that business will engage in social actions that are not mandated by law nor generally expected of business in an ethical sense" (p. 118). From this perspective, scholars have been interested in the philanthropic activities of businesses in the community, including donations and volunteerism (Crane & Matten, 2005). Some recent scholars (Birch, 2001) see CSR not so much as an external activity but instead as a core part of society. That is, business interests should not necessarily be separated from social interests in a society, as corporate citizenship is a metaphor for business participation in society (Moon, Crane, & Matten, 2005).

Scholars from this perspective, then, argue that corporations, similar to individuals, are citizens of their communities (local, national, and/or global) and, therefore, must attend to a diverse array of stakeholder interests, including community problems such as poverty, pollution, and racial discrimination (Eilbirt & Parker, 1973). They encourage a communitarian view of how businesses should act and see collaboration among business, government, and civil society as a necessity for the public good and the duty of a corporate citizen (Vidaver-Cohen & Altman, 2000). More recently, scholars have extended the citizenship metaphor to include corporations as grantors of citizenship itself (Crane et al., 2008).

Especially in nations in which governments are unstable or in situations where the nation-state is ambiguous (transborder issues, for instance), corporations can (and do) step in and act governmentally to help solve social and environmental problems in a form of quasi-governance. One broad example can be seen in the United Nations' Global Compact, a set of 10 principles that companies voluntarily sign up to. Although there has been criticism of the Global Compact, especially from NGOs, for a lack of enforcement or even auditing of adherence to the principles, the list of signatories is extensive and growing. This is arguably significant in issues such as human rights that may not be protected by national laws but are placed on the national and international agenda by the Global Compact and those businesses that agree to abide by it.

Business intervention over nation-states is more commonly found in the area of global environmental governance. The insurance industry worldwide, for example, has been a first mover in climate change mitigation, with many more industries now urging measures such as global emissions trading schemes. Other prominent examples take the form of private environmental governance and include the Forestry Stewardship Council and the Marine Stewardship Council (Falkner, 2003), with Unilever being instrumental in the latter not for altruistic reasons but to ensure sustainable supplies of a valuable resource.

The notion of *citizenship* evokes ethical assumptions regarding both individual rights and duties within a political environment. In the case of corporate citizenship, similar conceptions of *community* and the *common good* are also used. In the traditional Aristotelian sense, businesses are viewed as integral to society and, therefore, must also participate in it to create a common good. As Solomon (1992) explains, corporate responsibilities "are not the products of argument or implicit contracts, but intrinsic to their very existence as social entities" (p. 184). Others, such as Waddock and Smith (2000), go further to suggest that the ethical mandate is to build strong relationships with stakeholders in a manner that establishes mutual trust and respect. This respect and trust is rooted, according to Parry (1991), in the ethical premises of the three most commonly accepted approaches to citizenship: (1) minimalist, (2) communitarian, and (3) universal rights. In minimalist views, citizens (including, in this case, businesses) are merely residents of a jurisdiction with standard rights and duties and, as such, scholars focus on normative obligations. From a communitarian perspective, citizens fully participate in the community and are expected to adhere to basic rules, norms, and traditions; therefore, scholars seek to better understand the development of, and adherence to, such principles. Finally, from a universal rights view, scholars are interested in the degree to which businesses impact human dignity and agency. Most notably, Wal-Mart has faced considerable outcry and activism that is steeped in the public's belief that large corporations should be good citizens by maintaining the dignity and rights of its workers while also adhering to local, state, national, and international standards (e.g., tax and development laws). The charges against Wal-Mart over the years have been extensive (e.g., union busting, illegal and unfair labor conditions, exploitive global trade, community sprawl, corporate welfare), and in response, Wal-Mart has sought to position itself as a progressive, environmental company that seeks to collaborate with interested parties (e.g., land preservation with the National Fish and Wildlife Foundation) for the public good.

Stakeholder theory is an additional, widely used approach to CSR research common in the business and management literature. Scholars from this perspective argue that businesses should account for any individuals or groups who have a stake in it. From this perspective, "corporations have an obligation to constituent groups in society other than stockholders and beyond that prescribed by law or union contract" (Jones, 1980, pp. 59–60). In its early iterations, stakeholder theory was a new way of focusing on strategic management, with an emphasis on long-term financial success (Freeman, 1984). More recently, it has also been studied as a normative approach, in which management has a moral duty to not only protect the fiduciary health of the business but to also negotiate the multiple claims of conflicting stakeholders (Evan & Freeman, 1988). So, although the survival of the firm is central to stakeholder theory, stakeholder scholars also assume that the business should be managed for the benefit of all of its stakeholders, including customers, suppliers, owners, employees, and communities. In some versions of stakeholder theory, scholars argue that the corporate governance structure should include stakeholder representatives in decision making, since a range of stakeholders may be affected by the business.

Stakeholder theory has been based on two ethical principles, the *principle of corporate rights* and the *principle of corporate effects*, with both adhering to a Kantian emphasis on respect for humans. The former suggests that members of a corporation should not impair the legitimate right of others to self-determination. The latter extends this assumption further to argue that corporate actions should not negatively impact others. In this respect, one of the underlying principles of stakeholder theory is a distributive justice for all persons with a stake in the business. Beyond these ethical principles, stakeholder scholars in business and management have also drawn upon more expansive views of the theory to include feminist theory (Burton & Dunn, 1996), integrative social contracts theory (Donaldson & Dunfee, 1999), and common good theory (Argandona, 1998), among others. As such, stakeholder theory has been pluralistic enough to accommodate other ethical points of view.

A normative version of stakeholder theory, based in philosophy and ethical theories, is *stakeholder engagement*. Stakeholder engagement focuses on the nature of the relationship with stakeholders and is concerned with involving them in dialogue and decision making: "Partnering and engagement activities allow firms to build bridges with their stakeholders in the pursuit of common goals" (Andriof & Waddock, 2002, p. 36). Leaders coordinate and facilitate between stakeholders. This participative governance model leads to "more creativity, effecting new product development, greater efficiency and effectiveness in personal and organizational goal accomplishment, higher levels of mutual commitment, and great product and service customization" (Deetz, 2007, p. 276). Dialogue between partners allows corporations to become "just one more way we can live together" (Freeman & Liedtka, 1991, p. 97) and flourish. Starbucks is one company that has sought to more closely approximate stakeholder engagement. Similar to the other companies mentioned above, they have faced criticism from activists for their early use of "sweatshop coffee," nonsupport for organic coffee, and destruction of farming communities. More recently, however, they developed a "materiality matrix" in consultation with a range of stakeholders such as farmers, employees, and customers to identify business practices that are good for the company and good for the public. These include coffee purchasing practices, environmental impacts, sustainable growth, health and wellness, and employee satisfaction and well-being. Such examples of stakeholder engagement and collaboration are also undoubtedly more common outside of the U.S., particularly in northern European countries where corporate leaders are required, by law, to include diverse stakeholders, such as employees and unions, in board decision making.

We now turn to a more detailed discussion of how dialogue, and communication in general, has been studied within organizational communication. More specifically, we discuss the diverse range of conceptual discourses that help frame CSR research in organizational communication as a means to organize what is often a disparate array of studies. Doing so should help us recognize the theoretical and practical distinctions that CSR research in organizational communication offers as a contrast to business/management (for related examples of case studies, see May, 2013).

Discourses of Organizational Communication in Corporate Social Responsibility Research

As noted above, the theoretical debates circulating around CSR have been largely dominated by business and management scholars, but the range and scope of issues related to CSR (e.g., human rights, global labor conditions, climate change, stakeholder relations, corporate governance, socially responsible investing) indicate that no single discipline will be able to adequately address both the opportunities and challenges related to the phenomenon (May et al., 2007). In particular, few communication-based reviews of the CSR literature have been developed, even as a growing number of scholars have begun to study it. Over the last several years, many new scholars have entered the CSR debate, but few have sought to review the state of CSR scholarship in a manner that accounts for both its possibilities and its limitations. This section seeks to address that gap by exploring the emerging area of CSR research in organizational communication as scholars seek to study and shape organizing practices into the future.

In order to conceptualize CSR research in organizational communication, we draw on a categorization scheme developed by Deetz (2001), which focuses on the process of organizing through symbolic interaction rather than merely on communication within an organization. Similar to his theoretical conceptualization of organizational communication, this review focuses not so much on theories of organizational communication, *per se*, but in "producing a communication theory of organizations" (p. 5). His two-dimensional scheme was developed to direct scholars' attention to similarities and differences among research studies and, as a result, serves as a useful organizing structure for exploring studies of CSR within organizational communication.

According to Deetz, research can be distinguished by paying attention to two scholarly tensions: (1) the type of interaction a researcher prefers in studying subjects/participants, characterized as *local/emergent* versus *elite/a priori* conceptions, and (2) the extent to which the researcher focuses on either closure or indeterminacy in that action, characterized as *consensus* seeking versus *dissensus* seeking (see May, 2011, for a more detailed discussion). For Deetz (2001), these dimensions represent poles in a continuum and produce a series of organizational communication discourses that structure research assumptions and practices, which include normative, interpretive, critical, and dialogic research. We believe that using these discourses as a guide will help clarify key distinctions of CSR research among organizational communication scholars. In the following section, we apply Deetz's continuum of organizational communication discourses as a framework to review the CSR literature that has emerged within the field of organizational communication.

Normative CSR Research

As Deetz (2001) explains, normative studies of organizational communication approach organizations as "naturally existing objects open to description, prediction, and control" (p. 19). This modernist approach draws on economic metaphors and views the organization as a marketplace of ideas and practices that require intervention to produce structure and social order. Although normative organizational communication research was quite common for some time, the fairly recent emergence of CSR means that very few studies of CSR in this field have been conducted from a normative perspective. Normative research, in the business/management theories noted above, emphasize the codification of data and the search for regularity and normalization and, typically, include prescriptive claims.

The research is often organized topically and, within organizational communication, includes studies of phenomena such as information flow and channels, organizational climate, organizational structure, supervisor-subordinate communication, leadership and managerial styles, communication networks, and decision making. To date, normatively oriented scholars who remain interested in these topics have rarely connected them to CSR, except in a few limited examples. This is somewhat surprising, given the long tradition of normative research in organizational communication. The gap, however, has been filled by the broader realm of organization studies and, in part, may explain the lack of urgency to study CSR from a normative perspective. That task has already been taken up, quite successfully, by a wide range of organizational scholars in business/management (see Bartlett & Devin, 2011, for a more comprehensive explanation).

Given the influence of business/management on the normative scholarly tradition, it is not surprising that CSR studies will, at times, focus on the instrumental role of CSR communication in largely economic and/or managerial terms, such as *maximizing business returns* (Du, Bhattacharya, & Sen, 2010), *gaining legitimacy* (Bronn & Vidaver-Cohen, 2009), *strengthening corporate reputation* (Lewis, 2003), *improving integrity* (Waddock, 2001), *satisfying investors* (Hockerts & Moir, 2004), and *managing stakeholders* (Shumate & O'Connor, 2010). Such studies of CSR assume that organizations are naturally existing objects open to description, prediction, and control and in which managerial goals are largely unquestioned.

In the business/management literature, the long-standing, normative interest has been in CSP (see Orlitzky, 2008). CSR is seen as another example of the recent value shift (Paine, 2003) that aligns economic performance with social performance by doing well and good (Friedland, 2009). Just as communication is seen as a tool to serve business interests, so too is CSR seen as an instrumental means to strengthen competitive advantage (Porter & Kramer, 2003) and business innovation (Kanter, 2003). From this point of view, CSR embodies the principle of enlightened self-interest and can, ultimately, be profitable if managed according to shareholder interests (Keim, 1978).

Normative CSR research is not limited to a focus on profitability, however. As is common among normative studies that focus on unity, stability, and universal laws, another strand of organizational research also focuses on CSR standards (Fombrun, 2005), codes (Painter-Morland, 2006), and ethical principles (Svensson, Wood, Singh, & Callaghan, 2009). This strand of CSR research is often based on the assumption that standards, codes, and principles can serve as a risk management tool (Godfrey, 2005). These studies suggest that investment of resources in CSR initiatives may serve to strengthen brand and reputation and act as preventative measures against legal liability (Trevino, Weaver, Gibson, & Toffler, 1999).

One of the more significant, emerging trends in normative research has been the focus on CSR and stakeholders (Freeman, 1984). From a stakeholder perspective, CSR research focuses on the various obligations that corporations have to a diverse range of constituent groups, as an alternative to a primary responsibility to shareholders (Jones, 1980). Stakeholder scholars embrace a wide range of theoretical positions, including common good theory, integrative social contracts theory, the principle of fairness, and, more recently, feminist theory (see Mele, 2008, for a more detailed discussion). Regardless of the theoretical orientation, stakeholder scholars with a normative orientation have, historically, prioritized stakeholder management as a means to achieve positive business outcomes (Marcoux, 2003). As noted above, organizational scholars have recently extended the conception of stakeholder management to *stakeholder engagement*, which acknowledges a more active, collaborative role for communication among diverse parties in CSR programs (Morsing & Schultz, 2006). As a result, some of its newer manifestations may not necessarily fall under the rubric of normative research (see Deetz, 2007, for example).

A final thread of normative CSR research focuses on accepted norms for CSR and how they compare/contrast in various global contexts. These studies tend to be comparative and, typically, consider similarities and difference in CSR reporting based on place (Chambers, Chapple, Moon, & Sullivan, 2003). The focus of this research is to better understand the ways in which context, such as geographic location/nationality, either enables or constrains effective CSR reporting to a range of stakeholders. Consistent with the variable analytic tradition of normative research, CSR research from this tradition examines broad trends (Kolk, 2003), content analysis as a methodology (Jose & Lee, 2007), and global comparisons of cultural differences across countries (Idowu & Filho, 2009).

Via these threads of normative CSR research, organizational scholars tend to use *a priori* assumptions about the economic consequences of CSR to further explore the various instrumental functions of communication in CSR programs, emphasizing the role of persuasion, information transfer/exchange, and impact. A normative approach, then, allows organizational scholars interested in CSR to consider the applied communication skills necessary to accomplish CSR-related tasks, whether that be engaging stakeholders, developing shared global norms for business conduct, or reporting CSR practices.

Interpretive CSR Research

Interpretive organizational communication research, by contrast, focuses on social rather than economic dimensions of organizing and, as a result, explores how organizational realities are created, maintained, and transformed in/through informal, daily practices. Researchers from this orientation seek to understand the sensemaking activities of the persons they study as a kind of translation of participants' interests. To date, only a limited number of studies in organizational communication have taken an explicitly interpretive perspective on CSR. Given the earlier emergence and stabilization of CSR in many European countries, interpretive studies have emerged there more frequently than in the United States. Even though there has been a long tradition of organizational communication research that focuses on the social rather than economic views of organizational activities—based on phenomenological, hermeneutic, and symbolic interactionist traditions—organizational scholars, as a whole, have rarely focused on the sensemaking processes related to the informal dimensions of CSR. By contrast, most organizational communication research has taken an external vantage point, focusing on the practices that are readily available for public scrutiny (e.g., CSR reports, websites, public announcements and documents, public CSR initiatives). There are a number of potential reasons for this absence. First, since CSR is still relatively new, it can be difficult to identify the "location" of employees working on CSR, and in addition, they represent a very small pool of potential research subjects (at least among U.S. corporations). Second, few scholars have necessarily made the link between a company's CSR practices and the ways in which these practices may affect employees sensemaking. Because many organizational communication scholars remain skeptical of CSR, in general, they have shown less interest in how it impacts the day-to-day work experiences of employees, as is evidenced by the number of works described (below) from a critical perspective. Finally, the difficulty of gaining access to employees working on, or affected by, CSR initiatives may have limited the number of studies. As with other ethics-based research in organizations, even strong advocates of CSR within the business world may be concerned that their efforts will be portrayed negatively, particularly given public suspicion of CSR as a self-interested activity. According to one international survey, for example, more than half of citizens globally consider the social responsibilities of organizations to be more important than profits, yet less than a quarter of corporations meet those expectations.

Further, citizen concern over corporate conduct has begun to translate into action, as nearly two-thirds of consumers in North America state that they have punished (e.g., boycotted a company or product) a corporation for its irresponsible behavior (Conference Board, 2012).

Our review of the literature suggests that most interpretive studies of CSR tend to focus either on the attitudes (Burchell & Cook, 2006) or perceptions (Nielsen & Thomsen, 2009) of CSR among a range of employees, most typically managers. However, scholars have shown little to no interest in studying the attitudes and perception of rank-and-file employees to CSR and, instead, they tend to focus on executives and/or CSR directors. For example, some scholars (e.g., Swanson, 2008) have explored the role of ethical leadership in CSR initiatives, although most of the data tend to be anecdotal rather than empirical. Arvidsson (2010) studied the views of management teams in large companies as they tried to understand and react to an emergent set of practices around CSR. Similarly, Hine and Preuss (2009) examined the various perceptions of CSR among different groups of managers. Not surprisingly, managers dichotomized (ethics vs. business performance) what they saw as the critical operations of their companies and the discretionary actions of CSR. A notable exception is a Chinese case study that includes perspectives from interviews with employees and managers across a large, state-owned corporation (Zhao & Roper, 2011).

In another study that takes a largely interpretive approach, Morsing, Midttun, and Palmas (2007) explore the history of Scandinavian companies' integration of CSR into corporate strategies. Using companies such as SparNord, Novo Nordisk, and Lego as case studies, they report on the self-perceptions of CSR among managers in a range of companies. Much of their discussion is a historical description of CSR's evolution, but they also include an interpretive account of how managers changed their views of CSR over the years as they sought to develop a business case for it. As another example, Seitanidi (2009) used ethnography to explore how employees develop a sense of accountability for their actions as they formed and delivered a CSR initiative with nonprofit business partnerships. The in-depth analysis also offers insight on how communication among employees during a CSR initiative can strengthen participation and mutual responsibility for the success of collaborative CSR initiatives.

These studies are among the few to date that include the qualitative, emergent data-gathering methods common to interpretive research, and as a result, we have a limited understanding of how employees "take up" CSR in their day-to-day activities. Given the fairly long and well-established history of interpretive organizational communication research, the lack of research related to CSR is a glaring absence. In short, the dearth of interpretive research means we lack an important perspective on CSR—the insider's view.

Critical CSR Research

Critical studies view organizations as historical constructions that are brought about in/through power relations. As political sites for the negotiation of divergent and competing interests, organizations are the nexus for struggles over the use of resources, distribution of income, and opportunities for decision making and voice. Critical researchers seek out both overt and covert difference and dissensus in order to show how organizational practices have become naturalized and normalized to the benefit of some over others. While interpretive research focuses on internal dynamics and has an employee-centered emphasis, critical CSR studies often focus on broader sets of social, political, and economic conditions, with an eye toward critique and self-reflexivity. Blowfield (2005), however, has argued that CSR scholars, in general, have yet to "develop the means for internal critique and, as a result, have been unable to recognize their own assumptions, prejudices, and limitations" (p. 173). In response to this kind of criticism, organizational communication scholars have begun to consider legal (Seeger & Hipfel, 2007), economic (Aune, 2007), social (Breen, 2007; Deetz, 2007), and environmental (Livesey & Graham, 2007) dimensions of CSR. In addition, some scholars have sought to understand the importance of cultural context (Chavarria, 2007; Morsing et al., 2007; Sriramesh, Ng, Ting, & Wanyin, 2007). A recent *Management Communication Quarterly* forum opened up discussion of CSR in state-owned companies (Morsing, 2011; Roper & Schoenberger-Orgad, 2011).

Finally, organizational communication research on CSR has explored a range of communication-oriented topics, including governance (Deetz, 2007), regulation (Hearit, 2007), exploitation (Cloud, 2007), consumer activism (Kendall, Gill, & Cheney, 2007), development (Ganesh, 2007), and sustainability (Peterson & Norton, 2007), to name just a few. Regardless of the dimension, context, or topic, though, most scholars have taken a largely critical perspective toward CSR, sometimes articulating suspicion and, at other times, hope.

A Critical Discourse of Suspicion. Although some scholars have argued that CSR represents a constructive alternative to commonly held assumptions of business as usual (Kotler & Lee, 2005), critical organizational scholars have questioned not only the intent but also the process and outcome of CSR. These scholars have drawn on a range of critical, post-structuralist, and postmodern writers, including Foucault (Shamir, 2008), Habermas (Scherer & Palazzo, 2007), Derrida (Jones, 2003), and Levinas (Roberts, 2003), among others, to question the practices of CSR and the knowledge that has developed around it. Such authors pay particular attention to the intersection of power, knowledge, and discourse as means to further understand, analyze, and reconstruct corporate responsibilities.

As a starting point, Shamir (2008) proposes that today's neo-liberal epistemology has dissolved the distinction between the economy and society, with the *social* being subjugated to the mandates of the *economic*. In addition, Hanlon (2008) has argued that CSR practices have served to further limit citizen participation in politics and that, as a result, "CSR does not represent a challenge to business" but instead "further embeds capitalist social relations and a deeper opening up of social life to the dictates of the marketplace" (p. 157). Similarly, former Labor Secretary Robert Reich (2007) pursues a similar argument in his book, *Supercapitalism*, where he explains that "a kind of faux democracy has invaded capitalism" (p. 207). The focus on corporations as moral entities, he argues, distracts attention from creating laws that adequately govern and regulate them. CSR, in his view, has become a means to further marginalize democratic processes to create a productive yet sustainable way of life.

In their criticism of CSR, Munshi and Kurian (2007) also explain how its discourse conflates realms of life and privileges the economic over the social. Programs of CSR, they argue, further instantiate corporate power and, in general, fall short of their professed goals because of their omissions: "'corporate' overlooks the many proxies of corporations; 'social' ignores the political, including issues of gender and diversity; and 'responsibility' glosses over accountability" (p. 438). They argue that CSR research silences the voice of the subaltern—a group that is deliberately marginalized by ruling elites.

In a similar, emerging strand of research, scholars such as Kendall et al. (2007) suggest that efforts by consumers and activist groups to voice their concerns about corporate conduct must be understood as well. Actions directed against corporations as leverage for positive social change can range from conscientious consumption to campaigns to write letters, make phone calls, create alternative consumption venues (e.g., Worldstock.com, CraigsList, eBay), and, in more organized cases, to participate in boycotts or buycotts. In addition, large-scale community responses can also come in the form of demonstrations, protests, marches, and, in longer-term efforts, social movements. Other scholars have also explored not only how CSR has silenced discourse and public participation in democracy, but also how it has effectively managed decision making. For example, in their discussion of critical theory and CSR, Kuhn and Deetz (2008) describe how CSR-related values shape corporate decisions in three ways: managerial choices, routines, and reasoning processes; governmental regulation incentives, tax structures, and oversight; and consumption choices within market systems. However, these realms of communication and decision making, they contend, are too weak to bolster progressive CSR-based actions that could introduce more diverse values and reasoning processes. This propensity to limit or inhibit dissensus is also evident in McMillan's (2007) description of how discourses of managerialism are embedded in CSR in ways that are instrumental, exclusive, attributional, monological, and narcissistic.

In general, it appears that many critical organizational scholars agree with Banerjee (2008), who suggests that CSR is not as much a progressive trend as an ideological movement designed to further legitimize the power of large corporations. Critical theorists who draw upon a tradition of scholarly "suspicion," similar to those noted above, often argue that the rhetoric of CSR is rarely enacted in practice. More specifically, they argue that CSR initiatives can often obscure more deeply rooted contradictions in capitalism (Cloud, 2007) and that they may also pacify citizens who seek more fundamental, systemic change by interrogating corporate power. Addressing these broader, structural issues, they argue, offers the opportunity to redirect corporations toward processes of community engagement with multiple constituencies to create "public goods." From this skeptical perspective of suspicion, critical scholars studying CSR suggest that a radical rethinking of corporate practices may create positive outcomes for corporations and communities that collaborate to confront complex social, economic, and political problems—but not without a fundamental overhaul of systemic power inequities.

A Critical Discourse of Hope. Within the critical tradition of organizational research, scholars who focus on a discourse of hope offer a counterbalance to the inherent skepticism toward CSR among many critical scholars. Although she is primarily critical of CSR, McMillan (2007) does also point to the prospect for communication to create a mutual dwelling place that can transform corporate words and actions via dialogue, stakeholder engagement, accounting for human and social capital, and expanding the corporate gaze inward for self-reflection. Likewise, Kuhn and Deetz (2008) also encourage scholars to look for hopeful opportunities among CSR initiatives instead of the inevitable cynicism that may result from constant critique. As another example of a hopeful nod toward CSR, Scherer and Palazzo (2007) draw on Habermas's theory of deliberative democracy to argue for "democratic control on the public use of power" (p. 1109). Doing so, though, first requires that scholars recognize CSR as a political phenomenon and that the corporation is a political actor (Matten & Crane, 2005) amidst civil society.

In a chapter that explores whether CSR is merely fashionable or truly sustainable, Zorn and Collins (2007) explain that they are optimistic about the prospects of CSR because of public demands for communicative transparency and accountability in the face of climate change, finite resources, income inequality, and shifting demographics across the world. For them, organizational communication practices may legitimize the incremental change that is more common among business fads that, ultimately, become fully integrated into a company's operations. Livesey and Graham (2007) also accept the premise that corporate discourse can produce constructive, if unexpected and unintended, change. They use Butler's concept of performativity to explain how the corporate eco-talk and eco-collaborative storytelling by companies such as Shell and McDonald's bring into being the world of which they speak, revealing the power of discourse to not only affirm corporate power via CSR but also to transform it.

Another hopeful strand of CSR research explores challenges related to global human rights conditions. In one example, Stohl, Stohl, and Townsley (2007) provide a global perspective that seeks to frame CSR in a more expansive and less elite Western-centric frame. A global approach to CSR, they argue, has begun to mirror the historical evolution of the international human rights regime. In their work, they recommend a third generation of CSR that addresses proactive and positive responsibilities, in contrast to the more common first-generation approach that focused on what not to do. Scholars who focus on such global human rights issues remind us that CSR research needs to draw upon a bottom-up orientation that takes into account communicative practices in a long tradition of corporate colonialism and imperialism (Ganesh, Zoller, & Cheney, 2005). Considering practices of resistance to CSR provides hopeful opportunities to construct alternative CSR practices that may also serve the underprivileged and marginalized (D'Souza, 1990). Bendell and Bendell (2007) also offer hope that collaborative CSR initiatives among government, business, and NGOs may be a productive avenue for communication among different stakeholders to restructure corporate power and influence.

Some scholars who remain hopeful with regard to CSR also focus on corporate identity and brand. McIntosh (2007) has claimed, for example, that an emphasis on brand integrity may create the potential for reconstructing CSR in a manner that serves both business and community interests. He argues that brands such as Coke, Dove, and Toyota, for example, have the potential to expand global borders to address and, ultimately, transcend a wide range of human problems. According to McIntosh, brand integrity "is loyalty beyond reason . . . and is increasingly formulated on the basis of human rights, labor standards, environmental protection, and liberalized markets" in ways that may hold corporations accountable for their actions (p. 54).

Finally, other scholars have sought to provide a path to a hopeful future by strengthening accountability. Werhane (2007), for example, addresses the ongoing problems of corporate accountability and recommends that scholars identify the range and scope of actions that they expect of corporations, given their limited economic goals and means. More specifically, she proposes that organizational scholars focus on communication among various stakeholders that create interlocking obligations of companies, citizens, NGOs, civic societies, traditions, and cultures.

The scholars noted above retain a critical, skeptical orientation toward communication and CSR but seek to not only deconstruct CSR but also to reconstruct it in and through communication. They are likely to advocate for CSR initiatives that promote more humane labor conditions, stronger environmental sustainability, improved governance and transparency, and more alternatives for social auditing/investing. Not surprisingly, a number of firms and publications (e.g., CRO's Best Corporate Citizens) reward companies for their pro-social activities. But, for scholars within this critical tradition, such rewards may not necessarily translate into substantive change (Maclagan, 1999). What is needed, in addition, are communicative practices that focus not so much on consensus and agreement but on the dissensus and conflict that produces requisite variety and, in turn, on creative solutions that sustain mutual commitment and provide hope for a continual movement toward CSR programs that positively contribute to society.

Dialogic CSR Research

Similar to critical studies, dialogic scholars are often interested in domination in organizations. By contrast, though, dialogic research tends to focus on the micro practices of power and resistance and views them as fluid, dispersed, and interdependent. There are still a limited number of studies that take a dialogic approach, but the emergence of this orientation in communication studies more generally suggests that it will likely be more common in the near future. Similar to critical research on CSR, this approach is concerned with asymmetry and power in organizations, but there is a greater tendency to focus on micro practices, as well as the fluid and dispersed (rather than centralized) nature of power. Rather than viewing CSR as unified and coherent, dialogic scholars see it as complex, contradictory, and contested, such as when Morsing, Schultz, and Nielsen (2008) describe the common dilemma—or *catch-22*—of communicating CSR. The authors note that, regardless of the intent, corporate CSR initiatives are often viewed with suspicion by the general public. As a result, corporate leaders face the prospect of criticism for both engaging in—and not engaging in—CSR.

As an exemplar of dialogic CSR research, Waddock (2007) studied programs at companies such as Novartis and Cisco to explore the paradoxes of CSR (see also Bondy, 2008). She suggests that we have produced an economic system in which success means "continual growth and expansion, a focus on efficiency within a company (and externalizing costs whenever possible to society), and control over resources, markets, customer preferences and choices, and employees" (p. 76). Wal-Mart, she explains, is a prime example of the paradox, since it offers lower socioeconomic groups the opportunity to save money—allowing for greater discretionary household income—while at the same time destroying local business, paying low wages to contingent workers, and producing "sprawl-mart" or greater suburban sprawl. To control such complicated yet sociopathic tendencies (see Bakan, 2004), Waddock proposes that CSR be used to expand the commonly held view of businesses as mere economic engines to recognize their broader societal impact as well.

In addition to this kind of more-expansive cultural focus on CSR, Christensen (2007) argues that, to fully embrace CSR, "corporations need not only to open themselves to their surroundings, but also to look internally, become self-reflective, aware of their own practices, as well as their own communication" (p. 457). This kind of hyper-reflexivity is common to dialogic perspectives that invite readers to understand the polysemy of CSR discourse and its creative (and destructive) force. A renewed discourse of CSR for Christensen, then, requires working through the tensions of responsibility/regulation, responsibility/responsiveness, and responsibility/involvement in ways that acknowledge that language and reality are closely intertwined. Similar to Waddock, he recognizes how business beliefs and strategies tend to be dichotomized and, as a result, relegated to different spheres of the organization.

Also adopting a dialogic approach, Conrad and Abbott (2007) acknowledge the inherent tension between a company's internal practices and its management of public policy. Bounded by competing narratives of corporate progress and capitalist imperialism, today's CSR communication practices of corporations need to be understood in terms of public policy making. If we are to seriously consider the potential of CSR, they argue, we must carefully examine the ways in which corporate elites, in and through communication, influence not just the content but also the process of public policy making.

As is evident from the brief summary of several examples of dialogic research on CSR, this approach reminds us, as scholars, that we should not necessarily take language use—and the corporate practices that emerge from it—for granted. Dialogic research affirms that signifiers, such as *CSR*, can become self-referential, containing assumed meanings in much the same way that *development* has become its own referent, one that has evolved, over time, to be self-explanatory and neutral. Dialogic research, then, also allows us to consider what has been lost, negated, and silenced in the emergence of CSR itself. A genealogy of CSR, for example, might emphasize alternative conceptions of CSR, particularly among local forms of knowledge and experience that have been forgotten.

Dialectical Tensions in CSR Research

The above review reveals several dialectical tensions in CSR research among organizational communication scholars, including ethics/performance, agency/structure, and internal/external. First, the ethics/performance tension is one of the most common tensions among organizational communication research on CSR and represents the inherent, long-standing distinctions between scholars conducting dialogic and normative research. This tension is evident when comparing the normative tendency to see communication and CSR as instrumental tools to maximize corporate efficiency and productivity, on the one hand, and the dialogic propensity to view communication and CSR as emergent, evolving conditions of organizing that are complex and constantly being renegotiated, on the other hand. For years, research on ethics and responsibility has been dominated by two primary domains—moral philosophy, with its various ethical prescriptions, and the science of business/management, with its economic prescriptions. Scholars supporting the former have sought to question the basic assumptions of business practices, while scholars who stand behind the latter claim that business issues should not be considered in philosophical terms (see, e.g., Pearson, 1995). As Parker (1998) explains, "Much of the debate so far has been couched in terms of intellectual abstraction versus economic pragmatism, or as is it is often put more crudely, idealism versus realism" (p. 283). This tension between idealism and realism is at the heart of CSR research, not just in organizational communication but in all fields, and has the potential to create a scholarly wedge between advocates and critics of CSR. What is needed, then, is scholarship that can effectively handle the need to maintain optimism about CSR's potential and, simultaneously, to address the importance of questioning the limits and risks of CSR.

A second recurring tension in the organizational communication research on CSR is that between agency and structure. Similar to the ethics/performance tension, this dialectic has persisted for some time. In attempts to better understand this tension, social theorists have proposed two competing views of human action. The first perspective focuses on the environmental factors that constrain human communication. The second view of human action focuses on the ways in which humans are enabled by creating, sustaining, and transforming social realities in and through communication. The former, with its emphasis on *social system*, accounts for the situational impediments that are placed on human action while the latter, which prioritizes *social action*, considers humans to be creative, autonomous agents. All researchers must negotiate these competing poles—the extremes of fate (determinism) and freedom (voluntarism).

In terms of CSR research, the question revolves around the extent to which structural conditions or human agency are responsible for CSR programs and communication related to them. For some scholars, CSR represents a response to, if not support of, capitalist market forces in general and industry norms more specifically. For others, CSR initiatives are seen as innovative, creative endeavors that are reshaping the corporate landscape. One of the key challenges for organizational communication scholars, then, is to better understand how this "duality of structure" functions with regard to communication and CSR.

Finally, one of the most common tensions in CSR research in organizational communication is the link between *internal* and *external* dimensions of organizations (Cheney & Christensen, 2001). Historically, many scholars have assumed a container metaphor of organizational communication. From this point of view, communication oriented toward *external* audiences was regarded as outside the scope of *internal* organizational communication. As other chapters in this volume have indicated, however, the notion of organizational boundaries has been problematized and so-called internal and external communication no longer represent separate fields—either in theory or in practice (Alvesson, 1990). For example, in order to gain legitimacy in material and symbolic markets, corporations pursue a wide range of communication activities that do not neatly fall within either realm.

CSR research is at the complicated nexus of these internal/external boundaries. On the one hand, CSR initiatives are directed at external stakeholders. Not surprisingly, then, scholars of rhetoric and public relations have shown a great deal of interest in CSR. Yet CSR necessarily includes internal communication as well, given the ways in which it can become a part of the organization's operating discourse in addition to its general operations. A range of discussions and decisions within the organization regarding, for example, CSR strategy and implementation, precede the external communication of a company's CSR activities. In addition, organizational communication scholars have also increasingly focused their attention on broader sets of cultural discourses (Fairhurst & Putnam, 2004), exploring the ways in which discourses of excellence, innovation, and ethics have been utilized by organizations for a variety of purposes. Thus, the most interesting questions may be less related to differentiating between the types of communication and more to understanding the organizational processes of integrating internal and external communication to produce a seemingly coherent organizational identity. Such a focus on the tension between what we have historically (and mistakenly, some would argue) called *internal* and *external communication* directs us to more fully understand the degree to which CSR programs are embedded within an organization (and culture as a whole) or whether, by contrast, they are designed merely for public relations or risk management.

Directions for CSR Research

These three scholarly tensions create a number of interesting directions for future research. First, the ethics/performance tension offers opportunities to extend past research that is both hopeful and suspicious of CSR. Using a normative approach, there is still room for scholars to explore the most effective and efficient means of CSR communication, focusing on common features such as strategies, channels, processes, and audiences. Given its normative history, organizational communication should be able to offer prescriptive recommendations to guide organizational members in the development and implementation of CSR communication. From a dialogic perspective, we need studies that focus not so much on performance but, rather, on the ethical quandaries created by CSR, such as whether it ultimately produces a greater good through corporate influence or whether CSR merely replaces efforts within government and civil sectors that are better tailored to the needs of communities. Similarly, scholars should begin to study the common ethical dilemmas that leaders and managers face when confronted with their own values in relation to corporate values. In addition, studies are needed that account for alternative forms of organizing (e.g., the blurring of for-profit and nonprofit organizations) as well as the increasingly common collaborative relationships that have developed between corporations and NGOs, for example. Although much of the CSR research to date has been conducted from a critical perspective, more research is needed in this area that addresses the ways in which CSR has affected marginalized and impoverished groups. That is, we need scholars to consider not just whether there is a business case for CSR but whether there is also positive social impact on needy communities. Further studies that focus on corporate power and subaltern publics will help remedy this gap in the CSR research. In particular, there is an important place for scholars who are studying the ways in which consumer and activist voices can disrupt and, in some cases, alter, the logics of corporate decision making.

Second, the agency/structure tension is another productive avenue for research. Historically, CSR has been viewed largely as a discrete, autonomous, self-initiated practice in today's corporations. However, it is also clear that government and industry regulations and NGO and citizen scrutiny may have an impact on how businesses proceed with CSR. Future research should take into account these interorganizational relationships and how, if at all, they impact the nature and process of CSR communication. In particular, scholars may explore the network of relationships among corporations who engage in similar initiatives on a single cause, for example. Or, further, the emerging collaborative networks between corporations and nonprofits also merit further study, particularly as the boundaries between these organizational forms continue to blur. From a social action perspective, scholars should study specific cases of CSR innovation, whether at the macro, meso, or micro level of analysis. For example, we need to better understand how specific constraints to constructive CSR can be overcome by individual and collective action, via in-depth case studies. It is also crucial that some organizational communication scholars explore the recursive nature of agency/structure, taking into account how organizational rules and resources enable and constrain CSR communication and then, in turn, how corporate communication reproduces or alters organizational structures. An understanding of the reflexive tendencies of CSR practices will help us come to terms with their complexity.

Within the internal/external tension, organizational communication scholars need to simultaneously consider both the internal and external dimensions of CSR. As our review of the literature suggests, scholars have almost exclusively focused on external communication of CSR. To date, little research has been conducted on the specific employees engaged in CSR programs to understand their own sensemaking frameworks and practices. More specifically, because most of the interpretive research has been conducted on managers, CSR scholars should begin to focus their attention on employees of all levels within the organization. Ideally, though, researchers would also begin to explore the relationship between internal and external CSR communication. Scholars may want to consider the ways in which CSR programs impact corporate decision making, if at all. In addition, scholars should begin to focus not only on external features of CSR but they should also consider specific practices within organizations to determine whether the company is acting responsibly toward its own employees. Or, in a broader sense, researchers may choose to explore how cultural discourses of productivity, ethics, and responsibility are used in corporate CSR programs. The analysis of these discursive logics, rationales, and frameworks might provide more nuanced insights regarding whether corporations are, in fact, "walking the talk" of CSR.

Finally, we should note that interdisciplinary research on CSR is needed to account for both the strengths and limitations of various fields of study. In the future, the trend toward epistemological plurality is likely to continue as organizational communication scholars strengthen interdisciplinary ties to management and organization studies in particular. Organizational communication scholars may need to develop expertise in areas related to CSR practice, such as corporate law, third-world development, finance, sustainability, community organizing, global labor conditions, international governance, investing, and climate change. The potential range and scope of CSR practices suggest that we need to develop not just organizational expertise but also a set of related areas of expertise from other disciplines that will allow us to account for the unique and complex features of CSR in a competitive, rapidly changing global economy. Doing so will allow us to better understand both the opportunities and limits of CSR as a set of practices that are now fully embedded in organizations.

References

Ackerman, R. W., & Bauer, R. (1976). *Corporate social responsiveness*. Reston, VA: Reston Publishing Co.

Allen, C. (2009). *The caring face of business? A study of the discursive construction of the New Zealand Business for Social Responsibility* (Unpublished doctoral dissertation). University of Waikato, Hamilton, New Zealand.

Alvesson, M. (1990). Organization: From substance to image? *Organization Studies, 11*(3), 373–394.

Andriof, J., & Waddock, S. (2002). Unfolding stakeholder engagement. In J. Andriof, S. Waddock, B. Husted, & S. Sutherland Rahman (Eds.), *Unfolding stakeholder thinking* (pp. 19–42). Sheffield, UK: Greenleaf Publishing.

Argandona, A. (1998). The stakeholder theory and the common good. *Journal of Business Ethics, 17*(9/10), 1093–1112.

Arvidsson, S. (2010). Communication of corporate social responsibility: A study of the views of management teams in large companies. *Journal of Business Ethics, 96*(3), 339–354.

Aune, J. (2007). How to read Milton Friedman: Corporate social responsibility in today's capitalisms. In S. May, G. Cheney, & J. Roper (Eds.), *The debate over corporate social responsibility* (pp. 207–218). New York, NY: Oxford University Press.

Bakan, J. (2004). *The corporation: The pathological pursuit of profit and power*. London, England: Constable.

Banerjee, S. B. (2008). Corporate social responsibility: The good, the bad, and the ugly. *Critical Sociology, 34*(3), 391–407.

Bartlett, J. L, & Devin, B. (2011). Management, communication, and corporate social responsibility. In O. Ihlen, J. Bartlett, & S. May (Eds.), *Handbook of communication and corporate social responsibility* (pp. 47–66). Boston, MA: Wiley-Blackwell.

Bendell, J., & Bendell, M. (2007). Facing corporate power. In S. May, G. Cheney, & J. Roper (Eds.), *The debate over corporate social responsibility* (pp. 59–73). New York, NY: Oxford University Press.

Birch, D. (2001). Corporate citizenship: Rethinking business beyond social responsibility. In M. McIntosh (Ed.), *Perspectives on corporate citizenship* (pp. 53–65). Sheffield, England: Greenleaf.

Blowfield, M. (2005). Corporate social responsibility: The failing discipline and why it matters for international relations. *International Relations, 19*(2), 173–191.

Bondy, K. (2008). The paradox of power in CSR: A case study on implementation. *Journal of Business Ethics, 82*(2), 307–323.

Bowen, H. R. (1953). *Social responsibilities of the businessman*. New York, NY: Harper and Row.

Breen, M. (2007). Business, society, and its impacts on indigenous peoples. In S. May, G. Cheney, & J. Roper (Eds.), *The debate over corporate social responsibility* (pp. 292–304). New York, NY: Oxford University Press.

Bronn, P. S., & Vidaver-Cohen, D. (2009). Corporate motives for social initiative: Legitimacy, sustainability, or the bottom line? *Journal of Business Ethics, 87*(1), 91–109.

Burchell, J., & Cook. J. (2006). It's good to talk? Examining attitudes towards corporate social responsibility dialogue and engagement processes. *Business Ethics: A European Review, 15*(2), 154–170.

Burton, B. K., & Dunn, C. P. (1996). Feminist ethics as moral grounding for stakeholder theory. *Business Ethics Quarterly, 6*(2), 133–147.

Carroll, A. B. (1979). A three-dimensional conceptual model of corporate social responsibility performance. *Academy of Management Review, 4*(4), 497–505.

Carroll, A. B. (1999). Corporate social responsibility: Evolution of a definitional construct. *Business and Society, 38*(3), 268–295.

Carroll, A. B. (2004). Managing ethically with global stakeholders: A present and future challenge. *Academy of Management Executive, 18*(2), 114–120.

Chambers, E., Chapple, W., Moon, J., & Sullivan, M. (2003). *CSR in Asia: A seven country study of CSR website reporting*. Nottingham, UK: International Centre for Corporate Social Responsibility.

Chavarria, M. P. (2007). Corporate social responsibility in Mexico: An approximation from the point of view of communication. In S. May, G. Cheney, & J. Roper (Eds.), *The debate over corporate social responsibility* (pp. 135–144). New York, NY: Oxford University Press.

Cheney, G., & Christensen, L. G. (2001). Organizational identity: Linkages between internal and external communication. In L. Putnam & F. Jablin (Eds.), *The new handbook of organizational communication* (pp. 231–269). Thousand Oaks, CA: SAGE.

Cheney, G., May, S. K., & Munshi, D. (Eds.). (2011). *Handbook of communication ethics*. New York, NY: Routledge.

Cheney, G., Roper, J., & May, S. (Eds.). (2007). Overview. In S. May, G. Cheney, & J. Roper (Eds.), *The debate over corporate social responsibility* (pp. 3–14). New York, NY: Oxford University Press.

Christensen, L. (2007). The discourse of corporate social responsibility: Postmodern remarks. In S. May, G. Cheney, & J. Roper (Eds.), *The debate over corporate social responsibility* (pp. 448–458). New York, NY: Oxford University Press.

Cloud, D. (2007). Corporate social responsibility as oxymoron: Universalization and exploitation at Boeing. In S. May, G. Cheney, & J. Roper (Eds.), *The debate over corporate social responsibility* (pp. 219–231). New York, NY: Oxford University Press.

Conference Board. (2012). *Millennium poll on corporate social responsibility.* Toronto, Canada: Environics International Ltd.

Conrad, C., & Abbott, J. (2007). Corporate social responsibility and public policy making. In S. May, G. Cheney, & J. Roper (Eds.), *The debate over corporate social responsibility* (pp. 405–416). New York, NY: Oxford University Press.

Crable, R. E., & Vibbert, S. L. (1983). Mobil's epideictic advocacy: "Observations" of Prometheus-bound. *Communication Monographs, 50*(4), 380–394.

Crane, A., & Matten, D. (2005). Corporate citizenship: Missing the point or missing the boat? A reply to van Oosterhout. *Academy of Management Review, 30*(4), 681–684.

Crane, A., McWilliams, A., Matten, D., Moon, J., & Siegel, D. S. (Eds.). (2008). *The Oxford handbook of corporate social responsibility.* Oxford, UK: Oxford University Press.

Davis, K. (1960, Spring). Can business afford to ignore social responsibilities? *California Management Review, 2*, 70–76.

Davis, K. (1975). Five propositions for social responsibility. *Business Horizons, 18*(3), 19–24.

Deetz, S. (2001). Conceptual foundations. In F. Jablin & L. Putnam (Eds.), *The new handbook of organizational communication: Advances in theory, research, and methods* (pp. 3–46). Thousand Oaks, CA: SAGE.

Deetz, S. (2007). Corporate governance, corporate social responsibility, and communication. In S. May, G. Cheney, & J. Roper (Eds.), *The debate over corporate social responsibility* (pp. 267–278). New York, NY: Oxford University Press.

Donaldson, T., & Dunfee, T. W. (1999). *Ties that bind: A social contracts approach to business ethics.* Boston, MA: Harvard Business School Press.

D'Souza, V. (1990). *Development planning and structural inequalities: The response of the underprivileged.* New Delhi, India: SAGE.

Du, S., Bhattacharya, C. B., & Sen, S. (2010). Maximizing business returns to corporate social responsibility (CSR): The role of CSR communication. *International Journal of Management Reviews, 12*(1), 8–19.

Eilbirt, H., & Parker, I. R. (1973). The current status of corporate social responsibility. *Business Horizons, 16*(4), 5–14.

Evan, W. M., & Freeman, R. E. (1988). A stakeholder theory of the modern corporation: Kantian capitalism. In T. Beauchamp & N. Bowie (Eds.), *Ethical theory and business* (pp. 75–93). Englewood Cliffs, NJ: Prentice Hall.

Fairhurst, G., & Putnam, L. (2004). Organizations as discursive constructions. *Communication Theory, 14*(1), 5–26.

Falkner, R. (2003). Private environmental governance and international relations: Exploring the links. *Global Environmental Politics,* 3(2), 72–88.

Fombrun, C. J. (2005). Building corporate reputation through CSR initiatives: Evolving standards. *Corporate Reputation Review, 8*(1), 7–11.

Frederick, W. C. (2006). *Corporation be good: The story of corporate social responsibility.* Indianapolis, IN: Dog Ear Publishing.

Freeman, R. E. (1984). *Strategic management: A stakeholder approach.* Boston, MA: Pitman.

Freeman, R. E., & Liedtka, J. (1991). Corporate social responsibility: A critical approach. *Business Horizons, 34*(4), 92–96.

Friedland, J. (Ed.). (2009). *Doing good and well: The human face of the new capitalism.* Charlotte, NC: Information Age Publishing.

Friedman, M. (1970, September 13). The social responsibility of business is to increase its profits. *The New York Times Magazine*, pp. 32–33, 122, 126.

Ganesh, S. (2007). Sustainable development discourse and the global economy: Promoting responsibility, containing change. In S. May, G. Cheney, & J. Roper (Eds.), *The debate over corporate social responsibility* (pp. 379–390). New York, NY: Oxford University Press.

Ganesh, S., Zoller, H. M., & Cheney, C. (2005). Transforming resistance, broadening our boundaries: Critical organizational communication studies meets globalization from below. *Communication Monographs, 72*(2), 169–191.

Godfrey, P. (2005). The relationship between corporate philanthropy and shareholder wealth: A risk management perspective. *Academy of Management Review, 30*(4), 777–798.

Hanlon, G. (2008). Rethinking corporate social responsibility and the role of the firm: On the denial of politics. In A. Crane, A. McWilliams, D. Matten, J. Moon, & D. Siegel (Eds.), *The Oxford handbook of corporate social responsibility* (pp. 156–172). New York, NY: Oxford University Press.

Hearit, K. M. (2007). Corporate deception and fraud: The case for an ethical apologia. In S. May, G. Cheney, & J. Roper (Eds.), *The debate over corporate social responsibility* (pp. 167–176). New York, NY: Oxford University Press.

Hine, J., & Preuss, L. (2009). "Society is out there, organization is in here": On the perceptions of corporate social responsibility held by different managerial groups. *Journal of Business Ethics, 88*(2), 381–393.

Hockerts, K., & Moir. L. (2004). Communicating corporate social responsibility to investors: The changing role of the investor relations function. *Journal of Business Ethics, 52*(1), 85–98.

Idowu, S. O., & Filho, W. L. (Eds.). (2009). *Global practices of corporate social responsibility*. Berlin, Germany: Springer.

Jensen, M. C. (2002). Value maximization, stakeholder theory, and the corporate objective function. *Business Ethics Quarterly, 12*(2), 235–256.

Jones, C. (2003). As if business ethics were possible: Within such limits. *Organization, 10*(2), 223–248.

Jones, T. M. (1980, Spring). Corporate social responsibility revisited, redefined. *California Management Review, 22*(2), 59–67.

Jordan, T. (2001). *Shell, Greenpeace, and Brent Spar*. New York, NY: Palgrave.

Jose, A., & Lee. S. M. (2007). Environmental reporting of global corporations: A content analysis based on website disclosures. *Journal of Business Ethics, 72*(4), 307–321.

Kanter, R. M. (2003). From spare change to real change: The social sector as beta site for business innovation. In Harvard Business School, C. K. Prahalad, & M. E. Porter (Eds.), *Harvard Business Review on corporate social responsibility* (pp. 189–214). Boston, MA: Harvard Business School Publishing.

Keim, G. D. (1978). Corporate social responsibility: An assessment of the enlightened self-interest model. *Academy of Management Review, 3*(1), 32–40.

Kendall, B. E., Gill, R., & Cheney, G. (2007). Consumer activism and corporate social responsibility: How strong a connection? In S. May, G. Cheney, & J. Roper (Eds.), *The debate over corporate social responsibility* (pp. 241–266). New York, NY: Oxford University Press.

Kolk, A. (2003). Trends in sustainability reporting by the Fortune Global 250. *Business Strategy and the Environment, 12*(5), 279–291.

Kotler, P., & Lee, N. (2005). *Corporate social responsibility: Doing the most good for your company and your cause*. New York, NY: John Wiley.

Kuhn, T., & Deetz, S. (2008). Critical theory and corporate social responsibility: Can/should we get beyond cynical reasoning? In A. Crane, A. McWilliams, D. Matten, J. Moon, & D. Siegel (Eds.), *The Oxford handbook of corporate social responsibility* (pp. 173–196). New York, NY: Oxford University Press.

Lewis, S. (2003). Reputation and corporate social responsibility. *Journal of Communication Management, 7*(4), 356–364.

Livesey, S. M., & Graham, J. (2007). Greening of corporations? Eco-talk and the emerging social imaginary of sustainable development. In S. May, G. Cheney, & J. Roper (Eds.), *The debate over corporate social responsibility* (pp. 336–350). New York, NY: Oxford University Press.

Logsdon, J. M., & Wood, D. J. (2005). Global business citizenship and voluntary codes of ethical conduct. *Journal of Business Ethics, 59*(1/2), 55–67.

Maclagan, P. (1999). Corporate social responsibility as a participative process. *Business Ethics: A European Review, 8*(1), 43–49.

Marchand, R. (1998). *Creating the corporate soul: The rise of public relations and corporate imagery in American big business*. Berkeley: University of California Press.

Marcoux, A. M. (2003). A fiduciary argument against stakeholder theory. *Business Ethics Quarterly, 13*(1), 1–24.

Margolis, J. D., & Walsh, J. P. (2003). Misery loves companies: Rethinking social initiatives by business. *Administrative Science Quarterly, 48*(2), 268–305.

Matten, D., & Crane, A. (2005). Corporate citizenship: Toward an extended theoretical conceptualization. *Academy of Management Review, 30*(1), 166–179.

May, S. (2008). Reconsidering strategic corporate social responsibility: Public relations and ethical engagement of employees in a global economy. In

A. Zerfass, B. van Ruler, & K. Sriramesh (Eds.), *Public relations research: European and international perspectives and innovations* (pp. 365–383). Wiesbaden, Germany: VS Verlag für Sozialwissenschaften.

May, S. (2011). Organizational communication and corporate social responsibility. In O. Ihlen, J. Bartlett, & S. May (Eds.), *Handbook of communication and corporate social responsibility* (pp. 87–109). Boston, MA: Wiley-Blackwell.

May, S. (Ed.). (2013). *Case studies in organizational communication: Ethical perspectives and practices* (2nd ed.). Thousand Oaks, CA: SAGE.

May, S., Cheney, G., & Roper, J. (Eds.). (2007). *The debate over corporate social responsibility.* New York, NY: Oxford University Press.

McIntosh, M. (2007). Progressing from corporate social responsibility to brand integrity. In S. May, G. Cheney, & J. Roper (Eds.), *The debate over corporate social responsibility* (pp. 45–73). New York, NY: Oxford University Press.

McMillan, J. (2007). Why corporate social responsibility? Why now? How? In S. May, G. Cheney, & J. Roper (Eds.), *The debate over corporate social responsibility* (pp. 15–29). New York, NY: Oxford University Press.

Mele, D. (2008). Corporate social responsibility theories. In A. Crane, A. McWilliams, D. Matten, J. Moon, & D. Siegel (Eds.), *The Oxford handbook of corporate social responsibility* (pp. 47–82). New York, NY: Oxford University Press.

Moon, J., Crane, A., & Matten, D. (2005). Can corporations be citizens? Corporate citizenship as a metaphor for business participation in society. *Business Ethics Quarterly, 15*(3), 429–453.

Morsing, M. (2011). State-owned enterprises: A corporatization of governments? *Management Communication Quarterly, 25*(4), 710–717.

Morsing, M., Midttun, A., & Palmas, K. (2007). Corporate social responsibility in Scandinavia: A turn toward the business case? In S. May, G. Cheney, & J. Roper (Eds.), *The debate over corporate social responsibility* (pp. 87–104). New York, NY: Oxford University Press.

Morsing, M., & Schultz, M. (2006). Corporate social responsibility communication: Stakeholder information, response and involvement strategies. *Business Ethics: A European Review, 15*(4), 323–338.

Morsing, M., Schultz, M., & Nielsen, K. U. (2008). The "catch 22"of communicating CSR: Findings from a Danish study. *Journal of Marketing Communications, 14*(2), 97–111.

Munshi, D., & Kurian, P. (2007). The case of the subaltern public: A postcolonial investigation of corporate social responsibility's (o)missions. In S. May, G. Cheney, & J. Roper (Eds.), *The debate over corporate social responsibility* (pp. 438–447). New York, NY: Oxford University Press.

Nielsen, A. E., & Thomsen, C. (2009). CSR communication in small and medium-sized enterprises: A study of the attitudes and beliefs of middle managers. *Corporate Communications: An International Journal, 14*(2), 176–189.

Orlitzky, M. (2008). Corporate social performance and financial performance: A research synthesis. In A. Crane, A. McWilliams, D. Matten, J. Moon, & D. Siegel (Eds.), *The Oxford handbook of corporate social responsibility* (pp. 113–136). New York, NY: Oxford University Press.

Orlitzky, M., Schmidt, F. L., & Rynes, S. L. (2003). Corporate social and financial performance: A meta-analysis. *Organization Studies, 24*(3), 403–441.

Paine, L. S. (2003). *Value shift: Why companies must merge social and financial imperatives to achieve superior performance.* New York, NY: McGraw-Hill.

Painter-Morland, M. (2006). Triple bottom-line reporting as social grammar: Integrating corporate social responsibility and corporate codes of conduct. *Business Ethics: A European Review, 15*(4), 352–364.

Parker, M. (Ed.). (1998). *Ethics and organization.* London, England: SAGE.

Parry, G. (1991). Paths to citizenship. In U. Vogel & M. Moran (Eds.), *Frontiers of citizenship* (pp. 166–201). New York, NY: St. Martin's Press.

Pearson, G. (1995). *Integrity in organizations: An alternative business ethic.* New York, NY: McGraw-Hill.

Peterson, T. R., & Norton, T. (2007). Discourses of sustainability in today's public sphere. In S. May, G. Cheney, & J. Roper (Eds.), *The debate over corporate social responsibility* (pp. 351–364). New York, NY: Oxford University Press.

Porter, M. E., & Kramer, M. R. (2003). The competitive advantage of corporate philanthropy. In Harvard Business School, C. K. Prahalad, & M. E. Porter (Eds.), *Harvard Business Review on corporate social responsibility* (pp. 27–64). Boston, MA: Harvard Business School Publishing.

Porter, M. E., & Kramer, M. R. (2006, December). Strategy and society: The link between competitive advantage and corporate social responsibility. *Harvard Business Review*, 78–92.

Prahalad, C. K. (2003). Strategies for the bottom of the economic pyramid: India as a source of innovation. *Reflections: The SOL Journal, 3*(4), 6–18.

Preston, L. E., & Post, J. E. (1975). *Private management and public policy: The principle of public responsibility*. Englewood Cliffs, NJ: Prentice Hall.

Reich, R. (2007). *Supercapitalism: The transformation of business, democracy, and everyday life*. New York, NY: Alfred A. Knopf.

Roberts, J. (2003). The manufacture of corporate social responsibility: Constructing corporate sensibility. *Organization, 10*(2), 249–265.

Roper, J. (2005). Symmetrical communication: Excellent public relations or a strategy for hegemony? *Journal of Public Relations Research, 17*(1), 69–86.

Roper, J., & Schoenberger-Orgad, M. (2011). State-owned enterprises: Issues of accountability and legitimacy. *Management Communication Quarterly, 25*(4), 693–709.

Sahlin-Andersson, K. (2006). Corporate social responsibility: A trend and a movement, but of what and for what? *Corporate Governance, 6*(5), 595–608.

Sanborn, C. (2004). *La filantropía "realmente existente" en América Latina*. Bogotá, Colombia: Departamento de Ciencias Sociales y Políticas, Centro de Investigación de la Universidad del Pacífico.

Scherer, A. G., & Palazzo, G. (2007). Towards a political conception of corporate social responsibility: Business and society seen from a Habermasian perspective. *Academy of Management Review, 32*(4), 1096–1120.

Seeger, M. W., & Hipfel, S. J. (2007). Legal versus ethical arguments: Contexts for corporate social responsibility. In S. May, G. Cheney, & J. Roper (Eds.), *The debate over corporate social responsibility* (pp. 155–166). New York, NY: Oxford University Press.

Seitanidi, M. (2009). Employee involvement in implementing CSR in cross-sector social partnerships. *Corporate Reputation Review, 12,* 87–98.

Sethi, S. P. (1975). Dimensions of corporate social performance: An analytical framework. *California Management Review, 17*(3), 58–64.

Shamir, R. (2008). The age of responsibilization: On market-embedded morality. *Economy and Society, 37*(1), 1–19.

Shumate, M., & O'Connor, A. (2010). Corporate reporting on cross-sector alliances: The portfolio of NGO partners communicated on corporate websites. *Communication Monographs, 77*(2), 207–230.

Smith, W., & Higgins. M. (2000). Cause-related marketing: Ethics and the ecstatic. *Business and Society, 39*(3), 304–322.

Solomon, C. R. (1992). *Ethics and excellence: Cooperation and integrity in business*. New York, NY: Oxford University Press.

Sriramesh, K., Ng, C. W., Ting, S. T., & Wanyin, L. (2007). Corporate social responsibility and public relations: Perceptions and practices in Singapore. In S. May, G. Cheney, & J. Roper (Eds.), *The debate over corporate social responsibility* (pp. 119–134). New York, NY: Oxford University Press.

Stohl, M., Stohl, C., & Townsley, N. (2007). A new generation of global corporate social responsibility. In S. May, G. Cheney, & J. Roper (Eds.), *The debate over corporate social responsibility* (pp. 30–44). New York, NY: Oxford University Press.

Svensson, G., Wood, G., Singh, J., & Callaghan, M. (2009). Implementation, communication and benefits of corporate codes of ethics: An international and longitudinal approach for Australia, Canada, and Sweden. *Business Ethics: A European Review, 18*(4), 389–407.

Swanson, D. (2008). Top managers as drivers for corporate social responsibility. In A. Crane, A. McWilliams, D. Matten, J. Moon, & D. Siegel (Eds.), *The Oxford handbook of corporate social responsibility* (pp. 227–248). New York, NY: Oxford University Press.

Trevino, L. K., Weaver, G., Gibson, D., & Toffler, B. (1999). Managing ethics and legal compliance: What works and what hurts. *California Management Review, 41*(2), 131–151.

Vidaver-Cohen, D., & Altman, B. W. (2000). Concluding remarks: Corporate citizenship in the new millennium: Foundation for an architecture of excellence. *Business and Society Review, 105*(1), 145–168.

Vogel, D. (2006). *The market for virtue: The potential and limits of corporate social responsibility*. Washington, DC: Brookings Institute Press.

Waddock, S. (2001). Integrity and mindfulness: Foundations of corporate citizenship. In J. Andriof & M. McIntosh (Eds.), *Perspectives on corporate citizenship* (pp. 26–38). Sheffield, UK: Greenleaf Publishing.

Waddock, S. (2007). Corporate citizenship: The dark-side paradoxes of success. In S. May, G. Cheney, & J. Roper (Eds.), *The debate over corporate social responsibility* (pp. 74–86). New York, NY: Oxford University Press.

Waddock, S., & Smith, N. (2000). Relationships: The real challenge of corporate global citizenship. *Business and Society Review, 105*(1), 47–62.

Wartick, S. L., & Cochran, P. L. (1985). The evolution of the corporate social performance model. *The Academy of Management Review, 10*(4), 758–769.

Werhane, P. H. (2007). Corporate social responsibility/corporate moral responsibility: Is there a difference and the difference it makes. In S. May, G. Cheney, & J. Roper (Eds.), *The debate over corporate social responsibility* (pp. 459–474). New York, NY: Oxford University Press.

Windsor, D. (2006). Corporate social responsibility: Three key approaches. *Journal of Management Studies, 43*(1), 93–114.

Wood, D. J. (1991). Corporate social performance revisited. *Academy of Management Review, 16*(4), 691–718.

Zhao, L., & Roper, J. (2011). A Confucian approach to well-being and social capital. *Journal of Management Development, 30*(7/8), 740–752.

Zorn, T., & Collins, E. (2007). Is sustainability sustainable? CSR, sustainable business, and management fashion. In S. May, G. Cheney, & J. Roper (Eds.), *The debate over corporate social responsibility* (pp. 405–416). New York, NY: Oxford University Press.

Author Index

Subject Index

About the Editors

LINDA L. PUTNAM (Ph.D., University of Minnesota) is a Professor in the Department of Communication at the University of California, Santa Barbara. Her research interests include negotiation, organizational conflict, and organizational discourse analysis. She is the co-editor of 11 books and her published articles appear in such journals as *Management Communication Quarterly, Communication Monographs, Academy of Management Review, Human Relations, Organization Studies,* and *Negotiation Journal.* She is a distinguished scholar of the National Communication Association, a fellow of the International Communication Association, and the recipient of life-time achievement awards from the International Association for Conflict Management and *Management Communication Quarterly.* [Email: lputnam@comm.ucsb.edu]

DENNIS K. MUMBY (Ph.D., Southern Illinois University, Carbondale) is Professor of Communication Studies at The University of North Carolina at Chapel Hill. His research focuses on the relationships among discourse, power, and organizing. He is a Fellow of the International Communication Association, and a National Communication Association Distinguished Scholar. He has published 6 books and over 50 articles in the area of critical organization studies, and his work has appeared in journals such as *Academy of Management Review, Management Communication Quarterly, Communication Monographs, Discourse & Society,* and *Human Relations.* He is past chair of the Organizational Communication Division of NCA, and a 6-time winner of the division's annual research award. [Email: mumby@email.unc.edu]

About the Contributors

KAREN LEE ASHCRAFT (Ph.D., University of Colorado Boulder) is a Professor in the Department of Communication at the University of Colorado Boulder. Her research examines relations of gender, race, and other forms of difference in the context of organizing and working, with a particular interest in organizational forms and occupational identities as these entwine in the evolution and practice of professions. She co-authored the book *Reworking Gender* and has published in such outlets as *Academy of Management Review, Administrative Science Quarterly, Communication Theory*, and *Management Communication Quarterly*. [Email: karen.ashcraft@colorado.edu]

J. KEVIN BARGE (Ph.D., University of Kansas) is a Professor in the Department of Communi-cation at Texas A&M University. Kevin's major research interests center on developing a social constructionist approach to leadership, articulating the connections between appreciative practice and organizational change, as well as exploring the relationship between discourse and public deliberation, specifically practices that facilitate communities working through polarized and polarizing issues. He has published articles on leadership, dialogue, and organizational change in *The Academy of Management Review, Management Communication Quarterly, Human Relations, Communication Theory, Journal of Applied Communication Research*, and *Communication Monographs.* [Email: kbarge@tamu.edu]

JAMES R. BARKER (Ph.D., University of Colorado) is the Herbert S. Lamb Chair in Business Education and Professor of Organizational Behavior in the Rowe School of Business at Dalhousie University, Canada. His research focuses on the role of organizational communication in the development of safe and sustainable knowledge, innovation, and change initiatives and the consequences of these initiatives on organizational governance systems, markets, and practices. His articles appear in such journals as *Academy of Management Review, Human Relations, Organization Studies,* and *Management Communication Quarterly.* He is the immediate past Editor-in-Chief of *Management Communication Quarterly*. [Email: j.barker@dal.ca]

KIRSTEN J. BROADFOOT (Ph.D., University of Colorado at Boulder) is an Associate Professor in the School of Medicine at the University of Colorado Anschutz Medical Campus. Her research interests lie in postcolonial approaches to organizing and communicative practice, especially the 're-organizing' of medicine and clinical interaction, through culture, technology and relationship centered care. She is the author of *Living with Genetics: Recombining Health and Self in Modern Medicine,* and she has published in *Management Communication Quarterly, Journal of Applied Communication Research, New Media and Society, Women's Studies in Communication*, and *Journal of Broadcasting and Electronic Media.* [Email: Kirsten.broadfoot@ucdenver.edu]

BORIS H. J. M. BRUMMANS (Ph.D., Texas A&M University) is an Associate Professor in the Département de Communication at the Université de Montréal, Canada. His research interests include the communicative constitution of organizations, spiritual organizing, organizational conflict, and organizational ethnography. He has contributed chapters to several edited books and his articles appear in journals such as *Communication Monographs*, *Human Relations*, *Journal of International and Intercultural Communication*, *Management Communication Quarterly*, *Qualitative Inquiry*, and *Qualitative Communication Research*. [Email: boris.brummans@umontreal.ca]

PATRICE M. BUZZANELL (Ph.D., Purdue University) is a Professor in the Brian Lamb School of Communication and the School of Engineering Education. Co-editor of three books and author of over 130 articles and chapters, her research centers on the intersections of career, gender, and communication, particularly in STEM (science, technology, engineering, and math). Her research has appeared in such journals as *Communication Monographs*, *Management Communication Quarterly*, *Human Relations*, *Communication Theory*, *Human Communication Research*, and *Journal of Applied Communication Research*.. A fellow of the International Communication Association, she has received awards for her research, teaching/mentoring, and engagement. [Email: buzzanel@purdue.edu]

GEORGE CHENEY (Ph.D., Purdue University) is Professor of Communication Studies and Coordinator of Doctoral Education and Interdisciplinary Research in Communication and Information at Kent State University. Also, he is an adjunct professor at The University of Waikato, New Zealand, as well as at the universities of Utah and Texas-Austin. His research interests include identity at work, workplace participation/democracy, professional ethics, discourses of globalization and consumerism, business sustainability, dissent, and dialogue. He is the author, co-author or co-editor of ten books and has published more than 100 articles, chapters, reviews and editorials. Recognized for teaching, research, and community as well as academic service, he has lectured and consulted widely, including in Europe and Latin America as well as in New Zealand and the United States. [Email: gcheney@kent.edu]

LARS THØGER CHRISTENSEN (Ph.D., Odense University) is Professor of Communication and Organization at The Copenhagen Business School, Denmark. His research interests include organizational identity, corporate communication, branding, autocommunication, corporate social responsibility, and transparency and accountability, which he approaches from critical and postmodern perspectives. In addition to six books, his research articles appear in such venues as *Organization Studies*, *Human Relations*, *European Journal of Marketing*, *Organization, Consumption, Markets and Culture*, and *Communication Yearbook*. He has more than 15 years of experience in providing lectures, courses, counseling, and consultancy on strategic communication to public and private sector organizations. [Email: ltc.ikl@cbs.dk]

STACEY L. CONNAUGHTON (Ph.D., University of Texas at Austin) is an Associate Professor and Associate Head in the Brian Lamb School of Communication at Purdue University. Her research examines leadership and identification in geographically distributed contexts, particularly as these issues relate to virtual teams/organizations and political parties. Her research has been funded by the National Science Foundation, the Carnegie Foundation, and the Russell Sage Foundation. She has authored one book and her published articles appear in such journals as *Journal of Communication*, *Management Communication Quarterly*, *Small Group Research*, and *JASIST*. She is the Director of the Purdue Peace Project, a funded research initiative in West Africa. [Email: sconnaug@purdue.edu]

NOSHIR S. CONTRACTOR (Ph.D., University of Southern California) is the Jane S. & William J. White Professor of Behavioral Sciences at Northwestern University. He is investigating factors that lead to the formation, maintenance, and dissolution of dynamically linked social and knowledge networks in communities. His papers and articles have received Top Paper and Best Article awards from the International Communication Association and the National Communication Association. His co-authored book titled *Theories of Communication Networks* is translated in Chinese and received the Book of the Year award from the Organizational Communication Division of the National Communication Association. [Email: nosh@northwestern.edu]

FRANÇOIS COOREN (Ph.D., Université de Montréal) is a Professor and Chair of the Department of Communication at the Université de Montréal, Canada. His research interests include organizational communication, discourse analysis, and creativity. He is the author of two books, editor of four volumes, and his published articles appear in such journals as *Management Communication Quarterly, Communication Monographs, Journal of Communication, Human Relations, Organization,* and *Communication Theory.* He is a fellow and past president of the International Communication Association (ICA), and the recipient of several awards, including the Frederic M. Jablin Memorial Award for Contributions to the Organizational Communication division of the ICA. [Email: f.cooren@umontreal.ca]

STEPHANIE L. DAILEY (M.A., University of Texas at Austin) is a Doctoral Candidate in the Department of Communication Studies at the University of Texas at Austin. Her research interests include organizational identification and socialization, information seeking, the use of technology in organizations, and narratives. Her dissertation, which explores how individuals learn and identify with organizations before joining them, is funded by a National Science Foundation grant. The College of Communication at the University of Texas also awarded Stephanie the Jesse H. Jones Endowed Centennial Fellowship. Stephanie's published articles appear in *Management Communication Quarterly*, the *Academy of Management Review, Health Communication*, and *Communication Teacher*. [Email: Stephanie.Dailey@me.com]

STANLEY A. DEETZ (Ph.D., Ohio University) is Professor and President's Teaching Scholar, University of Colorado at Boulder, and Director of the Center for the Study of Conflict, Collaboration and Creative Governance, as well as Managing Director for Institutional Change in the Center for STEM (Science, Technology, Engineering and Math) Learning. He is the author or co-author of over 140 scholarly articles and author/editor of twelve books on collaborative interaction and organizational culture and change. He has served as a Senior Fulbright Scholar and is a National Communication Association Distinguished Scholar and an International Communication Association Past-President and Fellow. [Email: stanley.deetz@colorado.edu]

SARAH E. DEMPSEY (Ph.D., University of Colorado, Boulder) is an Associate Professor in the Department of Communication Studies at the University of North Carolina, Chapel Hill, where she teaches courses on organization, labor and globalization, food politics, and contemporary social theory. Her research has appeared in *Children's Geographies, Communication and Critical/Cultural Studies, Communication Monographs, Feminist Media Studies, Management Communication Quarterly*, and *Organization*. She also serves as an Associate Editor for *Culture and Organization*, and is currently working on a project on the politics of labor in the U.S. food system. [Email: sedempse@email.unc.edu]

MARYA L. DOERFEL (Ph.D., University at Buffalo) is an Associate Professor in the Department of Communication at Rutgers University. Her research interests include networked forms of organizing, disrupted networks, and interorganizational relationships. Her research has been funded by the National Science Foundation and her published articles appear in such journals as *Human Communication Research, Communication Monographs, New Media & Society, Management Communication Quarterly, Journal of Applied Communication Research, and Journal of the American Society for Information and Technology, International Journal for Intercultural Relations, and the International Journal of Conflict Management.* [Email: mdoerfel@rutgers.edu]

ELIZABETH K. EGER (M.A., Arizona State University) is a Doctoral Candidate in the Department of Communication at the University of Colorado. Her critical and qualitative organizational communication research focuses on contemporary work as both excessive and inaccessible, including scholarship on work's influence in our lives and on how difference is organized. Her organizational ethnographies include research with a university police department, a global innovation incubator, and a computing camp for girls of color. Her published work appears in venues such as the *Journal of Applied Communication Research* and *Celebrating Bud: A festschrift honoring the life and work of H.L. "Bud" Goodall, Jr.* [Email: elizabeth.eger@colorado.edu].

GAIL T. FAIRHURST (Ph.D., University of Oregon) is a Professor of Communication at the University of Cincinnati. Her research and writing interests are in leadership and organizational discourse analysis. She has published over 70 articles and chapters in communication and management outlets. She is the author of three books, including *Discursive Leadership: In Conversation with Leadership Psychology* (Sage, 2007) and *The Power of Framing: Challenging the Language of Leadership* (Jossey-Bass, 2011). She is a Fellow of the International Communication Association; a Distinguished Scholar of the National Communication Association; a Fulbright Scholar; and an Associate Editor for the journal, *Human Relations*. Her email is: fairhug@ucmail.uc.edu

JANET FULK (Ph.D., The Ohio State University) is a Professor of Communication in the Annenberg School for Communication and Journalism and Professor of Management and Organization the Marshall School of Business at University of Southern California. Her research, which has been sponsored by the National Science Foundation, centers on social aspects of knowledge and distributed intelligence, social media use, nongovernmental organizations, and online communities. She is a Fellow of the Academy of Management Association and the International Communication Association and holds lifetime achievement awards from the Academy of Management Association as well as publication awards from the National Communication Association. [email: fulk@usc.edu]

SHIV GANESH (Ph.D., Purdue University) is Professor of Communication at the School of Communication, Journalism and Marketing, Massey University, New Zealand. Shiv's research engages with substantive issues that arise from the intersection of communication processes with globalization, digital technologies, and civil society organizing. Specific studies he has published include such topics as technological transformations in collective action and social justice, dialogue and social change, volunteering and non-profit organizing, global aspects of the digital divide, and neoliberalism and entrepreneurship. His work has appeared in such outlets as *Communication Monographs, Human Relations, Management Communication Quarterly, Journal of Applied Communication Research*, and *Organization Studies*. [Email: S.N.Ganesh@massey.ac.nz]

MATTEA A. GARCIA (Ph.D., University of Illinois at Urbana-Champaign) is an Assistant Professor in the Department of Communication at Indiana State University. She also serves as the Director of Foundational Studies in Communication and leads the basic course. Her research interests include professions, professional identity, and institutional work. Currently, she is working on a project involving public safety officers' experiences of profession. Her work appears in *Management Communication Quarterly*. [Email: matteagarcia@gmail.com]

PATRICIA GEIST-MARTIN (Ph.D., Purdue University) is a Professor in the School of Communication at San Diego State University. Her research interests focus on narrative and negotiating identity, voice, ideology, and control in organizations, particularly in health and illness. She has published three books, *Communicating Health: Personal, Political, and Cultural Complexities* (2004) (with Eileen Berlin Ray and Barbara Sharf), *Courage of Conviction: Women's Words, Women's Wisdom* (1997) (with Linda A. M. Perry), and *Negotiating the Crisis: DRGs and the Transformation of Hospitals* (1992) (with Monica Hardesty). She has published over 60 articles and book chapters covering a wide range of topics related to gender, health, and negotiating identities. [Email: pgeist@mail.sdsu.edu]

JENNIFER L. GIBBS (Ph.D., University of Southern California) is an Associate Professor in the Department of Communication at Rutgers University. Her research interests include collaboration, knowledge sharing, and self-presentation in virtual and multicultural work contexts, such as global virtual teams and online communities. She has published articles in such journals as *Administrative Science*

Quarterly, Communication Research, Communication Yearbook, Human Relations, Journal of Computer-Mediated Communication, Journal of Social & Personal Relationships, and *Organization Science.* [Email: jgibbs@rutgers.edu]

ANDREA B. HOLLINGSHEAD (Ph.D., University of Illinois at Urbana-Champaign) is Professor of Communication in the Annenberg School of Communication and Journalism at the University of Southern California (USC). She holds joint appointments in the USC Marshall School of Business and the Department of Psychology. Her research focuses on the factors and processes that lead to knowledge sharing in groups. She has been a co- investigator on projects funded by the National Science Foundation. She has co-authored three books, *Research Methods for Studying Groups and Teams, Theories of Small Groups: Interdisciplinary Perspectives,* and *Groups Interacting with Technology* and has published many articles in communication, management, and psychology journals. [Email: aholling@usc.edu]

JOEL. O. IVERSON (Ph.D., Arizona State University) is an Associate Professor in the Department of Communication Studies at the University of Montana. His research interests include organizational knowledge, communicative constitution of organizations, and nonprofit organizations. He is the author of over fifteen articles and chapters and his published articles appear in such journals as *Management Communication Quarterly, Nonprofit and Voluntary Sector Quarterly, Journal of Applied Communication Research, and Nonprofit Management and Leadership.* His research uses structuration theory to explore the communicative enactment of organizations through multiple contexts including volunteers, nonprofit boards, communities of practice, and knowledge management systems. [Email: joel.iverson@umontana.edu]

JEFFREY W. KASSING (Ph.D., Kent State University) is Professor and Director of the School of Social and Behavioral Sciences at Arizona State University. His research interests include employee dissent, organizational democracy, workplace bullying, and superior-subordinate communication. He is the co-author of *Managing Risk in Communication Encounters: Strategies for the Workplace*, which received the Book of the Year Award from the Organizational Communication Division of the National Communication Association, and the author of *Dissent in Organizations*. His work also has appeared in *Management Communication Quarterly*, *Journal of Business Communication*, *Communication Studies*, *Communication Research Reports*, and *Communication Reports.* [Email: jkassing@asu.edu]

JOANN KEYTON (Ph.D., The Ohio State University) is a Professor in the Department of Communication at North Carolina State University. Her research interests include team dynamics, organizational culture, and research methods, especially the analysis of conversation in collaborative and decision-making contexts. She is the author of *Communication and Organizational Culture: A Key to Understanding Work Experiences,* and the author or co-editor of other organizational communication textbooks. She is Editor of *Small Group Research*, past editor of *Journal of Applied Communication,* and founding editor of *Communication Currents.* She is a founder of the Interdisciplinary Network for Group Research, and currently serves as its vice-chair. [Email: jkeyton@ncsu.edu]

ERIKA L. KIRBY (Ph.D., University of Nebraska) is a Professor in the Department of Communication Studies at Creighton University in Omaha, Nebraska. Her research interests emphasize *everyday intersections of working and personal life,* emphasizing how differing social identities (especially gender) assimilate into and collide with organizational structures. She co-edited the book *Gender Actualized* and her published articles appear in such journals as *Management Communication Quarterly, Communication Monographs, Journal of Applied Communication Research* and *Communication Yearbook*. She is Past-President of the Organization for the Study of Communication, Language, and Gender and a 2013 National Communication Association Hope Institute Scholar. [Email: ekirby@creighton.edu]

MICHAEL W. KRAMER (Ph.D., University of Texas at Austin) is Chair and Professor in the Department of Communication at the University of Oklahoma. His research interests include socialization/assimilation, leadership, and decision-making including volunteer settings. His books include *Managing Uncertainty in Organizational Communication, Organizational Socialization,* and *Volunteering and Communication.* He research has appeared in journals such as *Communication Monographs, Journal of Applied Communication Quarterly, Management Communication Quarterly, Academy of Management Journal, Leadership Quarterly,* and *Small Group Research.* He has received a variety of article and conference paper awards and three departmental and university teaching awards. [Email: mkramer@ou.edu]

KATHLEEN J. KRONE (Ph.D., The University of Texas at Austin) is a Professor in the Department of Communication Studies at the University of Nebraska, Lincoln. Her research examines organizations and the development of voice and her current projects focus on the management of international joint ventures as cooperative struggle and stakeholder participation in (non)institutionalized spaces. She co-edited the multi-volume reference *Organizational Communication,* and published articles that appear in *Management Communication Quarterly, Journal of International and Intercultural Communication,* and *Journal of Applied Communication Research.* She is a past chair of the Organizational Communication Division of the National Communication Association and past Forum Editor for *Management Communication Quarterly.* [Email: kkrone1@unl.edu]

TIMOTHY R. KUHN (Ph.D., Arizona State University) is Associate Professor in the Department of Communication at the University of Colorado Boulder and Visiting Fellow in the School of Economics and Management at Lund University (Sweden). Guided by efforts to reframe commercial firms in distinctly communicative terms, his research examines how knowledge, authority, identities, and conceptions of value emerge in the distributed, sociomaterial, and power-laden practices of communication. His work has appeared in *Academy of Management Review, Communication Monographs, Human Communication Research, Management Communication Quarterly, Organization,* and *Organization Studies,* among other outlets. [Email: tim.kuhn@colorado.edu]

JOHN C. LAMMERS (Ph.D., University of California-Davis) is a Professor in the Department of Communication and Director of the Health Communication Online Masters of Science Program at the University of Illinois at Urbana-Champaign. His research includes applications of institutional theory to communication among professionals and managers in health organizations. His work has appeared in *Management Communication Quarterly, Communication Theory, Health Communication,* the *Annals of Internal Medicine,* the *Annals of Emergency Medicine,* the *Handbook of Health Communication,* and *the Handbook Communication and Corporate Reputation.* Currently he is co-editing a special issue of the *Academy of Management Review* on institutions, communication, and cognition. [email: jclammer@illinois.edu]

PAUL M. LEONARDI (Ph.D., Stanford University) is the Pentair-Nugent Associate Professor at Northwestern University where he holds appointments in the departments of Communication Studies, Industrial Engineering & Management Sciences, and Management. His research focuses on knowledge sharing, informational technologies, and organizational structures and he is the author of *Car Crashes Without Cars: Lessons About Simulation Technology and Organizational Change From Automotive Design* (2012), and the co-editor of *Materiality and Organizing* (2012). His research has received awards from multiple associations, including the Academy of Management, the American Sociological Association, the Association for Information Systems, the International Communication Association, and the National Communication Association. [Email: Leonardi@northwestern.edu]

LAURIE K. LEWIS (Ph.D., University of California, Santa Barbara) is Professor and Chair in the

Department of Communication at Rutgers University. Dr. Lewis also serves as an Associate Editor for *Management Communication Quarterly*. Her research focuses on communication during organizational change processes. She is the author of the book, *Organizational Change: Creating Change through Strategic Communication*. She also has research interests in nonprofit collaboration and the management and experience of volunteering. [lewisl@rutgers.edu]

STEVEN K. MAY (Ph.D., University of Utah) is Associate Professor in the Department of Communication Studies at the University of North Carolina at Chapel Hill. His research interests include organizational ethics and corporate social responsibility, with particular attention to ethical practices of dialogue, transparency, participation, courage, and accountability. His edited books include *The Handbook of Communication Ethics*, *The Handbook of Communication and Corporate Social Responsibility*, *The Debate Over Corporate Social Responsibility*, *Case Studies in Organizational Communication: Ethical Perspectives and Practices* and *Engaging Organizational Communication Theory and Research: Multiple Perspectives*. His current book projects include *Corporate Social Responsibility: Virtue or Vice?* and *Working Identity*. [Email: skmay@email.unc.edu]

ROBERT D. MCPHEE (Ph. D., Michigan State University, 1978) is a Professor in the Hugh Downs School of Human Communication at Arizona State University. Among his specific research interests are structuration theory, the communicative constitution of organizations, organizational hierarchies, and organizational knowledge. He has served as Chair of the Organizational Communication Division of the National Communication Association (NCA), as Associate Editor of *Human Communication Research*, and as Book Review Editor of *Communication Theory*. His research has won the NCA Golden Anniversary Award and research awards from the NCA Organizational Communication Division.

KATHERINE MILLER (Ph.D., University of Southern California) is on the faculty of the Hugh Downs School of Human Communication at Arizona State University. Her research interests include organizational emotion, family caregiving, and historical and contemporary challenges of women in the workplace. She has written three books, served as editor of *Management Communication Quarterly* and *Communication Monographs* and is editor-elect of *Journal of Applied Communication Research*. She is the recipient of the Gerald Phillips Award for Applied Communication Scholarship from the National Communication Association and numerous other awards for research, teaching, and mentoring. [Email: kathymiller@asu.edu]

VERNON MILLER (Ph.D., University of Texas at Austin) is an Associate Professor in the Department of Communication and Department of Management at Michigan State University. His research focuses on the communicative aspects of the employment interview, organizational entry, and role negotiation and appears in journals such as *Journal of Applied Communication Research*, *Management Communication Quarterly*, *Human Communication Research*, and *Academy of Management Review*. He is the co-author of *Conversations about Job Performance: A Communication Perspective on the Appraisal Process* and the co-editor of *Meeting the Challenges of Human Resource Management: A Communication Perspective*. [vmiller@msu.edu]

DEBASHISH MUNSHI (Ph.D., University of Waikato) is a Professor in the Department of Management Communication at the University of Waikato, Hamilton, New Zealand. His research interests lie at the intersections of communication, diversity, sustainability, and ethics and much of his work is anchored in postcolonial theory. He is co-author or co-editor of three books, including the *Handbook of Communication Ethics*, and his articles have been published in a wide range of major international journals. He serves on the editorial boards of six communication journals – *Management Communication Quarterly*, *Journal of International and Intercultural Communication*, *Journal of Public Relations Research*, *Public Relations Inquiry*, *Review of Communication*, and *Public Understanding of Science*. [Email: munshi@waikato.ac.nz]

KAREN K. MYERS (Ph.D., Arizona State University) is an Associate Professor in the

Department of Communication at the University of California, Santa Barbara. She researches membership negotiation (organizational socialization, assimilation); vocational anticipatory socialization; workplace flexibility and work-life balance issues; organizational identification; and interaction between generational cohorts in the workplace. Myers frequently uses and is an advocate for mixed methods research. Her work has appeared in *Human Communication Research, Communication Monographs, Communication Theory, Management Communication Quarterly, Journal of Applied Communication Research, Human Relations,* and *Journal of Business and Psychology*. [Email: myers@comm.ucsb.edu]

PATRICIA PARKER (Ph.D., University of Texas at Austin) is Associate Professor of Communication Studies at the University of North Carolina at Chapel Hill, where she is Director of Faculty Diversity Initiatives for the College of Arts and Sciences. Her research explores questions about access, equity and participatory democracy at the intersections of race, gender, class and power in organization processes. She is the author of *Race, Gender, and Leadership* (2005), and her articles and book chapters appear in such venues as *Management Communication Quarterly, Leadership Quarterly, Journal of International and Intercultural Communication Research*, and *Handbook of Business Discourse*. She is the inaugural recipient (2010) of the Engaged Scholars Service Award from the Organizational Communication Division of the National Communication Association. [Email: psparker@email.unc.edu]

MARSHALL SCOTT POOLE (Ph.D., University of Wisconsin-Madison) is a Professor in the Department of Communication; Senior Research Scientist at the National Center for Supercomputing Applications; and Director of the Institute for Computing in the Humanities, Arts, and Social Sciences at the University of Illinois Urbana-Champaign. His research interests include group and organizational communication, information systems, collaboration technologies, organizational innovation, and theory construction. He has been named a Fellow of the International Communication Association, a Distinguished Scholar of the National Communication Association, and a recipient of the Steven A. Chaffee Career Productivity Award from the International Communication Association. [Email: mspoole@uiuc.edu]

RONALD E. RICE (Ph.D., Stanford University) is the Arthur N. Rupe Chair in the Social Effects of Mass Communication in the Department of Communication, and Co-Director of the Carsey-Wolf Center, at University of California, Santa Barbara. He is a past president of the International Communication Association (2006-2007), received a Fulbright Award to Finland (2006), was a Visiting University Professor at Nanyang Technological University in Singapore (2007-2010), and was given an Honorary Doctorate at University of Montreal. His research areas include network analysis, public communication campaigns, diffusion of innovations, social aspects of new media, and environmental communication. [Email: rrice@comm.ucsb.edu; website: http://www.comm.ucsb.edu/people/academic/ronald-e-rice]

DANIEL ROBICHAUD (Ph.D., Université de Montréal) is Associate Professor of Communication at the Université de Montréal, Canada. He has conducted postdoctoral research at the University of Colorado, Boulder and was a Visiting Professor at the University of Sydney. His research focuses on organizational communication, particularly the discursive properties of organizing processes in different contexts. He has published numerous articles in journals such as *The Academy of Management Review, Organization*, and *Communication Theory*. [Email: daniel.robichaud@umontreal.ca]

JULIET ROPER (Ph.D., University of Waikato) is Professor and Chair of Management Communication at the University of Waikato Management School. Her research interests include social and environmental aspects of sustainability and CSR, examining issues of cross sector engagement, issues management, public relations, and public policy. She is co-editor of *The Debate over Corporate Social Responsibility* (2007) and has more than 40 articles published in refereed European and US journals, including *Organization Studies, Journal of Applied*

Communication Research, Journal of Public Relations Research, Public Relations Review, Corporate Governance, Public Understanding of Science, Management Communication Quarterly, and *Work Employment and Society*. [Email: jroper@waikato .ac.nz]

PATRICIA M. SIAS (Ph.D., University of Texas at Austin) is Director of the McGuire Entrepreneurship Program at the University of Arizona's Eller College of Management. Her research centers on workplace relationships, uncertainty, and communication and innovation in entrepreneurial teams. She has published a book, numerous book chapters, and many articles in academic journals such *as Communication Monographs, Communication Research, Human Communication Research, Management Communication Quarterly,* and *The Journal of Social and Personal Relationships.* She has served on the editorial boards of many refereed journals and is currently an Associate Editor of *Management Communication Quarterly.* [Email: psias@email.arizona.edu]

DAVID R. SEIBOLD (Ph.D., Michigan State University) is Professor and Vice Chair in the Technology Management Program at the University of California, Santa Barbara. His research interests include team processes, management of innovation, and collaborative technologies. His articles have appeared in *Academy of Management Review, Journal of Organizational Change Management, Small Group Research, Management Communication Quarterly, Journal of Business Communication,* and *Business Communication Quarterly.* A former editor of the *Journal of Applied Communication Research,* he is a fellow of the International Communication Association, a distinguished scholar of the National Communication Association, and the recipient of career awards for scholarship, mentoring, and professional service. [Email: dseibold@engineering. ucsb.edu]

MICHELLE SHUMATE (Ph.D., University of Southern California) is an Associate Professor in the Department of Communication Studies and Director of the Network for Nonprofit and Social Impact at Northwestern University. Her research focuses on the dynamics of interorganizational networks designed to impact large social issues. Her published articles appear in such journals as *Management Communication Quarterly, Communication Monographs, Human Relations, Journal of Computer Mediated Communication, Human Communication Research,* and *Journal of Communication.* She was awarded a National Science Foundation CAREER award for her work on interorganizational networks and nonprofit capacity. [Email: shumate@northwestern.edu]

PATRICIA J. SOTIRIN (Ph.D., Purdue University) is a Professor of Communication in the Department of Humanities, Michigan Technological University. Her research interests include workplace discourse, qualitative methodologies, and feminist theory. She is co-author of two books and co-editor of one collection. Her published articles appear in such journals as *Organization, Qualitative Inquiry, Journal of Research Practice, Cultural Studies<->Critical Methodologies, Text and Performance Quarterly,* and *Women's Studies in Communication.* She is the editor of *Women and Language*, a past president of the Organization for the Study of Communication, Language, and Gender, and a past chair of the Ethnography Division of the National Communication Association. [email: pjsotiri@mtu .edu]

CYNTHIA STOHL (Ph.D., Purdue University) is a Professor in the Department of Communication at the University of California, Santa Barbara. Her research interests include globalization, network processes, and collective action. She is the author of two award-winning books published by Sage and Cambridge University Press. Her published articles appear in journals such as *Communication Theory, Management Communication Quarterly, Communication Monographs, Journal of Applied Communication Research, Journal of Business Ethics, Organization Studies,* and *Journal of Communication Management.* She is a distinguished scholar of the National Communication Association, a fellow of the International Communication Association, and is Past President of the International Communication Association [Email: cstohl@comm.ucsb.edu]

JAMES R. TAYLOR (Ph.D., University of Pennsylvania) founded the communication sciences program at the Université de Montréal, where he is now Emeritus Professor. His research has focused on the communicative construction of organization with special attention to the formative role of technology. Author or co-author of eight books (one, in press, on authority), he has published articles based on his research in four languages, English, French, Spanish and Portuguese. He has received top paper and book awards from both ICA and NCA and his book with co-author Elizabeth Van Every, *The Emergent Organization*, was the recipient of the 2013 ICA Fellows book award. [Email: jr.taylor@umontreal.ca).

SARAH J. TRACY (Ph.D., University of Colorado, 2000) is associate professor of organizational communication and director of The Project for Wellness and Work-life at Arizona State University. Her scholarly work examines emotional labor, identity, workplace bullying, compassion, engagement, and burnout and she is an expert in qualitative research methods. Her research has resulted in two books and over 40 monographs appearing in outlets such as *Management Communication Quarterly, Communication Theory, Journal of Management Studies, Human Communication Research, Qualitative Inquiry*, and *Journal of Applied Communication Research*. She has been acknowledged with disciplinary research awards and university teaching awards. [Email: Sarah@SarahJTracy.com]

VINCENT R. WALDRON (Ph.D., Ohio State University) is Professor of Communication Studies at Arizona State University. His research interests include relationship maintenance practices, the communication of emotion in work settings, and the forgiveness in personal and work relationships. He is author of four books, including *Communicating Emotion at Work* (Polity, 2012), *Managing Risk in Communication Encounters: Strategies for the Workplace* (Sage, 2010) with Jeffrey Kassing, and Risk in Communication Encounters: Strategies for the Workpalce *Communicating Forgiveness* (Sage, 2008) and *Marriage at Midlife* (Springer, 2009) with Douglas Kelley. His articles appear in *Management Communication Quarterly, Journal of Social and Personal Relationships*, and *Journal of Family Communication*, among other outlets. [Email: vincew@asu.edu]

KAY YOON (Ph.D., University of Illinois at Urbana-Champaign) is an Associate Professor in the College of Communication at DePaul University. Her areas of research include knowledge sharing in work teams, diversity management, and pedagogy and training for team processes. Her articles appear in *Social Psychological and Personality Science, Small Group Research, International Journal of Organizational Diversity, College Teaching, and Journal of Communication Engagement and Scholarship*. She has also contributed chapters to books in the areas of team cognition, organizational knowledge, and small group communication theories. [Email: kyoon4@depaul.edu]

HEATHER ZOLLER (Ph.D., Purdue University) is a Professor and Director of Graduate Studies in the Department of Communication at the University of Cincinnati. Her research interests focus on organizing and the politics of public health, including issues of power and participation in community organizing, health activism, and corporate issue management. Her research appears in journals such as *Management Communication Quarterly, Communication Monographs, Communication Theory*, and *Human Relations*. She co-edited the book, *Emerging Perspectives in Health Communication*. She is a former Associate Editor at Management Communication Quarterly and an incoming Senior Editor at Health Communication. [Email: heather.zoller@uc.edu]